Tennessee

HOLT McDOUGAL

Mathematics
Course 2

Jennie M. Bennett

Edward B. Burger

David J. Chard

Earlene J. Hall

Paul A. Kennedy

Freddie L. Renfro

Tom W. Roby

Janet K. Scheer

Bert K. Waits

HOLT McDOUGAL

 HOUGHTON MIFFLIN HARCOURT

Cover Photo: Colorful soap bubbles in wand

HMH/Sam Dudgeon

Printed in the U.S.A.

ISBN 978-0-547-47679-7

4 5 6 7 8 9 10 1421 19 18 17 16 15 14 13 12 11

4500311702

Jennie M. Bennett, Ed.D., is a recently retired mathematics teacher at Hartman Middle School in Houston, Texas. She is past president of the Benjamin Banneker Association, the former First Vice-President of NCSM, and a former board member of NCTM.

Edward B. Burger, Ph.D., is Professor of Mathematics and Chair at Williams College and is the author of numerous articles, books, and videos. He has won many prestigious writing and teaching awards offered by the Mathematical Association of America. In 2006, Dr. Burger was named Reader's Digest's "Best Math Teacher" in its "100 Best of America" issue. He has made numerous television and radio appearances and has given countless mathematical presentations around the world.

David J. Chard, Ph.D., is the Leon Simmons Dean of the School of Education and Human Development at Southern Methodist University. He is a Past President of the Division for Research at the Council for Exceptional Children, a member of the International Academy for Research on Learning Disabilities, and has been the Principal Investigator on numerous research projects for the U.S. Department of Education. He is the author of several research articles and books on instructional strategies for students struggling in school.

Earlene J. Hall, Ed.D., is the Middle School Mathematics Supervisor for the Detroit Public Schools district. She teaches graduate courses in Mathematics Leadership at University of Michigan Dearborn. Dr. Hall has traveled extensively throughout Africa and China and has made numerous presentations including topics such as Developing Standards Based Professional Development and Culture Centered Education. She was a member of the NCTM 2009 Yearbook Panel.

Paul A. Kennedy, Ph.D., is a professor in the Department of Mathematics at Colorado State University. Dr. Kennedy is a leader in mathematics education. His research focuses on developing algebraic thinking by using multiple representations and technology. He is the author of numerous publications.

Freddie L. Renfro, MA, has 35 years of experience in Texas education as a classroom teacher and director/coordinator of Mathematics PreK-12 for school districts in the Houston area. She has served as a reviewer and TXTEAM trainer for Texas Math Institutes and has presented at numerous math workshops.

Tom W. Roby, Ph.D., is Associate Professor of Mathematics and Director of the Quantitative Learning Center at the University of Connecticut. He founded and co-directed the Bay Area-based ACCLAIM professional development program. He also chaired the advisory board of the California Mathematics Project and reviewed content for the California Standards Tests.

Janet K. Scheer, Ph.D., Executive Director of Create A Vision™, is a motivational speaker and provides customized K-12 math staff development. She has taught and supervised internationally and nationally at all grade levels.

Bert K. Waits, Ph.D., is a Professor Emeritus of Mathematics at The Ohio State University and cofounder of T^3 (Teachers Teaching with Technology), a national professional development program. Dr. Waits is also a former board member of NCTM and an author of the original NCTM Standards.

TENNESSEE TEACHER REVIEWERS

Michael Clark
Math Teacher
Metropolitan Nashville Public
    Schools

Jill Haley
Math Teacher
Woodstock Middle School
Shelby County Schools

Janice Mosley
H.G. Hill Middle School
Nashville, TN

Vicki P. Petty
Oakland Middle School
Murfreesboro, TN

Janai Shelton
John F. Kennedy Middle School
Antioch, TN

Jaci E. Stewart
Williamson County Schools
Franklin, TN

FIELD TEST PARTICIPANTS

Wendy Black
Southmont Jr. High
Crawfordsville, IN

Barbara Broeckelman
Oakley Middle School
Oakley, KS

Cindy Bush
Riverside Middle School
Greer, SC

Cadian Collman
Cutler Ridge Middle School
Miami, FL

Dora Corcini
Eisenhower Middle School
Oregon, OH

Deborah Drinkwalter
Sedgefield Middle School
Goose Creek, SC

Susan Gomez
Glades Middle School
Miami, FL

LaChandra Hogan
Apollo Middle School
Hollywood, FL

Ty Inlow
Oakley Middle School
Oakley, KS

Leighton Jenkins
Glades Middle School
Miami, FL

Heather King
Clever Middle School
Clever, MO

Dianne Marrett
Pines Middle School
Pembroke Pines, FL

Angela J. McNeal
Audubon Middle School
Los Angeles, CA

Wendy Misner
Lakeland Middle School
LaGrange, IN

Vanessa Nance
Pines Middle School
Pembroke Pines, FL

Teresa Patterson
Damonte Ranch High School
Reno, NV

Traci Peters
Cario Middle School
Mount Pleasant, SC

Ashley Piatt
East Forsyth Middle School
Kernersville, NC

Jeannine Quigley
Wilbur Wright Middle School
Dayton, OH

Shioban Smith-Haye
Apollo Middle School
Hollywood, FL

Jill Snipes
Bunn Middle School
Bunn, NC

Cathy Spencer
Oakridge Junior High
Oakridge, OR

Connie Vaught
K.D. Waldo School
Aurora, IL

Shelley Weeks
Lewis Middle School
Valparaiso, FL

Jennie Woo
Gaithersburg Middle School
Gaitersburg, MD

Reggie Wright
West Hopkins School
Nebo, KY

PROGRAM REVIEWERS

TENNESSEE MATHEMATICS COURSE 2
Student Edition

Contents in Brief

Algebraic Reasoning

Learn It Online
Online Resources go.hrw.com,
keyword MS10 TOC Go

Tools for Success

Reading Math 5, 10, 42

Writing Math 9, 13, 15, 17, 22, 27, 33, 37, 41, 45, 51, 55

Vocabulary 6, 10, 14, 19, 24, 30, 38, 42, 48, 52

Know-It Notebook Chapter 1

Homework Help Online 8, 12, 16, 21, 26, 32, 36, 40, 44, 50, 54

Student Help 7, 14, 20, 24, 25, 38, 39

Countdown to TCAP Weeks 1, 2, 3

Test Prep and Spiral Review 9, 13, 17, 22, 27, 33, 37, 41, 45, 51, 55

Test Tackler 64

TCAP Test Prep 66

Integers and Rational Numbers

Learn It Online
Online Resources **go.hrw.com**,
keyword **MS10 TOC** **Go**

Tools for Success

 **Reading and Writing Math**

 **Study Skills**

 Test Prep

Reading Math 73, 123

Writing Math 71, 75, 77, 83, 95, 101, 104, 107, 111, 115, 121, 125, 129

Vocabulary 72, 104, 108, 112, 118, 122, 126

Know-It Notebook Chapter 2

Homework Help Online 74, 82, 88, 94, 106, 110, 114, 120, 124, 128

Student Help 72, 73, 76, 81, 86, 92, 100, 104, 119, 122, 126, 127

Countdown to TCAP Weeks 3, 4, 5, 6

Test Prep and Spiral Review 75, 83, 89, 95, 101, 107, 111, 115, 121, 125, 129

TCAP Test Prep 138

CHAPTER 3

Applying Rational Numbers

Learn It Online
Online Resources **go.hrw.com,**
keyword **MS10 TOC** Go

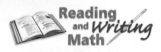

Writing Math 147, 151, 157, 163, 167, 173, 179, 183, 189, 192, 197
Vocabulary 144, 190

Study Skills

Know-It Notebook Chapter 3
Study Strategy 143
Homework Help Online 146, 150, 156, 162, 166, 172, 178, 182, 188, 192, 196
Student Help 144, 145, 149, 155, 160, 161, 164, 166, 167, 171, 176, 180, 181, 186, 194, 195, 205

Countdown to TCAP Weeks 6, 7, 8
Test Prep and Spiral Review 147, 151, 157, 163, 167, 173, 179, 183, 189, 193, 197
Test Tackler 206
TCAP Test Prep 208

Proportional Relationships

Learn It Online
Online Resources **go.hrw.com**,
keyword **MS10 TOC** Go

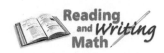

Reading Math 222, 237, 248

Writing Math 213, 221, 225, 229, 235, 239, 243, 248, 251, 255, 258

Vocabulary 214, 218, 222, 226, 240, 248, 252, 256

Know-It Notebook Chapter 4

Homework Help Online 216, 220, 224, 228, 234, 238, 242, 250, 254, 258

Student Help 215, 232, 236, 240, 249, 256

Countdown to TCAP Weeks 9, 10, 11

Test Prep and Spiral Review 217, 221, 225, 229, 235, 239, 243, 251, 255, 259

TCAP Test Prep 270

Graphs and Functions

Learn It Online
Online Resources **go.hrw.com**,
keyword MS10 TOC Go

Tools for Success

Reading Math 313, 318
Writing Math 275, 279, 283, 287, 299, 306, 312, 317
Vocabulary 276, 284, 288, 296, 300, 302, 308, 313, 318

Know-It Notebook Chapter 5
Homework Help Online 278, 282, 286, 290, 298, 304, 310, 316
Student Help 285, 297, 300, 303, 309, 310, 314, 315

Countdown to TCAP Weeks 11, 12
Test Prep and Spiral Review 279, 283, 287, 291, 299, 306, 312, 317
Test Tackler 328
TCAP Test Prep 330

Percents

Learn It Online
Online Resources **go.hrw.com**,
keyword **MS10 TOC** Go

Tools for Success

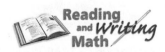

Reading Math 336, 359

Writing Math 338, 343, 347, 351, 355, 365

Vocabulary 336, 358, 362

Know-It Notebook Chapter 6

Study Strategy 335

Homework Help Online 337, 342, 346, 350, 354, 360, 364

Student Help 340, 344, 348, 353, 358

Countdown to TCAP Weeks 13, 14

Test Prep and Spiral Review 338, 343, 347, 351, 355, 361, 365

TCAP Test Prep 374

CHAPTER

7

Collecting, Displaying, and Analyzing Data

Learn It Online
Online Resources **go.hrw.com**,
keyword **MS10 TOC** **Go**

Tools for Success

Reading Math 379
Writing Math 384, 389, 393, 397, 401, 409, 415, 421, 431
Vocabulary 380, 385, 390, 394, 398, 406, 418, 422

Know-It Notebook Chapter 7
Homework Help Online 382, 388, 392, 396, 400, 408, 414, 420, 424, 430
Student Help 380, 381, 385, 387, 398, 406, 418, 419

Countdown to TCAP Weeks 14, 15, 16, 17
Test Prep and Spiral Review 384, 389, 393, 397, 401, 409, 415, 421, 425, 431
Test Tackler 440
TCAP Test Prep 442

Geometric Figures

Learn It Online
Online Resources go.hrw.com,
keyword MS10 TOC Go

Tools for Success

Reading Math 449, 455, 460, 461, 468, 474, 497

Writing Math 447, 451, 454, 457, 463, 471, 481, 485, 489, 495, 500, 507

Vocabulary 448, 454, 460, 468, 474, 478, 482, 486, 492, 496, 502, 504

Know-It Notebook Chapter 8

Homework Help Online 450, 456, 462, 470, 476, 480, 484, 488, 494, 498, 506

Student Help 448, 455, 475, 493, 498, 502

Countdown to TCAP Weeks 17, 18, 19

Test Prep and Spiral Review 451, 457, 463, 471, 477, 481, 485, 489, 495, 500, 507

TCAP Test Prep 518

CHAPTER 9

Measurement: Two-Dimensional Figures

Learn It Online
Online Resources **go.hrw.com**,
keyword **MS10 TOC** Go

Tools for Success

Reading Math 523, 540, 541, 558, 561

Writing Math 527, 533, 537, 539, 543, 549, 553, 559, 569

Vocabulary 524, 530, 536, 558, 562, 566

Know-It Notebook Chapter 9

Homework Help Online 526, 532, 536, 538, 542, 548, 552, 560, 568

Student Help 524, 531, 546, 547, 551, 562

Countdown to TCAP Weeks 19, 20, 21

Test Prep and Spiral Review 527, 533, 537, 539, 543, 549, 561, 569

Test Tackler 578

TCAP Test Prep 580

Measurement: Three-Dimensional Figures

Learn It Online
Online Resources **go.hrw.com**,
keyword MS10 TOC Go

Tools for Success

Reading and Writing Math

Reading Math 596
Writing Math 599, 603, 611, 617
Vocabulary 588, 592, 596, 607, 614

Study Skills

Know-It Notebook Chapter 10
Study Strategy 585
Homework Help Online 590, 598, 602, 610, 616, 623
Student Help 588, 601, 620, 621

Test Prep

Countdown to TCAP Weeks 22, 23
Test Prep and Spiral Review 591, 599, 603, 611, 617, 624
TCAP Test Prep 634

CHAPTER 11

Probability

Tennessee Mathematics Standards

Learn It Online
Online Resources go.hrw.com,
keyword MS10 TOC Go

Tools for Success

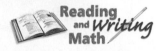

Reading Math 639, 645, 652, 666
Writing Math 641, 643, 644, 651, 655, 661, 669, 677
Vocabulary 640, 644, 648, 652, 658, 666, 670, 674

Know-It Notebook Chapter 11
Homework Help Online 642, 646, 650, 654, 660, 668, 672, 676
Student Help 653, 675

Countdown to TCAP Week 24
Test Prep and Spiral Review 643, 647, 651, 655, 661, 669, 673, 677
Test Tackler 686
TCAP Test Prep 688

Multi-Step Equations and Inequalities

Learn It Online
Online Resources **go.hrw.com**,
keyword **MS10 TOC** Go

Tools for Success

Reading Math 711

Writing Math 703, 707, 711, 712, 717, 721, 725

Vocabulary 710

Know-It Notebook Chapter 12

Study Strategy 693

Homework Help Online 698, 702, 706, 712, 716, 720, 724

Student Help 696, 700, 714, 715

Test Prep and Spiral Review 699, 703, 707, 713, 717, 721, 725

TCAP Test Prep 736

Unpacking *the* Standards

for Tennessee Grade Seven Mathematics

What are Tennessee Mathematics Standards?

The Tennessee Mathematics Standards are an intregral part of the Tennessee Mathematics Curriculum Framework. They outline what you should know and be able to do at each grade level. Your teacher uses the standards to design a course of instruction that will help you develop the skills and knowledge you need for success on standardized tests as well as in everyday life and the workplace.

How will I learn the Mathematics Standards?

Your textbook is closely aligned to the Tennessee Grade Seven Mathematics Standards. Every time you learn new information or practice a skill, you are mastering one of the mathematics standards.

Hernando Desoto Bridge

Thinkstock/Jupiterimages/Getty Images

Standard 1: Mathematical Processes

Themes

1. Mathematical Reasoning
2. Multiple Data Representations
3. Mathematical Symbols and Notation
4. Rounding and Estimation
5. Proportional Reasoning
6. Scale Factor
7. Patterns
8. Linear Functions

What it means to you

You can use mathematical reasoning to help you analyze patterns that represent real-world relationships. For example, you can write a relationship that can help you figure out the cost of renting a certain number of DVDs.

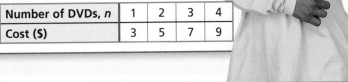

Number of DVDs, n	1	2	3	4
Cost ($)	3	5	7	9

Grade Level Expectations

GLE 0706.1.1 Use mathematical language, symbols, and definitions while developing mathematical reasoning.

GLE 0706.1.2 Apply and adapt a variety of appropriate strategies to problem solving, including estimation, and reasonableness of the solution.

GLE 0706.1.3 Develop independent reasoning to communicate mathematical ideas and derive algorithms and/or formulas.

GLE 0706.1.4 Move flexibly between concrete and abstract representations of mathematical ideas in order to solve problems, model mathematical ideas, and communicate solution strategies.

GLE 0706.1.5 Use mathematical ideas and processes in different settings to formulate patterns, analyze graphs, set up and solve problems and interpret solutions.

GLE 0706.1.6 Read and interpret the language of mathematics and use written/oral communication to express mathematical ideas precisely.

GLE 0706.1.7 Recognize the historical development of mathematics, mathematics in context, and the connections between mathematics and the real world.

GLE 0706.1.8 Use technologies/manipulatives appropriately to develop understanding of mathematical algorithms, to facilitate problem solving, and to create accurate and reliable models of mathematical concepts.

Checks for Understanding (Formative/Summative Assessment)

✓ **0706.1.1** Recognize common abbreviations (such as gcd/gcf and lcm).

✓ **0706.1.2** Recognize round-off error and the inaccuracies it introduces.

✓ **0706.1.3** Check answers both by estimation and by appropriate independent calculations, using calculators or computers judiciously.

✓ **0706.1.4** Recognize quantities that are inversely proportional (such as the relationship between the lengths of the base and the side of a rectangle with fixed area).

✓ **0706.1.5** Understand that a linear function in which $f(0) = 0$ is called a directly proportional relationship.

✓ **0706.1.6** Develop meaning of intercept and rate of change in contextual problems.

✓ **0706.1.7** Explain and demonstrate how scale in maps and drawings shows relative size and distance.

✓ **0706.1.8** Recognize the applications of scale factor by exploring blueprints, shadow measuring, and scale models.

✓ **0706.1.9** Use age-appropriate books, stories, and videos to convey ideas of mathematics.

✓ **0706.1.10** Model algebraic equations with manipulatives, technology, and pencil and paper.

✓ **0706.1.11** Translate from calculator notation to scientific/standard notation.

✓ **0706.1.12** Use dynamic geometry software to explore scale factor and similarity.

State Performance Indicators

SPI 0706.1.1 Use proportional reasoning to solve mixture/concentration problems.

SPI 0706.1.2 Generalize a variety of patterns to a symbolic rule from tables, graphs, or words.

SPI 0706.1.3 Recognize whether information given in a table, graph, or formula suggests a directly proportional, linear, inversely proportional, or other nonlinear relationship.

SPI 0706.1.4 Use scales to read maps.

Standard 2: Number & Operations

Themes

1. Properties of Rational Numbers
2. Operations with Rational Numbers
3. Operations with Integers
4. Square Roots and Cube Roots
5. Negative Exponents
6. Scientific Notation
7. Using Number Lines
8. Ratios, Rates, Proportions, and Percents

What it means to you

Expanding your knowledge of numbers to include rational numbers will help further your understanding of everyday occurrences that consist of numbers less than zero, fractions, decimals, and percents. For example, you can figure out how much money you will earn if you baby sit for 7 hours.

Number of Hours	2	3	5	7
Money earned	11	16.50	27.50	?

Grade Level Expectations

GLE 0706.2.1 Extend understandings of addition, subtraction, multiplication and division to integers.

GLE 0706.2.2 Understand and work with the properties of and operations on the system of rational numbers.

GLE 0706.2.3 Develop an understanding of and apply proportionality.

GLE 0706.2.4 Use ratios, rates and percents to solve single- and multi-step problems in various contexts.

GLE 0706.2.5 Understand and work with squares, cubes, square roots and cube roots.

GLE 0706.2.6 Introduce the concept of negative exponents.

GLE 0706.2.7 Understand and use scientific notation.

Checks for Understanding (Formative/Summative Assessment)

✓ **0706.2.1** Understand that the set of rational numbers includes any number that can be written as a ratio of two integers in which the denominator is not zero.

✓ **0706.2.2** Develop and analyze algorithms and compute efficiently with integers and rational numbers.

✓ **0706.2.3** Recognize that rational numbers satisfy the commutative and associative laws of addition and multiplication and the distributive law.

✓ **0706.2.4** Understand that a and −a are additive inverses and are located the same distance from zero on the number line; relate distance from zero to absolute value.

✓ **0706.2.5** Understand that $-(-a) = a$ for any number a.

✓ **0706.2.6** Use the number line to demonstrate addition and subtraction with integers.

✓ **0706.2.7** Write number sentences to solve contextual problems involving ratio and percent.

✓ **0706.2.8** Apply ratios, rates, proportions and percents (such as discounts, interest, taxes, tips, distance/rate/time, and percent increase or decrease).

✓ **0706.2.9** Efficiently compare and order rational numbers and roots of perfect squares/cubes; determine their approximate locations on a number line.

✓ **0706.2.10** Recognize that when a whole number is not a perfect square, then its square root is not rational and cannot be written as the ratio of two integers.

✓ **0706.2.11** Estimate square/cube roots and use calculators to find approximations.

✓ **0706.2.12** Recognize $\sqrt{mn} = \sqrt{m} \cdot \sqrt{n}$ and $(\sqrt{m})^2 = m$.

✓ **0706.2.13** Use the meaning of negative exponents to represent small numbers; translate between scientific and standard notation.

✓ **0706.2.14** Express numbers in scientific notation and recognize its importance in representing the magnitude of a number.

✓ **0706.2.15** Report results of calculations appropriately in a given context (i.e. using rules of rounding, degree of accuracy, and/or significant digits).

State Performance Indicators

SPI 0706.2.1 Simplify numerical expressions involving rational numbers.

SPI 0706.2.2 Compare rational numbers using appropriate inequality symbols.

SPI 0706.2.3 Use rational numbers and roots of perfect squares/cubes to solve contextual problems.

SPI 0706.2.4 Determine the approximate location of square/cube roots on a number line.

SPI 0706.2.5 Solve contextual problems that involve operations with integers.

SPI 0706.2.6 Express the ratio between two quantities as a percent, and a percent as a ratio or fraction.

SPI 0706.2.7 Use ratios and proportions to solve problems.

Standard 3: Algebra

Themes

1. Algebraic Expressions
2. Relations and Functions
3. Slope
4. Proportional Relationships
5. Linear Equations
6. Linear Inequalities

What it means to you

You can use linear equations and functions to analyze a variety of real-world situations. For example, you can graph the number of grams of protein in different numbers of cups of cooked rice to help figure out how your diet compares to the daily recommended values of protein.

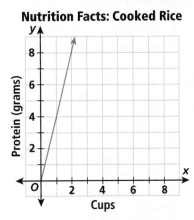

Nutrition Facts: Cooked Rice

Grade Level Expectations

GLE 0706.3.1 Recognize and generate equivalent forms for simple algebraic expressions.

GLE 0706.3.2 Understand and compare various representations of relations and functions.

GLE 0706.3.3 Understand the concept of function as a rule that assigns to a given input one and only one number (the output).

GLE 0706.3.4 Use function notation where $f(x)$ represents the output that the function f assigns to the input x.

GLE 0706.3.5 Understand and graph proportional relationships.

GLE 0706.3.6 Conceptualize the meanings of slope using various interpretations, representations, and contexts.

GLE 0706.3.7 Use mathematical models involving linear equations to analyze real-world phenomena.

GLE 0706.3.8 Use a variety of strategies to efficiently solve linear equations and inequalities.

Checks for Understanding (Formative/ Summative Assessment)

✓ **0706.3.1** Perform basic operations on linear expressions (including grouping, order of operations, exponents, simplifying and expanding).

✓ **0706.3.2** Represent and analyze mathematical situations using algebraic symbols.

✓ **0706.3.3** Identify a function from a written description, table, graph, rule, set of ordered pairs, and/or mapping.

✓ **0706.3.4** Make tables of inputs x and outputs $f(x)$ for a variety of rules that include rational numbers (including negative numbers) as inputs.

✓ **0706.3.5** Plot points to represent tables of linear function values.

✓ **0706.3.6** Understand that the graph of a linear function f is the set of points on a line representing the ordered pairs $(x, f(x))$.

✓ **0706.3.7** Distinguish proportional relationships ($y/x = k$, or $y = kx$) from other relationships, including inverse proportionality ($xy = k$, or $y = k/x$).

✓ **0706.3.8** Understand slope as the ratio of vertical change to horizontal change.

✓ **0706.3.9** Identify a function exhibiting a constant rate of change as a linear function and identify the slope as a unit rate.

✓ **0706.3.10** Solve problems involving unit rates (e.g., miles per hour, words per minute).

✓ **0706.3.11** Relate the features of a linear equation to a table and/or graph of the equation.

✓ **0706.3.12** Use linear equations to solve problems and interpret the meaning of slope, m, and the y-intercept, b, in $f(x) = mx + b$ in terms of the context.

✓ **0706.3.13** Given a graph that exhibits the intersection of a line and the y-axis, write a linear function in slope-intercept form: $y = mx + b$.

✓ **0706.3.14** Understand that when solving linear inequalities, multiplication or division by a negative reverses the inequality symbol.

State Performance Indicators

SPI 0706.3.1 Evaluate algebraic expressions involving rational values for coefficients and/or variables.

SPI 0706.3.2 Determine whether a relation (represented in various ways) is a function.

SPI 0706.3.3 Given a table of inputs x and outputs $f(x)$, identify the function rule and continue the pattern.

SPI 0706.3.4 Interpret the slope of a line as a unit rate given the graph of a proportional relationship.

SPI 0706.3.5 Represent proportional relationships with equations, tables and graphs.

SPI 0706.3.6 Solve linear equations with rational coefficients symbolically or graphically.

SPI 0706.3.7 Translate between verbal and symbolic representations of real-world phenomena involving linear equations.

SPI 0706.3.8 Solve contextual problems involving two-step linear equations.

SPI 0706.3.9 Solve linear inequalities in one variable with rational coefficients symbolically or graphically.

Standard 4: Geometry & Measurement

Themes

1. Similar Triangles
2. Scale Factor
3. Proportional Reasoning
4. Indirect Measurement
5. Area and Volume

What it means to you

You can use geometry skills to explore the properties, measurements, and relationships among figures. For example, you can use indirect measurement to find the height of a tree by comparing its shadow with the height and shadow of a known object.

16 ft   4 ft   2 ft

Grade Level Expectations

GLE 0706.4.1 Understand the application of proportionality with similar triangles.

GLE 0706.4.2 Apply proportionality to converting among different units of measurements to solve problems involving rates such as motion at a constant speed.

GLE 0706.4.3 Understand and use scale factor to describe the relationships between length, area, and volume.

GLE 0706.4.4 Understand and use ratios, derived quantities, and indirect measurements.

Checks for Understanding (Formative/ Summative Assessment)

✓ **0706.4.1** Solve problems involving indirect measurement such as finding the height of a building by comparing its shadow with the height and shadow of a known object.

✓ **0706.4.2** Use similar triangles and proportionality to find the lengths of unknown line segments in a triangle.

✓ **0706.4.3** Understand that if a scale factor describes how corresponding lengths in two similar objects are related, then the square of the scale factor describes how corresponding areas are related, and the cube of the scale factor describes how corresponding volumes are related.

✓ **0706.4.4** Compare angles, side lengths, perimeters and areas of similar shapes.

✓ **0706.4.5** Solve problems using ratio quantities: velocity (measured in units such as miles per hour), density (measured in units such as kilograms per liter), pressure (measured in units such as pounds per square foot), and population density (measured in units such as persons per square mile).

State Performance Indicators

SPI 0706.4.1 Solve contextual problems involving similar triangles.

SPI 0706.4.2 Use SSS, SAS, and AA to determine if two triangles are similar.

SPI 0706.4.3 Apply scale factor to solve problems involving area and volume.

Standard 5: Data Analysis, Statistics, & Probability

Themes

1. Data Representations

2. Measures of Center and Spread

3. Probability

What it means to you

Collecting, analyzing, and presenting data is an important part of mathematics and the real-world. Probability is often used in real-life to make predictions for the future. For example, if you spin the spinner 40 times, you can use probability to predict how many times the spinner will land on B.

Grade Level Expectations

GLE 0706.5.1 Collect, organize, and analyze both single- and two-variable data.

GLE 0706.5.2 Select, create, and use appropriate graphical representations of data.

GLE 0706.5.3 Formulate questions and design studies to collect data about a characteristic shared by two populations, or different characteristics within one population.

GLE 0706.5.4 Use descriptive statistics to summarize and compare data.

GLE 0706.5.5 Understand and apply basic concepts of probability.

Checks for Understanding (Formative/Summative Assessment)

✓ **0706.5.1** Create and interpret box-and-whisker plots and stem-and-leaf plots.

✓ **0706.5.2** Interpret and solve problems using information presented in various visual forms.

✓ **0706.5.3** Predict and compare the characteristics of two populations based on the analysis of sample data.

✓ **0706.5.4** Use proportional reasoning to make predictions about results of experiments and simulations.

✓ **0706.5.5** Evaluate the design of an experiment.

✓ **0706.5.6** Apply percentages to make and interpret histograms and circle graphs.

✓ **0706.5.7** Use a tree diagram or organized list to determine all possible outcomes of a simple probability experiment.

State Performance Indicators

SPI 0706.5.1 Interpret and employ various graphs and charts to represent data.

SPI 0706.5.2 Select suitable graph types (such as bar graphs, histograms, line graphs, circle graphs, box-and-whisker plots, and stem-and-leaf plots) and use them to create accurate representations of given data.

SPI 0706.5.3 Calculate and interpret the mean, median, upper-quartile, lower-quartile, and interquartile range of a set of data.

SPI 0706.5.4 Use theoretical probability to make predictions.

Holt McDougal Mathematics provides many opportunities for you to prepare for the Tennessee Comprehensive Assessment Program (TCAP) Achievement Test.

Countdown to TCAP

Use the Countdown to TCAP to practice for your test every day.

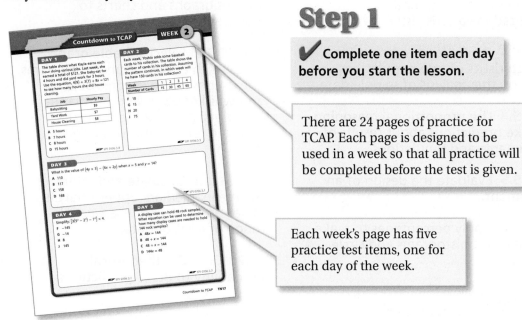

Step 1

✔ **Complete one item each day before you start the lesson.**

There are 24 pages of practice for TCAP. Each page is designed to be used in a week so that all practice will be completed before the test is given.

Each week's page has five practice test items, one for each day of the week.

Step 2

✔ **Preview the standards before you start the lesson.**

TN Tennessee Mathematics Standards

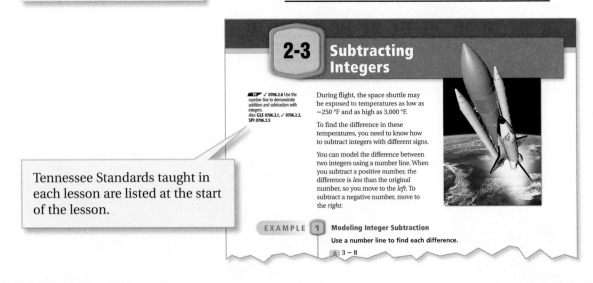

Tennessee Standards taught in each lesson are listed at the start of the lesson.

2-3 Subtracting Integers

TN ✓ 0706.2.6 Use the number line to demonstrate addition and subtraction with integers. *Also* GLE 0706.2.1, ✓ 0706.2.2, SPI 0706.2.5

During flight, the space shuttle may be exposed to temperatures as low as −250 °F and as high as 3,000 °F.

To find the difference in these temperatures, you need to know how to subtract integers with different signs.

You can model the difference between two integers using a number line. When you subtract a positive number, the difference is *less* than the original number, so you move to the *left*. To subtract a negative number, move to the *right*.

EXAMPLE 1 Modeling Integer Subtraction

Use a number line to find each difference.

A 3 − 8

Test Prep and Spiral Review

Use the Test Prep and Spiral Review for constant review of standards taught in the current and previous lessons.

Step 3

✔ Keep your skills fresh by practicing the standards daily.

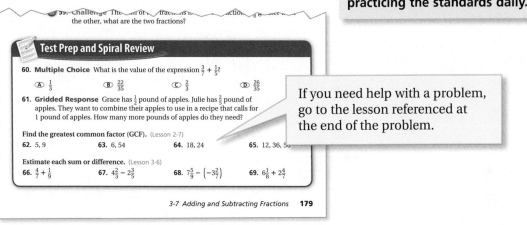

59. Challenge The ~~sum of two~~ fractions is ~~a fraction greater than~~ the other, what are the two fractions?

Test Prep and Spiral Review

60. Multiple Choice What is the value of the expression $\frac{3}{7} + \frac{1}{5}$?

Ⓐ $\frac{1}{3}$ Ⓑ $\frac{22}{35}$ Ⓒ $\frac{2}{3}$ Ⓓ $\frac{26}{35}$

61. Gridded Response Grace has $\frac{1}{2}$ pound of apples. Julie has $\frac{2}{5}$ pound of apples. They want to combine their apples to use in a recipe that calls for 1 pound of apples. How many more pounds of apples do they need?

Find the greatest common factor (GCF). (Lesson 2-7)

62. 5, 9 **63.** 6, 54 **64.** 18, 24 **65.** 12, 36, 5~~0~~

Estimate each sum or difference. (Lesson 3-6)

66. $\frac{4}{7} + \frac{1}{9}$ **67.** $4\frac{2}{3} - 2\frac{3}{5}$ **68.** $7\frac{5}{9} - \left(-3\frac{2}{7}\right)$ **69.** $6\frac{1}{8} + 2\frac{4}{7}$

3-7 Adding and Subtracting Fractions **179**

If you need help with a problem, go to the lesson referenced at the end of the problem.

TCAP Test Prep

Use the TCAP Test Prep for review of standards taught in the current and previous chapters.

Step 4

✔ After finishing each chapter, review your knowledge of the standards.

CHAPTER 5
TCAP Test Prep

Learn It Online State Test Practice go.hrw.com. Keyword: MS10 TestPrep

Cumulative Assessment, Chapters 1–5
Multiple Choice

1. Which inequality is not true?

   A $\frac{4}{9} < \frac{1}{2}$ C $\frac{11}{12} > \frac{1}{3}$

   B $\frac{11}{24} < \frac{3}{4}$ D $\frac{2}{3} > \frac{5}{6}$

2. Brandi is writing a paper for class. Which expression represents the number of pages she will write on the nth day?

Day	Pages Written
1	1.25
2	3.25
3	5.25
4	7.25
n	

   F $n + 1.25$
   G $n - 1.25$
   H $2n + 0.75$
   J $2n - 0.75$

3. A triangular garden has side lengths of 3 yards and 5 yards. The included angle is 60°. Tell which set of measurements could be the corresponding parts of a similar triangular garden.

   A side lengths of 1.5 yards and 2.5 yards; included angle is 30°

   B side lengths of 1.5 yards and 2.5 yards; included angle is 60°

   C side lengths of 6 yards and 11 yards; included angle is 30°

   D side lengths of 6 yards and 11 yards; included angle is 60°

4. On a map the distance between Aceville and Beetown is 4.7 inches. The map scale is 1 in:15 mi. How should the proportions be set up to find the actual distance between Aceville and Beetown?

   F $\frac{1 \text{ in.}}{4.7 \text{ in.}} = \frac{x \text{ mi}}{15 \text{ mi}}$

   G $\frac{1 \text{ in.}}{x \text{ mi}} = \frac{4.7 \text{ in.}}{15 \text{ mi}}$

   H $\frac{1 \text{ in.}}{15 \text{ mi}} = \frac{4.7 \text{ in.}}{x \text{ mi}}$

   J $\frac{4.7 \text{ in.}}{1 \text{ in.}} = \frac{15 \text{ mi}}{x \text{ mi}}$

5. A recipe that makes 2 cups of guacamole dip calls for $1\frac{1}{3}$ cups of mashed avocados. How much avocado is needed to make 4 cups of dip with this recipe?

   A 3.25 cups C 3.75 cups
   B 3.5 cups D 4 cups

6. Which ordered pair is not a solution of $y = 5x - 4$?

   F (2, 6) H (1, 0)
   G (0, −4) J (−1, −9)

7. Write an equation in function notation for the given situation.

   An apple orchard charges a $2 admission fee and $3 per basket of apples picked.

   A $f(x) = 2x + 3$
   B $f(x) = 2x + x$
   C $f(x) = 3x + 3$
   D $f(x) = 3x + 2$

...can be used ...om degrees ...Celsius (C). ...is equivalent

...°C

...°C

...next 28 ...nt-lifting ...pend a total ...Patrick is at ...unt of time ...ns will he be

...5

...3

...the point on

Process Standards Practice
Short Response

51. A teacher discussed 112 of the 164 pages of the textbook. What portion of the pages did the teacher discuss? Write your answer as a decimal rounded to the nearest thousandth and as a fraction in simplest form.

52. A bag of nickels and quarters contains four times as many nickels as quarters. The total value of the coins in the bag is $1.35.

    a. How many nickels are in the bag?

    b. How many quarters are in the bag?

53. Describe in what order you would perform the operations to find the value of $(4 \cdot 4 - 6)^2 + (5 \cdot 7)$.

54. A recipe calls for $\frac{2}{3}$ cup flour and $\frac{3}{4}$ cup butter. Does the recipe require more flour or butter? Is this still true if the recipe is doubled? Explain how you determined your answer.

Extended Response

E1. A bus travels at an average rate of 50 miles per hour from Nashville, Tennessee, to El Paso, Texas. To find the distance y traveled in x hours, use the equation $y = 50x$.

    a. Make a table of ordered pairs using the domain $x = 1, 2, 3, 4,$ and 5.

    b. Graph the solutions from the table of ordered pairs on a coordinate plane.

    c. Brett leaves Nashville by bus at 6:00 A.M. He needs to be in El Paso by 5:00 A.M. the following day. If Nashville is 1,100 miles from El Paso, will Brett make it on time? Explain how you determined your answer.

330 *Chapter 5 Graphs and Functions*

Cumulative Assessment, Chapters 1–5 **331**

These pages include practice with multiple choice items as seen on the TCAP Achievement Test. They also include short response and extended response items.

DAY 1

Simplify: $[2(4 - 7)^3] - 13$.

A -67

B -54

C 41

D 54

SPI 0706.2.1

DAY 2

Simplify: $17 + (3 \times 15) \div (-3) \times 2^2$.

F -43

G -13

H 13

J 43

SPI 0706.2.1

DAY 3

Which rule describes this pattern?

x	3	4	5	6	7
y	23	31	39	41	55

A $y = 8x - 1$

B $y = 6x + 2$

C $y = x^2$

D $y = 4x + 4$

SPI 0706.1.2

DAY 4

What is the value of the expression $\frac{2}{3} jk + 14$, when $j = 7$ and $k = 6$?

F 28

G 42

H 84

J 112

SPI 0706.3.1

DAY 5

What expression describes the nth term of the following sequence?

1, 3, 5, 7, ...

A $2n - 1$

B $2n + 1$

C $3n - 1$

D $5n - 2$

SPI 0706.1.2

DAY 1

The table shows what Kayla earns each hour doing various jobs. Last week, she earned a total of $121. She baby-sat for 4 hours and did yard work for 3 hours. Use the equation, $4(9) + 3(7) + 8x = 121$ to see how many hours she did house cleaning.

Job	Hourly Pay
Babysitting	$9
Yard Work	$7
House Cleaning	$8

A 5 hours

B 7 hours

C 8 hours

D 15 hours

TN SPI 0706.3.8

DAY 2

Each week, Yoshio adds some baseball cards to his collection. The table shows the number of cards in his collection. Assuming the pattern continues, in which week will he have 150 cards in his collection?

Week	1	2	3	4
Number of Cards	15	30	45	60

F 10

G 15

H 20

J 75

TN SPI 0706.3.3

DAY 3

What is the value of $(4y \times 3) - (6x + 2y)$ when $x = 5$ and $y = 14$?

A 110

B 117

C 158

D 168

TN SPI 0706.3.1

DAY 4

Simplify: $[3(5^2 - 2^3) - 7^2] \times 4$.

F -145

G -14

H 8

J 145

TN SPI 0706.2.1

DAY 5

A display case can hold 48 rock samples. What equation can be used to determine how many display cases are needed to hold 144 rock samples?

A $48x = 144$

B $48 + x = 144$

C $48 \div x = 144$

D $144x = 48$

TN SPI 0706.3.7

DAY 1

What is the value of $3t^2 \div 3^3$ when $t = 6$?

A 3

B 4

C 12

D 27

TN SPI 0706.3.1

DAY 2

A flat contains 30 eggs. A baker bought 18 flats of eggs. This is 7 more flats than he bought last week. Use the equation $30(18) = x + 7(30)$ to find how many eggs he bought last week.

F 210

G 330

H 540

J 750

TN SPI 0706.3.8

DAY 3

What is the value of $8a + (7b - c^3)$ when $a = 6$, $b = 3$, and $c = 2$?

A 35

B 41

C 61

D 65

TN SPI 0706.3.1

DAY 4

Sajeeh uses plastic chips to make the pattern shown here. What expression can he use to find the number of chips in row n?

Row 1 ●
Row 2 ●●●●
Row 3 ●●●●●●●●●

F n

G $n + 1$

H $2n$

J n^2

TN SPI 0706.1.2

DAY 5

Tamiko uses tiles to create the pattern shown here. How many tiles does she need to make Stage n of the pattern?

Stage 1   Stage 2   Stage 3

A $2n$ C n^2

B $n + 3$ D $4(n - 1)$

TN SPI 0706.1.2

DAY 1

On a winter day, the temperature at noon is −3 °F. The temperature drops 2 °F every hour. What is the temperature at 5 PM?

A −5 °F

B −8 °F

C −10 °F

D −13 °F

TN SPI 0706.2.5

DAY 2

An explorer descends to the deepest part of a cave. Then she ascends 25 feet per minute. After 3 minutes, she is at −195 feet. What is the depth of the cave?

F −100 feet

G −170 feet

H −220 feet

J −270 feet

TN SPI 0706.2.5

DAY 3

The table shows the ingredients for Mrs. Washington's vegetable soup. If she wants to keep the proportions the same, how many cups of water should she add if she uses 4 cans of whole tomatoes?

Ingredients	Amount
Potatoes	2 lb
Whole Tomatoes	3 cans
Water	5 cups
Mixed Vegetables	4 cans
Beef Bouillon	4 TB

A 3 cups

B 5 cups

C $6\frac{2}{3}$ cups

D $7\frac{1}{3}$ cups

TN SPI 0706.2.7

DAY 4

Bill's Plumbing charges $85 for a service call. The hourly rate is $42 per hour. Which equation represents the cost, c, of a service call the lasts h hours?

F $h = 85 + 42c$

G $c = 85 + 42h$

H $85 = 42h + c$

J $2c = 85h$

TN SPI 0706.3.7

DAY 5

A contestant on a game show started with 200 points. He answered 3 questions correctly for 50 points each. He answered 4 questions incorrectly and lost 100 points for each. What was his final score?

A −150   C 50

B −50   D 150

TN SPI 0706.2.5

Countdown to TCAP

WEEK 5

DAY 1

What is the value of the expression $4(7x + 5y)$, when $x = 9$ and $y = 7$?

A 98

B 292

C 392

D 398

TN SPI 0706.3.1

DAY 2

Simplify: $(11 \times 2^3) + (11 + 4^2) - 17^2$.

F -174

G -25

H 17

J 25

TN SPI 0706.2.1

DAY 3

Martha creates different shades of color when she paints. The table shows the ratios for 8 grams of pigment that she mixes with white to get a desired shade. If Martha wants to keep the proportions the same, how many grams of white should she add to 12 grams of red to get the desired shade?

A $4\frac{1}{2}$ g

B 5 g

C $5\frac{1}{2}$ g

D 7 g

Pigment (8 g)	White Added (g)
Blue	2
Green	5
Red	3
Yellow	4
Black	6

TN SPI 0706.1.1

DAY 4

Solve the equation for t: $5 + 4t = \frac{2t}{8}$.

F $t = -\frac{4}{3}$

G $t = -\frac{3}{4}$

H $t = \frac{3}{4}$

J $t = \frac{4}{3}$

TN SPI 0706.3.6

DAY 5

Which expression has the greatest value?

A $3^2 + 4 \times 5 - 3$

B $(3^2 + 4) \times 5 - 3$

C $3^2 + (4 \times 5) - 3$

D $3^2 + 4 \times (5 - 3)$

TN SPI 0706.2.1

DAY 1

Solve the equation for x: $\frac{1}{2}x - 23 = 12x$.

A $x = -3.8$

B $x = -2$

C $x = -1.84$

D $x = 1.5$

TN SPI 0706.3.6

DAY 2

The temperature inside a freezer is 29°F. The temperature decreases at the rate of 6°F per hour. What equation gives a linear function for the temperature y inside the freezer after x hours?

F $y = 29x - 6$

G $y = 6x - 29$

H $y = 6 - 29x$

J $y = 29 - 6x$

TN SPI 0706.3.7

DAY 3

Kilroy works at a coffee shop where he pumps mocha flavoring into coffee. The table below shows the number of pumps of mocha that he puts into different sizes of coffee.

Coffee	Number of Mocha Pumps
8 oz	2
12 oz	3
16 oz	4

To keep the same proportion, how many pumps of mocha should Kilroy put into an 18-oz travel coffee mug?

A 4.5   C 5.5

B 5   D 6

TN SPI 0706.1.1

DAY 4

Solve the equation for k: $3k - 2 = \frac{k}{7}$.

F $k = -1\frac{3}{7}$

G $k = -\frac{7}{10}$

H $k = \frac{7}{10}$

J $k = 1\frac{3}{7}$

TN SPI 0706.3.6

DAY 5

Solve $-27 \geq -3s$.

A $s \leq 9$

B $s \leq -9$

C $s \geq 9$

D $s \geq -9$

TN SPI 0706.3.9

DAY 1

Brad had $530.45 in his checking account. He wrote checks for $16.50 and $95.68. He also made a deposit of $19.13. What is the approximate final balance in his account?

A $400

B $440

C $480

D $500

SPI 0706.2.3

DAY 2

If it takes 5 buses to carry 225 passengers, how many passengers will 3 buses carry?

F 45

G 135

H 170

J 222

SPI 0706.2.7

DAY 3

Lauren drives 3.2 km farther than Cara, and Cara drives 4.9 km farther than Vance. If Lauren drives a total of 15.3 km, what equation can you use to find the distance d that Vance drives?

A $15.3 = d + 8.1$

B $15.3 = 3.2d$

C $3.2 = 4.9 + d + 15.3$

D $8.1 = 15.3 + d$

SPI 0706.3.7

DAY 4

To make different amounts of lemonade, Ms. Siekman uses different combinations of lemon juice and water as shown in the table below.

Water (c)	Lemon juice (oz)
3	4
7.5	10
12	16
$22\frac{1}{2}$	30

To keep the same concentration, how many ounces of lemon juice should Ms. Siekman add if she uses 15 cups of water?

F 12

G 15

H 18

J 20

SPI 0706.1.1

DAY 5

Which point represents the location of $\sqrt{36}$?

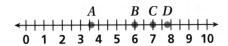

A A

B B

C C

D D

SPI 0706.2.4

DAY 1

The table shows the number of students in four different classes at Park Street Middle School who take the bus to school. Which inequality is true?

Class	A	B	C	D
Students Who Take Bus	$\frac{15}{20}$	$\frac{20}{25}$	$\frac{12}{18}$	$\frac{12}{24}$

A $\frac{20}{25} < \frac{12}{18}$

B $\frac{12}{18} < \frac{15}{20}$

C $\frac{15}{20} > \frac{20}{25}$

D $\frac{12}{24} > \frac{12}{18}$

TN SPI 0706.2.2

DAY 2

Which point represents the location of $\sqrt[3]{64}$?

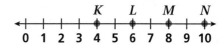

F K

G L

H M

J N

TN SPI 0706.2.4

DAY 3

A company that manufactures softballs packages each softball individually in a box that is in the shape of a cube. The volume of the box is 216 cubic inches. If the volume of a cube is found using the formula s^3, where s is the side length, what is the side length of the box?

A 4 inches

B 5 inches

C 6 inches

D 7 inches

TN SPI 0706.2.3

DAY 4

Margie weaved a square rug. The area is shown below. What is the perimeter of the rug?

2,025 cm²

F 45 cm   H 180 cm

G 90 cm   J 506 cm

TN SPI 0706.2.3

DAY 5

Which relation is a not function?

A $(-2, 5), (-1, 2), (0, 6), (2, -4)$

B $(-2, 5), (-1, 7), (-1, -8), (3, 4)$

C $(-2, 1), (-1, 1), (0, 1), (1, 1)$

D $(-2, -2), (-1, 5), (0, 7), (1, 7)$

TN SPI 0706.3.2

DAY 1

Which symbol makes the statement true?

$-\dfrac{5}{8}$ ▮ -0.6

A $>$

B $<$

C $\geq$

D $=$

SPI 0706.2.2

DAY 2

The volume of a room that is in the shape of a rectangular prism is 2400 cubic feet. What is the volume of a similar room that is larger by a scale factor of 2?

F 1200 cubic feet

G 4800 cubic feet

H 9600 cubic feet

J 19,200 cubic feet

SPI 0706.4.3

DAY 3

Alicia volunteers at an animal shelter where a new litter of kittens was born. The weight of each kitten is shown below.

Which number sentence is not true?

A $\dfrac{7}{8} > \dfrac{1}{2}$

B $\dfrac{11}{12} < \dfrac{7}{8}$

C $\dfrac{4}{6} > \dfrac{3}{5}$

D $\dfrac{1}{2} < \dfrac{3}{5}$

Kitten	Weight (lbs)
Brown	$\dfrac{7}{8}$
White	$\dfrac{4}{6}$
Spotted	$\dfrac{1}{2}$
Striped	$\dfrac{11}{12}$
Orange	$\dfrac{3}{5}$

SPI 0706.2.2

DAY 4

Alice mixes her own potting soil. The table below shows the amounts of each ingredient.

Ingredient	Amount (cups)
Sand	8 c
Peat	5 c
Pumice	4 c

To keep the same concentrations of each ingredient in the mix, how many cups of peat should Alice add if she uses 40 cups of sand?

F 22 c

G 23 c

H 24 c

J 25 c

SPI 0706.1.1

DAY 5

Sherri surveyed the ages of children who visited the doctor's office on Tuesday. Which stem-and-leaf plot correctly represents this data set?

12, 9, 8, 15, 10, 13, 12

A 0 | 8 9
   1 | 10 12 13 15

B 0 | 8 9
   1 | 0 2 2 3 5

C 0 | 8 9
   1 | 0 2 3 5

D 0 | 8 9 0
   1 | 2 2 3 5

SPI 0706.5.1

DAY 1

Which symbol makes the statement true?

-4.05 ⬛ -4.5

A $>$

B $<$

C $\geq$

D $=$

TN SPI 0706.2.2

DAY 2

Which description allows you to find the cost of renting n DVDs?

Number of DVDs, n	1	2	3	4
Cost ($)	3	5	7	9

F Multiply n by 3.

G Add 2 to n.

H Multiply n by 2, then add 1.

J Add 1 to n, then multiply by 2.

TN SPI 0706.1.2

DAY 3

The scale factor for a map is 1 cm:200 km. On the map, Boston is about 1.5 centimeters from New York. How far is Boston from New York?

A 150 kilometers

B 200 kilometers

C 300 kilometers

D 350 kilometers

TN SPI 0706.1.4

DAY 4

Which of the triangles are similar?

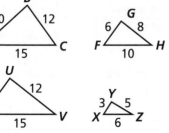

F △ABC and △FGH   **H** △TUV and △XYZ

G △FGH and △TUV   **J** △XYZ and △ABC

TN SPI 0706.4.1

DAY 5

Which point represents the location of $\sqrt[3]{27}$?

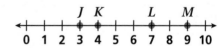

A J

B K

C L

D M

TN SPI 0706.2.4

DAY 1

Which proves the two triangles are similar?

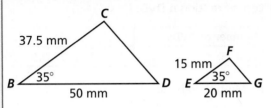

A SSS Similarity Theorem

B SAS Similarity Theorem

C AA Similarity Postulate

D ASA Similarity Postulate

TN SPI 0706.4.2

DAY 2

Solve $-4x \leq 64$.

F $x \geq -16$

G $x \geq 16$

H $x \leq -16$

J $x \leq 16$

TN SPI 0706.3.9

DAY 3

The Taipei 101 skyscraper has some of the world's fastest elevators. The table shows the distance the building's elevators can travel in various amount of time. How long does it take an elevators to travel 660 feet?

A 10 seconds   C 15 seconds

B 12 seconds   D 20 seconds

Taipei 101 Elevators	
Time (s)	Distance (ft)
3	165
5	275
8	440

TN SPI 0706.2.7

DAY 4

Angelo makes different amounts of play dough with flour and water. What is the missing value?

Flour (c)	$\frac{1}{2}$	1	?	4
Water (c)	$\frac{1}{4}$	$\frac{1}{2}$	$1\frac{1}{2}$	2

F $3\frac{1}{2}$

G 3

H $2\frac{1}{2}$

J 2

TN SPI 0706.3.5

DAY 5

Cameron baked 24 muffins for a party. The table below shows the number of muffins each guest will get in muffins are divided equally among the guests.

Number of Guests	2	3	4	6	8
Number of Muffins Per Guest	12	8	6	4	3

Which best describes this relationship?

A linear

B exponential

C inversely proportional

D directly proportional

TN SPI 0706.1.3

DAY 1

Mapledale and Concord are 70 kilometers apart. What will be the distance on a map with a scale of 0.5 cm: 20 km?

A $1\frac{1}{2}$ cm   C 2 cm

B $1\frac{3}{4}$ cm   D $2\frac{1}{2}$ cm

TN SPI 0706.1.4

DAY 2

Mikela practices piano 3 out of 5 days. What percent of the days does she practice?

F 35%   H 55%

G 50%   J 60%

TN SPI 0706.2.6

DAY 3

Omar enlarged a photograph, by a scale factor of $2\frac{1}{2}$. What is the area of the enlarged photograph?

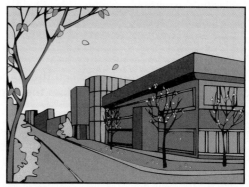

6.4 in.

4.4 in.

A 30.4 square inches   C 70.4 square inches

B 54.0 square inches   D 174 square inches

TN SPI 0706.4.3

DAY 4

Jamal is selling tickets for the school play. He makes a graph to represent the ticket prices.

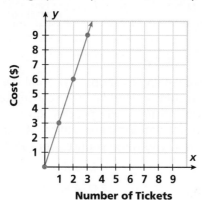

Number of Tickets

What is the unit rate per ticket?

F $2   H $5

G $3   J $6

TN SPI 0706.3.4

DAY 5

The shadow of a 4-foot-tall mailbox is 2 feet long. If the shadow of a tree is 16 feet long, what is the height of the tree?

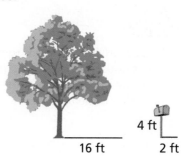

4 ft

16 ft   2 ft

A 18 feet   C 32 feet

B 24 feet   D 64 feet

TN SPI 0706.4.1

DAY 1

Which proves the two triangles are similar?

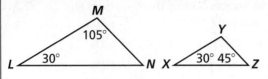

A SAS Similarity Theorem

B SSS Similarity Theorem

C ASA Similarity Postulate

D AA Similarity Postulate

TN SPI 0706.4.2

DAY 2

Waldorf and Summerville are 5 inches apart on a map. The scale of the map is 1 in:40 mi. Janelle drives from Waldorf to Summerville at an average speed of 50 miles per hour. How long does the trip take?

F 2 hours

G 4 hours

H 6 hours

J 8 hours

TN SPI 0706.1.4

DAY 3

The graph shows the relationship between the number of cups of rice cooked and the number of grams of protein. What does the slope of the line represent?

A the total number of cups of cooked rice

B the total number of grams of protein

C the number of cups of rice per gram of protein

D the number of grams of protein per cup of rice

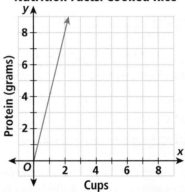

Nutrition Facts: Cooked Rice

TN SPI 0706.3.4

DAY 4

Ronnie plans on driving 110 miles to his grandmother's house. He looks on a map and measures the distance of 5 inches. What is the scale on the map?

F 1 in.: 11 mi

G 1 in.: 22 mi

H 1 in.: 55 mi

J 1 in.: 110 mi

TN SPI 0706.1.4

DAY 5

At a frozen yogurt shop, 50% of all the yogurts sold on Monday were chocolate yogurts and 10% were peach yogurts. If 20 peach yogurts were sold on Monday, how many chocolate yogurts were sold?

A 50   C 200

B 100   D 400

TN SPI 0706.2.7

DAY 1

Rodney cut two similar triangular pendants from a piece of fabric.

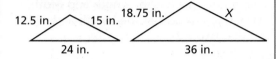

What is the length of x?

A 12 in.

B 15 in.

C 18.5 in.

D 22.5 in.

SPI 0706.4.1

DAY 2

The graph shows the distance that Terri walks over time.

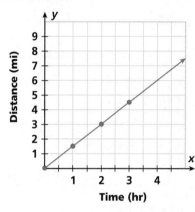

How fast does Terri travel?

F 1.5 mi/hr   **H** 2.5 mi/hr

G 2 mi/hr   **J** 3 mi/hr

SPI 0706.3.4

DAY 3

Which proves the two triangles are similar?

A SAS Similarity Theorem

B SSS Similarity Theorem

C AA Similarity Postulate

D The two triangles are not similar.

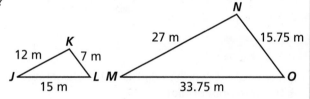

SPI 0706.4.2

DAY 4

April is standing next to a tree. The length of April's shadow is 4 feet, and the length of the tree's shadow is 32 feet. If April is 5 feet tall, how tall is the tree?

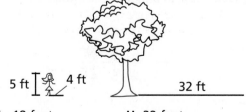

F 18 feet   **H** 32 feet

G 24 feet   **J** 40 feet

SPI 0706.4.1

DAY 5

A bike rental company charges an hourly rate to rent a bike. Tamika wrote the equation $y = 6.5x$ to represent the bike rental charges, with x as the number of hours a bike is rented. What does the 6.5 represent?

A the daily charge

B the total cost

C a one-time fee

D the hourly rate

SPI 0706.3.4

DAY 1

The graph shows the weight of Annie's kitten over time.

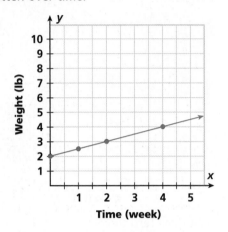

At what rate does the kitten gain weight?

A $\frac{1}{2}$ lb per week

C $1\frac{1}{2}$ lb per week

B 1 lb per week

D 2 lb per week

TN SPI 0706.3.4

DAY 2

Jim wants a rectangular garden with 200 square feet. The graph shows some of the options he has for length and width. Which best describes the length and width of the garden?

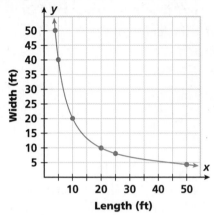

F directly proportional

G inversely proportional

H linear

J There is no relationship.

TN SPI 0706.1.3

DAY 3

Jenny wrote down the heights of her classmates in inches and put her data in a box-and-whisker plot.

What is the interquartile range of her data?

A 12 inches

C 42 inches

B 22 inches

D 52 inches

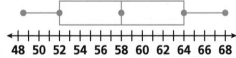

TN SPI 0706.5.3

DAY 4

Nina made a table showing the amount of money she earns for the time she baby sits.

Number of Hours	2	3	5	7
Money earned	11	16.50	27.50	?

If she baby sits for 7 hours, how much will she earn?

F $27.50

H $38.50

G $33.50

J $43.50

TN SPI 0706.3.5

DAY 5

Which is greatest for this set of data–the mean, median, mode, or range?

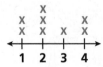

A mean

C mode

B median

D range

TN SPI 0706.5.3

DAY 1

Coco studies each day after school. She spends equal amounts of time studying science and language arts, and always works on math homework for 50 minutes. On Tuesday, Coco decides to do homework for 2 hours. Use the equation $50 + 2x = 120$. How much time does work on science?

A 30 minutes

B 35 minutes

C 70 minutes

D 75 minutes

SPI 0706.3.8

DAY 2

What kind of data is most likely represented by this plot?

Stems	Leaves
7	2 2 4 4 5 7
8	1 3 5 5 7 8 8 8 9
9	0 2

Key: 7|2 means 72

F cost of a movie ticket at local theaters

G average height (in.) of students in a class

H average daily temperatures at the beach

J ages of students in a 7th grade class

SPI 0706.5.1

DAY 3

The graph shows the number of species at the Paignton Zoo in England. Which category accounts for about 10% of the species?

A Invertebrates

B Fish

C Birds

D Mammals

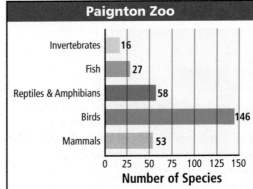

SPI 0706.5.1

DAY 4

Kenia receives a weekly allowance of $15. This week she has $8.25 left after buying lunches for $2.25. Use the equation, $15 = 8.25 + 2.25x$ to find how many times she bought lunch.

F 3

G 4

H 5

J 6

SPI 0706.3.8

DAY 5

According to a 2007 survey, 17% of people with an email account check their email just once per day. If 680 of the people surveyed said they checked their email just once per day, how many people were surveyed?

A 116   C 2400

B 796   D 4000

SPI 0706.2.7

DAY 1

Which point represents the location of $\sqrt{81}$?

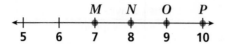

A M

B N

C O

D V

TN SPI 0706.2.4

DAY 2

Jackson works at a car rental office that charges a one-time fee of $40 plus $0.35 a mile to rent a car. He wrote the equation, $y = 0.35x + 40$, where x is the number of days a car is rented.

Which best describes the relationship in the equation?

F linear

G nonlinear

H inversely proportional

J directly proportional

TN SPI 0706.1.3

DAY 3

Which proves the two triangles are similar?

A The two triangles are not similar.

B SSS Similarity Theorem

C AA Similarity Postulate

D SAS Similarity Theorem

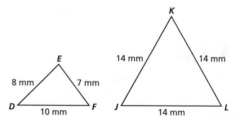

TN SPI 0706.4.2

DAY 4

Jason recorded the number of cardinals he saw each month during his nature hikes. What is the mean number of cardinals Jason saw? Round your answer to the nearest whole number.

Stems	Leaves
0	6 6 8 9
1	2 4 5 8 8 8 9
2	1

Key: 0|6 means 6

F 6

G 14

H 15

J 18

TN SPI 0706.5.3

DAY 5

The graph shows the number of words Lawrence types over a period of time.

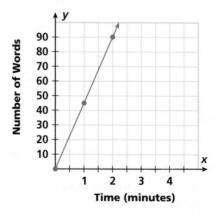

How many words does Lawrence type per minute?

A 30 words per min   C 40 words per min

B 35 words per min   D 45 words per min

TN SPI 0706.3.4

DAY 1

What inequality is graphed on the number line?

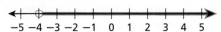

A $2x < -8$

B $2x \leq -8$

C $2x \geq -8$

D $2x > -8$

TN SPI 0706.3.9

DAY 2

Jacob made a graph to show how much water to use to dilute a cleaning solution.

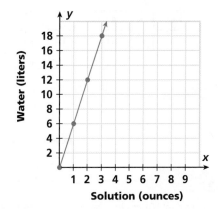

What is the rate of water per ounce of solution mixed by Jacob?

F 2 liters per ounce

G 3 liters per ounce

H 6 liters per ounce

J 12 liters per ounce

TN SPI 0706.3.4

DAY 3

Michelle's teacher drew two triangles on the board. How can Michelle prove $\triangle ABC$ is similar to $\triangle XYZ$?

A SAS Similarity Theorem

B SSS Similarity Theorem

C AA Similarity Postulate

D ASA Similarity Postulate

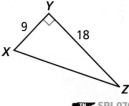

TN SPI 0706.4.2

DAY 4

Katrina volunteers for an organization that makes blankets for newborn babies. She is able to quilt 3 blankets every 14 days. Which equation can she use to see how many quilts she can make in 30 days?

F $\dfrac{3}{14} = \dfrac{30}{x}$ H $\dfrac{3}{x} = \dfrac{30}{14}$

G $\dfrac{3}{14} = \dfrac{x}{30}$ J $\dfrac{x}{14} = \dfrac{3}{30}$

TN SPI 0706.3.5

DAY 5

Marco bought bags of party favors for a birthday party. Each bag held 32 favors. Marco decided to give each of his 10 guests 12 favors. Use the equation, $12 = \dfrac{32x}{10}$ to find how many bags of favors, x, that Marco should buy. Round to the next whole number.

A 2   C 4

B 3   D 5

TN SPI 0706.3.8

DAY 1

What equation describes the relationship shown in the table?

x	5	6	7	8
y	8	10	12	14

A $y = x + 3$ **C** $y = -x + 13$

B $y = 3x - 7$ **D** $y = 2x - 2$

TN SPI 0706.3.3

DAY 2

Marietta works at a fruit market. In a display she puts 50% more oranges than apples. The ratio of apple to oranges is $x{:}y$. What is x when y is 3?

F 2

G 3

H 4

J 5

TN SPI 0706.2.6

DAY 3

Which of the following best describes the relationship shown in the graph?

A directly proportional

B inversely proportional

C linear

D nonlinear

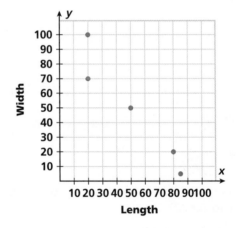

TN SPI 0706.1.3

DAY 4

The surface area of a rectangular prism is 729 square meters. What is the surface area of a similar prism that has edge lengths that are larger by a scale factor of 3?

F 243 square meters

G 1458 square meters

H 4374 square meters

J 6561 square meters

TN SPI 0706.4.3

DAY 5

The surface area of a tissue box is 160 square inches. What is the surface area of a similar box that has edge lengths that are smaller by a scale factor of $\frac{1}{4}$?

A 8 square inches

B 10 square inches

C 40 square inches

D 80 square inches

TN SPI 0706.4.3

DAY 1

Mr. Kurtman recorded the number of students absent each day for a month and then placed the information into the box-and-whisker plot below.

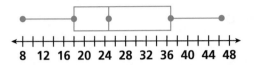

8 12 16 20 24 28 32 36 40 44 48

What is the lower Quartile, Q_1, of the data?

A 8 students

B 18 students

C 20 students

D 26 students

TN SPI 0706.5.3

DAY 2

A florist did a survey to see what type of flowers her customers prefer. The florist wants to share the results with the shop owner so she put the results in a circle graph. Of the 150 customers surveyed, 36 chose tulips. What percentage of the circle graph should the florist label tulips?

F 18%

G 20%

H 24%

J 36%

TN SPI 0706.5.2

DAY 3

Which point represents the location of $\sqrt[3]{125}$?

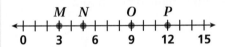

0   3   6   9   12   15

A *M*

B *N*

C *O*

D *P*

TN SPI 0706.2.4

DAY 4

A bakery makes 2 pans of brownies for every 12 cupcakes. What is this ratio written as a fraction?

F $\frac{1}{3}$

G $\frac{2}{3}$

H $\frac{1}{4}$

J $\frac{1}{6}$

TN SPI 0706.2.7

DAY 5

Four shovels of sand are mixed with 5 shovels of gravel to make cement. About how many shovels of gravel are needed for 45 shovels of sand?

A 20

B 55

C 45

D 75

TN SPI 0706.1.1

DAY 1

Which table does not represent a proportional relationship?

A
x	−7	−3	1	3	4
y	−14	−6	2	6	8

B
x	−2	1	3	4	5
y	−1	−0.5	1.5	2	10

C
x	0	1	3	5	7
y	1	2	4	6	8

D
x	−7	−3	0	1	12
y	−49	−21	0	7	84

SPI 0706.3.5

DAY 2

Which point represents the location of $\sqrt{9}$?

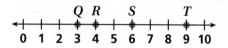

F   Q

G   R

H   S

J   T

SPI 0706.2.3

DAY 3

Tyler spins a spinner that has four equal sections. Three of the sections are blue and one of the sections is red. If Tyler spins the spinner 60 times, how many times should he expect the spinner to land on blue?

A   15

B   30

C   45

D   60

SPI 0706.5.4

DAY 4

Which relation is not a function?

F 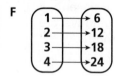   H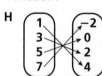

G 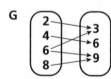   J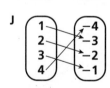

SPI 0706.3.2

DAY 5

Chang asked his classmates how many siblings they each have. He wants to put the results in a graph to share with the class. Which graph is the best choice?

A   A bar graph because it displays and compares categories.

B   A line graph because it shows the change over time.

C   A histogram because it displays and compares data in individual intervals.

D   A stem-and-leaf plot because it organizes and compares frequencies.

SPI 0706.5.2

DAY 1

According to the histogram below, how many students were surveyed?

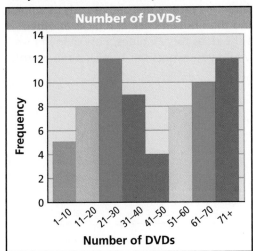

Number of DVDs

A 12

B 14

C 68

D 70

TN SPI 0706.5.1

DAY 2

Bruce and Jhang conduct a science experiment where they measure the temperature of a solution every minute as it boils. Their results show that the temperature of the solution decreases as the time increases. They decide to put their results in a data display. Which statement should they consider when choosing their graph?

F A stem-and-leaf plot would group the temperatures in intervals.

G A circle graph would show the percent of minutes the temperature was unchanged.

H A bar graph would show the type of solution and the maximum temperature it reached.

J A line graph would show the temperature changes over time.

TN SPI 0706.5.2

DAY 3

Sonia and Zachary are renting ice skates. The price of the rental for each of them is $5 plus $2 per hour. They rent skates for the same amount of time and together they spend a total of $26. Which equation can you solve to find the number of hours for which they rented the skates?

A $5x + 2 = 26$

B $2x + 5 = 26$

C $10x + 4 = 26$

D $4x + 10 = 26$

TN SPI 0706.3.7

DAY 4

Max is conducting an experiment where he will spin this spinner.

If he spins the spinner 40 times, how often would you expect the spinner to land on B?

F 3 times

G 8 times

H 15 times

J 18 times

TN SPI 0706.5.4

DAY 5

Which relation represents a function?

A {(−2, −7), (−1, −5), (0, −3), (0, −1)}

B {(−2, −1), (−1, 3), (0, −3), (−1, −1)}

C {(−2, 5), (−1, 2), (0, 1), (1, 2)}

D {(−2, 0), (−1, 1), (1, 2), (1, 5)}

TN SPI 0706.3.2

DAY 1

What is the rule for the pattern in the table below?

x	1	2	3	4
y	1	4	7	10

A $y = 2x + 2$

B $y = 3x - 2$

C $y = \frac{x}{2} \cdot 5$

D $y = 2x + 1$

SPI 0706.3.3

DAY 2

There is a bag with 8 black marbles, 8 red marbles, and 4 yellow marbles. Beatrice randomly picks a marble, records its color, and then puts it back and picks another. If she does this 25 times, how many times would you expect her to pick a red marble?

F   8

G   10

H   12

J   16

SPI 0706.5.4

DAY 3

Which number line shows the solution to $\frac{x}{7} \geq -7$?

A
```
←+——+——+——+——⊕——+——+——+——+——+——→
 -51  -50  -49  -48  -47  -46
```

B
```
←══════════════●——+——+——+——→
  46   47   48   49   50   51
```

C
```
←══════════════⊕——+——+——+——→
  46   47   48   49   50   51
```

D
```
←+——+——+——+——●——+——+——+——+——+——→
 -51  -50  -49  -48  -47  -46
```

SPI 0706.3.9

DAY 4

Which values for the domain will make this a function?

x					
y	-4	-1	0	2	7

F $\{-3, -2, 4, 5\}$

G $\{-3, 1, -3, 4, 5\}$

H $\{1, -2, 4, 5\}$

J $\{-3, 1, -2, 4, 5\}$

SPI 0706.3.2

DAY 5

Which point represents the location of $\sqrt[3]{512}$?

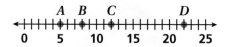

A   A

B   B

C   C

D   D

SPI 0706.2.3

DAY 1

Mackenzie rolls a number cube 50 times. How many times would you expect her to roll a number less than 4?

A 10

B 15

C 20

D 25

SPI 0706.5.4

DAY 2

Ivy's Fresh Eggs transports its eggs in crates. How many crates will 8 trucks carry?

Trucks	2	3	4	5
Crates	80	120	160	200

F 220

G 280

H 320

J 360

SPI 0706.3.3

DAY 3

Which expression best represents the value of y?

x	2	4	6	8	10
y	1	2	3	4	5

A $x - 1$

B $2x$

C $\dfrac{x}{2}$

D $x + 1$

SPI 0706.3.3

DAY 4

Mrs. Minato's math class took a test yesterday. Any student who scored below 76 will have to take a make-up test. How many students in the class will **not** have to take the make-up test?

Stems	Leaves
9	2 4 4 6
8	0 0 3 4 7 9
7	2 2 5 6
6	3 8

Key: 9|2 means 92

F 5   H 11

G 7   J 16

SPI 0706.5.1

DAY 5

Bob will spin this spinner 24 times.

How often would you expect the spinner to land on a triangle or star?

A 10 times

B 12 times

C 15 times

D 16 times

SPI 0706.5.4

ARE YOU READY?

Pre-Course Test

✓ Round Whole Numbers

Round each number to the nearest ten and nearest hundred.

1. 6,752

2. 31,817

✓ Order Whole Numbers

Order the numbers from least to greatest.

3. 35, 53, 49, 41, 11, 20

4. 60, 331, 600, 532, 218, 311

✓ Factors

List all the factors of each number.

5. 18

6. 125

✓ Number Patterns

Find the next three numbers in the pattern.

7. 85, 78, 71, 64, . . .

8. $-12, 24, -48, 96, . . .$

✓ Round Decimals

Round each number to the nearest whole number and nearest tenth.

9. 4.82

10. 26.19

✓ Simplify Fractions

Write each fraction in simplest form.

11. $\frac{4}{16}$

12. $\frac{6}{27}$

✓ Write an Improper Fraction as a Mixed Number

Write each improper fraction as a mixed number.

13. $\frac{17}{6}$

14. $\frac{27}{8}$

✓ Write Equivalent Fractions

Find two fractions that are equivalent to each fraction.

15. $\frac{5}{7}$

16. $\frac{14}{19}$

✓ Write Fractions as Decimals

Write each fraction as a decimal.

17. $\frac{28}{100}$

18. $\frac{9}{20}$

✓ Percents and Decimals

Write each decimal as a percent.

19. 0.7

20. 1.15

Write each percent as a decimal.

21. 20%

22. 8%

✓ Whole Number Operations

Add or subtract.

23. $58 + 39$

24. $217 - 81$

✓ Use Repeated Multiplication

Find each product.

25. $7 \times 7 \times 7 \times 7$

26. $20 \times 20 \times 20 \times 20$

Multiply Fractions

Multiply. Write each answer in simplest form.

27. $\frac{7}{9} \times \frac{3}{5}$

28. $\frac{25}{40} \times \frac{18}{100}$

Find the Percent of a Number

Solve.

29. What is 50% of 44?

30. What is 20% of 85?

31. What is 72% of 75?

Order of Operations

Simplify.

32. $7 + 6 \times 3 - 1$

33. $4^3 \div (21 - 19)$

34. $\frac{(9 - 3)^2}{4} \cdot 7$

Evaluate Expressions

Evaluate each expression.

35. $\frac{2g}{h} \cdot 3$ for $g = -16$ and $h = 24$

36. $5(a + b) + 21$ for $a = 15$ and $b = -27$

Inverse Operations

Solve.

37. $w + 28 = 41$

38. $x - 21 = 56$

39. $12y = 72$

40. $\frac{z}{52} = 4$

Solve Proportions

Solve each proportion.

41. $\frac{t}{4} = \frac{39}{52}$

42. $\frac{3}{q} = \frac{24}{56}$

Graph Ordered Pairs

Use the coordinate plane below. Write the ordered pair for each point.

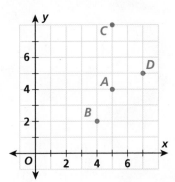

43. point A

44. point B

45. point C

46. point D

Areas of Squares, Rectangles, Triangles

Find the area of each figure.

47.

6.8 cm

12 cm

48.

5 ft

11 ft

Area of Circles

Find the area of each circle to the nearest tenth. Use 3.14 for π.

49.

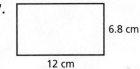

6.2 ft

50.

11 yd

Additional Topics

Simplifying Square Roots

TN ✓ 0706.2.12 Recognize $\sqrt{mn} = \sqrt{m} \cdot \sqrt{n}$ and $(\sqrt{m})^2 = m$.

Use with Lesson 9-7

An important property of square roots states that the square root of a product is equal to the product of the square roots of the factors. To see what this means, you can enter $\sqrt{8 \cdot 3}$ on your calculator and compare this to the value of $\sqrt{8} \cdot \sqrt{3}$. The values are the same, which shows that $\sqrt{8 \cdot 3} = \sqrt{8} \cdot \sqrt{3}$.

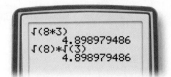

SIMPLIFYING SQUARE ROOTS	
Algebra	**Numbers**
For any nonnegative numbers m and n, $\sqrt{mn} = \sqrt{m} \cdot \sqrt{n}$.	$\sqrt{10} = \sqrt{2 \cdot 5} = \sqrt{2} \cdot \sqrt{5}$

EXAMPLE 1 **Simplifying Square Roots**

Simplify.

A $\sqrt{65}$

$\sqrt{65} = \sqrt{5 \cdot 13}$ *Factor 65.*

$\phantom{\sqrt{65}} = \sqrt{5} \cdot \sqrt{13}$ *Use $\sqrt{mn} = \sqrt{m} \cdot \sqrt{n}$.*

B $\sqrt{45}$

$\sqrt{45} = \sqrt{9 \cdot 5}$ *9 is a perfect-square factor of 45.*

$\phantom{\sqrt{45}} = \sqrt{9} \cdot \sqrt{5}$ *Use $\sqrt{mn} = \sqrt{m} \cdot \sqrt{n}$.*

$\phantom{\sqrt{45}} = 3\sqrt{5}$ *$\sqrt{9} = \sqrt{3}$*

C $\sqrt{700}$

$\sqrt{700} = \sqrt{100 \cdot 7}$ *100 is the greatest perfect-square factor.*

$\phantom{\sqrt{700}} = \sqrt{100} \cdot \sqrt{7}$ *Use $\sqrt{mn} = \sqrt{m} \cdot \sqrt{n}$.*

$\phantom{\sqrt{700}} = 10\sqrt{7}$ *$\sqrt{100} = 10$*

> **Helpful Hint**
>
> When simplifying square roots, it is often easiest to start by finding the greatest factor of the number under the radical sign that is a perfect square.

When you find the square root of a nonnegative number and then square the result, you end up with the number you started with.

SQUARING SQUARE ROOTS	
Algebra	**Numbers**
For any nonnegative number m, $(\sqrt{m})^2 = m$.	$(\sqrt{9})^2 = (3)^2 = 9$

EXAMPLE 2 Squaring Square Roots

Simplify.

A $(\sqrt{36})^2$

$(\sqrt{36})^2 = (6)^2$ *Perform operations within parentheses. 36 is a*

$\qquad\qquad = 36$ *perfect square. $\sqrt{36} = 6$. Then square the number.*

B $(\sqrt{17})^2$

$(\sqrt{17})^2 = 17$ *17 is not a perfect square; use $(\sqrt{m})^2 = m$.*

Exercises

Simplify.

1. $\sqrt{14}$

2. $\sqrt{33}$

3. $\sqrt{12}$

4. $\sqrt{18}$

5. $\sqrt{50}$

6. $\sqrt{80}$

7. $\sqrt{21}$

8. $\sqrt{128}$

9. $\sqrt{28}$

10. $\sqrt{125}$

11. $\sqrt{300}$

12. $\sqrt{243}$

13. $\sqrt{245}$

14. $\sqrt{96}$

15. $\sqrt{275}$

16. $\sqrt{360}$

17. $(\sqrt{11})^2$

18. $(\sqrt{25})^2$

19. $(\sqrt{38})^2$

20. $(\sqrt{72})^2$

21. $(\sqrt{144})^2$

22. $(\sqrt{87})^2$

23. $(2\sqrt{7})^2$

24. $(3\sqrt{2})^2$

Use the fact that $\sqrt{mn} = \sqrt{m} \cdot \sqrt{n}$ to write each expression as a single square root. Then simplify if possible.

25. $\sqrt{2} \cdot \sqrt{8}$

26. $\sqrt{32} \cdot \sqrt{2}$

27. $\sqrt{3} \cdot \sqrt{12}$

28. $\sqrt{5} \cdot \sqrt{15}$

29. $\sqrt{3} \cdot \sqrt{6}$

30. $\sqrt{15} \cdot \sqrt{3}$

31. $\sqrt{6} \cdot \sqrt{12}$

32. $\sqrt{10} \cdot \sqrt{20}$

33. A square flower bed has an area of 128 square feet.

    a. Write the length of a side of the flower bed as a simplified square root.

    b. Explain how you know that each side of the flower bed is longer than 8 feet.

34. A computer monitor's screen has a length ℓ of 14 inches and a width w of 12 inches. By the Pythagorean Theorem, the length of the diagonal is $d = \sqrt{\ell^2 + w^2}$. Use this to find the length of the diagonal of the screen. Write your answer as a simplified square root.

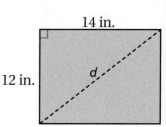

35. **Critical Thinking** Suppose you know that $\sqrt{5}$ is approximately 2.2. Explain how you can use this fact to help you estimate the value of $\sqrt{20}$.

36. **Critical Thinking** Explain how you can determine which is greater without using a calculator, $\sqrt{7} \cdot \sqrt{21}$ or $6\sqrt{3}$.

A-1 Simplifying Square Roots   **AT3**

Cubes of Numbers

TN ✓ GLE 0706.2.5 Understand and work with…cubes…

Use with Lesson 10-2

Recall that the square of a number is the number raised to the second power. It is called a *square* because it represents the area of a square with side lengths equal to the number. For example, the drawing shows that 9 is the square of 3, or $3^2 = 9$.

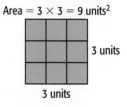

Area = $3 \times 3 = 9$ units^2

3 units

3 units

Similarly, a *cube of a number* is the number raised to the third power. It is called a cube because it represents the volume of a cube with edge lengths equal to the number. The drawing shows that 27 is the cube of 3, or $3^3 = 27$.

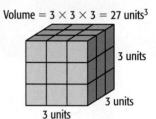

Volume = $3 \times 3 \times 3 = 27$ units^3

3 units

3 units

3 units

EXAMPLE 1

Finding Cubes of Numbers

Find the cube of each number.

A -7

$(-7)^3$ *Raise the number to the third power.*

$(-7) \cdot (-7) \cdot (-7)$ *Write in expanded form. Multiply.*

$49 \cdot (-7)$

-343

The cube of -7 is -343.

B $\dfrac{1}{3}$

$\left(\dfrac{1}{3}\right)^3$ *Raise the number to the third power.*

$\dfrac{1}{3} \times \dfrac{1}{3} \times \dfrac{1}{3}$ *Write in expanded form.*

$\dfrac{1}{9} \times \dfrac{1}{3}$ *Multiply.*

$\dfrac{1}{27}$

The cube of $\frac{1}{3}$ is $\frac{1}{27}$.

EXAMPLE 2

Evaluating Expressions Containing Cubes

Evaluate $2x^3 - 5x$ for $x = -6$.

$2 \cdot (-6)^3 - 5 \cdot (-6)$ *Substitute –6 for x.*

$2 \cdot (-216) - 5 \cdot (-6)$ *Evaluate the power: $(-6) \cdot (-6) \cdot (-6) = -216$.*

$-432 - (-30)$ *Multiply.*

$-432 + 30$ *To subtract, add the opposite.*

-402 *Add.*

EXAMPLE 3 Art Application

Pablo wants to build a large cube out of
small multi-colored cubes. He wants each
edge of the large cube to be made up of
8 small cubes. How many small cubes will
Pablo need?

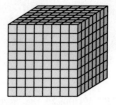

Since each edge of the cube will be made of 8 cubes, the
total number of cubes needed will be 8 cubed.

$8^3 = 8 \cdot 8 \cdot 8$

$= 64 \cdot 8$

$= 512$

Pablo will need 512 cubes.

Exercises

Find the cube of each number.

1. 4   **2.** -5 **3.** $\frac{1}{2}$ **4.** 10

5. 0.3   **6.** 15   **7.** -3 **8.** $\frac{1}{6}$

9. 12   **10.** 0.8   **11.** $\frac{2}{3}$ **12.** $-\frac{1}{9}$

Evaluate each expression for the given values of the variables.

13. $x^3 + x^2 + x$ for $x = 8$ **14.** $4(y^3 + 10) - 9y$ for $y = 10$

15. $5x^3 - x^2$ for $x = -5$ **16.** $-2a^3 - 4a$ for $a = \frac{1}{2}$

17. $\frac{4}{3}r^3 + \frac{1}{3}r^2$ for $r = 9$ **18.** $a^3 - b^3$ for $a = 5$ and $b = -2$

19. Critical Thinking Sebastian has 72 centimeter cubes. He wants to build a larger
cube that uses exactly those 72 cubes. Is this possible? Explain.

20. Tara has stacked up many cubic boxes to form
a large cube as shown.

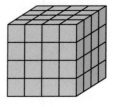

   a. How many boxes are in the stack?

   b. Each box has a volume of 2.5 cubic feet. What is
the total volume of the stack of boxes?

   c. Critical Thinking To fit the most boxes into a storage container, Tara needs
to increase the stack so it is 5 boxes wide, 5 boxes deep, and 5 boxes tall. How
many more boxes does Tara need?

Cube Roots

TN SPI 0706.2.3 Use...roots of perfect... cubes to solve contextual problems.

SPI 0706.2.4 Determine the approximate location of... cube roots on a number line.

✓ **0706.2.11** Estimate...cube roots and use calculators to find approximations.

Also **GLE 0706.2.5**

Use with Lesson 10-2

Recall that the cube of a number is the number raised to the third power. It is called a cube because it represents the volume of a cube with edge lengths equal to that number.

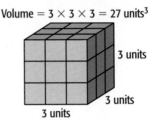

Volume = $3 \times 3 \times 3 = 27$ units^3

3 units
3 units
3 units

Finding a cube root is the inverse of cubing a number. A number raised to the third power to form a product is a *cube root* of that product. 3 is a cube root of 27 because $3^3 = 27$. The symbol $\sqrt[3]{}$ means "cube root." Since $3^3 = 27$, $\sqrt[3]{27} = 3$.

A *perfect cube* is a number whose cube root is an integer. Some perfect cubes are shown in the table.

1	8	27	64	125	216	343	512	729	1000
1^3	2^3	3^3	4^3	5^3	6^3	7^3	8^3	9^3	10^3

EXAMPLE 1

Finding Cube Roots of Perfect Cubes

Find each cube root.

A $\sqrt[3]{64}$

$$\sqrt[3]{64} = \sqrt[3]{4^3} = 4$$ *Think: What number cubed equals 64?*

Check $4^3 = 4 \cdot 4 \cdot 4 = 64$ ✓

B $\sqrt[3]{729}$

$$\sqrt[3]{729} = \sqrt[3]{9^3}$$ *Think: What number cubed equals 729?*
$$= 9$$

Check $9^3 = 9 \cdot 9 \cdot 9 = 729$ ✓

C $\sqrt[3]{-27}$

$$\sqrt[3]{-27} = \sqrt[3]{(-3)^3}$$ *Think: What number cubed equals −27?*
$$= -3$$

Check $(-3)^3 = (-3) \cdot (-3) \cdot (-3)$
$$= 9 \cdot (-3)$$
$$= -27$$ ✓

Cube roots of numbers that are not perfect cubes, such as 25, are not integers. You can use a calculator to approximate $\sqrt[3]{25}$ as 2.924017... Without a calculator you can use cube roots of perfect cubes to estimate the cube roots of other numbers.

EXAMPLE 2

Estimating Cube Roots

Find the two integers that $\sqrt[3]{43}$ lies between.

Find the two consecutive perfect cubes that 622 lies between.

$$3^3 = 27 \text{ and } 4^3 = 64$$

43 is between 27 and 64, so $\sqrt[3]{43}$ is between 3 and 4.

Check: Use a calculator to find the approximate cube root of 43. Press **MATH** and select **4:** $\sqrt[3]{}$ from the menu. Then enter 43 **)** **ENTER** .

$$\sqrt[3]{43} \approx 3.5$$

EXAMPLE 3

Ordering Cube Roots

Graph the list of numbers on a number line. Then order the numbers from least to greatest.

$2.6, \frac{1}{2}, \sqrt[3]{8}, -1.3, \sqrt{9}$

To help place the numbers on the number line, write all the numbers in decimal form.

$2.6 \qquad \frac{1}{2} = 0.5 \qquad \sqrt[3]{8} = 2.0 \qquad -1.3 \qquad \sqrt{9} = 3.0$

Now graph the numbers on the number line.

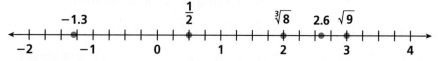

The numbers appear on the number line from left to right as least to greatest.

$-1.3, \frac{1}{2}, \sqrt[3]{8}, 2.6, \sqrt{9}$

EXAMPLE 4 **Art Application**

An artist has created a sculpture in the shape of a cube. The cube has a volume of 125 cubic feet. If the artist wants to wrap the sculpture, what is the minimum amount of wrapping paper he will need to cover all 6 faces?

Remember!

The face of a cube is a square and the area of a square is s^2 or $s \cdot s$, where s is the length of the side of the square.

$$\sqrt[3]{125} = \sqrt[3]{5^3}$$

$$= 5 \text{ ft}$$

Find the cube root of 125 to find the length of each edge of the cube.

$$5 \cdot 5 = 25 \text{ ft}^2$$

Find the surface area of one face of the cube by using the edge length.

$$25 \cdot 6 = 150 \text{ ft}^2$$

There are 6 faces on a cube.

The total surface area of the cube is 150 square feet. The minimum amount of wrapping paper needed to cover all 6 faces is 150 square feet.

Exercises

Find each cube root.

1. $\sqrt[3]{216}$ 2. $\sqrt[3]{1}$ 3. $\sqrt[3]{-729}$ 4. $\sqrt[3]{1000}$

Find the two integers that each cube root lies between.

5. $\sqrt[3]{99}$ 6. $\sqrt[3]{872}$ 7. $\sqrt[3]{13}$ 8. $\sqrt[3]{126}$

9. Graph $\sqrt[3]{64}$, -1.5, $\frac{3}{4}$, $\sqrt{4}$, 1.7 on a number line. Then order the numbers from least to greatest.

10. A wooden cube has a volume of 8 cubic feet. The cube is to be covered on 5 faces with leather to create an ottoman. What is the amount of leather needed to cover all 5 faces?

11. Rusty bought a cube-shaped aquarium. The total surface area of the aquarium is 864 square inches. What is the volume of the aquarium?

Compare the expressions. Write $>$, $<$, or $=$.

12. $\sqrt[3]{512}$ ▨ $\sqrt{144}$ 13. 2^3 ▨ $\sqrt[3]{8}$ 14. 1^{10} ▨ $\sqrt[3]{1}$

15. -5 ▨ $\sqrt[3]{-125}$ 16. 9.5 ▨ $\sqrt[3]{1000}$ 17. $\sqrt[3]{65}$ ▨ 3

18. Jacob is building a small garden wall out of concrete cubes. The base layer cubes have a volume of 1,728 cubic inches. The next 3 layers will be built out of cubes that have a volume of 512 cubic inches. How tall will the finished wall be?

19. **Critical Thinking** Explain why you cannot take the square root of a negative number but you can take the cube root of a negative number.

Relations and Functions

TN ▶ **SPI 0706.3.2** Determine whether a relation (represented in various ways) is a function.

✓ **0706.3.3** Identify a function from a written description, table, graph, rule, set of ordered pairs, and/or mapping.

Also **GLE 0706.3.2, GLE 0706.3.3**

Use with Lesson 5-3

A *relation* is a set of ordered pairs. The *domain* of a relation is the set of *x*-values of the ordered pairs. The *range* of a relation is the set of *y*-values of the ordered pairs.

Relations can be represented in several different ways such as in tables, mapping diagrams, graphs, and equations. The relation {(1, 2), (2, 4), (3, 6)} can be expressed in the following forms.

Table

x	y
1	2
2	4
3	6

Mapping Diagram

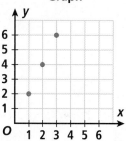

Equation

Function Rule

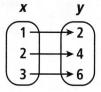

$$y = 2x$$

Output   Input

Graph

EXAMPLE 1   Multiple Representations of Relations

Express the relation {(0, 1), (2, 3), (4, 7), (5, 9)}, as a table, as a graph, and as a mapping diagram.

Table

x	y
0	1
2	3
4	7
5	9

Write all the x-values in one column and all their corresponding y-values in another.

Graph

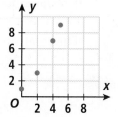

Use the x- and y-values to plot the ordered pairs.

Mapping Diagram

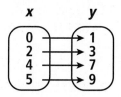

Write all the x-values under "x" and all y-values under "y." Draw an arrow from each x-value to its corresponding y-value.

There is a special type of relation called a *function*. A function pairs each domain value x with exactly one range value y. The x-value is also known as the input and the y-value is the output. If the relation has an input value that is paired with more than one output value, then the relation is not a function.

Function
Each input gives only one output.

Not a Function
One input gives more than one output.

EXAMPLE 2 **Identifying Functions**

Determine whether each relation represents a function.

A $\{(-4, -19), (-2, -7), (3, 23), (6, 41)\}$

$\{(-4, -19), (-2, -7), (3, 23), (6, 41)\}$ *Each input x has only one output y.*

The relation is a function.

B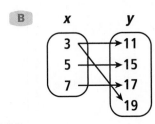

Each input value does not have exactly one output. The x-value 3 has output values of 11 and 19.

The relation is not a function.

C

x	y
−2	13
−1	4
0	1
2	13

Each input x has only one output y. Even though 13 appears twice, it is paired with different inputs.

The relation is a function.

D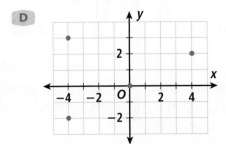

Each input value does not have exactly one output. The x-value −4 has output values of −2 and 3.

The relation is not a function.

EXAMPLE **3** **Identifying Functions from Written Descriptions**

Reading Math

Another term that means *paired with* is *maps*. The first element stated is the input and the second is the output.

A **A coach assigns different numbers to each player on the football team. Is the relation that maps players to numbers a function?**

Since each player is given a different number, the relation that maps players to numbers is a function.

B **In the United States Senate each U.S. state is represented by two senators. Is the relation that maps states to senators a function?**

Since each state is represented by two different senators, the relation that maps states to senators is not a function.

Exercises

Express each relation as a table, as a graph, and as a mapping diagram.

1. $\{(-2, 5), (0, 10), (1, 7), (2, 5)\}$ **2.** $\{(-6, -5), (-5, 0), (1, -2), (3, 5)\}$

Determine whether each relation represents a function.

3.

x	y
−1	−2
−1	7
5	18
10	20

4.
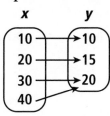

5.
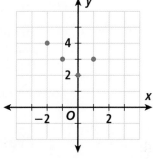

6. Each person in a class of 10 people is assigned a letter from A through E. Is the relation that maps letters to people a function?

7. Each person in a group of 5 people is assigned either the letter A or letter B. Is the relation that maps people to letters a function?

8. An equation for determining the number of eggs y in x dozen eggs is $y = 12x$. Does this equation represent a function? Explain.

Each set of ordered pairs represents a function. Find 3 more ordered pairs that can be included in each set so that the set still represents a function.

9. $\{(1, 6), (2, 8), (3, 10), (4, 12)\}$ **10.** $\{(1, 6), (2, 7), (3, 8), (4, 9)\}$

11. A bike shop rents bikes for $8 an hour with a maximum charge of $40. Express the relation between the number of hours x and the cost y as a set of ordered pairs and find the cost to rent a bike for 1, 2, 3, 4, 5, and 6 hours. Is this relation a function? Explain.

12. Critical Thinking A teacher asks Carlie to graph points that form the capital letter C on a coordinate plane. He asks Vivienne to do the same thing for the capital letter V. Which student's graph represents a function? Explain.

13. Challenge Draw a mapping diagram using the values 1, 2, 3, 4, and 4 that represents a function. Then use the same values to draw a mapping diagram that does not represent a function.

Writing and Evaluating Functions

TN **SPI 0706.3.3** Given a table of inputs *x* and outputs *f(x)*, identify the function rule and continue the pattern.

✓ **0706.3.4** Make tables of inputs *x* and outputs *f(x)* for a variety of rules that include rational numbers (including negative numbers) as inputs.

Also **GLE 0706.3.4**

Use with Lesson 5-3

Bridget charges $7 an hour for dog walking. The amount Bridget is paid is $7 times the number of hours she works. This relationship can be shown as a *linear function*. A linear function is a function that can be described by a linear equation.

One way to write a linear function is by using *function notation*. If *x* represents the input value of a function and *y* represents the output value, then the function notation of *y* is *f(x)*, where *f* names the function.

The amount Bridget earns, *y*, can be written as $y = 7x$, where *x* is the number of hours she works. This function can be written in function notation by substituting *f(x)* for *y*: $f(x) = 7x$.

Reading Math

f(x) is read as "*f* of *x*."

If Bridget wanted to know how much she would earn by working 3 hours, she could input 3 for *x* and find the output. This is called *evaluating the function*.

Output value   Input value

$$f(x) = 7x$$

f of *x* equals 7 times *x*.

Output value   Input value

$$f(3) = 7(3) = 21$$

f of 3 equals 7 times 3, or 21.

EXAMPLE 1

Evaluating Functions

Find the output for each input.

A $f(x) = 1.5x$

Input	Rule	Output	
x	**1.5x**	*f(x)*	
−1	1.5(−1)	−1.5	Substitute −1 for x. Then simplify.
0	1.5(0)	0	Substitute 0 for x. Then simplify.
1.5	1.5(1.5)	2.25	Substitute 1.5 for x. Then simplify.

B $f(x) = -3x + 2$

Input	Rule	Output	
x	**−3x + 2**	*f(x)*	
−5	−3(−5) + 2	17	Substitute −5 for x. Then simplify.
1	−3(1) + 2	−1	Substitute 1 for x. Then simplify.
10	−3(10) + 2	−28	Substitute 10 for x. Then simplify.

By finding a pattern between the inputs and outputs of a function you can write a function rule that will continue the pattern.

EXAMPLE 2

Writing Equations from Function Tables

Determine a relationship between the input and output values in the table. Write an equation in function notation to describe the relationship. Then find the missing values.

x	-2	-1	0	1	2	3
$f(x)$	-6	-3	0	3	▉	▉

Compare x and f(x) to find a relationship.
List any possible relationships.

Relationship 1: $-2 - 4 = -6$
Relationship 2: $-2 \cdot 3 = -6$

Determine which relationship works for the remaining values in the table.

$-1 - 4 \neq -3$ ✗ $-1 \cdot 3 = -3$ ✓
$0 - 4 \neq 0$ ✗ $0 \cdot 3 = 0$ ✓
$1 - 4 \neq 3$ ✗ $1 \cdot 3 = 3$ ✓

The second relationship works.
Use the relationship to write an equation for the function table.

The value of $f(x)$ is 3 times the value of x.
$$f(x) = \quad 3x$$

Use the equation to find the next two values in the table.

$f(2) = 3(2) = 6$ $f(3) = 3(3) = 9$

EXAMPLE 3

Real-World Application

A lawyer charges a $50 retainer fee plus a set fee per hour for his services. The table shows his total fee for different number of hours worked. If he continues to charge the same amount per hour, what would it cost to hire the lawyer for 8 hours?

Number of Hours	Total Fee ($)
0	50
2	350
4	650
5	800

Write an equation describing the relationship in the table.
Total fee = $150 times number of hours worked plus $50
$$f(x) = \quad 150x \quad + \quad 50$$

Use the equation to find out how much the lawyer will charge for 8 hours of work.

$f(x) = 150x + 50$

$f(8) = 150(8) + 50$ *Substitute 8 for x.*
$= 1{,}200 + 50 = 1{,}250$ *Simplify.*

The lawyer will charge $1,250 for 8 hours of work.

Exercises

Find the output for each input.

1. $f(x) = \frac{1}{2}x$

Input	Rule	Output
x	$\frac{1}{2}x$	$f(x)$
–2	■	■
1	■	■
4	■	■

2. $f(x) = -3.5x + 1.54$

Input	Rule	Output
x	$-3.5x + 1.5$	$f(x)$
–5	■	■
–2.5	■	■
8	■	■

Determine a relationship between the input and output values in the table. Write an equation in function notation to describe the relationship. Then find the missing values.

3.

x	–2	–1	0	1	2	3
$f(x)$	–1	1	3	5	■	■

4.

x	–2	–1	0	1	2	3
$f(x)$	7	6	5	4	■	■

5. Ralphie got a $100 signing bonus at his new job. He earns the same amount of money per hour. The table shows how much Ralphie earns at the end of different numbers of hours. If he continues to earn the same amount of money per hour, how much will he have earned after working 40 hours?

Number of Hours	Total Earned ($)
0	100
3	175
5	225
7	275

Write an equation in function notation for the given situations.

6. Khloe pays a fee of $5 per month plus $0.05 per text she sends.

7. A county fair charges a $3 admission fee and $1 for each game played.

8. A taxi charges a flat rate of $1.50 and $0.95 for each mile traveled.

Write an equation for a function that gives the values in each table and then find the missing terms.

9.

x	–1	0	1	2	5	7
$f(x)$	■	2.1	3.1	■	7.1	■

10.

x	–3	0	3	6	9	12
$f(x)$	–1	0	1	■	3	4

11. Kim runs the same circular route once a week for 4 weeks. Her times for running the route are shown in the table. If this pattern continues, what function rule can represent the time, in minutes, that it will take Kim to run the route in week n?

Week	Time (min)
1	60
2	58
3	56
4	54

Back-to-Back Stem-and-Leaf Plots

TN ✓ **0706.5.2** Interpret and solve problems using information presented in various visual forms.

Also **GLE 0706.5.4**

Use with Lesson 7-1

A *back-to-back stem-and-leaf plot* can be used to compare two sets of data. One set of data is shown on the left side of the stems, and one set of data is shown on the right side. Leaves on the left side are read in reverse. In the example shown, the first value in data set A is 18. The first value in data set B is 23.

Data Set A		Data Set B
8	1	
8 3 1 1	2	3 4 4 6
2	3	1 4

Key: 8|1| means 18
|2|3 means 23

EXAMPLE **1** **Creating a Back-to-Back Stem-and-Leaf Plot**

Use the given data to make a back-to-back stem-and-leaf plot.

Daily Temperatures in Ten Cities	
Low (°F)	52 56 47 67 71 52 67 61 56 51
High (°F)	56 76 68 82 95 59 89 68 71 65

Low Temperatures		High Temperatures
7	4	
6 6 2 2 1	5	6 9
7 7 1	6	5 8 8
1	7	1 6
	8	2 9
	9	5

Key: 1|5| means 51
|6|5 means 65

Group the data by tens digits. Then order the data from least to greatest. Write the tens digits in the stems column. Then write the ones digit for each data value as the leaves. Include a key for both data sets.

Back-to-back stem-and-leaf plots make it easy to analyze and compare two data sets. You can see the general shape of a data set and identify clusters, gaps, and symmetry. In Example 1, you might notice that the low temperatures are clustered around the 50s and 60s while the high temperatures are more spread out over a greater range.

EXAMPLE **2** **Comparing Back-to-Back Stem-and-Leaf Plots**

Use the back-to-back stem-and-leaf plot to answer each question.

Ages of people on a school bus		Ages of people on a city bus
9 9 9 8 8	0	
4 4 3 3 3 2 2 2 2 1 1 0	1	6 8
	2	1 4 4
	3	3 3 7 9
6	4	1 2 6
	5	5 8

Key: 2|1| means 12
|4|1 means 41

Use the back-to-back stem-and-leaf plot to answer each question.

A **Find the median and mode(s) of each data set.**

median of school bus data: 12
median of city bus data: 35

The median is the middle value.

modes of school bus data: 9, 12, and 13
modes of city bus data: 24 and 33

The modes are the most frequent values.

B **Compare the data sets.**

The school bus data is clustered around the 0s and 10s, which means that most people riding the school bus are children or teenagers. There is a large gap between the values 14 and 46, which is an outlier.

In general the city bus data values are much higher. The median is also much higher. The city bus data is symmetrical around the 30s. There are no gaps or clusters, so the data is more evenly spread out.

Exercises

1. The table shows the scores of the last 11 basketball games for two teams.

Points Scored in Last 11 Basketball Games	
Rockets	92 77 89 86 103 108 84 86 113 115 93
Lakers	107 108 86 119 113 125 92 98 116 122 88

a. Make a back-to-back stem-and-leaf plot of the data.

b. Find the medians and modes. Then compare the data sets.

c. **Critical Thinking** The two teams are playing their next game against each other. Who do you think will win? Justify your answer.

2. The back-to-back stem-and-leaf plot shows the ages of the audiences in two different movie theaters.

Theater 1		Theater 2
9 9 8 7 7 6 4	0	
2 1 1 0 0 0	1	8 8 9 9 9
	2	0 1 1 1 1 3 3 4 7
5 4 2 1 1 1 0	3	2
0	4	

Key: 2|1| means 12
|3|2 means 32

a. Find the medians and modes of the audiences in both theaters.

b. Compare the data sets.

c. **Critical Thinking** What type of movie might be showing in each theater? Justify your answer.

ADDITIONAL TOPIC

A-7

Comparing Samples and Populations

 TN ✓ **0706.5.3** Predict and compare the characteristics of two populations based on the analysis of sample data.

Use with Lesson 7-8

Recall that a population is the entire group of objects or individuals considered for a survey. A sample is a part of the population. You can use data from samples to make comparisons and predictions about populations.

EXAMPLE **1** | **Comparing Samples**

According to the U.S. Census Bureau, about 23% of all adults in the United States visited an art museum in the past year. Nicole surveys a random sample of adults in two towns. Compare the samples with the national percent.

Art Museum Attendance		
Sample	Visited an Art Museum	Did Not Visit an Art Museum
Town A	23	27
Town B	11	39

For each sample, find the percent of adults who visited an art museum.

Town A: $\dfrac{\text{number of adults who visited an art museum}}{\text{total number of adults in sample}} = \dfrac{23}{23 + 27} = \dfrac{23}{50} = 46\%$

Town B: $\dfrac{\text{number of adults who visited an art museum}}{\text{total number of adults in sample}} = \dfrac{11}{11 + 39} = \dfrac{11}{50} = 22\%$

The data suggest that attendance at art museums in Town B is close to the national percent, while attendance at art museums in Town A is greater than the national percent.

EXAMPLE **2** | **Making Predictions**

The table shows the adult populations of the two towns from Example 1. Predict which town had a greater number of adult visitors to art museums.

Town Populations	
Town	Adult Population
Town A	20,500
Town B	48,200

Helpful Hint

Even though Town B's percentage was less than Town A's in Example 1, it can still have more adult visitors because its population was greater.

For each town, predict the number of adults who visited an art museum.

Town A: 46% of 20,500   *Use the percent found in Example 1.*

$0.46 \cdot 20,500 = 9,430$ *Write the percent as a decimal and multiply.*

Town B: 22% of 48,200   *Use the percent found in Example 1.*

$0.22 \cdot 48,200 = 10,604$ *Write the percent as a decimal and multiply.*

The data suggest that Town B had a greater number of adult visitors to art museums than Town A.

Exercises

About 74% of all middle school students in the United States participate in after-school sports. Malik surveys a random sample of students at two middle schools.

Participation in After-School Sports		
Sample	Participates	Does Not Participate
School A	18	7
School B	18	12

1. Compare the samples with the national percent.

2. School A has 480 students. School B has 510 students. Predict which school has a greater number of students who participate in after-school sports.

A store receives two shipments of MP3 players. A manager checks a random sample of MP3 players from each shipment.

MP3 Players		
Sample	Defective	Not Defective
Shipment A	2	48
Shipment B	3	147

3. The goal is for no more than 2% of the MP3 players in any shipment to be defective. Compare the samples to the goal.

4. Shipment A contains 450 MP3 players. Shipment B contains 650 MP3 players. Predict which shipment has a greater number of defective MP3 players.

About 87% of all employees in the United States drive to work. Naomi surveys a random sample of employees at two companies.

Driving to Work		
Sample	Drives to Work	Does Not Drive to Work
Company A	21	4
Company B	124	76

5. Compare the samples with the national percent.

6. Company A has 1,242 employees. Company B has 1,529 employees. Which company's parking lot do you think should have a greater number of parking spots? Why?

Crunch-O's Cereal is packaged at three factories. The goal is for 40% of the boxes of the cereal to contain a coupon. A manager checks a random sample of boxes from all three factories.

Crunch-O's Cereal		
Sample	Boxes that Contain Coupons	Sample Size
Factory A	75	200
Factory B	123	300
Factory C	98	350

7. Based on the samples, which factory came closest to the goal?

8. Each factory produces 12,000 boxes of cereal per day. Predict the total number of coupons that are packaged in the boxes each day.

Triangle Similarity: AA, SAS, and SSS

TN SPI 0706.4.2 Use SSS, SAS, and AA to determine if two triangles are similar.

Use with Lesson 4-8

Recall that two figures are similar if their corresponding angle measures are equal *and* if the ratios of the lengths of their corresponding sides are proportional.

To prove that two triangles are similar, it is not necessary to show that both of these conditions are always true. Triangles can be considered similar if they meet any of the following conditions:

Angle-Angle (AA) Similarity	Two triangles are similar if two pairs of corresponding angles are congruent.	$\angle D \cong \angle A$; $\angle E \cong \angle B$ 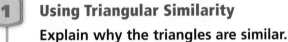
Side-Angle-Side (SAS) Similarity	Two triangles are similar if the ratios of two pairs of corresponding sides are proportional and the corresponding included angles are congruent.	$\dfrac{12}{6} = \dfrac{24}{12}$; $\angle U \cong \angle X$ 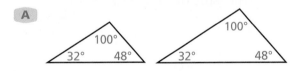
Side-Side-Side (SSS) Similarity	Two triangles are similar if the ratios of all pairs of corresponding sides are proportional.	$\dfrac{12}{18} = \dfrac{5}{7.5}$; $\dfrac{12}{18} = \dfrac{13}{19.5}$; $\dfrac{13}{19.5} = \dfrac{5}{7.5}$ 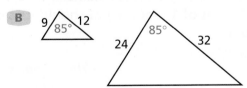

EXAMPLE **1** **Using Triangular Similarity**

Explain why the triangles are similar.

A

All corresponding angles are congruent since corresponding angle measures are equal: 32° = 32°, 48° = 48°, and 100° = 100°.

Since two pairs of corresponding angle measures are equal, the triangles are similar by AA similarity.

B

The ratios of two pairs of corresponding sides are proportional: $\frac{9}{24} = \frac{12}{32}$. The corresponding included angles are congruent since both measure 85°.

Since the ratios of two pairs of corresponding sides are proportional and the included angles are congruent, the triangles are similar by SAS similarity.

EXAMPLE **2**   **Finding Missing Measures in Similar Triangles**

Explain why the given triangles are similar. Then find the missing measure.

A

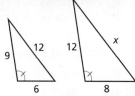

The ratios of two pairs of corresponding sides are proportional: $\frac{9}{12} = \frac{6}{8}$.
The corresponding included angles are marked as being congruent.

Since the ratio of two pairs of corresponding sides are proportional and the included angles are congruent, the triangles are similar by SAS similarity.

Find the missing value.

$$\frac{9}{12} = \frac{12}{x}$$

$$9x = 144$$

$$x = 16$$

Since the triangles are similar, the ratios of all pairs of corresponding sides are proportional.
Set up a proportion that includes the missing side. Solve for x.

The missing side length of the triangle is 16.

B

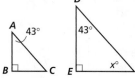

The corresponding angles are congruent since corresponding angle measures are equal: 43° = 43° and 90° = 90°.

Since two pairs of corresponding angles are congruent, the triangles are similar by AA similarity.

Find the missing value.

$$90 + 43 + x = 180$$

$$133 + x = 180$$

$$x = 47$$

The sum of the measure of the angles in a triangle is 180°. Simplify.

Solve for x.

The measure of $\angle F = 47°$.

EXAMPLE **3**   **Sailing Application**

The mainsail on Desmond's sailboat is in the shape of a right triangle. It has a height of 20 feet and a side length of 10 feet. If he wants to buy another mainsail that is similar to the original with a height of 16 feet, what should its side length and included angle be?

Draw a diagram.

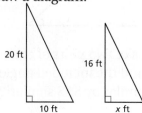

The triangles are similar; so the ratios of the two corresponding sides must be equal and the included angles must be congruent by SAS similarity.
The included angle on the smaller triangle is 90°.

$$\frac{20}{16} = \frac{10}{x}$$

$$20x = 160$$

$$x = 8$$

Since the triangles are similar, the ratio of all pairs of corresponding sides are equal. Set up a proportion that includes the missing side. Solve for x.

The side length of the similar mainsail is 8 feet and the included angle is 90°.

Exercises

Explain why the triangles are similar.

1.

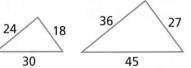

2.

Explain why the given triangles are similar. Then find the missing measure.

3.

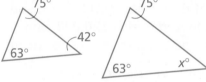

4.

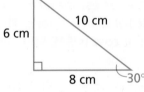

5. Charlotte is cutting out triangular shaped pieces of cloth with side lengths of 3 in., 5.2 in., and 6 in. If she wants to cut out a similar triangle with corresponding sides of 9 in. and 15.6 in., what will be the length of the third side?

6. An isosceles triangle has two sides that are 27 cm long and a base that is 18 cm long. A similar isosceles triangle has a base that is 24 cm. How long are the two sides?

7. A triangle has side lengths of 8 feet and 10 feet. The included angle is 30°. Tell which set(s) of measurements could be the corresponding parts of side lengths and included angle for a similar triangle.

   a. side lengths of 4 feet and 5 feet; included angle: 30°

   b. side lengths of 10 feet and 12.5 feet; included angle: 60°

   c. side lengths of 18 feet and 22.5 feet; included angle: 30°

   d. side lengths of 20 feet and 24.5 feet; included angle: 60°

8. **Challenge** Are all equilateral triangles similar? Explain.

Relative Error

TN ✓ 0706.2.15 Report results of calculations appropriately in a given context (i.e. ... degree of accuracy, ...).

Use with Lesson 9-1

You can describe how far an estimate is from the actual value by calculating the *actual error* and the *relative error*.

The actual error (or absolute error) is the absolute value of the difference between the estimated value and the actual value. Actual error is sometimes referred to as the magnitude of the error.

$$\text{actual error} = |\text{estimated value} - \text{actual value}|$$

The relative error takes the size of the numbers into account by converting the error into a percent.

$$\text{relative error} = \frac{\text{actual error}}{\text{actual value}}, \text{written as a percent}$$

EXAMPLE 1 Estimating Costs

A landscaper estimates the cost of new trees, shrubs, and sod to plant for a small park. The estimated cost is $20,000, and the actual cost is $18,500. Find the actual and relative error of the estimate.

Actual error $= |\text{estimated value} - \text{actual value}|$
$= |20,000 - 18,500|$
$= |1,500|$ or $1,500

Relative error $= \frac{\text{actual error}}{\text{actual value}} = \frac{1,500}{18,500} \approx 0.081 = 8.1\%$

The actual error of the estimate is $1,500 and the relative error of the estimate is 8.1%.

In some cases, the relative error is a better indicator of the accuracy of an estimate than the actual error.

EXAMPLE 2 Arts Application

Samir and Julie are putting on a school play. Samir is in charge of building the sets and Julie is in charge of the costumes. The table shows their estimates for their projects and the actual costs. Whose estimate was more accurate?

	Estimated Cost ($)	Actual Cost ($)
Samir	350.00	375.00
Julie	165.00	145.00

Find the actual and relative error for both estimates.

Samir's actual error $= |350 - 375|$
$= |-25| = 25.00 *Actual error = |estimated value − actual value|*

Samir's relative error $= \dfrac{25}{375}$ *Relative error* $= \dfrac{actual\ error}{actual\ value}$

$\approx 0.067 = 6.7\%$

Julie's actual error $= |165 - 145|$ *Actual error = |estimated*
$= |20| = \$20.00$ *value – actual value|*

Julie's relative error $= \dfrac{20}{145}$
$\approx 0.138 = 13.8\%$ *Relative error* $= \dfrac{actual\ error}{actual\ value}$

Julie's actual error of $20.00 is less than Samir's error of $25.00, but because the cost of Samir's project is almost three times the cost of Julie's project, his relative error is smaller. Samir's estimate is more accurate.

Exercises

1. Sandy estimated how much money two fundraising races would raise. The table shows her estimate and the actual amounts raised. Calculate the actual and relative error for each race.

Race	Estimated Amount Raised ($)	Actual Amount Raised ($)
10-K	5,000	5,600
5-miler	5,600	5,500

2. Sasha and Brian are estimating the populations of their hometowns. Sasha lives in Buffalo, NY, and Brian lives in Schenectady, NY. Their estimates and the actual values from the 2005 census are given in the table. Whose estimate is more accurate? Explain.

	Estimated Population	Actual Population
Sasha	270,000	279,745
Brian	55,000	61,280

3. Marcus and Erin are laying out a tennis court. A regulation tennis court is 78 feet long and 27 feet wide. Marcus marks the length of the court as 75 feet and Erin marks the width at 25 feet. Whose measurement is more accurate? Explain. (*Hint*: Substitute 78 feet and 27 feet as the actual measurements in the relative error formula.)

4. Determine if two different estimates for the same actual value can have the same actual errors.

5. **Critical Thinking** What does it mean when the relative error is greater than 100%? What does this mean about the estimated value?

6. **Write About It** Describe the difference between actual error and relative error. Give a real-world example of when the actual error is more important than the relative error, and give an example when the opposite is true.

Explore Similarity

TN ✓ 0706.1.12 Use dynamic geometry software to explore scale factor and similarity.

You can use dynamic geometry software to explore the connections among similarity, scale factor, and dilations.

Activity 1

1. Use geometry software to construct a triangle. Label the vertices *A*, *B*, and *C*. Then use the software to measure each side and angle of △*ABC*.

2. Plot a point in the interior of the triangle and label it *D*. Select *D* and choose Mark Center from the Transform menu. Then select the triangle, choose Dilate from the Transform menu, and use the default settings. Label the vertices of the new triangle *A'*, *B'*, and *C'*. Use the software to measure each side and angle of △*A'B'C'*.

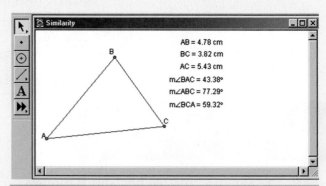

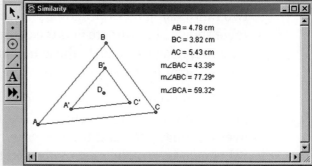

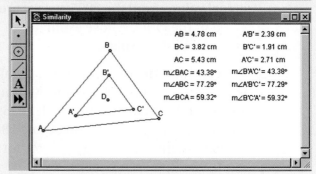

Think and Discuss

1. Change the shape of △*ABC*. Look for relationships that change and relationships that remain the same. What can you conclude about △*ABC* and △*A'B'C'*? Why?

2. What is the scale factor of the dilation? How is this related to the ratio of corresponding side lengths of the triangles?

3. Move point *D*, the center of dilation. When point *D* is inside △*ABC*, what must be true about the location of △*A'B'C'*?

1. Repeat the steps of the activity. This time, choose Dilate from the Transform menu and enter $\frac{3}{2}$ as the fixed ratio.

   a. How is this dilation different from the dilation in the Activity 1?

   b. How do the side lengths of the dilated triangle compare to the side lengths of your original triangle?

   c. What do you think would happen if you repeated the steps but entered $\frac{1}{1}$ as the fixed ratio for the dilation?

Activity 2

1. Use geometry software to construct a quadrilateral. Label the vertices *A*, *B*, *C*, and *D*. Then use the software to measure each side and angle of the quadrilateral. Plot a point in the interior of the quadrilateral and label it point *E*.

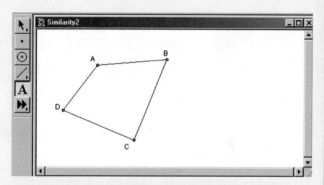

2. Predict what will happen if you use point *E* as the center of dilation to dilate quadrilateral *ABCD* with a scale factor of $\frac{1}{3}$. How will the sides and angles of the dilated quadrilateral compare to those of quadrilateral *ABCD*? Use the software to check your prediction. Enter $\frac{1}{3}$ as the fixed ratio for this dilation.

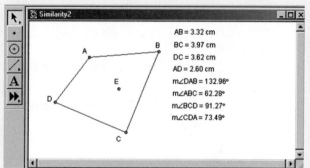

Think and Discuss

1. Suppose you use point *E* as the center of dilation to dilate quadrilateral *ABCD* with a scale factor of 3. How do you think the dilated quadrilateral will compare to quadrilateral *ABCD*?

Try This

A student used software to dilate △ *RST* as shown at right. Use the figure for 1–3.

1. What scale factor did the student use for the dilation? Explain how you know.

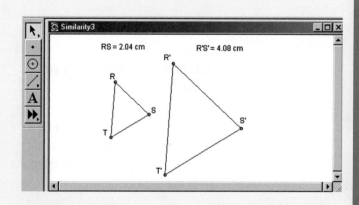

2. The center of the dilation is not shown in the figure. Do you think the center of dilation was inside or outside △ *RST*? Why?

3. How does the measure of ∠*S'* compare to the measure of ∠*S*? Why?

Focus on Problem Solving

The Problem Solving Process

In order to be a good problem solver, you first need a good problem-solving process. A process or strategy will help you to understand the problem, to work through a solution, and to check that your answer makes sense. The process used in this book is detailed below.

UNDERSTAND the Problem

- **What are you asked to find?** Restate the problem in your own words.
- **What information is given?** Identify the important facts in the problem.
- **What information do you need?** Determine which facts are needed to solve the problem.
- **Is all the information given?** Determine whether all the facts are given.

Make a PLAN

- **Have you ever solved a similar problem?** Think about other problems like this that you successfully solved.
- **What strategy or strategies can you use?** Determine a strategy that you can use and how you will use it.

SOLVE

- **Follow your plan.** Show the steps in your solution. Write your answer as a complete sentence.

LOOK BACK

- **Have you answered the question?** Be sure that you answered the question that is being asked.
- **Is your answer reasonable?** Your answer should make sense in the context of the problem.
- **Is there another strategy you could use?** Solving the problem using another strategy is a good way to check your work.
- **Did you learn anything while solving this problem that could help you solve similar problems in the future?** Try to remember the problems you have solved and the strategies you used to solve them.

Using the Problem Solving Process

During summer vacation, Ricardo will go to space camp and then to visit his relatives. He will be gone for 5 weeks and 4 days and will spend 11 more days with his relatives than at space camp. How long will Ricardo stay at each place?

UNDERSTAND the Problem

List the important information.

- Ricardo will be gone for 5 weeks and 4 days.
- He will spend 11 more days with his relatives than at space camp.

The answer will be how long Ricardo stays at each place.

Make a PLAN

You can **draw a diagram** to show how long he will stay at each place. Use boxes for the length of each stay. The length of each box will represent the length of each stay.

SOLVE

Think: There are 7 days in a week, so 5 weeks and 4 days is a total of 39 days. Your diagram might look like this:

Relatives	? days	11 days

Space camp	? days

$= 39$ days

$39 - 11 = 28$ *Subtract 11 days from the total number of days.*
$28 \div 2 = 14$ *Divide this number by 2 for the 2 places he visits.*

Relatives	14 days	11 days

$= 25$ days

Space camp	14 days

$= 14$ days

So Ricardo will stay with his relatives for 25 days and at space camp for 14 days.

LOOK BACK

Twenty-five days is 11 days longer than 14 days. The total length of the two stays is $25 + 14 = 39$ days, or 5 weeks and 4 days. This solution fits the information given in the problem.

CHAPTER 1

Algebraic Reasoning

Chapter Focus

- Use properties of arithmetic and properties of equality.
- Write and solve equations to solve problems.

Why Learn This?

Yellowstone National Park was created by Congress in 1872. An algebraic expression can model the current age of the park.

 Learn It Online
Chapter Project Online **go.hrw.com**
keyword **MS10 Ch1** **Go**

Are You Ready?

 **Vocabulary**

Choose the best term from the list to complete each sentence.

1. The operation that gives the quotient of two numbers is ___?___ .

2. The ___?___ of the digit 3 in 4,903,672 is thousands.

3. The operation that gives the product of two numbers is ___?___ .

4. In the equation 15 ÷ 3 = 5, the ___?___ is 5.

division

multiplication

place value

product

quotient

Complete these exercises to review skills you will need for this chapter.

✓ **Find Place Value**

Give the place value of the digit 4 in each number.

5. 4,092
6. 608,241
7. 7,040,000
8. 4,556,890,100
9. 3,408,289
10. 34,506,123
11. 500,986,402
12. 3,540,277,009

✓ **Use Repeated Multiplication**

Find each product.

13. $2 \cdot 2 \cdot 2$
14. $9 \cdot 9 \cdot 9 \cdot 9$
15. $14 \cdot 14 \cdot 14$
16. $10 \cdot 10 \cdot 10 \cdot 10$
17. $3 \cdot 3 \cdot 5 \cdot 5$
18. $2 \cdot 2 \cdot 5 \cdot 7$
19. $3 \cdot 3 \cdot 11 \cdot 11$
20. $5 \cdot 10 \cdot 10 \cdot 10$

✓ **Division Facts**

Find each quotient.

21. $49 \div 7$
22. $54 \div 9$
23. $96 \div 12$
24. $88 \div 8$
25. $42 \div 6$
26. $65 \div 5$
27. $39 \div 3$
28. $121 \div 11$

✓ **Whole Number Operations**

Add, subtract, multiply, or divide.

29. $\begin{array}{r} 425 \\ + 12 \\ \hline \end{array}$
30. $\begin{array}{r} 619 \\ + 254 \\ \hline \end{array}$
31. $\begin{array}{r} 62 \\ - 47 \\ \hline \end{array}$
32. $\begin{array}{r} 373 \\ + 86 \\ \hline \end{array}$
33. $\begin{array}{r} 62 \\ \times 42 \\ \hline \end{array}$
34. $\begin{array}{r} 122 \\ \times 15 \\ \hline \end{array}$
35. $7\overline{)623}$
36. $24\overline{)149}$

Where You've Been

Previously, you

- used order of operations to simplify whole number expressions without exponents.
- used multiplication and division to solve problems involving whole numbers.
- wrote large numbers in standard form.

In This Chapter

You will study

- simplifying numerical expressions involving order of operations and exponents.
- using concrete models to solve equations.
- writing numbers in scientific notation.

Where You're Going

You can use the skills learned in this chapter

- to express distances and sizes of objects in scientific fields such as astronomy and biology.
- to solve problems in math and science classes such as Algebra and Physics.

Key Vocabulary/Vocabulario

algebraic expression	expresión algebraica
Associative Property	propiedad asociativa
Commutative Property	propiedad conmutativa
Distributive Property	propiedad distributiva
equation	ecuación
exponent	exponente
numerical expression	expresión numérica
order of operations	orden de las operaciones
term	término
variable	variable

Vocabulary Connections

To become familiar with some of the vocabulary terms in the chapter, consider the following. You may refer to the chapter, the glossary, or a dictionary if you like.

1. The words *equation, equal,* and *equator* all begin with the Latin root *equa-,* meaning "level." How can the Latin root word help you define **equation**?

2. The word *numerical* means "of numbers." How might a **numerical expression** differ from an expression such as "the sum of two and five"?

3. When something is *variable,* it has the ability to change. In mathematics, a **variable** is an algebraic symbol. What special property do you think this type of symbol has?

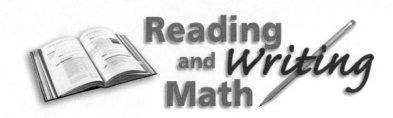

TN English/Language Arts
GLE 0701.6.2 Analyze the organizational structures of informational texts.

Reading Strategy: Use Your Book for Success

Understanding how your textbook is organized will help you locate and use helpful information.

As you read through an example problem, pay attention to the **margin notes**, such as Helpful Hints, Reading Math notes, and Caution notes. These notes will help you understand concepts and avoid common mistakes.

Reading Math

Read -4^3 as "-4 to the 3rd power or -4 cubed".

Writing Math

A repeating decimal can be written with a bar over the digits

Helpful Hint

In Example 1A, parentheses are not needed because

Caution!

An open circle means that the corresponding value

The **glossary** is found in the back of your textbook. Use it to find definitions and examples of unfamiliar words or properties.

The **index** is located at the end of your textbook. Use it to find the page where a particular concept is taught.

The **Skills Bank** is found in the back of your textbook. These pages review concepts from previous math courses.

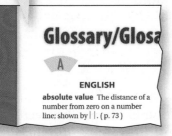

Glossary/Glosa

A

ENGLISH

absolute value The distance of a number from zero on a number line; shown by | |. (p. 73)

Index . . .

A

Absolute value, 73
Accuracy, 524
Acute angles, 454

Skills Bank . . .

Read and Write D

When reading and writing a dec to know the place value of the d

Try This

Use your textbook for the following problems.

1. Use the index to find the page where *exponent* is defined.

2. In Lesson 1-8, what does the Remember box, located in the margin of page 39, remind you about the perimeter of a figure?

3. Use the glossary to find the definition of each term: *order of operations, numerical expression, equation.*

4. Where can you review how to read and write decimals?

1-1 Numbers and Patterns

TN **GLE 0706.1.5** Use mathematical ideas and processes in different settings to formulate patterns, analyze graphs, set up and solve problems and interpret solutions.

Vocabulary

conjecture

Each year, football teams battle for the state championship. The table shows the number of teams in each round of a division's football playoffs. You can look for a pattern to find out how many teams are in rounds 5 and 6.

Football Playoffs						
Round	1	2	3	4	5	6
Number of Teams	64	32	16	8	▢	▢

EXAMPLE 1 **Identifying and Extending Number Patterns**

Identify a possible pattern. Use the pattern to write the next three numbers.

A 64, 32, 16, 8, ▢, ▢, ▢, . . .

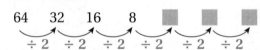

A pattern is to divide each number by 2 to get the next number.

$8 \div 2 = 4$ $4 \div 2 = 2$ $2 \div 2 = 1$

The next three numbers will be 4, 2, and 1.

B 51, 44, 37, 30, ▢, ▢, ▢, . . .

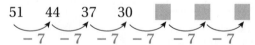

A pattern is to subtract 7 from each number to get the next number.

$30 - 7 = 23$ $23 - 7 = 16$ $16 - 7 = 9$

The next three numbers will be 23, 16, and 9.

C 2, 3, 5, 8, 12, ▢, ▢, ▢, . . .

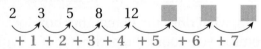

A pattern is to add one more than you did the time before.

$12 + 5 = 17$ $17 + 6 = 23$ $23 + 7 = 30$

The next three numbers will be 17, 23, and 30.

Video **Lesson Tutorials Online** my.hrw.com

EXAMPLE **2** **Identifying and Extending Geometric Patterns**

Identify a possible pattern. Use the pattern to draw the next three figures.

A

The pattern is alternating squares and circles with triangles between them.
The next three figures will be   .

B

The pattern is to shade every other triangle in a clockwise direction.
The next three figures will be   .

Helpful Hint

For more on conjectures, see Skills Bank p. SB12.

You can analyze patterns to make *conjectures*. A **conjecture** is a statement believed to be true.

EXAMPLE **3** **Using Tables to Identify and Extend Patterns**

Make a table that shows the number of triangles in each figure. Then make a conjecture about the number of triangles in the fifth figure of the pattern.
Complete the table, and use drawings to justify your answer.

  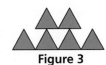

Figure 1   Figure 2   Figure 3

Figure	1	2	3	4	5
Number of Triangles	2	4	6	8	10

+2 +2 +2 +2

The pattern is to add 2 triangles each time.

Figure 4 has 6 + 2 = 8 triangles.

Figure 5 has 8 + 2 = 10 triangles.

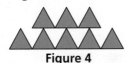 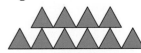

Figure 4

Figure 5

Think and Discuss

1. **Describe** two different number patterns that begin with 3, 6, . . .

2. **Tell** when it would be useful to make a table to help you identify and extend a pattern.

GUIDED PRACTICE

See Example 1   Identify a possible pattern. Use the pattern to write the next three numbers.

1. 6, 14, 22, 30, ▪, ▪, ▪, . . .

2. 1, 3, 9, 27, ▪, ▪, ▪, . . .

3. 59, 50, 41, 32, ▪, ▪, ▪, . . .

4. 8, 9, 11, 14, ▪, ▪, ▪, . . .

See Example 2   Identify a possible pattern. Use the pattern to draw the next three figures.

5.

6.

See Example 3   **7.** Make a table that shows the number of green triangles in each figure. Then make a conjecture about the number of green triangles in the fifth figure of the pattern. Complete the table, and use drawings to justify your answer.

Figure 1   Figure 2   Figure 3

INDEPENDENT PRACTICE

See Example 1   Identify a possible pattern. Use the pattern to write the next three numbers.

8. 27, 24, 21, 18, ▪, ▪, ▪, . . .

9. 4,096, 1,024, 256, 64, ▪, ▪, ▪, . . .

10. 1, 3, 7, 13, 21, ▪, ▪, ▪, . . .

11. 14, 37, 60, 83, ▪, ▪, ▪, . . .

See Example 2   Identify a possible pattern. Use the pattern to draw the next three figures.

12. ■ △ ● ■ △ ●

13. ⬡ ⬡ ⬡ ⬡

See Example 3   **14.** Make a table that shows the number of dots in each figure. Then make a conjecture about the numer of dots in the sixth figure of the pattern. Complete the table, and use drawings to justify your answer.

Figure 1   Figure 2   Figure 3   Figure 4

PRACTICE AND PROBLEM SOLVING

Extra Practice
See page EP2.

Use the rule to write the first five numbers in each pattern.

15. Start with 7; add 16 to each number to get the next number.

16. Start with 96; divide each number by 2 to get the next number.

17. Start with 50; subtract 2, then 4, then 6, and so on, to get the next number.

18. Critical Thinking Suppose the pattern 3, 6, 9, 12, 15 . . . is continued forever. Will the number 100 appear in the pattern? Why or why not?

Identify a possible pattern. Use the pattern to find the missing numbers.

19. 3, 12, ▢, 192, 768, ▢, ▢, …

20. 61, 55, ▢, 43, ▢, ▢, 25, …

21. ▢, ▢, 19, 27, 35, ▢, 51, …

22. 2, ▢, 8, ▢, 32, 64, ▢, …

23. Health The table shows the target heart rate during exercise for athletes of different ages. Assuming the pattern continues, what is the target heart rate for a 40-year-old athlete? a 65-year-old athlete?

Target Heart Rate	
Age	Heart Rate (beats per minute)
20	150
25	146
30	142
35	138

Draw the next three figures in each pattern.

24. ▷1 , △5 , ◁9 , ▽13 , ▷17 , △21 , , …

25. ●4 , ▪5 , ▲7 , ●10 , ▪14 , ▲19 , ●25 , , …

26. Social Studies In the ancient Mayan civilization, people used a number system based on bars and dots. Several numbers are shown below. Look for a pattern and write the number 18 in the Mayan system.

```
 ••      •••   ———   •••   •••
——   —   ——   ———   ———
  3    5    8    10   13   15
```

? 27. What's the Error? A student was asked to write the next three numbers in the pattern 96, 48, 24, 12, … . The student's response was 6, 2, 1. Describe and correct the student's error.

✐ 28. Write About It A school chess club meets every Tuesday during the month of March. March 1 falls on a Sunday. Explain how to use a number pattern to find all the dates when the club meets.

★ 29. Challenge Find the 83rd number in the pattern 5, 10, 15, 20, 25, … .

Test Prep and Spiral Review

30. Multiple Choice Which is the missing number in the pattern 2, 6, ▢, 54, 162, … ?

Ⓐ 10   Ⓑ 18   Ⓒ 30   Ⓓ 48

31. Gridded Response Find the next number in the pattern 9, 11, 15, 21, 29, 39, … .

Round each number to the nearest ten. (Previous course)

32. 61   **33.** 88   **34.** 105   **35.** 2,019   **36.** 11,403

Round each number to the nearest hundred. (Previous course)

37. 91   **38.** 543   **39.** 952   **40.** 4,050   **41.** 23,093

A DNA molecule makes a copy of itself by splitting in half. Each half becomes a molecule that is identical to the original. The molecules continue to split so that the two become four, the four become eight, and so on.

Each time DNA copies itself, the number of molecules doubles. After four copies, the number of molecules is $2 \cdot 2 \cdot 2 \cdot 2 = 16$.

This multiplication can also be written as a **power**, using a base and an *exponent*. The **exponent** tells how many times to use the **base** as a factor.

The structure of DNA can be compared to a twisted ladder.

Vocabulary

power

exponent

base

Reading Math

Read 2^4 as "the fourth power of 2" or "2 to the fourth power."

$$2 \cdot 2 \cdot 2 \cdot 2 = 2^4 = 16$$

Exponent

Base

EXAMPLE 1 **Evaluating Powers**

Interactivities Online ▶

Find each value.

A 5^2

$5^2 = 5 \cdot 5$ *Use 5 as a factor 2 times.*

    $= 25$

B 2^6

$2^6 = 2 \cdot 2 \cdot 2 \cdot 2 \cdot 2 \cdot 2$ *Use 2 as a factor 6 times.*

    $= 64$

C 25^1

$25^1 = 25$ *Any number to the first power is equal to that number.*

Any number to the zero power, except zero, is equal to 1.

$6^0 = 1$ $10^0 = 1$ $19^0 = 1$

Zero to the zero power is *undefined,* meaning that it does not exist.

To express a whole number as a power, write the number as the product of equal factors. Then write the product using the base and an exponent. For example, $10{,}000 = 10 \cdot 10 \cdot 10 \cdot 10 = 10^4$.

EXAMPLE 2 **Expressing Whole Numbers as Powers**

Write each number using an exponent and the given base.

A **49, base 7**

$49 = 7 \cdot 7$ *7 is used as a factor 2 times.*

    $= 7^2$

B **81, base 3**

$81 = 3 \cdot 3 \cdot 3 \cdot 3$ *3 is used as a factor 4 times.*

    $= 3^4$

EXAMPLE 3 *Earth Science Application*

Earth Science

An earthquake measuring 7.2 on the Richter scale struck Duzce, Turkey, on November 12, 1999.

The Richter scale measures an earthquake's strength, or magnitude. Each category in the table is 10 times stronger than the next lower category. For example, a large earthquake is 10 times stronger than a moderate earthquake. How many times stronger is a great earthquake than a moderate one?

Earthquake Strength	
Category	Magnitude
Moderate	5
Large	6
Major	7
Great	8

An earthquake with a magnitude of 6 is 10 times stronger than one with a magnitude of 5.

An earthquake with a magnitude of 7 is 10 times stronger than one with a magnitude of 6.

An earthquake with a magnitude of 8 is 10 times stronger than one with a magnitude of 7.

$$10 \cdot 10 \cdot 10 = 10^3 = 1{,}000$$

A great earthquake is 1,000 times stronger than a moderate one.

Think and Discuss

1. Describe a relationship between 3^5 and 3^6.

2. Tell which power of 8 is equal to 2^6. Explain.

3. Explain why any number to the first power is equal to that number.

Learn It Online
Homework Help Online **go.hrw.com**,
keyword MS10 1-2 **Go**
Exercises 1–30, 37, 39, 41, 45,
49, 51, 55

GUIDED PRACTICE

See Example **1**   Find each value.

1. 2^5 **2.** 3^3 **3.** 6^2 **4.** 9^1 **5.** 10^6

See Example **2**   Write each number using an exponent and the given base.

6. 25, base 5 **7.** 16, base 4 **8.** 27, base 3 **9.** 100, base 10

See Example **3**   **10. Earth Science** On the Richter scale, a great earthquake is 10 times stronger than a major one, and a major one is 10 times stronger than a large one. How many times stronger is a great earthquake than a large one?

INDEPENDENT PRACTICE

See Example **1**   Find each value.

11. 11^2 **12.** 3^5 **13.** 8^3 **14.** 4^3 **15.** 3^4

16. 2^5 **17.** 5^1 **18.** 2^3 **19.** 5^3 **20.** 30^1

See Example **2**   Write each number using an exponent and the given base.

21. 81, base 9 **22.** 4, base 4 **23.** 64, base 4

24. 1, base 7 **25.** 32, base 2 **26.** 128, base 2

27. 1,600, base 40 **28.** 2,500, base 50 **29.** 100,000, base 10

See Example **3**   **30.** In a game, a contestant had a starting score of one point. He tripled his score every turn for four turns. Write his score after four turns as a power. Then find his score.

PRACTICE AND PROBLEM SOLVING

Extra Practice
See page EP2.

Give two ways to represent each number using powers.

31. 81 **32.** 16 **33.** 64 **34.** 729 **35.** 625

Compare. Write <, >, or =.

36. 4^2 ▢ 15 **37.** 2^3 ▢ 3^2 **38.** 64 ▢ 4^3 **39.** 8^3 ▢ 7^4

40. 10,000 ▢ 10^5 **41.** 6^5 ▢ 3,000 **42.** 9^3 ▢ 3^6 **43.** 5^4 ▢ 17^0

44. To find the volume of a cube, find the third power of the length of an edge of the cube. What is the volume of a cube that is 6 inches long on an edge?

45. Patterns Domingo decided to save $0.03 the first day and to triple the amount he saves each day. How much will he save on the seventh day?

46. Life Science A newborn panda cub weighs an average of 4 ounces. How many ounces might a one-year-old panda weigh if its weight increases by the power of 5 in one year?

47. Social Studies If the populations of the cities in the table double every 10 years, what will their populations be in 2034?

48. Critical Thinking Explain why $6^3 \neq 3^6$.

City	Population (2004)
Yuma, AZ	86,070
Phoenix, AZ	1,421,298

49. Hobbies Malia is making a quilt with a pattern of rings. In the center ring, she uses four stars. In each of the next three rings, she uses three times as many stars as in the one before. How many stars does she use in the fourth ring? Write the answer using a power and find its value.

Order each set of numbers from least to greatest.

50. 29, 2^3, 6^2, 16^0, 3^5

51. 4^3, 33, 6^2, 5^3, 10^1

52. 7^2, 2^4, 80, 10^2, 1^8

53. 2, 1^8, 3^4, 16^1, 0

54. 5^2, 21, 11^2, 13^1, 1^9

55. 2^5, 3^3, 9, 5^2, 8^1

56. Two weeks before Jackie's birthday her parents gave her one penny. They plan to double the amount of pennies she receives each day until her birthday. Use exponents to write a pattern that represents the number of pennies Jackie receives the first 5 days. Then use the pattern to predict how many pennies she will receive on her birthday.

57. Life Science The cells of some kinds of bacteria divide every 30 minutes. If you begin with a single cell, how many cells will there be after 1 hour? 2 hours? 3 hours?

58. What's the Error? A student wrote 64 as $8 \cdot 2$. What was the student's error?

59. Write About It Is 2^5 greater than or less than 3^3? Explain your answer.

60. Challenge What is the length of the edge of a cube if its volume is 1,000 cubic meters?

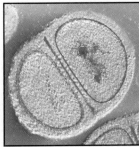

Bacteria divide by pinching in two. This process is called binary fission.

Test Prep and Spiral Review

61. Multiple Choice What is the value of 4^6?

  (A) 24   (B) 1,024   (C) 4,096   (D) 16,384

62. Multiple Choice Which of the following is NOT equal to 64?

  (F) 6^4 (G) 4^3 (H) 2^6 (J) 8^2

63. Gridded Response Simplify $2^3 + 3^2$.

Simplify. (Previous course)

64. $15 + 27 + 5 + 3 + 11 + 16 + 7 + 4$

65. $2 + 6 + 5 + 7 + 100 + 1 + 75$

Identify a possible pattern. Use the pattern to write the next three numbers. (Lesson 1-1)

66. 100, 91, 82, 73, 64, . . .

67. 17, 19, 22, 26, 31, . . .

68. 2, 6, 18, 54, 162, . . .

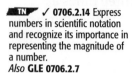 ✓ **0706.2.14** Express numbers in scientific notation and recognize its importance in representing the magnitude of a number. *Also* **GLE 0706.2.7**

The distance from Venus to the Sun is greater than 100,000,000 kilometers. You can write this number as a power of ten by using a base of ten and an exponent.

$$10 \cdot 10 \cdot 10 \cdot 10 \cdot 10 \cdot 10 \cdot 10 \cdot 10 = 10^8$$

Power of ten

Vocabulary

scientific notation

The table shows several powers of ten.

Interactivities Online ▶

Power of 10	Meaning	Value
10^1	10	10
10^2	$10 \cdot 10$	100
10^3	$10 \cdot 10 \cdot 10$	1,000
10^4	$10 \cdot 10 \cdot 10 \cdot 10$	10,000

You can find the product of a number and a power of ten by multiplying or by moving the decimal point of the number. For powers of ten with positive exponents, move the decimal point to the right.

EXAMPLE 1 **Multiplying by Powers of Ten**

Multiply $137 \cdot 10^3$.

A **Method 1: Evaluate the power.**

$137 \cdot 10^3 = 137 \cdot (10 \cdot 10 \cdot 10)$ *Multiply 10 by itself 3 times.*

$= 137 \cdot 1,000$ *Multiply.*

$= 137,000$

B **Method 2: Use mental math.**

$137 \cdot 10^3 = 137.000$ *Move the decimal point 3 places.*

$= 137,000$ 3 places *(You will need to add 3 zeros.)*

Remember!

A factor is a number that is multiplied by another number to get a product. See Skills Bank p. SB6.

Scientific notation is a kind of shorthand that can be used to write numbers. Numbers expressed in scientific notation are written as the product of two factors.

Video **Lesson Tutorials Online** my.hrw.com

In scientific notation, 17,900,000 is written as

$$1.79 \times 10^7$$

A number greater than or equal to 1 but less than 10

A power of 10

EXAMPLE 2 **Writing Numbers in Scientific Notation**

Write 9,580,000 in scientific notation.

$9,580,000 = 9,\underset{\frown}{580,000}.$ *Move the decimal point to get a number between 1 and 10.*

$= 9.58 \times 10^6$ *The exponent is equal to the number of places the decimal point is moved.*

EXAMPLE 3 **Writing Numbers in Standard Form**

Pluto is about 3.7×10^9 miles from the Sun. Write this distance in standard form.

$3.7 \times 10^9 = 3.\underset{\frown}{700000000}$ *Since the exponent is 9, move the decimal point 9 places to the right.*

$= 3,700,000,000$

Pluto is about 3,700,000,000 miles from the Sun.

EXAMPLE 4 **Comparing Numbers in Scientific Notation**

Mercury is 9.17×10^7 kilometers from Earth. Jupiter is 6.287×10^8 kilometers from Earth. Which planet is closer to Earth?

To compare numbers written in scientific notation, first compare the exponents. If the exponents are equal, then compare the decimal portion of the numbers.

Mercury: 9.17×10^7 km

Jupiter: 6.287×10^8 km   *Compare the exponents.*

Notice that $7 < 8$. So $9.17 \times 10^7 < 6.287 \times 10^8$.

Mercury is closer to Earth than Jupiter.

Think and Discuss

1. Tell whether 15×10^9 is in scientific notation. Explain.

2. Compare 4×10^3 and 3×10^4. Explain how you know which is greater.

GUIDED PRACTICE

See Example **1** **Multiply.**

1. $15 \cdot 10^2$ **2.** $12 \cdot 10^4$ **3.** $208 \cdot 10^3$ **4.** $113 \cdot 10^7$

See Example **2** **Write each number in scientific notation.**

5. 3,600,000   **6.** 214,000   **7.** 8,000,000,000   **8.** 42,000

See Example **3**   **9.** A drop of water contains about 2.0×10^{21} molecules. Write this number in standard form.

See Example **4**   **10.** **Astronomy** The diameter of Neptune is 4.9528×10^7 meters. The diameter of Mars is 6.7868×10^6 meters. Which planet has the larger diameter?

INDEPENDENT PRACTICE

See Example **1** **Multiply.**

11. $21 \cdot 10^2$ **12.** $8 \cdot 10^4$ **13.** $25 \cdot 10^5$ **14.** $40 \cdot 10^4$

15. $268 \cdot 10^3$ **16.** $550 \cdot 10^7$ **17.** $2{,}115 \cdot 10^5$ **18.** $70{,}030 \cdot 10^1$

See Example **2** **Write each number in scientific notation.**

19. 428,000   **20.** 1,610,000   **21.** 3,000,000,000   **22.** 60,100

23. 52.000   **24.** $29.8 \cdot 10^7$ **25.** 8,900,000   **26.** $500 \cdot 10^3$

See Example **3**   **27.** **History** Ancient Egyptians hammered gold into sheets so thin that it took 3.67×10^5 sheets to make a pile 2.5 centimeters high. Write the number of sheets in standard form.

See Example **4**   **28.** **Astronomy** Mars is 7.83×10^7 kilometers from Earth. Venus is 4.14×10^7 kilometers from Earth. Which planet is closer to Earth?

PRACTICE AND PROBLEM SOLVING

Extra Practice
See page EP2.

Find the missing number or numbers.

29. $24{,}500 = 2.45 \times 10^{\blacksquare}$ **30.** $16{,}800 = \blacksquare \times 10^4$ **31.** $\blacksquare = 3.40 \times 10^2$

32. $280{,}000 = 2.8 \times 10^{\blacksquare}$ **33.** $5.4 \times 10^8 = \blacksquare$ **34.** $60{,}000{,}000 = \blacksquare \times 10^{\blacksquare}$

Tell whether each number is written in scientific notation. Then order the numbers from least to greatest.

35. 43.7×10^6 **36.** 1×10^7 **37.** 2.9×10^7 **38.** 305×10^6

39. **Physical Science** In a vacuum, light travels at a speed of about nine hundred and eighty million feet per second. Write this speed in scientific notation.

40. The earliest rocks native to Earth formed during the Archean eon. Calculate the length of this eon. Write your answer in scientific notation.

41. Dinosaurs lived during the Mesozoic era. Calculate the length of the Mesozoic era. Write your answer in scientific notation.

42. Tropites were prehistoric marine animals whose fossil remains can be used to date the rock formations in which they are found. Such fossils are known as *index fossils*. Tropites lived between 2.08×10^8 and 2.30×10^8 years ago. During what geologic time period did they live?

43. ✐ **Write About It** Explain why scientific notation is especially useful in earth science.

44. ⭐ **Challenge** We live in the Holocene epoch. Write the age of this epoch in scientific notation.

Geologic Time Scale		
Eon	**Era**	**Period**
Phanerozoic (540 mya*–present)	**Cenozoic** (65 mya–present)	**Quaternary** (1.8 mya–present) Holocene epoch (11,000 yrs ago–present) Pleistocene epoch (1.8 mya–11,000 yrs ago) **Tertiary** (65 mya–1.8 mya) Pliocene epoch (5.3 mya–1.8 mya) Miocene epoch (23.8 mya–5.3 mya) Oligocene epoch (33.7 mya–23.8 mya) Eocene epoch (54.8 mya–33.7 mya) Paleocene epoch (65 mya–54.8 mya)
	Mesozoic (248 mya–65 mya)	Cretaceous (144 mya–65 mya) Jurassic (206 mya–144 mya) Triassic (248 mya–206 mya)
	Paleozoic (540 mya–248 mya)	Permian (290 mya–248 mya) Pennsylvanian (323 mya–290 mya) Mississippian (354 mya–323 mya) Devonian (417 mya–354 mya) Silurian (443 mya–417 mya) Ordovician (490 mya–443 mya) Cambrian (540 mya–490 mya)
Proterozoic (2,500 mya–540 mya)		
Archean (3,800 mya–2,500 mya)		
Hadean (4,600 mya–3,800 mya)		

*mya = million years ago

Test Prep and Spiral Review

45. Multiple Choice Kaylee wrote in her dinosaur report that the Jurassic period was 1.75×10^8 years ago. According to Kaylee's report, how many years ago was the Jurassic period?

Ⓐ 1,750,000　　Ⓑ 17,500,000　　Ⓒ 175,000,000　　Ⓓ 17,500,000,000

46. Multiple Choice What is 2,430,000 in scientific notation?

Ⓕ 243×10^4　　Ⓖ 24.3×10^5　　Ⓗ 2.43×10^5　　Ⓙ 2.43×10^6

Identify a possible pattern. Use the pattern to write the next three numbers. (Lesson 1-1)

47. 19, 16, 13, 10, ▮, ▮, ▮, . . .　　　　**48.** 5, 15, 45, 135, ▮, ▮, ▮, . . .

Write each number using an exponent and the given base. (Lesson 1-2)

49. 625, base 5　　　　**50.** 512, base 8　　　　**51.** 512, base 2

Technology LAB 1-3

Use with Lesson 1-3

TN ✓ **0706.1.11** Translate from calculator notation to scientific/standard notation.
Also **GLE 0706.2.7**

Scientific Notation with a Calculator

Learn It Online
Lab Resources Online **go.hrw.com**,
keyword **MS10 Lab1** **Go**

Scientists often have to work with very large numbers. For example, the Andromeda Galaxy contains over 200,000,000,000 stars. Scientific notation is a compact way of expressing large numbers such as this.

Activity

1 Show 200,000,000,000 in scientific notation.

Enter 200,000,000,000 on your graphing calculator. Then press **ENTER**.

2 E 11 on the calculator display means 2×10^{11}, which is 200,000,000,000 in scientific notation. Your calculator automatically puts very large numbers into scientific notation.

You can use the **EE** function to enter 2×10^{11} directly into the calculator. Enter 2×10^{11} by pressing 2 **2nd** **EE ,** 11 **ENTER**.

2 Simplify $2.31 \times 10^4 \div 525$.

Enter 2.31×10^4 into your calculator in scientific notation, and then divide by 525. To do this, press 2.31 **2nd** **EE ,** **4** **÷** 525 **ENTER**.
Your answer should be 44.

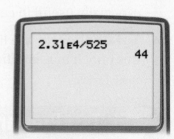

Think and Discuss

1. Explain how scientific notation and calculator notation are similar. What could the "E" possibly stand for in calculator notation?

Try This

Use the calculator to write each number in scientific notation.

1. 6,500,000

2. 15,000,000

3. 360,000,000,000

Simplify each expression, and express your answer in scientific notation.

4. $8.4 \times 10^6 \div 300$

5. $9 \times 10^3 - 900$

6. $2.5 \times 10^9 \times 10$

7. $3 \times 10^2 + 6000$

8. $2.85 \times 10^8 \div 95$

9. $1.5 \times 10^7 \div 150$

TN ✓ **0706.2.2** Develop and analyze algorithms and compute efficiently with integers and rational numbers. *Also* ✓ **0706.3.1**

To assemble the correct product, directions must be followed in the correct order. In mathematics, some tasks must also be done in a certain order.

A **numerical expression** is made up of numbers and operations. When simplifying a numerical expression, rules must be followed so that everyone gets the same answer. That is why mathematicians have agreed upon the **order of operations**.

Vocabulary

numerical expression

order of operations

Interactivities Online ▶

ORDER OF OPERATIONS

1. Perform operations within grouping symbols.
2. Evaluate powers.
3. Multiply and divide in order from left to right.
4. Add and subtract in order from left to right.

EXAMPLE **1** **Using the Order of Operations**

Simplify each expression. Use the order of operations to justify your answer.

A $27 - 18 \div 6$

$27 - 18 \div 6$	*Divide.*
$27 - 3$	*Subtract.*
24	

B $36 - 18 \div 2 \cdot 3 + 8$

$36 - 18 \div 2 \cdot 3 + 8$	*Divide and multiply from left to right.*
$36 - 9 \cdot 3 + 8$	
$36 - 27 + 8$	*Subtract and add from left to right.*
$9 + 8$	
17	

C $5 + 6^2 \cdot 10$

$5 + 6^2 \cdot 10$	*Evaluate the power.*
$5 + 36 \cdot 10$	*Multiply.*
$5 + 360$	*Add.*
365	

EXAMPLE 2 **Using the Order of Operations with Grouping Symbols**

Simplify each expression.

A $36 - (2 \cdot 6) \div 3$

$36 - (2 \cdot 6) \div 3$	*Perform the operation in parentheses.*
$36 - 12 \div 3$	*Divide.*
$36 - 4$	*Subtract.*
32	

Helpful Hint

When an expression has a set of grouping symbols within a second set of grouping symbols, begin with the innermost set.

B $[(4 + 12 \div 4) - 2]^3$

$[(4 + 12 \div 4) - 2]^3$	*The parentheses are inside the brackets,*
$[(4 + 3) - 2]^3$	*so perform the operations inside the*
$[7 - 2]^3$	*parentheses first.*
5^3	
125	

EXAMPLE 3 *Career Application*

Maria works part-time in a law office, where she earns \$20 per hour. The table shows the number of hours she worked last week. Simplify the expression $(6 + 5 \cdot 3) \cdot 20$ to find out how much money Maria earned last week.

Day	Hours
Monday	6
Tuesday	5
Wednesday	5
Thursday	5

$(6 + 5 \cdot 3) \cdot 20$	*Perform the operations in parentheses.*
$(6 + 15) \cdot 20$	*Add.*
$21 \cdot 20$	*Multiply.*
420	

Maria earned \$420 last week.

Think and Discuss

1. Apply the order of operations to determine if the expressions $3 + 4^2$ and $(3 + 4)^2$ have the same value.

2. Give the correct order of operations for simplifying $(5 + 3 \cdot 20) \div 13 + 3^2$.

3. Determine where grouping symbols should be inserted in the expression $3 + 9 - 4 \cdot 2$ so that its value is 13.

Video **Lesson Tutorials Online** my.hrw.com

Learn It Online
Homework Help Online go.hrw.com,
keyword MS10 1-4 Go
Exercises 1–18, 21, 23, 27, 29, 33, 35, 37

GUIDED PRACTICE

See Example 1 **Simplify each expression. Use the order of operations to justify your answer.**

1. $43 + 16 \div 4$

2. $28 - 4 \cdot 3 \div 6 + 4$

3. $25 - 4^2 \div 8$

See Example 2 **4.** $26 - (7 \cdot 3) + 2$

5. $(3^2 + 11) \div 5$

6. $32 + 6(4 - 2^2) + 8$

See Example 3 **7. Career** Caleb earns $10 per hour. He worked 4 hours on Monday, Wednesday, and Friday. He worked 8 hours on Tuesday and Thursday. Simplify the expression $(3 \cdot 4 + 2 \cdot 8) \cdot 10$ to find out how much Caleb earned in all.

INDEPENDENT PRACTICE

See Example 1 **Simplify each expression. Use the order of operations to justify your answer.**

8. $3 + 7 \cdot 5 - 1$

9. $5 \cdot 9 - 3$

10. $3 - 2 + 6 \cdot 2^2$

See Example 2 **11.** $(3 \cdot 3 - 3)^2 \div 3 + 3$

12. $2^5 - (4 \cdot 5 + 3)$

13. $(3 \div 3) + 3 \cdot (3^3 - 3)$

14. $4^3 \div 8 - 2$

15. $(8 - 2)^2 \cdot (8 - 1)^2 \div 3$

16. $9{,}234 \div [3 \cdot 3(1 + 8^3)]$

See Example 3 **17. Consumer Math** Maki paid a $14 basic fee plus $25 a day to rent a car. Simplify the expression $14 + 5 \cdot 25$ to find out how much it cost her to rent the car for 5 days.

18. Consumer Math Enrico spent $20 per square yard for carpet and $35 for a carpet pad. Simplify the expression $35 + 20(12^2 \div 9)$ to find out how much Enrico spent to carpet a 12 ft by 12 ft room.

PRACTICE AND PROBLEM SOLVING

Extra Practice
See page EP3.

Simplify each expression.

19. $90 - 36 \times 2$

20. $16 + 14 \div 2 - 7$

21. $64 \div 2^2 + 4$

22. $(4.5 \times 10^2) + (6 \div 3)$

23. $(9 - 4)^2 - 12 \times 2$

24. $[1 + (2 + 5)^2] \times 2$

Compare. Write <, >, or =.

25. $8 \cdot 3 - 2 \ \blacksquare\ 8 \cdot (3 - 2)$

26. $(6 + 10) \div 2 \ \blacksquare\ 6 + 10 \div 2$

27. $12 \div 3 \cdot 4 \ \blacksquare\ 12 \div (3 \cdot 4)$

28. $18 + 6 - 2 \ \blacksquare\ 18 + (6 - 2)$

29. $[6(8 - 3) + 2] \ \blacksquare\ 6(8 - 3) + 2$

30. $(18 - 14) \div (2 + 2) \ \blacksquare\ 18 - 14 \div 2 + 2$

Critical Thinking Insert grouping symbols to make each statement true.

31. $4 \cdot 8 - 3 = 20$

32. $5 + 9 - 3 \div 2 = 8$

33. $12 - 2^2 \div 5 = 20$

34. $4 \cdot 2 + 6 = 32$

35. $4 + 6 - 3 \div 7 = 1$

36. $9 \cdot 8 - 6 \div 3 = 6$

37. Bertha earned $8.00 per hour for 4 hours babysitting and $10.00 per hour for 5 hours painting a room. Simplify the expression $8 \cdot 4 + 10 \cdot 5$ to find out how much Bertha earned in all.

38. Consumer Math Mike bought a painting for $512. He sold it at an antique auction for 4 times the amount that he paid for it, and then he purchased another painting with half of the profit that he made. Simplify the expression $(512 \cdot 4 - 512) \div 2$ to find how much Mike paid for the second painting.

39. Multi-Step Anelise bought four shirts and two pairs of jeans. She paid $6 in sales tax.

    a. Write an expression that shows how much she spent on shirts.

    b. Write an expression that shows how much she spent on jeans.

    c. Write and evaluate an expression to show how much she spent on clothes, including sales tax.

40. Choose a Strategy There are four children in a family. The sum of the squares of the ages of the three youngest children equals the square of the age of the oldest child. How old are the children?

    (A) 1, 4, 8, 9   (B) 1, 3, 6, 12   (C) 4, 5, 8, 10   (D) 2, 3, 8, 16

41. Write About It Describe the order in which you would perform the operations to find the correct value of $[(2 + 4)^2 - 2 \cdot 3] \div 6$.

42. Challenge Use the numbers 3, 5, 6, 2, 54, and 5 in that order to write an expression that has a value of 100.

Test Prep and Spiral Review

43. Multiple Choice Which operation should be performed first to simplify the expression $18 - 1 \cdot 9 \div 3 + 8$?

    (A) Addition   (B) Subtraction   (C) Multiplication   (D) Division

44. Multiple Choice Which expression does NOT simplify to 81?

    (F) $9 \cdot (4 + 5)$ (G) $7 + 16 \cdot 4 + 10$ (H) $3 \cdot 25 + 2$ (J) $10^2 - 4 \cdot 5 + 1$

45. Multiple Choice Quinton bought 2 pairs of jeans for $30 each and 3 pairs of socks for $5 each. Which expression can be simplified to determine the total amount Quinton paid for the jeans and socks?

    (A) $2 \cdot 3(30 + 5)$ (B) $(2 + 3) \cdot (30 + 5)$ (C) $2 \cdot (30 + 5) \cdot 3$ (D) $2 \cdot 30 + 3 \cdot 5$

Find each value. (Lesson 1-2)

46. 8^6 **47.** 9^3 **48.** 4^5 **49.** 3^3 **50.** 7^1

Multiply. (Lesson 1-3)

51. $612 \cdot 10^3$ **52.** $43.8 \cdot 10^6$ **53.** $590 \cdot 10^5$ **54.** $3.1 \cdot 10^7$ **55.** $1.91 \cdot 10^2$

Explore Order of Operations

Use with Lesson 1-4

TN ✓ **0706.2.2** Develop and analyze algorithms and compute efficiently with integers and rational numbers. *Also* **GLE 0706.1.8,** ✓ **0706.3.1**

Learn It Online
Lab Resources Online **go.hrw.com,**
keyword MS10 Lab1 Go

REMEMBER

The order of operations
1. Perform operations within grouping symbols.
2. Evaluate powers.
3. Multiply and divide in order from left to right.
4. Add and subtract in order from left to right.

Many calculators have an x^2 key that allows you to find the square of a number. On calculators that do not have this key, or to use exponents other than 2, you can use the caret key, $\wedge$.

For example, to evaluate 3^5, press 3 $\wedge$ 5, and then press ENTER.

Activity

1 Simplify $4 \cdot 2^3$ using paper and pencil. Then check your answer with a calculator.

First simplify the expression using paper and pencil: $4 \cdot 2^3 = 4 \cdot 8 = 32$.

Then simplify $4 \cdot 2^3$ using your calculator.

Notice that the calculator automatically evaluates the power first. If you want to perform the multiplication first, you must put that operation inside parentheses.

2 Use a calculator to simplify $\dfrac{(2 + 5 \cdot 4)^3}{4^2}$.

Think and Discuss

1. Is $2 + 5 \cdot 4^3 + 4^2$ equivalent to $(2 + 5 \cdot 4^3) + 4^2$? Explain.

Try This

Simplify each expression with pencil and paper. Check your answers with a calculator.

1. $3 \cdot 2^3 + 5$ **2.** $3 \cdot (2^3 + 5)$ **3.** $(3 \cdot 2)^2$ **4.** $3 \cdot 2^2$ **5.** $2^{(3 \cdot 2)}$

Use a calculator to simplify each expression. Round your answers to the nearest hundredth.

6. $(2.1 + 5.6 \cdot 4^3) \div 6^4$ **7.** $[(2.1 + 5.6) \cdot 4^3] \div 6^4$ **8.** $[(8.6 - 1.5) \div 2^3] \div 5^2$

TN ✓ **0706.2.3** Recognize that rational numbers satisfy the commutative and associative laws of addition and multiplication and the distributive law. *Also* ✓ **0706.3.1**

In Lesson 1-4 you learned how to use the order of operations to simplify numerical expressions. The following properties of numbers are also useful when you simplify expressions.

Vocabulary

Commutative Property

Associative Property

Identity Property

Distributive Property

Commutative Property		
Words	Numbers	Algebra
You can add numbers in any order and multiply numbers in any order.	$3 + 8 = 8 + 3$ $5 \cdot 7 = 7 \cdot 5$	$a + b = b + a$ $ab = ba$

Associative Property		
Words	Numbers	Algebra
When you add or multiply, you can group the numbers together in any combination.	$(4 + 5) + 1 = 4 + (5 + 1)$ $(9 \cdot 2) \cdot 6 = 9 \cdot (2 \cdot 6)$	$(a + b) + c = a + (b + c)$ $(a \cdot b) \cdot c = a \cdot (b \cdot c)$

Identity Property		
Words	Numbers	Algebra
The sum of 0 and any number is the number. The product of 1 and any number is the number.	$4 + 0 = 4$ $8 \cdot 1 = 8$	$a + 0 = a$ $a \cdot 1 = a$

Helpful Hint

For more on properties, see Skills Bank p. SB2.

EXAMPLE 1 **Identifying Properties of Addition and Multiplication**

Tell which property is represented.

A $2 + (7 + 8) = (2 + 7) + 8$

$2 + (7 + 8) = (2 + 7) + 8$ *The numbers are regrouped.*

Associative Property

B $25 \cdot 1 = 25$

$25 \cdot 1 = 25$ *One of the factors is 1.*

Identity Property

C $xy = yx$

$xy = yx$ *The order of the variables is switched.*

Commutative Property

Video **Lesson Tutorials Online** my.hrw.com

You can use properties and mental math to rearrange or regroup numbers into combinations that are easier to work with.

EXAMPLE **2** **Using Properties to Simplify Expressions**

Simplify each expression. Justify each step.

A $12 + 19 + 18$

$$
\begin{aligned}
12 + 19 + 18 &= 19 + 12 + 18 & \textit{Commutative Property} \\
&= 19 + (12 + 18) & \textit{Associative Property} \\
&= 19 + 30 & \textit{Add.} \\
&= 49
\end{aligned}
$$

B $25 \cdot 13 \cdot 4$

$$
\begin{aligned}
25 \cdot 13 \cdot 4 &= 25 \cdot 4 \cdot 13 & \textit{Commutative Property} \\
&= (25 \cdot 4) \cdot 13 & \textit{Associative Property} \\
&= 100 \cdot 13 & \textit{Multiply.} \\
&= 1,300
\end{aligned}
$$

You can use the Distributive Property to multiply numbers mentally by breaking apart one of the numbers and writing it as a sum or difference.

Remember!

Multiplication can be written as $a(b + c)$ or $a \cdot (b + c)$.

Distributive Property		
Numbers	$6(9 + 14) = 6 \cdot 9 + 6 \cdot 14$	$8(5 - 2) = 8 \cdot 5 - 8 \cdot 2$
Algebra	$a(b + c) = ab + ac$	$a(b - c) = ab - ac$

EXAMPLE **3** **Using the Distributive Property to Multiply Mentally**

Use the Distributive Property to find 7(29).

Method 1

$$
\begin{aligned}
7(29) &= 7(20 + 9) & \textit{Rewrite 29.} \\
&= (7 \cdot 20) + (7 \cdot 9) & \textit{Use the Distributive} \\
& & \textit{Property.} \\
&= 140 + 63 & \textit{Multiply.} \\
&= 203 & \textit{Simplify.}
\end{aligned}
$$

Method 2

$$
\begin{aligned}
7(29) &= 7(30 - 1) \\
&= (7 \cdot 30) - (7 \cdot 1) \\
&= 210 - 7 \\
&= 203
\end{aligned}
$$

Think and Discuss

1. Describe two different ways to simplify the expression $7 \cdot (3 + 9)$.

2. Explain how the Distributive Property can help you find $6 \cdot 102$ using mental math.

Exercises

Learn It Online
Homework Help Online **go.hrw.com**,
keyword **MS10 1-5** **Go**
Exercises 1–36, 41, 47, 49, 51, 53

GUIDED PRACTICE

See Example **1** Tell which property is represented.

1. $1 + (6 + 7) = (1 + 6) + 7$ **2.** $1 \cdot 10 = 10$ **3.** $3 \cdot 5 = 5 \cdot 3$

4. $6 + 0 = 6$ **5.** $4 \cdot (4 \cdot 2) = (4 \cdot 4) \cdot 2$ **6.** $x + y = y + x$

See Example **2** Simplify each expression. Justify each step.

7. $8 + 23 + 2$ **8.** $2 \cdot (17 \cdot 5)$ **9.** $(25 \cdot 11) \cdot 4$

10. $17 + 29 + 3$ **11.** $16 + (17 + 14)$ **12.** $5 \cdot 19 \cdot 20$

See Example **3** Use the Distributive Property to find each product.

13. $2(19)$ **14.** $5(31)$ **15.** $(22)2$

16. $(13)6$ **17.** $8(26)$ **18.** $(34)6$

INDEPENDENT PRACTICE

See Example **1** Tell which property is represented.

19. $1 + 0 = 1$ **20.** $xyz = x \cdot (yz)$ **21.** $9 + (9 + 0) = (9 + 9) + 0$

22. $11 + 25 = 25 + 11$ **23.** $7 \cdot 1 = 7$ **24.** $16 \cdot 4 = 4 \cdot 16$

See Example **2** Simplify each expression. Justify each step.

25. $50 \cdot 16 \cdot 2$ **26.** $9 + 34 + 1$ **27.** $4 \cdot (25 \cdot 9)$

28. $27 + 28 + 3$ **29.** $20 + (63 + 80)$ **30.** $25 + 17 + 75$

See Example **3** Use the Distributive Property to find each product.

31. $9(15)$ **32.** $(14)5$ **33.** $3(58)$

34. $10(42)$ **35.** $(23)4$ **36.** $(16)5$

PRACTICE AND PROBLEM SOLVING

Extra Practice
See page EP3.

Write an example of each property using whole numbers.

37. Commutative Property   **38.** Identity Property

39. Associative Property   **40.** Distributive Property

41. Architecture The figure shows the floor plan for a studio loft. To find the area of the loft, the architect multiplies the length and the width: $(14 + 8) \cdot 10$. Use the Distributive Property to find the area of the loft.

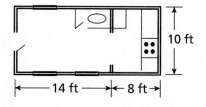

Simplify each expression. Justify each step.

42. $32 + 26 + 43$ **43.** $50 \cdot 45 \cdot 2^2$ **44.** $5 + 16 + 5^2$ **45.** $35 \cdot 25 \cdot 20$

Complete each equation. Then tell which property is represented.

46. $5 + 16 = 16 +$ ▢

47. $15 \cdot 1 =$ ▢

48. ▢ $\cdot (4 + 7) = 3 \cdot 4 + 3 \cdot 7$

49. $20 +$ ▢ $= 20$

50. $2 \cdot$ ▢ $\cdot 9 = (2 \cdot 13) \cdot 9$

51. $8 + ($ ▢ $+ 4) = (8 + 8) + 4$

52. $2 \cdot (6 + 1) = 2 \cdot$ ▢ $+ 2 \cdot 1$

53. $(12 - 9) \cdot$ ▢ $= 12 \cdot 2 - 9 \cdot 2$

54. Sports Janice wants to know the total number of games won by the Denver Nuggets basketball team over the three seasons shown in the table. What expression should she simplify? Explain how she can use mental math and the properties of this lesson to simplify the expression.

Denver Nuggets		
Season	Won	Lost
2001–02	27	55
2002–03	17	65
2003–04	43	39

 55. What's the Error? A student simplified the expression $6 \cdot (9 + 12)$ as shown. What is the student's error?

$6 \cdot (9 + 12) = 6 \cdot 9 + 12$
$= 54 + 12$
$= 66$

 56. Write About It Do you think there is a Commutative Property of Subtraction? Give an example to justify your answer.

⭐ **57. Challenge** Use the Distributive Property to simplify $\frac{1}{6} \cdot (36 + \frac{1}{2})$.

Test Prep and Spiral Review

58. Multiple Choice Which is an example of the Associative Property?

Ⓐ $4 + 0 = 4$

Ⓒ $5 + 7 = 7 + 5$

Ⓑ $9 + 8 + 2 = 9 + (8 + 2)$

Ⓓ $5 \cdot (12 + 3) = 5 \cdot 12 + 5 \cdot 3$

59. Multiple Choice Which property is $2 \cdot (3 + 7) = (2 \cdot 3) + (2 \cdot 7)$ an example of?

Ⓕ Associative   Ⓖ Commutative   Ⓗ Distributive   Ⓙ Identity

60. Short Response Show how to use the Distributive Property to simplify the expression $8(27)$.

Write each number using an exponent and the given base. (Lesson 1-2)

61. 36, base 6   **62.** 64, base 2   **63.** 9, base 3   **64.** 1,000, base 10

Simplify each expression. (Lesson 1-4)

65. $25 + 5 - (6^2 - 7)$ **66.** $3^3 - (6 + 3)$ **67.** $(4^2 + 5) \div 7$ **68.** $(5 - 3)^2 \div (3^2 - 7)$

Quiz for Lessons 1-1 Through 1-5

1-1 Numbers and Patterns

Identify a possible pattern. Use the pattern to write the next three numbers or figures.

1. 8, 15, 22, 29, . . .   **2.** 79, 66, 53, 40, . . .   **3.** 21, 36, 51, 66, . . .

4.

5. Make a table that shows the number of squares in each figure. Then make a conjecture about the number of squares in the fifth figure of the pattern. Complete the table, and use drawings to justify your answer.

Figure 1   Figure 2   Figure 3

1-2 Exponents

Find each value.

6. 8^4 **7.** 7^3 **8.** 4^5 **9.** 6^2

10. The number of bacteria in a sample doubles every hour. How many bacteria cells will there be after 8 hours if there is one cell at the beginning? Write your answer as a power.

1-3 Scientific Notation

Multiply.

11. $456 \cdot 10^5$ **12.** $9.3 \cdot 10^2$ **13.** $0.36 \cdot 10^8$

Write each number in scientific notation.

14. 8,400,000   **15.** 521,000,000   **16.** 29,000

17. In May 2005, the world's population was over 6,446,000,000 and was increasing by 140 people each minute! Write this population in scientific notation.

1-4 Order of Operations

Simplify each expression.

18. $8 - 14 \div (9 - 2)$ **19.** $54 - 6 \cdot 3 + 4^2$ **20.** $4 - 24 \div 2^3$ **21.** $4(3 + 2)^2 - 9$

1-5 Properties of Numbers

Simplify each expression. Justify each step.

22. $29 + 50 + 21$ **23.** $5 \cdot 18 \cdot 20$ **24.** $34 + 62 + 36$ **25.** $3 \cdot 11 \cdot 20$

Focus on Problem Solving

Solve

• **Choose an operation: multiplication or division**

To solve a word problem, you must determine which mathematical operation you can use to find the answer. One way of doing this is to determine the action the problem is asking you to take. If you are putting equal parts together, then you need to multiply. If you are separating something into equal parts, then you need to divide.

Decide what action each problem is asking you to take, and tell whether you must multiply or divide. Then explain your decision.

1 Judy plays the flute in the band. She practices for 3 hours every week. Judy practices only half as long as Angie, who plays the clarinet. How long does Angie practice playing the clarinet each week?

2 Each year, members of the band and choir are invited to join the bell ensemble for the winter performance. There are 18 bells in the bell ensemble. This year, each student has 3 bells to play. How many students are in the bell ensemble this year?

3 For every percussion instrument in the band, there are 4 wind instruments. If there are 48 wind instruments in the band, how many percussion instruments are there?

4 A group of 4 people singing together in harmony is called a quartet. At a state competition for high school choir students, 7 quartets from different schools competed. How many students competed in the quartet competition?

TN SPI 0706.3.1 Evaluate algebraic expressions involving rational values for coefficients and/or variables.
Also GLE 0706.3.1, ✓ 0706.3.1 ✓ 0706.3.2

Harrison Ford was born in 1942. You can find out what year Harrison turned 18 by adding 18 to the year he was born.

$$1942 + 18$$

Vocabulary

variable

constant

algebraic expression

evaluate

In algebra, letters are often used to represent numbers. You can use a letter such as *a* to represent Harrison Ford's age. When he turns *a* years old, the year will be

$$1942 + a.$$

The letter *a* has a value that can change, or vary. When a letter represents a number that can vary, it is called a **variable**. The year 1942 is a **constant** because the number cannot change.

An **algebraic expression** consists of one or more variables. It usually contains constants and operations. For example, $1942 + a$ is an algebraic expression for the year Harrison Ford turns a certain age.

Age	Year born + age	= year at age
18	1942 + 18	1960
25	1942 + 25	1967
36	1942 + 36	1978
63	1942 + 63	2005
a	1942 + *a*	

To **evaluate** an algebraic expression, substitute a number for the variable.

EXAMPLE 1 **Evaluating Algebraic Expressions**

Evaluate *n* + 7 for each value of *n*.

A $n = 3$ $n + 7$
            $3 + 7$ *Substitute 3 for n.*
              10 *Add.*

Interactivities Online ▶

B $n = 5$ $n + 7$
            $5 + 7$ *Substitute 5 for n.*
              12 *Add.*

Multiplication and division of variables can be written in several ways, as shown in the table.

When evaluating expressions, use the order of operations.

Multiplication		Division	
$7t$ $7 \cdot t$		$\dfrac{q}{2}$	$q/2$
$7(t)$ $7 \times t$		$q \div 2$	
ab $a \cdot b$		$\dfrac{s}{r}$	s/r
$a(b)$ $a \times b$		$s \div r$	

EXAMPLE 2

Evaluating Algebraic Expressions Involving Order of Operations

Evaluate each expression for the given value of the variable.

A $3x - 2$ for $x = 5$

$3(5) - 2$	*Substitute 5 for x.*
$15 - 2$	*Multiply.*
13	*Subtract*

B $n \div 2 + n$ for $n = 4$

$4 \div 2 + 4$	*Substitute 4 for n.*
$2 + 4$	*Divide.*
6	*Add.*

C $6y^2 + 2y$ for $y = 2$

$6(2)^2 + 2(2)$	*Substitute 2 for y.*
$6(4) + 2(2)$	*Evaluate the power.*
$24 + 4$	*Multiply.*
28	*Add.*

EXAMPLE 3

Evaluating Algebraic Expressions with Two Variables

Evaluate $\dfrac{3}{n} + 2m$ for $n = 3$ and $m = 4$.

$\dfrac{3}{n} + 2m$	
$\dfrac{3}{3} + 2(4)$	*Substitute 3 for n and 4 for m.*
$1 + 8$	*Divide and multiply from left to right.*
9	*Add.*

Think and Discuss

1. Write each expression another way.   **a.** $12x$ **b.** $\dfrac{4}{y}$ **c.** $\dfrac{3xy}{2}$

2. Explain the difference between a variable and a constant.

Learn It Online
Homework Help Online **go.hrw.com**,
keyword MS10 1-6 Go
Exercises 1–21, 23, 25, 27, 29, 31, 33, 35

GUIDED PRACTICE

See Example 1 Evaluate $n + 9$ for each value of n.

1. $n = 3$ **2.** $n = 2$ **3.** $n = 11$

See Example 2 Evaluate each expression for the given value of the variable.

4. $2x - 3$ for $x = 4$ **5.** $n \div 3 + n$ for $n = 6$ **6.** $5y^2 + 3y$ for $y = 2$

See Example 3 Evaluate each expression for the given values of the variables.

7. $\frac{8}{n} + 3m$ for $n = 2$ and $m = 5$ **8.** $5a - 3b + 5$ for $a = 4$ and $b = 3$

INDEPENDENT PRACTICE

See Example 1 Evaluate $n + 5$ for each value of n.

9. $n = 17$ **10.** $n = 9$ **11.** $n = 0$

See Example 2 Evaluate each expression for the given value of the variable.

12. $5y - 1$ for $y = 3$ **13.** $10b - 9$ for $b = 2$ **14.** $p \div 7 + p$ for $p = 14$

15. $n \div 5 + n$ for $n = 20$ **16.** $3x^2 + 2x$ for $x = 10$ **17.** $3c^2 - 5c$ for $c = 3$

See Example 3 Evaluate each expression for the given values of the variables.

18. $\frac{12}{n} + 7m$ for $n = 6$ and $m = 4$ **19.** $7p - 2t + 3$ for $p = 6$ and $t = 2$

20. $9 - \frac{3x}{4} + 20y$ for $x = 4$ and $y = 5$ **21.** $r^2 + 15k$ for $r = 15$ and $k = 5$

PRACTICE AND PROBLEM SOLVING

Extra Practice
See page EP3.

Evaluate each expression for the given values of the variables.

22. $20x - 10$ for $x = 4$ **23.** $4d^2 - 3d$ for $d = 2$

24. $22p \div 11 + p$ for $p = 3$ **25.** $q + q^2 + q \div 2$ for $q = 4$

26. $\frac{16}{k} + 7h$ for $k = 8$ and $h = 2$ **27.** $f \div 3 + f$ for $f = 18$

28. $3t \div 3 + t$ for $t = 13$ **29.** $9 + 3p - 5t + 3$ for $p = 2$ and $t = 1$

30. $108 - 12j + j$ for $j = 9$ **31.** $3m^3 + \frac{y}{5}$ for $m = 2$ and $y = 35$

32. The expression $60m$ gives the number of seconds in m minutes. Evaluate $60m$ for $m = 7$. How many seconds are there in 7 minutes?

33. Money Betsy has n quarters. You can use the expression $0.25n$ to find the total value of her coins in dollars. What is the value of 18 quarters?

34. Physical Science A color TV has a power rating of 200 watts. The expression $200t$ gives the power used by t color TV sets. Evaluate $200t$ for $t = 13$. How much power is used by 13 TV sets?

35. **Physical Science** The expression $1.8c + 32$ can be used to convert a temperature in degrees Celsius c to degrees Fahrenheit. What is the temperature in degrees Fahrenheit if the temperature is 30 °C?

36. **Physical Science** The graph shows the changes of state for water.

    a. What is the boiling point of water in degrees Celsius?

    b. Use the expression $1.8c + 32$ to find the boiling point of water in degrees Fahrenheit.

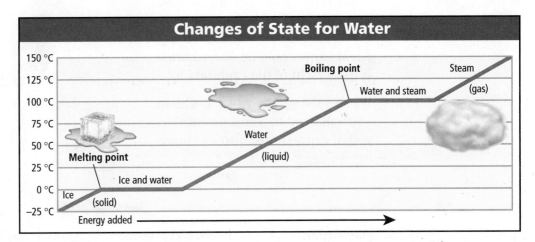

Changes of State for Water

37. **What's the Error?** A student was asked to identify the variable in the expression $72x + 8$. The student answered $72x$. What was the student's error?

38. **Write About It** Explain why letters such as x, p, and n used in algebraic expressions are called variables. Use examples to illustrate your response.

39. **Challenge** Evaluate the expression $\frac{x + y}{y - x}$ for $x = 6$ and $y = 8$.

Test Prep and Spiral Review

40. **Multiple Choice** Which expression does NOT equal 15?

    Ⓐ $3t$ for $t = 5$ Ⓑ $3 + t$ for $t = 12$ Ⓒ $t \div 3$ for $t = 60$ Ⓓ $t - 10$ for $t = 25$

41. **Multiple Choice** A group of 11 students go rock climbing at a local gym. It costs $12 per student plus $4 for each shoe rental. If only 8 students rent shoes, what is the total cost for the group to go climbing? Use the expression $12x + 4y$, where x represents the total number of students and y represents the number of students who rent shoes.

    Ⓕ $132   Ⓖ $140   Ⓗ $164   Ⓙ $176

Write each number in scientific notation. (Lesson 1-3)

42. 102.45   43. 62,100,000   44. 769,000   45. 800,000

Use the Distributive Property to find each product. (Lesson 1-5)

46. $5(16)$ 47. $(17)4$ 48. $7(23)$ 49. $(29)3$

TN ✓ **0706.3.2** Represent and analyze mathematical situations using algebraic symbols.

Although they are closely related, a Great Dane weighs about 40 times as much as a Chihuahua. An expression for the weight of the Great Dane could be 40*c*, where *c* is the weight of the Chihuahua.

When solving real-world problems, you will need to translate words, or verbal expressions, into algebraic expressions.

Interactivities Online ▶

Operation	Verbal Expressions	Algebraic Expression
✚	• add 3 to a number • a number plus 3 • the sum of a number and 3 • 3 more than a number • a number increased by 3	$n + 3$
▬	• subtract 12 from a number • a number minus 12 • the difference of a number and 12 • 12 less than a number • a number decreased by 12 • take away 12 from a number • a number less 12	$x - 12$
✖	• 2 times a number • 2 multiplied by a number • the product of 2 and a number	$2m$ or $2 \cdot m$
➗	• 6 divided into a number • a number divided by 6 • the quotient of a number and 6	$a \div 6$ or $\frac{a}{6}$

EXAMPLE **1** **Translating Verbal Expressions into Algebraic Expressions**

Write each phrase as an algebraic expression.

A **the product of 20 and *t***
product means "multiply"
$20t$

B **24 less than a number**
less than means "subtract from"
$n - 24$

Video **Lesson Tutorials Online** my.hrw.com

Write each phrase as an algebraic expression.

C **4 times the sum of a number and 2**

4 times the sum of a number and 2

4   ·   n + 2

$4(n + 2)$

D **the sum of 4 times a number and 2**

the sum of 4 times a number and 2

4   · n   + 2

$4n + 2$

When solving real-world problems, you may need to determine the action to know which operation to use.

Action	Operation
Put parts together	Add
Put equal parts together	Multiply
Find how much more or less	Subtract
Separate into equal parts	Divide

E X A M P L E **2** **Translating Real-World Problems into Algebraic Expressions**

A Jed reads *p* pages each day of a 200-page book. Write an algebraic expression for how many days it will take Jed to read the book.

You need to *separate* the total number of pages *into equal parts*. This involves division.

$$\frac{\text{total number of pages}}{\text{pages read each day}} = \frac{200}{p}$$

B To rent a certain car for a day costs $84 plus $0.29 for every mile the car is driven. Write an algebraic expression to show how much it costs to rent the car for a day.

The cost includes $0.29 per mile. Use *m* for the number of miles.

Multiply to *put equal parts together:* $0.29m$

In addition to the fee per mile, the cost includes a flat fee of $84.

Add to *put parts together:* $84 + 0.29m$

Think and Discuss

1. Write three different verbal expressions that can be represented by $2 - y$.

2. Explain how you would determine which operation to use to find the number of chairs in 6 rows of 100 chairs each.

Exercises

GUIDED PRACTICE

See Example **1**   **Write each phrase as an algebraic expression.**

1. the product of 7 and p

2. 3 less than a number

3. 12 divided into a number

4. 3 times the sum of a number and 5

See Example **2**   **5.** Carly spends \$5 for n notebooks. Write an algebraic expression to represent the cost of one notebook.

6. A company charges \$46 for cable TV installation and \$21 per month for basic cable service. Write an algebraic expression to represent the total cost of m months of basic cable service, including installation.

INDEPENDENT PRACTICE

See Example **1**   **Write each phrase as an algebraic expression.**

7. the sum of 5 and a number

8. 2 less than a number

9. the quotient of a number and 8

10. 9 times a number

11. 10 less than the product of a number and 3

See Example **2**   **12.** Video Express sells used tapes. Marta bought v tapes for \$45. Write an algebraic expression for the average cost of each tape.

13. A 5-foot pine tree was planted and grew 2 feet each year. Write an algebraic expression for the height of the tree after t years.

PRACTICE AND PROBLEM SOLVING

Extra Practice
See page EP3.

Write each phrase as an algebraic expression.

14. m plus the product of 6 and n

15. the quotient of 23 and u minus t

16. 14 less than the quantity k times 6

17. 2 times the sum of y and 5

18. the quotient of 100 and the quantity 6 plus w

19. 35 multiplied by the quantity r less 45

20. **Multi-Step** An ice machine can produce 17 pounds of ice in one hour.

   a. Write an algebraic expression to describe the number of pounds of ice produced in n hours.

   b. How many pounds of ice can the machine produce in 4 hours?

21. **Career** Karen earns \$65,000 a year as an optometrist. She received a bonus of b dollars last year and expects to get double that amount as a bonus this year. Write an algebraic expression to show the total amount Karen expects to earn this year.

Write a verbal expression for each algebraic expression.

22. $h + 3$ **23.** $90 \div y$ **24.** $s - 405$ **25.** $16t$

26. $5(a - 8)$ **27.** $4p - 10$ **28.** $(r + 1) \div 14$ **29.** $\frac{m}{15} + 3$

Life Science

Reddish-brown spots appear on the leaves and fruit of plants infested by rust mites.

30. Life Science Tiny and harmless, follicle mites live in our eyebrows and eyelashes. They are relatives of spiders and like spiders, they have eight legs. Write an algebraic expression for the number of legs in m mites.

Nutrition The table shows the estimated number of grams of carbohydrates commonly found in various types of foods.

31. Write an algebraic expression for the number of grams of carbohydrates in y pieces of fruit and 1 cup of skim milk.

32. How many grams of carbohydrates are in a sandwich made from t ounces of lean meat and 2 slices of bread?

Food	Carbohydrates
1 c skim milk	12 g
1 piece of fruit	15 g
1 slice of bread	15 g
1 oz lean meat	0 g

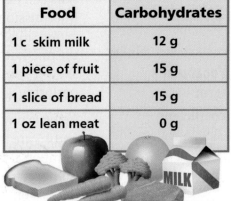

33. What's the Question? Al has twice as many baseball cards as Frank and four times as many football cards as Joe. The expression $2x + 4y$ can be used to show the total number of baseball and football cards Al has. If the answer is y, then what is the question?

34. Write About It If you are asked to compare two numbers, what two operations might you use? Why?

35. Challenge In 2006, one U.S. dollar was equivalent, on average, to $1.134 in Canadian dollars. Write an algebraic expression for the number of U.S. dollars you could get for n Canadian dollars.

Test Prep and Spiral Review

36. Multiple Choice Which verbal expression does NOT represent $9 - x$?

(A) x less than nine

(C) subtract x from nine

(B) x decreased by nine

(D) the difference of nine and x

37. Short Response A room at the Oak Creek Inn costs $104 per night for two people. There is a $19 charge for each extra person. Write an algebraic expression that shows the cost per night for a family of four staying at the inn. Then evaluate your expression for 3 nights.

Simplify each expression. (Lesson 1-4)

38. $6 + 4 \div 2$ **39.** $9 \cdot 1 - 4$ **40.** $5^2 - 3$ **41.** $24 \div 3 + 3^3$

42. Evaluate $b - a^2$ for $a = 2$ and $b = 9$. (Lesson 1-6)

TN ✓ **0706.3.1** Perform basic operations on linear expressions (including grouping, order of operations, exponents, simplifying and expanding)
Also ✓ **0706.3.2**

Vocabulary

term

coefficient

Individual skits at the talent show can last up to x minutes each, and group skits can last up to y minutes each. Intermission will be 15 minutes. The expression $7x + 9y + 15$ represents the maximum length of the talent show if 7 individuals and 9 groups perform.

In the expression $7x + 9y + 15$, $7x$, $9y$, and 15 are *terms*. A **term** can be a number, a variable, or a product of numbers and variables. Terms in an expression are separated by plus or minus signs.

Caution!

A variable by itself, such as y, has a coefficient of 1. So $y = 1y$.

In the term $7x$, 7 is called the *coefficient*. A **coefficient** is a number that is multiplied by a variable in an algebraic expression.

Coefficient →  ← Variable

Like terms are terms with the same variables raised to the same exponents. The coefficients do not have to be the same. Constants, like 5, $\frac{1}{2}$, and 3.2, are also like terms.

Like Terms	$3x$ and $2x$	w and $\frac{w}{7}$	5 and 1.8
Unlike Terms	$5x^2$ and $2x$ *The exponents are different.*	$6a$ and $6b$ *The variables are different.*	3.2 and n *Only one term contains a variable.*

EXAMPLE 1 **Identifying Like Terms**

Identify like terms in the list.

$$5a \quad \frac{t}{2} \quad 3y^2 \quad 7t \quad x^2 \quad 4z \quad k \quad 4.5y^2 \quad 2t \quad \frac{2}{3}a$$

Look for like variables with like powers.

Helpful Hint

Use different shapes or colors to indicate sets of like terms.

$$\boxed{5a} \quad \boxed{\frac{t}{2}} \quad \boxed{3y^2} \quad \boxed{7t} \quad x^2 \quad 4z \quad k \quad \boxed{4.5y^2} \quad \boxed{2t} \quad \boxed{\frac{2}{3}a}$$

Like terms: $5a$ and $\frac{2}{3}a$ $\frac{t}{2}$, $7t$, and $2t$ $3y^2$ and $4.5y^2$

To simplify an algebraic expression that contains like terms, combine the terms. Combining like terms is like grouping similar objects.

$$4x \quad + \quad 5x \quad = \quad 9x$$

To combine like terms that have variables, add or subtract the coefficients.

EXAMPLE 2   **Simplifying Algebraic Expressions**

Simplify. Justify your steps using the Commutative, Associative, and Distributive Properties when necessary.

A   **$7x + 2x$**

$7x + 2x$ *7x and 2x are like terms.*

$\quad 9x$ *Add the coefficients.*

B   **$5x^3 + 3y + 7x^3 - 2y - 4x^2$**

$5x^3 + 3y + 7x^3 - 2y - 4x^2$ *Identify like terms.*

$5x^3 + 7x^3 + 3y - 2y - 4x^2$ *Commutative Property*

$(5x^3 + 7x^3) + (3y - 2y) - 4x^2$ *Associative Property*

$\quad 12x^3 + y - 4x^2$ *Add or subtract the coefficients.*

C   **$2(a + 2a^2) + 2b$**

$2(a + 2a^2) + 2b$

$2a + 4a^2 + 2b$ *Distributive Property*

There are no like terms to combine.

EXAMPLE 3   *Geometry Application*

Remember!

To find the perimeter of a figure, add the lengths of the sides.

Write an expression for the perimeter of the rectangle. Then simplify the expression.

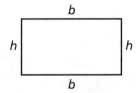

$b + h + b + h$ *Write an expression using the side lengths.*

$(b + b) + (h + h)$ *Identify and group like terms.*

$\quad 2b + 2h$ *Add the coefficients.*

Think and Discuss

1. Explain whether $5x$, $5x^2$, and $5x^3$ are like terms.

2. Explain how you know when an expression cannot be simplified.

Learn It Online
Homework Help Online **go.hrw.com,**
keyword MS10 1-8 (Go)
Exercises 1–17, 19, 21, 23, 25, 29

GUIDED PRACTICE

See Example ① **Identify like terms in each list.**

1. $6b$ $5x^2$ $4x^3$ $\dfrac{b}{2}$ x^2 $2e$

2. $12a^2$ $4x^3$ b $4a^2$ $3.5x^3$ $\dfrac{5}{6}b$

See Example ② **Simplify. Justify your steps using the Commutative, Associative, and Distributive Properties when necessary.**

3. $5x + 3x$

4. $6a^2 - a^2 + 16$

5. $4a^2 + 5a + 14b$

See Example ③ **6. Geometry** Write an expression for the perimeter of the rectangle. Then simplify the expression.

INDEPENDENT PRACTICE

See Example ① **Identify like terms in each list.**

7. $2b$ b^6 b x^4 $3b^6$ $2x^2$

8. 6 $2n$ $3n^2$ $6m^2$ $\dfrac{n}{4}$ 7

9. $10k^2$ m 3^3 $\dfrac{p}{6}$ $2m$ 2

10. 6^3 y^3 $3y^2$ 6^2 y $5y^3$

See Example ② **Simplify. Justify your steps using the Commutative, Associative, and Distributive Properties when necessary.**

11. $3a + 2b + 5a$

12. $5b + 7b + 10$

13. $a + 2b + 2a + b + 2c$

14. $y + 4 + 2x + 3y$

15. $q^2 + 2q + 2q^2$

16. $18 + 2d^3 + d + 3d$

See Example ③ **17. Geometry** Write an expression for the perimeter of the given figure. Then simplify the expression.

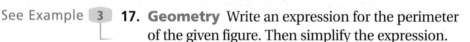

PRACTICE AND PROBLEM SOLVING

Extra Practice
See page EP4.

Simplify each expression.

18. $4x + 5x$

19. $32y - 5y$

20. $4c^2 + 5c + 2c$

21. $5d^2 - 3d^2 + d$

22. $5f^2 + 2f + f^2$

23. $7x + 8x^2 - 3y$

24. $3(p + 9q - 2 + 9) + 14p$

25. $6b + 6b^2 + 4b^3$

26. $2(a^2 + 2b + 2a^2) + b + 2c$

27. Geometry Write an expression for the perimeter of the given triangle. Then evaluate the perimeter when n is 1, 2, 3, 4, and 5.

n	1	2	3	4	5
Perimeter					

Business

The winner of each year's National Best Bagger Competition gets a bag-shaped trophy and a cash prize.

28. Critical Thinking Determine whether the expression $9m^2 + k$ is equal to $7m^2 + 2(2k - m^2) + 5k$. Use properties to justify your answer.

29. Multi-Step Brad makes d dollars per hour as a cook at a deli. The table shows the number of hours he worked each week in June.

Hours Brad Worked	
Week	**Hours**
1	21.5
2	23
3	15.5
4	19

   a. Write and simplify an expression for the amount of money Brad earned in June.

   b. Evaluate your expression from part **a** for d = $9.50.

   c. What does your answer to part **b** represent?

30. Business Ashley earns $8 per hour working at a grocery store. Last week she worked h hours bagging groceries and twice as many hours stocking shelves. Write and simplify an expression for the amount Ashley earned.

31. Critical Thinking The terms $3x$, $23x^2$, $6y^2$, $2x$, y^2 and one other term can be written in an expression which, when simplified, equals $5x + 7y^2$. Identify the term missing from the list and write the expression.

32. What's the Question? At one store, a pair of jeans costs $29 and a shirt costs $25. At another store, the same kind of jeans costs $26 and the same kind of shirt costs $20. The answer is $29j - 26j + 25s - 20s = 3j + 5s$. What is the question?

33. Write About It Describe the steps for simplifying the expression $2x + 3 + 5x - 15$.

34. Challenge A rectangle has a width of $x + 2$ and a length of $3x + 1$. Write and simplify an expression for the perimeter of the rectangle.

Test Prep and Spiral Review

35. Multiple Choice Translate "six times the sum of x and y" and "five less than y." Which algebraic expression represents the sum of these two verbal expressions?

   (A) $6x + 5$ (B) $6x + 2y - 5$ (C) $6x + 5y + 5$ (D) $6x + 7y - 5$

36. Multiple Choice The side length of a square is $2x + 3$. Which expression represents the perimeter of the square?

   (F) $2x + 12$ (G) $4x + 6$ (H) $6x + 7$ (J) $8x + 12$

37. The budget for the 2006 movie *Superman Returns* was about two hundred and sixty-eight million dollars. Write this amount in scientific notation. (Lesson 1-3)

Evaluate the expression $9y - 3$ for each given value of the variable. (Lesson 1-6)

38. $y = 2$ **39.** $y = 6$ **40.** $y = 10$ **41.** $y = 18$

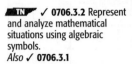

1-9 # Equations and Their Solutions

TN ✓ **0706.3.2** Represent and analyze mathematical situations using algebraic symbols.
Also ✓ **0706.3.1**

Ella has 22 songs on her MP3 player. This is 9 more than Kay has.

This situation can be written as an *equation*. An **equation** is a mathematical statement that two expressions are equal in value.

Vocabulary

equation

solution

An equation is like a balanced scale.

Interactivities Online ▶

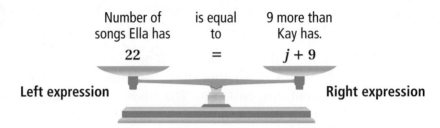

| Number of songs Ella has | is equal to | 9 more than Kay has. |
| 22 | = | $j + 9$ |

Left expression   **Right expression**

Just as the weights on both sides of a balanced scale are exactly the same, the expressions on both sides of an equation represent exactly the same value.

When an equation contains a variable, a value of the variable that makes the statement true is called a **solution** of the equation.

Reading Math

The symbol ≠ means "is not equal to."

$22 = j + 9$ $j = 13$ is a solution because $22 = 13 + 9$.

$22 = j + 9$ $j = 15$ is not a solution because $22 ≠ 15 + 9$.

EXAMPLE 1   **Determining Whether a Number Is a Solution of an Equation**

Determine whether the given value of the variable is a solution.

A $18 = s - 7; s = 11$

$18 = s - 7$

$18 \overset{?}{=} 11 - 7$ *Substitute 11 for s.*

$18 \overset{?}{=} 4$ ✗

11 **is not** a solution of $18 = s - 7$.

B $w + 17 = 23; w = 6$

$w + 17 = 23$

$6 + 17 \overset{?}{=} 23$ *Substitute 6 for w.*

$23 \overset{?}{=} 23$ ✔

6 **is** a solution of $w + 17 = 23$.

EXAMPLE 2 **Writing an Equation to Determine Whether a Number Is a Solution**

Tyler wants to buy a new skateboard. He has $57, which is $38 less than he needs. Does the skateboard cost $90 or $95?

You can write an equation to find the price of the skateboard. If s represents the price of the skateboard, then $s - 38 = 57$.

$90

$s - 38 = 57$

$90 - 38 \overset{?}{=} 57$ *Substitute 90 for s.*

$52 \overset{?}{=} 57$ ✗

$95

$s - 38 = 57$

$95 - 38 \overset{?}{=} 57$ *Substitute 95 for s.*

$57 \overset{?}{=} 57$ ✔

The skateboard costs $95.

EXAMPLE 3 **Deriving a Real-World Situation from an Equation**

Which problem situation best matches the equation $3x + 4 = 22$?

Situation A:

Harvey spent $22 at the gas station. He paid $4 per gallon for gas and $3 for snacks. How many gallons of gas did Harvey buy?

The variable x represents the number of gallons of gas that Harvey bought.

$$\$4 \text{ per gallon} \longrightarrow 4x$$

Since $4x$ is not a term in the given equation, Situation A does not match the equation.

Situation B:

Harvey spent $22 at the gas station. He paid $3 per gallon for gas and $4 for snacks. How many gallons of gas did Harvey buy?

$$\$3 \text{ per gallon} \longrightarrow 3x$$
$$\$4 \text{ on snacks} \longrightarrow + 4$$

Harvey spent $22 in all, so $3x + 4 = 22$. Situation B matches the equation.

Think and Discuss

1. **Compare** equations with expressions.

2. **Give an example** of an equation whose solution is 5.

Learn It Online
Homework Help Online **go.hrw.com**,
keyword MS10 1-9 Go
Exercises 1–13, 15, 17, 19, 21, 23, 25

GUIDED PRACTICE

See Example **1** Determine whether the given value of the variable is a solution.

1. $19 = x + 4$; $x = 23$ **2.** $6n = 78$; $n = 13$ **3.** $k \div 3 = 14$; $k = 42$

See Example **2** **4.** Mavis wants to buy a book. She has $25, which is $9 less than she needs. Does the book cost $34 or $38?

See Example **3** **5.** Which problem situation best matches the equation $10 + 2x = 16$?

Situation A: Angie bought peaches for $2 per pound and laundry detergent for $10. She spent a total of $16. How many pounds of peaches did Angie buy?

Situation B: Angie bought peaches for $10 per pound and laundry detergent for $2. She spent a total of $16. How many pounds of peaches did Angie buy?

INDEPENDENT PRACTICE

See Example **1** Determine whether the given value of the variable is a solution.

6. $r - 12 = 25$; $r = 37$ **7.** $39 \div x = 13$; $x = 4$ **8.** $21 = m + 9$; $m = 11$

9. $\frac{a}{18} = 7$; $a = 126$ **10.** $16f = 48$; $f = 3$ **11.** $71 - y = 26$; $y = 47$

See Example **2** **12.** Curtis wants to buy a new snowboard. He has $119, which is $56 less than he needs. Does the snowboard cost $165 or $175?

See Example **3** **13.** Which problem situation best matches the equation $2m + 10 = 18$?

Situation A: A taxi service charges a $2 fee, plus $18 per mile. Jeremy paid the driver $10. How many miles did Jeremy ride in the taxi?

Situation B: A taxi service charges a $10 fee, plus $2 per mile. Jeremy paid the driver $18. How many miles did Jeremy ride in the taxi?

PRACTICE AND PROBLEM SOLVING

Extra Practice
See page EP4.

Determine whether the given value of the variable is a solution.

14. $j = 6$ for $15 - j = 21$ **15.** $x = 36$ for $48 = x + 12$

16. $m = 18$ for $16 = 34 - m$ **17.** $k = 23$ for $17 + k = 40$

18. $y = 8$ for $9y + 2 = 74$ **19.** $c = 12$ for $100 - 2c = 86$

20. $q = 13$ for $5q + 7 - q = 51$ **21.** $w = 15$ for $13w - 2 - 6w = 103$

22. $t = 12$ for $3(50 - t) - 10t = 104$ **23.** $r = 21$ for $4r - 8 + 9r - 1 = 264$

24. **Hobbies** Monique has a collection of stamps from 6 different countries. Jeremy has stamps from 3 fewer countries than Monique does. Write an equation showing this, using j as the number of countries from which Jeremy has stamps.

25. The diagram shows approximate elevations for different climate zones in the Colorado Rockies. Use the diagram to write an equation that shows the vertical distance d from the summit of Mount Evans (14,264 ft) to the tree line, which marks the beginning of the alpine tundra zone.

West ⟵	East ⟶
	Alpine tundra, above 10,500 ft
Tree line	Subalpine, 9,000–10,500 ft
	Montane forest, 7,500–9,000 ft
Piñon-Juniper, 7,000–9,000 ft	Foothills, 5,500–7,500 ft
Semidesert, 5,500–7,000 ft	Great Plains, 3,000–5,500 ft

Source: Colorado Mall

26. The top wind speed of an F5 tornado, the strongest known kind of tornado, is 246 mi/h faster than the top wind speed of an F1 tornado, the weakest kind of tornado. The top wind speed of an F1 tornado is 72 mi/h. Is the top wind speed of an F5 tornado 174 mi/h, 218 mi/h, or 318 mi/h?

27. ⬤ **Write a Problem** The mean surface temperature of Earth increased about 1 °F from 1861 to 1998. In 1998, the mean surface temperature was about 60 °F. Use these data to write a problem involving an equation with a variable.

28. ⭐ **Challenge** In the 1980s, about 9.3×10^4 acres of tropical forests were destroyed each year due to deforestation. About how many acres of tropical forests were destroyed during the 1980s?

Maroon Lake and Maroon Bells in the Colorado Rockies

Test Prep and Spiral Review

29. Multiple Choice Jack's rectangular bedroom has a length of 10 feet. He used the formula $A = 10w$ to find the area of his room. He found that his bedroom had an area of 150 square feet. What was the width of his bedroom?

Ⓐ 15 feet   Ⓑ 25 feet   Ⓒ 30 feet   Ⓓ 15,000 feet

30. Multiple Choice The number of seventh-graders at Pecos Middle School is 316. This is 27 more than the number of eighth-graders. How many eighth-graders are enrolled?

Ⓕ 289   Ⓖ 291   Ⓗ 299   Ⓙ 343

Write each number in scientific notation. (Lesson 1-3)

31. 10,850,000   **32.** 627,000   **33.** 9,040,000

Tell which property is represented. (Lesson 1-5)

34. $(7 + 5) + 3 = 7 + (5 + 3)$ **35.** $181 + 0 = 181$ **36.** $bc = cb$

Model Solving Equations

Use with Lessons 1-10 and 1-11

Learn It Online
Lab Resources Online **go.hrw.com**,
keyword MS10 Lab1 Go

TN ✓ **0706.1.10** Model algebraic
equations with manipulatives, technology,
and pencil and paper.
Also **GLE 0706.3.8**

KEY

1 = 1   x = variable

OR

+ = 1   + = variable

REMEMBER

- In an equation, the expressions on both sides of the equal sign are equivalent.
- A variable can have any value that makes the equation true.

You can use balance scales and algebra tiles to model and solve equations.

Activity

1 Use a balance scale to model and solve the equation $3 + x = 11$.

a. On the left side of the scale, place 3 unit weights and one variable weight. On the right side, place 11 unit weights. This models $3 + x = 11$.

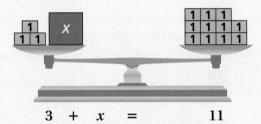

$$3 + x = 11$$

b. Remove 3 of the unit weights from each side of the scale to leave the variable weight by itself on one side.

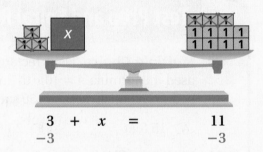

$$3 + x = 11$$
$$-3 \qquad\qquad -3$$

c. Count the remaining unit weights on the right side of the scale. This number represents the solution of the equation.

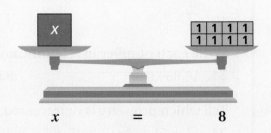

$$x = 8$$

The model shows that if $3 + x = 11$, then $x = 8$.

2 Use algebra tiles to model and solve the equation $3y = 15$.

a. On the left side of the mat, place 3 variable tiles. On the right side, place 15 unit tiles. This models $3y = 15$.

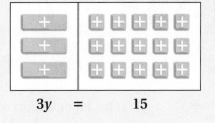

$$3y \quad = \quad 15$$

b. Since there are 3 variable tiles, divide the tiles on each side of the mat into 3 equal groups.

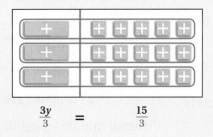

$$\frac{3y}{3} \quad = \quad \frac{15}{3}$$

c. Count the number of unit tiles in one of the groups. This number represents the solution of the equation.

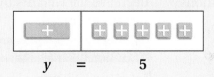

$$y \quad = \quad 5$$

The model shows that if $3y = 15$, then $y = 5$.

To check your solutions, substitute the variable in each equation with your solution. If the resulting equation is true, your solution is correct.

$3 + x = 11$

$3 + 8 \overset{?}{=} 11$

$11 \overset{?}{=} 11$ ✔

$3y = 15$

$3 \cdot 5 \overset{?}{=} 15$

$15 \overset{?}{=} 15$ ✔

Think and Discuss

1. What operation did you use to solve the equation $3 + x = 11$ in **1**? What operation did you use to solve $3y = 15$ in **2**?

2. Compare using a balance scale and weights with using a mat and algebra tiles. Which method of modeling equations is more helpful to you? Explain.

Try This

Use a balance scale or algebra tiles to model and solve each equation.

1. $4x = 16$ **2.** $3 + 5 = n$ **3.** $5r = 15$ **4.** $n + 7 = 12$

5. $y + 6 = 13$ **6.** $8 = 2r$ **7.** $9 = 7 + w$ **8.** $18 = 6p$

 **1-10** **Solving Equations by Adding or Subtracting**

TN ✓ **0706.1.10** Model algebraic equations with manipulatives, technology, and pencil and paper. *Also* **GLE 0706.3.8**, ✓ **0706.3.2**

To solve an equation means to find a solution to the equation. To do this, isolate the variable—that is, get the variable alone on one side of the equal sign.

$$x = 8 - 5 \qquad\qquad x + 5 = 8$$
$$7 - 3 = y \qquad\qquad 7 = 3 + y$$

The variables are isolated.   The variables are *not* isolated.

Recall that an equation is like a balanced scale. If you increase or decrease the weights by the same amount on both sides, the scale will remain balanced.

Vocabulary

Addition Property of Equality

inverse operations

Subtraction Property of Equality

Interactivities Online ▶

ADDITION PROPERTY OF EQUALITY		
Words	**Numbers**	**Algebra**
You can add the same amount to both sides of an equation, and the statement will still be true.	$2 + 3 = 5$ $\underline{+4 \qquad +4}$ $2 + 7 = 9$	$x = y$ $\underline{+z \qquad +z}$ $x + z = y + z$

Use *inverse operations* when isolating a variable. Addition and subtraction are **inverse operations**, which means that they "undo" each other.

$$2\boxed{+5}=7 \longleftrightarrow 7\boxed{-5}=2$$

EXAMPLE **1** **Using the Addition Property of Equality**

Solve the equation $x - 8 = 17$. Check your answer.

$$x - 8 = 17 \qquad \textit{Think: 8 is \textbf{subtracted} from x, so}$$
$$\underline{+8 \qquad +8} \qquad \textit{\textbf{add} 8 to both sides to isolate x.}$$
$$x = 25$$

Check

$$x - 8 = 17$$
$$25 - 8 \overset{?}{=} 17 \qquad \textit{Substitute 25 for x.}$$
$$17 \overset{?}{=} 17 \checkmark \qquad \textit{25 is a solution.}$$

Video **Lesson Tutorials Online** my.hrw.com

SUBTRACTION PROPERTY OF EQUALITY		

Words	Numbers	Algebra
You can subtract the same amount from both sides of an equation, and the statement will still be true.	$4 + 7 = 11$ $\underline{-3 \quad\quad -3}$ $4 + 4 = 8$	$x = y$ $\underline{-z \quad\quad\quad -z}$ $x - z = y - z$

EXAMPLE 2 **Using the Subtraction Property of Equality**

Solve the equation $a + 5 = 11$. Check your answer.

$a + 5 = 11$ *Think: 5 is added to a, so*
$\underline{-5 \quad -5}$ *subtract 5 from both sides to isolate a.*
$a \quad = \quad 6$

Check

$a + 5 = 11$
$6 + 5 \overset{?}{=} 11$ *Substitute 6 for a.*
$11 \overset{?}{=} 11 \checkmark$ *6 is a solution.*

EXAMPLE 3 *Sports Application*

Michael Jordan's highest point total for a single game was 69. The entire team scored 117 points in that game. How many points did his teammates score?

Let p represent the points scored by the rest of the team.

Jordan's points	+	Teammates' points	=	Final score
69	+	p	=	117

$69 + p = 117$
$\underline{-69 \quad\quad\quad -69}$ *Subtract 69 from both sides to isolate p.*
$p = 48$

His teammates scored 48 points.

Think and Discuss

1. **Explain** how to decide which operation to use in order to isolate the variable in an equation.

2. **Describe** what would happen if a number were added or subtracted on one side of an equation but not on the other side.

Exercises

Learn It Online
Homework Help Online **go.hrw.com,**
keyword MS10 1-10 Go
Exercises 1–24, 25, 27, 29, 31,
35, 37, 39

GUIDED PRACTICE

See Example 1   Solve each equation. Check your answer.

1. $r - 77 = 99$ **2.** $102 = v - 66$ **3.** $x - 22 = 66$

See Example 2   **4.** $d + 83 = 92$ **5.** $45 = 36 + f$ **6.** $987 = 16 + m$

See Example 3   **7.** After a gain of 9 yards, your team has gained a total of 23 yards. How many yards had your team gained before the 9-yard gain?

INDEPENDENT PRACTICE

See Example 1   Solve each equation. Check your answer.

8. $n - 36 = 17$ **9.** $t - 28 = 54$ **10.** $p - 56 = 12$

11. $b - 41 = 26$ **12.** $m - 51 = 23$ **13.** $k - 22 = 101$

See Example 2   **14.** $x + 15 = 43$ **15.** $w + 19 = 62$ **16.** $a + 14 = 38$

17. $110 = s + 65$ **18.** $x + 47 = 82$ **19.** $18 + j = 94$

20. $97 = t + 45$ **21.** $q + 13 = 112$ **22.** $44 = 16 + n$

See Example 3   **23.** Hank is on a field trip. He has to travel 56 miles to reach his destination. He has traveled 18 miles so far. How much farther does he have to travel?

24. Sandy read 8 books in April. If her book club requires her to read 6 books each month, how many more books did she read than what was required?

PRACTICE AND PROBLEM SOLVING

Extra Practice
See page EP4.

Solve each equation. Check your answer. Tell which property you used.

25. $p - 7 = 3$ **26.** $n + 17 = 98$ **27.** $23 + b = 75$

28. $356 = y - 219$ **29.** $105 = a + 60$ **30.** $g - 720 = 159$

31. $651 + c = 800$ **32.** $f - 63 = 937$ **33.** $59 + m = 258$

34. $16 = h - 125$ **35.** $s + 841 = 1,000$ **36.** $711 = q - 800$

37. $63 + x = 902$ **38.** $z - 712 = 54$ **39.** $120 = w + 41$

40. **Physical Science** An object weighs less when it is in water. This is because water exerts a buoyant force on the object. The weight of an object out of water is equal to the object's weight in water plus the buoyant force of the water. Suppose an object weighs 103 pounds out of water and 55 pounds in water. Write and solve an equation to find the buoyant force of the water.

41. **Banking** After Lana deposited a check for $65, her new account balance was $315. Write and solve an equation to find the amount that was in Lana's account before the deposit.

42. Music Jason wants to buy the trumpet advertised in the classified ads. He has saved $156. Using the information from the ad, write and solve an equation to find how much more money he needs to buy the trumpet.

 43. What's the Error? Describe and correct the error.
$x = 50$ for $(8 + 4)2 + x = 26$

44. Write About It Explain how you know whether to add or subtract to solve an equation.

45. Challenge Kwan keeps a record of his football team's gains and losses on each play of the game. The record is shown in the table. Find the missing information by writing and solving an equation.

Play	Play Gain/Loss	Overall Gain/Loss
1st down	Gain of 2 yards	Gain of 2 yards
2nd down	Loss of 5 yards	Loss of 3 yards
3rd down	Gain of 7 yards	Gain of 4 yards
4th down		Loss of 7 yards

Test Prep and Spiral Review

46. Gridded Response Morgan has read 78 pages of *Treasure Island*. The book has 203 pages. How many pages of the book does Morgan have left to read?

47. Multiple Choice Which problem situation best represents the equation $42 - x = 7$?

Ⓐ Craig is 42 years old. His brother is 7 years older than he is. How old is Craig's brother?

Ⓑ Dylan has 42 days to finish his science fair project. How many weeks does he have left to finish his project?

Ⓒ The total lunch bill for a group of 7 friends is $42. If the friends split the cost of the meal evenly, how much should each person pay?

Ⓓ Each student in the Anderson Junior High Spanish Club has paid for a club T-shirt. If there are 42 students in the club and only 7 shirts are left to be picked up, how many students have already picked up their shirts?

Write each phrase as an algebraic expression. (Lesson 1-7)

48. the product of 16 and n **49.** 17 decreased by k **50.** 8 times the sum of x and 4

Simplify each expression. (Lesson 1-8)

51. $6(2 + 2n) + 3n$ **52.** $4x - 7y + x$ **53.** $8 + 3t + 2(4t)$

Solving Equations by Multiplying or Dividing

TN ✓ **0706.1.10** Model algebraic equations with manipulatives, technology, and pencil and paper.
Also **GLE 0706.3.8,** ✓ **0706.3.2**

Like addition and subtraction, multiplication and division are inverse operations. They "undo" each other.

$$2 \cdot 5 = 10$$
$$10 \div 5 = 2$$

Vocabulary

Multiplication Property of Equality

Division Property of Equality

Interactivities Online ▶

MULTIPLICATION PROPERTY OF EQUALITY		
Words	**Numbers**	**Algebra**
You can multiply both sides of an equation by the same number, and the statement will still be true.	$3 \cdot 4 = 12$ $2 \cdot 3 \cdot 4 = 2 \cdot 12$ $6 \cdot 4 = 24$	$x = y$ $zx = zy$

If a variable is divided by a number, you can often use multiplication to isolate the variable. Multiply both sides of the equation by the number.

E X A M P L E **Using the Multiplication Property of Equality**

Solve the equation $\frac{x}{7} = 20$. Check your answer.

$$\frac{x}{7} = 20$$

$$(7)\frac{x}{7} = 20(7) \qquad \textit{Think: x is \textbf{divided} by 7, so \textbf{multiply} both sides by 7 to isolate x.}$$

$$x = 140$$

Check

$$\frac{x}{7} = 20$$

$$\frac{140}{7} \overset{?}{=} 20 \qquad \textit{Substitute 140 for x.}$$

$$20 \overset{?}{=} 20 ✔ \qquad \textit{140 is a solution.}$$

DIVISION PROPERTY OF EQUALITY		
Words	**Numbers**	**Algebra**
You can divide both sides of an equation by the same nonzero number, and the statement will still be true.	$5 \cdot 6 = 30$ $\frac{5 \cdot 6}{3} = \frac{30}{3}$ $5 \cdot \frac{6}{3} = 10$ $5 \cdot 2 = 10$	$x = y$ $\frac{x}{z} = \frac{y}{z}$ $z \neq 0$

Video **Lesson Tutorials Online** my.hrw.com

If a variable is multiplied by a number, you can often use division to isolate the variable. Divide both sides of the equation by the number.

E X A M P L E **Using the Division Property of Equality**

Solve the equation 240 = 4z. Check your answer.

$240 = 4z$ *Think: z is **multiplied** by 4, so*

$\dfrac{240}{4} = \dfrac{4z}{4}$ ***divide** both sides by 4 to isolate z.*

$60 = z$

Check

$240 = 4z$

$240 \overset{?}{=} 4\,(60)$ *Substitute 60 for z.*

$240 \overset{?}{=} 240 \checkmark$ *60 is a solution.*

E X A M P L E **3** *Health Application*

In 2005, Lance Armstrong won his seventh consecutive Tour de France. He is the first person to win the 2,051-mile bicycle race more than five years in a row.

If you count your heartbeats for 10 seconds and multiply that number by 6, you can find your heart rate in beats per minute. Lance Armstrong, who won the Tour de France seven years in a row, from 1999 to 2005, has a resting heart rate of 30 beats per minute. How many times does his heart beat in 10 seconds?

Use the given information to write an equation, where b is the number of heartbeats in 10 seconds.

Beats in 10 s	·	6	=	beats per minute
b	·	6	=	30

$6b = 30$ *Think: b is **multiplied** by 6, so*

$\dfrac{6b}{6} = \dfrac{30}{6}$ ***divide** both sides by 6 to isolate b.*

$b = 5$

Lance Armstrong's heart beats 5 times in 10 seconds.

Think and Discuss

1. **Explain** how to check your solution to an equation.

2. **Describe** how to solve $13x = 91$.

3. When you solve $5p = 35$, will p be greater than 35 or less than 35? **Explain** your answer.

4. When you solve $\dfrac{p}{5} = 35$, will p be greater than 35 or less than 35? **Explain** your answer.

Learn It Online
Homework Help Online **go.hrw.com,**
keyword **MS10 1-11** Go
Exercises 1–20, 21, 27, 31, 33, 35, 41, 43

GUIDED PRACTICE

See Example 1   Solve each equation. Check your answer.

1. $\frac{s}{77} = 11$ 2. $b \div 25 = 4$ 3. $y \div 8 = 5$

See Example 2   4. $72 = 8x$ 5. $3c = 96$ 6. $x \cdot 18 = 18$

See Example 3   7. On Friday nights, a local bowling alley charges $5 per person to bowl all night. If Carol and her friends paid a total of $45 to bowl, how many people were in their group?

INDEPENDENT PRACTICE

See Example 1   Solve each equation. Check your answer.

8. $12 = s \div 4$ 9. $\frac{k}{18} = 72$ 10. $13 = \frac{z}{5}$

11. $\frac{c}{5} = 35$ 12. $\frac{w}{11} = 22$ 13. $17 = n \div 18$

See Example 2   14. $17x = 85$ 15. $63 = 3p$ 16. $6u = 222$

17. $97a = 194$ 18. $9q = 108$ 19. $495 = 11d$

See Example 3   20. It costs $6 per ticket for groups of ten or more people to see a minor league baseball game. If Albert's group paid a total of $162 for game tickets, how many people were in the group?

PRACTICE AND PROBLEM SOLVING

Extra Practice
See page EP4.

Solve each equation. Check your answer.

21. $9 = g \div 3$ 22. $150 = 3j$ 23. $68 = m - 42$

24. $7r = 84$ 25. $5x = 35$ 26. $9 = \frac{s}{38}$

27. $b + 33 = 95$ 28. $\frac{p}{15} = 6$ 29. $12f = 240$

30. $504 = c - 212$ 31. $8a = 288$ 32. $157 + q = 269$

33. $21 = d \div 2$ 34. $\frac{h}{20} = 83$ 35. $r - 92 = 215$

Multi-Step Translate each sentence into an equation. Then solve the equation.

36. A number d divided by 4 equals 3.

37. The sum of 7 and a number n is 15.

38. The product of a number b and 5 is 250.

39. Twelve is the difference of a number q and 8.

40. **Consumer Math** Nine weeks from now Susan hopes to buy a bicycle that costs $180. How much money must she save per week?

41. **School** A school club is collecting toys for a children's charity. There are 18 students in the club. The goal is to collect 216 toys. Each member will collect the same number of toys. How many toys should each member collect?

42. **Travel** Lissa drove from Los Angeles to New York City and averaged 45 miles per hour. Her driving time totaled 62 hours. Write and solve an equation to find the distance Lissa traveled.

43. **Business** A store rents space in a building at a cost of $19 per square foot. If the store is 700 square feet, how much is the rent?

44. Ms. Ryan asked her students to name their favorite fruit. If 6 times as many people like bananas as like peaches, how many people like peaches?

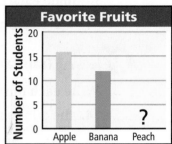

45. **What's the Error?** For the equation $7x = 56$, a student found the value of x to be 392. What was the student's error?

46. **Write About It** How do you know whether to use multiplication or division to solve an equation?

47. **Challenge** In a survey, 8,690,000 college students were asked about their electronic equipment usage. The results are as follows: 7,299,600 use a TV, 6,604,400 use a DVD, 3,389,100 use a video game system, 3,041,500 use a VCR, and x students use an MP3 player. If you multiply the number of students who use MP3 players by 5 and divide by 3, you get the total number of students represented in the survey. Write and solve an equation to find the number of students who use MP3 players.

Test Prep and Spiral Review

48. **Multiple Choice** Mr. Tomkins borrowed $1,200 to buy a computer. He wants to repay the loan in 8 equal payments. How much will each payment be?

   (A) $80   (B) $100   (C) $150   (D) $200

49. **Multiple Choice** Solve the equation $16x = 208$.

   (F) $x = 11$ (G) $x = 12$ (H) $x = 13$ (J) $x = 14$

50. **Extended Response** It costs $18 per ticket for groups of 20 or more people to enter an amusement park. If Celia's group paid a total of $414 to enter, how many people were in her group?

Determine whether the given value of the variable is a solution. (Lesson 1-9)

51. $x + 34 = 48$; $x = 14$ 52. $d - 87 = 77$; $d = 10$

Solve each equation. (Lesson 1-10)

53. $76 + n = 115$ 54. $j - 97 = 145$ 55. $t - 123 = 455$ 56. $a + 39 = 86$

Quiz for Lessons 1-6 Through 1-11

1-6 Variables and Algebraic Expressions

Evaluate each expression for the given values of the variable.

1. $7(x + 4)$ for $x = 5$ **2.** $11 - n \div 3$ for $n = 6$ **3.** $p + 6t^2$ for $p = 11$ and $t = 3$

1-7 Translating Words into Math

Write each phrase as an algebraic expression.

4. the quotient of a number and 15   **5.** a number decreased by 13

6. 10 times the difference of p and 2   **7.** 3 plus the product of a number and 8

8. A long-distance phone company charges a $2.95 monthly fee plus $0.14 for each minute. Write an algebraic expression to show the cost of calling for t minutes in one month.

1-8 Simplifying Algebraic Expressions

Simplify each expression. Justify your steps.

9. $2y + 5y^2 - 2y^2$ **10.** $x + 4 + 7x + 9$ **11.** $10 + 9b - 6a - b$

12. Write an expression for the perimeter of the given figure. Then simplify the expression.

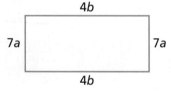

1-9 Equations and Their Solutions

Determine whether the given value of the variable is a solution.

13. $22 - x = 7$; $x = 15$ **14.** $\frac{56}{r} = 8$; $r = 9$ **15.** $m + 19 = 47$; $m = 28$

16. Last month Sue spent $147 on groceries. This month she spent $29 more on groceries than last month. Did Sue spend $118 or $176 on groceries this month?

1-10 Solving Equations by Adding or Subtracting

Solve each equation.

17. $g - 4 = 13$ **18.** $20 = 7 + p$ **19.** $t - 18 = 6$ **20.** $m + 34 = 53$

1-11 Solving Equations by Multiplying or Dividing

Solve each equation.

21. $\frac{k}{8} = 7$ **22.** $3b = 39$ **23.** $n \div 16 = 7$ **24.** $330 = 22x$

25. A water jug holds 128 fluid ounces. How many 8-ounce servings of water does the jug hold?

Real-World CONNECTIONS

CHAPTER 1

Willis Tower When it was completed in 1973, the Willis Tower, formerly named the Sears Tower, in Chicago became the tallest building in the United States. The tower's Skydeck on the 103rd floor offers an incredible view that attracts 1.3 million visitors per year. The express elevators to the Skydeck are among the fastest in the world.

ILLINOIS

Chicago

For 1–4, use the table.

1. The table shows the distance the Skydeck elevators travel in seconds. Describe the pattern in the table.

2. Find the distance an elevator can travel in 7 seconds. Explain how you found the distance.

3. Write an expression that gives the distance an elevator travels in *s* seconds.

4. The Skydeck is 1,353 feet above ground. Write and solve an equation to find out about how long it takes an elevator to go from the ground to the Skydeck.

Skydeck Elevators	
Time (s)	Distance (ft)
1	27
2	54
3	81
4	108

5. The Willis Tower has 1.61×10^4 windows. The Empire State Building in New York has 6.5×10^3 windows. Which building has more windows? How many more windows does it have?

6. Approximately 2.5×10^4 people enter the Willis Tower each day. About how many people enter the building during a typical work week from Monday to Friday?

Real-World Connections

Game Time

Jumping Beans

You will need a grid that is 4 squares by 6 squares. Each square must be large enough to contain a bean. Mark off a 3-square by 3-square section of the grid. Place nine beans in the nine spaces, as shown below.

You must move all nine beans to the nine marked-off squares in the fewest number of moves.

Follow the rules below to move the beans.

1 You may move to any empty square in any direction.

2 You may jump over another bean in any direction to an empty square.

3 You may jump over other beans as many times as you like.

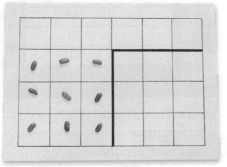 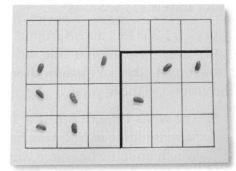

Moving all the beans in ten moves is not too difficult, but can you do it in nine moves?

Trading Spaces

The purpose of the game is to replace the red counters with the yellow counters, and the yellow counters with the red counters, in the fewest moves possible. The counters must be moved one at a time in an L-shape. No two counters may occupy the same square.

A complete copy of the rules and a game board are available online.

Learn It Online
Game Time Extra **go.hrw.com**,
keyword MS10 Games Go

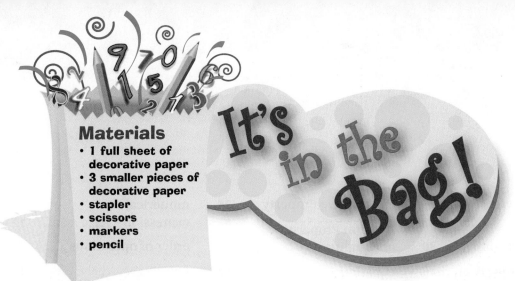

Materials
- 1 full sheet of decorative paper
- 3 smaller pieces of decorative paper
- stapler
- scissors
- markers
- pencil

It's in the Bag!

PROJECT **Step-by-Step Algebra**

This "step book" is a great place to record sample algebra problems.

Directions

1 Lay the $11\frac{1}{2}$-by-$7\frac{3}{4}$ inch sheet of paper in front of you. Fold it down $2\frac{1}{2}$ inches from the top and make a crease. **Figure A**

2 Slide the $7\frac{1}{4}$-by-$7\frac{3}{4}$-inch sheet of paper under the flap of the first piece. Do the same with the $5\frac{1}{2}$-by-$7\frac{3}{4}$-inch and $3\frac{3}{4}$-by-$7\frac{3}{4}$-inch sheets of paper to make a step book. Staple all of the sheets together at the top. **Figure B**

3 Use a pencil to divide the three middle sheets into thirds. Then cut up from the bottom along the lines you drew to make slits in these three sheets. **Figure C**

4 On the top step of your booklet, write the number and title of the chapter.

Taking Note of the Math

Label each of the steps in your booklet with important concepts from the chapter: "Using Exponents," "Expressing Numbers in Scientific Notation," and so on. On the bottom sheet, write "Solving Equations." Write sample problems from the chapter on the appropriate steps.

A

B

C

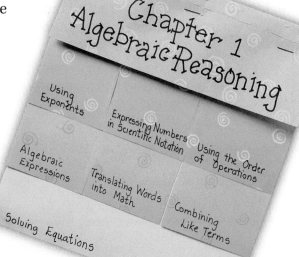

Chapter 1 Algebraic Reasoning

Using Exponents

Expressing Numbers in Scientific Notation

Using the Order of Operations

Algebraic Expressions

Translating Words into Math

Combining Like Terms

Solving Equations

Study Guide: Review

Vocabulary

Addition Property
of Equality 48

algebraic expression 30

Associative Property 24

base.................. 10

coefficient.............. 38

Commutative
Property 24

conjecture 7

constant 30

Distributive Property ... 25

Division Property
of Equality 52

equation 42

evaluate 30

exponent 10

Identity Property 24

inverse operations 48

Multiplication
Property of Equality 52

numerical
expression 19

order of operations 19

power 10

scientific notation 14

solution 42

Subtraction Property
of Equality 49

term 38

variable 30

Complete the sentences below with vocabulary words from the list above.

1. The __?__ tells how many times to use the __?__ as a factor.

2. A(n) __?__ is a mathematical phrase made up of numbers and operations.

3. A(n) __?__ is a mathematical statement that two expressions are equal in value.

4. A(n) __?__ consists of constants, variables, and operations.

EXAMPLES

EXERCISES

1-1 Numbers and Patterns (pp. 6–9)

■ Identify a possible pattern. Use the pattern to write the next three numbers.

2, 8, 14, 20, . . .
2 + 6 = 8   8 + 6 = 14   14 + 6 = 20
A possible pattern is to add 6 each time.
20 + 6 = 26   26 + 6 = 32   32 + 6 = 38

Identify a possible pattern. Use the pattern to write the next three numbers.

5. 6, 10, 14, 18, . . .   **6.** 15, 35, 55, 75, . . .

7. 7, 14, 21, 28, . . .   **8.** 8, 40, 200, 1,000, . . .

9. 41, 37, 33, 29, . . . **10.** 68, 61, 54, 47, . . .

1-2 Exponents (pp. 10–13)

■ Find the value of 4^3.
$4^3 = 4 \cdot 4 \cdot 4 = 64$

Find each value.

11. 9^2 **12.** 10^1 **13.** 2^7 **14.** 1^7 **15.** 11^2

1-3 **Scientific Notation** (pp. 14–17)

■ Multiply $157 \cdot 10^4$.

$157 \cdot 10^4 = 1570000$
$= 1,570,000$

Multiply.

16. $144 \cdot 10^2$ **17.** $1.32 \cdot 10^3$ **18.** $22 \cdot 10^7$

Write each number in scientific notation.

19. 48,000   **20.** 7,020,000   **21.** 149,000

22. In 2006 the population of Switzerland was about 7.507×10^6. Write this population in standard form.

1-4 **Order of Operations** (pp. 19–22)

■ Simplify $150 - (18 + 6) \cdot 5$.

$150 - (18 + 6) \cdot 5$ *Perform the operation in parentheses.*

$150 - 24 \cdot 5$ *Multiply.*

$150 - 120$ *Subtract.*

30

Simplify each expression.

23. $2 + (9 - 6) \div 3$ **24.** $12 \cdot 3^2 - 5$

25. $11 + 2 \cdot 5 - (9 + 7)$ **26.** $75 \div 5^2 + 8^2$

27. Lola decides to join a 15 mile walk-a-thon. Her parents give her $3 for each mile walked and her brother gives her $10. Simplify the expression $3 \cdot 15 + 10$ to find out how much money she raised.

1-5 **Properties of Numbers** (pp. 24–27)

■ Tell which property is represented.

$(10 \cdot 13) \cdot 28 = 10 \cdot (13 \cdot 28)$
Associative Property

Tell which property is represented.

28. $42 + 17 = 17 + 42$

29. $m + 0 = m$

30. $6 \cdot (x - 5) = 6 \cdot x - 6 \cdot 5$

Simplify each expression. Justify each step.

31. $28 + 15 + 22$ **32.** $20 \cdot 23 \cdot 5$

1-6 **Variables and Algebraic Expressions** (pp. 30–33)

■ Evaluate $5a - 6b + 7$ for $a = 4$ and $b = 3$.

$5a - 6b + 7$
$5(4) - 6(3) + 7$
$20 - 18 + 7$
9

Evaluate each expression for the given values of the variables.

33. $4x - 5$ for $x = 6$

34. $8y^3 + 3y$ for $y = 4$

35. $\frac{n}{5} + 6m - 3$ for $n = 5$ and $m = 2$

Study Guide: Review

1-7 Translating Words into Math (pp. 34–37)

■ Write as an algebraic expression.

5 times the sum of a number and 6
$5(n + 6)$

Write as an algebraic expression.

36. 4 divided by the sum of a number and 12

37. 2 times the difference of t and 11

38. Missy spent \$32 on s shirts. Write an algebraic expression to represent the cost of one shirt.

1-8 Simplifying Algebraic Expressions (pp. 38–41)

■ Simplify the expression.

$4x^3 + 5y + 8x^3 - 4y - 5x^2$
$4x^3 + 5y + 8x^3 - 4y - 5x^2$
$\quad 12x^3 + y - 5x^2$

Simplify each expression.

39. $7b^2 + 8 + 3b^2$

40. $12a^2 + 4 + 3a^2 - 2$

41. $x^2 + x^3 + x^4 + 5x^2$

1-9 Equations and Their Solutions (pp. 42–45)

■ Determine whether 22 is a solution.

$24 = s - 13$
$24 \overset{?}{=} 22 - 13$
$24 \overset{?}{=} 9$ ✗   *22 is not a solution.*

Determine whether the given value of the variable is a solution.

42. $\frac{b}{12} = 3; b = 48$

43. $36 = n - 12; n = 48$

44. $9x = 117; x = 12$

1-10 Solving Equations by Adding or Subtracting (pp. 48–51)

■ Solve the equation. Then check.

$\begin{aligned} b + 12 &= 16 \\ -12 &\;\; -12 \\ b &= 4 \end{aligned}$

$\begin{aligned} b + 12 &\overset{?}{=} 16 \\ 4 + 12 &\overset{?}{=} 16 \\ 16 &\overset{?}{=} 16 \;✔ \end{aligned}$

Solve each equation. Then check.

45. $8 + b = 16$ **46.** $20 = n - 12$

47. $27 + c = 45$ **48.** $t - 68 = 44$

1-11 Solving Equations by Multiplying or Dividing (pp. 52–55)

■ Solve the equation. Then check.

$2r = 12$
$\frac{2r}{2} = \frac{12}{2}$
$r = 6$

$2r = 12$
$2(6) \overset{?}{=} 12$
$12 \overset{?}{=} 12$ ✔

Solve each equation. Then check.

49. $n \div 12 = 6$ **50.** $3p = 27$

51. $\frac{d}{14} = 7$ **52.** $6x = 78$

53. Lee charges \$8 per hour to baby-sit. Last month she earned \$136. How many hours did Lee baby-sit last month?

Chapter Test

Identify a possible pattern. Use the pattern to write the next three numbers.

1. 24, 32, 40, 48, . . . **2.** 6, 18, 54, 162, . . . **3.** 64, 58, 52, 46, . . . **4.** 13, 30, 47, 64, . . .

Find each value.

5. 6^2 **6.** 7^5 **7.** 8^6 **8.** 3^5

Multiply.

9. $148 \cdot 10^2$ **10.** $56.3 \cdot 10^3$ **11.** $6.89 \cdot 10^4$ **12.** $7.5 \cdot 10^4$

Write each number in scientific notation.

13. 406,000,000 **14.** 1,905,000 **15.** 22,400 **16.** 500,000

17. The deepest point in the Atlantic Ocean is the Milwaukee Depth lying at a depth of 2.7493×10^4 feet. Write this depth in standard form.

Simplify each expression.

18. $18 \cdot 3 \div 3^3$ **19.** $36 + 16 - 50$ **20.** $149 - (2^8 - 200)$ **21.** $(4 \div 2) \cdot 9 + 11$

Tell which property is represented.

22. $0 + 45 = 45$ **23.** $(r + s) + t = r + (s + t)$ **24.** $84 \cdot 3 = 3 \cdot 84$

Evaluate each expression for the given values of the variables.

25. $4a + 6b + 7$ for $a = 2$ and $b = 3$ **26.** $7y^2 + 7y$ for $y = 3$

Write each phrase as an algebraic expression.

27. a number increased by 12 **28.** the quotient of a number and 7

29. 5 less than the product of 7 and s **30.** the difference between 3 times x and 4

Simplify each expression. Justify your steps.

31. $b + 2 + 5b$ **32.** $16 + 5b + 3b + 9$ **33.** $5a + 6t + 9 + 2a$

34. To join the gym Halle must pay a \$75 enrollment fee and \$32 per month. Write an algebraic expression to represent the total cost of m months at the gym, including the enrollment fee.

Solve each equation.

35. $x + 9 = 19$ **36.** $21 = y - 20$ **37.** $m - 54 = 72$ **38.** $136 = y + 114$

39. $16 = \dfrac{y}{3}$ **40.** $102 = 17y$ **41.** $\dfrac{r}{7} = 1{,}400$ **42.** $6x = 42$

43. A caterer charged \$15 per person to prepare a meal for a banquet. If the total catering charge for the banquet was \$1,530, how many people attended?

Multiple Choice: Eliminate Answer Choices

With some multiple-choice test items, you can use mental math or number sense to quickly eliminate some of the answer choices before you begin solving the problem.

EXAMPLE 1

Which is the solution to the equation $x + 7 = 15$?

(A) $x = 22$ (B) $x = 15$ (C) $x = 8$ (D) $x = 7$

READ the question. Then try to **eliminate** some of the answer choices.

Use number sense:
When you add, you get a greater number than what you started with. Since $x + 7 = 15$, 15 must be greater than x, or x must be less than 15. Since 22 and 15 are not less than 15, you can eliminate answer choices A and B.

The correct answer choice is C.

EXAMPLE 2

What is the value of the expression $18x + 6$ for $x = 5$?

(F) 90 (G) 96 (H) 191 (J) 198

LOOK at the choices. Then try to **eliminate** some of the answer choices.

Use mental math:
Estimate the value of the expression. Round 18 to 20 to make the multiplication easier.

$20x + 6$
$20(5) + 6$ *Substitute 5 for x.*
106 *Multiply. Then add.*

Because you rounded up, the value of the expression should be less than 106. You can eliminate choices H and J because they are too large.

The correct answer choice is G.

Test Tackler

Before you work a test question, use mental math to help you decide if there are answer choices that you can eliminate right away.

Read each test item and answer the questions that follow.

Item A
During the August back-to-school sale, 2 pairs of shoes cost $34, a shirt costs $15, and a pair of pants costs $27. Janet bought 2 pairs of shoes, 4 shirts, and 4 pairs of pants and then paid an additional $7 for tax. Which expression shows the total that Janet spent?

(A) $34 + 4(15 + 27)$

(B) $34 + 4(15 + 27) + 7$

(C) $4(34 + 15 + 27) + 7$

(D) $34 + 15 + 4 \cdot 27$

1. Can any of the answer choices be eliminated immediately? If so, which choices and why?

2. Describe how you can determine the correct answer from the remaining choices.

Item B
Anthony saved $1 from his first paycheck, $2 from his second paycheck, then $4, $8, and so on. How much money did Anthony save from his tenth paycheck?

(F) $10   (H) $512

(G) $16   (J) $1,023

3. Are there any answer choices you can eliminate immediately? If so, which choices and why?

4. What common error was made in finding answer choice F?

Item C
Craig has three weeks to read an 850-page book. Which equation can be used to find the number of pages Craig has to read each day?

(A) $\frac{x}{3} = 850$ (C) $3x = 850$

(B) $21x = 850$ (D) $\frac{x}{21} = 850$

5. Describe how to use number sense to eliminate at least one answer choice.

6. What common error was made in finding answer choice D?

Item D
What value of t makes the following equation true?

$$22t = 132$$

(F) 6   (H) 154

(G) 110   (J) 2,904

7. Which choices can be eliminated by using number sense? Explain.

8. What common error was made in finding answer choice J?

9. Describe how you could check your answer to this problem.

Item E
What is the value of the expression $(1 + 2)^2 + 14 \div 2 + 5$?

(A) 0   (C) 17

(B) 11   (D) 21

10. Use mental math to quickly eliminate one answer choice. Explain your choice.

11. What common error was made in finding answer choice B?

12. What common error was made in finding answer choice C?

TCAP
Test Prep

Learn It Online
State Test Practice **go.hrw.com**,
keyword MS10 TestPrep Go

Cumulative Assessment, Chapter 1

Multiple Choice

1. Which expression has a value of 74 when $x = 10$, $y = 8$, and $z = 12$?

  A $4xyz$ **C** $2xz - 3y$

  B $x + 5y + 2z$ **D** $6xyz + 8$

2. Which of the following does <u>not</u> have a value of 27?

  F 3^3 **H** $3 \times 3 + 18$

  G $3^2 + 3 \times 7$ **J** $9^2 \div 3$

3. A contractor charges $22 to install one miniblind. How much does the contractor charge to install m miniblinds?

  A $22m$ **C** $22 + m$

  B $\frac{m}{22}$ **D** $\frac{22}{m}$

4. Which of the following is an example of the Commutative Property?

  F $20 + 10 = 2(10 + 5)$

  G $20 + 10 = 10 + 20$

  H $5 + (20 + 10) = (5 + 20) + 10$

  J $20 + 0 = 20$

5. Which expression simplifies to $9x + 3$ when you combine like terms?

  A $10x^2 - x^2 - 3$

  B $3x + 7 - 4 + 3x$

  C $18 + 4x - 15 + 5x$

  D $7x^2 + 2x + 6 - 3$

6. Which expression is equivalent to 8×92?

  F $8 \times 90 + 8 \times 2$

  G $8 + (90 + 2)$

  H $8 \times 90 + 2$

  J $8 \times 90 \times 2$

7. Tia maps out her jogging route as shown in the table. How many miles does Tia plan to jog?

Tia's Jogging Route	
Street	**Miles**
1st to Park	0.42
Park to Windsor	1.12
Windsor to East	0.56
East to Manor	1.4
Manor to Vane	1.25
Vane to 1st	0.35

  A 4.2 mi   **C** 5.1 mi

  B 4.89 mi   **D** 6.7 mi

8. Audrey spent $\frac{14}{30}$ of June visiting her grandparents. Which of the following is the fraction $\frac{14}{30}$ <u>not</u> equal to?

  F $\frac{7}{15}$ **H** $\frac{21}{45}$

  G $0.9\overline{3}$ **J** $0.4\overline{6}$

9. A writer spends $144.75 on 5 ink cartridges. Which equation can be used to find the cost c of one ink cartridge?

  A $5c = 144.75$

  B $\frac{c}{144.75} = 5$

  C $5 + c = 144.75$

  D $144.75 - c = 5$

10. Marc spends $78 for n shirts. Which expression can be used to represent the cost of one shirt?

  F $\frac{n}{78}$ **H** $\frac{78}{n}$

  G $78n$ **J** $78 + n$

11. Which situation <u>best</u> matches the expression $0.29x + 2$?

   A A taxi company charges a $2.00 flat fee plus $0.29 for every mile.

   B Jimmy ran 0.29 miles, stopped to rest, and then ran 2 more miles.

   C There are 0.29 grams of calcium in 2 servings of Hearty Health Cereal.

   D Amy bought 2 pieces of gum for $0.29 each.

12. Which of the following should be performed first to simplify this expression?

   $$16 \cdot 2 + (20 \div 5) - 3^2 \div 3 + 1$$

   F $3^2 \div 3$

   G $20 \div 5$

   H $16 \cdot 2$

   J $3 + 1$

 When you read a word problem, cross out any information that is not needed to solve the problem.

13. Charlie ate $\frac{5}{8}$ of a pizza. The only mushrooms on the pizza were on $\frac{1}{5}$ of what Charlie ate. How much of the pizza was covered with mushrooms?

   A $\frac{1}{8}$ pizza

   B $\frac{5}{13}$ pizza

   C $\frac{1}{5}$ pizza

   D $3\frac{1}{8}$ pizzas

14. What is the value of the expression $3^2 \times (2 + 3 \times 4) - 5$?

   F 13

   G 18

   H 81

   J 121

Process Standards Practice
Short Response

S1. Luke can swim 25 laps in one hour. Write an algebraic expression to show how many laps Luke can swim in h hours. How many hours will it take Luke to swim 100 laps?

S2. An aerobics instructor teaches a 45-minute class at 9:30 A.M., three times a week. She dedicates 12 minutes during each class to stretching. The rest of the class consists of aerobic dance. How many minutes of each class does the instructor spend teaching aerobic dance? Write and solve an equation to explain how you found your answer.

S3. Ike and Joe ran the same distance but took different routes. Ike ran 3 blocks east and 7 blocks south. Joe ran 4 blocks west and then turned north. How far north did Joe run? Show your work.

Extended Response

E1. The Raiders and the Hornets are buying new uniforms for their baseball teams. Each team member will receive a new cap, a jersey, and a pair of pants.

Uniform Costs		
	Raiders	Hornets
Cap	$15	$15
Jersey	$75	$70
Pants	$60	$70

   a. Let r represent the number of Raiders team members, and let h represent the number of Hornets team members. For each team, write an expression that gives the total cost of the team's uniforms.

   b. If the Raiders and the Hornets both have 12 team members, how much will each team spend on uniforms? Which team will spend the most, and by how much? Show your work.

Integers and Rational Numbers

Chapter Focus
• Add, subtract, multiply and divide intergers.
• Find prime factorizations.
• Express factions as decimals.

Why Learn This?

Integers are commonly used to describe temperatures. In many parts of the world, winter temperatures are often negative integers, meaning it is colder than 0°.

 Learn It Online
Chapter Project Online **go.hrw.com**,
keyword MS10 Ch2

Learn It Online
Resources Online **go.hrw.com**,
keyword **MS10 AYR2** **Go**

✓ Vocabulary

Choose the best term from the list to complete each sentence.

1. To __?__ a number on a number line, mark and label the point that corresponds to that number.

2. The expression $1 < 3 < 5$ tells the __?__ of these three numbers on a number line.

3. A(n) __?__ is a mathematical statement showing two things are equal.

4. Each number in the set 0, 1, 2, 3, 4, 5, 6, 7, ... is a(n) __?__.

5. To __?__ an equation, find a value that makes it true.

whole number

expression

graph

solve

equation

order

Complete these exercises to review skills you will need for this chapter.

✓ Order of Operations

Simplify.

6. $7 + 9 - 5 \cdot 2$

7. $12 \cdot 3 - 4 \cdot 5$

8. $115 - 15 \cdot 3 + 9(8 - 2)$

9. $20 \cdot 5 \cdot 2(7 + 1) \div 4$

10. $300 + 6(5 - 3) - 11$

11. $14 - 13 + 9 \cdot 2$

✓ Find Multiples

Find the first five multiples of each number.

12. 2

13. 9

14. 15

15. 1

16. 101

17. 54

18. 326

19. 1,024

✓ Find Factors

List all the factors of each number.

20. 8

21. 22

22. 36

23. 50

24. 108

25. 84

26. 256

27. 630

✓ Use Inverse Operations to Solve Equations

Solve.

28. $n + 3 = 10$

29. $x - 4 = 16$

30. $9p = 63$

31. $\frac{t}{5} = 80$

32. $x - 3 = 14$

33. $\frac{q}{3} = 21$

34. $9 + r = 91$

35. $15p = 45$

Study Guide: Preview

Where You've Been

Previously, you

- compared and ordered non-negative rational numbers.

- generated equivalent forms of rational numbers including whole numbers, fractions, and decimals.

- used integers to represent real-life situations.

In This Chapter

You will study

- comparing and ordering integers and rational numbers.

- converting between fractions and decimals mentally, on paper, and with a calculator.

- using models to add, subtract, multiply, and divide integers.

- finding the prime factorization, greatest common factor, and least common multiple.

Where You're Going

You can use the skills learned in this chapter

- to express negative numbers related to scientific fields such as marine biology or meteorology.

- to find equivalent measures.

Key Vocabulary/Vocabulario

equivalent fraction	fracción equivalente
greatest common factor (GCF)	máximo común divisor (MCD)
integer	entero
least common multiple (LCM)	mínimo común múltiplo (MCM)
prime factorization	factorización prima
rational number	número racional
relatively prime	primo relativo
repeating decimal	decimal periódico
terminating decimal	decimal finito

Vocabulary Connections

To become familiar with some of the vocabulary terms in the chapter, consider the following. You may refer to the chapter, the glossary, or a dictionary if you like.

1. The word *common* means "belonging to or shared by two things." How can you use this definition to explain what the **least common multiple** of two numbers is?

2. When something is relative, it is "carried back" to or compared to certain values. A *prime* number is only divisible by itself and one. If two numbers are **relatively prime** and neither are prime numbers, how do you think they relate to each other?

3. A decimal is a number that has digits to the right of the decimal point. What might you predict about those digits in a **repeating decimal**?

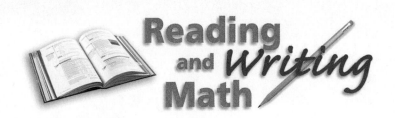

Writing Strategy: Translate Between Words and Math

As you read a real-world math problem, look for key words to help you translate between the words and the math.

Example

At FunZone the cost to play laser tag is $8 per game. The cost to play miniature golf is $5 per game. The one-time admission fee to the park is $3. Jonna wants to play both laser tag and miniature golf. Write an algebraic expression to find the total amount Jonna would pay to play ℓ laser tag games and m golf games at FunZone.

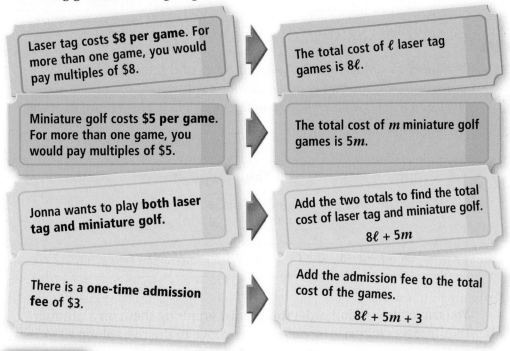

Laser tag costs **$8 per game**. For more than one game, you would pay multiples of $8. → The total cost of ℓ laser tag games is 8ℓ.

Miniature golf costs **$5 per game**. For more than one game, you would pay multiples of $5. → The total cost of m miniature golf games is $5m$.

Jonna wants to play **both laser tag and miniature golf**. → Add the two totals to find the total cost of laser tag and miniature golf.
$$8\ell + 5m$$

There is a **one-time admission fee of $3**. → Add the admission fee to the total cost of the games.
$$8\ell + 5m + 3$$

Try This

Write an algebraic expression that describes the situation. Explain why you chose each operation in the expression.

1. School supplies are half-price at Bargain Mart this week. The original prices were $2 per package of pens and $4 per notebook. Cally buys 1 package of pens and n notebooks. How much does Cally spend?

2. Fred has f cookies, and Gary has g cookies. Fred and Gary each eat 3 cookies. How many total cookies are left?

Integers and Rational Numbers **71**

2-1 Integers

TN ✓ **0706.2.4** Understand that *a* and −*a* are additive inverses and are located the same distance from zero on the number line; relate distance from zero to absolute value. *Also* ✓ **0706.2.5**

The **opposite**, or **additive inverse**, of a number is the same distance from 0 on a number line as the original number, but on the other side of 0. Zero is its own opposite.

Vocabulary

opposite

additive inverse

integer

absolute value

−4 and 4 are opposites.

−4   4

$$\xleftarrow{\quad} \overset{-5\ -4\ -3\ -2\ -1\quad 0\quad 1\quad 2\quad 3\quad 4\quad 5}{\rule{0pt}{0pt}} \xrightarrow{\quad}$$

Negative integers   Positive integers

0 is neither positive nor negative.

Dr. Sylvia Earle holds the world record for the deepest solo dive.

Remember!

The whole numbers are the natural numbers and zero: 0, 1, 2, 3, ...

The **integers** are the set of whole numbers and their opposites. By using integers, you can express elevations above, below, and at sea level. Sea level has an elevation of 0 feet. Sylvia Earle's record dive was to an elevation of −1,250 feet.

EXAMPLE 1 **Graphing Integers and Their Opposites on a Number Line**

Graph the integer −3 and its opposite on a number line.

3 units   3 units

$$\xleftarrow{\quad} \overset{-5\ -4\ -3\ -2\ -1\quad 0\quad 1\quad 2\quad 3\quad 4\quad 5}{\rule{0pt}{0pt}} \xrightarrow{\quad}$$

The opposite of −3 is 3.

You can compare and order integers by graphing them on a number line. Integers increase in value as you move to the right along a number line. They decrease in value as you move to the left.

EXAMPLE 2 **Comparing Integers Using a Number Line**

Compare the integers. Use < or >.

A 2 ▢ −2

$$\xleftarrow{\quad} \overset{-4\ -3\ -2\ -1\quad 0\quad 1\quad 2\quad 3\quad 4}{\rule{0pt}{0pt}} \xrightarrow{\quad}$$

Remember!

The symbol < means "is less than," and the symbol > means "is greater than."

2 is farther to the right than −2, so 2 > −2.

Compare the integers. Use < or >.

B −10 ▮ −7

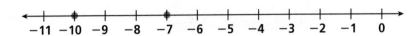

−10 is farther to the left than −7, so −10 < −7.

EXAMPLE 3 **Ordering Integers Using a Number Line**

Use a number line to order the integers −2, 5, −4, 1, −1, and 0 from least to greatest.

Graph the integers on a number line. Then read them from left to right.

The numbers in order from least to greatest are −4, −2, −1, 0, 1, and 5.

Helpful Hint

For more on absolute value, see Skills Bank p. SB16.

A number's **absolute value** is its distance from 0 on a number line. Since distance can never be negative, absolute values are never negative. They are always positive or zero.

EXAMPLE 4 **Finding Absolute Value**

Reading Math

The symbol | | is read as "the absolute value of." For example, |−3| means "the absolute value of −3."

Use a number line to find each absolute value.

A |7|

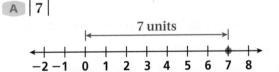

7 is 7 units from 0, so |7| = 7.

B |−4|

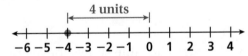

−4 is 4 units from 0, so |−4| = 4.

Think and Discuss

1. **Tell** which number is greater: −4,500 or −10,000.

2. **Name** the greatest negative integer and the least nonnegative integer. Then compare the absolute values of these integers.

Learn It Online
Homework Help Online **go.hrw.com**,
keyword [MS10 2-1] [Go]
Exercises 1–30, 31, 33, 35, 37, 39, 41, 45

GUIDED PRACTICE

See Example **1** Graph each integer and its opposite on a number line.

   1. 2   **2.** −9   **3.** −1   **4.** 6

See Example **2** Compare the integers. Use < or >.

   5. 5 ■ −5   **6.** −9 ■ −18   **7.** −21 ■ −17   **8.** −12 ■ 12

See Example **3** Use a number line to order the integers from least to greatest.

   9. 6, −3, −1, −5, 4   **10.** 8, −2, 7, 1, −8   **11.** −6, −4, 3, 0, 1

See Example **4** Use a number line to find each absolute value.

   12. $|-2|$ **13.** $|8|$ **14.** $|-7|$ **15.** $|-10|$

INDEPENDENT PRACTICE

See Example **1** Graph each integer and its opposite on a number line.

   16. −4   **17.** 10   **18.** −12   **19.** 7

See Example **2** Compare the integers. Use < or >.

   20. −14 ■ −7   **21.** 9 ■ −9   **22.** −12 ■ 12   **23.** −31 ■ −27

See Example **3** Use a number line to order the integers from least to greatest.

   24. −3, 2, −5, −6, 5   **25.** −7, −9, −2, 0, −5   **26.** 3, −6, 9, −1, −2

See Example **4** Use a number line to find each absolute value.

   27. $|-16|$ **28.** $|12|$ **29.** $|-20|$ **30.** $|15|$

PRACTICE AND PROBLEM SOLVING

Extra Practice
See page EP5.

Compare. Write <, >, or =.

   31. −25 ■ 25   **32.** 18 ■ −55   **33.** $|-21|$ ■ 21   **34.** −9 ■ −27

   35. 34 ■ $|34|$ **36.** 64 ■ $|-75|$ **37.** $|-3|$ ■ $|3|$ **38.** −100 ■ −82

39. Earth Science The table shows the average temperatures in Vostok, Antarctica from March to October. List the months in order from coldest to warmest.

Month	Mar	Apr	May	Jun	Jul	Aug	Sep	Oct
Temperature (°F)	−72	−84	−86	−85	−88	−90	−87	−71

40. What is the opposite of $|32|$?   **41.** What is the opposite of $|-29|$?

42. Business A company reported a net loss of $2,000,000 during its first year. In its second year it reported a profit of $5,000,000. Write each amount as an integer.

In wakeboarding, a rider uses the waves created by a boat, the wake, to jump into the air and perform tricks such as rolls and flips.

43. Critical Thinking Give an example in which a negative number has a greater absolute value than a positive number.

44. Social Studies Lines of latitude are imaginary lines that circle the globe in an east-west direction. They measure distances north and south of the equator. The equator represents 0° latitude.

   a. What latitude is opposite of 30° north latitude?

   b. How do these latitudes' distances from the equator compare?

Sports The graph shows how participation in several sports changed between 1999 and 2000 in the United States.

45. By about what percent did participation in racquetball increase or decrease?

46. By about what percent did participation in wall climbing increase or decrease?

47. What's the Error? At 9 A.M. the outside temperature was −3 °F. By noon, the temperature was −12 °F. A newscaster said that it was getting warmer outside. Why is this incorrect?

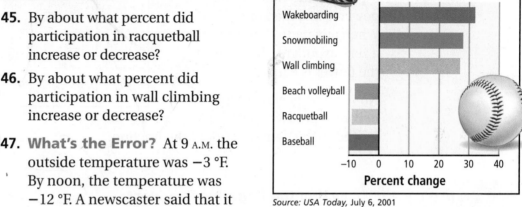

Popular Recreational Sports

Group sports declined in 1999 as Americans turned to individual sports.

Wakeboarding
Snowmobiling
Wall climbing
Beach volleyball
Racquetball
Baseball

−10 0 10 20 30 40
Percent change

Source: USA Today, July 6, 2001

48. Write About It Explain how to compare two integers.

49. Challenge What values can x have if $|x| = 11$?

Test Prep and Spiral Review

50. Multiple Choice Which list shows the integers in order from least to greatest?

  Ⓐ −5, −6, −7, 2, 3 Ⓑ 2, 3, −5, −6, −7 Ⓒ −7, −6, −5, 2, 3 Ⓓ 3, 2, −7, −6, −5

51. Multiple Choice The table shows the average temperatures in Barrow, Alaska, for several months. In which month is the average temperature lowest?

  Ⓕ January   Ⓗ May

  Ⓖ March   Ⓙ July

Monthly Temperatures	
January	−12 °F
March	−13 °F
May	20 °F
July	40 °F

Write each number in scientific notation. (Lesson 1-3)

52. 400,000   **53.** 1,802,300   **54.** $59.7 \cdot 10^3$ **55.** $800 \cdot 10^6$

Use the Distributive Property to find each product. (Lesson 1-5)

56. 3(12)   **57.** 2(56)   **58.** (27)6   **59.** (34)5

Negative Exponents

TN ✓ **0706.2.13** Use the meaning of negative exponents to represent small numbers; translate between scientific and standard notation.
Also **GLE 0706.2.6, GLE 0706.2.7,** ✓ **0706.2.14**

When a natural number has a positive exponent, the value of the power is greater than or equal to 1. When a natural number has a negative exponent, the value of the power is less than or equal to 1. When any natural number has a zero exponent, the value of the power is equal to 1.

Notice: The negative exponent becomes positive when it is moved to the denominator of the fraction.

Power	Meaning	Value
10^2	$10 \cdot 10$	100
10^1	10	10
10^0	1	1
10^{-1}	$\frac{1}{10^1}$	$\frac{1}{10}$ or 0.1
10^{-2}	$\frac{1}{10} \cdot \frac{1}{10}$ or $\frac{1}{10^2}$	$\frac{1}{100}$ or 0.01
10^{-3}	$\frac{1}{10} \cdot \frac{1}{10} \cdot \frac{1}{10}$ or $\frac{1}{10^3}$	$\frac{1}{1000}$ or 0.001

EXAMPLE **Evaluating Negative Exponents**

Evaluate 10^{-4}.

$10^{-4} = \dfrac{1}{10^4}$　　*Write the fraction with a positive exponent in the denominator.*

$= \dfrac{1}{10,000}$　　*Evaluate the power.*

$= 0.0001$　　*Write the decimal form.*

In Chapter 1, you learned to write large numbers in scientific notation using powers of ten with positive exponents. In the same way, you can write very small numbers in scientific notation using powers of ten with negative exponents.

EXAMPLE **Writing Small Numbers in Scientific Notation**

Write 0.000065 in scientific notation.

$0.000065 = 0.000065$　　*Move the decimal point 5 places to the right.*

$= 6.5 \times 0.00001$　　*Write as a product of two factors.*

$= 6.5 \times 10^{-5}$　　*Write the exponential form. Since the decimal point was moved 5 places, the exponent is −5.*

Remember!

Move the decimal point to get a number that is greater than or equal to 1 and less than 10.

EXAMPLE **3**

Writing Small Numbers in Standard Form

Write 3.4×10^{-6} in standard form.

$3.4 \times 10^{-6} = 0\underset{\sim}{000003}.4$ *Since the exponent is −6, move the decimal point 6 places to the left.*

$= 0.0000034$

When comparing numbers in scientific notation, you may need to compare only the powers of ten to see which value is greater.

EXAMPLE **4**

Comparing Numbers Using Scientific Notation

Compare. Write <, >, or =.

A 3.7×10^{-8} ▢ 6.1×10^{-12}

$10^{-8} > 10^{-12}$ *Compare the powers of ten.*

Since $10^{-8} > 10^{-12}$, $3.7 \times 10^{-8} > 6.1 \times 10^{-12}$.

B 4.9×10^{-5} ▢ 7.3×10^{-5}

$10^{-5} = 10^{-5}$ *Compare the powers of ten.*

Since the powers of ten are equal, compare the decimals.

$4.9 < 7.3$ *4 is less than 7.*

Since $4.9 < 7.3$, $4.9 \times 10^{-5} < 7.3 \times 10^{-5}$.

EXTENSION

Exercises

Find each value.

1. 10^{-8} **2.** 10^{-6} **3.** 10^{-5} **4.** 10^{-10} **5.** 10^{-7}

Write each number in scientific notation or standard form.

6. 0.00000021   **7.** 0.00086   **8.** 0.0000000066   **9.** 0.007

10. 0.0009   **11.** 0.0453   **12.** 0.0701   **13.** 0.00003021

14. 5.8×10^{-9} **15.** 4.5×10^{-5} **16.** 3.2×10^{-3} **17.** 1.4×10^{-11}

18. 2.77×10^{-1} **19.** 9.06×10^{-2} **20.** 7×10^{-10} **21.** 8×10^{-8}

Compare. Write <, >, or =.

22. 7.6×10^{-1} ▢ 7.7×10^{-1} **23.** 8.2×10^{-7} ▢ 8.1×10^{-6}

24. 2.8×10^{-6} ▢ 2.8×10^{-7} **25.** 5.5×10^{-2} ▢ 2.2×10^{-5}

 26. Write About It Explain the effect that a zero exponent has on a power.

Hands-on LAB 2-2

Model Integer Addition

Use with Lesson 2-2

Learn It Online
Lab Resources Online **go.hrw.com**,
keyword **MS10 Lab2** **Go**

TN **GLE 0706.1.8** Use technologies/manipulatives appropriately to develop understanding of mathematical algorithms, to facilitate problem solving, and to create accurate and reliable models of mathematical concepts.
Also **GLE 0706.2.1**

KEY
🟡 = 1
🔴 = −1
🟡 + 🔴 = 0

REMEMBER
• Adding or subtracting zero does not change the value of an expression.

You can model integer addition by using integer chips. Yellow chips represent positive numbers and red chips represent negative numbers.

Activity

When you model adding numbers with the same sign, you can count the total number of chips to find the sum.

   *The total number of positive chips is 7.*

   *The total number of negative chips is 7.*

$3 + 4 = 7$

$-3 + (-4) = -7$

1 Use integer chips to find each sum.

a. $2 + 4$ **b.** $-2 + (-4)$ **c.** $6 + 3$ **d.** $-5 + (-4)$

When you model adding numbers with different signs, you cannot count the chips to find their sum.

🟡 + 🟡 = 2 and 🔴 + 🔴 = −2

but 🟡 + 🔴 = 0   *A red chip and a yellow chip make a neutral pair.*

When you model adding a positive and a negative number, you need to remove all of the neutral pairs that you can find—that is, all pairs of 1 red chip and 1 yellow chip. These pairs have a value of zero, so they do not affect the sum.

$3 + (-4) = $ ■

You cannot just count the colored chips to find their sum.

Before you count the chips, you need to remove all of the zero pairs.

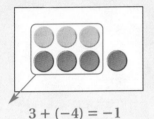

When you remove the zero pairs, there is one red chip left. So the sum of the chips is −1.

$3 + (-4) = -1$

2 Use integer chips to find each sum.

a. $4 + (-6)$ b. $-5 + 2$ c. $7 + (-3)$ d. $-6 + 3$

Think and Discuss

1. Will $8 + (-3)$ and $-3 + 8$ give the same answer? Why or why not?

2. If you have more red chips than yellow chips in a group, is the sum of the chips positive or negative?

3. If you have more yellow chips than red chips in a group, is the sum of the chips positive or negative?

4. **Make a Conjecture** Make a conjecture for the sign of the answer when negative and positive integers are added. Give examples.

Try This

Use integer chips to find each sum.

1. $4 + (-7)$ 2. $-5 + (-4)$ 3. $-5 + 1$ 4. $6 + (-4)$

Write the addition problems modeled below.

5.

6.

7.

8.

Adding Integers

TN ✓ 0706.2.6 Use the number line to demonstrate addition and subtraction with integers.
Also **GLE 0706.2.1**, ✓ 0706.2.2, SPI 0706.2.5, SPI 0706.3.1

The math team wanted to raise money for a trip to Washington, D.C. They began by estimating their income and expenses.

Income items are positive, and expenses are negative. By adding all your income and expenses, you can find your total earnings or losses.

One way to add integers is by using a number line.

Club Ledger

Estimated Income and Expenses

Description	Amount
Car wash supplies	–$25.00
Car wash earnings	$300.00
Bake sale supplies	–$50.00
Bake sale earnings	$250.00

EXAMPLE **1** **Modeling Integer Addition**

Interactivities Online ▶

Use a number line to find each sum.

A $-3 + (-6)$

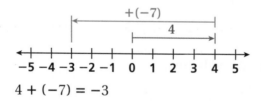

$-3 + (-6) = -9$

Start at 0. Move left 3 units. Then move left 6 more units.

B $4 + (-7)$

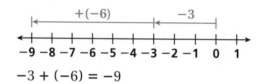

$4 + (-7) = -3$

Start at 0. Move right 4 units. Then move left 7 units.

You can also use absolute value to add integers.

Adding Integers

To add two integers with the same sign, find the sum of their absolute values. Use the sign of the two integers.

To add two integers with different signs, find the difference of their absolute values. Use the sign of the integer with the greater absolute value.

Video **Lesson Tutorials Online** my.hrw.com

EXAMPLE 2 **Adding Integers Using Absolute Values**

Find each sum.

A $-7 + (-4)$

The signs are the **same**. Find the **sum** of the absolute values.

$-7 + (-4)$ *Think: 7 + 4 = 11.*
-11 *Use the sign of the two integers.*

Helpful Hint

When adding integers, think: If the signs are the *same*, find the *sum*.
If the signs are *different*, find the *difference*.

B $-8 + 6$

The signs are **different**. Find the **difference** of the absolute values.

$-8 + 6$ *Think: 8 − 6 = 2.*
-2 *Use the sign of the integer with the greater absolute value.*

EXAMPLE 3 **Evaluating Expressions with Integers**

Evaluate $a + b$ for $a = 6$ and $b = -10$.

$a + b$
$6 + (-10)$ *Substitute 6 for **a** and −10 for **b**.*
               *The signs are **different**. Think: 10 − 6 = 4.*
-4 *Use the sign of the integer with the greater absolute value (**negative**).*

EXAMPLE 4 *Banking Application*

The math team's income from a car wash was $300, including tips. Supply expenses were $25. Use integer addition to find the team's total profit or loss.

$300 + (-25)$ *Use negative for the expenses.*
$300 - 25$ *Find the difference of the absolute values.*
275 *The answer is positive.*
The team earned $275.

Think and Discuss

1. **Explain** whether $-7 + 2$ is the same as $7 + (-2)$.

2. **Use** the Commutative Property to write an expression that is equivalent to $3 + (-5)$.

Learn It Online
Homework Help Online **go.hrw.com**,
keyword MS10 2-2 Go
Exercises 1–32, 33, 37, 39, 43, 47, 49, 51

GUIDED PRACTICE

See Example 1   **Use a number line to find each sum.**

1. $9 + 3$ **2.** $-4 + (-2)$ **3.** $7 + (-9)$ **4.** $-3 + 6$

See Example 2   **Find each sum.**

5. $7 + 8$ **6.** $-1 + (-12)$ **7.** $-25 + 10$ **8.** $31 + (-20)$

See Example 3   **Evaluate $a + b$ for the given values.**

9. $a = 5, b = -17$ **10.** $a = 8, b = -8$ **11.** $a = -4, b = -16$

See Example 4   **12. Sports** A football team gains 8 yards on one play and then loses 13 yards on the next. Use integer addition to find the team's total yardage.

INDEPENDENT PRACTICE

See Example 1   **Use a number line to find each sum.**

13. $-16 + 7$ **14.** $-5 + (-1)$ **15.** $4 + 9$ **16.** $-7 + 8$

17. $10 + (-3)$ **18.** $-20 + 2$ **19.** $-12 + (-5)$ **20.** $-9 + 6$

See Example 2   **Find each sum.**

21. $-13 + (-6)$ **22.** $14 + 25$ **23.** $-22 + 6$ **24.** $35 + (-50)$

25. $-81 + (-7)$ **26.** $28 + (-3)$ **27.** $-70 + 15$ **28.** $-18 + (-62)$

See Example 3   **Evaluate $c + d$ for the given values.**

29. $c = 6, d = -20$ **30.** $c = -8, d = -21$ **31.** $c = -45, d = 32$

See Example 4   **32.** The temperature dropped 17 °F in 6 hours. The final temperature was −3 °F. Use integer addition to find the starting temperature.

PRACTICE AND PROBLEM SOLVING

Extra Practice
See page EP5.

Find each sum.

33. $-8 + (-5)$ **34.** $14 + (-7)$ **35.** $-41 + 15$

36. $-22 + (-18) + 22$ **37.** $27 + (-29) + 16$ **38.** $-30 + 71 + (-70)$

Compare. Write $<$, $>$, or $=$.

39. $-23 + 18 \ \blacksquare \ -41$ **40.** $59 + (-59) \ \blacksquare \ 0$ **41.** $31 + (-20) \ \blacksquare \ 9$

42. $-24 + (-24) \ \blacksquare \ 48$ **43.** $25 + (-70) \ \blacksquare \ -95$ **44.** $16 + (-40) \ \blacksquare \ -24$

45. Personal Finance Cody made deposits of $45, $18, and $27 into his checking account. He then wrote checks for $21 and $93. Write an expression to show the change in Cody's account. Then simplify the expression.

Evaluate each expression for $w = -12$, $x = 10$, and $y = -7$.

46. $7 + y$ **47.** $-4 + w$ **48.** $w + y$ **49.** $x + y$ **50.** $w + x$

51. **Recreation** Hikers along the Appalachian Trail camped overnight at Horns Pond, at an elevation of 3,100 ft. Then they hiked along the ridge of the Bigelow Mountains to West Peak, which is one of Maine's highest peaks. Use the diagram to determine the elevation of West Peak.

The Appalachian Trail extends about 2,160 miles from Maine to Georgia. It takes about 5 to 7 months to hike the entire trail.

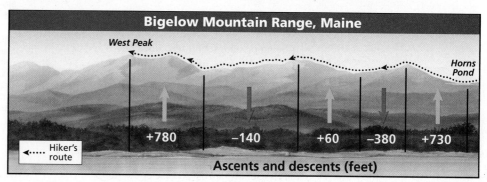

52. **Multi-Step** Hector and Luis are playing a game. In the game, each player starts with 0 points, and the player with the most points at the end wins. Hector gains 5 points, loses 3, loses 2, and then gains 3. Luis loses 5 points, gains 1, gains 5, and then loses 3. Determine the final scores by modeling the problem on a number line. Then tell who wins the game and by how much.

53. **What's the Question?** The temperature was $-8\,°\text{F}$ at 6 A.M. and rose $15\,°\text{F}$ by 9 A.M. The answer is $7\,°\text{F}$. What is the question?

54. **Write About It** Compare the method used to add integers with the same sign and the method used to add integers with different signs.

55. **Challenge** A business had losses of $225 million, $75 million, and $375 million and profits of $15 million and $125 million. How much was its overall profit or loss?

Test Prep and Spiral Review

56. **Multiple Choice** Which expression is represented by the model?

Ⓐ $-4 + (-1)$ Ⓒ $-4 + 3$

Ⓑ $-4 + 0$ Ⓓ $-4 + 4$

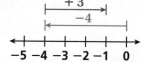

57. **Multiple Choice** Which expression has the greatest value?

Ⓕ $-4 + 8$ Ⓖ $-2 + (-3)$ Ⓗ $1 + 2$ Ⓙ $4 + (-6)$

Simplify each expression. (Lesson 1-4)

58. $2 + 5 \cdot 2 - 3$ **59.** $3^3 - (6 \cdot 4) + 1$ **60.** $30 - 5 \cdot (3 + 2)$ **61.** $15 - 3 \cdot 2^2 + 1$

Compare. Write <, >, or =. (Lesson 2-1)

62. $-14 \ \blacksquare\ -12$ **63.** $|-4| \ \blacksquare\ 3$ **64.** $|-6| \ \blacksquare\ 6$ **65.** $-9 \ \blacksquare\ -11$

Hands-on LAB 2-3

Model Integer Subtraction

Use with Lesson 2-3

Learn It Online
Lab Resources Online **go.hrw.com**,
keyword MS10 Lab2 Go

TN GLE 0706.1.8 Use technologies/
manipulatives appropriately to develop
understanding of mathematical algorithms,
to facilitate problem solving, and to
create accurate and reliable models of
mathematical concepts.
Also GLE 0706.2.1

KEY	REMEMBER
○ = 1 ● = −1 ○ + ● = 0	• Adding or subtracting zero does not change the value of an expression.

You can model integer subtraction by using integer chips.

Activity

These groups of chips show three different ways of modeling 2.

1 Show two other ways of modeling 2.

These groups of chips show two different ways of modeling −2.

2 Show two other ways of modeling −2.

You can model subtraction problems involving two integers with the
same sign by taking away chips.

$$8 - 3 = 5$$ $$-8 - (-3) = -5$$

3 Use integer chips to find each difference.

   a. $6 - 5$ **b.** $-6 - (-5)$ **c.** $10 - 7$ **d.** $-7 - (-4)$

To model subtraction problems involving two integers with different signs, such as $-6 - 3$, you will need to add zero pairs before you can take chips away.

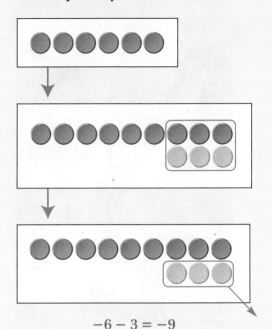

Use 6 red chips to represent -6.

Since you cannot take away 3 yellow chips, add 3 yellow chips paired with 3 red chips.

Now you can take away 3 yellow chips.

$$-6 - 3 = -9$$

4 Use integer chips to find each difference.

a. $-6 - 5$ **b.** $5 - (-6)$ **c.** $4 - 7$ **d.** $-2 - (-3)$

Think and Discuss

1. How could you model the expression $0 - 5$?

2. When you add zero pairs to model subtraction using chips, does it matter how many zero pairs you add?

3. Would $2 - 3$ have the same answer as $3 - 2$? Why or why not?

4. **Make a Conjecture** Make a conjecture for the sign of the answer when a positive integer is subtracted from a negative integer. Give examples.

Try This

Use integer chips to find each difference.

1. $4 - 2$ **2.** $-4 - (-2)$ **3.** $-2 - (-3)$

4. $3 - 4$ **5.** $2 - 3$ **6.** $0 - 3$

7. $5 - 3$ **8.** $-3 - (-5)$ **9.** $6 - (-4)$

Subtracting Integers

TN ✓ **0706.2.6** Use the number line to demonstrate addition and subtraction with integers.
Also **GLE 0706.2.1**, ✓ **0706.2.2**, **SPI 0706.2.5**

During flight, the space shuttle may be exposed to temperatures as low as −250 °F and as high as 3,000 °F.

To find the difference in these temperatures, you need to know how to subtract integers with different signs.

You can model the difference between two integers using a number line. When you subtract a positive number, the difference is *less* than the original number, so you move to the *left*. To subtract a negative number, move to the *right*.

EXAMPLE 1 **Modeling Integer Subtraction**

Use a number line to find each difference.

A 3 − 8

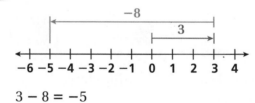

$3 - 8 = -5$

Start at 0.
Move right 3 units.
To subtract 8,
move to the left.

Helpful Hint

If the number being subtracted is less than the number it is subtracted from, the answer will be positive. If the number being subtracted is greater, the answer will be negative.

B −4 − 2

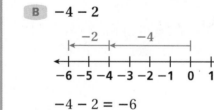

$-4 - 2 = -6$

Start at 0.
Move left 4 units.
To subtract 2,
move to the left.

C 2 − (−3)

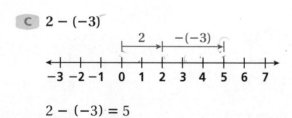

$2 - (-3) = 5$

Start at 0.
Move right 2 units.
To subtract −3,
move to the right.

Addition and subtraction are inverse operations—they "undo" each other. Instead of subtracting a number, you can *add its opposite*.

EXAMPLE 2 Subtracting Integers by Adding the Opposite

Interactivities Online ▶

Find each difference.

A $5 - 9$

$5 - 9 = 5 + (-9)$ *Add the opposite of 9.*

$\quad\quad = -4$

B $-9 - (-2)$

$-9 - (-2) = -9 + 2$ *Add the opposite of −2.*

$\quad\quad\quad = -7$

C $-4 - 3$

$-4 - 3 = -4 + (-3)$ *Add the opposite of 3.*

$\quad\quad\quad = -7$

EXAMPLE 3 Evaluating Expressions with Integers

Evaluate $a - b$ for each set of values.

A $a = -6, b = 7$

$a - b$

$-6 - 7 = -6 + (-7)$ *Substitute for a and b. Add the opposite*

$\quad\quad\quad = -13$ *of 7.*

B $a = 14, b = -9$

$a - b$

$14 - (-9) = 14 + 9$ *Substitute for a and b. Add the opposite*

$\quad\quad\quad = 23$ *of −9.*

EXAMPLE 4 *Temperature Application*

Find the difference between 3,000 °F and −250 °F, the temperatures the space shuttle must endure.

$3,000 - (-250)$

$3,000 + 250 = 3,250$ *Add the opposite of −250.*

The difference in temperatures the shuttle must endure is 3,250 °F.

Think and Discuss

1. **Suppose** you subtract one negative integer from another. Will your answer be greater than or less than the number you started with?

2. **Tell** whether you can reverse the order of integers when subtracting and still get the same answer. Why or why not?

2-3

Exercises

Learn It Online
Homework Help Online **go.hrw.com**,
keyword [MS10 2-3] (Go)
Exercises 1–35, 39 41, 43, 45,
47, 51, 53

GUIDED PRACTICE

See Example **1**   Use a number line to find each difference.

1. $4 - 7$ **2.** $-6 - 5$ **3.** $2 - (-4)$ **4.** $-8 - (-2)$

See Example **2**   Find each difference.

5. $6 - 10$ **6.** $-3 - (-8)$ **7.** $-1 - 9$ **8.** $-12 - (-2)$

See Example **3**   Evaluate $a - b$ for each set of values.

9. $a = 5, b = -2$ **10.** $a = -8, b = 6$ **11.** $a = 4, b = 18$

See Example **4**   **12.** In 1980, in Great Falls, Montana, the temperature rose from -32 °F to 15 °F in seven minutes. How much did the temperature increase?

INDEPENDENT PRACTICE

See Example **1**   Use a number line to find each difference.

13. $7 - 12$ **14.** $-5 - (-9)$ **15.** $2 - (-6)$ **16.** $7 - (-8)$

17. $9 - (-3)$ **18.** $-4 - 10$ **19.** $8 - (-8)$ **20.** $-3 - (-3)$

See Example **2**   Find each difference.

21. $-22 - (-5)$ **22.** $-4 - 21$ **23.** $27 - 19$ **24.** $-10 - (-7)$

25. $30 - (-20)$ **26.** $-15 - 15$ **27.** $12 - (-6)$ **28.** $-31 - 15$

See Example **3**   Evaluate $a - b$ for each set of values.

29. $a = 9, b = -7$ **30.** $a = -11, b = 2$ **31.** $a = -2, b = 3$

32. $a = 8, b = 19$ **33.** $a = -10, b = 10$ **34.** $a = -4, b = -15$

See Example **4**   **35.** In 1918, in Granville, North Dakota, the temperature rose from -33 °F to 50 °F in 12 hours. How much did the temperature increase?

PRACTICE AND PROBLEM SOLVING

Extra Practice
See page EP5.

Simplify.

36. $2 - 8$ **37.** $-5 - 9$ **38.** $15 - 12 - 8$

39. $6 + (-5) - 3$ **40.** $1 - 8 + (-6)$ **41.** $4 - (-7) - 9$

42. $(2 - 3) - (5 - 6)$ **43.** $5 - (-8) - (-3)$ **44.** $10 - 12 + 2$

Evaluate each expression for $m = -5$, $n = 8$, and $p = -14$.

45. $m - n + p$ **46.** $n - m - p$ **47.** $p - m - n$ **48.** $m + n - p$

49. Patterns Find the next three numbers in the pattern 7, 3, -1, -5, -9, ... Then describe the pattern.

50. The temperature of Mercury can be as high as 873 °F. The temperature of Pluto is about −393 °F. What is the difference between these temperatures?

51. One side of Mercury always faces the Sun. The temperature on this side can reach 873 °F. The temperature on the other side can be as low as −361 °F. What is the difference between the two temperatures?

52. Earth's moon rotates relative to the Sun about once a month. The side facing the Sun at a given time can be as hot as 224 °F. The side away from the Sun can be as cold as −307 °F. What is the difference between these temperatures?

53. The highest recorded temperature on Earth is 136 °F. The lowest is −129 °F. What is the difference between these temperatures?

Use the graph for Exercises 54 and 55.

54. How much deeper is the deepest canyon on Mars than the deepest canyon on Venus?

55. ⭐ **Challenge** What is the difference between Earth's highest mountain and its deepest ocean canyon? What is the difference between Mars' highest mountain and its deepest canyon? Which difference is greater? How much greater is it?

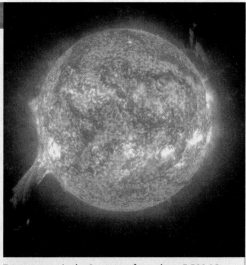

Temperatures in the Sun range from about 5,500 °C at its surface to more than 15 million °C at its core.

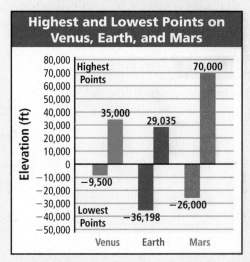

Test Prep and Spiral Review

56. Multiple Choice Which expression does NOT have a value of −3?

Ⓐ −2 − 1   Ⓑ 10 − 13   Ⓒ 5 − (−8)   Ⓓ −4 − (−1)

57. Extended Response If $m = -2$ and $n = 4$, which expression has the least absolute value: $m + n$, $n - m$, or $m - n$? Explain your answer.

Evaluate each expression for the given values of the variables. (Lesson 1-6)

58. $3x - 5$ for $x = 2$

59. $2n^2 + n$ for $n = 1$

60. $4y^2 - 3y$ for $y = 2$

61. $4a + 7$ for $a = 3$

62. $x^2 + 9$ for $x = 1$

63. $5z + z^2$ for $z = 3$

64. Sports In three plays, a football team gained 10 yards, lost 22 yards, and gained 15 yards. Use integer addition to find the team's total yardage for the three plays. (Lesson 2-2)

Model Integer Multiplication and Division

Use with Lesson 2-4

Learn It Online
Lab Resources Online **go.hrw.com**,
keyword **MS10 Lab2** **Go**

TN **GLE 0706.1.8** Use technologies/ manipulatives appropriately to develop understanding of mathematical algorithms, to facilitate problem solving, and to create accurate and reliable models of mathematical concepts. *Also* **GLE 0706.2.1**

KEY

= 1

= −1

+ = 0

REMEMBER
- The Commutative Property states that two numbers can be multiplied in any order without changing the product.
- Multiplication is repeated addition.
- Multiplication and division are inverse operations.

You can model integer multiplication and division by using integer chips.

Activity 1

Use integer chips to model $3 \cdot (-5)$.

Think: $3 \cdot (-5)$ means 3 groups of −5.

Arrange 3 groups of 5 red chips.
There are a total of 15 red chips.

$3 \cdot (-5) = -15$

1 Use integer chips to find each product.

a. $2 \cdot (-2)$ **b.** $3 \cdot (-6)$ **c.** $5 \cdot (-4)$ **d.** $6 \cdot (-3)$

Use integer chips to model $-4 \cdot 2$.

Using the Commutative Property, you can write $-4 \cdot 2$ as $2 \cdot (-4)$.

Think: $2 \cdot (-4)$ means 2 groups of −4.

Arrange 2 groups of 4 red chips.
There are a total of 8 red chips.

$-4 \cdot 2 = -8$

2 Use integer chips to find each product.

a. $-6 \cdot 5$ **b.** $-4 \cdot 6$ **c.** $-3 \cdot 4$ **d.** $-2 \cdot 3$

Think and Discuss

1. What is the sign of the product when you multiply two positive numbers? a negative and a positive number? two negative numbers?

2. If 12 were the answer to a multiplication problem, list all of the possible factors that are integers.

Try This

Use integer chips to find each product.

1. $4 \cdot (-5)$
2. $-3 \cdot 2$
3. $1 \cdot (-6)$
4. $-5 \cdot 2$

5. On days that Kathy has swimming lessons, she spends $2.00 of her allowance on snacks. Last week, Kathy had swimming lessons on Monday, Wednesday, and Friday. How much of her allowance did Kathy spend on snacks last week? Use integer chips to model the situation and solve the problem.

Activity 2

Use integer chips to model $-15 \div 3$.

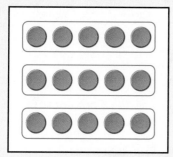

Think: −15 is separated into 3 equal groups.

Arrange 15 red chips into 3 equal groups.

There are 5 red chips in each group.

$$-15 \div 3 = -5$$

1 Use integer chips to find each quotient.

a. $-20 \div 5$
b. $-18 \div 6$
c. $-12 \div 4$
d. $-24 \div 8$

Think and Discuss

1. What is the sign of the answer when you divide two negative integers? a negative integer by a positive integer? a positive integer by a negative integer?

2. How are multiplication and division of integers related?

Try This

Use integer chips to find each quotient.

1. $-21 \div 7$
2. $-12 \div 4$
3. $-8 \div 2$
4. $-10 \div 5$

5. Ty spent $18 of his allowance at the arcade. He hit baseballs, played pinball, and played video games. Each of these activities cost the same amount at the arcade. How much did each activity cost? Use integer chips to model the situation and solve the problem.

2-4 Multiplying and Dividing Integers

TN SPI 0706.2.5 Solve contextual problems that involve operations with integers. *Also* ✓ 0706.2.2

You can think of multiplication as repeated addition.

$$3 \cdot 2 = 2 + 2 + 2 = 6$$
$$3 \cdot (-2) = (-2) + (-2) + (-2) = -6$$

EXAMPLE 1 **Multiplying Integers Using Repeated Addition**

Interactivities Online ▶

Use a number line to find each product.

A $3 \cdot (-3)$

$+(-3) \quad +(-3) \quad +(-3)$

-10 -9 -8 -7 -6 -5 -4 -3 -2 -1 0 1

Think: Start at 0.
Add -3 three times.

$3 \cdot (-3) = -9$

B $-4 \cdot 2$

$-4 \cdot 2 = 2 \cdot (-4)$

Use the Commutative Property.

$+(-4) \quad +(-4)$

-10 -9 -8 -7 -6 -5 -4 -3 -2 -1 0 1

Think: Start at 0.
Add -4 two times.

$-4 \cdot 2 = -8$

The patterns below suggest that when the signs of two integers are different, their product or quotient is negative. The patterns also suggest that the product or quotient of two negative integers is positive.

Remember!

Multiplication and division are inverse operations. They "undo" each other. Notice how these operations undo each other in the patterns shown.

$$-3 \cdot \quad 2 = -6$$
$$-3 \cdot \quad 1 = -3$$
$$-3 \cdot \quad 0 = \quad 0$$
$$-3 \cdot (-1) = \quad 3$$
$$-3 \cdot (-2) = \quad ´6$$

$$-6 \div (-3) = \quad 2$$
$$-3 \div (-3) = \quad 1$$
$$0 \div (-3) = \quad 0$$
$$3 \div (-3) = -1$$
$$6 \div (-3) = -2$$

Multiplying and Dividing Two Integers	
If the signs are:	**Your answer will be:**
the same ⟶	positive
different ⟶	negative

Video **Lesson Tutorials Online** my.hrw.com

EXAMPLE 2 **Multiplying Integers**

Find each product.

A $-4 \cdot (-2)$

$-4 \cdot (-2)$ *Both signs are*
                  negative, so the
     8   *product is positive.*

B $-3 \cdot 6$

$-3 \cdot 6$ *The signs are*
               different, so the
   -18 *product is negative.*

EXAMPLE 3 **Dividing Integers**

Find each quotient.

A $72 \div (-9)$ *The signs are*
$72 \div (-9)$ *different, so the*
   -8 *quotient is negative.*

B $-100 \div (-5)$ *The signs are the*
$-100 \div (-5)$ *same, so the*
     20   *quotient is positive.*

Zero divided by any number is zero, but you cannot find an answer for division by zero. For example, $-6 \div 0 \neq 0$, because $0 \cdot 0 \neq -6$. We say that division by zero is undefined.

EXAMPLE 4 *Sports Application*

A football team must move the ball forward at least 10 yards from its starting point to make a first down. If the team has 2 losses of 3 yards each and a gain of 14 yards, does the team make a first down?

Add the total loss to the gain to find how far the ball moved forward.

$2 \cdot (-3) + 14$ *Multiply -3 by 2 to find the total loss;*
                       then add the gain of 14.

$-6 + 14$ *Use the order of operations. Multiply first.*

8   *Then add.*

The team moved the ball forward 8 yards, so it did not make a first down.

Think and Discuss

1. **List** at least four different multiplication examples that have 24 as their product. Use both positive and negative integers.

2. **Explain** why the rules for multiplying integers make sense.

Learn It Online
Homework Help Online **go.hrw.com,**
keyword MS10 2-4 **Go**
Exercises 1–34, 35, 37, 39, 41,
43, 45, 47

GUIDED PRACTICE

See Example **1** Use a number line to find each product.

1. $5 \cdot (-3)$ **2.** $5 \cdot (-2)$ **3.** $-3 \cdot 5$ **4.** $-4 \cdot 6$

See Example **2** Find each product.

5. $-5 \cdot (-3)$ **6.** $-2 \cdot 5$ **7.** $3 \cdot (-5)$ **8.** $-7 \cdot (-4)$

See Example **3** Find each quotient.

9. $32 \div (-4)$ **10.** $-18 \div 3$ **11.** $-20 \div (-5)$ **12.** $49 \div (-7)$

13. $-63 \div (-9)$ **14.** $-50 \div 10$ **15.** $63 \div 0$ **16.** $-45 \div (-5)$

See Example **4** **17.** Angelina hiked along a 2,250-foot mountain trail. She stopped 5 times along the way to rest, walking the same distance between each stop. How far did Angelina hike before the first stop?

INDEPENDENT PRACTICE

See Example **1** Use a number line to find each product.

18. $2 \cdot (-1)$ **19.** $-5 \cdot 2$ **20.** $-4 \cdot 2$ **21.** $3 \cdot (-4)$

See Example **2** Find each product.

22. $4 \cdot (-6)$ **23.** $-6 \cdot (-8)$ **24.** $-8 \cdot 4$ **25.** $-5 \cdot (-7)$

See Example **3** Find each quotient.

26. $48 \div (-6)$ **27.** $-35 \div (-5)$ **28.** $-16 \div 4$ **29.** $-64 \div 8$

30. $-42 \div 0$ **31.** $81 \div (-9)$ **32.** $-77 \div 11$ **33.** $27 \div (-3)$

See Example **4** **34.** A scuba diver descended below the ocean's surface in 35-foot intervals as he examined a coral reef. He dove to a total depth of 140 feet. In how many intervals did the diver make his descent?

PRACTICE AND PROBLEM SOLVING

Extra Practice
See page EP5.

Find each product or quotient.

35. $-4 \cdot 10$ **36.** $-3 \div 0$ **37.** $-45 \div 15$ **38.** $-3 \cdot 4 \cdot (-1)$

39. $-500 \div (-10)$ **40.** $5 \cdot (-4) \cdot (-2)$ **41.** $225 \div (-75)$ **42.** $0 \div (-3)$

Evaluate each expression for $a = -5$, $b = 6$, and $c = -12$.

43. $-2c + b$ **44.** $4a - b$ **45.** $ab + c$ **46.** $ac \div b$

47. Earth Science A scuba diver is swimming at a depth of -12 feet in the Flower Garden Banks National Marine Sanctuary. She dives down to a coral reef that is at five times this depth. What is the depth of the coral reef?

Simplify each expression. Justify your steps using the Commutative, Associative, and Distributive Properties when necessary.

48. $(-3)^2$

49. $-(-2 + 1)$

50. $8 + (-5)^3 + 7$

51. $(-1)^5 \cdot (9 + 3)$

52. $29 - (-7) - 3$

53. $-4 \cdot 14 \cdot (-25)$

54. $25 - (-2) \cdot 4^2$

55. $8 - (6 \div (-2))$

56. Earth Science The table shows the depths of major caves in the United States. Approximately how many times deeper is Jewel Cave than Kartchner Caverns?

Depths of Major U.S. Caves	
Cave	Depth (ft)
Carlsbad Caverns	−1,022
Caverns of Sonora	−150
Ellison's Cave	−1,000
Jewel Cave	−696
Kartchner Caverns	−137
Mammoth Cave	−379

Source: NSS U.S.A. Long Cave List

Personal Finance Does each person end up with more or less money than he started with? By how much?

57. Kevin spends $24 a day for 3 days.

58. Devin earns $15 a day for 5 days.

59. Evan spends $20 a day for 3 days. Then he earns $18 a day for 4 days.

? 60. What's the Error? A student writes, "The quotient of an integer divided by an integer of the opposite sign has the sign of the integer with the greater absolute value." What is the student's error?

✍ 61. Write About It Explain how to find the product and the quotient of two integers.

★ 62. Challenge Use > or < to compare $-2 \cdot (-1) \cdot 4 \cdot 2 \cdot (-3)$ and $-1 + (-2) + 4 + (-25) + (-10)$.

Test Prep and Spiral Review

63. Multiple Choice Which of the expressions are equal to −20?

I $-2 \cdot 10$ **II** $-40 \div (-2)$ **III** $-5 \cdot (-2)^2$ **IV** $-4 \cdot 2 - 12$

Ⓐ I only   Ⓑ I and II   Ⓒ I, III, and IV   Ⓓ I, II, III, IV

64. Multiple Choice Which expression has a value that is greater than the value of $-25 \div (-5)$?

Ⓕ $36 \div (-6)$ Ⓖ $-100 \div 10$ Ⓗ $-50 \div (-10)$ Ⓙ $-45 \div (-5)$

Write each phrase as an algebraic expression. (Lesson 1-7)

65. the sum of a number and 6

66. the product of −3 and a number

67. 4 less than twice a number

68. 5 more than a number divided by 3

Find each difference. (Lesson 2-3)

69. $3 - (-2)$

70. $-5 - 6$

71. $6 - 8$

72. $2 - (-7)$

Model Integer Equations

Use with Lesson 2-5

Learn It Online
Lab Resources Online **go.hrw.com**,
keyword **MS10 Lab2** **Go**

TN ✓ **0706.1.10** Model algebraic
equations with manipulatives, technology,
and pencil and paper.
Also **GLE 0706.1.8, GLE 0706.3.8**

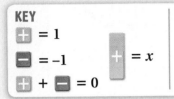

KEY

+ = 1

− = −1

+ + − = 0

+ = x

REMEMBER

- Adding or subtracting zero does not change the value of an expression.

You can use algebra tiles to model and solve equations.

Activity

To solve the equation $x + 2 = 3$, you need to get x alone on one side of the equal sign. You can add or remove tiles as long as you add the same amount or remove the same amount on both sides.

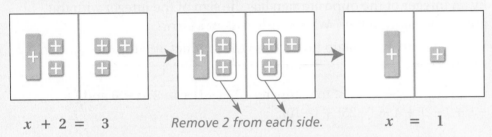

$x + 2 = 3$ *Remove 2 from each side.* $x = 1$

1 Use algebra tiles to model and solve each equation.

a. $x + 3 = 5$ **b.** $x + 4 = 9$ **c.** $x + 5 = 8$ **d.** $x + 6 = 6$

The equation $x + 6 = 4$ is more difficult to model because there are not enough tiles on the right side of the mat to remove 6 from each side.

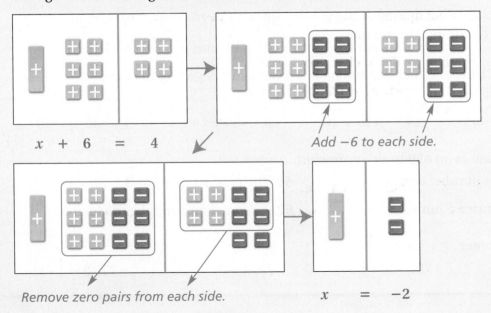

$x + 6 = 4$ *Add −6 to each side.*

Remove zero pairs from each side. $x = -2$

2 Use algebra tiles to model and solve each equation.

    a. $x + 5 = 3$ **b.** $x + 4 = 2$ **c.** $x + 7 = -3$ **d.** $x + 6 = -2$

When modeling an equation that involves subtraction, such as $x - 6 = 2$, you must first rewrite the equation as an addition equation. For example, the equation $x - 6 = 2$ can be rewritten as $x + (-6) = 2$.

Modeling equations that involve addition of negative numbers is similar to modeling equations that involve addition of positive numbers.

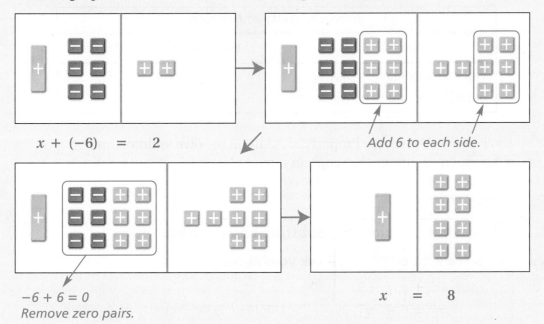

$x + (-6) = 2$

Add 6 to each side.

$-6 + 6 = 0$
Remove zero pairs.

$x = 8$

3 Use algebra tiles to model and solve each equation.

    a. $x - 4 = 3$ **b.** $x - 2 = 8$ **c.** $x - 5 = -5$ **d.** $x - 7 = 0$

Think and Discuss

1. When you remove tiles, what operation are you modeling? When you add tiles, what operation are you modeling?

2. How can you use the original model to check your solution?

3. To model $x - 6 = 2$, you must rewrite the equation as $x + (-6) = 2$. Why are you allowed to do this?

Try This

Use algebra tiles to model and solve each equation.

1. $x + 7 = 10$ **2.** $x - 5 = -8$ **3.** $x + (-5) = -4$ **4.** $x - 2 = 1$

5. $x + 4 = 8$ **6.** $x + 3 = -2$ **7.** $x + (-1) = 9$ **8.** $x - 7 = -6$

Solving Equations Containing Integers

TN SPI 0706.2.5 Solve contextual problems that involve operations with integers.
Also ✓ 0706.1.10, GLE 0706.2.1, ✓ 0706.2.2

Recall that the sum of a number and its opposite is 0. This is called the Inverse Property of Addition.

Inverse Property of Addition		
Words	**Numbers**	**Algebra**
The sum of a number and its opposite, or additive inverse, is 0.	$3 + (-3) = 0$	$a + (-a) = 0$

You can use the Inverse Property of Addition to solve addition and subtraction equations that contain integers, such as $-3 + y = -5$.

EXAMPLE 1 Solving Addition and Subtraction Equations

Interactivities Online ▶

Solve each equation. Check your answer.

A $-3 + y = -5$

$$-3 + y = -5$$ *Use the Inverse Property of Addition.*
$$\underline{+\,3 \qquad\quad +\,3}$$ *Add 3 to both sides.*
$$y = -2$$

Check $-3 + y = -5$
$$-3 + (-2) \overset{?}{=} -5$$ *Substitute –2 for y.*
$$-5 \overset{?}{=} -5 ✔$$ *True.*

B $n + 3 = -10$

$$n + 3 = -10$$ *Use the Inverse Property of Addition.*
$$\underline{+\,(-3) \quad +\,(-3)}$$ *Add –3 to both sides.*
$$n = -13$$

Check $n + 3 = -10$
$$-13 + 3 \overset{?}{=} -10$$ *Substitute –13 for n.*
$$-10 \overset{?}{=} -10 ✔$$ *True.*

C $x - 8 = -32$

$$x - 8 = -32$$ *Use the Inverse Property of Addition.*
$$\underline{+\,8 \quad +\,8}$$ *Add 8 to both sides.*
$$x = -24$$

Check $x - 8 = -32$
$$-24 - 8 \overset{?}{=} -32$$ *Substitute –24 for x.*
$$-32 \overset{?}{=} -32 ✔$$ *True.*

In Chapter 1, you used inverse operations to solve multiplication and division equations. You can also use inverse operations to solve multiplication and division equations that contain integers.

EXAMPLE **2**

Solving Multiplication and Division Equations

Solve each equation. Check your answer.

A $\frac{a}{-3} = 9$

$$(-3)\left(\frac{a}{-3}\right) = (-3)9 \qquad \textit{Multiply both sides by -3.}$$

$$a = -27$$

Check $\frac{a}{-3} = 9$

$$\frac{-27}{-3} \stackrel{?}{=} 9 \qquad \textit{Substitute -27 for a.}$$

$$9 \stackrel{?}{=} 9 ✔ \qquad \textit{True.}$$

B $-120 = 6x$

$$\frac{-120}{6} = \frac{6x}{6} \qquad \textit{Divide both sides by 6.}$$

$$-20 = x$$

Check $-120 = 6x$

$$-120 \stackrel{?}{=} 6(-20) \qquad \textit{Substitute -20 for x.}$$

$$-120 \stackrel{?}{=} -120 ✔ \qquad \textit{True.}$$

EXAMPLE **3**

Business Application

A shoe manufacturer made a profit of $800 million. This amount is $200 million more than last year's profit. What was last year's profit?

Let *p* represent last year's profit (in millions of dollars).

This year's profit	is	$200 million	more than	last year's profit.
800	=	200	+	*p*

$$800 = 200 + p$$
$$\underline{-200 \quad -200}$$
$$600 = \qquad p \qquad \text{Last year's profit was \$600 million.}$$

Think and Discuss

1. Tell what value of *n* makes $-n + 32$ equal to zero.

2. Explain why you would or would not multiply both sides of an equation by 0 to solve it.

Exercises

Learn It Online
Homework Help Online **go.hrw.com**,
keyword MS10 2-5 Go
Exercises 1–20, 23, 25, 31, 33, 35, 37, 43

GUIDED PRACTICE

Solve each equation. Check your answer.

See Example **1**
1. $w - 6 = -2$
2. $x + 5 = -7$
3. $k = -18 + 11$

See Example **2**
4. $\frac{n}{-4} = 2$
5. $-240 = 8y$
6. $-5a = 300$

See Example **3**
7. **Business** Last year, a chain of electronics stores had a loss of $45 million. This year the loss is $12 million more than last year's loss. What is this year's loss?

INDEPENDENT PRACTICE

Solve each equation. Check your answer.

See Example **1**
8. $b - 7 = -16$
9. $k + 6 = 3$
10. $s + 2 = -4$
11. $v + 14 = 10$
12. $c + 8 = -20$
13. $a - 25 = -5$

See Example **2**
14. $9c = -99$
15. $\frac{t}{8} = -4$
16. $-16 = 2z$
17. $\frac{n}{-5} = -30$
18. $200 = -25p$
19. $\frac{\ell}{12} = 12$

See Example **3**
20. The temperature in Nome, Alaska, was $-50\,°F$. This was $18\,°F$ less than the temperature in Anchorage, Alaska, on the same day. What was the temperature in Anchorage?

PRACTICE AND PROBLEM SOLVING

Extra Practice
See page EP6.

Solve each equation. Check your answer.

21. $9y = 900$
22. $d - 15 = 45$
23. $j + 56 = -7$

24. $\frac{s}{-20} = 7$
25. $-85 = -5c$
26. $v - 39 = -16$

27. $11y = -121$
28. $\frac{n}{36} = 9$
29. $w + 41 = 0$

30. $\frac{r}{238} = 8$
31. $-23 = x + 35$
32. $0 = -15m$

33. $4x = 2 + 14$
34. $c + c + c = 6$
35. $t - 3 = 4 + 2$

36. **Geometry** The three angles of a triangle have equal measures. The sum of their measures is $180°$. What is the measure of each angle?

37. **Sports** Herb has 42 days to prepare for a cross-country race. During his training, he will run a total of 126 miles. If Herb runs the same distance every day, how many miles will he run each day?

38. **Multi-Step** Jared bought one share of stock for $225.
    a. He sold the stock for a profit of $55. What was the selling price of the stock?
    b. The price of the stock dropped $40 the day after Jared sold it. At what price would Jared have sold it if he had waited until then?

Translate each sentence into an equation. Then solve the equation.

39. The sum of -13 and a number p is 8.

40. A number x divided by 4 is -7.

41. 9 less than a number t is -22.

42. **Physical Science** On the Kelvin temperature scale, pure water boils at 373 K. The difference between the boiling point and the freezing point of water on this scale is 100 K. What is the freezing point of water?

Recreation The graph shows the most popular travel destinations over Labor Day weekend. Use the graph for Exercises 43 and 44.

43. Which destination was 5 times more popular than theme or amusement parks?

44. According to the graph, the mountains were as popular as state or national parks and what other destination combined?

Top Labor Day Destinations

Destination	%
Cities	23%
Oceans or beaches	20%
Towns or rural areas	19%
Mountains	14%
Lakes	8%
State or national parks	6%
Theme or amusement parks	4%
Other	6%

Source: AAA

45. **Choose a Strategy** Matthew (M) earns $23 less a week than his sister Allie (A). Their combined salaries are $93. How much does each of them earn per week?

    Ⓐ *A*: $35; *M*: $12   Ⓑ *A*: $35; *M*: $58   Ⓒ *A*: $58; *M*: $35

46. **Write About It** Explain how to isolate a variable in an equation.

47. **Challenge** Write an equation that includes the variable p and the numbers 5, 3, and 31 so that the solution is $p = 16$.

Test Prep and Spiral Review

48. Multiple Choice Solve $-15m = 60$.

    Ⓐ $m = -4$ Ⓑ $m = 5$ Ⓒ $m = 45$ Ⓓ $m = 75$

49. Multiple Choice For which equation does $x = 2$?

    Ⓕ $-3x = 6$ Ⓖ $x + 3 = -5$ Ⓗ $x + x = 4$ Ⓙ $\frac{x}{4} = -8$

Identify a possible pattern. Use the pattern to write the next three numbers. (Lesson 1-1)

50. $26, 21, 16, 11, 6, \ldots$ **51.** $1, 2, 4, 8, 16, \ldots$ **52.** $1, 4, 3, 6, 5, \ldots$

Compare. Write <, >, or =. (Lessons 2-1, 2-2, and 2-3)

53. -5 ▮ -8 **54.** 4 ▮ $|-4|$ **55.** $|-7|$ ▮ $|-9|$

56. -10 ▮ $|-10|$ **57.** $-7 - 8$ ▮ -15 **58.** -12 ▮ $10 + (-12)$

Quiz for Lessons 2-1 Through 2-5

✓ **2-1** **Integers**

Compare the integers. Use < or > .

1. 5 ▦ −8

2. −2 ▦ −6

3. −4 ▦ 3

4. Use a number line to order the integers −7, 3, 6, −1, 0, 5, −4, and 7 from least to greatest.

Use a number line to find each absolute value.

5. |−23|

6. |17|

7. |−10|

✓ **2-2** **Adding Integers**

Find each sum.

8. −6 + 3

9. 5 + (−9)

10. −7 + (−11)

Evaluate $p + t$ for the given values.

11. $p = 5, t = -18$

12. $p = -4, t = -13$

13. $p = -37, t = 39$

✓ **2-3** **Subtracting Integers**

Find each difference.

14. −21 − (−7)

15. 9 − (−11)

16. 6 − 17

17. When Cai traveled from New Orleans, Louisiana, to the Ozark Mountains in Arkansas, the elevation changed from 7 ft below sea level to 2,314 ft above sea level. How much did the elevation increase?

✓ **2-4** **Multiplying and Dividing Integers**

Find each product or quotient.

18. −7 · 3

19. 30 ÷ (−15)

20. −5 · (−9)

21. After reaching the top of a cliff, a rock climber descended the rock face using a 65 ft rope. The distance to the base of the cliff was 585 ft. How many rope lengths did it take the climber to complete her descent?

✓ **2-5** **Solving Equations Containing Integers**

Solve each equation. Check your answer.

22. $3x = 30$

23. $k - 25 = 50$

24. $y + 16 = -8$

25. This year, 72 students completed projects for the science fair. This was 23 more students than last year. How many students completed projects for the science fair last year?

Focus on Problem Solving

Make a Plan

• **Choose a method of computation**

When you know the operation you must use and you know exactly which numbers to use, a calculator might be the easiest way to solve a problem. Sometimes, such as when the numbers are small or are multiples of 10, it may be quicker to use mental math.

Sometimes, you have to write the numbers to see how they relate in an equation. When you are working an equation, using a pencil and paper is the simplest method to use because you can see each step as you go.

For each problem, tell whether you would use a calculator, mental math, or pencil and paper to solve it. Explain your answer. Then solve the problem.

1 A scouting troop is collecting aluminum cans to raise money for charity. Their goal is to collect 3,000 cans in 6 months. If they set a goal to collect an equal number of cans each month, how many cans can they expect to collect each month?

2 The Grand Canyon is 29,000 meters wide at its widest point. The Empire State Building, located in New York City, is 381 meters tall. Laid end to end, about how many Empire State Buildings would fit across the Grand Canyon at its widest point?

3 On a piano keyboard, all but one of the black keys are arranged in groups so that there are 7 groups with 2 black keys each and 7 groups with 3 black keys each. How many black keys are there on a piano?

4 Some wind chimes are made of rods. The rods are usually of different lengths, producing different sounds. The frequency (which determines the pitch) of the sound is measured in hertz (Hz). If one rod on a chime has a frequency of 55 Hz and another rod has a frequency that is twice that of the first rod's, what is the frequency of the second rod?

In the Chinese zodiac, each year is named by one of twelve animals. The years are named in an established order that repeats every twelve years. 2011 is the Year of Rabbit, and 2012 is the Year of the Dragon. 2011 is a *prime number*. 2012 is a *composite number*.

A **prime number** is a whole number greater than 1 that has exactly two factors, 1 and itself. Three is a prime number because its only factors are 1 and 3.

Vocabulary

prime number

composite number

prime factorization

A **composite number** is a whole number that has more than two factors. Six is a composite number because it has more than two factors—1, 2, 3, and 6. The number 1 has exactly one factor and is neither prime nor composite.

EXAMPLE 1 Identifying Prime and Composite Numbers

Helpful Hint

For a review of factors, see Skills Bank p. SB6.

Tell whether each number is prime or composite.

A 19

The factors of 19 are 1 and 19.

So 19 is prime.

B 20

The factors of 20 are 1, 2, 4, 5, 10, and 20.

So 20 is composite.

A composite number can be written as the product of its prime factors. This is called the **prime factorization** of the number. You can use a factor tree to find the prime factors of a composite number.

EXAMPLE 2 Using a Factor Tree to Find Prime Factorization

Writing Math

You can write prime factorizations by using exponents. The exponent tells how many times to use the base as a factor.

Write the prime factorization of each number.

A 36

Write 36 as the product of two factors.

Continue factoring until all factors are prime.

The prime factorization of 36 is $2 \cdot 2 \cdot 3 \cdot 3$, or $2^2 \cdot 3^2$.

Write the prime factorization of each number.

B 280

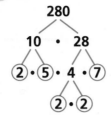

Write 280 as the product of two factors.

Continue factoring until all factors are prime.

The prime factorization of 280 is 2 · 2 · 2 · 5 · 7, or 2^3 · 5 · 7.

You can also use a step diagram to find a prime factorization. At each step, divide by a prime factor until the quotient is 1.

EXAMPLE 3 **Using a Step Diagram to Find Prime Factorization**

Write the prime factorization of each number.

A 252

```
2 | 252
2 | 126
  3 | 63
    3 | 21
      7 | 7
          1
```

Divide 252 by 2. Write the quotient below 252. Keep dividing by a prime factor.

Stop when the quotient is 1.

The prime factorization of 252 is 2 · 2 · 3 · 3 · 7, or 2^2 · 3^2 · 7.

B 495

```
3 | 495
  3 | 165
    5 | 55
     11 | 11
          1
```

Divide 495 by 3.
Keep dividing by a prime factor.

Stop when the quotient is 1.

The prime factorization of 495 is 3 · 3 · 5 · 11, or 3^2 · 5 · 11.

There is only one prime factorization for any given composite number (except for different orders of the factors). Example 3B began by dividing 495 by 3, the smallest prime factor of 495. Beginning with any prime factor of 495 gives the same result.

```
5 | 495
  3 | 99
    3 | 33
     11 | 11
          1
```

```
11 | 495
   3 | 45
     5 | 15
       3 | 3
           1
```

Think and Discuss

1. **Explain** how to decide whether 47 is prime.

2. **Compare** prime numbers and composite numbers.

GUIDED PRACTICE

See Example 1 Tell whether each number is prime or composite.

1. 7   **2.** 15   **3.** 49   **4.** 12

Write the prime factorization of each number.

See Example 2

5. 16   **6.** 54   **7.** 81   **8.** 105

```
      16                 54                 81                105
     /  \               /  \               /  \              /  \
   4  •  4            6  •  9            9  •  ?           5  •  ?
  /\    /\           /\    /\           /\    /\          /\   /\
 ?•?  ?•?          ?•?  ?•?          ?•?  ?•?          ?•? ?•?
```

9. 18   **10.** 26   **11.** 45   **12.** 80

See Example 3 **13.** 250   **14.** 190   **15.** 100   **16.** 360

17. 639   **18.** 414   **19.** 1,000   **20.** 140

INDEPENDENT PRACTICE

See Example 1 Tell whether each number is prime or composite.

21. 31   **22.** 18   **23.** 67   **24.** 8

25. 77   **26.** 5   **27.** 9   **28.** 113

Write the prime factorization of each number.

See Example 2 **29.** 68   **30.** 75   **31.** 120   **32.** 150

33. 135   **34.** 48   **35.** 154   **36.** 210

37. 800   **38.** 310   **39.** 625   **40.** 2,000

See Example 3 **41.** 315   **42.** 728   **43.** 189   **44.** 396

45. 242   **46.** 700   **47.** 187   **48.** 884

49. 1,225   **50.** 288   **51.** 360   **52.** 1,152

PRACTICE AND PROBLEM SOLVING

Extra Practice
See page EP6.

Complete the prime factorization for each composite number.

53. $180 = 2^2 \cdot \blacksquare \cdot 5$ **54.** $462 = 2 \cdot 3 \cdot 7 \cdot \blacksquare$ **55.** $1,575 = 3^2 \cdot \blacksquare \cdot 7$

56. $117 = 3^2 \cdot \blacksquare$ **57.** $144 = \blacksquare \cdot 3^2$ **58.** $13,000 = 2^3 \cdot \blacksquare \cdot 13$

59. Critical Thinking One way to factor 64 is $1 \cdot 64$.

  a. What other ways can 64 be written as the product of two factors?

  b. How many prime factorizations of 64 are there?

60. Critical Thinking If the prime factors of a number are all the prime numbers less than 10 and no factor is repeated, what is the number?

61. A number n is a prime factor of 28 and 63. What is the number?

62. If you were born in one of the years listed in the table, was your birth year a composite number? List five composite numbers in the table.

Chinese Zodiac			
Animal Sign	**Years**	**Animal Sign**	**Years**
Horse	1990, 2002	Rat	1996, 2008
Ram	1991, 2003	Ox	1997, 2009
Monkey	1992, 2004	Tiger	1998, 2010
Rooster	1993, 2005	Rabbit	1999, 2011
Dog	1994, 2006	Dragon	2000, 2012
Boar	1995, 2007	Snake	2001, 2013

63. Business Eric is catering a party for 152 people. He wants to seat the same number of people at each table. He also wants more than 2 people but fewer than 10 people at a table. How many people can he seat at each table?

64. Write a Problem Using the information in the table, write a problem using prime factorization that includes the number of calories per serving of the melons.

65. Write About It Describe how to use factor trees to find a prime factorization.

66. Challenge Find the smallest number that is divisible by 2, 3, 4, 5, 6, 7, 8, 9, and 10.

Fruit	Calories per Serving
Cantaloupe	66
Watermelon	15
Honeydew	42

Test Prep and Spiral Review

67. Multiple Choice Which is the prime factorization of 75?

    (A) $3^2 \cdot 5$ (B) $3 \cdot 5^2$ (C) $3^2 \cdot 5^2$ (D) $3 \cdot 5^3$

68. Multiple Choice Write the composite number for $2 \cdot 3^3 \cdot 5^2$.

    (F) 84   (G) 180   (H) 450   (J) 1,350

69. Short Response Create two different factor trees for 120. Then write the prime factorization for 120.

Multiply. (Lesson 1-3)

70. $2.45 \cdot 10^3$ **71.** $58.7 \cdot 10^1$ **72.** $200 \cdot 10^2$ **73.** $1,480 \cdot 10^4$

Solve each equation. Check your answer. (Lesson 2-5)

74. $3x = -6$ **75.** $y - 4 = -3$ **76.** $z + 4 = 3 - 5$ **77.** $0 = -4x$

Greetest Common Factor

TN ✓ 0706.1.1 Recognize common abbreviations (such as gcd/gcf and lcm).

When getting ready for his birthday party, David used the *greatest common factor* to make matching favor bags. The **greatest common factor (GCF)** of two or more whole numbers is the greatest whole number that divides evenly into each number.

Vocabulary

greatest common factor (GCF)

One way to find the GCF of two or more numbers is to list all the factors of each number. The GCF is the greatest factor that appears in all the lists.

EXAMPLE 1 | **Using a List to Find the GCF**

Find the greatest common factor (GCF) of 24, 36, and 48.

Factors of 24: 1, 2, 3, 4, 6, 8, ⑫, 24

Factors of 36: 1, 2, 3, 4, 6, 9, ⑫, 18, 36

Factors of 48: 1, 2, 3, 4, 6, 8, ⑫, 16, 24, 48

The GCF is 12.

List all the factors of each number.

Circle the greatest factor that is in all the lists.

A second way to find the GCF is to use prime factorization.

EXAMPLE 2 | **Using Prime Factorization to Find the GCF**

Find the greatest common factor (GCF).

A 60, 45

$60 = 2 \cdot 2 \cdot ③ \cdot ⑤$

$45 = ③ \cdot 3 \cdot ⑤$

Write the prime factorization of each number and circle the prime factors common to all the numbers.

$3 \cdot 5 = 15$

Multiply the common prime factors.

The GCF is 15.

B 504, 132, 96, 60

$504 = ②\cdot②\cdot 2 \cdot ③\cdot 3 \cdot 7$

$132 = ②\cdot②\cdot ③\cdot 11$

$96 = ②\cdot②\cdot 2 \cdot 2 \cdot 2 \cdot ③$

$60 = ②\cdot②\cdot ③\cdot 5$

Write the prime factorization of each number and circle the prime factors common to all the numbers.

$2 \cdot 2 \cdot 3 = 12$

Multiply the common prime factors.

The GCF is 12.

Video **Lesson Tutorials Online** my.hrw.com

EXAMPLE  3 **PROBLEM SOLVING APPLICATION**

David is making favor bags
for his birthday party.
He has 50 confetti eggs
and 30 noisemakers. What is the
greatest number of matching
favor bags he can make
using all of the confetti eggs
and noisemakers?

1 Understand the Problem

Rewrite the question as a statement.
• Find the greatest number of favor bags David can make.
List the **important information:**
• There are 50 confetti eggs.
• There are 30 noisemakers.
• Each favor bag must have the same number of eggs
  and the same number of noisemakers.
The **answer** will be the GCF of 50 and 30.

2 Make a Plan

You can write the prime factorizations of 50 and 30 to find the GCF.

3 Solve

$50 = ②\cdot⑤\cdot 5$
$30 = ②\cdot 3 \cdot⑤$ *Multiply the prime factors that are*
$2 \cdot 5 = 10$ *common to both 50 and 30.*
David can make 10 favor bags.

4 Look Back

If David makes 10 favor bags, each one will have
5 confetti eggs and 3 noisemakers, with nothing left over.

Think and Discuss

1. Tell what the letters GCF stand for and explain what the GCF
   of two numbers is.

2. Discuss whether the GCF of two numbers could be a
   prime number.

3. Explain whether every factor of the GCF of two numbers
   is also a factor of each number. Give an example.

2-7

Exercises

Learn It Online
Homework Help Online **go.hrw.com,**
keyword MS10 2-7 Go
Exercises 1–20, 23, 25, 29, 33,
35, 37, 39

GUIDED PRACTICE

Find the greatest common factor (GCF).

See Example 1   **1.** 30, 42   **2.** 36, 45   **3.** 24, 36, 60, 84

See Example 2   **4.** 60, 231   **5.** 12, 28   **6.** 20, 40, 50, 120

See Example 3   **7.** The Math Club members are preparing identical welcome kits for the sixth-graders. They have 60 pencils and 48 memo pads. What is the greatest number of kits they can prepare using all of the pencils and memo pads?

INDEPENDENT PRACTICE

Find the greatest common factor (GCF).

See Example 1   **8.** 60, 126   **9.** 12, 36   **10.** 75, 90

     11. 22, 121   **12.** 28, 42   **13.** 38, 76

See Example 2   **14.** 28, 60   **15.** 54, 80   **16.** 30, 45, 60, 105

     17. 26, 52   **18.** 11, 44, 77   **19.** 18, 27, 36, 48

See Example 3   **20.** Hetty is making identical gift baskets for the Senior Citizens Center. She has 39 small soap bars and 26 small bottles of lotion. What is the greatest number of baskets she can make using all of the soap bars and bottles of lotion?

PRACTICE AND PROBLEM SOLVING

Extra Practice
See page EP6.

Find the greatest common factor (GCF).

21. 5, 7   **22.** 12, 15   **23.** 4, 6

24. 9, 11   **25.** 22, 44, 66   **26.** 77, 121

27. 80, 120   **28.** 20, 28   **29.** 2, 3, 4, 5, 7

30. 4, 6, 10, 22   **31.** 14, 21, 35, 70   **32.** 6, 10, 11, 14

33. 6, 15, 33, 48   **34.** 18, 45, 63, 81   **35.** 13, 39, 52, 78

36. Critical Thinking Which pair of numbers has a GCF that is a prime number, 48 and 90 or 105 and 56?

37. Museum employees are preparing an exhibit of ancient coins. They have 49 copper coins and 35 silver coins to arrange on shelves. Each shelf will have the same number of copper coins and the same number of silver coins. How many shelves will the employees need for this exhibit?

38. Multi-Step Todd and Elizabeth are making treat bags for the hospital volunteers. They have baked 56 shortbread cookies and 84 lemon bars. What is the greatest number of bags they can make if all volunteers receive identical treat bags? How many cookies and how many lemon bars will each bag contain?

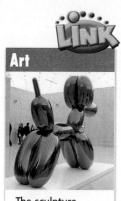

39. School Some of the students in the Math Club signed up to bring food and drinks to a party.

  a. If each club member gets the same amount of each item at the party, how many students are in the Math Club?

  b. How many carrots, pizza slices, cans of juice, and apples can each club member have at the party?

Food and Drink Sign-up Sheet		
Student	**Item**	**Amount**
Macy	Apples	14
Paul	Pizza slices	21
Christie	Juice boxes	7
Peter	Carrot sticks	35

40. Art A gallery is displaying a collection of 12 sculptures and 20 paintings by local artists. The exhibit is arranged into as many sections as possible so that each section has the same number of sculptures and the same number of paintings. How many sections are in the exhibit?

 41. What's the Error? A student used these factor trees to find the GCF of 50 and 70. The student decided that the GCF is 5. Explain the student's error and give the correct GCF.

 42. Write About It The GCF of 1,274 and 1,365 is 91, or $7 \cdot 13$. Are 7, 13, and 91 factors of both 1,274 and 1,365? Explain.

43. Challenge Find three *composite* numbers that have a GCF of 1.

Test Prep and Spiral Review

44. Multiple Choice Which pair of numbers has a greatest common factor that is NOT a prime number?

  (A) 15, 20   (B) 18, 30   (C) 24, 75   (D) 6, 10

45. Gridded Response What is the greatest common factor of 28 and 91?

Find each value. (Lesson 1-2)

46. 10^3 **47.** 13^1 **48.** 6^3 **49.** 3^4

Use a number line to find each sum or difference. (Lessons 2-2 and 2-3)

50. $-5 + (-3)$ **51.** $2 - 7$ **52.** $4 + (-8)$ **53.** $-3 - (-5)$

Complete the prime factorization for each composite number. (Lesson 2-6)

54. $100 = \blacksquare \cdot 5^2$ **55.** $147 = 3 \cdot \blacksquare$ **56.** $270 = 2 \cdot 3^3 \cdot \blacksquare$ **57.** $140 = \blacksquare \cdot 5 \cdot 7$

✓ 0706.1.1 Recognize common abbreviations (such as gcd/gcf and lcm).

Vocabulary

multiple

least common multiple (LCM)

The maintenance schedule on Kendra's pickup truck shows that the tires should be rotated every 7,500 miles and that the oil filter should be replaced every 5,000 miles. What is the lowest mileage at which both services are due at the same time? To find the answer, you can use *least common multiples.*

A **multiple** of a number is the product of that number and a nonzero whole number. Some multiples of 7,500 and 5,000 are as follows:

7,500: 7,500, 15,000, 22,500, 30,000, 37,500, 45,000, . . .
5,000: 5,000, 10,000, 15,000, 20,000, 25,000, 30,000, . . .

A common multiple of two or more numbers is a number that is a multiple of each of the given numbers. So 15,000 and 30,000 are common multiples of 7,500 and 5,000.

The **least common multiple (LCM)** of two or more numbers is the common multiple with the least value. The LCM of 7,500 and 5,000 is 15,000. This is the lowest mileage at which both services are due at the same time.

EXAMPLE 1 **Using a List to Find the LCM**

Find the least common multiple (LCM).

A **3, 5**
Multiples of 3: 3, 6, 9, 12, ⑮, 18   *List multiples of each number.*
Multiples of 5: 5, 10, ⑮, 20, 25   *Find the least value that*
The LCM is 15.   *is in both lists.*

B **4, 6, 12**
Multiples of 4: 4, 8, ⑫, 16, 20, 24, 28 *List multiples of each number.*
Multiples of 6: 6, ⑫, 18, 24, 30   *Find the least value that*
Multiples of 12: ⑫, 24, 36, 48   *is in all the lists.*
The LCM is 12.

Sometimes, listing the multiples of numbers is not the easiest way to find the LCM. For example, the LCM of 78 and 110 is 4,290. You would have to list 55 multiples of 78 and 39 multiples of 110 to reach 4,290!

EXAMPLE 2 **Using Prime Factorization to Find the LCM**

Find the least common multiple (LCM).

A **78, 110**

$78 = ②\cdot 3 \cdot 13$ — *Write the prime factorization of each number.*

$110 = ②\cdot 5 \cdot 11$ — *Circle any common prime factors.*

②, 3, 13, 5, 11 — *List the prime factors of the numbers. Use each circled factor only once.*

$2 \cdot 3 \cdot 5 \cdot 11 \cdot 13$ — *Multiply the factors in the list.*

The LCM is 4,290.

B **6, 27, 45**

$6 = 2 \cdot ③$ — *Write the prime factorization of each number.*

$27 = ③\cdot ③\cdot 3$ — *Circle any prime factors that are common to at*

$45 = ③\cdot ③\cdot 5$ — *least 2 numbers.*

2, ③ ③, 3, 5 — *List the prime factors of the numbers. Use each circled factor only once.*

$2 \cdot 3^3 \cdot 5$ — *Multiply the factors in the list.*

The LCM is 270.

EXAMPLE 3 *Recreation Application*

Charla and her little brother are walking laps on a track. Charla walks one lap every 4 minutes, and her brother walks one lap every 6 minutes. They start together. In how many minutes will they be together at the starting line again?

Find the LCM of 4 and 6.

$4 = ②\cdot 2$

$6 = ②\cdot 3$

The LCM is ②$\cdot 2 \cdot 3 = 12$.

They will be together at the starting line in 12 minutes.

Think and Discuss

1. Tell what the letters LCM stand for and explain what the LCM of two numbers is.

2. Describe a way to remember the difference between GCF and LCM.

Exercises

Learn It Online
Homework Help Online **go.hrw.com**,
keyword MS10 2-8 Go
Exercises 1–21, 23, 25, 27, 29, 31, 33, 37

GUIDED PRACTICE

Find the least common multiple (LCM).

See Example **1** **1.** 4, 7 **2.** 14, 21, 28 **3.** 4, 8, 12, 16

See Example **2** **4.** 30, 48 **5.** 3, 9, 15 **6.** 10, 40, 50

See Example **3** **7.** Jerry and his dad are walking around the track. Jerry completes one lap every 8 minutes. His dad completes one lap every 6 minutes. They start together. In how many minutes will they be together at the starting line again?

INDEPENDENT PRACTICE

Find the least common multiple (LCM).

See Example **1** **8.** 6, 9 **9.** 8, 12 **10.** 15, 20

11. 6, 14 **12.** 18, 27 **13.** 8, 10, 12

See Example **2** **14.** 6, 27 **15.** 16, 20 **16.** 12, 15, 22

17. 10, 15, 18, 20 **18.** 11, 22, 44 **19.** 8, 12, 18, 20

See Example **3** **20. Recreation** On her bicycle, Anna circles the block every 4 minutes. Her brother, on his scooter, circles the block every 10 minutes. They start out together. In how many minutes will they meet again at the starting point?

21. Rod helped his mom plant a vegetable garden. Rod planted a row every 30 minutes, and his mom planted a row every 20 minutes. If they started together, how long will it be before they both finish a row at the same time?

PRACTICE AND PROBLEM SOLVING

Extra Practice
See page EP7.

Find the least common multiple (LCM).

22. 3, 7 **23.** 4, 6 **24.** 9, 12

25. 22, 44, 66 **26.** 80, 120 **27.** 10, 18

28. 3, 5, 7 **29.** 3, 6, 12 **30.** 5, 7, 9

31. 24, 36, 48 **32.** 2, 3, 4, 5 **33.** 14, 21, 35, 70

34. Jack mows the lawn every three weeks and washes the car every two weeks. If he does both today, how many days will pass before he does them both on the same day again?

35. Critical Thinking Is it possible for two numbers to have the same LCM and GCF? Explain.

36. Multi-Step Milli jogs every day, bikes every 3 days, and swims once a week. She does all three activities on October 3. On what date will she next perform all three activities?

The Mayan, the Chinese, and the standard western calendar are all based on cycles.

37. The Mayan ceremonial calendar, or *tzolkin*, was 260 days long. It was composed of two independent cycles, a 13-day cycle and a 20-day cycle. At the beginning of the calendar, both cycles are at day 1. Will both cycles be at day 1 at the same time again before the 260 days are over? If so, when?

38. The Chinese calendar has 12 months of 30 days each and 6-day weeks. The Chinese New Year begins on the first day of a month and the first day of a week. Will the first day of a month and the first day of a week occur again at the same time before the 360-day year is over? If so, when? Explain your answer.

39. ✍ **Write About It** The Julian Date calendar assigns each day a unique number. It begins on day 0 and adds 1 for each new day. So JD 2266296, or October 12, 1492, is 2,266,296 days from the beginning of the calendar. What are some advantages of using the Julian Date calendar? What are some advantages of using calendars that are based on cycles?

40. ⭐ **Challenge** The Mayan Long Count calendar used the naming system at right. Assuming the calendar began on JD 584285, express JD 2266296 in terms of the Mayan Long Count calendar. Start by finding the number of pictun that had passed up to that date.

Mayan Long Count Calendar
1 Pictun = 20 Baktun = 2,880,000 days
1 Baktun = 20 Katun = 144,000 days
1 Katun = 20 Tun = 7,200 days
1 Tun = 18 Winal = 360 days
1 Winal = 20 Kin = 20 days
1 Kin = 1 day

Test Prep and Spiral Review

41. Multiple Choice Which is the least common multiple of 4 and 10?

   Ⓐ 2   Ⓑ 10   Ⓒ 20   Ⓓ 40

42. Multiple Choice Which pair of numbers has a least common multiple of 150?

   Ⓕ 10, 15   Ⓖ 150, 300   Ⓗ 2, 300   Ⓙ 15, 50

Simplify each expression. (Lesson 1-8)

43. $3c + 2c - 2$ **44.** $5x + 3x^2 - 2x$ **45.** $7u + 3v - 4$ **46.** $m + 1 - 6m$

Find the greatest common factor (GCF). (Lesson 2-7)

47. 12, 28   **48.** 16, 24   **49.** 15, 75   **50.** 28, 70

Ready To Go On?

Learn It Online
Resources Online **go.hrw.com,**
keyword MS10 RTGO2B Go

Quiz for Lessons 2-6 Through 2-8

 2-6 Prime Factorization

Complete each factor tree to find the prime factorization.

1. 24
6 • 4
? • ? • ? • ?

2. 140
14 • 10
? • ? • ? • ?

3. 45
3 • ?
3 • ? • ?

4. 42
? • ?
3 • 7 • ?

Write the prime factorization of each number.

5. 96   **6.** 125   **7.** 99

8. 105   **9.** 324   **10.** 500

 2-7 Greatest Common Factor

Find the greatest common factor (GCF).

11. 66, 96   **12.** 18, 27, 45   **13.** 16, 28, 44

14. 14, 28, 56   **15.** 85, 102   **16.** 76, 95

17. 52, 91, 104   **18.** 30, 75, 90   **19.** 118, 116

20. Yasmin and Jon have volunteered to prepare snacks for the first-grade field trip. They have 63 carrot sticks and 105 strawberries. What is the greatest number of identical snacks they can prepare using all of the carrot sticks and strawberries?

 2-8 Least Common Multiple

Find the least common multiple (LCM).

21. 35, 40   **22.** 8, 25   **23.** 64, 72

24. 12, 20   **25.** 21, 33   **26.** 6, 30

27. 20, 42   **28.** 9, 13   **29.** 14, 18

30. Eddie goes jogging every other day, lifts weights every third day, and swims every fourth day. If Eddie begins all three activities on Monday, how many days will it be before he does all three activities on the same day again?

31. Sean and his mom start running around a 1-mile track at the same time. Sean runs 1 mile every 8 minutes. His mom runs 1 mile every 10 minutes. In how many minutes will they be together at the starting line again?

Focus on Problem Solving

Look Back

• **Check that your answer is reasonable**

In some situations, such as when you are looking for an estimate or completing a multiple-choice question, check to see whether a solution or answer is reasonably accurate. One way to do this is by rounding the numbers to the nearest multiple of 10 or 100, depending on how large the numbers are. Sometimes it is useful to round one number up and another down.

 Read each problem, and determine whether the given solution is too high, is too low, or appears to be correct. Explain your answer.

① The cheerleading team is preparing to host a spaghetti dinner as a fund-raising project. They have set up and decorated 54 tables in the gymnasium. Each table can seat 8 people. How many people can be seated at the spaghetti dinner?

Solution: 432 people

② The cheerleaders need to raise $4,260 to attend a cheerleader camp. How much money must they charge each person if they are expecting 400 people at the spaghetti dinner?

Solution: $4

③ To help out the fund-raising project, local restaurants have offered $25 gift certificates to give as door prizes. One gift certificate will be given for each door prize, and there will be six door prizes in all. What is the total value of all of the gift certificates given by the restaurants?

Solution: $250

④ The total cost of hosting the spaghetti dinner will be about $270. If the cheerleaders make $3,280 in ticket sales, how much money will they have after paying for the spaghetti dinner?

Solution: $3,000

⑤ Eighteen cheerleaders and two coaches plan to attend the camp. If each person will have an equal share of the $4,260 expense money, how much money will each person have?

Solution: $562

Equivalent Fractions and Mixed Numbers

In some recipes the amounts of ingredients are given as fractions, and sometimes those amounts don't equal the fractions on a measuring cup. Knowing how fractions relate to each other can be very helpful.

Different fractions can name the same number.

Vocabulary

equivalent fractions

relatively prime

 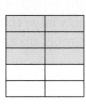 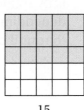

$$\frac{3}{5} \quad = \quad \frac{6}{10} \quad = \quad \frac{15}{25}$$

In the diagram, $\frac{3}{5} = \frac{6}{10} = \frac{15}{25}$. These are called **equivalent fractions** because they are different expressions for the same nonzero number.

To create fractions equivalent to a given fraction, multiply or divide the numerator and denominator by the same number.

EXAMPLE 1 **Finding Equivalent Fractions**

Find two fractions equivalent to $\frac{14}{16}$.

$$\frac{14}{16} = \frac{14 \cdot 2}{16 \cdot 2} = \frac{28}{32} \qquad \textit{Multiply the numerator and denominator by 2.}$$

$$\frac{14}{16} = \frac{14 \div 2}{16 \div 2} = \frac{7}{8} \qquad \textit{Divide the numerator and denominator by 2.}$$

The fractions $\frac{7}{8}$, $\frac{14}{16}$, and $\frac{28}{32}$ in Example 1 are equivalent, but only $\frac{7}{8}$ is in simplest form. A fraction is in simplest form when the numerator and denominator are *relatively prime*. **Relatively prime** numbers have no common factors other than 1.

EXAMPLE 2 **Writing Fractions in Simplest Form**

Write the fraction $\frac{24}{36}$ in simplest form.

Find the GCF of 24 and 36.

$24 = 2 \cdot 2 \cdot 2 \cdot 3$ *The GCF is $2 \cdot 2 \cdot 3 = 12$.*

$36 = 2 \cdot 2 \cdot 3 \cdot 3$

$\frac{24}{36} = \frac{24 \div 12}{36 \div 12} = \frac{2}{3}$ *Divide the numerator and denominator by 12.*

Video **Lesson Tutorials Online** my.hrw.com

To determine if two fractions are equivalent, find a common denominator and compare the numerators.

EXAMPLE 3 **Determining Whether Fractions Are Equivalent**

Determine whether the fractions in each pair are equivalent.

A $\frac{6}{8}$ and $\frac{9}{12}$

Both fractions can be written with a denominator of 4.

$$\frac{6}{8} = \frac{6 \div 2}{8 \div 2} = \frac{3}{4} \qquad\qquad \frac{9}{12} = \frac{9 \div 3}{12 \div 3} = \frac{3}{4}$$

The numerators are equal, so the fractions are equivalent.

B $\frac{18}{15}$ and $\frac{25}{20}$

Both fractions can be written with a denominator of 60.

$$\frac{18}{15} = \frac{18 \cdot 4}{15 \cdot 4} = \frac{72}{60} \qquad\qquad \frac{25}{20} = \frac{25 \cdot 3}{20 \cdot 3} = \frac{75}{60}$$

The numerators are *not* equal, so the fractions are *not* equivalent.

Remember!

An improper fraction is a fraction whose numerator is greater than or equal to the denominator.

$\frac{8}{5}$ is an **improper fraction**. Its numerator is greater than its denominator.

$$\frac{8}{5} = 1\frac{3}{5}$$

$1\frac{3}{5}$ is a **mixed number**. It contains both a whole number and a fraction.

EXAMPLE 4 **Converting Between Improper Fractions and Mixed Numbers**

A Write $\frac{21}{4}$ as a mixed number.

First divide the numerator by the denominator.

$$\frac{21}{4} = 21 \div 4 = 5\text{R}1 = 5\frac{1}{4}$$

Use the quotient and remainder to write the mixed number.

B Write $4\frac{2}{3}$ as an improper fraction.

First multiply the denominator and whole number, and then add the numerator.

 $= \frac{3 \cdot 4 + 2}{3} = \frac{14}{3}$

Use the result to write the improper fraction.

Think and Discuss

1. Explain a process for finding common denominators.

2. Describe how to convert between improper fractions and mixed numbers.

Exercises

GUIDED PRACTICE

See Example 1   Find two fractions equivalent to the given fraction.

1. $\frac{21}{42}$ **2.** $\frac{33}{55}$ **3.** $\frac{10}{12}$ **4.** $\frac{15}{40}$

See Example 2   Write each fraction in simplest form.

5. $\frac{13}{26}$ **6.** $\frac{54}{72}$ **7.** $\frac{12}{15}$ **8.** $\frac{36}{42}$

See Example 3   Determine whether the fractions in each pair are equivalent.

9. $\frac{3}{9}$ and $\frac{6}{8}$ **10.** $\frac{10}{12}$ and $\frac{20}{24}$ **11.** $\frac{8}{6}$ and $\frac{20}{15}$ **12.** $\frac{15}{8}$ and $\frac{19}{12}$

See Example 4   Write each as a mixed number.

13. $\frac{15}{4}$ **14.** $\frac{22}{5}$ **15.** $\frac{17}{13}$ **16.** $\frac{14}{3}$

Write each as an improper fraction.

17. $6\frac{1}{5}$ **18.** $1\frac{11}{12}$ **19.** $7\frac{3}{5}$ **20.** $2\frac{7}{16}$

INDEPENDENT PRACTICE

See Example 1   Find two fractions equivalent to the given fraction.

21. $\frac{18}{20}$ **22.** $\frac{25}{50}$ **23.** $\frac{9}{15}$ **24.** $\frac{42}{70}$

See Example 2   Write each fraction in simplest form.

25. $\frac{63}{81}$ **26.** $\frac{14}{21}$ **27.** $\frac{34}{48}$ **28.** $\frac{100}{250}$

See Example 3   Determine whether the fractions in each pair are equivalent.

29. $\frac{5}{10}$ and $\frac{14}{28}$ **30.** $\frac{15}{20}$ and $\frac{20}{24}$ **31.** $\frac{125}{100}$ and $\frac{40}{32}$ **32.** $\frac{10}{5}$ and $\frac{18}{8}$

33. $\frac{2}{3}$ and $\frac{12}{18}$ **34.** $\frac{8}{12}$ and $\frac{24}{36}$ **35.** $\frac{54}{99}$ and $\frac{84}{132}$ **36.** $\frac{25}{15}$ and $\frac{175}{75}$

See Example 4   Write each as a mixed number.

37. $\frac{19}{3}$ **38.** $\frac{13}{9}$ **39.** $\frac{81}{11}$ **40.** $\frac{71}{8}$

Write each as an improper fraction.

41. $25\frac{3}{5}$ **42.** $4\frac{7}{16}$ **43.** $9\frac{2}{3}$ **44.** $4\frac{16}{31}$

PRACTICE AND PROBLEM SOLVING

Extra Practice
See page EP7.

45. Personal Finance Every month, Adrian pays for his own long-distance calls made on the family phone. Last month, 15 of the 60 minutes of long-distance charges were Adrian's, and he paid $2.50 of the $12 long-distance bill. Did Adrian pay his fair share?

Write a fraction equivalent to the given number.

46. 8   **47.** $6\frac{1}{2}$ **48.** $2\frac{2}{3}$ **49.** $\frac{8}{21}$ **50.** $9\frac{8}{11}$

51. $\frac{55}{10}$ **52.** 101   **53.** $6\frac{15}{21}$ **54.** $\frac{475}{75}$ **55.** $11\frac{23}{50}$

Find the equivalent pair of fractions in each set.

56. $\frac{6}{15}, \frac{21}{35}, \frac{3}{5}$ **57.** $\frac{7}{12}, \frac{12}{20}, \frac{6}{10}$ **58.** $\frac{2}{3}, \frac{12}{15}, \frac{20}{30}, \frac{15}{24}$ **59.** $\frac{7}{4}, \frac{9}{5}, \frac{32}{20}, \frac{72}{40}$

There are 12 inches in 1 foot. Write a mixed number to represent each measurement in feet. (Example: 14 inches = $1\frac{2}{12}$ feet or $1\frac{1}{6}$ feet)

60. 25 inches   **61.** 100 inches   **62.** 362 inches   **63.** 42 inches

64. Social Studies A dollar bill is $15\frac{7}{10}$ centimeters long and $6\frac{13}{20}$ centimeters wide. Write each number as an improper fraction.

 65. Food A bakery uses $37\frac{1}{2}$ cups of flour to make 25 loaves of bread each day. Write a fraction that shows how many $\frac{1}{4}$ cups of flour are used to make bread each day at the bakery.

 66. Write a Problem Cal made the graph at right. Use the graph to write a problem involving fractions.

 67. Write About It Draw a diagram to show how you can use division to write $\frac{25}{3}$ as a mixed number. Explain your diagram.

 68. Challenge Kenichi spent $\frac{2}{5}$ of his $100 birthday check on clothes. How much did Kenichi's new clothes cost?

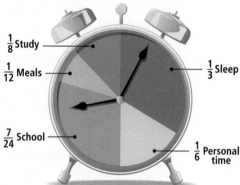

How Cal Spends His Day

$\frac{1}{8}$ Study
$\frac{1}{12}$ Meals
$\frac{7}{24}$ School
$\frac{1}{3}$ Sleep
$\frac{1}{6}$ Personal time

Test Prep and Spiral Review

69. Multiple Choice Which improper fraction is NOT equivalent to $2\frac{1}{2}$?

Ⓐ $\frac{5}{2}$ Ⓑ $\frac{10}{4}$ Ⓒ $\frac{20}{6}$ Ⓓ $\frac{25}{10}$

70. Multiple Choice Which fraction is equivalent to $\frac{5}{6}$?

Ⓕ $\frac{20}{24}$ Ⓖ $\frac{10}{18}$ Ⓗ $\frac{6}{7}$ Ⓙ $\frac{6}{5}$

71. Short Response Maria needs $\frac{4}{3}$ cups of flour, $\frac{11}{4}$ cups of water, and $\frac{3}{2}$ tablespoons of sugar. Write each of these measures as a mixed number.

Solve each equation. Check your answer. (Lessons 1-10 and 1-11)

72. $5b = 25$ **73.** $6 + y = 18$ **74.** $k - 57 = 119$ **75.** $\frac{z}{4} = 20$

Find the least common multiple (LCM). (Lesson 2-8)

76. 2, 3, 4   **77.** 9, 15   **78.** 15, 20   **79.** 3, 7, 8

Equivalent Fractions and Decimals

In baseball, a player's batting average compares the number of hits with the number of times the player has been at bat. The statistics below are for the 2006 Major League Baseball season.

Vocabulary

terminating decimal

repeating decimal

Player	Hits	At Bats	Hits At Bats	Batting Average (thousandths)
Miguel Cabrera	195	576	$\frac{195}{576}$	$195 \div 576 \approx 0.339$
Ichiro Suzuki	224	695	$\frac{224}{695}$	$224 \div 695 \approx 0.322$

To convert a fraction to a decimal, divide the numerator by the denominator.

EXAMPLE 1 **Writing Fractions as Decimals**

Write each fraction as a decimal. Round to the nearest hundredth, if necessary.

A $\frac{3}{4}$

$$
\begin{array}{r}
0.75 \\
4)\overline{3.00} \\
-28 \\
\hline
20 \\
-20 \\
\hline
0
\end{array}
$$

$\frac{3}{4} = 0.75$

B $\frac{6}{5}$

$$
\begin{array}{r}
1.2 \\
5)\overline{6.0} \\
-5 \\
\hline
10 \\
-10 \\
\hline
0
\end{array}
$$

$\frac{6}{5} = 1.2$

C $\frac{1}{3}$

$$
\begin{array}{r}
0.333\ldots \\
3)\overline{1.000} \\
-9 \\
\hline
10 \\
-9 \\
\hline
10 \\
-9 \\
\hline
1
\end{array}
$$

$\frac{1}{3} = 0.333\ldots$
≈ 0.33

Helpful Hint

You can use a calculator to check your division:

$3 \div 4 = 0.75$
$6 \div 5 = 1.2$
$1 \div 3 = 0.333\ldots$

The decimals 0.75 and 1.2 in Example 1 are **terminating decimals** because the decimals come to an end. The decimal $0.333\ldots$ is a **repeating decimal** because the decimal repeats a pattern forever. You can also write a repeating decimal with a bar over the repeating part.

$0.333\ldots = 0.\overline{3}$ $0.8333\ldots = 0.8\overline{3}$ $0.727272\ldots = 0.\overline{72}$

Video   **Lesson Tutorials Online**   my.hrw.com

You can use place value to write some fractions as decimals.

EXAMPLE 2 **Using Mental Math to Write Fractions as Decimals**

Write each fraction as a decimal.

A $\frac{2}{5}$

$\frac{2}{5} \times \frac{2}{2} = \frac{4}{10}$ *Multiply to get a power of ten in the denominator.*

$= 0.4$

B $\frac{7}{25}$

$\frac{7}{25} \times \frac{4}{4} = \frac{28}{100}$ *Multiply to get a power of ten in the denominator.*

$= 0.28$

You can also use place value to write a terminating decimal as a fraction. Use the place value of the last digit to the right of the decimal point as the denominator of the fraction.

EXAMPLE 3 **Writing Decimals as Fractions**

Write each decimal as a fraction in simplest form.

Reading Math

You read the decimal 0.036 as "thirty-six thousandths."

A 0.036

$0.036 = \frac{36}{1,000}$ *6 is in the thousandths place.*

$= \frac{36 \div 4}{1,000 \div 4}$

$= \frac{9}{250}$

B 1.28

$1.28 = \frac{128}{100}$ *8 is in the hundredths place.*

$= \frac{128 \div 4}{100 \div 4}$

$= \frac{32}{25}$, or $1\frac{7}{25}$

EXAMPLE 4 **Sports Application**

During a football game, Albert completed 23 of the 27 passes he attempted. Find his completion rate to the nearest thousandth.

Fraction	What the Calculator Shows	Completion Rate
$\frac{23}{27}$	23 ÷ 27 ENTER .8518518519	0.852

His completion rate is 0.852.

Think and Discuss

1. Tell how to write a fraction as a decimal.

2. Explain how to use place value to convert 0.2048 to a fraction.

Exercises

GUIDED PRACTICE

See Example 1 Write each fraction as a decimal. Round to the nearest hundredth, if necessary.

1. $\frac{4}{7}$ **2.** $\frac{21}{8}$ **3.** $\frac{11}{6}$ **4.** $\frac{7}{9}$

See Example 2 Write each fraction as a decimal.

5. $\frac{3}{25}$ **6.** $\frac{7}{10}$ **7.** $\frac{1}{20}$ **8.** $\frac{3}{5}$

See Example 3 Write each decimal as a fraction in simplest form.

9. 0.008 **10.** −0.6 **11.** −2.05 **12.** 3.75

See Example 4 **13. Sports** After sweeping the Baltimore Orioles at home in 2001, the Seattle Mariners had a record of 103 wins out of 143 games played. Find the Mariners' winning rate. Write your answer as a decimal rounded to the nearest thousandth.

INDEPENDENT PRACTICE

See Example 1 Write each fraction as a decimal. Round to the nearest hundredth, if necessary.

14. $\frac{9}{10}$ **15.** $\frac{32}{5}$ **16.** $\frac{18}{25}$ **17.** $\frac{7}{8}$

18. $\frac{16}{11}$ **19.** $\frac{500}{500}$ **20.** $\frac{17}{3}$ **21.** $\frac{23}{12}$

See Example 2 Write each fraction as a decimal.

22. $\frac{5}{4}$ **23.** $\frac{4}{5}$ **24.** $\frac{15}{25}$ **25.** $\frac{11}{20}$

See Example 3 Write each decimal as a fraction in simplest form.

26. 0.45 **27.** 0.01 **28.** −0.25 **29.** −0.08

30. 1.8 **31.** 15.25 **32.** 5.09 **33.** 8.375

See Example 4 **34. School** On a test, Caleb answered 73 out of 86 questions correctly. What portion of his answers was correct? Write your answer as a decimal rounded to the nearest thousandth.

PRACTICE AND PROBLEM SOLVING

Extra Practice
See page EP7.

Give two numbers equivalent to each fraction or decimal.

35. $8\frac{3}{4}$ **36.** 0.66 **37.** 5.05 **38.** $\frac{8}{25}$

39. 15.35 **40.** $8\frac{3}{8}$ **41.** $4\frac{3}{1,000}$ **42.** $3\frac{1}{3}$

Determine whether the numbers in each pair are equivalent.

43. $\frac{3}{4}$ and 0.75 **44.** $\frac{7}{20}$ and 0.45 **45.** $\frac{11}{21}$ and 0.55 **46.** 0.8 and $\frac{4}{5}$

47. 0.275 and $\frac{11}{40}$ **48.** $1\frac{21}{25}$ and 1.72 **49.** 0.74 and $\frac{16}{25}$ **50.** 0.35 and $\frac{7}{20}$

Use the table for Exercises 51 and 52.

XYZ Stock Values (October 2006)				
Date	Open	High	Low	Close
Oct 16	17.89	18.05	17.5	17.8
Oct 17	18.01	18.04	17.15	17.95
Oct 18	17.84	18.55	17.81	18.20

51. Write the highest value of stock XYZ for each day as a mixed number in simplest form.

52. On which date did the price of stock XYZ change by $\frac{9}{25}$ of a dollar between the open and close of the day?

Traders watch the stock prices change from the floor of a stock exchange.

53. ✒ **Write About It** Until recently, prices of stocks were expressed as mixed numbers, such as $24\frac{15}{32}$ dollars. The denominators of such fractions were multiples of 2, such as 2, 4, 6, 8, and so forth. Today, the prices are expressed as decimals to the nearest hundredth, such as 32.35 dollars.

  a. What are some advantages of using decimals instead of fractions?

  b. The old ticker-tape machine punched stock prices onto a tape. Perhaps because fractions could not be shown using the machine, the prices were punched as decimals. Write some decimal equivalents of fractions that the machine might print.

Before the days of computer technology, ticker-tape machines were used to punch the stock prices onto paper strands.

54. ⭐ **Challenge** Write $\frac{1}{9}$ and $\frac{2}{9}$ as decimals. Use the results to predict the decimal equivalent of $\frac{8}{9}$.

Test Prep and Spiral Review

55. Multiple Choice Which is NOT equivalent to 0.35?

Ⓐ $\frac{35}{100}$ Ⓑ $\frac{7}{20}$ Ⓒ $\frac{14}{40}$ Ⓓ $\frac{25}{80}$

56. Gridded Response Write $\frac{6}{17}$ as a decimal rounded to the nearest hundredth.

Determine whether the given value of the variable is a solution. (Lesson 1-9)

57. $x = 2$ for $3x - 4 = 1$ **58.** $x = 3$ for $5x + 4 = 19$ **59.** $x = 14$ for $9(4 + x) = 162$

Write each as an improper fraction. (Lesson 2-9)

60. $4\frac{1}{5}$ **61.** $3\frac{1}{4}$ **62.** $1\frac{2}{3}$ **63.** $6\frac{1}{4}$

TN SPI 0706.2.2 Compare rational numbers using appropriate inequality symbols.
Also ✓ 0706.2.1, ✓ 0706.2.9

Vocabulary

rational number

Which is greater, $\frac{7}{9}$ or $\frac{2}{9}$?

To compare fractions with the same denominator, just compare the numerators.

$\frac{7}{9} > \frac{2}{9}$ because $7 > 2$.

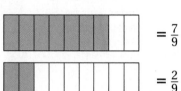 $= \frac{7}{9}$

$= \frac{2}{9}$

To compare fractions with unlike denominators, first write equivalent fractions with common denominators. Then compare the numerators.

"I would like an extra-large pizza with $\frac{1}{2}$ pepperoni, $\frac{4}{5}$ sausuage, $\frac{3}{8}$ anchovies on the pepperoni side, $\frac{5}{11}$ pineapple, $\frac{2}{13}$ doggie treats, $\frac{1}{16}$ catnip . . . and extra cheese."

EXAMPLE 1 **Comparing Fractions**

Compare the fractions. Write < or >.

A $\frac{5}{6}$ ☐ $\frac{7}{10}$

The LCM of the denominators 6 and 10 is 30.

$\frac{5}{6} = \frac{5 \cdot 5}{6 \cdot 5} = \frac{25}{30}$ *Write equivalent fractions with 30 as the denominator.*

$\frac{7}{10} = \frac{7 \cdot 3}{10 \cdot 3} = \frac{21}{30}$

$\frac{25}{30} > \frac{21}{30}$, and so $\frac{5}{6} > \frac{7}{10}$.   *Compare the numerators.*

B $-\frac{3}{5}$ ☐ $-\frac{5}{9}$

Both fractions can be written with a denominator of 45.

$-\frac{3}{5} = \frac{-3 \cdot 9}{5 \cdot 9} = \frac{-27}{45}$ *Write equivalent fractions with 45 as the denominator. Put the negative signs in the numerators.*

$-\frac{5}{9} = \frac{-5 \cdot 5}{9 \cdot 5} = \frac{-25}{45}$

$\frac{-27}{45} < \frac{-25}{45}$, and so $-\frac{3}{5} < -\frac{5}{9}$.

Helpful Hint

A fraction less than 0 can be written as $-\frac{3}{5}$, $\frac{-3}{5}$, or $\frac{3}{-5}$.

To compare decimals, line up the decimal points and compare digits from left to right until you find the place where the digits are different.

EXAMPLE 2 **Comparing Decimals**

Compare the decimals. Write < or >.

A 0.81 ▨ 0.84

0.81
↕
0.84

Line up the decimal points.
The tenths are the same.
Compare the hundredths: 1 < 4.

Since 0.01 < 0.04, 0.81 < 0.84.

B $0.\overline{34}$ ▨ 0.342

$0.\overline{34} = 0.3434\ldots$
↕
0.342

$0.\overline{34}$ is a repeating decimal.
Line up the decimal points.
The tenths and hundredths are the same.
Compare the thousandths: 3 > 2.

Since 0.003 > 0.002, $0.\overline{34}$ > 0.342.

A **rational number** is a number that can be written as a fraction with an integer for its numerator and a nonzero integer for its denominator. When rational numbers are written in a variety of forms, you can compare the numbers by writing them all in the same form.

EXAMPLE 3 **Ordering Fractions and Decimals**

Order $\frac{3}{5}$, $0.\overline{77}$, −0.1, and $1\frac{1}{5}$ from least to greatest.

$\frac{3}{5} = 0.60$ $0.\overline{77} \approx 0.78$ *Write as decimals with the same number of places.*

$-0.1 = -0.10$ $1\frac{1}{5} = 1.20$

Graph the numbers on a number line.

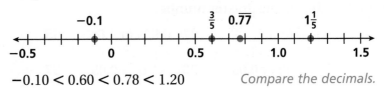

Remember!

The values on a number line increase as you move from left to right.

$-0.10 < 0.60 < 0.78 < 1.20$ *Compare the decimals.*

From least to greatest, the numbers are -0.1, $\frac{3}{5}$, $0.\overline{77}$, and $1\frac{1}{5}$.

Think and Discuss

1. Tell how to compare two fractions with different denominators.

2. Explain why −0.31 is greater than −0.325 even though 2 > 1.

Learn It Online
Homework Help Online **go.hrw.com,**
keyword MS10 2-11 **Go**
Exercises 1–30, 31, 33, 35, 37, 41

GUIDED PRACTICE

See Example **1** Compare the fractions. Write $<$ or $>$.

1. $\frac{3}{5}$ ▨ $\frac{4}{5}$ **2.** $-\frac{5}{8}$ ▨ $-\frac{7}{8}$ **3.** $-\frac{2}{3}$ ▨ $-\frac{4}{7}$ **4.** $3\frac{4}{5}$ ▨ $3\frac{2}{3}$

See Example **2** Compare the decimals. Write $<$ or $>$.

5. 0.622 ▨ 0.625 **6.** 0.405 ▨ $0.\overline{45}$ **7.** -3.822 ▨ -3.819

See Example **3** Order the numbers from least to greatest.

8. $0.\overline{55}, \frac{3}{4}, 0.505$ **9.** $2.5, 2.05, -\frac{13}{5}$ **10.** $\frac{5}{8}, -0.875, 0.877$

INDEPENDENT PRACTICE

See Example **1** Compare the fractions. Write $<$ or $>$.

11. $\frac{6}{11}$ ▨ $\frac{7}{11}$ **12.** $-\frac{5}{9}$ ▨ $-\frac{6}{9}$ **13.** $-\frac{5}{6}$ ▨ $-\frac{8}{9}$ **14.** $10\frac{3}{4}$ ▨ $10\frac{3}{5}$

15. $\frac{5}{7}$ ▨ $\frac{2}{7}$ **16.** $-\frac{3}{4}$ ▨ $\frac{1}{4}$ **17.** $\frac{7}{4}$ ▨ $-\frac{1}{4}$ **18.** $-\frac{2}{3}$ ▨ $\frac{4}{3}$

See Example **2** Compare the decimals. Write $<$ or $>$.

19. 3.8 ▨ 3.6 **20.** 0.088 ▨ 0.109 **21.** $4.\overline{26}$ ▨ 4.266

22. -1.902 ▨ 0.920 **23.** -0.7 ▨ -0.07 **24.** $3.\overline{08}$ ▨ 3.808

See Example **3** Order the numbers from least to greatest.

25. $0.7, 0.755, \frac{5}{8}$ **26.** $1.82, 1.6, 1\frac{4}{5}$ **27.** $-2.25, 2.05, \frac{21}{10}$

28. $-3.\overline{02}, -3.02, 1\frac{1}{2}$ **29.** $2.88, -2.98, -2\frac{9}{10}$ **30.** $\frac{5}{6}, \frac{4}{5}, 0.82$

PRACTICE AND PROBLEM SOLVING

Extra Practice
See page EP7.

Choose the greater number.

31. $\frac{3}{4}$ or 0.7 **32.** 0.999 or 1.0 **33.** $\frac{7}{8}$ or $\frac{13}{20}$ **34.** -0.93 or 0.2

35. 0.32 or 0.088 **36.** $-\frac{1}{2}$ or -0.05 **37.** $-\frac{9}{10}$ or $-\frac{7}{8}$ **38.** 23.44 or 23

39. Earth Science Density is a measure of mass in a specific unit of space. The mean densities (in g/cm³) of the planets of our solar system are given in the table below. Rearrange the planets from least to most dense.

Planet	Density	Planet	Density	Planet	Density
Mercury	5.43	Mars	3.93	Uranus	1.32
Venus	5.20	Jupiter	1.32	Neptune	1.64
Earth	5.52	Saturn	0.69	Pluto*	2.05

*designated a dwarf planet in 2006

Life Science

Algae that grows in sloths' fur make them look slightly green. This helps them blend into the trees and stay out of sight from predators.

40. Multi-Step Twenty-four karat gold is considered pure.

 a. Angie's necklace is 22-karat gold. What is its purity as a fraction?

 b. Luke's ring is 0.75 gold. If Angie's necklace and Luke's ring weigh the same amount, which contains more gold?

41. Life Science Sloths are tree-dwelling animals that live in South and Central America. They generally sleep about $\frac{3}{4}$ of a 24-hour day. Humans sleep an average of 8 hours each day. Which sleep the most each day, sloths or humans?

42. Ecology Of Beatrice's total household water use, $\frac{5}{9}$ is for bathing, toilet flushing, and laundry. How does her water use for these purposes compare with that shown in the graph?

43. What's the Error? A recipe for a large cake called for $4\frac{1}{2}$ cups of flour. The chef added 10 one-half cupfuls of flour to the mixture. What was the chef's error?

44. Write About It Explain how to compare a mixed number with a decimal.

Average Daily Household Use of Water

$\frac{3}{5}$ Bathing, toilet flushing, laundry

$\frac{8}{25}$ Lawn watering, car washing, pool maintenance

$\frac{2}{25}$ Drinking, cooking, washing dishes, running garbage disposal

45. Challenge Scientists estimate that Earth is approximately 4.6 billion years old. We are currently in what is called the Phanerozoic eon, which has made up about $\frac{7}{60}$ of the time that Earth has existed. The first eon, called the Hadean, made up approximately 0.175 of the time Earth has existed. Which eon represents the most time?

Test Prep and Spiral Review

46. Multiple Choice Which number is the greatest?

 Ⓐ 0.71   Ⓑ $\frac{5}{8}$ Ⓒ 0.65   Ⓓ $\frac{5}{7}$

47. Multiple Choice Which shows the order of the animals from fastest to slowest?

 Ⓕ Spider, tortoise, snail, sloth

 Ⓖ Snail, sloth, tortoise, spider

 Ⓗ Tortoise, spider, snail, sloth

 Ⓙ Spider, tortoise, sloth, snail

Maximum Speed (mi/h)				
Animal	Snail	Tortoise	Spider	Sloth
Speed	0.03	0.17	1.17	0.15

Compare. Write <, >, or =. (Lesson 2-1)

48. |−14| ▊ −12   **49.** −7 ▊ −8   **50.** −4 ▊ 0   **51.** 3 ▊ −5

Simplify. (Lessons 2-2 and 2-3)

52. −13 + 51   **53.** 142 − (−27)   **54.** −118 − (−57)   **55.** −27 + 84

CHAPTER
2

SECTION 2C

 **Ready To Go On?**

 **Learn It Online**
Resources Online **go.hrw.com,**
keyword MS10 RTGO2C Go

Quiz for Lessons 2-9 Through 2-11

✓ **2-9** **Equivalent Fractions and Mixed Numbers**

Determine whether the fractions in each pair are equivalent.

1. $\frac{3}{4}$ and $\frac{2}{3}$ **2.** $\frac{3}{12}$ and $\frac{4}{16}$ **3.** $\frac{7}{25}$ and $\frac{6}{20}$ **4.** $\frac{5}{9}$ and $\frac{25}{45}$

5. There are $2\frac{54}{100}$ centimeters in an inch. When asked to write this value as an improper fraction, Aimee wrote $\frac{127}{50}$. Was she correct? Explain.

✓ **2-10** **Equivalent Fractions and Decimals**

Write each fraction as a decimal. Round to the nearest hundredth, if necessary.

6. $\frac{7}{10}$ **7.** $\frac{5}{8}$ **8.** $\frac{2}{3}$ **9.** $\frac{14}{15}$

Write each decimal as a fraction in simplest form.

10. 0.22   **11.** −0.135   **12.** −4.06   **13.** 0.07

14. In one 30-gram serving of snack crackers, there are 24 grams of carbohydrates. What fraction of a serving is made up of carbohydrates? Write your answer as a fraction and as a decimal.

15. During a softball game, Sara threw 70 pitches. Of those pitches, 29 were strikes. What portion of the pitches that Sara threw were strikes? Write your answer as a decimal rounded to the nearest thousandth.

✓ **2-11** **Comparing and Ordering Rational Numbers**

Compare the fractions. Write < or >.

16. $\frac{3}{7}$ ■ $\frac{2}{4}$ **17.** $-\frac{1}{8}$ ■ $-\frac{2}{11}$ **18.** $\frac{5}{4}$ ■ $\frac{4}{5}$ **19.** $-1\frac{2}{3}$ ■ $\frac{1}{2}$

Compare the decimals. Write < or >.

20. 0.521 ■ 0.524   **21.** 2.05 ■ −2.50   **22.** 3.001 ■ 3.010   **23.** −0.26 ■ −0.626

Order the numbers from least to greatest.

24. $\frac{3}{7}$, −0.372, $-\frac{2}{3}$, 0.5   **25.** $2\frac{9}{11}$, $\frac{4}{5}$, 2.91, 0.9

26. −5.36, 2.36, $-5\frac{1}{3}$, $-2\frac{3}{6}$ **27.** 8.75, $\frac{7}{8}$, 0.8, $\frac{8}{7}$

28. Rafael measured the rainfall at his house for 3 days. On Sunday, it rained $\frac{2}{5}$ in. On Monday, it rained $\frac{5}{8}$ in. On Wednesday, it rained 0.57 in. List the days in order from the least to the greatest amount of rainfall.

Real-World CONNECTIONS

Amphibians and Reptiles of Arizona   The desert climate of Arizona makes the state an ideal habitat for amphibians and reptiles. In fact, the state has more than 140 different species of lizards, turtles, snakes, frogs, and toads. Visitors to the state may even see one of the 11 species of rattlesnakes found in Arizona.

ARIZONA

1. Most reptiles can survive only in temperatures between –4 °C and 36 °C. What is the difference between these temperatures?

2. In Arizona, there are 28 species of amphibians and 52 species of snakes. An employee at a museum is arranging photos of these species on a wall. The photos will be placed in rows. Each row will have the same number of species of amphibians and the same number of species of snakes.

Gila monster

   a. The employee wants to make as many rows of photos as possible. How many rows can the employee make?

   b. How many photos of amphibians will be in each row? How many photos of snakes will be in each row?

For 3–5, use the table.

3. Write the length of the Gila monster as a decimal.

4. Write the length of the desert iguana as a mixed number in simplest form.

5. List the five species of lizards in order from shortest to longest. Explain how you put the species in order.

Lizards of Arizona	
Species	**Length (cm)**
Gila Monster	$35\frac{3}{5}$
Desert Iguana	14.6
Great Plains Skink	$\frac{133}{10}$
Common Chuckwalla	22.9
Zebra-Tailed Lizard	$\frac{51}{5}$

Real-World Connections

Game Time

Magic Squares

A magic square is a grid with numbers, such that the numbers in each row, column, and diagonal have the same "magic" sum. Test the square at right to see an example of this.

You can use a magic square to do some amazing calculations. Cover a block of four squares (2 × 2) with a piece of paper. There is a way you can find the sum of these squares without looking at them. Try to find it. (*Hint:* What number in the magic square can you subtract from the magic sum to give you the sum of the numbers in the block? Where is that number located?)

Here's the answer: To find the sum of any block of four numbers, take 65 (the magic sum) and subtract from it the number that is diagonally two squares away from a corner of the block.

18	10	22	14	1
12	4	16	8	25
6	23	15	2	19
5	17	9	21	13
24	11	3	20	7

$$65 - 21 = 44$$

18	10	22	14	1
12	4	16	8	25
6	23	15	2	19
5	17	9	21	13
24	11	3	20	7

$$65 - 1 = 64$$

The number you subtract must fall on an extension of a diagonal of the block. For each block that you choose, there will be only one direction you can go.

Try to create a 3 × 3 magic square with the numbers 1–9.

Modified Tic-Tac-Toe

The board has a row of nine squares numbered 1 through 9. Players take turns selecting squares. The goal of the game is for a player to select squares such that any three of the player's squares add up to 15. The game can also be played with a board numbered 1 through 16 and a sum goal of 34.

A complete copy of the rules and a game board are available online.

Learn It Online
Game Time Extra **go.hrw.com,**
keyword MS10 Games Go

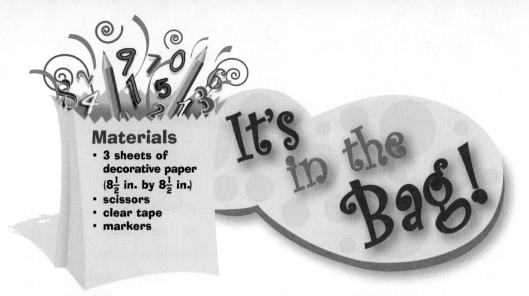

Materials
- **3 sheets of decorative paper** (8½ in. by 8½ in.)
- **scissors**
- **clear tape**
- **markers**

It's in the Bag!

PROJECT **Flipping Over Integers and Rational Numbers**

Create your own flip-flop-fold book and use it to write definitions, sample problems, and practice exercises.

Directions

1 Stack the sheets of decorative paper. Fold the stack into quarters and then unfold it. Use scissors to make a slit from the edge of the stack to the center of the stack along the left-hand crease. **Figure A**

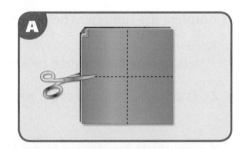

2 Place the stack in front of you with the slit on the left side. Fold the top left square over to the right side of the stack. **Figure B**

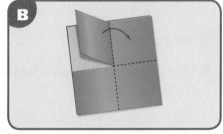

3 Now fold down the top two squares from the top right corner. Along the slit, tape the bottom left square to the top left square. **Figure C**

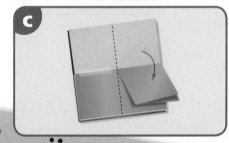

4 Continue folding around the stack, always in a clockwise direction. When you get to the second layer, tape the slit in the same place as before.

Taking Note of the Math

Unfold your completed booklet. This time, as you flip the pages, add definitions, sample problems, practice exercises, or any other notes you need to help you study the material in the chapter.

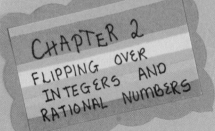

CHAPTER 2
FLIPPING OVER
INTEGERS AND
RATIONAL NUMBERS

Study Guide: Review

Vocabulary

absolute value 73

additive inverse 72

composite number 104

equivalent fractions ... 118

greatest common
factor (GCF) 108

integer 72

least common
multiple (LCM) 112

multiple 112

opposite 72

prime
factorization 104

prime number 104

rational number 127

relatively prime 118

repeating decimal 122

terminating decimal ...122

Complete the sentences below with vocabulary words from the list above.

1. A(n) ___?___ can be written as the ratio of one ___?___ to another and can be represented by a repeating or ___?___.

2. The ___?___ are the set of whole numbers and their ___?___(s).

EXAMPLES

EXERCISES

2-1 Integers (pp. 72–75)

■ Use a number line to order the integers from least to greatest.

$3, 4, -2, 1, -3$

$-3, -2, 1, 3, 4$

Compare the integers. Use < or >.

3. -8 ⬛ -15 **4.** -7 ⬛ 7

Use a number line to order the integers from least to greatest.

5. $-6, 4, 0, -2, 5$ **6.** $8, -3, 2, -8, 1$

Use a number line to find each absolute value.

7. $|0|$ **8.** $|-17|$ **9.** $|6|$

2-2 Adding Integers (pp. 80–83)

■ Find the sum.

$-7 + (-11)$

$-7 + (-11)$ *The signs are the same.*

-18

Find each sum.

10. $-8 + 5$ **11.** $7 + (-6)$

12. $-16 + (-40)$ **13.** $-9 + 18$

14. $-2 + 16 + (-4)$ **15.** $12 + (-18) + 1$

16. The temperature was $-9\,°F$ at 5 A.M. and rose 20° by 10 A.M. What was the temperature at 10 A.M.?

2-3 Subtracting Integers (pp. 86–89)

■ Find the difference.

$-5 - (-3)$

$-5 + 3 = -2$ *Add the opposite of −3.*

Find each difference.

17. $8 - 2$ **18.** $10 - 19$

19. $-6 - (-5)$ **20.** $-5 - 4$

21. $6 - (-5) - 8$ **22.** $10 - (-3) - (-1)$

2-4 Multiplying and Dividing Integers (pp. 92–95)

Find each product or quotient.

■ $12 \cdot (-3)$ *The signs are different, so*
   -36 *the product is negative.*

■ $-16 \div (-4)$ *The signs are the same, so*
   4 *the quotient is positive.*

Find each product or quotient.

23. $5 \cdot (-10)$ **24.** $-27 \div (-9)$

25. $-2 \cdot (-8)$ **26.** $-40 \div 20$

27. $-3 \cdot 4$ **28.** $45 \div (-15)$

2-5 Solving Equations Containing Integers (pp. 98–101)

Solve.

■ $\begin{aligned} x - 12 &= 4 \\ \underline{+12} \quad &\underline{+12} \\ x &= 16 \end{aligned}$ *Add 12 to each side.*

■ $\begin{aligned} -10 &= -2f \\ \frac{-10}{-2} &= \frac{-2f}{-2} \\ 5 &= f \end{aligned}$ *Divide each side by −2.*

Solve.

29. $7y = 70$ **30.** $d - 8 = 6$

31. $j + 23 = -3$ **32.** $\frac{n}{36} = 2$

33. $-26 = -2c$ **34.** $28 = -7m$

35. A scuba diver is at the −30 foot level. How many feet will she have to rise to be at the −12 foot level?

2-6 Prime Factorization (pp. 104–107)

Write the prime factorization of 56.

■ $56 = 8 \cdot 7 = 2 \cdot 2 \cdot 2 \cdot 7$, or $2^3 \cdot 7$

Write the prime factorization.

36. 88   **37.** 27   **38.** 162   **39.** 96

40. Find two composite numbers that each have prime factors with a sum of 10.

2-7 Greatest Common Factor (pp. 108–111)

■ Find the GCF of 32 and 12.

Factors of 32: 1, 2, ④, 8, 16, 32
Factors of 12: 1, 2, 3, ④, 6, 12
The GCF is 4.

Find the greatest common factor.

41. 120, 210   **42.** 81, 132

43. 36, 60, 96   **44.** 220, 440, 880

Study Guide: Review

2-8 **Least Common Multiple** (pp. 112–115)

■ **Find the LCM of 8 and 10.**

Multiples of 8: 8, 16, 24, 32, ④⓪
Multiples of 10: 10, 20, 30, ④⓪
The LCM is 40.

Find the least common multiple.

45. 5, 12   **46.** 4, 32   **47.** 3, 27

48. 15, 18   **49.** 6, 12   **50.** 5, 7, 9

51. Two tour buses leave the visitor's center at 10:00 A.M. Bus A returns to the visitors' center every 60 minutes. Bus B returns every 45 minutes. At what time will the buses be together again at the center?

2-9 **Equivalent Fractions and Mixed Numbers** (pp. 118–121)

■ **Write $5\frac{2}{3}$ as an improper fraction.**

$5\frac{2}{3} = \frac{3 \cdot 5 + 2}{3} = \frac{17}{3}$

■ **Write $\frac{17}{4}$ as a mixed number.**

$\frac{17}{4} = 17 \div 4 = 4 \text{ R}1 = 4\frac{1}{4}$ *Divide the numerator by the denominator.*

Write each as an improper fraction.

52. $4\frac{1}{5}$ **53.** $3\frac{1}{6}$ **54.** $10\frac{3}{4}$

Write each as a mixed number.

55. $\frac{10}{3}$ **56.** $\frac{5}{2}$ **57.** $\frac{17}{7}$

Find two fractions equivalent to the given fraction.

58. $\frac{16}{18}$ **59.** $\frac{21}{24}$ **60.** $\frac{48}{63}$

2-10 **Equivalent Fractions and Decimals** (pp. 122–125)

■ **Write 0.75 as a fraction in simplest form.**

$0.75 = \frac{75}{100} = \frac{75 \div 25}{100 \div 25} = \frac{3}{4}$

■ **Write $\frac{5}{4}$ as a decimal.**

$\frac{5}{4} = 5 \div 4 = 1.25$

Write each decimal as a fraction in simplest form.

61. 0.25   **62.** −0.004   **63.** 0.05

Write each fraction as a decimal.

64. $\frac{7}{2}$ **65.** $\frac{3}{5}$ **66.** $\frac{2}{3}$

2-11 **Comparing and Ordering Rational Numbers** (pp. 126–129)

■ **Compare. Write < or >.**

$-\frac{3}{4} \ \blacksquare \ -\frac{2}{3}$

$-\frac{3}{4} \cdot \frac{3}{3} \ \blacksquare \ -\frac{2}{3} \cdot \frac{4}{4}$ *Write as fractions with common denominators.*

$-\frac{9}{12} < -\frac{8}{12}$

Compare. Write < or > .

67. $\frac{4}{5} \ \blacksquare \ 0.81$ **68.** $0.22 \ \blacksquare \ \frac{3}{20}$

69. $-\frac{3}{5} \ \blacksquare \ -1.5$ **70.** $1\frac{1}{8} \ \blacksquare \ 1\frac{2}{9}$

71. Order $\frac{6}{13}$, 0.58, −0.55, and $\frac{1}{2}$ from least to greatest.

Chapter Test

Use a number line to order the integers from least to greatest.

1. $-4, 3, -2, 0, 1$ **2.** $7, -6, 5, -8, -3$

Use a number line to find each absolute value.

3. $|11|$ **4.** $|-5|$ **5.** $|-74|$ **6.** $|-1|$

Find each sum, difference, product, or quotient.

7. $-7 + (-3)$ **8.** $-6 - 3$ **9.** $17 - (-9) - 8$ **10.** $102 + (-97) + 3$

11. $-3 \cdot 20$ **12.** $-36 \div 12$ **13.** $-400 \div (-10)$ **14.** $-5 \cdot (-2) \cdot 9$

Solve.

15. $w - 4 = -6$ **16.** $x + 5 = -5$ **17.** $-6a = 60$ **18.** $\frac{n}{-4} = 12$

19. Kathryn's tennis team has won 52 matches. Her team has won 9 more matches than Rebecca's team. How many matches has Rebecca's team won this season?

Write the prime factorization of each number.

20. 30   **21.** 66   **22.** 78   **23.** 110

Find the greatest common factor (GCF).

24. 18, 27, 45   **25.** 16, 28, 44   **26.** 14, 28, 56   **27.** 24, 36, 64

Find the least common multiple (LCM).

28. 24, 36, 64   **29.** 24, 72, 144   **30.** 12, 15, 36   **31.** 9, 16, 25

Determine whether the fractions in each pair are equivalent.

32. $\frac{6}{12}$ and $\frac{13}{26}$ **33.** $\frac{17}{20}$ and $\frac{20}{24}$ **34.** $\frac{30}{24}$ and $\frac{35}{28}$ **35.** $\frac{5}{3}$ and $\frac{8}{5}$

Write each fraction as a decimal. Write each decimal as a fraction in simplest form.

36. $\frac{3}{50}$ **37.** $\frac{25}{10}$ **38.** 3.15   **39.** 0.004

40. The Drama Club has 52 members. Of these members, 18 are in the seventh grade. What fraction of the Drama Club is made up of seventh-graders? Write your answer as a fraction and a decimal. Round the decimal to the nearest thousandth.

Compare. Write < or >.

41. $\frac{2}{3}$ ■ 0.62   **42.** 1.5 ■ $1\frac{6}{20}$ **43.** $-\frac{9}{7}$ ■ -1 **44.** $\frac{11}{5}$ ■ $1\frac{2}{3}$

Cumulative Assessment, Chapters 1–2

Multiple Choice

1. During a week in January in Cleveland, Ohio, the daily high temperatures were −4 °F, −2 °F, −12 °F, 5 °F, 12 °F, 16 °F, and 20 °F. Which expression can be used to find the difference between the highest temperature of the week and the lowest temperature of the week?

   A 20 − 2
   B 20 − (−2)
   C 20 − 12
   D 20 − (−12)

2. Compare the fractions.

   $$2\frac{4}{7} \blacksquare 2\frac{3}{4}$$

   F >
   G <
   H =
   J ≈

3. The fraction $\frac{3}{5}$ is found between which pair of fractions on a number line?

   A $\frac{1}{2}$ and $\frac{2}{10}$
   B $\frac{1}{2}$ and $\frac{7}{10}$
   C $\frac{3}{10}$ and $\frac{5}{15}$
   D $\frac{3}{10}$ and $\frac{8}{15}$

4. Maxie earns $210 a week working as a lifeguard. After she gets paid, she gives each of her three sisters $20, and her mom $120 for her car payment. Which equation can be used to find p, the amount of money Maxie has left after she pays her mom and sisters?

   F $p = 210 − (3 \times 20) − 120$
   G $p = 210 − 20 − 120$
   H $p = 120 − (3 \times 20) − 120$
   J $p = 3 \times (210 − 20 − 120)$

5. Which expression can be used to represent a pattern in the table?

x	?
−3	4
−5	2
−7	0
−9	−2

   A $x + 2$
   B $−2x$
   C $x − (−7)$
   D $x − 7$

6. Which of the following shows a list of numbers in order from least to greatest?

   F −1.05, −2.55, −3.05
   G −2.75, $2\frac{5}{6}$, 2.50
   H −0.05, −0.01, $3\frac{1}{4}$
   J $−1\frac{2}{8}$, $−1\frac{4}{8}$, 1.05

7. Which of the following is an example of the Associative Property?

   A 5 + (4 + 1) = (5 + 4) + 1
   B 32 + (2 + 11) = 32 + (11 + 2)
   C (2 × 10) + (2 × 4) = 2 × 14
   D 4(2 × 7) = (4 × 2) + (4 × 7)

8. There are 100 centimeters in 1 meter. Which mixed number represents 625 centimeters in meters?

   F $6\frac{1}{4}$ meters
   G $6\frac{2}{4}$ meters
   H $6\frac{2}{5}$ meters
   J $6\frac{3}{5}$ meters

9. Evaluate $a - b$ for $a = -5$ and $b = 3$.

    A −8   **C** 2

    B −2   **D** 8

10. Simplify the expression $(-5)^2 - 3 \cdot 4$.

    F −112   **H** 13

    G −37   **J** 88

 HOT TIP! If you are unsure how to solve a problem, look at the answer choices. They may give you a clue to the solution method.

11. Find the missing value in the table.

t	$-t + 3 \cdot 5$
5	10
10	?

    A −35   **C** 25

    B 5   **D** 65

Paul and Clara went rock climbing. Paul started at the top of a cliff, 80 feet above the ground. He climbed down 50 feet and then climbed up 23 feet to rest on a ledge. Clara started at the ground, climbed up 80 feet, and then climbed down 15 feet to rest on a different ledge. Use this information for items 12 and 13.

12. How far above the ground was Paul when he was resting?

    F 23 feet   **H** 53 feet

    G 50 feet   **J** 73 feet

13. Each climber's distance traveled is the sum of the distances climbed up and down. What was Clara's total distance traveled?

    A 30 feet   **C** 73 feet

    B 65 feet   **D** 95 feet

Process Standards Practice
Short Response

S1. The sponsors of the marching band provided 128 sandwiches for a picnic. After the picnic, s sandwiches were left.

  a. Write an expression that shows how many sandwiches were handed out.

  b. Evaluate your expression for $s = 15$. What does your answer represent?

S2. Casey said the solution to the equation $x + 42 = 65$ is 107. Identify the error that Casey made. Explain why this answer is unreasonable. Show how to solve this equation correctly. Explain your work.

Extended Response

E1. Mary's allowance is based on the amount of time that she spends practicing different activities each week. This week Mary spent 12 hours practicing and earned $12.00.

  a. Mary spent the following amounts of time on each activity: $\frac{1}{5}$ practicing flute, $\frac{1}{6}$ studying Spanish, $\frac{1}{3}$ playing soccer, and $\frac{3}{10}$ studying math. Write an equivalent decimal for the amount of time that she spent on each activity. Round to the nearest hundredth, if necessary.

  b. For each activity, Mary earned the same fraction of her allowance as the time spent on a particular activity. This week, she was paid $2.00 for studying Spanish. Was this the correct amount? Explain how you know.

  c. Order the amount of time that Mary spent practicing each activity from least to greatest.

  d. Next week Mary plans to spend 0.45 of her time studying math. Write this amount as a fraction in simplest form.

CHAPTER 3
Applying Rational Numbers

Chapter Focus
- Add, subtract, multiply and divide rational numbers.
- Solve equations containing fractions.

Why Learn This?

By using operations with decimals, you can determine statistics for football players and teams.

Learn It Online
Chapter Project Online go.hrw.com,
keyword MS10 Ch3 Go

✓ Vocabulary

Choose the best term from the list to complete each sentence.

1. A(n) __?__ is a number that is written using the base-ten place value system.

2. An example of a(n) __?__ is $\frac{14}{5}$.

3. A(n) __?__ is a number that represents a part of a whole.

decimal

fraction

improper fraction

mixed number

simplest form

Complete these exercises to review the skills you will need for this chapter.

✓ Simplify Fractions

Write each fraction in simplest form.

4. $\frac{24}{40}$ 5. $\frac{64}{84}$ 6. $\frac{66}{78}$ 7. $\frac{64}{192}$

8. $\frac{21}{35}$ 9. $\frac{11}{99}$ 10. $\frac{16}{36}$ 11. $\frac{20}{30}$

✓ Write Mixed Numbers as Fractions

Write each mixed number as an improper fraction.

12. $7\frac{1}{2}$ 13. $2\frac{5}{6}$ 14. $1\frac{14}{15}$ 15. $3\frac{2}{11}$

16. $3\frac{7}{8}$ 17. $8\frac{4}{9}$ 18. $4\frac{1}{7}$ 19. $5\frac{9}{10}$

✓ Write Fractions as Mixed Numbers

Write each improper fraction as a mixed number.

20. $\frac{23}{6}$ 21. $\frac{17}{3}$ 22. $\frac{29}{7}$ 23. $\frac{39}{4}$

24. $\frac{48}{5}$ 25. $\frac{82}{9}$ 26. $\frac{69}{4}$ 27. $\frac{35}{8}$

✓ Add, Subtract, Multiply, or Divide Integers

Find each sum, difference, product, or quotient.

28. $-11 + (-24)$ 29. $-11 - 7$ 30. $-4 \cdot (-10)$

31. $-22 \div (-11)$ 32. $23 + (-30)$ 33. $-33 - 74$

34. $-62 \cdot (-34)$ 35. $84 \div (-12)$ 36. $-26 - 18$

Study Guide: Preview

Where You've Been

Previously, you

- added, subtracted, multiplied, and divided whole numbers.
- used models to solve equations with whole numbers.

In This Chapter

You will study

- using models to represent multiplication and division situations involving fractions and decimals.
- using addition, subtraction, multiplication, and division to solve problems involving fractions and decimals.
- solving equations with rational numbers.

Where You're Going

You can use the skills learned in this chapter

- to estimate total cost when purchasing several items at the grocery store.
- to find measurements in fields such as carpentry.

Key Vocabulary/Vocabulario

compatible numbers	números compatibles
reciprocal	recíproco

Vocabulary Connections

To become familiar with some of the vocabulary terms in the chapter, consider the following. You may refer to the chapter, the glossary, or a dictionary if you like.

1. When two things are compatible, they make a good match. You can match a fraction with a number that is easier to work with, such as 1, $\frac{1}{2}$, or 0, by rounding up or down. How could you use these **compatible numbers** to estimate the sums and differences of fractions?

2. When fractions are **reciprocals** of each other, they have a special relationship. The fractions $\frac{3}{5}$ and $\frac{5}{3}$ are reciprocals of each other. What do you think the relationship between reciprocals is?

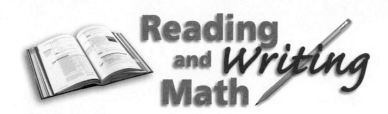

Reading and Writing Math

TN **English/Language Arts**
✓ **0701.4.2** Take and organize notes on what is known and what needs to be researched about the topic.

Study Strategy: Use Your Notes Effectively

Taking notes helps you understand and remember information from your textbook and lessons in class. Listed below are some steps for effectively using your notes before and after class.

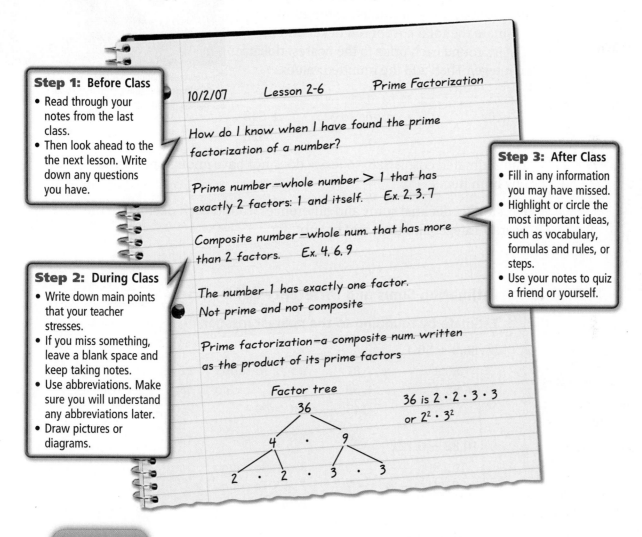

Step 1: Before Class
- Read through your notes from the last class.
- Then look ahead to the the next lesson. Write down any questions you have.

Step 2: During Class
- Write down main points that your teacher stresses.
- If you miss something, leave a blank space and keep taking notes.
- Use abbreviations. Make sure you will understand any abbreviations later.
- Draw pictures or diagrams.

Step 3: After Class
- Fill in any information you may have missed.
- Highlight or circle the most important ideas, such as vocabulary, formulas and rules, or steps.
- Use your notes to quiz a friend or yourself.

10/2/07 Lesson 2-6 Prime Factorization

How do I know when I have found the prime factorization of a number?

Prime number – whole number > 1 that has exactly 2 factors: 1 and itself. Ex. 2, 3, 7

Composite number – whole num. that has more than 2 factors. Ex. 4, 6, 9

The number 1 has exactly one factor. Not prime and not composite

Prime factorization – a composite num. written as the product of its prime factors

Factor tree
36
4 · 9
2 · 2 · 3 · 3

36 is $2 \cdot 2 \cdot 3 \cdot 3$ or $2^2 \cdot 3^2$

Try This

1. Look at the next lesson in your textbook. Think about how the new vocabulary terms relate to previous lessons. Write down any questions you have.

2. With a classmate, compare the notes you took during the last class. Are there differences in the main points that you each recorded? Then brainstorm two ways you can improve your note-taking skills.

Estimating with Decimals

TN GLE 0706.1.2 Apply and adapt a variety of appropriate strategies to problem solving, including estimation, and reasonableness of the solution. *Also* ✓ 0706.1.2, SPI 0706.2.3

Vocabulary
compatible numbers

Jessie earned $26.00 for baby-sitting. She wants to use the money to buy a ticket to an aquarium for $14.75 and a souvenir T-shirt for $13.20.

To find out if Jessie has enough money to buy both items, you can use estimation. To estimate the total cost of the ticket and the T-shirt, round each price to the nearest dollar, or integer. Then add the rounded values.

The Georgia Aquarium in Atlanta, GA, is the world's largest aquarium, with more than 8.1 million gallons of water.

$14.75	*7 > 5, so round to $15.*	$15
$13.20	*2 < 5, so round to $13.*	+ $13
		$28

The estimated cost is $28, so Jessie does not have enough money to buy both items.

To estimate decimal sums and differences, round each decimal to the nearest integer and then add or subtract.

EXAMPLE 1

Estimating Sums and Differences of Decimals

Estimate by rounding to the nearest integer.

A 86.9 + 58.4

86.9	⟶	87	*9 > 5, so round to 87.*
+ 58.4	⟶	+ 58	*4 < 5, so round to 58.*
		145	⟵ *Estimate*

B 10.38 − 6.721

10.38	⟶	10	*3 < 5, so round to 10.*
− 6.721	⟶	− 7	*7 > 5, so round to 7.*
		3	⟵ *Estimate*

C −26.3 + 15.195

−26.3	⟶	−26	*3 < 5, so round to −26.*
+ 15.195	⟶	+ 15	*1 < 5, so round to 15.*
		−11	⟵ *Estimate*

> **Remember!**
>
> To round to the nearest integer, look at the digit in the tenths place. If it is greater than or equal to 5, round to the next integer. If it is less than 5, keep the same integer. See Skills Bank p. SB1.

You can use *compatible numbers* when estimating. **Compatible numbers** are numbers that are close to the given numbers that make estimation easier.

[Video] **Lesson Tutorials Online** my.hrw.com

Guidelines for Using Compatible Numbers	
When multiplying . . .	**When dividing . . .**
round numbers to the nearest nonzero integer or to numbers that are easy to multiply.	round numbers so that they divide without leaving a remainder.

EXAMPLE 2 **Estimating Products and Quotients of Decimals**

Use compatible numbers to estimate.

A $32.66 \cdot 7.69$

$$
\begin{array}{rcl}
32.66 & \longrightarrow & 30 \\
\times\ 7.69 & \longrightarrow & \times\ 8 \\
\hline
 & & 240
\end{array}
$$

Round to the nearest multiple of 10.
6 > 5, so round to 8.
← *Estimate*

> **Remember!**
>
> A prime number has exactly two factors, 1 and itself. So the factors of 37 are 1 and 37.

B $36.5 \div (-8.241)$

$$
\begin{array}{rcl}
36.5 & \longrightarrow & 36 \\
-8.241 & \longrightarrow & -9 \\
\end{array}
$$
$$36 \div (-9) = -4$$

37 is a prime number, so round to 36.
−9 divides into 36 without a remainder.
← *Estimate*

When you solve problems, using an estimate can help you decide whether your answer is reasonable.

EXAMPLE 3 *School Application*

On a math test, a student worked the problem 6.2$\overline{)55.9}$ and got the answer 0.9. Use estimation to check whether the answer is reasonable.

$$
\begin{array}{rcl}
6.2 & \longrightarrow & 6 \\
55.9 & \longrightarrow & 60 \\
\end{array}
$$
$$60 \div 6 = 10$$

2 < 5, so round to 6.
6 divides into 60 without a remainder.
← *Estimate*

The estimate is more than ten times the student's answer, so 0.9 is not a reasonable answer.

> **Think and Discuss**
>
> **1. Explain** whether your estimate will be greater than or less than the actual answer when you round both numbers down in an addition or multiplication problem.
>
> **2. Describe** a situation in which you would want your estimate to be greater than the actual amount.

Exercises

GUIDED PRACTICE

See Example **1**   **Estimate by rounding to the nearest integer.**

1. $37.2 + 25.83$ **2.** $18.256 - 5.71$ **3.** $-9.916 + 12.4$

See Example **2**   **Use compatible numbers to estimate.**

4. $8.09 \cdot 28.32$ **5.** $-3.45 \cdot 73.6$ **6.** $41.9 \div 6.391$

See Example **3**   **7. School** A student worked the problem $35.8 \cdot 9.3$. The student's answer was 3,329.4. Use estimation to check whether this answer is reasonable.

INDEPENDENT PRACTICE

See Example **1**   **Estimate by rounding to the nearest integer.**

8. $5.982 + 37.1$ **9.** $68.2 + 23.67$ **10.** $-36.8 + 14.217$

11. $15.23 - 6.835$ **12.** $6.88 + (-8.1)$ **13.** $80.38 - 24.592$

See Example **2**   **Use compatible numbers to estimate.**

14. $51.38 \cdot 4.33$ **15.** $46.72 \div 9.24$ **16.** $32.91 \cdot 6.28$

17. $-3.45 \cdot 43.91$ **18.** $2.81 \cdot (-79.2)$ **19.** $28.22 \div 3.156$

See Example **3**   **20.** Ann has a piece of rope that is 12.35 m long. She wants to cut it into smaller pieces that are each 3.6 m long. She thinks she will get about 3 smaller pieces of rope. Use estimation to check whether her assumption is reasonable.

PRACTICE AND PROBLEM SOLVING

Extra Practice
See page EP8.

Estimate.

21. $5.921 - 13.2$ **22.** $-7.98 - 8.1$ **23.** $-42.25 + (-17.091)$

24. $98.6 + 43.921$ **25.** $4.69 \cdot (-18.33)$ **26.** $62.84 - 35.169$

27. $-48.28 + 11.901$ **28.** $31.53 \div (-4.12)$ **29.** $35.9 - 24.71$

30. $69.7 - 7.81$ **31.** $-6.56 \cdot 14.2$ **32.** $4.513 + 72.45$

33. $-8.9 \cdot (-24.1)$ **34.** $6.92 \cdot (-3.714)$ **35.** $-78.3 \div (-6.25)$

36. Jo needs 10 lb of ground beef for a party. She has packages that weigh 4.23 lb and 5.09 lb. Does she have enough?

37. Consumer Math Ramón saves $8.35 each week. He wants to buy a video game that costs $61.95. For about how many weeks will Ramón have to save his money before he can buy the video game?

38. Multi-Step Tickets at a local movie theater cost $7.50 each. A large bucket of popcorn at the theater costs $4.19, and a large soda costs $3.74. Estimate the amount that 3 friends spent at the theater when they saw one movie, shared one large bucket of popcorn, and had one large soda each.

39. Transportation Kayla stopped for gasoline at a station that was charging $2.719 per gallon. If Kayla had $14.75 in cash, approximately how many gallons of gas could she buy?

40. Social Studies The circle graph shows the languages spoken in Canada.

a. Which language do approximately 60% of Canadians speak?

b. What is the approximate difference between the percent of people who speak English and the percent who speak French?

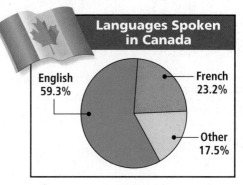

Languages Spoken in Canada

English 59.3%
French 23.2%
Other 17.5%

41. Astronomy Jupiter is 5.20 astronomical units (AU) from the Sun. Neptune is almost 6 times as far from the Sun as Jupiter is. Estimate Neptune's distance from the Sun in astronomical units.

42. Sports Scott must earn a total of 27 points to advance to the final round in an ice-skating competition. He earns scores of 5.9, 5.8, 6.0, 5.8, and 6.0. Scott estimates that his total score will allow him to advance. Is his estimate reasonable? Explain.

 43. Write a Problem Write a problem that can be solved by estimating with decimals.

 44. Write About It Explain how an estimate helps you decide whether an answer is reasonable.

 45. Challenge Estimate. $6.35 - 15.512 + 8.744 - 4.19 - 72.7 + 25.008$

Test Prep and Spiral Review

46. Multiple Choice Which is the best estimate for $24.976 \div (-4.893)$?

Ⓐ 20   Ⓑ −6   Ⓒ −5   Ⓓ 2

47. Multiple Choice Steve is saving $10.50 from his allowance each week to buy a printer that costs $150. Which is the best estimate of the number of weeks he will have to save his money until he can buy the printer?

Ⓕ 5 weeks   Ⓖ 10 weeks   Ⓗ 12 weeks   Ⓙ 15 weeks

48. Short Response Joe's restaurant bill was $16.84. He had $20 in his wallet. Explain how to use rounding to estimate whether Joe had enough money to leave a $2.75 tip.

Simplify each expression. (Lessons 2-3 and 2-4)

49. $-5 + 4 - 2$

50. $16 \cdot (-3) + 12$

51. $28 - (-2) \cdot (-3)$

52. $-90 - (-6) \cdot (-8)$

53. $-7 - 3 - 1$

54. $-10 \cdot (-5) + 2$

Adding and Subtracting Decimals

TN SPI 0706.2.1 Simplify numerical expressions involving rational numbers.
Also ✓ 0706.1.3, GLE 0706.2.2, SPI 0706.2.3

One of the coolest summers on record in the Midwest was in 1992. The average summertime temperature that year was 66.8 °F. Normally, the average temperature is 4 °F higher than it was in 1992.

To find the normal average summertime temperature in the Midwest, you can add 66.8 °F and 4 °F.

<u>Interactivities Online</u> ▶

$$\begin{array}{r} 66.8 \\ + 4.0 \\ \hline 70.8 \end{array}$$

Use zero as a placeholder so that both numbers have the same number of digits after their decimal points.

Add each column just as you would add integers.

Line up the decimal points.

The normal average summertime temperature in the Midwest is 70.8 °F.

EXAMPLE **Adding Decimals**

Add. Estimate to check whether each answer is reasonable.

A **3.62 + 18.57**

$$\begin{array}{r} 3.62 \\ + 18.57 \\ \hline 22.19 \end{array}$$

Line up the decimal points.

Add.

Estimate

4 + 19 = 23   *22.19 is a reasonable answer.*

B **9 + 3.245**

$$\begin{array}{r} 9.000 \\ + 3.245 \\ \hline 12.245 \end{array}$$

Use zeros as placeholders.
Line up the decimal points.
Add.

Estimate

9 + 3 = 12   *12.245 is a reasonable answer.*

Video **Lesson Tutorials Online** my.hrw.com

Add. Estimate to check whether each answer is reasonable.

C −5.78 + (−18.3)

$$-5.78 + (-18.3)$$

5.78	*Think: 5.78 + 18.3.*
+ 18.30	*Line up the decimal points.*
	Use zero as a placeholder.
24.08	*Add.*
−5.78 + (−18.3) = −24.08	*Use the sign of the two numbers.*

Estimate

−6 + (−18) = −24   *−24.08 is a reasonable answer.*

EXAMPLE 2

Subtracting Decimals

Subtract.

A 12.49 − 7.25

12.49	*Line up the decimal points.*
− 7.25	
5.24	*Subtract.*

Caution!

You will need to regroup numbers in order to subtract in Example 2B.

B 14 − 7.32

13 9 10	
1̶4̶.0̶0̶	*Use zeros as placeholders.*
− 7.32	*Line up the decimal points.*
6.68	*Subtract.*

EXAMPLE 3

Transportation Application

During one month in the United States, 492.23 million commuter trips were taken on buses, and 26.331 million commuter trips were taken on light rail. How many more trips were taken on buses than on light rail? Estimate to check whether your answer is reasonable.

492.230	*Use zero as a placeholder.*
− 26.331	*Line up the decimal points.*
465.899	*Subtract.*

Estimate

490 − 30 = 460   *465.899 is a reasonable answer.*

465.899 million more trips were taken on buses than on light rail.

Think and Discuss

1. **Tell** whether the addition is correct. If it is not, explain why not.

12.3
+ 4.68
5.91

2. **Describe** how you can check an answer when adding and subtracting decimals.

Exercises

Learn It Online
Homework Help Online **go.hrw.com,**
keyword MS10 3-2 Go
Exercises 1–27, 29, 31, 33, 35, 37, 39, 43

GUIDED PRACTICE

See Example **1**   **Add. Estimate to check whether each answer is reasonable.**

1. $5.37 + 16.45$ **2.** $2.46 + 11.99$ **3.** $7 + 5.826$ **4.** $-5.62 + (-12.9)$

See Example **2**   **Subtract.**

5. $7.89 - 5.91$ **6.** $17 - 4.12$ **7.** $4.97 - 3.2$ **8.** $9 - 1.03$

See Example **3**   **9.** In 1990, international visitors to the United States spent $58.3 billion. In 1999, international visitors spent $95.5 billion. By how much did spending by international visitors increase from 1990 to 1999?

INDEPENDENT PRACTICE

See Example **1**   **Add. Estimate to check whether each answer is reasonable.**

10. $7.82 + 31.23$ **11.** $5.98 + 12.99$ **12.** $4.917 + 12$ **13.** $-9.82 + (-15.7)$

14. $6 + 9.33$ **15.** $10.022 + 0.11$ **16.** $8 + 1.071$ **17.** $-3.29 + (-12.6)$

See Example **2**   **Subtract.**

18. $5.45 - 3.21$ **19.** $12.87 - 3.86$ **20.** $15.39 - 2.6$ **21.** $21.04 - 4.99$

22. $5 - 0.53$ **23.** $14 - 8.9$ **24.** $41 - 9.85$ **25.** $33 - 10.23$

See Example **3**   **26.** Angela runs her first lap around the track in 4.35 minutes and her second lap in 3.9 minutes. What is her total time for the two laps?

27. A jeweler has 122.83 grams of silver. He uses 45.7 grams of the silver to make a necklace and earrings. How much silver does he have left?

PRACTICE AND PROBLEM SOLVING

Extra Practice
See page EP8.

Add or subtract. Estimate to check whether each answer is reasonable.

28. $-7.238 + 6.9$ **29.** $4.16 - 9.043$ **30.** $-2.09 - 15.271$

31. $5.23 - (-9.1)$ **32.** $-123 - 2.55$ **33.** $5.29 - 3.37$

34. $32.6 - (-15.86)$ **35.** $-32.7 + 62.82$ **36.** $-51 + 81.623$

37. $5.9 - 10 + 2.84$ **38.** $-4.2 + 2.3 - 0.7$ **39.** $-8.3 + 5.38 - 0.537$

40. Multi-Step Students at Hill Middle School plan to run a total of 2,462 mi, which is the distance from Los Angeles to New York City. So far, the sixth grade has run 273.5 mi, the seventh grade has run 275.8 mi, and the eighth grade has run 270.2 mi. How many more miles must the students run to reach their goal?

41. Critical Thinking Why must you line up the decimal points when adding and subtracting decimals?

Weather The graph shows the five coolest summers recorded in the Midwest. The average summertime temperature in the Midwest is 70.8 °F.

42. How much warmer was the average summertime temperature in 1950 than in 1915?

43. In what year was the temperature 4.4 °F cooler than the average summertime temperature in the Midwest?

Egg-drop competitions challenge students to build devices that will protect eggs when they are dropped from as high as 100 ft.

44. **Physical Science** To float in water, an object must have a density of less than 1 gram per milliliter. The density of a fresh egg is about 1.2 grams per milliliter. If the density of a spoiled egg is about 0.3 grams per milliliter less than that of a fresh egg, what is the density of a spoiled egg? How can you use water to tell whether an egg is spoiled?

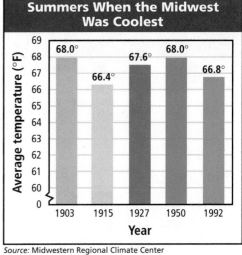

Summers When the Midwest Was Coolest

68.0° (1903)   66.4° (1915)   67.6° (1927)   68.0° (1950)   66.8° (1992)

Source: Midwestern Regional Climate Center

45. **Choose a Strategy** How much larger in area is Agua Fria than Pompeys Pillar?

  Ⓐ 6.6 thousand acres

  Ⓑ 20.1 thousand acres

  Ⓒ 70.59 thousand acres

  Ⓓ 71.049 thousand acres

National Monument	Area (thousand acres)
Agua Fria	71.1
Pompeys Pillar	0.051

46. **Write About It** Explain how to find the sum or difference of two decimals.

47. **Challenge** Find the missing number. $5.11 + 6.9 - 15.3 + \blacksquare = 20$

Test Prep and Spiral Review

48. Multiple Choice In the 1900 Olympic Games, the 200-meter dash was won in 22.20 seconds. In 2000, the 200-meter dash was won in 20.09 seconds. How many seconds faster was the winning time in the 2000 Olympics?

  Ⓐ 1.10 seconds   Ⓑ 2.11 seconds   Ⓒ 2.29 seconds   Ⓓ 4.83 seconds

49. Multiple Choice John left school with $2.38. He found a quarter on his way home and then stopped to buy a banana for $0.89. How much money did he have when he got home?

  Ⓕ $1.24   Ⓖ $1.74   Ⓗ $3.02   Ⓙ $3.52

Solve each equation. Check your answer. (Lesson 2-5)

50. $x - 8 = -22$ **51.** $-3y = -45$ **52.** $\frac{z}{2} = -8$ **53.** $29 = -10 + p$

Estimate. (Lesson 3-1)

54. $15.85 \div 4.01$ **55.** $18.95 + 3.21$ **56.** $44.217 - 19.876$ **57.** $21.43 \cdot 1.57$

Model Decimal Multiplication

3-3

Use with Lesson 3-3

Learn It Online
Lab Resources Online **go.hrw.com**,
keyword MS10 Lab3 Go

TN **SPI 0706.2.1** Simplify numerical expressions involving rational numbers. *Also* **GLE 0706.1.4, GLE 0706.1.8, GLE 0706.2.2**

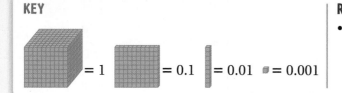

KEY

= 1   = 0.1   = 0.01   = 0.001

REMEMBER
- When using base-ten blocks, always use the largest value block possible.

You can use base-ten blocks to model multiplying decimals by whole numbers.

Activity 1

1 Use base-ten blocks to find $3 \cdot 0.1$.

Multiplication is repeated addition, so $3 \cdot 0.1 = 0.1 + 0.1 + 0.1$.

$$3 \cdot 0.1 = 0.3$$

2 Use base-ten blocks to find $5 \cdot 0.03$.

$$5 \cdot 0.03 = 0.03 + 0.03 + 0.03 + 0.03 + 0.03$$

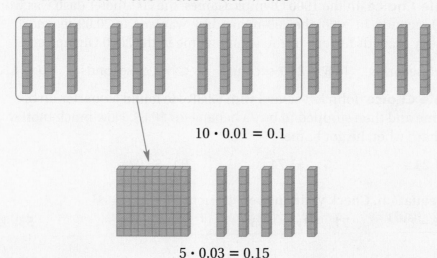

$$10 \cdot 0.01 = 0.1$$

$$5 \cdot 0.03 = 0.15$$

Think and Discuss

1. Why can't you use base-ten blocks to model multiplying a decimal by a decimal?

2. Is the product of a decimal between 0 and 1 and a whole number less than or greater than the whole number? Explain.

Try This

Use base-ten blocks to find each product.

1. 4 · 0.5   **2.** 2 · 0.04   **3.** 3 · 0.16   **4.** 6 · 0.2

5. 3 · 0.33   **6.** 0.25 · 5   **7.** 0.42 · 3   **8.** 1.1 · 4

You can use decimal grids to model multiplying decimals by decimals.

Activity 2

1 Use a decimal grid to find 0. 4 · 0.7.

| Shade 0.4 horizontally. | | Shade 0.7 vertically. | | The area where the shaded regions overlap is the answer. |

 × =

0.4   ×   0.7   =   0.28

Think and Discuss

1. Explain the steps you would take to model 0.5 · 0.5 with a decimal grid.

2. How could you use decimal grids to model multiplying a decimal by a whole number?

Try This

Use decimal grids to find each product.

1. 0.6 · 0.6   **2.** 0.5 · 0.4   **3.** 0.3 · 0.8

4. 0.2 · 0.8   **5.** 3 · 0.3   **6.** 0.8 · 0.8

7. 2 · 0.5   **8.** 0.1 · 0.9   **9.** 0.1 · 0.1

3-3 Multiplying Decimals

TN SPI 0706.2.1 Simplify numerical expressions involving rational numbers.
Also ✓ 0706.1.3, GLE 0706.2.2, SPI 0706.2.3

You can use decimal grids to model multiplication of decimals. Each large square represents 1. Each row and column represents 0.1. Each small square represents 0.01. The area where the shading overlaps shows the product of the two decimals.

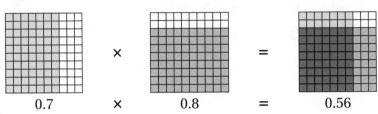

| 0.7 | × | 0.8 | = | 0.56 |

Interactivities Online ▶

To multiply decimals, multiply as you would with integers. To place the decimal point in the product, count the number of decimal places in each factor. The product should have the same number of decimal places as the sum of the decimal places in the factors.

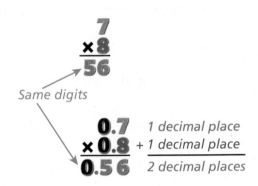

$$\begin{array}{r} 7 \\ \times\, 8 \\ \hline 56 \end{array}$$

Same digits

$$\begin{array}{r} 0.7 \\ \times\, 0.8 \\ \hline 0.56 \end{array}$$
1 decimal place
+ 1 decimal place
2 decimal places

EXAMPLE 1   Multiplying Integers by Decimals

Multiply.

A 6 · 0.1

$$\begin{array}{r} 6 \\ \times\, 0.1 \\ \hline 0.6 \end{array}$$

0 decimal places
1 decimal place
0 + 1 = 1 decimal place

B −2 · 0.04

$$\begin{array}{r} -2 \\ \times\, 0.04 \\ \hline -0.08 \end{array}$$

0 decimal places
2 decimal places
0 + 2 = 2 decimal places. Use zero as a placeholder.

C 1.25 · 23

$$\begin{array}{r} 1.25 \\ \times\, 23 \\ \hline 3\,75 \\ +\, 25\,00 \\ \hline 28.75 \end{array}$$

2 decimal places
0 decimal places

2 + 0 = 2 decimal places

EXAMPLE 2 Multiplying Decimals by Decimals

Multiply. Estimate to check whether each answer is reasonable.

A $1.2 \cdot 1.6$

$$
\begin{array}{rl}
1.2 & \text{1 decimal place} \\
\times\ 1.6 & \text{1 decimal place} \\
\hline
72 & \\
\underline{120} & \\
1.92 & \text{1 + 1 = 2 decimal places}
\end{array}
$$

Estimate

$1 \cdot 2 = 2$ *1.92 is a reasonable answer.*

B $-2.78 \cdot 0.8$

$$
\begin{array}{rl}
-2.78 & \text{2 decimal places} \\
\times\ 0.8 & \text{1 decimal place} \\
\hline
-2.224 & \text{2 + 1 = 3 decimal places}
\end{array}
$$

Estimate

$-3 \cdot 1 = -3$ *−2.224 is a reasonable answer.*

EXAMPLE 3 *Nutrition Application*

On average, Americans eat 0.25 lb of peanut butter per month. How many pounds of peanut butter are eaten by the approximately 302 million Americans living in the United States per month?

$$
\begin{array}{rl}
302 & \text{0 decimal places} \\
\times\ 0.25 & \text{2 decimal places} \\
\hline
1510 & \\
\underline{6040} & \\
75.50 & \text{0 + 2 = 2 decimal places}
\end{array}
$$

Estimate

$300 \cdot 0.3 = 90$ *75.50 is a reasonable answer.*

Approximately 75.50 million (75,500,000) pounds of peanut butter are eaten by Americans each month.

Think and Discuss

1. **Explain** whether the multiplication $2.1 \cdot 3.3 = 69.3$ is correct.

2. **Compare** multiplying integers with multiplying decimals.

3-3 Exercises

Learn It Online
Homework Help Online **go.hrw.com**,
keyword MS10 3-3 Go
Exercises 1–27, 31, 33, 37, 39, 41, 43, 47

GUIDED PRACTICE

See Example 1 **Multiply.**

1. $-9 \cdot 0.4$ **2.** $3 \cdot 0.2$ **3.** $0.06 \cdot 3$ **4.** $-0.5 \cdot 2$

See Example 2 **Multiply. Estimate to check whether each answer is reasonable.**

5. $1.7 \cdot 1.2$ **6.** $2.6 \cdot 0.4$ **7.** $1.5 \cdot (-0.21)$ **8.** $-0.4 \cdot 1.17$

See Example 3 **9.** If Carla is able to drive her car 24.03 miles on one gallon of gas, how far could she drive on 13.93 gallons of gas?

INDEPENDENT PRACTICE

See Example 1 **Multiply.**

10. $8 \cdot 0.6$ **11.** $5 \cdot 0.07$ **12.** $-3 \cdot 2.7$ **13.** $0.8 \cdot 4$

14. $6 \cdot 4.9$ **15.** $1.7 \cdot (-12)$ **16.** $43 \cdot 2.11$ **17.** $-7 \cdot (-1.3)$

See Example 2 **Multiply. Estimate to check whether each answer is reasonable.**

18. $2.4 \cdot 3.2$ **19.** $2.8 \cdot 1.6$ **20.** $5.3 \cdot 4.6$ **21.** $4.02 \cdot 0.7$

22. $-5.14 \cdot 0.03$ **23.** $1.04 \cdot (-8.9)$ **24.** $4.31 \cdot (-9.5)$ **25.** $-6.1 \cdot (-1.01)$

See Example 3 **26.** Nicholas bicycled 15.8 kilometers each day for 18 days last month. How many kilometers did he bicycle last month?

27. While walking, Lara averaged 3.63 miles per hour. How far did she walk in 1.5 hours?

PRACTICE AND PROBLEM SOLVING

Extra Practice
See page EP8.

Multiply. Estimate to check whether each answer is reasonable.

28. $-9.6 \cdot 2.05$ **29.** $0.07 \cdot 0.03$ **30.** $4 \cdot 4.15$

31. $-1.08 \cdot (-0.4)$ **32.** $1.46 \cdot (-0.06)$ **33.** $-3.2 \cdot 0.9$

34. $-325.9 \cdot 1.5$ **35.** $14.7 \cdot 0.13$ **36.** $-28.5 \cdot (-1.07)$

37. $-7.02 \cdot (-0.05)$ **38.** $1.104 \cdot (-0.7)$ **39.** $0.072 \cdot 0.12$

40. Multi-Step Bo earns $8.95 per hour plus commission. Last week, he worked 32.5 hours and earned $28.75 in commission. How much money did Bo earn last week?

41. Weather As a hurricane increases in intensity, the air pressure within its eye decreases. In a Category 5 hurricane, which is the most intense, the air pressure measures approximately 27.16 inches of mercury. In a Category 1 hurricane, which is the least intense, the air pressure is about 1.066 times that of a Category 5 hurricane. What is the air pressure within the eye of a Category 1 hurricane? Round your answer to the nearest hundredth.

42. Estimation The graph shows the results of a survey about river recreation activities.

a. A report claimed that about 3 times as many people enjoyed canoeing in 1999–2000 than in 1994–1995. According to the graph, is this claim reasonable?

b. Suppose a future survey shows that 6 times as many people enjoyed kayaking in 2016–2017 than in 1999–2000. About how many people reported that they enjoyed kayaking in 2016–2017?

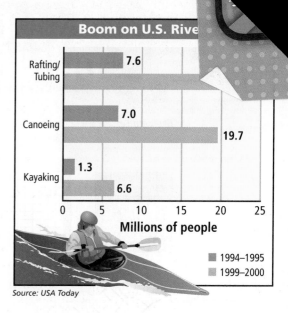

Boom on U.S. Rive

Rafting/Tubing 7.6

Canoeing 7.0 19.7

Kayaking 1.3 6.6

0 5 10 15 20 25
Millions of people

■ 1994–1995
■ 1999–2000

Source: USA Today

Multiply. Estimate to check whether each answer is reasonable.

43. $0.3 \cdot 2.8 \cdot (-10.6)$

44. $1.3 \cdot (-4.2) \cdot (-3.94)$

45. $0.6 \cdot (-0.9) \cdot 0.05$

46. $-6.5 \cdot (-1.02) \cdot (-12.6)$

47. $-22.08 \cdot (-5.6) \cdot 9.9$

48. $-63.75 \cdot 13.46 \cdot 7.8$

49. What's the Question? In a collection, each rock sample has a mass of 4.35 kilograms. There are a dozen rocks in the collection. If the answer is 52.2 kilograms, what is the question?

50. Write About It How do the products $4.3 \cdot 0.56$ and $0.43 \cdot 5.6$ compare? Explain.

51. Challenge Evaluate $(0.2)^5$.

Test Prep and Spiral Review

52. Multiple Choice Which expression is equal to -4.3?

Ⓐ $0.8 \cdot (-5.375)$　　Ⓑ $-1.2 \cdot (-3.6)$　　Ⓒ $-0.75 \cdot 5.6$　　Ⓓ $2.2 \cdot (-1.9)$

53. Gridded Response Julia walked 1.8 mi each day from Monday through Friday. On Saturday, she walked 2.3 mi. How many miles did she walk in all?

Write the prime factorization of each number. (Lesson 2-6)

54. 20　　　　**55.** 35　　　　**56.** 120　　　　**57.** 64

Add or subtract. Estimate to check whether each answer is reasonable. (Lesson 3-2)

58. $-4.875 + 3.62$　　**59.** $5.83 - (-2.74)$　　**60.** $6.32 + (-3.62)$　　**61.** $-8.34 - (-4.6)$

62. $9.3 + 5.88$　　**63.** $32.08 - 12.37$　　**64.** $19 - 6.92$　　**65.** $-75.25 + 6.382$

Model Decimal Division

Use with Lesson 3-4

Learn It Online
Lab Resources Online **go.hrw.com**,
keyword **MS10 Lab3** **Go**

TN **SPI 0706.2.1** Simplify numerical expressions involving rational numbers. *Also* **GLE 0706.1.4**

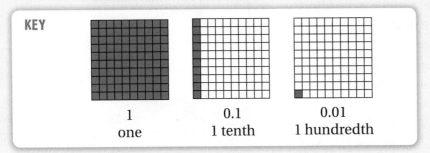

KEY

| 1 | 0.1 | 0.01 |
| one | 1 tenth | 1 hundredth |

You can use decimal grids to model dividing decimals by integers and by decimals.

Activity

1 Use a decimal grid to find 0.6 ÷ 2.

Shade 6 columns to represent 0.6.

Divide the 6 columns into 2 equal groups.

There are 3 columns, or 30 squares, in each group. 3 columns = 0.3

0.6 ÷ 2 = 0.3

2 Use decimal grids to find 2.25 ÷ 5.

Shade 2 grids and 25 squares of a third grid to represent 2.25.

Divide the grids and squares into 5 equal groups. Use scissors to cut apart the grids. Think: 225 squares ÷ 5 = 45 squares.

There are 45 squares, or 4.5 columns, in each group. 4.5 columns = 0.45

2.25 ÷ 5 = 0.45

3 Use decimal grids to find $0.8 \div 0.4$.

Shade 8 columns to represent 0.8.

Divide the 8 columns into groups that each contain 0.4 of a decimal grid, or 4 columns.

There are 2 groups that each contain 0.4 of a grid.
$0.8 \div 0.4 = 2$

4 Use decimal grids to find $3.9 \div 1.3$.

Shade 3 grids and 90 squares of a fourth grid to represent 3.9.

Divide the grids and squares into groups that each contain 1.3 of a decimal grid, or 13 columns.

There are 3 groups that each contain 1.3 grids.
$3.9 \div 1.3 = 3$

Think and Discuss

1. Explain why you think division is or is not commutative.

2. How is dividing a decimal by a whole number different from dividing a decimal by another decimal?

Try This

Use decimal grids to find each quotient.

1. $0.8 \div 4$ **2.** $0.6 \div 4$ **3.** $0.9 \div 0.3$ **4.** $0.6 \div 0.4$

5. $4.5 \div 9$ **6.** $1.35 \div 3$ **7.** $3.6 \div 1.2$ **8.** $4.2 \div 2.1$

TN ▶ **SPI 0706.2.1** Simplify numerical expressions involving rational numbers.
Also ✓ **0706.1.3, GLE 0706.2.2,** ✓ **0706.2.3, SPI 0706.2.3**

Sandy and her family traveled from Columbus, Ohio, to Chicago, Illinois, to visit Millennium Park. They used 14.95 gallons of gas for their 358.8-mile drive.

To find the number of miles per gallon the car got, you will need to divide a decimal by a decimal.

When you divide two numbers, you can multiply *both numbers* by the same power of ten without changing the final answer.

Multiply both 0.6 and 0.3 by 10: $0.6 \cdot 10 = 6$ and $0.3 \cdot 10 = 3$

$$0.6 \div 0.3 = 2 \quad \text{and} \quad 6 \div 3 = 2$$

By multiplying both numbers by the same power of ten, you can make the divisor an integer. Dividing by an integer is much easier than dividing by a decimal.

EXAMPLE 1 **Dividing Decimals by Decimals**

Divide.

Helpful Hint

Multiply both numbers by the least power of ten that will make the divisor an integer.

A $4.32 \div 3.6$

$4.32 \div 3.6 = 43.2 \div 36$

$$
\begin{array}{r}
1.2 \\
36\overline{)43.2} \\
-36 \\
\hline
7\,2 \\
-7\,2 \\
\hline
0
\end{array}
$$

Multiply both numbers by 10 to make the divisor an integer. Divide as with whole numbers.

B $12.95 \div (-1.25)$

$12.95 \div (-1.25) = 1295 \div (-125)$

$$
\begin{array}{r}
10.36 \\
125\overline{)1{,}295.00} \\
-1\,25 \\
\hline
45\,0 \\
-37\,5 \\
\hline
7\,50 \\
-7\,50 \\
\hline
0
\end{array}
$$

$12.95 \div (-1.25) = -10.36$

Multiply both numbers by 100 to make the divisor an integer.

Use zeros as placeholders. Divide as with whole numbers.

The signs are different.

EXAMPLE 2 **Dividing Integers by Decimals**

Divide. Estimate to check whether each answer is reasonable.

A $9 \div 1.25$

$9.00 \div 1.25 = 900 \div 125$

Multiply both numbers by 100 to make the divisor an integer.

$$
\begin{array}{r}
7.2 \\
125)\overline{900.0} \\
-875 \\
\hline
25\ 0 \\
-25\ 0 \\
\hline
0
\end{array}
$$

Use zero as a placeholder. Divide as with whole numbers.

Estimate $9 \div 1 = 9$

7.2 is a reasonable answer.

B $-12 \div (-1.6)$

$-12.0 \div (-1.6) = -120 \div (-16)$

Multiply both numbers by 10 to make the divisor an integer.

$$
\begin{array}{r}
7.5 \\
16)\overline{120.0} \\
-112 \\
\hline
8\ 0 \\
-8\ 0 \\
\hline
0
\end{array}
$$

Divide as with whole numbers.

$-12 \div (-1.6) = 7.5$

The signs are the same.

Estimate $-12 \div (-2) = 6$

7.5 is a reasonable answer.

EXAMPLE 3 *Transportation Application*

If Sandy and her family used 14.95 gallons of gas to drive 358.8 miles, how many miles per gallon did the car get?

$358.80 \div 14.95 = 35,880 \div 1,495$

Multiply both numbers by 100 to make the divisor an integer.

$$
\begin{array}{r}
24 \\
1,495)\overline{35,880} \\
-29\ 90 \\
\hline
5\ 980 \\
-5\ 980 \\
\hline
0
\end{array}
$$

Divide as with whole numbers.

Helpful Hint

To calculate miles per gallon, divide the number of miles driven by the number of gallons of gas used.

The car got 24 miles per gallon.

Think and Discuss

1. Explain whether $4.27 \div 0.7$ is the same as $427 \div 7$.

2. Explain how to divide an integer by a decimal.

Learn It Online
Homework Help Online **go.hrw.com**,
keyword **MS10 3-4** **Go**
Exercises 1–27, 31, 33, 35, 37, 39, 41

GUIDED PRACTICE

See Example **1** **Divide.**

1. $3.78 \div 4.2$

2. $13.3 \div (-0.38)$

3. $14.49 \div 3.15$

4. $1.06 \div 0.2$

5. $-9.76 \div 3.05$

6. $263.16 \div (-21.5)$

See Example **2** **Divide. Estimate to check whether each answer is reasonable.**

7. $3 \div 1.2$

8. $84 \div 2.4$

9. $36 \div (-2.25)$

10. $24 \div (-1.2)$

11. $-18 \div 3.75$

12. $189 \div 8.4$

See Example **3** **13. Transportation** Samuel used 14.35 gallons of gas to drive his car 401.8 miles. How many miles per gallon did he get?

INDEPENDENT PRACTICE

See Example **1** **Divide.**

14. $81.27 \div 0.03$

15. $-0.408 \div 3.4$

16. $38.5 \div (-5.5)$

17. $-1.12 \div 0.08$

18. $27.82 \div 2.6$

19. $14.7 \div 3.5$

See Example **2** **Divide. Estimate to check whether each answer is reasonable.**

20. $35 \div (-2.5)$

21. $361 \div 7.6$

22. $63 \div (-4.2)$

23. $5 \div 1.25$

24. $14 \div 2.5$

25. $-78 \div 1.6$

See Example **3** **26. Transportation** Lonnie used 26.75 gallons of gas to drive his truck 508.25 miles. How many miles per gallon did he get?

27. Mitchell walked 8.5 laps in 20.4 minutes. If he walked each lap at the same pace, how long did it take him to walk one full lap?

PRACTICE AND PROBLEM SOLVING

Extra Practice
See page EP8.

Divide. Estimate to check whether each answer is reasonable.

28. $-24 \div 0.32$

29. $153 \div 6.8$

30. $-2.58 \div (-4.3)$

31. $4.12 \div (-10.3)$

32. $-17.85 \div 17$

33. $64 \div 2.56$

Simplify each expression. Justify your steps using the Commutative, Associative, and Distributive Properties when neccessary.

34. $2^2 \cdot (6.8 \div 3.4) \cdot 5$

35. $11.7 \div (0.7 + 0.6) \cdot 2$

36. $4 \cdot 5(0.6 + 0.2) \cdot 0.25$

37. $(1.6 \div 3.2) \cdot (4.2 + 8.6)$

38. Critical Thinking A car loan totaling $13,456.44 is to be paid off in 36 equal monthly payments. Lin Yao can afford no more than $350 per month. Can she afford the loan? Explain.

39. Earth Science Glaciers form when snow accumulates faster than it melts and thus becomes compacted into ice under the weight of more snow. Once the ice reaches a thickness of about 18 m, it begins to flow. If ice were to accumulate at a rate of 0.0072 m per year, how long would it take to start flowing?

40. Critical Thinking Explain why using estimation to check the answer to $56.21457 \div 7$ is useful.

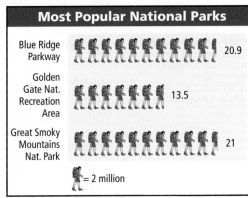

41. Recreation The graph shows the approximate number of total visits to the three most visited U.S. national parks in 2006. What was the average number of visits to these three parks? Round your answer to the nearest hundredth.

Source: National Park Service

42. Write a Problem Find some supermarket advertisements. Use the ads to write a problem that can be solved by dividing a decimal by a whole number.

43. Write About It Can you use the Commutative Property when dividing decimals? Explain.

44. Challenge Use a calculator to simplify the expression $(2^3 \cdot 7.5 + 3.69) \div 48.25 \div [1.04 - (0.08 \cdot 2)]$.

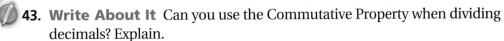

Test Prep and Spiral Review

45. Multiple Choice Which expression is NOT equal to -1.34?

Ⓐ $-6.7 \div 5$ Ⓑ $16.08 \div (-12)$ Ⓒ $-12.06 \div (-9)$ Ⓓ $-22.78 \div 17$

46. Multiple Choice A deli is selling 5 sandwiches for $5.55, including tax. A school spent $83.25 on roast beef sandwiches for its 25 football players. How many sandwiches did each player get?

Ⓕ 1 Ⓖ 2 Ⓗ 3 Ⓙ 5

47. Gridded Response Rujuta spent a total of $49.65 on 5 CDs. What was the average cost in dollars for each CD?

Simplify each expression. (Lesson 1-4)

48. $2 + 6 \cdot 2$

49. $3^2 - 8 \cdot 0$

50. $(2 - 1)^5 + 3 \cdot 2^2$

51. $10 - (5 - 3)^2 + 4 \div 2$

52. $2^5 \div (7 + 1)$

53. $6 - 2 \cdot 3 + 5$

Multiply. Estimate to check whether each answer is reasonable. (Lesson 3-3)

54. $-2.75 \cdot 6.34$

55. $0.2 \cdot (-4.6) \cdot (-2.3)$

56. $1.3 \cdot (-6.7)$

57. $-6.87 \cdot (-2.65)$

58. $9 \cdot 4.26$

59. $7.13 \cdot (-14)$

Solving Equations Containing Decimals

TN ✓ **0706.1.10** Model algebraic equations with manipulatives, technology, and pencil and paper.
Also **SPI 0706.2.3, GLE 0706.3.8, ✓ 0706.3.2**

Students in a physical education class were running 40-yard dashes as part of a fitness test. The slowest time in the class was 3.84 seconds slower than the fastest time of 7.2 seconds.

<u>Interactivities Online</u> ▶

You can write an equation to represent this situation. The slowest time *s* minus 3.84 is equal to the fastest time of 7.2 seconds.

$$s - 3.84 = 7.2$$

EXAMPLE 1 Solving Equations by Adding or Subtracting

Solve. Justify your steps.

Remember!

You can solve an equation by performing the same operation on both sides of the equation to isolate the variable.

A $s - 3.84 = 7.2$

$$
\begin{array}{rl}
s - 3.84 = & 7.20 \\
\underline{+\ 3.84} & \underline{+\ 3.84} \\
s = & 11.04
\end{array}
$$

Use the Addition Property of Equality.
Add 3.84 to both sides.

B $y + 20.51 = 26$

$$
\begin{array}{rl}
y + 20.51 = & 26.\overset{5\ \ 9\ 10}{\cancel{00}} \\
\underline{-\ 20.51} & \underline{-\ 20.51} \\
y = & 5.49
\end{array}
$$

Use the Subtraction Property of Equality.
Subtract 20.51 from both sides.

EXAMPLE 2 Solving Equations by Multiplying or Dividing

Solve. Justify your steps.

A $\dfrac{w}{3.9} = 1.2$

$$\frac{w}{3.9} = 1.2$$

$$\frac{w}{3.9} \cdot 3.9 = 1.2 \cdot 3.9$$

$$w = 4.68$$

Use the Multiplication Property of Equality.
Multiply by 3.9 on both sides.

B $4 = 1.6c$

$$4 = 1.6c$$

$$\frac{4}{1.6} = \frac{1.6c}{1.6}$$

$$\frac{4}{1.6} = c$$

$$2.5 = c$$

Use the Division Property of Equality.
Divide by 1.6 on both sides.

Think: 4 ÷ 1.6 = 40 ÷ 16.

Video **Lesson Tutorials Online** my.hrw.com

EXAMPLE 3

PROBLEM SOLVING

...VING APPLICATION

Yanc... ...buy a new snowboard that costs $396.00. If she earns $... ...ur at work, how many hours must she work to earn enou... ...y to buy the snowboard?

 Understand ...blem

Rewrite the questi... ...statement.
- Find the number ... ...rs Yancey must work to earn $396.00.

List the **important information**:
- Yancey earns $8.25 per hour.
- Yancey needs $396.00 to buy a snowboard.

 Make a Plan

Yancey's pay is equal to her hourly pay times the number of hours she works. Since you know how much money she needs to earn, you can write an equation with h being the number of hours.

$$8.25h = 396$$

 Solve

$$8.25h = 396$$

$$\frac{8.25h}{8.25} = \frac{396}{8.25}$$ *Use the Division Property of Equality.*

$$h = 48$$

Yancey must work 48 hours.

4 Look Back

You can round 8.25 to 8 and 396 to 400 to estimate how many hours Yancey needs to work.

$$400 \div 8 = 50$$

So 48 hours is a reasonable answer.

Think and Discuss

1. Describe how to solve the equation $-1.25 + x = 1.25$. Then solve.

2. Explain how you can tell if 1.01 is a solution of $10s = -10.1$ without solving the equation.

Learn It Online
Homework Help Online **go.hrw.com,**
keyword MS10 3-5 Go
Exercises 1–23, 29, 33, 35, 39,
41, 43, 45

GUIDED PRACTICE

See Example 1 | Solve. Justify your steps.

1. $w - 5.8 = 1.2$ **2.** $x + 9.15 = 17$

3. $k + 3.91 = 28$ **4.** $n - 1.35 = 19.9$

See Example 2 | **5.** $\frac{b}{1.4} = 3.6$ **6.** $\frac{x}{0.8} = 7.2$

7. $3.1t = 27.9$ **8.** $7.5 = 5y$

See Example 3 | **9. Consumer Math** Jeff bought a sandwich and a salad for lunch. His total bill was \$7.10. The salad cost \$2.85. How much did the sandwich cost?

INDEPENDENT PRACTICE

See Example 1 | Solve. Justify your steps.

10. $v + 0.84 = 6$ **11.** $c - 32.56 = 12$ **12.** $d - 14.25 = -23.9$

13. $3.52 + a = 8.6$ **14.** $w - 9.01 = 12.6$ **15.** $p + 30.34 = -22.87$

See Example 2 | **16.** $3.2c = 8$ **17.** $72 = 4.5z$ **18.** $21.8x = -124.26$

19. $\frac{w}{2.8} = 4.2$ **20.** $\frac{m}{0.19} = 12$ **21.** $\frac{a}{21.23} = -3.5$

See Example 3 | **22.** At the fair, 25 food tickets cost \$31.25. What is the cost of each ticket?

23. To climb the rock wall at the fair, you must have 5 ride tickets. If each ticket costs \$1.50, how much does it cost to climb the rock wall?

PRACTICE AND PROBLEM SOLVING

Extra Practice
See page EP9.

Solve. Justify your steps.

24. $1.2y = -1.44$ **25.** $\frac{n}{8.2} = -0.6$ **26.** $w - 4.1 = -5$

27. $r + 0.48 = 1.2$ **28.** $x - 5.2 = -7.3$ **29.** $1.05 = -7m$

30. $a + 0.81 = -6.3$ **31.** $60k = 54$ **32.** $\frac{h}{-7.1} = 0.62$

33. $\frac{t}{-0.18} = -5.2$ **34.** $7.9 = d + 12.7$ **35.** $-1.8 + v = -3.8$

36. $-k = 287.658$ **37.** $-n = -12.254$ **38.** $0.64f = 12.8$

39. $15.217 - j = 4.11$ **40.** $-2.1 = p + (-9.3)$ **41.** $\frac{27.3}{g} = 54.6$

42. The Drama Club at Smith Valley Middle School is selling cookie dough in order to raise money for costumes. If each tub of cookie dough costs \$4.75, how many tubs must members sell to make \$570.00?

43. Consumer Math Gregory bought a computer desk at a thrift store for \$38. The regular price of a similar desk at a furniture store is 4.5 times as much. What is the regular price of the desk at the furniture store?

44. **Physical Science** Pennies minted, or created, before 1982 are made mostly of copper and have a density of 8.85 g/cm^3. Because of an increase in the cost of copper, the density of pennies made after 1982 is 1.71 g/cm^3 less. What is the density of pennies minted today?

45. **Social Studies** The table shows the most common European ancestral origins of Americans (in millions), according to a Census 2000 supplementary survey. In addition, 19.6 million people stated that their ancestry was "American."

Ancestral Origins of Americans	
European Ancestry	**Number (millions)**
English	28.3
French	9.8
German	46.5
Irish	33.1
Italian	15.9
Polish	9.1
Scottish	5.4

a. How many people claimed ancestry from the countries listed, according to the survey?

b. If the data were placed in order from greatest to least, between which two nationalities would "American" ancestry be placed?

46. **What's the Error?** A student's solution to the equation $m + 0.63 = 5$ was $m = 5.63$. What is the error? What is the correct solution?

47. **Write About It** Compare the process of solving equations containing integers with the process of solving equations containing decimals.

48. **Challenge** Solve the equation $-2.8 + (b - 1.7) = -0.6 \cdot 9.4$.

Test Prep and Spiral Review

49. **Multiple Choice** What is the solution to the equation $-4.55 + x = 6.32$?

   Ⓐ $x = -1.39$ Ⓑ $x = 1.77$ Ⓒ $x = 10.87$ Ⓓ $x = 28.76$

50. **Multiple Choice** The pep squad is selling tickets for a raffle. The tickets are $0.25 each or 5 for $1.00. Julie bought a pack of 5 tickets. Which equation can be used to find how much Julie paid per ticket?

   Ⓕ $5x = 0.25$ Ⓖ $0.25x = 1.00$ Ⓗ $5x = 1.00$ Ⓙ $1.00x = 0.25$

51. **Extended Response** Write a word problem that the equation $6.25x = 125$ can be used to solve. Solve the problem and explain what the solution means.

Write each number in scientific notation. (Lesson 1-3)

52. 340,000   53. 6,000,000   54. $32.4 \cdot 10^2$

Simplify each expression. (Lesson 3-4)

55. $6.3 \div 2.1 - 1.5$ 56. $4 \cdot 5.1 \div 2 + 3.6$ 57. $(1.6 + 3.8) \div 1.8$

58. $(-5.4 + 3.6) \div 0.9$ 59. $-4.5 \div 0.6 \cdot (-1.2)$ 60. $5.8 + 3.2 \div (-6.4)$

Ready To Go On?

Learn It Online
Resources Online **go.hrw.com,**
keyword **MS10 RTGO3A** Go

Quiz for Lessons 3-1 Through 3-5

3-1 Estimating with Decimals

Estimate.

1. $163.2 \cdot 5.4$ **2.** $37.19 + 100.94$ **3.** $376.82 - 139.28$ **4.** $33.19 \div 8.18$

5. Brad worked the homework problem 119.67 m $\div 10.43$ m. His answer was 11.47 m. Use estimation to check whether this answer is reasonable.

3-2 Adding and Subtracting Decimals

Add or subtract.

6. $4.73 + 29.68$ **7.** $-6.89 - (-29.4)$ **8.** $23.58 - 8.36$ **9.** $-15 + (-9.44)$

3-3 Multiplying Decimals

Multiply.

10. $3.4 \cdot 9.6$ **11.** $-2.66 \cdot 0.9$ **12.** $-7 \cdot (-0.06)$ **13.** $6.94 \cdot (-24)$

14. Cami can run 7.02 miles per hour. How many miles can she run in 1.75 hours? Round your answer to the nearest hundredth.

3-4 Dividing Decimals

Divide.

15. $55 \div 12.5$ **16.** $-126.45 \div (-4.5)$ **17.** $-3.3 \div 0.11$ **18.** $-36 \div (-0.9)$

19. $10.4 \div (-0.8)$ **20.** $18 \div 2.4$ **21.** $-45.6 \div 12$ **22.** $-99.36 \div (-4)$

23. Cynthia ran 17.5 laps in 38.5 minutes. If she ran each lap at the same pace, how long did it take her to run one full lap?

24. A jewelry store sold a 7.4-gram gold necklace for $\$162.18$. How much was the necklace worth per gram? Round your answer to the nearest tenth.

3-5 Solving Equations Containing Decimals

Solve.

25. $3.4 + n = 8$ **26.** $x - 1.75 = -19$ **27.** $-3.5 = -5x$ **28.** $10.1 = \frac{s}{8}$

29. Pablo earns $\$5.50$ per hour. His friend Raymond earns 1.2 times as much. How much does Raymond earn per hour?

Focus on Problem Solving

Look Back

- **Does your solution answer the question in the problem?**

Sometimes, before you solve a problem, you first need to use the given data to find additional information. Any time you find a solution for a problem, you should ask yourself if your solution answers the question being asked, or if it just gives you the information you need to find the final answer.

Read each problem, and determine whether the given solution answers the question in the problem. Explain your answer.

1 At one store, a new CD costs $15.99. At a second store, the same CD costs 0.75 as much. About how much does the second store charge?

Solution: The second store charges about $12.00.

2 Bobbie is 1.4 feet shorter than her older sister. If Bobbie's sister is 5.5 feet tall, how tall is Bobbie?

Solution:
Bobbie is 4.1 feet tall.

3 Juanita ran the 100-yard dash 1.12 seconds faster than Kellie. Kellie's time was 0.8 seconds faster than Rachel's. If Rachel's time was 15.3 seconds, what was Juanita's time?

Solution: Kellie's time was 14.5 seconds.

4 The playscape at a local park is located in a triangular sandpit. Side A of the sandpit is 2 meters longer than side B. Side B is twice as long as side C. If side C is 6 meters long, how long is side A?

Solution: Side B is 12 meters long.

5 Both Tyrone and Albert walk to and from school every day. Albert has to walk 1.25 miles farther than Tyrone does each way. If Tyrone's house is 0.6 mi from school, how far do the two boys walk altogether?

Solution: Albert lives 1.85 mi from school.

Estimating with Fractions

TN GLE 0706.1.2 Apply and adapt a variety of appropriate strategies to problem solving, including estimation, and reasonableness of the solution. *Also* SPI 0706.2.3

One of the largest cheese wheels ever produced was made in Alkmaar, Netherlands, and weighed about $1{,}250\frac{1}{50}$ lb. About how much heavier was this than the average cheese wheel, which may weigh about 6 lb?

Sometimes, when solving problems, you may not need an exact answer. To estimate sums and differences of fractions and mixed numbers, round each fraction to 0, $\frac{1}{2}$, or 1. You can use a number line to help.

Interactivities Online ▶

$\frac{2}{5}$ is closer to $\frac{1}{2}$ than to 0.

You can also round fractions by comparing numerators with denominators.

Benchmarks for Rounding Fractions		
Round to **0** if the numerator is much smaller than the denominator.	Round to $\frac{1}{2}$ if the numerator is about half the denominator.	Round to **1** if the numerator is nearly equal to the denominator.
Examples: $\frac{1}{9}, \frac{3}{20}, \frac{2}{11}$	Examples: $\frac{2}{5}, \frac{5}{12}, \frac{7}{13}$	Examples: $\frac{8}{9}, \frac{23}{25}, \frac{97}{100}$

EXAMPLE 1 *Measurement Application*

One of the largest wheels of cheese ever made weighed about $1{,}250\frac{1}{50}$ lb. Estimate how much more this wheel of cheese weighed than an average 6 lb wheel.

$1{,}250\frac{1}{50} - 6$

$1{,}250\frac{1}{50} \longrightarrow 1{,}250$ *Round the mixed number.*

$1{,}250 - 6 = 1{,}244$ *Subtract.*

The cheese wheel weighed about 1,244 lb more than an average cheese wheel.

    Video **Lesson Tutorials Online** my.hrw.com

EXAMPLE **2** **Estimating Sums and Differences**

Estimate each sum or difference.

A $\frac{4}{7} - \frac{13}{16}$

$\frac{4}{7} \longrightarrow \frac{1}{2}$ $\frac{13}{16} \longrightarrow 1$ *Round each fraction.*

$\frac{1}{2} - 1 = -\frac{1}{2}$ *Subtract.*

Helpful Hint

Round $\frac{1}{3}$ to $\frac{1}{2}$ since it is closer to $\frac{1}{2}$ than 0.

B $3\frac{3}{8} + 3\frac{1}{3}$

$3\frac{3}{8} \longrightarrow 3\frac{1}{2}$ $3\frac{1}{3} \longrightarrow 3\frac{1}{2}$ *Round each mixed number.*

$3\frac{1}{2} + 3\frac{1}{2} = 7$ *Add.*

C $5\frac{7}{8} + \left(-\frac{2}{5}\right)$

$5\frac{7}{8} \longrightarrow 6$ $-\frac{2}{5} \longrightarrow -\frac{1}{2}$ *Round each number.*

$6 + \left(-\frac{1}{2}\right) = 5\frac{1}{2}$ *Add.*

You can estimate products and quotients of mixed numbers by rounding to the nearest whole number. If the fraction in a mixed number is greater than or equal to $\frac{1}{2}$, round the mixed number up to the next whole number. If the fraction is less than $\frac{1}{2}$, round down to a whole number by dropping the fraction.

EXAMPLE **3** **Estimating Products and Quotients**

Estimate each product or quotient.

A $4\frac{2}{7} \cdot 6\frac{9}{10}$

$4\frac{2}{7} \longrightarrow 4$ $6\frac{9}{10} \longrightarrow 7$ *Round each mixed number to the nearest whole number.*

$4 \cdot 7 = 28$ *Multiply.*

B $11\frac{3}{4} \div 2\frac{1}{5}$

$11\frac{3}{4} \longrightarrow 12$ $2\frac{1}{5} \longrightarrow 2$ *Round each mixed number to the nearest whole number.*

$12 \div 2 = 6$ *Divide.*

Think and Discuss

1. Demonstrate how to round $\frac{5}{12}$ and $5\frac{1}{5}$.

2. Explain how you know that $25\frac{5}{8} \cdot 5\frac{1}{10} > 125$.

3-6 **Exercises**

Learn It Online
Homework Help Online **go.hrw.com**,
keyword MS10 3-6 Go
Exercises 1–26, 27, 29, 31, 35,
37, 39, 43

GUIDED PRACTICE

See Example 1   **1.** The length of a large SUV is $18\frac{9}{10}$ feet, and the length of a small SUV is $15\frac{1}{8}$ feet. Estimate how much longer the large SUV is than the small SUV.

See Example 2   **Estimate each sum or difference.**

2. $\frac{5}{6} + \frac{5}{12}$ **3.** $\frac{15}{16} - \frac{4}{5}$ **4.** $2\frac{1}{6} + 3\frac{6}{11}$ **5.** $5\frac{2}{7} - 2\frac{7}{9}$

See Example 3   **Estimate each product or quotient.**

6. $1\frac{3}{25} \cdot 9\frac{6}{7}$ **7.** $21\frac{2}{7} \div 7\frac{1}{3}$ **8.** $31\frac{7}{8} \div 4\frac{1}{5}$ **9.** $12\frac{2}{5} \cdot 3\frac{6}{9}$

INDEPENDENT PRACTICE

See Example 1   **10. Measurement** Sarah's bedroom is $14\frac{5}{6}$ feet long and $12\frac{1}{4}$ feet wide. Estimate the difference between the length and width of Sarah's bedroom.

See Example 2   **Estimate each sum or difference.**

11. $\frac{4}{9} + \frac{3}{5}$ **12.** $2\frac{5}{9} + 1\frac{7}{8}$ **13.** $8\frac{3}{4} - 6\frac{2}{5}$ **14.** $6\frac{1}{3} + \left(-\frac{5}{6}\right)$

15. $\frac{7}{8} - \frac{2}{5}$ **16.** $15\frac{1}{7} - 10\frac{8}{9}$ **17.** $8\frac{7}{15} + 2\frac{7}{8}$ **18.** $\frac{4}{5} + 7\frac{1}{8}$

See Example 3   **Estimate each product or quotient.**

19. $23\frac{5}{7} \div 3\frac{6}{9}$ **20.** $10\frac{2}{5} \div 4\frac{5}{8}$ **21.** $2\frac{1}{8} \cdot 14\frac{5}{6}$ **22.** $7\frac{9}{10} \cdot 11\frac{3}{4}$

23. $5\frac{3}{5} \div 2\frac{2}{3}$ **24.** $12\frac{4}{6} \cdot 3\frac{2}{7}$ **25.** $8\frac{1}{4} \div 1\frac{7}{8}$ **26.** $15\frac{12}{15} \cdot 1\frac{5}{7}$

PRACTICE AND PROBLEM SOLVING

Extra Practice
See page EP9.

Estimate each sum, difference, product, or quotient.

27. $\frac{7}{9} - \frac{3}{8}$ **28.** $\frac{3}{5} + \frac{6}{7}$ **29.** $2\frac{5}{7} \cdot 8\frac{3}{11}$ **30.** $16\frac{7}{20} \div 3\frac{8}{9}$

31. $-1\frac{3}{5} \cdot 4\frac{6}{13}$ **32.** $5\frac{3}{5} - 4\frac{1}{3}$ **33.** $3\frac{7}{8} + \frac{2}{15}$ **34.** $19\frac{5}{7} \div \left(-5\frac{2}{5}\right)$

35. $\frac{3}{8} + 3\frac{5}{7} + 6\frac{7}{8}$ **36.** $8\frac{4}{5} + 6\frac{1}{12} + 3\frac{2}{5}$ **37.** $14\frac{2}{3} + 1\frac{7}{9} - 11\frac{14}{29}$

38. Kevin has $3\frac{3}{4}$ pounds of pecans and $6\frac{2}{3}$ pounds of walnuts. About how many more pounds of walnuts than pecans does Kevin have?

39. Business October 19, 1987, is known as Black Monday because the stock market fell 508 points. Xerox stock began the day at $\$70\frac{1}{8}$ and finished at $\$56\frac{1}{4}$. Approximately how far did Xerox's stock price fall during the day?

40. Recreation Monica and Paul hiked $5\frac{3}{8}$ miles on Saturday and $4\frac{9}{10}$ miles on Sunday. Estimate the number of miles Monica and Paul hiked.

41. Critical Thinking If you round a divisor down, is the quotient going to be less than or greater than the actual quotient? Explain.

Life Science The diagram shows the wingspans of different species of birds. Use the diagram for Exercises 42 and 43.

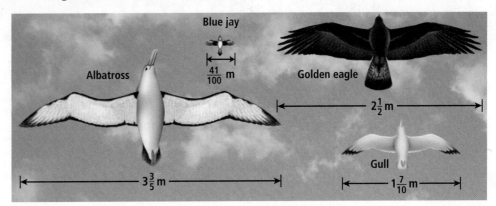

42. Approximately how much longer is the wingspan of an albatross than the wingspan of a gull?

43. Approximately how much longer is the wingspan of a golden eagle than the wingspan of a blue jay?

44. **Write a Problem** Using mixed numbers, write a problem in which an estimate is enough to solve the problem.

45. **Write About It** How is estimating fractions or mixed numbers similar to rounding whole numbers?

46. **Challenge** Suppose you had bought 10 shares of Xerox stock on October 16, 1987, for $73 per share and sold them at the end of the day on October 19, 1987, for $56\frac{1}{4}$ per share. Approximately how much money would you have lost?

Test Prep and Spiral Review

47. **Multiple Choice** For which of the following would 2 be the best estimate?

ⓐ $8\frac{7}{9} \cdot 4\frac{2}{5}$ ⓑ $4\frac{1}{5} \div 2\frac{5}{9}$ ⓒ $8\frac{7}{9} \cdot 2\frac{1}{5}$ ⓓ $8\frac{1}{9} \div 4\frac{2}{5}$

48. **Multiple Choice** The table shows the distance Maria biked each day last week.

Day	Mon	Tue	Wed	Thu	Fri	Sat	Sun
Distance (mi)	$12\frac{3}{8}$	$9\frac{11}{15}$	$3\frac{1}{4}$	$8\frac{1}{2}$	0	$4\frac{3}{4}$	$5\frac{2}{5}$

Which is the best estimate for the total distance Maria biked last week?

ⓕ 40 mi ⓖ 44 mi ⓗ 48 mi ⓙ 52 mi

Solve each equation. Check your answer. (Lessons 1-10 and 1-11)

49. $x + 16 = 43$ 50. $y - 32 = 14$ 51. $5m = 65$ 52. $\frac{n}{3} = 18$

Solve. (Lesson 3-5)

53. $-7.1x = -46.15$ 54. $8.7 = y + (-4.6)$ 55. $\frac{q}{-5.4} = 3.6$ 56. $r - 4 = -31.2$

Hands-On LAB 3-7

Model Fraction Addition and Subtraction

Use with Lesson 3-7

Learn It Online
Lab Resources Online **go.hrw.com**,
keyword MS10 Lab3 Go

Fraction bars can be used to model addition and subtraction of fractions.

TN SPI 0706.2.1 Simplify numerical expressions involving rational numbers. *Also* GLE 0706.1.4, GLE 0706.1.8, GLE 0706.2.2

Activity

You can use fraction bars to find $\frac{3}{8} + \frac{2}{8}$.

Use fraction bars to represent both fractions. Place the fraction bars side by side.

$$\frac{3}{8} + \frac{2}{8} = \frac{5}{8}$$

1 Use fraction bars to find each sum.

a. $\frac{1}{3} + \frac{1}{3}$ **b.** $\frac{2}{4} + \frac{1}{4}$ **c.** $\frac{3}{12} + \frac{2}{12}$ **d.** $\frac{1}{5} + \frac{2}{5}$

You can use fraction bars to find $\frac{1}{3} + \frac{1}{4}$.

Use fraction bars to represent both fractions. Place the fraction bars side by side. Which kind of fraction bar placed side by side will fit below $\frac{1}{3}$ and $\frac{1}{4}$? (*Hint:* What is the LCM of 3 and 4?)

$$\frac{1}{3} + \frac{1}{4} = \frac{7}{12}$$

2 Use fraction bars to find each sum.

a. $\frac{1}{2} + \frac{1}{3}$ **b.** $\frac{1}{2} + \frac{1}{4}$ **c.** $\frac{1}{3} + \frac{1}{6}$ **d.** $\frac{1}{4} + \frac{1}{6}$

You can use fraction bars to find $\frac{1}{3} + \frac{5}{6}$.

Use fraction bars to represent both fractions. Place the fraction bars side by side. Which kind of fraction bar placed side by side will fit below $\frac{1}{3}$ and $\frac{5}{6}$? (*Hint:* What is the LCM of 3 and 6?)

$$\frac{1}{3} + \frac{5}{6} = \frac{7}{6}$$

When the sum is an improper fraction, you can use the 1 bar along with fraction bars to find the mixed-number equivalent.

$$\frac{7}{6} = 1\frac{1}{6}$$

3 Use fraction bars to find each sum.

a. $\frac{3}{4} + \frac{3}{4}$ b. $\frac{2}{3} + \frac{1}{2}$ c. $\frac{5}{6} + \frac{1}{4}$ d. $\frac{3}{8} + \frac{3}{4}$

You can use fraction bars to find $\frac{2}{3} - \frac{1}{2}$.

Place a $\frac{1}{2}$ bar beneath bars that show $\frac{2}{3}$, and find which fraction fills in the remaining space.

$$\frac{2}{3} - \frac{1}{2} = \frac{1}{6}$$

4 Use fraction bars to find each difference.

a. $\frac{2}{3} - \frac{1}{3}$ b. $\frac{1}{4} - \frac{1}{6}$ c. $\frac{1}{2} - \frac{1}{3}$ d. $\frac{3}{4} - \frac{2}{3}$

Think and Discuss

1. Model and solve $\frac{3}{4} - \frac{1}{6}$. Explain your steps.

2. Two students solved $\frac{1}{4} + \frac{1}{3}$ in different ways. One got $\frac{7}{12}$ for the answer, and the other got $\frac{2}{7}$. Use models to show which student is correct.

3. Find three different ways to model $\frac{1}{2} + \frac{1}{4}$.

4. If you add two proper fractions, do you always get a sum that is greater than one? Explain.

Try This

Use fraction bars to find each sum or difference.

1. $\frac{1}{2} + \frac{1}{2}$ 2. $\frac{2}{3} + \frac{1}{6}$ 3. $\frac{1}{4} + \frac{1}{6}$ 4. $\frac{1}{3} + \frac{7}{12}$

5. $\frac{5}{12} - \frac{1}{3}$ 6. $\frac{1}{2} - \frac{1}{4}$ 7. $\frac{3}{4} - \frac{1}{6}$ 8. $\frac{2}{3} - \frac{1}{4}$

9. You ate $\frac{1}{4}$ of a pizza for lunch and $\frac{5}{8}$ of the pizza for dinner. How much of the pizza did you eat in all?

10. It is $\frac{5}{6}$ mile from your home to the library. After walking $\frac{3}{4}$ mile, you stop to visit a friend. How much farther must you walk to reach the library?

Adding and Subtracting Fractions

TN SPI 0706.2.1 Simplify
numerical expressions involving
rational numbers.
Also ✓ 0706.1.1, ✓ 0706.1.3,
GLE 0706.2.2, SPI 0706.2.3

From January 1 to March 14 of any given year, Earth completes approximately $\frac{1}{5}$ of its circular orbit around the Sun, while Venus completes approximately $\frac{1}{3}$ of its orbit. To find out how much more of its orbit Venus completes than Earth, you need to subtract fractions.

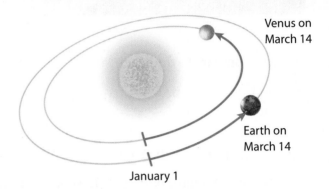

Venus on March 14

Earth on March 14

January 1

E X A M P L E **1** **Adding and Subtracting Fractions with Like Denominators**

Add or subtract. Write each answer in simplest form.

A $\frac{3}{10} + \frac{1}{10}$

$$\frac{3}{10} + \frac{1}{10} = \frac{3+1}{10}$$ *Add the numerators and keep the common denominator.*

$$= \frac{4}{10} = \frac{2}{5}$$ *Simplify.*

B $\frac{7}{9} - \frac{4}{9}$

$$\frac{7}{9} - \frac{4}{9} = \frac{7-4}{9}$$ *Subtract the numerators and keep the common denominator.*

$$= \frac{3}{9} = \frac{1}{3}$$ *Simplify.*

To add or subtract fractions with different denominators, you must rewrite the fractions with a common denominator.

Two Ways to Find a Common Denominator	
Method 1: Find the LCM (least common multiple) of the denominators.	**Method 2:** Multiply the denominators.
$\frac{1}{2} + \frac{1}{4} = \frac{1 \cdot 2}{2 \cdot 2} + \frac{1}{4}$ *The LCM of the denominators is 4.*	$\frac{1}{2} + \frac{1}{4} = \frac{1 \cdot 4}{2 \cdot 4} + \frac{1 \cdot 2}{4 \cdot 2}$ *Multiply the denominators.*
$\frac{2}{4} + \frac{1}{4} = \frac{3}{4}$	$\frac{4}{8} + \frac{2}{8} = \frac{6}{8} = \frac{3}{4}$

Helpful Hint

The LCM of two denominators is the lowest common denominator (LCD) of the fractions.

Video **Lesson Tutorials Online** my.hrw.com

EXAMPLE 2

Adding and Subtracting Fractions with Unlike Denominators

Add or subtract. Write each answer in simplest form.

A $\frac{3}{8} + \frac{5}{12}$

$$\frac{3}{8} + \frac{5}{12} = \frac{3 \cdot 3}{8 \cdot 3} + \frac{5 \cdot 2}{12 \cdot 2}$$ *The LCM of the denominators is 24.*

$$= \frac{9}{24} + \frac{10}{24} = \frac{19}{24}$$ *Write equivalent fractions. Add.*

Estimate $\frac{1}{2} + \frac{1}{2} = 1$ $\frac{19}{24}$ *is a reasonable answer.*

B $\frac{1}{10} - \frac{5}{8}$

$$\frac{1}{10} - \frac{5}{8} = \frac{1 \cdot 4}{10 \cdot 4} - \frac{5 \cdot 5}{8 \cdot 5}$$ *The LCM of the denominators is 40.*

$$= \frac{4}{40} - \frac{25}{40} = -\frac{21}{40}$$ *Write equivalent fractions. Subtract.*

Estimate $0 - \frac{1}{2} = -\frac{1}{2}$ $-\frac{21}{40}$ *is a reasonable answer.*

C $-\frac{2}{3} + \frac{7}{8}$

$$-\frac{2}{3} + \frac{7}{8} = -\frac{2 \cdot 8}{3 \cdot 8} + \frac{7 \cdot 3}{8 \cdot 3}$$ *Multiply the denominators.*

$$= -\frac{16}{24} + \frac{21}{24} = \frac{5}{24}$$ *Write equivalent fractions. Add.*

Estimate $-1 + 1 = 0$ $\frac{5}{24}$ *is a reasonable answer.*

EXAMPLE 3

Astronomy Application

From January 1 to March 14, Earth completes about $\frac{1}{5}$ of its orbit, while Venus completes about $\frac{1}{3}$ of its orbit. How much more of its orbit does Venus complete than Earth?

$$\frac{1}{3} - \frac{1}{5} = \frac{1 \cdot 5}{3 \cdot 5} - \frac{1 \cdot 3}{5 \cdot 3}$$ *The LCM of the denominators is 15.*

$$= \frac{5}{15} - \frac{3}{15}$$ *Write equivalent fractions.*

$$= \frac{2}{15}$$ *Subtract.*

Venus completes $\frac{2}{15}$ more of its orbit than Earth does.

Think and Discuss

1. Describe the process for subtracting fractions with different denominators.

2. Explain whether $\frac{3}{4} + \frac{2}{3} = \frac{5}{7}$ is correct.

3-7 Adding and Subtracting Fractions **177**

3-7 **Exercises**

Learn It Online
Homework Help Online **go.hrw.com**,
keyword | MS10 3-7 | Go
Exercises 1–27, 29, 31, 37, 47,
49, 51, 55

GUIDED PRACTICE

See Example 1   Add or subtract. Write each answer in simplest form.

1. $\frac{2}{3} - \frac{1}{3}$ 2. $\frac{1}{12} + \frac{1}{12}$ 3. $\frac{16}{21} - \frac{7}{21}$ 4. $\frac{4}{17} + \frac{11}{17}$

See Example 2   5. $\frac{1}{6} + \frac{1}{3}$ 6. $\frac{9}{10} - \frac{3}{4}$ 7. $\frac{2}{3} + \frac{1}{8}$ 8. $\frac{5}{8} - \frac{3}{10}$

See Example 3   9. Parker spends $\frac{1}{4}$ of his earnings on rent and $\frac{1}{6}$ on entertainment. How much more of his earnings does Parker spend on rent than on entertainment?

INDEPENDENT PRACTICE

See Example 1   Add or subtract. Write each answer in simplest form.

10. $\frac{2}{3} + \frac{1}{3}$ 11. $\frac{3}{20} + \frac{7}{20}$ 12. $\frac{5}{8} + \frac{7}{8}$ 13. $\frac{6}{15} + \frac{3}{15}$

14. $\frac{7}{12} - \frac{5}{12}$ 15. $\frac{5}{6} - \frac{1}{6}$ 16. $\frac{8}{9} - \frac{5}{9}$ 17. $\frac{9}{25} - \frac{4}{25}$

See Example 2   18. $\frac{1}{5} + \frac{2}{3}$ 19. $\frac{1}{6} + \frac{1}{12}$ 20. $\frac{5}{6} + \frac{3}{4}$ 21. $\frac{1}{2} + \frac{2}{8}$

22. $\frac{21}{24} - \frac{1}{2}$ 23. $\frac{3}{4} - \frac{11}{12}$ 24. $\frac{1}{2} - \frac{2}{7}$ 25. $\frac{7}{10} - \frac{1}{6}$

See Example 3   26. Seana picked $\frac{3}{4}$ quart of blackberries. She ate $\frac{1}{12}$ quart. How much was left?

27. Armando lives $\frac{2}{3}$ mi from his school. If he has walked $\frac{1}{2}$ mi already this morning, how much farther must he walk to get to his school?

PRACTICE AND PROBLEM SOLVING

Extra Practice
See page EP9.

Find each sum or difference. Write your answer in simplest form.

28. $\frac{4}{5} + \frac{6}{7}$ 29. $\frac{5}{6} - \frac{1}{9}$ 30. $\frac{1}{2} - \frac{3}{4}$ 31. $\frac{2}{3} + \frac{2}{15}$

32. $\frac{5}{7} + \frac{1}{3}$ 33. $\frac{1}{2} - \frac{7}{12}$ 34. $\frac{3}{4} + \frac{2}{5}$ 35. $\frac{9}{14} - \frac{1}{7}$

36. $\frac{7}{8} + \frac{2}{3} + \frac{5}{6}$ 37. $\frac{3}{5} + \frac{1}{10} - \frac{3}{4}$ 38. $\frac{3}{10} + \frac{5}{8} + \frac{1}{5}$ 39. $\frac{2}{5} - \frac{1}{6} + \frac{7}{10}$

40. $-\frac{1}{2} + \frac{3}{8} + \frac{2}{7}$ 41. $\frac{1}{3} + \frac{3}{7} - \frac{1}{9}$ 42. $\frac{2}{9} - \frac{7}{18} + \frac{1}{6}$ 43. $\frac{2}{15} + \frac{4}{9} + \frac{1}{3}$

44. $\frac{9}{35} - \frac{4}{7} - \frac{5}{14}$ 45. $\frac{1}{3} - \frac{5}{7} + \frac{8}{21}$ 46. $-\frac{2}{9} - \frac{1}{12} - \frac{7}{18}$ 47. $-\frac{2}{3} + \frac{4}{5} + \frac{5}{8}$

48. **Cooking** One fruit salad recipe calls for $\frac{1}{2}$ cup of sugar. Another recipe calls for 2 tablespoons of sugar. Since 1 tablespoon is $\frac{1}{16}$ cup, how much more sugar does the first recipe require?

49. It took Earl $\frac{1}{2}$ hour to do his science homework and $\frac{1}{3}$ hour to do his math homework. How long did Earl work on homework?

50. **Music** In music written in 4/4 time, a half note lasts for $\frac{1}{2}$ measure and an eighth note lasts for $\frac{1}{8}$ measure. In terms of a musical measure, what is the difference in the duration of the two notes?

Fitness Four friends had a competition to see how far they could walk while spinning a hoop around their waists. The table shows how far each friend walked. Use the table for Exercises 51–53.

Person	Distance (mi)
Rosalyn	$\frac{1}{8}$
Cai	$\frac{3}{4}$
Lauren	$\frac{2}{3}$
Janna	$\frac{7}{10}$

51. How much farther did Lauren walk than Rosalyn?

52. What is the combined distance that Cai and Rosalyn walked?

53. Who walked farther, Janna or Cai?

54. Measurement A shrew weighs $\frac{3}{16}$ lb. A hamster weighs $\frac{1}{4}$ lb.

   a. How many more pounds does a hamster weigh than a shrew?

   b. There are 16 oz in 1 lb. How many more ounces does the hamster weigh than the shrew?

55. Multi-Step To make $\frac{3}{4}$ lb of mixed nuts, how many pounds of cashews would you add to $\frac{1}{8}$ lb of almonds and $\frac{1}{4}$ lb of peanuts?

56. Make a Conjecture Suppose the pattern $1, \frac{7}{8}, \frac{3}{4}, \frac{5}{8}, \frac{1}{2} \dots$ is continued forever. Make a conjecture about the rest of the numbers in the pattern.

57. Write a Problem Use facts you find in a newspaper or magazine to write a problem that can be solved using addition or subtraction of fractions.

58. Write About It Explain the steps you use to add or subtract fractions that have different denominators.

59. Challenge The sum of two fractions is 1. If one fraction is $\frac{3}{8}$ greater than the other, what are the two fractions?

Test Prep and Spiral Review

60. Multiple Choice What is the value of the expression $\frac{3}{7} + \frac{1}{5}$?

  Ⓐ $\frac{1}{3}$ Ⓑ $\frac{22}{35}$ Ⓒ $\frac{2}{3}$ Ⓓ $\frac{26}{35}$

61. Gridded Response Grace has $\frac{1}{2}$ pound of apples. Julie has $\frac{2}{5}$ pound of apples. They want to combine their apples to use in a recipe that calls for 1 pound of apples. How many more pounds of apples do they need?

Find the greatest common factor (GCF). (Lesson 2-7)

62. 5, 9   **63.** 6, 54   **64.** 18, 24   **65.** 12, 36, 50

Estimate each sum or difference. (Lesson 3-6)

66. $\frac{4}{7} + \frac{1}{9}$ **67.** $4\frac{2}{3} - 2\frac{3}{5}$ **68.** $7\frac{5}{9} - \left(-3\frac{2}{7}\right)$ **69.** $6\frac{1}{8} + 2\frac{4}{7}$

Adding and Subtracting Mixed Numbers

TN SPI 0706.2.1 Simplify numerical expressions involving rational numbers. *Also* GLE 0706.2.2, SPI 0706.2.3

Beetles can be found all over the world in a fabulous variety of shapes, sizes, and colors. The giraffe beetle from Madagascar can grow about $6\frac{2}{5}$ centimeters longer than the giant green fruit beetle can. The giant green fruit beetle can grow up to $1\frac{1}{5}$ centimeters long. To find the maximum length of the giraffe beetle, you can add $6\frac{2}{5}$ and $1\frac{1}{5}$.

EXAMPLE 1 *Measurement Application*

The giraffe beetle can grow about $6\frac{2}{5}$ centimeters longer than the giant green fruit beetle can. The giant green fruit beetle can grow up to $1\frac{1}{5}$ centimeters long. What is the maximum length of the giraffe beetle?

$$6\frac{2}{5} + 1\frac{1}{5} = 7 + \frac{3}{5} \qquad \textit{Add the fractions, and then add the integers.}$$

$$= 7\frac{3}{5} \qquad \textit{Add.}$$

The maximum length of the giraffe beetle is $7\frac{3}{5}$ centimeters.

EXAMPLE 2 **Adding Mixed Numbers**

Add. Write each answer in simplest form.

Helpful Hint

Add the fractions first in case an improper fraction needs to be rewritten.

A $3\frac{4}{5} + 4\frac{2}{5}$

$$3\frac{4}{5} + 4\frac{2}{5} = 7 + \frac{6}{5} \qquad \textit{Add the fractions, and then add the integers.}$$

$$= 7 + 1\frac{1}{5} \qquad \textit{Rewrite the improper fraction as a mixed number.}$$

$$= 8\frac{1}{5} \qquad \textit{Add.}$$

B $1\frac{2}{15} + 7\frac{1}{6}$

$$1\frac{2}{15} + 7\frac{1}{6} = 1\frac{4}{30} + 7\frac{5}{30} \qquad \textit{Find a common denominator.}$$

$$= 8 + \frac{9}{30} \qquad \textit{Add the fractions, and then add the integers.}$$

$$= 8\frac{9}{30} = 8\frac{3}{10} \qquad \textit{Add. Then simplify.}$$

Video **Lesson Tutorials Online** my.hrw.com

Sometimes, when you subtract mixed numbers, the fraction portion of the first number is less than the fraction portion of the second number. In these cases, you must regroup before subtracting.

REGROUPING MIXED NUMBERS	
Words	**Numbers**
Regroup.	$7\frac{1}{8} = 6 + 1 + \frac{1}{8}$
Rewrite 1 as a fraction with a common denominator.	$= 6 + \frac{8}{8} + \frac{1}{8}$
Add.	$= 6\frac{9}{8}$

Remember!

Any fraction in which the numerator and denominator are the same is equal to 1.

EXAMPLE 3 **Subtracting Mixed Numbers**

Subtract. Write each answer in simplest form.

A $10\frac{7}{9} - 4\frac{2}{9}$

$10\frac{7}{9} - 4\frac{2}{9} = 6\frac{5}{9}$ *Subtract the fractions, and then subtract the integers.*

B $12\frac{7}{8} - 5\frac{17}{24}$

$12\frac{7}{8} - 5\frac{17}{24} = 12\frac{21}{24} - 5\frac{17}{24}$ *Find a common denominator.*

$= 7\frac{4}{24}$ *Subtract the fractions, and then subtract the integers.*

$= 7\frac{1}{6}$ *Simplify.*

C $72\frac{3}{5} - 63\frac{4}{5}$

$72\frac{3}{5} - 63\frac{4}{5} = 71\frac{8}{5} - 63\frac{4}{5}$ *Regroup.* $72\frac{3}{5} = 71 + \frac{5}{5} + \frac{3}{5}$

$= 8\frac{4}{5}$ *Subtract the fractions, and then subtract the integers.*

Think and Discuss

1. Explain whether it is possible for the sum of two mixed numbers to be a whole number.

2. Explain whether $2\frac{3}{5} + 1\frac{3}{5} = 3\frac{6}{5}$ is correct. Is there another way to write the answer?

3. Demonstrate how to regroup to simplify $6\frac{2}{5} - 4\frac{3}{5}$.

Exercises

Learn It Online
Homework Help Online **go.hrw.com,**
keyword MS10 3-8 Go
Exercises 1–26, 27, 31, 33, 37,
41, 43, 45

GUIDED PRACTICE

See Example 1

1. **Measurement** Chrystelle's mother is $1\frac{2}{3}$ ft taller than Chrystelle. If Chrystelle is $3\frac{1}{2}$ ft tall, how tall is her mother?

See Example 2

Add. Write each answer in simplest form.

2. $3\frac{2}{5} + 4\frac{1}{5}$
3. $2\frac{7}{8} + 3\frac{3}{4}$
4. $1\frac{8}{9} + 4\frac{4}{9}$
5. $5\frac{1}{2} + 2\frac{1}{4}$

See Example 3

Subtract. Write each answer in simplest form.

6. $6\frac{2}{3} - 5\frac{1}{3}$
7. $8\frac{1}{6} - 2\frac{5}{6}$
8. $3\frac{2}{3} - 2\frac{3}{4}$
9. $7\frac{5}{8} - 3\frac{2}{5}$

INDEPENDENT PRACTICE

See Example 1

10. **Sports** The track at Daytona International Speedway is $\frac{24}{25}$ mi longer than the track at Atlanta Motor Speedway. If the track at Atlanta is $1\frac{27}{50}$ mi long, how long is the track at Daytona?

See Example 2

Add. Write each answer in simplest form.

11. $6\frac{1}{4} + 8\frac{3}{4}$
12. $3\frac{3}{5} + 7\frac{4}{5}$
13. $3\frac{5}{6} + 1\frac{5}{6}$
14. $2\frac{3}{5} + 4\frac{1}{3}$

15. $2\frac{3}{10} + 4\frac{1}{2}$
16. $6\frac{1}{8} + 8\frac{9}{10}$
17. $6\frac{1}{6} + 5\frac{3}{10}$
18. $1\frac{2}{5} + 9\frac{1}{4}$

See Example 3

Subtract. Write each answer in simplest form.

19. $2\frac{1}{14} - 1\frac{3}{14}$
20. $4\frac{5}{12} - 1\frac{7}{12}$
21. $8 - 2\frac{3}{4}$
22. $7\frac{3}{4} - 5\frac{2}{3}$

23. $8\frac{3}{4} - 6\frac{2}{5}$
24. $3\frac{1}{3} - 2\frac{5}{8}$
25. $4\frac{2}{5} - 3\frac{1}{2}$
26. $11 - 6\frac{5}{9}$

PRACTICE AND PROBLEM SOLVING

Extra Practice
See page EP9.

Add or subtract. Write each answer in simplest form.

27. $7\frac{1}{3} + 8\frac{1}{5}$
28. $14\frac{3}{5} - 8\frac{1}{2}$
29. $9\frac{1}{6} + 4\frac{6}{9}$
30. $21\frac{8}{12} - 3\frac{1}{2}$

31. $3\frac{5}{8} + 2\frac{7}{12}$
32. $25\frac{1}{3} + 3\frac{5}{6}$
33. $1\frac{7}{9} - \frac{17}{18}$
34. $3\frac{1}{2} + 5\frac{1}{4}$

35. $1\frac{7}{15} + 2\frac{7}{10}$
36. $12\frac{4}{6} - \frac{2}{5}$
37. $4\frac{2}{3} + 1\frac{7}{8} + 3\frac{1}{2}$
38. $5\frac{1}{6} + 8\frac{2}{3} - 9\frac{1}{2}$

Compare. Write <, >, or =.

39. $12\frac{1}{4} - 10\frac{3}{4}$ ▨ $5\frac{1}{2} - 3\frac{7}{10}$
40. $4\frac{1}{2} + 3\frac{4}{5}$ ▨ $4\frac{5}{7} + 3\frac{1}{2}$

41. $13\frac{3}{4} - 2\frac{3}{8}$ ▨ $5\frac{5}{6} + 4\frac{2}{9}$
42. $4\frac{1}{3} - 2\frac{1}{4}$ ▨ $3\frac{1}{4} - 1\frac{1}{6}$

43. The liquid ingredients in a recipe are water and olive oil. The recipe calls for $3\frac{1}{2}$ cups of water and $1\frac{1}{8}$ cups of olive oil. How many cups of liquid ingredients are included in the recipe?

Travel The table shows the distances in miles between four cities. To find the distance between two cities, locate the square where the row for one city and the column for the other city intersect.

	Atherton	Baily	Charleston	Dixon
Atherton	✕	$40\frac{2}{3}$	$100\frac{5}{6}$	$16\frac{1}{2}$
Baily	$40\frac{2}{3}$	✕	$210\frac{3}{8}$	$30\frac{2}{3}$
Charleston	$100\frac{5}{6}$	$210\frac{3}{8}$	✕	$98\frac{3}{4}$
Dixon	$16\frac{1}{2}$	$30\frac{2}{3}$	$98\frac{3}{4}$	✕

44. How much farther is it from Charleston to Dixon than from Atherton to Baily?

45. If you drove from Charleston to Atherton and then from Atherton to Dixon, how far would you drive?

46. Agriculture In 2003, the United States imported $\frac{97}{100}$ of its tulip bulbs from the Netherlands and $\frac{1}{50}$ of its tulip bulbs from New Zealand. What fraction more of tulip imports came from the Netherlands?

47. Recreation Kathy wants to hike to Candle Lake. The waterfall trail is $1\frac{2}{3}$ miles long, and the meadow trail is $1\frac{5}{6}$ miles long. Which route is shorter and by how much?

48. Choose a Strategy Spiro needs to draw a 6-inch-long line. He does not have a ruler, but he has sheets of notebook paper that are $8\frac{1}{2}$ in. wide and 11 in. long. Describe how Spiro can use the notebook paper to measure 6 in.

49. Write About It Explain why it is sometimes necessary to regroup a mixed number when subtracting.

50. Challenge Todd had d pounds of nails. He sold $3\frac{1}{2}$ pounds on Monday and $5\frac{2}{3}$ pounds on Tuesday. Write an expression to show how many pounds he had left and then simplify it.

Test Prep and Spiral Review

51. Multiple Choice Which expression is NOT equal to $2\frac{7}{8}$?

Ⓐ $1\frac{1}{2} + 1\frac{3}{8}$ Ⓑ $5\frac{15}{16} - 3\frac{1}{16}$ Ⓒ $6 - 3\frac{1}{8}$ Ⓓ $1\frac{1}{8} + 1\frac{1}{4}$

52. Short Response Where Maddie lives, there is a $5\frac{1}{2}$-cent state sales tax, a $1\frac{3}{4}$-cent county sales tax, and a $\frac{3}{4}$-cent city sales tax. The total sales tax is the sum of the state, county, and city sales taxes. What is the total sales tax where Maddie lives? Show your work.

Find each sum. (Lesson 2-2)

53. $-3 + 9$ **54.** $6 + (-15)$ **55.** $-4 + (-8)$ **56.** $-11 + 5$

Find each sum or difference. Write your answer in simplest form. (Lesson 3-7)

57. $\frac{2}{5} + \frac{7}{20}$ **58.** $\frac{3}{7} - \frac{1}{3}$ **59.** $\frac{3}{4} + \frac{7}{18}$ **60.** $\frac{1}{3} - \frac{4}{5}$

Model Fraction Multiplication and Division

3-9

Use with Lessons 3-9 and 3-10

Learn It Online
Lab Resources Online **go.hrw.com**,
keyword **MS10 Lab3** **Go**

TN SPI 0706.2.1 Simplify numerical expressions involving rational numbers. *Also* **GLE 0706.1.4, GLE 0706.1.8, GLE 0706.2.2**

You can use grids to model fraction multiplication and division.

Activity 1

Use a grid to model $\frac{3}{4} \cdot \frac{1}{2}$.

Think of $\frac{3}{4} \cdot \frac{1}{2}$ as $\frac{3}{4}$ of $\frac{1}{2}$.

Model $\frac{1}{2}$ by shading half of a grid.

The denominator tells you to divide the grid into 2 parts.
The numerator tells you how many parts to shade.

Divide the grid into 4 equal horizontal sections.

Use a different color to shade $\frac{3}{4}$ of the same grid.

The denominator tells you to divide the grid into 4 parts.
The numerator tells you how many parts to shade.

What fraction of the whole is shaded?

To find the numerator, think: How many parts overlap?
To find the denominator, think: How many total parts are there?

$\frac{3}{4} \cdot \frac{1}{2} = \frac{3}{8}$

Think and Discuss

1. Are $\frac{2}{3} \cdot \frac{1}{5}$ and $\frac{1}{5} \cdot \frac{2}{3}$ modeled the same way? Explain.

2. When you multiply a positive fraction by a positive fraction, the product is less than either factor. Why?

Use a grid to find each product.

1. $\frac{1}{2} \cdot \frac{1}{2}$
2. $\frac{3}{4} \cdot \frac{2}{3}$
3. $\frac{5}{8} \cdot \frac{1}{3}$
4. $\frac{2}{5} \cdot \frac{5}{6}$

Activity 2

Use grids to model $4\frac{1}{3} \div \frac{2}{3}$.

Divide 5 grids into thirds. Shade 4 grids and $\frac{1}{3}$ of a fifth grid to represent $4\frac{1}{3}$.

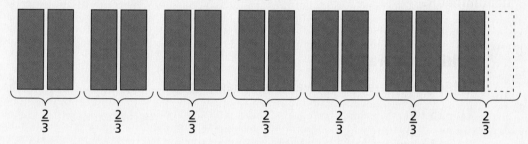

Think: How many groups of $\frac{2}{3}$ are in $4\frac{1}{3}$?

Divide the shaded grids into equal groups of 2.

There are 6 groups of $\frac{2}{3}$, with $\frac{1}{3}$ left over. This piece is $\frac{1}{2}$ of a group of $\frac{2}{3}$.

Thus there are $6 + \frac{1}{2}$ groups of $\frac{2}{3}$ in $4\frac{1}{3}$.

$4\frac{1}{3} \div \frac{2}{3} = 6\frac{1}{2}$

Think and Discuss

1. Are $\frac{3}{4} \div \frac{1}{6}$ and $\frac{1}{6} \div \frac{3}{4}$ modeled the same way? Explain.

2. When you divide fractions, is the quotient greater than or less than the dividend and the divisor? Explain.

Try This

Use grids to find each quotient.

1. $\frac{7}{12} \div \frac{1}{6}$
2. $\frac{4}{5} \div \frac{3}{10}$
3. $\frac{2}{3} \div \frac{4}{9}$
4. $3\frac{2}{5} \div \frac{3}{5}$

TN SPI 0706.2.1 Simplify numerical expressions involving rational numbers. *Also* GLE 0706.2.2, SPI 0706.2.3

The original Sunshine Skyway Bridge connecting St. Petersburg and Palmetto, Florida, opened in 1954 and had a toll of $1.75. The current Sunshine Skyway Bridge opened in 1987, replacing the original. In 2007, the toll for a car crossing the bridge was $\frac{4}{7}$ of the toll in 1954. To find the toll in 2007, you will need to multiply the toll in 1954 by a fraction.

To multiply fractions, multiply the numerators to find the product's numerator. Then multiply the denominators to find the product's denominator.

EXAMPLE 1 **Multiplying Fractions**

Multiply. Write each answer in simplest form.

A $-15 \cdot \frac{2}{3}$

$-15 \cdot \frac{2}{3} = -\frac{15}{1} \cdot \frac{2}{3}$ *Write –15 as a fraction.*

$= -\frac{\overset{5}{\cancel{15}} \cdot 2}{1 \cdot \cancel{3}_{1}}$ *Simplify.*

$= -\frac{10}{1}$ *Multiply numerators. Multiply denominators.*

$= -10$

Helpful Hint

The product of two positive proper fractions is less than either fraction.

B $\frac{1}{4} \cdot \frac{4}{5}$

$\frac{1}{4} \cdot \frac{4}{5} = \frac{1 \cdot \cancel{4}^{1}}{{}_{1}\cancel{4} \cdot 5}$ *Simplify.*

$= \frac{1}{5}$ *Multiply numerators. Multiply denominators.*

C $\frac{3}{4} \cdot \left(-\frac{1}{2}\right)$

$\frac{3}{4} \cdot \left(-\frac{1}{2}\right) = -\frac{3 \cdot 1}{4 \cdot 2}$ *The signs are different, so the answer will be negative.*

$= -\frac{3}{8}$ *Multiply numerators. Multiply denominators.*

EXAMPLE 2 **Multiplying Mixed Numbers**

Multiply. Write each answer in simplest form.

A $8 \cdot 2\frac{3}{4}$

$8 \cdot 2\frac{3}{4} = \frac{8}{1} \cdot \frac{11}{4}$ *Write mixed numbers as improper fractions.*

$= \frac{\overset{2}{\cancel{8}} \cdot 11}{1 \cdot \cancel{4}_1}$ *Simplify.*

$= \frac{22}{1} = 22$ *Multiply numerators. Multiply denominators.*

B $\frac{1}{3} \cdot 4\frac{1}{2}$

$\frac{1}{3} \cdot 4\frac{1}{2} = \frac{1}{3} \cdot \frac{9}{2}$ *Write the mixed number as an improper fraction.*

$= \frac{1 \cdot \overset{3}{\cancel{9}}}{_1\cancel{3} \cdot 2}$ *Simplify.*

$= \frac{3}{2}$ or $1\frac{1}{2}$ *Multiply numerators. Multiply denominators.*

C $3\frac{3}{5} \cdot 1\frac{1}{12}$

$3\frac{3}{5} \cdot 1\frac{1}{12} = \frac{18}{5} \cdot \frac{13}{12}$ *Write mixed numbers as improper fractions.*

$= \frac{\overset{3}{\cancel{18}} \cdot 13}{5 \cdot \cancel{12}_2}$ *Simplify.*

$= \frac{39}{10}$ or $3\frac{9}{10}$ *Multiply numerators. Multiply denominators.*

EXAMPLE 3 *Transportation Application*

In 1954, the Sunshine Skyway Bridge toll for a car was $1.75. In 2007, the toll was $\frac{4}{7}$ of the toll in 1954. What was the toll in 2007?

$1.75 \cdot \frac{4}{7} = 1\frac{75}{100} = 1\frac{3}{4} \cdot \frac{4}{7}$ *Write the decimal as a fraction.*

$= \frac{7}{4} \cdot \frac{4}{7}$ *Write the mixed number as an improper fraction.*

$= \frac{\overset{1}{\cancel{7}} \cdot \overset{1}{\cancel{4}}}{_1\cancel{4} \cdot \cancel{7}_1}$ *Simplify.*

$= \frac{1}{1} = 1$ *Multiply numerators. Multiply denominators.*

The Sunshine Skyway Bridge toll for a car was $1.00 in 2007.

Think and Discuss

1. Describe how to multiply a mixed number and a fraction.

2. Explain why $\frac{1}{2} \cdot \frac{1}{3} \cdot \frac{1}{4} = \frac{1}{24}$ is or is not correct.

3. Explain why you may want to simplify before multiplying $\frac{2}{3} \cdot \frac{3}{4}$. What answer will you get if you don't simplify first?

Exercises

Learn It Online
Homework Help Online **go.hrw.com**,
keyword MS10 3-9 Go
Exercises 1–27, 33, 39, 43, 45,
49, 53, 55

GUIDED PRACTICE

See Example 1   **Multiply. Write each answer in simplest form.**

1. $-8 \cdot \frac{3}{4}$ **2.** $\frac{2}{3} \cdot \frac{3}{5}$ **3.** $\frac{1}{4} \cdot \left(-\frac{2}{3}\right)$ **4.** $\frac{3}{5} \cdot (-15)$

See Example 2   **5.** $4 \cdot 3\frac{1}{2}$ **6.** $\frac{4}{9} \cdot 5\frac{2}{5}$ **7.** $1\frac{1}{2} \cdot 1\frac{5}{9}$ **8.** $2\frac{6}{7} \cdot (-7)$

See Example 3   **9.** On average, people spend $\frac{1}{4}$ of the time they sleep in a dream state. If Maxwell slept 10 hours last night, how much time did he spend dreaming? Write your answer in simplest form.

INDEPENDENT PRACTICE

See Example 1   **Multiply. Write each answer in simplest form.**

10. $5 \cdot \frac{1}{8}$ **11.** $4 \cdot \frac{1}{8}$ **12.** $3 \cdot \frac{5}{8}$ **13.** $6 \cdot \frac{2}{3}$

14. $\frac{2}{5} \cdot \frac{5}{7}$ **15.** $\frac{3}{8} \cdot \frac{2}{3}$ **16.** $\frac{1}{2} \cdot \left(-\frac{4}{9}\right)$ **17.** $-\frac{5}{6} \cdot \frac{2}{3}$

See Example 2   **18.** $7\frac{1}{2} \cdot 2\frac{2}{5}$ **19.** $6 \cdot 7\frac{2}{5}$ **20.** $2\frac{4}{7} \cdot \frac{1}{6}$ **21.** $2\frac{5}{8} \cdot 6\frac{2}{3}$

22. $\frac{2}{3} \cdot 2\frac{91}{4}$ **23.** $1\frac{1}{2} \cdot 1\frac{5}{9}$ **24.** $7 \cdot 5\frac{1}{8}$ **25.** $3\frac{3}{4} \cdot 2\frac{1}{5}$

See Example 3   **26.** Sherry spent 4 hours exercising last week. If $\frac{5}{6}$ of the time was spent jogging, how much time did she spend jogging? Write your answer in simplest form.

27. **Measurement** A cookie recipe calls for $\frac{1}{3}$ tsp of salt for 1 batch. Doreen is making cookies for a school bake sale and wants to bake 5 batches. How much salt does she need? Write your answer in simplest form.

PRACTICE AND PROBLEM SOLVING

Extra Practice
See page EP10.

Multiply. Write each answer in simplest form.

28. $\frac{5}{8} \cdot \frac{4}{5}$ **29.** $4\frac{3}{7} \cdot \frac{5}{6}$ **30.** $-\frac{2}{3} \cdot 6$ **31.** $2 \cdot \frac{1}{6}$

32. $\frac{1}{8} \cdot 5$ **33.** $-\frac{3}{4} \cdot \frac{2}{9}$ **34.** $4\frac{2}{3} \cdot 2\frac{4}{7}$ **35.** $-\frac{4}{9} \cdot \left(-\frac{3}{16}\right)$

36. $3\frac{1}{2} \cdot 5$ **37.** $\frac{1}{2} \cdot \frac{2}{3} \cdot \frac{3}{5}$ **38.** $\frac{6}{7} \cdot 5$ **39.** $1\frac{1}{2} \cdot \frac{3}{5} \cdot \frac{7}{9}$

40. $-\frac{2}{3} \cdot 1\frac{1}{2} \cdot \frac{2}{3}$ **41.** $\frac{8}{9} \cdot \frac{3}{11} \cdot \frac{33}{40}$ **42.** $\frac{1}{6} \cdot 6 \cdot 8\frac{2}{3}$ **43.** $-\frac{8}{9} \cdot \left(-1\frac{1}{8}\right)$

Complete each multiplication sentence.

44. $\frac{1}{2} \cdot \blacksquare = \frac{3}{16}$ **45.** $\frac{2}{3} \cdot \blacksquare = \frac{1}{2}$ **46.** $\frac{\blacksquare}{3} \cdot \frac{5}{8} = \frac{5}{12}$ **47.** $\frac{3}{5} \cdot \frac{\blacksquare}{7} = \frac{3}{7}$

48. $\frac{5}{6} \cdot \frac{3}{\blacksquare} = \frac{1}{4}$ **49.** $\frac{4}{\blacksquare} \cdot \frac{4}{5} = \frac{8}{15}$ **50.** $\frac{2}{3} \cdot \frac{9}{\blacksquare} = \frac{3}{11}$ **51.** $\frac{\blacksquare}{15} \cdot \frac{3}{5} = \frac{1}{25}$

52. **Measurement** A standard paper clip is $1\frac{1}{4}$ in. long. If you laid 75 paper clips end to end, how long would the line of paper clips be?

53. Physical Science The weight of an object on the moon is $\frac{1}{6}$ its weight on Earth. If a bowling ball weighs $12\frac{1}{2}$ pounds on Earth, how much would it weigh on the moon?

54. In a survey, 200 students were asked what most influenced them to download songs. The results are shown in the circle graph.

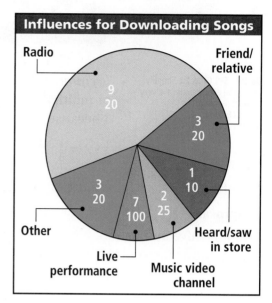

Influences for Downloading Songs

  a. How many students said radio most influenced them?

  b. How many more students were influenced by radio than by a music video channel?

  c. How many said a friend or relative influenced them or they heard the song in a store?

55. The Mississippi River flows at a rate of 2 miles per hour. If Eduardo floats down the river in a boat for $5\frac{2}{3}$ hours, how far will he travel?

56. Choose a Strategy What is the product of $\frac{1}{2} \cdot \frac{2}{3} \cdot \frac{3}{4} \cdot \frac{4}{5}$?

  (A) $\frac{1}{5}$ (B) 5   (C) $\frac{1}{20}$ (D) $\frac{3}{5}$

57. Write About It Two positive proper fractions are multiplied. Is the product less than or greater than one? Explain.

58. Challenge Write three multiplication problems to show that the product of two fractions can be less than, equal to, or greater than 1.

Test Prep and Spiral Review

59. Multiple Choice Which expression is greater than $5\frac{5}{8}$?

  (A) $8 \cdot \frac{9}{16}$ (B) $-\frac{7}{9} \cdot \left(-8\frac{2}{7}\right)$ (C) $3\frac{1}{2} \cdot \frac{5}{7}$ (D) $-\frac{3}{7} \cdot \frac{14}{27}$

60. Multiple Choice The weight of an object on Mars is about $\frac{3}{8}$ its weight on Earth. If Sam weighs 85 pounds on Earth, how much would he weigh on Mars?

  (F) 11 pounds   (G) $31\frac{7}{8}$ pounds   (H) $120\frac{4}{5}$ pounds   (J) $226\frac{2}{3}$ pounds

Use a number line to order the integers from least to greatest. (Lesson 2-1)

61. $-7, 5, -3, 0, 4$ **62.** $-5, -10, -15, -20, 0$ **63.** $9, -9, -4, 1, -1$

Add or subtract. Write each answer in simplest form. (Lesson 3-8)

64. $4\frac{3}{5} + 2\frac{1}{5}$ **65.** $2\frac{3}{4} - 1\frac{1}{3}$ **66.** $5\frac{1}{7} + 3\frac{5}{14}$ **67.** $4\frac{5}{6} + 2\frac{5}{8}$

3-10 Dividing Fractions and Mixed Numbers

TN SPI 0706.2.1 Simplify numerical expressions involving rational numbers.
Also GLE 0706.2.2, SPI 0706.2.3

Reciprocals can help you divide by fractions. Two numbers are **reciprocals** or **multiplicative inverses** if their product is 1. The reciprocal of $\frac{1}{3}$ is 3 because

$$\frac{1}{3} \cdot 3 = \frac{1}{3} \cdot \frac{3}{1} = \frac{3}{3} = 1.$$

Dividing by a number is the same as multiplying by its reciprocal.

Vocabulary

reciprocal

multiplicative inverse

Reciprocals

$$6 \div 3 = 2 \qquad 6 \cdot \frac{1}{3} = 2$$

Same answer

Interactivities Online ▶ You can use this rule to divide by fractions.

EXAMPLE 1 Dividing Fractions

Divide. Write each answer in simplest form.

A $\frac{2}{3} \div \frac{1}{5}$

$\frac{2}{3} \div \frac{1}{5} = \frac{2}{3} \cdot \frac{5}{1}$ *Multiply by the reciprocal of $\frac{1}{5}$.*

$= \frac{2 \cdot 5}{3 \cdot 1}$

$= \frac{10}{3}$ or $3\frac{1}{3}$

B $\frac{3}{5} \div 6$

$\frac{3}{5} \div 6 = \frac{3}{5} \cdot \frac{1}{6}$ *Multiply by the reciprocal of 6.*

$= \frac{{}^{1}3 \cdot 1}{5 \cdot 6_{2}}$ *Simplify.*

$= \frac{1}{10}$

EXAMPLE 2 Dividing Mixed Numbers

Divide. Write each answer in simplest form.

A $4\frac{1}{3} \div 2\frac{1}{2}$

$4\frac{1}{3} \div 2\frac{1}{2} = \frac{13}{3} \div \frac{5}{2}$ *Write mixed numbers as improper fractions.*

$= \frac{13}{3} \cdot \frac{2}{5}$ *Multiply by the reciprocal of $\frac{5}{2}$.*

$= \frac{26}{15}$ or $1\frac{11}{15}$

Video **Lesson Tutorials Online** my.hrw.com

Divide. Write each answer in simplest form.

B $\frac{5}{6} \div 7\frac{1}{7}$

$\frac{5}{6} \div 7\frac{1}{7} = \frac{5}{6} \div \frac{50}{7}$ *Write $7\frac{1}{7}$ as an improper fraction.*

$= \frac{5}{6} \cdot \frac{7}{50}$ *Multiply by the reciprocal of $\frac{50}{7}$.*

$= \frac{\overset{1}{\cancel{5}} \cdot 7}{6 \cdot \underset{10}{\cancel{50}}}$ *Simplify.*

$= \frac{7}{60}$

C $4\frac{4}{5} \div \frac{6}{7}$

$4\frac{4}{5} \div \frac{6}{7} = \frac{24}{5} \div \frac{6}{7}$ *Write $4\frac{4}{5}$ as an improper fraction.*

$= \frac{24}{5} \cdot \frac{7}{6}$ *Multiply by the reciprocal of $\frac{6}{7}$.*

$= \frac{\overset{4}{\cancel{24}} \cdot 7}{5 \cdot \underset{1}{\cancel{6}}}$ *Simplify.*

$= \frac{28}{5}$ or $5\frac{3}{5}$

EXAMPLE 3   *Social Studies Application*

Use the bar graph to determine how many times longer a $100 bill is expected to stay in circulation than a $1 bill.

The life span of a $1 bill is $1\frac{1}{2}$ years. The life span of a $100 bill is 9 years.

Think: How many $1\frac{1}{2}$'s are there in 9?

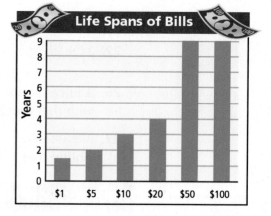

$9 \div 1\frac{1}{2} = \frac{9}{1} \div \frac{3}{2}$ *Write both numbers as improper fractions.*

$= \frac{9}{1} \cdot \frac{2}{3}$ *Multiply by the reciprocal of $\frac{3}{2}$.*

$= \frac{\overset{3}{\cancel{9}} \cdot 2}{1 \cdot \underset{1}{\cancel{3}}}$ *Simplify.*

$= \frac{6}{1}$ or 6

A $100 bill is expected to stay in circulation 6 times longer than a $1 bill.

Think and Discuss

1. Explain whether $\frac{1}{2} \div \frac{2}{3}$ is the same as $2 \cdot \frac{2}{3}$.

2. Compare the steps used in multiplying mixed numbers with those used in dividing mixed numbers.

3-10

Exercises

Learn It Online
Homework Help Online **go.hrw.com**,
keyword **MS10 3-10** (Go)
Exercises 1–27, 29, 31, 33, 35, 37, 43, 47

GUIDED PRACTICE

See Example **1** **Divide. Write each answer in simplest form.**

1. $6 \div \frac{1}{3}$ **2.** $\frac{3}{5} \div \frac{3}{4}$ **3.** $\frac{3}{4} \div 8$ **4.** $-\frac{5}{9} \div \frac{2}{5}$

See Example **2** **5.** $\frac{5}{6} \div 3\frac{1}{3}$ **6.** $5\frac{5}{8} \div 4\frac{1}{2}$ **7.** $10\frac{4}{5} \div 5\frac{2}{5}$ **8.** $2\frac{1}{10} \div \frac{3}{5}$

See Example **3** **9.** Kareem has $12\frac{1}{2}$ yards of material. A cape for a play takes $3\frac{5}{6}$ yards. How many capes can Kareem make with the material?

INDEPENDENT PRACTICE

See Example **1** **Divide. Write each answer in simplest form.**

10. $2 \div \frac{7}{8}$ **11.** $10 \div \frac{5}{9}$ **12.** $\frac{3}{4} \div \frac{6}{7}$ **13.** $\frac{7}{8} \div \frac{1}{5}$

14. $\frac{8}{9} \div \frac{1}{4}$ **15.** $\frac{4}{9} \div 12$ **16.** $\frac{9}{10} \div 6$ **17.** $-16 \div \frac{2}{5}$

See Example **2** **18.** $\frac{7}{11} \div 4\frac{1}{5}$ **19.** $\frac{3}{4} \div 2\frac{1}{10}$ **20.** $22\frac{1}{2} \div 4\frac{2}{7}$ **21.** $-10\frac{1}{2} \div \frac{3}{4}$

22. $3\frac{5}{7} \div 9\frac{1}{7}$ **23.** $14\frac{2}{3} \div 1\frac{1}{6}$ **24.** $7\frac{7}{10} \div 2\frac{2}{5}$ **25.** $8\frac{2}{5} \div \frac{7}{8}$

See Example **3** **26.** A juicer holds $43\frac{3}{4}$ pints of juice. How many $2\frac{1}{2}$-pint bottles can be filled with that much juice?

27. **Measurement** How many $24\frac{1}{2}$ in. pieces of ribbon can be cut from a roll of ribbon that is 147 in. long?

PRACTICE AND PROBLEM SOLVING

Extra Practice
See page EP10.

Evaluate. Write each answer in simplest form.

28. $6\frac{2}{3} \div \frac{7}{9}$ **29.** $-1\frac{7}{11} \div \left(\frac{9}{11}\right)$ **30.** $\frac{2}{3} \div \frac{8}{9}$ **31.** $-1\frac{3}{5} \div 2\frac{1}{2}$

32. $\frac{1}{2} \div 4\frac{3}{4}$ **33.** $\left(2\frac{3}{4} + 3\frac{2}{3}\right) \div \frac{11}{18}$ **34.** $\left(\frac{1}{2} + \frac{2}{3}\right) \div 1\frac{1}{2}$ **35.** $\frac{4}{5} \cdot \frac{3}{8} \div \frac{9}{10}$

36. $\frac{1}{2}\left(\frac{3}{5} - \frac{2}{15}\right) + \frac{2}{9} \div \frac{1}{3}$ **37.** $\frac{3}{7} \div \frac{15}{28} \div \left(-\frac{4}{5}\right)$ **38.** $\frac{7}{8} \div 2\frac{1}{10}$

39. $\frac{2}{3} \div \left(\frac{5}{6} + \frac{1}{12}\right) - 2 \cdot \frac{1}{2}$ **40.** $\frac{3}{4} + \frac{3}{20} \div \frac{2}{5} \cdot \frac{7}{8} - 1$ **41.** $\left(\frac{1}{2}\right)^2 + \frac{1}{3} \div \frac{1}{6} - \frac{1}{4}$

42. Three friends will be driving to an amusement park that is $226\frac{4}{5}$ mi from their town. If each friend drives the same distance, how far will each drive? Explain how you decided which operation to use to solve this problem.

43. **Multi-Step** How many $\frac{1}{4}$ lb hamburger patties can be made from a $10\frac{1}{4}$ lb package and an $11\frac{1}{2}$ lb package of ground meat?

 44. **Write About It** Explain what it means to divide $\frac{2}{3}$ by $\frac{1}{3}$. Use a model in your explanation.

45. **Multi-Step** The students in Mr. Park's woodworking class are making birdhouses. The plans call for the side pieces of the birdhouses to be $7\frac{1}{4}$ inches long. If Mr. Park has 6 boards that are $50\frac{3}{4}$ inches long, how many side pieces can be cut?

46. **Critical Thinking** Brandy is stamping circles from a strip of aluminum. If each circle is $1\frac{1}{4}$ inches tall, how many circles can she get from an $8\frac{3}{4}$-inch by $1\frac{1}{4}$-inch strip of aluminum?

47. For his drafting class, Manuel is drawing plans for a bookcase. Because he wants his drawing to be $\frac{1}{4}$ the actual size of the bookcase, Manuel must divide each measurement of the bookcase by 4. If the bookcase will be $3\frac{2}{3}$ feet wide, how wide will Manuel's drawing be?

48. The table shows the total number of hours that the students in each of Mrs. Anwar's 5 industrial arts classes took to complete their final projects. If the third-period class has 17 students, how many hours did each student in that class work on average?

Period	Hours
1st	$200\frac{1}{2}$
2nd	$179\frac{2}{5}$
3rd	$199\frac{3}{4}$
5th	$190\frac{3}{4}$
6th	$180\frac{1}{4}$

49. ⭐ **Challenge** Alexandra is cutting wood stencils to spell her first name with capital letters. Her first step is to cut a square of wood that is $3\frac{1}{2}$ in. long on a side for each letter in her name. Will Alexandra be able to make all of the letters of her name from a single piece of wood that is $7\frac{1}{2}$ in. wide and 18 in. long? Explain your answer.

Test Prep and Spiral Review

50. **Multiple Choice** Which expression is NOT equivalent to $2\frac{2}{3} \div 1\frac{5}{8}$?

   (A) $\frac{8}{3} \cdot \frac{8}{13}$ (B) $2\frac{2}{3} \div \frac{13}{8}$ (C) $\frac{8}{3} \div \frac{13}{8}$ (D) $\frac{8}{3} \cdot 1\frac{5}{8}$

51. **Multiple Choice** What is the value of the expression $\frac{3}{5} \cdot \frac{1}{6} \div \frac{2}{5}$?

   (F) $\frac{1}{25}$ (G) $\frac{1}{4}$ (H) $\frac{15}{22}$ (J) 25

52. **Gridded Response** Each cat at the animal shelter gets $\frac{3}{4}$ c of food every day. If Alysse has $16\frac{1}{2}$ c of cat food, how many cats can she feed?

Find the least common multiple (LCM). (Lesson 2-8)

53. 2, 15   54. 6, 8   55. 4, 6, 18   56. 3, 4, 8

Multiply. Write each answer in simplest form. (Lesson 3-9)

57. $-\frac{2}{15} \cdot \frac{5}{8}$ 58. $1\frac{7}{20} \cdot 6$ 59. $1\frac{2}{7} \cdot 2\frac{3}{4}$ 60. $\frac{1}{8} \cdot 6 \cdot 2\frac{5}{9}$

Solving Equations Containing Fractions

TN ✓ **0706.1.10** Model algebraic equations with manipulatives, technology, and pencil and paper. *Also* **SPI 0706.2.3, GLE 0706.3.8,** ✓ **0706.3.2**

Gold classified as 24 karat is pure gold, while gold classified as 18 karat is only $\frac{3}{4}$ pure. The remaining $\frac{1}{4}$ of 18-karat gold is made up of one or more different metals, such as silver, copper, or zinc.

Equations can help you determine the amounts of metals in different kinds of gold. The goal when solving equations that contain fractions is the same as when working with other kinds of numbers—*to isolate the variable* on one side of the equation.

EXAMPLE 1 Solving Equations by Adding or Subtracting

Solve. Write each answer in simplest form.

A $x - \frac{1}{5} = \frac{3}{5}$

$$x - \frac{1}{5} = \frac{3}{5}$$

$$x - \frac{1}{5} + \frac{1}{5} = \frac{3}{5} + \frac{1}{5} \qquad \text{\textit{Use the Addition Property of Equality.}}$$

$$x = \frac{4}{5} \qquad \text{\textit{Add.}}$$

B $\frac{7}{18} + u = -\frac{14}{27}$

$$\frac{7}{18} + u = -\frac{14}{27}$$

$$\frac{7}{18} + u - \frac{7}{18} = -\frac{14}{27} - \frac{7}{18} \qquad \text{\textit{Use the Subtraction Property of Equality.}}$$

$$u = -\frac{28}{54} - \frac{21}{54} \qquad \text{\textit{Find a common denominator.}}$$

$$u = -\frac{49}{54} \qquad \text{\textit{Subtract.}}$$

Helpful Hint

You can also isolate the variable *y* by adding the opposite of $\frac{7}{18}, -\frac{7}{18},$ to both sides.

Recall that the product of a nonzero number and its reciprocal is 1. This is called the Multiplicative Inverse Property.

Multiplicative Inverse Property		
Words	**Numbers**	**Algebra**
The product of a nonzero number and its reciprocal, or multiplicative inverse, is one.	$\frac{4}{5} \cdot \frac{5}{4} = 1$	$\frac{a}{b} \cdot \frac{b}{a} = 1$

You can use the Multiplicative Inverse Property to solve multiplication equations that contain fractions and whole numbers.

[Video] **Lesson Tutorials Online** my.hrw.com

EXAMPLE 2 Solving Equations by Multiplying

Solve. Write each answer in simplest form.

A $\frac{2}{3}x = \frac{4}{5}$

$$\frac{2}{3}x = \frac{4}{5}$$ *Use the Multiplicative Inverse Property.*

$$\frac{2}{3}x \cdot \frac{3}{2} = \frac{\overset{2}{\cancel{4}}}{5} \cdot \frac{3}{\cancel{2}_1}$$ *Multiply by the reciprocal of $\frac{2}{3}$. Then simplify.*

$$x = \frac{6}{5} \text{ or } 1\frac{1}{5}$$

B $3y = \frac{6}{7}$

$$3y = \frac{6}{7}$$ *Use the Multiplicative Inverse Property.*

$$3y \cdot \frac{1}{3} = \frac{\overset{2}{\cancel{6}}}{7} \cdot \frac{1}{\cancel{3}_1}$$ *Multiply by the reciprocal of 3. Then simplify.*

$$y = \frac{2}{7}$$

> **Caution!**
>
> To undo multiplying by $\frac{2}{3}$, you must divide by $\frac{2}{3}$ or multiply by its reciprocal, $\frac{3}{2}$.

EXAMPLE 3 *Physical Science Application*

Pink gold is made of pure gold, silver, and copper. There is $\frac{11}{20}$ more pure gold than copper in pink gold. If pink gold is $\frac{3}{4}$ pure gold, what portion of pink gold is copper?

Let c represent the amount of copper in pink gold.

$$c + \frac{11}{20} = \frac{3}{4}$$ *Write an equation.*

$$c + \frac{11}{20} - \frac{11}{20} = \frac{3}{4} - \frac{11}{20}$$ *Subtract to isolate c.*

$$c = \frac{15}{20} - \frac{11}{20}$$ *Find a common denominator.*

$$c = \frac{4}{20}$$ *Subtract.*

$$c = \frac{1}{5}$$ *Simplify.*

Pink gold is $\frac{1}{5}$ copper.

Think and Discuss

1. **Show** the first step you would use to solve $m + 3\frac{5}{8} = 12\frac{1}{2}$.

2. **Describe** how to decide whether $\frac{2}{3}$ is a solution of $\frac{7}{8}y = \frac{3}{5}$.

3. **Explain** why solving $\frac{2}{5}c = \frac{8}{9}$ by multiplying both sides by $\frac{5}{2}$ is the same as solving it by dividing both sides by $\frac{2}{5}$.

Exercises

Learn It Online
Homework Help Online **go.hrw.com**,
keyword MS7 3-11 Go
Exercises 1–20, 27, 31, 33, 35, 39, 41, 43

GUIDED PRACTICE

See Example **1** Solve. Write each answer in simplest form.

1. $a - \frac{1}{2} = \frac{1}{4}$

2. $m + \frac{1}{6} = \frac{5}{6}$

3. $p - \frac{2}{3} = \frac{5}{6}$

See Example **2** **4.** $\frac{1}{5}x = 8$

5. $\frac{2}{3}r = \frac{3}{5}$

6. $3w = \frac{3}{7}$

See Example **3** **7.** Kara has $\frac{3}{8}$ cup less oatmeal than she needs for a cookie recipe. If she has $\frac{3}{4}$ cup of oatmeal, how much oatmeal does she need?

INDEPENDENT PRACTICE

See Example **1** Solve. Write each answer in simplest form.

8. $n - \frac{1}{5} = \frac{3}{5}$

9. $t - \frac{3}{8} = \frac{1}{4}$

10. $s - \frac{7}{24} = \frac{1}{3}$

11. $x + \frac{2}{3} = 2\frac{7}{8}$

12. $h + \frac{7}{10} = \frac{7}{10}$

13. $y + \frac{5}{6} = \frac{19}{20}$

See Example **2** **14.** $\frac{1}{5}x = 4$

15. $\frac{1}{4}w = \frac{1}{8}$

16. $5y = \frac{3}{10}$

17. $6z = \frac{1}{2}$

18. $\frac{5}{8}x = \frac{2}{5}$

19. $\frac{5}{8}n = 1\frac{1}{5}$

See Example **3** **20.** **Earth Science** Carbon-14 has a half-life of 5,730 years. After 17,190 years, $\frac{1}{8}$ of the carbon-14 in a sample will be left. If 5 grams of carbon-14 are left after 17,190 years, how much was in the original sample?

PRACTICE AND PROBLEM SOLVING

Extra Practice
See page EP10.

Solve. Write each answer in simplest form.

21. $\frac{4}{5}t = \frac{1}{5}$

22. $m - \frac{1}{2} = \frac{2}{3}$

23. $\frac{1}{8}w = \frac{3}{4}$

24. $\frac{8}{9} + t = \frac{17}{18}$

25. $\frac{5}{3}x = 1$

26. $j + \frac{5}{8} = \frac{11}{16}$

27. $\frac{4}{3}n = 3\frac{1}{5}$

28. $z + \frac{1}{6} = 3\frac{9}{15}$

29. $\frac{3}{4}y = \frac{3}{8}$

30. $-\frac{5}{26} + m = -\frac{7}{13}$

31. $-\frac{8}{77} + r = -\frac{1}{11}$

32. $y - \frac{3}{4} = -\frac{9}{20}$

33. $h - \frac{3}{8} = -\frac{11}{24}$

34. $-\frac{5}{36}t = -\frac{5}{16}$

35. $-\frac{8}{13}v = -\frac{6}{13}$

36. $4\frac{6}{7} + p = 5\frac{1}{4}$

37. $d - 5\frac{1}{8} = 9\frac{3}{10}$

38. $6\frac{8}{21}k = 13\frac{1}{3}$

39. **Food** Each person in Finland drinks an average of $24\frac{1}{4}$ lb of coffee per year. This is $13\frac{1}{16}$ lb more than the average person in Italy consumes. On average, how much coffee does an Italian drink each year?

40. **Weather** Yuma, Arizona, receives $102\frac{1}{100}$ fewer inches of rain each year than Quillayute, Washington, which receives $105\frac{9}{50}$ inches per year. (*Source: National Weather Service*). How much rain does Yuma get in one year?

41. Life Science Scientists have discovered $1\frac{1}{2}$ million species of animals. This is estimated to be $\frac{1}{10}$ the total number of species thought to exist. About how many species do scientists think exist?

42. History The circle graph shows the birthplaces of the United States' presidents who were in office between 1789 and 1845.

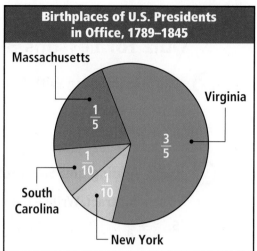

Birthplaces of U.S. Presidents in Office, 1789–1845

Massachusetts $\frac{1}{5}$
Virginia $\frac{3}{5}$
South Carolina $\frac{1}{10}$
$\frac{1}{10}$
New York

  a. If six of the presidents represented in the graph were born in Virginia, how many presidents are represented in the graph?

  b. Based on your answer to **a**, how many of the presidents were born in Massachusetts?

Architecture

The Chase Tower is the tallest skyscraper in Indiana. The two spires bring the building's height to 830 feet. One of the spires functions as a communications antenna, while the other is simply decorative.

43. Architecture In Indianapolis, the Market Tower has $\frac{2}{3}$ as many stories as the Chase Tower. If the Market Tower has 32 stories, how many stories does the Chase Tower have?

44. Multi-Step Each week, Jennifer saves $\frac{1}{5}$ of her allowance and spends some of the rest on lunches. This week, she had $\frac{2}{15}$ of her allowance left after buying her lunch each day. What fraction of her allowance did she spend on lunches?

45. What's the Error? A student solved $\frac{3}{5}x = \frac{2}{3}$ and got $x = \frac{2}{5}$. Find the error.

46. Write About It Solve $3\frac{1}{3}z = 1\frac{1}{2}$. Explain why you need to write mixed numbers as improper fractions when multiplying and dividing.

47. Challenge Solve $\frac{3}{5}w = 0.9$. Write your answer as a fraction and as a decimal.

Test Prep and Spiral Review

48. Multiple Choice Which value of y is the solution to the equation $y - \frac{7}{8} = \frac{3}{5}$?

  A $y = -\frac{11}{40}$ **B** $y = \frac{10}{13}$ **C** $y = 1\frac{19}{40}$ **D** $y = 2$

49. Multiple Choice Which equation has the solution $x = -\frac{2}{5}$?

  F $\frac{2}{5}x = -1$ **G** $-\frac{3}{4}x = \frac{6}{20}$ **H** $-\frac{4}{7} + x = \frac{2}{3}$ **J** $x - 3\frac{5}{7} = 3\frac{1}{2}$

Order the numbers from least to greatest. (Lesson 2-11)

50. $-0.61, -\frac{3}{5}, -\frac{4}{3}, -1.25$ **51.** $3.25, 3\frac{2}{10}, 3, 3.02$ **52.** $\frac{1}{2}, -0.2, -\frac{7}{10}, 0.04$

Estimate. (Lesson 3-1)

53. $5.87 - 7.01$ **54.** $4.0387 + (-2.13)$ **55.** $6.785 \cdot 3.01$

Quiz for Lessons 3-6 Through 3-11

3-6 Estimating with Fractions

Estimate each sum, difference, product, or quotient.

1. $\frac{3}{4} - \frac{2}{9}$

2. $-\frac{2}{7} + 5\frac{6}{11}$

3. $4\frac{9}{15} \cdot 3\frac{1}{4}$

4. $9\frac{7}{9} \div 4\frac{3}{5}$

3-7 Adding and Subtracting Fractions

Add or subtract. Write each answer in simplest form.

5. $\frac{5}{8} + \frac{1}{8}$

6. $\frac{14}{15} - \frac{11}{15}$

7. $-\frac{1}{3} + \frac{6}{9}$

8. $\frac{5}{8} - \frac{2}{3}$

3-8 Adding and Subtracting Mixed Numbers

Add or subtract. Write each answer in simplest form.

9. $6\frac{1}{9} + 2\frac{2}{9}$

10. $1\frac{3}{6} + 7\frac{2}{3}$

11. $5\frac{5}{8} - 3\frac{1}{8}$

12. $8\frac{1}{12} - 3\frac{1}{4}$

13. A mother giraffe is $13\frac{7}{10}$ ft tall. She is $5\frac{1}{2}$ ft taller than her young giraffe. How tall is the young giraffe?

3-9 Multiplying Fractions and Mixed Numbers

Multiply. Write each answer in simplest form.

14. $-12 \cdot \frac{5}{6}$

15. $\frac{5}{14} \cdot \frac{7}{10}$

16. $8\frac{4}{5} \cdot \frac{10}{11}$

17. $10\frac{5}{12} \cdot 1\frac{3}{5}$

18. A recipe calls for $1\frac{1}{3}$ cups flour. Tom is making $2\frac{1}{2}$ times the recipe for his family reunion. How much flour does he need? Write your answer in simplest form.

3-10 Dividing Fractions and Mixed Numbers

Divide. Write each answer in simplest form.

19. $\frac{1}{6} \div \frac{5}{6}$

20. $\frac{2}{3} \div 4$

21. $5\frac{3}{5} \div \frac{4}{5}$

22. $4\frac{2}{7} \div 1\frac{1}{5}$

23. Nina has $9\frac{3}{7}$ yards of material. She needs $1\frac{4}{7}$ yards to make a pillow case. How many pillow cases can Nina make with the material?

3-11 Solving Equations Containing Fractions

Solve. Write each answer in simplest form.

24. $x - \frac{2}{3} = \frac{2}{15}$

25. $\frac{4}{9} = -2q$

26. $\frac{1}{6}m = \frac{1}{9}$

27. $\frac{3}{8} + p = -\frac{1}{6}$

28. A recipe for Uncle Frank's homemade hush puppies calls for $\frac{1}{8}$ teaspoon of cayenne pepper. The recipe calls for 6 times as much salt as it does cayenne pepper. How much salt does Uncle Frank's recipe require?

CHAPTER 3

Real-World CONNECTIONS

Civil Rights in Education Heritage Trail The roots of free public education in the United States can be traced to southern Virginia. A self-guided driving tour of the area takes visitors to more than 40 schools, libraries, and other sites that played a key role in the story of civil rights in education.

VIRGINIA

The Wilson family is driving the Civil Rights in Education Heritage Trail. Use the map to solve these problems about their trip.

1. The Wilsons drive from Appomattox to Petersburg on the first day of their trip. How many miles do they drive?

2. On the second day of the trip, they drive from Petersburg to South Hill. How much farther do they drive on the first day than on the second day?

3. The distance from South Boston to Halifax is $\frac{1}{6}$ of the distance from Farmville to Nottoway. What is the distance from South Boston to Halifax?

4. The entire trip from Appomattox to Halifax is 202.1 miles. The Wilsons' car gets 21.5 miles to the gallon. How many gallons of gas will they use for the trip?

5. Gas costs $3.65 per gallon. How much will gas cost for the entire trip?

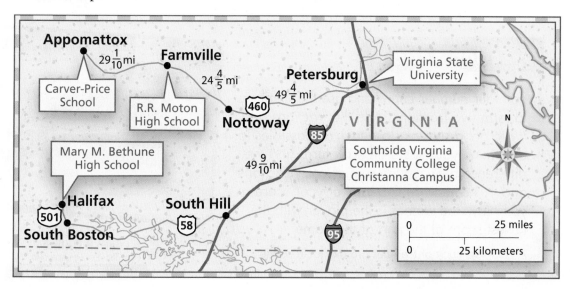

Real-World Connections

Real-World Connections **199**

Game Time

Number Patterns

The numbers one through ten form the pattern below. Each arrow indicates some kind of relationship between the two numbers. Four relates to itself. Can you figure out what the pattern is?

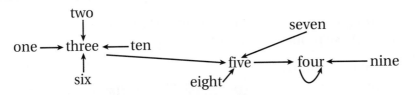

The Spanish numbers *uno* through *diez* form a similar pattern. In this case, *cinco* relates to itself.

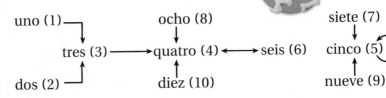

Other interesting number patterns involve cyclic numbers. Cyclic numbers sometimes occur when a fraction converts to a repeating nonterminating decimal. One of the most interesting cyclic numbers is produced by converting the fraction $\frac{1}{7}$ to a decimal.

$\frac{1}{7} = 0.142857142857142\ldots$

Multiplying 142857 by the numbers 1–6 produces the same digits in a different order.

$1 \cdot 142857 = 142857$ $3 \cdot 142857 = 428571$ $5 \cdot 142857 = 714285$

$2 \cdot 142857 = 285714$ $4 \cdot 142857 = 571428$ $6 \cdot 142857 = 857142$

Fraction Action

Roll four number cubes and use the numbers to form two fractions. Add the fractions and try to get a sum as close to 1 as possible. To determine your score on each turn, find the difference between the sum of your fractions and 1. Keep a running total of your score as you play. The winner is the player with the lowest score at the end of the game.

A complete copy of the rules are available online.

Learn It Online
Game Time Extra **go.hrw.com**,
keyword MS10 Games Go

Materials
- file folder
- ruler
- pencil
- scissors
- markers

It's in the Bag!

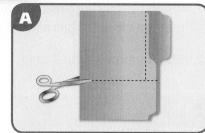
A

PROJECT **Operation Slide Through**

Slide notes through the frame to review key concepts about operations with rational numbers.

Directions

❶ Keep the file folder closed throughout the project. Cut off a $3\frac{1}{2}$-inch strip from the bottom of the folder. Trim the remaining folder so that is has no tabs and measures 8 inches by 8 inches. **Figure A**

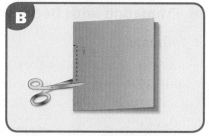
B

❷ Cut out a thin notch about 4 inches long along the middle of the folded edge. **Figure B**

❸ Cut a $3\frac{3}{4}$-inch slit about 2 inches to the right of the notch. Make another slit, also $3\frac{3}{4}$ inches long, about 3 inches to the right of the first slit. **Figure C**

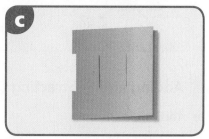
C

❹ Weave the $3\frac{1}{2}$-inch strip of the folder into the notch, through the first slit, and into the second slit. **Figure D**

Taking Note of the Math

As you pull the strip through the frame, divide the strip into several sections. Use each section to record vocabulary and practice problems from the chapter.

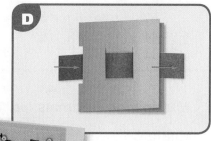
D

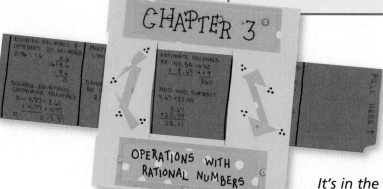

Vocabulary

compatible numbers 144

multiplicative inverse 190

reciprocal 190

Complete the sentences below with vocabulary words from the list above.

1. When estimating products or quotients, you can use ____?____ that are close to the original numbers and easy to use.

2. The fractions $\frac{3}{8}$ and $\frac{8}{3}$ are ____?____ because they multiply to give 1.

EXAMPLES

EXERCISES

3-1 Estimating with Decimals (pp. 144–147)

■ **Estimate.**

$$\begin{array}{r} 63.28 \longrightarrow 63 \\ + 16.52 \longrightarrow + 17 \\ \hline 80 \end{array}$$ *Round each decimal to the nearest integer.*

$$\begin{array}{r} 43.55 \longrightarrow 40 \\ \times 8.65 \longrightarrow \times 9 \\ \hline 360 \end{array}$$ *Use compatible numbers.*

Estimate.

3. $54.4 + 55.99$

4. $11.48 - 5.6$

5. $24.77 \cdot 3.45$

6. $37.8 \div 9.3$

7. Helen saves $7.85 each week. She wants to buy a TV that costs $163.15. For about how many weeks will Helen have to save her money before she can buy the TV?

3-2 Adding and Subtracting Decimals (pp. 148–151)

■ **Add.**

$5.67 + 22.44$

$$\begin{array}{r} 5.67 \\ + 22.44 \\ \hline 28.11 \end{array}$$

Line up the decimal points.

Add.

Add or subtract.

8. $4.99 + 22.89$

9. $-6.7 + (-44.5)$

10. $18.09 - 11.87$

11. $47 + 5.902$

12. $23 - 8.905$

13. $4.68 + 31.2$

3-3 Multiplying Decimals (pp. 154–157)

■ **Multiply.**

$1.44 \cdot 0.6$

$$\begin{array}{r} 1.44 \\ \times 0.6 \\ \hline 0.864 \end{array}$$

2 decimal places
1 decimal place
2 + 1 = 3 decimal places

Multiply.

14. $7 \cdot 0.5$

15. $-4.3 \cdot 9$

16. $4.55 \cdot 8.9$

17. $7.88 \cdot 7.65$

18. $63.4 \cdot 1.22$

19. $-9.9 \cdot 1.9$

20. Fred buys 4 shirts at $9.52 per shirt. How much did Fred spend?

3-4 Dividing Decimals (pp. 160–163)

■ **Divide.**

$7 \div 2.8$

$$\begin{array}{r} 2.5 \\ 28\overline{)70.0} \\ \underline{56} \\ 140 \\ \underline{140} \\ 0 \end{array}$$

Multiply both numbers by 10 to make the divisior an integer.

■ **Divide.**

$0.96 \div 1.6$

$$\begin{array}{r} 0.6 \\ 16\overline{)9.6} \\ \underline{-9\,6} \\ 0 \end{array}$$

Multiply both numbers by 10 to make the divisor an integer.

Divide.

21. $16 \div 3.2$ **22.** $50 \div (-1.25)$

23. $48 \div 0.06$ **24.** $31 \div (-6.2)$

25. $78 \div (-12.5)$ **26.** $816 \div 2.4$

27. $7.65 \div 1.7$ **28.** $9.483 \div (-8.7)$

29. $126.28 \div (-8.2)$ **30.** $2.5 \div (-0.005)$

31. $9 \div 4.5$ **32.** $13 \div 3.25$

33. In qualifying for an auto race, one driver had lap speeds of 195.3 mi/h, 190.456 mi/h, 193.557 mi/h, and 192.757 mi/h. What was the driver's average speed for these four laps?

3-5 Solving Equations Containing Decimals (pp. 164–167)

■ **Solve.**

$$\begin{array}{rl} n - 4.77 = & 8.60 \\ \underline{+\ 4.77} & \underline{+\ 4.77} \\ n = & 13.37 \end{array}$$

Add to isolate n.

Solve.

34. $x + 40.44 = 30$ **35.** $\frac{s}{1.07} = 100$

36. $0.8n = 0.0056$ **37.** $k - 8 = 0.64$

38. $3.65 + e = -1.4$ **39.** $\frac{w}{-0.2} = 15.4$

40. Sam wants to buy a new wakeboard that costs \$434. If he makes \$7.75 per hour, how many hours must he work to earn enough money for the wakeboard?

3-6 Estimating with Fractions (pp. 170–173)

■ **Estimate.**

$7\frac{3}{4} - 4\frac{1}{3}$

$7\frac{3}{4} \longrightarrow 8 \qquad 4\frac{1}{3} \longrightarrow 4\frac{1}{2}$

$8 - 4\frac{1}{2} = 3\frac{1}{2}$

$11\frac{7}{12} \div 3\frac{2}{5}$

$11\frac{7}{12} \longrightarrow 12 \qquad 3\frac{2}{5} \longrightarrow 3$

$12 \div 3 = 4$

Estimate each sum, difference, product, or quotient.

41. $11\frac{1}{7} + 12\frac{3}{4}$ **42.** $5\frac{5}{7} - 13\frac{10}{17}$

43. $9\frac{7}{8} + \left(-7\frac{1}{13}\right)$ **44.** $11\frac{8}{9} - 11\frac{1}{20}$

45. $5\frac{13}{20} \cdot 4\frac{1}{2}$ **46.** $-6\frac{1}{4} \div \left(-1\frac{5}{8}\right)$

47. Sara ran $2\frac{1}{3}$ laps on Monday and $7\frac{3}{4}$ laps on Friday. About how many more laps did Sara run on Friday?

Study Guide: Review

3-7 **Adding and Subtracting Fractions** (pp. 176–179)

■ Add.

$\frac{1}{3} + \frac{2}{5} = \frac{5}{15} + \frac{6}{15}$ *Write equivalent fractions using a*

$= \frac{11}{15}$ *common denominator.*

Add or subtract. Write each answer in simplest form.

48. $\frac{3}{4} - \frac{1}{3}$ **49.** $\frac{1}{4} + \frac{3}{5}$

50. $\frac{4}{11} + \frac{4}{44}$ **51.** $\frac{4}{9} - \frac{1}{3}$

3-8 **Adding and Subtracting Mixed Numbers** (pp. 180–183)

■ Add.

$1\frac{1}{3} + 2\frac{1}{2} = 1\frac{2}{6} + 2\frac{3}{6}$ *Add the integers, and then add the*

$= 3 + \frac{5}{6}$ *fractions.*

$= 3\frac{5}{6}$

Add or subtract. Write each answer in simplest form.

52. $3\frac{7}{8} + 2\frac{1}{3}$ **53.** $2\frac{1}{4} + 1\frac{1}{12}$

54. $8\frac{1}{2} - 2\frac{1}{4}$ **55.** $11\frac{3}{4} - 10\frac{1}{3}$

3-9 **Multiplying Fractions and Mixed Numbers** (pp. 186–189)

■ Multiply. Write the answer in simplest form.

$4\frac{1}{2} \cdot 5\frac{3}{4} = \frac{9}{2} \cdot \frac{23}{4}$

$= \frac{207}{8}$ or $25\frac{7}{8}$

Multiply. Write each answer in simplest form.

56. $1\frac{2}{3} \cdot 4\frac{1}{2}$ **57.** $\frac{4}{5} \cdot 2\frac{3}{10}$

58. $4\frac{6}{7} \cdot 3\frac{5}{9}$ **59.** $3\frac{4}{7} \cdot 1\frac{3}{4}$

3-10 **Dividing Fractions and Mixed Numbers** (pp. 190–193)

■ Divide.

$\frac{3}{4} \div \frac{2}{5} = \frac{3}{4} \cdot \frac{5}{2}$ *Multiply by the reciprocal of $\frac{2}{5}$.*

$= \frac{15}{8}$ or $1\frac{7}{8}$

Divide. Write each answer in simplest form.

60. $\frac{1}{3} \div 6\frac{1}{4}$ **61.** $\frac{1}{2} \div 3\frac{3}{4}$

62. $\frac{11}{13} \div \frac{11}{13}$ **63.** $2\frac{7}{8} \div 1\frac{1}{2}$

64. A 21-inch long loaf of bread is cut into $\frac{3}{4}$-inch slices. How many slices will there be?

3-11 **Solving Equations Containing Fractions** (pp. 194–197)

■ Solve. Write the answer in simplest form.

$\frac{1}{4}x = \frac{1}{6}$

$\frac{4}{1} \cdot \frac{1}{4}x = \frac{1}{6} \cdot \frac{4}{1}$ *Multiply by the reciprocal of $\frac{1}{4}$.*

$x = \frac{4}{6} = \frac{2}{3}$

Solve. Write each answer in simplest form.

65. $\frac{1}{5}x = \frac{1}{3}$ **66.** $\frac{1}{3} + y = \frac{2}{5}$

67. $\frac{1}{6}x = \frac{2}{7}$ **68.** $\frac{2}{7} + x = \frac{3}{4}$

69. Ty had $2\frac{1}{2}$ cups of oil and used $\frac{3}{4}$ cup for a recipe. How many cups of oil are left?

Study Guide: Review

Estimate.

1. $19.95 + 21.36$ 2. $49.17 - 5.88$ 3. $3.21 \cdot 16.78$ 4. $49.1 \div 5.6$

Add or subtract.

5. $3.086 + 6.152$ 6. $5.91 + 12.8$ 7. $3.1 - 2.076$ 8. $14.75 - 6.926$

Multiply or divide.

9. $3.25 \cdot 24$ 10. $-3.79 \cdot 0.9$ 11. $32 \div 1.6$ 12. $3.57 \div (-0.7)$

Solve.

13. $w - 5.3 = 7.6$ 14. $4.9 = c + 3.7$ 15. $b \div 1.8 = 2.1$ 16. $4.3h = 81.7$

Estimate each sum, difference, product, or quotient.

17. $\frac{3}{4} + \frac{3}{8}$ 18. $5\frac{7}{8} - 3\frac{1}{4}$ 19. $6\frac{5}{7} \cdot 2\frac{2}{9}$ 20. $8\frac{1}{5} \div 3\frac{9}{10}$

Add or subtract. Write each answer in simplest form.

21. $\frac{3}{10} + \frac{2}{5}$ 22. $\frac{11}{16} - \frac{7}{8}$ 23. $7\frac{1}{3} + 5\frac{11}{12}$ 24. $9 - 3\frac{2}{5}$

Multiply or divide. Write each answer in simplest form.

25. $5 \cdot 4\frac{1}{3}$ 26. $2\frac{7}{10} \cdot 2\frac{2}{3}$ 27. $\frac{3}{10} \div \frac{4}{5}$ 28. $2\frac{1}{5} \div 1\frac{5}{6}$

29. A recipe calls for $4\frac{4}{5}$ tbsp of butter. Nasim is making $3\frac{1}{3}$ times the recipe for his soccer team. How much butter does he need? Write your answer in simplest form.

30. Brianna has $11\frac{2}{3}$ cups of milk. She needs $1\frac{1}{6}$ cups of milk to make a pot of hot cocoa. How many pots of hot cocoa can Brianna make?

Solve. Write each answer in simplest form.

31. $\frac{1}{5}a = \frac{1}{8}$ 32. $\frac{1}{4}c = 980$ 33. $-\frac{7}{9} + w = \frac{2}{3}$ 34. $z - \frac{5}{13} = \frac{6}{7}$

35. Alan finished his homework in $1\frac{1}{2}$ hours. It took Jimmy $\frac{3}{4}$ of an hour longer than Alan to finish his homework. How long did it take Jimmy to finish his homework?

36. Mya played in two softball games one afternoon. The first game lasted 42 min. The second game lasted $1\frac{2}{3}$ times longer than the first game. How long did Mya's second game last?

Chapter Test

Test Tackler
STANDARDIZED TEST STRATEGIES

Gridded Response: Write Gridded Responses

When responding to a test item that requires you to place your answer in a grid, you must fill in the grid on your answer sheet correctly, or the item will be marked as incorrect.

EXAMPLE 1

Gridded Response: Solve the equation 0.23 + r = 1.42.

$$
\begin{aligned}
0.23 + r &= 1.42 \\
- 0.23 & \quad - 0.23 \\
r &= 1.19
\end{aligned}
$$

- Using a pencil, write your answer in the answer boxes at the top of the grid. Put the first digit of your answer in the leftmost box, or put the last digit of your answer in the rightmost box. On some grids, the fraction bar and the decimal point have a designated box.

- Put only one digit or symbol in each box. Do not leave a blank box in the middle of an answer.

- Shade the bubble for each digit or symbol in the same column as in the answer box.

EXAMPLE 2

Gridded Response: Divide. $3 \div 1\frac{4}{5}$

$$
3 \div 1\frac{4}{5} = \frac{3}{1} \div \frac{9}{5}
$$

$$
= \frac{3}{1} \cdot \frac{5}{9}
$$

$$
= \frac{15}{9} = \frac{5}{3} = 1\frac{2}{3} = 1.\overline{6}
$$

The answer simplifies to $\frac{5}{3}$, $1\frac{2}{3}$, or $1.\overline{6}$.

- Mixed numbers and repeating decimals cannot be gridded, so you must grid the answer as $\frac{5}{3}$.

- Write your answer in the answer boxes at the top of the grid.

- Put only one digit or symbol in each box. Do not leave a blank box in the middle of an answer.

- Shade the bubble for each digit or symbol in the same column as in the answer box.

If you get a negative answer to a gridded response item, rework the problem carefully. Response grids do not include negative signs, so if you get a negative answer, you probably made a math error.

Read each statement, and then answer the questions that follow.

Sample A
A student correctly solved an equation for *x* and got 42 as a result. Then the student filled in the grid as shown.

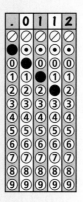

1. What error did the student make when filling in the grid?

2. Explain a second method of filling in the answer correctly.

Sample B
A student correctly multiplied 0.16 and 0.07. Then the student filled in the grid as shown.

3. What error did the student make when filling in the grid?

4. Explain how to fill in the answer correctly.

Sample C
A student subtracted −12 from 5 and got an answer of −17. Then the student filled in the grid as shown.

5. What error did the student make when finding the answer?

6. Explain why you cannot fill in a negative number on a grid.

7. Explain how to fill in the answer to 5 − (−12) correctly.

Sample D
A student correctly simplified $\frac{5}{6} + \frac{11}{12}$ and got $1\frac{9}{12}$ as a result. Then the student filled in the grid as shown.

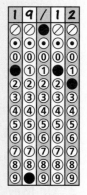

8. What answer is shown in the grid?

9. Explain why you cannot show a mixed number in a grid.

10. Write two equivalent forms of the answer $1\frac{9}{12}$ that could be filled in the grid correctly.

TCAP
Test Prep

Learn It Online
State Test Practice **go.hrw.com**,
keyword MS10 TestPrep Go

Cumulative Assessment, Chapters 1–3

Multiple Choice

1. Evaluate $m + n$ when $m = -4.7$ and $n = -2.4$.

   A −7.1   C 2.3

   B −2.3   D 7.1

2. Ahmed had $7.50 in his bank account on Sunday. The table shows his account activity for each day last week. What was the balance in Ahmed's account on Friday?

Day	Deposit	Withdrawal
Monday	$25.25	none
Tuesday	none	−$108.13
Wednesday	$65.25	none
Thursday	$32.17	none
Friday	none	−$101.50

   F −$86.96   H $0

   G −$79.46   J $96.46

3. On May 5, Teri made three $50 ATM deposits. On May 6, she made two $100 ATM withdrawals. On May 7, she made two $60 deposits. After these last deposits, she had $1012 in her account. How much money did Teri have before she made the deposits on May 5?

   A $822   C $1,002

   B $942   D $1,082

4. What is the value of $5\frac{2}{3} \div \frac{3}{9}$?

   F 17   H 10

   G $\frac{17}{9}$ J $5\frac{1}{3}$

5. A certain video game scores each correct answer as +15 points and each incorrect answer as −20 points. Garrett answers 7 questions correctly and answers 5 questions incorrectly. What is his final score?

   A −5   C 15

   B 5   D 20

6. A personal trainer expects his clients to be able to do $35 + 20w$ sit-ups a day, where w is the number of weeks the person has been training. If a client has been training for 5.5 weeks, how many sit-ups should the person be able to do?

   F 60   H 135

   G 75   J 145

7. Daisy the bulldog weighs $45\frac{13}{16}$ pounds. Henry the beagle weighs $21\frac{3}{4}$ pounds. How many more pounds does Daisy weigh than Henry?

   A $23\frac{15}{16}$ pounds

   B $24\frac{5}{6}$ pounds

   C $24\frac{1}{16}$ pounds

   D $67\frac{9}{16}$ pounds

8. Joel threw a ball $24\frac{2}{9}$ yards. Jamil threw the ball $33\frac{10}{11}$ yards. How much farther did Jamil throw the ball than Joel?

   F $7\frac{8}{11}$ yards   H $10\frac{11}{99}$ yards

   G $9\frac{68}{99}$ yards   J $58\frac{13}{99}$ yards

9. Which model **best** represents the expression $\frac{6}{8} \times \frac{1}{2}$?

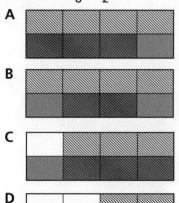

A

B

C

D

10. Webster built a shelf that can hold 87 pounds to showcase his model airplanes. He has already placed 34.8 pounds on this shelf. If each remaining model weighs 5.8 pounds, how many more models can this shelf hold?

    F 706

    G 303

    H 21

    J 9

11. Frieda earns $5.85 per hour. Use the expression $5.85x$ to find the amount of money Frieda earns working x hours. How many dollars does Frieda earn if she works 2.4 hours?

    A $8.25

    B $10

    C $14.04

    D $20.40

Process Standards Practice

Short Response

S1. Louise is staying on the 22nd floor of a hotel. Her mother is staying on the 43rd floor. Louise wants to visit her mother, but the elevator is temporarily out of service. Write and solve an equation to find the number of floors that Louise must climb if she takes the stairs.

S2. Mari bought 3 packages of colored paper. She used $\frac{3}{4}$ of a package to make greeting cards and used $1\frac{1}{6}$ packages for an art project. She gave $\frac{2}{3}$ of a package to her brother. How much colored paper does Mari have left? Show the steps you used to find the answer.

S3. A building proposal calls for 6 acres of land to be divided into $\frac{3}{4}$-acre lots. How many lots can be made? Explain your answer.

Extended Response

E1. A high school is hosting a triple-jump competition. In this event, athletes make three leaps in a row to try to cover the greatest distance.

   a. Tony's first two jumps were $11\frac{2}{3}$ ft and $11\frac{1}{2}$ ft. His total distance was 44 ft. Write and solve an equation to find the length of his final jump.

   b. Candice's three jumps were all the same length. Her total distance was 38 ft. What was the length of each of her jumps?

   c. The lengths of Davis's jumps were 11.6 ft, $11\frac{1}{4}$ ft, and $11\frac{2}{3}$ ft. Plot these lengths on a number line. What was the farthest distance he jumped? How much farther was this distance than the shortest distance Davis jumped?

CHAPTER 4

Proportional Relationships

Why Learn This?

Proportions can be used to find the heights of objects that are too tall to measure directly, such as a lighthouse.

 Learn It Online
Chapter Project Online **go.hrw.com**,
keyword **MS10 Ch4** **Go**

 Chapter Focus
• Use proportionality to solve problems, including problems involving similar objects, units of measurement, and rates.

✓ Vocabulary

Choose the best term from the list to complete each sentence.

1. A(n) __?__ states that two expressions are equivalent.

2. To __?__ an expression is to substitute a number for the variable and simplify.

3. A value of the variable in an equation that makes the statement true is a(n) __?__ of the equation.

4. A(n) __?__ is a number that can be written as a ratio of two integers.

equation

evaluate

irrational number

rational number

solution

Complete these exercises to review skills you will need for this chapter.

✓ Evaluate Expressions

Evaluate each expression.

5. $x + 5$ for $x = -18$

6. $-9y$ for $y = 13$

7. $\frac{z}{-6}$ for $z = 96$

8. $w - 9$ for $w = -13$

9. $-3z + 1$ for $z = 4$

10. $3w + 9$ for $w = 7$

11. $5 - \frac{y}{3}$ for $y = -3$

12. $x^2 + 1$ for $x = -2$

✓ Solve Equations

Solve each equation.

13. $y + 14 = -3$

14. $-4y = -72$

15. $y - 6 = 39$

16. $\frac{y}{3} = -9$

17. $56 = 8y$

18. $26 = y + 2$

19. $25 - y = 7$

20. $\frac{121}{y} = 11$

21. $-72 = 3y$

22. $25 = \frac{150}{y}$

23. $15 + y = 4$

24. $-120 = -2y$

✓ Number Patterns

Find the next three numbers in the pattern.

25. $95, 112, 129, 146, \ldots$

26. $85, 65, 60, 40, 35, \ldots$

27. $20, 20, 100, 100, 500, \ldots$

28. $12, 14, 17, 21, 26, \ldots$

29. $1, 3, 5, 7, \ldots$

30. $-19, -12, -5, 2, \ldots$

31. $5, -10, 20, -40, 80, \ldots$

32. $0, -10, -5, -15, -10, \ldots$

Where You've Been

Previously, you

- used ratios to describe proportional situations.
- used ratios to make predictions in proportional situations.
- used tables to describe proportional relationships involving conversions.

In This Chapter

You will study

- using division to find unit rates and ratios in proportional relationships.
- estimating and finding solutions to application problems involving proportional relationships.
- generating formulas involving unit conversions.
- using critical attributes to define similarity.
- using ratios and proportions in scale drawings and scale models.

Where You're Going

You can use the skills learned in this chapter

- to read and interpret maps.
- to find heights of objects that are too tall to measure.

Key Vocabulary/Vocabulario

corresponding angles	ángulos correspondientes
corresponding sides	lados correspondientes
equivalent ratios	razones equivalentes
proportion	proporción
rate	tasa
ratio	razón
scale	escala
scale drawing	dibujo a escala
scale model	modelo a escala
similar	semejante

Vocabulary Connections

To become familiar with some of the vocabulary terms in the chapter, consider the following. You may refer to the chapter, the glossary, or a dictionary if you like.

1. "Miles per hour," "students per class," and "Calories per serving" are all examples of *rates*. What other rates can you think of? How would you describe a **rate** to someone if you couldn't use examples in your explanation?

2. You can select a gear ratio on a bicycle for maximum speed. Think of other examples where the word **ratio** is used. What do these examples have in common?

3. *Similar* means "having characteristics in common." If two triangles are **similar**, what might they have in common?

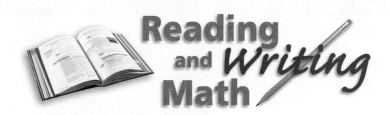

Writing Strategy: Use Your Own Words

TN ▶ **English/Language Arts**
✓ **0701.3.14** Edit to craft a tone that is appropriate for the topic and audience, and supports the purpose.

Using your own words to explain a concept can help you understand the concept. For example, learning how to solve equations might seem difficult if the textbook does not explain solving equations in the same way that you would.

As you work through each lesson:

- Identify the important ideas from the explanation in the book.

- Use your own words to explain these ideas.

What Sara Reads

An **equation** is a mathematical statement that two expressions are equal in value.

When an equation contains a variable, a value of the variable that makes the statement true is called a **solution** of the equation.

If a variable is multiplied by a number, you can often use division to isolate the variable. Divide both sides of the equation by the number.

What Sara Writes

An <u>equation</u> has an equal sign to show that two expressions are equal to each other.

The <u>solution</u> of an equation that has a variable in it is the number that the variable is equal to.

When the variable is multiplied by a number, you can undo the multiplication and get the variable alone by dividing both sides of the equation by the number.

 Try This

Rewrite each sentence in your own words.

1. When solving addition equations involving integers, isolate the variable by adding opposites.

2. When you solve equations that have one operation, you use an inverse operation to isolate the variable.

Reading and Writing Math

4-1 Ratios

TN **SPI 0706.2.7** Use ratios and proportions to solve problems. *Also* **GLE 0706.2.4**, ✓ **0706.2.8**, ✓ **0706.4.5**

Vocabulary

ratio

In basketball practice, Kathlene made 17 baskets in 25 attempts. She compared the number of baskets she made to the total number of attempts she made by using the *ratio* $\frac{17}{25}$. A **ratio** is a comparison of two quantities by division.

Kathlene can write her ratio of baskets made to attempts in three different ways.

$$\frac{17}{25} \qquad 17 \text{ to } 25 \qquad 17\!:\!25$$

EXAMPLE **1** **Writing Ratios**

A basket of fruit contains 6 apples, 4 bananas, and 3 oranges. Write each ratio in all three forms.

A **bananas to apples**

$$\frac{\text{number of bananas}}{\text{number of apples}} = \frac{4}{6} \qquad \textit{There are 4 bananas and 6 apples.}$$

The ratio of bananas to apples can be written as $\frac{4}{6}$, 4 to 6, or 4:6.

B **bananas and apples to oranges**

$$\frac{\text{number of bananas and apples}}{\text{number of oranges}} = \frac{4+6}{3} = \frac{10}{3}$$

The ratio of bananas and apples to oranges can be written as $\frac{10}{3}$, 10 to 3, or 10:3.

C **oranges to total pieces of fruit**

$$\frac{\text{number of oranges}}{\text{number of total pieces of fruit}} = \frac{3}{6+4+3} = \frac{3}{13}$$

The ratio of oranges to total pieces of fruit can be written as $\frac{3}{13}$, 3 to 13, or 3:13.

Video **Lesson Tutorials Online** my.hrw.com

Sometimes a ratio can be simplified. To simplify a ratio, first write it in fraction form and then simplify the fraction.

EXAMPLE 2 **Writing Ratios in Simplest Form**

Remember!

A fraction is in simplest form when the GCF of the numerator and denominator is 1.

At Franklin Middle School, there are 252 students in the seventh grade and 9 seventh-grade teachers. Write the ratio of students to teachers in simplest form.

$$\frac{\text{students}}{\text{teachers}} = \frac{252}{9} \qquad \textit{Write the ratio as a fraction.}$$

$$= \frac{252 \div 9}{9 \div 9} \qquad \textit{Simplify.}$$

$$= \frac{28}{1} \qquad \textit{For every 28 students, there is 1 teacher.}$$

The ratio of students to teachers is 28 to 1.

To compare ratios, write them as fractions with common denominators. Then compare the numerators.

EXAMPLE 3 **Comparing Ratios**

Tell whether the wallet size photo or the portrait size photo has the greater ratio of width to length.

	Width (in.)	Length (in.)
Wallet	3.5	5
Personal	4	6
Desk	5	7
Portrait	8	10

Wallet: $\dfrac{\text{width (in.)}}{\text{length (in.)}} = \dfrac{3.5}{5}$ *Write the ratios as fractions with common denominators.*

Portrait: $\dfrac{\text{width (in.)}}{\text{length (in.)}} = \dfrac{8}{10} = \dfrac{4}{5}$

Because $4 > 3.5$ and the denominators are the same, the portrait size photo has the greater ratio of width to length.

Think and Discuss

1. **Explain** why the ratio $\frac{10}{3}$ in Example 1B is not written as a mixed number.

2. **Tell** how to simplify a ratio.

3. **Explain** how to compare two ratios.

Learn It Online
Homework Help Online **go.hrw.com**,
keyword MS10 4-1 **Go**
Exercises 1–10, 11, 15, 17, 19

GUIDED PRACTICE

See Example 1
Sun-Li has 10 blue marbles, 3 red marbles, and 17 white marbles. Write each ratio in all three forms.

1. blue marbles to red marbles

2. red marbles to total marbles

See Example 2
3. In a 40-gallon aquarium, there are 21 neon tetras and 7 zebra danio fish. Write the ratio of neon tetras to zebra danio fish in simplest form.

See Example 3
4. Tell whose DVD collection has the greater ratio of comedy movies to adventure movies.

	Joseph	Yolanda
Comedy	5	7
Adventure	3	5

INDEPENDENT PRACTICE

See Example 1
A soccer league has 25 sixth-graders, 30 seventh-graders, and 15 eighth-graders. Write each ratio in all three forms.

5. 6th-graders to 7th-graders

6. 6th-graders to total students

7. 7th-graders to 8th-graders

8. 7th- and 8th-graders to 6th-graders

See Example 2
9. Thirty-six people auditioned for a play, and 9 people got roles. Write the ratio in simplest form of the number of people who auditioned to the number of people who got roles.

See Example 3
10. Tell whose bag of nut mix has the greater ratio of peanuts to total nuts.

	Dina	Don
Almonds	6	11
Cashews	8	7
Peanuts	10	18

PRACTICE AND PROBLEM SOLVING

Extra Practice
See page EP11.

Use the table for Exercises 11–13.

11. Tell whether group 1 or group 2 has the greater ratio of the number of people for an open-campus lunch to the number of people with no opinion.

Opinions on Open-Campus Lunch			
	Group 1	Group 2	Group 3
For	9	10	12
Against	14	16	16
No Opinion	5	6	8

12. Which group has the least ratio of the number of people against an open-campus lunch to the total number of survey responses?

13. **Estimation** For each group, is the ratio of the number of people for an open-campus lunch to the number of people against it less than or greater than $\frac{1}{2}$?

The pressure of water at different depths can be measured in *atmospheres,* or atm. The water pressure on a scuba diver increases as the diver descends below the surface. Use the table for Exercises 14–20.

Write each ratio in all three forms.

14. pressure at −33 ft to pressure at surface

15. pressure at −66 ft to pressure at surface

16. pressure at −99 ft to pressure at surface

17. pressure at −66 ft to pressure at −33 ft

18. pressure at −99 ft to pressure at −66 ft

19. Tell whether the ratio of pressure at −66 ft to pressure at −33 ft is greater than or less than the ratio of pressure at −99 ft to pressure at −66 ft.

20. ⭐ **Challenge** Compare the ratio of the beginning pressure and the new pressure when a scuba diver goes from −33 ft to −66 ft and when the diver goes from the surface to −33 ft. Are these ratios of pressures less than or greater than the ratio of pressure when the diver goes from −66 ft to −99 ft? Use ratios to explain.

Pressure Experienced by Diver	
Depth (ft)	Pressure (atm)
0	1
−33	2
−66	3
−99	4

Test Prep and Spiral Review

21. Multiple Choice Johnson Middle School has 125 sixth-graders, 150 seventh-graders, and 100 eighth-graders. Which statement is NOT true?

(A) The ratio of sixth-graders to seventh-graders is 5 to 6.

(B) The ratio of eighth-graders to seventh-graders is 3:2.

(C) The ratio of sixth-graders to students in all three grades is 1:3.

(D) The ratio of eighth-graders to students in all three grades is 4 to 15.

22. Short Response A pancake recipe calls for 4 cups of pancake mix for every 3 cups of milk. A biscuit recipe calls for 2 cups of biscuit mix for every 1 cup of milk. Which recipe has a greater ratio of mix to milk? Explain.

Solve. (Lesson 3-5)

23. $1.23 + x = -5.47$ **24.** $3.8y = 27.36$ **25.** $v - 3.8 = 4.7$

26. On Monday Jessika ran $3\frac{1}{2}$ miles. On Wednesday she ran $4\frac{1}{3}$ miles. How much farther did Jessika run on Wednesday? (Lesson 3-7)

4-2 Rates

TN SPI 0706.2.7 Use ratios and proportions to solve problems.
Also GLE 0706.2.4, ✓ 0706.2.7, ✓ 0706.2.8, ✓ 0706.3.10, GLE 0706.4.4

Vocabulary

rate

unit rate

The Lawsons are going camping at Rainbow Falls, which is 288 miles from their home. They would like to reach the campground in 6 hours. What should their average speed be in miles per hour?

In order to answer the question above, you need to find the family's *rate* of travel. A **rate** is a ratio that compares two quantities measured in different units.

The Lawson family's rate is $\frac{288 \text{ miles}}{6 \text{ hours}}$.

A **unit rate** is a rate whose denominator is 1 when it is written as a fraction. To change a rate to a unit rate, first write the rate as a fraction and then divide both the numerator and denominator by the denominator.

EXAMPLE 1 | **Finding Unit Rates**

Interactivities Online ▶

A During exercise, Sonia's heart beats 675 times in 5 minutes. How many times does it beat per minute?

$\frac{675 \text{ beats}}{5 \text{ minutes}}$ *Write a rate that compares heart beats and time.*

$\frac{675 \text{ beats} \div 5}{5 \text{ minutes} \div 5}$ *Divide the numerator and denominator by 5.*

$\frac{135 \text{ beats}}{1 \text{ minute}}$ *Simplify.*

Sonia's heart beats 135 times per minute.

B To make 4 large pizza pockets, Paul needs 14 cups of broccoli. How much broccoli does he need for 1 large pizza pocket?

$\frac{14 \text{ cups broccoli}}{4 \text{ pizza pockets}}$ *Write a rate that compares cups to pockets.*

$\frac{14 \text{ cups broccoli} \div 4}{4 \text{ pizza pockets} \div 4}$ *Divide the numerator and denominator by 4.*

$\frac{3.5 \text{ cups broccoli}}{1 \text{ pizza pocket}}$ *Simplify.*

Paul needs 3.5 cups of broccoli to make 1 large pizza pocket.

    Video **Lesson Tutorials Online** my.hrw.com

An average rate of speed is the ratio of distance traveled to time. The ratio is a rate because the units being compared are different.

EXAMPLE 2 **Finding Average Speed**

The Lawsons want to drive 288 miles to Rainbow Falls in 6 hours. What should their average speed be in miles per hour?

$\dfrac{288 \text{ miles}}{6 \text{ hours}}$ *Write the rate as a fraction.*

$\dfrac{288 \text{ miles} \div 6}{6 \text{ hours} \div 6} = \dfrac{48 \text{ miles}}{1 \text{ hour}}$ *Divide the numerator and denominator by the denominator.*

Their average speed should be 48 miles per hour.

A unit price is the price of one unit of an item. The unit used depends on how the item is sold. The table shows some examples.

Type of Item	Examples of Units
Liquid	Fluid ounces, quarts, gallons, liters
Solid	Ounces, pounds, grams, kilograms
Any item	Bottle, container, carton

EXAMPLE 3 *Consumer Math Application*

The Lawsons stop at a roadside farmers' market. The market offers lemonade in three sizes. Which size lemonade has the lowest price per fluid ounce?

Size	Price
12 fl oz	$0.89
18 fl oz	$1.69
24 fl oz	$2.09

Divide the price by the number of fluid ounces (fl oz) to find the unit price of each size.

$\dfrac{\$0.89}{12 \text{ fl oz}} \approx \dfrac{\$0.07}{\text{fl oz}}$ $\dfrac{\$1.69}{18 \text{ fl oz}} \approx \dfrac{\$0.09}{\text{fl oz}}$ $\dfrac{\$2.09}{24 \text{ fl oz}} \approx \dfrac{\$0.09}{\text{fl oz}}$

Since $0.07 < $0.09, the 12 fl oz lemonade has the lowest price per fluid ounce.

Think and Discuss

1. Explain how you can tell whether a rate represents a unit rate.

2. Suppose a store offers cereal with a unit price of $0.15 per ounce. Another store offers cereal with a unit price of $0.18 per ounce. Before determining which is the better buy, what variables must you consider?

GUIDED PRACTICE

See Example **1**   **1.** A faucet leaks 668 milliliters of water in 8 minutes. How many milliliters of water does the faucet leak per minute?

2. A recipe for 6 muffins calls for 360 grams of oat flakes. How many grams of oat flakes are needed for each muffin?

See Example **2**   **3.** An airliner makes a 2,748-mile flight in 6 hours. What is the airliner's average rate of speed in miles per hour?

See Example **3**   **4. Consumer Math** During a car trip, the Webers buy gasoline at three different stations. At the first station, they pay $18.63 for 9 gallons of gas. At the second, they pay $29.54 for 14 gallons. At the third, they pay $33.44 for 16 gallons. Which station offers the lowest price per gallon?

INDEPENDENT PRACTICE

See Example **1**   **5.** An after-school job pays $116.25 for 15 hours of work. How much money does the job pay per hour?

6. It took Samantha 324 minutes to cook an 18 lb turkey. How many minutes per pound did it take to cook the turkey?

See Example **2**   **7. Sports** The first Indianapolis 500 auto race took place in 1911. The winning car covered the 500 miles in 6.7 hours. What was the winning car's average rate of speed in miles per hour?

See Example **3**   **8. Consumer Math** A supermarket sells orange juice in three sizes. The 32 fl oz container costs $1.99, the 64 fl oz container costs $3.69, and the 96 fl oz container costs $5.85. Which size orange juice has the lowest price per fluid ounce?

PRACTICE AND PROBLEM SOLVING

Extra Practice
See page EP11.

Find each unit rate. Round to the nearest hundredth, if necessary.

9. 9 runs in 3 games   **10.** $207,000 for 1,800 ft^2 **11.** $2,010 in 6 mo

12. 52 songs on 4 CDs   **13.** 226 mi on 12 gal   **14.** 324 words in 6 min

15. 12 hr for $69   **16.** 6 lb for $12.96   **17.** 488 mi in 4 trips

18. 220 m in 20 s   **19.** 1.5 mi in 39 min   **20.** 24,000 km in 1.5 hr

21. In Grant Middle School, each class has an equal number of students. There are 38 classes and a total of 1,026 students. Write a rate that describes the distribution of students in the classes at Grant. What is the unit rate?

22. Estimation Use estimation to determine which is the better buy: 450 minutes of phone time for $49.99 or 800 minutes for $62.99.

Find each unit price. Then decide which is the better buy.

23. $\frac{\$2.52}{42 \text{ oz}}$ or $\frac{\$3.64}{52 \text{ oz}}$

24. $\frac{\$28.40}{8 \text{ yd}}$ or $\frac{\$55.50}{15 \text{ yd}}$

25. $\frac{\$8.28}{0.3 \text{ m}}$ or $\frac{\$13.00}{0.4 \text{ m}}$

26. **Sports** At the track meet, Justin won the 100-meter race in 12.61 seconds. Shawn won the 200-meter race in 26.38 seconds. Which runner ran at a faster average rate?

27. **Social Studies** The population density of a country is the average number of people per unit of area. Write the population densities of the countries in the map at right as unit rates. Round your answers to the nearest person per square mile. Then rank the countries from least population density to greatest population density.

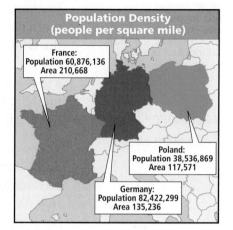

**Population Density
(people per square mile)**

France:
Population 60,876,136
Area 210,668

Poland:
Population 38,536,869
Area 117,571

Germany:
Population 82,422,299
Area 135,236

28. **Write a Problem** A store sells paper towels in packs of 6 and packs of 8. Use this information to write a problem about comparing unit rates.

29. **Write About It** Michael Jordan has the highest scoring average in NBA history. During his career, he played in 1,072 games and scored a total of 32,292 points. Explain how to find a unit rate to describe his scoring average. What is the unit rate?

30. **Challenge** Mike fills his car's gas tank with 20 gallons of regular gas at $2.01 per gallon. His car averages 25 miles per gallon. Serena fills her car's tank with 15 gallons of premium gas at $2.29 per gallon. Her car averages 30 miles per gallon. Compare the drivers' unit costs of driving one mile.

Test Prep and Spiral Review

31. **Multiple Choice** What is the unit price of a 16-ounce box of cereal that sells for $2.48?

   Ⓐ $0.14   Ⓑ $0.15   Ⓒ $0.0155   Ⓓ $0.155

32. **Short Response** A carpenter needs 3 minutes to make 5 cuts in a board. Each cut takes the same length of time. At what rate is the carpenter cutting?

Multiply. Estimate to check whether each answer is reasonable. (Lesson 3-3)

33. $-4.87 \cdot (-2.4)$

34. $-6.2 \cdot 130$

35. $0.65 \cdot (-2.07)$

36. Julita's walking stick is $3\frac{2}{3}$ feet long, and Toni's walking stick is $3\frac{3}{8}$ feet long. Whose walking stick is longer and by how much? (Lesson 3-8)

TN SPI 0706.2.7 Use ratios and proportions to solve problems.
Also GLE 0706.2.3, ✓ 0706.2.8, GLE 0706.3.8, GLE 0706.4.4

Vocabulary

equivalent ratios

proportion

Students in Mr. Howell's math class are measuring the width w and the length ℓ of their faces. The ratio of ℓ to w is 6 inches to 4 inches for Jean and 21 centimeters to 14 centimeters for Pat.

Oval face: $\frac{\ell}{w} \approx \frac{3}{2}$

These ratios can be written as $\frac{6}{4}$ and $\frac{21}{14}$. Since both ratios simplify to $\frac{3}{2}$, they are equivalent. **Equivalent ratios** are ratios that name the same comparison.

An equation stating that two ratios are equivalent is called a **proportion**. The equation, or proportion, below states that the ratios $\frac{6}{4}$ and $\frac{21}{14}$ are equivalent.

Round face: $\ell \approx w$

$$\frac{6}{4} = \frac{21}{14}$$

If two ratios are equivalent, they are said to be *proportional*, or *in proportion*.

> **Reading Math**
>
> Read the proportion $\frac{6}{4} = \frac{21}{14}$ by saying "six is to four as twenty-one is to fourteen."

EXAMPLE **1** **Comparing Ratios in Simplest Form**

Determine whether the ratios are proportional.

A $\frac{2}{7}, \frac{6}{21}$

$\frac{2}{7}$ *$\frac{2}{7}$ is already in simplest form.*

$\frac{6}{21} = \frac{6 \div 3}{21 \div 3} = \frac{2}{7}$ *Simplify $\frac{6}{21}$.*

Since $\frac{2}{7} = \frac{2}{7}$, the ratios are proportional.

B $\frac{8}{24}, \frac{6}{20}$

$\frac{8}{24} = \frac{8 \div 8}{24 \div 8} = \frac{1}{3}$ *Simplify $\frac{8}{24}$.*

$\frac{6}{20} = \frac{6 \div 2}{20 \div 2} = \frac{3}{10}$ *Simplify $\frac{6}{20}$.*

Since $\frac{1}{3} \neq \frac{3}{10}$, the ratios are *not* proportional.

EXAMPLE 2 Comparing Ratios Using a Common Denominator

Use the data in the table to determine whether the ratios of oats to water are proportional for both servings of oatmeal.

Servings of Oatmeal	Cups of Oats	Cups of Water
8	2	4
12	3	6

Write the ratios of oats to water for 8 servings and for 12 servings.

Ratio of oats to water, 8 servings: $\frac{2}{4}$ *Write the ratio as a fraction.*

Ratio of oats to water, 12 servings: $\frac{3}{6}$ *Write the ratio as a fraction.*

$$\frac{2}{4} = \frac{2 \cdot 6}{4 \cdot 6} = \frac{12}{24}$$

$$\frac{3}{6} = \frac{3 \cdot 4}{6 \cdot 4} = \frac{12}{24}$$

Write the fractions with a common denominator, such as 24.

Since both ratios are equal to $\frac{12}{24}$, they are proportional.

You can find an equivalent ratio by multiplying or dividing both terms of a ratio by the same number.

EXAMPLE 3 Finding Equivalent Ratios and Writing Proportions

Find a ratio equivalent to each ratio. Then use the ratios to write a proportion.

A $\frac{8}{14}$

$$\frac{8}{14} = \frac{8 \cdot 20}{14 \cdot 20} = \frac{160}{280}$$ *Multiply both terms by any number, such as 20.*

$$\frac{8}{14} = \frac{160}{280}$$ *Write a proportion.*

B $\frac{4}{18}$

$$\frac{4}{18} = \frac{4 \div 2}{18 \div 2} = \frac{2}{9}$$ *Divide both terms by a common factor, such as 2.*

$$\frac{4}{18} = \frac{2}{9}$$ *Write a proportion.*

Life Science LINK

The ratios of the sizes of the segments of a nautilus shell are approximately equal to the *golden ratio*, 1.618.... This ratio can be found in many places in nature.

Think and Discuss

1. **Explain** why the ratios in Example 1B are not proportional.

2. **Describe** what it means for ratios to be proportional.

3. **Give an example** of a proportion. Then tell how you know it is a proportion.

GUIDED PRACTICE

See Example 1 — Determine whether the ratios are proportional.

1. $\frac{2}{3}, \frac{4}{6}$ **2.** $\frac{5}{10}, \frac{8}{18}$ **3.** $\frac{9}{12}, \frac{15}{20}$ **4.** $\frac{3}{4}, \frac{8}{12}$

See Example 2 **5.** $\frac{10}{12}, \frac{15}{18}$ **6.** $\frac{6}{9}, \frac{8}{12}$ **7.** $\frac{3}{4}, \frac{5}{6}$ **8.** $\frac{4}{6}, \frac{6}{9}$

See Example 3 — Find a ratio equivalent to each ratio. Then use the ratios to write a proportion.

9. $\frac{1}{3}$ **10.** $\frac{9}{21}$ **11.** $\frac{8}{3}$ **12.** $\frac{10}{4}$

INDEPENDENT PRACTICE

See Example 1 — Determine whether the ratios are proportional.

13. $\frac{5}{8}, \frac{7}{14}$ **14.** $\frac{8}{24}, \frac{10}{30}$ **15.** $\frac{18}{20}, \frac{81}{180}$ **16.** $\frac{15}{20}, \frac{27}{35}$

See Example 2 **17.** $\frac{2}{3}, \frac{4}{9}$ **18.** $\frac{18}{12}, \frac{15}{10}$ **19.** $\frac{7}{8}, \frac{14}{24}$ **20.** $\frac{18}{54}, \frac{10}{30}$

See Example 3 — Find a ratio equivalent to each ratio. Then use the ratios to write a proportion.

21. $\frac{5}{9}$ **22.** $\frac{27}{60}$ **23.** $\frac{6}{15}$ **24.** $\frac{121}{99}$

25. $\frac{11}{13}$ **26.** $\frac{5}{22}$ **27.** $\frac{78}{104}$ **28.** $\frac{27}{72}$

PRACTICE AND PROBLEM SOLVING

Extra Practice
See page EP11.

Complete each table of equivalent ratios.

29.

angelfish	4	8		20
tiger fish		6	18	

30.

squares	2	4	6	8
circles		16		

Find two ratios equivalent to each given ratio.

31. 3 to 7   **32.** 6:2   **33.** $\frac{5}{12}$ **34.** 8:4

35. 6 to 9   **36.** $\frac{10}{50}$ **37.** 10:4   **38.** 1 to 10

39. Ecology If you recycle one aluminum can, you save enough energy to run a TV for four hours.

  a. Write the ratio of cans to hours.

  b. Marti's class recycled enough aluminum cans to run a TV for 2,080 hours. Did the class recycle 545 cans? Justify your answer using equivalent ratios.

40. Critical Thinking The ratio of girls to boys riding a bus is 15:12. If the driver drops off the same number of girls as boys at the next stop, does the ratio of girls to boys remain 15:12? Explain.

41. Critical Thinking Write all possible proportions using only the numbers 1, 2, and 4.

42. School Last year in Kerry's school, the ratio of students to teachers was 22:1. Write an equivalent ratio to show how many students and teachers there could have been at Kerry's school.

43. Life Science Students in a biology class visited four different ponds to determine whether salamanders and frogs were inhabiting the area.

Pond	Number of Salamanders	Number of Frogs
Cypress Pond	8	5
Mill Pond	15	10
Clear Pond	3	2
Gill Pond	2	7

    a. What was the ratio of salamanders to frogs in Cypress Pond?

    b. In which two ponds was the ratio of salamanders to frogs the same?

44. Marcus earned $230 for 40 hours of work. Phillip earned $192 for 32 hours of work. Are these pay rates proportional? Explain.

45. What's the Error? A student wrote the proportion $\frac{13}{20} = \frac{26}{60}$. What did the student do wrong?

46. Write About It Explain two different ways to determine if two ratios are proportional.

47. Challenge A skydiver jumps out of an airplane. After 0.8 second, she has fallen 100 feet. After 3.1 seconds, she has fallen 500 feet. Is the rate (in feet per second) at which she falls the first 100 feet proportional to the rate at which she falls the next 400 feet? Explain.

Test Prep and Spiral Review

48. Multiple Choice Which ratio is NOT equivalent to $\frac{32}{48}$?

   A $\frac{2}{3}$ **B** $\frac{8}{12}$ **C** $\frac{64}{96}$ **D** $\frac{128}{144}$

49. Multiple Choice Which ratio can form a proportion with $\frac{5}{6}$?

   F $\frac{13}{18}$ **G** $\frac{25}{36}$ **H** $\frac{70}{84}$ **J** $\frac{95}{102}$

Divide. Estimate to check whether each answer is reasonable. (Lesson 3-4)

50. $14.35 \div 0.7$ **51.** $-9 \div 2.4$ **52.** $12.505 \div 3.05$ **53.** $427 \div (-5.6)$

Compare. Write <, >, or =. (Lesson 4-1)

54. 3:5 ▮ 12:15   **55.** 33:66 ▮ 1:3   **56.** 9:24 ▮ 3:8   **57.** 15:7 ▮ 8:3

TN SPI 0706.2.7 Use ratios and proportions to solve problems.
Also ✓ 0706.1.3, SPI 0706.1.1, GLE 0706.2.3, GLE 0706.3.8, GLE 0706.4.4, ✓ 0706.4.5

Vocabulary

cross product

Interactivities Online ▶

Density is a ratio that compares a substance's mass to its volume. If you are given the density of ice, you can find the mass of 3 mL of ice by solving a proportion.

For two ratios, the product of the first term in one ratio and the second term in the other is a **cross product**. If the cross products are equal, then the ratios form a proportion.

$$\frac{2}{5} \times \frac{6}{15}$$

$5 \cdot 6 = 30$

$2 \cdot 15 = 30$

Ice floats in water because the density of ice is less than the density of water.

CROSS PRODUCTS

In the proportion $\frac{a}{b} = \frac{c}{d}$, where $b \neq 0$ and $d \neq 0$, the cross products, $a \cdot d$ and $b \cdot c$, are equal.

You can use cross products to solve proportions with variables.

EXAMPLE 1   **Solving Proportions Using Cross Products**

Use cross products to solve the proportion $\frac{p}{6} = \frac{10}{3}$.

$$\frac{p}{6} \times \frac{10}{3}$$

$10 \cdot 6 = p \cdot 3$ *The cross products are equal.*

$60 = 3p$ *Multiply.*

$\frac{60}{3} = \frac{3p}{3}$ *Divide each side by 3.*

$20 = p$

It is important to set up proportions correctly. Each ratio must compare corresponding quantities in the same order. Suppose a boat travels 16 miles in 4 hours and 8 miles in x hours at the same speed. Either of these proportions could represent this situation.

Trip 1 ⟶ $\boxed{\frac{16 \text{ mi}}{4 \text{ h}}} = \boxed{\frac{8 \text{ mi}}{x \text{ h}}}$ ⟵ Trip 2 $\frac{\boxed{16 \text{ mi} \quad 4 \text{ h}}}{\boxed{8 \text{ mi} \quad x \text{ h}}}$ ⟵ Trip 1
⟵ Trip 2

EXAMPLE 2 **PROBLEM SOLVING APPLICATION**

PROBLEM SOLVING

Density is the ratio of a substance's mass to its volume. The density of ice is 0.92 g/mL. What is the mass of 3 mL of ice?

1. Understand the Problem

Rewrite the question as a statement.
- Find the mass, in grams, of 3 mL of ice.

List the **important information:**

- density $= \dfrac{\text{mass (g)}}{\text{volume (mL)}}$

- density of ice $= \dfrac{0.92 \text{ g}}{1 \text{ mL}}$

2. Make a Plan

Set up a proportion using the given information. Let m represent the mass of 3 mL of ice.

$$\dfrac{0.92 \text{ g}}{1 \text{ mL}} = \dfrac{m}{3 \text{ mL}} \quad \begin{array}{l} \leftarrow mass \\ \leftarrow volume \end{array}$$

3. Solve

Solve the proportion.

$$\dfrac{0.92}{1} \diagup\!\!\!\!\diagdown \dfrac{m}{3} \qquad \text{Write the proportion.}$$

$$m \cdot 1 = 0.92 \cdot 3 \qquad \text{The cross products are equal.}$$

$$m = 2.76 \qquad\qquad \text{Multiply.}$$

The mass of 3 mL of ice is 2.76 g.

4. Look Back

Since the density of ice is 0.92 g/mL, each milliliter of ice has a mass of a little less than 1 g. So 3 mL of ice should have a mass of a little less than 3 g. Since 2.76 is a little less than 3, the answer is reasonable.

Think and Discuss

1. **Explain** how the term *cross product* can help you remember how to solve a proportion.

2. **Describe** the error in these steps: $\frac{2}{3} = \frac{x}{12}$; $2x = 36$; $x = 18$.

3. **Show** how to use cross products to decide whether the ratios 6:45 and 2:15 are proportional.

Exercises

Learn It Online
Homework Help Online **go.hrw.com,**
keyword MS10 4-4 Go
Exercises 1–15, 29, 31, 33, 35, 37, 39

GUIDED PRACTICE

See Example 1 **Use cross products to solve each proportion.**

1. $\frac{6}{10} = \frac{36}{x}$ 2. $\frac{4}{7} = \frac{5}{p}$ 3. $\frac{12.3}{m} = \frac{75}{100}$ 4. $\frac{t}{42} = \frac{1.5}{3}$

See Example 2 **5.** A stack of 2,450 one-dollar bills weighs 5 pounds. How much does a stack of 1,470 one-dollar bills weigh?

INDEPENDENT PRACTICE

See Example 1 **Use cross products to solve each proportion.**

6. $\frac{4}{36} = \frac{x}{180}$ 7. $\frac{7}{84} = \frac{12}{h}$ 8. $\frac{3}{24} = \frac{r}{52}$ 9. $\frac{5}{140} = \frac{12}{v}$

10. $\frac{45}{x} = \frac{15}{3}$ 11. $\frac{t}{6} = \frac{96}{16}$ 12. $\frac{2}{5} = \frac{s}{12}$ 13. $\frac{14}{n} = \frac{5}{8}$

See Example 2 **14.** Euro coins come in eight denominations. One denomination is the one-euro coin, which is worth 100 cents. A stack of 10 one-euro coins is 21.25 millimeters tall. How tall would a stack of 45 one-euro coins be? Round your answer to the nearest hundredth of a millimeter.

15. There are 18.5 ounces of soup in a can. This is equivalent to 524 grams. Jenna has 8 ounces of soup. How many grams does she have? Round your answer to the nearest whole gram.

PRACTICE AND PROBLEM SOLVING

Extra Practice
See page EP11.

Solve each proportion. Then find another equivalent ratio.

16. $\frac{4}{h} = \frac{12}{24}$ 17. $\frac{x}{15} = \frac{12}{90}$ 18. $\frac{39}{4} = \frac{t}{12}$ 19. $\frac{5.5}{6} = \frac{16.5}{w}$

20. $\frac{1}{3} = \frac{y}{25.5}$ 21. $\frac{18}{x} = \frac{1}{5}$ 22. $\frac{m}{4} = \frac{175}{20}$ 23. $\frac{8.7}{2} = \frac{q}{4}$

24. $\frac{r}{84} = \frac{32.5}{182}$ 25. $\frac{76}{304} = \frac{81}{k}$ 26. $\frac{9}{500} = \frac{p}{2,500}$ 27. $\frac{5}{j} = \frac{6}{19.8}$

28. A certain shade of paint is made by mixing 5 parts blue paint with 2 parts white paint. To get the correct shade, how many quarts of white paint should be mixed with 8.5 quarts of blue paint?

29. Measurement If you put an object that has a mass of 40 grams on one side of a balance scale, you would have to put about 18 U.S. dimes on the other side to balance the weight. About how many dimes would balance the weight of a 50-gram object?

30. Sandra drove 126.2 miles in 2 hours at a constant speed. Use a proportion to find how long it would take her to drive 189.3 miles at the same speed.

31. Multi-Step In June, a camp has 325 campers and 26 counselors. In July, 265 campers leave and 215 new campers arrive. How many counselors does the camp need in July to keep an equivalent ratio of campers to counselors?

This catfish was 7 feet, 7 inches long and weighed 212 pounds! She was caught and re-released in the River Ebro, near Barcelona, Spain.

Arrange each set of numbers to form a proportion.

32. 10, 6, 30, 18   **33.** 4, 6, 10, 15   **34.** 12, 21, 7, 4

35. 75, 4, 3, 100   **36.** 30, 42, 5, 7   **37.** 5, 90, 108, 6

38. Life Science On Monday a marine biologist took a random sample of 50 fish from a pond and tagged them. On Tuesday she took a new sample of 100 fish. Among them were 4 fish that had been tagged on Monday.

    a. What comparison does the ratio $\frac{4}{100}$ represent?

    b. What ratio represents the number of fish tagged on Monday to n, the total number of fish in the pond?

    c. Use a proportion to estimate the number of fish in the pond.

39. Chemistry The table shows the type and number of atoms in one molecule of citric acid. Use a proportion to find the number of oxygen atoms in 15 molecules of citric acid.

Composition of Citric Acid	
Type of Atom	**Number of Atoms**
Carbon	6
Hydrogen	8
Oxygen	7

40. Earth Science You can find your distance from a thunderstorm by counting the number of seconds between a lightning flash and the thunder. For example, if the time difference is 21 s, then the storm is about 7 km away. About how far away is a storm if the time difference is 9 s?

41. What's the Question? There are 20 grams of protein in 3 ounces of sautéed fish. If the answer is 9 ounces, what is the question?

42. Write About It Give an example from your own life that can be described using a ratio. Then tell how a proportion can give you additional information.

43. Challenge Use the Multiplication Property of Equality and the proportion $\frac{a}{b} = \frac{c}{d}$ to show that the cross product rule works for all proportions.

Test Prep and Spiral Review

44. Multiple Choice Which proportion is correct?

   Ⓐ $\frac{4}{8} = \frac{6}{10}$ Ⓑ $\frac{2}{7} = \frac{10}{15}$ Ⓒ $\frac{7}{14} = \frac{15}{30}$ Ⓓ $\frac{16}{25} = \frac{13}{18}$

45. Gridded Response Find a ratio to complete the proportion $\frac{2}{3} = \frac{?}{?}$ so that the cross products are equal to 12. Grid your answer in the form of a fraction.

Estimate. (Lesson 3-1)

46. $16.21 - 14.87$ **47.** $3.82 \cdot (-4.97)$ **48.** $-8.7 \cdot (-20.1)$

Find each unit rate. (Lesson 4-2)

49. 128 miles in 2 hours   **50.** 9 books in 6 weeks   **51.** $114 in 12 hours

CHAPTER
4
SECTION 4A

Ready To Go On?

Learn It Online
Resources Online **go.hrw.com**,
keyword MS10 RTGO4A Go

Quiz for Lessons 4-1 Through 4-4

4-1 Ratios

1. The 2007 record for the University of North Carolina softball team was 46 wins to 21 losses. Write the ratio of wins to losses in all three forms.

2. A concession stand sold 14 strawberry, 18 banana, 8 grape, and 6 orange fruit drinks during a game. Tell whether the ratio of strawberry to orange drinks or the ratio of banana to grape drinks is greater.

4-2 Rates

Find each unit rate. Round to the nearest hundredth, if necessary.

3. $140 for 18 ft^2

4. 346 mi on 22 gal

5. 14 lb for $2.99

6. Shaunti drove 621 miles in 11.5 hours. What was her average speed in miles per hour?

7. A grocery store sells a 7 oz bag of raisins for $1.10 and a 9 oz bag of raisins for $1.46. Which size bag has the lower price per ounce?

4-3 Identifying and Writing Proportions

Find a ratio equivalent to each ratio. Then use the ratios to write a proportion.

8. $\frac{10}{16}$

9. $\frac{21}{28}$

10. $\frac{12}{25}$

11. $\frac{40}{48}$

12. Ryan earned $272 for 40 hours of work. Jonathan earned $224 for 32 hours of work. Are these pay rates proportional? Explain.

13. On a given day, the ratio of dollars to euros was approximately 1:0.735. Is the ratio 20 to 14.70 an equivalent ratio? Explain.

4-4 Solving Proportions

Use cross products to solve each proportion.

14. $\frac{n}{8} = \frac{15}{4}$

15. $\frac{20}{t} = \frac{2.5}{6}$

16. $\frac{6}{11} = \frac{0.12}{z}$

17. $\frac{15}{24} = \frac{x}{10}$

18. One human year is said to be about 7 dog years. Cliff's dog is 5.5 years old in human years. Estimate his dog's age in dog years.

Focus on Problem Solving

Make a Plan

Plan

• **Choose a problem-solving strategy**

The following are strategies that you might choose to help you solve a problem:

- Make a table
- Find a pattern
- Make an organized list
- Work backward
- Use a Venn diagram
- Draw a diagram
- Guess and test
- Use logical reasoning
- Solve a simpler problem
- Make a model

Tell which strategy from the list above you would use to solve each problem. Explain your choice.

1 A recipe for blueberry muffins calls for 1 cup of milk and 1.5 cups of blueberries. Ashley wants to make more muffins than the recipe yields. In Ashley's muffin batter, there are 4.5 cups of blueberries. If she is using the recipe as a guide, how many cups of milk will she need?

2 There are 32 students in Samantha's math class. Of those students 18 are boys. Write the ratio in simplest form of the number of girls in Samantha's class to the number of boys.

3 Jeremy is the oldest of four brothers. Each of the four boys gets an allowance for doing chores at home each week. The amount of money each boy receives depends on his age. Jeremy is 13 years old, and he gets $12.75. His 11-year-old brother gets $11.25, and his 9-year-old brother gets $9.75. How much money does his 7-year-old brother get?

4 According to an article in a medical journal, a healthful diet should include a ratio of 2.5 servings of meat to 4 servings of vegetables. If you eat 7 servings of meat per week, how many servings of vegetables should you eat?

4-5 Customary Measurements

TN SPI 0706.2.7 Use ratios and proportions to solve problems. *Also* GLE 0706.2.3, GLE 0706.2.4, ✓ 0706.2.7, ✓ 0706.2.8, GLE 0706.4.2

The king cobra is one of the world's most poisonous snakes. Just 2 fluid ounces of the snake's venom is enough to kill a 2-ton elephant.

You can use the following benchmarks to help you understand fluid ounces, tons, and other customary units of measure.

Helpful Hint

For more on measurements, see the table of measures on the inside back cover.

	Customary Unit	Benchmark
Length	Inch (in.)	Length of a small paper clip
	Foot (ft)	Length of a standard sheet of paper
	Mile (mi)	Length of 4 laps around a track
Weight	Ounce (oz)	Weight of a slice of bread
	Pound (lb)	Weight of 3 apples
	Ton	Weight of a buffalo
Capacity	Fluid ounce (fl oz)	Amount of water in 2 tablespoons
	Cup (c)	Capacity of a standard measuring cup
	Gallon (gal)	Capacity of a large milk jug

EXAMPLE 1 **Choosing the Appropriate Customary Unit**

Choose the most appropriate customary unit for each measurement. Justify your answer.

A the length of a rug

Feet—the length of a rug is about the length of several sheets of paper.

B the weight of a magazine

Ounces—the weight of a magazine is about the weight of several slices of bread.

C the capacity of an aquarium

Gallons—the capacity of an aquarium is about the capacity of several large milk jugs.

Video **Lesson Tutorials Online** my.hrw.com

The following table shows some common equivalent customary units. You can use equivalent measures to convert units of measure.

Length	Weight	Capacity
12 inches (in.) = 1 foot (ft) 3 feet = 1 yard (yd) 5,280 feet = 1 mile (mi) 1,760 yards = 1 mile (mi)	16 ounces (oz) = 1 pound (lb) 2,000 pounds = 1 ton	8 fluid ounces (fl oz) = 1 cup (c) 2 cups = 1 pint (pt) 2 pints = 1 quart (qt) 4 quarts = 1 gallon (gal)

EXAMPLE 2

Converting Customary Units

Convert 19 c to fluid ounces.

Method 1: Use a proportion.

Write a proportion using a ratio of equivalent measures.

$$\frac{\text{fluid ounces}}{\text{cups}} \longrightarrow \frac{8}{1} = \frac{x}{19}$$

$$8 \cdot 19 = 1 \cdot x$$

$$152 = x$$

Method 2: Multiply by 1.

Multiply by a ratio equal to 1, and divide out the units.

$$19 \text{ c} = \frac{19\ \cancel{c}}{1} \times \frac{8 \text{ fl oz}}{1\ \cancel{c}}$$

$$= \frac{19 \cdot 8 \text{ fl oz}}{1}$$

$$= 152 \text{ fl oz}$$

Nineteen cups is equal to 152 fluid ounces.

EXAMPLE 3

Adding or Subtracting Mixed Units of Measure

A carpenter has a wooden post that is 4 ft long. She cuts 17 in. off the end of the post. What is the length of the remaining post?

First convert 4 ft to inches.

$$\frac{\text{inches}}{\text{feet}} \longrightarrow \frac{12}{1} = \frac{x}{4}$$ *Write a proportion using 1 ft = 12 in.*

$$x = 48 \text{ in.}$$

The carpenter cuts off 17 in., so subtract 17 in.

$$4 \text{ ft} - 17 \text{ in.} = 48 \text{ in.} - 17 \text{ in.}$$

$$= 31 \text{ in.}$$

Write the answer in feet and inches.

$$31 \text{ in.} \times \frac{1 \text{ ft}}{12 \text{ in.}} = \frac{31}{12} \text{ ft}$$ *Multiply by a ratio equal to 1.*

$$= 2\frac{7}{12} \text{ ft, or 2 ft 7 in.}$$

Think and Discuss

1. Describe an object that you would weigh in ounces.

2. Explain how to convert yards to feet and feet to yards.

Video **Lesson Tutorials Online** my.hrw.com

4-5 Customary Measurements **233**

Learn It Online
Homework Help Online **go.hrw.com**,
keyword MS10 4-5 (Go)
Exercises 1–18, 19, 23, 25, 29, 31, 35, 37

GUIDED PRACTICE

See Example 1 Choose the most appropriate customary unit for each measurement. Justify your answer.

1. the width of a sidewalk

2. the amount of water in a pool

3. the weight of a truck

4. the distance across Lake Erie

See Example 2 Convert each measure.

5. 12 gal to quarts

6. 8 mi to feet

7. 72 oz to pounds

8. 3.5 c to fluid ounces

See Example 3 **9.** A pitcher contains 4 c of pancake batter. A cook pours out 5 fl oz of the batter to make a pancake. How much batter remains in the pitcher?

INDEPENDENT PRACTICE

See Example 1 Choose the most appropriate customary unit for each measurement. Justify your answer.

10. the weight of a watermelon

11. the wingspan of a sparrow

12. the capacity of a soup bowl

13. the height of an office building

See Example 2 Convert each measure.

14. 28 pt to quarts

15. 15,840 ft to miles

16. 5.4 tons to pounds

17. $6\frac{1}{4}$ ft to inches

See Example 3 **18.** A sculptor has a 3 lb block of clay. He adds 24 oz of clay to the block in order to make a sculpture. What is the total weight of the clay before he begins sculpting?

PRACTICE AND PROBLEM SOLVING

Extra Practice
See page EP12.

Compare. Write <, >, or =.

19. 6 yd ▢ 12 ft

20. 80 oz ▢ 5 lb

21. 18 in. ▢ 3 ft

22. 5 tons ▢ 12,000 lb

23. 8 gal ▢ 30 qt

24. 6.5 c ▢ 52 fl oz

25. 10,000 ft ▢ 2 mi

26. 20 pt ▢ 40 c

27. 1 gal ▢ 18 c

Helpful Hint

For more on units of time see Skills Bank p. SB8.

28. Grayson has 3 music lessons each week. Each lesson is 45 minutes long. How many total hours will he spend in music lessons in 1 year?

29. **Earth Science** The average depth of the Pacific Ocean is 12,925 feet. How deep is this in miles, rounded to the nearest tenth of a mile?

Order each set of measures from least to greatest.

30. 8 ft; 2 yd; 60 in.

31. 5 qt; 2 gal; 12 pt; 8 c

32. $\frac{1}{2}$ ton; 8,000 oz; 430 lb

33. 2.5 mi; 12,000 ft; 5,000 yd

34. 63 fl oz; 7 c; 1.5 qt

35. 9.5 yd; 32.5 ft; 380 in.

36. Agriculture In one year, the United States produced nearly 895 million pounds of pumpkins. How many ounces were produced by the state with the lowest production shown in the table?

U.S. Pumpkin Production	
State	Pumpkins (million pounds)
California	180
Illinois	364
New York	114
Pennsylvania	109

37. Multi-Step A marathon is a race that is 26 miles 385 yards long. What is the length of a marathon in yards?

38. Estimation In 2007, $1 was approximately equal to 1.052 Canadian dollars. About how many Canadian dollars equaled $25?

39. Critical Thinking Explain why it makes sense to divide when you convert a measurement to a larger unit.

40. What's the Error? A student converted 480 ft to inches as follows. What did the student do wrong? What is the correct answer?

$$\frac{1 \text{ ft}}{12 \text{ in.}} = \frac{x}{480 \text{ ft}}$$

41. Write About It Explain how to convert 1.2 tons to ounces.

42. Challenge A dollar bill is approximately 6 in. long. A radio station gives away a prize consisting of a mile-long string of dollar bills. What is the approximate value of the prize?

Test Prep and Spiral Review

43. Multiple Choice Which measure is the same as 32 quarts?

Ⓐ 64 pt   Ⓑ 128 gal   Ⓒ 16 c   Ⓓ 512 fl oz

44. Multiple Choice Judy has 3 yards of ribbon. She cuts off 16 inches of the ribbon to wrap a package. How much ribbon does she have left?

Ⓕ 1 ft 8 in.   Ⓖ 4 ft 8 in.   Ⓗ 7 ft 8 in.   Ⓙ 10 ft 4 in.

45. A store sells a television for $486.50. That price is 3.5 times what the store paid. What was the store's cost? (Lesson 3-5)

Determine whether the ratios are proportional. (Lesson 4-3)

46. $\frac{20}{45}, \frac{8}{18}$

47. $\frac{6}{5}, \frac{5}{6}$

48. $\frac{11}{44}, \frac{7}{28}$

49. $\frac{9}{6}, \frac{27}{20}$

Metric Measurements

TN SPI 0706.2.7 Use ratios and proportions to solve problems.
Also **GLE 0706.2.3, GLE 0706.2.4,** ✓ **0706.2.7,** ✓ **0706.2.8**

The Micro Flying Robot II is the world's lightest helicopter. Produced in Japan in 2004, the robot is 85 millimeters tall and has a mass of 8.6 grams.

You can use the following benchmarks to help you understand millimeters, grams, and other metric units.

Helpful Hint

For more on metric units, see Skills Bank p. SB7.

	Metric Unit	Benchmark
Length	Millimeter (mm)	Thickness of a dime
	Centimeter (cm)	Width of your little finger
	Meter (m)	Width of a doorway
	Kilometer (km)	Length of 10 football fields
Mass	Milligram (mg)	Mass of a grain of sand
	Gram (g)	Mass of a small paperclip
	Kilogram (kg)	Mass of a textbook
Capacity	Milliliter (mL)	Amount of liquid in an eyedropper
	Liter (L)	Amount of water in a large water bottle
	Kiloliter (kL)	Capacity of 2 large refrigerators

EXAMPLE 1 Choosing the Appropriate Metric Unit

Choose the most appropriate metric unit for each measurement. Justify your answer.

A **The length of a car**

Meters—the length of a car is about the width of several doorways.

B **The mass of a skateboard**

Kilograms—the mass of a skateboard is about the mass of several textbooks.

C **The recommended dose of a cough syrup**

Milliliters—one dose of cough syrup is about the amount of liquid in several eyedroppers.

Video **Lesson Tutorials Online** my.hrw.com

The table shows how metric units are based on powers of 10.

$10^3 = 1,000$	$10^2 = 100$	$10^1 = 10$	$10^0 = 1$	$\frac{1}{10^1} = 0.1$	$\frac{1}{10^2} = 0.01$	$\frac{1}{10^3} = 0.001$
Thousands	Hundreds	Tens	Ones	Tenths	Hundredths	Thousandths
Kilo-	Hecto-	Deca-	Base unit	Deci-	Centi-	Milli-

Prefixes:
Milli- means "thousandth"
Centi- means "hundredth"
Kilo- means "thousand"

To convert metric units, multiply or divide by a power of 10. Multiply to convert to a smaller unit and divide to convert to a larger unit.

EXAMPLE 2 **Converting Metric Units**

Convert each measure.

A 510 cm to meters

510 cm = (510 ÷ 100) m *100 cm = 1 m, so divide by 100.*

= 5.1 m *Since $100 = 10^2$, move the decimal point 2 places left: 510.*

B 2.3 L to milliliters

2.3 L = (2.3 × 1,000) mL *1 L = 1,000 mL, so multiply by 1,000.*

= 2,300 mL *Since $1,000 = 10^3$, move the decimal point 3 places right: 2.300*

EXAMPLE 3 **Using Unit Conversion to Make Comparisons**

Mai and Brian are measuring the mass of rocks in their earth science class. Mai's rock has a mass of 480 g. Brian's rock has a mass of 0.05 kg. Whose rock has the greater mass? How much greater is its mass?

$\frac{480}{x} = \frac{1,000}{1}$ *Write a proportion.*

$480 = 1,000x$ *The cross products are equal.*

$0.48 = x$ *480 g = 0.48 kg*

Since 0.48 kg > 0.05 kg, Mai's rock has the greater mass.

$0.48 - 0.05 = 0.43$ *Subtract to find how much greater the mass of Mai's rock is.*

The mass of Mai's rock is 0.43 kg greater than the mass of Brian's rock.

Think and Discuss

1. Tell how the metric system relates to the base-10 number system.

2. Explain why it makes sense to multiply when you convert to a smaller unit.

Learn It Online
Homework Help Online **go.hrw.com**,
keyword MS10 4-6 Go
Exercises 1–18, 23, 25, 29, 35, 37, 39

GUIDED PRACTICE

See Example 1 **Choose the most appropriate metric unit for each measurement. Justify your answer.**

1. The mass of a pumpkin

2. The amount of water in a pond

3. The length of an eagle's beak

4. The mass of a penny

See Example 2 **Convert each measure.**

5. 12 kg to grams

6. 4.3 m to centimeters

7. 0.7 mm to centimeters

8. 3,200 mL to liters

See Example 3 **9.** On Sunday, Li ran 0.8 km. On Monday, she ran 720 m. On which day did Li run farther? How much farther?

INDEPENDENT PRACTICE

See Example 1 **Choose the most appropriate metric unit for each measurement. Justify your answer.**

10. The capacity of a teacup

11. The mass of 10 grains of salt

12. The height of a palm tree

13. The distance between your eyes

See Example 2 **Convert each measure.**

14. 0.067 L to milliliters

15. 1.4 m to kilometers

16. 900 mg to grams

17. 355 cm to millimeters

See Example 3 **18.** Carmen pours 75 mL of water into a beaker. Nick pours 0.75 L of water into a different beaker. Who has the greater amount of water? How much greater?

PRACTICE AND PROBLEM SOLVING

Extra Practice
See page EP12.

Convert each measure.

19. 1.995 m = ▢ cm

20. 0.00004 kg = ▢ g

21. 2,050 kL = ▢ L

22. 0.002 mL = ▢ L

23. 3.7 mm = ▢ cm

24. 61.8 g = ▢ mg

Compare. Write <, >, or =.

25. 0.1 cm ▢ 1 mm

26. 25 g ▢ 3,000 mg

27. 340 mg ▢ 0.4 g

28. 0.05 kL ▢ 5 L

29. 0.3 mL ▢ 0.005 L

30. 1.3 kg ▢ 1,300 g

31. Art The *Mona Lisa* by Leonardo da Vinci is 77 cm tall. *Starry Night* by Vincent Van Gogh is 0.73 m tall. Which is the taller painting? How much taller is it?

Write each set of measures in order from least to greatest.

32. 0.005 kL; 4.1 L; 6,300 mL

33. 1.5 m; 1,200 mm; 130 cm

34. 4,000 mg; 50 kg; 70 g

35. 9.03 g; 0.0008 kg; 1,000 mg

36. Measurement Use a ruler to measure the line segment at right in centimeters. Then give the length of the segment in millimeters and meters.

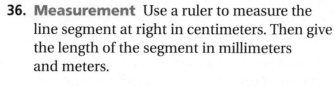

Life Science

Bats consume up to 25% of their mass at each feeding.

Life Science The table gives information about several species of Vesper, or Evening, bats. Use the table for Exercises 37 and 38.

37. Which bat has the greatest mass?

38. Which bat has a longer wingspread, the Red Bat or the Big Brown Bat? How much longer is its wingspread?

U.S. Vesper Bats		
Name	**Wingspread**	**Mass**
Red Bat	0.3 m	10.9 g
Silver-Haired Bat	28.7 cm	8,500 mg
Big Brown Bat	317 mm	0.01 kg

39. Critical Thinking One milliliter of water has a mass of 1 gram. What is the mass of a liter of water?

40. What's the Error? A student converted 45 grams to milligrams as shown below. Explain the student's error.

$$45 \text{ g} = (45 \div 1{,}000) \text{ mg} = 0.045 \text{ mg}$$

41. Write About It Explain how to decide whether milligrams, grams, or kilograms are the most appropriate unit for measuring the mass of an object.

42. Challenge A decimeter is $\frac{1}{10}$ of a meter. Explain how to convert millimeters to decimeters.

Test Prep and Spiral Review

43. Multiple Choice Which of these is the same as 0.4 grams?

  Ⓐ 0.0004 mg   Ⓑ 0.004 mg   Ⓒ 400 mg   Ⓓ 4,000 mg

44. Short Response Which has a greater capacity, a measuring cup that holds 250 milliliters or a measuring cup that holds 0.5 liters? Justify your answer.

Find each value. (Lesson 1-2)

45. 9^2 **46.** 12^0 **47.** 2^7 **48.** 7^3 **49.** 3^4

Use cross products to solve each proportion. (Lesson 4-4)

50. $\frac{80}{x} = \frac{1000}{20}$ **51.** $\frac{a}{5.24} = \frac{28}{2}$ **52.** $\frac{8}{25} = \frac{m}{15}$ **53.** $\frac{2.4}{4} = \frac{8.1}{n}$

Dimensional Analysis

TN SPI 0706.2.7 Use
ratios and proportions to solve
problems.
Also **GLE 0706.2.3, GLE 0706.2.4,**
✓ **0706.2.7,** ✓ **0706.2.8,**
GLE 0706.4.2, GLE 0706.4.4,
✓ **0706.4.5**

A **unit conversion factor** is a fraction in which the numerator and denominator represent the same quantity in different units. For example, $\frac{5,280 \text{ ft}}{1 \text{ mi}}$ is a unit conversion factor. Because 1 mi = 5,280 ft, the conversion factor can be simplified to 1.

Vocabulary

unit conversion
factor

$$\frac{5,280 \text{ ft}}{1 \text{ mi}} = \frac{5,280 \text{ ft}}{5,280 \text{ ft}} = 1$$

Interactivities Online ▶

You can use a unit conversion factor to change, or convert, measurements from one unit to another. Choosing an appropriate conversion factor is called *dimensional analysis*.

EXAMPLE 1   Using Conversion Factors to Solve Problems

A As you go deeper underground, the earth's temperature increases. In some places, it may increase by 25 °C per kilometer. Find this rate in degrees per meter.

Convert the rate 25 °C per *kilometer* to degrees per *meter*.

Helpful Hint

In Example 1A, "1 km" appears to divide out, leaving "degrees per meter," which are the units asked for. Use this strategy of "dividing out" units when converting rates.

$\frac{25 \, ^\circ\text{C}}{1 \text{ km}} \cdot \frac{1 \text{ km}}{1000 \text{ m}}$ *To convert the second quantity in a rate, multiply by a conversion factor with that unit in the first quantity.*

$\frac{25 \, ^\circ\text{C}}{1000 \text{ m}}$ *Divide out like units.* $\frac{^\circ\text{C}}{\cancel{\text{km}}} \cdot \frac{\cancel{\text{km}}}{\text{m}} = \frac{^\circ\text{C}}{\text{m}}$

$\frac{0.025 \, ^\circ\text{C}}{1 \text{ m}}$ *Divide 25 °C by 1000 m.*

The rate is 0.025°C per meter.

B In the United States in 2003, the average person drank about 22 gallons of milk. Find this rate in quarts per month.

Convert the rate 22 *gallons* per *year* to *quarts* per *month*.

$\frac{22 \text{ gal}}{1 \text{ yr}} \cdot \frac{4 \text{ qt}}{1 \text{ gal}} \cdot \frac{1 \text{ yr}}{12 \text{ mo}}$ *To convert, multiply by conversion factors with those units.*

$\frac{22 \cdot 4 \text{ qt}}{12 \text{ mo}}$ *Divide out like units.* $\frac{\cancel{\text{gal}}}{\cancel{\text{yr}}} \cdot \frac{\text{qt}}{\cancel{\text{gal}}} \cdot \frac{\cancel{\text{yr}}}{\text{mo}} = \frac{\text{qt}}{\text{mo}}$

$\frac{88 \text{ qt}}{12 \text{ mo}}$ *Multiply.*

$\frac{7.3 \text{ qt}}{1 \text{ mo}}$ *Simplify.*

The rate is about 7.3 quarts per month.

EXAMPLE 2 **Converting Between Metric and Customary Units**

One inch is 2.54 centimeters. A bookmark has a length of 18 centimeters. What is the length of the bookmark in inches, rounded to the nearest inch?

$$\frac{\text{inches}}{\text{centimeters}} \longrightarrow \frac{1}{2.54} = \frac{x}{18}$$ *Write a proportion using 1 in. = 2.54 cm.*

$$1 \cdot 18 = 2.54 \cdot x$$ *The cross products are equal.*

$$18 = 2.54x$$ *Multiply.*

$$\frac{18}{2.54} = \frac{2.54x}{2.54}$$ *Divide each side by 2.54.*

$$7 \approx x$$ *Round to the nearest whole number.*

The bookmark is about 7 inches long.

EXAMPLE 3 *Sports Application*

A football player runs from his team's 9-yard line to his team's 44-yard line in 7 seconds. Find the player's average speed in yards per second. Use dimensional analysis to check the reasonableness of your answer.

$$\text{Average speed} = \frac{\text{total distance}}{\text{total time}}$$

$$= \frac{35 \text{ yards}}{7 \text{ seconds}}$$ *The player runs $44 - 9 = 35$ yards in 7 seconds.*

$$\frac{35 \text{ yards} \div 7}{7 \text{ seconds} \div 7} = \frac{5 \text{ yards}}{1 \text{ second}}$$ *Divide to find yards per second.*

The player's average speed is 5 yards per second.

Convert yd/s to mi/h to see if the answer is reasonable.

$$\frac{1 \text{ mi}}{5280 \text{ ft}} \cdot \frac{3 \text{ ft}}{1 \text{ yd}} = \frac{3 \text{ mi}}{5280 \text{ yd}} = \frac{1 \text{ mi}}{1760 \text{ yd}}$$ *Convert miles to yards.*

$$\frac{5 \text{ yd}}{1 \text{ s}} \cdot \frac{1 \text{ mi}}{1760 \text{ yd}} \cdot \frac{3600 \text{ s}}{1 \text{ h}}$$ *Set up the conversion factors.*

$$= \frac{5 \text{ yd}}{1 \text{ s}} \cdot \frac{1 \text{ mi}}{1760 \text{ yd}} \cdot \frac{3600 \text{ s}}{1 \text{ h}}$$ *Divide out like units.*

$$= \frac{5 \cdot 1 \text{ mi} \cdot 3600}{1 \cdot 1760 \cdot 1 \text{ h}} \approx 10.2 \text{ mi/h}$$ *Multiply. Then simplify.*

The player's average speed is approximately 10.2 mi/h, which is a reasonable speed for a football player to run a short distance.

Think and Discuss

1. Tell whether you get an equivalent rate when you multiply a rate by a conversion factor. Explain.

2. Compare the process of converting feet to inches with the process of converting feet per minute to inches per second.

Learn It Online
Homework Help Online **go.hrw.com**,
keyword MS10 4-7 **Go**
Exercises 1–8, 9, 11, 13, 15

GUIDED PRACTICE

See Example 1. The maxmimum speed of the Tupolev Tu-144 airliner is 694 m/s. Find this rate in kilometers per second.

2. Ali's car uses 12 gallons of gas each week. Find this rate in quarts per year.

See Example 3. One lap around the Daytona Speedway is 2.5 miles. To the nearest hundredth, how many kilometers is this? (*Hint:* 1 mi ≈ 1.609 km)

See Example 4. Martin begins driving to work at 8:15 A.M. He drives 18 miles and arrives at his office at 8:39 A.M. Find Martin's average speed in miles per minute. Use dimensional analysis to check the reasonableness of your answer.

INDEPENDENT PRACTICE

See Example 1 5. Lydia wrote $4\frac{1}{2}$ pages of her science report in one hour. What was her writing rate in pages per minute?

6. An Olympic athlete can run 110 yards in 10 seconds. How fast in miles per hour can the athlete run?

See Example 2 7. One lap around the Talladega Speedway is about 4.3 km. To the nearest tenth, how many miles is one lap around the speedway? (*Hint:* 1 mi ≈ 1.609 km)

See Example 3 8. There are markers every 1000 feet along the side of a road. While driving, Sonya passes marker number 8 at 3:10 P.M. and marker number 20 at 3:14 P.M. Find Sonya's average speed in feet per minute. Use dimensional analysis to check the reasonableness of your answer.

PRACTICE AND PROBLEM SOLVING

Extra Practice
See page EP12.

Use conversion factors to find each of the following.

9. concert tickets sold in an hour at a rate of 6 tickets sold per minute

10. miles jogged in 1 hour at an average rate of 8.5 feet per second

11. calls made in a 3 day telephone fund-raiser at a rate of 10 calls per hour

12. **Estimation** In England, a commonly used unit of measure is the *stone*. One stone is equivalent to 14 pounds. Jonathan weighs 95 pounds. About how many stones does he weigh? Round to the nearest tenth of a stone.

13. One pound approximately equals 0.454 kilograms. Water weighs about 62.4 lb per cubic foot. About how much does water weigh in kilograms per cubic foot? Round to the nearest tenth.

14. Ellie added 600 liters of water into a pool in one hour. One liter approximately equals 1.0567 quarts. How many quarts of water per minute did she add? Round to the nearest tenth.

15. **Life Science** The Outer Bay exhibit at the Monterey Bay Aquarium holds about 1,000,000 gallons of sea water. How many days would it take to fill the exhibit at a rate of 1 gallon per second?

16. **Money** Fencing costs $3.75 per foot. Bryan wants to enclose his rectangular garden, which measures 6 yards by 4 yards. How much will fencing for the garden cost?

17. **Life Science** A cheetah can run as fast as 70 miles per hour. To the nearest hundredth, what is the cheetah's speed in kilometers per minute?

18. **Transportation** Your car gets 32 miles per gallon of gasoline. Gasoline costs $3 per gallon. How many kilometers can you travel on $30?

19. **Choose a Strategy** Which unit conversion factor should you use to convert 56 square feet to square yards?

    a. $\dfrac{3\text{ sq ft}}{1\text{ sq yd}}$ **b.** $\dfrac{6\text{ sq ft}}{1\text{ sq yd}}$ **c.** $\dfrac{9\text{ sq ft}}{1\text{ sq yd}}$ **d.** $\dfrac{12\text{ sq ft}}{1\text{ sq yd}}$

20. **What's the Error?** To convert 5.6 kg to pounds, a student wrote $\dfrac{5.6\text{ kg}}{1\text{ lb}} \cdot \dfrac{1\text{ kg}}{2.2\text{ lb}}$. What error did the student make?

21. **Write About It** Give an example when you would use customary instead of metric measurements, or describe a situation when you would use metric instead of customary measurements.

 22. **Challenge** Convert each measure. (*Hint:* 1 oz = 28.35 g)

    a. 8 oz = ▮ g   **c.** 198.45 g = ▮ oz

    b. 538.65 g = ▮ lb   **d.** 1.5625 lb = ▮ g

Test Prep and Spiral Review

23. **Multiple Choice** A company rents boats for $9 per hour. How much per minute is this?

    Ⓐ $0.15   Ⓑ $0.25   Ⓒ $0.54   Ⓓ $1.05

24. **Multiple Choice** How many square yards are in 27 square feet?

    Ⓕ 3 square yards   Ⓗ 81 square yards

    Ⓖ 9 square yards   Ⓙ 243 square yards

25. **Short Response** Show how to convert 1.5 quarts per pound to liters per kilogram. Round each step to the nearest hundredth. (*Hint:* 1L ≈ 1.06 qt, 1 kg ≈ 2.2 lb)

Evaluate each expression for the given value of the variable. (Lesson 1-6)

26. $2x - 3$ for $x = -1$ 27. $3a + 1$ for $a = 3$ 28. $3c^2 - 1$ for $c = -3$

Multiply. Write each answer in simplest form. (Lesson 3-9)

29. $12 \cdot \dfrac{3}{4}$ 30. $\dfrac{2}{5} \cdot \left(-\dfrac{1}{4}\right)$ 31. $3\dfrac{2}{3} \cdot \dfrac{1}{2}$ 32. $\dfrac{4}{6} \cdot 10 \cdot 7\dfrac{1}{2}$

CHAPTER

4

SECTION 4B

Ready To Go On?

Learn It Online
Resources Online **go.hrw.com**,
keyword MS10 RTGO4B Go

Quiz for Lessons 4-5 Through 4-7

✓ 4-5 Customary Measurements

Convert each measure.

1. 7 lb to ounces

2. 15 qt to pints

3. 3 mi to feet

4. 20 fl oz to cups

5. 39 ft to yards

6. 7,000 lb to tons

7. Mara and Andrew are baking cornbread to serve 30 people. They pour 3 cups of milk into the batter and then add 18 more fluid ounces. How much milk did they use?

8. Gabrielle has 3 gal of paint. She uses 9 qt to paint her bedroom. How much paint does she have left?

✓ 4-6 Metric Measurements

Convert each measure.

9. 17.3 kg to grams

10. 540 mL to liters

11. 0.46 cm to millimeters

12. 172 L to kiloliters

13. 0.36 km to meters

14. 54.4 mg to grams

15. Cat ran in the 400-meter dash and the 800-meter run. Hilo ran in the 2-kilometer cross-country race. All together, who ran the farthest, Cat or Hilo? How much farther?

16. Luis and Sara collected rainwater over three days. Luis collected 7.6 liters of rainwater, and Sara collected 7,060 milliliters. Who collected more rainwater, Luis or Sara? How much more?

✓ 4-7 Dimensional Analysis

17. A yellow jacket can fly 4.5 meters in 9 seconds. What is this rate in meters per minute?

18. The average U.S. citizen throws away about 1,606 lb of trash each year. Find this rate in pounds per month, to the nearest tenth.

19. One gallon is about 3.79 liters. A car has a 55-liter gas tank. What is the capacity of the tank in gallons, rounded to the nearest tenth of a gallon?

20. A 1-pound weight has a mass of about 0.45 kilogram. What is the mass in kilograms of a sculpture that weighs 570 pounds? Round your answer to the nearest tenth of a kilogram.

21. A football player runs from his team's 12-yard line to his team's 36-yard line in 6 seconds. Find the player's average speed in yards per second. Use dimensional analysis to check the reasonableness of your answer.

Ready to Go On?

Focus on Problem Solving

Solve

• Choose an operation: multiplication or division

When you are converting units, think about whether the number in the answer will be greater than or less than the number given in the question. This will help you decide whether to multiply or divide when changing the units.

Tell whether you would multiply or divide by the conversion factor to solve each problem. Then solve the problem.

1 A pontoon built to look like a duck was part of a 2007 project. The giant yellow duck floated the Loire River in France. Its dimensions were 26 × 20 × 32 meters. Find the dimensions of the duck in feet. Round to the nearest hundredth. (*Hint:* 1 m ≈ 3.28 ft)

2 The length of a rectangle is 8 cm, and its width is 5 cm less than its length. A larger rectangle with dimensions that are proportional to those of the first has a length of 24 cm. What is the width of the larger rectangle in meters?

3 One of the world's largest cheeseburgers was made in Thailand. The cheeseburger weighed 73.6 pounds. It was 23.5 inches in diameter and 13.75 inches in height.

a. Find the weight of the cheeseburger in kilograms. (*Hint:* 1 lb ≈ 2.2 kg)

b. Find its dimensions in centimeters. (*Hint:* 1 in. ≈ 2.54 cm)

4 Some of the ingredients for the cheeseburger are listed in the table. Find the missing measures. Round to the nearest hundredth, if necessary.

Cheeseburger Ingredients	Size
Beef	25 kg = ▉ lb
Mustard	$1\frac{1}{2}$ cups = ▉ mL (1 cup ≈ 236.59 mL)
Ketchup	1 cup = ▉ fluid oz

Hands-On LAB

4-8

Make Similar Figures

Use with Lesson 4-8

Learn It Online
Lab Resources Online **go.hrw.com**,
keyword **MS10 Lab4** **Go**

TN ✓ **0706.4.4** Compare
angles, side lengths, perimeters
and areas of similar shapes.
Also **GLE 0706.1.4**

Similar figures are figures that have the same shape but not necessarily the same size. You can make similar rectangles by increasing or decreasing both dimensions of a rectangle while keeping the ratios of the side lengths proportional. Modeling similar rectangles using square tiles can help you solve proportions.

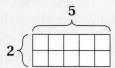

Activity

A rectangle made of square tiles measures 5 tiles long and 2 tiles wide. What is the length of a similar rectangle whose width is 6 tiles?

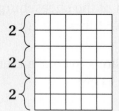

Use tiles to make a 5 × 2 rectangle.

Add tiles to increase the width of the rectangle to 6 tiles.

Notice that there are now 3 sets of 2 tiles along the width of the rectangle because 2 × 3 = 6.

The width of the new rectangle is three times greater than the width of the original rectangle. To keep the ratios of the side measures proportional, the length must also be three times greater than the length of the original rectangle.

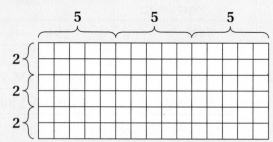

5 × 3 = 15

Add tiles to increase the length of the rectangle to 15 tiles.

The length of the similar rectangle is 15 tiles.

246 *Chapter 4 Proportional Relationships*

To check your answer, you can use ratios.

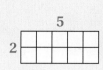

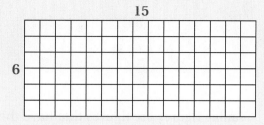

$\frac{2}{6} \stackrel{?}{=} \frac{5}{15}$ *Write ratios using the corresponding side lengths.*

$\frac{1}{3} \stackrel{?}{=} \frac{1}{3}$ ✔   *Simplify each ratio.*

1 Use square tiles to model similar figures with the given dimensions. Then find the missing dimension of each similar rectangle.

   a. The original rectangle is 4 tiles wide by 3 tiles long.
   The similar rectangle is 8 tiles wide by x tiles long.

   b. The original rectangle is 8 tiles wide by 10 tiles long.
   The similar rectangle is x tiles wide by 15 tiles long.

   c. The original rectangle is 3 tiles wide by 7 tiles long.
   The similar rectangle is 9 tiles wide by x tiles long.

Think and Discuss

1. Sarah wants to increase the size of her rectangular backyard patio. Why must she change both dimensions of the patio to create a patio similar to the original?

2. In a backyard, a rectangular plot of land that is 5 yd × 8 yd is used to grow tomatoes. The homeowner wants to decrease this plot to 4 yd × 6 yd. Will the new plot be similar to the original? Why or why not?

Try This

1. A rectangle is 3 meters long and 11 meters wide. What is the width of a similar rectangle whose length is 9 meters?

2. A rectangle is 6 feet long and 12 feet wide. What is the length of a similar rectangle whose width is 4 feet?

Use square tiles to model similar rectangles to solve each proportion.

3. $\frac{4}{5} = \frac{8}{x}$ **4.** $\frac{5}{9} = \frac{h}{18}$ **5.** $\frac{2}{y} = \frac{6}{18}$ **6.** $\frac{1}{t} = \frac{4}{16}$

7. $\frac{2}{3} = \frac{8}{m}$ **8.** $\frac{9}{12} = \frac{p}{4}$ **9.** $\frac{6}{r} = \frac{9}{15}$ **10.** $\frac{k}{12} = \frac{7}{6}$

Similar Figures and Proportions

TN GLE 0706.4.1 Understand the application of proportionality with similar triangles.
Also **GLE 0706.2.3,** ✓ **0706.4.4,** **SPI 0706.4.1**

Use Additional Topic A-8 with this lesson.

Vocabulary

similar

corresponding sides

corresponding angles

Similar figures are figures that have the same shape but not necessarily the same size. The symbol ~ means "is similar to."

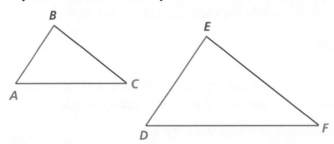

Corresponding angles of two or more similar polygons are in the same relative position. **Corresponding sides** of two or more similar polygons are in the same relative position. When naming similar figures, list the corresponding angles in the same order. For the triangles above, $\triangle ABC \sim \triangle DEF$.

SIMILAR FIGURES
Two figures are similar if • the measures of their corresponding angles are equal. • the ratios of the lengths of their corresponding sides are proportional.

EXAMPLE 1 Determining Whether Two Triangles Are Similar

Reading Math

A side of a figure can be named by its endpoints with a bar above, such as $\overline{AB}$. Without the bar, the letters indicate the *length* of the side.

Tell whether the triangles are similar.

The corresponding angles of the figures have equal measures.

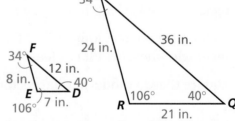

$\overline{DE}$ corresponds to $\overline{QR}$.
$\overline{EF}$ corresponds to $\overline{RS}$.
$\overline{DF}$ corresponds to $\overline{QS}$.

$\dfrac{DE}{QR} \stackrel{?}{=} \dfrac{EF}{RS} \stackrel{?}{=} \dfrac{DF}{QS}$ *Write ratios using the corresponding sides.*

$\dfrac{7}{21} \stackrel{?}{=} \dfrac{8}{24} \stackrel{?}{=} \dfrac{12}{36}$ *Substitute the lengths of the sides.*

$\dfrac{1}{3} = \dfrac{1}{3} = \dfrac{1}{3}$ *Simplify each ratio.*

Since the measures of the corresponding angles are equal and the ratios of the corresponding sides are equivalent, the triangles are similar.

Video **Lesson Tutorials Online** my.hrw.com

Helpful Hint

For more on similar triangles, see page SB20 in the Skills Bank.

With triangles, if the corresponding side lengths are all proportional, then the corresponding angles *must* have equal measures. With figures that have four or more sides, if the corresponding side lengths are all proportional, then the corresponding angles *may or may not* have equal angle measures.

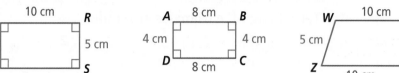

ABCD and QRST
are similar.

ABCD and WXYZ
are not similar.

E X A M P L E ② **Determining Whether Two Four-Sided Figures Are Similar**

Tell whether the figures are similar.

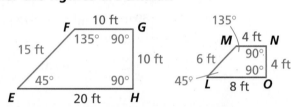

The corresponding angles of the figures have equal measures. Write each set of corresponding sides as a ratio.

$\frac{EF}{LM}$ $\overline{EF}$ corresponds to $\overline{LM}$. $\frac{FG}{MN}$ $\overline{FG}$ corresponds to $\overline{MN}$.

$\frac{GH}{NO}$ $\overline{GH}$ corresponds to $\overline{NO}$. $\frac{EH}{LO}$ $\overline{EH}$ corresponds to $\overline{LO}$.

Determine whether the ratios of the lengths of the corresponding sides are proportional.

$\frac{EF}{LM} \overset{?}{=} \frac{FG}{MN} \overset{?}{=} \frac{GH}{NO} \overset{?}{=} \frac{EH}{LO}$ *Write ratios using the corresponding sides.*

$\frac{15}{6} \overset{?}{=} \frac{10}{4} \overset{?}{=} \frac{10}{4} \overset{?}{=} \frac{20}{8}$ *Substitute the lengths of the sides.*

$\frac{5}{2} = \frac{5}{2} = \frac{5}{2} = \frac{5}{2}$ *Write the ratios in simplest form.*

Since the measures of the corresponding angles are equal and the ratios of the corresponding sides are equivalent, *EFGH ~ LMNO*.

Think and Discuss

1. **Identify** the corresponding angles of △*JKL* and △*UTS*.

2. **Explain** whether all rectangles are similar. Give specific examples to justify your answer.

GUIDED PRACTICE

See Example **1** Tell whether the triangles are similar.

1.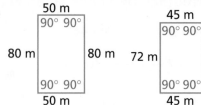

2.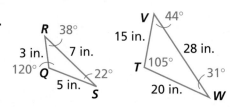

See Example **2** Tell whether the figures are similar.

3.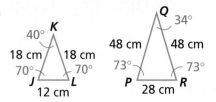

4.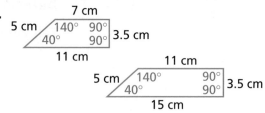

INDEPENDENT PRACTICE

See Example **1** Tell whether the triangles are similar.

5.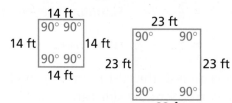

6.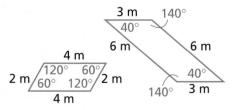

See Example **2** Tell whether the figures are similar.

7.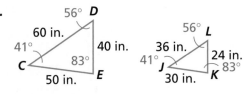

8.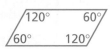

PRACTICE AND PROBLEM SOLVING

Extra Practice
See page EP13.

9. Tell whether the parallelogram and trapezoid could be similar. Explain your answer.

10. Kia wants similar prints in small and large sizes of a favorite photo. The photo lab sells prints in these sizes: 3 in. × 5 in., 4 in. × 6 in., 8 in. × 18 in., 9 in. × 20 in., and 16 in. × 24 in. Which could she order to get similar prints?

Tell whether the triangles are similar.

11.

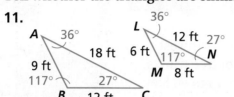

12.

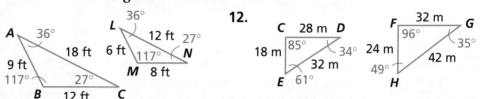

The figure shows a 12 ft by 15 ft rectangle divided into four rectangular parts. Explain whether the rectangles in each pair are similar.

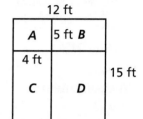

13. rectangle *A* and the original rectangle

14. rectangle *C* and rectangle *B*

15. the original rectangle and rectangle *D*

Critical Thinking For Exercises 16–19, justify your answers using words or drawings.

16. Are all squares similar? 17. Are all parallelograms similar?

18. Are all rectangles similar? 19. Are all right triangles similar?

20. **Choose a Strategy** What number gives the same result when multiplied by 6 as it does when 6 is added to it?

21. **Write About It** Tell how to decide whether two figures are similar.

22. **Challenge** Two triangles are similar. The ratio of the lengths of the corresponding sides is $\frac{5}{4}$. The length of one side of the larger triangle is 40 feet. What is the length of the corresponding side of the smaller triangle?

Test Prep and Spiral Review

23. **Multiple Choice** Luis wants to make a deck that is similar to one that is 10 feet long and 8 feet wide. Luis's deck must be 18 feet long. What must its width be?

   (A) 20 feet   (B) 16 feet   (C) 14.4 feet   (D) 22.5 feet

24. **Short Response** A real dollar bill measures 2.61 inches by 6.14 inches. A play dollar bill measures 3.61 inches by 7.14 inches. Is the play money similar to the real money? Explain your answer.

Multiply. Write each answer in simplest form. (Lesson 3-9)

25. $-\frac{3}{4} \cdot 14$ 26. $2\frac{1}{8} \cdot (-5)$ 27. $\frac{1}{4} \cdot 1\frac{7}{8} \cdot 3\frac{1}{5}$

28. Tell whether 5:3 or 12:7 is a greater ratio. (Lesson 4-1)

Using Similar Figures

TN ✓ 0706.4.1 Solve problems involving indirect measurement such as finding the height of a building by comparing its shadow with the height and shadow of a known object. *Also* **GLE 0706.2.3, GLE 0706.4.1, GLE 0706.4.4,** ✓ **0706.4.2, SPI 0706.4.1**

Vocabulary

indirect
  measurement

Native Americans of the Northwest carved totem poles out of tree trunks. These poles could stand up to 80 feet tall. Totem poles include carvings of animal figures, such as bears and eagles, which symbolize traits of the family or clan who built them.

Measuring the heights of tall objects, like some totem poles, cannot be done by using a ruler or yardstick. Instead, you can use *indirect measurement*.

Interactivities Online ▶ **Indirect measurement** is a method of using proportions to find an unknown length or distance in similar figures.

EXAMPLE **1** **Finding Unknown Measures in Similar Figures**

△*ABC* ~ △*JKL*. Find the unknown measures.

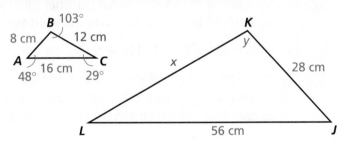

Step 1 Find *x*.

$$\frac{AB}{JK} = \frac{BC}{KL}$$ *Write a proportion using corresponding sides.*

$$\frac{8}{28} = \frac{12}{x}$$ *Substitute the lengths of the sides.*

$8 \cdot x = 28 \cdot 12$ *Find the cross products.*

$8x = 336$ *Multiply.*

$$\frac{8x}{8} = \frac{336}{8}$$ *Divide each side by 8.*

$x = 42$

KL is 42 centimeters.

Step 2 Find *y*.

∠*K* corresponds to ∠*B*.   *Corresponding angles of similar triangles have equal angle measures.*

$y = 103°$

Video **Lesson Tutorials Online** my.hrw.com

EXAMPLE 2 **Measurement Application**

A volleyball court is a rectangle that is similar in shape to an Olympic-sized pool. Find the width of the pool.

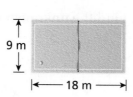

9 m

|← 18 m →|

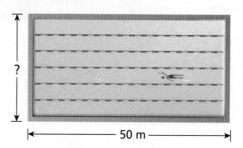

?

|← 50 m →|

Let w = the width of the pool.

$\frac{18}{50} = \frac{9}{w}$ *Write a proportion using corresponding side lengths.*

$18 \cdot w = 50 \cdot 9$ *Find the cross products.*

$18w = 450$ *Multiply.*

$\frac{18w}{18} = \frac{450}{18}$ *Divide each side by 18.*

$w = 25$

The pool is 25 meters wide.

EXAMPLE 3 **Estimating with Indirect Measurement**

Estimate the height of the totem pole shown at right.

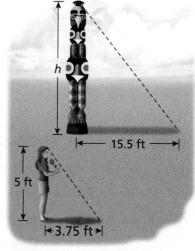

$\frac{h}{5} = \frac{15.5}{3.75}$ *Write a proportion.*

$\frac{h}{5} \approx \frac{16}{4}$ *Use compatible numbers to estimate.*

$\frac{h}{5} \approx 4$ *Simplify.*

$5 \cdot \frac{h}{5} \approx 5 \cdot 4$ *Multiply each side by 5.*

$h \approx 20$

The totem pole is about 20 feet tall.

h

|← 15.5 ft →|

5 ft

|←3.75 ft→|

Think and Discuss

1. Write another proportion that could be used to find the value of x in Example 1.

2. Name two objects that it would make sense to measure using indirect measurement.

GUIDED PRACTICE

See Example **1** $\triangle XYZ \sim \triangle PQR$ in each pair. Find the unknown measures.

1.
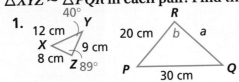

2.
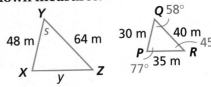

See Example **2** **3.** The rectangular gardens at right are similar in shape. How wide is the smaller garden?

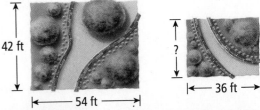

See Example **3** **4.** A water tower casts a shadow that is 21 ft long. A tree casts a shadow that is 8 ft long. Estimate the height of the water tower.

INDEPENDENT PRACTICE

See Example **1** $\triangle ABC \sim \triangle DEF$ in each pair. Find the unknown measures.

5.
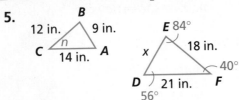

6.
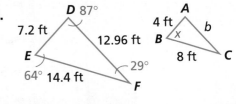

See Example **2** **7.** The movie still and its projected image at right are similar. What is the height of the projected image to the nearest hundredth of an inch?

See Example **3** **8.** A cactus casts a shadow that is 14 ft 7 in. long. A gate nearby casts a shadow that is 5 ft long. Estimate the height of the cactus.

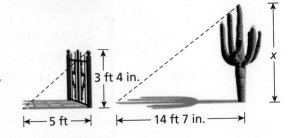

Extra Practice
See page EP13.

9. A building with a height of 14 m casts a shadow that is 16 m long while a taller building casts a 24 m long shadow. What is the height of the taller building?

10. Two common envelope sizes are $3\frac{1}{2}$ in. × $6\frac{1}{2}$ in. and 4 in. × $9\frac{1}{2}$ in. Are these envelopes similar? Explain.

11. **Art** An art class has painted a mural composed of brightly colored geometric shapes. All of the right triangles in the design are similar to the red right triangle. Find the heights of the three other right triangles in the mural. Round your answers to the nearest tenth.

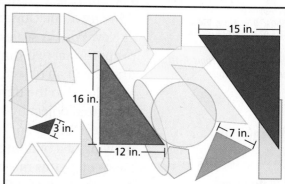

 12. **Write a Problem** Write a problem that can be solved using indirect measurement.

 13. **Write About It** Assume you know the side lengths of one triangle and the length of one side of a second similar triangle. Explain how to use the properties of similar figures to find the unknown lengths in the second triangle.

14. **Challenge** $\triangle ABE \sim \triangle ACD$. What is the value of y in the diagram?

Test Prep and Spiral Review

15. **Multiple Choice** Find the unknown length in the similar figures.

   Ⓐ 10 cm   Ⓒ 15 cm
   Ⓑ 12 cm   Ⓓ 18 cm

16. **Gridded Response** A building casts a 16-foot shadow. A 6-foot man standing next to the building casts a 2.5-foot shadow. What is the height, in feet, of the building?

Write each phrase as an algebraic expression. (Lesson 1-7)

17. the product of 18 and y 18. 5 less than a number   19. 12 divided by z

Choose the most appropriate customary unit for each measurement. Justify your answer. (Lesson 4-5)

20. weight of a cell phone   21. height of a cat   22. capacity of a gas tank

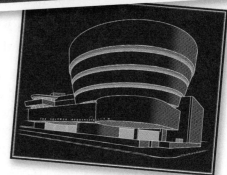

TN SPI 0706.1.4 Use scales to read maps.
Also ✓ 0706.1.7, ✓ 0706.1.8, GLE 0706.2.3, GLE 0706.4.3

Use Additional Topic A-10 with this lesson.

Vocabulary

scale drawing

scale factor

scale model

scale

Interactivities Online ▶

The drawing at right shows a *scale drawing* of the Guggenheim Museum in New York. A **scale drawing** is a proportional two-dimensional drawing of an object. Its dimensions are related to the dimensions of the actual object by a ratio called the **scale factor**. For example, if a drawing of a building has a scale factor of $\frac{1}{87}$, this means that each dimension of the drawing is $\frac{1}{87}$ of the corresponding dimension of the actual building.

A **scale model** is a proportional three-dimensional model of an object. A **scale** is the ratio between two sets of measurements. Scales can use the same units or different units. Both scale drawings and scale models can be smaller or larger than the objects they represent.

EXAMPLE 1 Finding a Scale Factor

Identify the scale factor.

	Race Car	Model
Length (in.)	132	11
Height (in.)	66	5.5

Caution! //////

A scale factor is always the ratio of the model's dimensions to the actual object's dimensions.

You can use the lengths *or* heights to find the scale factor.

$\dfrac{\text{model length}}{\text{race car length}} = \dfrac{11}{132} = \dfrac{1}{12}$ *Write a ratio. Then simplify.*

$\dfrac{\text{model height}}{\text{race car height}} = \dfrac{5.5}{66} = \dfrac{1}{12}$

The scale factor is $\frac{1}{12}$. This is reasonable because $\frac{1}{10}$ the length of the race car is 13.2 in. The length of the model is 11 in., which is less than 13.2 in., and $\frac{1}{12}$ is less than $\frac{1}{10}$.

EXAMPLE 2 Using Scale Factors to Find Unknown Lengths

A photograph of Rene Magritte's painting *The Schoolmaster* has dimensions 5.4 cm and 4 cm. The scale factor is $\frac{1}{15}$. Find the size of the actual painting.

Think: $\frac{\text{photo}}{\text{painting}} = \frac{1}{15}$

$\frac{5.4}{\ell} = \frac{1}{15}$ *Write a proportion to find the length ℓ.*

$\ell = 5.4 \cdot 15$ *Find the cross products.*

$\ell = 81$ cm   *Multiply.*

$\frac{4}{w} = \frac{1}{15}$ *Write a proportion to find the width w.*

$w = 4 \cdot 15$ *Find the cross products.*

$w = 60$ cm   *Multiply.*

The painting is 81 cm long and 60 cm wide.

EXAMPLE 3 *Measurement Application*

On a map of Florida, the distance between Hialeah and Tampa is 10.5 cm. The map scale is 3 cm:128 km. What is the actual distance *d* between these two cities?

Think: $\frac{\text{map distance}}{\text{actual distance}} = \frac{3}{128}$

$\frac{3}{128} = \frac{10.5}{d}$ *Write a proportion.*

$3 \cdot d = 128 \cdot 10.5$ *Find the cross products.*

$3d = 1{,}344$

$\frac{3d}{3} = \frac{1{,}344}{3}$ *Divide both sides by 3.*

$d = 448$ km

The distance between the cities is 448 km.

Think and Discuss

1. **Explain** how you can tell whether a model with a scale factor of $\frac{5}{3}$ is larger or smaller than the original object.

2. **Describe** how to find the scale factor if an antenna is 60 feet long and a scale drawing shows the length as 1 foot long.

Exercises

GUIDED PRACTICE

See Example 1 — **Identify the scale factor.**

1.

	Grizzly Bear	Model
Height (in.)	84	6

2.

	Moray Eel	Model
Length (ft)	5	$1\frac{1}{2}$

See Example 2 — **3.** In a photograph, a sculpture is 4.2 cm tall and 2.5 cm wide. The scale factor is $\frac{1}{16}$. Find the size of the actual sculpture.

See Example 3 — **4.** Ms. Jackson is driving from South Bend to Indianapolis. She measures a distance of 4.3 cm between the cities on her Indiana road map. The map scale is 1 cm:48 km. What is the actual distance between these two cities?

INDEPENDENT PRACTICE

See Example 1 — **Identify the scale factor.**

5.

	Eagle	Model
Wingspan (in.)	90	6

6.

	Dolphin	Model
Length (cm)	260	13

See Example 2 — **7.** On a scale drawing, a tree is $6\frac{3}{4}$ inches tall. The scale factor is $\frac{1}{20}$. Find the height of the actual tree.

See Example 3 — **8. Measurement** On a road map of Virginia, the distance from Alexandria to Roanoke is 7.6 cm. The map scale is 2 cm:80 km. What is the actual distance between these two cities?

PRACTICE AND PROBLEM SOLVING

Extra Practice
See page EP13.

The scale factor of each model is 1:12. Find the missing dimensions.

	Item	Actual Dimensions	Model Dimensions
9.	Lamp	Height: ▪	Height: $1\frac{1}{3}$ in.
10.	Couch	Height: 32 in. Length: 69 in.	Height: ▪ Length: ▪
11.	Table	Height: ▪ Width: ▪ Length: ▪	Height: 6.25 cm Width: 11.75 cm Length: 20 cm

12. An artist transferred a rectangular design 13 cm long and 6 cm wide to a similar canvas 260 cm long and 120 cm wide. What is the scale factor?

13. Critical Thinking A countertop is 18 ft long. How long is it on a scale drawing with the scale 1 in:3 yd?

 14. Write About It A scale for a scale drawing is 10 cm:1 mm. Which will be larger, the actual object or the scale drawing? Explain.

Use the map for Exercises 15–16.

15. In 1863, Confederate troops marched from Chambersburg to Gettysburg in search of badly needed shoes. Use the ruler and the scale of the map to estimate how far the Confederate soldiers, many of whom were barefoot, marched.

Mason Dixon Line

1 inch = 10 miles

16. Before the Civil War, the Mason-Dixon Line was considered the dividing line between the North and the South. Gettysburg is about 8.1 miles north of the Mason-Dixon Line. How far apart in inches are Gettysburg and the Mason-Dixon Line on the map?

17. Multi-Step Toby is making a scale model of the battlefield at Fredericksburg. The area he wants to model measures about 11 mi by 7.5 mi. He plans to put the model on a 3.25 ft by 3.25 ft square table. On each side of the model he wants to leave at least 3 in. between the model and the table edges. What is the largest scale he can use?

18. ⭐ Challenge A map of Vicksburg, Mississippi, has a scale of "1 mile to the inch." The map has been reduced so that 5 inches on the original map appears as 1.5 inches on the reduced map. The distance between two points on the reduced map is 1.75 inches. What is the actual distance in miles?

President Abraham Lincoln, Major Allan Pinkerton, and General John A. McCleland, October 1862.

Test Prep and Spiral Review

19. Multiple Choice On a scale model with a scale of $\frac{1}{16}$, the height of a shed is 7 inches. What is the approximate height of the actual shed?

Ⓐ 2 feet   Ⓑ 9 feet   Ⓒ 58 feet   Ⓓ 112 feet

20. Gridded Response On a map, the scale is 3 centimeters:120 kilometers. The distance between two cities on the map is 6.8 centimeters. What is the distance between the actual cities in kilometers?

Order the numbers from least to greatest. (Lesson 2-11)

21. $\frac{4}{7}$, 0.41, 0.054   **22.** $\frac{1}{4}$, 0.2, −1.2   **23.** 0.7, $\frac{7}{9}$, $\frac{7}{11}$ **24.** 0.3, $-\frac{5}{6}$, 0.32

Divide. Estimate to check whether each answer is reasonable. (Lesson 3-4)

25. 0.32 ÷ 5   **26.** 78.57 ÷ 9   **27.** 40.5 ÷ 15   **28.** 29.68 ÷ 28

Make Scale Drawings and Models

Use with Lesson 4-10

Learn It Online
Lab Resources Online **go.hrw.com**,
keyword **MS10 Lab4** **Go**

Scale drawings and scale models are used in mapmaking, construction, and other trades. You can create scale drawings and models using graph paper. If you measure carefully and convert your measurements correctly, your scale drawings and models will be similar to the actual objects they represent.

TN ✓ **0706.1.7** Explain and demonstrate how scale in maps and drawings shows relative size and distance.
Also ✓ **0706.1.8, GLE 0706.2.3**

Activity 1

Make a scale drawing of a classroom and items with the following dimensions.

Classroom	6 Student Desks	Teacher's Desk	Aquarium
12 ft × 20 ft	2 ft × 3 ft	2 ft × 6 ft	5 ft × 2 ft

1 You can use graph paper for your drawing. When making a scale drawing, you can use any scale you wish. For this activity, use a scale in which 2 squares represent 1 foot. To convert each measurement, multiply the number of feet by 2.

2 This means that the room measures 24 squares (2 · 12 ft) by 40 squares (2 · 20 ft). Convert the other measurements in the table using the same scale.

Classroom	6 Student Desks	Teacher's Desk	Aquarium
24 sq × 40 sq	4 sq × 6 sq	4 sq × 12 sq	10 sq × 4 sq

3 Now sketch the room and items on graph paper. Place the items anywhere in the room you wish.

Think and Discuss

1. Write ratios to compare the widths and lengths of the actual classroom and the drawing. Can you make a proportion with your ratios? Explain.

2. Describe how your drawing would change if you used a scale in which 1 square represents 2 feet.

Try This

1. Measure the dimensions of your classroom as well as some items in the room. Then make a scale drawing. Explain the scale you used.

Activity 2

Make a scale model of a school gym whose floor is 20 meters × 32 meters and whose walls are 12 meters tall.

1 You can use graph paper for your model. For this activity, use a scale in which 1 square represents 2 meters. To convert each measurement, divide the number of meters by 2.

2 The two longer sides of the gym floor are 16 squares (32 m ÷ 2). The other two sides are 10 squares (20 m ÷ 2). The walls are 6 squares (12 m ÷ 2) tall.

	Floor Length	Floor Width	Wall Height
Actual	20 m	32 m	12 m
Model	10 squares	16 squares	6 squares

3 Sketch the walls on graph paper as shown. Then cut them out and tape them together to make an open rectangular box to represent the gym.

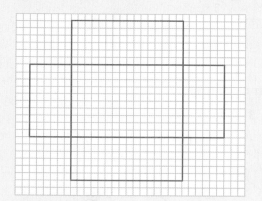 

Think and Discuss

1. A different gym has a floor that is 120 feet × 75 feet and a height of 45 feet. A model of the gym has a height of 9 squares. What are the dimensions of the model's floor? What scale was used to create this model?

Try This

1. Make a scale model of the building shown. Explain the scale you used to create your model.

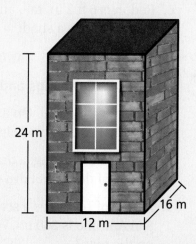

24 m

12 m

16 m

Quiz for Lessons 4-8 Through 4-10

 4-8 **Similar Figures and Proportions**

1. Tell whether the triangles are similar.

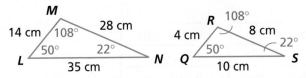

2. Tell whether the figures are similar.

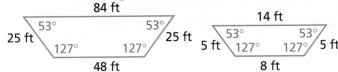

 4-9 **Using Similar Figures**

△*ABC* ~ △*XYZ* in each pair. Find the unknown measures.

3.

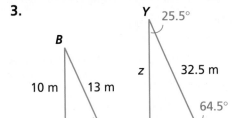

4.

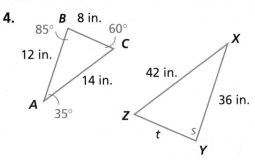

5. Reynaldo drew a rectangular design that was 6 in. wide and 8 in. long. He used a copy machine to enlarge the rectangular design so that the width was 10 in. What was the length of the enlarged design?

6. Redon is 6 ft 2 in. tall, and his shadow is 4 ft 1 in. long. At the same time, a building casts a shadow that is 19 ft 10 in. long. Estimate the height of the building.

 4-10 **Scale Drawings and Scale Models**

7. An actor is 6 ft tall. On a billboard for a new movie, the actor's picture is enlarged so that his height is 16.8 ft. What is the scale factor?

8. On a scale drawing, a driveway is 6 in. long. The scale factor is $\frac{1}{24}$. Find the length of the actual driveway.

9. A map of Texas has a scale of 1 in:65 mi. The distance from Dallas to San Antonio is 260 mi. What is the distance in inches between these two cities on the map?

Real-World CONNECTIONS

Paul Bunyan Statues According to legend, Paul Bunyan was a giant lumberjack whose footsteps created Minnesota's ten thousand lakes. Statues honoring this mythical figure can be found throughout the state. One of the largest, in Brainerd, stands 26 feet tall and can greet you by name!

MINNESOTA

1. A tourist who is 1.8 m tall stands next to the statue of Paul Bunyan in Bemidji, MN. He measures the length of his shadow and the shadow cast by the statue. The measurements are shown in the figure. What is the height of the statue?

2. Show how to use dimensional analysis to convert the height of the statue to feet. Round to the nearest foot. (*Hint*: 1 m = 3.28 ft)

3. The Bemidji statue includes Paul Bunyan's companion, Babe, the Blue Ox. The statue's horns are 14 feet across. The statue was made using the dimensions of an actual ox and a scale of 3:1. What was the length of the horns of the actual ox?

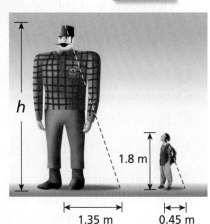

h

1.8 m

1.35 m 0.45 m

4. The kneeling Paul Bunyan statue in Akeley, MN, is 25 feet tall. The ratio of the statue's height to its width is 17:11. What is the width of the statue to the nearest tenth of a foot?

5. A souvenir of the Akeley statue is made using the scale 2 in:5 ft. What is the height of the souvenir?

BEMIDJI
PAUL
BUNYAN
1937

Game Time

Water Works

You have three glasses: a 3-ounce glass, a 5-ounce glass, and an 8-ounce glass. The 8-ounce glass is full of water, and the other two glasses are empty. By pouring water from one glass to another, how can you get exactly 6 ounces of water in one of the glasses? The step-by-step solution is described below.

1 Pour the water from the 8 oz glass into the 5 oz glass.

2 Pour the water from the 5 oz glass into the 3 oz glass.

3 Pour the water from the 3 oz glass into the 8 oz glass.

You now have 6 ounces of water in the 8-ounce glass.

Start again, but this time try to get exactly 4 ounces of water in one glass. (*Hint:* Find a way to get 1 ounce of water. Start by pouring water into the 3-ounce glass.)

Next, using 3-ounce, 8-ounce, and 11-ounce glasses, try to get exactly 9 ounces of water in one glass. Start with the 11-ounce glass full of water. (*Hint:* Start by pouring water into the 8-ounce glass.)

Look at the sizes of the glasses in each problem. The volume of the third glass is the sum of the volumes of the first two glasses: $3 + 5 = 8$ and $3 + 8 = 11$. Using any amounts for the two smaller glasses, and starting with the largest glass full, you can get any multiple of the smaller glass's volume. Try it and see.

Concentration

Each card in a deck of cards has a ratio on one side. Place each card face down. Each player or team takes a turn flipping over two cards. If the ratios on the cards are equivalent, the player or team can keep the pair. If not, the next player or team flips two cards. After every card has been turned over, the player or team with the most pairs wins.

A complete copy of the rules and the game pieces are available online.

Learn It Online
Game Time Extra **go.hrw.com**,
keyword MS10 Games **Go**

Materials
- 2 paper plates
- scissors
- markers

It's in the Bag!

PROJECT **Paper Plate Proportions**

Serve up some proportions on this book made from paper plates.

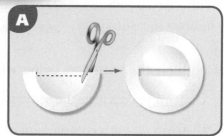
A

❶ Fold one of the paper plates in half. Cut out a narrow rectangle along the folded edge. The rectangle should be as long as the diameter of plate's inner circle. When you open the plate, you will have a narrow window in the center. **Figure A**

B

❷ Fold the second paper plate in half and then unfold it. Cut slits on both sides of the crease beginning from the edge of the plate to the inner circle. **Figure B**

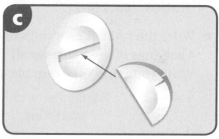
C

❸ Roll up the plate with the slits so that the two slits touch each other. Then slide this plate into the narrow window in the other plate. **Figure C**

❹ When the rolled-up plate is halfway through the window, unroll it so that the slits fit on the sides of the window. **Figure D**

D

❺ Close the book so that all the plates are folded in half.

Taking Note of the Math

Write the number and name of the chapter on the cover of the book. Then review the chapter, using the inside pages to take notes on ratios, rates, proportions, and similar figures.

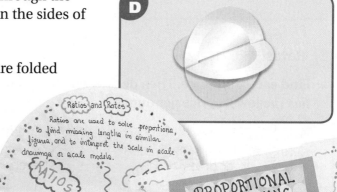

CHAPTER

4

Study Guide: Review

Study Guide: Review

Vocabulary

corresponding angles .. 248	proportion 222	scale factor 256
corresponding sides ... 248	rate 218	scale model 256
cross product 226	ratio 214	similar 248
equivalent ratios 222	scale 256	unit conversion factor .. 240
indirect measurement . 252	scale drawing 256	unit rate 218

Complete the sentences below with vocabulary words from the list above.

1. __?__ figures have the same shape but not necessarily the same size.

2. A(n) __?__ is a comparison of two numbers, and a(n) __?__ is a ratio that compares two quantities measured in different units.

3. The ratio used to enlarge or reduce similar figures is a(n) __?__.

EXAMPLES

EXERCISES

4-1 Ratios (pp. 214–217)

■ Write the ratio of 2 servings of bread to 4 servings of vegetables in all three forms. Write your answers in simplest form.

$\frac{2}{4} = \frac{1}{2}$ *Write the ratio 2 to 4 in simplest form.*

$\frac{1}{2}$, 1 to 2, 1:2

There are 3 red, 7 blue, and 5 yellow balloons.

4. Write the ratio of blue balloons to total balloons in all three forms. Write your answer in simplest form.

5. Tell whether the ratio of red to blue balloons or the ratio of yellow balloons to total balloons is greater.

4-2 Rates (pp. 218–221)

■ Find each unit price. Then decide which has the lowest price per ounce.

$\frac{\$2.70}{5 \text{ oz}}$ or $\frac{\$4.32}{12 \text{ oz}}$

$\frac{\$2.70}{5 \text{ oz}} = \frac{\$0.54}{\text{oz}}$ and $\frac{\$4.32}{12 \text{ oz}} = \frac{\$0.36}{\text{oz}}$

Since $0.36 < 0.54$, $\frac{\$4.32}{12 \text{ oz}}$ has the lowest price per ounce.

Find each unit rate.

6. 540 ft in 90 s   7. 436 mi in 4 hr

Find each unit price. Then decide which is the better buy.

8. $\frac{\$56}{25 \text{ gal}}$ or $\frac{\$32.05}{15 \text{ gal}}$ 9. $\frac{\$160}{5 \text{ g}}$ or $\frac{\$315}{9 \text{ g}}$

10. Beatríz earned $197.50 for 25 hours of work. How much money did she earn per hour?

4-3 Identifying and Writing Proportions (pp. 222–225)

■ Determine if $\frac{5}{12}$ and $\frac{3}{9}$ are proportional.

$\frac{5}{12}$ $\frac{5}{12}$ *is already in simplest form.*

$\frac{3}{9} = \frac{1}{3}$ *Simplify $\frac{3}{9}$.*

$\frac{5}{12} \neq \frac{1}{3}$ *The ratios are not proportional.*

Determine if the ratios are proportional.

11. $\frac{9}{27}, \frac{6}{20}$ **12.** $\frac{15}{25}, \frac{20}{30}$ **13.** $\frac{21}{14}, \frac{18}{12}$

Find a ratio equivalent to the given ratio. Then use the ratios to write a proportion.

14. $\frac{10}{12}$ **15.** $\frac{45}{50}$ **16.** $\frac{9}{15}$

4-4 Solving Proportions (pp. 226–229)

■ Use cross products to solve $\frac{p}{8} = \frac{10}{21}$.

$\frac{p}{8} = \frac{10}{12}$

$p \cdot 12 = 8 \cdot 10$ *Multiply the cross*

$12p = 80$ *products.*

$\frac{12p}{12} = \frac{80}{12}$ *Divide each side by 12.*

$p = \frac{20}{3}$, or $6\frac{2}{3}$

Use cross products to solve each proportion.

17. $\frac{4}{6} = \frac{n}{3}$ **18.** $\frac{2}{a} = \frac{5}{15}$

19. $\frac{b}{1.5} = \frac{8}{3}$ **20.** $\frac{16}{11} = \frac{96}{x}$

21. $\frac{2}{y} = \frac{1}{5}$ **22.** $\frac{7}{2} = \frac{70}{w}$

4-5 Customary Measurements (pp. 232–235)

■ Convert 5 mi to feet.

$\frac{\text{feet}}{\text{miles}} \longrightarrow \frac{5{,}280}{1} = \frac{x}{5}$

$x = 5{,}280 \cdot 5 = 26{,}400$ ft

Convert each measure.

23. 32 fl oz to pt   **24.** 1.5 T to lb

25. Manda has 4 yards of fabric. She cuts off 29 inches. What is the length of the remaining fabric?

4-6 Metric Measurements (pp. 236–239)

■ Convert 63 m to centimeters.

63 m $= (63 \times 100)$ cm   *100 cm $= 1$ m*

$= 6{,}300$ cm

Convert each measure.

26. 18 L to mL   **27.** 720 mg to g

28. 5.3 km to m   **29.** 0.6 cm to mm

4-7 Dimensional Analysis (pp. 240–243)

■ Amil can run 12 kilometers in 1 hour. How many meters can he run at this pace in 1 minute?

km to m: $= \frac{1{,}000 \text{ m}}{1 \text{ km}}$ h to min: $= \frac{1 \text{ h}}{60 \text{ min}}$

$\frac{12 \text{ km}}{1 \text{ h}} \cdot \frac{1{,}000 \text{ m}}{1 \text{ km}} \cdot \frac{1 \text{ h}}{60 \text{ min}} = \frac{12 \cdot 1{,}000 \text{ m}}{60 \text{ min}} = \frac{200 \text{ m}}{1 \text{ min}}$

Use conversion factors to find each rate.

30. 162 lb/yr to lb/mo

31. 1,232 ft/min to mi/h

32. While driving, Abby passed mile marker 130 at 3:10 P.M. and mile marker 170 at 4:00 P.M. Find Abby's average speed in miles per minute.

Study Guide: Review

4-8 **Similar Figures and Proportions** (pp. 248–251)

- **Tell whether the figures are similar.**

  The corresponding angles of the figures have equal measures.

  $$\frac{5}{30} \stackrel{?}{=} \frac{3}{18} \stackrel{?}{=} \frac{5}{30} \stackrel{?}{=} \frac{3}{18}$$

  $$\frac{1}{6} = \frac{1}{6} = \frac{1}{6} = \frac{1}{6}$$

  The ratios of the corresponding sides are equivalent. The figures are similar.

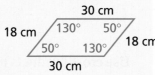

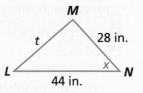

Tell whether the figures are similar.

33.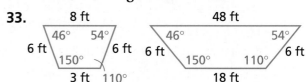

34.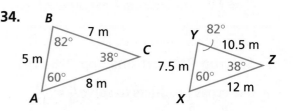

4-9 **Using Similar Figures** (pp. 252–255)

- **$\triangle ABC \sim \triangle LMN$. Find the unknown measures.**

  $$\frac{AB}{LM} = \frac{AC}{LN}$$

  $$\frac{8}{t} = \frac{11}{44}$$

  $$8 \cdot 44 = t \cdot 11$$

  $$352 = 11t$$

  $$\frac{352}{11} = \frac{11t}{11}$$

  $$32 \text{ in.} = t$$

  $\angle N$ corresponds to $\angle C$.

  $$x = 46°$$

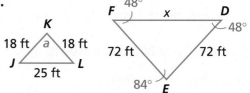

$\triangle JKL \sim \triangle DEF$. Find the unknown measures.

35.

36. A rectangular photo frame is 24 cm long and 9 cm wide. A frame that is similar in shape is 3 cm wide. Find the length of the frame.

37. A tree casts a $30\frac{1}{2}$ ft shadow at the time of day when a 2 ft stake casts a $7\frac{2}{3}$ ft shadow. Estimate the height of the tree.

4-10 **Scale Drawings and Scale Models** (pp. 256–259)

- **A model boat is 4 inches long. The scale factor is $\frac{1}{24}$. How long is the actual boat?**

  $$\frac{\text{model}}{\text{boat}} = \frac{1}{24}$$

  $$\frac{4}{n} = \frac{1}{24} \qquad \textit{Write a proportion.}$$

  $$4 \cdot 24 = n \cdot 1 \qquad \textit{Find the cross products.}$$

  $$96 = n \qquad \textit{Solve.}$$

  The boat is 96 inches long.

38. The Wright brothers' *Flyer* had a 484-inch wingspan. Carla bought a model of the plane with a scale factor of $\frac{1}{40}$. What is the model's wingspan?

39. The distance from Austin to Houston on a map is 4.3 inches. The map scale is 1 inch:38 miles. What is the actual distance?

1. Stan found 12 pennies, 15 nickels, 7 dimes, and 5 quarters. Tell whether the ratio of pennies to quarters or the ratio of nickels to dimes is greater.

2. Lenny sold 576 tacos in 48 hours. What was Lenny's average rate of taco sales?

3. A store sells a 5 lb box of detergent for $5.25 and a 10 lb box of detergent for $9.75. Which size box has the lowest price per pound?

Find a ratio equivalent to each ratio. Then use the ratios to write a proportion.

4. $\frac{22}{30}$

5. $\frac{7}{9}$

6. $\frac{18}{54}$

7. $\frac{10}{17}$

Use cross products to solve each proportion.

8. $\frac{9}{12} = \frac{m}{6}$

9. $\frac{x}{2} = \frac{18}{6}$

10. $\frac{3}{7} = \frac{21}{t}$

11. $\frac{5}{p} = \frac{10}{2}$

12. A certain salsa is made with 6 parts tomato and 2 parts bell pepper. To correctly make the recipe, how many cups of tomato should be combined with 1.5 cups of bell pepper?

Convert each measure or rate.

13. 13,200 ft to mi

14. 3.5 lb to oz

15. 6.12 km to m

16. 57 L to kL

17. 828 lb/yr to lb/mo

18. 4.25 L/h to mL/h

19. Some world-class race walkers can walk 9 miles per hour. What is this rate in feet per minute?

20. One pound is about 2.2 kilograms. Jefferson's dog weighs 40 lb. What is the mass of his dog in kilograms?

Tell whether the figures are similar.

21.

22.

$\triangle WYZ \sim \triangle MNO$ in each pair. Find the unknown measures.

23.

24.

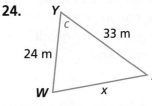

25. A scale model of a building is 8 in. by 12 in. The scale is 1 in:15 ft. What are the dimensions of the actual building?

26. The distance from Portland to Seaside is 75 mi. What is the distance in inches between the two towns on a map whose scale is $1\frac{1}{4}$ in:25 mi?

CHAPTER 4

TCAP
Test Prep

Learn It Online
State Test Practice **go.hrw.com,**
keyword MS10 TestPrep Go

Cumulative Assessment, Chapters 1–4

Multiple Choice

1. What is the unknown length *b* in similar triangles *ABC* and *DEF*?

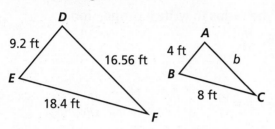

   A 7.2 feet   **C** 4 feet

   B 6 feet   **D** 5.6 feet

2. The total length of the Golden Gate Bridge in San Francisco, California, is 8,981 feet. A car is traveling at a speed of 45 miles per hour. How many minutes will it take the car to cross the bridge?

   F 0.04 minute   **H** 1.7 minutes

   G 1.28 minutes   **J** 2.27 minutes

3. What is the product of −3.1 and 6.9?

   A −21.39

   B −13.0

   C 13.0

   D 21.39

4. A hot air balloon descends 38.5 meters in 22 seconds. If the balloon continues to descend at this rate, how long will it take to descend 125 meters?

   F 25.25 seconds

   G 86.5 seconds

   H 71.43 seconds

   J 218.75 seconds

5. Which value completes the table of equivalent ratios?

Microphones	3	9	15	36
Karaoke Machines	1	3	?	12

   A 5   **C** 8

   B 7   **D** 9

6. On a baseball field, the distance from home plate to the pitcher's mound is $60\frac{1}{2}$ feet. The distance from home plate to second base is about $127\frac{7}{24}$ feet. What is the difference between the two distances?

   F $61\frac{1}{3}$ feet   **H** $66\frac{19}{24}$ feet

   G $66\frac{5}{6}$ feet   **J** $66\frac{5}{24}$ feet

7. What is the value of the expression $\frac{2h + 2}{3}$ if $h = 3.5$?

   A 2.5

   B 3

   C 7.5

   D 9

8. A football weighs about $\frac{3}{20}$ kilogram. A coach has 15 footballs in a large bag. Which is the <u>best</u> description of the total weight of the footballs?

   F Not quite 3 kilograms

   G A little more than 2 kilograms

   H Almost 1 kilogram

   J Between 1 and 2 kilograms

9. The scale on a map is 1 centimeter: 70 kilometers. The distance between two cities on the map is 8.2 centimeters. Which is the best estimate of the actual distance?

 A 85 kilometers

 B 471 kilometers

 C 117 kilometers

 D 574 kilometers

10. On a scale drawing, a cell phone tower is 1.25 feet tall. The scale factor is $\frac{1}{150}$. What is the height of the actual cell phone tower?

 F 37.5 feet

 G 120 feet

 H 148 feet

 J 187.5 feet

When a diagram or graph is not provided, quickly sketch one to clarify the information provided in the test item.

11. The Liberty Bell, a symbol of freedom in the United States, weighs 2,080 pounds. If 1 pound is approximately 0.45 kilograms, about how many kilograms does the Liberty Bell weigh?

 A 462 kg

 B 936 kg

 C 4,622 kg

 D 9,360 kg

12. Evaluate: $-51.03 \div (-8.1)$.

 F -59.13 H 0.16

 G -42.93 J 6.3

13. A scale drawing of a rectangular garden has a length of 4 inches and a width of 2.5 inches. The scale is 1 inch:3 feet. What is the perimeter of the actual garden in feet?

 A 7.5 feet   C 39 feet

 B 12 feet   D 90 feet

Process Standards Practice

Short Response

S1. Jana began the month with $102.50 in her checking account. During the month, she deposited $8.50 that she earned from baby-sitting, withdrew $9.75 to buy a CD, deposited $5.00 that her aunt gave her, and withdrew $6.50 for a movie ticket. Using compatible numbers, write and evaluate an expression to estimate the balance in Jana's account at the end of the month.

S2. A lamppost casts a shadow that is 18 feet long. At the same time of day, Alyce casts a shadow that is 4.2 feet long. Alyce is 5.3 feet tall. Draw a picture of the situation. Set up and solve a proportion to find the height of the lamppost to the nearest foot. Show your work.

Extended Response

E1. Riley is drawing a map of the state of Virginia. From east to west, the greatest distance across the state is about 430 miles. From north to south, the greatest distance is about 200 miles.

 a. Riley is using a map scale of 1 inch: 24 miles. Find the length of the map from east to west and the length from north to south. Round your answers to the nearest tenth.

 b. The length between two cities on Riley's map is 9 inches. What is the actual distance between the cities in miles?

 c. About how many minutes will it take for an airplane traveling at a speed of 520 miles per hour to fly from east to west across the widest part of Virginia? Show your work.

Graphs and Functions

Why Learn This?

You can use linear equations to represent how far a sailboat moving at a constant rate has traveled after a certain amount of time.

Learn It Online
Chapter Project Online go.hrw.com,
keyword MS10 Ch5 Go

Chapter Focus
- Graph linear relationships and identify the slope of the line.
- Identify proportional relationships ($y = kx$).

Are You Ready?

✓ Vocabulary

Choose the best term from the list to complete each sentence.

1. A(n) __?__ is a number that represents a part of a whole.

2. A closed figure with three sides is called a(n) __?__.

3. Two fractions are __?__ if they represent the same number.

4. One way to compare two fractions is to first find a(n) __?__.

common
denominator

equivalent

fraction

quadrilateral

triangle

Complete these exercises to review skills you will need for this Chapter.

✓ Write Equivalent Fractions

Find two fractions that are equivalent to each fraction.

5. $\frac{2}{5}$
6. $\frac{7}{11}$
7. $\frac{25}{100}$
8. $\frac{4}{6}$

9. $\frac{5}{17}$
10. $\frac{15}{23}$
11. $\frac{24}{78}$
12. $\frac{150}{325}$

✓ Compare Fractions

Compare. Write < or >.

13. $\frac{5}{6}$ ▮ $\frac{2}{3}$
14. $\frac{3}{8}$ ▮ $\frac{2}{5}$
15. $\frac{6}{11}$ ▮ $\frac{1}{4}$
16. $\frac{5}{8}$ ▮ $\frac{11}{12}$

17. $\frac{8}{9}$ ▮ $\frac{12}{13}$
18. $\frac{5}{11}$ ▮ $\frac{7}{21}$
19. $\frac{4}{10}$ ▮ $\frac{3}{7}$
20. $\frac{3}{4}$ ▮ $\frac{2}{9}$

✓ Solve Multiplication Equations

Solve each equation.

21. $3x = 12$
22. $15t = 75$
23. $2y = 14$
24. $7m = 84$

25. $25c = 125$
26. $16f = 320$
27. $11n = 121$
28. $53y = 318$

✓ Multiply Fractions

Solve. Write each answer in simplest form.

29. $\frac{2}{3} \cdot \frac{5}{7}$
30. $\frac{12}{16} \cdot \frac{3}{9}$
31. $\frac{4}{9} \cdot \frac{18}{24}$
32. $\frac{1}{56} \cdot \frac{50}{200}$

33. $\frac{1}{5} \cdot \frac{5}{9}$
34. $\frac{7}{8} \cdot \frac{4}{3}$
35. $\frac{25}{100} \cdot \frac{30}{90}$
36. $\frac{46}{91} \cdot \frac{3}{6}$

Study Guide: Preview

Where You've Been

Previously, you

- graphed ordered pairs of non-negative rational numbers on a coordinate plane.

- used tables to generate formulas representing relationships.

- formulated equations from problem situations.

In This Chapter

You will study

- plotting and identifying ordered pairs of integers on a coordinate plane.

- graphing to demonstrate relationships between data sets.

- describing the relationship between the terms in a sequence and their positions in a sequence.

- formulating problem situations when given a simple equation.

Where You're Going

You can use the skills learned in this chapter

- to sketch or interpret a graph that shows how a measurement such as distance, speed, cost, or temperature changes over time.

- to interpret patterns and make predictions in science, business, and personal finance.

Key Vocabulary/Vocabulario

coordinate plane	plano cartesiano
function	función
linear equation	ecuación lineal
linear function	función lineal
ordered pair	par ordenado
origin	origen
quadrant	cuadrante
sequence	secuencia
x-axis	eje x
y-axis	eje y

Vocabulary Connections

To become familiar with some of the vocabulary terms in the chapter, consider the following. You may refer to the chapter, the glossary, or a dictionary if you like.

1. A **sequence** is an ordered list of numbers, such as 2, 4, 6, and 8. Can you make up a sequence with a pattern and describe the pattern?

2. The word "linear" comes from the word *line*. What do you think the graph of a **linear equation** looks like?

3. An *origin* is the point at which something begins. Can you describe where to begin when you plot a point on a coordinate plane? Can you guess why the point where the x-axis and y-axis cross is called the **origin** ?

4. *Quadrupeds* are animals with four feet, and a *quadrilateral* is a four-sided figure. A coordinate plane has sections called **quadrants** . What does this word imply about the number of sections in a coordinate plane?

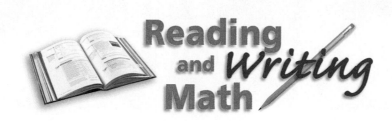

TN ◤ **English/Language Arts**
✓ **0701.4.12** Present a body of well-developed and specific facts and information pertinent to the topic, developed as a series of paragraphs which support the topic.

Writing Strategy:
Write a Convincing Argument

A convincing argument or explanation should include the following:

• The problem restated in your own words

• A short response

• Evidence to support the response

• A summary statement

 Example

✎ **Write About It**
Explain how to find the next three integers in the pattern -43, -40, -37, -34, ...

Step 1 **Identify the goal.**

Explain how to find the next three integers in the pattern -43, -40, -37, -34, ...

Step 2 **Provide a short response.**

As the pattern continues, the integers increase in value. Find the amount of increase from one integer to the next. Then add that amount to the last integer in the pattern. Follow this step two more times to get the next three integers in the pattern.

Step 3 **Provide evidence to support your response.**

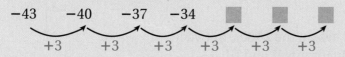

Find the amount of increase from one integer to the next.

$-34 + 3 = -31$ $-31 + 3 = -28$ $-28 + 3 = -25$

The next three integers are -31, -28, and -25.

The pattern is to add 3 to each integer to get the next integer.

Step 4 **Summarize your argument.**

To find the next three integers in the pattern -43, -40, -37, -34, . . . , find the amount that is added to each integer to get the next integer in the pattern.

Try This

Write a convincing argument using the method above.

1. Explain how to find the next three integers in the pattern 0, -2, -4, -6, ...

2. Explain how to find the seventh integer in the pattern -18, -13, -8, -3, ...

Reading and Writing Math

The Coordinate Plane

TN GLE 0706.1.1 Use mathematical language, symbols, and definitions while developing mathematical reasoning.

A **coordinate plane** is a plane containing a horizontal number line, the **x-axis**, and a vertical number line, the **y-axis**. The intersection of these axes is called the **origin**.

The axes divide the coordinate plane into four regions called **quadrants**, which are numbered I, II, III, and IV.

Vocabulary

coordinate plane

x-axis, y-axis

origin

quadrant

ordered pair

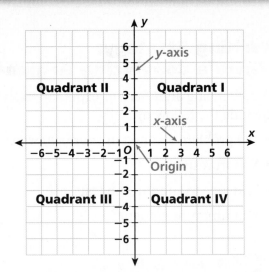

E X A M P L E   **1**   **Identifying Quadrants on a Coordinate Plane**

Identify the quadrant that contains each point.

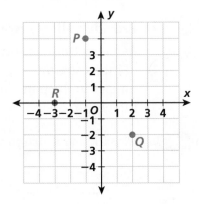

A *P*

   P lies in Quadrant II.

B *Q*

   Q lies in Quadrant IV.

C *R*

   R lies on the *x*-axis, between Quadrants II and III.

An **ordered pair** is a pair of numbers that can be used to locate a point on a coordinate plane. The two numbers that form the ordered pair are called coordinates. The origin is identified by the ordered pair (0,0).

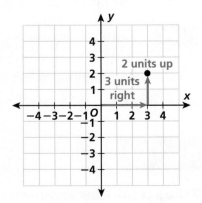

Ordered pair

(3, 2)

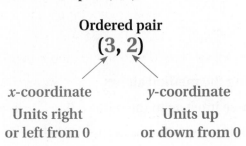

x-coordinate

Units right
or left from 0

y-coordinate

Units up
or down from 0

[Video] **Lesson Tutorials Online**   my.hrw.com

EXAMPLE 2 **Plotting Points on a Coordinate Plane**

Plot each point on a coordinate plane.

A *G* (2, 5)

Start at the origin. Move 2 units right and 5 units up.

B *N* (−3, −4)

Start at the origin. Move 3 units left and 4 units down.

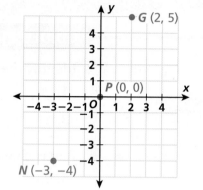

C *P* (0, 0)

Point P is at the origin.

EXAMPLE 3 **Identifying Points on a Coordinate Plane**

Give the coordinates of each point.

A *J*

Start at the origin. Point J is 3 units right and 2 units down.

The coordinates of *J* are (3, −2).

B *K*

Start at the origin. Point K is 2 units left and 4 units up.

The coordinates of *K* are (−2, 4).

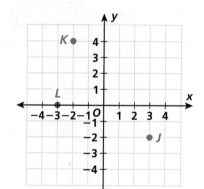

C *L*

Start at the origin. Point L is 3 units left on the x-axis.

The coordinates of *L* are (−3, 0).

Think and Discuss

1. **Explain** whether point (4, 5) is the same as point (5, 4).

2. **Name** the *x*-coordinate of a point on the *y*-axis. Name the *y*-coordinate of a point on the *x*-axis.

3. **Suppose** the equator represents the *x*-axis on a map of Earth and a line called the *prime meridian,* which passes through England, represents the *y*-axis. Starting at the origin, which of these directions —east, west, north, and south—are positive? Which are negative?

Learn It Online
Homework Help Online **go.hrw.com,**
keyword MS10 5-1 Go
Exercises 1–26, 27, 29, 33

GUIDED PRACTICE

See Example 1   **Identify the quadrant that contains each point.**

    1. A **2.** B

    3. C **4.** D

See Example 2   **Plot each point on a coordinate plane.**

    5. $E(-1, 2)$ **6.** $N(2, -4)$

    7. $H(-3, -4)$ **8.** $T(5, 0)$

See Example 3   **Give the coordinates of each point.**

    9. J **10.** P

    11. S **12.** M

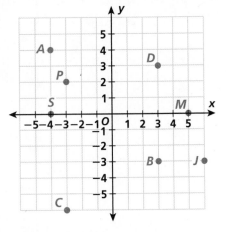

INDEPENDENT PRACTICE

See Example 1   **Identify the quadrant that contains each point.**

    13. F **14.** J

    15. K **16.** E

See Example 2   **Plot each point on a coordinate plane.**

    17. $A(-1, 1)$ **18.** $M(2, -2)$

    19. $W(-5, -5)$ **20.** $G(0, -3)$

See Example 3   **Give the coordinates of each point.**

    21. Q **22.** V

    23. R **24.** P

    25. S **26.** L

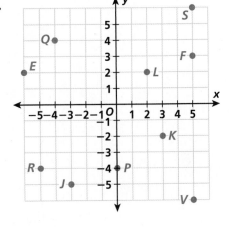

PRACTICE AND PROBLEM SOLVING

Extra Practice
See page EP14.

Graph each set of ordered pairs. Then connect the points, identify the figure created, and name the quadrants in which it is located.

27. $(-8, 1); (4, 3); (-3, 6)$ **28.** $(-8, -2); (-1, -2); (-1, 3); (-8, 3)$

Identify the quadrant of each point described below.

29. The x-coordinate and the y-coordinate are both negative.

30. The x-coordinate is negative and the y-coordinate is positive.

31. The x-coordinate is positive and the y-coordinate is negative.

32. What point is 5 units left and 2 units down from point $(1, 2)$?

33. What point is 9 units right and 3 units up from point (3, 4)?

34. What point is 4 units left and and 7 units up from point (−2, −4)?

35. What point is 10 units right and and 1 unit down from point (−10, 1)?

36. **Critical Thinking** After being moved 6 units right and 4 units down, a point is located at (6, 1). What were the original coordinates of the point?

37. **Weather** The map shows the path of Hurricane Rita. Estimate to the nearest integer the coordinates of the storm for each of the times below.

   a. when Rita first became a hurricane

   b. when Rita made landfall in the United States

   c. when Rita weakened to a tropical depression

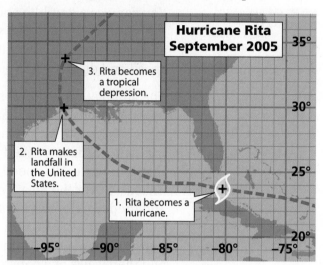

38. **What's the Error?** To plot (−12, 1), a student started at (0, 0) and moved 12 units right and 1 unit down. What did the student do wrong?

39. **Write About It** Why is order important when graphing an ordered pair on a coordinate plane?

40. **Challenge** Armand and Kayla started jogging from the same point. Armand jogged 4 miles south and 6 miles east. Kayla jogged west and 4 miles south. If they were 11 miles apart when they stopped, how far west did Kayla jog?

Test Prep and Spiral Review

41. **Multiple Choice** Which of the following points lie within the circle graphed at right?

    (A) (2, 6)   (B) (−4, 4)   (C) (0, −4)   (D) (−6, 6)

42. **Multiple Choice** Which point on the *x*-axis is the same distance from the origin as (0, −3)?

    (F) (0, 3)   (G) (3, 0)   (H) (3, −3)   (J) (−3, 3)

Find each sum. (Lesson 2-2)

43. −17 + 11

44. 29 + 8

45. 40 + (−64)

46. −55 + (−32)

Divide. Write each answer in simplest form. (Lesson 3-10)

47. $8 \div 1\frac{1}{4}$

48. $\frac{3}{5} \div \frac{6}{15}$

49. $2\frac{1}{3} \div 1\frac{2}{3}$

50. $\frac{5}{8} \div \frac{3}{4}$

Interpreting Graphs

TN GLE 0706.1.5 Use
mathematical ideas and
processes in different settings
to formulate patterns, analyze
graphs, set up and solve
problems and interpret solutions.

You can use a graph to show the relationship between speed and time, time and distance, or speed and distance.

The graph at right shows the varying speeds at which Emma exercises her horse. The horse walks at a constant speed for the first 10 minutes. Its speed increases over the next 7 minutes, and then it gallops at a constant rate for 20 minutes. Then it slows down over the next 3 minutes and then walks at a constant pace for 10 minutes.

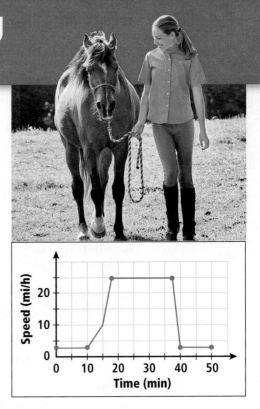

EXAMPLE 1 **Relating Graphs to Situations**

Jenny leaves home and drives to the beach. She stays at the beach all day before driving back home. Which graph best shows the situation?

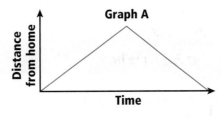

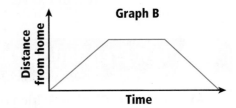

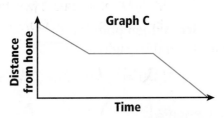

As Jenny drives to the beach, her distance from home *increases*. While she is at the beach, her distance from home is *constant*. As she drives home, her distance from home *decreases*. The answer is graph B.

Video **Lesson Tutorials Online** my.hrw.com

EXAMPLE 2 **PROBLEM SOLVING APPLICATION**

Maili and Katrina traveled 10 miles from Maili's house to the movie theater. They watched a movie, and then they traveled 5 miles farther to a restaurant to eat lunch. After eating they returned to Maili's house. Sketch a graph to show the distance from Maili's house compared to time. Use your graph to find the total distance traveled.

1 Understand the Problem

The answer will be the total distance that Katrina and Maili traveled.

List the **important information**:

• The friends traveled 10 miles from Maili's house to the theater.

• They traveled an additional 5 miles and then ate lunch.

• They returned to Maili's house.

2 Make a Plan

Sketch a graph that represents the situation. Then use the graph to find the total distance Katrina and Maili traveled.

3 Solve

The distance from Maili's house increases from 0 to 10 miles when the friends travel to the theater. The distance does not change while the friends watch the movie and eat lunch. The distance increases from 10 to 15 miles when they go to the restaurant. The distance decreases from 15 to 0 miles when they return home.

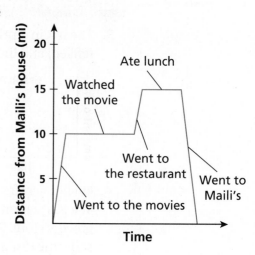

Maili and Katrina traveled a total of 30 miles.

4 Look Back

The theater is 10 miles away, so the friends must have traveled twice that distance just to go to the theater and return. The answer, 30 miles, is reasonable since it is greater than 20 miles.

Think and Discuss

1. Explain the meaning of a horizontal segment on a graph that compares distance to time.

2. Describe a real-world situation that could be represented by a graph that has connected lines or curves.

Learn It Online
Homework Help Online go.hrw.com,
keyword MS10 5-2 Go
Exercises 1–4, 7, 9

GUIDED PRACTICE

See Example 1

1. The temperature of an ice cube increases until it starts to melt. While it melts, its temperature stays constant. Which graph best shows the situation?

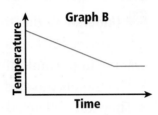 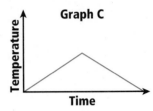

See Example 2

2. Mike and Claudia rode a bus 15 miles from home to a wildlife park. They waited in line to ride a train, which took them on a 3-mile ride around the park. After the train ride, they ate lunch, and then they rode the bus home. Sketch a graph to show the distance from their home compared to time. Use your graph to find the total distance traveled.

INDEPENDENT PRACTICE

See Example 1

3. The ink in a printer is used until the ink cartridge is empty. The cartridge is refilled, and the ink is used up again. Which graph best shows the situation?

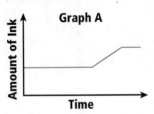 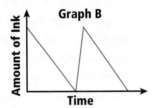 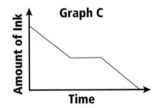

See Example 2

4. On her way from home to the grocery store, a 6-mile trip, Veronica stopped at a gas station to buy gas. After filling her tank, she continued to the grocery store. She then returned home after shopping. Sketch a graph to show the distance from Veronica's home compared to time. Use your graph to find the total distance traveled.

PRACTICE AND PROBLEM SOLVING

Extra Practice
See page EP14.

5. Describe a situation that fits the graph at right.

6. Lynn jogged for 2.5 miles. Then she walked a little while before stopping to stretch. Sketch a graph to show Lynn's speed compared to time.

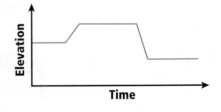

7. On his way to the library, Jeff runs two blocks and then walks three more blocks. Sketch a graph to show the distance Jeff travels compared to time.

8. Critical Thinking The graph at right shows high school enrollment, including future projections.

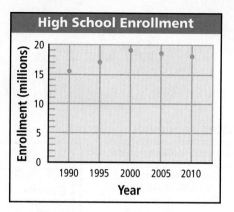

High School Enrollment

a. Describe what is happening in the graph.

b. Does it make sense to connect the points in the graph? Explain.

c. Graphs that are not connected are called *discrete*. Describe another situation where the graph that shows the situation would be discrete.

 9. Choose a Strategy Three bananas were given to two mothers who were with their daughters. Each person had a banana to eat. How is that possible?

10. Write About It A driver sets his car's cruise control to 55 mi/h. Describe a graph that shows the car's speed compared to time. Then describe a second graph that shows the distance traveled compared to time.

11. Challenge The graph at right shows the temperature of an oven after the oven is turned on. Explain what the graph shows.

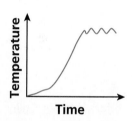

Test Prep and Spiral Review

12. Multiple Choice How does speed compare to time in the graph at right?

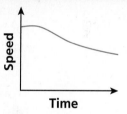

 Ⓐ It increases. Ⓒ It stays the same.

 Ⓑ It decreases. Ⓓ It fluctuates.

13. Short Response Keisha takes a big drink from a bottle of water. She sets the bottle down to tie her shoe and then picks up the bottle to take a small sip of water. Sketch a graph to show the amount of water in the bottle over time.

Find each absolute value. (Lesson 2-1)

14. $|9|$ **15.** $|-3|$ **16.** $|-15|$ **17.** $|0|$ **18.** $|5|$

Find the greatest common factor. (Lesson 2-7)

19. 12, 45 **20.** 33, 110 **21.** 6, 81 **22.** 24, 36

Divide. Estimate to check whether each answer is reasonable. (Lesson 3-4)

23. $48.6 \div 6$ **24.** $31.5 \div (-5)$

25. $-8.32 \div 4$ **26.** $-74.1 \div 6$

Functions, Tables, and Graphs

TN ✓ **0706.3.4** Make
tables of inputs *x* and outputs *f(x)*
for a variety of rules that include
rational numbers (including
negative numbers) as inputs.
Also **GLE 0706.3.2, GLE 0706.3.3,**
✓ **0706.3.5**

*Use Additional Topics A-4
and A-5 with this lesson.*

Vocabulary

function

input

output

When you slip on ice, your foot kicks paddle (A), lowering finger (B), snapping turtle (C) extends neck to bite finger, opening ice tongs (D) and dropping pillow (E), thus allowing you to fall on something soft.

Rube Goldberg, a famous cartoonist, invented machines that perform ordinary tasks in extraordinary ways. Each machine operates according to a rule, or a set of steps, to produce a particular *output*.

In mathematics, a **function** operates according to a rule to produce exactly one output value for each input value. The **input** is the value substituted into the function. The **output** is the value that results from the substitution of a given input into the function.

Interactivities Online ▶

A function can be represented by a rule written in words, such as "double the number and then add nine to the result," or by an equation with two variables. One variable represents the input, and the other represents the output.

Function Rule

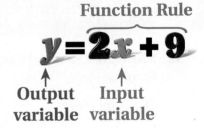

$$y = 2x + 9$$

Output variable   Input variable

You can use a table to organize and display the input and output values of a function.

E X A M P L E ① **Completing a Function Table**

Find the output for each input.

Ⓐ $y = 4x - 2$

Input	Rule	Output	
x	4*x* − 2	*y*	
−1	4(−1) − 2	−6	*Substitute −1 for x. Then simplify.*
0	4(0) − 2	−2	*Substitute 0 for x. Then simplify.*
3	4(3) − 2	10	*Substitute 3 for x. Then simplify.*

Video **Lesson Tutorials Online** my.hrw.com

Find the output for each input.

B $y = 6x^2$

Input	Rule	Output
x	$6x^2$	y
-5	$6(-5)^2$	150
0	$6(0)^2$	0
5	$6(5)^2$	150

Substitute −5 for x. Then simplify.

Substitute 0 for x. Then simplify.

Substitute 5 for x. Then simplify.

You can also use a graph to represent a function. The corresponding input and output values together form unique ordered pairs.

EXAMPLE 2 **Graphing Functions Using Ordered Pairs**

Make a function table, and graph the resulting ordered pairs.

A $y = 2x$

Input	Rule	Output	Ordered Pair
x	$2x$	y	(x, y)
-2	$2(-2)$	-4	$(-2, -4)$
-1	$2(-1)$	-2	$(-1, -2)$
0	$2(0)$	0	$(0, 0)$
1	$2(1)$	2	$(1, 2)$
2	$2(2)$	4	$(2, 4)$

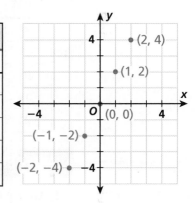

B $y = x^2$

Input	Rule	Output	Ordered Pair
x	x^2	y	(x, y)
-2	$(-2)^2$	4	$(-2, 4)$
-1	$(-1)^2$	1	$(-1, 1)$
0	$(0)^2$	0	$(0, 0)$
1	$(1)^2$	1	$(1, 1)$
2	$(2)^2$	4	$(2, 4)$

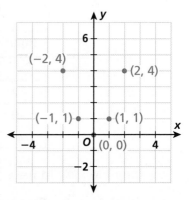

Think and Discuss

1. Describe how a function works like a machine.

2. Give an example of a rule that takes an input value of 4 and produces an output value of 10.

GUIDED PRACTICE

See Example 1   Find the output for each input.

1. $y = 2x + 1$

Input	Rule	Output
x	$2x + 1$	y
-3	▨	▨
0	▨	▨
1	▨	▨

2. $y = -x + 3$

Input	Rule	Output
x	$-x + 3$	y
-2	▨	▨
0	▨	▨
2	▨	▨

3. $y = 2x^2$

Input	Rule	Output
x	$2x^2$	y
-5	▨	▨
1	▨	▨
3	▨	▨

See Example 2   Make a function table, and graph the resulting ordered pairs.

4. $y = 3x - 2$

Input	Rule	Output	Ordered Pair
x	$3x - 2$	y	(x, y)
-1	▨	▨	▨
0	▨	▨	▨
1	▨	▨	▨
2	▨	▨	▨

5. $y = x^2 + 2$

Input	Rule	Output	Ordered Pair
x	$x^2 + 2$	y	(x, y)
-1	▨	▨	▨
0	▨	▨	▨
1	▨	▨	▨
2	▨	▨	▨

INDEPENDENT PRACTICE

See Example 1   Find the output for each input.

6. $y = -2x$

Input	Rule	Output
x	$-2x$	y
-2	▨	▨
-0	▨	▨
4	▨	▨

7. $y = 3x + 2$

Input	Rule	Output
x	$3x + 2$	y
-3	▨	▨
-1	▨	▨
2	▨	▨

8. $y = 3x^2$

Input	Rule	Output
x	$3x^2$	y
-10	▨	▨
-6	▨	▨
-2	▨	▨

See Example 2   Make a function table, and graph the resulting ordered pairs.

9. $y = x \div 2$

Input	Rule	Output	Ordered Pair
x	$x \div 2$	y	(x, y)
-1	▨	▨	▨
0	▨	▨	▨
1	▨	▨	▨
2	▨	▨	▨

10. $y = x^2 - 4$

Input	Rule	Output	Ordered Pair
x	$x^2 - 4$	y	(x, y)
-1	▨	▨	▨
0	▨	▨	▨
1	▨	▨	▨
2	▨	▨	▨

Extra Practice
See page EP14.

11. Weather The Northeast gets an average of 11.66 inches of rain in the summer.

   a. Write an equation that can be used to find y, the difference in rainfall between the average amount of summer rainfall and x, a given year's summer rainfall.

   b. Make a function table using each year's summer rainfall data.

12. Physical Science The equation $F = \frac{9}{5}C + 32$ gives the Fahrenheit temperature F for a given Celsius temperature C. Make a function table for the values $C = -20°, -5°, 0°, 20°,$ and $100°$.

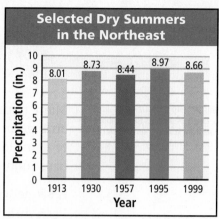

Source: USA Today, August 17, 2001

13. What's the Error? What is the error in the function table at right?

14. Write About It Explain how to make a function table for $y = 2x + 11$.

15. Challenge Mountain Rental charges a \$25 deposit plus \$10 per hour to rent a bicycle. Write an equation that gives the cost y to rent a bike for x hours. Then write the ordered pairs for $x = \frac{1}{2}, 5,$ and $8\frac{1}{2}$.

x	$y = -x - 5$	y
-2	$y = -(-2) - 5$	-7
-1	$y = -(-1) - 5$	-6
0	$y = -(0) - 5$	-5
1	$y = -(1) - 5$	-6
2	$y = -(2) - 5$	-7

Test Prep and Spiral Review

16. Multiple Choice Which table shows correct input and output values for the function $y = -2x + 3$?

Ⓐ
x	y
-1	-1
0	0

Ⓑ
x	y
-3	-2
-2	-1

Ⓒ
x	y
-5	-7
-1	1

Ⓓ
x	y
-3	9
-1	5

17. Multiple Choice Which function matches the function table?

Ⓕ $y = x + 3$ Ⓗ $y = 5x + 1$

Ⓖ $y = x^2 + 7$ Ⓙ $y = x^3 + 3$

x	0	1	2
y	3	4	11

Simplify. (Lesson 2-3)

18. $43 - (-18)$ **19.** $3 - (-2) - (5 + 1)$ **20.** $-4 - 8 - (-3)$

Solve. Write each answer in simplest form. (Lesson 3-11)

21. $\frac{1}{7}x = \frac{6}{7}$ **22.** $4z = \frac{4}{5}$ **23.** $\frac{6}{9}y = 3$ **24.** $\frac{1}{10}x = \frac{7}{8}$

TN SPI 0706.1.2 Generalize a variety of patterns to a symbolic rule from tables, graphs, or words. *Also* ✓ 0706.3.3, ✓ 0706.3.4

Many natural things, such as the arrangement of seeds in the head of a sunflower, follow the pattern of sequences.

A **sequence** is an ordered list of numbers. Each number in a sequence is called a **term**. When the sequence follows a pattern, the terms in the sequence are the output values of a function, and the value of each term depends on its position in the sequence.

Vocabulary

sequence

term

arithmetic sequence

common difference

geometric sequence

You can use a variable, such as n, to represent a number's position in a sequence.

n (position in the sequence)	1	2	3	4
y (value of term)	2	4	6	8

+2 +2 +2

In an **arithmetic sequence**, the terms of the sequence differ by the same nonzero number. This difference is called the **common difference**. In a **geometric sequence**, each term is multiplied by the same amount to get the next term in the sequence.

EXAMPLE 1 **Identifying Patterns in Sequences**

Tell whether each sequence of y-values is arithmetic or geometric. Then find y when $n = 5$.

A

n	1	2	3	4	5
y	−12	−5	2	9	■

In the sequence 7 is added to each term.

$9 + 7 = 16$ *Add 7 to the fourth term.*

The sequence is arithmetic. When $n = 5$, $y = 16$.

B

n	1	2	3	4	5
y	4	−12	36	−108	■

In the sequence each term is multiplied by −3.

$-108 \cdot (-3) = 324$ *Multiply the fourth term by −3.*

The sequence is geometric. When $n = 5$, $y = 324$.

Video **Lesson Tutorials Online** my.hrw.com

EXAMPLE **2** **Identifying Functions in Sequences**

Write a function that describes each sequence.

A 2, 4, 6, 8, . . .

Make a function table.

n	Rule	y
1	1 · 2	2
2	2 · 2	4
3	3 · 2	6
4	4 · 2	8

Multiply n by 2.

The function $y = 2n$ describes this sequence.

B 4, 5, 6, 7, . . .

Make a function table.

n	Rule	y
1	1 + 3	4
2	2 + 3	5
3	3 + 3	6
4	4 + 3	7

Add 3 to n.

The function $y = n + 3$ describes this sequence.

EXAMPLE **3** **Using Functions to Extend Sequences**

Sara has one week to read a book. She plans to increase the number of chapters that she reads each day. Her plan is to read 3 chapters on Sunday, 5 on Monday, 7 on Tuesday, and 9 on Wednesday. Write a function that describes the sequence. Then use the function to predict how many chapters Sara will read on Saturday.

Write the number of chapters she reads each day: 3, 5, 7, 9, . . .
Make a function table.

n	Rule	y
1	1 · 2 + 1	3
2	2 · 2 + 1	5
3	3 · 2 + 1	7
4	4 · 2 + 1	9

Multiply n by 2. Then add 1.

$y = 2n + 1$ *Write the function.*

Saturday corresponds to $n = 7$. When $n = 7$, $y = 2 \cdot 7 + 1 = 15$. Sara plans to read 15 chapters on Saturday.

Think and Discuss

1. **Give an example** of a sequence involving addition, and give the rule you used.

2. **Describe** how to find a pattern in the sequence 1, 4, 16, 64, ...

Learn It Online
Homework Help Online **go.hrw.com,**
keyword MS10 5-4 **Go**
Exercises 1–16, 21, 25

GUIDED PRACTICE

See Example **1** Tell whether each sequence of *y*-values is arithmetic or geometric. Then find *y* when *n* = 5.

1.

n	1	2	3	4	5
y	−4	9	22	35	▓

2.

n	1	2	3	4	5
y	8	4	2	1	▓

See Example **2** Write a function that describes each sequence.

3. 3, 6, 9, 12, . . .   **4.** 3, 4, 5, 6, . . .   **5.** 0, 1, 2, 3, . . .   **6.** 5, 10, 15, 20, . . .

See Example **3** **7.** In March, WaterWorks recorded $195 in swimsuit sales. The store recorded $390 in sales in April, $585 in May, and $780 in June. Write a function that describes the sequence. Then use the function to predict the store's swimsuit sales in July.

INDEPENDENT PRACTICE

See Example **1** Tell whether each sequence of *y*-values is arithmetic or geometric. Then find *y* when *n* = 5.

8.

n	1	2	3	4	5
y	13	26	52	104	▓

9.

n	1	2	3	4	5
y	14	30	46	62	▓

See Example **2** Write a function that describes each sequence.

10. 5, 6, 7, 8, . . .   **11.** 7, 14, 21, 28, . . .   **12.** −2, −1, 0, 1, . . .

13. 20, 40, 60, 80, . . .   **14.** $\frac{1}{2}$, 1, $\frac{3}{2}$, 2, . . .   **15.** 1.5, 2.5, 3.5, 4.5, . . .

See Example **3** **16.** The number of seats in the first row of a concert hall is 6. The second row has 9 seats, the third row has 12 seats, and the fourth row has 15 seats. Write a function to describe the sequence. Then use the function to predict the number of seats in the eighth row.

PRACTICE AND PROBLEM SOLVING

Extra Practice
See page EP14.

Write a rule for each sequence in words. Then find the next three terms.

17. 35, 70, 105, 140, . . .   **18.** 0.7, 1.7, 2.7, 3.7, . . .   **19.** $\frac{3}{2}$, $\frac{5}{2}$, $\frac{7}{2}$, $\frac{9}{2}$, . . .

20. −1, 0, 1, 2, . . .   **21.** $\frac{1}{3}$, $\frac{2}{3}$, 1, $\frac{4}{3}$, . . .   **22.** 6, 11, 16, 21, . . .

Write a function that describes each sequence. Use the function to find the tenth term in the sequence.

23. 0.5, 1.5, 2.5, 3.5, . . .   **24.** 0, 2, 4, 6, . . .   **25.** 5, 8, 11, 14, . . .

26. 3, 8, 13, 18, . . .   **27.** 1, 3, 5, 7, . . .   **28.** 6, 10, 14, 18, . . .

Computer Science

Computer programmers use functions to create designs known as *fractals*. A fractal is a *self-similar* pattern, which means that each part of the pattern is similar to the whole pattern. Fractals are created by repeating a set of steps, called *iterations*.

29. Below is part of a famous fractal called the Cantor set. In each iteration, part of a line segment is removed, resulting in twice as many segments as before. The table lists the number of line segments that result from the iterations shown. Find a function that describes the sequence.

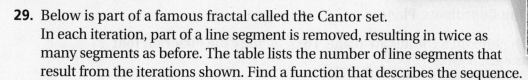

Iteration (*n*)	Number of Segments (*y*)
1	2
2	4
3	8

30. **Multi-Step** These are the first three iterations of the Sierpinski triangle. In each iteration, a certain number of smaller triangles are cut out of the larger triangle.

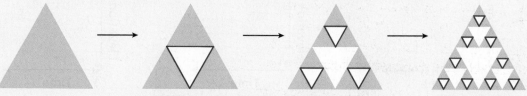

Iteration 1
1 triangle removed

Iteration 2
3 more triangles removed

Iteration 3
9 more triangles removed

Create a table to list the number of yellow triangles that exist after each iteration. Then find a function that describes the sequence.

31. ⭐ **Challenge** Find a function that describes the number of triangles removed in each iteration of the Sierpinski triangle.

Test Prep and Spiral Review

32. **Multiple Choice** Which function describes the sequence 1, 4, 7, 10, . . . ?

    Ⓐ $y = 3n$ Ⓑ $y = n + 3$ Ⓒ $y = 3n - 2$ Ⓓ $y = 2n$

33. **Extended Response** Create a sequence, and then write a function that describes it. Use the function to find the ninth term in the sequence.

Find each value. (Lesson 1-2)

34. 15^2 35. 10^7 36. 7^4 37. 9^3

Find each product. (Lesson 2-4)

38. $-16 \cdot 2$ 39. $-40 \cdot (-5)$ 40. $4 \cdot (-11)$ 41. $-5 \cdot (-21)$

 **Ready To Go On?**

Quiz for Lessons 5-1 Through 5-4

✓ **5-1** **The Coordinate Plane**

Plot each point on a coordinate plane. Then identify the quadrant that contains each point.

1. $W(1, 5)$　　　**2.** $X(5, -3)$　　　**3.** $Y(-1, -5)$　　　**4.** $Z(-8, 2)$

✓ **5-2** **Interpreting Graphs**

5. Raj climbs to the top of a cliff. He descends a little bit to another cliff, and then he begins to climb again. Which graph best shows the situation?

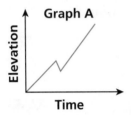
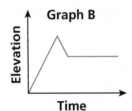
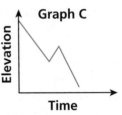

6. Ty walks 1 mile to the mall. An hour later, he walks $\frac{1}{2}$ mile farther to a park and eats lunch. Then he walks home. Sketch a graph to show the distance Ty traveled compared to time. Use your graph to find the total distance traveled.

✓ **5-3** **Functions, Tables, and Graphs**

Make a function table, and graph the resulting ordered pairs.

7. $y = -6x$　　　**8.** $y = 4x - 3$　　　**9.** $y = 4x^2$　　　**10.** $-2x + 4$

✓ **5-4** **Sequences**

Tell whether the sequence of y-values is arithmetic or geometric. Then find y when $n = 5$.

11.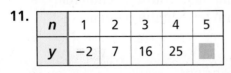

n	1	2	3	4	5
y	-2	7	16	25	

12.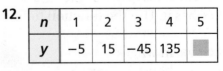

n	1	2	3	4	5
y	-5	15	-45	135	

Write a function that describes each sequence. Use the function to find the eleventh term in the sequence.

13. $1, 2, 3, 4, \ldots$　　　**14.** $4, 8, 12, 16, \ldots$　　　**15.** $11, 21, 31, 41, \ldots$　　　**16.** $1, 4, 9, 16, \ldots$

Focus on Problem Solving

 Understand the Problem

• **Sequence and prioritize information**

When you are reading a math problem, putting events in order, or in *sequence*, can help you understand the problem better. It helps to *prioritize* the information when you put it in order. To prioritize, you decide which of the information in your list is most important. The most important information has highest priority.

 Use the information in the list or table to answer each question.

1 The list at right shows all of the things that Roderick has to do on Saturday. He starts the day without any money.

  a. Which two activities on Roderick's list must be done before any of the other activities? Do these two activities have higher or lower priority?

  b. Is there more than one way that he can order his activities? Explain.

  c. List the order in which Roderick's activities could occur on Saturday.

> **Saturday Activities**
> - Attend birthday party at 4 P.M.
> - Buy gift - either a CD for $18 or a computer game for $25.
> - Get haircut at 2 P.M.; pay $16.
> - Mow Mrs. Mayberry's lawn before 10 A.M.; earn $15.
> - Mow Mr. Boyar's lawn and trim hedge anytime after 10 A.M.; earn $25.

2 Tara and her family will visit Ocean World Park from 9:30 to 4:00. They want to see the waterskiing show at 10:00. Each show in the park is 50 minutes long. The time they choose to eat lunch will depend on the schedule they choose for seeing the shows.

  a. Which of the information given in the paragraph above has the highest priority? Which has the lowest priority?

  b. List the order in which they can see all of the shows, including the time they will see each.

  c. At what time should they plan to have lunch?

Show Times at Ocean World Park	
9:00, 12:00	Underwater acrobats
9:00, 3:00	Whale acts
10:00, 2:00	Dolphin acts
10:00, 1:00	Waterskiing
11:00, 4:00	Aquarium tour

Explore Linear Functions

5-5

Use with Lesson 5-5

Learn It Online
Lab Resources Online **go.hrw.com,**
keyword MS10 Lab5 **Go**

TN **SPI 0706.1.2** Generalize a variety of patterns to a symbolic rule from tables, graphs, or words.
Also ✓ **0706.3.3,** ✓ **0706.3.4**

When the graph of a function is a line or a set of points that lie on a line, the function is *linear*. You can use patterns to explore linear functions.

Activity

1 The perimeter of a 1-inch-long square tile is 4 inches. Place 2 tiles together side by side. The perimeter of this figure is 6 inches.

1 in.

1 in. ☐ 1 in.

1 in.

2 in.

1 in. ☐☐ 1 in.

2 in.

   a. Complete the table at right by adding tiles side by side and finding the perimeter of each new figure.

   b. If *x* equals the number of tiles, what is the difference between consecutive *x*-values? If *y* equals the perimeter, what is the difference between consecutive *y*-values? How do these differences compare?

   c. Graph the ordered pairs from your table on a coordinate plane. Is the graph linear? What does the table indicate about this function?

Number of Tiles	Perimeter (in.)
1	4
2	6
3	☐
4	☐
5	☐

2 Draw the pattern at right and complete the next two sets of dots in the pattern.

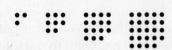

   a. Complete the table at right. Let *x* equal the number of dots in the top row of each set. Let *y* equal the total number of dots in the set.

   b. What is the difference between consecutive *x*-values? What is the difference between consecutive *y*-values? How do these differences compare?

   c. Graph the ordered pairs on a coordinate plane. Is the graph linear? What does the table indicate about this function?

x	y
2	3
3	☐
4	☐
5	☐
6	☐

3 Use square tiles to model rectangles with the following dimensions: 2×1, 2×2, 2×3, 2×4, and 2×5. The first three rectangles are shown.

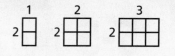

a. Find the perimeter and area of each rectangle. Complete the table at right. Let x equal perimeter and y equal area. (To find the area of a rectangle, multiply its length by its width. The areas of the first two rectangles are shown in the table.)

b. What is the difference between consecutive x-values? What is the difference between consecutive y-values? How do these differences compare?

c. Using what you have observed in **❶** and **❷**, tell whether the relationship between x and y in the table is linear.

Rectangle	Perimeter x	Area y
2 × 1	◼	2
2 × 2	◼	4
2 × 3	◼	◼
2 × 4	◼	◼
2 × 5	◼	◼

d. Graph the ordered pairs from your table on a coordinate plane. Does the shape of your graph agree with your answer to **c**?

Think and Discuss

1. How can you tell by looking at a function table whether the graph of the function is a line?

2. Is $y = x^2$ a linear function? Explain your answer.

Try This

1. Use square tiles to model each of the patterns shown below.

2. Model the next two sets in each pattern using square tiles.

3. Complete each table.

4. Graph the ordered pairs in each table, and then tell whether the function is linear.

Pattern 1

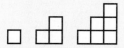

Pattern 2

Pattern 3

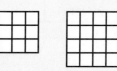

Number of Tiles x	Perimeter y
◼	4
◼	8
◼	12
◼	◼
◼	◼

Perimeter x	Area y
8	◼
12	◼
16	◼
◼	◼
◼	◼

Perimeter x	Area y
4	◼
6	◼
8	◼
◼	◼
◼	◼

TN SPI 0706.3.7 Translate between verbal and symbolic representations of real-world phenomena involving linear equations. *Also* SPI 0706.1.2, GLE 0706.3.2, GLE 0706.3.7, GLE 0706.3.8, ✓ 0706.3.4, ✓ 0706.3.5, ✓ 0706.3.6, ✓ 0706.3.11, SPI 0706.3.5, SPI 0706.3.6

Vocabulary

linear equation

linear function

The graph below shows how far a kayak travels down a river if the kayak is moving at a rate of 2 miles per hour. The graph is linear because all of the points fall on a line. It is part of the graph of a *linear equation*.

A **linear equation** is an equation whose graph is a line. The solutions of a linear equation are the points that make up its graph. Linear equations and linear graphs can be different representations of *linear functions*. A **linear function** is a function whose graph is a nonvertical line.

Only two points are needed to draw the graph of a linear function. However, graphing a third point serves as a check. You can use a function table to find each ordered pair.

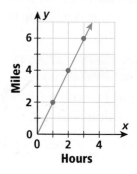

EXAMPLE 1 **Graphing Linear Functions**

Graph the linear function $y = 2x + 1$.

Input	Rule	Output	Ordered Pair
x	$2x + 1$	y	(x, y)
-1	$2(-1) + 1$	-1	$(-1, -1)$
0	$2(0) + 1$	1	$(0, 1)$
1	$2(1) + 1$	3	$(1, 3)$

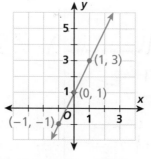

Place each ordered pair on the coordinate grid. Then connect the points to form a line.

Video **LESSON TUTORIALS ONLINE** my.hrw.com

EXAMPLE 2 *Physical Science Application*

For every degree that temperature increases on the Celsius scale, the temperature increases by 1.8 degrees on the Fahrenheit scale. When the temperature is 0 °C, it is 32 °F. Write a linear function that describes the relationship between the Celsius and Fahrenheit scales. Then make a graph to show the relationship.

Let x represent the input, which is the temperature in degrees Celsius. Let y represent the output, which is the temperature in degrees Fahrenheit.

The function is $y = 1.8x + 32$.

Make a function table. Include a column for the rule.

Remember!

The solutions to a function lie on the line.

Input	Rule	Output
x	$1.8x + 32$	y
0	$1.8(0) + 32$	32
15	$1.8(15) + 32$	59
30	$1.8(30) + 32$	86

Multiply the input by 1.8 and then add 32.

Graph the ordered pairs (0, 32), (15, 59), and (30, 86) from your table. Connect the points to form a line.

Check

Substitute the ordered pairs into the function $y = 1.8x + 32$.

$32 \stackrel{?}{=} 1.8(0) + 32$ $59 \stackrel{?}{=} 1.8(15) + 32$

$32 \stackrel{?}{=} 32$ ✔ $59 \stackrel{?}{=} 59$ ✔

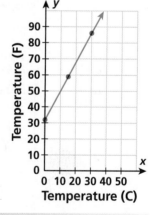

Since each output y depends on the input x, y is called the *dependent variable* and x is called the *independent variable*.

Think and Discuss

1. Describe how a linear equation is related to a linear graph.

2. Explain how to use a graph to find the output value of a linear function for a given input value.

Learn It Online
Homework Help Online **go.hrw.com**,
keyword MS10 5-5 Go
Exercises 1–8, 9, 11

GUIDED PRACTICE

See Example 1   **Graph each linear function.**

1. $y = x + 3$

Input	Rule	Output	Ordered Pair
x	x + 3	y	(x, y)
−2	■	■	■
0	■	■	■
2	■	■	■

2. $y = 2x - 2$

Input	Rule	Output	Ordered Pair
x	2x − 2	y	(x, y)
−1	■	■	■
0	■	■	■
1	■	■	■

See Example 2   **3.** A water tanker is used to fill a community pool. The tanker pumps 750 gallons of water per hour. Write a linear function that describes the amount of water in the pool over time. Then make a graph to show the amount of water in the pool over the first 6 hours.

INDEPENDENT PRACTICE

See Example 1   **Graph each linear function.**

4. $y = -x - 2$

Input	Rule	Output	Ordered Pair
x	−x − 2	y	(x, y)
0	■	■	■
1	■	■	■
2	■	■	■

5. $y = x - 1$

Input	Rule	Output	Ordered Pair
x	x − 1	y	(x, y)
3	■	■	■
4	■	■	■
5	■	■	■

6. $y = 3x - 1$

Input	Rule	Output	Ordered Pair
x	3x − 1	y	(x, y)
−4	■	■	■
0	■	■	■
4	■	■	■

7. $y = 2x + 3$

Input	Rule	Output	Ordered Pair
x	2x + 3	y	(x, y)
−2	■	■	■
−1	■	■	■
0	■	■	■

See Example 2   **8. Physical Science** The temperature of a liquid is increasing at the rate of 3 °C per hour. When Joe begins measuring the temperature, it is 40 °C. Write a linear function that describes the temperature of the liquid over time. Then make a graph to show the temperature over the first 12 hours.

PRACTICE AND PROBLEM SOLVING

Extra Practice
See page EP15.

Environment

The Mauna Loa Observatory is located on Mauna Loa volcano, the largest volcano on Earth. Its most recent eruption occurred in 1984.

9. **Earth Science** The water level in a well is 100 m. Water is seeping into the well and raising the water level by 10 cm per year. Water is also draining out of the well at a rate of 2 m per year. What will the water level be in 10 years?

10. **Multi-Step** Graph the function $y = -2x + 1$. If the ordered pair $(x, -5)$ lies on the graph of the function, what is the value of x? Use your graph to find the answer.

11. **Environment** The Mauna Loa Observatory in Hawaii has been monitoring carbon dioxide levels in the atmosphere since 1957.

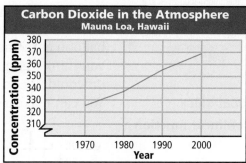

Carbon Dioxide in the Atmosphere
Mauna Loa, Hawaii

a. The graph is approximately linear. About how many parts per million (ppm) were added each 10-year period?

b. Given the parts per million in 2000 shown on the graph, about how many parts per million do you predict there will be in 2020?

12. **What's the Question?** Tron used the equation $y = 100 + 25x$ to track his savings y after x months. If the answer is $250, what is the question?

13. **Write About It** Explain how to graph $y = 2x - 5$.

14. **Challenge** Certain bacteria divide every 30 minutes. You can use the function $y = 2^x$ to find the number of bacteria after each half-hour period, where x is the number of half-hour periods. Make a table of values for $x = 1, 2, 3, 4,$ and 5. Graph the points. How does the graph differ from those you have seen so far in this lesson?

Test Prep and Spiral Review

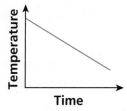

15. **Multiple Choice** The graph of which linear function passes through the origin?

Ⓐ $y = x + 2$ Ⓑ $y = 3x$ Ⓒ $y = x - 1$ Ⓓ $y = 2x + 4$

16. **Short Response** Simon graphed the linear function $y = -x + 3$ at right. Explain his error, and graph $y = -x + 3$ correctly on a coordinate grid.

17. Tell a story that fits the graph. (Lesson 5-2)

Write a function that describes each sequence. (Lesson 5-4)

18. 15, 10, 5, 0, . . .

19. −4, −2, 0, 2, . . .

20. 0.2, 1.2, 2.2, 3.2, . . .

5-5 Graphing Linear Functions **299**

Nonlinear Functions

TN **SPI 0706.1.3** Recognize whether information given in a table, graph, or formula suggests a directly proportional, linear, inversely proportional, or other nonlinear relationship.
Also ✓ **0706.3.3**

Vocabulary

nonlinear function

As you inflate a balloon, its volume increases. The table at right shows the increase in volume of a round balloon as its radius changes. Do you think a graph of the data would or would not be a straight line? You can make a graph to find out.

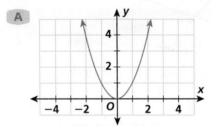

Radius (in.)	Volume (in³)
1	4.19
2	33.52
3	113.13
4	268.16
5	523.75

A **nonlinear function** is a function whose graph is not a straight line.

EXAMPLE 1 **Identifying Graphs of Nonlinear Functions**

Tell whether the graph is linear or nonlinear.

A

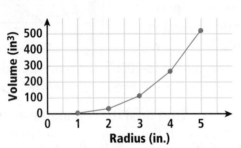

The graph is not a straight line, so it is nonlinear.

B

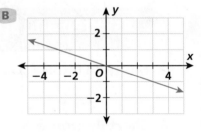

The graph is a straight line, so it is linear.

Helpful Hint

Exponential and quadratic functions are nonlinear. For information on these relationships, see pp. SB18–SB19 in the Skills Bank.

You can use a function table to determine whether ordered pairs describe a linear or a nonlinear relationship.

For a function that has a linear relationship, when the difference between each successive input value is constant, the difference between each corresponding output value is *constant*.

For a function that has a nonlinear relationship, when the difference between each successive input value is constant, the difference between each corresponding output value *varies*.

EXAMPLE 2

Identifying Nonlinear Relationships in Function Tables

Tell whether the function represented in each table has a linear or nonlinear relationship.

A

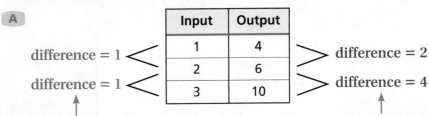

difference = 1

difference = 1

Input	Output
1	4
2	6
3	10

difference = 2

difference = 4

The difference is constant.   *The difference varies.*

The function represented in the table has a nonlinear relationship.

B

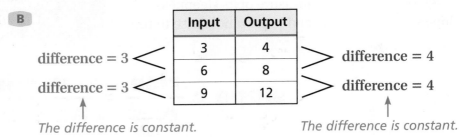

difference = 3

difference = 3

Input	Output
3	4
6	8
9	12

difference = 4

difference = 4

The difference is constant.   *The difference is constant.*

The function represented in the table has a linear relationship.

EXTENSION

Exercises

Tell whether the graph is linear or nonlinear.

1.
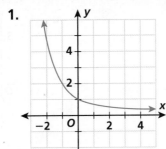

2.
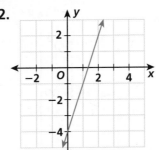

3.
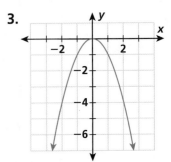

Tell whether the function represented in each table has a linear or nonlinear relationship.

4.

Input	Output
2	5
4	7
6	9

5.

Input	Output
1	6
2	9
3	14

6.

Input	Output
4	25
8	36
12	49

Slope and Rates of Change

TN SPI 0706.3.4 Interpret the slope of a line as a unit rate given the graph of a proportional relationship.
Also ✓ 0706.1.6, GLE 0706.3.6, GLE 0706.3.7, GLE 0706.3.8, ✓ 0706.3.8, ✓ 0706.3.9, SPI 0706.3.6, SPI 0706.3.7

Vocabulary

slope

rate of change

Baldwin Street, located in Dunedin, New Zealand, is considered one of the world's steepest streets. The *slope* of the street is about $\frac{1}{3}$.

The **slope** of a line is a measure of its steepness and is the ratio of rise to run:

$$\text{slope} = \frac{\text{rise}}{\text{run}} = \frac{\text{vertical change}}{\text{horizontal change}}$$

If a line rises from left to right, its slope is positive. If a line falls from left to right, its slope is negative.

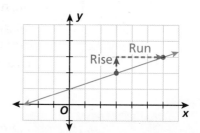

EXAMPLE **1** **Identifying the Slope of the Line**

Tell whether the slope is positive or negative. Then find the slope.

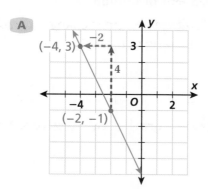

A

The line falls from left to right.

The slope is negative.

$\text{slope} = \frac{\text{rise}}{\text{run}}$

$= \frac{4}{-2}$ *The rise is 4.*

$= -2$ *The run is –2.*

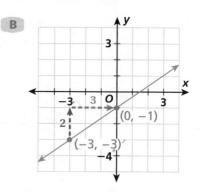

B

The line rises from left to right.

The slope is positive.

$\text{slope} = \frac{\text{rise}}{\text{run}}$

$= \frac{2}{3}$ *The rise is 2.*

    The run is 3.

Video **Lesson Tutorials Online** my.hrw.com

You can graph a line if you know its slope and one of its points.

EXAMPLE 2 **Using Slope and a Point to Graph a Line**

Use the given slope and point to graph each line.

Helpful Hint

Slope of a line can be represented as a unit rate. For example, $-\frac{3}{4}$ can be thought of as a rise of $-\frac{3}{4}$ to a run of 1.

A $-\frac{3}{4}$; $(-3, 2)$

$\text{slope} = \frac{\text{rise}}{\text{run}} = \frac{-3}{4}$ or $\frac{3}{-4}$

From point $(-3, 2)$, move 3 units down and 4 units right, or move 3 units up and 4 units left. Mark the points, and draw a line through the two points.

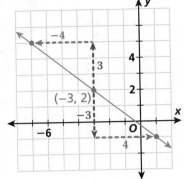

B 3; $(-1, -2)$

$3 = \frac{3}{1}$ *Write the slope as a fraction.*

$\text{slope} = \frac{\text{rise}}{\text{run}} = \frac{3}{1}$

From point $(-1, -2)$, move 3 units up and 1 unit right. Mark the points, and draw a line through the two points.

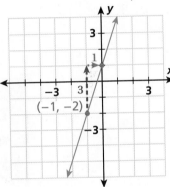

The ratio of two quantities that change, such as slope, is a **rate of change**.

A *constant rate of change* describes changes of the same amount during equal intervals. Linear functions have a constant rate of change. The graph of a constant rate of change is a line.

A *variable rate of change* describes changes of a different amount during equal intervals. The graph of a variable rate of change is not a line.

EXAMPLE 3 **Identifying Rates of Change in Graphs**

Tell whether each graph shows a constant or variable rate of change.

A

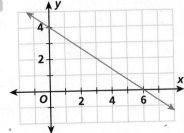

The graph is a line, so the rate of change is constant.

B

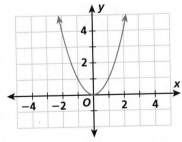

The graph is not a line, so the rate of change is variable.

EXAMPLE **4**   **Using Rate of Change to Solve Problems**

The graph shows the distance a bicyclist travels over time. Does the bicyclist travel at a constant or variable speed? How fast does the bicyclist travel?

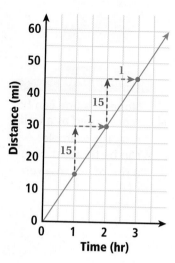

The graph is a line, so the bicyclist is traveling at a constant speed.

The amount of distance is the rise, and the amount of time is the run. You can find the speed by finding the slope.

$$\text{slope (speed)} = \frac{\text{rise (distance)}}{\text{run (time)}} = \frac{15}{1}$$

The bicyclist travels at 15 miles per hour.

Think and Discuss

1. Describe a line with a negative slope.

2. Compare constant and variable rates of change.

3. Give an example of a real-world situation involving a rate of change.

5-6 Exercises

Learn It Online
Homework Help Online **go.hrw.com,**
keyword MS10 5-6 **Go**
Exercises 1–20, 21, 25, 29

GUIDED PRACTICE

See Example **1**   Tell whether the slope is positive or negative. Then find the slope.

1.
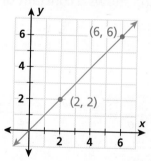

2.
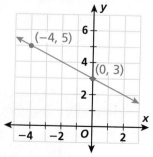

See Example **2**   Use the given slope and point to graph each line.

3. 3; $(4, -2)$ **4.** -2; $(-3, -2)$ **5.** $-\frac{1}{4}$; $(0, 5)$ **6.** $\frac{3}{2}$; $(-1, 1)$

See Example 3 **Tell whether each graph shows a constant or variable rate of change.**

7.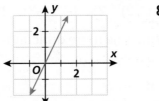

8.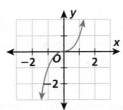

9.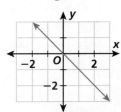

See Example 4 **10.** The graph shows the distance a trout swims over time. Does the trout swim at a constant or variable speed? How fast does the trout swim?

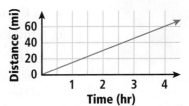

INDEPENDENT PRACTICE

See Example 1 **Tell whether the slope is positive or negative. Then find the slope.**

11.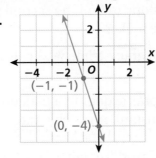

12.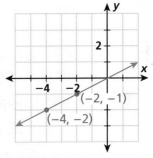

See Example 2 **Use the given slope and point to graph each line.**

13. -1; $(-1, 4)$ **14.** 4; $(-1, -3)$ **15.** $\frac{3}{5}$; $(3, -1)$ **16.** $\frac{2}{3}$; $(0, 5)$

See Example 3 **Tell whether each graph shows a constant or variable rate of change.**

17.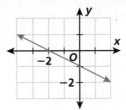

18.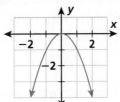

19.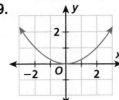

See Example 4 **20.** The graph shows the amount of rain that falls over time. Does the rain fall at a constant or variable rate? How much rain falls per hour?

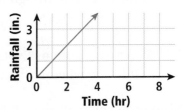

PRACTICE AND PROBLEM SOLVING

Extra Practice
See page EP15.

21. Multi-Step A line has a slope of 5 and passes through the points $(4, 3)$ and $(2, y)$. What is the value of y?

22. A line passes through the origin and has a slope of $-\frac{3}{2}$. Through which quadrants does the line pass?

Agriculture

This water tower can be seen in Poteet, Texas, where the Poteet Strawberry Festival® is held every April. Known as the "Strawberry Capital of Texas," Poteet produces 40% of Texas' strawberries.

Graph the line containing the two points, and then find the slope.

23. $(-2, 13), (1, 4)$ **24.** $(-2, -6), (2, 2)$ **25.** $(-2, -3), (2, 3)$ **26.** $(2, -3), (3, -5)$

27. Explain whether you think it would be more difficult to run up a hill with a slope of $\frac{1}{3}$ or a hill with a slope of $\frac{3}{4}$.

28. Agriculture The graph at right shows the cost per pound of buying strawberries.

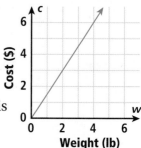

  a. Is the cost per pound a constant or variable rate?

  b. Find the slope of the line.

  c. Remember, a unit rate is a rate whose denominator is one. Using the slope from part **b**, find the unit rate of the line. What does it tell you?

29. Critical Thinking A line has a negative slope. Explain how the y-values of the line change as the x-values increase.

30. What's the Error? Kyle graphed a line, given a slope of $-\frac{4}{3}$ and the point $(2, 3)$. When he used the slope to find the second point, he found $(5, 7)$. What error did Kyle make?

31. Write About It Explain how to graph a line when given the slope and one of the points on the line.

32. Challenge The population of prairie dogs in a park doubles every year. Does this population show a constant or variable rate of change? Explain.

Test Prep and Spiral Review

33. Multiple Choice To graph a line, Caelyn plotted the point $(2, 1)$ and then used the slope $-\frac{1}{2}$ to find another point on the line. Which point could be the other point on the line that Caelyn found?

  Ⓐ $(1, 3)$ Ⓑ $(4, 0)$ Ⓒ $(1, -1)$ Ⓓ $(0, 0)$

34. Multiple Choice A line has a positive slope and passes through the point $(-1, 2)$. Through which quadrant can the line NOT pass?

  Ⓕ Quadrant I   Ⓖ Quadrant II   Ⓗ Quadrant III   Ⓙ Quadrant IV

35. Short Response Explain how you can use three points on a graph to determine whether the rate of change is constant or variable.

Find each value. (Lesson 1-2)

36. 3^5 **37.** 5^3 **38.** 4^1 **39.** 10^5

Write a rule for each sequence in words. Then find the next three terms.
(Lesson 5-3)

40. $3.7, 3.2, 2.7, 2.2, \ldots$ **41.** $-\frac{3}{2}, 0, \frac{3}{2}, 3, \ldots$ **42.** $3, -1, \frac{1}{3}, -\frac{1}{9}, \ldots$

Generate Formulas to Convert Units

5-6

Use with Lesson 5-6

TN **GLE 0706.1.3** Develop independent reasoning to communicate mathematical ideas and derive algorithms and/or formulas.

Learn It Online
Lab Resources Online **go.hrw.com**,
keyword MS10 Lab5 Go

Activity

Publishers, editors, and graphic designers measure lengths in *picas*. Measure each of the following line segments to the nearest inch, and record your results in the table.

Segment	Length (in.)	Length (picas)	Ratio of Picas to Inches
1	■	6	■
2	■	12	■
3	■	24	■
4	■	30	■
5	■	36	■

① ——————

② ——————————

③ ————————————————

④ ——————————————————————

⑤ ————————————————————————————

Think and Discuss

1. **Make a Conjecture** Make a conjecture about the relationship between picas and inches.

2. Use your conjecture to write a formula relating inches n to picas p.

3. How many picas wide is a sheet of paper that is $8\frac{1}{2}$ in. wide?

Try This

Using inches for *x*-coordinates and picas for *y*-coordinates, write ordered pairs for the data in the table. Then plot the points and draw a graph.

1. What shape is the graph?

2. Use the graph to find the number of picas that is equal to 3 inches.

3. Use the graph to find the number of inches that is equal to 27 picas.

4. A designer is laying out a page in a magazine. The dimensions of a photo are 18 picas by 15 picas. She doubles the dimensions of the photo. What are the new dimensions of the photo in inches?

TN ✓ **0706.3.12** Use linear equations to solve problems and interpret the meaning of slope, *m*, and the *y*-intercept, *b*, in *f(x)* = *mx* + *b* in terms of the context. *Also* ✓ **0706.1.6, SPI 0706.1.2, GLE 0706.3.6, GLE 0706.3.7, GLE 0706.3.8,** ✓ **0706.3.11,** ✓ **0706.3.13, SPI 0706.3.6, SPI 0706.3.7**

Vocabulary

x-intercept

y-intercept

slope-intercept form

Tom wants to see how far he can drive on one tank of gas in his new hybrid car. He starts with a full tank of 12 gallons of gas and averages 45 miles per gallon. The graph shows the relationship between number of gallons of gas and distance traveled.

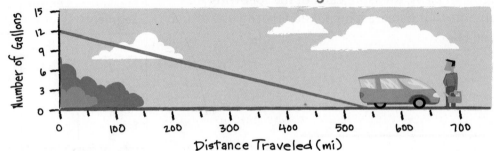

The points where the line intersects the axes can help you understand more about the line.

The **x-intercept** of a line is the *x*-coordinate of the point where the line intersects the *x*-axis. The *y*-coordinate of this point is always 0.

The **y-intercept** of a line is the *y*-coordinate of the point where the line intersects the *y*-axis. The *x*-coordinate of this point is always 0.

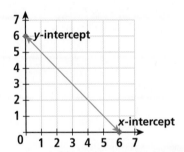

EXAMPLE 1 Finding *x*- and *y*-Intercepts

Find the *x*- and *y*-intercepts.

A

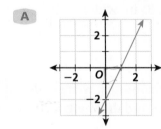

The line intersects the x-axis at (1, 0).
The *x*-intercept is 1.
The line intersects the y-axis at (0, –2).
The *y*-intercept is –2.

B

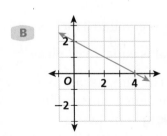

The line intersects the x-axis at (4, 0).
The *x*-intercept is 4.
The line intersects the y-axis at (0, 2).
The *y*-intercept is 2.

Video **Lesson Tutorials Online** my.hrw.com

If you know the slope of a line and the *y*-intercept, you can write an equation that describes the line. Recall from Lesson 5-6 that the slope of a line is the ratio of rise to run.

The linear equation $y = mx + b$ is written in **slope-intercept form**, where *m* is the *slope* and *b* is the *y*-intercept of the line.

Slope   y-intercept

$$y = mx + b$$

EXAMPLE 2 **Graphing by Using Slope and *y*-Intercept**

Graph each equation.

A $y = \frac{2}{3}x + 1$

Step 1: Find *m* and *b*.

$\quad y = \frac{2}{3}x + 1 \qquad m = \frac{2}{3} \quad b = 1$

Step 2: Plot (0, 1).

Step 3: Use the slope $\frac{2}{3}$ to plot at least 1 more point on the line.

Step 4: Draw a line through the points.

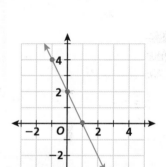

> **Remember!**
>
> Since the *y*-intercept is 1, the point (0, 1) is a point on the line.

B $2x + y = 2$

Step 1: Find *m* and *b*. $\quad$ *2x + y = 2 is not in*

$\quad\quad 2x + y = \;\; 2 \qquad$ *the form y = mx + b,*

$\quad\quad \underline{-2x \quad\quad\quad -2x} \qquad$ *so solve for y.*

$\quad\quad\quad\quad y = 2 - 2x$

$\quad\quad\quad\quad y = -2x + 2$

$\quad\quad\quad\quad m = -2 \quad b = 2$

Step 2: Plot (0, 2).

Step 3: Use the slope -2 to plot at least 1 more point on the line.

Step 4: Draw a line through the points.

EXAMPLE 3 **Writing an Equation in Slope-Intercept Form**

Write the equation of the line in slope-intercept form.

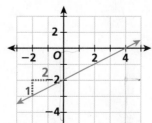

$m = \frac{\text{rise}}{\text{run}} = \frac{1}{2}$ *The line rises from left to right, so the slope is positive.*

$b = -2$ *The line intersects the y-axis at (0, –2), so the y-intercept is –2.*

$y = \frac{1}{2}x - 2$ *Substitute for m and b.*

EXAMPLE 4 **Using Slope-Intercept Form**

Remember!

A constant rate of change describes a linear function.

Rea's house is 350 meters from her friend's house. Rea walks to her friend's house at a constant rate of 50 meters per minute. The linear equation $y = -50x + 350$ represents the distance y that Rea has left to walk after x minutes. Graph the equation, and then identify the x- and y-intercepts and describe their meanings.

Use the slope and y-intercept to graph the equation.

Plot (0, 350). Use the slope −50 to plot the line down to the x-axis.

The y-intercept is 350. This represents the total distance in meters that Rea has to walk.

The x-intercept is 7. This represents the time in minutes it takes Rea to walk the 350 meters.

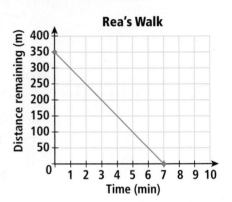

Think and Discuss

1. Explain how to find the slope and y-intercept of the line $y = 2x - 4$.

2. Describe how to graph the equation $y = -\frac{1}{2}x + 6$.

5-7 **Exercises**

Learn It Online
Homework Help Online **go.hrw.com**,
keyword **MS10 5-7** Go
Exercises 1–22, 25, 31, 35

GUIDED PRACTICE

See Example 1 **Find the x- and y-intercepts.**

1.

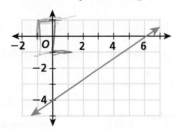

2.

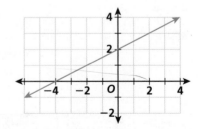

See Example 2 **Graph each equation.**

3. $y = \frac{1}{2}x - 2$ **4.** $y + 4 = -x$ **5.** $y = -\frac{3}{4}x + 1$ **6.** $y - 2x = -5$

See Example 3 **Write the equation of each line in slope-intercept form.**

7.

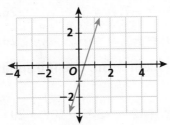

8.

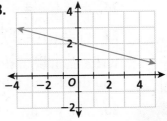

See Example 4 **9.** Pete walks down a 280 ft hill at a constant rate of 70 ft per minute. The linear equation $y = -70x + 280$ represents the distance y Pete has to walk. Graph the equation, and then identify the x- and y-intercepts and describe their meanings.

INDEPENDENT PRACTICE

See Example 1 **Find the x- and y-intercepts.**

10.

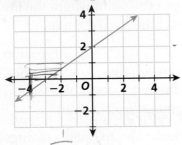

11.

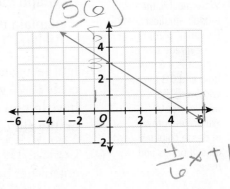

See Example 2 **Graph each equation.**

12. $y = 5x + 3$ **13.** $y = -\frac{1}{3}x - 6$ **14.** $y - 4x = -2$ **15.** $y = -x + 3$

16. $y = \frac{3}{4}x - 5$ **17.** $y - 2 = 7x$ **18.** $y + \frac{4}{5}x = 4$ **19.** $y = 2x - 5$

See Example 3 **Write the equation of each line in slope-intercept form.**

20.

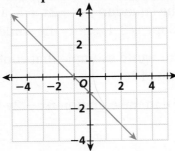

21.

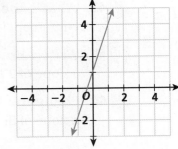

See Example 4 **22.** Fred slides down a 200 ft water slide at a constant rate of 10 ft per second. The linear equation $y = -10x + 200$ represents the distance y that Fred has to slide. Graph the equation, and then identify the x- and y-intercepts and describe their meanings.

PRACTICE AND PROBLEM SOLVING

Extra Practice
See page EP15. **23.** An airplane is cruising at an altitude of 35,000 feet. It begins to descend for landing at a rate of 700 feet per minute. Write an equation that represents the distance y the airplane has left to descend. Find the slope and x- and y-intercepts. What does each intercept represent?

Use the following values to write an equation in slope-intercept form.

24. $m = \frac{1}{2}, b = 6$ **25.** $m = -7, b = 5$ **26.** $m = 1, b = -5$

27. $m = 4, b = 2$ **28.** $m = -\frac{3}{8}, b = -2$ **29.** $m = -1, b = 0$

Write each equation in slope-intercept form. Use the equation to find the slope and the x- and y-intercepts.

30. $2x + y = 8$ **31.** $4y = -3x - 12$ **32.** $-10y = 20x - 30$ **33.** $x + y = 4$

34. $-x + y = 15$ **35.** $y + 30 = 15x$ **36.** $8y = 4x - 16$ **37.** $x + y = 0$

Life Science

Watermeal is the world's smallest flowering plant. The average size of a plant is 0.6 mm long and 0.3 mm wide, and they have no roots. Watermeal grows in dense colonies on still ponds and rivers.

38. Life Science Shelley buys a house plant from a nursery. When she brings it home, it is 5 cm high. The plant grows 2 centimeters each day.

  a. Write an equation expressing this relation, where H is the height of the plant and d represents the number of days.

  b. Graph the linear function.

  c. Explain the significance of the point where the line meets the y-axis. Will the line ever intersect the x-axis? Explain.

39. Jani receives a gift card to her favorite smoothie shop for $30. Each smoothie costs $2.75 with tax. Write an equation to represent the amount y she will have left on the card after buying x smoothies. Does she have enough money on the gift card to buy 11 smoothies? Explain.

40. Critical Thinking Hayden decides to open a savings account using $25 she got for her birthday. Each week she deposits $25. Write an equation in slope-intercept form to represent the amount of money in her bank account. Is there an x- and y-intercept? If so, what are they, and what does each represent?

41. Make a Conjecture Make a conjecture about the y-intercept of a line of the form $y = mx$.

42. What's the Error? For the equation $y = -2x + 3$, a student says the y-intercept is -2 and the slope is 3. Identify the student's error.

43. Write About It Give a real-world example that could represent a line with a slope of 2 and a y-intercept of 10.

44. Challenge What value of n in the equation $nx - 2y = 4$ would give the line a slope of 8?

Test Prep and Spiral Review

45. Multiple Choice Which equation does NOT represent a line with an x-intercept of 3?

Ⓐ $y = -2x + 6$ Ⓑ $y = -\frac{1}{3}x + 1$ Ⓒ $y = \frac{2}{3}x - 2$ Ⓓ $y = 3x - 1$

46. Short Response Graph the equation $y = -\frac{2}{3}x + 2$. Find the x- and y-intercepts.

47. A car travels 150 miles in 3 hours. What is the unit rate of speed per hour? (Lesson 4-1)

48. Tell whether the ratios $\frac{6}{9}$ and $\frac{26}{36}$ are proportional. (Lesson 4-2)

TN SPI 0706.3.5 Represent proportional relationships with equations, tables and graphs. *Also* ✓ 0706.1.5, ✓ 0706.1.6, SPI 0706.1.2, SPI 0706.1.3, GLE 0706.3.5, GLE 0706.3.6, GLE 0706.3.7, GLE 0706.3.8, ✓ 0706.3.2, ✓ 0706.3.5, ✓ 0706.3.7, SPI 0706.3.6, SPI 0706.3.7

Vocabulary

direct variation

constant of variation

Reading Math

You can read direct variation as "*y* varies directly as *x*" or "*y* is directly proportional to *x*" or "*y* varies with *x*."

An Eastern box turtle can travel at a speed of about 18 feet per minute. The chart shows the distance an Eastern box turtle can travel when moving at a constant speed.

The distance traveled is found by multiplying time by 18. Distance and time are directly proportional.

Time (min)	1	2	3	4
Distance (ft)	18	36	54	72

Direct variation is a linear relationship between two variables that can be written in the form $y = kx$ or $k = \frac{y}{x}$, where $k \neq 0$. The fixed number k in a direct variation equation is the **constant of variation**.

$$y = kx \qquad k = \frac{y}{x}$$

To check whether an equation represents a direct variation, solve for *y*. If the equation can be written as $y = kx$, then it represents a direct variation.

EXAMPLE 1 Identifying a Direct Variation from an Equation

Tell whether each equation represents a direct variation. If so, identify the constant of variation.

A $2y = x$

$\frac{2y}{2} = \frac{x}{2}$ *Solve the equation for y. Divide both sides by 2.*

$y = \frac{1}{2}x$ *Write $\frac{x}{2}$ as $\frac{1}{2}x$.*

The equation is in the form $y = kx$, so the original equation $2y = x$ is a direct variation. The constant of variation is $\frac{1}{2}$.

B $y + 1 = 2x$

$y + 1 = 2x$ *Solve the equation for y. Subtract 1 from both sides.*

$\underline{-1 \qquad -1}$

$y = 2x - 1$

The equation is not in the form $y = kx$, so $y + 1 = 2x$ is not a direct variation.

The equation $y = kx$ can be solved for the constant of variation, $k = \frac{y}{x}$. If $\frac{y}{x}$ is the same for all ordered pairs in a set of data, then the data set represents a direct variation. To write a direct variation equation for a set of data, substitute the value of $\frac{y}{x}$ for k in $y = kx$.

EXAMPLE 2 Identifying a Direct Variation from a Table

Tell whether each set of data represents a direct variation. If so, identify the constant of variation and then write the direct variation equation.

Helpful Hint

In a direct variation where k is positive, when x increases, y also increases; when x decreases, y also decreases.

A

Weight (lb)	1	2	3
Price ($)	3	6	9

Find $\frac{y}{x}$ for each ordered pair.

$$\frac{y}{x} = \frac{3}{1} = 3 \qquad \frac{y}{x} = \frac{6}{2} = 3 \qquad \frac{y}{x} = \frac{9}{3} = 3$$

$k = 3$ for each ordered pair.

The data represent a direct variation where $k = 3$. The equation is $y = 3x$.

B

Constant Speed (mi/h)	10	20	30
Time (h)		3	1.5	1

Find $\frac{y}{x}$ for each ordered pair.

$$\frac{y}{x} = \frac{3}{10} \qquad \frac{y}{x} = \frac{1.5}{20} = \frac{3}{40} \qquad \frac{y}{x} = \frac{1}{30} = \frac{1}{30}$$

k is not the same for each ordered pair.

The data do not represent a direct variation.

The graph of any direct variation is a straight line that passes through the origin, (0, 0). The slope of a line of direct variation is the constant of variation, k.

EXAMPLE 3 Identifying a Direct Variation from a Graph

Tell whether each graph represents a direct variation. If so, identify the constant of variation and then write the direct variation equation.

A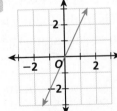

B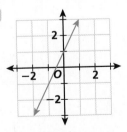

The graph is a line through (0, 0). This is a direct variation. The slope of the line is 2, so $k = 2$. The equation is $y = 2x$.

The line does not pass through (0, 0). This is not a direct variation.

Helpful Hint

In a direct variation, the slope, k, represents a constant rate of change.

Video **Lesson Tutorials Online** my.hrw.com

EXAMPLE 4 *Life Science Application*

An Eastern box turtle travels on the ground at a speed of about 18 feet per minute.

a. Write a direct variation equation for the distance *y* an Eastern box turtle travels in *x* minutes.

distance	=	18 feet per minute	times	number of minutes
y	=	18	•	*x*

Use the formula y = kx.

$$y = 18x \qquad \textit{k = 18}$$

b. Graph the data.

Make a table. Since time cannot be negative, use nonnegative numbers for *x*.

x	*y* = 18*x*	*y*	(*x, y*)
0	*y* = 18(0)	0	(0, 0)
1	*y* = 18(1)	18	(1, 18)
2	*y* = 18(2)	36	(2, 36)

Use the ordered pairs to plot the points on a coordinate plane. Connect the points in a straight line. Label the axes.

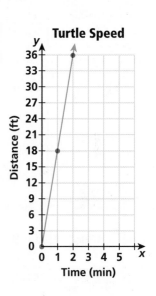

Turtle Speed

Check

$y = 18x$ is in slope-intercept form with $m = 18$ and $b = 0$. The graph shows a slope of 18 and a *y*-intercept of 0.

c. How long does it take an Eastern box turtle to travel 162 feet?

Find the value of *x* when *y* = 162.

$$y = 18x \qquad \textit{Write the equation for the direct variation.}$$
$$162 = 18x \qquad \textit{Substitute 162 for y.}$$
$$\frac{162}{18} = \frac{18x}{18} \qquad \textit{Divide both sides by 18.}$$
$$9 = x$$

It will take an Eastern box turtle 9 minutes to travel 162 feet.

Helpful Hint

In this problem the variable *x* represents time and *y* represents distance, so 162 will be substituted for *y*.

Think and Discuss

1. Explain how to use a table of data to check whether the relationship between two variables is a direct variation.

2. Describe how to recognize a direct variation from an equation, from a table, and from a graph.

3. Discuss why every direct variation equation is a linear equation, but not every linear equation is a direct variation equation.

GUIDED PRACTICE

See Example 1 Tell whether each equation represents a direct variation. If so, identify the constant of variation.

1. $y = 5x + 8$ 　　2. $y = 3.6x$ 　　3. $8y = 2x$ 　　4. $x = 3y + 1$

See Example 2 Tell whether each set of data or graph represents a direct variation. If so, identify the constant of variation and then write the direct variation equation.

5.
Number of Boxes	2	3	4
Rolls of Tape Needed	1	2	5

6.
x	2	4	8
y	3	7	15

See Example 3 7.

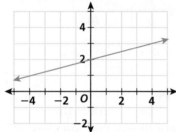

8.

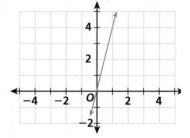

See Example 4 **9. Physical Science** Belinda's garden hose sprays about 4 gallons of water each minute.

　　a. Write a direct variation equation for the number of gallons y Belinda uses during x minutes of watering her garden.

　　b. Graph the data.

　　c. How many gallons of water does Belinda use in 20 minutes?

INDEPENDENT PRACTICE

See Example 1 Tell whether each equation represents a direct variation. If so, identify the constant of variation.

10. $y = \dfrac{x}{7}$ 　　11. $\dfrac{y}{x} = \dfrac{2}{3}$ 　　12. $3y = 15 - 6x$ 　　13. $3xy = 9x$

See Example 2 Tell whether each set of data or graph represents a direct variation. If so, identify the constant of variation and then write the direct variation equation.

14.
x	7	8	9
y	0.5	1.2	1.5

15.
Cans of Food	2	4	6
Dinners Made	4	8	12

See Example 3 16.

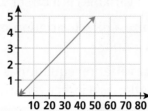

17.

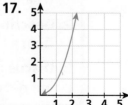

See Example 4

18. Physical Science Neil Armstrong's weight on the moon was about $\frac{1}{6}$ his weight on Earth.

    a. Write a direct variation equation for the number of pounds y an object on the moon weighs if the object weighs x pounds on Earth.

    b. Graph the data.

    c. Li would weigh 24 pounds on the moon. What does he weigh on Earth?

PRACTICE AND PROBLEM SOLVING

Extra Practice
See page EP15.

Life Science

Sea snakes are found in warm waters ranging from the Indian Ocean to the Pacific. They do not have gills and must surface regularly to breathe.

Write an equation for the direct variation that includes each point.

19. (7, 2)   **20.** (6, 30)   **21.** (4, 8)   **22.** (17, 31)

23. If y varies directly as x, and $y = 8$ when $x = 2$, find y when $x = 10$.

24. Is a direct variation a function? Explain.

Tell whether each relationship is a direct variation. Explain.

25. pay per hour and the number of hours worked

26. pay per hour and the number of hours worked, including a \$100 bonus

27. Life Science A sea snake can swim at a rate of 60 meters per minute. How far can a sea snake swim in half an hour?

28. Critical Thinking If you double an x-value in a direct variation equation, will the y-value double? Explain your answer.

29. What's the Error? Phil says that the graph represents a direct variation because it passes through the origin. What's the error?

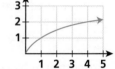

30. Write About It Compare the graphs of a direct variation equation with a slope of 3 and an equation with the same slope and a y-intercept of 2.

31. Challenge Explain why the graph of a line that does not pass through the origin cannot be a direct variation.

Test Prep and Spiral Review

32. Multiple Choice Which equation does NOT show direct variation?

    Ⓐ $y = 16x$ Ⓑ $y - 19 = x - 19$ Ⓒ $20y = x$ Ⓓ $y = 25$

33. Short Response Ron buys 5 pounds of apples for \$3.25. Write a direct variation equation for the cost y of x pounds of apples. Find the cost of 21 lbs of apples.

Add. Write each answer in simplest form. (Lesson 3-8)

34. $1\frac{1}{5} + 3\frac{3}{5}$ **35.** $7\frac{2}{3} + 8\frac{2}{3}$ **36.** $9\frac{1}{4} + 6\frac{2}{3}$ **37.** $4\frac{7}{10} + 3\frac{1}{8}$

Plot each point on a coordinate plane. (Lesson 5-1)

38. $A(-4, 1)$ **39.** $B(0, 3)$ **40.** $C(2, -2)$ **41.** $D(-1, 4)$

Inverse Variation

TN **SPI 0706.1.3** Recognize whether information given in a table, graph, or formula suggests a directly proportional, linear, inversely proportional, or other nonlinear relationship.
Also ✓ **0706.1.4,** ✓ **0706.3.7**

Vocabulary

inverse variation

Inverse variation is a relationship between two variables that can be written in the form $y = \frac{k}{x}$, or $xy = k$, where k is a nonzero constant and $x \neq 0$.

$$y = \frac{k}{x} \qquad xy = k$$

In an inverse variation, the product of x and y is constant.

EXAMPLE **1** **Identifying an Inverse Variation**

Tell whether each relationship is an inverse variation. Explain.

A

x	2	3	4
y	12	8	6

Find the product of xy.

$2(12) = 24 \quad 3(8) = 24 \quad 4(6) = 24$ *Substitute for x and y.*

The product for xy is constant, so the relationship is an inverse variation with $k = 24$.

B

x	5	7	9
y	80	75	70

Find the product of xy.

$5(80) = 400 \quad 7(75) = 525 \quad 9(70) = 630$

The product for xy is not constant, so the relationship is not an inverse variation.

Reading Math

You can read inverse variation as "y varies inversely as x" or "y is inversely proportional to x."

EXAMPLE **2** *Geometry Application*

David is building a rectangular flowerbed. He has soil to cover 48 square feet. The flowerbed can be 4, 6, or 12 feet long. For each length x, find the width of the flowerbed y to use all the soil.

The area A of the flowerbed is a constant k. The length x times the width y must equal the area, 48. The equation $xy = 48$ is an inverse variation.

$xy = k$	$xy = k$	$xy = k$	*Use xy = k.*
$4y = 48$	$6y = 48$	$12y = 48$	*Substitute for x and k.*
$y = 12$	$y = 8$	$y = 4$	*Solve for y.*

David can build a flowerbed that is 4 ft long by 12 ft wide, 6 ft long by 8 ft wide, or 12 ft long by 4 ft wide.

An inverse variation can also be identified by its graph. Since k is a nonzero constant, $xy \neq 0$. Therefore, neither x nor y can equal 0, and no solution points will be on the x-axis or y-axis.

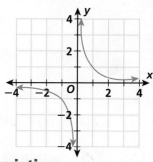

EXAMPLE **Identifying a Graph of an Inverse Variation**

Tell whether each graph represents an inverse variation. Explain.

A

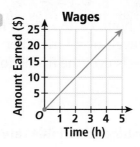

Identify points on the graph. Use the equation $xy = k$.
$(1)5 = 5$, $(3)15 = 45$, $(5)25 = 125$
The values of k are not constant. The graph does not represent an inverse variation.

B

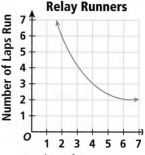

Identity points on the graph. Use the equation $xy = k$.
$(2)6 = 12$, $(3)4 = 12$, $(4)3 = 12$
The values of k are constant. The graph represents an inverse variation.

EXTENSION

Exercises

Determine whether each set of data shows inverse or direct variation.

1.

2.

3. If x and y show inverse variation, and you know that $y = 10$ when $x = 6$, find y when $x = 12$.

4. You are on a trip to a museum that is 120 miles away. You know that if you travel 60 miles per hour, you will arrive in 2 hours. How long will the trip take if you travel at 30 miles per hour?

5. **Write About It** Explain the difference between a direct variation and an inverse variation.

6. **Critical Thinking** The definition of inverse variation says that k is a nonzero constant. What would $y = \frac{k}{x}$ represent if k were 0?

Quiz for Lessons 5-5 Through 5-8

5-5 Graphing Linear Functions

Graph each linear function.

1. $y = x - 4$ **2.** $y = 2x - 5$ **3.** $y = -x + 7$ **4.** $y = -2x + 1$

5. A freight train travels 50 miles per hour. Write a linear function that describes the distance the train travels over time. Then make a graph to show the distance the train travels over the first 9 hours.

5-6 Slope and Rates of Change

Tell whether each graph shows a constant or variable rate of change. If constant, find the slope.

6.
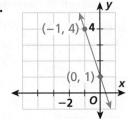

7.
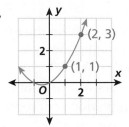

8.
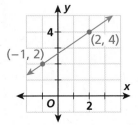

5-7 Slope-Intercept Form

Write the equation of the line in slope-intercept form.

9.
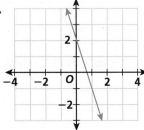

10.
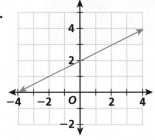

11.
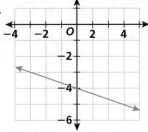

12. A skier skis down a 108-meter ramp at a constant rate of 27 m per second. The linear equation $y = -27x + 108$ represents the distance y the skier has left to ski. Graph the equation and then identify the x- and y-intercepts and describe their meanings.

5-8 Direct Variation

Tell whether each set of data represents a direct variation. If so, identify the constant of variation, and then write the direct variation equation.

13.

Weight (lb)	1	2	3
Price ($)	1.50	3.00	4.50

14.

x	1	2	3
y	4	5	7

The Alabama National Fair Where can you see trapeze acts, a cheerleading competition, and racing pigs all in one place? Since the 1950s, the annual Alabama National Fair has brought all of this—and much more—to the Agricultural Center and Fairgrounds in Montgomery.

ALABAMA

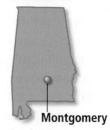

Montgomery

A teacher is planning to take some of her students to the fair.

1. The Alabama National Fair has one admission fee for adults and a different fee for students. The table can be used to determine how much it will cost for the teacher and her students to attend the fair. Complete the table.

2. What is the fair's admission fee for adults? What is the fair's admission fee for students?

3. Suppose x represents the number of students that the teacher brings to the fair and y represents the total cost. Write a function that describes the data in the table.

4. Use the function you wrote in Problem 3 to find the total cost of bringing 14 students to the fair.

5. Make a graph that shows the total cost as a function of the number of students.

6. What is the slope of the line in your graph?

7. A county fair offers admission to a teacher and any number of students for $85. For what number of students would it be less expensive for the teacher to take her students to the county fair than the Alabama National Fair?

ADMIT ONE

Number of Students	Rule	Total Cost
0		$9
1	9 + 7(1)	$16
2		$23
3	9 + 7(3)	
4		$37
6	9 + 7(6)	
8		$65
12		

Game Time

Clothes Encounters

Five students from the same math class met to study for an upcoming test. They sat around a circular table with seat 1 and seat 5 next to each other. No two students were wearing the same color of shirt or the same type of shoes. From the clues provided, determine where each student sat, each student's shirt color, and what type of shoes each student was wearing.

❶ The girls' shoes were sandals, flip-flops, and boots.

❷ Robin, wearing a blue shirt, was sitting next to the person wearing the green shirt. She was not sitting next to the person wearing the orange shirt.

❸ Lila was sitting between the person wearing sandals and the person in the yellow shirt.

❹ The boy who was wearing the tennis shoes was wearing the orange shirt.

❺ April had on flip-flops and was sitting between Lila and Charles.

❻ Glenn was wearing loafers, but his shirt was not brown.

❼ Robin sat in seat 1.

You can use a chart like the one below to organize the information given. Put X's in the spaces where the information is false and O's in the spaces where the information is true. Some of the information from the first two clues has been included on the chart already. You will need to read through the clues several times and use logic to complete the chart.

	Seat 1	Seat 2	Seat 3	Seat 4	Seat 5	Blue shirt	Green shirt	Orange shirt	Yellow shirt	Brown shirt	Sandals	Flip-flops	Boots	Tennis shoes	Loafers
Lila					X									X	X
Robin					O	O	X	X	X	X				X	X
April					X									X	X
Charles					X										
Glenn					X										

Materials
- **6 sheets of unlined paper**
- **scissors**
- **markers**

It's in the Bag!

A

PROJECT **Graphs and Functions Fold-A-Books**

These handy books will store your notes from each lesson of the chapter.

Directions

1 Fold a sheet of paper in half down the middle. Then open the paper and lay it flat so it forms a peak. **Figure A**

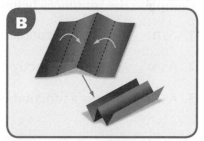
B

2 Fold the left and right edges to the crease in the middle. When you're done, the paper will be folded into four sections, accordion-style. **Figure B**

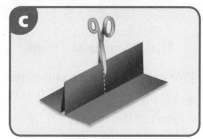
C

3 Pinch the middle sections together. Use scissors to cut a slit down the center of these sections, stopping when you get to the folds. **Figure C**

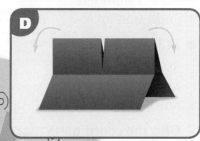
D

4 Hold the paper on either side of the slit. As you open the slit, the paper will form a four-page book. **Figure D**

5 Crease the top edges and fold the book closed. Repeat all the steps to make five more books.

Taking Note of the Math

On the cover of each book, write the number and name of a lesson from the chapter. Use the remaining pages to take notes on the lesson.

CHAPTER 5 Graphs & Functions

Lesson 5-4 Sequences

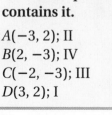

Vocabulary

arithmetic sequence ... 288	linear equation 296	slope 302
common difference 288	linear function 296	slope-intercept form ... 309
constant of variation ... 313	ordered pair 276	term 288
coordinate plane 276	origin 276	x-axis 276
direct variation 313	output 284	x-intercept 308
function 284	quadrant 276	y-axis 276
geometric sequence 288	rate of change 303	y-intercept 308
input 284	sequence 288	

Complete the sentences below with vocabulary words from the list above.

1. A(n) ___?___ is an ordered list of numbers.

2. A(n) ___?___ gives exactly one output for every input.

3. A(n) ___?___ is a function whose graph is a nonvertical line.

EXAMPLES

EXERCISES

5-1 The Coordinate Plane (pp. 276–279)

Plot each point on a coordinate plane.

■ $M(-3, 1)$
Start at the origin.
Move 3 units left
and 1 unit up.

■ $R(3, -4)$
Start at the origin.
Move 3 units right
and 4 units down.

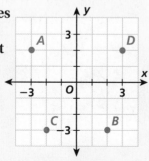

■ Give the coordinates
of each point and
tell which quadrant
contains it.

$A(-3, 2)$; II
$B(2, -3)$; IV
$C(-2, -3)$; III
$D(3, 2)$; I

Plot each point on a coordinate plane.

4. $A(4, 2)$ **5.** $B(-4, -2)$

6. $C(-2, 4)$ **7.** $D(2, -4)$

Give the coordinates of each point and tell
which quadrant contains it.

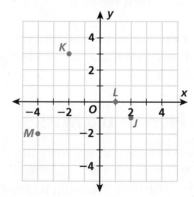

8. J **9.** K **10.** L **11.** M

EXAMPLES

EXERCISES

5-2 Interpreting Graphs (pp. 280–283)

■ Ari visits his grandmother, who lives 45 miles away. After the visit, he returns home, stopping for gas along the way. Sketch a graph to show the distance Ari traveled compared to time. Use your graph to find the total distance traveled.

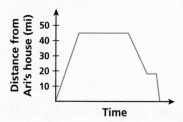

The graph increases from 0 to 45 miles and then decreases from 45 to 0 miles. The distance does not change while Ari visits his grandmother and stops for gas. Ari traveled a total of 90 miles.

12. Amanda walks 1.5 miles to school in the morning. After school, she walks 0.5 mile to the public library. After she has chosen her books, she walks 2 miles home. Sketch a graph to show the distance Amanda traveled compared to time. Use your graph to find the total distance traveled.

13. Joel rides his bike to the park, 12 miles away, to meet his friends. He then rides an additional 6 miles to the grocery store and then 18 miles back home. Sketch a graph to show the distance Joel traveled compared to time. Use your graph to find the total distance traveled.

5-3 Functions, Tables, and Graphs (pp. 284–287)

■ Find the output for each input.

$y = 3x + 4$

Input	Rule	Output
x	$3x + 4$	y
-1	$3(-1) + 4$	1
0	$3(0) + 4$	4
2	$3(2) + 4$	10

Find the output for each input.

14. $y = x^2 - 1$

Input	Rule	Output
x	$x^2 - 1$	y
-2	▪	▪
3	▪	▪
5	▪	▪

5-4 Sequences (pp. 288–291)

■ Write a function that describes the sequence. Use the function to find the eighth term in the sequence.

3, 6, 9, 12, . . .

n	Rule	y
1	$1 \cdot 3$	3
2	$2 \cdot 3$	6
3	$3 \cdot 3$	9
4	$4 \cdot 3$	12

Function: $y = 3n$
When $n = 8$, $y = 24$.

Write a function that describes each sequence. Use the function to find the eighth term in the sequence.

15. 25, 50, 75, 100, . . .

16. $-3, -2, -1, 0, . . .$

17. $-4, -1, 2, 5, . . .$

18. 4, 6, 8, 10, . . .

5-5 **Graphing Linear Functions** (pp. 296–299)

■ Graph the linear function $y = -x + 2$.

Input	Output	Ordered Pair
x	y	(x, y)
-1	3	$(-1, 3)$
0	2	$(0, 2)$
2	0	$(2, 0)$

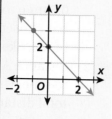

Graph each linear function.

19. $y = 2x - 1$

20. $y = -3x$

21. $y = x - 3$

22. $y = 2x + 4$

23. $y = x - 6$

24. $y = 3x - 9$

5-6 **Slope and Rates of Change** (pp. 302–306)

■ Tell whether the graph shows a constant or variable rate of change. If constant, find the slope.

The graph is a line, so the rate of change is constant.

$$\text{slope} = \frac{\text{rise}}{\text{run}}$$

$$= \frac{-4}{1} = -4$$

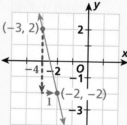

Tell whether each graph shows a constant or variable rate of change. If constant, find the slope.

25.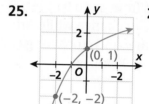

26.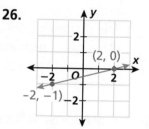

5-7 **Slope-Intercept Form** (pp. 308–312)

■ Write the equation of the line in slope-intercept form.

Find m and b.

$m = -\frac{1}{4}$; $b = -2$

Substitute.

$y = -\frac{1}{4}x - 2$

27. Write the equation of the line in slope-intercept form.

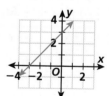

28. Graph $y = -\frac{3}{2}x + 4$.

5-8 **Direct Variation** (pp. 313–317)

■ Tell whether each equation represents a direct variation. If so, identify the constant of variation.

$3y = x$

$\frac{3y}{3} = \frac{x}{3}$ *Solve the equation for y.*

$y = \frac{1}{3}x$ *Divide by 3 on both sides.*

The constant of variation is $\frac{1}{3}$.

Tell whether the set of data represents a direct variation. If so, identify the constant of variation and then write the direct variation equation.

29.

x	1	2	3
y	18	36	54

30.

x	1	2	3
y	4	7	10

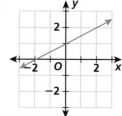

Chapter Test

Plot each point on a coordinate plane. Then identify the quadrant that contains each point.

1. $L(4, -3)$ **2.** $M(-5, 2)$ **3.** $N(7, 1)$ **4.** $O(-7, -2)$

5. Ian jogs 4 miles to the lake and then rests for 30 min before jogging home. Sketch a graph to show the distance Ian traveled compared to time. Use your graph to find the total distance traveled.

Write a function that describes each sequence. Use the function to find the eleventh term in the sequence.

6. 1, 3, 5, 7 . . .   **7.** 11, 21, 31, 41 . . .   **8.** 0, 3, 8, 15 . . .

Make a table of values to graph each linear function.

9. $y = 3x - 4$ **10.** $y = x - 8$ **11.** $y = 2x + 7$ **12.** $y = -x + 1$

Tell whether each graph shows a constant or variable rate of change. If constant, find the slope.

13.

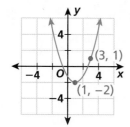

14.

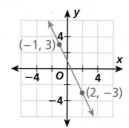

Write the equation of each line in slope-intercept form.

15.

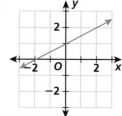

16.

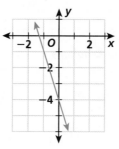

17. Paula walks up a 520-meter hill at a pace of 40 meters per minute. The linear equation $y = -40x + 520$ represents the distance y that Paula has left to walk after x minutes. Graph the equation, and then identify the x- and y-intercepts and describe their meanings.

Tell whether each equation represents a direct variation. If so, identify the constant of variation.

18. $5y = 10x$ **19.** $y - 3 = x$ **20.** $x + y = 4$ **21.** $-7x = y$

Test Tackler
STANDARDIZED TEST STRATEGIES

Extended Response: Understand the Scores

Extended-response test items usually involve multiple steps and require a detailed explanation. The items are scored using a 4-point rubric. A complete and correct response is worth 4 points, a partial response is worth 2 to 3 points, an incorrect response with no work shown is worth 1 point, and no response at all is worth 0 points.

EXAMPLE 1

Extended Response A 10-pound bag of apples costs $4. Write and solve a proportion to find how much a 15-pound bag of apples would cost at the same rate. Explain how the increase in weight is related to the increase in cost.

Here are examples of how different responses were scored using the scoring rubric shown.

4-point response:

Let c = the cost of the 15 lb bag.

$$\frac{10 \text{ pounds}}{\$4} = \frac{15 \text{ pounds}}{c}$$

$$10 \cdot c = 4 \cdot 15$$

$$\frac{10c}{10} = \frac{60}{10}$$

$$c = 6$$

The 15 lb bag costs $6.

For every additional 5 pounds, the cost increases by 2 dollars.

3-point response:

Let c = the cost of the 15 lb bag.

$$\frac{10 \text{ pounds}}{\$4} = \frac{15 \text{ pounds}}{c}$$

$$10 \cdot c = 4 \cdot 15$$

$$\frac{10c}{10} = \frac{60}{10}$$

$$c = 6$$

The 15 lb bag costs $6.

For every additional 5 pounds, the cost increases by 6 dollars.

The proportion is set up and solved correctly, and all work is shown, but the explanation is incorrect.

2-point response:

Let c = the cost of the apples.

$$\frac{10 \text{ pounds}}{\$4} = \frac{c}{15 \text{ pounds}}$$

$$10 \cdot 15 = 4 \cdot c$$

$$\frac{150}{4} = \frac{4c}{4}$$

$$37.5 = c$$

The proportion is set up incorrectly, and no explanation is given.

1-point response:

$$37.5 = c$$

The answer is incorrect, no work is shown, and no explanation is given.

EXAMPLE **3** **Writing Percents as Decimals**

Write each percent as a decimal.

A **43%**

Method 1: Use pencil and paper.

$43\% = \dfrac{43}{100}$ *Write the percent as a fraction.*

$= 0.43$ *Divide 43 by 100.*

B **30.75%**

Method 2: Use mental math.

$30.75\% = 0.3075$ *Move the decimal point two places to the left.*

Think and Discuss

1. Tell in your own words what *percent* means.

6-1 Exercises

Learn It Online
Homework Help Online **go.hrw.com**,
keyword MS10 6-1 Go
Exercises 1–26, 33, 35

GUIDED PRACTICE

See Example **1** Write the percent modeled by each grid.

 1.   2.   3.

See Example **2** Write each percent as a fraction in simplest form.

4. 65%   **5.** 82%   **6.** 12%   **7.** 38%   **8.** 75%

See Example **3** Write each percent as a decimal.

9. 22%   **10.** 51%   **11.** 8.07%   **12.** 1.6%   **13.** 11%

INDEPENDENT PRACTICE

See Example **1** Write the percent modeled by each grid.

 14.   15.   16.

See Example 2 **Write each percent as a fraction in simplest form.**

17. 55%   **18.** 34%   **19.** 83%   **20.** 53%   **21.** 81%

See Example 3 **Write each percent as a decimal.**

22. 48%   **23.** 9.8%   **24.** 30.2%   **25.** 66.3%   **26.** 8.39%

PRACTICE AND PROBLEM SOLVING

Extra Practice
See page EP16.

Write each percent as a fraction in simplest form and as a decimal.

27. 2.70%   **28.** 7.6%   **29.** 44%   **30.** 3.148%   **31.** 10.5%

Compare. Write <, >, or =.

32. $\frac{18}{100}$ ▮ 22%   **33.** $\frac{35}{52}$ ▮ 72%   **34.** $\frac{10}{50}$ ▮ 22%   **35.** $\frac{11}{20}$ ▮ 56%

36. 41% ▮ $\frac{13}{30}$ **37.** $\frac{17}{20}$ ▮ 85%   **38.** $\frac{3}{5}$ ▮ 60%   **39.** 15% ▮ $\frac{4}{30}$

40. Multi-Step A nutrition label states that one serving of tortilla chips contains 7 grams of fat and 11% of the recommended daily allowance (RDA) of fat.

  a. Write a ratio that represents the percent RDA of fat in one serving of tortilla chips.

  b. Use the ratio from part **a** to write and solve a proportion to determine how many grams of fat are in the recommended daily allowance.

41. Choose a Strategy During class, Brad finished 63% of his homework, and Liz completed $\frac{5}{7}$ of her homework. Who must finish a greater percent of homework at home?

42. Write About It Compare ratios and percents. How are they alike? How are they different?

43. Challenge Write each of the following as a percent: 0.4 and 0.03.

Test Prep and Spiral Review

44. Multiple Choice Which inequality is a true statement?

  Ⓐ 24% > $\frac{1}{4}$ Ⓑ 0.76 < 76%   Ⓒ 8% < 0.8   Ⓓ $\frac{1}{5}$ < 5%

45. Short Response Nineteen out of the 25 students on Sean's team sold mugs, and 68% of the students on Chi's team sold caps. Which team had a greater percent of students participate in the fundraiser?

Estimate each sum or difference. (Lesson 3-6)

46. $\frac{7}{8} - \frac{3}{7}$ **47.** $6\frac{1}{10} + 5\frac{7}{9}$ **48.** $5\frac{2}{3} - \left(-\frac{3}{4}\right)$ **49.** $\frac{5}{12} + 2\frac{4}{5}$

Plot each point on a coordinate plane. (Lesson 5-1)

50. $A(2, 3)$ **51.** $B(-1, 4)$ **52.** $C(-2, -6)$ **53.** $D(0, -3)$

Hands-on LAB
6-1

Model Percents

Use with Lesson 6-1

Learn It Online
Lab Resources Online **go.hrw.com**,
keyword MS10 Lab6 Go

TN ▶ **SPI 0706.2.6** Express the ratio between two quantities as a percent, and a percent as a ratio or fraction. *Also* **GLE 0706.1.4, GLE 0706.1.8,** ✓ **0706.2.8**

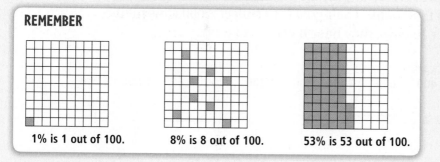

REMEMBER

1% is 1 out of 100.　　8% is 8 out of 100.　　53% is 53 out of 100.

Percents less than 1% represent numbers less than 0.01, or $\frac{1}{100}$. Percents greater than 100% represent numbers greater than 1. You can use 10-by-10 grids to model percents less than 1 or greater than 100.

Activity 1

1 Use 10-by-10 grids to model 132%.

 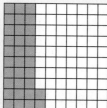

Think: 132% means 132 out of 100.

Shade 100 squares plus 32 squares to model 132%.

2 Use a 10-by-10 grid to model 0.5%.

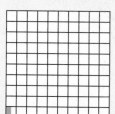

Think: One square equals 1%, so $\frac{1}{2}$ of one square equals 0.5%.

Shade $\frac{1}{2}$ of one square to model 0.5%.

Think and Discuss

1. Explain how to model 36.75% on a 10-by-10 grid.

2. How can you model 0.7%? Explain your answer.

Try This

Use 10-by-10 grids to model each percent.

1. 280%　　　2. $16\frac{1}{2}$%　　　3. 0.25%　　　4. 65%　　　5. 140.75%

TN **SPI 0706.2.6** Express the ratio between two quantities as a percent, and a percent as a ratio or fraction.
Also **GLE 0706.1.8, GLE 0706.2.4,** ✓ **0706.2.7,** ✓ **0706.2.8,** ✓ **0706.2.9**

The students at Westview Middle School are collecting cans of food for the local food bank. Their goal is to collect 2,000 cans in one month. After 10 days, they have 800 cans of food.

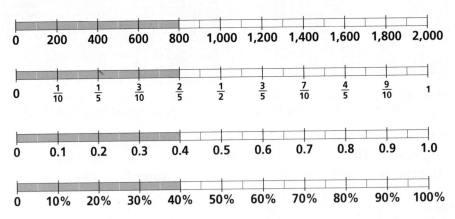

Interactivities Online ▶ The models show that 800 out of 2,000 can be written as $\frac{800}{2,000}$, $\frac{2}{5}$, 0.4, or 40%. The students have reached 40% of their goal.

EXAMPLE 1 Writing Decimals as Percents

Write 0.2 as a percent.

Method 1: Use pencil and paper.

$0.2 = \frac{2}{10} = \frac{20}{100}$ *Write the decimal as a fraction with a denominator of 100.*

$= 20\%$ *Write the numerator with a percent sign.*

Method 2: Use mental math.

$0.20 = 20.0\%$
$= 20\%$ *Move the decimal point two places to the right and add a percent sign.*

EXAMPLE 2 Writing Fractions as Percents

Write $\frac{4}{5}$ as a percent.

Method 1: Use pencil and paper.

$\frac{4}{5} = 4 \div 5$ *Use division to write the fraction as a decimal.*

$= 0.8$
$= 0.80$
$= 80\%$ *Write the decimal as a percent.*

Method 2: Use mental math.

$\frac{4 \cdot 20}{5 \cdot 20} = \frac{80}{100}$ *Write an equivalent fraction with a denominator of 100.*

$= 80\%$ *Write the numerator with a percent sign.*

Remember!

To divide 4 by 5, use long division and place a decimal point followed by a zero after the 4.

$\begin{array}{r} 0.8 \\ 5\overline{)4.0} \end{array}$

Video **Lesson Tutorials Online** my.hrw.com

EXAMPLE **3** | **Ordering Rational Numbers**

Order $1\frac{4}{5}$, $0.\overline{33}$, -1.6, 3, $2\frac{1}{5}$, and 70.2% from least to greatest.

Step 1 Write the numbers as decimals with the same number of decimal places.

$$1\frac{4}{5} = 1.8 \qquad 0.\overline{33} \approx 0.3 \qquad -1.6 = -1.6$$
$$3 = 3.0 \qquad 2\frac{1}{5} = 2.2 \qquad 70.2\% \approx 0.7$$

Step 2 Graph the numbers on a number line.

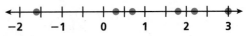

Step 3 Compare the decimals.

$$-1.6 < 0.3 < 0.7 < 1.8 < 2.2 < 3.0$$

From least to greatest, the numbers are: -1.6, $0.\overline{33}$, 70.2%, $1\frac{4}{5}$, $2\frac{1}{5}$, 3

EXAMPLE **4** | **Choosing a Method of Computation**

Decide whether using pencil and paper, mental math, or a calculator is most useful when solving the following problem. Then solve.

In a survey, 55 people were asked whether they prefer cats or dogs. Twenty-nine people said they prefer cats. What percent of the people surveyed said they prefer cats?

29 out of 55 $= \frac{29}{55}$ *Think: Since 29 ÷ 55 does not divide evenly, pencil and paper is not a good choice.*

Think: Since the denominator is not a factor of 100, mental math is not a good choice.

Using a calculator is the best method.

29 ÷ 55 ENTER [0.5272727273]

$0.5272727273 = 52.72727273\%$ *Write the decimal as a percent.*

 $\approx 52.7\%$ *Round to the nearest tenth of a percent.*

About 52.7% of the people surveyed said they prefer cats.

Think and Discuss

1. Describe two methods you could use to write $\frac{3}{4}$ as a percent.

2. Write the ratio 25:100 as a fraction, as a decimal, and as a percent.

Learn It Online
Homework Help Online **go.hrw.com**,
keyword **MS10 6-2** **Go**
Exercises 1–35, 37, 39, 41

GUIDED PRACTICE

See Example **1** Write each decimal as a percent.

1. 0.6　　　**2.** 0.32　　　**3.** 0.544　　　**4.** 0.06　　　**5.** 0.087

See Example **2** Write each fraction as a percent.

6. $\frac{1}{4}$　　**7.** $\frac{3}{25}$　　**8.** $\frac{11}{20}$　　**9.** $\frac{7}{40}$　　**10.** $\frac{5}{8}$

See Example **3** Order the numbers from least to greatest.

11. $0.\overline{5}, 50\%, \frac{11}{20}$　　　　　**12.** $\frac{7}{8}, -0.9, 90\%$

13. $10\%, 1\%, -\frac{1}{10}$　　　　**14.** $-0.8, \frac{4}{5}, 8\%$

15. $72\%, \frac{35}{54}, 0.\overline{6}$　　　　**16.** $-\frac{1}{2}, 5\%, -0.05$

See Example **4** **17.** Decide whether using pencil and paper, mental math, or a calculator is most useful when solving the following problem. Then solve.

In a survey, 50 students were asked whether they prefer pepperoni pizza or cheese pizza. Twenty students said they prefer cheese pizza. What percent of the students surveyed said they prefer cheese pizza?

INDEPENDENT PRACTICE

See Example **1** Write each decimal as a percent.

18. 0.15　　　**19.** 0.83　　　**20.** 0.325　　　**21.** 0.081　　　**22.** 0.42

See Example **2** Write each fraction as a percent.

23. $\frac{3}{4}$　　**24.** $\frac{2}{5}$　　**25.** $\frac{3}{8}$　　**26.** $\frac{3}{16}$　　**27.** $\frac{7}{25}$

See Example **3** Order the numbers from least to greatest.

28. $0.\overline{6}, 6\%, \frac{3}{5}$　　　　　**29.** $-\frac{2}{3}, -0.7, 7\%$

30. $\frac{8}{3}, 30\%, 3$　　　　　**31.** $-0.1, 1\%, -\frac{1}{9}$

32. $2\%, \frac{5}{4}, 1.\overline{1}$　　　　**33.** $-\frac{1}{6}, -0.01, 2\%$

See Example **4** Decide whether using pencil and paper, mental math, or a calculator is most useful when solving each of the following problems. Then solve.

34. In a theme-park survey, 75 visitors were asked whether they prefer the Ferris wheel or the roller coaster. Thirty visitors prefer the Ferris wheel. What percent of the visitors surveyed said they prefer the Ferris wheel?

35. In a survey, 65 students were asked whether they prefer television sitcoms or dramas. Thirteen students prefer dramas. What percent of the students surveyed prefer dramas?

Extra Practice
See page EP16.

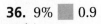

Life Science

One of the world's largest flowers, the Titan arum, is native to the Sumatran rain forests. These flowers can grow to over 6 feet tall; the tallest ever recorded was over 10 feet tall.

Compare. Write <, >, or =.

36. 9% ▨ 0.9

37. 45% ▨ $\frac{2}{5}$

38. 0.037 ▨ 37%

39. $\frac{7}{12}$ ▨ 60%

40. Life Science Rain forests are home to 90,000 of the 250,000 identified plant species in the world. What percent of the world's identified plant species are found in rain forests?

41. Multi-Step One-half of the 900 students at Jefferson Middle School are boys. One-tenth of the boys are in the band, and one-fifth of those play the trumpet. What percent of the students at Jefferson are boys who play the trumpet in the band?

Use the table for Exercises 42–45.

42. What percent of the championship appearances did Dudley win?

43. Write the schools in order from least portion of games won to greatest portion of games won.

44. Which school won 5 out of 6 games?

45. Estimate the percent of the games Wallace-Rose Hill lost.

North Carolina Men's Basketball Championship Appearances	
School Name	**Portion of Games Won**
Cummings	$0.8\overline{3}$
Dudley	0.6
North Mecklenburg	$0.\overline{3}$
Wakefield	1.0
Wallace-Rose Hill	$0.\overline{6}$

46. What's the Error? A student wrote $\frac{2}{5}$ as 0.4%. What was the error?

47. Write About It Describe two ways to change a fraction to a percent.

48. Challenge A desert area's average rainfall is 12 inches a year. This year the area received 15 inches of rain. What percent of the average rainfall amount is 15 inches?

Test Prep and Spiral Review

49. Multiple Choice Which value is NOT equivalent to 45%?

Ⓐ $\frac{9}{20}$ Ⓑ 0.45   Ⓒ $\frac{45}{100}$ Ⓓ 0.045

50. Short Response Melanie's room measures 10 ft by 12 ft. Her rug covers 90 ft². Explain how to determine the percent of floor covered by the rug.

Make a function table for $x = -2, -1, 0, 1,$ and 2. (Lesson 5-3)

51. $y = 5x + 2$ **52.** $y = -2x$ **53.** $y = -\frac{2}{3}x - 4$

54. The actual length of a room is 6 m. The scale factor of a model is 1:15. What is the length of the room in the model? (Lesson 4-10)

Estimating with Percents

TN ✓ 0706.2.7 Write number sentences to solve contextual problems involving ratio and percent. *Also* **GLE 0706.1.2, GLE 0706.2.4,** ✓ **0706.2.8, SPI 0706.2.7**

A basketball at Hoops Haven costs $14.99. Cam's Sports is offering the same basketball at 20% off the regular price of $19.99. To find out which store is offering the better deal on the basketball, you can use estimation.

The table shows common percents and their fraction equivalents. You can estimate the percent of a number by substituting a fraction that is close to a given percent.

Percent	10%	20%	25%	$33\frac{1}{3}$%	50%	$66\frac{2}{3}$%
Fraction	$\frac{1}{10}$	$\frac{1}{5}$	$\frac{1}{4}$	$\frac{1}{3}$	$\frac{1}{2}$	$\frac{2}{3}$

EXAMPLE 1   Using Fractions to Estimate Percents

Use a fraction to estimate 48% of 79.

Remember!

Compatible numbers are close to the numbers in a problem and help you use mental math to find a solution.

48% of $79 \approx \frac{1}{2} \cdot 79$ *Think: 48% is about 50% and 50% is equivalent to $\frac{1}{2}$.*

$\approx \frac{1}{2} \cdot 80$ *Change 79 to a compatible number.*

≈ 40 *Multiply.*

48% of 79 is about 40.

EXAMPLE 2   *Consumer Math Application*

Cam's Sports is offering 20% off a basketball that costs $19.99. The same basketball costs $14.99 at Hoops Haven. Which store offers the better deal?

First find the discount on the basketball at Cam's Sports.

20% of $\$19.99 = \frac{1}{5} \cdot \$19.99$ *Think: 20% is equivalent to $\frac{1}{5}$.*

$\approx \frac{1}{5} \cdot \$20$ *Change $19.99 to a compatible number.*

$\approx \$4$ *Multiply.*

The discount is approximately $4. Since $20 − $4 = $16, the $14.99 basketball at Hoops Haven is the better deal.

Video Lesson Tutorials Online   my.hrw.com

Another way to estimate percents is to find 1% or 10% of a number. You can do this by moving the decimal point in the number.

1% of 45: 45.0   10% of 45: 45.0

= 0.45   = 4.5

To find 1% of a number,   *To find 10% of a number,*
move the decimal point   *move the decimal point*
two places to the left.   *one place to the left.*

EXAMPLE **3** **Estimating with Simple Percents**

Use 1% or 10% to estimate the percent of each number.

A **3% of 59**

59 is about 60, so find 3% of 60.

1% of 60 = 60.0 = 0.60
3% of 60 = 3 · 0.60 = 1.8   *3% equals 3 · 1%.*

3% of 59 is about 1.8.

B **18% of 45**

18% is about 20%, so find 20% of 45.

10% of 45 = 45.0 = 4.5
20% of 45 = 2 · 4.5 = 9.0   *20% equals 2 · 10%.*

18% of 45 is about 9.

EXAMPLE **4** *Consumer Math Application*

Eric and Selena spent $25.85 for their meals at a restaurant. About how much money should they leave for a 15% tip?

Since $25.85 is about $26, find 15% of $26.

15% = 10% + 5%   *Think: 15% is 10% plus 5%.*
10% of $26 = $2.60
5% of $26 = $2.60 ÷ 2 = $1.30   *5% is $\frac{1}{2}$ of 10%, so divide $2.60 by 2.*
$2.60 + $1.30 = $3.90   *Add the 10% and 5% estimates.*

Eric and Selena should leave about $3.90 for a 15% tip.

Think and Discuss

1. Describe two ways to estimate 51% of 88.

2. Explain why you might divide by 7 or multiply by $\frac{1}{7}$ to estimate a 15% tip.

3. Give an example of a situation in which an estimate of a percent is sufficient and a situation in which an exact percent is necessary.

Learn It Online
Homework Help Online **go.hrw.com**,
keyword MS10 6-3 Go
Exercises 1–28, 37, 39

GUIDED PRACTICE

See Example **1** Use a fraction to estimate the percent of each number.

1. 30% of 86   **2.** 52% of 83   **3.** 10% of 48   **4.** 27% of 63

See Example **2** **5.** Darden has $35. He finds a backpack on sale for 35% off the regular price of $43.99. Does Darden have enough to buy the backpack? Explain.

See Example **3** Use 1% or 10% to estimate the percent of each number.

6. 5% of 82   **7.** 39% of 19   **8.** 21% of 68   **9.** 7% of 109

See Example **4** **10.** Mrs. Coronado spent $23 on a manicure. About how much money should she leave for a 15% tip?

INDEPENDENT PRACTICE

See Example **1** Use a fraction to estimate the percent of each number.

11. 8% of 261   **12.** 34% of 93   **13.** 53% of 142   **14.** 23% of 98

15. 51% of 432   **16.** 18% of 42   **17.** 11% of 132   **18.** 54% of 39

See Example **2** **19.** **Consumer Math** A pair of shoes at The Value Store costs $20. Fancy Feet has the same shoes on sale for 25% off the regular price of $23.99. Which store offers the better price on the shoes?

See Example **3** Use 1% or 10% to estimate the percent of each number.

20. 41% of 16   **21.** 8% of 310   **22.** 83% of 70   **23.** 2% of 634

24. 58% of 81   **25.** 24% of 49   **26.** 11% of 99   **27.** 63% of 39

See Example **4** **28.** Marc's lunch cost $8.92. He wants to leave a 15% tip for the service. About how much should his tip be?

PRACTICE AND PROBLEM SOLVING

Extra Practice
See page EP16.

Estimate.

29. 31% of 180   **30.** 18% of 150   **31.** 3% of 96   **32.** 2% of 198

33. 78% of 90   **34.** 52% of 234   **35.** 19% of 75   **36.** 4% of 311

37. The new package of Marti's Snacks contains 20% more snack mix than the old package. There were 22 ounces of snack mix in the old package. About how many ounces are in the new package?

38. Frameworks charges $60.85 for framing. Including the 7% sales tax, about how much will it cost to have a painting framed?

39. **Multi-Step** Camden's lunch cost $11.67, and he left a $2.00 tip. About how much more than 15% of the bill did Camden leave for the tip?

40. Sports Last season, Ali had a hit 19.3% of the times he came to bat. If Ali batted 82 times last season, about how many hits did he have?

41. Business The graph shows the results of a survey about the Internet. The number of people interviewed was 391.

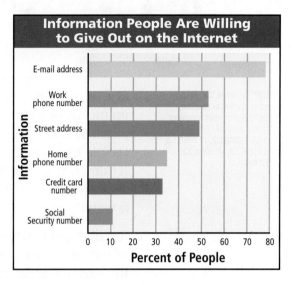

a. Estimate the number of people willing to give out their e-mail address.

b. Estimate the number of people not willing to give out their credit card number.

42. Estimation Sandi earns $43,000 per year. This year, she plans to spend about 27% of her income on rent.

a. About how much does Sandi plan to spend on rent this year?

b. About how much does she plan to spend on rent each month?

43. Write a Problem Use information from the graph in Exercise 41 to write a problem that can be solved by using estimation of a percent.

44. Write About It Explain why it might be important to know whether your estimate of a percent is too high or too low. Give an example.

45. Challenge Use the graph from Exercise 41 to estimate how many more people will give out their work phone number than their Social Security number. Show your work using two different methods.

Test Prep and Spiral Review

46. Multiple Choice About 65% of the people answering a survey said that they have read a "blog," or Web log, online. Sixty-six people were surveyed. Which is the best estimate of the number of people surveyed who have read a blog?

(A) 30   (B) 35   (C) 45   (D) 50

47. Short Response Ryan's dinner bill is $35.00. He wants to leave a 15% tip. Explain how to use mental math to determine how much he should leave as a tip.

Find each product. (Lesson 3-3)

48. $0.8 \cdot 96$ **49.** $30 \cdot 0.04$ **50.** $1.6 \cdot 900$ **51.** $0.005 \cdot 75$

52. Brandi's room was painted in a color that is a blend of 3 parts red paint and 2 parts white paint. How many quarts of white paint does Brandi need to mix with 6 quarts of red paint to match the paint in her room? (Lesson 4-4)

Percent of a Number

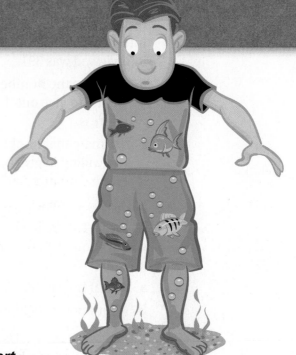

TN ✓ 0706.2.7 Write number sentences to solve contextual problems involving ratio and percent.
Also GLE 0706.1.2, ✓ 0706.1.3, GLE 0706.2.4, ✓ 0706.2.8, SPI 0706.2.7

The human body is made up mostly of water. In fact, about 67% of a person's total (100%) body weight is water. If Cameron weighs 90 pounds, about how much of his weight is water?

Recall that a percent is a part of 100. Since you want to know the part of Cameron's body that is water, you can set up and solve a proportion to find the answer.

Interactivities Online ▶   Part → $\dfrac{67}{100} = \dfrac{n}{90}$ ← Part
Whole →   ← Whole

EXAMPLE **Using Proportions to Find Percents of Numbers**

Find the percent of each number.

A **67% of 90**

$\dfrac{67}{100} = \dfrac{n}{90}$	*Write a proportion.*
$67 \cdot 90 = 100 \cdot n$	*Set the cross products equal.*
$6{,}030 = 100n$	*Multiply.*
$\dfrac{6{,}030}{100} = \dfrac{100n}{100}$	*Divide each side by 100 to isolate the variable.*
$60.3 = n$	

67% of 90 is 60.3.

B **145% of 210**

$\dfrac{145}{100} = \dfrac{n}{210}$	*Write a proportion.*
$145 \cdot 210 = 100 \cdot n$	*Set the cross products equal.*
$30{,}450 = 100n$	*Multiply.*
$\dfrac{30{,}450}{100} = \dfrac{100n}{100}$	*Divide each side by 100 to isolate the variable.*
$304.5 = n$	

145% of 210 is 304.5.

> **Helpful Hint**
>
> When solving a problem with a percent greater than 100%, the *part* will be greater than the *whole*.

Video **Lesson Tutorials Online** my.hrw.com

In addition to using proportions, you can find the percent of a number by using decimal equivalents.

EXAMPLE 2   **Using Decimal Equivalents to Find Percents of Numbers**

Find the percent of each number. Check whether your answer is reasonable.

A **8% of 50**

   $8\% \text{ of } 50 = 0.08 \cdot 50$ *Write the percent as a decimal.*
   $\qquad\qquad\ = 4$ *Multiply.*

   Model
   Since 10% of 50 is 5,
   a reasonable answer
   for 8% of 50 is 4.

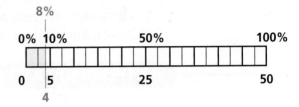

B **0.5% of 36**

   $0.5\% \text{ of } 36 = 0.005 \cdot 36$ *Write the percent as a decimal.*
   $\qquad\qquad\quad\ = 0.18$ *Multiply.*

   Estimate
   1% of 40 = 0.4, so 0.5% of 40 is half of 0.4, or 0.2. Thus 0.18 is a reasonable answer.

EXAMPLE 3   *Geography Application*

Earth's total land area is about 57,308,738 mi². The land area of Asia is about 30% of this total. What is the approximate land area of Asia to the nearest square mile?

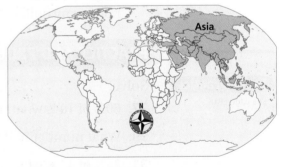

Find 30% of 57,308,738.
0.30 · 57,308,738   *Write the percent as a decimal.*
= 17,192,621.4   *Multiply.*

The land area of Asia is about 17,192,621 mi².

Think and Discuss

1. **Explain** how to set up a proportion to find 150% of a number.

2. **Describe** a situation in which you might need to find a percent of a number.

6-4 Exercises

Learn It Online

Homework Help Online go.hrw.com, keyword MS10 6-4 **Go**
Exercises 1–26, 31, 33, 37, 39, 41, 43, 45

GUIDED PRACTICE

See Example 1 — Find the percent of each number.
1. 30% of 80 **2.** 38% of 400 **3.** 200% of 10 **4.** 180% of 90

See Example 2 — Find the percent of each number. Check whether your answer is reasonable.
5. 16% of 50 **6.** 7% of 200 **7.** 47% of 900 **8.** 40% of 75

See Example 3 — **9.** Of the 450 students at Miller Middle School, 38% ride the bus to school. How many students ride the bus to school?

INDEPENDENT PRACTICE

See Example 1 — Find the percent of each number.
10. 80% of 35 **11.** 16% of 70 **12.** 150% of 80 **13.** 118% of 3,000
14. 5% of 58 **15.** 1% of 4 **16.** 103% of 50 **17.** 225% of 8

See Example 2 — Find the percent of each number. Check whether your answer is reasonable.
18. 9% of 40 **19.** 20% of 65 **20.** 36% of 50 **21.** 2.9% of 60
22. 5% of 12 **23.** 220% of 18 **24.** 0.2% of 160 **25.** 155% of 8

See Example 3 — **26.** In 2004, there were 19,396 bulldogs registered by the American Kennel Club. Approximately 86% of this number were registered in 2003. About how many bulldogs were registered in 2003?

PRACTICE AND PROBLEM SOLVING

Extra Practice
See page EP16.

Solve.
27. 60% of 10 is what number? **28.** What number is 25% of 160?
29. What number is 15% of 30? **30.** 10% of 84 is what number?
31. 25% of 47 is what number? **32.** What number is 59% of 20?
33. What number is 125% of 4,100? **34.** 150% of 150 is what number?

Find the percent of each number. If necessary, round to the nearest tenth.
35. 160% of 50 **36.** 350% of 20 **37.** 480% of 25 **38.** 115% of 200
39. 18% of 3.4 **40.** 0.9% of 43 **41.** 98% of 4.3 **42.** 1.22% of 56

43. Consumer Math Fun Tees is offering a 30% discount on all merchandise. Find the amount of discount on a T-shirt that was originally priced at $15.99.

44. Multi-Step Shoe Style is discounting everything in the store by 25%. What is the sale price of a pair of flip-flops that was originally priced at $10?

350 *Chapter 6 Percents*

45. Nutrition The United States Department of Agriculture recommends that women should eat 25 g of fiber each day. A granola bar provides 9% of that amount. How many grams of fiber does it contain?

46. Physical Science The percent of pure gold in 14-karat gold is about 58.3%. A 14-karat gold ring weighs 5.6 grams. About how many grams of pure gold are in the ring?

47. Earth Science The apparent magnitude of the star Mimosa is 1.25. Spica, another star, has an apparent magnitude that is 78.4% of Mimosa's. What is Spica's apparent magnitude?

48. Multi-Step Trahn purchased a pair of slacks for $39.95 and a jacket for $64.00. The sales tax rate on his purchases was 5.5%. Find the total cost of Trahn's purchases, including sales tax.

49. The graph shows the results of a student survey about computers. Use the graph to predict how many students in your class have a computer at home.

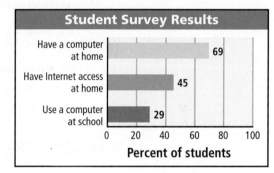

50. What's the Error? A student used the proportion $\frac{n}{100} = \frac{5}{26}$ to find 5% of 26. What did the student do wrong?

51. Write About It Describe two ways to find 18% of 40.

52. Challenge François's starting pay was $6.25 per hour. During his annual review, he received a 5% raise. Find François's pay raise to the nearest cent and the amount he will earn with his raise. Then find 105% of $6.25. What can you conclude?

Test Prep and Spiral Review

53. Multiple Choice Of the 875 students enrolled at Sycamore Valley Middle School, 48% are boys. How many of the students are boys?

Ⓐ 250   Ⓑ 310   Ⓒ 420   Ⓓ 440

54. Gridded Response A children's multivitamin has 80% of the recommended daily allowance of zinc. The recommended daily allowance is 15 mg. How many milligrams of zinc does the vitamin provide?

Find each unit rate. (Lesson 4-2)

55. Monica buys 3 pounds of peaches for $5.25. What is the cost per pound?

56. Kevin types 295 words in 5 minutes. At what rate does Kevin type?

Write each decimal as a percent. (Lesson 6-2)

57. 0.0125   **58.** 0.26   **59.** 0.389   **60.** 0.099   **61.** 0.407

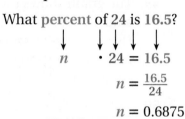

6-5 Solving Percent Problems

TN ✓ **0706.2.7** Write number sentences to solve contextual problems involving ratio and percent.
Also **GLE 0706.2.4**, ✓ **0706.2.8**, **SPI 0706.2.7**, **GLE 0706.3.8**

Sloths may seem lazy, but their extremely slow movement helps them seem almost invisible to predators. Sloths sleep an average of 16.5 hours per day. To find out what percent of a 24-hour day 16.5 hours is, you can use a proportion or an equation.

Proportion method

$$Part \rightarrow \frac{n}{100} = \frac{16.5}{24} \leftarrow Part$$
$$Whole \rightarrow \qquad\qquad \leftarrow Whole$$

$$n \cdot 24 = 100 \cdot 16.5$$
$$24n = 1{,}650$$
$$n = 68.75$$

Equation method

What **percent** of 24 is 16.5?
$$\downarrow \qquad \downarrow \quad \downarrow \quad \downarrow$$
$$n \qquad \cdot 24 = 16.5$$
$$n = \frac{16.5}{24}$$
$$n = 0.6875$$

Sloths spend about **69%** of the day sleeping!

EXAMPLE **1** **Using Proportions to Solve Problems with Percents**

Solve.

A **What percent of 90 is 45?**

$$\frac{n}{100} = \frac{45}{90} \qquad \textit{Write a proportion.}$$
$$n \cdot 90 = 100 \cdot 45 \qquad \textit{Set the cross products equal.}$$
$$90n = 4{,}500 \qquad \textit{Multiply.}$$
$$\frac{90n}{90} = \frac{4{,}500}{90} \qquad \textit{Divide each side by 90 to isolate the variable.}$$
$$n = 50$$

50% of 90 is 45.

B **12 is 8% of what number?**

$$\frac{8}{100} = \frac{12}{n} \qquad \textit{Write a proportion.}$$
$$8 \cdot n = 100 \cdot 12 \qquad \textit{Set the cross products equal.}$$
$$8n = 1{,}200 \qquad \textit{Multiply.}$$
$$\frac{8n}{8} = \frac{1{,}200}{8} \qquad \textit{Divide each side by 8 to isolate the variable.}$$
$$n = 150$$

12 is 8% of 150.

Video **Lesson Tutorials Online** my.hrw.com

EXAMPLE **2** **Using Equations to Solve Problems with Percents**

Solve.

A **What percent of 75 is 105?**

$n \cdot 75 = 105$ *Write an equation.*

$\dfrac{n \cdot 75}{75} = \dfrac{105}{75}$ *Divide each side by 75 to isolate the variable.*

$n = 1.4$

$n = 140\%$ *Write the decimal as a percent.*

140% of 75 is 105.

B **48 is 20% of what number?**

$48 = 20\% \cdot n$ *Write an equation.*

$48 = 0.2 \cdot n$ *Write 20% as a decimal.*

$\dfrac{48}{0.2} = \dfrac{0.2 \cdot n}{0.2}$ *Divide each side by 0.2 to isolate the variable.*

$240 = n$

48 is 20% of 240.

EXAMPLE **3** **Finding Sales Tax**

Helpful Hint

The *sales tax rate* is the percent used to calculate sales tax.

Ravi bought a T-shirt with a retail sales price of $12 and paid $0.99 sales tax. What is the sales tax rate where Ravi bought the T-shirt?

Restate the question: What percent of $12 is $0.99?

$\dfrac{n}{100} = \dfrac{0.99}{12}$ *Write a proportion.*

$n \cdot 12 = 100 \cdot 0.99$ *Set the cross products equal.*

$12n = 99$ *Multiply.*

$\dfrac{12n}{12} = \dfrac{99}{12}$ *Divide each side by 12.*

$n = 8.25$

8.25% of $12 is $0.99. The sales tax rate where Ravi bought the T-shirt is 8.25%.

Think and Discuss

1. Describe two methods for solving percent problems.

2. Explain whether you prefer to use the proportion method or the equation method when solving percent problems.

3. Tell what the first step is in solving a sales tax problem.

Learn It Online
Homework Help Online **go.hrw.com**,
keyword MS10 6-5   Go
Exercises 1–22, 23, 25, 27, 29,
31, 35, 39

GUIDED PRACTICE

Solve.

See Example 1
1. What percent of 100 is 25?

2. What percent of 5 is 4?

3. 6 is 10% of what number?

4. 8 is 20% of what number?

See Example 2
5. What percent of 50 is 9?

6. What percent of 30 is 27?

7. 7 is 14% of what number?

8. 30 is 15% of what number?

See Example 3
9. The sales tax on a $120 skateboard at Surf 'n' Skate is $9.60. What is the sales tax rate?

INDEPENDENT PRACTICE

Solve.

See Example 1
10. What percent of 60 is 40?

11. What percent of 48 is 16?

12. What percent of 45 is 9?

13. What percent of 6 is 18?

14. 56 is 140% of what number?

15. 45 is 20% of what number?

See Example 2
16. What percent of 80 is 10?

17. What percent of 12.4 is 12.4?

18. 18 is 15% of what number?

19. 9 is 30% of what number?

20. 210% of what number is 147?

21. 8.8 is 40% of what number?

See Example 3
22. A 12-pack of cinnamon-scented pencils sells for $3.00 at a school booster club sale. What is the sales tax rate if the total cost of the pencils is $3.21?

PRACTICE AND PROBLEM SOLVING

Extra Practice
See page EP17.

Solve. Round to the nearest tenth, if necessary.

23. 5 is what percent of 9?

24. What is 45% of 39?

25. 55 is 80% of what number?

26. 12 is what percent of 19?

27. What is 155% of 50?

28. 5.8 is 0.9% of what number?

29. 36% of what number is 57?

30. What percent of 64 is 40?

31. Multi-Step The advertised cost of admission to a water park in a nearby city is $25 per student. A student paid $30 for admission and received $3.75 in change. What is the sales tax rate in that city?

32. Consumer Math The table shows the cost of sunscreen purchased in Beach City and Desert City with and without sales tax. Which city has a greater sales tax rate? Give the sales tax rate for each city.

	Cost	Cost + Tax
Beach City	$10	$10.83
Desert City	$5	$5.42

Music

The viola family is made up of the cello, violin, and viola. Of the three instruments, the cello is the largest.

33. **Critical Thinking** What number is always used when you set up a proportion to solve a percent problem? Explain.

34. **Health** The circle graph shows the approximate distribution of blood types among people in the United States.

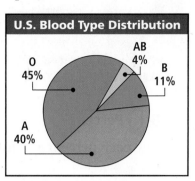

U.S. Blood Type Distribution

O 45%

AB 4%

B 11%

A 40%

   a. In a survey, 126 people had type O blood. Predict how many people were surveyed.

   b. How many of the people surveyed had type AB blood?

 35. **Music** Beethoven wrote 9 trios for the piano, violin, and cello. These trios make up 20% of the chamber music pieces Beethoven wrote. How many pieces of chamber music did he write?

36. **History** The length of Abraham Lincoln's first inaugural speech was 3,635 words. The length of his second inaugural speech was about 19.3% of the length of his first speech. About how long was Lincoln's second speech?

37. **What's the Question?** The first lap of an auto race is 2,500 m. This is 10% of the total race distance. The answer is 10. What is the question?

38. **Write About It** If 35 is 110% of a number, is the number greater than or less than 35? Explain.

39. **Challenge** Kayleen has been offered two jobs. The first job offers an annual salary of $32,000. The second job offers an annual salary of $10,000 plus 8% commission on all of her sales. How much money per month would Kayleen need to make in sales to earn enough commission to make more money at the second job?

Test Prep and Spiral Review

40. **Multiple Choice** Thirty children from an after-school club went to the matinee. This is 20% of the children in the club. How many children are in the club?

    Ⓐ 6   Ⓑ 67   Ⓒ 150   Ⓓ 600

41. **Gridded Response** Jason saves 30% of his monthly paycheck for college. He earned $250 last month. How many dollars did he save for college?

Divide. (Lesson 3-4)

42. $-3.92 \div 7$ 43. $10.68 \div 3$ 44. $23.2 \div 0.2$ 45. $19.52 \div 6.1$

Find the percent of each number. If necessary, round to the nearest hundredth. (Lesson 6-4)

46. 45% of 26   47. 22% of 30   48. 15% of 17   49. 68% of 98

Quiz for Lessons 6-1 Through 6-5

 **6-1** Percents

Write each percent as a fraction in simplest form.

1. 9%   **2.** 43%   **3.** 5%   **4.** 18%

Write each percent as a decimal.

5. 22%   **6.** 90%   **7.** 29%   **8.** 5%

 **6-2** Fractions, Decimals, and Percents

Write each decimal as a percent.

9. 0.85   **10.** 0.026   **11.** 0.1111   **12.** 0.56

Write each fraction as a percent. Round to the nearest tenth of a percent, if necessary.

13. $\frac{14}{81}$ **14.** $\frac{25}{52}$ **15.** $\frac{55}{78}$ **16.** $\frac{13}{32}$

 **6-3** Estimating with Percents

Estimate.

17. 49% of 46   **18.** 9% of 25   **19.** 36% of 150   **20.** 5% of 60

21. 18% of 80   **22.** 26% of 115   **23.** 91% of 300   **24.** 42% of 197

25. Carlton spent $21.85 on lunch for himself and a friend. About how much should he leave for a 15% tip?

 **6-4** Percent of a Number

Find the percent of each number.

26. 25% of 84   **27.** 52% of 300   **28.** 0.5% of 40   **29.** 160% of 450

30. 41% of 122   **31.** 178% of 35   **32.** 29% of 88   **33.** 80% of 176

34. Students get a 15% discount off the original prices at the Everything Fluorescent store during its back-to-school sale. Find the amount of discount on fluorescent notebooks originally priced at $7.99.

 **6-5** Solving Percent Problems

Solve. Round to the nearest tenth, if necessary.

35. 14 is 44% of what number?   **36.** 22 is what percent of 900?

37. 99 is what percent of 396?   **38.** 75 is 24% of what number?

39. The sales tax on a $105 digital camera is $7.15. What is the sales tax rate?

Focus on Problem Solving

Plan

Make a Plan

• **Estimate or find an exact answer**

Sometimes an estimate is sufficient when you are solving a problem. Other times you need to find an exact answer. Before you try to solve a problem, you should decide whether an estimate will be sufficient. Usually if a problem includes the word *about*, then you can estimate the answer.

Read each problem. Decide whether you need an exact answer or whether you can solve the problem with an estimate. Explain how you know.

1. Barry has $21.50 left from his allowance. He wants to buy a book for $5.85 and a CD for $14.99. Assuming these prices include tax, does Barry have enough money left to buy both the book and the CD?

2. Last weekend Valerie practiced playing the drums for 3 hours. This is 40% of the total time she spent practicing last week. How much time did Valerie spend practicing last week?

3. Amber is shopping for a winter coat. She finds one that costs $157. The coat is on sale and is discounted 25% today only. About how much money will Amber save if she buys the coat today?

4. Marcus is planning a budget. He plans to spend less than 35% of his allowance each week on entertainment. Last week Marcus spent $7.42 on entertainment. If Marcus gets $20.00 each week, did he stay within his budget?

5. An upright piano is on sale for 20% off the original price. The original price is $9,840. What is the sale price?

6. The Mapleton Middle School band has 41 students. Six of the students in the band play percussion instruments. Do more than 15% of the students play percussion instruments?

Percent of Change

TN ✓ 0706.2.8 Apply ratios, rates, proportions and percents (such as discounts, interest, taxes, tips, distance/rate/time, and percent increase or decrease). *Also* **GLE 0706.2.4**, ✓ **0706.2.7**, **SPI 0706.2.7**

According to the U.S. Consumer Product Safety Commission, emergency rooms treated more than 50,000 skateboarding injuries in 2000. This was a 67% decrease from the peak of 150,000 skateboarding injuries in 1977.

Vocabulary

percent of change

percent of increase

percent of decrease

A percent can be used to describe an amount of change. The **percent of change** is the amount, stated as a percent, that a number increases or decreases. If the amount goes up, it is a **percent of increase**. If the amount goes down, it is a **percent of decrease**.

You can find the percent of change by using the following formula.

$$\text{percent of change} = \frac{\text{amount of change}}{\text{original amount}}$$

EXAMPLE 1 Finding Percent of Change

Find each percent of change. Round answers to the nearest tenth of a percent, if necessary.

Helpful Hint

When a number is decreased, subtract the new amount from the original amount to find the amount of change. When a number is increased, subtract the original amount from the new amount.

A 27 is decreased to 20.

$27 - 20 = 7$ *Find the amount of change.*

$\text{percent of change} = \frac{7}{27}$ *Substitute values into formula.*

≈ 0.259259 *Divide.*

$\approx 25.9\%$ *Write as a percent. Round.*

The percent of decrease is about 25.9%.

B 32 is increased to 67.

$67 - 32 = 35$ *Find the amount of change.*

$\text{percent of change} = \frac{35}{32}$ *Substitute values into formula.*

$= 1.09375$ *Divide.*

$\approx 109.4\%$ *Write as a percent. Round.*

The percent of increase is about 109.4%.

Video **Lesson Tutorials Online** my.hrw.com

EXAMPLE 2 **Using Percent of Change**

The regular price of an MP3 player at TechSource is $79.99. This week the MP3 player is on sale for 25% off. What is the sale price?

Step 1 Find the amount of the discount.

$$\frac{25}{100} = \frac{d}{\$79.99}$$ *Write a proportion.*

$$25 \cdot \$79.99 = 100d$$ *Set the cross products equal.*

$$\frac{1999.75}{100} = \frac{100d}{100}$$ *Multiply. Then divide each side by 100.*

$$\$20.00 \approx d$$

The amount of the discount d is $20.00.

Step 2 Find the sale price.

regular price	−	amount of discount	=	sale price
$79.99	−	$20.00	=	$59.99

The sale price is $59.99.

EXAMPLE 3 *Business Application*

Reading Math

The amount of increase is also called the *markup*.

Winter Wonders buys snow globes from a manufacturer for $9.20 each and sells them at a 95% increase in price. What is the retail price of the snow globes?

Step 1 Find the amount n of increase.

$95\% \cdot 9.20 = n$ *Think: 95% of $9.20 is what number?*

$0.95 \cdot 9.20 = n$ *Write the percent as a decimal.*

$8.74 = n$

Step 2 Find the retail price.

wholesale price	+	amount of increase	=	retail price
$9.20	+	$8.74	=	$17.94

The retail price of the snow globes is $17.94 each.

Think and Discuss

1. **Explain** what is meant by a 100% decrease.

2. **Give an example** in which the amount of increase or markup is greater than the original amount. What do you know about the percent of increase?

Learn It Online
Homework Help Online **go.hrw.com**,
keyword MS10 6-6 Go
Exercises 1–12, 13, 15, 17, 19,
21, 23, 25

GUIDED PRACTICE

See Example **Find each percent of change. Round answers to the nearest tenth of a percent, if necessary.**

1. 25 is decreased to 18.

2. 36 is increased to 84.

3. 62 is decreased to 52.

4. 28 is increased to 96.

See Example 2 **5.** The regular price of a sweater is $42.99. It is on sale for 20% off. Find the sale price.

See Example 3 **6. Business** The retail price of a pair of shoes is a 98% increase from its wholesale price. The wholesale price of the shoes is $12.50. What is the retail price?

INDEPENDENT PRACTICE

See Example **Find each percent of change. Round answers to the nearest tenth of a percent, if necessary.**

7. 72 is decreased to 45.

8. 55 is increased to 90.

9. 180 is decreased to 140.

10. 230 is increased to 250.

See Example 2 **11.** A skateboard that sells for $65 is on sale for 15% off. Find the sale price.

See Example 3 **12. Business** A jeweler buys a ring from an artisan for $85. He sells the ring in his store at a 135% increase in price. What is the retail price of the ring?

PRACTICE AND PROBLEM SOLVING

Extra Practice
See page EP17.

Find each percent of change, amount of increase, or amount of decrease. Round answers to the nearest tenth, if necessary.

13. $8.80 is increased to $17.60.

14. 6.2 is decreased to 5.9.

15. 39.2 is increased to 56.3.

16. $325 is decreased to $100.

17. 75 is decreased by 40%.

18. 28 is increased by 150%.

19. A water tank holds 45 gallons of water. A new water tank can hold 25% more water. What is the capacity of the new water tank?

20. Business Marla makes stretchy beaded purses and sells them to Bangles 'n' Beads for $7 each. Bangles 'n' Beads makes a profit of 28% on each purse. Find the retail price of the purses.

21. Multi-Step A store is discounting all of its stock. The original price of a pair of sunglasses was $44.95. The sale price is $26.97. At this discount, what was the original price of a bathing suit that has a sale price of $28.95?

22. Critical Thinking Explain why a change in price from $20 to $10 is a 50% decrease, but a change in price from $10 to $20 is a 100% markup.

23. The information at right shows the expenses for the Kramer family for one year.

    a. The Kramers spent $2,905 on auto expenses. What was their income for the year?

    b. How much money was spent on household expenses?

    c. The Kramers pay $14,400 per year on their mortgage. What percent of their household expenses is this? Round your answer to the nearest tenth.

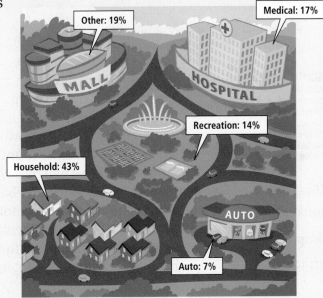

Other: 19%

Medical: 17%

Recreation: 14%

Household: 43%

Auto: 7%

24. United States health expenses were $428.7 billion in 1985 and $991.4 billion in 1995. What was the percent of increase in health expenses during this ten-year period? Round your answer to the nearest tenth of a percent.

25. In 1990, the total amount of energy consumed for transportation in the United States was 22,540 trillion British thermal units (Btu). From 1950 to 1990, there was a 165% increase in energy consumed for transportation. About how many Btu of energy were consumed in 1950?

26. ⭐ **Challenge** In 1960, 21.5% of U.S. households did not have a telephone. This statistic decreased by 75.8% between 1960 and 1990. In 1990, what percent of U.S. households had a telephone?

Test Prep and Spiral Review

27. **Multiple Choice** Find the percent of change if the price of a 20-ounce bottle of water increases from $0.85 to $1.25. Round to the nearest tenth.

    Ⓐ 47.1%   Ⓑ 40.0%   Ⓒ 32.0%   Ⓓ 1.7%

28. **Extended Response** A store buys jeans from the manufacturer for $30 each and sells them at a 50% markup in price. At the end of the season, the store puts the jeans on sale for 50% off. Is the sale price $30? Explain your reasoning.

Write each mixed number as an improper fraction. (Lesson 2-9)

29. $3\frac{2}{9}$ **30.** $6\frac{2}{3}$ **31.** $7\frac{1}{4}$ **32.** $3\frac{2}{5}$ **33.** $24\frac{1}{3}$

Convert each measure. (Lesson 4-5)

34. 34 mi to feet   **35.** 52 oz to pounds   **36.** 164 lb to tons

Simple Interest

TN ✓ **0706.2.8** Apply ratios, rates, proportions and percents (such as discounts, interest, taxes, tips, distance/rate/time, and percent increase or decrease). *Also* **GLE 0706.1.2, GLE 0706.2.4,** ✓ **0706.2.7**

Vocabulary

interest

simple interest

principal

When you keep money in a savings account, your money earns *interest*. **Interest** is an amount of money that is charged for borrowing or using money, or an amount of money that is earned by saving money. For example, the bank pays you interest to use your money to conduct its business. Likewise, when you borrow money from the bank, the bank collects interest that is paid annually on its loan to you.

One type of interest, called **simple interest**, is money paid only on the *principal*. The **principal** is the amount of money deposited or borrowed. To solve problems involving simple interest that is paid annually, you can use the following formula.

Interest ⟶ Rate of interest per year (as a decimal) ⟶

$$I = P \cdot r \cdot t$$

Principal ⟶   ⟵ Time in years that the money earns interest

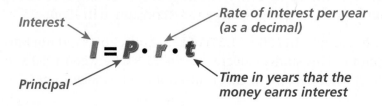

EXAMPLE **1** **Using the Simple Interest Formula**

Find each missing value.

A $I = $ ▮, $P = \$225$, $r = 3\%$, $t = 2$ years

$I = P \cdot r \cdot t$

$I = 225 \cdot 0.03 \cdot 2$ *Substitute. Use 0.03 for 3%.*

$I = 13.5$ *Multiply.*

The simple interest is $13.50.

B $I = \$300$, $P = \$1,000$, $r = $ ▮, $t = 5$ years

$I = P \cdot r \cdot t$

$300 = 1,000 \cdot r \cdot 5$ *Substitute.*

$300 = 5,000r$ *Multiply.*

$\dfrac{300}{5,000} = \dfrac{5,000r}{5,000}$ *Divide each side by 5,000.*

$0.06 = r$

The interest rate is 6%.

Video Lesson Tutorials Online   my.hrw.com

EXAMPLE 2

PROBLEM SOLVING APPLICATION

Olivia deposits $7,000 in an account that earns 7% simple interest paid annually. About how long will it take for her account balance to reach $8,000?

1 **Understand the Problem**

Rewrite the question as a statement:

• Find the number of years it will take for the balance to reach $8,000.

List the **important information:**

• The principal is $7,000.

• The interest rate is 7%.

• Her account balance will be $8,000.

2 **Make a Plan**

Olivia's account balance A includes the principal plus the interest: $A = P + I$. Once you solve for I, you can use $I = P \cdot r \cdot t$ to find the time.

3 **Solve**

$$A = P + I$$
$$8{,}000 = 7{,}000 + I \qquad \text{Substitute.}$$
$$\underline{-7{,}000 \quad -7{,}000} \qquad \text{Subtract 7,000 from each side.}$$
$$1{,}000 = \qquad\quad I$$

$$I = P \cdot r \cdot t$$
$$1{,}000 = 7{,}000 \cdot 0.07 \cdot t \qquad \text{Substitute. Use 0.07 for 7\%.}$$
$$1{,}000 = 490t \qquad \text{Multiply.}$$
$$\frac{1{,}000}{490} = \frac{490t}{490} \qquad \text{Divide each side by 490.}$$
$$2.04 \approx t$$

It will take just over 2 years.

4 **Look Back**

The account earns 7% of $7,000, which is $490, per year. So after 2 years, the interest will be $980, giving a total balance of $7,980. An answer of just over 2 years to reach $8,000 makes sense.

Think and Discuss

1. Write the value of t in the annual simple interest formula for a time period of 6 months.

2. Show how to find r if $I = \$10$, $P = \$100$, and $t = 2$ years.

Learn It Online
Homework Help Online **go.hrw.com**,
keyword MS10 6-7 Go
Exercises 1–13, 15, 17, 19, 21, 23

GUIDED PRACTICE

See Example 1 **Find each missing value.**

1. $I = \blacksquare$, $P = \$300$, $r = 4\%$, $t = 2$ years

2. $I = \blacksquare$, $P = \$500$, $r = 2\%$, $t = 1$ year

3. $I = \$120$, $P = \blacksquare$, $r = 6\%$, $t = 5$ years

4. $I = \$240$, $P = \$4,000$, $r = \blacksquare$, $t = 2$ years

See Example 2 5. Scott deposits \$8,000 in an account that earns 6% simple interest paid annually. How long will it be before the total amount is \$10,000?

INDEPENDENT PRACTICE

See Example 1 **Find each missing value.**

6. $I = \blacksquare$, $P = \$600$, $r = 7\%$, $t = 2$ years

7. $I = \blacksquare$, $P = \$12,000$, $r = 3\%$, $t = 9$ years

8. $I = \$364$, $P = \$1,300$, $r = \blacksquare$, $t = 7$ years

9. $I = \$440$, $P = \blacksquare$, $r = 5\%$, $t = 4$ years

10. $I = \$455$, $P = \blacksquare$, $r = 7\%$, $t = 5$ years

11. $I = \$231$, $P = \$700$, $r = \blacksquare$, $t = 3$ years

See Example 2 12. Broderick deposits \$6,000 in an account that earns 5.5% simple interest paid annually. How long will it be before the total amount is \$9,000?

13. Teresa deposits \$4,000 in an account that earns 7% simple interest paid annually. How long will it be before the total amount is \$6,500?

PRACTICE AND PROBLEM SOLVING

Extra Practice
See page EP17.

Complete the table.

	Principal	Interest Rate	Time	Annual Simple Interest
14.	$2,455	3%	$\blacksquare$	$441.90
15.	$\blacksquare$	4.25%	3 years	$663
16.	$18,500	$\blacksquare$	42 months	$1,942.50
17.	$425.50	5%	10 years	$\blacksquare$
18.	$\blacksquare$	6%	3 years	$2,952

19. **Finance** How many years will it take for \$4,000 to double at an annual simple interest rate of 5%?

20. **Banking** After 2 years, an account earning annual simple interest held \$585.75. The original deposit was \$550. What was the interest rate?

Use the graph for Exercises 21–23.

Art

The 1907 painting *Portrait of Adele Bloch-Bauer I* by the Austrian artist Gustav Klimt recently sold for $135 million, making it among the most expensive paintings ever sold.

21. How much more interest was earned on $8,000 deposited for 6 months in a statement savings account than in a passbook savings account?

22. How much money was lost on $5,000 invested in S&P 500 stocks for one year?

23. Compare the returns on $12,000 invested in the high-yield 1-year CD and the Dow Jones industrials for one year.

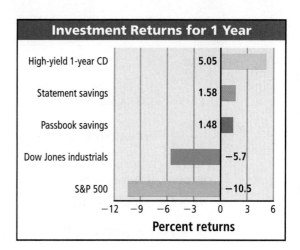

24. **Art** Alexandra can buy an artist's-work-and-storage furniture set from her art instructor. She would buy it on credit for $5,000 at an annual simple interest rate of 4% for 3 years. She can purchase a similar furniture set online for $5,500 plus a $295 shipping and handling fee. Including interest, which set costs less? How much would Alexandra pay for the set?

25. Write a Problem Use the graph in Exercises 21–23 to write a problem that can be solved by using the simple interest formula.

26. **Write About It** Explain whether you would pay more annual simple interest on a loan if you used plan A or plan B.

Plan A: $1,500 for 8 years at 6%   **Plan B:** $1,500 for 6 years at 8%

27. **Challenge** The Jacksons are opening a savings account for their child's college education. In 18 years, they will need about $134,000. If the account earns 6% simple interest annually, how much money must the Jacksons invest now to cover the cost of the college education?

Test Prep and Spiral Review

28. Multiple Choice Julian deposits $4,500 in a bank account that pays 3% simple interest annually. How much interest will he earn in 5 years?

(A) $135   (B) $485   (C) $675   (D) $5,175

29. Short Response Susan deposits $3,000 in the bank at 6.5% annual simple interest. How long will it be before she has $3,500 in the bank?

30. Small book covers are $1\frac{1}{3}$ ft long. How many book covers can be made out of 40 ft of book cover material? (Lesson 3-10)

Find each percent of change. Round answers to the nearest tenth of a percent, if necessary. (Lesson 6-6)

31. 154 is increased to 200.   **32.** 95 is decreased to 75.   **33.** 88 is increased to 170.

 **Ready To Go On?**

Quiz for Lessons 6-6 Through 6-7

☑ **6-6** **Percent of Change**

Find each percent of change. Round answers to the nearest tenth of a percent, if necessary.

1. 37 is decreased to 17.

2. 121 is increased to 321.

3. 89 is decreased to 84.

4. 45 is increased to 60.

5. 61 is decreased to 33.

6. 86 is increased to 95.

When customers purchase a contract for cell phone service, providers often include the phone at a discounted price. Prices for cell phones from On-the-Go Cellular are listed in the table. Use the table for problems 7–9.

On-the-Go Cellular Phones	
Regular Price	Price with 2-year Contract
$49	Free
$99	$39.60
$149	$47.68
$189	$52.92
$229	$57.25

7. Find the percent discount on the $99 phone with a 2-year contract.

8. Find the percent discount on the $149 phone with a 2-year contract.

9. What happens to the percent discount that On-the-Go Cellular gives on its phones as the price of the phone increases?

10. Since Frank is increasing the distance of his daily runs, he needs to carry more water. His current water bottle holds 16 ounces. Frank's new bottle holds 25% more water than his current bottle. What is the capacity of Frank's new water bottle?

☑ **6-7** **Simple Interest**

Find each missing value.

11. $I = $ ▨, $P = \$750$, $r = 4\%$, $t = 3$ years

12. $I = \$120$, $P = $ ▨, $r = 3\%$, $t = 5$ years

13. $I = \$180$, $P = \$1500$, $r = $ ▨, $t = 2$ years

14. $I = \$220$, $P = \$680$, $r = 8\%$, $t = $ ▨

15. Leslie wants to deposit $10,000 in an account that earns 5% simple interest paid annually so that she will have $12,000 when she starts college. How long will it take her account to reach $12,000?

16. Harrison deposits $345 in a savings account that earns 4.2% simple interest paid annually. How long will it take for the total amount in the account to reach $410?

Corn Nebraska's nickname is the Cornhusker State, which seems appropriate because corn is Nebraska's top crop in terms of acres and dollar value. In 2007, nearly 1.5 billion bushels of corn were harvested in the state.

NEBRASKA

For 1–2, use the table.

1. The recommended daily allowance (RDA) of carbohydrates for a teenage girl is 130 grams.

   a. What percent of the RDA of carbohydrates does a teenage girl consume by eating an ear of corn? Round to the nearest percent.

   b. Write the percent as a decimal and as a fraction.

Nutrition Facts	
Serving Size: One medium ear of corn	
Amount per serving	
Calories	78
Carbohydrates	17 g
Protein	3 g
Fat	1.1 g
Dietary Fiber	2.5 g

2. A student's dinner included a medium ear of corn. The corn provided 12% of the Calories in the meal. How many Calories did the student consume at dinner?

3. In 2007, 9.4 million acres of corn were planted in Nebraska. In the United States, 93.6 million acres of corn were planted. Estimate the percent of all corn in the United States that was planted in Nebraska. Explain how you made the estimate.

4. The 9.4 million acres of corn planted in Nebraska in 2007 was an 11% increase from the amount of corn planted in the state in 2006.

   a. How many acres of corn were planted in Nebraska in 2006?

   b. Suppose 10 million acres of corn were planted in Nebraska in 2008. Find the percent increase from 2007 to 2008. Round to the nearest percent.

Real-World Connections

Game Time

Lighten Up

On a digital clock, up to seven light bulbs make up each digit on the display. You can label each light bulb as shown below.

If each number were lit up for the same amount of time, you could find out which light bulb is lit the greatest percent of the time. You could also find out which light bulb is lit the least percent of the time.

For each number 0–9, list the letters of the light bulbs that are used when that number is showing. The first few numbers have been done for you.

Once you have determined which bulbs are lit for each number, count how many times each bulb is lit. What percent of the time is each bulb lit? What does this tell you about which bulb will burn out first?

Percent Bingo

Use the bingo cards with numbers and percents provided online. The caller has a collection of percent problems. The caller reads a problem. Then the players solve the problem, and the solution is a number or a percent. If players have the solution on their card, they mark it off. Normal bingo rules apply. You can win with a horizontal, vertical, or diagonal row.

A complete copy of the rules and game pieces is available online.

Learn It Online
Game Time Extra **go.hrw.com**,
keyword MS10 Games Go

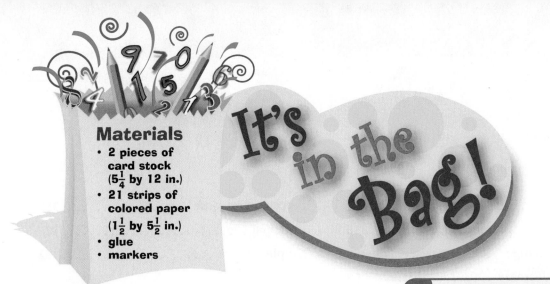

Materials
- 2 pieces of card stock ($5\frac{1}{4}$ by 12 in.)
- 21 strips of colored paper ($1\frac{1}{2}$ by $5\frac{1}{2}$ in.)
- glue
- markers

PROJECT **Percent Strips**

This colorful booklet holds questions and answers about percents.

Directions

1 Fold one piece of card stock in half. Cut along the crease to make two rectangles that are each $5\frac{1}{4}$ inches by 6 inches. You will use these later as covers for your booklet.

2 On the other piece of card stock, make accordion folds about $\frac{3}{4}$-inch wide. When you are done, there should be 16 panels. These panels will be the pages of your booklet. **Figure A**

3 Fold up the accordion strip. Glue the covers to the top and bottom panels of the strip. **Figure B**

4 Open the front cover. Glue a strip of colored paper to the top and bottom of the first page. **Figure C**

5 Turn the page. Glue a strip of colored paper to the back of the first page between the other two strips. **Figure D**

6 Glue strips to the other pages in the same way.

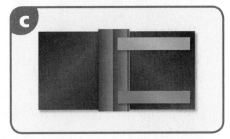

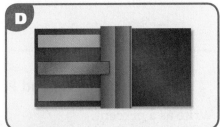

Putting the Math into Action

Write a question about percents on the front of each strip. Write the answer on the back. Trade books with another student and put your knowledge of percents to the test.

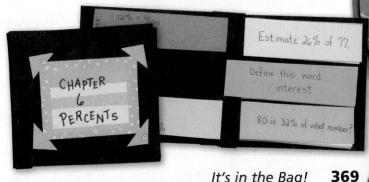

CHAPTER

6

Study Guide: Review

Study Guide: Review

Vocabulary

interest 362
percent 336
percent of change 358
percent of decrease 358

percent of increase 358
principal 362
simple interest 362

Complete the sentences below with vocabulary words from the list above.

1. __?__ is an amount that is collected or paid for the use of money. The equation $I = P \cdot r \cdot t$ is used for calculating __?__ paid annually. The letter P represents the __?__ and the letter r represents the annual rate.

2. The ratio of an amount of increase to the original amount is the __?__.

3. The ratio of an amount of decrease to the original amount is the __?__.

4. A (n) __?__ is a ratio whose denominator is 100.

EXAMPLES

EXERCISES

6-1 Percents (pp. 336–338)

■ Write **12%** as a fraction in simplest form and as a decimal.

$$12\% = \frac{12}{100} \qquad\qquad 12\% = \frac{12}{100}$$

$$= \frac{12 \div 4}{100 \div 4} \qquad\qquad = 0.12$$

$$= \frac{3}{25}$$

Write each percent as a fraction in simplest form and as a decimal.

5. 78% **6.** 40%

7. 5% **8.** 16%

9. 65% **10.** 89%

6-2 Fractions, Decimals, and Percents (pp. 340–343)

Write as a percent.

■ $\frac{7}{8}$ ■ **0.82**

$$\frac{7}{8} = 7 \div 8 \qquad\qquad 0.82 = \frac{82}{100}$$

$$= 0.875 \qquad\qquad\quad = 82\%$$

$$= 87.5\%$$

Write as a percent. Round to the nearest tenth of a percent, if necessary.

11. $\frac{3}{5}$ **12.** $\frac{1}{6}$

13. 0.09 **14.** 0.8

15. $\frac{2}{3}$ **16.** 0.0056

17. Order $0.\overline{33}$, -2.6, $2\frac{3}{5}$, and 30% from least to greatest.

370 *Chapter 6 Percents*

6-3 **Estimating with Percents** (pp. 344–347)

■ Estimate 26% of 77.

26% of 77 $\approx \frac{1}{4} \cdot 77$ *26% is about 25% and 25% is equivalent to $\frac{1}{4}$.*

$\approx \frac{1}{4} \cdot 80$ *Change 77 to 80.*

≈ 20 *Multiply.*

26% of 77 is about 20.

Estimate.

18. 22% of 44   **19.** 74% of 120

20. 43% of 64   **21.** 31% of 97

22. 49% of 82   **23.** 6% of 53

24. Byron and Kate's dinner cost $18.23. About how much money should they leave for a 15% tip?

25. Salvador's lunch cost $9.85, and he left a $2.00 tip. About how much more than 15% of the bill did Salvador leave for the tip?

6-4 **Percent of a Number** (pp. 348–351)

■ Find the percent of the number.

125% of 610

$\frac{125}{100} = \frac{n}{610}$ *Write a proportion.*

$125 \cdot 610 = 100 \cdot n$ *Cross products*

$76{,}250 = 100n$ *Multiply.*

$\frac{76{,}250}{100} = \frac{100n}{100}$ *Divide each side by 100.*

$762.5 = n$

125% of 610 is 762.5.

Find the percent of each number.

26. 16% of 425   **27.** 48% of 50

28. 7% of 63   **29.** 96% of 125

30. 130% of 21   **31.** 72% of 75

32. Canyon Middle School has 1,247 students. About 38% of the students are in the seventh grade. About how many seventh-graders currently attend Canyon Middle School?

6-5 **Solving Percent Problems** (pp. 352–355)

■ Solve.

80 is 32% of what number?

$80 = 32\% \cdot n$ *Write an equation.*

$80 = 0.32 \cdot n$ *Write 32% as a decimal.*

$\frac{80}{0.32} = \frac{0.32 \cdot n}{0.32}$ *Divide each side by 0.32.*

$250 = n$

80 is 32% of 250.

Solve.

33. 20% of what number is 25?

34. 4 is what percent of 50?

35. 30 is 250% of what number?

36. What percent of 96 is 36?

37. 6 is 75% of what number?

38. 200 is what percent of 720?

39. The sales tax on a $25 shirt purchased at a store in Oak Park is $1.99. What is the sales tax rate in Oak Park?

40. Jaclyn paid a sales tax of $10.03 on a camera. The tax rate in her state is 8%. About how much did the camera cost?

Study Guide: Review

6-6 **Percent of Change** (pp. 358–361)

Find each percent of change. Round answers to the nearest tenth of a percent, if necessary.

■ **25 is decreased to 16.**

$25 - 16 = 9$ *Find the amount of change.*

$$\text{percent of change} = \frac{9}{25}$$

$$= 0.36$$

$$= 36\%$$

The percent of decrease is 36%.

■ **13.5 is increased to 27.**

$27 - 13.5 = 13.5$ *Find the amount of change.*

$$\text{percent of change} = \frac{13.5}{13.5}$$

$$= 1$$

$$= 100\%$$

The percent of increase is 100%.

Find each percent of change. Round answers to the nearest tenth of a percent, if necessary.

41. 54 is increased to 81.

42. 14 is decreased to 12.

43. 110 is increased to 143.

44. 90 is decreased to 15.2.

45. 26 is increased to 32.

46. 84 is decreased to 21.

47. The regular price of a new pair of skis is $245. This week the skis are on sale for 15% off. Find the sale price.

48. In 2006 the mean annual earnings for a person with a high school diploma was $31,071. A person with a bachelor's degree earned an average of $56,788 per year. What is the percent of increase to the nearest tenth?

6-7 **Simple Interest** (pp. 362–365)

Find each missing value.

■ $I = \blacksquare$, $P = \$545$, $r = 1.5\%$, $t = 2$ years

$I = P \cdot r \cdot t$ *Substitute.*

$I = 545 \cdot 0.015 \cdot 2$ *Multiply.*

$I = 16.35$

The simple interest is $16.35.

■ $I = \$825$, $P = \blacksquare$, $r = 6\%$, $t = 11$ years

$I = P \cdot r \cdot t$ *Substitute.*

$825 = P \cdot 0.06 \cdot 11$ *Multiply.*

$825 = P \cdot 0.66$

$\dfrac{825}{0.66} = \dfrac{P \cdot 0.66}{0.66}$ *Divide each side by 0.66.*

$1,250 = P$

The principal is $1,250.

Find each missing value.

49. $I = \blacksquare$, $P = \$1,000$, $r = 3\%$, $t = 6$ months

50. $I = \$452.16$, $P = \$1,256$, $r = 12\%$, $t = \blacksquare$

51. $I = \blacksquare$, $P = \$675$, $r = 4.5\%$, $t = 8$ years

52. $I = \$555.75$, $P = \$950$, $r = \blacksquare$, $t = 15$ years

53. $I = \$172.50$, $P = \blacksquare$, $r = 5\%$, $t = 18$ months

54. Craig deposits $1,000 in a savings account that earns 5% simple interest paid annually. How long will it take for the total amount in his account to reach $1,350?

55. Zach deposits $755 in an account that earns 4.2% simple interest paid annually. How long will it take for the total amount in the account to reach $1,050?

Chapter Test

Write each percent as a fraction in simplest form and as a decimal.

1. 95%   **2.** 37.5%   **3.** 4%   **4.** 0.01%

Write as a percent. Round to the nearest tenth of a percent, if necessary.

5. 0.75   **6.** 0.12   **7.** 0.8   **8.** 0.0039

9. $\frac{3}{10}$ **10.** $\frac{9}{20}$ **11.** $\frac{5}{16}$ **12.** $\frac{7}{21}$

Estimate.

13. 48% of 8   **14.** 3% of 119   **15.** 26% of 32   **16.** 76% of 280

17. The Pattersons spent $47.89 for a meal at a restaurant. About how much should they leave for a 15% tip?

Find the percent of each number.

18. 90% of 200   **19.** 35% of 210   **20.** 16% of 85

21. 250% of 30   **22.** 38% of 11   **23.** 5% of 145

Solve.

24. 36 is what percent of 150?   **25.** What percent of 145 is 29?

26. 51 is what percent of 340?   **27.** 36 is 40% of what number?

28. 70 is 14% of what number?   **29.** 25 is 20% of what number?

30. Hampton Middle School is expecting 376 seventh-graders next year. This is 40% of the expected school enrollment. How many students are expected to enroll in the school next year?

Find each percent of change. Round answers to the nearest tenth, if necessary.

31. 30 is increased to 45.   **32.** 115 is decreased to 46.

33. 116 is increased to 145.   **34.** 129 is decreased to 32.

35. A community theater sold 8,500 tickets to performances during its first year. By its tenth year, ticket sales had increased by 34%. How many tickets did the theater sell during its tenth year?

Find each missing value.

36. $I = $ ▆, $P = \$500$, $r = 5\%$, $t = 1$ year   **37.** $I = \$702$, $P = \$1,200$, $r = 3.9\%$, $t = $ ▆

38. $I = \$468$, $P = \$900$, $r = $ ▆, $t = 8$ years   **39.** $I = \$37.50$, $P = $ ▆, $r = 10\%$, $t = 6$ months

40. Kate invested $3,500 at a 5% simple interest rate. How many years will it take for the original amount to double?

Cumulative Assessment, Chapters 1–6

Multiple Choice

1. Violet is creating a quilt using similar triangles. The pattern she is using for two of the triangles is shown below. Which ratio corresponds to the triangles?

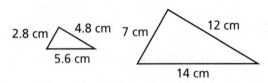

2.8 cm 4.8 cm 7 cm 12 cm
5.6 cm 14 cm

A $\frac{4.2}{1}$ **C** $\frac{1}{2}$

B $\frac{2.5}{1}$ **D** $\frac{1}{4}$

2. Which of the following is <u>not</u> equivalent to 12%?

F 0.012   **H** 0.12

G $\frac{12}{100}$ **J** $\frac{3}{25}$

3. The table below shows the amount of money Mika will receive for each item she sells. What type of relationship is described in the table?

Item Sold	Commission ($)
0	0.00
1	1.25
2	2.50
3	3.75
4	5.00

A direct variation

B exponential

C inverse variation

D non-proportional

4. Which point is <u>not</u> on the graph of $y = 2x - 3$?

F $(0, -3)$ **H** $(-2, -7)$

G $(2, 1)$ **J** $(-1, -2)$

5. A baseball coach has a rule that for every time a player strikes out, that player has to do 12 push ups. If Cal strikes out 27 times, how many push ups will he be required to do?

A 15 push ups   **C** 152 push ups

B 39 push ups   **D** 324 push ups

6. A basketball goal that usually sells for $825 goes on sale for $650. What is the percent of decrease, to the nearest whole percent?

F 12%   **H** 27%

G 21%   **J** 79%

7. In Oregon, about 40 of the state's nearly 1,000 public water systems add fluoride to their water. What percent best represents this situation?

A 0.4%   **C** 40%

B 4%   **D** 400%

8. The number of whooping cranes wintering in Texas reached an all time high in 2004 at 213. The lowest number ever recorded was 15 whooping cranes in 1941. What is the percent of increase of whooping cranes wintering in Texas from 1941 to 2004?

F 7%   **H** 198%

G 91%   **J** 1,320%

9. What is the value of $8\frac{2}{5} - 2\frac{3}{4}$?

A $5\frac{9}{20}$ **C** $6\frac{1}{9}$

B $5\frac{13}{20}$ **D** $6\frac{7}{20}$

10. Which point would make the relation <u>not</u> a function?

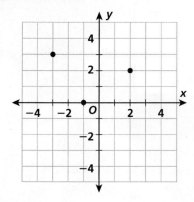

F $(-3, 0)$ **H** $(3, 3)$

G $(1, 2)$ **J** $(-2, 0)$

 HOT TIP! Make sure that your answer makes sense before marking it as your response. Reread the question and determine whether your answer is reasonable.

11. Sylas finished a 100-meter freestyle swim in 80.35 seconds. The winner of the race finished in 79.22 seconds. How many seconds faster was the winning time than Sylas's time?

A 0.13 second

B 1 second

C 1.13 seconds

D 13 seconds

12. What is the decimal equivalent of 65%?

F 0.065

G 0.65

H 6.5

J 65

Process Standards Practice

Short Response

S1. The graph shows the number of boys and the number of girls who participated in a talent show.

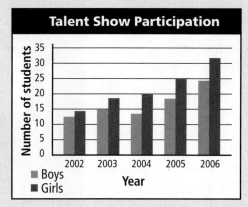

a. What is the approximate percent of increase of girls participating in the talent show from 2002 to 2005?

b. What percent of students participating in the talent show in 2006 were boys? Explain how you found your answer.

S2. A homemaker association has 134 members. If 31 of these members are experts in canning vegetables, are more or less than 25% of the members canning experts? Explain how you know.

Extended Response

E1. Riley and Louie each have $5,000 to invest. They both invest at a 2.5% simple interest rate.

a. Riley keeps her money invested for 7 years. How much interest will she earn? How much will her investment be worth?

b. What is the value of Louie's investment if he invests for 3 years, then removes and spends $1,000, and then invests what is remaining for 4 more years at a rate of 4%?

c. Using the information from parts **a** and **b**, who has more money in 7 years, Louie or Riley? Explain your reasoning.

Collecting, Displaying, and Analyzing Data

Chapter Focus
- Make and interpret graphs, such as histograms and circle graphs.
- Make estimates relating to a population based on a sample.

Why Learn This?

Biologists can take random samples of a wildlife population, such as sea lions, to make estimates about population growth or infectious diseases that might affect the group.

Learn It Online
Chapter Project Online **go.hrw.com**,
keyword MS10 Ch 7 **Go**

☑ Vocabulary

Choose the best term from the list to complete each sentence.

circle

frequency

interval

line segment

scale

1. A part of a line consisting of two endpoints and all points between those endpoints is called a(n) __?__.

2. A(n) __?__ is the amount of space between the marked values on the __?__ of a graph.

3. The number of times an item occurs is called its __?__.

Complete these exercises to review skills you will need for this chapter.

☑ Order Whole Numbers

Order the numbers from least to greatest.

4. 45, 23, 65, 15, 42, 18

5. 103, 105, 102, 118, 87, 104

6. 56, 65, 24, 19, 76, 33, 82

7. 8, 3, 6, 2, 5, 9, 3, 4, 2

☑ Whole Number Operations

Add or subtract.

8. $18 + 26$

9. $23 + 17$

10. $75 + 37$

11. $98 + 64$

12. $133 - 35$

13. $54 - 29$

14. $200 - 88$

15. $1,055 - 899$

☑ Locate Points on a Number Line

Copy the number line. Then graph each number.

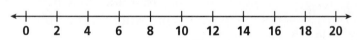

16. 15

17. 2

18. 18

19. 7

☑ Read a Table

Use the data in the table for Exercises 20 and 21.

20. Which animal is the fastest?

21. Which animal is faster, a rabbit or a zebra?

Top Speeds of Some Animals	
Animal	**Speed (mi/h)**
Elephant	25
Lion	50
Rabbit	35
Zebra	40

Study Guide: Preview

Where You've Been

Previously, you

- used an appropriate representation for displaying data.

- identified mean, median, mode, and range of a set of data.

- solved problems by collecting, organizing, and displaying data.

In This Chapter

You will study

- selecting an appropriate representation for displaying relationships among data.

- choosing among mean, median, mode, or range to describe a set of data.

- making inferences and convincing arguments based on analysis of data.

Where You're Going

You can use the skills learned in this chapter

- to analyze trends and make business and marketing decisions.

- to strengthen a persuasive argument by presenting data and trends in visual displays.

Key Vocabulary/Vocabulario

bar graph	gráfica de barras
circle graph	gráfica circular
frequency table	tabla de frecuencia
line graph	gráfica lineal
line plot	diagrama de acumulación
mean	media
median	mediana
mode	moda
scatter plot	diagrama de dispersión
stem-and-leaf plot	diagrama de tallo y hojas

Vocabulary Connections

To become familiar with some of the vocabulary terms in the chapter, consider the following. You may refer to the chapter, the glossary, or a dictionary if you like.

1. The word *median* comes from the Latin word *medius*, meaning "middle." What is the **median** value in a set of data? What other words come from this Latin root?

2. *Scatter* can mean "to spread out" or "to occur at random." What might the data points on a **scatter plot** look like?

3. *Frequency* is a measure of how often an event occurs or the number of like objects that are in a group. What do you think a **frequency table** might show?

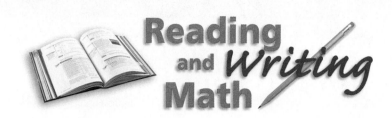 

CHAPTER
7

TN English/Language Arts
GLE 0701.6.1 Comprehend and summarize the main ideas and supporting details of informational texts.

Reading Strategy: Read a Lesson for Understanding

Before you begin reading a lesson, find out what its main focus, or objective, is. Each lesson is centered on a specific objective, which is located at the top of the first page of the lesson. Reading with the objective in mind will help guide you through the lesson material. You can use the following tips to help you follow the math as you read.

> Identify the objective of the lesson. Then skim through the lesson to get a sense of where the objective is covered.

"How do I find the percent of a number?"

> As you read through the lesson, write down any questions, problems, or trouble spots you may have.

Find the percent of each number.

8% of 50

8% of 50 = 0.08 · 50   *Write the percent as a decimal.*

= 4   *Multiply.*

> Work through each example, as the examples help demonstrate the objectives.

Think and Discuss

1. Explain how to set up a proportion to find 150% of a number.

> Check your understanding of the lesson by answering the Think and Discuss questions.

Try This

Use Lesson 6-1 in your textbook to answer each question.

1. What is the objective of the lesson?

2. What new terms are defined in the lesson?

3. What skills are being taught in Example 3 of the lesson?

4. Which parts of the lesson can you use to answer Think and Discuss question 1?

Collecting, Displaying, and Analyzing Data **379**

7-1 Frequency Tables, Stem-and-Leaf Plots, and Line Plots

TN SPI 0706.5.1 Interpret and employ various graphs and charts to represent data.
Also GLE 0706.5.1, ✓ 0706.5.1, ✓ 0706.5.2, SPI 0706.5.2

Use Additional Topic A-6 with this lesson.

Vocabulary

frequency table

cumulative frequency

stem-and-leaf plot

line plot

> **Remember!**
>
> The frequency of a data value is the number of times it occurs.

IMAX® theaters, with their huge screens and powerful sound systems, make viewers feel as if they are in the middle of the action.

To see how common it is for an IMAX movie to attract such a large number of viewers, you could use a *frequency table*. A **frequency table** is a way to organize data values into categories or groups. By including a **cumulative frequency** column in your table, you can keep a running total of the number of data items.

EXAMPLE 1

Organizing and Interpreting Data in a Frequency Table

The list shows box office receipts in millions of dollars for 20 IMAX films. Make a cumulative frequency table of the data. How many films earned under $40 million?

76, 51, 41, 38, 18, 17, 16, 15, 13, 13, 12, 12, 10, 10, 6, 5, 5, 4, 4, 2

Step 1: Choose a scale that includes all of the data values. Then separate the scale into equal intervals.

Step 2: Find the number of data values in each interval. Write these numbers in the "Frequency" column.

Step 3: Find the cumulative frequency for each row by adding all the frequency values that are above or in that row.

IMAX Films		
Receipts ($ million)	Frequency	Cumulative Frequency
0–19	16	16
20–39	1	17
40–59	2	19
60–79	1	20

The number of films that earned under $40 million is the cumulative frequency of the first two rows: 17.

A **stem-and-leaf plot** uses the digits of each number to organize and display a set of data. Each *leaf* on the plot represents the right-hand digit in a data value, and each *stem* represents the remaining left-hand digits. The key shows the values of the data on the plot.

Stems	Leaves
2	4 7 9
3	0 6

Key: 2|7 means 27

EXAMPLE 2

Organizing and Interpreting Data in a Stem-and-Leaf Plot

The table shows the number of minutes students spent doing their Spanish homework. Make a stem-and-leaf plot of the data. Then find the number of students who studied longer than 45 minutes.

Minutes Spent Doing Homework					
38	48	45	32	29	48
32	45	36	22	21	64
35	45	47	26	43	29

Step 1: Order the data from least to greatest. Since the data values range from 21 to 64, use tens digits for the stems and ones digits for the leaves.

Step 2: List the stems from least to greatest on the plot.

Step 3: List the leaves for each stem from least to greatest.

Step 4: Add a key and title the graph.

Minutes Spent Doing Homework

The stems are the tens digits.

Stems	Leaves
2	1 2 6 9 9
3	2 2 5 6 8
4	3 5 5 5 7 8 8
5	
6	4

Key: 3|2 means 32

The stem 5 has no leaves, so there are no data values in the 50's.

The leaves are the ones digits.

The entries in the second row represent the data values 32, 32, 35, 36, and 38.

One student studied for **47** minutes, 2 students studied for **48** minutes, and 1 student studied for **64** minutes.

A total of 4 students studied longer than 45 minutes.

Similar to a stem-and-leaf plot, a **line plot** can be used to show how many times each data value occurs. Line plots use a number line and **X**'s to show frequency. By looking at a line plot, you can quickly see the *distribution*, or spread, of the data.

EXAMPLE 3

Organizing and Interpreting Data in a Line Plot

Make a line plot of the data. How many miles per day did Trey run most often?

Number of Miles Trey Ran Each Day During Training								
5	6	5	5	3	5	4	4	6
8	6	3	4	3	2	16	12	12

Step 1: The data values range from 2 to 16. Draw a number line that includes this range.

Step 2: Put an **X** above the number on the number line that corresponds to the number of miles Trey ran each day.

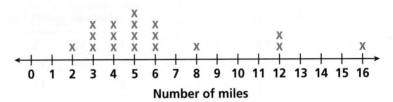

The greatest number of **X**'s appear above the number 5. This means that Trey ran 5 miles most often.

Think and Discuss

1. Tell which you would use to determine the number of data values in a set: a cumulative frequency table or a stem-and-leaf plot. Explain.

7-1 Exercises

Learn It Online
Homework Help Online **go.hrw.com,**
keyword   MS10 7-1   **Go**
Exercises 1–6, 7, 9, 11

GUIDED PRACTICE

Number of Electoral Votes for Select States (2004)											
CA	55	GA	15	IN	11	MI	17	NY	31	PA	21
NJ	15	IL	21	KY	8	NC	15	OH	20	TX	34

See Example 1
1. Make a cumulative frequency table of the data. How many of the states had fewer than 20 electoral votes in 2004?

See Example 2
2. Make a stem-and-leaf plot of the data. How many of the states had more than 30 electoral votes in 2004?

See Example 3
3. Make a line plot of the data. For the states shown, what was the most common number of electoral votes in 2004?

The table shows the ages of the first 18 U.S. presidents when they took office.

President	Age	President	Age	President	Age
Washington	57	Jackson	61	Fillmore	50
Adams	61	Van Buren	54	Pierce	48
Jefferson	57	Harrison	68	Buchanan	65
Madison	57	Tyler	51	Lincoln	52
Monroe	58	Polk	49	Johnson	56
Adams	57	Taylor	64	Grant	46

See Example ①
4. Make a cumulative frequency table of the data. How many of the presidents were under the age of 65 when they took office?

See Example ②
5. Make a stem-and-leaf plot of the data. How many of the presidents were in their 40s when they took office?

See Example ③
6. Make a line plot of the data. What was the most common age at which the presidents took office?

PRACTICE AND PROBLEM SOLVING

Extra Practice
See page EP18.

Use the stem-and-leaf plot for Exercises 7–9.

7. What is the least data value?
   What is the greatest data value?

8. Which data value occurs most often?

9. **Critical Thinking** Which of the following is most likely the source of the data in the stem-and-leaf plot?

   (A) Shoe sizes of 12 middle school students

   (B) Number of hours 12 adults exercised in one month

   (C) Number of boxes of cereal per household at one time

   (D) Monthly temperatures in degrees Fahrenheit in Chicago, Illinois

Stems	Leaves
0	4 6 6 9
1	2 5 8 8 8
2	0 3
3	1

Key: 1|2 means 12

10. **Earth Science** The table shows the masses of the largest meteorites found on Earth.

Largest Meteorites			
Meteorite	**Mass (kg)**	**Meteorite**	**Mass (kg)**
Armanty	23.5	Chupaderos	14
Bacubirito	22	Hoba	60
Campo del Cielo	15	Mbosi	16
Cape York (Agpalilik)	20	Mundrabilla	12
Cape York (Ahnighito)	31	Willamette	15

a. Use the data in the table to make a line plot.

b. How many of the meteorites have a mass of 15 kilograms or greater?

The map shows the number of critically endangered animal species in each country in South America. A species is critically endangered when it faces a very high risk of extinction in the wild in the near future.

Golden Lion Tamarin

11. Which country has the fewest critically endangered species? Which has the most?

12. Make a cumulative frequency table of the data. How many countries have fewer than 20 critically endangered species?

13. Make a stem-and-leaf plot of the data.

14. **Write About It** Explain how changing the size of the intervals you used in Exercise 12 affects your cumulative frequency table.

15. ⭐ **Challenge** In a recent year, the number of endangered animal species in the United States was 190. Show how to represent this number on a stem-and-leaf plot.

Numbers of Critically Endangered Animal Species in South America

Guyana 7
Venezuela 30
Suriname 7
French Guiana 8
Colombia 74
Ecuador 74
Peru 35
Bolivia 9
Brazil 60
Paraguay 5
Chile 15
Uruguay 6
Argentina 11

Source: International Union for Conservation of Nature and Natural Resources

Test Prep and Spiral Review

Use the data for Exercises 16 and 17.

16. **Multiple Choice** How many stems would a stem-and-leaf plot of the data in the table have?

    (A) 1
    (B) 2
    (C) 3
    (D) 4

20	30	9	25	28
8	11	12	7	18
33	26	10	9	2

17. **Extended Response** Make a stem-and-leaf plot and a line plot of the data in the table. Which data display best shows the distribution of data? Explain.

18. Maria has 18 yards of fabric. A pillowcase takes $1\frac{1}{5}$ yards. How many pillowcases can Maria make with the fabric? (Lesson 3-10)

Find each unit rate. Round to the nearest hundredth if necessary. (Lesson 4-2)

19. 12 hr for $102
20. $2,289 in 7 mo
21. 48 points in 3 games

Mean, Median, Mode, and Range

TN SPI 0706.5.3 Calculate and interpret the mean, median, upper-quartile, lower-quartile, and interquartile range of a set of data.
Also **GLE 0706.5.1**, ✓ **0706.5.2**

To crack secret messages in code, you can list the number of times each symbol of the code appears in the message. The symbol that appears the most often represents the *mode*, which likely corresponds to the letter *e*.

The mode, along with the *mean* and the *median*, is a measure of *central tendency* used to represent the "middle" of a data set.

• The **mean** is the sum of the data values divided by the number of data items.

• The **median** is the middle value of an odd number of data items arranged in order. For an even number of data items, the median is the mean of the two middle values.

• The **mode** is the value or values that occur most often. When all the data values occur the same number of times, there is no mode.

The **range** of a set of data is the difference between the greatest and least values.

Vocabulary

mean

median

mode

range

outlier

EXAMPLE 1 · Finding the Mean, Median, Mode, and Range of a Data Set

Interactivities Online ▶

Find the mean, median, mode, and range of the data set.

$$2, 1, 8, 0, 2, 4, 3, 4$$

mean:

$2 + 1 + 8 + 0 + 2 + 4 + 3 + 4 = 24$	*Add the values.*
$24 \div 8 = 3$	*Divide the sum by the number of items.*
The mean is 3.	

Helpful Hint

The mean is sometimes called the *average*.

median:

0, 1, 2, 2, 3, 4, 4, 8	*Arrange the values in order.*
$\frac{2 + 3}{2} = 2.5$	*There are two middle values, so find the mean of these values.*
The median is 2.5.	

mode:

0, 1, 2, 2, 3, 4, 4, 8	*The values 2 and 4 occur twice.*
The modes are 2 and 4.	

range: $8 - 0 = 8$ *Subtract the least value from*
The range is 8.   *the greatest value.*

Often one measure of central tendency is more appropriate for describing a set of data than another measure is. Think about what each measure tells you about the data. Then choose the measure that best answers the question being asked.

EXAMPLE 2   **Choosing the Best Measure to Describe a Set of Data**

The line plot shows the number of hours 15 people exercised in one week. Which measure of central tendency best describes these data? Justify your answer.

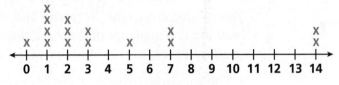

Number of hours

mean:

$$\frac{0+1+1+1+1+2+2+2+3+3+5+7+7+14+14}{15} = \frac{63}{15} = 4.2$$

The mean is 4.2.

Most of the people exercised fewer than 4 hours, so the mean does not describe the data set best.

median:

0, 1, 1, 1, 1, 2, 2, 2, 3, 3, 5, 7, 7, 14, 14

The median is 2.

The median best describes the data set because a majority of the data is clustered around the data value 2.

mode:

The greatest number of **X**'s occur above the number 1 on the line plot.

The mode is 1.

The mode represents only 4 of the 15 people. The mode does not describe the entire data set.

In the data set in Example 2, the value 14 is much greater than the other values in the set. An extreme value such as this is called an **outlier**. Outliers can greatly affect the mean of a data set.

Measure	Most Useful When
mean	the data are spread fairly evenly
median	the data set has an outlier
mode	the data involve a subject in which many data points of one value are important, such as election results

EXAMPLE 3 Exploring the Effects of Outliers on Measures of Central Tendency

The table shows the number of art pieces created by students in a glass-blowing workshop. Identify the outlier in the data set, and determine how the outlier affects the mean, median, and mode of the data. Then tell which measure of central tendency best describes the data with and without the outlier.

Name	Number of Pieces
Suzanne	5
Glen	1
Charissa	3
Eileen	4
Hermann	14
Tom	2

The outlier is 14.

Without the Outlier

mean:

$$\frac{5 + 1 + 3 + 4 + 2}{5} = 3$$

The mean is 3.

With the Outlier

mean:

$$\frac{5 + 1 + 3 + 4 + 14 + 2}{6} \approx 4.8$$

The mean is about 4.8.

The outlier increases the mean of the data by about 1.8.

median:

1, 2, 3, 4, 5

The median is 3.

median:

1, 2, 3, 4, 5, 14

$$\frac{3 + 4}{2} = 3.5$$

The median is 3.5.

The outlier increases the median of the data by 0.5.

mode:

There is no mode.

mode:

There is no mode.

The outlier does not change the mode of the data.

The median best describes the data with the outlier. The mean and median best describe the data without the outlier.

Caution!

Since all the data values occur the same number of times, the set has no mode.

Think and Discuss

1. Describe a situation in which the mean would best describe a data set.

2. Tell which measure of central tendency must be a data value.

3. Explain how an outlier affects the mean, median, and mode of a data set.

Learn It Online
Homework Help Online **go.hrw.com,**
keyword MS10 7-2 Go
Exercises 1–11, 13, 15

GUIDED PRACTICE

See Example 1 Find the mean, median, mode, and range of each data set.

1. 5, 30, 35, 20, 5, 25, 20

2. 44, 68, 48, 61, 59, 48, 63, 49

See Example 2 3. The line plot shows cooking temperatures required by different recipes. Which measure of central tendency best describes the data? Justify your answer.

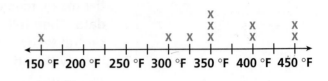

See Example 3 4. The table shows the number of glasses of water consumed in one day. Identify the outlier in the data set. Then determine how the outlier affects the mean, median, and mode of the data. Then tell which measure of central tendency best describes the data with and without the outlier.

Water Consumption							
Name	Randy	Lori	Anita	Jana	Sonya	Victor	Mark	Jorge
Glasses	4	12	3	1	4	7	5	4

INDEPENDENT PRACTICE

See Example 1 Find the mean, median, mode, and range of each data set.

5. 92, 88, 65, 68, 76, 90, 84, 88, 93, 89

6. 23, 43, 5, 3, 4, 14, 24, 15, 15, 13

7. 2.0, 4.4, 6.2, 3.2, 4.4, 6.2, 3.7

8. 13.1, 7.5, 3.9, 4.8, 17.1, 14.6, 8.3, 3.9

See Example 2 9. The line plot shows the number of letters in the spellings of the 12 months. Which measure of central tendency best describes the data set? Justify your answer.

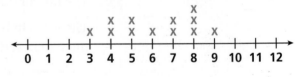

See Example 3 Identify the outlier in each data set. Then determine how the outlier affects the mean, median, and mode of the data. Then tell which measure of central tendency best describes the data with and without the outlier.

10. 13, 18, 20, 5, 15, 20, 13, 20

11. 45, 48, 63, 85, 151, 47, 88, 44, 68

PRACTICE AND PROBLEM SOLVING

Extra Practice
See page EP18.

12. **Health** Based on the data from three annual checkups, Jon's mean height is 62 in. At the first two checkups Jon's height was 58 in. and 61 in. What was his height at the third checkup?

Sports

The Leadville Trail 100 Mountain Bicycle Race is a 100-mile mountain-bike race held in Leadville, Colorado. Bikers climb over 12,000 ft throughout the Sawatch Range. In 2007, David Wiens won his fifth straight race.

13. Find the mean, median, and mode of the data displayed in the line plot. Then determine how the outlier affects the mean.

```
                              x
              x    x         x
      x   x x  x x  x x x               x
    +--+--+--+--+--+--+--+--+--+--+--+--+
    0  2  4  6  8  10 12 14 16 18 20 22
```

14. Critical Thinking The values in a data set are 95, 93, 91, 95, 100, 99, and 92. What value can be added to the set so that the mean, median, and mode remain the same?

15. Sports The ages of the participants in a mountain bike race are 14, 23, 20, 24, 26, 17, 21, 31, 27, 25, 14, and 28. Make a stem-and-leaf plot of the data and find the mean, median, and mode. Which measure of central tendency best represents the ages of the participants? Explain.

16. Estimation The table shows the monthly rainfall in inches for six months. Estimate the mean, median, and range of the data.

Month	Rainfall (in.)
Jan	4.33 ⑥
Feb	1.62 ③
Mar	2.17 ④
Apr	0.56 ①
May	3.35 ⑤
Jun	1.14 ②

17. What's the Question? The values in a data set are 10, 7, 9, 5, 13, 10, 7, 14, 8, and 11. What is the question about central tendency that gives the answer 9.5 for the data set?

18. Write About It Which measure of central tendency is most often affected by including an outlier? Explain.

0.56, 1.14, 1.62, 2.17

19. Challenge Pick a measure of central tendency that describes each situation. Explain your choice.

a. the number of siblings in a family   **b.** the number of days in a month

Test Prep and Spiral Review

20. Multiple Choice What is the mean of the winning scores shown in the table?

Masters Tournament Winning Scores					
Year	2001	2002	2003	2004	2005
Score	272	276	281	279	276

Ⓐ 276   Ⓒ 282.1

Ⓑ 276.8   Ⓓ 285

21. Multiple Choice In which data set are the mean, median, and mode all the same number?

Ⓕ 6, 2, 5, 4, 3, 4, 1   Ⓗ 2, 3, 7, 3, 8, 3, 2

Ⓖ 4, 2, 2, 1, 3, 2, 3   Ⓙ 4, 3, 4, 3, 4, 6, 4

22. Brett deposits $4,000 in an account that earns 4.5% simple interest. How long will it be before the total amount is $4,800? (Lesson 6-7)

23. Make a stem-and-leaf plot of the following data: 48, 60, 57, 62, 43, 62, 45, and 51. (Lesson 7-1)

Bar Graphs and Histograms

TN SPI 0706.5.1 Interpret and employ various graphs and charts to represent data.
Also GLE 0706.5.1, GLE 0706.5.4, ✓ 0706.5.2, SPI 0706.5.2

Vocabulary
bar graph

double-bar graph

histogram

Hundreds of different languages are spoken around the world. The graph shows the numbers of native speakers of four languages.

A **bar graph** can be used to display and compare data. The scale of a bar graph should include all the data values and be easily divided into equal intervals.

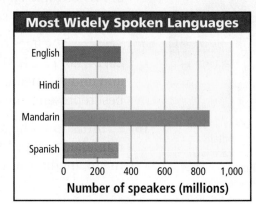

Most Widely Spoken Languages

Number of speakers (millions)

EXAMPLE 1 **Interpreting a Bar Graph**

Use the bar graph to answer each question.

A **Which language has the most native speakers?**

The bar for Mandarin is the longest, so Mandarin has the most native speakers.

B **About how many more people speak Mandarin than speak Hindi?**

About 500 million more people speak Mandarin than speak Hindi.

You can use a **double-bar graph** to compare two related sets of data.

EXAMPLE 2 **Making a Double-Bar Graph**

The table shows the life expectancies of people in three Central American countries. Make a double-bar graph of the data.

Country	Male	Female
El Salvador	67	74
Honduras	63	66
Nicaragua	65	70

Step 1: Choose a scale and interval for the vertical axis.

Step 2: Draw a pair of bars for each country's data. Use different colors to show males and females.

Step 3: Label the axes and give the graph a title.

Step 4: Make a key to show what each bar represents.

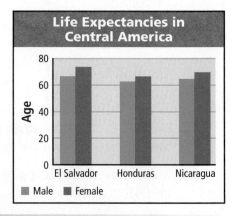

Life Expectancies in Central America

Age

El Salvador   Honduras   Nicaragua

■ Male ■ Female

Video **Lesson Tutorials Online**

A **histogram** is a bar graph that shows the frequency of data within equal intervals. There is no space between the bars in a histogram.

EXAMPLE 3 Making a Histogram

The table below shows survey results about the number of CDs students own. Make a histogram of the data.

Number of CDs									
1	///	5	卌 /	9	卌 /	13	卌 ////	17	卌 ////
2	//	6	///	10	卌 卌	14	卌 卌 /	18	卌 //
3	卌	7	卌 ///	11	卌 卌 /	15	卌 卌 /	19	//
4	卌 /	8	卌 //	12	卌 卌	16	卌 卌 /	20	卌 /

Step 1: Make a frequency table of the data. Be sure to use a scale that includes all of the data values and separate the scale into equal intervals. Use these intervals on the horizontal axis of your histogram.

Number of CDs	Frequency
1–5	22
6–10	34
11–15	52
16–20	35

Step 2: Choose an appropriate scale and interval for the vertical axis. The greatest value on the scale should be at least as great as the greatest frequency.

Step 3: Draw a bar for each interval. The height of the bar is the frequency for that interval. Bars must touch but not overlap.

Step 4: Label the axes and give the graph a title.

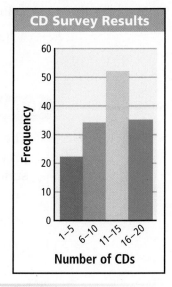

Think and Discuss

1. **Explain** how to use the frequency table in Example 3 to find the number of students surveyed.

2. **Explain** why you might use a double-bar graph instead of two separate bar graphs to display data.

3. **Describe** the similarities and differences between a bar graph and a histogram.

Learn It Online
Homework Help Online **go.hrw.com**,
keyword **MS10 7-3** **Go**
Exercises 1–10, 11, 17

GUIDED PRACTICE

See Example 1 The bar graph shows the average amount of fresh fruit consumed per person in the United States in 1997. Use the graph for Exercises 1–3.

1. Which fruit was eaten the least?

2. About how many pounds of apples were eaten per person?

3. About how many more pounds of bananas than pounds of oranges were eaten per person?

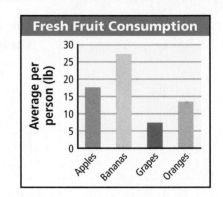

See Example 2 4. The table shows national average SAT scores for three years. Make a double-bar graph of the data.

See Example 3 5. The list below shows the ages of musicians in a local orchestra. Make a histogram of the data.

Year	Verbal	Math
1980	502	492
1990	500	501
2000	505	514

14, 35, 22, 18, 49, 38, 30, 27, 45, 19, 35, 46, 27, 21, 32, 30

INDEPENDENT PRACTICE

See Example 1 The bar graph shows the maximum precipitation in 24 hours for several states. Use the graph for Exercises 6–8.

6. Which state received the most precipitation in 24 hours?

7. About how many inches of precipitation did Virginia receive?

8. About how many more inches of precipitation did Oklahoma receive than Indiana?

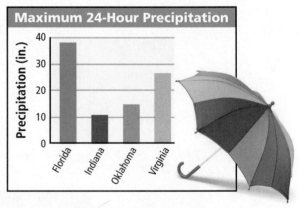

See Example 2 9. The table shows the average annual income per capita for three U.S. states. Make a double-bar graph of the data.

See Example 3 10. The list below shows the results of a typing test in words per minute. Make a histogram of the data.

State	2000	2005
Alabama	$23,521	$29,136
Indiana	$26,933	$31,276
Ohio	$27,977	$32,478

Extra Practice
See page EP18.

62, 55, 68, 47, 50, 41, 62, 39, 54, 70, 56, 47, 71, 55, 60, 42

In 1896 and 1900, William McKinley, a Republican, and William Jennings Bryan, a Democrat, ran for president of the United States. The table shows the number of electoral votes each man received in these elections.

William
Jennings Bryan

11. Use the data in the table to make a double-bar graph. Label the horizontal axis with the years.

Candidate	1896	1900
McKinley	271	292
Bryan	176	155

12. Estimation In 1896, about how many more electoral votes did McKinley get than Bryan?

13. The frequency table shows the number of years the first 42 presidents spent in office. Find the median and mode of the data.

Years in Office	Frequency
0–2	7
3–5	22
6–8	12
9–11	0
12–14	1

14. Use the frequency table to make a histogram. What percent of the presidents spent 12–14 years in office?

 William McKinley   3.35

15. ✐ **Write About It** What does your histogram show you about the number of years the presidents spent in office?

Test Prep and Spiral Review

Use the graph for Exercises 16 and 17.

16. Multiple Choice In which year did the Democrats get the fewest number of electoral votes?

Ⓐ 1988   Ⓒ 2000

Ⓑ 1996   Ⓓ 2004

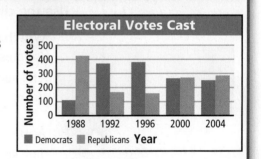

Electoral Votes Cast

■ Democrats ■ Republicans **Year**

17. Gridded Response In which year was the difference between the number of electoral votes for the Republicans and Democrats the least?

Determine whether the ratios are proportional. (Lesson 4-3)

18. $\frac{10}{24}, \frac{15}{36}$ **19.** $\frac{5}{22}, \frac{10}{27}$ **20.** $\frac{2}{20}, \frac{3}{30}$ **21.** $\frac{72}{96}, \frac{9}{12}$

Find the mean, median, mode, and range of each data set. (Lesson 7-2)

22. 42, 29, 49, 32, 19   **23.** 15, 34, 26, 15, 21, 30   **24.** 4, 3, 3, 3, 3, 4, 1

Reading and Interpreting Circle Graphs

TN SPI 0706.5.1 Interpret and employ various graphs and charts to represent data. *Also* **GLE 0706.5.1, GLE 0706.5.2,** ✓ **0706.5.2,** ✓ **0706.5.6, SPI 0706.5.2**

A **circle graph,** also called a pie chart, shows how a set of data is divided into parts. The entire circle contains 100% of the data. Each **sector,** or slice, of the circle represents one part of the entire data set.

Vocabulary

circle graph

sector

The circle graph compares the number of species in each group of echinoderms. Echinoderms are marine animals that live on the ocean floor. The name *echinoderm* means "spiny-skinned."

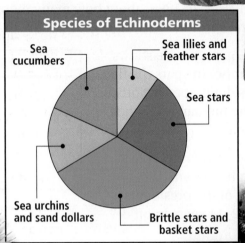

Species of Echinoderms

Sea cucumbers

Sea lilies and feather stars

Sea stars

Sea urchins and sand dollars

Brittle stars and basket stars

EXAMPLE 1 · *Life Science Application*

Use the circle graph to answer each question.

A **Which group of echinoderms includes the greatest number of species?**

The sector for brittle stars and basket stars is the largest, so this group includes the greatest number of species.

B **Approximately what percent of echinoderm species are sea stars?**

The sector for sea stars makes up about one-fourth of the circle. Since the circle shows 100% of the data, about one-fourth of 100%, or 25%, of echinoderm species are sea stars.

C **Which group is made up of fewer species—sea cucumbers or sea urchins and sand dollars?**

The sector for sea urchins and sand dollars is smaller than the sector for sea cucumbers. This means there are fewer species of sea urchins and sand dollars than species of sea cucumbers.

Video **Lesson Tutorials Online**

EXAMPLE **2** **Interpreting Circle Graphs**

Leon surveyed 30 people about pet ownership. The circle graph shows his results. Use the graph to answer each question.

A How many people do not own pets?

The circle graph shows that 50% of the 30 people do not own pets.

50% of 30 = 0.5 · 30

= 15

Fifteen people do not own pets.

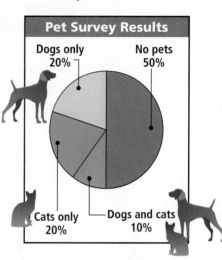

Pet Survey Results

Dogs only 20%

No pets 50%

Cats only 20%

Dogs and cats 10%

B How many people own cats only?

The circle graph shows that 20% of the 30 people own cats only.

20% of 30 = 0.2 · 30

= 6

Six people own cats only.

EXAMPLE **3** **Choosing an Appropriate Graph**

4.33

Decide whether a bar graph or a circle graph would best display the information. Explain your answer.

A the percent of a nation's electricity supply generated by each of several fuel sources

A circle graph is the better choice because it makes it easy to see what part of the nation's electricity comes from each fuel source.

B the number of visitors to Shenandoah National Park in each of the last five years

A bar graph is the better choice because it makes it easy to see how the number of visitors has changed over the years.

C the comparison between the time spent in math class and the total time spent in school each day

A circle graph is the better choice because the sector that represents the time spent in math class could be compared to the entire circle, which represents the total time spent in school.

Recreation LINK

Shenandoah National Park, located near Waynesboro, Virginia, covers 199,017 acres. The highest mountain in the park is Hawksbill Mountain, standing at 4,050 ft.

Think and Discuss

1. Describe two ways a circle graph can be used to compare data.

2. Compare the use of circle graphs with the use of bar graphs to display data.

GUIDED PRACTICE

The circle graph shows the estimated spending on advertising in 2000. Use the graph for Exercises 1–3.

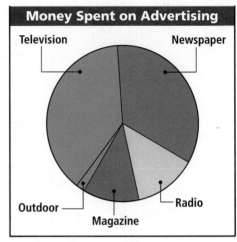

Money Spent on Advertising

Source: USA Today

See Example **1** **1.** On which type of advertising was the least amount of money spent?

2. Approximately what percent of spending was on radio and magazine advertising?

See Example **2** **3.** Television and magazine advertising made up about 50% of all advertising spending in 2000. If the total amount spent was $100,000, about how much was spent on television and magazine advertising?

See Example **3** Decide whether a bar graph or a circle graph would best display the information. Explain your answer.

4. the lengths of the five longest rivers in the world

5. the percent of citizens who voted for each candidate in an election

INDEPENDENT PRACTICE

The circle graph shows the results of a survey of 100 teens who were asked about their favorite sports. Use the graph for Exercises 6–8.

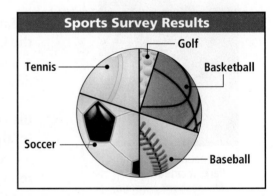

Sports Survey Results

See Example **1** **6.** Did more teens pick basketball or tennis as their favorite sport?

7. Approximately what percent of teens picked soccer as their favorite sport?

See Example **2** **8.** According to the survey, 5% of teens chose golf. What is the number of teens who chose golf?

See Example **3** Decide whether a bar graph or a circle graph would best display the information. Explain your answer.

9. the number of calories eaten at breakfast compared with the total number of calories eaten in one day

10. the number of inches of rain that fell each month in Honolulu, Hawaii, during one year

Extra Practice
See page EP18.

Geography The circle graph shows the percent of Earth's land area covered by each continent. Use the graph for Exercises 11–13.

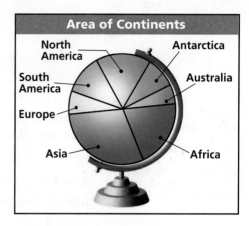

Area of Continents

11. List the continents in order of size, from largest to smallest.

12. Approximately what percent of Earth's total land area is Asia?

13. Approximately what percent of Earth's total land area is North America and South America combined?

14. **Critical Thinking** A group of 200 students were asked how they like to spend their free time. Of the students surveyed, 47% said they like to play on the computer, 59% said they like to go to the mall, 38% said they like to go to the movies, and 41% said they like to play sports. Can you make a circle graph to display this data? Explain.

15. **What's the Error?** The table shows the types of pets owned by a group of students. A circle graph of the data shows that 25% of the students surveyed own a dog. Why is the graph incorrect?

Pet	Number of Students
Cat	JHT JHT JHT
Dog	JHT JHT I
Fish	JHT
Other	JHT

16. **Write About It** What math skills do you use when interpreting information in a circle graph?

17. **Challenge** Earth's total land area is approximately 57,900,000 square miles. Antarctica is almost 10% of the total area. What is the approximate land area of Antarctica in square miles?

Test Prep and Spiral Review

Use the graph for Exercises 18 and 19.

18. **Multiple Choice** Approximately what percent of the medals won by the United States were gold?

 Ⓐ 25% Ⓑ 40% Ⓒ 50% Ⓓ 75%

19. **Short Response** The United States won a total of 502 medals in the Summer Olympics from 1988 to 2004. About how many of these were bronze medals? Show your work.

20. José has an American flag that measures 10 inches by 19 inches. He paints a picture of a flag that is 60 inches by 114 inches. Will his painted flag be similar to the American flag? (Lesson 4-8)

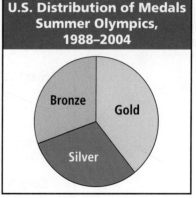

U.S. Distribution of Medals Summer Olympics, 1988–2004

Compare. Write <, >, or =. (Lesson 6-2)

21. 0.1 ▨ 0.09

22. 1.71 ▨ $\frac{24}{11}$

23. 1.25 ▨ 125%

24. 32.5 ▨ 69%

Box-and-Whisker Plots

TN SPI 0706.5.3 Calculate and interpret the mean, median, upper-quartile, lower-quartile, and interquartile range of a set of data.
Also GLE 0706.5.1, GLE 0706.5.4, ✓ 0706.5.1, ✓ 0706.5.2, SPI 0706.5.1, SPI 0706.5.2

Vocabulary

box-and-whisker plot

lower quartile

upper quartile

interquartile range

Carson is planning a deep-sea fishing trip. He chooses a fishing charter based on the number of fish caught on different charters.

A **box-and-whisker plot** uses a number line to show the distribution of a set of data.

To make a box-and-whisker plot, first divide the data into four parts using *quartiles*. The median, or *middle quartile*, divides the data into a lower half and an upper half. The median of the lower half is the **lower quartile**, and the median of the upper half is the **upper quartile** .

EXAMPLE 1

Making a Box-and-Whisker Plot

Use the data to make a box-and-whisker plot.

26, 17, 21, 23, 19, 28, 17, 20, 29

Step 1: Order the data from least to greatest. Then find the least and greatest values, the median, and the lower and upper quartiles.

Caution!

To find the median of a data set with an even number of values, find the mean of the two middle values.

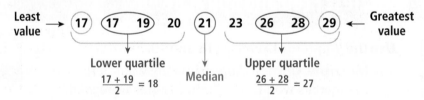

Least value → (17) (17 19) 20 (21) 23 (26 28) (29) ← Greatest value

Lower quartile
$\frac{17 + 19}{2} = 18$

Median

Upper quartile
$\frac{26 + 28}{2} = 27$

Step 2: Draw a number line. Above the number line, plot a point for each value in Step 1.

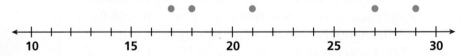

Step 3: Draw a box from the lower to the upper quartile. Inside the box, draw a vertical line through the median. Then draw the "whiskers" from the box to the least and greatest values.

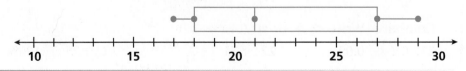

Video Lesson Tutorials Online

The **interquartile range** of a data set is the difference between the lower and upper quartiles. It tells how large the spread of data around the median is.

You can use a box-and-whisker plot to analyze how data in a set are distributed. You can also use box-and-whisker plots to help you compare two sets of data.

EXAMPLE **2** **Comparing Box-and-Whisker Plots**

The box-and-whisker plots below show the distribution of the number of fish caught per trip by two fishing charters.

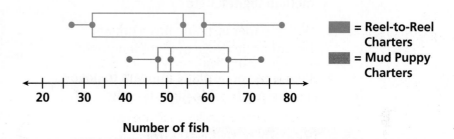

= Reel-to-Reel Charters
= Mud Puppy Charters

Number of fish

A **Which fishing charter has a greater median?**

The median number of fish caught on Reel-to-Reel Charters, about 54, is greater than the median number of fish caught on Mud Puppy Charters, about 51.

B **Which fishing charter has a greater interquartile range?**

The length of the box in a box-and-whisker plot indicates the interquartile range. Reel-to-Reel Charters has a longer box, so it has a greater interquartile range.

C **Which fishing charter appears to be more predictable in the number of fish that might be caught on a fishing trip?**

The range and interquartile range are smaller for Mud Puppy Charters, which means that there is less variation in the data. So the number of fish caught on Mud Puppy Charters is more predictable.

Think and Discuss

1. Describe what you can tell about a data set from a box-and-whisker plot.

2. Explain how the range and the interquartile range of a set of data are different. Which measure tells you more about central tendency?

Learn It Online
Homework Help Online **go.hrw.com**,
keyword MS10 7-5 Go
Exercises 1–8, 9, 11, 19

GUIDED PRACTICE

See Example **1** Use the data to make a box-and-whisker plot.

1. 46   35   46   38   37   33   49   42   35   40   37

See Example **2** Use the box-and-whisker plots of inches flown by two different paper airplanes for Exercises 2–4.

2. Which paper airplane has a greater median flight length?

3. Which paper airplane has a greater interquartile range of flight lengths?

4. Which paper airplane appears to have a more predictable flight length?

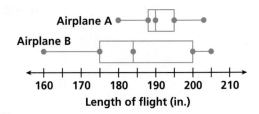

INDEPENDENT PRACTICE

See Example **1** Use the data to make a box-and-whisker plot.

5. 81   73   88   85   81   72   86   72   79   75   76

See Example **2** Use the box-and-whisker plots of apartment rental costs in two different cities for Exercises 6–8.

6. Which city has a greater median apartment rental cost?

7. Which city has a greater interquartile range of apartment rental costs?

8. Which city appears to have a more predictable apartment rental cost?

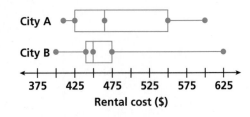

PRACTICE AND PROBLEM SOLVING

Extra Practice
See page EP9.

The points scored per game by a basketball player are shown below. Use the data for Exercises 9–11.

12   7   15   23   10   18   39   15   20   8   13

9. Make two box-and-whisker plots of the data on the same number line: one plot with the outlier and one plot without the outlier.

10. How does the outlier affect the interquartile range of the data?

11. Which is affected more by the outlier: the range or the interquartile range?

12. Make a box-and-whisker plot of the data shown in the line plot.

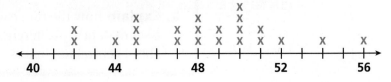

13. **Sports** The table shows the countries that were the top 15 medal winners in the 2004 Olympics.

Country	Medals	Country	Medals	Country	Medals
USA	103	Russia	92	China	63
Australia	49	Germany	48	Japan	37
France	33	Italy	32	Britain	30
Korea	30	Cuba	27	Ukraine	23
Netherlands	22	Romania	19	Spain	19

   a. Make a box-and-whisker plot of the data.

   b. Describe the distribution of the number of medals won.

14. **Measurement** The stem-and-leaf plot shows the heights in inches of a class of seventh graders.

   a. Make a box-and-whisker plot of the data.

   b. Three-fourths of the students are taller than what height?

   c. Three-fourths of the students are shorter than what height?

Student Heights

Stems	Leaves
5	3 5 6 6 8 8 8 9 9
6	0 0 1 1 1 1 1 2 2 2 4

Key: 5|3 means 53

15. **What's the Error?** Using the data 2, 9, 5, 14, 8, 13, 7, 5, and 8, a student found the upper quartile to be 9. What did the student do wrong?

16. **Write About It** Two box-and-whisker plots have the same median and equally long whiskers. If the box of one plot is longer, what can you say about the difference between the two data sets?

17. **Challenge** An outlier is defined to be at least 1.5 times the interquartile range. Name the value that would be considered an outlier in the data set 1, 2, 4, 2, 1, 0, 6, 8, 1, 6, and 2.

Test Prep and Spiral Review

Use the graph for Exercises 18 and 19.

18. **Multiple Choice** What is the difference between the interquartile ranges for the two data sets?

   Ⓐ 21   Ⓒ 9

   Ⓑ 18   Ⓓ 0

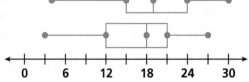

19. **Gridded Response** What is the lower quartile of the box-and-whisker plot with the greater range?

20. A tree casts a 21.25 ft shadow, while a 6 ft tall man casts a 10.5 ft shadow. Estimate the height of the tree. (Lesson 4-9)

21. Mari spent $24.69 on lunch with her mom. About how much should she leave for a 15% tip? (Lesson 6-3)

Technology LAB 7-5

Explore Box-and-Whisker Plots

Use with Lesson 7-5

Learn It Online
Lab Resources Online **go.hrw.com**,
keyword MS10 Lab7 **Go**

You can use a graphing calculator to analyze data in box-and-whisker plots.

TN **SPI 0706.5.3** Calculate and interpret the mean, median, upper-quartile, lower-quartile, and interquartile range of a set of data.
Also **GLE 0706.5.1, GLE 0706.5.3, GLE 0706.5.4, ✓ 0706.5.1, ✓ 0706.5.2, SPI 0706.5.1, SPI 0706.5.2**

Activity 1

Ms. Garza's math class took a statewide math test. The data below are the scores of her 19 students.

79, 80, 61, 66, 74, 92, 88, 75, 93, 61, 77, 94, 25, 79, 86, 85, 48, 99, 80

Use a graphing calculator to make a box-and-whisker plot of the data.

To make a list of the scores, press **STAT** and choose **Edit**. Enter each value under List 1 (L1).

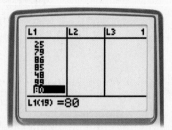

Use the **STAT PLOT** editor to set up the box-and-whisker plot.

Press **2nd** **Y=** (STAT PLOT). Press **ENTER** to select **Plot1**. Turn the plot **On** and use the arrow to select the plot type. The box-and-whisker plot is the fifth type shown.

The plot's values will come from the values listed in L1, so **Xlist: L1** should be visible. The **Freq** should also be set at 1.

Press **ZOOM** and select **9: ZoomStat** to display the plot. Press **TRACE** and use the arrows to see the values of the least value **(minX)**, greatest value **(maxX)**, median **(Med)**, and lower **(Q1)** and upper **(Q3)** quartiles.

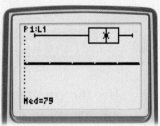

Think and Discuss

1. What five values do you need to construct a box-and-whisker plot? What values must you find before you can identify the upper and lower quartiles?

2. What does the box-and-whisker plot tell you about the data?

Try This

1. Survey your classmates to find the number of U.S. states that each student has visited. Use your calculator to make a box-and-whisker plot of the data.

2. Identify the least value, greatest value, range, median, lower quartile and upper quartile. What is the range between the upper and lower quartile?

Ray surveys 15 seventh-grade students and 15 teachers at his school to find the number of hours they sleep at night. The table shows the results.

	Average Number of Hours of Sleep Per Night
Students	9, 7, 10, 6, 11, 7, 9, 10, 10, 7, 9, 10, 8, 9, 11
Teachers	7, 6, 8, 9, 8, 7, 10, 6, 7, 9, 6, 7, 5, 7, 8

Use a graphing calculator to make a box-and-whisker plot for each set of data.

Enter the first set of student data in L1.

Press ▸ to move right into the L2 column.
Enter the teacher data.

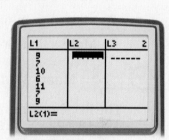

Set up **Plot1** as shown in Activity 1. Repeat the steps to set up **Plot2**.
Set the **Xlist** to L2 by pressing [2nd] [2].

Press [ZOOM] and select **9: ZoomStat** to display both box-and-whisker plots. Press [TRACE] to display the statistics and use the left and right arrows to move along the plots. Use the up and down arrows to move between plots. The display in the left corner tells which plot (P1 or P2) and which list (L1 or L2) the statistics are for.

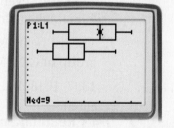

Think and Discuss

1. How can you use the box-and-whisker plots to compare the ranges of the data sets?

2. **Make a Conjecture** What do the graphs tell you about the sleeping habits of students and teachers?

Try This

1. Survey the boys and the girls in your class to find how many minutes they each talk on the phone. Use your calculator to make separate box-and-whisker plots for each set of data.

2. What are the least and greatest values and the median and lower and upper quartile for each box and-whisker-plot?

3. Are there any differences in the plots? What do these differences tell you about boys talking on the phone as compared to girls?

Quiz for Lessons 7-1 Through 7-5

7-1 Frequency Tables, Stem-and-Leaf Plots, and Line Plots

The list shows the top speeds of various land animals.

42 55 62 48 65 51 47 59 67 61 49 54 55 52 44

1. Make a cumulative frequency table of the data.

2. Make a stem-and-leaf plot of the data.

3. Make a line plot of the data.

7-2 Mean, Median, Mode, and Range

The list shows the life spans in years of vampire bats in captivity.

18 22 5 21 19 21 17 3 19 20 29 18 17

4. Find the mean, median, mode, and range of the data. Round your answers to the nearest tenth of a year.

5. Which measure of central tendency best represents the data? Explain.

7-3 Bar Graphs and Histograms

6. The table shows the numbers of students in the sixth and seventh grades who participated in school fairs. Make a double-bar graph of the data.

7. The list below shows the numbers of tracks on a group of CDs. Make a histogram of the data.

13, 7, 10, 8, 15, 17, 22, 9, 11, 10, 16, 12, 9, 20

School Fair Participation		
Fair	Sixth Grade	Seventh Grade
Book	55	76
Health	69	58
Science	74	98

7-4 Reading and Interpreting Circle Graphs

Use the circle graph for problems 8 and 9.

8. Approximately what percent of students picked cheese as their favorite topping?

9. Out of 200 students, 25% picked pepperoni as their favorite pizza topping. How many students picked pepperoni?

Favorite Pizza Toppings

Cheese, Pepperoni, Green peppers, Sausage, Mushrooms

7-5 Box-and-Whisker Plots

10. Make a box-and-whisker plot of the data 14, 8, 13, 20, 15, 17, 1, 12, 18, and 10.

11. On the same number line, make a box-and-whisker plot of the data 3, 8, 5, 12, 6, 18, 14, 8, 15, and 11.

12. Which box-and-whisker plot has a greater interquartile range?

Focus on Problem Solving

Solve

• **Choose an operation: addition or subtraction**

In order to decide whether to add or subtract to solve a problem, you need to determine what action is taking place in the problem. If you are combining or putting together numbers, you need to add. If you are taking away or finding how far apart two numbers are, you need to subtract.

Determine the action in each problem. Then determine which operation could be used to solve the problem. Use the table for problems 5 and 6.

1 Betty, Raymond, and Helen ran a three-person relay race. Their individual times were 48 seconds, 55 seconds, and 51 seconds. What was their total time?

2 The Scots pine and the sessile oak are trees native to Northern Ireland. The height of a mature Scots pine is 111 feet, and the height of a mature sessile oak is 90 feet. How much taller is the Scots pine than the sessile oak?

3 Mr. Hutchins has $35.00 to buy supplies for his social studies class. He wants to buy items that cost $19.75, $8.49, and $7.10. Does Mr. Hutchins have enough money to buy all of the supplies?

4 The running time for the 1998 movie *Antz* is 83 minutes. Jordan has watched 25 minutes of the movie. How many minutes does he have left to watch?

Sizes of Marine Mammals	
Mammal	**Weight (kg)**
Killer whale	3,600
Manatee	400
Sea lion	200
Walrus	750

5 The table gives the approximate weights of four marine mammals. How much more does the killer whale weigh than the sea lion?

6 Find the total weight of the manatee, the sea lion, and the walrus. Do these three mammals together weigh more or less than the killer whale?

7-6 Line Graphs

TN SPI 0706.5.1 Interpret and employ various graphs and charts to represent data. *Also* **GLE 0706.5.1, GLE 0706.5.4,** ✓ **0706.5.2, SPI 0706.5.2**

You can use a *line graph* to show how data changes over a period of time. In a **line graph**, line segments are used to connect data points on a coordinate grid. The result is a visual record of change.

Line graphs can be used for a variety of reasons, including showing the growth of a dog over time.

Vocabulary

line graph

double-line graph

EXAMPLE 1   Making a Line Graph

Make a line graph of the data in the table. Use the graph to determine during which 2-month period the puppy's weight increased the most.

Age (mo)	Weight (lb)
0	0.2
2	1.7
4	3.8
6	5.1
8	6.0
10	6.7
12	7.2

Step 1: Determine the scale and interval for each axis. Place units of time on the horizontal axis.

Helpful Hint

To plot each point, start at zero. Move *right* for the time and *up* for the weight.

Step 2: Plot a point for each pair of values. Connect the points using line segments.

Step 3: Label the axes and give the graph a title.

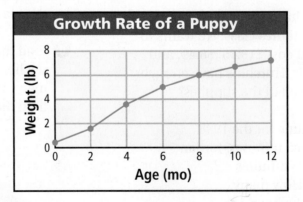

The graph shows the steepest line segment between 2 and 4 months. This means the puppy's weight increased most between 2 and 4 months.

Video **Lesson Tutorials Online**

You can use a line graph to estimate values between data points.

EXAMPLE 2 **Using a Line Graph to Estimate Data**

Use the graph to estimate the population of Florida in 1990.

To estimate the population in 1990, find the point on the line between 1980 and 2000 that corresponds to 1990.

The graph shows about 12.5 million. In fact, the population was 12.9 million in 1990.

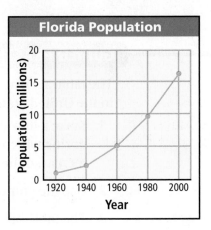

A **double-line graph** shows change over time for two sets of data.

EXAMPLE 3 **Making a Double-Line Graph**

The table shows the normal daily temperatures in degrees Fahrenheit in two Alaskan cities. Make a double-line graph of the data.

Month	Nome	Anchorage
Jan	7	15
Feb	4	19
Mar	9	26
Apr	18	36
May	36	47
Jun	46	54

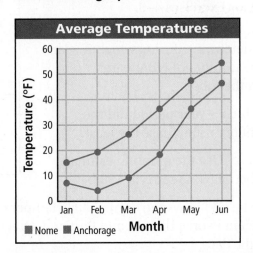

Plot a point for each temperature in Nome and connect the points. Then, using a different color, plot a point for each temperature in Anchorage and connect the points. Make a key to show what each line represents.

Think and Discuss

1. **Describe** how a line graph would look for a set of data that increases and then decreases over time.

2. **Give an example** of a situation that can be described by a double-line graph in which the two sets of data intersect at least once.

Exercises

GUIDED PRACTICE

The table at right shows average movie theater ticket prices in the United States. Use the table for Exercises 1 and 2.

Year	Price ($)
1965	1.01
1970	1.55
1975	2.05
1980	2.69
1985	3.55
1990	4.23
1995	4.35
2000	5.39
2005	6.41

See Example 1 **1.** Make a line graph of the data. Use the graph to determine during which 5-year period the average ticket price increased the least.

See Example 2 **2.** Use the graph to estimate the average ticket price in 1997.

See Example 3 **3.** The table below shows the amount of apple juice and raw apples in pounds consumed per person in the United States. Make a double-line graph of the data.

	2001	2002	2003	2004	2005
Apple Juice	21.4	21.3	21.4	23.1	24.0
Raw Apples	17.5	15.6	16.0	16.9	19.1

INDEPENDENT PRACTICE

The table at right shows the number of teams in the National Basketball Association (NBA). Use the table for Exercises 4–6.

Year	Teams
1965	9
1970	14
1975	18
1980	22
1985	23
1990	27
1995	27
2000	29
2005	30

See Example 1 **4.** Make a line graph of the data. Use the graph to determine during which 5-year period the number of NBA teams increased the most.

5. During which 5-year period did the number of teams increase the least?

See Example 2 **6. Estimation** Use the graph to estimate the number of NBA teams in 1988.

See Example 3 **7.** The table below shows the normal daily temperatures in degrees Fahrenheit in Peoria, Illinois, and Portland, Oregon. Make a double-line graph of the data.

	Jul	Aug	Sept	Oct	Nov	Dec
Peoria	76	73	66	54	41	27
Portland	68	69	63	55	46	40

PRACTICE AND PROBLEM SOLVING

Extra Practice
See page EP19.

8. Critical Thinking Explain how the intervals on the vertical axis of a line graph affect the look of the graph.

Wildfires can also be started naturally by lightning or lava. Fires can start when the lava flow ignites the vegetation. This is common in Hawaii.

9. Life Science The table shows the numbers of endangered species of vertebrates for selected years between 1998 and 2004.

	1998	2000	2002	2003	2004
Number of Species (thousands)	3.31	3.51	3.52	3.52	5.19

a. Make a line graph of the data in the table.

b. Estimate the number of endangered species of vertebrates in 1999.

10. Earth Science The graph shows the number of acres burned by wildfires in the United States from 2001 to 2006.

a. During which years did wildfires burn more than 8 million acres?

b. Explain whether the graph would be useful in predicting future data.

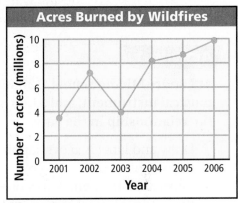

Source: National Interagency Fire Center

11. What's the Error? Denise makes a line plot to display how her town's population has changed over 10 years. Explain which type of graph would be more appropriate.

12. Write About It Explain the benefit of drawing a double-line graph rather than two single-line graphs for related sets of data.

13. Challenge A line graph shows that a town's population was 4,500 in 1980, 5,300 in 1990, and 6,100 in 2000. Assuming the population continues to grow at the same rate, what population will the line graph show in 2010?

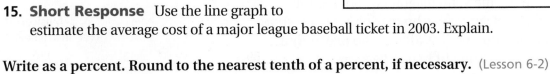

Test Prep and Spiral Review

Use the graph for Exercises 14 and 15.

14. Multiple Choice During which period did the average cost of a major league baseball ticket increase the most?

   Ⓐ 1991–1993   Ⓒ 1997–2001

   Ⓑ 1993–1997   Ⓓ 2001–2005

15. Short Response Use the line graph to estimate the average cost of a major league baseball ticket in 2003. Explain.

Write as a percent. Round to the nearest tenth of a percent, if necessary. (Lesson 6-2)

16. 0.15   **17.** 1.36   **18.** $\frac{2}{3}$ **19.** $\frac{11}{20}$

20. Decide whether a bar graph or a circle graph would best display the average temperature for each day of one week. Explain your answer. (Lesson 7-4)

Hands-On LAB 7-6

Use Venn Diagrams to Display Collected Data

Use with Lesson 7-6

Learn It Online
Lab Resources Online **go.hrw.com**,
keyword **MS10 Lab7** Go

TN SPI 0706.5.1 Interpret and employ various graphs and charts to represent data. *Also* **GLE 0706.5.1, GLE 0706.5.2, GLE 0706.5.3, ✓ 0706.5.2**

You can use a Venn diagram to display relationships in data. Use ovals, circles, or other shapes to represent individual data sets.

Activity 1

At Landry Middle School, 127 students play a team sport, 145 play a musical instrument, and 31 do both. Make a Venn diagram to display the relationship in the data.

1 Draw and label two overlapping circles to represent the sets of students who play a team sport and a musical instrument. Label one "Team sport" and the other "Musical instrument."

Team sport   Musical instrument

2 Write "31" in the area where the circles overlap. This is the number of students who play a musical instrument and a team sport.

3 To find the number of students who play a team sport *only*, begin with the number of students who play a team sport, 127, and subtract the number of students who do both, 31.

team sport − both = team sport *only*

127 − 31 = 96

Use the same process to find the number of students who play a musical instrument *only*.

musical instrument − both = musical instrument *only*

145 − 31 = 114

4 Complete the Venn diagram by adding the number of students who play *only* a team sport and the number of students who play *only* a musical instrument to the diagram.

Team Sport 96   31   Musical Instrument 114

Think and Discuss

1. Explain why some of the numbers that were given in Activity 1, such as 127 and 145, do not appear in the Venn diagram.

2. Describe a Venn diagram that has three individual data sets. How many overlapping areas does it have?

Try This

Responding to a survey about favorite foods, 60 people said they like pasta, 45 said they like chicken, and 70 said they like hot dogs. Also, 15 people said they like both chicken and pasta, 22 said they like both hot dogs and chicken, and 17 said they like both hot dogs and pasta. Only 8 people said they like all 3 foods.

1. How many people like only pasta?

2. How many people like only chicken?

3. How many people like only hot dogs?

4. Make a Venn diagram to show the relationships in the data.

Activity 2

1 Interview your classmates to find out what kinds of movies they like (for example, action, comedy, drama, and horror).

2 Make a Venn diagram to show the relationships in the collected data.

Think and Discuss

1. Tell how many individual sets and how many overlapping areas a Venn diagram of the movie data will have.

2. Describe what a Venn diagram of student ages might look like. Would there be any overlapping sets? Explain.

Try This

1. Interview your classmates to find out what kinds of sports they like to play. Make a Venn diagram to show the relationships in the data.

2. The Venn diagram shows the types of exercise that some students do.

   a. How many students were surveyed?

   b. How many students jog?

   c. How many students like to both bike and walk?

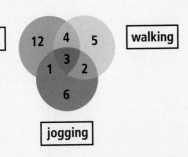

Choosing an Appropriate Display

TN **SPI 0706.5.2** Select suitable graph types (such as bar graphs, histograms, line graphs, circle graphs, box-and-whisker plots, and stem-and-leaf plots) and use them to create accurate representations of given data. *Also* **GLE 0706.5.2,** ✓ **0706.5.2**

On a field trip to a butterfly park, students recorded the number of species of each butterfly family they saw. Which type of graph would best display the data they collected?

There are several ways to display data. Some types of displays are more appropriate than others, depending on how the data is to be analyzed.

 Use a **bar graph** to display and compare data.

 Use a **circle graph** to show how a set of data is divided into parts.

 Use a **Venn diagram** to show relationships between two or more data sets.

 Use a **line plot** to show the frequency of values.

 Use a **line graph** to show how data change over a period of time.

 Use a **stem-and-leaf plot** to show how often data values occur and how they are distributed.

EXAMPLE **1** **Choosing an Appropriate Display**

A The students want to create a display to show the number of species of each butterfly family they saw. Choose the type of graph that would best represent the data in the table. Explain.

Butterfly Family	Number of Species
Gossamer-wing	7
Skippers	10
Swallowtails	5
Whites and sulphurs	4

There are distinct categories showing the number of species seen in each butterfly family.

A bar graph can be used to display data in categories.

B The students want to create a display to show the population of butterflies in the park for the past few years. Choose the type of graph that would best represent this data. Explain.

A line graph would best represent data that gives population over time.

Video **Lesson Tutorials Online**

EXAMPLE 2 **Identifying the Most Appropriate Display**

The table shows the amount of time the students spent at the different exhibits at the butterfly park. Explain why each display does or does not appropriately represent the data.

Exhibit	Time (min)
Butterflies	60
Insects	45
Invertebrates	30
Birds	15

A

Stems	Leaves
1	5
2	
3	0
4	5
5	
6	0

A stem-and-leaf plot shows how often data values occur and how they are distributed.

Key: 2|0 means 20

There are only four data values, and how often they occur and how they are distributed are not important.

B

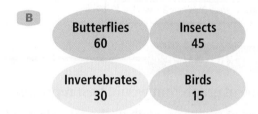

A Venn diagram shows the relationship between two or more data sets.

There is no relationship among the times spent at each exhibit.

C

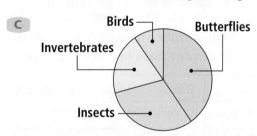

A circle graph shows how a set of data is divided into parts.

This circle graph appropriately shows the proportionate amount of time spent at each exhibit.

D

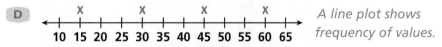

A line plot shows frequency of values.

How often the data values occur is not important.

Think and Discuss

1. **Explain** how data displayed in a stem-and-leaf plot and data displayed in a line plot are similar.

2. **Describe** a set of data that could best be displayed in a line graph.

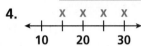

Learn It Online
Homework Help Online **go.hrw.com**,
keyword MS10 7-7 Go
Exercises 1–8, 15

GUIDED PRACTICE

See Example **1** **Choose the type of graph that would best represent each type of data.**

1. the prices of the five top-selling 42-inch plasma televisions

2. the height of a person from birth to age 21

See Example **2** **The table shows Keiffer's earnings for a month. Explain why each display does or does not appropriately represent the data.**

Week	1	2	3	4
Earnings ($)	20	30	15	25

3.

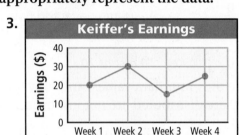

4.

```
      x  x  x  x
  <--+--+--+--+-->
     10    20    30
```

INDEPENDENT PRACTICE

See Example **1** **Choose the type of graph that would best represent each type of data.**

5. the number of tracks on each of the 50 CDs in a CD collection

6. the number of runners in a marathon for the last five years

See Example **2** **The table shows the number of people who participate in various activities. Explain why each display does or does not appropriately represent the data.**

Activity	Biking	Hiking	Skating	Jogging
Number of People	35	20	25	15

7.

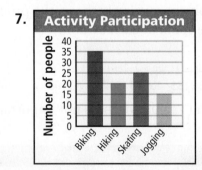

8.

Stems	Leaves
1	5
2	0 5
3	5

Key: 1|5 means 15

PRACTICE AND PROBLEM SOLVING

Extra Practice
See page EP19.

9. The data gives the number of books 25 students read last summer.
7, 10, 8, 6, 0, 5, 3, 8, 12, 7, 2, 5, 9, 10, 15, 8, 3, 1, 0, 4, 7, 10, 8, 2, 11
Make the type of graph that would best represent the data.

10. **Nutrition** The table shows the amount of protein per serving in various foods. Draw two different displays to represent the data. Explain your choices.

Food	Protein (g)
Egg	6
Milk	8
Cheese	24
Roast beef	28

11. Yoko wants to use a stem-and-leaf plot to show the growth of the sweet peas that she planted last year. She measured how much the vines grew each month. Explain why Yoko's display choice may or may not best represent the data.

12. **Life Science** Komodo Dragons are the world's largest lizard species. The table shows the weights of some adult male Komodo Dragons. Make the type of graph that would best represent the information.

Weight (lb)	Frequency
161–170	4
171–180	8
181–190	12
191–200	11
201–210	7

13. **Choose a Strategy** Five friends worked together on a project. Matti, Jerad, and Stu all worked the same length of time. Tisha worked a total of 3 hours, which was equal to the total amount of time that Matti, Jerad, and Stu worked. Pablo and Matti together worked $\frac{1}{2}$ of the total amount of time that the five friends worked. Make the type of graph that would best represent the information.

14. **Write About It** Is a circle graph always appropriate to represent data stated in percents? Explain your answer.

15. **Challenge** The table shows the results of a survey of 50 people about their favorite color. What type of display would you choose to represent the data of those who chose blue, green, or red? Explain.

Color	Blue	Yellow	Green	Red	Other
Number	14	4	6	14	12

Test Prep and Spiral Review

16. **Multiple Choice** Which type of display would be most appropriate to compare the monthly rainfall for five cities?

    (A) Line graph   (B) Bar graph   (C) Circle graph   (D) Stem-and-leaf plot

17. **Extended Response** Nathan's family budgets $1,000 a month for expenses. They budget $250 for food, $500 for rent, $150 for transportation, and $100 for utilities. Tell which type of graph would best represent the data, justify your response, and draw the display.

Write each decimal as a percent. (Lesson 6-2)

18. 0.27   19. 0.9   20. 0.02   21. 0.406

22. Of the 75 campers at Happy Trails Summer Camp, 36% are scheduled to go horseback riding on Tuesdays. How many campers are scheduled to go horseback riding on Tuesdays? (Lesson 6-4)

Use Technology to Display Data

Learn It Online
Lab Resources Online **go.hrw.com**,
keyword **MS10 Lab7** **Go**

There are several ways to display data, including bar graphs, line graphs, and circle graphs. A spreadsheet provides a quick way to create these graphs.

TN **SPI 0706.5.2** Select suitable graph types (such as bar graphs, histograms, line graphs, circle graphs, box-and-whisker plots, and stem-and-leaf plots) and use them to create accurate representations of given data. *Also* **GLE 0706.5.2, GLE 0706.5.3, ✓ 0706.5.2**

Activity

Use a spreadsheet to display the Kennedy Middle School Student Council budget shown in the table at right.

Student Council Budget	
Activity	**Amount ($)**
Assemblies	275
Dances	587
Spring Festival	412
Awards Banquet	384
Other	250

1 Open the spreadsheet program, and enter the data as shown below. Enter the activities in column A and the amount budgeted in column B. Include the column titles in row 1.

	A	B	C
1	Activity	Amount ($)	
2	Assemblies	275	
3	Dances	587	
4	Spring Festival	412	
5	Awards Banquet	384	
6	Other	250	
7			

2 Highlight the data by clicking on cell A1 and dragging the cursor to cell B6. Click the Chart Wizard icon . Then click **FINISH** to choose the first type of column graph.

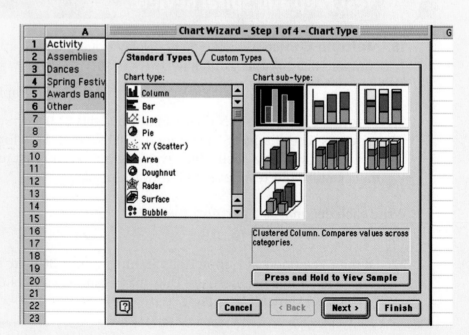

3 The bar graph of the data appears as shown. Resize or reposition the graph, if necessary.

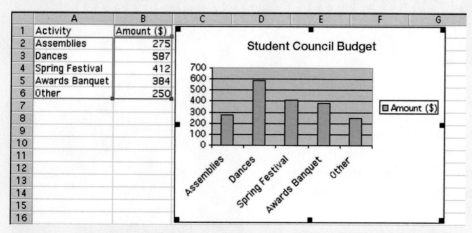

To see a circle graph of the data, select the bar graph (as shown above). Click the Chart Wizard icon and choose "Pie," which is the circle graph. Then click **FINISH** to choose the first type of circle graph.

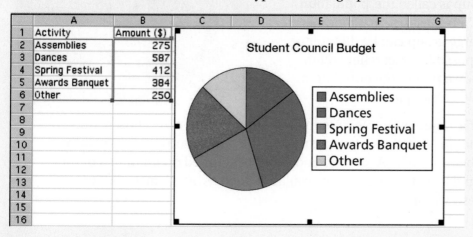

Think and Discuss

1. Which graph best displays the Student Council budget? Why?

2. Would a line graph be an appropriate display of the Student Council budget data? Explain.

Try This

1. The table shows the number of points scored by members of a girls' basketball team in one season. Use a spreadsheet to create a bar graph and a circle graph of the data.

Player	Ana	Angel	Mary	Nia	Tina	Zoe
Points Scored	201	145	89	40	21	8

2. Which type of graph is a better display of the data? Why?

3. Formulate a question and survey your classmates. Use the Chart Wizard to make the graph that best displays your data. Which type of graph did you use? Why?

TN **GLE 0706.5.3** Formulate questions and design studies to collect data about a characteristic shared by two populations, or different characteristics within one population.

Use Additional Topic A-7 with this lesson.

Vocabulary

population

sample

random sample

convenience sample

biased sample

In 2002, there were claims that Chronic Wasting Disease (CWD), or Mad Elk Disease, was spreading westward across North America. In order to verify claims such as these, the elk population had to be tested.

When information is gathered about a group, such as all the elk in North America, the entire group is called the **population**. Because testing each member of a large group can be difficult or impossible, researchers often study a part of the population, called a **sample**.

Helpful Hint

A random sample is more likely to be representative of a population than a convenience sample is.

For a **random sample**, members of the population are chosen at random. This gives every member of the population an equal chance of being chosen. A **convenience sample** is based on members of the population that are readily available, such as 30 elk in a wildlife preservation area.

EXAMPLE 1 Analyzing Sampling Methods

Determine which sampling method will better represent the entire population. Justify your answer.

Football Game: Student Attendance	
Sampling Method	**Results of Survey**
Arnie surveys 80 students by randomly choosing names from the school directory.	62% attend football games
Vic surveys 28 students that were sitting near him during lunch.	81% attend football games

Arnie's method produces results that better represent the entire student population because he uses a random sample.

Vic's method produces results that are not as representative of the entire student population because he uses a convenience sample.

A **biased sample** does not fairly represent the population. A study of 50 elk belonging to a breeder could be biased because the breeder's elk might be less likely to have Mad Elk Disease than elk in the wild.

EXAMPLE 2 **Identifying Potentially Biased Samples**

Determine whether each sample may be biased. Explain.

A The first 50 people exiting a movie are surveyed to find out what type of movie people in the town like to see.

The sample is biased. It is likely that not everyone in the town likes to see the same type of movie that those 50 people just saw.

B A librarian randomly chooses 100 books from the library's database to calculate the average length of a library book.

The sample is not biased. It is a random sample.

Given data about a random sample, you can use proportional reasoning to make predictions or verify claims about the entire population.

EXAMPLE 3 **Verifying Claims Based on Statistical Data**

A biologist estimates that more than 700 of the 4,500 elk at a wildlife preserve are infected with a parasite. A random sample of 50 elk shows that 8 of them are infected. Determine whether the biologist's estimate is likely to be accurate.

Set up a proportion to predict the total number of infected elk.

$$\frac{\text{infected elk in sample}}{\text{size of sample}} = \frac{\text{infected elk in population}}{\text{size of population}}$$

$$\frac{8}{50} = \frac{x}{4,500} \qquad \textit{Let x represent the number of infected elk at the preserve.}$$

$$8 \cdot 4,500 = 50 \cdot x \qquad \textit{The cross products are equal.}$$

$$36,000 = 50x \qquad \textit{Multiply.}$$

$$\frac{36,000}{50} = \frac{50x}{50} \qquad \textit{Divide each side by 50.}$$

$$720 = x$$

Based on the sample, you can predict that there are 720 infected elk at the preserve. The biologist's estimate is likely to be accurate.

> **Remember!**
>
> In the proportion $\frac{a}{b} = \frac{c}{d}$, the cross products, $a \cdot d$ and $b \cdot c$ are equal.

Think and Discuss

1. **Describe** a situation in which you would want to use a sample rather than survey the entire population.

2. **Explain** why it might be difficult to obtain a truly random sample of a very large population.

Learn It Online
Homework Help Online **go.hrw.com,**
keyword **MS10 7-8** **Go**
Exercises 1–8, 9, 11

GUIDED PRACTICE

See Example **1**

1. Determine which sampling method will better represent the entire population. Justify your answer.

Lone Star Cars: Customer Satisfaction	
Sampling Method	**Results of Survey**
Nadia surveys 200 customers on the car lot one Saturday morning.	92% are satisfied
Daria mails surveys to 100 randomly-selected customers.	68% are satisfied

See Example **2**

Determine whether each sample may be biased. Explain.

2. A company randomly selects 500 customers from its computer database and then surveys those customers to find out how they like their service.

3. A city-hall employee surveys 100 customers at a restaurant to learn about the jobs and salaries of city residents.

See Example **3**

4. A factory produces 150,000 light bulbs per day. The manager of the factory estimates that fewer than 1,000 defective bulbs are produced each day. In a random sample of 250 light bulbs, there are 2 defective bulbs. Determine whether the manager's estimate is likely to be accurate. Explain.

INDEPENDENT PRACTICE

See Example **1**

5. Determine which sampling method will better represent the entire population. Justify your answer.

Midville Morning News: Subscription Renewals	
Sampling Method	**Results of Survey**
Suzanne surveys 80 subscribers in her neighborhood.	61% intend to renew subscription
Vonetta telephones 150 randomly-selected subscribers.	82% intend to renew subscription

See Example **2**

Determine whether each sample may be biased. Explain.

6. A disc jockey asks the first 10 listeners who call in if they liked the last song that was played.

7. Members of a polling organization survey 700 registered voters by randomly choosing names from a list of all registered voters.

See Example **3**

8. A university has 30,600 students. In a random sample of 240 students, 20 speak three or more languages. Predict the number of students at the university who speak three or more languages.

PRACTICE AND PROBLEM SOLVING

Extra Practice
See page EP19.

Life Science

North American fruit flies are known to damage cherries, apples, and blueberries. In the Mediterranean, fruit flies are a threat to citrus fruits.

Explain whether you would survey the entire population or use a sample.

9. You want to know the favorite painters of employees at a local art museum.

10. You want to know the types of calculators used by middle school students across the country.

11. You want to know how many hours per week the students in your social studies class spend on their homework.

12. **Life Science** A biologist chooses a random sample of 50 out of 750 fruit flies. She finds that 2 of them have mutated genes causing deformed wings. The biologist claims that approximately 30 of the 750 fruit flies have deformed wings. Do you agree? Explain.

13. A *biased question* is one that leads people to a certain answer. Kelly decides to use a random sampling to determine her classmates' favorite color. She asks, "Is green your favorite color?" Is this question biased? If so, give an example of an unbiased question.

14. **Critical Thinking** Explain why surveying 100 people who are listed in the phone book may not be a random sample.

15. **Write About It** Suppose you want to know whether the seventh-grade students at your school spend more time watching TV or using a computer. How might you choose a random sample from the population?

16. **Challenge** A manager at XQJ Software surveyed 200 company employees to find out how many of the employees walk to work. The results are shown in the table. Do you think the manager chose a random sample? Why or why not?

Employees at XQJ Software		
	Total Number	Number Who Walk
Population	9,200	300
Sample	200	40

Test Prep and Spiral Review

17. **Multiple Choice** Banneker Middle School has 580 students. Wei surveys a random sample of 30 students and finds that 12 of them have pet dogs. How many students at the school are likely to have pet dogs?

Ⓐ 116 Ⓑ 232 Ⓒ 290 Ⓓ 360

18. **Short Response** Give an example of a biased sample. Explain why it is biased.

Write each percent as a decimal. (Lesson 6-1)

19. 52% 20. 7% 21. 110% 22. 0.4%

Find the percent of each number. (Lesson 6-4)

23. 11% of 50 24. 48% of 600 25. 0.5% of 82 26. 210% of 16

Scatter Plots

TN SPI 0706.5.1 Interpret and employ various graphs and charts to represent data. *Also* **GLE 0706.5.1**, ✓ **0706.5.2**

Vocabulary

scatter plot

correlation

positive correlation

negative correlation

no correlation

The supersaurus, one of the largest known dinosaurs, could weigh as much as 55 tons and grow as long as 100 feet from head to tail. The tyrannosaurus, a large meat-eating dinosaur, was about one-third the length of the supersaurus.

Two sets of data, such as the length and the weight of dinosaurs, may be related. To find out, you can make a *scatter plot* of the data values in each set. A **scatter plot** has two number lines, called *axes*—one for each set of data values. Each point on the scatter plot represents a pair of data values. These points may appear to be scattered or may cluster in the shape of a line or a curve.

EXAMPLE 1 **Making a Scatter Plot**

Use the data to make a scatter plot. Describe the relationship between the data sets.

Step 1: Determine the scale and interval for each axis. Place units of length on the horizontal axis and units of weight on the vertical axis.

Step 2: Plot a point for each pair of values.

Step 3: Label the axes and title the graph.

The scatter plot shows that a dinosaur's weight tends to increase as its length increases.

Name	Length (ft)	Weight (tons)
Triceratops	30	6
Tyrannosaurus	39	7
Euhelopus	50	25
Brachiosaurus	82	50
Supersaurus	100	55

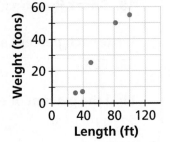

Dinosaur Sizes

Video **Lesson Tutorials Online**

A **correlation** is the description of the relationship between two data sets. There are three correlations that can describe data displayed in a scatter plot.

Positive Correlation	Negative Correlation	No Correlation
	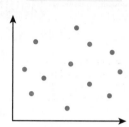	
The values in both data sets increase at the same time.	The values in one data set increase as the values in the other set decrease.	The values in both data sets show no pattern.

EXAMPLE 2 Determining Relationships Between Two Sets of Data

Write *positive correlation, negative correlation,* or *no correlation* to describe each relationship. Explain.

A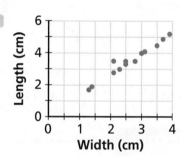

The graph shows that as width increases, length increases. So the graph shows a positive correlation.

B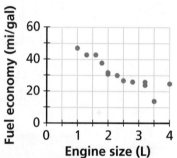

The graph shows that as engine size increases, fuel economy decreases. So the graph shows a negative correlation.

C the ages of people and the number of pets they own

The number of pets a person owns is not related to the person's age. So there seems to be no correlation between the data sets.

Think and Discuss

1. Describe the type of correlation you would expect between the number of absences in a class and the grades in the class.

2. Give an example of a relationship between two sets of data that shows a negative correlation.

GUIDED PRACTICE

See Example **1**

1. The table shows the typical weights (in kilograms) and heart rates (in beats per minute) of several mammals. Use the data to make a scatter plot. Describe the relationship between the data sets.

Mammal	Weight	Heart Rate
Ferret	0.6	360 ·
Human	70	70
Llama	185	75
Red deer	110	80
Rhesus monkey	10	160

See Example **2**

Write *positive correlation, negative correlation,* or *no correlation* to describe each relationship. Explain.

2. **Math Score and Shoe Size**

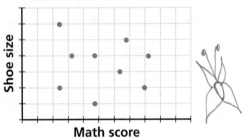

3. **Work Experience**

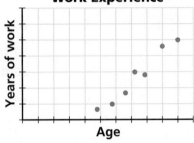

4. the time it takes to drive 100 miles and the driving speed

INDEPENDENT PRACTICE

See Example **1**

5. The table shows solar energy cell capacity (in megawatts) over several years. Use the data to make a scatter plot. Describe the relationship between the data sets.

Year	Capacity	Year	Capacity
1990	13.8	1993	21.0
1991	14.9	1994	26.1
1992	15.6	1995	31.1

See Example **2**

Write *positive correlation, negative correlation,* or *no correlation* to describe each relationship. Explain.

6. **Sales**

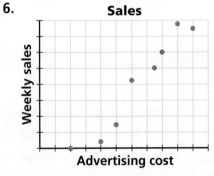

7. **Car's Mileage and Value**

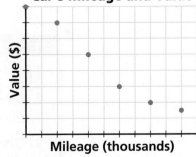

Extra Practice
See page EP19.

8. the number of students in a district and the number of buses in the district

Critical Thinking For Exercises 9–11, tell whether you would expect a positive correlation, a negative correlation, or no correlation. Explain your answers.

9. the average temperature of a location and the amount of rainfall it receives each year

10. the latitude of a location and the amount of snow it receives each year

11. the number of hours of daylight and the amount of rainfall in a day

12. The table shows the approximate latitude and average temperature for several locations in the Southern Hemisphere. Construct a scatter plot of the data. What can you conclude from this data?

Fief Mountains, Antarctica

San Rafael Falls, Ecuador

13. ⭐ **Challenge** A location's elevation is negatively correlated to its average temperature and positively correlated to the amount of snow it receives. What kind of correlation would you expect between temperature and the amount of snowfall? Explain.

Location	Latitude	Temperature
Quito, Ecuador	0° S	55 °F
Melbourne, Australia	38° S	43 °F
Tucuman, Argentina	27° S	57 °F
Tananarive, Madagascar	19° S	60 °F
Halley Research Station, Antarctica	76° S	20 °F

 Test Prep and Spiral Review

14. **Multiple Choice** Use the scatter plot to determine which statements are true.

 I   The data shows a positive correlation.

 II The data shows a negative correlation.

 III The data shows no correlation.

 IV As the years increase, the prize money increases.

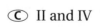

Ⓐ I only   Ⓑ I and IV   Ⓒ II and IV   Ⓓ III only

15. **Short Response** Give an example of two data sets that you would expect to have a positive correlation. Explain your answer.

Find the percent of each number. If necessary, round to the nearest tenth. (Lesson 6-4)

16. 95% of 80   17. 120% of 63   18. 62% of 14   19. 7% of 50

20. The regular price of a computer monitor at the electronics store is $499. This month the monitor is on sale for 15% off. Find the sale price of the monitor. (Lesson 6-6)

Technology LAB

7-9

Use after Lesson 7-9

Samples and Lines of Best Fit

TN SPI 0706.5.1 Interpret and employ various graphs and charts to represent data. *Also* **GLE 0706.3.7, ✓ 0706.5.2**

Learn It Online
Lab Resources Online **go.hrw.com**, keyword MS10 Lab7 Go

You can use a graphing calculator to display relationships between variables in a scatter plot.

Activity 1

1 Survey at least 30 students in your grade to find the following information. Record your data in a table like the one below. (Your table will have at least 30 rows of data.) For **L5**, use numbers for the month. For example, enter "1" for January, "2" for February, etc.

L1 Height (in.)	L2 Age (yr)	L3 Length of Foot (in.)	L4 Length of Forearm (in.)	L5 Month of Birth
66	12	11	10	3
63	13	8	9	10
65	12	10	9.5	7

2 Press `STAT` `ENTER` to enter all the data into a graphing calculator.

3 Create a scatter plot for height and length of foot.

   a. Press `2nd` `Y=` `ENTER` for **Plot 1**.
   (above Y=: **STAT PLOT**)

   b. Select **On,** and use the arrow keys to select the scatter plot for **Type**.

   c. Use the down arrow to move the cursor to **Xlist**. Press `2nd` 1 to select **L1**.

   d. Move the cursor to **Ylist**. Press `2nd` 3 to select **L3**.

   e. Press `ZOOM` and then **9: ZoomStat** to view your graph.

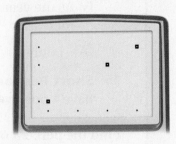

Think and Discuss

1. Describe the relationship between height and length of foot that is shown in the scatter plot from Activity 1.

2. What relationships would you expect to see between the other variables in the table?

1. Create a scatter plot of each of the other pairs of variables in your data-collection table. Which variables show a positive correlation? a negative correlation? no correlation?

A **line of best fit** is a straight line that comes closest to the points on a scatter plot. You can create a line of best fit on the calculator.

Activity 2

1 Follow the steps from Activity 1, part 3 to display a scatter plot that shows the relationship between height and length of forearm.

2 Use TRACE to move the cursor between points on the graph. Use the coordinates of two points to estimate the slope of a line that would best fit through the data points on the graph.

3 Press STAT and then use the right arrow key to select **CALC 4: LinReg (*ax* + *b*)**. Then press 2nd 1 , 2nd 4 ENTER to find the equation of the line of best fit.

4 Press Y= VARS 5: **Statistics**.... Use the right arrow key to select **EQ 1: RegEQ** and press ENTER to put the equation for the line of best fit into the equation editor.

5 Press GRAPH to see the line of best fit graphed with the data points on the scatter plot.

Think and Discuss

1. Discuss how estimating the line of best fit gets easier the more data points you have.

2. Explain whether the sample from your class is representative of the population.

3. What type of correlation does the line of best fit help show? What is the relationship between these two variables?

Try This

1. **a.** Press 2nd STAT MATH 3: **mean** (2nd 1 ENTER to find the mean height of your 30 classmates.

   b. Calculate the mean height of three students from the original survey who sit closest to you. What kind of sample is this? How does the mean height of this sample compare to the mean of the population from part **a**? Explain why they might be different.

   c. Calculate the mean height of 15 students from the original survey. How does this number compare with the mean of the population? Is it closer to the mean than the answer you got in part **b**?

TN ➤ **SPI 0706.5.1** Interpret and employ various graphs and charts to represent data. *Also ✓* **0706.5.2**

Interactivities Online ▶

Advertisements and news articles often use data to support a point. Sometimes the data is presented in a way that influences how the data is interpreted. A data display that distorts information in order to persuade can be *misleading*.

An axis in a graph can be "broken" to make the graph easier to read. However, a broken axis can also be misleading. In the graph at right, the cost per text message with Company B looks like it is twice as much as the cost with Company A. In fact, the difference is only $0.01 per text message.

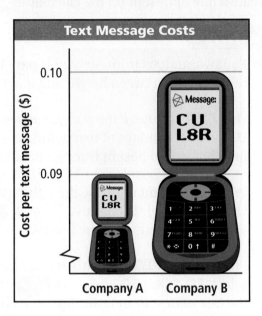

Text Message Costs

Cost per text message ($)

0.10

0.09

Company A   Company B

EXAMPLE 1 *Social Studies Application*

Both bar graphs show the percent of people in California, Maryland, Michigan, and Washington who use seat belts. Which graph could be misleading? Why?

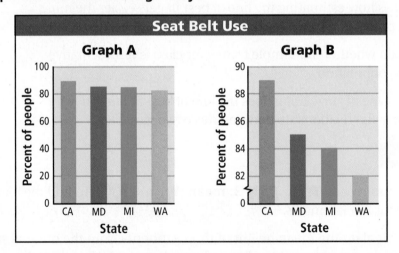

Seat Belt Use

Graph A

Percent of people

100
80
60
40
20
0

CA MD MI WA

State

Graph B

Percent of people

90
88
86
84
82
0

CA MD MI WA

State

Graph B could be misleading. Because the vertical axis on graph B is broken, it appears that the percent of people in California who wear seat belts is twice as great as the percent in Michigan. In fact, it is only 5% greater. People might conclude from graph B that the percent of people in California who wear seat belts is much greater than the percents in the other states.

EXAMPLE 2 **Analyzing Misleading Graphs**

Explain why each graph could be misleading.

Sports LINK

At the 1988 Summer Olympics Jackie Joyner-Kersee earned gold medals in the long jump and heptathlon events. A heptathlon consists of seven separate events given over the course of two days.

A

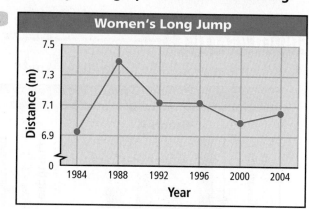

Women's Long Jump

Distance (m)
7.5
7.3
7.1
6.9
0
1984 1988 1992 1996 2000 2004
Year

Because the vertical axis is broken, the distance jumped in 1988 appears to be over two times as far as in 1984. In fact, the distance jumped in 1988 is less than 0.5 meter greater than in the other years.

B

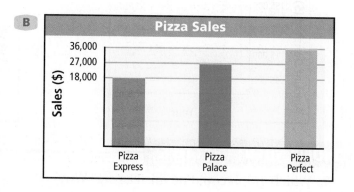

Pizza Sales

Sales ($)
36,000
27,000
18,000

Pizza
Express

Pizza
Palace

Pizza
Perfect

The scale of the graph is wrong. Equal distances on the vertical axis should represent equal intervals of numbers, but in this graph, the first $18,000 in sales is larger than the next $18,000. Because of this, you can't tell from the bars that Pizza Perfect's sales were twice those of Pizza Express.

Think and Discuss

1. Explain how to use the scale of a graph to decide if the graph is misleading.

2. Describe what might indicate that a graph is misleading.

3. Give an example of a situation in which a misleading graph might be used to persuade readers.

Learn It Online
Homework Help Online go.hrw.com,
keyword MS10 7-10 Go
Exercises 1–6, 7

GUIDED PRACTICE

See Example 1

1. Which graph could be misleading? Why?

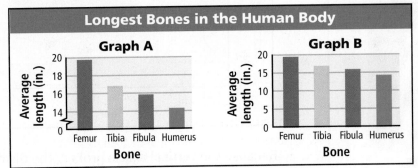

Longest Bones in the Human Body

Graph A — Average length (in.): Femur, Tibia, Fibula, Humerus

Graph B — Average length (in.): Femur, Tibia, Fibula, Humerus

See Example 2

Explain why each graph could be misleading.

2. Fund-raising Donations

3. Kite Sales

INDEPENDENT PRACTICE

See Example 1

4. Which graph could be misleading? Why?

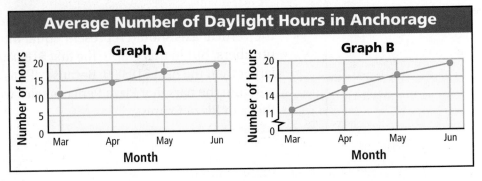

Average Number of Daylight Hours in Anchorage

Graph A — Number of hours: Mar, Apr, May, Jun

Graph B — Number of hours: Mar, Apr, May, Jun

See Example 2

Explain why each graph could be misleading.

5. CD Sales

6. Threatened Birds

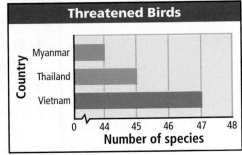

Extra Practice
See page EP19.

7. Business Explain why the graphs below are misleading. Then tell how you can redraw them so that they are not misleading.

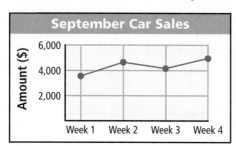

8. Social Studies The Appalachian Trail is a 2,160-mile footpath that runs from Maine to Georgia. The bar graph shows the number of miles of trail in three states. Redraw the graph so that it is not misleading. Then compare the two graphs.

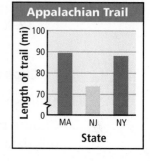

9. Choose a Strategy Tanya had $1.19 in coins. None of the coins were dollars or 50-cent pieces. Josie asked Tanya for change for a dollar, but she did not have the correct change. Which coins did Tanya have?

10. Write About It Why is it important to closely examine graphs in ads?

11. Challenge A company asked 10 people about their favorite brand of toothpaste. Three people chose Sparkle, one chose Smile, and six chose Purely White. An advertisement for Sparkle states, "Three times as many people prefer Sparkle over Smile!" Explain why this statement is misleading.

Test Prep and Spiral Review

Use the graph for Exercises 12 and 13.

12. Multiple Choice Which statement is NOT a reason that the graph is misleading?

  Ⓐ Broken interval on the vertical axis

  Ⓑ The title

  Ⓒ Vertical scale is not small enough

  Ⓓ Intervals are not equal

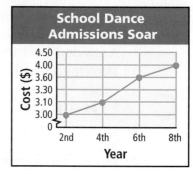

13. Short Response Redraw the graph so that it is not misleading.

Solve. Write each answer in simplest form. (Lesson 3-11)

14. $\frac{3}{5}x = \frac{1}{5}$ **15.** $x + \frac{2}{3} = \frac{5}{6}$ **16.** $-\frac{1}{8}x = \frac{3}{4}$ **17.** $x - \frac{3}{8} = -\frac{5}{6}$

Write *positive*, *negative*, or *no correlation* to describe each relationship. (Lesson 7-9)

18. height and test scores   **19.** speed of a car and time required to travel a distance

 **Ready To Go On?**

Quiz for Lessons 7-6 Through 7-10

 7-6 **Line Graphs**

The table shows the value of a truck as its mileage increases.

1. Make a line graph of the data.

2. Use the graph to estimate the value of the truck when it has 12,000 miles.

Mileage (thousands)	Value of Truck ($)
0	20,000
20	18,000
40	14,000
60	11,000
80	10,000

7-7 **Choosing an Appropriate Display**

The table shows worldwide earthquake frequency.

3. Choose the type of graph that would best display this data.

4. Create the graph that would best display the data.

Earthquake Frequency	
Category	Annual Frequency
Great	1
Major	18
Strong	120
Moderate	800

 7-8 **Populations and Samples**

Determine whether each sample may be biased. Explain.

5. Rickie surveys people at an amusement park to find out the average size of people's immediate family.

6. Theo surveys every fourth person entering a grocery store to find out the average number of pets in people's homes.

7. A biologist estimates that there are 1,800 fish in a quarry. To test this estimate, a student caught 150 fish from the quarry, tagged them, and released them. A few days later, the student caught 50 fish and noted that 4 were tagged. Determine whether the biologist's estimate is likely to be accurate.

7-9 **Scatter Plots**

8. Use the data to make a scatter plot.

9. Write *positive correlation, negative correlation,* or *no correlation* to describe the relationship between the data sets.

Cost ($)	2	3	4	5
Number of Purchases	12	8	6	3

7-10 **Misleading Graphs**

10. Which graph is misleading? Explain.

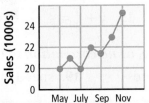

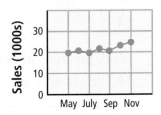

The Utah Jazz In 1979, the New Orleans Jazz moved to Salt Lake City, giving the state of Utah its first professional sports team. Since then, the Jazz have appeared frequently in the National Basketball Association's postseason playoffs.

UTAH

Salt Lake City

For 1–5, use the table.

1. Make a stem-and-leaf plot to display the number of wins.

2. Find the mean, median, mode, and range of the data.

3. Which season, if any, was an outlier? How does removing this season from the data set affect the mean, median, and mode?

4. A sports writer wants to present a graph that shows how the number of wins changed over time.

   a. Which type of graph should the writer use? Why?

   b. Make the graph.

   c. In general, what does the graph tell you about the team?

5. Make a box-and-whisker plot of the data.

Wins by the Utah Jazz	
Season	**Wins**
1999–2000	55
2000–2001	53
2001–2002	46
2002–2003	47
2003–2004	42
2004–2005	26
2005–2006	41
2006–2007	51

Real-World Connections

433

Game Time

Code Breaker

A *cryptogram* is a message written in code. One of the most common types of codes is a substitution code, in which each letter of a text is replaced with a different letter. The table shows one way to replace the letters in a text to make a coded message.

Original Letter	A	B	C	D	E	F	G	H	I	J	K	L	M
Code Letter	J	E	O	H	K	A	U	B	L	Y	V	G	P
Original Letter	N	O	P	Q	R	S	T	U	V	W	X	Y	Z
Code Letter	X	N	S	D	Z	Q	M	W	C	R	F	T	I

With this code, the word MATH is written PJMB. You can also use the table as a key to decode messages. Try decoding the following message.

J EJZ UZJSB OJX EK WQKH MN HLQSGJT HJMJ.

Suppose you want to crack a substitution code but are not given the key. You can use letter frequencies to help you. The bar graph below shows the number of times each letter of the English language is likely to appear in a text of 100 letters.

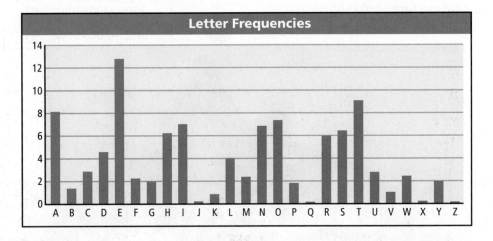

From the graph, you can see that E is the mode. In a coded text, the letter that appears most frequently is likely to represent the letter E. The letter that appears the second most frequently is likely to represent the letter T. Count the number of times each letter appears in the following message. Then use the letter frequencies and a bit of guesswork to decode the message. (*Hint:* In this code, P represents the letter M.)

KSQ PQUR, KSQ PQHGUR, URH KSQ PXHQ KQWW VXE DXPQKSGRT UCXEK U DQK XZ HUKU.

Materials
- card stock
- scissors
- glue
- colored paper
- magnetic strip
- tape
- empty CD case
- graph paper
- stapler

It's in the Bag!

PROJECT **Graph Match**

Use an empty CD case to make a magnetic matching game about different types of graphs.

Directions

❶ Trim the card stock to $4\frac{1}{2}$ inches by 5 inches. On the card stock, write "Match the Name and Number" and list the numbers 1 through 5 as shown. Cut small rectangles from the magnetic strip and glue these next to the numbers. **Figure A**

❷ Glue colored paper to the rest of the magnetic strip. Write the names of five different types of graphs on the strip. Cut these apart to form magnetic rectangles with the names of the graphs. **Figure B**

❸ Put a magnetic name of a graph next to each number on the card stock. Then tape the card stock to the inside back cover of an empty CD case. **Figure C**

❹ Cut out five squares of graph paper that are each $4\frac{1}{2}$ inches by $4\frac{1}{2}$ inches. Label the squares 1 through 5. Draw a different type of graph on each square, making sure to match the types that are named on the magnetic rectangles.

❺ Staple the graphs together to make a booklet. Insert the booklet into the cover of the CD case.

Putting the Math into Action

Exchange your game with a partner. Can you match each graph with its name?

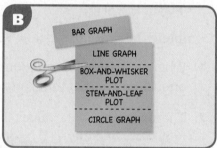

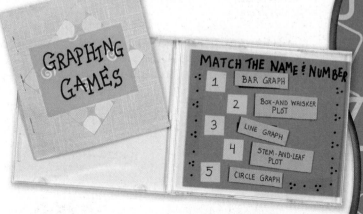

Study Guide: Review

Vocabulary

Complete the sentences below with vocabulary words from the list above.

1. When gathering information about a (n) ___?___, researchers often study part of the group, called a (n) ___?___.

2. The sum of the data values divided by the number of data items is called the ___?___ of the data.

EXAMPLES

EXERCISES

7-1 Frequency Tables, Stem-and-Leaf Plots, and Line Plots (pp. 380–384)

■ Make a line plot of the data.

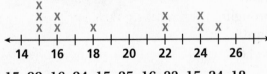

15, 22, 16, 24, 15, 25, 16, 22, 15, 24, 18

Use the data set 35, 29, 14, 19, 32, 25, 27, 16, and 8 for Exercises 3 through 5.

3. Make a cumulative frequency table.

4. Make a stem-and-leaf plot of the data.

5. Make a line plot of the data.

7-2 Mean, Median, Mode, and Range (pp. 385–389)

■ Find the mean, median, mode, and range of the data set 3, 7, 10, 2, and 3.

Mean: $3 + 7 + 10 + 2 + 3 = 25$ $\frac{25}{5} = 5$

Median: 2, 3, 3, 7, 10

Mode: 3   Range: $10 - 2 = 8$

Find the mean, median, mode, and range of each data set.

6. 324, 233, 324, 399, 233, 299

7. 48, 39, 27, 52, 45, 47, 49, 37

8. When is the median the most useful measure of central tendency?

7-3 **Bar Graphs and Histograms** (pp. 390–393)

■ Make a bar graph of the chess club's results: W, L, W, W, L, W, L, L, W, W, W, L, W.

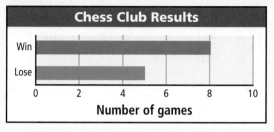

Chess Club Results

9. Make a double-bar graph of the data.

Favorite Pet	Girls	Boys
Cat	42	31
Dog	36	52
Fish	3	10
Other	19	7

7-4 **Reading and Interpreting Circle Graphs** (pp. 394–397)

■ About what percent of people said yellow was their favorite color?
about 25%

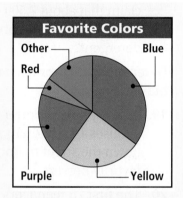

Favorite Colors

Use the circle graph at left for Exercises 10 and 11.

10. Did more people choose purple or yellow as their favorite color?

11. Out of the 100 people surveyed, 35% chose blue as their favorite color. How many people chose blue?

12. Decide whether a bar graph or a circle graph would best display the percent of U.S. citizens living in different countries.

7-5 **Box-and-Whisker Plots** (pp. 398–401)

■ Use the data to make a box-and-whisker plot: 14, 10, 23, 16, 21, 26, 23, 17, and 25.

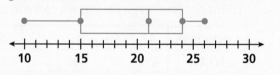

Use the following data for Exercises 13–14: 33, 38, 43, 30, 29, 40, 51, 27, 42, 23, and 31.

13. Make a box-and-whisker plot.

14. What is the interquartile range?

7-6 **Line Graphs** (pp. 406–409)

■ Make a line graph of the rainfall data: Apr, 5 in.; May, 3 in.; Jun, 4 in.; Jul, 1 in.

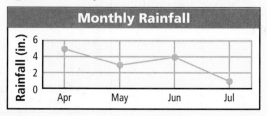

Monthly Rainfall

15. Make a double-line graph of the data in the table.

U.S. Open Winning Scores					
	1995	1996	1997	1998	1999
Men	280	278	276	280	279
Women	278	272	274	290	272

Study Guide: Review

7-7 **Choosing an Appropriate Display** (pp. 412–415)

■ Choose the type of graph that would best represent the population of a town over a 10-year period.

Line graph

Choose the type of graph that would best represent these data.

16. number of dogs in a kennel each day

17. number of exports from different countries

7-8 **Populations and Samples** (pp. 418–421)

■ In a random sample of 50 pigeons at a park, 4 are found to have a beak deformation. Is it reasonable to claim that about 20 of the pigeon population of 2,000 have this deformation? Explain.

No; $\frac{4}{50}$ is not closely proportional to $\frac{20}{2,000}$.

18. Fourteen out of 35 people surveyed prefer Brand X detergent. Is it reasonable for the store manager to claim that about 2,500 of the town's 6,000 residents will prefer Brand X detergent?

Determine whether each sample may be biased. Explain

19. A newspaper reporter randomly chooses 100 different people walking down the street to find out their favorite dessert.

20. The first 25 teenagers exiting a clothing store are surveyed to find out what types of clothes teenagers like to buy.

7-9 **Scatter Plots** (pp. 422–425)

■ Write *positive*, *negative*, or *no correlation* to describe the relationship between date of birth and eye color.

There seems to be no correlation between the data sets.

21. Use the data to make a scatter plot. Write *positive*, *negative*, or *no correlation*.

Customers	47	56	35	75	25
Sales ($)	495	501	490	520	375

7-10 **Misleading Graphs** (pp. 428–431)

■ Explain why the graph could be misleading.

The vertical axis is broken, so it appears that A's sales are twice more than B's.

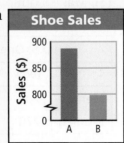

22. Explain why the graph could be misleading.

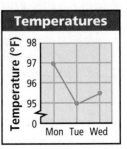

Study Guide: Review

Use the data set 12, 18, 12, 22, 28, 23, 32, 10, 29, and 36 for problems 1–8.

1. Find the mean, median, mode, and range of the data set.

2. How would the outlier 57 affect the measures of central tendency?

3. Make a cumulative frequency table of the data.

4. Make a stem-and-leaf plot of the data.

5. Make a line plot of the data.　　6. Make a histogram of the data.

7. Make a box-and-whisker plot of the data.　　8. What is the interquartile range?

Use the table for problems 9 and 10.

9. The table shows the weight in pounds of several mammals. Make a double-bar graph of the data.

10. Which mammal shows the greatest weight difference between the male and the female?

Mammal	Male	Female
Gorilla	450	200
Lion	400	300
Tiger	420	300

Use the circle graph for problems 11 and 12.

11. Approximately what percent of the students are seventh-graders?

12. If the school population is 1,200 students, are more than 500 students in eighth grade? Explain.

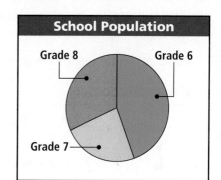

Use the table for problems 13 and 14.

13. The table shows passenger car fuel rates in miles per gallon for several years. Make a line graph of the data. During which 2-year period did the fuel rate decrease?

Year	2000	2002	2004	2006
Rate	21.0	20.7	21.2	21.6

14. Estimate the fuel rate in 2005.

15. What type of graph would best display student attendance at various sporting events?

For problems 16 and 17, write *positive correlation, negative correlation,* or *no correlation* to describe each relationship.

16. size of hand and typing speed

17. height from which an object is dropped and time it takes to hit the ground

18. Explain why the graph at right could be misleading.

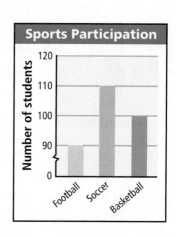

CHAPTER

7

Test Tackler

STANDARDIZED TEST STRATEGIES

Short Response: Write Short Responses

Short-response test items are designed to test your understanding of a math concept. In your response, you usually have to show your work and explain your answer. Scores are based on a 2-point scoring chart called a rubric.

EXAMPLE 1

Short Response The following data represents the number of hours Leann studied each day after school for her history test.

$$0, 1, 0, 1, 5, 3, 4$$

Find the mean, median, and mode for the data set. Which measure of central tendency best represents the data? Explain your answer.

Here are some responses scored using the 2-point rubric.

2-point response:

$\dfrac{0 + 1 + 0 + 1 + 5 + 3 + 4}{7} = 2$ The mean is 2.

0 0 1 ①3 4 5   The median is 1.

⓪ ⓪① ① 3 4 5   The modes are 0 and 1.

The measure of central tendency that best represents the data is the mean, because it shows the average number of hours that Leann studied before her test.

1-point response:

$\dfrac{0 + 1 + 0 + 1 + 5 + 3 + 4}{7} = 2$ The mean is 2.

0 0 1 ①3 4 5   The median is 1.

⓪ ⓪① ① 3 4 5   The modes are 0 and 1.

0-point response:

The mean is 2, the median is 2, and the mode is 0.

Scoring Rubric

2 points: The student correctly answers the question, shows all work, and provides a complete and correct explanation.

1 point: The student correctly answers the question but does not show all work or does not provide a complete explanation; or the student makes minor errors resulting in an incorrect solution but shows all work and provides a complete explanation.

0 points: The student gives an incorrect answer and shows no work or explanation, or the student gives no response.

Notice that there is no explanation given about the measure of central tendency that best represents the data.

Notice that the answer is incorrect and there is no explanation.

440   *Chapter 7 Collecting, Displaying, and Analyzing Data*

Underline or highlight what you are being asked to do in each question. Be sure to explain how you get your answer in complete sentences.

Read each test item and use the scoring rubric to answer the questions that follow.

Item A
Short Response The box-and-whisker plot shows the height in inches of seventh-grade students. Describe the spread of the data.

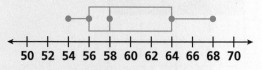

50 52 54 56 58 60 62 64 66 68 70

Student's Answer

> There are more students between 58 and 70 inches tall than there are between 50 and 58 inches tall because the third quartile is farther from the median than the first quartile is.

1. What score should the student's answer receive? Explain your reasoning.

2. What additional information, if any, should the student's answer include in order to receive full credit?

Item B
Short Response Explain the type of graph you would use to represent the number of each type of car sold at a car dealership in May.

Student's Answer

> I would use a bar graph to show how many of each car model was sold during the month.

3. What score should the student's answer receive? Explain your reasoning.

4. What additional information, if any, should the student's answer include in order to receive full credit?

Item C
Short Response Create a scatter plot of the data and describe the correlation between the outside temperature and the number of people at the public pool.

Temperature (°F)	70	75	80	85	90
Number of People	20	22	40	46	67

Student's Answer

> There is a positive correlation between the temperature and the number of people at the public pool because as it gets hotter, more people want to go swimming.

5. What score should the student's answer receive? Explain your reasoning.

6. What additional information, if any, should the student's answer include in order to receive full credit?

Item D
Short Response A survey was conducted to determine which age group attended the most movies in November. Fifteen people at a movie theater were asked their age, and their responses are as follows: 6, 10, 34, 22, 46, 11, 62, 14, 14, 5, 23, 25, 17, 18, and 55. Make a cumulative frequency table of the data. Then explain which group saw the most movies.

Student's Answer

Age Groups	Frequency	Cumulative Frequency
0–13	4	4
14–26	7	11
27–40	1	12
41–54	1	13
55–68	2	15

7. What score should the student's answer receive? Explain your reasoning.

8. What additional information, if any, should the student's answer include in order to receive full credit?

CHAPTER

7

TCAP
Test Prep

Learn It Online
State Test Practice **go.hrw.com**,
keyword MS10 TestPrep Go

Cumulative Assessment, Chapters 1–7

Multiple Choice

1. Which expression is true for the data set? 15, 18, 13, 15, 16, 14

   A Mean < mode

   B Median > mean

   C Median = mean

   D Median = mode

2. What is the first step to complete in simplifying this expression?

   $\frac{2}{5} + [3 - 5(2)] \div 6$

   F Multiply 5 and 2.

   G Divide by 6.

   H Subtract 5 from 3.

   J Divide 2 by 5.

3. What is the slope of the line shown?

   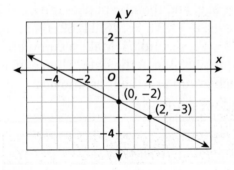

   (0, −2)

   (2, −3)

   A $\frac{1}{2}$ C 2

   B $-\frac{2}{1}$ D $-\frac{1}{2}$

4. On Monday the temperature was −13 °F. On Tuesday the temperature rose 7 °F. What was the temperature on Tuesday?

   F −20 °F   H −6 °F

   G −8 °F   J 7 °F

5. Which rule describes the ordered pairs in the table?

x	y
1	1
2	4
3	7
4	10

   A $y = 4x - 3$

   B $y = 2x + 1$

   C $y = 3x - 2$

   D $y = \frac{1}{2}x + 3$

6. Evaluate $x(7 - y)$ for $x = 3.1$ and $y = -10$.

   F −9.3

   G −3.9

   H 5.5

   J 52.7

7. What is the mode of the data given in the stem-and-leaf plot?

Stems	Leaves
6	1 2 2 5 9
7	0 4 6 7 8
8	3 3 3 5 6

   Key: 7|0 means 70

   A 25

   B 62

   C 76

   D 83

8. Which statement is best supported by the data?

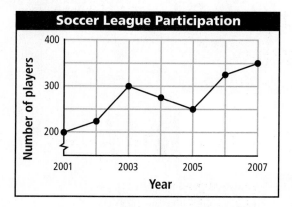

Soccer League Participation

F More students played soccer in 2005 than in 2002.

G From 2001–2007, soccer participation increased by 100%.

H From 2002–2006, soccer participation decreased by 144%.

J Participation increased between 2004 and 2005.

Read a graph or diagram as closely as you read the actual test question. These visual aids contain important information.

9. To the nearest hundredth, what is the difference between the median and the mean of the data set?

14, 11, 14, 11, 13, 12, 9, 15, 16

A 0.02   **C** 2.22

B 0.22   **D** 22.01

10. What value represents the upper quartile of the data in the box-and-whisker plot below?

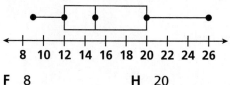

F 8   **H** 20

G 12   **J** 26

Process Standards Practice

Short Response

S1. The graph shows the results of a survey. Aaron read the graph and determined that more than $\frac{1}{5}$ of the students chose drama as their favorite type of movie. Do you agree with Aaron? Why or why not?

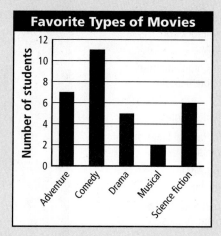

Favorite Types of Movies

S2. A land developer purchases 120 acres of land and plans to divide one part into five 5-acre lots, another part into two 10-acre lots, and the rest into $\frac{1}{2}$-acre lots. Each lot will be sold for a future home site. How many total lots can the developer plan to sell?

Extended Response

E1. Mr. Parker wants to identify the types of activities in which high school students participate after school, so he surveys the twelfth-graders in his science classes. The table shows the results of the survey.

Activity	Boys	Girls
Play sports	36	24
Talk to friends	6	30
Do homework	15	18
Work	5	4

a. Use the data in the table to construct a double-bar graph.

b. What is the mean number of girls per activity? Show your work.

c. What type of sample is used? Is this sample representative of the population? Explain.

CHAPTER
8

Geometric Figures

Chapter Focus
- Use facts about distance and angles to analyze figures.
- Find unknown measures of angles.

Why Learn This?

The deck of the Brooklyn Bridge is suspended by vertical cables. Reinforcement cables intersect the suspenders and form geometric shapes such as quadrilaterals.

Learn It Online
Chapter Project Online **go.hrw.com**,
keyword MS10 Ch8 Go

Are You Ready?

Learn It Online
Resources Online **go.hrw.com**,
keyword MS10 AYR8 [Go]

✓ Vocabulary

Choose the best term from the list to complete each sentence.

1. An equation showing that two ratios are equal is a(n) __?__.
2. The coordinates of a point on a grid are written as a(n) __?__.
3. A(n) __?__ is a special ratio that compares a number to 100 and uses the symbol %.
4. The number −3 is a(n) __?__.

decimal
integer
percent
proportion
ordered pair

Complete these exercises to review skills you will need for this chapter.

✓ Percents and Decimals

Write each decimal as a percent.

5. 0.77   6. 0.06   7. 0.9   8. 1.04

Write each percent as a decimal.

9. 42%   10. 80%   11. 1%   12. 131%

✓ Find the Percent of a Number

Solve.

13. What is 10% of 40?   14. What is 12% of 100?   15. What is 99% of 60?

16. What is 100% of 81?   17. What is 45% of 360?   18. What is 55% of 1,024?

✓ Inverse Operations

Use the inverse operation to write an equation. Solve.

19. $45 + n = 97$ 20. $n - 18 = 100$ 21. $n - 72 = 91$ 22. $n + 23 = 55$

23. $5 \times t = 105$ 24. $b \div 13 = 8$ 25. $k \times 18 = 90$ 26. $d \div 7 = 8$

✓ Graph Ordered Pairs

Use the coordinate plane at right. Write the ordered pair for each point.

27. point A 28. point B

29. point C 30. point D

31. point E 32. point F

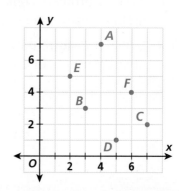

Where You've Been

Previously, you

- identified angle and line relationships.

- identified similar figures.

- graphed points on a coordinate plane.

In This Chapter

You will study

- classifying pairs of angles as complementary or supplementary.

- classifying triangles and quadrilaterals.

- graphing translations and reflections on a coordinate plane.

- using congruence and similarity to solve problems.

Where You're Going

You can use the skills learned in this chapter

- to solve problems related to architecture and engineering.

- to use transformations to create patterns in art classes.

Key Vocabulary/Vocabulario

angle	ángulo
congruent	congruentes
image	imagen
line symmetry	simetría axial
parallel lines	rectas paralelas
perpendicular lines	rectas perpendiculares
polygon	polígono
rotation	rotación
transformation	transformación
vertex	vértice

Vocabulary Connections

To become familiar with some of the vocabulary terms in the chapter, consider the following. You may refer to the chapter, the glossary, or a dictionary if you like.

1. *Congruent* comes from the Latin word *congruere*, meaning "to agree or correspond." If two figures are **congruent**, do you think they look the same or different?

2. *Polygon* comes from the Greek words *polus*, meaning "many," and *gonia*, meaning "angle." What do you think a shape called a **polygon** includes?

3. *Rotation* can mean "the act of spinning or turning." How do you think a figure is moved when you perform a **rotation** on it?

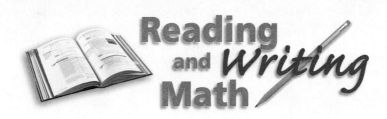

Reading and Writing Math

TN English/Language Arts
GLE 0701.6.1 Comprehend and summarize the main ideas and supporting details of informational texts.

Writing Strategy: Keep a Math Journal

Keeping a math journal can help you improve your writing and reasoning skills and help you make sense of math topics that might be confusing.

You can use your journal to reflect on what you have learned in class or to summarize important concepts and vocabulary. Most important, though, your math journal can help you see your progress throughout the year.

Journal Entry: Read the entry Lydia wrote in her math journal about similar figures.

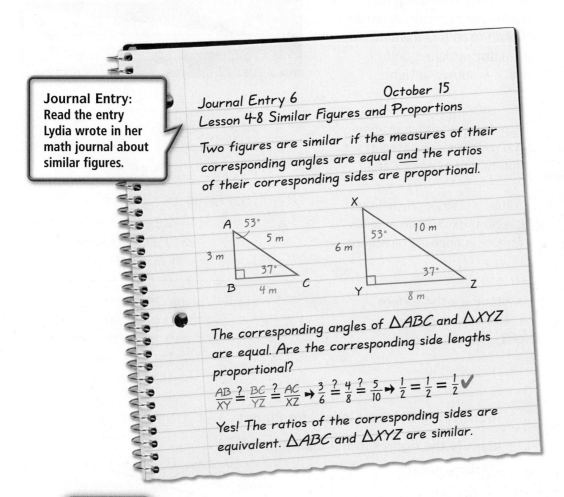

Journal Entry 6   October 15
Lesson 4-8 Similar Figures and Proportions

Two figures are similar if the measures of their corresponding angles are equal <u>and</u> the ratios of their corresponding sides are proportional.

The corresponding angles of $\triangle ABC$ and $\triangle XYZ$ are equal. Are the corresponding side lengths proportional?

$$\frac{AB}{XY} \overset{?}{=} \frac{BC}{YZ} \overset{?}{=} \frac{AC}{XZ} \rightarrow \frac{3}{6} \overset{?}{=} \frac{4}{8} \overset{?}{=} \frac{5}{10} \rightarrow \frac{1}{2} = \frac{1}{2} = \frac{1}{2} \checkmark$$

Yes! The ratios of the corresponding sides are equivalent. $\triangle ABC$ and $\triangle XYZ$ are similar.

Try This

Begin a math journal. Make an entry every day for one week. Use the following ideas to begin your entries. Be sure to date each entry.

• What I already know about this lesson is . . .

• The skills I need to be successful in this lesson are . . .

• What challenges did I have? How did I handle these challenges?

Building Blocks of Geometry

Points, *lines*, and *planes* are the most basic figures of geometry. Other geometric figures, such as *line segments* and *rays*, are defined in terms of these building blocks.

Artists often use basic geometric figures when creating their works. For example, Auguste Herbin used *line segments* in his painting called *Eight I*, which is shown at right.

Vocabulary

point

line

plane

ray

line segment

congruent

Helpful Hint

A number line is an example of a line, and a coordinate plane is an example of a plane.

A **point** is an exact location. It is usually represented as a dot, but it has no size at all.	• *A*	point *A* *Use a capital letter to name a point.*
A **line** is a straight path that has no thickness and extends forever in opposite directions.	ℓ ← • • → *X* *Y*	$\overleftrightarrow{XY}$, $\overleftrightarrow{YX}$, or ℓ *Use two points on the line or a lowercase letter to name a line.*
A **plane** is a flat surface that has no thickness and extends forever.	*Q*• *S*• *R*•	plane *QRS* *Use three points in any order, not on the same line, to name a plane.*

EXAMPLE **1** **Identifying Points, Lines, and Planes**

Identify the figures in the diagram.

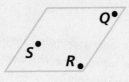

A three points

A, E, and *D* *Choose any three points.*

B two lines

$\overleftrightarrow{BD}$, $\overleftrightarrow{CE}$ *Choose any two points on a line to name a line.*

C a plane

plane *ABC* *Choose any three points not on the same line to name a plane.*

Video **Lesson Tutorials Online** my.hrw.com

A **ray** is a part of a line. It has one endpoint and extends forever in one direction.

$\overrightarrow{GH}$
Name the endpoint first when naming a ray.

A **line segment** is a part of a line or a ray that extends from one endpoint to another.

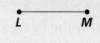

$\overline{LM}$ or $\overline{ML}$
Use the endpoints to name a line segment.

EXAMPLE **2** **Identifying Line Segments and Rays**

Identify the figures in the diagram.

A **three rays**
$\overrightarrow{RQ}$, $\overrightarrow{RT}$, and $\overrightarrow{SQ}$ *Name the endpoint of a ray first.*

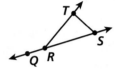

B **three line segments**
$\overline{RQ}$, $\overline{QS}$, and $\overline{ST}$ *Use the endpoints in any order to name a line segment.*

Figures are **congruent** if they have the same shape and size. Line segments are congruent if they have the same length.

You can use tick marks to indicate congruent line segments. In the triangle at right, line segments *AB* and *BC* are congruent.

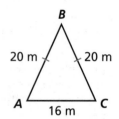

EXAMPLE **3** **Identifying Congruent Line Segments**

Identify the line segments that are congruent in the figure.

Reading Math
The symbol ≅ means "is congruent to."

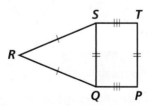

$\overline{QR} \cong \overline{SR}$ *One tick mark*
$\overline{QS} \cong \overline{PT}$ *Two tick marks*
$\overline{QP} \cong \overline{ST}$ *Three tick marks*

Think and Discuss

1. Explain why a line and a plane can be named in more than two ways. How many ways can a line segment be named?

2. Explain why it is important to choose three points that are not on the same line when naming a plane.

Learn It Online
Homework Help Online **go.hrw.com**,
keyword MS10 8-1 **Go**
Exercises 1–12, 21

GUIDED PRACTICE

See Example 1 **Identify the figures in the diagram.**

1. three points

2. two lines

3. a plane

See Example 2 4. three rays

5. three line segments

See Example 3 6. Identify the line segments that are congruent in the figure.

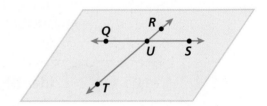

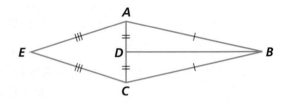

INDEPENDENT PRACTICE

See Example 1 **Identify the figures in the diagram.**

7. three points

8. two lines

9. a plane

See Example 2 10. three rays

11. three line segments

See Example 3 12. Identify the line segments that are congruent in the figure.

PRACTICE AND PROBLEM SOLVING

Extra Practice
See page EP20.

13. Identify the points, lines, line segments, and rays that are represented in the illustration, and tell what plane each is in. Some figures may be in more than one plane.

14. **Critical Thinking** How many different line segments can be named in the figure below? Name each segment.

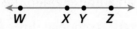

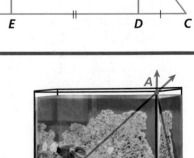

15. Draw a diagram in which a plane, 5 points, 4 rays, and 2 lines can be identified. Then identify these figures.

Art LINK

16. The artwork at right, by Diana Ong, is called *Blocs*.

  a. Copy the line segments in the artwork. Add tick marks to show line segments that appear to be congruent.

  b. Label the endpoints of the segments, including the points of intersection. Then name four pairs of line segments that appear to be congruent.

17. Draw a figure that includes at least three sets of congruent line segments. Label the endpoints and use notation to tell which line segments are congruent.

18. **Critical Thinking** Can two endpoints be shared by two different line segments? Make a drawing to illustrate your answer.

19. **Write About It** Explain the difference between a line, a line segment, and a ray. Is it possible to estimate the length of any of these figures? If so, tell which ones and why.

20. **Challenge** The sandstone sculpture at right, by Georges Vantongerloo, is called *Interrelation of Volumes*. Explain whether two separate faces on the front of the sculpture could be in the same plane.

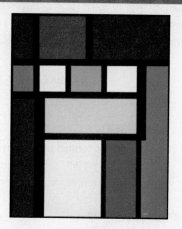

Test Prep and Spiral Review

21. **Multiple Choice** Identify the line segments that are congruent in the figure.

  I $\overline{AB}, \overline{BC}$ II $\overline{AB}, \overline{CD}$

  III $\overline{BC}, \overline{CD}$ IV $\overline{BC}, \overline{AD}$

  Ⓐ I only   Ⓑ I and III   Ⓒ II and IV   Ⓓ II only

22. **Short Response** Draw a plane that contains each of the following: points *A*, *B*, and *C*; line segment *AB*; ray *BC*; and line *AC*.

Find each product or quotient. (Lesson 2-4)

23. $-48 \div (-3)$ 24. $-2 \cdot (-6)$ 25. $-56 \div 8$ 26. $5 \cdot (-13)$

Find each percent of change. Round answers to the nearest tenth of a percent, if necessary. (Lesson 6-6)

27. 85 is decreased to 60. 28. 35 is increased to 120. 29. 6 is decreased to 1.

Hands-On LAB 8-2

Explore Complementary and Supplementary Angles

Use with Lesson 8-2

Learn It Online
Lab Resources Online **go.hrw.com**,
keyword **MS10 Lab8** **Go**

> **REMEMBER**
> • An angle is formed by two rays with a common endpoint, called the vertex.

Activity 1

You can use a *protractor* to measure angles in units called *degrees*. Find the measure of ∠AVB.

1 Place the center point of the protractor on the vertex of the angle.

2 Place the protractor so that $\overrightarrow{AV}$ passes through the 0° mark.

3 Using the scale that starts with 0° along $\overrightarrow{AV}$, read the measure where $\overrightarrow{VB}$ crosses the scale. The measure of ∠AVB is 50°.

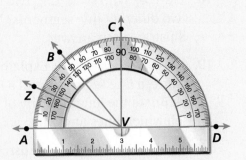

Think and Discuss

1. Explain how to find the measure of ∠BVC without moving the protractor.

Try This

Use the protractor in Activity 1 to find the measure of each angle.

1. ∠AVC   **2.** ∠AVZ   **3.** ∠DVC

Activity 2

Copy and measure each pair of angles.

Type of Angle Pair	Examples	Nonexamples
Complementary	**1.** ![angle A B]	**2.** ![angle C D]
	3. ![angle E F]	**4.** ![angle G H]

Type of Angle Pair	Examples	Nonexamples
Supplementary	5. I J	6. K L 7. M N	8. O P

Think and Discuss

1. **Make a Conjecture** For each type of angle pair, complementary and supplementary, make a conjecture about how the angle measurements are related.

Try This

Use a protractor to measure each of the angle pairs below. Tell whether the angle pairs are complementary, supplementary, or neither.

1.

2.

3.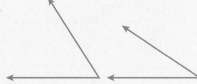

4.

5. **Make a Conjecture** The two angles in Exercise 4 form a straight angle. Make a conjecture about the number of degrees in a straight angle.

6. Use a protractor to find four pairs of complementary angles and four pairs of supplementary angles in the figure at right.

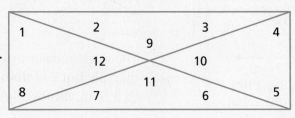

As an airplane takes off, the path of the airplane forms an *angle* with the ground.

An **angle** is formed by two rays with a common endpoint. The two rays are the sides of the angle. The common endpoint is the **vertex**.

Angles are measured in degrees (°). An angle's measure determines the type of angle it is.

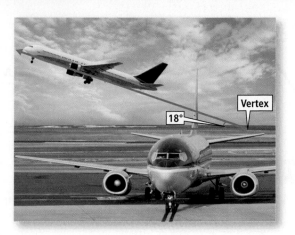

Vertex
18°

Vocabulary

angle
vertex
right angle
acute angle
obtuse angle
straight angle
complementary angles
supplementary angles

Interactivities Online ▶

A **right angle** is an angle that measures exactly 90°. The symbol ⌐ indicates a right angle.

An **acute angle** is an angle that measures greater than 0° and less than 90°.

An **obtuse angle** is an angle that measures greater than 90° but less than 180°.

A **straight angle** is an angle that measures exactly 180°.

EXAMPLE 1 **Classifying Angles**

Tell whether each angle is acute, right, obtuse, or straight.

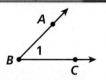
A

The angle measures greater than 90° but less than 180°, so it is an obtuse angle.

B

The angle measures less than 90°, so it is an acute angle.

If the sum of the measures of two angles is 90°, then the angles are **complementary angles**. If the sum of the measures of two angles is 180°, then the angles are **supplementary angles**.

Video **Lesson Tutorials Online** my.hrw.com

EXAMPLE 2 **Identifying Complementary and Supplementary Angles**

Use the diagram to tell whether the angles are complementary, supplementary, or neither.

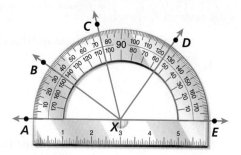

A ∠*DXE* and ∠*AXB*

m∠*DXE* = 55° and m∠*AXB* = 35°

Since 55° + 35° = 90°, ∠*DXE* and ∠*AXB* are complementary.

B ∠*DXE* and ∠*BXC*

m∠*DXE* = 55°. To find m∠*BXC*, start with the measure that $\overrightarrow{XC}$ crosses, 75°, and subtract the measure that $\overrightarrow{XB}$ crosses, 35°. m∠*BXC* = 75° − 35° = 40°.

Since 55° + 40° = 95°, ∠*DXE* and ∠*BXC* are neither complementary nor supplementary.

C ∠*AXC* and ∠*CXE*

m∠*AXC* = 75° and m∠*CXE* = 105°

Since 75° + 105° = 180°, ∠*AXC* and ∠*CXE* are supplementary.

EXAMPLE 3 **Finding Angle Measures**

Angles *R* and *V* are supplementary. If m∠*R* is 67°, what is m∠*V*?

Since ∠*R* and ∠*V* are supplementary, m∠*R* + m∠*V* = 180°.

$$m\angle R + m\angle V = 180°$$
$$67° + m\angle V = 180°$$ *Substitute 67° for m∠R.*
$$\underline{-67° \qquad\qquad -67°}$$ *Subtract 67° from both sides.*
$$m\angle V = 113°$$

The measure of ∠*V* is 113°.

Think and Discuss

1. **Describe** three different ways to classify an angle.

2. **Explain** how to find the measure of ∠*P* if ∠*P* and ∠*Q* are complementary angles and m∠*Q* = 25°.

Learn It Online
Homework Help Online **go.hrw.com**,
keyword MS10 8-2 Go
Exercises 1–18, 19, 21, 23

GUIDED PRACTICE

See Example **1** Tell whether each angle is acute, right, obtuse, or straight.

1.

2.

3.

See Example **2** Use the diagram to tell whether the angles are complementary, supplementary, or neither.

4. ∠AXB and ∠BXC

5. ∠BXC and ∠DXE

6. ∠DXE and ∠AXD

7. ∠CXD and ∠AXB

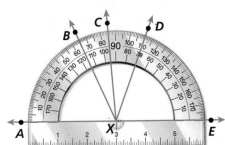

See Example **3** **8.** Angles L and P are complementary. If m∠P is 34°, what is m∠L?

9. Angles B and C are supplementary. If m∠B is 119°, what is m∠C?

INDEPENDENT PRACTICE

See Example **1** Tell whether each angle is acute, right, obtuse, or straight.

10.

11.

12.

See Example **2** Use the diagram to tell whether the angles are complementary, supplementary, or neither.

13. ∠NZO and ∠MZN

14. ∠MZN and ∠OZP

15. ∠LZN and ∠NZP

16. ∠NZO and ∠LZM

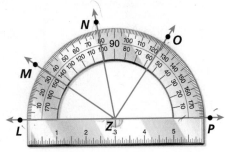

See Example **3** **17.** Angles F and O are supplementary. If m∠F is 85°, what is m∠O?

18. Angles J and K are complementary. If m∠K is 22°, what is m∠J?

PRACTICE AND PROBLEM SOLVING

Extra Practice
See page EP20.

Classify each pair of angles as complementary or supplementary. Then find the unknown angle measure.

19.

28°   x

20.

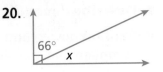

66°

x

21.

134°

x

22. **Critical Thinking** The hands of a clock form an acute angle at 1:00. What type of angle is formed at 6:00? at 3:00? at 5:00?

23. **Geography** Imaginary curves around Earth show distances in degrees from the equator and Prime Meridian. On a flat map, these curves are displayed as horizontal lines (latitude) and vertical lines (longitude).

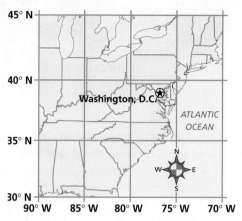

   a. What type of angle is formed where a line of latitude and a line of longitude cross?

   b. Estimate the latitude and longitude of Washington, D.C.

24. **What's the Error?** A student states that when the sum of two angles equals the measure of a straight angle, the two angles are complementary. Explain why the student is incorrect.

25. **Write About It** Explain why two obtuse angles cannot be supplementary to one another.

26. **Challenge** Find m∠BAC in the figure.

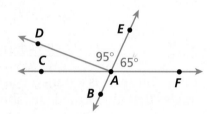

Test Prep and Spiral Review

Use the diagram for Exercises 27 and 28.

27. **Multiple Choice** Which statement is NOT true?

   Ⓐ ∠BAC is acute.

   Ⓑ ∠DAE is a right angle.

   Ⓒ ∠FAE and ∠EAD are complementary angles.

   Ⓓ ∠FAD and ∠DAC are supplementary angles.

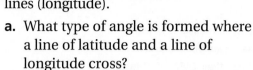

28. **Multiple Choice** What is the measure of ∠FAD?

   Ⓕ 30°   Ⓖ 120°   Ⓗ 150°   Ⓙ 180°

Find the mean, median, mode, and range of each data set. (Lesson 7-2)

29. 6, 3, 5, 6, 8   **30.** 14, 18, 10, 20, 23   **31.** 41, 35, 29, 41, 58, 24

32. Identify and name the figure at right. (Lesson 8-1)

Explore Parallel Lines and Transversals

8-3A

Use with Lesson 8-3

Learn It Online
Lab Resources Online **go.hrw.com**,
keyword MS10 Lab8 Go

> **REMEMBER**
> - Two angles are supplementary if the sum of their measures is 180°.
> - Angles with measures greater than 0° but less than 90° are acute.
> - Angles with measures greater than 90° but less than 180° are obtuse.

Parallel lines are lines in the same plane that never cross. When two parallel lines are intersected by a third line, the angles formed have special relationships. This third line is called a *transversal*.

In San Francisco, California, many streets are parallel such as Lombard St. and Broadway.

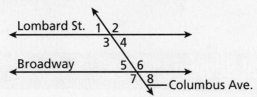

Columbus Ave. is a transversal that runs diagonally across them. The eight angles that are formed are labeled on the diagram below.

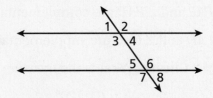

Activity

1. Copy the table below. Then use a protractor to measure angles 1–8 in the diagram. Write these measures in your table.

Angle Number	Angle Measure
1	
2	
3	
4	
5	
6	
7	
8	

2 Use the table you completed and the corresponding diagram for the following problems.

    a. Angles inside the parallel lines are *interior angles*. Name them.

    b. Angles outside the parallel lines are *exterior angles*. Name them.

    c. Angles 3 and 6 and angles 4 and 5 are *alternate interior angles*. What do you notice about the measures of angles 3 and 6? What do you notice about the measures of angles 4 and 5?

    d. Angles 2 and 7 and angles 1 and 8 are *alternate exterior angles*. How do the measures of each pair of alternate exterior angles compare?

    e. Angles 1 and 5 are *corresponding angles* because they are in the same position relative to the parallel lines. How do the measures of angles 1 and 5 compare? Name another set of corresponding angles.

    f. **Make a Conjecture** What conjectures can you make about the measures of alternate interior angles? alternate exterior angles? corresponding angles?

Think and Discuss

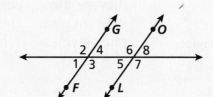

1. $\overleftrightarrow{FG}$ and $\overleftrightarrow{LO}$ are parallel. Tell what you know about the angles that are labeled 1 through 8.

2. Angle 2 measures 125°. What are the measures of angles 1, 3, 4, 5, 6, 7, and 8?

3. A transversal intersects two parallel lines and one of the angles formed measures 90°. Compare the measures of the remaining angles formed by the three lines.

Try This

Use a protractor to measure one angle in each diagram. Then find the measures of all the other angles without using a protractor. Tell how to find each angle measure.

1.

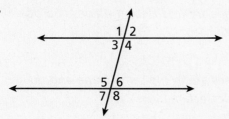

2.

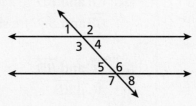

3.

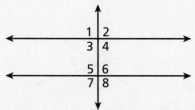

4.

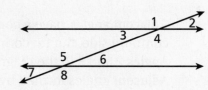

Line and Angle Relationships

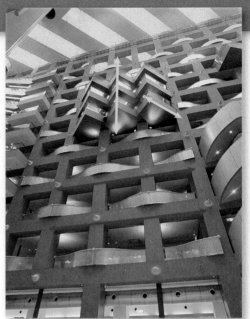

When lines, line segments, or rays intersect, they form angles. If the angles formed by two intersecting lines measure 90°, the lines are **perpendicular lines**.

Some lines in the same plane do not intersect at all. These lines are **parallel lines**. Segments and rays that are parts of parallel lines are also parallel. The blue lines in the photograph are parallel.

Skew lines do not intersect, and yet they are also not parallel. They lie in different planes. The yellow lines in the photograph are skew.

Vocabulary

perpendicular lines

parallel lines

skew lines

adjacent angles

vertical angles

transversal

EXAMPLE 1 Identifying Parallel, Perpendicular, and Skew Lines

Interactivities Online ▶

Tell whether the lines in the figure appear parallel, perpendicular, or skew.

A $\overleftrightarrow{AB}$ and $\overleftrightarrow{AC}$
$\overleftrightarrow{AB} \perp \overleftrightarrow{AC}$

The lines appear to intersect to form right angles.

Reading Math

The symbol $\perp$ means "is perpendicular to." The symbol $\parallel$ means "is parallel to."

B $\overleftrightarrow{CE}$ and $\overleftrightarrow{BD}$
$\overleftrightarrow{CE}$ and $\overleftrightarrow{BD}$ are skew.

The lines are in different planes and do not intersect.

C $\overleftrightarrow{AC}$ and $\overleftrightarrow{BD}$
$\overleftrightarrow{AC} \parallel \overleftrightarrow{BD}$

The lines are in the same plane and do not intersect.

Adjacent angles have a common vertex and a common side, but no common interior points. Angles 2 and 3 in the diagram are adjacent. Adjacent angles formed by two intersecting lines are supplementary.

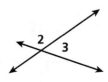

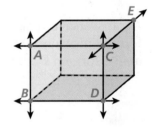

Video Lesson Tutorials Online   my.hrw.com

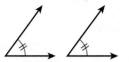

Reading Math

Angles with the same number of tick marks are congruent.

Vertical angles are the opposite angles formed by two intersecting lines. Angles 1 and 3 in the diagram are vertical angles. Vertical angles have the same measure, so they are congruent.

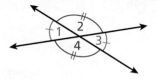

A **transversal** is a line that intersects two or more lines that lie in the same plane. Transversals to parallel lines form special angle pairs.

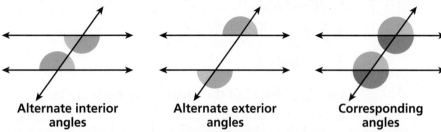

Alternate interior angles   Alternate exterior angles   Corresponding angles

PROPERTIES OF TRANSVERSALS TO PARALLEL LINES

If two parallel lines are intersected by a transversal,
- corresponding angles are congruent,
- alternate interior angles are congruent,
- and alternate exterior angles are congruent.

EXAMPLE 2 **Using Angle Relationships to Find Angle Measures**

Line *n* ∥ line *p*. Find the measure of each angle.

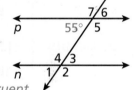

A ∠6

$m\angle 6 = 55°$ *Vertical angles are congruent.*

B ∠1

$m\angle 1 = 55°$ *Corresponding angles are congruent.*

C ∠7

$$m\angle 7 + 55° = 180°$$ *Adjacent angles formed by two*
$$\underline{\quad -55° \quad -55°}$$ *intersecting lines are supplementary.*
$$m\angle 7 \quad = \quad 125°$$

D ∠3

$m\angle 3 = 55°$ *Alternate interior angles are congruent.*

Think and Discuss

1. Draw a pair of parallel lines intersected by a transversal. Use tick marks to indicate the congruent angles.

2. Give some examples in which parallel, perpendicular, and skew relationships can be seen in the real world.

Learn It Online
Homework Help Online **go.hrw.com,**
keyword **MS10 8-3** **Go**
Exercises 1–12, 13, 15, 17, 19, 21, 23

GUIDED PRACTICE

See Example **1** Tell whether the lines appear parallel, perpendicular, or skew.

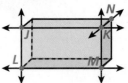

1. $\overleftrightarrow{JL}$ and $\overleftrightarrow{KM}$

2. $\overleftrightarrow{LM}$ and $\overleftrightarrow{KN}$

3. $\overleftrightarrow{LM}$ and $\overleftrightarrow{KM}$

See Example **2** Line $r \parallel$ line s. Find the measure of each angle.

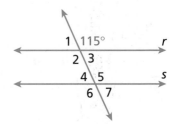

4. $\angle 5$

5. $\angle 2$

6. $\angle 6$

INDEPENDENT PRACTICE

See Example **1** Tell whether the lines appear parallel, perpendicular, or skew.

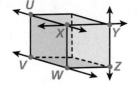

7. $\overleftrightarrow{UX}$ and $\overleftrightarrow{YZ}$

8. $\overleftrightarrow{YZ}$ and $\overleftrightarrow{XY}$

9. $\overleftrightarrow{UX}$ and $\overleftrightarrow{VW}$

See Example **2** Line $k \parallel$ line m. Find the measure of each angle.

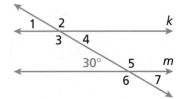

10. $\angle 1$

11. $\angle 4$

12. $\angle 6$

PRACTICE AND PROBLEM SOLVING

Extra Practice
See page EP20.

For Exercises 13–16, use the figure to complete each statement.

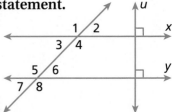

13. Lines x and y are ___?___.

14. Lines u and x are ___?___.

15. $\angle 3$ and $\angle 4$ are ___?___. They are also ___?___.

16. $\angle 2$ and $\angle 7$ are ___?___. They are also ___?___.

17. Critical Thinking A pair of complementary angles are congruent. What is the measure of each angle?

18. Multi-Step Two lines intersect to form four angles. The measure of one angle is 27°. Draw a diagram to show the measures of the other three angles. Explain your answer.

Tell whether each statement is always, sometimes, or never true.

19. Adjacent angles are congruent.

20. Intersecting lines are skew.

21. Vertical angles are congruent.

22. Parallel lines intersect.

23. Construction In the diagram of the partial wall frame shown, the vertical beams are parallel.

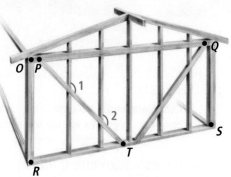

    a. Angle *ORT* measures 90°. How are $\overline{OR}$ and $\overline{RS}$ related?

    b. $\overline{PT}$ crosses two vertical crossbeams. What word describes $\overline{PT}$?

    c. How are ∠1 and ∠2 related?

24. Critical Thinking Two lines intersect to form congruent adjacent angles. What can you say about the two lines?

 25. Choose a Strategy Trace the dots in the figure. Draw all the lines that connect three dots. How many pairs of perpendicular lines have you drawn?

    Ⓐ 8   Ⓑ 9   Ⓒ 10   Ⓓ 14

26. Write About It Use the definition of a straight angle to explain why adjacent angles formed by two intersecting lines are supplementary.

27. Challenge The lines in the parking lot appear to be parallel. How could you check that the lines are parallel?

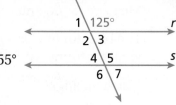

Test Prep and Spiral Review

Use the diagram for Exercises 28 and 29. Line *r* ∥ line *s*.

28. Multiple Choice What is the measure of ∠3?

    Ⓐ 125°   Ⓑ 75°   Ⓒ 65°   Ⓓ 55°

29. Multiple Choice What is the measure of ∠6?

    Ⓕ 125°   Ⓖ 75°   Ⓗ 65°   Ⓙ 55°

Add or subtract. Estimate to check whether each answer is reasonable. (Lesson 3-2)

30. $3.583 - (-2.759)$ **31.** $-9.43 + 7.68$ **32.** $-1.03 + (-0.081)$

Classify each pair of angles as complementary or supplementary. Then find the unknown angle measure. (Lesson 8-2)

33.

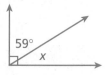

34.

35.

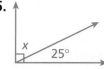

Construct Bisectors and Congruent Angles

8-3B

Use with Lesson 8-3

REMEMBER
- Congruent angles have the same measure, and congruent segments are the same length.

To bisect a segment or an angle is to divide it into two congruent parts. You can bisect segments and angles, and construct congruent angles without using a protractor or ruler. Instead, you can use a compass and a straightedge.

Activity

1. Construct a perpendicular bisector of a line segment.

   a. Draw a line segment $\overline{JS}$ on a piece of paper.

   b. Place your compass on endpoint J and, using an opening that is greater than half the length of $\overline{JS}$, draw an arc that intersects $\overline{JS}$.

   c. Place your compass on endpoint S and draw an arc using the same opening as you did in Step **b**. The arc should intersect the first arc at both ends.

   d. Draw a line to connect the intersections of the arcs. Label the intersection of $\overline{JS}$ and the line point K.

   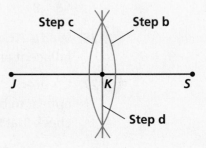

   Measure $\overline{JS}$, $\overline{JK}$, and $\overline{KS}$. What do you notice?

   The bisector of $\overline{JS}$ is a *perpendicular* bisector because all of the angles it forms with $\overline{JS}$ measure 90°.

2. Bisect an angle.

   a. Draw an acute angle *GHE* on a piece of paper. Label the vertex *H*.

   b. Place the point of your compass on *H* and draw an arc through both sides of the angle. Label points *G* and *E* where the arc crosses each side of the angle.

   c. Without changing your compass opening, draw intersecting arcs from point *G* and point *E*. Label the point of intersection *D*.

   d. Draw $\overrightarrow{HD}$.

   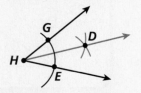

   Use your protractor to measure angles *GHE*, *GHD*, and *DHE*. What do you notice?

3 Construct congruent angles.

a. Draw ∠ABM on your paper.

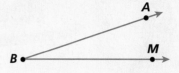

b. To construct an angle congruent to ∠ABM,
begin by drawing a ray, and label its endpoint C.

c. With your compass point on B,
draw an arc through ∠ABM.

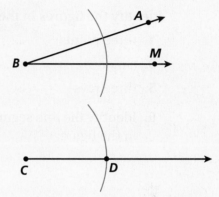

d. With the same compass opening, place the
compass point on C and draw an arc through
the ray. Label point D where the arc crosses the ray.

e. With your compass, measure the arc in ∠ABM.

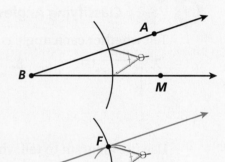

f. With the same opening, place your compass point
on D, and draw another arc intersecting the first one.
Label the intersection F. Draw $\overrightarrow{CF}$.

Use your protractor to measure ∠ABM and ∠FCD.
What do you find?

Think and Discuss

1. How many bisectors would you use to divide an angle into four
equal parts?

2. An 88° angle is bisected, and then each of the two angles formed are
bisected. What is the measure of each of the smaller angles formed?

Try This

Use a compass and a straightedge to perform each construction.

1. Draw and bisect a line segment.

2. Trace and then bisect ∠GOB.

3. Draw an angle congruent to ∠GOB.

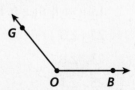

Ready To Go On?

Quiz for Lessons 8-1 Through 8-3

✓ **8-1** **Building Blocks of Geometry**

Identify the figures in the diagram.

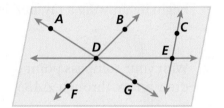

1. three points
2. three lines
3. a plane
4. three line segments
5. three rays

6. Identify the line segments that are congruent in the figure.

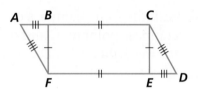

✓ **8-2** **Classifying Angles**

Tell whether each angle is acute, right, obtuse, or straight.

7.   8.   9.   10.

Use the diagram to tell whether the angles are complementary, supplementary, or neither.

11. ∠DXE and ∠AXD   12. ∠AXB and ∠CXD
13. ∠DXE and ∠AXB   14. ∠BXC and ∠DXE

15. Angles *R* and *S* are complementary. If m∠S is 17°, what is m∠R?

16. Angles *D* and *F* are supplementary. If m∠D is 45°, what is m∠F?

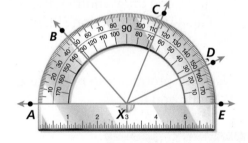

✓ **8-3** **Line and Angle Relationships**

Tell whether the lines appear parallel, perpendicular, or skew.

17. $\overleftrightarrow{KL}$ and $\overleftrightarrow{MN}$ 18. $\overleftrightarrow{JL}$ and $\overleftrightarrow{MN}$
19. $\overleftrightarrow{KL}$ and $\overleftrightarrow{JL}$ 20. $\overleftrightarrow{IJ}$ and $\overleftrightarrow{MN}$

Line *a* ∥ line *b*. Find the measure of each angle.

21. ∠3   22. ∠4
23. ∠8   24. ∠6
25. ∠1   26. ∠5

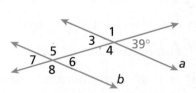

Focus on Problem Solving

Understand the Problem

• **Restate the problem in your own words**

By writing a problem in your own words, you may understand it better. Before writing the problem, you may need to reread it several times, perhaps aloud, so that you can hear yourself saying the words.

Once you have written the problem in your own words, check to make sure you included all of the necessary information to solve it.

Write each problem in your own words. Check to make sure you have included all of the information needed to solve the problem.

① The diagram shows a ray of light being reflected off a mirror. The angle of reflection is congruent to the angle of incidence. Use the diagram to find the measure of the obtuse angle formed by the reflected light.

② At the intersection shown, the turn from northbound Main Street left onto Jefferson Street is dangerous because the turn is too sharp. City planners have decided to change the road to increase the angle of the turn. Explain how the measures of angles 1, 3, and 4 change as the measure of angle 2 increases.

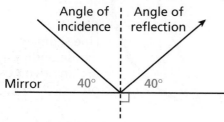

③ Parallel lines *s* and *t* are intersected by a transversal *r*. The obtuse angles formed by lines *s* and *t* measure 134°. Find the measure of the acute angles formed by the intersection of lines *t* and *r*.

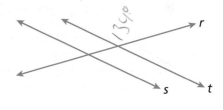

④ Many fashion designers use basic geometric shapes and patterns in their textile designs. In the textile design shown, angles 1 and 2 are formed by two intersecting lines. Find the measures of ∠1 and ∠2 if the angle adjacent to ∠2 measures 88°.

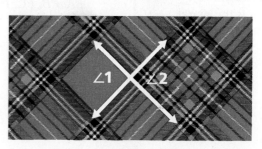

8-4 Properties of Circles

Completed in 1893 for the Chicago World's Fair, the first Ferris wheel could carry up to 2,160 people. George Ferris relied on the idea of a *circle* when he modeled his design on a bicycle wheel.

A **circle** is the set of all points in a plane that are the same distance from a given point, called the **center of a circle**.

A circle is named by its center. For example, if point *A* is the center of a circle, then the name of the circle is circle *A*. There are special names for the different parts of a circle.

Navy Pier Ferris Wheel, Chicago, Illinois

Vocabulary

circle

center of a circle

arc

radius

diameter

chord

central angle

sector

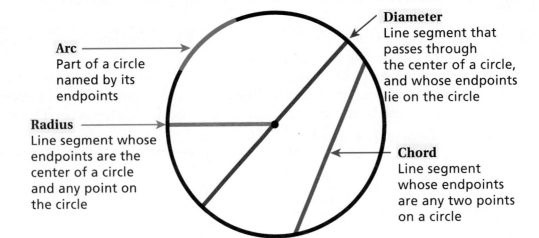

Arc
Part of a circle named by its endpoints

Radius
Line segment whose endpoints are the center of a circle and any point on the circle

Diameter
Line segment that passes through the center of a circle, and whose endpoints lie on the circle

Chord
Line segment whose endpoints are any two points on a circle

EXAMPLE 1 Identifying Parts of Circles

Name the parts of circle *P*.

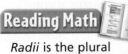
Radii is the plural form of *radius*.

A radii
$\overline{PA}$, $\overline{PB}$, $\overline{PC}$, $\overline{PD}$

B diameter
$\overline{BD}$

C chords
$\overline{AD}$, $\overline{DC}$, $\overline{AB}$, $\overline{BC}$, $\overline{BD}$

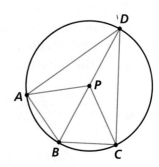

Video Lesson Tutorials Online my.hrw.com

A **central angle** of a circle is an angle formed by two radii. A **sector** of a circle is the part of the circle enclosed by two radii and an arc connecting them.

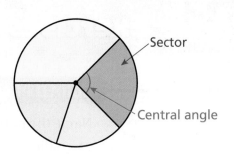

Sector

Central angle

The sum of the measures of all of the nonoverlapping central angles in a circle is 360°. We say that there are 360° in a circle.

EXAMPLE **2**

PROBLEM SOLVING

PROBLEM SOLVING APPLICATION

The circle graph shows the results of a survey to determine how people feel about keeping the penny. Find the central angle measure of the sector that shows the percent of people who are against keeping the penny.

Keep the Penny?

Uncertain 3%
Against 32%
For 65%

Source: USA Today

1 Understand the Problem

List the **important information:**

• The percent of people who are against keeping the penny is 32%.

2 Make a Plan

The central angle measure of the sector that represents those people against keeping the penny is 32% of the angle measure of the whole circle. The angle measure of a circle is 360°. Since the sector is 32% of the circle graph, the central angle measure is 32% of 360°.

32% of 360° = 0.32 · 360°

3 Solve

0.32 · 360° = 115.2°   *Multiply.*

The central angle of the sector measures 115.2°.

4 Look Back

The 32% sector is about one-third of the graph, and 120° is one-third of 360°. Since 115.2° is close to 120°, the answer is reasonable.

Think and Discuss

1. **Explain** why a diameter is a chord but a radius is not.

2. **Draw** a circle with a central angle of 90°.

Learn It Online
Homework Help Online **go.hrw.com**,
keyword MS10 8-4 Go
Exercises 1–8, 9, 11, 13

GUIDED PRACTICE

See Example **1** Name the parts of circle *O*.

1. radii

2. diameter

3. chords

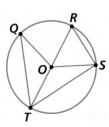

See Example **2** 4. The circle graph shows the results of a survey in which the following question was asked: "If you had to describe your office environment as a type of television show, which would it be?" Find the central angle measure of the sector that shows the percent of people who described their workplace as a courtroom drama.

Describe Your Workplace

Real-life survivors 38%
Soap opera 27%
Medical emergency 18%
Science fiction 7%
Courtroom drama 10%

Source: USA Today

INDEPENDENT PRACTICE

See Example **1** Name the parts of circle *C*.

5. radii

6. diameters

7. chords

See Example **2** 8. The circle graph shows the areas from which the United States imports bananas. Find the central angle measure of the sector that shows the percent of banana imports from South America.

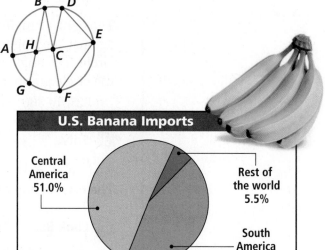

U.S. Banana Imports

Central America 51.0%
Rest of the world 5.5%
South America 43.5%

Source: US Bureau of the Census Trade Data

PRACTICE AND PROBLEM SOLVING

Extra Practice
See page EP21.

9. What is the distance between the centers of the circles at right?

10. A circle is divided into five equal sectors. Find the measure of the central angle of each sector.

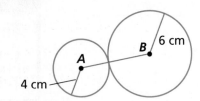

6 cm

B

A

4 cm

Surveys The results of a survey asking "What word(s) do you use to address a group of two or more people?" are shown in the graph. Use the graph for Exercises 11 and 12.

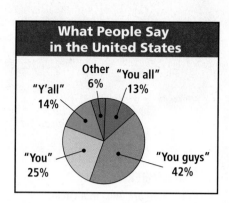

What People Say in the United States

Other 6%
"You all" 13%
"Y'all" 14%
"You" 25%
"You guys" 42%

11. Find the central angle measure of the sector that shows the percent of people who say "you guys" to address two or more people.

12. Find the central angle measure of the sector that shows the percent of people who say "y'all" to address two or more people.

13. If $\overline{AB} \parallel \overline{CD}$ in the circle at right, what is the measure of $\angle 1$? Explain your answer.

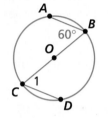

14. **Write a Problem** Find a circle graph in your science or social studies textbook. Use the graph to write a problem that can be solved by finding the central angle measure of one of the sectors of the circle.

15. **Write About It** Compare central angles of a circle with sectors of a circle.

16. **Challenge** Find the angle measure between the minute and hour hands on the clock at right.

Test Prep and Spiral Review

Use the figure for Exercises 17 and 18.

17. **Multiple Choice** Which statement is NOT true about the figure?

Ⓐ $\overline{GI}$ is a diameter of the circle.

Ⓑ $\overline{GI}$ is a chord of the circle.

Ⓒ $\angle GFH$ is a central angle of the circle.

Ⓓ $\angle GFH$ and $\angle JFI$ are supplementary angles.

18. **Gridded Response** The diameter of the circle is perpendicular to radius *HF*. What is the measure of $\angle HFI$ in degrees?

Estimate. (Lesson 6-3)

19. 28% of 150

20. 21% of 90

21. 2% of 55

22. 53% of 72

Use the alphabet at right. (Lesson 8-3)

23. Identify the letters that appear to have parallel lines.

24. Identify the letters that appear to have perpendicular lines.

ABCDEFGH
IJKLMN
OPQRST
UVWXYZ

Construct Circle Graphs

Use with Lesson 8-4

Learn It Online
Lab Resources Online **go.hrw.com**,
keyword MS10 Lab8 Go

REMEMBER
• There are 360° in a circle.
• A radius is a line segment with one endpoint at the center of a circle and the other endpoint on the circle.

A circle graph can be used to compare data that are parts of a whole.

Activity

You can make a circle graph using information from a table.

At Booker Middle School, a survey was conducted to find the percent of students who favor certain types of books. The results are shown in the table below.

To make a circle graph, you need to find the size of each part of your graph. Each part is a *sector*.

To find the size of a sector, you must find the measure of its angle. You do this by finding what percent of the whole circle that sector represents.

Find the size of each sector.

a. Copy the table at right.

b. Find a decimal equivalent for each percent given, and fill in the decimal column of your table.

c. Find the fraction equivalent for each percent given, and fill in the fraction column of your table.

d. Find the angle measure of each sector by setting up a proportion with each fraction.

$$\frac{1}{4} = \frac{x}{360°}$$

$$4x = 360°$$

$$x = 90° \quad \text{\textit{The measure of a sector that is } } \frac{1}{4} \text{ \textit{of a circle is 90°.}}$$

Fill in the last column of your table. Use a calculator to check by multiplying each decimal by 360°.

Students' Favorite Types of Books				
Type of Book	**Percent**	**Decimal**	**Fraction**	**Degrees**
Mysteries	35%			
Science Fiction	25%	0.25	$\frac{1}{4}$	
Sports	20%			
Biographies	15%			
Humor	5%			

Follow the steps below to draw a circle graph.

a. Using a compass, draw a circle. Using a straightedge, draw one radius.

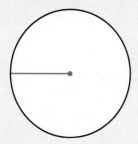

b. Use a protractor to measure the angle of the first sector. Draw the angle.

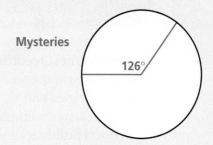

Mysteries 126°

c. Use a protractor to measure the angle of the next sector. Draw the angle.

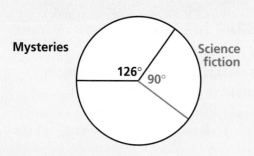

Mysteries 126° 90° Science fiction

d. Continue until your graph is complete. Label each sector with its name and percent.

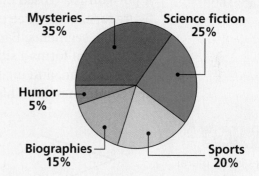

Mysteries 35% Science fiction 25% Humor 5% Biographies 15% Sports 20%

Think and Discuss

1. Total each column in the table from the beginning of the activity. What do you notice?

2. What type of data would you want to display using a circle graph?

3. How does the size of each sector of your circle graph relate to the percent, the decimal, and the fraction in your table?

Try This

1. Complete the table below and use the information to make a circle graph.

How Alan Spends His Free Time				
Activity	Percent	Decimal	Fraction	Degrees
Playing sports	35%			
Reading	25%			
Working on computer	40%			

2. Ask your classmates a survey question. Organize the data in a table, and then use the data to make a circle graph.

From the earliest recorded time, geometric shapes, such as triangles and rectangles, have been used to decorate buildings and works of art.

The Kalachakra sand mandala is made entirely of colored sand.

Vocabulary

polygon

regular polygon

Triangles and rectangles are examples of *polygons*. A **polygon** is a closed plane figure formed by three or more line segments. Each line segment forms a side of the polygon, and meets, but does not cross, another line segment at a common point. This common point is a vertex of a polygon.

Reading Math

Vertices is the plural form of *vertex*.

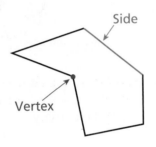

Side

Vertex

The polygon at left has six sides and six vertices.

EXAMPLE **1** **Identifying Polygons**

Determine whether each figure is a polygon. If it is not, explain why not.

A

The figure is a polygon. It is a closed figure with 5 sides.

B

The figure is not a polygon. It is not a closed figure.

C

The figure is not a polygon. Not all of the sides of the figure are line segments.

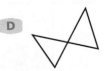

D

The figure is not a polygon. There are line segments in the figure that cross.

Video Lesson Tutorials Online my.hrw.com

Polygons are classified by the number of sides and angles they have.

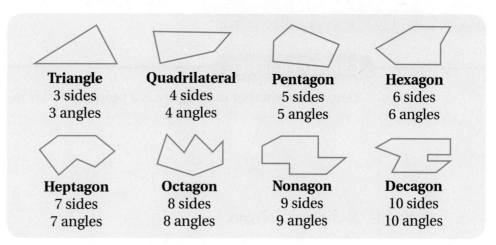

Triangle
3 sides
3 angles

Quadrilateral
4 sides
4 angles

Pentagon
5 sides
5 angles

Hexagon
6 sides
6 angles

Heptagon
7 sides
7 angles

Octagon
8 sides
8 angles

Nonagon
9 sides
9 angles

Decagon
10 sides
10 angles

EXAMPLE 2 **Classifying Polygons**

Name each polygon.

A

10 sides,
10 angles

Decagon

B

6 sides,
6 angles

Hexagon

A **regular polygon** is a polygon in which all sides are congruent and all angles are congruent. If a polygon is not regular, it is called irregular.

EXAMPLE 3 **Identifying and Classifying Regular Polygons**

Name each polygon, and tell whether it is a regular polygon. If it is not, explain why not.

Caution!

A polygon with congruent sides is not necessarily a regular polygon. Its angles must also be congruent.

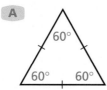

A

60°

60°   60°

The figure has congruent angles and congruent sides. It is a regular triangle.

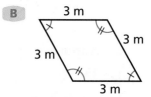

B

3 m

3 m

3 m

3 m

The figure is a quadrilateral. It is an irregular polygon because not all of the angles are congruent.

Think and Discuss

1. Explain why a circle is not a polygon.

2. Name three reasons why a figure would not be a polygon.

Learn It Online
Homework Help Online go.hrw.com,
keyword MS10 8-5 Go
Exercises 1–18, 21, 23

GUIDED PRACTICE

Determine whether each figure is a polygon. If it is not, explain why not.

See Example 1

1.

2.

3.

See Example 2 **Name each polygon.**

4.

5.

6.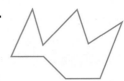

See Example 3 **Name each polygon, and tell whether it is a regular polygon. If it is not, explain why not.**

7.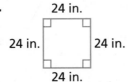
24 in.
24 in. 24 in.
24 in.

8.

9.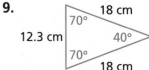
18 cm
70°
12.3 cm 40°
70°
18 cm

INDEPENDENT PRACTICE

See Example 1 **Determine whether each figure is a polygon. If it is not, explain why not.**

10.

11.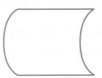

12.

See Example 2 **Name each polygon.**

13.

14.

15.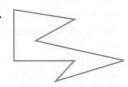

See Example 3 **Name each polygon, and tell whether it is a regular polygon. If it is not, explain why not.**

Extra Practice
See page EP21.

16.

17.
130°
5 ft 2 ft
100°
3 ft 110°
4 ft
110°
5 ft

18.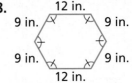
12 in.
9 in. 9 in.
9 in. 9 in.
12 in.

Quilting is an art form that has existed in many countries for hundreds of years. Some cultures record their histories and traditions through the colors and patterns in quilts.

19. The design of the quilt at right is made of triangles.

    a. Name two other polygons in the pattern.

    b. Which of the polygons in the pattern appear to be regular?

Use the photograph of the star quilt for Exercises 20 and 21.

20. The large star in the quilt pattern is made of smaller shapes stitched together. These smaller shapes are all the same type of polygon. What type of polygon are the smaller shapes?

21. A polygon can be named by the number of its sides followed by *-gon*. For example, a polygon with 14 sides is called a 14-gon. What is the name of the large star-shaped polygon on the quilt?

22. ⭐ **Challenge** The quilt at right has a modern design. Find and copy one of each type of polygon, from a triangle up to a decagon, onto your paper from the design. Write the name of each polygon next to its drawing.

Test Prep and Spiral Review

23. Multiple Choice What is true about the figure?

    Ⓐ It is a polygon.   Ⓒ It is a quadrilateral.

    Ⓑ It is a regular polygon.   Ⓓ It is a nonagon.

24. Short Response Draw an example of a figure that is NOT a polygon. Explain why it is not a polygon.

Write a function that describes each sequence. (Lesson 5-4)

25. 4, 7, 10, 13,…   **26.** −1, 1, 3, 5,…   **27.** 2.3, 3.3, 4.3, 5.3,…

Solve. Round answers to the nearest tenth, if necessary. (Lesson 6-5)

28. 8 is what percent of 15?   **29.** What is 35% of 58?

30. 63 is 25% of what number?   **31.** 22 is what percent of 85?

Classifying Triangles

A harnessed rider uses the triangle-shaped control bar on a hang glider to steer. The framework of most hang gliders is made up of many types of triangles. One way to classify triangles is by the lengths of their sides. Another way is by the measures of their angles.

Vocabulary

scalene triangle

isosceles triangle

equilateral triangle

acute triangle

obtuse triangle

right triangle

Triangles classified by sides

A **scalene triangle** has no congruent sides.

An **isosceles triangle** has at least 2 congruent sides.

In an **equilateral triangle**, all of the sides are congruent.

Triangles classified by angles

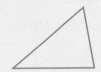 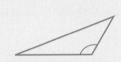

In an **acute triangle**, all of the angles are acute.

An **obtuse triangle** has exactly one obtuse angle.

A **right triangle** has exactly one right angle.

EXAMPLE **1** **Classifying Triangles**

Classify each triangle according to its sides and angles.

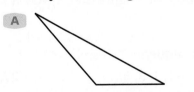

A

scalene   *No congruent sides*
obtuse   *One obtuse angle*

This is a scalene obtuse triangle.

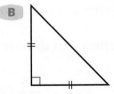

B

isosceles   *Two congruent sides*
right   *One right angle*

This is an isosceles right triangle.

Video **Lesson Tutorials Online** my.hrw.com

Classify each triangle according to its sides and angles.

scalene   *No congruent sides*
right   *One right angle*

This is a scalene right triangle.

isosceles   *Two congruent sides*
obtuse   *One obtuse angle*

This is an isosceles obtuse triangle.

EXAMPLE 2 **Identifying Triangles**

Identify the different types of triangles in the figure, and determine how many of each there are.

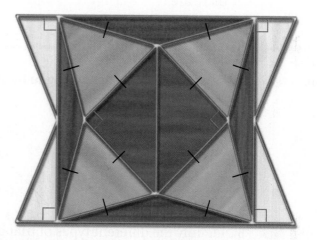

Type	How Many	Colors	Type	How Many	Colors
Scalene	4	Yellow	Right	6	Purple, yellow
Isosceles	10	Green, pink, purple	Obtuse	4	Green
Equilateral	4	Pink	Acute	4	Pink

Think and Discuss

1. Draw an isosceles acute triangle and an isosceles obtuse triangle.

2. Draw a triangle that is right and scalene.

3. Explain why any equilateral triangle is also an isosceles triangle, but not all isosceles triangles are equilateral triangles.

Learn It Online
Homework Help Online **go.hrw.com**,
keyword MS10 8-6 (Go)
Exercises 1–8, 9, 11, 13, 15, 17, 19, 21

GUIDED PRACTICE

See Example 1 Classify each triangle according to its sides and angles.

1.

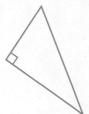

2.

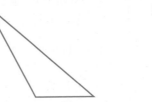

3.

See Example 2 **4.** Identify the different types of triangles in the figure, and determine how many of each there are.

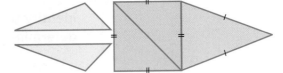

INDEPENDENT PRACTICE

See Example 1 Classify each triangle according to its sides and angles.

5.

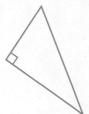

6.

7.

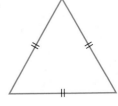

See Example 2 **8.** Identify the different types of triangles in the figure, and determine how many of each there are.

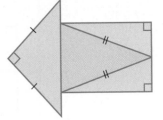

PRACTICE AND PROBLEM SOLVING

Extra Practice
See page EP21.

Classify each triangle according to the lengths of its sides.

9. 6 ft, 9 ft, 12 ft   **10.** 2 in., 2 in., 2 in.   **11.** 7.4 mi, 7.4 mi, 4 mi

Classify each triangle according to the measures of its angles.

12. 105°, 38°, 37°   **13.** 45°, 90°, 45°   **14.** 40°, 60°, 80°

15. Multi-Step The sum of the lengths of the sides of △ABC is 25 inches. The lengths of sides $\overline{AB}$ and $\overline{BC}$ are 9 inches and 8 inches. Find the length of side $\overline{AC}$ and classify the triangle.

16. Draw a square. Divide it into two triangles. Describe the triangles.

Classify each triangle according to its sides and angles.

17.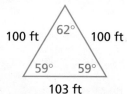
100 ft   62°   100 ft
59°   59°
103 ft

18.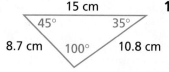
15 cm
45°   35°
8.7 cm   100°   10.8 cm

19.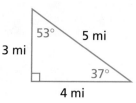
53°   5 mi
3 mi
37°
4 mi

20. **Geology** Each face of a topaz crystal is a triangle whose sides are all different lengths. What kind of triangle is each face of a topaz crystal?

21. **Architecture** The Washington Monument is an obelisk, the top of which is a pyramid. The pyramid has four triangular faces. The bottom edge of each face measures 10.5 m. The other edges of each face measure 17.0 m. What kind of triangle is each face of the pyramid?

22. **Critical Thinking** A line segment connects each vertex of a regular octagon to the vertex opposite it. How many triangles are within the octagon? What type of triangles are they?

23. **Choose a Strategy** How many triangles are in the figure?
    (A) 6   (B) 9   (C) 10   (D) 13

24. **Write About It** Is it possible for an equilateral triangle to be obtuse? Explain your answer.

25. **Challenge** The centers of circles A, B, C, D, and E are connected by line segments. Classify each triangle in the figure, given that the diameter of circle D is 4 and $DE = 5$, $BD = 6$, $CB = 8$, and $AC = 8$.

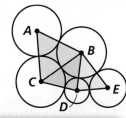

Test Prep and Spiral Review

26. **Multiple Choice** Based on the angle measures given, which triangle is NOT acute?

    (A) 60°, 60°, 60°   (B) 90°, 45°, 45°   (C) 54°, 54°, 72°   (D) 75°, 45°, 60°

27. **Multiple Choice** Which of the following best describes the triangle?

    (F) Scalene, right triangle   (H) Isosceles, obtuse triangle
    (G) Isosceles, acute triangle   (J) Equilateral, acute triangle

    124°
    28°   28°

28. Order the numbers $\frac{3}{7}$, -0.4, 2.3, and $1\frac{3}{10}$ from least to greatest. (Lesson 2-11)

Name each polygon, and tell whether it is a regular polygon. If it is not, explain why not. (Lesson 8-5)

29.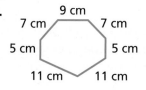
9 cm
7 cm   7 cm
5 cm   5 cm
11 cm   11 cm

30.

31.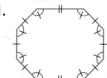

Classifying Quadrilaterals

College campuses are often built around an open space called a "quad" or "quadrangle." A quadrangle is a four-sided enclosure, or a quadrilateral.

Some quadrilaterals have properties that classify them as *special quadrilaterals*.

The Liberal Arts Quadrangle at the University of Washington, Seattle

Vocabulary

parallelogram

rectangle

rhombus

square

trapezoid

Interactivities Online ▶

Parallelogram		Opposite sides are parallel and congruent. Opposite angles are congruent.
Rectangle		Parallelogram with four right angles.
Rhombus		Parallelogram with four congruent sides.
Square		Parallelogram with four congruent sides and four right angles.
Trapezoid		Exactly one pair of opposite sides is parallel.

Quadrilaterals can have more than one name because the special quadrilaterals sometimes share properties.

EXAMPLE 1 **Classifying Quadrilaterals**

Give all of the names that apply to each quadrilateral. Then give the name that best describes it.

A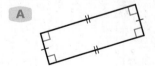

The figure has opposite sides that are parallel, so it is a parallelogram. It has four right angles, so it is also a rectangle.

Rectangle best describes this quadrilateral.

Video **Lesson Tutorials Online** my.hrw.com

Give all of the names that apply to each quadrilateral. Then give the name that best describes it.

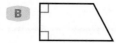 **B**

The figure has exactly one pair of opposite sides that is parallel, so it is a trapezoid.

Trapezoid best describes this quadrilateral.

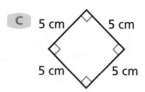 **C** 5 cm 5 cm 5 cm 5 cm

The figure has two pairs of opposite sides that are parallel, so it is a parallelogram. It has four right angles, so it is also a rectangle. It has four congruent sides, so it is also a rhombus and a square.

Square best describes this quadrilateral.

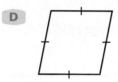 **D**

The figure has two pairs of opposite sides that are parallel, so it is a parallelogram. It has four congruent sides, so it is a rhombus. It does not have four right angles, so it is not a rectangle or a square.

Rhombus best describes this quadrilateral.

EXAMPLE **2** **Drawing Quadrilaterals**

Draw each figure. If it is not possible to draw, explain why.

A a parallelogram that is not a rhombus

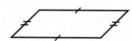

The figure has two pairs of parallel sides, but all sides are not congruent.

B a trapezoid that is also a rectangle

A trapezoid has exactly one pair of opposite sides that is parallel, but a rectangle has two pairs of opposite sides that are parallel. It is not possible to draw this figure.

Think and Discuss

1. Describe how you can decide whether a rhombus is also a square. Use drawings to justify your answer.

2. Draw a Venn diagram to show how the properties of the five quadrilaterals relate.

8-7 **Exercises**

Learn It Online
Homework Help Online **go.hrw.com**,
keyword MS10 8-7 Go
Exercises 1–13, 15, 17, 19, 21,
23, 25

GUIDED PRACTICE

See Example 1 **Give all of the names that apply to each quadrilateral. Then give the name that best describes it.**

1.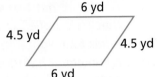
6 yd
4.5 yd
4.5 yd
6 yd

2.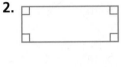

3.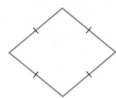

See Example 2 **Draw each figure. If it is not possible to draw, explain why.**

4. a rectangle that is not a square

5. a parallelogram that is also a trapezoid

INDEPENDENT PRACTICE

See Example 1 **Give all of the names that apply to each quadrilateral. Then give the name that best describes it.**

6.

7.

8.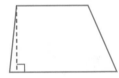

9.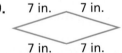
7 in. 7 in.
7 in. 7 in.

10.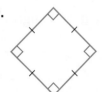

11.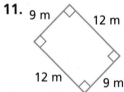
9 m 12 m
12 m 9 m

See Example 2 **Draw each figure. If it is not possible to draw, explain why.**

12. a parallelogram that is also a rhombus

13. a rhombus that is not a square

PRACTICE AND PROBLEM SOLVING

Extra Practice
See page EP21.

Name the types of quadrilaterals that have each property.

14. four right angles

15. two pairs of opposite, parallel sides

16. four congruent sides

17. opposite sides that are congruent

18. Describe how to construct a parallelogram from the figure at right, and then complete the construction.

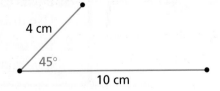
4 cm
45°
10 cm

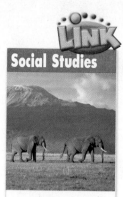
Tell whether each statement is true or false. Explain your answer.

19. All squares are rhombuses.

20. All rectangles are parallelograms.

21. All squares are rectangles.

22. All rhombuses are rectangles.

23. Some trapezoids are squares.

24. Some rectangles are squares.

25. Social Studies Name the polygons made by each color in the flag of Tanzania. Give the specific names of any quadrilaterals you find.

26. Graph the points $A(-2, -2)$, $B(4, 1)$, $C(3, 4)$, and $D(-1, 2)$, and draw line segments to connect the points. What kind of quadrilateral did you draw?

27. Bandon Highway is being built perpendicular to Avenue A and Avenue B, which are parallel. What kinds of polygons could be made by adding a fourth road?

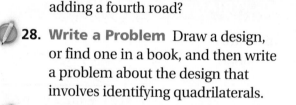

28. Write a Problem Draw a design, or find one in a book, and then write a problem about the design that involves identifying quadrilaterals.

29. Write About It Quadrilaterals can be found on many college campuses. Describe two special quadrilaterals that you commonly find in the world around you.

30. Challenge The coordinates of three vertices of a parallelogram are $(-1, 1)$, $(2, 1)$, and $(0, -4)$. What are the coordinates of the fourth vertex?

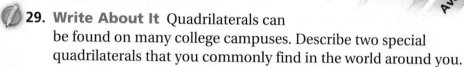

Test Prep and Spiral Review

31. Multiple Choice Which statement is NOT true?

  (A) All rhombuses are parallelograms.

  (C) Some trapezoids are rectangles.

  (B) All squares are rectangles.

  (D) Some rhombuses are squares.

32. Extended Response Graph the points $A(-1, 5)$, $B(4, 3)$, $C(2, -2)$, and $D(-3, 0)$. Draw segments AB, BC, CD, and AD, and give all of the names that apply to the quadrilateral. Then give the name that best describes it.

Use the data set 43, 28, 33, 49, 18, 44, 57, 34, 40, 57 for Exercises 33 and 34. (Lesson 7-1)

33. Make a stem-and-leaf plot of the data.

34. Make a cumulative frequency table of the data.

Classify each triangle according to the measures of its angles. (Lesson 8-6)

35. $50°, 50°, 80°$ **36.** $40°, 50°, 90°$ **37.** $20°, 30°, 130°$ **38.** $20°, 60°, 100°$

Angles in Polygons

If you tear off the corners of a triangle and put them together, you will find that they form a straight angle. This suggests that the sum of the measures of the angles in a triangle is 180°.

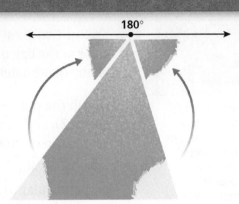
180°

Vocabulary

diagonal

TRIANGLE SUM RULE
The sum of the measures of the angles in a triangle is 180°. 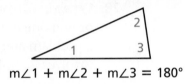 $m\angle 1 + m\angle 2 + m\angle 3 = 180°$

E X A M P L E 1 | **Finding an Angle Measure in a Triangle**

Find the unknown angle measure in the triangle.

$25° + 37° + x = 180°$ *The sum of the angle measures in a triangle is 180°.*

$\begin{array}{r} 62° + x = 180° \\ -62° \quad\quad -62° \\ \hline x = 118° \end{array}$ *Combine like terms.*
Subtract 62° from both sides.

The unknown angle measure is 118°.

Interactivities Online ▶ The sum of the angle measures in any four-sided figure can be found by dividing the figure into two triangles. You can divide the figure by drawing a *diagonal*. A **diagonal** is a line segment that connects two non-adjacent vertices of a polygon. Since the sum of the angle measures in each triangle is 180°, the sum of the angle measures in a four-sided figure is 2 · 180°, or 360°.

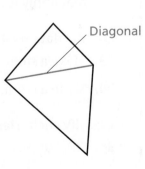
Diagonal

Video **Lesson Tutorials Online** my.hrw.com

SUM OF THE ANGLES OF A QUADRILATERAL

The sum of the measures of the angles in a quadrilateral is 360°.

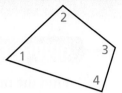

m∠1 + m∠2 + m∠3 + m∠4 = 360°

EXAMPLE **2**

Finding an Angle Measure in a Quadrilateral

Find the unknown angle measure in the quadrilateral.

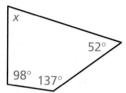

$$98° + 137° + 52° + x = 360°$$ *The sum of the angle measures is 360°.*

$$287° + x = 360°$$ *Combine like terms.*

$$-287° \qquad -287°$$ *Subtract 287° from both sides.*

$$x = 73°$$

The unknown angle measure is 73°.

In a convex polygon, all diagonals can be drawn within the interior of the figure. By dividing any convex polygon into triangles, you can find the sum of its interior angle measures.

EXAMPLE **3**

Drawing Triangles to Find the Sum of Interior Angles

Divide the polygon into triangles to find the sum of its angle measures.

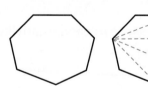

There are 5 triangles.

$5 \cdot 180° = 900°$

The sum of the angle measures of a heptagon is 900°.

Think and Discuss

1. **Explain** how to find the measure of an angle in a triangle when the measures of the two other angles are known.

2. **Determine** for which polygon the sum of the angle measures is greater, a pentagon or an octagon.

3. **Explain** how the measure of each angle in a regular polygon changes as the number of sides increases.

GUIDED PRACTICE

See Example ① Find the unknown angle measure in each triangle.

1.

2.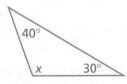

3.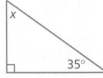

See Example ② Find the unknown angle measure in each quadrilateral .

4.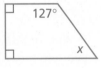

5.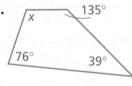

6.

See Example ③ Divide each polygon into triangles to find the sum of its angle measures.

7.

8.

9.

INDEPENDENT PRACTICE

See Example ① Find the unknown angle measure in each triangle.

10.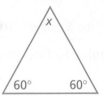

11.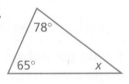

12.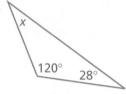

See Example ② Find the unknown angle measure in each quadrilateral.

13.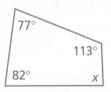

14.

15.

See Example ③ Divide each polygon into triangles to find the sum of its angle measures.

16.

17.

18.

PRACTICE AND PROBLEM SOLVING

Extra Practice
See page EP21.

19. Earth Science A sundial consists of a circular base and a right triangle mounted upright on the base. One acute angle in the right triangle is 52°. What is the measure of the other acute angle?

Find the measure of the third angle in each triangle, given two angle measures. Then classify the triangle.

20. 56°, 101°   **21.** 18°, 63°   **22.** 62°, 58°   **23.** 41°, 49°

24. Multi-Step Each outer wall of the Pentagon in Washington, D.C., measures 921 feet. What is the measure of each angle made by the Pentagon's outer walls?

25. Critical Thinking A truss bridge is supported by triangular frames. If every triangular frame in a truss bridge is an isosceles right triangle, what is the measure of each angle in one of the frames? (*Hint:* Two of the angles in each frame are congruent.)

26. Make a Conjecture Use what you have learned to write a formula for finding the sum of interior angle measures in polygons with five or more sides.

? 27. What's the Error? A student finds the sum of the angle measures in an octagon by multiplying 7 · 180°. What is the student's error?

28. Write About It Explain how to find the sum of the angle measures in a quadrilateral by dividing the quadrilateral into triangles.

★ 29. Challenge The angle between the lines of sight from a lighthouse to a tugboat and to a cargo ship is 27°. The angle between the lines of sight at the cargo ship is twice the angle between the lines of sight at the tugboat. What are the angles at the tugboat and at the cargo ship?

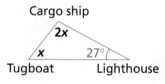

Test Prep and Spiral Review

30. Multiple Choice A triangle has three congruent angles. What is the measure of each angle?

Ⓐ 50°   Ⓑ 60°   Ⓒ 75°   Ⓓ 100°

31. Gridded Response Two angles of a triangle measure 58° and 42°. What is the measure, in degrees, of the third angle of the triangle?

Solve each proportion. (Lesson 4-4)

32. $\frac{x}{3} = \frac{30}{18}$ **33.** $\frac{8}{p} = \frac{24}{27}$ **34.** $\frac{4}{3} = \frac{t}{21}$ **35.** $\frac{0.5}{1.8} = \frac{n}{9}$

Name the types of quadrilaterals that have each property. (Lesson 8-7)

36. two pairs of opposite, congruent sides   **37.** four congruent sides

Quiz for Lessons 8-4 Through 8-8

8-4 Properties of Circles

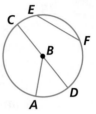

Name the parts of circle *B*.

1. radii   **2.** diameter   **3.** chords

4. A circle is divided into 6 equal sectors. Find the measure of the central angle of each sector.

8-5 Classifying Polygons

Name each polygon, and tell whether it is a regular polygon. If it is not, explain why not.

5.

6.

7.

8.

  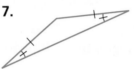

8-6 Classifying Triangles

Classify each triangle according to its sides and angles.

9.   **10.**   **11.**   **12.**

8-7 Classifying Quadrilaterals

Give all of the names that apply to each quadrilateral. Then give the name that best describes it.

13.   **14.**   **15.**   **16.**

   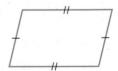

8-8 Angles in Polygons

Find the unknown angle measure in each figure.

17.   **18.**   **19.**   **20.**

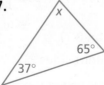 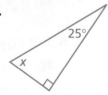 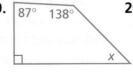

Focus on Problem Solving

Understand the Problem

• **Understand the words in the problem**

Words that you do not understand can sometimes make a simple problem seem difficult. Some of those words, such as the names of things or persons, may not even be necessary to solve the problem. If a problem contains an unfamiliar name, or one that you cannot pronounce, you can substitute another word for it. If a word that you don't understand is necessary to solve the problem, look the word up to find its meaning.

Read each problem, and make a list of unusual or unfamiliar words. If a word is not necessary to solve the problem, replace it with a familiar one. If a word is necessary, look up the word and write its meaning.

1 Using a pair of calipers, Mr. Papadimitriou measures the diameter of an ancient Greek amphora to be 17.8 cm at its widest point. What is the radius of the amphora at this point?

2 Joseph wants to plant gloxinia and hydrangeas in two similar rectangular gardens. The length of one garden is 5 ft, and the width is 4 ft. The other garden's length is 20 ft. What is the width of the second garden?

3 Mr. Manityche is sailing his catamaran from Kaua'i to Ni'ihau, a distance of about 12 nautical miles. If his speed averages 10 knots, how long will the trip take him?

4 Aimee's lepidoptera collection includes a butterfly with dots that appear to form a scalene triangle on each wing. What is the sum of the angles of each triangle on the butterfly's wings?

5 Students in a physics class use wire and resistors to build a Wheatstone bridge. Each side of their rhombus-shaped design is 2 cm long. What angle measures would the design have to have for its shape to be a square?

8-9 Congruent Figures

Originally rolled and twisted by hand, pretzels today are primarily manufactured in production lines. After the dough is mixed, automated machines stamp the dough into consistent forms. These forms are the same shape and size. Recall from Lesson 8-1 that congruent figures are the same shape and size. The automation of the production line process ensures that the pretzels are congruent.

Vocabulary

Side-Side-Side Rule

One way to determine whether figures are congruent is to see whether one figure will fit exactly over the other one.

EXAMPLE 1 **Identifying Congruent Figures in the Real World**

Identify any congruent figures.

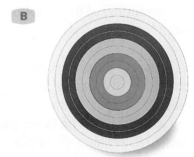

A

The squares on a checkerboard are congruent. The checkers are also congruent.

B

The rings on a target are not congruent. Each ring is larger than the one inside of it.

If all of the corresponding sides and angles of two polygons are congruent, then the polygons are congruent. For triangles, if the corresponding sides are congruent, then the corresponding angles will always be congruent. This is called the **Side-Side-Side Rule**. Because of this rule, when determining whether triangles are congruent, you only need to determine whether the sides are congruent.

Video **Lesson Tutorials Online** my.hrw.com

EXAMPLE 2

Identifying Congruent Triangles

The scale factor of congruent figures is 1. Notice that in Example 2 the ratio of corresponding sides is $\frac{3}{3} = \frac{4}{4} = \frac{5}{5} = 1$.

Determine whether the triangles are congruent.

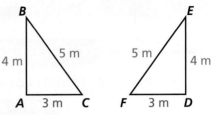

$AC = 3$ m	$DF = 3$ m
$AB = 4$ m	$DE = 4$ m
$BC = 5$ m	$EF = 5$ m

By the Side-Side-Side Rule, $\triangle ABC$ is congruent to $\triangle DEF$, or $\triangle ABC \cong \triangle DEF$. If you flip one triangle, it will fit exactly over the other.

For polygons with more than three sides, it is not enough to compare the measures of their sides. For example, the corresponding sides of the figures below are congruent, but the figures are not congruent.

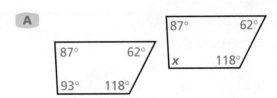

If you know that two figures are congruent, you can find missing measures in the figures.

EXAMPLE 3

Using Congruence to Find Unknown Measures

Determine the unknown measure in each set of congruent polygons.

A

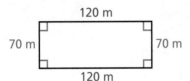

The corresponding angles of congruent polygons are congruent.

The unknown angle measure is 93°.

B

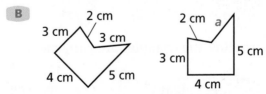

The corresponding sides of congruent polygons are congruent.

The unknown side length is 3 cm.

Think and Discuss

1. **Draw** an illustration to explain whether an isosceles triangle can be congruent to a right triangle.

2. **Explain** why congruent figures are always similar figures.

Exercises

Learn It Online
Homework Help Online **go.hrw.com,**
keyword **MS10 8-9** Go
Exercises 1–14, 15, 17, 19

GUIDED PRACTICE

See Example 1 **Identify any congruent figures.**

1.

2.

3.

See Example 2 **Determine whether the triangles are congruent.**

4.

5.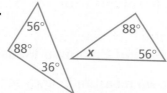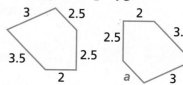

See Example 3 **Determine the unknown measure in each set of congruent polygons.**

6.

7.

INDEPENDENT PRACTICE

See Example 1 **Identify any congruent figures.**

8.

9.

10.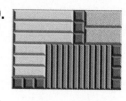

See Example 2 **Determine whether the triangles are congruent.**

11.

12.

See Example 3 **Determine the unknown measures in each set of congruent polygons.**

13.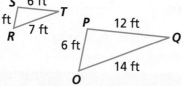

14.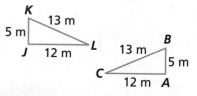

Extra Practice
See page EP22.

Tell the minimum amount of information needed to determine whether the figures are congruent.

15. two triangles **16.** two squares **17.** two rectangles **18.** two pentagons

19. Surveying In the figure, trees *A* and *B* are on opposite sides of the stream. Jamil wants to string a rope from one tree to the other. Triangles *ABC* and *DEC* are congruent. What is the distance between the trees?

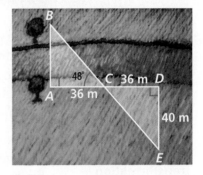

20. Hobbies In the quilt block, which figures appear congruent?

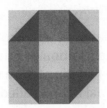

21. Choose a Strategy Anji and her brother Art walked to school along the routes in the figure. They started at 7:40 A.M. and walked at the same rate. Who arrived first?
ⓐ Anji ⓑ Art ⓒ They arrived at the same time.

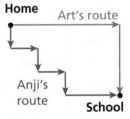

22. Write About It Are similar triangles always congruent? Explain.

23. Challenge If all of the angles in two triangles have the same measure, are the triangles necessarily congruent? Explain.

Test Prep and Spiral Review

24. Multiple Choice Which figures are congruent?

 Ⓐ   Ⓑ   Ⓒ  Ⓓ

25. Multiple Choice Determine the unknown measure in the set of congruent triangles.

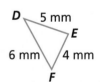

ⓕ 4 mm ⓗ 6 mm
ⓖ 5 mm ⓙ Cannot be determined

Plot each point on a coordinate plane. (Lesson 5-1)

26. $A(-4, 3)$ **27.** $B(1, -4)$ **28.** $C(-2, 0)$ **29.** $D(3, 2)$

Find the measure of the third angle in each triangle, given two angle measures. Then classify the triangle. (Lesson 8-8)

30. 25°, 48° **31.** 125°, 30° **32.** 60°, 60° **33.** 72°, 18°

Translations, Reflections, and Rotations

In the photograph, Sasha Cohen is performing a *layback spin*. She is holding her body in one position while she rotates. This is an example of a *transformation*.

In mathematics, a **transformation** changes the position or orientation of a figure. The resulting figure is the **image** of the original figure, called the **preimage**. Images resulting from the transformations described below are congruent to the preimages.

Vocabulary

transformation

image

preimage

translation

reflection

line of reflection

rotation

Types of Transformations

Translation	Reflection	Rotation

| The figure slides along a straight line without turning. | The figure flips across a **line of reflection,** creating a mirror image. | The figure turns around a fixed point. |

EXAMPLE 1 **Identifying Types of Transformations**

Identify each type of transformation.

A

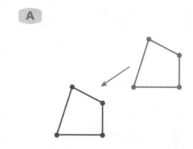

The figure slides along a straight line.
It is a translation.

B

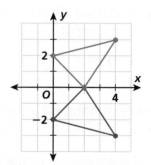

The figure flips across the x-axis.
It is a reflection.

Video **Lesson Tutorials Online** my.hrw.com

In a translation, the preimage slides *a* units right or left and *b* units up or down. A translation to the right or up is positive. A translation to the left or down is negative.

$$(x, y) \rightarrow (x + a, y + b)$$

EXAMPLE 2 **Graphing Translations on a Coordinate Plane**

Graph the translation of △*ABC* 6 units right and 4 units down. Write the coordinates of the vertices of the image.

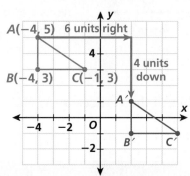

Each vertex is moved 6 units right and 4 units down.

△*ABC*	(x + 6, y + (−4))	△*A'B'C'*
A(−4, 5)	(−4 + 6, 5 + (−4))	A'(2, 1)
B(−4, 3)	(−4 + 6, 3 + (−4))	B'(2, −1)
C(−1, 3)	(−1 + 6, 3 + (−4))	C'(5, −1)

The coordinates of the vertices of △*A'B'C'* are *A'*(2, 1), *B'*(2, −1), and *C'*(5, −1).

In a reflection across the *x*-axis, $(x, y) \rightarrow (x, -y)$.
In a reflection across the *y*-axis, $(x, y) \rightarrow (-x, y)$.

EXAMPLE 3 **Graphing Reflections on a Coordinate Plane**

Graph the reflection of each figure across the indicated axis. Write the coordinates of the vertices of each image.

A *x*-axis

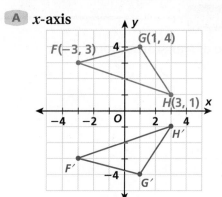

B *y*-axis

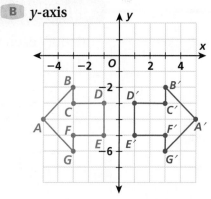

x-coordinates → same
y-coordinates → opposites

x-coordinates → opposites
y-coordinates → same

The coordinates of the vertices of △*F'G'H'* are *F'*(−3, −3), *G'*(1, −4), and *H'*(3, −1).

The coordinates of the vertices of the image are *A'*(5, −4), *B'*(3, −2), *C'*(3, −3), *D'*(1, −3), *E'*(1, −5), *F'*(3, −5), and *G'*(3, −6).

EXAMPLE 4 **Graphing Rotations on a Coordinate Plane**

Triangle *JKL* has vertices *J*(0, 0), *K*(0, −3), and *L*(4, −3). Rotate △*JKL* 90° counterclockwise about the origin. Write the coordinates of the vertices of the image.

Helpful Hint

The point that a figure rotates around may be on the figure or away from the figure.

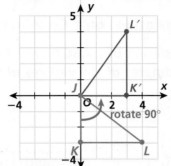

The corresponding sides, $\overline{JK}$ and $\overline{JK'}$, make a 90° angle.

Notice that vertex *K* is 3 units below the origin, and vertex *K'* is 3 units to the right of the origin.

The coordinates of the vertices of △*JK'L'* are *J*(0, 0), *K'*(3, 0), and *L'*(3, 4).

Think and Discuss

1. Explain how a figure skater might perform a translation and a rotation at the same time.

8-10 Exercises

Learn It Online
Homework Help Online **go.hrw.com**,
keyword **MS10 8-10** **Go**
Exercises 1–14, 17

GUIDED PRACTICE

See Example **1** **Identify each type of transformation.**

1.

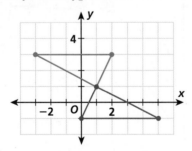

2.

See Example **2** **Graph each translation. Write the coordinates of the vertices of each image.**

3. 2 units left and 3 units up

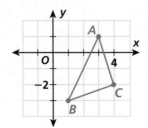

4. 3 units right and 4 units down

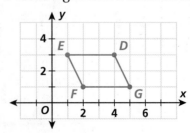

Graph the reflection of each figure across the indicated axis. Write the coordinates of the vertices of each image.

5. *x*-axis

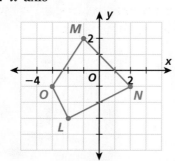

6. *y*-axis

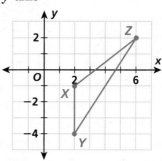

See Example 4 **7.** Triangle *LMN* has vertices *L*(0, 0), *M*(−3, 0), and *N*(1, 4). Rotate △*LMN* 180° about the origin. Write the coordinates of the vertices of the image.

INDEPENDENT PRACTICE

See Example 1 Identify each type of transformation.

8.

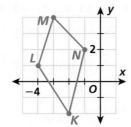

9.

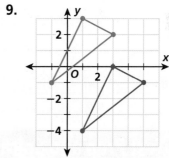

See Example 2 Graph each translation. Write the coordinates of the vertices of each image.

10. 5 units right and 1 unit down

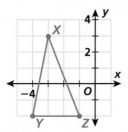

11. 4 units left and 3 units up

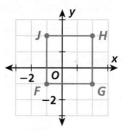

See Example 3 Graph the reflection of each figure across the indicated axis. Write the coordinates of the vertices of each image.

12. *y*-axis

13. *x*-axis

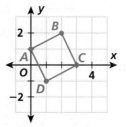

Extra Practice
See page EP22.

See Example 4 **14.** Triangle *MNL* has vertices *M*(0, 4), *N*(3, 3), and *L*(0, 0). Rotate △*MNL* 90° counterclockwise about the origin. Write the coordinates of the vertices of the image.

Social Studies

The Native American art pieces in the photos show combinations of transformations. Use the photos for Exercises 15 and 16.

15. ✐ **Write About It** The Navajo blanket at right has a design based on a sand painting. The two people in the design are standing next to a stalk of corn, which the Native Americans called *maize*. The red, white, and black stripes represent a rainbow. Tell how the design shows reflections. Also explain what parts of the design do not show reflections.

16. ⭐ **Challenge** What part of the bead design in the saddle bag at right can be described as three separate transformations? Draw diagrams to illustrate your answer.

Test Prep and Spiral Review

17. **Multiple Choice** What will be the coordinates of point *X* after a translation 2 units down and 3 units to the right?

    Ⓐ (0, 1)   Ⓑ (1, 0)   Ⓒ (−1, 0)   Ⓓ (0, −1)

18. **Short Response** Triangle *ABC* has vertices *A*(−4, 0), *B*(0, 0), and *C*(0, 5). Rotate △*ABC* 90° clockwise around the origin. Draw △*ABC* and its image. Write the coordinates of the vertices of the image.

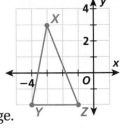

Use the box-and-whisker plot for Exercises 19 and 20. (Lesson 7-5)

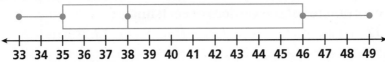

33 34 35 36 37 38 39 40 41 42 43 44 45 46 47 48 49

19. What is the median of the data?   20. What is the range of the data?

Determine the unknown measure in each set of congruent polygons. (Lesson 8-9)

21.

22.

Technology LAB

8-10

Use with Lesson 8-10

Explore Transformations

Learn It Online
Lab Resources Online **go.hrw.com**,
keyword MS10 Lab8 Go

You can use geometry software to perform transformations of geometric figures.

Activity

1 Use your dynamic geometry software to construct a 5-sided polygon like the one below. Label the vertices *A, B, C, D,* and *E.* Use the translation tool to translate the polygon 2 units right and $\frac{1}{2}$ unit up.

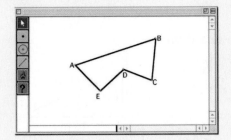 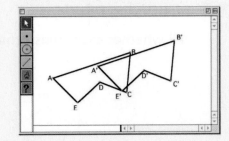

2 Start with the polygon from **1**. Use the rotation tool to rotate the polygon 30° and then 150°, both about the vertex *C.*

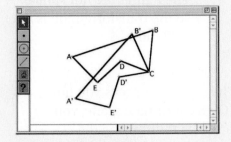 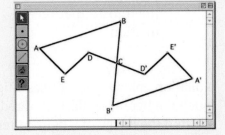

Think and Discuss

1. Rotate a triangle 30° about a point outside the triangle. Can this image be found by combining a vertical translation (slide up or down) and a horizontal translation (slide left or right) of the preimage?

2. After what angle of rotation will the rotated image of a figure have the same orientation as the preimage?

Try This

1. Construct a quadrilateral *ABCD* using the geometry software.

   a. Translate the figure 2 units right and 1 unit up.

   b. Rotate the figure 30°, 45°, and 60°.

Dilations

You can use computer software to *dilate* an image, such as a photograph. A **dilation** is a transformation that changes the size, but not the shape, of a figure. After a dilation, the image of a figure is similar to the preimage.

Vocabulary

dilation

EXAMPLE 1 Identifying Dilations

Tell whether each transformation is a dilation.

Remember!

Similar figures have the same shape but not necessarily the same size.

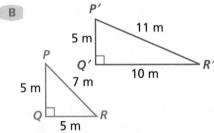

A

The figures are similar, so the transformation is a dilation.

B

The figures are not similar, so the transformation is not a dilation.

A dilation enlarges or reduces a figure. The scale factor tells you how much the figure is enlarged or reduced. On a coordinate plane, you can find the image of a figure after a dilation by multiplying the coordinates of the vertices by the scale factor.

EXAMPLE 2 Using a Dilation to Enlarge a Figure

Draw the image of △*ABC* after a dilation by a scale factor of 2.

Write the coordinates of the vertices of △*ABC*. Then multiply the coordinates by 2 to find the coordinates of the vertices of △*A′B′C′*.

$A(1, 3) \rightarrow A'(1 \cdot 2, 3 \cdot 2) = A'(2, 6)$
$B(4, 3) \rightarrow B'(4 \cdot 2, 3 \cdot 2) = B'(8, 6)$
$C(4, 1) \rightarrow C'(4 \cdot 2, 1 \cdot 2) = C'(8, 2)$
Plot A', B', and C' and draw △*A′B′C′*.

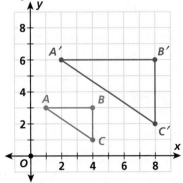

EXAMPLE 3 **Using a Dilation to Reduce a Figure**

Draw the image of △*DEF* after a dilation by a scale factor of $\frac{1}{3}$.

Write the coordinates of the vertices of △*DEF*. Then multiply the coordinates by $\frac{1}{3}$ to find the coordinates of the vertices of △*D'E'F'*.

$D(3, 3) \rightarrow D'\left(3 \cdot \frac{1}{3}, 3 \cdot \frac{1}{3}\right) = D'(1, 1)$

$E(9, 6) \rightarrow E'\left(9 \cdot \frac{1}{3}, 6 \cdot \frac{1}{3}\right) = E'(3, 2)$

$F(6, 0) \rightarrow F'\left(6 \cdot \frac{1}{3}, 0 \cdot \frac{1}{3}\right) = F'(2, 0)$

Plot D', E', and F' and draw △*D'E'F'*.

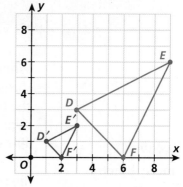

EXTENSION

Exercises

Tell whether each transformation is a dilation.

1.

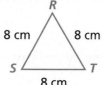

8 cm   8 cm
8 cm

6 cm   9.2 cm
7 cm

2.

 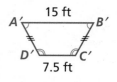

6 ft
3 ft

15 ft
7.5 ft

Draw the image of each figure after a dilation by the given scale factor.

3. scale factor 3

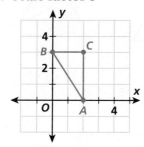

4. scale factor 2

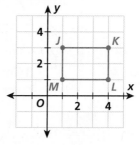

5. scale factor $\frac{1}{2}$

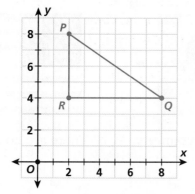

6. scale factor $\frac{1}{3}$

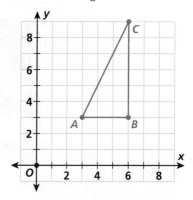

Lesson 8-10 Extension **503**

When you can draw a line through a plane figure so that the two halves are reflections of each other, the figure has **line symmetry**. The line of reflection is called the **line of symmetry**. The reflections you created in Lesson 8-10 have line symmetry.

Vocabulary

line symmetry

line of symmetry

asymmetry

rotational symmetry

center of rotation

Many architects and artists use symmetry in their buildings. The structure of the Puerta de Europa towers in Madrid, Spain, is symmetrical. You can draw a line of symmetry between the towers.

When a figure is not symmetrical, it has **asymmetry**, or is asymmetrical.

EXAMPLE 1 Identifying Line Symmetry

Decide whether each figure has line symmetry. If it does, draw all the lines of symmetry.

3 lines of symmetry

4 lines of symmetry

EXAMPLE 2 *Social Studies Application*

Find all the lines of symmetry in each flag.

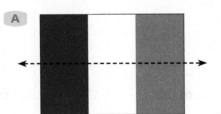 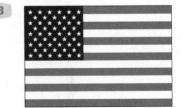

There is 1 line of symmetry.   There are no lines of symmetry.

Video Lesson Tutorials Online   my.hrw.com

When you rotate a figure, you can create a figure with *rotational symmetry*. A figure has **rotational symmetry** if, when it is rotated less than 360° around a central point, it coincides with itself. The central point is called the **center of rotation**.

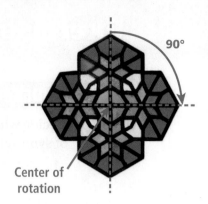

90°

Center of rotation

If the stained glass window at right is rotated 90°, as shown, the image looks the same as the original stained glass window. Therefore the window has rotational symmetry.

EXAMPLE 3 | **Identifying Rotational Symmetry**

Tell how many times each figure will show rotational symmetry within one full rotation.

A

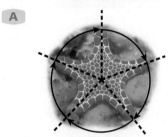

The starfish will show rotational symmetry 5 times within a 360° rotation.

Draw lines from the center of the figure out through identical places in the figure.

Count the number of lines drawn.

B

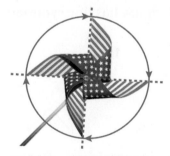

The pinwheel will show rotational symmetry 4 times within a 360° rotation.

Draw lines from the center of the figure out through identical places in the figure.

Count the number of lines drawn.

Think and Discuss

1. **Draw** a figure that does not have rotational symmetry.

2. **Determine** whether an equilateral triangle has rotational symmetry. If so, tell how many times it shows rotational symmetry within one full rotation.

Exercises

GUIDED PRACTICE

See Example 1 **Decide whether each figure has line symmetry. If it does, draw all the lines of symmetry.**

1.

2.

3.

See Example 2 **Find all the lines of symmetry in each flag.**

4.

5.

6.

See Example 3 **Tell how many times each figure will show rotational symmetry within one full rotation.**

7.

8.

9.

INDEPENDENT PRACTICE

See Example 1 **Decide whether each figure has line symmetry. If it does, draw all the lines of symmetry.**

10.

11.

12.

See Example 2 **Find all the lines of symmetry in each flag.**

13.

14.

15.

See Example 3 **Tell how many times each figure will show rotational symmetry within one full rotation.**

16.

17.

18.

Extra Practice
See page EP22.

19. Critical Thinking Which regular polygon shows rotational symmetry 9 times within one full rotation?

20. Nature How many lines of symmetry, if any, does the snowflake have? How many times, if any, will the snowflake show rotational symmetry within one full rotation?

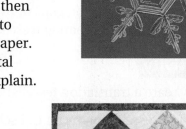

21. Fold a piece of paper in half vertically and then in half horizontally. Cut or tear a design into one of the folded edges. Then unfold the paper. Does the design have a vertical or horizontal line of symmetry? rotational symmetry? Explain.

22. Art Tell how many times the quilt design shows rotational symmetry in one full rotation if you consider only the shape of the design. Then tell how many times the image shows rotational symmetry if you consider both the shape and the colors in the design.

 23. What's the Question? Marla drew a square on the chalkboard. As an answer to Marla's question about symmetry, Rob said "90°." What question did Marla ask?

24. Write About It Explain why an angle of rotation must be less than 360° for a figure to have rotational symmetry.

25. Challenge Print a word in capital letters, using only letters that have horizontal lines of symmetry. Print another word using only capital letters that have vertical lines of symmetry.

Test Prep and Spiral Review

26. Multiple Choice How many lines of symmetry does the figure have?

    (A) None   (B) 1   (C) 2   (D) 4

27. Gridded Response How many times will the figure show rotational symmetry within one full rotation?

28. A bridge in an architectural model is 22 cm long. The model scale is 2 cm:30 m. Find the length of the actual bridge. (Lesson 4-10)

Triangle *JKL* has vertices *J*(−3, −1), *K*(−1, −1), and *L*(−1, −4). Write the coordinates of the vertices of the triangle after each transformation. (Lesson 8-10)

29. Translate the triangle 4 units right and 2 units down.

30. Reflect the triangle across the *y*-axis.

Hands-On LAB 8-11

Create Tessellations

Use with Lessons 8-10 and 8-11

Tessellations are patterns of identical shapes that completely cover a plane with no gaps or overlaps. The artist M. C. Escher created many fascinating tessellations.

Learn It Online
Lab Resources Online **go.hrw.com**,
keyword MS10 Lab8 Go

Activity

① Create a translation tessellation.

The tessellation by M. C. Escher shown at right is an example of a *translation tessellation*. To create your own translation tessellation, follow the steps below.

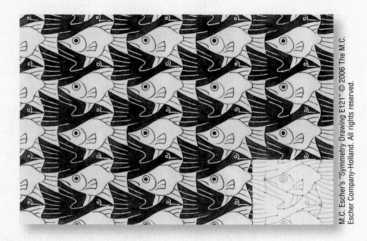

a. Start by drawing a square, rectangle, or other parallelogram. Replace one side of the parallelogram with a curve, as shown.

b. Translate the curve to the opposite side of the parallelogram.

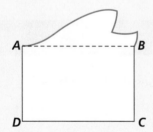

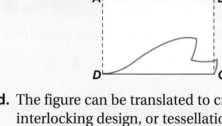

c. Repeat steps **a** and **b** for the other two sides of your parallelogram.

d. The figure can be translated to create an interlocking design, or tessellation. You can add details to your figure or divide it into two or more parts, as shown below.

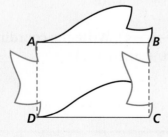

2 Create a rotation tessellation.

The tessellation by M. C. Escher shown at right is an example of a *rotation tessellation*. To create your own rotation tessellation, follow the steps below.

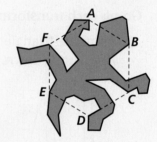

a. Start with a regular hexagon. Replace one side of the hexagon with a curve. Rotate the curve about point *B* so that the endpoint at point *A* is moved to point *C*.

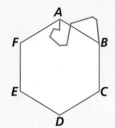 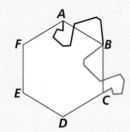

b. Replace side $\overline{CD}$ with a new curve, and rotate it about point *D* to replace side $\overline{DE}$.

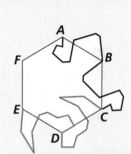

c. Replace side $\overline{EF}$ with a new curve, and rotate it about point *F* to replace side $\overline{FA}$.

The figure can be rotated and fitted together with copies of itself to create an interlocking design, or tessellation. You can add details to your figure, if desired.

Think and Discuss

1. Explain why the two types of tessellations in this activity are known as translation and rotation tessellations.

Try This

1. Create your own design for a translation or rotation tessellation.

2. Cut out copies of your design from **1** and fit them together to fill a space with your pattern.

CHAPTER

8

SECTION 8C

Learn It Online
Resources Online **go.hrw.com,**
keyword MS10 RTGO8C Go

Quiz for Lessons 8-9 Through 8-11

 8-9 **Congruent Figures**

Determine whether the triangles are congruent.

1.

A — 10 ft — B — 20 ft — C, 25 ft

D — 10 ft — E, 25 ft — 20 ft — F

2.

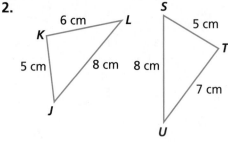

3. Determine the unknown measure in
the pair of congruent polygons.

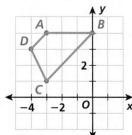 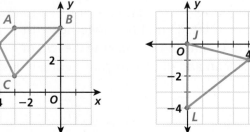

Ready to Go On?

 8-10 **Translations, Reflections, and Rotations**

Graph each transformation. Write the coordinates of the vertices of each image.

4. Translate triangle
RST 5 units down.

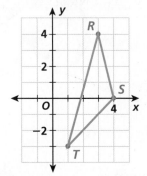

5. Reflect the figure
across the *x*-axis.

6. Rotate triangle *JKL* 90°
clockwise about the origin.

 8-11 **Symmetry**

7. Decide whether the figure has line
symmetry. If it does, draw all the
lines of symmetry.

8. Tell how many times the figure will
show rotational symmetry within
one full rotation.

510 *Chapter 8 Geometric Figures*

Piscataqua River Bridge The first bridge over the Piscataqua River, built in 1794, was the longest bridge in the world. The modern bridge, completed in 1971, is not the world's longest, but it is well known for its elegant symmetric design. The bridge connects Kittery, Maine with Portsmouth, New Hampshire.

MAINE

Kittery

1. Does the Piscataqua River Bridge have any lines of symmetry? If so, make a simple sketch of the bridge and draw all of its lines of symmetry.

For 2–7, use the diagram.

2. ∠1 and ∠2 are supplementary. Given that m∠1 is 78°, what is m∠2?

3. Classify △AEF according to its angles. Then measure the sides with a ruler, and classify the triangle according to its sides.

4. Quadrilateral *AEFD* is a trapezoid. What can you conclude about $\overline{AD}$ and $\overline{EF}$?

5. What can you say about ∠1 and ∠EAD? Why?

6. Find m∠EAD.

7. Given that m ∠DFE is 96°, find m∠3. Explain how you found the angle measure.

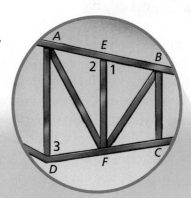

Real-World Connections

Game Time

Networks

A network is a figure that uses vertices and segments to show how objects are connected. You can use a network to show distances between cities. In the network at right, the vertices identify four cities in North Carolina, and the segments show the distances in miles between the cities.

Greensboro — 85 — Raleigh
94 215 127
98
Charlotte — 197 — Wilmington

You can use the network to find the shortest route from Charlotte to the other three cities and back to Charlotte. First find all the possible routes. Then find the distance in miles for each route. One route has been identified below.

CGWRC $94 + 215 + 127 + 98 = 534$

Which is the shortest route, and what is the distance?

Color Craze

You can use rhombus-shaped tiles to build a variety of polygons. Each side of a tile is a different color. Build each design by matching the same-colored sides of tiles. Then see if you can create your own designs with the tiles. Try to make designs that have line or rotational symmetry.

A complete set of tiles is available online.

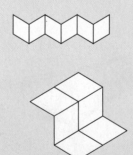
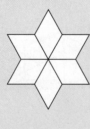

Learn It Online
Game Time Extra **go.hrw.com**,
keyword MS10 Games Go

Materials
- 6 sheets of construction paper
- card stock
- scissors
- hole punch
- 4 electrical ties
- white paper
- markers

It's in the Bag!

PROJECT ▸ **Brochure Book of Geometric Figures**

Make an organizer to hold brochures that summarize each lesson of the chapter.

Directions

① Start with sheets of construction paper that are 12 inches by 18 inches. Fold one sheet in half to make it 12 inches by 9 inches and then in half again to make it 6 inches by 9 inches. **Figure A**

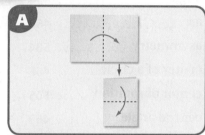

② Hold the paper with the folds at the bottom and on the right-hand side. Turn the top left-hand corner back and under to form a pocket. **Figure B**

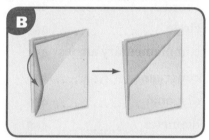

③ Turn the whole thing over and fold the top right-hand corner back and under to form a pocket. Repeat steps 1–3 with the other sheets of construction paper.

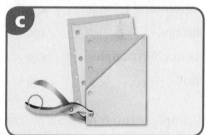

④ Cut out two pieces of card stock that are 6 inches by 9 inches. Punch four equally spaced holes down the length of each piece. Similarly, punch four equally spaced holes on each pocket as shown. **Figure C**

⑤ Stack the six pockets and put the card stock covers on the front and back of the stack. Insert electrical ties into the holes to hold everything together.

Taking Note of the Math

Fold sheets of plain white paper into thirds like a brochure. Use the brochures to take notes on the lessons of the chapter. Store the brochures in the pockets of your organizer.

Study Guide: Review

Study Guide: Review

Vocabulary

acute angle 454	line of reflection 496	right angle 454
acute triangle 478	line of symmetry 504	right triangle 478
adjacent angles 460	line segment 449	rotation 496
angle 454	line symmetry 504	rotational symmetry .. 505
arc 468	obtuse angle 454	scalene triangle 478
asymmetry 504	obtuse triangle 478	sector 469
center of a circle 468	parallel lines 460	Side-Side-Side Rule ... 492
center of rotation 505	parallelogram 482	skew lines 460
central angle 469	perpendicular lines ... 460	square 482
chord 468	plane 448	straight angle 454
circle 468	point 448	supplementary angles 454
complementary angles 454	polygon 474	transformation 496
congruent 449	preimage 496	translation 496
diagonal 486	radius 468	transversal 461
diameter 468	ray 449	trapezoid 482
equilateral triangle ... 478	rectangle 482	vertex 454
image 496	reflection 496	vertical angles 461
isosceles triangle 478	regular polygon 475	
line 448	rhombus 482	

Complete the sentences below with vocabulary words from the list above.

1. Every equilateral triangle is also a(n) __?__ triangle.

2. Lines in the same plane that do not intersect are __?__.

3. A line segment whose endpoints are any two points on a circle is a(n) __?__.

EXAMPLES

EXERCISES

8-1 **Building Blocks of Geometry** (pp. 448–451)

Identify the figures in the diagram.

■ points: *A, B, C* ■ lines: $\overleftrightarrow{AB}$
■ planes: *ABC* ■ rays: $\overrightarrow{BA}$; $\overrightarrow{AB}$
■ line segments: $\overline{AB}$; $\overline{BC}$

Identify the figures in the diagram.

4. points **5.** lines
6. planes **7.** rays
8. line segments

8-2 Classifying Angles (pp. 454–457)

■ Tell whether the angle is acute, right, obtuse, or straight.

The angle is a right angle.

Tell whether each angle is acute, right, obtuse, or straight.

9.

10.

8-3 Line and Angle Relationships (pp. 460–463)

■ Tell whether the lines appear parallel, perpendicular, or skew.

perpendicular

Tell whether the lines appear parallel, perpendicular, or skew.

11.

12.
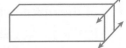

■ Line *a* ∥ line *b*. Find the measure of ∠4. Corresponding angles are congruent.
m∠4 = 74°

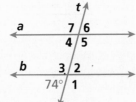

For Exercises 13–16, use the figure at left. Find the measure of each angle.

13. ∠2   14. ∠3

15. ∠5   16. ∠6

8-4 Properties of Circles (pp. 468–471)

Name the parts of circle *D*.

■ radii: $\overline{DB}$, $\overline{DC}$, $\overline{DE}$
■ diameter: $\overline{EB}$
■ chords: $\overline{AB}$, $\overline{EB}$, $\overline{EF}$

Name the parts of circle *F*.

17. radii
18. diameter
19. chords

8-5 Classifying Polygons (pp. 474–477)

■ Tell whether the figure is a regular polygon. If it is not, explain why not.
No, all the angles in the polygon are not congruent.

Tell whether each figure is a regular polygon. If it is not, explain why not.

20.

21.

8-6 Classifying Triangles (pp. 478–481)

■ Classify the triangle according to its sides and angles.

Isosceles right

Classify each triangle according to its sides and angles.

22.
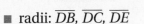

23.

EXAMPLES

EXERCISES

8-7 Classifying Quadrilaterals (pp. 482–485)

■ Give all of the names that apply to the quadrilateral. Then give the name that best describes it.

trapezoid; trapezoid

Give all of the names that apply to each quadrilateral. Then give the name that best describes it.

24. 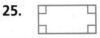 **25.**

8-8 Angles in Polygons (pp. 486–489)

■ Find the measure of the unknown angle.

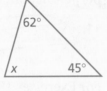

$62° + 45° + x = 180°$
$107° + x = 180°$
$x = 73°$

Find the measure of each unknown angle.

26. 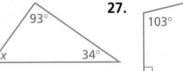 **27.**

8-9 Congruent Figures (pp. 492–495)

■ Determine the unknown measure in the set of congruent polygons.

The angle measures 53°.

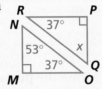

28. Determine the unknown measures in the set of congruent polygons.

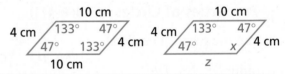

8-10 Translations, Reflections, and Rotations (pp. 496–500)

■ Graph the translation. Write the coordinates of the vertices of the image.

Translate △ABC 1 unit right and 3 units down.

△A′B′C′ has vertices A′(3, 1), B′(5, 3), and C′(5, 1).

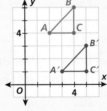

Graph the translation. Write the coordinates of the vertices of the image.

29. Translate △BCD 2 units left and 4 units down.

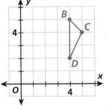

8-11 Symmetry (pp. 504–507)

■ Find all the lines of symmetry in the flag.

The flag has four lines of symmetry.

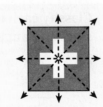

30. Find all the lines of symmetry in the flag.

Study Guide: Review

Chapter Test

Identify the figures in the diagram.

1. 4 points   **2.** 3 lines   **3.** a plane

4. 5 line segments   **5.** 6 rays

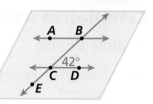

Line *AB* ∥ line *CD* in the diagram. Find the measure of each angle and tell whether the angle is acute, right, obtuse, or straight.

6. ∠*ABC*   **7.** ∠*BCE*   **8.** ∠*DCE*

Tell whether the lines appear parallel, perpendicular, or skew.

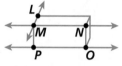

9. $\overleftrightarrow{MN}$ and $\overleftrightarrow{PO}$ **10.** $\overleftrightarrow{LM}$ and $\overleftrightarrow{PO}$ **11.** $\overleftrightarrow{NO}$ and $\overleftrightarrow{MN}$

Name the parts of circle *E*.

12. radii   **13.** chords   **14.** diameter

Tell whether each figure is a regular polygon. If it is not, explain why not.

15.   **16.**   **17.**

Classify each triangle according to its sides and angles.

18.   **19.**   **20.**

Give all the names that apply to each quadrilateral. Then give the name that best describes it.

21.    **22.**    **23.**

Find the measure of each unknown angle.

24.    **25.**   **26.**

27. Determine the unknown measure in the set of congruent polygons.

28. The vertices of △*ABC* have the coordinates *A*(−1, −3), *B*(−4, −1), and *C*(−1, −1). Graph the triangle after a translation 3 units left. Write the coordinates of the vertices of the image.

Find all the lines of symmetry in each flag.

29.   **30.**

Chapter Test

CHAPTER

8

TCAP
Test Prep

Learn It Online
State Test Practice **go.hrw.com**,
keyword MS10 TestPrep Go

Cumulative Assessment, Chapters 1–8

Multiple Choice

1. Which graph represents a direct variation?

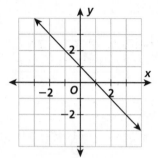

A

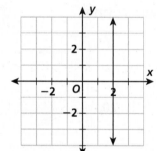

B

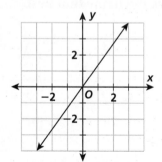

C

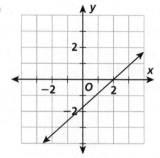

D

2. A store sells two dozen rolls of toilet paper for $4.84. What is the unit rate for one roll of toilet paper?

   F $0.13/roll of toilet paper

   G $0.20/roll of toilet paper

   H $0.40/roll of toilet paper

   J $1.21/roll of toilet paper

3. Nolan spent $\frac{1}{2}$ hour traveling to his orthodontist appointment, $\frac{3}{5}$ hour at his appointment, and $\frac{3}{4}$ hour traveling home. What is the total amount of time Nolan spent for this appointment?

   A $\frac{7}{11}$ hour

   B $\frac{37}{60}$ hour

   C $1\frac{17}{20}$ hours

   D $\frac{13}{5}$ hours

4. What is the value of the expression $-4x^2y - y$ for $x = -2$ and $y = -5$?

   F -85

   G -80

   H 75

   J 85

5. Which ratios form a proportion?

   A $\frac{4}{8}$ and $\frac{3}{6}$

   B $\frac{4}{12}$ and $\frac{6}{15}$

   C $\frac{4}{10}$ and $\frac{6}{16}$

   D $\frac{2}{3}$ and $\frac{5}{8}$

6. The graph shows how Amy spends her earnings each month. Amy earned $100 in May. How much did she spend on transportation and clothing combined?

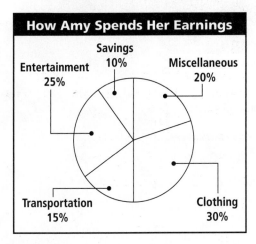

How Amy Spends Her Earnings

Savings 10%
Entertainment 25%
Miscellaneous 20%
Transportation 15%
Clothing 30%

F $15	**H** $45
G $30	**J** $55

HOT TIP! The incorrect answer choices in a multiple-choice test item are called distracters. They are the results of common mistakes. Be sure to check your work!

7. Which linear function is graphed below?

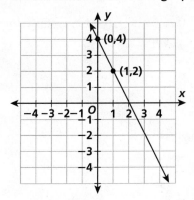

(0,4)
(1,2)

A $y = -2x + 4$

B $y = -2x - 4$

C $y = 2x + 4$

D $y = 2x - 4$

Process Standards Practice

Short Response

S1. Triangle *ABC*, with vertices *A*(2, 3), *B*(4, 0), and *C*(0, 0), is translated 2 units left and 6 units down to form triangle *A'B'C'*.

   a. On a coordinate plane, draw and label triangle *ABC* and triangle *A'B'C'*.

   b. Give the coordinates of the vertices of triangle *A'B'C'*.

S2. Taylor's goal is to spend less than 35% of her allowance each month on cell phone bills. Last month, Taylor spent $45 on cell phone bills. If she gets $120 each month as her allowance, did she achieve her goal? Explain your answer.

S3. Consider the sequence 4, 8, 12, 16, 20, ...

   a. Write a rule for the sequence. Use *n* to represent the position of the term in the sequence.

   b. What is the 8th term in the sequence?

Extended Response

E1. Four of the angles in a pentagon measure 74°, 111°, 145°, and 95°.

   a. How many sides and how many angles does a pentagon have?

   b. Is the pentagon a regular pentagon? How do you know?

   c. What is the sum of the angle measures of a pentagon? Include a drawing as part of your answer.

   d. Write and solve an equation to determine the missing angle measure of the pentagon.

Measurement: Two-Dimensional Figures

Chapter Focus

- Solve problems involving area and circumference of circles.
- Investigate the areas of similar figures.

Why Learn This?

The perimeter and area of garden beds can be determined by measuring their lengths and widths and then using a formula.

 Learn It Online
Chapter Project Online **go.hrw.com**,
keyword MS10 Ch9 Go

Are You Ready?

✓ Vocabulary

Choose the best term from the list to complete each sentence.

1. A (n) __?__ is a quadrilateral with exactly one pair of parallel sides.

2. A (n) __?__ is a four-sided figure with opposite sides that are congruent and parallel.

3. The __?__ of a circle is one-half the __?__ of the circle.

> diameter
>
> parallelogram
>
> radius
>
> right triangle
>
> trapezoid

Complete these exercises to review skills you will need for this chapter.

✓ Round Whole Numbers

Round each number to the nearest ten and nearest hundred.

4. 1,535 5. 294 6. 30,758 7. 497

✓ Round Decimals

Round each number to the nearest whole number and nearest tenth.

8. 6.18 9. 10.50 10. 513.93 11. 29.06

✓ Multiply with Decimals

Multiply.

12. $5.63 \cdot 8$ 13. $9.67 \cdot 4.3$ 14. $8.34 \cdot 16$ 15. $6.08 \cdot 0.56$

16. $0.82 \cdot 21$ 17. $2.74 \cdot 6.6$ 18. $40 \cdot 9.54$ 19. $0.33 \cdot 0.08$

✓ Order of Operations

Simplify each expression.

20. $2 \cdot 9 + 2 \cdot 6$ 21. $2(15 + 8)$ 22. $4 \cdot 6.8 + 7 \cdot 9.3$

23. $14(25.9 + 13.6)$ 24. $(27.3 + 0.7) \div 2^2$ 25. $5 \cdot 3^3 - 8.02$

26. $(63 \div 7) \cdot 4^2$ 27. $1.1 + 3 \cdot 4.3$ 28. $66 \cdot [5 + (3 + 3)^2]$

✓ Identify Polygons

Name each figure.

29. 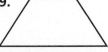 30.   31.

Measurement: Two-Dimensional Figures   **521**

Where You've Been

Previously, you

- found the perimeter or circumference of geometric figures.

- explored customary and metric units of measure.

- used proportions to convert measurements within the customary system and within the metric system.

In This Chapter

You will study

- comparing perimeter and circumference with the area of geometric figures.

- finding the area of parallelograms, triangles, trapezoids, and circles.

- finding the area of irregular figures.

- using powers, roots, and the Pythagorean Theorem to find missing measures.

Where You're Going

You can use the skills learned in this chapter

- to create an architectural floor plan.

- to design a building access ramp that meets government regulations.

Key Vocabulary/Vocabulario

area	área
circumference	circunferencia
hypotenuse	hipotenusa
perfect square	cuadrado perfecto
perimeter	perímetro
Pythagorean Theorem	Teorema de Pitágoras
square root	raíz cuadrada

Vocabulary Connections

To become familiar with some of the vocabulary terms in the chapter, consider the following. You may refer to the chapter, the glossary, or a dictionary if you like.

1. The *square root* of a number is one of the two equal factors of the number. For example, 3 is a square root because $3 \cdot 3 = 9$. How might picturing plant roots help you remember the meaning of **square root**?

2. The word *perimeter* comes from the Greek roots *peri,* meaning "all around," and *metron,* meaning "measure." What do the Greek roots tell you about the **perimeter** of a geometric figure?

3. To *square a number* means "to multiply the number by itself," as in $2 \cdot 2$. Keeping this idea of *square* in mind, what do you think a **perfect square** might be?

4. The word *circumference* comes from the Latin word *circumferre,* meaning "to carry around." How does the Latin meaning help you define the **circumference** of a circle?

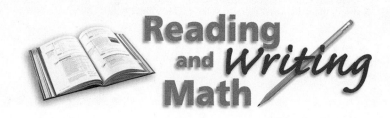 

Reading and Writing Math

TN English/Language Arts **SPI 0701.6.4** Interpret factual, quantitative, technical, or mathematical information presented in text features (e.g., maps, charts, graphs, time lines, tables, and diagrams).

Reading Strategy: Read and Interpret Graphics

Figures, diagrams, tables, and graphs provide important data. Knowing how to read these graphics will help you understand and solve related problems.

Similar Figures

$\triangle ABC$ and $\triangle JKL$ are similar.

8 cm
12 cm
B
A
C
16 cm
K
x
28 cm
L
56 cm
J

How to Read

Read all labels.
$AB = 8$ cm; $AC = 16$ cm; $BC = 12$ cm; $JK = 28$ cm; $JL = 56$ cm; $KL = x$ cm; $\angle A$ corresponds to $\angle J$.

Be careful about what you assume.
You may think $\overline{AB}$ corresponds to $\overline{LK}$, but this is not so. Since $\angle A$ corresponds to $\angle J$, you know $\overline{AB}$ corresponds to $\overline{JK}$.

Double-Bar Graph

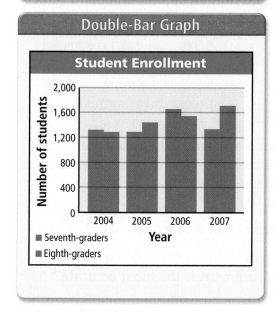

How to Read

Read the title of the graph and any special notes.
Blue indicates seventh-graders. Purple indicates eighth-graders.

Read each axis label and note the intervals of each scale.
x-axis—year increases by 1.
y-axis—enrollment increases by 400 students.

Determine what information is presented.
student enrollment for seventh- and eighth-graders per year

Try This

Look up each graphic in your textbook and answer the following questions.

1. Lesson 4-8 Exercise 1: Which side of the smaller triangle corresponds to $\overline{BC}$? Which angle corresponds to $\angle EDF$?

2. Lesson 7-3 Example 1: By what interval does the *x*-axis scale increase? About how many people speak Hindi?

Reading and Writing Math

Accuracy and Precision

TN ✓ **0706.2.15** Report
results of calculations appropriately
in a given context (i.e. using rules
of rounding, degree of accuracy,
and/or significant digits).
Also **GLE 0706.1.7**

*Use Additional Topic A-9
with this lesson.*

Vocabulary

precision

accuracy

Ancient Greeks used measurements taken during lunar eclipses to determine that the Moon was an average distance of 240,000 miles from Earth. Modern astronomers place the average distance at 238,855 miles.

Although the measurements are relatively close, modern astronomers measure with greater *precision*. **Precision** is the level of detail an instrument can measure.

The smaller the unit an instrument can measure, the more precise its measurements will be. For example, a millimeter ruler has greater precision than a centimeter ruler.

EXAMPLE 1 Judging Precision of Measurements

Choose the more precise measurement in each pair.

A 25 in.
2 ft
An inch is a smaller unit than a foot.

25 in. is the more precise measurement.

B 4 qt
4.3 qt
One tenth of a quart is a smaller unit than a quart.

4.3 qt is the more precise measurement.

Helpful Hint

You can measure length only to the precision level of the tool you are using.

In the real world, no measurement is exact and all measurements are approximations. **Accuracy** is the closeness of any given measurement or value to the actual measurement or value.

EXAMPLE 2 Measuring to Varying Degrees of Accuracy

Measure the length of the paper clip to the nearest half, fourth, and eighth inch. Which measurement is the most accurate? Explain.

Length to the nearest half inch: 1 in.

Length to the nearest fourth inch: $1\frac{1}{4}$ in.

Length to the nearest eighth inch: $1\frac{2}{8}$ in. = $1\frac{1}{4}$ in.

Measuring to the nearest fourth and to the nearest eighth both result in $1\frac{1}{4}$ in. Although measuring to the nearest eighth involves greater precision, both measurements are equally accurate because they are equally close to the actual value.

Since measurements are only as precise as the tool being used, in some cases you may need to estimate measurements beyond the level of precision provided by the instrument.

EXAMPLE 3 **Estimating Measures**

Estimate each measurement.

A

The weight of the potatoes is halfway between the 5 lb and 10 lb mark.

$10 - 5 = 5$ *Find the difference between the marks.*

$\frac{1}{2} \cdot 5 = 2.5$ *Find half of 5 lb.*

$5 + 2.5 = 7.5 \text{ lb}$ *Add the two weights together to find the weight of the potatoes.*

The weight of the potatoes is about 7.5 lb.

B

The amount of juice in the cup is about a fourth of the way between 2 fl oz and 4 fl oz.

$4 - 2 = 2$ *Find the difference between the marks.*

$\frac{1}{4} \cdot 2 = \frac{1}{2}$ *Find one fourth of 2 fl oz.*

$2 + \frac{1}{2} = 2\frac{1}{2} \text{ fl oz}$ *Add the two amounts together to find the number of fl oz of juice.*

The amount of liquid in the cup is about $2\frac{1}{2}$ fl oz.

Think and Discuss

1. **Find** the most precise measurement for the paper clip in Example 2.

2. **Explain whether** measuring to the nearest $\frac{1}{2}$ in. or to the nearest $\frac{1}{4}$ in. would give the more accurate measurement for a nail that is $3\frac{5}{8}$ inches in length.

Learn It Online
Homework Help Online **go.hrw.com**,
keyword MS10 9-1 Go
Exercises 1–13, 15, 19, 21

GUIDED PRACTICE

See Example **1** Choose the more precise measurement in each pair.

1. 5,281 yd
3 mi

2. 1.05 g
1.1 g

3. 205 lb
205.5 lb

4. 1 ft
5 in.

See Example **2** **5.** Measure to the nearest half, fourth, and eighth inch. Which measurement is the most accurate? Explain.

See Example **3** **6.** Estimate the mass of the backpack.

INDEPENDENT PRACTICE

See Example **1** Choose the more precise measurement in each pair.

7. 1.2 mm
1 mm

8. 15 fl oz
$1\frac{1}{2}$ c

9. $5\frac{1}{2}$ ft
$5\frac{1}{4}$ ft

10. 300g
13 kg

See Example **2** **11.** Measure to the nearest half, fourth, and eighth inch. Which measurement is the most accurate? Explain.

See Example **3** Estimate each measurement.

12.

13.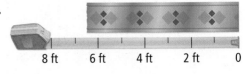

8 ft   6 ft   4 ft   2 ft   0

PRACTICE AND PROBLEM SOLVING

Extra Practice
See page EP23.

Choose the more precise unit in each pair.

14. liter or millimeter

15. ounce or pound

16. quart or fluid ounce

17. **Critical Thinking** The prefix *deca* means ten. The prefix *deci* means tenth. Would the length of an object be more accurate if measured in decameters or decimeters? Explain.

Estimate the measure of each angle.

18.

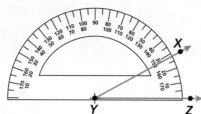

19.

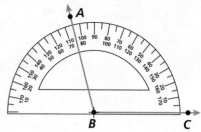

20. Estimation Estimate and then measure the width of a hallway at your school. Give your answer measured to the nearest meter and centimeter.

Find the greatest precision for each scale shown.

21.

22.

23. Critical Thinking Rita wants to center a poster on the wall of her room. The tools available to her to help her measure include a ruler, a measuring tape, and a meter stick. Which tool or tools should she choose? Explain.

24. What's the Error? Shia says that 4.25 m is a more precise measure than 4.2 mm. What is his error?

25. Write About It Give an example of when an accurate measurement is important and when an estimate will do.

26. Challenge The weight limit for vehicles on a bridge is 40 tons. The weight of a loaded truck is estimated at 40 tons. Should the truck be allowed to cross the bridge? Explain.

Test Prep and Spiral Review

27. Multiple Choice Which is the most precise measurement?

(A) 1 mile   (B) 1,758 yards   (C) 5,281 feet   (D) 63,355 inches

28. Short Response Kylie is measuring the thickness of a nickel. Which unit, inches or millimeters, would give her the more precise measurement? Explain.

For Exercises 29–30, tell whether you would expect a positive correlation, a negative correlation, or no correlation. (Lesson 7-9)

29. the price of a car and the number of windows it has

30. the speed a car travels and the amount of time it takes to go 100 miles

Determine whether each figure is a polygon. If it is not, explain why. (Lesson 8-5)

31.   **32.**   **33.**

Hands-on LAB 9-2

Explore Perimeter & Circumference

Use with Lesson 9-2

The distance around a figure is its perimeter. You can use a loop of string to explore the dimensions of a rectangle with a perimeter of 18 inches.

Learn It Online
Lab Resources Online **go.hrw.com**,
keyword **MS10 Lab9** Go

TN ✓ 0706.2.2 Develop and analyze algorithms and compute efficiently with integers and rational numbers.

Activity 1

1 Cut a piece of string that is slightly longer than 18 inches. Tie the ends together to form an 18-inch loop.

2 Make the loop into a rectangle by placing it around four push pins on a corkboard. Both the length and the width of the rectangle should be a whole number of inches.

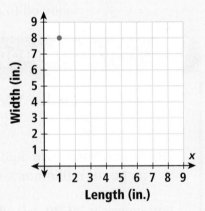

3 Make different rectangles with whole-number lengths and widths. Record the lengths and widths in a table.

Length (in.)	1	2	3	■	■	■	■	■
Width (in.)	8	■	■	■	■	■	■	■

4 Graph the data in your table by plotting points on a coordinate plane like the one shown.

Think and Discuss

1. What pattern is made by the points on your graph?

2. How is the sum of the length and width of each rectangle related to the rectangle's perimeter of 18 inches?

3. Suppose a rectangle has length ℓ and width w. Write a rule that you can use to find the rectangle's perimeter.

Try This

Use the rule you discovered to find the perimeter of each rectangle.

1.
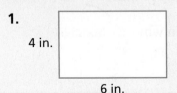
4 in.
6 in.

2.
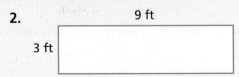
9 ft
3 ft

3.
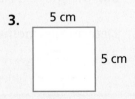
5 cm
5 cm

The perimeter of a circle is called the *circumference.* You can explore the relationship between a circle's circumference and its diameter by measuring some circles.

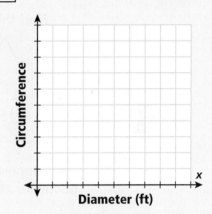

Diameter

Circumference

Activity 2

1 Four students should stand in a circle with their arms outstretched, as shown in the diagram.

2 Another student should find the diameter of the circle by measuring the distance across the middle of the circle with a tape measure.

3 The student should also find the circumference of the circle by measuring the distance around the circle from fingertip to fingertip across the backs of the students.

4 Record the diameter and circumference in a table like the one below.

Diameter	■	■	■	■	■
Circumference	■	■	■	■	■

5 Add one or more students to the circle and repeat the process. Record the diameter and circumference for at least five different circles.

6 Graph the data in your table by plotting points on a coordinate plane like the one shown.

Think and Discuss

1. **Make a Conjecture** In general, what do you notice about the points on your graph? What shape or pattern do they seem to form?

2. Calculate the ratio of the circumference to the diameter for each of the data points. Then calculate the mean of these ratios. For any circle, the ratio of the circumference to the diameter is a constant, known as *pi* (π). Give an estimate for π based on your findings.

Try This

1. For a circle with circumference *C* and diameter *d*, the ratio of the circumference to the diameter is $\frac{C}{d} = \pi$. Use this to write a formula that you can use to find the circumference of a circle when you know its diameter.

2. Use your estimate for the value of π to find the approximate circumference of the circle at right.

d = 4 cm

In volleyball, the player serving must hit the ball over the net but keep it within the court's sidelines and end lines. The two sidelines on a volleyball court are each 18 meters long, and the two end lines are each 9 meters long. Together, the four lines form the *perimeter* of the court.

Vocabulary

perimeter

circumference

pi

Perimeter is the distance around a geometric figure. To find the perimeter P of a rectangular volleyball court, you can add the lengths of its sides. Perimeter is measured in units of length.

EXAMPLE 1 Finding the Perimeter of a Polygon

Find the perimeter.

9 cm, 12 cm, 11 cm

$$P = 9 + 12 + 11 \qquad \textit{Use the side lengths.}$$
$$P = 32 \qquad \textit{Add.}$$

The perimeter of the triangle is 32 cm.

Since opposite sides of a rectangle are equal in length, you can find the perimeter of a rectangle by using a formula.

Interactivities Online ▶

PERIMETER OF A RECTANGLE		
The perimeter P of a rectangle is the sum of twice its length ℓ and twice its width w.	$P = 2\ell + 2w$	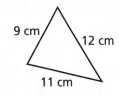

EXAMPLE 2 Using Properties of a Rectangle to Find Perimeter

Find the perimeter.

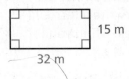
15 m
32 m

$$P = 2\ell + 2w \qquad \textit{Use the formula.}$$
$$P = (2 \cdot 32) + (2 \cdot 15) \qquad \textit{Substitute for } \ell \textit{ and } w.$$
$$P = 64 + 30 \qquad \textit{Multiply.}$$
$$P = 94 \qquad \textit{Add.}$$

The perimeter of the rectangle is 94 m.

Video **Lesson Tutorials Online**

The distance around a circle is called **circumference**. For every circle, the ratio of circumference C to diameter d is the same. This ratio, $\frac{C}{d}$, is represented by the Greek letter π, called **pi**. Pi is approximately equal to 3.14 or $\frac{22}{7}$. By solving the equation $\frac{C}{d} = \pi$ for C, you get the formula for circumference.

CIRCUMFERENCE OF A CIRCLE		
The circumference C of a circle is π times the diameter d, or 2π times the radius r.	$C = \pi d$ or $C = 2\pi r$	Radius — Diameter — Circumference

EXAMPLE 3 Finding the Circumference of a Circle

Find the circumference of each circle to the nearest tenth, if necessary. Use 3.14 or $\frac{22}{7}$ for π.

Helpful Hint

If the diameter or radius of a circle is a multiple of 7, use $\frac{22}{7}$ for π.

$C \approx \frac{22}{\underset{1}{7}} \cdot \frac{\overset{3}{21}}{1} \approx 66$

A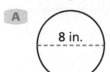
8 in.

$C = \pi d$ *You know the diameter.*
$C \approx 3.14 \cdot 8$ *Substitute 3.14 for π and 8 for d.*
$C \approx 25.12$ *Multiply.*

The circumference of the circle is about 25.1 in.

B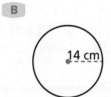
14 cm

$C = 2\pi r$ *You know the radius.*
$C \approx 2 \cdot \frac{22}{7} \cdot 14$ *Substitute $\frac{22}{7}$ for π and 14 for r.*
$C \approx 88$ *Multiply.*

The circumference of the circle is about 88 cm.

EXAMPLE 4 *Design Application*

Lily is drawing plans for a circular fountain. The circumference of the fountain is 63 ft. What is its approximate diameter?

$C = \pi d$ *You know the circumference.*
$63 \approx 3.14 \cdot d$ *Substitute 3.14 for π and 63 for C.*
$\frac{63}{3.14} \approx \frac{3.14 \cdot d}{3.14}$ *Divide both sides by 3.14 to isolate the variable.*
$20 \approx d$

The diameter of the fountain is about 20 ft.

Think and Discuss

1. Describe two ways to find the perimeter of a volleyball court.

2. Explain how to use the formula $C = \pi d$ to find the circumference of a circle if you know the radius.

Exercises

Learn It Online
Homework Help Online **go.hrw.com**,
keyword MS10 9-2 Go
Exercises 1–20, 21, 23

GUIDED PRACTICE

Find each perimeter.

See Example **1**

1.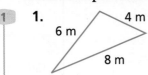

2.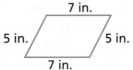

3.

See Example **2**

4.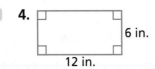

5.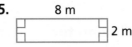

6.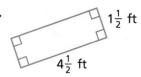

See Example **3**   **Find the circumference of each circle to the nearest tenth, if necessary. Use 3.14 or $\frac{22}{7}$ for π.**

7. 12 m

8. 3 ft

9. 21 in.

See Example **4**   **10.** A Ferris wheel has a circumference of 440 feet. What is the approximate diameter of the Ferris wheel? Use 3.14 for π.

INDEPENDENT PRACTICE

Find each perimeter.

See Example **1**   **11.**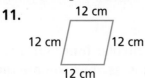

12.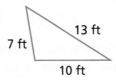

13.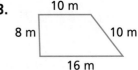

See Example **2**   **14.**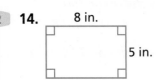

15.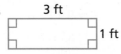

16.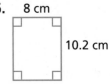

See Example **3**   **Find the circumference of each circle to the nearest tenth, if necessary. Use 3.14 or $\frac{22}{7}$ for π.**

17. 35 cm

18. 3 m

19. 5.1 in.

See Example **4**   **20.** The circumference of Kayla's bicycle wheel is 91 inches. What is the approximate diameter of her bicycle wheel? Use 3.14 for π.

Extra Practice
See page EP23.

Architecture

The U.S. Capitol Rotunda is 96 ft in diameter and rises 180 ft 3 in. to the canopy. The rotunda contains many historical paintings, including the Frieze of American History and several memorial statues.

Find each missing measurement to the nearest tenth. Use 3.14 for π.

21. $r = \blacksquare$; $d = \blacksquare$; $C = 17.8$ m

22. $r = 6.7$ yd; $d = \blacksquare$; $C = \blacksquare$

23. $r = \blacksquare$; $d = 10.6$ in.; $C = \blacksquare$

24. $r = \blacksquare$; $d = \blacksquare$; $C = \pi$

25. Critical Thinking Ben is placing rope lights around the edge of a circular patio with a 24.2 ft diameter. The lights are in lengths of 57 inches. How many strands of lights does he need to surround the patio edge?

26. Geography The map shows the distances in miles between the airports on the Big Island of Hawaii. A pilot flies from Kailua-Kona to Waimea to Hilo and back to Kailua-Kona. How far does he travel?

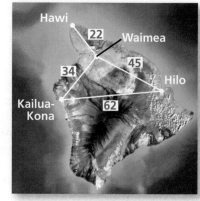

27. Architecture The Capitol Rotunda connects the House and Senate sides of the U.S. Capitol. The rotunda is 180 feet tall and has a circumference of about 301.5 feet. What is its approximate diameter, to the nearest foot?

28. Describe how you could use a piece of string to find the perimeter or circumference of an object.

29. Write a Problem Write a problem about finding the perimeter or circumference of an object in your school or classroom.

30. Write About It Explain how to find the width of a rectangle if you know its perimeter and length.

31. Challenge The perimeter of a regular nonagon is $25\frac{1}{2}$ in. What is the length of one side of the nonagon?

Test Prep and Spiral Review

32. Multiple Choice Which is the best estimate for the circumference of a circle with a diameter of 15 inches?

(A) 18.1 inches   (B) 23.6 inches   (C) 32.5 inches   (D) 47.1 inches

33. Gridded Response John is building a dog pen that is 6 feet by 8 feet. How many feet of fencing material will he need to go all the way around the pen?

Solve. (Lesson 6-5)

34. 18 is 20% of what number?

35. 78% of 65 is what number?

Choose the more precise measure in each pair. (Lesson 9-1)

36. 4 ft, 1 yd   **37.** 2 cm, 21 mm   **38.** $5\frac{1}{2}$ in., $5\frac{1}{4}$ in.   **39.** 37 g, 37.0 g

Explore Area of Polygons

9-3

Use with Lessons 9-3, 9-4 and 9-5

Learn It Online
Lab Resources Online **go.hrw.com**,
keyword **MS10 Lab9** **Go**

TN ✓ **0706.2.2** Develop and analyze
algorithms and compute efficiently with
integers and rational numbers.

You can use a parallelogram to find the area of a triangle or a trapezoid. To do so, you must first know how to find the area of a parallelogram.

Activity 1

1 On a sheet of graph paper, draw a parallelogram with a base of 10 units and a height of 6 units.

2 Cut out the parallelogram. Then cut a right triangle off the end of the parallelogram by cutting along the altitude.

3 Move the triangle to the other side of the figure to make a rectangle.

4 How is the area of the parallelogram related to the area of the rectangle?

5 What are the length and width of the rectangle? What is the area of the rectangle?

6 Find the area of the parallelogram.

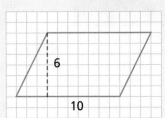

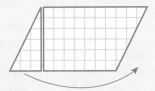

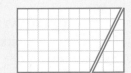

Think and Discuss

1. How are the length and width of the rectangle related to the base and height of the parallelogram?

2. Suppose a parallelogram has base *b* and height *h*. Write a formula for the area of the parallelogram.

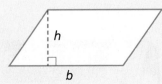

Try This

1. Does your formula work for any parallelogram? If so, show how to use the formula to find the area of the parallelogram at right.

2. Explain what must be true about the areas of the parallelograms below.

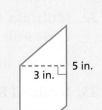

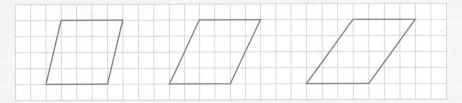

Activity 2

1 On a sheet of graph paper, draw a triangle with a base of 7 units and a height of 4 units.

2 Cut out the triangle. Then use the triangle to trace and cut out a second triangle that is congruent to it.

3 Arrange the two triangles to form a parallelogram.

4 How is the area of the triangle related to the area of the parallelogram?

5 Find the areas of the parallelogram and the triangle.

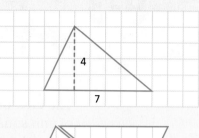

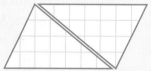

Think and Discuss

1. How are the base and height of the triangle related to the base and height of the parallelogram?

2. Suppose a triangle has base b and height h. Write a formula for the area of the triangle.

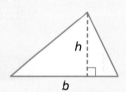

Try This

1. Find the area of a triangle with a base of 10 ft and a height of 5 ft.

Activity 3

1 On a sheet of graph paper, draw a trapezoid with bases 4 units and 8 units long and a height of 3 units.

2 Cut out the trapezoid. Then use the trapezoid to trace and cut out a second trapezoid that is congruent to it.

3 Arrange the two trapezoids to form a parallelogram.

4 How is the area of the trapezoid related to the area of the parallelogram?

5 Find the areas of the parallelogram and the trapezoid.

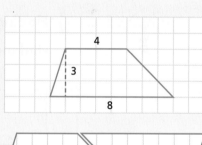

Think and Discuss

1. What is the length of the base of the parallelogram at right? What is the parallelogram's area?

2. What is the area of one of the trapezoids in the figure?

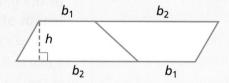

Try This

1. Find the area of a trapezoid with bases 4 in. and 6 in. and a height of 8 in.

The **area** of a figure is the number of unit squares needed to cover the figure. Area is measured in units of length squared, or square units. For example, the area of a chessboard can be measured in square inches. The area of a lawn chessboard is much larger than a regular chessboard, so it can be measured in square feet or square yards.

Vocabulary
area

AREA OF A RECTANGLE		
The area A of a rectangle is the product of its length ℓ and its width w.	$A = \ell w$	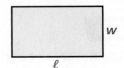

EXAMPLE 1 Finding the Area of a Rectangle

Find the area of the rectangle.

7.5 ft

10 ft

$A = \ell w$ — *Use the formula.*

$A = 10 \cdot 7.5$ — *Substitute for ℓ and w.*

$A = 75$ — *Multiply.*

The area of the rectangle is 75 ft².

EXAMPLE 2 Finding Length or Width of a Rectangle

Bethany and her dad are planting a rectangular garden. The area of the garden is 1,080 ft², and the width is 24 ft. What is the length of the garden?

$A = \ell w$ — *Use the formula for the area of a rectangle.*

$1,080 = \ell \cdot 24$ — *Substitute 1,080 for A and 24 for w.*

$\dfrac{1,080}{24} = \dfrac{\ell \cdot 24}{24}$ — *Divide both sides by 24 to isolate ℓ.*

$45 = \ell$

The length of the garden is 45 ft.

Video **Lesson Tutorials Online**

The base of a parallelogram is the length of one side. Its height is the perpendicular distance from the base to the opposite side.

AREA OF A PARALLELOGRAM		
The area A of a parallelogram is the product of its base b and its height h.	$A = bh$	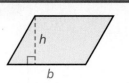

EXAMPLE **3** **Finding the Area of a Parallelogram**

Find the area of the parallelogram.

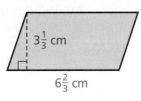
$3\frac{1}{3}$ cm

$6\frac{2}{3}$ cm

$A = bh$ *Use the formula.*

$A = 6\frac{2}{3} \cdot 3\frac{1}{3}$ *Substitute for b and h.*

$A = \frac{20}{3} \cdot \frac{10}{3}$ *Convert to improper fractions.*

$A = \frac{200}{9}$ or $22\frac{2}{9}$ *Multiply.*

The area of the parallelogram is $22\frac{2}{9}$ cm^2.

EXAMPLE **4** *Landscaping Application*

Birgit and Mark are building a rectangular patio measuring 9 yd by 7 yd. How many square feet of tile will they need?

First draw and label a diagram. Look at the units. The patio is measured in yards, but the answer should be in square feet.

$9 \text{ yd} \cdot \frac{3 \text{ ft}}{1 \text{ yd}} = 27 \text{ ft}$ *Convert yards to feet by using a unit conversion factor.*

7 yd
9 yd

$7 \text{ yd} \cdot \frac{3 \text{ ft}}{1 \text{ yd}} = 21 \text{ ft}$

Now find the area of the patio in square feet.

$A = \ell w$ *Use the formula for the area of a rectangle.*

$A = 27 \cdot 21$ *Substitute 27 for ℓ and 21 for w.*

$A = 567$ *Multiply.*

Birgit and Mark need 567 ft^2 of tile.

Think and Discuss

1. Write a formula for the area of a square, using an exponent.

2. Explain why the area of a nonrectangular parallelogram with side lengths 5 in. and 3 in. is not 15 in^2.

Exercises

GUIDED PRACTICE

See Example 1 **Find the area of each rectangle.**

1.
8 ft
4.2 ft

2.
3 m
7 m

3.
16.4 cm
9 cm

See Example 2 **4.** Kara wants a rug for her bedroom. She knows the area of her bedroom is 132 ft². The length of her room is 12 ft. What is the width of Kara's bedroom?

See Example 3 **Find the area of each parallelogram.**

5.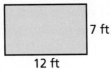
6 in.
8 in.

6.
4 cm
$2\frac{4}{5}$ cm

7.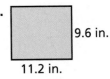
4.4 m
6.5 m

See Example 4 **8.** Anna is mowing a rectangular field measuring 120 yd by 66 yd. How many square feet will Anna mow?

INDEPENDENT PRACTICE

See Example 1 **Find the area of each rectangle.**

9.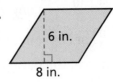
7 ft
12 ft

10.
$15\frac{1}{2}$ in.
$8\frac{1}{2}$ in.

11.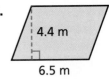
9.6 in.
11.2 in.

See Example 2 **12.** James and Linda are fencing a rectangular area of the yard for their dog. The width of the dog yard is 4.5 m. Its area is 67.5 m². What is the length of the dog yard?

See Example 3 **Find the area of each parallelogram.**

13.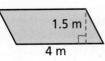
1.5 m
4 m

14.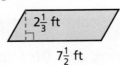
$2\frac{1}{3}$ ft
$7\frac{1}{2}$ ft

15.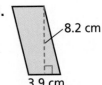
8.2 cm
3.9 cm

See Example 4 **16.** Abby is painting rectangular blocks on her bathroom walls. Each block is 15 in. by 18 in. What is the area of one block in square feet?

Extra Practice
See page EP23.

Find the area of each polygon.

17. rectangle: $\ell = 9$ yd; $w = 8$ yd

18. parallelogram: $b = 7$ m; $h = 4.2$ m

Graph the polygon with the given vertices. Identify the polygon and then find its area.

19. $(2, 0)$, $(2, -2)$, $(9, 0)$, $(9, -2)$

20. $(4, 1)$, $(4, 7)$, $(8, 4)$, $(8, 10)$

21. Art Without the frame, *Icarus* by Henri Matisse measures about 42 cm by 64 cm. The width of the frame is 8 cm.

    a. Find the perimeter and area of the painting.

    b. What is the total area covered by the painting and the frame?

② 22. What's the Error? Pete says the area of a 3 cm by 4 cm rectangle is 12 cm. What is his error?

② 23. Choose a Strategy The area of a parallelogram is 84 cm². If the base is 5 cm longer than the height, what is the length of the base?

    Ⓐ 5 cm   Ⓑ 7 cm   Ⓒ 12 cm   Ⓓ 14 cm

Icarus by Henri Matisse

✏ 24. Write About It A rectangle and a parallelogram have sides that measure 3 m, 4 m, 3 m, and 4 m. Do the figures have the same area? Explain.

☆ 25. Challenge Two parallelograms have the same base length, but the height of the first is half that of the second. What is the ratio of the area of the first parallelogram to that of the second? What would the ratio be if both the height and the base of the first parallelogram were half those of the second?

Test Prep and Spiral Review

26. Multiple Choice Find the area of the parallelogram.

    Ⓐ 13 in²   Ⓑ 26 in²   Ⓒ 40 in²   Ⓓ 56 in²

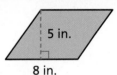

5 in.

8 in.

27. Extended Response Kiana is helping her dad build a deck. The plans they have are for a 6-foot-by-8-foot deck, but her dad wants a deck that has twice as much area. He suggests doubling the length of each side of the deck. Will this double the area? If not, suggest another method for doubling the area of the deck.

Tell whether each angle is acute, obtuse, right or straight. (Lesson 8-2)

28.   **29.**   **30.**   **31.**

Find the perimeter of each rectangle, given the dimensions. (Lesson 9-2)

32. 6 in. by 12 in.   **33.** 2 m by 8 m   **34.** 16 cm by 3 cm   **35.** $4\frac{4}{5}$ ft by $1\frac{3}{8}$ ft

The Bermuda Triangle is a triangular region of the Atlantic Ocean in which a number of aircraft and ships have mysteriously disappeared. To find the area of this region, you could use the formula for the area of a triangle.

Reading Math

An *altitude* of a triangle is a segment that represents the height.

The base of a triangle can be any side. The height of a triangle is the perpendicular distance from the base to the opposite vertex.

AREA OF A TRIANGLE		
The area A of a triangle is half the product of its base b and its height h.	$A = \frac{1}{2}bh$	

EXAMPLE 1 **Finding the Area of a Triangle**

Find the area of each triangle.

A

$A = \frac{1}{2}bh$ *Use the formula.*

$A = \frac{1}{2}(4 \cdot 3)$ *Substitute 4 for b and 3 for h.*

$A = 6$

The area of the triangle is 6 square units.

B

$A = \frac{1}{2}bh$ *Use the formula.*

$A = \frac{1}{2}(6 \cdot 5)$ *Substitute 6 for b and 5 for h.*

$A = 15$

The area of the triangle is 15 square units.

The two parallel sides of a trapezoid are its bases, b_1 and b_2. The height of a trapezoid is the perpendicular distance between the bases.

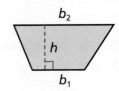

Video **Lesson Tutorials Online**

<table>
<tr><td colspan="3" align="center">**AREA OF A TRAPEZOID**</td></tr>
<tr>
<td>The area of a trapezoid is half its height multiplied by the sum of the lengths of its two bases.</td>
<td>$A = \frac{1}{2}h(b_1 + b_2)$</td>
<td></td>
</tr>
</table>

EXAMPLE **2** | **Finding the Area of a Trapezoid**

Reading Math

In the term b_1, the number 1 is called a *subscript*. It is read as "*b*-one" or "*b* sub-one."

Find the area of each trapezoid.

A

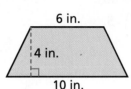

6 in.
4 in.
10 in.

$A = \frac{1}{2}h(b_1 + b_2)$ — *Use the formula.*

$A = \frac{1}{2} \cdot 4(10 + 6)$ — *Substitute.*

$A = \frac{1}{2} \cdot 4(16)$ — *Add.*

$A = 32$ — *Multiply.*

The area of the trapezoid is 32 in^2.

B

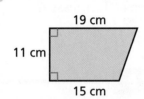

19 cm
11 cm
15 cm

$A = \frac{1}{2}h(b_1 + b_2)$ — *Use the formula.*

$A = \frac{1}{2} \cdot 11(15 + 19)$ — *Substitute.*

$A = \frac{1}{2} \cdot 11(34)$ — *Add.*

$A = 187$ — *Multiply.*

The area of the trapezoid is 187 cm^2.

EXAMPLE **3** | *Geography Application*

The state of Nevada is shaped somewhat like a trapezoid. What is the approximate area of Nevada?

320 mi
200 mi — Carson City
NEVADA
475 mi

$A = \frac{1}{2}h(b_1 + b_2)$ — *Use the formula.*

$A = \frac{1}{2} \cdot 320(200 + 475)$ — *Substitute.*

$A = \frac{1}{2} \cdot 320(675)$ — *Add.*

$A = 108,000$ — *Multiply.*

The area of Nevada is approximately 108,000 square miles.

Think and Discuss

1. Tell how to use the sides of a right triangle to find its area.

2. Explain how to find the area of a trapezoid.

Learn It Online
Homework Help Online **go.hrw.com**,
keyword MS10 9-4 **Go**
Exercises 1–14, 15, 17, 19, 21

GUIDED PRACTICE

See Example **1**   Find the area of each triangle.

1.
7
8

2.
4
6

3.
7
11.2

See Example **2**   Find the area of each trapezoid.

4.
2.5 cm
2 cm
4 cm

5.
6 m
8 m
10 m

6.
12 ft
6 ft
6 ft

See Example **3**   **7.** The state of Tennessee is shaped
somewhat like a trapezoid. What
is the approximate area of Tennessee?

442 mi
Nashville
TENNESSEE
115 mi
350 mi

INDEPENDENT PRACTICE

See Example **1**   Find the area of each triangle.

8.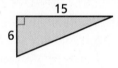
15
6

9.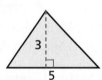
3
5

10.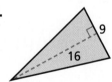
9
16

See Example **2**   Find the area of each trapezoid.

11.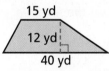
15 yd
12 yd
40 yd

12.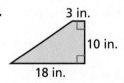
3 in.
10 in.
18 in.

13.
3 cm
10 cm
5 cm

See Example **3**   **14.** The state of New Hampshire is shaped somewhat
like a right triangle. What is the approximate
area of New Hampshire?

NEW
HAMPSHIRE
160 mi
Concord
85 mi

Extra Practice
See page EP23.

Find the missing measurement of each triangle.

15. $b = 8$ cm
$h = $ ■
$A = 18$ cm^2

16. $b = 16$ ft
$h = 0.7$ ft
$A = $ ■

17. $b = $ ■
$h = 95$ in.
$A = 1,045$ in^2

Graph the polygon with the given vertices. Identify the polygon and then find its area.

18. $(1, 2), (4, 5), (8, 2), (8, 5)$

19. $(1, -6), (5, -1), (7, -6)$

20. $(2, 3), (2, 10), (7, 6), (7, 8)$

21. $(3, 0), (3, 4), (-3, 0)$

22. What is the height of a trapezoid with an area of 9 m^2 and bases that measure 2.4 m and 3.6 m?

23. **Multi-Step** The state of Colorado is somewhat rectangular in shape. Estimate the perimeter and area of Colorado.

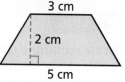
365 mi
276 mi
Denver ★
COLORADO

24. **What's the Error?** A student says the area of the triangle shown at right is 33 cm^2. Explain why the student is incorrect.

6 cm
11 cm

25. **Write About It** Explain how to use the formulas for the area of a rectangle and the area of a triangle to estimate the area of Nevada.

26. **Challenge** The state of North Dakota is trapezoidal in shape and has an area of 70,704 mi^2. If the southern border is 359 mi and the distance between the northern border and the southern border is 210 mi, what is the approximate length of the northern border?

Test Prep and Spiral Review

27. **Multiple Choice** Find the area of the trapezoid.

ⓐ 8 cm^2

ⓑ 16 cm^2

ⓒ 17 cm^2

ⓓ 30 cm^2

3 cm
2 cm
5 cm

28. **Short Response** Graph the triangle with vertices $(0, 0), (2, 3)$, and $(6, 0)$. Then find the area of the triangle.

Find the measure of the third angle in each triangle, given two angle measures. (Lesson 8-8)

29. $45°, 45°$

30. $71°, 57°$

31. $103°, 28°$

32. $62°, 19°$

33. Justin is laying a tile floor in a room that measures 5 yd by 6 yd. How many square feet of tile does he need? (Lesson 9-3)

Compare Perimeter and Area of Similar Figures

Use with Lesson 9-4

Learn It Online
Lab Resources Online **go.hrw.com**,
keyword MS10 Lab9 **Go**

TN ✓ **0706.4.3** Understand that if a scale factor describes how corresponding lengths in two similar objects are related, then the square of the scale factor describes how corresponding areas are related, and the cube of the scale factor describes how corresponding volumes are related.
Also **GLE 0706.4.3**, ✓ **0706.4.4**, SPI **0706.4.3**

REMEMBER
- Two figures are similar when the measures of the corresponding angles are equal and the ratios of the corresponding sides are equivalent.
- A scale factor is the ratio used to enlarge or reduce similar figures.

Activity 1

1. On graph paper, use a ruler to draw two rectangles.
   Rectangle A: $\ell = 3$ in., $w = 2$ in.
   Rectangle B: $\ell = 6$ in., $w = 4$ in.

2. Use rectangles **A** and **B** to complete the first two columns of the table.

3. Complete the third column by calculating the ratios for each row.

	Rectangle A	Rectangle B	$\dfrac{\text{Rectangle B}}{\text{Rectangle A}}$
Length (in.)	▪	▪	▪
Width (in.)	▪	▪	▪
Perimeter (in.)	▪	▪	▪
Area (in²)	▪	▪	▪

Think and Discuss

1. Identify the scale factor between rectangles **A** and **B**. Which ratios in the table are the same as the scale factor?

Try This

Draw rectangle C with $\ell = 1.5$ in., $w = 1$ in.

1. Complete a table similar to the table in Activity 1 for rectangles **A** and **C**.

2. **Make a Conjecture** Make a conjecture about the relationship between scale factor and perimeter for any similar rectangles.

3. **Make a Conjecture** Based on the information in the tables, how do you think the ratio of the areas of similar rectangles is related to the scale factor? (*Hint:* Area is measured in *square* units.)

Activity 2

1. Draw and label two isosceles triangles as shown in the diagram.

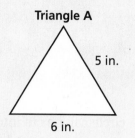

Triangle A

5 in.

Triangle B

2.5 in.

6 in.

3 in.

2. Complete the table. Use a ruler to measure the height of the triangle.

3. Complete the third column by calculating the ratios for each row.

	Triangle A	Triangle B	Triangle B / Triangle A
Base length (in.)	■	■	■
Side length (in.)	■	■	■
Height (in.)	■	■	■
Perimeter (in.)	■	■	■
Area (in²)	■	■	■

Think and Discuss

1. **Make a Conjecture** Based on your results from Activity 1 and the information in the table, make a conjecture about the relationship between the perimeters of two similar figures.

2. **Make a Conjecture** Based on your results from Activity 1 and the information in the table, make a conjecture about the relationship between the areas of two similar figures.

3. **Make a Prediction** Predict what will happen to the area of a triangle if the lengths of all its sides are multiplied by 4.

Try This

A rectangle has a perimeter of 30 in. and an area of 50 in². Find the perimeter and area of each similar rectangle with the given scale factor.

1. scale factor = 6

2. scale factor = 10

3. scale factor = $\frac{1}{2}$

4. **Critical Thinking** Do you think the relationship between the scale factor and perimeter and area will be true for ANY two similar polygons? Explain.

A circle can be cut into equal-sized sectors and arranged to resemble a parallelogram. The height h of the parallelogram is equal to the radius r of the circle, and the base b of the parallelogram is equal to one-half the circumference C of the circle. So the area of the parallelogram can be written as

$A = bh$, or $A = \frac{1}{2}Cr$.

Since $C = 2\pi r$, $A = \frac{1}{2}(2\pi r)r = \pi r^2$.

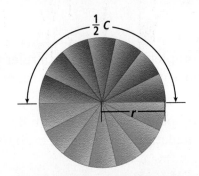

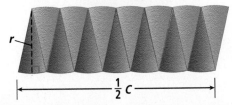

AREA OF A CIRCLE		
The area A of a circle is the product of π and the square of the circle's radius r.	$A = \pi r^2$	

EXAMPLE 1   Finding the Area of a Circle

Find the area of each circle to the nearest tenth. Use 3.14 for π.

A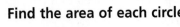
3 m

$A = \pi r^2$ *Use the formula.*
$A \approx 3.14 \cdot 3^2$ *Substitute. Use 3 for r.*
$A \approx 3.14 \cdot 9$ *Evaluate the power.*
$A \approx 28.26$ *Multiply.*

The area of the circle is about 28.3 m^2.

B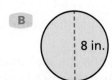
8 in.

$A = \pi r^2$ *Use the formula.*
$A \approx 3.14 \cdot 4^2$ *Substitute. Use 4 for r.*
$A \approx 3.14 \cdot 16$ *Evaluate the power.*
$A \approx 50.24$ *Multiply.*

The area of the circle is about 50.2 in^2.

EXAMPLE 2 *Social Studies Application*

Social Studies LINK

Nomads in Mongolia carried their homes wherever they roamed. These homes, called *yurts*, were made of wood and felt.

A group of historians are building a yurt to display at a local multicultural fair. The yurt has a height of 8 feet 9 inches at its center, and it has a circular floor of radius 7 feet. What is the area of the floor of the yurt? Use $\frac{22}{7}$ for π.

$A = \pi r^2$ *Use the formula for the area of a circle.*

$A \approx \frac{22}{7} \cdot 7^2$ *Substitute. Use 7 for r.*

$A \approx \frac{22}{\cancel{7}_1} \cdot \cancel{49}^7$ *Evaluate the power. Then simplify.*

$A \approx 22 \cdot 7$

$A \approx 154$ *Multiply.*

The area of the floor of the yurt is about 154 ft².

EXAMPLE 3 *Measurement Application*

Helpful Hint

To estimate the area of a circle, you can square the radius and multiply by 3.

Use a centimeter ruler to measure the radius of the circle. Then find the area of the shaded region of the circle. Use 3.14 for π. Round your answer to the nearest tenth.

First measure the radius of the circle: It measures 1.8 cm.

Now find the area of the entire circle.

$A = \pi r^2$ *Use the formula for the area of a circle.*

$A \approx 3.14 \cdot 1.8^2$ *Substitute. Use 1.8 for r and 3.14 for π.*

$A \approx 3.14 \cdot 3.24$ *Evaluate the power.*

$A \approx 10.1736$ *Multiply.*

Set up a proportion.

$\frac{1}{4} = \frac{x}{10.1736}$ *The shaded area is $\frac{1}{4}$ of the circle.*

$4x = 10.1736$ *The cross products are equal.*

$\frac{4x}{4} = \frac{10.1736}{4}$ *Divide each side by 4 to isolate the variable.*

$x = 2.5434$

The area of the shaded region of the circle is about 2.5 cm².

Think and Discuss

1. Compare finding the area of a circle when given the radius with finding the area when given the diameter.

2. Give an example of a circular object in your classroom. Tell how you could estimate the area of the object, and then estimate.

Learn It Online
Homework Help Online **go.hrw.com**,
keyword **MS10 9-5** **Go**
Exercises 1–12, 13, 15, 17, 19, 21

GUIDED PRACTICE

See Example **1** Find the area of each circle to the nearest tenth. Use 3.14 for π.

1.
5 in.

2.
16 cm

3.
20 yd

4.
1.1 m

See Example **2** **5.** The most popular pizza at Sam's Pizza is the 14-inch pepperoni pizza. What is the area of a pizza with a diameter of 14 inches? Use $\frac{22}{7}$ for π.

See Example **3** **6.** **Measurement** Use a centimeter ruler to measure the diameter of the circle. Then find the area of the shaded region of the circle. Use 3.14 for π. Round your answer to the nearest tenth.

INDEPENDENT PRACTICE

See Example **1** Find the area of each circle to the nearest tenth. Use 3.14 for π.

7.
3 in.

8.
16 ft

9.
6.4 yd

10.
15 cm

See Example **2** **11.** A wheel has a radius of 14 centimeters. What is the area of the wheel? Use $\frac{22}{7}$ for π.

See Example **3** **12.** **Measurement** Use a centimeter ruler to measure the radius of the circle. Then find the area of the shaded region of the circle. Use 3.14 for π. Round your answer to the nearest tenth.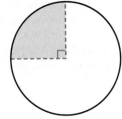

PRACTICE AND PROBLEM SOLVING

Extra Practice
See page EP23.

13. A radio station broadcasts a signal over an area with a 75-mile radius. What is the area of the region that receives the radio signal?

14. A circular flower bed in Kay's backyard has a diameter of 8 feet. What is the area of the flower bed? Round your answer to the nearest tenth.

15. A company is manufacturing aluminum lids. The radius of each lid is 3 cm. What is the area of one lid? Round your answer to the nearest tenth.

Given the radius or diameter, find the circumference and area of each circle to the nearest tenth. Use 3.14 for π.

16. $r = 7$ m   **17.** $d = 18$ in.   **18.** $d = 24$ ft   **19.** $r = 6.4$ cm

Given the area, find the radius of each circle. Use 3.14 for π.

20. $A = 113.04$ cm^2 **21.** $A = 3.14$ ft^2 **22.** $A = 28.26$ in^2

23. A hiker was last seen near a fire tower in the Catalina Mountains. Searchers are dispatched to the surrounding area to find the missing hiker.

    a. Assume the hiker could walk in any direction at a rate of 3 miles per hour. How large an area would searchers have to cover if the hiker was last seen 2 hours ago? Use 3.14 for π. Round your answer to the nearest square mile.

    b. How much additional area would the searchers have to cover if the hiker was last seen 3 hours ago?

24. Physical Science The tower of a wind turbine is about the height of a 20-story building. Each turbine can produce 24 megawatt-hours of electricity in one day. Find the area covered by the turbine when it is rotating. Use 3.14 for π. Round your answer to the nearest tenth.

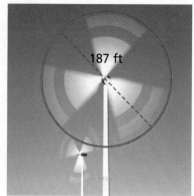

187 ft

25. Critical Thinking Two circles have the same radius. Is the combined area of the two circles the same as the area of a circle with twice the radius?

? 26. What's the Question? Chang painted half of a free-throw circle that has a diameter of 12 ft. The answer is 56.52 ft². What is the question?

27. Write About It Describe how to find the area of a circle when given only the circumference of the circle.

28. Challenge How does the area of a circle change if you multiply the radius by a factor of n, where n is a whole number?

Test Prep and Spiral Review

29. Multiple Choice The area of a circle is 30 square feet. A second circle has a radius that is 2 feet shorter than that of the first circle. What is the area, to the nearest tenth, of the second circle? Use 3.14 for π.

    Ⓐ 3.7 square feet   Ⓑ 10.0 square feet   Ⓒ 38.0 square feet   Ⓓ 179.2 square feet

30. Short Response A pizza parlor offers a large pizza with a 12-inch diameter. It also offers a "mega" pizza with a 24-inch diameter. The slogan used to advertise the mega pizza is "Twice the pizza of a large, and twice the fun." Is the mega pizza twice as big as the large? If not, how much bigger is it? Explain.

Line a ∥ line b. Use the diagram to find each angle measure. (Lesson 8-3)

31. m∠1   **32.** m∠2   **33.** m∠3

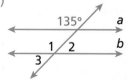

Graph the polygon with the given vertices. Identify the polygon and then find its area. (Lesson 9-4)

34. (−1, 1), (0, 4), (4, 1)   **35.** (−3, 3), (2, 3), (1, −1), (−1, −1)

Area of Irregular Figures

A **composite figure** is made up of simple geometric shapes, such as triangles and rectangles. You can find the area of composite and other irregular figures by separating them into non-overlapping familiar figures. The sum of the areas of these figures is the area of the entire figure. You can also estimate the area of an irregular figure by using graph paper.

EXAMPLE **1** **Estimating the Area of an Irregular Figure**

Vocabulary
composite figure

Estimate the area of the figure. Each square represents 1 ft².

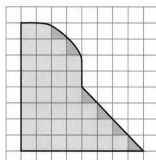

Count the number of filled or almost-filled squares: 35 yellow squares.

Count the number of squares that are about half-filled: 6 blue squares.

Add the number of filled squares plus $\frac{1}{2}$ the number of half-filled squares: $35 + \left(\frac{1}{2} \cdot 6\right) = 35 + 3 = 38.$

The area of the figure is about 38 ft².

EXAMPLE **2** **Finding the Area of a Composite Figure**

Find the area of the figure. Use 3.14 for π.

Step 1: Separate the figure into smaller, familiar figures.

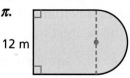
12 m
12 m

Step 2: Find the area of each smaller figure.

Area of the square:
$A = s^2$
$A = 12^2 = 144$

Area of the semicircle:
$A = \frac{1}{2}(\pi r^2)$
$A \approx \frac{1}{2}(3.14 \cdot 6^2)$
$A \approx \frac{1}{2}(113.04) \approx 56.52$

Helpful Hint

The area of a semicircle is $\frac{1}{2}$ the area of a circle.
$A = \frac{1}{2}(\pi r^2)$

Step 3: Add the areas to find the total area.
$A \approx 144 + 56.52 = 200.52$

The area of the figure is about 200.52 m².

Video Lesson Tutorials Online

EXAMPLE **3** **PROBLEM SOLVING APPLICATION**

Chandra wants to carpet the floor of her closet. A floor plan of the closet is shown at right. How much carpet does she need?

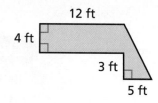

1 **Understand the Problem**

Rewrite the question as a statement:
• Find the amount of carpet needed to cover the floor of the closet.

List the **important information:**
• The floor of the closet is a composite figure.
• The amount of carpet needed is equal to the area of the floor.

2 **Make a Plan**

Find the area of the floor by separating the figure into familiar figures: a rectangle and a triangle. Then add the areas of the rectangle and triangle to find the total area.

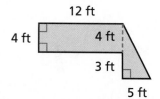

> **Helpful Hint**
>
> There are often several different ways to separate an irregular figure into familiar figures.

3 **Solve**

Find the area of each smaller figure.

Area of the rectangle:

$A = \ell w$

$A = 12 \cdot 4$

$A = 48 \text{ ft}^2$

Area of the triangle:

$A = \frac{1}{2}bh$

$A = \frac{1}{2}(5)(3 + 4)$

$A = \frac{1}{2}(35) = 17.5 \text{ ft}^2$

Add the areas to find the total area. $A = 48 + 17.5 = 65.5$

Chandra needs 65.5 ft² of carpet.

4 **Look Back**

The area of the closet floor must be greater than the area of the rectangle (48 ft²), so the answer is reasonable.

Think and Discuss

1. Describe two different ways to find the area of the irregular figure at right.

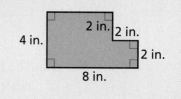

2. Explain how dividing the figure into two rectangles with a horizontal line would affect its area and perimeter.

GUIDED PRACTICE

See Example 1   Estimate the area of each figure. Each square represents 1 ft².

1.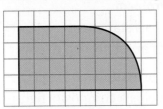

2.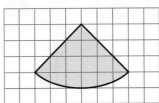

See Example 2   Find the area of each figure. Use 3.14 for π.

3.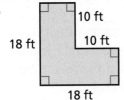

4.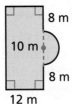

5.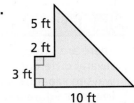

See Example 3   **6.** Luis has a model train set. The layout of the track is shown at right. How much artificial grass does Luis need in order to fill the interior of the layout? Use 3.14 for π.

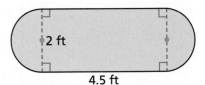

INDEPENDENT PRACTICE

See Example 1   Estimate the area of each figure. Each square represents 1 ft².

7.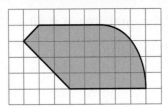

8.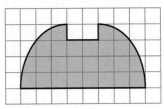

See Example 2   Find the area of each figure. Use 3.14 for π.

9.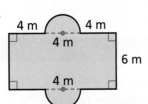

10.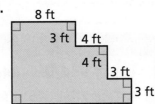

11.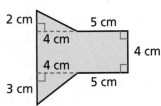

See Example 3   **12.** The figure shows the floor plan for a gallery of a museum. The ceiling of the gallery is to be covered with soundproofing material. How much material is needed? Use 3.14 for π.

PRACTICE AND PROBLEM SOLVING

Extra Practice
See page EP24.

Find the area and perimeter of each figure. Use 3.14 for π.

13.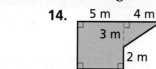

14.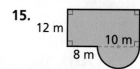

15.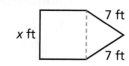

16. **Critical Thinking** Will the area and perimeter change for the figure in Exercise 14 if the triangle part is reflected to the left side? Explain.

17. **Critical Thinking** The figure at right is made up of an isosceles triangle and a square. The perimeter of the figure is 44 feet. What is the value of x?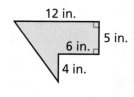

18. **Multi-Step** A figure has vertices $A(-8, 5)$, $B(-4, 5)$, $C(-4, 2)$, $D(3, 2)$, $E(3, -2)$, $F(6, -2)$, $G(6, -4)$, and $H(-8, -4)$. Graph the figure on a coordinate plane. Then find the area and perimeter of the figure.

19. **Choose a Strategy** A figure is formed by combining a square and a triangle. Its total area is 32.5 m². The area of the triangle is 7.5 m². What is the length of each side of the square?

20. **Write About It** Describe how to find the area of the composite figure at right.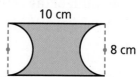

21. **Challenge** Find the area and perimeter of the figure at right. Use 3.14 for π.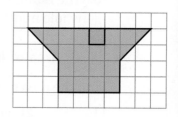

Test Prep and Spiral Review

22. **Multiple Choice** A rectangle is formed by two congruent right triangles. The area of each triangle is 6 in². Each side of the rectangle is a whole number of inches. Which of these CANNOT be the perimeter of the rectangle?

Ⓐ 26 in.　　　Ⓑ 24 in.　　　Ⓒ 16 in.　　　Ⓓ 14 in.

23. **Extended Response** The shaded area of the garden represents a patch of carrots. Veronica estimates that she will get about 12 carrots from this patch. Veronica is going to plant the rest of her garden with carrots. Estimate the total number of carrots she can expect to grow. Show your work.

∠1 and ∠2 are complementary angles. Find m∠2. (Lesson 8-2)

24. m∠1 = 33°　　25. m∠1 = 46°　　26. m∠1 = 60°　　27. m∠1 = 25.5°

Given the diameter, find the area of each circle to the nearest tenth. Use 3.14 for π. (Lesson 9-5)

28. $d = 30$ m　　29. $d = 5.5$ cm　　30. $d = 18$ in.　　31. $d = 11$ ft

Ready To Go On?

Learn It Online
Resources Online **go.hrw.com**,
keyword **MS10 RTGO9A** **Go**

Quiz for Lessons 9-1 Through 9-6

9-1 | Accuracy and Precision

Choose the more precise measurement in each pair.

1. 5 in.
56 ft

2. 6c
8 fl oz

9-2 | Perimeter and Circumference

3. Find the perimeter of the figure at right.

4. If the circumference of a wheel is 94 cm, what is its approximate diameter?

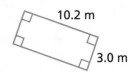
10.2 m
3.0 m

9-3 | Area of Parallelograms

5. The area of a rectangular courtyard is 1,508 m², and the length is 52 m. What is the width of the courtyard?

6. Jackson's kitchen is 8 yd by 3 yd. What is the area of his kitchen in square feet?

9-4 | Area of Triangles and Trapezoids

7. Find the area of the trapezoid at right.

8. A triangle has an area of 45 cm² and a base of 12.5 cm. What is the height of the triangle?

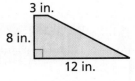
3 in.
8 in.
12 in.

9-5 | Area of Circles

9. Find the area of the circle to the nearest tenth. Use 3.14 or $\frac{22}{7}$ for π.

10. The radius of a clock face is $8\frac{3}{4}$ in. What is its area to the nearest whole number?

28 ft

9-6 | Area of Irregular Figures

Find the area of each figure to the nearest tenth if necessary. Use 3.14 for π.

11.
21 cm
21 cm
6 cm
6 cm

12.
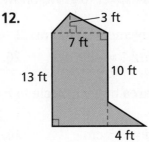
3 ft
7 ft
13 ft
10 ft
4 ft

13.
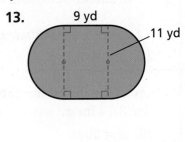
9 yd
11 yd

Focus on Problem Solving

 Understand the Problem

• Identify too much or too little information

Problems involving real-world situations sometimes give too much or too little information. Before solving these types of problems, you must decide what information is necessary and whether you have all the necessary information.

If the problem gives too much information, identify which of the facts are really needed to solve the problem. If the problem gives too little information, determine what additional information is required to solve the problem.

 Copy each problem and underline the information you need to solve it. If necessary information is missing, write down what additional information is required.

1. Mrs. Wong wants to put a fence around her garden. One side of her garden measures 8 feet. Another side measures 5 feet. What length of fencing does Mrs. Wong need to enclose her garden?

2. Two sides of a triangle measure 17 inches and 13 inches. The perimeter of the triangle is 45 inches. What is the length in feet of the third side of the triangle? (There are 12 inches in 1 foot.)

3. During swim practice, Peggy swims 2 laps each of freestyle and backstroke. The dimensions of the pool are 25 meters by 50 meters. What is the area of the pool?

4. Each afternoon, Molly walks her dog two times around the park. The park is a rectangle that is 315 yards long. How far does Molly walk her dog each afternoon?

5. A trapezoid has bases that measure 12 meters and 18 meters and one side that measures 9 meters. The trapezoid has no right angles. What is the area of the trapezoid?

Hands-on LAB 9-7

Explore Square Roots and Perfect Squares

Use with Lesson 9-7

Learn It Online
Lab Resources Online **go.hrw.com**,
keyword MS10 Lab9 Go

TN ✓ **0706.2.11** Estimate square/cube roots and use calculators to find approximations.

You can use geometric models such as tiles or graph paper to represent squares and square roots.

Activity 1

1. Copy the three square arrangements below on graph paper. Continue the pattern until you have drawn 10 square arrangements.

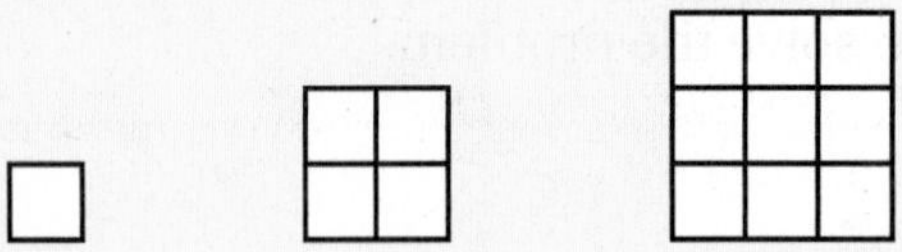

2. Copy and complete the table below. In the first column, write the number of small squares in each figure you drew. To complete the second column, use a calculator to find the square root.

(To find the square root of 4, press 2nd $\sqrt{\ }$ x^2 4) ENTER .)

Total Number of Small Squares	Square Root
1	1
4	2
9	3

3. Shade in one column of each square arrangement that you drew in 1.

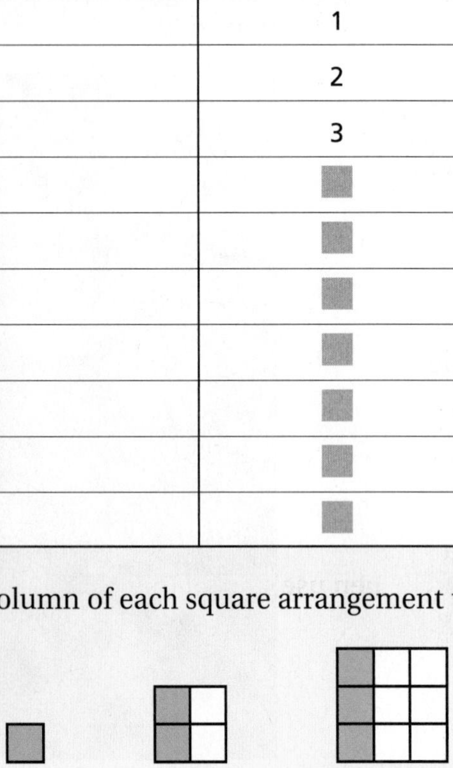

Think and Discuss

1. How does the square root relate to the total number of small squares in a figure?

2. How does the square root in the table relate to the shaded portion of each figure?

Try This

Use graph paper to find each square root.

1. 121   **2.** 144   **3.** 196

Activity 2

Follow the steps below to estimate $\sqrt{14}$.

① On graph paper, use one color to draw the smallest possible square arrangement using at least 14 small squares.

② On the same arrangement, draw the largest possible square arrangement using less than 14 small squares.

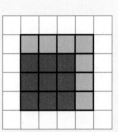

③ Count the number of squares in each arrangement. Notice that 14 is between these numbers.

Number in small arrangement   *Number in large arrangement*

9   <   14   <   16

④ Use a calculator to find $\sqrt{14}$ to the nearest tenth. $\sqrt{14} = 3.7$. Use inequality symbols to compare the square roots of 9, 14, and 16.

$$\sqrt{9} < \sqrt{14} < \sqrt{16}$$

$3 < 3.7 < 4$ *The square root of 9 is less than the square root of 14, which is less than the square root of 16.*

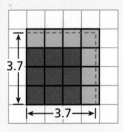

⑤ Use dashed lines on the figure to sketch a square that is 3.7 units on each side.

Think and Discuss

1. Describe how to use two numbers to estimate the square roots of nonperfect squares without using a calculator.

2. Explain how you can use graph paper to estimate $\sqrt{19}$.

3. Name three numbers that have square roots between 5 and 6.

Try This

Use graph paper to estimate each square root. Then use a calculator to find the square root to the nearest tenth.

1. $\sqrt{19}$ **2.** $\sqrt{10}$ **3.** $\sqrt{28}$ **4.** $\sqrt{35}$

Squares and Square Roots

TN **GLE 0706.2.5**
Understand and work with
squares, cubes, square roots
and cube roots.
Also ✓ **0706.2.11**

*Use Additional Topic A-1
with this lesson.*

A square with sides that measure
3 units each has an area of 3 • 3,
or 3^2. Notice that the area of the square
is represented by a power in which the
base is the side length and the
exponent is 2. A power in which the
exponent is 2 is called a *square*.

Exponent

Base

EXAMPLE **1**

Vocabulary

perfect square

square root

radical sign

Finding Squares of Numbers

Find each square.

A 6^2

Method 1: Use a model.

$A = \ell w$

$A = 6 \cdot 6$

$A = 36$

The square of 6 is 36.

B 14^2

Method 2: Use a calculator.

Press 14 $\boxed{x^2}$ $\boxed{\text{ENTER}}$.

$14^2 = 196$

The square of 14 is 196.

A **perfect square** is the square of a whole number. The number 36 is a
perfect square because $36 = 6^2$ and 6 is a whole number.

Reading Math

$\sqrt{16} = 4$ is read as
"The square root of
16 is 4."

The **square root** of a number is one of the two
equal factors of the number. Four is a square
root of 16 because $4 \cdot 4 = 16$. The symbol for a
square root is $\sqrt{}$, which is called a **radical sign** .

EXAMPLE **2**

Finding Square Roots of Perfect Squares

Find each square root.

A $\sqrt{64}$

Method 1: Use a model.

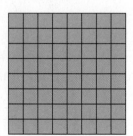

The square root of 64 is 8.

Video Lesson Tutorials Online

Find each square root.

B $\sqrt{324}$

> **Method 2: Use a calculator.** Press 2nd 324 ENTER.
>
> $$\sqrt{324} = 18$$
>
> The square root of 324 is 18.

You can use perfect squares to estimate the square roots of nonperfect squares.

EXAMPLE 3 **Estimating Square Roots**

Estimate $\sqrt{30}$ to the nearest whole number. Use a calculator to check your answer.

$1, 4, 9, 16, 25, 36, \ldots$	*List some perfect squares.*
$25 < 30 < 36$	*Find the perfect squares nearest 30.*
$\sqrt{25} < \sqrt{30} < \sqrt{36}$	
$5 < \sqrt{30} < 6$	*Find the square roots of 25 and 36.*
$\sqrt{30} \approx 5$	*30 is closer to 25 than to 36.*

Check

$\sqrt{30} \approx 5.477225575$	*Use a calculator to approximate $\sqrt{30}$.*
	5 is a reasonable estimate.

EXAMPLE 4 *Recreation Application*

While searching for a lost hiker, a helicopter pilot covers a square area of 150 mi². What is the approximate length of each side of the square area? Round your answer to the nearest mile.

The length of each side of the square is $\sqrt{150}$.

$144 < 150 < 169$	*Find the perfect squares nearest 150.*
$\sqrt{144} < \sqrt{150} < \sqrt{169}$	
$12 < \sqrt{150} < 13$	*Find the square roots of 144 and 169.*
$\sqrt{150} \approx 12$	*150 is closer to 144 than to 169.*

Each side of the search area is about 12 miles long.

Think and Discuss

1. Explain how to estimate $\sqrt{75}$.

2. Explain how you might find the square root of 3^2.

Learn It Online

Homework Help Online **go.hrw.com**,
keyword MS10 9-7 Go
Exercises 1–26, 29, 31, 37, 41,
47, 49, 51

GUIDED PRACTICE

See Example 1 **Find each square.**

1. 4^2 **2.** 17^2 **3.** 9^2 **4.** 15^2

See Example 2 **Find each square root.**

5. $\sqrt{400}$ **6.** $\sqrt{9}$ **7.** $\sqrt{144}$ **8.** $\sqrt{529}$

See Example 3 **Estimate each square root to the nearest whole number. Use a calculator to check your answer.**

9. $\sqrt{20}$ **10.** $\sqrt{45}$ **11.** $\sqrt{84}$ **12.** $\sqrt{58}$

See Example 4 **13.** A Coast Guard ship patrols an area of 125 square miles. The area the ship patrols is a square. About how long is each side of the area? Round your answer to the nearest mile.

INDEPENDENT PRACTICE

See Example 1 **Find each square.**

14. 3^2 **15.** 16^2 **16.** 8^2 **17.** 11^2

See Example 2 **Find each square root.**

18. $\sqrt{361}$ **19.** $\sqrt{16}$ **20.** $\sqrt{169}$ **21.** $\sqrt{441}$

See Example 3 **Estimate each square root to the nearest whole number. Use a calculator to check your answer.**

22. $\sqrt{12}$ **23.** $\sqrt{39}$ **24.** $\sqrt{73}$ **25.** $\sqrt{109}$

See Example 4 **26.** The area of a square field is 200 ft². What is the approximate length of each side of the field? Round your answer to the nearest foot.

PRACTICE AND PROBLEM SOLVING

Extra Practice
See page EP24.

Estimate each square root to the nearest whole number.

27. $\sqrt{6}$ **28.** $\sqrt{180}$ **29.** $\sqrt{145}$ **30.** $\sqrt{216}$

31. $\sqrt{300}$ **32.** $\sqrt{420}$ **33.** $\sqrt{700}$ **34.** $\sqrt{1,500}$

Use a calculator to find each square root to the nearest tenth.

35. $\sqrt{44}$ **36.** $\sqrt{253}$ **37.** $\sqrt{87}$ **38.** $\sqrt{125}$

39. $\sqrt{380}$ **40.** $\sqrt{94}$ **41.** $\sqrt{202}$ **42.** $\sqrt{571}$

43. Critical Thinking An artist is making two square stained-glass windows. One window has a perimeter of 48 inches. The other has an area of 110 square inches. Which window is bigger? Explain.

Earth Science

When looking out towards the horizon, it appears to be flat. The curvature of the Earth cannot be seen except at a great distance.

Given the area, find the missing value for each circle. Use 3.14 for π.

44. $A = 706.9 \text{ m}^2$; $r = $ ▮

45. $A = 615.44 \text{ yd}^2$; $C = $ ▮

46. $A = 28.26 \text{ ft}^2$; $d = $ ▮

47. $A = 3.14 \text{ in}^2$; $r = $ ▮

Order the numbers from least to greatest.

48. $\sqrt{49}$, $\frac{17}{3}$, 6.5, 8, $\frac{25}{4}$

49. $5\frac{2}{3}$, $\sqrt{25}$, 3^2, 7.15, $\frac{29}{4}$

50. Find the perimeter of a square whose area is 49 square inches.

51. **Earth Science** The formula $D = 3.56 \cdot \sqrt{A}$ gives the distance D in kilometers to the horizon from an airplane flying at an altitude A in meters. If a pilot is flying at an altitude of 1,800 m, about how far away is the horizon? Round your answer to the nearest kilometer.

52. **Multi-Step** For his new room, Darien's grandmother gave him a handmade quilt. The quilt is made up of 16 squares set in 4 rows of 4. The area of each square is 324 in². What are the dimensions of the quilt in inches?

? 53. **Choose a Strategy** The figure shows how two squares can be formed by drawing only seven lines. Show how two squares can be formed by drawing only six lines.

54. **Write About It** Explain the difference between finding the square of a number and finding the square root of a number. Use models and numbers in your explanation.

55. **Challenge** Find the value of $\sqrt{5^2 + 12^2}$.

Test Prep and Spiral Review

56. Multiple Choice Which model represents 5^2?

Ⓐ

Ⓑ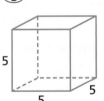

Ⓒ

Ⓓ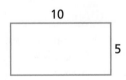

57. Multiple Choice Estimate the value of $\sqrt{87}$ to the nearest whole number.

Ⓕ 9   Ⓖ 10   Ⓗ 11   Ⓙ 12

Classify each triangle according to the lengths of its sides. (Lesson 8-6)

58. 2 in., 3 in., 4 in.

59. 5 cm, 5 cm, 5 cm

60. 8 ft, 6 ft, 8 ft

Given the radius or diameter, find the circumference and area of each circle to the nearest tenth. Use 3.14 for π. (Lesson 9-5)

61. $r = 11$ in.

62. $d = 25$ cm

63. $r = 3$ ft

Identifying and Graphing Irrational Numbers

TN SPI 0706.2.4 Determine the approximate location of square/cube roots on a number line.
Also ✓ 0706.2.9, ✓ 0706.2.10

Recall from Lesson 2-11 that a rational number can be written as a fraction with integers for its numerator and denominator. When rational numbers are written in decimal form, the decimal may be terminating or nonterminating. If a rational number is nonterminating, then it has a repeating pattern.

Vocabulary

irrational numbers

real numbers

A decimal that is nonterminating with no repeating pattern is an **irrational number**. For example, $\sqrt{2} = 1.4142135\ldots$, which does not terminate or repeat.

The set of **real numbers** consists of the set of rational numbers and the set of irrational numbers.

Real Numbers

Rational numbers	Irrational numbers
Integers	
Whole numbers	

EXAMPLE **1**   **Identifying Rational and Irrational Numbers**

Identify each number as rational or irrational. Justify your answer.

A $\frac{2}{5}$

$\frac{2}{5} = 0.4$ *Write the number in decimal form.*

Because its decimal form is terminating, $\frac{2}{5}$ is rational.

B $\frac{5}{6}$

$\frac{5}{6} = 0.8333\ldots$, or $0.8\overline{3}$ *Write the number in decimal form.*

Because its decimal form is nonterminating and repeating, $\frac{5}{6}$ is rational.

C $\sqrt{16}$

$\sqrt{16} = 4$ *Write the number in decimal form.*

Because its decimal form is terminating, $\sqrt{16}$ is rational.

D $\sqrt{7}$

$\sqrt{7} = 2.645751311\ldots$ *Write the number in decimal form.*

There is no pattern in the decimal form of $\sqrt{7}$. It is a nonterminating, nonrepeating decimal. So $\sqrt{7}$ is irrational.

Remember!

By definition, any ratio of integers is a rational number.

Every point on the number line corresponds to a real number, either a rational number or an irrational number. Between every two real numbers there is always another real number.

EXAMPLE 2

Graphing Rational and Irrational Numbers

Graph the list of numbers on a number line. Then order the numbers from least to greatest.

$1.4, \sqrt{5}, \frac{3}{8}, \pi, -\frac{2}{3}, \sqrt{4}, \sqrt{16}$

Write all the numbers in decimal form, and then graph them.

$1.4, \; \sqrt{5} \approx 2.236, \frac{3}{8} = 0.375, \pi \approx 3.14, -\frac{2}{3} = -0.\overline{6}, \; \sqrt{4} = 2.0, \; \sqrt{16} = 4.0$

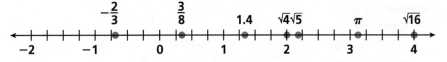

From left to right on the number line, the numbers appear from least to greatest: $-\frac{2}{3} < \frac{3}{8} < 1.4 < \sqrt{4} < \sqrt{5} < \pi < \sqrt{16}$.

EXTENSION

Exercises

Identify each number as rational or irrational. Justify your answer.

1. $\sqrt{8}$ **2.** $\frac{5}{11}$ **3.** $\frac{7}{8}$ **4.** $\sqrt{36}$

5. $\frac{3}{13}$ **6.** $\sqrt{14}$ **7.** 2.800 **8.** $\frac{5}{6}$

9. $\sqrt{5}$ **10.** $\frac{6}{24}$ **11.** $\frac{10}{33}$ **12.** $\sqrt{18}$

Graph each list of numbers on a number line. Then order the numbers from least to greatest.

13. $2.6, 0.5, \sqrt{3}, -\frac{7}{10}, \frac{1}{3}$ **14.** $\sqrt{12}, \frac{3}{8}, -0.65, \frac{5}{9}, \sqrt{11}$

15. $-1.3, \sqrt{15}, 3.1, -\frac{2}{5}, \sqrt{4}$ **16.** $-2.1, -\frac{9}{10}, \sqrt{1}, -1.5, \sqrt{9}$

Name the two perfect squares that each square root lies between. Then graph the square root on a number line, and justify its placement.

17. $\sqrt{34}$ **18.** $\sqrt{46}$ **19.** $\sqrt{14}$ **20.** $\sqrt{6}$

21. $\sqrt{99}$ **22.** $\sqrt{63}$ **23.** $\sqrt{71}$ **24.** $\sqrt{13}$

? **25. What's the Error?** A classmate tells you that the square root of any number is irrational. Explain why the classmate is incorrect.

Hands-on LAB 9-8

Explore the Pythagorean Theorem

Use with Lesson 9-8

Learn It Online
Lab Resources Online **go.hrw.com**,
keyword MS10 Lab9 **Go**

TN **GLE 0706.2.5** Understand and work with squares, cubes, square roots and cube roots.
Also **GLE 0706.1.4, ✓ 0706.2.2**

An important and famous relationship in mathematics, known as the Pythagorean Theorem, involves the three sides of a right triangle. Recall that a right triangle is a triangle that has one right angle. If you know the lengths of two sides of a right triangle, you can find the length of the third side.

Activity 1

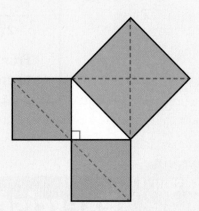

1 The drawing at right shows an isosceles right triangle and three squares. Make your own drawing similar to the one shown. (Recall that an isosceles right triangle has two congruent sides and a right angle.)

Cut out the two smaller squares of your drawing, then cut those squares in half along a diagonal. Fit the pieces of the smaller squares on top of the blue square.

Think and Discuss

1. What can you tell about the relationship between the areas of the squares?

2a. How does the side length of a square relate to the area of the square?

b. How do the side lengths of the triangle in your drawing relate to the areas of the squares around it?

c. Write an equation that shows the relationship between the lengths of the sides of the triangle in your drawing. Use the variables a and b to represent the lengths of the two shorter sides of your triangle, and c to represent the length of the longest side.

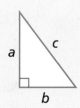

Try This

1. Repeat Activity 1 for other isosceles right triangles. Is the relationship that you found true for the areas of the squares around each triangle?

Activity 2

1 On graph paper, draw a segment that is 3 units long. At one end of this segment, draw a perpendicular segment that is 4 units long. Draw a third segment to form a triangle. Cut out the triangle.

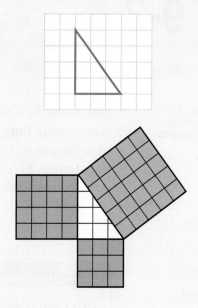

Cut out a 3-by-3 square and a 4-by-4 square from the same graph paper. Place the edges of the squares against the corresponding sides of the right triangle.

Cut the two squares into individual squares or strips. Arrange the squares into a large square along the third side of the triangle.

Think and Discuss

1. What is the area of each of the three squares? What relationship is there between the areas of the small squares and the area of the large square?

2. What is the length of the third side of the triangle?

3. Substitute the side lengths of your triangle into the equation you wrote in Think and Discuss Problem **2c** in Activity 1. What do you find?

4. Do you think the relationship is true for triangles that are not right triangles?

Try This

1. Use graph paper to cut out three squares with sides that are 3 units, 4 units, and 6 units long. Fit the squares together to form a triangle as shown at right. Is the relationship between the areas of the red squares and the area of the blue square the same as the relationship shown in Activity 2? Explain.

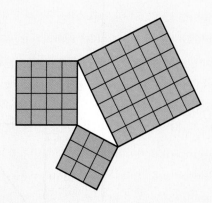

2. If you know the lengths of the two short sides of a right triangle are 9 and 12, can you find the length of the longest side? Show your work.

3. If you know the length of the longest side of a right triangle and the length of one of the shorter sides, how would you find the length of the third side?

TN GLE 0706.2.5
Understand and work with squares, cubes, square roots and cube roots.
Also **GLE 0706.1.7**

One of the first people to recognize the relationship between the sides of a right triangle was the Greek mathematician Pythagoras. This special relationship is called the *Pythagorean Theorem*.

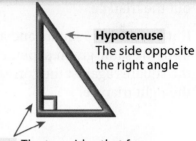

Hypotenuse
The side opposite the right angle

Legs The two sides that form the right angle in a right triangle

Vocabulary

leg

hypotenuse

Pythagorean Theorem

Interactivities Online ▶

PYTHAGOREAN THEOREM		
In a right triangle, the sum of the squares of the lengths of the legs is equal to the square of the length of the hypotenuse.	$a^2 + b^2 = c^2$	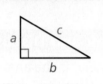

You can use the Pythagorean Theorem to find the length of any side of a right triangle.

EXAMPLE 1 Calculating the Length of a Side of a Right Triangle

Use the Pythagorean Theorem to find each missing measure.

A

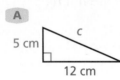

$$a^2 + b^2 = c^2 \qquad \text{Use the Pythagorean Theorem.}$$
$$5^2 + 12^2 = c^2 \qquad \text{Substitute for } a \text{ and } b.$$
$$25 + 144 = c^2 \qquad \text{Evaluate the powers.}$$
$$169 = c^2 \qquad \text{Add.}$$
$$\sqrt{169} = \sqrt{c^2} \qquad \text{Take the square root of both sides.}$$
$$13 = c$$

The length of the hypotenuse is 13 cm.

B

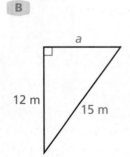

$$a^2 + b^2 = c^2 \qquad \text{Use the Pythagorean Theorem.}$$
$$a^2 + 12^2 = 15^2 \qquad \text{Substitute for } b \text{ and } c.$$
$$a^2 + 144 = 225 \qquad \text{Evaluate the powers.}$$
$$\underline{\quad -144 \quad -144} \qquad \text{Subtract 144 from both sides.}$$
$$a^2 \quad = \quad 81$$
$$\sqrt{a^2} = \sqrt{81} \qquad \text{Take the square root of both sides.}$$
$$a = 9$$

The length of the leg is 9 m.

Video **Lesson Tutorials Online**

EXAMPLE **2** PROBLEM SOLVING APPLICATION

A regulation baseball diamond is a square with sides that measure 90 feet. About how far is it from home plate to second base? Round your answer to the nearest tenth.

1 **Understand the Problem**

Rewrite the question as a statement.
• Find the distance from home plate to second base.

List the **important information:**
• Drawing a segment between home plate and second base divides the diamond into two right triangles.
• The angle at first base is the right angle, so the segment between home plate and second base is the hypotenuse.
• The base lines are legs, and they are each 90 feet long.

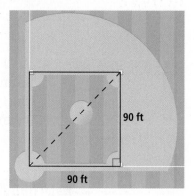

2 **Make a Plan**

You can use the Pythagorean Theorem to write an equation.

3 **Solve**

$$a^2 + b^2 = c^2$$ *Use the Pythagorean Theorem.*
$$90^2 + 90^2 = c^2$$ *Substitute for the known variables.*
$$8,100 + 8,100 = c^2$$ *Evaluate the powers.*
$$16,200 = c^2$$ *Add.*
$$127.279 \approx c$$ *Take the square root of both sides.*
$$127.3 \approx c$$ *Round.*

The distance from home plate to second base is about 127.3 ft.

4 **Look Back**

The hypotenuse is the longest side of a right triangle. Since the distance from home plate to second base is greater than the distance between the bases, the answer is reasonable.

Think and Discuss

1. **Explain** whether it is ever possible to use the Pythagorean Theorem to find an unknown side length of a scalene triangle.
2. **Demonstrate** whether a leg of a right triangle can be longer than the hypotenuse.

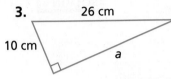
GUIDED PRACTICE

See Example **1** Use the Pythagorean Theorem to find each missing measure.

1.
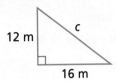
12 m   c
16 m

2.
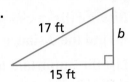
17 ft   b
15 ft

3.
26 cm
10 cm   a

See Example **2** **4.** A 10 ft ladder is leaning against a wall. If the ladder is 5 ft from the base of the wall, how far above the ground does the ladder touch the wall? Round your answer to the nearest tenth.

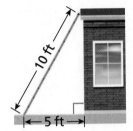
10 ft   5 ft

INDEPENDENT PRACTICE

See Example **1** Use the Pythagorean Theorem to find each missing measure.

5.
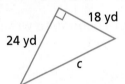
18 yd
24 yd
c

6.
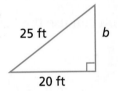
25 ft   b
20 ft

7.
30 in.
34 in.   a

See Example **2** **8.** James rides his bike 15 miles west. Then he turns north and rides another 15 miles before he stops to rest. How far is James from his starting point when he stops to rest? Round your answer to the nearest tenth.

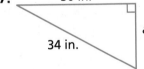
15 mi
15 mi

PRACTICE AND PROBLEM SOLVING

Extra Practice
See page EP24.

The lengths of two sides of a right triangle are given. Find the length of the third side to the nearest tenth.

9. legs: 5 ft and 8 ft

10. leg: 10 mm; hypotenuse: 15 mm

11. leg: 19 m; hypotenuse: 31 m

12. legs: 21 yd and 20 yd

13. legs: 13.5 in. and 18 in.

14. leg: 13 cm; hypotenuse: 18 cm

15. **Critical Thinking** The *converse* of a statement is formed by exchanging the hypothesis and the conclusion. So the converse of the Pythagorean Theorem states that if the sum of the squares of the lengths of two sides of the triangle is equal to the square of the length of the third side, then the triangle is a right triangle. Determine if the given lengths form right triangles.

a. 3, 4, 5   **b.** 6, 8, 10   **c.** 9, 15, 17   **d.** 7, 24, 25

16. Ancient Egyptians built pyramids to serve as tombs for their kings. One pyramid, called Menkaure, has a square base with an area of about 12,100 m².

  a. What is the length of each side of the base?

  b. What is the length of a diagonal of the base? Round your answer to the nearest tenth.

17. The photograph shows the Pyramid of Khafre in Egypt. Each side of its square base is about 214 meters long. Each triangular side is an isosceles triangle with a height of about 179 meters. What is the area of one side of the pyramid?

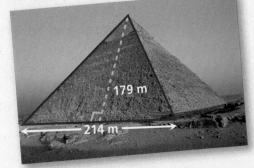
179 m
214 m

18. Use the Pythagorean Theorem to find the distance from one corner of the Pyramid of Khafre to its peak. Round your answer to the nearest tenth.

19. **Multi-Step** The pyramids were constructed using a unit of measurement called a cubit. There are about 21 inches in 1 cubit. If the height of a pyramid is 471 feet, what is its height in cubits?

20. **Write About It** Given a right triangle, explain how you know which values to substitute into the equation $a^2 + b^2 = c^2$.

21. **Challenge** The pyramid at right has a square base. Find the height of the pyramid to the nearest tenth.

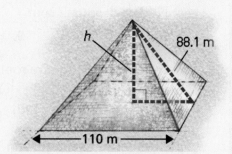
h
88.1 m
110 m

Test Prep and Spiral Review

22. Multiple Choice Find the missing measure to the nearest tenth.

  Ⓐ 3.6 m   **Ⓒ** 11.8 m

  Ⓑ 9.2 m   **Ⓓ** 85 m

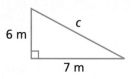
c
6 m
7 m

23. Gridded Response A 10-foot ladder is leaning against a wall. The bottom of the ladder is 2 feet away from the bottom of the wall. To the nearest tenth, how many feet up the wall will the ladder reach?

Find the measure of the angle formed by the hour and minute hands of a clock at each time. (Lesson 8-4)

24. 6:00   **25.** 3:00   **26.** 5:00   **27.** 2:00

Estimate each square root to the nearest whole number. (Lesson 9-7)

28. $\sqrt{140}$ **29.** $\sqrt{60}$ **30.** $\sqrt{200}$ **31.** $\sqrt{30}$

Quiz for Lessons 9-7 Through 9-8

 9-7 **Squares and Square Roots**

Find each square.

1. 21^2 **2.** 7^2 **3.** 12^2 **4.** 13^2

Name the square and the square root represented by each model.

5. 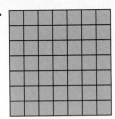   **6.**    **7.**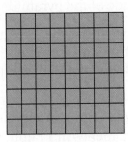

Find each square root.

8. $\sqrt{841}$ **9.** $\sqrt{1,089}$ **10.** $\sqrt{81}$ **11.** $\sqrt{576}$

Estimate each square root to the nearest whole number.
Use a calculator to check your answer.

12. $\sqrt{40}$ **13.** $\sqrt{85}$ **14.** $\sqrt{12}$ **15.** $\sqrt{33}$

 **9-8** **The Pythagorean Theorem**

Use the Pythagorean Theorem to find each missing measure.

16.
c / 8 cm / 6 cm

17.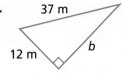
37 m / 12 m / b

18.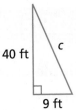
40 ft / c / 9 ft

19. Thomas likes to jog at Memorial Park. The running trail he follows is in the shape of a right triangle. He knows one leg of the path is 1.8 miles, and the other leg is 3.2 miles. What is the distance of the third side of the trail to the nearest tenth of a mile?

20. Audrey built a ramp for the set of the new musical at her school. The height of the ramp is 8 feet, and the hypotenuse is 17 feet. What is the length of the ramp's base?

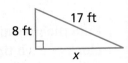
17 ft / 8 ft / x

The lengths of two sides of a right triangle are given. Find the length of the third side to the nearest tenth.

21. leg: 14.3 m; hypotenuse: 22 m   **22.** legs: 10 yd and 24 yd

23. legs: 12.4 in. and 9.0 in.   **24.** leg: 2.5 cm; hypotenuse: 8 cm

The Eiteljorg Museum of American Indians and Western Art

INDIANA

Indianapolis

The Eiteljorg Museum of American Indians and Western Art in Indianapolis is one of only two museums east of the Mississippi River dedicated to Native American and Western art. The building's unique design was inspired by the landscape and architecture of the American Southwest.

For 1–3, use the table.

1. To prepare for an event, an employee is placing strings of lights around the circumference of Clowes Sculpture Court.

   a. What is the total length of the lights that are needed? (Assume the strings will be hung so that there is no slack.) Use 3.14 for π, and round your answer to the nearest foot.

Galleries at the Eiteljorg Museum of American Indians and Western Art		
Gallery	**Shape**	**Dimensions**
Gund Gallery of Western Art	Square	Length: 80 ft
Art of the American West Gallery	Rectangle	Length: 112 ft Width: 80 ft
Clowes Sculpture Court	Circle	Diameter: 80 ft

   b. Lights are available in 20-foot strings. How many strings should the employee order?

2. The floor of the Gund Gallery of 80 Western Art and the Art of the American West Gallery are covered with carpeting. How much more carpeting is needed for the Art of the American West Gallery than for the Gund Gallery of Western Art?

3. During the event, the wire for a microphone runs in a straight line from one corner of the Art of the American West Gallery to the opposite corner. How long is the wire? Round to the nearest foot. Include a diagram and an explanation of how you found the length of the wire.

Real-World Connections

Game Time

Shape Up

Rectangles

The square below has been divided into four rectangles. The areas of two of the rectangles are given. If the length of each of the segments in the diagram is an integer, what is the area of the original square?

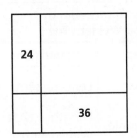

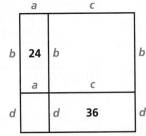

(*Hint:* Remember $a + c = b + d$.)

Use different lengths and a different answer to create your own version of this puzzle.

Circles

What is the maximum number of times that six circles of the same size can intersect? To find the answer, start by drawing two circles that are the same size. What is the greatest number of times they can intersect? Add another circle, and another, and so on.

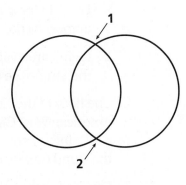

Circles and Squares

Two players start with a sequence of circles and squares. Before beginning the game, each player chooses whether to be a "circle" or a "square." The goal of the game is to have the final remaining shape be the shape you chose to be. Shapes are removed from the sequence according to the following rules: On each move, a player selects two shapes. If the shapes are identical, they are replaced with one square. If the shapes are different, they are replaced with one circle.

Learn It Online
Game Time Extra **go.hrw.com**,
keyword MS10 Games Go

A complete copy of the rules and game pieces are available online.

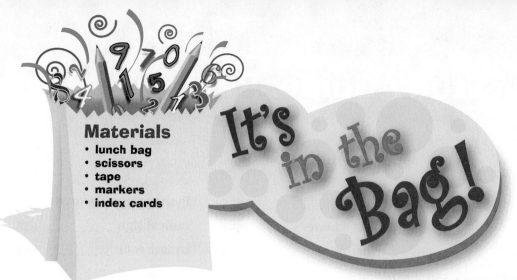

Materials
- lunch bag
- scissors
- tape
- markers
- index cards

It's in the Bag!

PROJECT **Bag o' Measurement**

This bag of index cards will help you organize your notes on measuring two-dimensional figures.

1. Hold the lunch bag with the flap facing you at the top. Cut a thin strip from the flap as shown. **Figure A**

2. Cut along the sides of the flap so you can open it up. Then use your scissors to round off the corners at the top of the flap. **Figure B**

3. Fold up the bottom part of the flap. Then trim this part of the flap by cutting out a trapezoid as shown. **Figure C**

4. Cut another trapezoid from the bottom edge of the bag by cutting through all the layers. Then fold up the bottom of the bag to make two pockets, one below the other. **Figure D**

5. Tape the sides of the bag together to close the pockets. Fold down the flap and label it with the number and title of the chapter.

Taking Note of the Math

Use index cards to record measurement formulas, the Pythagorean Theorem, and other important facts from the chapter. Store the cards in the pockets of the bag.

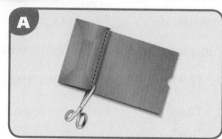

A

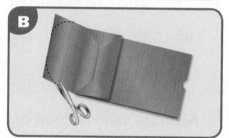

B

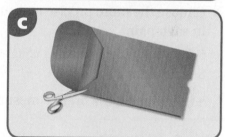

C

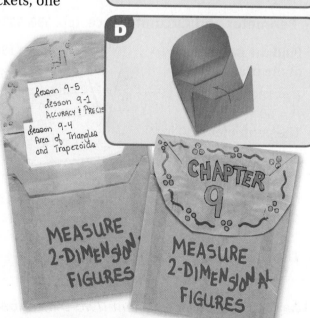

D

Lesson 9-5
Lesson 9-1
ACCURACY & PRECIS
Lesson 9-4
Area of Triangles
and Trapezoids

MEASURE
2-DIMENSIONAL
FIGURES

CHAPTER 9

MEASURE
2-DIMENSIONAL
FIGURES

Study Guide: Review

Vocabulary

accuracy 524
area 536
circumference 531
composite figure 550
hypotenuse 566

leg 566
perfect square 558
perimeter 530
pi 531
precision 524

Pythagorean Theorem . 566
radical sign 558
square root 558

Complete the sentences below with vocabulary words from the list above.

1. The longest side of a right triangle is called the ___?___.

2. The ___?___ is the distance around a circle.

3. ___?___ is the level of detail an instrument can measure.

4. A(n) ___?___ is one of the two equal factors of a number.

EXAMPLES

EXERCISES

9-1 Accuracy and Precision (pp. 524–527)

■ **Choose the more precise measurement in each pair.**

5 in.   *One tenth of an inch is a smaller*
5.8 in.   *unit than an inch.*

5.8 in. is the more precise mesurement.

Choose the more precise measurement in each pair.

5. 1.4 kg, 3 kg   6. 703 ft, 2 mi

7. 30 lb, $30\frac{1}{4}$ lb   8. 78 g, 7.8 g

9. 90 cm, 9 m   10. 204 gal, 204 qt

9-2 Perimeter and Circumference (pp. 530–533)

■ **Find the perimeter of the triangle.**

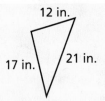

$P = 12 + 17 + 21$
$P = 50$
The perimeter is 50 in.

■ **Find the circumference of the circle. Use 3.14 for π.**

$C = 2\pi r$
$C \approx 2 \cdot 3.14 \cdot 5$
$C \approx 31.4$
The circumference is about 31.4 cm.

Find the perimeter of each polygon.

11.
     24 m
12 m   15 m
     32 m

12.
     24.9 cm
              15.8 cm

Find the circumference of each circle to the nearest tenth. Use 3.14 for π.

13.

13 ft

14.

7.8 in.

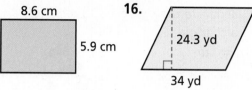
9-3 Area of Parallelograms (pp. 536–539)

■ **Find the area of the rectangle.**

14 in.

8.6 in.

$A = \ell w$
$A = 14 \cdot 8.6$
$A = 120.4$
The area of the rectangle is 120.4 in^2.

Find the area of each polygon.

15.

8.6 cm

5.9 cm

16.

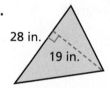

24.3 yd

34 yd

17. Rose is drawing a portrait for her art class. She is using a sheet of paper that is 6 inches wide and 12 inches long. What is the area of the art paper in square inches?

9-4 Area of Triangles and Trapezoids (pp. 540–543)

■ **Find the area of the triangle.**

2.9 m

4.8 m

$A = \frac{1}{2}bh$
$A = \frac{1}{2}(4.8 \cdot 2.9)$
$A = \frac{1}{2}(13.92)$
$A = 6.96$
The area of the triangle is 6.96 m^2.

Find the area of each polygon.

18.

28 in.

19 in.

19. 7.6 cm

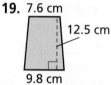

12.5 cm

9.8 cm

20.

8 yd

$12\frac{1}{2}$ yd

21. 67 in.

42 in.

36 in.

22. Josie is painting a mural that has 2 triangles each with a base of 12 m and a height of 4 m. How much area will she cover when she paints them?

9-5 Area of Circles (pp. 546–549)

■ **Find the area of the circle to the nearest tenth. Use 3.14 for π.**

5 in.

$A = \pi r^2$
$A \approx 3.14 \cdot 5^2$
$A \approx 3.14 \cdot 25$
$A \approx 78.5$
The area of the circle is about 78.5 in^2.

Find the area of each circle to the nearest tenth. Use 3.14 for π.

23.

3.4 m

24.

17 ft

25. The minute hand on a clock is 9 inches long. What is the area of the circle the minute hand covers after one hour? Give your answer in square inches.

Study Guide: Review

9-6 **Area of Irregular Figures** (pp. 550–553)

■ **Find the area of the irregular figure.**

Separate the figure into a rectangle and a triangle.

$A = \ell w$

$\quad = 4 \cdot 8 = 32 \text{ m}^2$

$A = \frac{1}{2}bh$

$\quad = \frac{1}{2}(3 \cdot 4) = 6 \text{ m}^2$

$A = 32 + 6 = 38 \text{ m}^2$

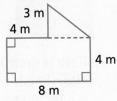

3 m
4 m
4 m
8 m

Find the area of each figure. Use 3.14 for π.

26.

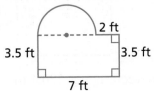

2 ft
3.5 ft   3.5 ft
7 ft

27.

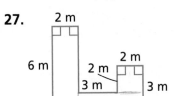

2 m
6 m   2 m   2 m
3 m   3 m

9-7 **Squares and Square Roots** (pp. 558–561)

■ **Estimate $\sqrt{71}$ to the nearest whole number.**

$64 < 71 < 81$ *Find the perfect squares nearest 71.*

$\sqrt{64} < \sqrt{71} < \sqrt{81}$

$8 < \sqrt{71} < 9$ *Find the square roots of 64 and 81.*

Since 71 is closer to 64 than to 81, $\sqrt{71} \approx 8$.

Estimate each square root to the nearest whole number.

28. $\sqrt{29}$ **29.** $\sqrt{92}$

30. $\sqrt{106}$ **31.** $\sqrt{150}$

32. The area of Rita's square vegetable garden is 265 ft². What is the length of each side of the garden to the nearest foot?

9-8 **Pythagorean Theorem** (pp. 566–569)

■ **Use the Pythagorean Theorem to find the missing measure.**

$a^2 + b^2 = c^2$

$9^2 + 12^2 = c^2$

$81 + 144 = c^2$

$225 = c^2$

$\sqrt{225} = \sqrt{c^2}$

$15 = c$

The hypotenuse is 15 in.

9 in.
c
12 in.

Use the Pythagorean Theorem to find each missing measure.

33.

c
16 cm
30 cm

34.

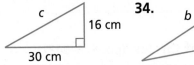

b   25
65 ft

35.

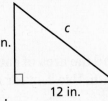

4.8 m
a
5.2 m

36.

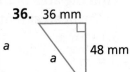

36 mm
48 mm
a

37. A 5 ft pole is leaning against a wall. If the pole is 2 ft from the base of the wall, how far above the ground does the pole touch the wall? Round your answer to the nearest tenth.

Study Guide: Review

Chapter Test

Choose the more precise measurement in each pair.

1. 80 m, 7.9 cm

2. 18 yd, 5 mi

3. 500 lb, 18 oz

4. Find the perimeter of the trapezoid.

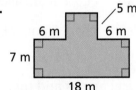

5. The opening of a playscape tunnel has a circumference of 25 ft. What is the radius of the tunnel to the nearest tenth?

Find the area of each figure.

6.

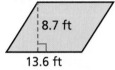

7.

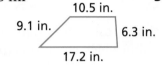

8.

9. The area of a rectangular computer lab is 660 ft², and the width is 22 ft. What is the length of the computer lab?

10. The area of a circular fountain is 66 cm². What is its radius to the nearest tenth?

11. The area of a triangle is 40 m², and the base is 10 m. What is the height?

Use the diagram for Items 12 and 13.

12. Find the circumference of the circle to the nearest tenth.

13. Find the area of the circle to the nearest tenth.

Find each square or square root.

14. 15^2

15. 23^2

16. $\sqrt{1,600}$

17. $\sqrt{961}$

18. The tiles of Sara's new floor are black and white as shown. What is the missing length to the nearest tenth?

19. Triangle Park has a trail that follows the path of a right triangle. One leg of the trail is 2.1 miles, and the other leg is 3.0 miles. What is the distance of the third side of the trail to the nearest tenth of a mile?

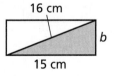

Use the diagram at right for Items 20 and 21.

20. Use the Pythagorean Theorem to find the missing measure.

21. Find the area of the triangle.

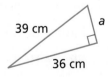

Test Tackler
STANDARDIZED TEST STRATEGIES

Test Tackler

Multiple Choice: Context-Based Test Items

Sometimes a multiple-choice test item requires you to use information in the answer choices to determine which choice fits the context of the problem.

EXAMPLE 1

Which statement is supported by the figure?

Ⓐ ∠1 and ∠4 are supplementary. Ⓒ The measure of ∠7 is 35°.

Ⓑ ∠3 and ∠2 are vertical angles. Ⓓ ∠5 and ∠6 are congruent.

Read each answer choice to find the best answer.

Choice A: ∠1 and ∠4 are vertical angles and therefore, congruent. Congruent angles are supplementary only if they are right angles. ∠1 and ∠4 measure 35°.

Choice B: ∠3 and ∠2 are vertical angles. This is the correct answer choice.

Choice C: The measure of ∠7 cannot be 35° because ∠7 is supplementary to a 35° angle. Therefore, ∠7 has a measure of 145°.

Choice D: ∠5 and ∠6 are supplementary angles but not right angles. Supplementary angles are congruent only if they are both right angles.

EXAMPLE 2

Which two figures have the same area?

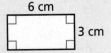

Figure I

Figure II

6 cm / 4 cm / 3 cm

Figure III

3 cm / 6 cm

Figure IV

Ⓕ Figure I and Figure II   Ⓗ Figure II and Figure III

Ⓖ Figure I and Figure III   Ⓙ Figure I and Figure IV

Find the areas of all four figures and compare them.

Figure I: $3 \cdot 6 = 18 \text{ cm}^2$ **Figure III:** $\frac{1}{2} \cdot 4(3 + 6) = 18 \text{ cm}^2$

Figure II: $3 \cdot 9 = 27 \text{ cm}^2$ **Figure IV:** $\frac{1}{2} \cdot 6 \cdot 3 = 9 \text{ cm}^2$

Figures I and III have the same area. Choice G is correct.

Do not choose an answer until you have read all of the answer choices.

Read each test item and answer the questions that follow.

Item A

The area of the square is 16 cm^2. Which of the following is NOT correct about the circle?

Ⓐ $C = 4\pi$ cm

Ⓑ $A = 16\pi$ cm^2

Ⓒ $d = 4$ cm

Ⓓ $r = 2$ cm

1. Since only one answer choice has incorrect information, why can you automatically eliminate answer choices C and D?

2. How can you find the side length of the square? What does the side length tell you about the circle?

3. Use your answer to Problem 2 to determine whether answer choice A has correct information.

4. How can you tell that choice B is the correct answer?

Item B

Which figure is an acute isosceles triangle?

5. What is an acute triangle?

6. What is an isosceles triangle?

7. Why is choice F incorrect?

Item C

Which graph represents a reflection across the x-axis?

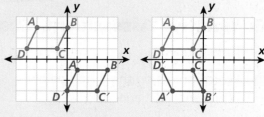

8. Which answer choices do NOT show reflections?

9. What is a reflection across the x-axis?

Item D

The area of the trapezoid is 30 in^2. Which equation CANNOT be used to find the height of the trapezoid?

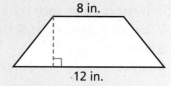

Ⓕ $30 = \frac{1}{2}(8 + 12)h$

Ⓖ $60 = (8 + 12)h$

Ⓗ $30 = \frac{1}{2}(8 - 12)h$

Ⓙ $\frac{1}{2}(8 + 12)h = 30$

10. What is the formula for the area of a trapezoid?

11. What steps would you take to solve the formula for h?

TCAP Test Prep

Cumulative Assessment, Chapters 1–9

Multiple Choice

1. Which points on the graph below represent $\sqrt{10}$ and $\sqrt{4}$?

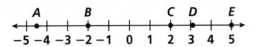

  A A and C   **C** B and E

  B C and D   **D** B and D

2. Explain why the triangles are similar. Then find the missing measure.

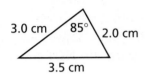 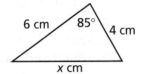

  F SSS; 0.7 cm

  G SAS; 7 cm

  H AA; 0.7 cm

  J AAS; 7 cm

3. A quilt is made with 10 square pieces of fabric. If the area of each square piece is 169 square inches, what is the length of each square piece?

  A 12 inches

  B 13 inches

  C 14 inches

  D 15 inches

4. A color printer is designed to print 8 pages per minute. How many pages can the printer print in 13 minutes?

  F 1.6 pages

  G 21 pages

  H 84 pages

  J 104 pages

5. Seventy percent of historical figures pictured on U.S. currency do not have facial hair. What is the fraction equivalent of this value?

  A $\dfrac{7}{1,000}$ **C** $\dfrac{7}{10}$

  B $\dfrac{7}{100}$ **D** $\dfrac{70}{1}$

6. Which equation describes the graph?

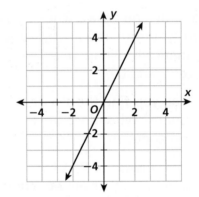

  F $y = x - 2$ **H** $y = 2x$

  G $y = x + 2$ **J** $y = -2x$

For Items 7 and 8, use the table below.

x	−2	−1	0	1	2
f(x)	−1	0	1	2	

7. Determine a relationship between the input and output values.

  A $f(x) = x + 1$

  B $f(x) = x - 1$

  C $f(x) = 2x + 1$

  D $f(x) = 2x - 1$

8. Find the missing value in the table.

  F −2   **H** 3

  G 1   **J** 5

9. Paul plans to build a fence around the perimeter of his property. How much fencing does he need?

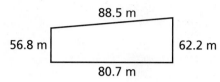

A 288.2 m   **C** 4,583.7 m

B 294.6 m   **D** 5,504.7 m

 When you are making graphs of data make sure that you calculated with the correct numbers that were given.

10. A birdwatcher keeps track of how many birds she sees each time she goes bird watching. She has seen 12, 18, 23, 23, 17, 11, 16, 22, and 30 birds on her last nine outings. Which box-and-whisker plot shows the same information?

F
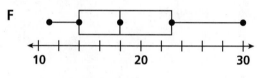

G
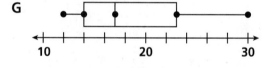

H
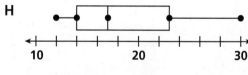

J
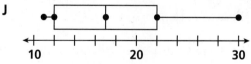

11. A turnstile counted 1040 people who entered a zoo in a 4-hour period. Which proportion can be used to find how many people p entered in an 8-hour period at the same hourly rate?

A $\dfrac{4}{1040} = \dfrac{p}{8}$ **C** $\dfrac{4}{p} = \dfrac{8}{1040}$

B $\dfrac{1040}{4} = \dfrac{p}{8}$ **D** $\dfrac{4}{1040} = \dfrac{12}{p}$

Process Standards Practice

Short Response

S1. The tennis team had a pizza party at the end of the season. The 17 team members spent a total of $51.95 on pizza and $6.70 on drinks. What is the average amount each team member spent for the party? Show your work.

S2. Laurie wants to paste a circular photo onto a rectangular piece of cardboard. The area of the photo is 50.24 in². What are the smallest possible dimensions the piece of cardboard can have and still hold the entire photo? Use 3.14 for π and explain your answer.

S3. Find the perimeter and area of a rectangle with length 12 m and width 7 m. Then find the side length of a square that has the same area as the rectangle. Round your answers to the nearest meter, and show your work.

Extended Response

E1. Use $\triangle ABC$ and $\triangle STU$ for the following problems.

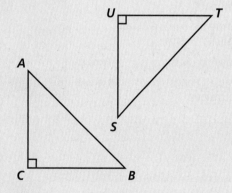

a. If $AB = 17$ m and $AC = 8$ m, what theorem can you use to find CB? Find CB, and show your work.

b. If $ST = 10$ m and $\triangle ABC$ is similar to $\triangle STU$, what ratio can you use to find SU and UT? Show how to find SU and UT to the nearest tenth of a meter.

c. Find the difference in the areas of the two triangles.

Measurement: Three-Dimensional Figures

Chapter Focus
- Find volume and surface area of prisms and cylinders.
- Investigate the volumes of similar figures.

Why Learn This?

Artists and architects make careful measurements to construct three-dimensional figures, such as the glass pyramid at the Louvre Museum in Paris, France.

Learn It Online
Chapter Project Online **go.hrw.com**,
keyword MS10 Ch10 Go

Are You Ready?

✓ Vocabulary

Choose the best term from the list to complete each sentence.

1. A polygon with six sides is called a(n) __?__.
2. __?__ figures are the same size and shape.
3. A(n) __?__ is a ratio that relates the dimensions of two similar objects.
4. The formula for the __?__ of a circle can be written as πd or $2\pi r$.
5. __?__ figures are the same shape but not necessarily the same size.
6. A polygon with five sides is called a(n) __?__.

area

circumference

congruent

hexagon

pentagon

scale factor

similar

Complete these exercises to review skills you will need for this chapter.

✓ Area of Squares, Rectangles, Triangles

Find the area of each figure.

7.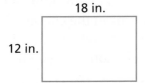
18 in.
12 in.

8.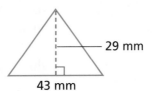
29 mm
43 mm

9.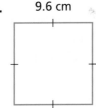
9.6 cm

✓ Area of Circles

Find the area of each circle to the nearest tenth. Use 3.14 for π.

10.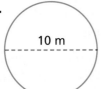
10 m

11.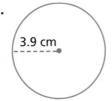
3.9 cm

12.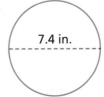
7.4 in.

✓ Find the Cube of a Number

Find each value.

13. 3^3
14. 8^3
15. 2.5^3
16. 6.2^3
17. 10^3
18. 5.9^3
19. 800^3
20. 98^3

Where You've Been

Previously, you

- found the area of polygons and irregular figures.

- compared the relationship between a figure's perimeter and its area.

In This Chapter

You will study

- finding the volume of prisms, cylinders, pyramids, and cones.

- using nets and formulas to find the surface area of prisms, cylinders, pyramids, and cones.

- finding the volume and surface area of similar three-dimensional figures.

Where You're Going

You can use the skills learned in this chapter

- to determine the amount of materials needed to build a doghouse.

- to convert dimensions of a model to real-world dimensions.

Key Vocabulary/Vocabulario

base of a three-dimensional figure	base de una figura tridimensional
cylinder	cilindro
edge	arista
face	cara
net	plantilla
polyhedron	poliedro
prism	prisma
surface area	área total
vertex of a polyhedron	vértice de un poliedro
volume	volumen

Vocabulary Connections

To become familiar with some of the vocabulary terms in the chapter, consider the following. You may refer to the chapter, the glossary, or a dictionary if you like.

1. Note the Spanish translation of *surface area* in the table above. What does the term *área total* tell you about the meaning of **surface area**?

2. The word *edge* comes from the Latin word *acer*, meaning "sharp." How does the Latin root help you define an **edge** of a three-dimensional figure?

3. The word *vertex* can mean "peak" or "highest point." What part of a cone or pyramid is the **vertex**?

4. The word *prism* comes from the Greek word *priein*, meaning "to saw." How might you describe a **prism** in terms of something sawn or cut off?

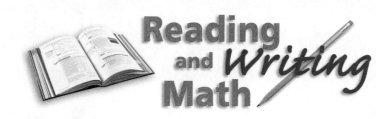

TN English/Language Arts
GLE 0701.6.1 Comprehend and summarize the main ideas and supporting details of informational texts.

Study Strategy: Learn and Use Formulas

Throughout this chapter, you will be introduced to many formulas. Although memorizing these formulas is helpful, understanding the concepts on which they are based will help you to re-create the formula if you happen to forget.

One way to memorize a formula is to use flash cards. Write the formula on an index card and review it often. Include a diagram and an example. Add any notes that you choose, such as when to use the formula.

In Lesson 9-3, you learned the formula for area of a rectangle.

Sample Flash Card

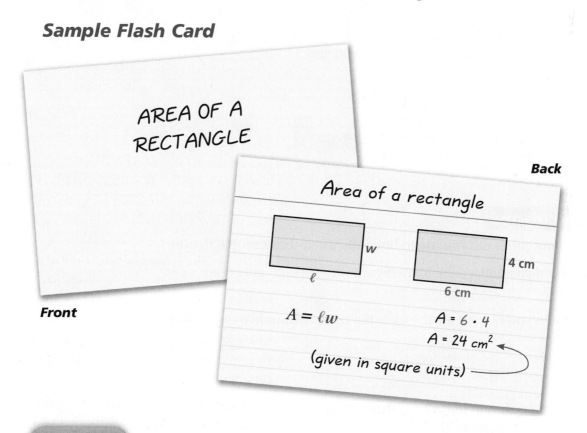

Back

Area of a rectangle

$A = \ell w$

$A = 6 \cdot 4$

$A = 24 \ cm^2$

(given in square units)

Front

AREA OF A RECTANGLE

Try This

1. Create flash cards for some of the formulas from the previous chapters.

2. Describe a plan to help you memorize the formulas in Chapters 9 and 10.

Sketch Three-Dimensional Figures from Different Views

Use with Lesson 10-1

Three-dimensional figures often look different from different points of view. You can use centimeter cubes to help you visualize and sketch three-dimensional figures.

Activity 1

1 Use centimeter cubes to build the three-dimensional figure at right.

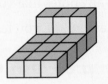

2 Now view the figure from the front and draw what you see. Then view the figure from the top and draw what you see. Finally, view the figure from the side and draw what you see.

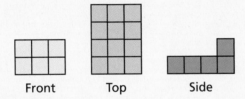

Front   Top   Side

Think and Discuss

1. How many cubes did you use to build the three-dimensional figure?

2. How could you add a cube to the figure without changing the top view?

3. How could you remove a cube from the figure without changing the side view?

Try This

Use centimeter cubes to build each three-dimensional figure. Then sketch the front, top, and side views.

1.

2.

3.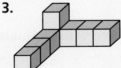

4.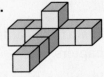

Activity 2

1 Use centimeter cubes to build a figure that has the front, top, and side views shown.

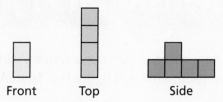

Front   Top   Side

2 You can build the figure by first making a simple figure that matches the front view.

3 Now add cubes so that the figure matches the top view.

4 Finally, remove cubes so that the figure matches the side view. Check that the front and top views are still correct for the figure that you built.

Think and Discuss

1. Discuss whether there is another step-by-step method for building the above figure. If so, is the final result the same?

Try This

The front, top, and side views of a figure are shown. Use centimeter cubes to build the figure. Then sketch the figure.

1.

Front   Top   Side

2.

Front   Top   Side

3. The views below represent a three-dimensional figure that cannot be built from cubes. Determine which three-dimensional figure matches the views.

Front   Top   Side

A   B   C   D

Introduction to Three-Dimensional Figures

Three-dimensional figures have three dimensions: length, width, and height. A flat surface of a three-dimensional figure is a **face**. An **edge** is where two faces meet.

A **polyhedron** is a three-dimensional figure whose faces are all polygons. A **vertex** of a polyhedron is a point where three or more edges meet. The face that is used to name a polyhedron is a **base**.

A *prism* has two bases, and a *pyramid* has one base.

Vocabulary

face

edge

polyhedron

vertex

base

prism

pyramid

cylinder

cone

sphere

Prisms	Pyramids
A **prism** is a polyhedron that has two parallel, congruent bases. The bases can be any polygon. The other faces are parallelograms.	A **pyramid** is a polyhedron that has one base. The base can be any polygon. The other faces are triangles.
Vertex 2 bases Edge	Vertex 1 base Edge

EXAMPLE **1** **Naming Prisms and Pyramids**

Identify the bases and faces of each figure. Then name the figure.

Interactivities Online ▶

A
There are two rectangular bases.
There are four other rectangular faces.
The figure is a rectangular prism.

B
There is one rectangular base.
There are four triangular faces.
The figure is a rectangular pyramid.

C
There are two triangular bases.
There are three rectangular faces.
The figure is a triangular prism.

Remember!

A polygon with six sides is called a hexagon.

D
There is one hexagonal base.
There are six triangular faces.
The figure is a hexagonal pyramid.

Video Lesson Tutorials Online

Other three-dimensional figures include *cylinders, cones,* and *spheres.* These figures are not polyhedrons because they are not made of faces that are all polygons.

Cylinders	Cones	Spheres
A **cylinder** has two parallel, congruent bases that are circles. 2 bases	A **cone** has one base that is a circle and a surface that comes to a point called the vertex. Vertex 1 base	A **sphere** has a surface made up of all the points that are the same distance from a given point.

You can use properties to classify three-dimensional figures.

EXAMPLE 2 **Classifying Three-Dimensional Figures**

Classify each figure as a polyhedron or not a polyhedron. Then name the figure.

A  *The faces are all polygons, so the figure is a polyhedron.*
There is one triangular base.
The figure is a triangular pyramid.

B  *The faces are not all polygons, so the figure is not a polyhedron.*
There are two circular bases.
The figure is a cylinder.

C  *The faces are not all polygons, so the figure is not a polyhedron.*
There is one circular base.
The figure is a cone.

Think and Discuss

1. Explain how to identify a prism or a pyramid.

2. Compare and contrast cylinders and prisms. How are they alike? How are they different?

Learn It Online
Homework Help Online **go.hrw.com**,
keyword MS10 10-1 Go
Exercises 1–12, 13, 15, 19, 21

GUIDED PRACTICE

See Example **1** Identify the bases and faces of each figure. Then name the figure.

1.

2.

3.

See Example **2** Classify each figure as a polyhedron or not a polyhedron. Then name the figure.

4.

5.

6.

INDEPENDENT PRACTICE

See Example **1** Identify the bases and faces of each figure. Then name the figure.

7.

8.

9.

See Example **2** Classify each figure as a polyhedron or not a polyhedron. Then name the figure.

10.

11.

12.

PRACTICE AND PROBLEM SOLVING

Extra Practice
See page EP25.

Identify the three-dimensional figure described.

13. two parallel, congruent square bases and four other polygonal faces

14. two parallel, congruent circular bases and one curved surface

15. one triangular base and three other triangular faces

16. all points on the surface are the same distance from a given point

Name two examples of the three-dimensional figure described.

17. two parallel, congruent bases   **18.** one base

19. The structures in the photo at right are tombs of ancient Egyptian kings. No one knows exactly when the tombs were built, but some archaeologists think the first one might have been built around 2780 B.C.E. Name the shape of the ancient Egyptian structures.

2600 B.C.E.
Ancient Egyptian structures at Giza

20. The Parthenon was built around 440 B.C.E. by the ancient Greeks. Its purpose was to house a statue of Athena, the Greek goddess of wisdom. Describe the three-dimensional shapes you see in the structure.

440 B.C.E.
Parthenon

21. The Leaning Tower of Pisa began to lean as it was being built. To keep the tower from falling over, the upper sections (floors) were built slightly off center so that the tower would curve away from the way it was leaning. What shape is each section of the tower?

22. ⭐ **Challenge** The stainless steel structure at right, called the Unisphere, became the symbol of the New York World's Fair of 1964–1965. Explain why the structure is not a sphere.

1173
Leaning Tower of Pisa

1964
Unisphere

Test Prep and Spiral Review

23. Multiple Choice Which figure has six rectangular faces?

Ⓐ Rectangular prism

Ⓒ Triangular pyramid

Ⓑ Triangular prism

Ⓓ Rectangular pyramid

24. Multiple Choice Which figure does NOT have two congruent bases?

Ⓕ Cube

Ⓖ Pyramid

Ⓗ Prism

Ⓙ Cylinder

Estimate each sum. (Lesson 3-6)

25. $\frac{2}{5} + \frac{3}{8}$

26. $\frac{1}{16} + \frac{4}{9}$

27. $\frac{7}{9} + \frac{11}{12}$

28. $\frac{1}{10} + \frac{1}{16}$

29. A store sells two sizes of detergent: 300 ounces for $21.63 and 100 ounces for $6.99. Which size detergent has the lowest price per ounce? (Lesson 4-2)

Cross Sections

When a three-dimensional figure and a plane intersect, the intersection is called a **cross section**. A three-dimensional figure can have many different cross sections. For example, when you cut an orange in half, the cross section that is exposed depends on the direction of the cut.

Vocabulary

cross section

EXAMPLE 1 **Identifying Cross Sections**

Identify the cross section that best matches the given figure.

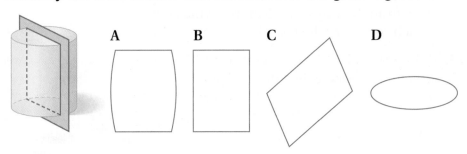

A B C D

The bases of the cylinder are parallel, so the cross section must contain a pair of parallel lines. The bases of the cylinder meet the lateral surface at right angles, so the cross section must contain right angles. The best choice is **B**.

EXAMPLE 2 **Sketching and Describing Cross Sections**

Sketch and describe the cross section of a cone that is cut parallel to its base.

The base of a cone is a circle. Any cross section made by cutting the cone parallel to the base will also be a circle.

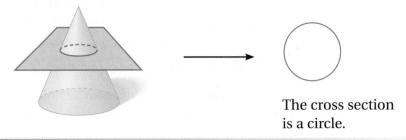

The cross section is a circle.

You can form three-dimensional figures by translating or rotating a cross section through space.

EXAMPLE 3 Describing Three-Dimensional Figures Formed by Transformations

Describe the three-dimensional figure formed by rotating an isosceles triangle around its line of symmetry.

Draw an isosceles triangle and its line of symmetry. Visualize rotating the triangle through space around the line. The resulting three-dimensional figure is a cone.

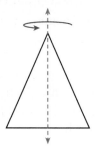 

EXTENSION

Exercises

1. Identify the cross section that best matches the given figure.

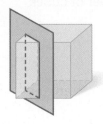 Ⓐ   Ⓑ   Ⓒ   Ⓓ

Sketch and describe each cross section.

2. a cylinder that is cut parallel to its bases

3. a cube that is cut parallel to one of its faces

Describe the three-dimensional figure formed by each transformation.

4. a rectangle that is rotated around a line of symmetry

5. a circle that is translated perpendicularly to the plane in which it lies (*Hint:* Imagine lifting a circle that is lying on a table straight upward.)

6. A sculptor has a block of clay in the shape of a rectangular prism. She uses a piece of wire to cut the clay, and the resulting cross section is a square. Make a sketch showing the prism and how the sculptor may have cut the clay.

Hands-on LAB

Explore the Volume of Prisms and Cylinders

10-2

Use with Lesson 10-2

Learn It Online
Lab Resources Online **go.hrw.com**,
keyword MS10 Lab10 Go

The volume of a three-dimensional figure is the number of cubes that it can hold. One cube represents one cubic unit of volume.

Activity 1

1 Use centimeter cubes to build the rectangular prism shown. What are the length, width, and height of the prism? How many cubes does the prism hold?

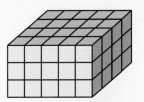

2 You can find out how many cubes the prism holds without counting every cube. First look at the prism from above. How can you find the number of cubes in the top layer without counting every cube?

Top

3 Now look at the prism from the side. How many layers does the prism have? How can you use this to find the total number of cubes in the prism?

Side

Think and Discuss

1. Describe a shortcut for finding the number of cubes in a rectangular prism.

2. **Make a Conjecture** Suppose you know the area of the base of a prism and the height of the prism. How can you find the prism's volume?

3. Let the area of the base of a prism be *B* and the height of the prism be *h*. Write a formula for the prism's volume *V*.

Try This

Use the formula you discovered to find the volume of each prism.

1.
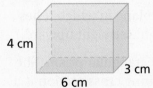
4 cm
6 cm
3 cm

2.
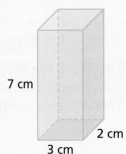
7 cm
3 cm
2 cm

3.
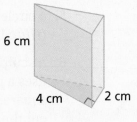
6 cm
4 cm
2 cm

1 You can use a process similar to that in Activity 1 to develop the formula for the volume of a cylinder. You will need an empty soup can or other cylindrical container. Remove one of the bases.

2 Arrange centimeter cubes in a single layer at the bottom of the cylinder. Fit as many cubes into the layer as possible. How many cubes are in this layer?

3 To find how many layers of cubes would fit in the cylinder, make a stack of cubes along the inside of the cylinder. How many layers would fit in the cylinder?

4 How can you use what you know to find the approximate number of cubes that would fit in the cylinder?

Think and Discuss

1. Make a Conjecture Suppose you know the area of the base of a cylinder and the height of the cylinder. How can you find the cylinder's volume?

2. Let the area of the base of a cylinder be B and the height of the cylinder be h. Write a formula for the cylinder's volume V.

3. The base of a cylinder is a circle with radius r. How can you find the area of the base? How can you use this in your formula for the volume of a cylinder?

Try This

Use the formula you discovered to find the volume of each cylinder. Use 3.14 for π and round to the nearest tenth.

1.

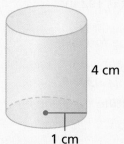

4 cm

1 cm

2.

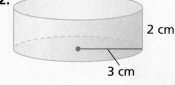

2 cm

3 cm

3.

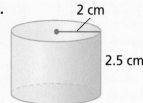

2 cm

2.5 cm

Volume of Prisms and Cylinders

TN *Use Additional Topics A-2 and A-3 with this lesson.*

Any three-dimensional figure can be filled completely with congruent cubes and parts of cubes. The **volume** of a three-dimensional figure is the number of cubes it can hold. Each cube represents a unit of measure called a cubic unit.

To find the volume of a rectangular prism, you can count cubes or multiply the lengths of the edges.

Vocabulary
volume

Interactivities Online ▶

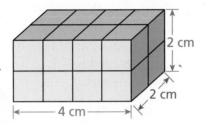

$$4 \text{ cm} \cdot 2 \text{ cm} \cdot 2 \text{ cm} = 16 \text{ cm}^3$$

length · width · height = volume

area of · height = volume
base

The volume of a prism is the area of its base times its height.

VOLUME OF A PRISM		
The volume V of a prism is the area of its base B times its height h.	$V = Bh$	←Height→
		← Base →

EXAMPLE **1** **Using a Formula to Find the Volume of a Prism**

Find the volume of each figure.

Reading Math

Any unit of measurement with an exponent of 3 is a cubic unit. For example, m³ means "cubic meter," and in³ means "cubic inch."

A

12 in.
8 in.
2 in.

$V = Bh$ *Use the formula.*
            The base is a rectangle: $B = 8 \cdot 2 = 16$.
$V = 16 \cdot 12$ *Substitute for B and h.*
$V = 192$ *Multiply.*

The volume of the cereal box is 192 in³.

B

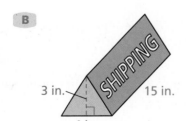

SHIPPING

3 in.
15 in.
4 in.

$V = Bh$ *Use the formula.*
            The base is a triangle:
            $B = \frac{1}{2} \cdot 4 \cdot 3 = 6$.
$V = 6 \cdot 15$ *Substitute for B and h.*
$V = 90$ *Multiply.*

The volume of the shipping carton is 90 in³.

Finding the volume of a cylinder is similar to finding the volume of a prism.

VOLUME OF A CYLINDER		
The volume V of a cylinder is the area of its base B times its height h.	$V = Bh$ or $V = \pi r^2 h$	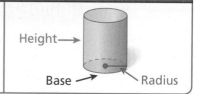 Height→ Base→ ⌐Radius

EXAMPLE 2

Using a Formula to Find the Volume of a Cylinder

A can of shoe polish is shaped like a cylinder. Find its volume to the nearest tenth. Use 3.14 for π.

$V = Bh$ *Use the formula.*

The base is a circle: $B = \pi \cdot 4^2 \approx 50.24 \text{ cm}^2$.

$V \approx 50.24 \cdot 5$ *Substitute for B and h.*

$V \approx 251.2$ *Multiply.*

The volume of the shoe polish can is about 251.2 cm^3.

8 cm

5 cm

A three-dimensional composite figure is made up of two or more simpler three-dimensional figures. To find the volume of a three-dimensional composite figure, add the volumes of the simpler figures.

EXAMPLE 3

Finding the Volume of a Composite Figure

Find the volume of the composite figure to the nearest tenth. Use 3.14 for π.

volume of composite figure	=	volume of prism	+	volume of cylinder
V	=	Bh	+	$\pi r^2 h$
V	$\approx$	$(7)(4)(5)$	+	$(3.14)(2)^2(3)$
V	$\approx$	140	+	37.68
V	$\approx$		177.68	

The volume of the composite figure is about 177.7 ft^3.

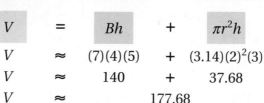

2 ft
3 ft
5 ft
4 ft
7 ft

Think and Discuss

1. **Explain** what a cubic unit is. What units would you use for the volume of a figure measured in yards?

2. **Compare and contrast** the formulas for volume of a prism and volume of a cylinder. How are they alike? How are they different?

GUIDED PRACTICE

See Example 1   **Find the volume of each figure.**

1.

5 in.
6 in.
8 in.

2.
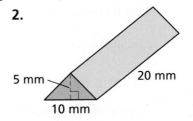
5 mm
20 mm
10 mm

3.

3.5 in.
2.25 in.
0.5 in.

See Example 2   **4.** A can of tomato paste is shaped like a cylinder. It is 4 cm wide and 6 cm tall. Find its volume to the nearest tenth. Use 3.14 for π.

See Example 3   **Find the volume of each composite figure to the nearest tenth. Use 3.14 for π.**

5.
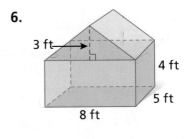
3 m
5 m
6 m
2 m
7 m

6.
3 ft
4 ft
5 ft
8 ft

INDEPENDENT PRACTICE

See Example 1   **Find the volume of each figure.**

7.
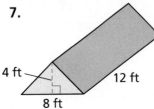
4 ft
12 ft
8 ft

8.
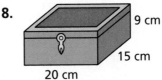
9 cm
15 cm
20 cm

9.
5.6 in.
6 in.
0.4 in.

See Example 2   **10.** A paper towel roll is shaped like a cylinder. It is 4 cm wide and 28 cm tall. Find its volume to the nearest tenth. Use 3.14 for π.

See Example 3   **Find the volume of each composite figure to the nearest tenth. Use 3.14 for π.**

11.
5 in.
5 in.
6 in.
5 in.

12.
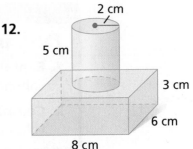
2 cm
5 cm
3 cm
6 cm
8 cm

Extra Practice

See page EP25.

13. **Multi-Step** The base of a triangular prism is a right triangle with hypotenuse 10 m long and one leg 6 m long. If the height of the prism is 12 m, what is the volume of the prism?

14. A cylindrical candle has a radius of 1.5 in. and a height of 4 in. What is the volume of the candle in cubic inches? in cubic centimeters? Use 3.14 for π and round your answers to the nearest hundredth. (*Hint:* $1 \text{ in}^3 \approx 16.38 \text{ cm}^3$)

15. **Recreation** The tent shown is in the shape of a triangular prism. How many cubic feet of space are in the tent?

16. **What's the Error?** A student said the volume of a cylinder with a 3-inch diameter is two times the volume of a cylinder with the same height and a 1.5-inch radius. What is the error?

17. **Write About It** Explain the similarities and differences between finding the volume of a cylinder and finding the volume of a triangular prism.

18. **Challenge** Find the volume, to the nearest tenth, of the material that makes up the pipe shown. Use 3.14 for π.

Test Prep and Spiral Review

19. **Multiple Choice** What is the volume of a triangular prism that is 10 in. long, 7 in. wide, and 4 in. high?

Ⓐ 110 in³   Ⓑ 140 in³   Ⓒ 205 in³   Ⓓ 280 in³

20. **Multiple Choice** Which figures have the same volume?

I   II   III

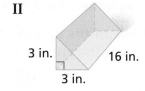   

Ⓕ I and II   Ⓖ I and III   Ⓗ II and III   Ⓙ I, II, and III

Find the simple interest. (Lesson 6-7)

21. $P = \$3{,}600$; $r = 5\%$; $t = 1.5$ years

22. $P = \$10{,}000$; $r = 3.2\%$; $t = 2$ years

23. Students collected data on the number of visitors to an amusement park over a period of 30 days. Choose the type of graph that would best represent the data. (Lesson 7-7)

Suppose you have a square-pyramid-shaped container and a square-prism-shaped container, and the bases and heights are the same size. If you pour sand from the pyramid into the prism, it appears that the prism holds three times as much sand as the pyramid.

In fact, the volume of a pyramid is exactly one-third the volume of a prism with the same height and a congruent base.

The height of a pyramid is the perpendicular distance from the pyramid's base to the vertex opposite the base.

VOLUME OF A PYRAMID		
The volume V of a pyramid is one-third the area of its base B times its height h.	$V = \frac{1}{3}Bh$	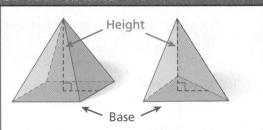

EXAMPLE **1** **Finding the Volume of a Pyramid**

Find the volume of the pyramid to the nearest tenth. Estimate to check whether the answer is reasonable.

A

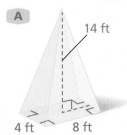

14 ft

4 ft   8 ft

$V = \frac{1}{3}Bh$ *Use the formula.*

The base is a rectangle, so $B = 4 \cdot 8 = 32$.

$V = \frac{1}{3} \cdot 32 \cdot 14$ *Substitute for B and h.*

$V \approx 149.3 \text{ ft}^3$ *Multiply.*

Estimate $V \approx \frac{1}{3} \cdot 30 \cdot 15$ *Round the measurements.*

$\approx 150 \text{ ft}^3$ *The answer is reasonable.*

Find the volume of the pyramid to the nearest tenth. Estimate to check whether the answer is reasonable.

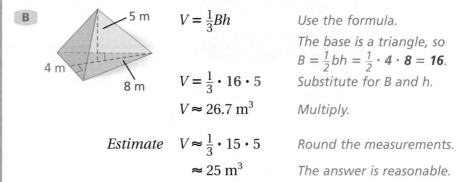

B

$V = \frac{1}{3}Bh$ *Use the formula.*

The base is a triangle, so
$B = \frac{1}{2}bh = \frac{1}{2} \cdot 4 \cdot 8 = \mathbf{16}$.

$V = \frac{1}{3} \cdot \mathbf{16} \cdot 5$ *Substitute for B and h.*

$V \approx 26.7 \text{ m}^3$ *Multiply.*

Estimate $V \approx \frac{1}{3} \cdot 15 \cdot 5$ *Round the measurements.*

            $\approx 25 \text{ m}^3$ *The answer is reasonable.*

Similar to the relationship between volumes of prisms and pyramids, the volume of a cone is one-third the volume of a cylinder with the same height and a congruent base.

VOLUME OF A CONE		
The volume *V* of a cone is one-third the area of its base *B* times its height *h*.	$V = \frac{1}{3}Bh$ or $V = \frac{1}{3}\pi r^2 h$	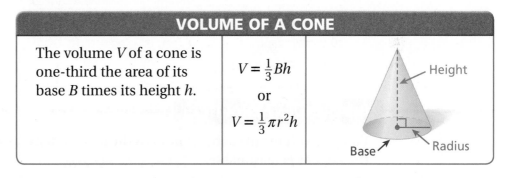

E X A M P L E   2   **Finding the Volume of a Cone**

Find the volume of the cone to the nearest tenth. Use 3.14 for π. Estimate to check whether the answer is reasonable.

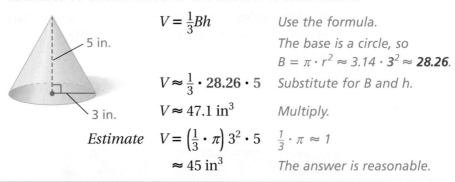

Helpful Hint

To estimate the volume of a cone, round π to 3 so that $\frac{1}{3} \cdot \pi$ becomes $\frac{1}{3} \cdot 3$, which is 1.

$V = \frac{1}{3}Bh$ *Use the formula.*

The base is a circle, so
$B = \pi \cdot r^2 \approx 3.14 \cdot 3^2 \approx \mathbf{28.26}$.

$V \approx \frac{1}{3} \cdot 28.26 \cdot 5$ *Substitute for B and h.*

$V \approx 47.1 \text{ in}^3$ *Multiply.*

Estimate $V = \left(\frac{1}{3} \cdot \pi\right) 3^2 \cdot 5$ $\frac{1}{3} \cdot \pi \approx 1$

            $\approx 45 \text{ in}^3$ *The answer is reasonable.*

Think and Discuss

1. Explain how to find the volume of a cone given the diameter of the base and the height of the cone.

2. Compare and contrast the formulas for volume of a pyramid and volume of a cone. How are they alike? How are they different?

Exercises

Learn It Online
Homework Help Online **go.hrw.com,**
keyword MS10 10-3 Go
Exercises 1–12, 13, 15, 17

GUIDED PRACTICE

See Example 1 Find the volume of each pyramid to the nearest tenth. Estimate to check whether the answer is reasonable.

1.
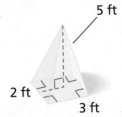
5 ft
2 ft
3 ft

2.
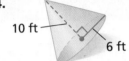
7 cm
5 cm
6 cm

3.

6 m
4 m
4 m

See Example 2 Find the volume of each cone to the nearest tenth. Use 3.14 for π. Estimate to check whether the answer is reasonable.

4.

10 ft
6 ft

5.
4 in.
2 in.

6.

5 m
9 m

INDEPENDENT PRACTICE

See Example 1 Find the volume of each pyramid to the nearest tenth. Estimate to check whether the answer is reasonable.

7.

8 in.
6 in.
11 in.

8.
6 ft
$B = 22.5 \text{ ft}^2$

9.
30 mm
18 mm   15 mm

See Example 2 Find the volume of each cone to the nearest tenth. Use 3.14 for π. Estimate to check whether the answer is reasonable.

10.

5 in.   3 in.

11.
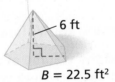
12.3 cm
15 cm

12.

12 m
25 m

PRACTICE AND PROBLEM SOLVING

Extra Practice
See page EP25.

Find the volume of each figure to the nearest tenth. Use 3.14 for π.

13. a 7 ft tall rectangular pyramid with base 4 ft by 5 ft

14. a cone with radius 8 yd and height 12 yd

15. **Multi-Step** Find the volume of an 8 in. tall right triangular pyramid with a base hypotenuse of 5 in. and base leg of 3 in.

16. **Architecture** The steeple on a building is a square pyramid with a base area of 12 square feet and a height of 15 feet. How many cubic feet of concrete was used to make the steeple?

17. Multi-Step A snack bar sells popcorn in the containers shown at right.

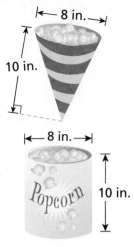

|← 8 in. →|

10 in.

|← 8 in. →|

Popcorn

10 in.

a. Based on the formulas for volume of a cylinder and a cone, how many times as much popcorn does the larger container hold?

b. How many cubic inches of popcorn, to the nearest tenth, does the cone-shaped container hold? Use 3.14 for π.

c. How many cubic inches of popcorn does the cylinder-shaped container hold? Use 3.14 for π.

d. Do your answers to parts **b** and **c** confirm your answer to part **a**? If not, find the error.

18. Critical Thinking Write a proportion of volumes for the given figures.

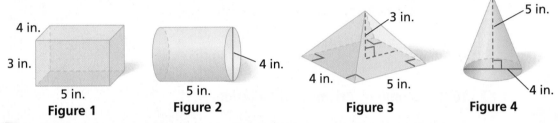

4 in.

3 in.

5 in.
Figure 1

4 in.

5 in.
Figure 2

3 in.

4 in. 5 in.
Figure 3

5 in.

4 in.
Figure 4

19. What's the Question? The answer is: The volume of figure A is $\frac{1}{3}$ the volume of figure B. What's the question?

20. Write About It Compare finding the volume of a cylinder with finding the volume of a cone that has the same height and base.

21. Challenge What effect does doubling the radius of a cone's base have on the cone's volume?

Test Prep and Spiral Review

22. Multiple Choice Which is the best estimate for the volume of a cone with a radius of 5 cm and a height of 8 cm?

(A) 40 cm³   (B) 80 cm³   (C) 200 cm³   (D) 800 cm³

23. Short Response A rectangular prism and a square pyramid both have a square base with side lengths of 5 inches and heights of 7 inches. Find the volume of each figure. Then explain the relationship between the volume of the prism and the volume of the pyramid.

Name the types of quadrilaterals that have each property. (Lesson 8-7)

24. four congruent sides

25. two sets of parallel sides

Find the volume of each figure to the nearest tenth. Use 3.14 for π. (Lesson 10-2)

26. cylinder: $d = 6$ m, $h = 8$ m

27. triangular prism: $B = 22$ ft², $h = 5$ ft

Ready To Go On?

Quiz for Lessons 10-1 Through 10-3

✓ **10-1** Introduction to Three-Dimensional Figures

Classify each figure as a polyhedron or not a polyhedron. Then name the figure.

1.

2.

3.

✓ **10-2** Volume of Prisms and Cylinders

4. A box is shaped like a rectangular prism. It is 6 ft long, 2 ft wide, and 3 ft high. Find its volume.

5. A can is shaped like a cylinder. It is 5.2 cm wide and 2.3 cm tall. Find its volume to the nearest tenth. Use 3.14 for π.

Find the volume of each composite figure to the nearest tenth. Use 3.14 for π.

6.
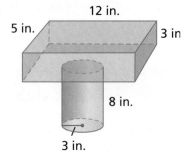
12 in.
5 in.
3 in
8 in.
3 in.

7.
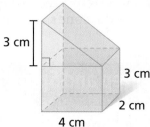
3 cm
3 cm
2 cm
4 cm

✓ **10-3** Volume of Pyramids and Cones

Find the volume of each figure to the nearest tenth. Use 3.14 for π.

8.
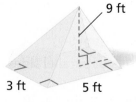
9 ft
3 ft
5 ft

9.
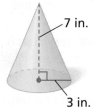
7 in.
3 in.

10.
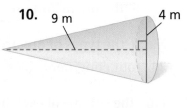
9 m
4 m

11. A cone has a radius of 2.5 cm and a height of 14 cm. What is the volume of the cone to the nearest hundredth? Use 3.14 for π.

Focus on Problem Solving

 Solve

• **Choose an operation**

When choosing an operation to use when solving a problem, you need to decide which action the problem is asking you to take. If you are asked to combine numbers, then you need to add. If you are asked to take away numbers or to find the difference between two numbers, then you need to subtract. You need to use multiplication when you put equal parts together and division when you separate something into equal parts.

 Determine the action in each problem. Then tell which operation should be used to solve the problem. Explain your choice.

1 Jeremy filled a sugar cone completely full of frozen yogurt and then put one scoop of frozen yogurt on top. The volume of Jeremy's cone is about 20.93 in^3, and the volume of the scoop that Jeremy used is about 16.75 in^3. About how much frozen yogurt, in cubic inches, did Jeremy use?

2 The volume of a cylinder equals the combined volumes of three cones that each have the same height and base size as the cylinder. What is the volume of a cylinder if a cone of the same height and base size has a volume of 45.2 cm^3?

3 The biology class at Jefferson High School takes care of a family of turtles that is kept in a glass tank with water, rocks, and plants. The volume of the tank is 2.75 cubic feet. At the end of the year, the baby turtles will have grown and will be moved into a tank that is 6.15 cubic feet. How much greater will the volume of the new tank be than that of the old tank?

4 Brianna is adding a second section to her hamster cage. The two sections will be connected by a tunnel that is made of 4 cylindrical parts, all the same size. If the volume of the tunnel is 56.52 cubic inches, what is the volume of each part of the tunnel?

Use Nets to Build Prisms and Cylinders

10-4

Use with Lesson 10-4

A net is a pattern of two-dimensional figures that can be folded to make a three-dimensional figure. You can use $\frac{1}{4}$-inch graph paper to help you make nets.

Activity

1 Use a net to construct a rectangular prism.

   a. Draw the net at right on a piece of graph paper. Each rectangle is 10 squares by 4 squares. The two squares are 4 small squares on each side.

   b. Cut out the net. Fold the net along the edges of each rectangle to make a rectangular prism. Tape the edges to hold them in place.

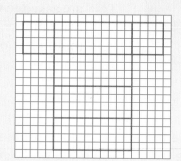

2 Use a net to construct a cylinder.

   a. Draw the net at right on a piece of graph paper. The rectangle is 25 squares by 8 squares. Use a compass to make the circles. Each circle has a radius of 4 squares.

   b. Cut out the net. Fold the net as shown to make a cylinder. Tape the edges to hold them in place.

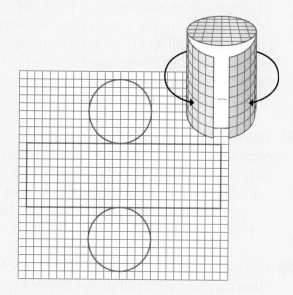

Think and Discuss

1. What are the dimensions, in inches, of the rectangular prism that you built?

2. What is the height, in inches, of the cylinder that you built? What is the cylinder's radius?

Try This

1. Use a net to construct a rectangular prism that is 1 inch by 2 inches by 3 inches.

2. Use a net to construct a cylinder with a height of 1 inch and a radius of $\frac{1}{2}$ in. (*Hint:* The length of the rectangle in the net must match the circumference of the circles, so the length should be $2\pi r = 2\pi\left(\frac{1}{2}\right) \approx 3.14$ inches.)

10-4 Surface Area of Prisms and Cylinders

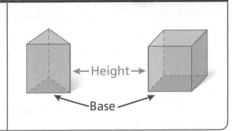

If you remove the surface from a three-dimensional figure and lay it out flat, the pattern you make is called a **net**.

Nets allow you to see all the surfaces of a solid at one time. You can use nets to help you find the *surface area* of a three-dimensional figure. **Surface area** is the sum of the areas of all of the surfaces of a figure expressed in square units.

Vocabulary

net

surface area

lateral face

lateral area

The **lateral faces** of a prism are parallelograms that connect the bases. The **lateral area** of a prism is the sum of the areas of the lateral faces.

Interactivities Online ▶ The net of a prism can be drawn so that the lateral faces form a rectangle with the same height as the prism. The length of the rectangle is equal to the perimeter of the base of the prism.

$P = a + b + c$

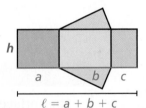

$\ell = a + b + c$

SURFACE AREA OF A PRISM		
The surface area S of a prism is twice the base area B plus the lateral area L. The lateral area is the base perimeter P times the height h.	$S = 2B + L$ or $S = 2B + Ph$	←Height→ Base

EXAMPLE 1 **Finding the Surface Area of a Prism**

Find the surface area of the prism.

$S = 2B + Ph$ *Use the formula.*

$S = 2(8)(12) + (40)(6)$ *Substitute.*
                        $P = 2(8) + 2(12) = 40$

$S = 192 + 240$ *Multiply.*

$S = 432$ *Add.*

6 in. 12 in. 8 in.

The surface area of the prism is 432 in^2.

Video   **LESSON TUTORIALS ONLINE**   <u>my.hrw.com</u>   *10-4 Surface Area of Prisms and Cylinders*   **607**

Find the surface area of the prism.

B

$S = 2B + Ph$ *Use the formula.*

$S = 2\left(\frac{1}{2}bh\right) + Ph$ $B = \frac{1}{2}bh$

$S = 2\left(\frac{1}{2}\right)(8)(3) + 18(7)$ *Substitute.* $P = 8 + 5 + 5 = 18$

$S = 24 + 126$ *Multiply.*

$S = 150$ *Add.*

The area is 150 ft^2.

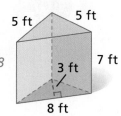

The lateral area of a cylinder is the curved surface that connects the two bases. The net of a cylinder can be drawn so that the lateral area forms a rectangle with the same height as the cylinder. The length of the rectangle is equal to the circumference of the base of the cylinder.

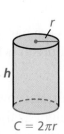

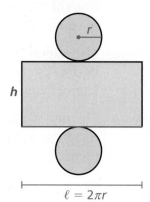

$C = 2\pi r$

$\ell = 2\pi r$

SURFACE AREA OF A CYLINDER

The surface area S of a cylinder is twice the base area B plus the lateral area L. The lateral area is the base circumference $2\pi r$ times the height h.	$S = 2B + L$ or $S = 2\pi r^2 + 2\pi rh$	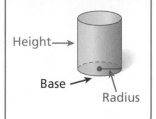

EXAMPLE **2**   **Finding the Surface Area of a Cylinder**

Find the surface area of the cylinder to the nearest tenth. Use 3.14 for π.

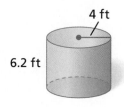

$S = 2\pi r^2 + 2\pi rh$ *Use the formula.*

$S \approx 2(3.14)(4^2) + 2(3.14)(4)(6.2)$ *Substitute.*

$S \approx 100.48 + 155.744$ *Multiply.*

$S \approx 256.224$ *Add.*

$S \approx 256.2$ *Round.*

The surface area of the cylinder is about 256.2 ft^2.

EXAMPLE 3

PROBLEM SOLVING

PROBLEM SOLVING APPLICATION

The treasure chest is a composite figure. What is the surface area of the chest to the nearest square foot?

1 Understand the Problem

- The chest is a rectangular prism and one-half of a cylinder.
- The base of the chest is 3 ft by 4 ft and the height is 2 ft.
- The radius of the cylinder is 1.5 ft and the height is 4 ft.

2 Make a Plan

Draw nets of the figures and shade the parts that show the surface area of the chest.

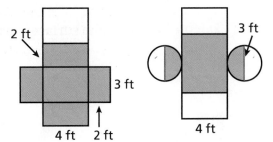

3 Solve

Find the surface area of the shaded part of the prism.

$$S = B + Ph \qquad \text{\textit{Use only one base.}}$$
$$= (4)(3) + 14(2) \qquad \text{\textit{Substitute.}}$$
$$= 12 + 28 = 40$$

Find the surface area of half of the cylinder.

$$S = \frac{1}{2}(2\pi r^2 + 2\pi rh) \qquad \text{\textit{Use only one-half the cylinder.}}$$
$$\approx \frac{1}{2}[2(3.14)(1.5^2) + 2(3.14)(1.5)(4)] \quad \text{\textit{Substitute. Use 3.14 for }} \pi.$$
$$\approx \frac{1}{2}(14.13 + 37.68)$$
$$\approx \frac{1}{2}(51.81) = 25.905$$

Add to find the total surface area: $40 + 25.905 = 65.905$.

The surface area of the treasure chest is about 66 ft^2.

4 Look Back

The surface area of the chest should be just less than the surface area of a rectangular prism with the same base and a height of 3.5 ft.

$$S = 2B + Ph = 2(12) + 14(3.5) = 73 \text{ ft}^2$$

66 ft^2 is just less than 73 ft^2, so the answer is reasonable.

Think and Discuss

1. Explain how you would find the surface area of an open-top box that is shaped like a rectangular prism.

GUIDED PRACTICE

See Example 1 **Find the surface area of each prism.**

1.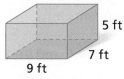
5 ft
7 ft
9 ft

2. 10 cm 8 cm
2.5 cm
8 cm
6 cm

See Example 2 **Find the surface area of each cylinder to the nearest tenth. Use 3.14 for π.**

3.
3 m
10 m

4. 15 in.
5 in.

See Example 3 **5.** What is the surface area of the breadbox to the nearest square inch? Check your answer for reasonableness.

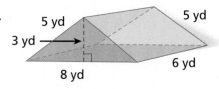
8 in.
16 in.
BREAD
⊢ 8 in. + 8 in. ⊣

INDEPENDENT PRACTICE

See Example 1 **Find the surface area of each prism.**

6.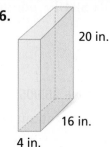
20 in.
16 in.
4 in.

7. 5 yd 5 yd
3 yd
6 yd
8 yd

See Example 2 **Find the surface area of each cylinder to the nearest tenth. Use 3.14 for π.**

8.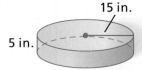
6 in.
15 in.

9. 18.5 cm
1.5 cm

See Example 3 **10.** What is the surface area of the milk carton to the nearest square inch? Check your answer for reasonableness.

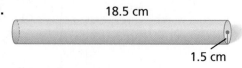
2 in.
MILK
12 in.
4 in.
4 in.

11. A cannery packs tuna into metal cans like the one shown. Round your answers to the nearest tenth, if necessary. Use 3.14 for π.

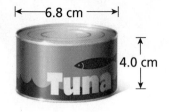

|←——6.8 cm——→|

4.0 cm

  a. Draw and label a net for the cylinder.

  b. About how many square centimeters of metal are used to make each can?

  c. The label for each can goes all the way around the can. About how many square centimeters of paper are needed for each label?

12. The table shows the dimensions of three boxes that are rectangular prisms.

	Length	Width	Depth
Box 1	3 in.	8 in.	9 in.
Box 2	4 in.	6 in.	9 in.
Box 3	6 in.	6 in.	6 in.

  a. Find the volume of each box.

  b. Which box requires the least material to wrap?

  c. **Make a Conjecture** For rectangular prisms of equal volume, what is true of the edge lengths that give the least surface area?

 13. **Choose a Strategy** A cylinder has a circumference of 20π cm and a height that is one-half the radius of the cylinder. What is the surface area of the cylinder? Give your answer in terms of π.

14. **Write About It** Explain how you would find the side lengths of a cube with a surface area of 512 ft^2.

15. **Challenge** Find the surface area of the rectangular prism shown with a rectangular-prism-shaped hole all the way through it.

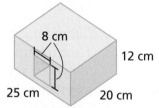

8 cm

12 cm

25 cm

20 cm

Test Prep and Spiral Review

16. Multiple Choice Find the surface area of the prism.

  Ⓐ 286 in^2

  Ⓑ 310 in^2

  Ⓒ 708 in^2

  Ⓓ 1,232 in^2

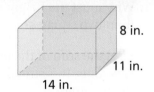

8 in.

11 in.

14 in.

17. Gridded Response Find the number of square centimeters in the surface area of a cylinder with a 5 cm radius and a 15 cm height. Use 3.14 for π.

Find the measure of the third angle in each triangle, given two angle measures. (Lesson 8-8)

18. 83°, 28°   **19.** 65°, 36°   **20.** 22°, 102°

Find the volume of each figure.

21. a 4 in. tall rectangular prism with base 7 in. by 8 in. (Lesson 10-2)

22. a 9 cm tall square pyramid with base 6 cm by 6 cm (Lesson 10-3)

Hands-on LAB

10-5

Explore the Surface Areas of Pyramids and Cones

Use with Lesson 10-5

You can use nets to estimate the surface areas of pyramids and cones.

Activity 1

Use a net to construct a square pyramid.

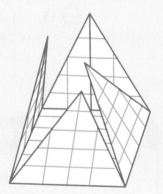

a. Draw a 4-by-4 square on a piece of graph paper. This square is the base of the pyramid.

b. The other four faces of the pyramid are triangles. To draw the triangles, find the midpoint of each side of the square. Draw a perpendicular line segment that is 5 squares long from the midpoint of each side away from the square. These are the heights of the triangular faces.

c. Use a straightedge to connect the endpoint of the height to the endpoints of the base for each triangle.

d. Cut out the net. Fold the net along the sides of the square. Then fold the triangles toward each other so they meet to make a square pyramid. Tape the faces of the pyramid together to hold them in place.

Think and Discuss

1. Why must the height of each triangle in the activity be greater than two squares?

2. Find the sum of the lengths of the bases of the four triangles. How does this sum compare to the perimeter of the base of the pyramid?

Try This

1. Estimate the area of each face of the pyramid by counting the squares. Add the areas to find the approximate surface area of the pyramid.

2. Use formulas from Chapter 9 to calculate the area of each figure in the net. What is the sum of these areas? How does this sum compare to your estimate?

3. Use a net to construct a square pyramid with dimensions different from the one in the activity. Then estimate the surface area of the pyramid.

Activity 2

Use a net to construct a cone.

a. Draw a line segment that is 2 squares long on a piece of graph paper. This segment is the radius of the base of your cone. Use a compass to draw a circle with this radius.

b. Use a compass to draw a second circle with a radius of 3 squares that touches the first circle at only one point.

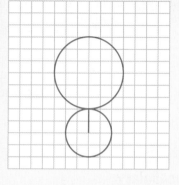

c. Lay a string around the edge of the smaller circle. Cut the string so that it is exactly the length of the smaller circle's circumference.

d. Now lay the piece of string around the edge of the larger circle. Place the middle of the string at the point where the two circles touch. Make a point at each end of the string where it lies on the larger circle. Connect each mark to the center of the circle with a line segment. Erase the part of the circle not formed using the string.

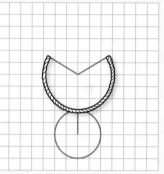

e. Cut out the net. Tape the edges from the larger circle to make the curved surface of the cone. Then tape the smaller circle to the open end of the curved surface to make your cone.

Think and Discuss

1. Why must the radius of the second circle be greater than the radius of the first circle?

2. Explain how the edge length of the curved surface of the cone is related to the circumference of the smaller circle.

Try This

1. Estimate the area of each surface of the cone by counting the squares. Add the areas to find the approximate surface area of the cone.

2. Use a net to construct a cone with dimensions different from the one in the activity. Then estimate the surface area of the cone.

The base of a **regular pyramid** is a regular polygon, and the other faces are congruent isosceles triangles.

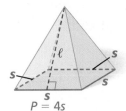

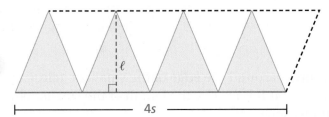

Vocabulary

regular pyramid

slant height of a pyramid

slant height of a cone

The diagram shows a square pyramid. The blue dashed line labeled ℓ is the **slant height of the pyramid**, the distance from the vertex opposite the base to the midpoint of an edge of the base.

The lateral faces of a regular pyramid can be arranged to cover half of a parallelogram. The height of the parallelogram is equal to the slant height of the pyramid. The base of the parallelogram is equal to the perimeter of the base of the pyramid.

SURFACE AREA OF A PYRAMID		
The surface area S of a regular pyramid is the base area B plus the lateral area L. The lateral area is one-half the base perimeter P times the slant height ℓ.	$S = B + L$ or $S = B + \frac{1}{2}P\ell$	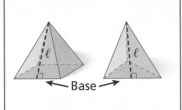 ← Base →

EXAMPLE 1 Finding the Surface Area of a Pyramid

Find the surface area of each pyramid.

A

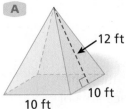

12 ft

10 ft

10 ft

$S = B + \frac{1}{2}P\ell$	*Use the formula.*
$S = \ell w + \frac{1}{2}P\ell$	*$B = \ell w$*
$S = (10)(10) + \frac{1}{2}(40)(12)$	*Substitute. $P = 4(10) = 40$*
$S = 100 + 240$	*Multiply.*
$S = 340$	*Add.*

The surface area is 340 square feet.

Video **Lesson Tutorials Online**

Find the surface area of each pyramid.

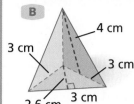

$S = B + \frac{1}{2}P\ell$ *Use the formula.*

$S = \frac{1}{2}bh + \frac{1}{2}P\ell$ $B = \frac{1}{2}bh$

$S = \frac{1}{2}(3)(2.6) + \frac{1}{2}(9)(4)$ *Substitute. P = 3(3) = 9*

$S = 3.9 + 18$ *Multiply.*

$S = 21.9$ *Add.*

The surface area is 21.9 square centimeters.

The diagram shows a cone and its net. The blue dashed line is the **slant height of the cone**, the distance from the vertex to a point on the edge of the base.

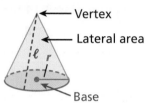

Finding the surface area of a cone is similar to finding the surface area of a pyramid. The distance around the cone's base is the circumference of a circle ($C = 2\pi r$), so you can substitute circumference for perimeter in the surface area formula $S = B + \frac{1}{2}P\ell$.

SURFACE AREA OF A CONE		
The surface area S of a cone is the area of the circular base B plus the lateral area L. The lateral area is π times the radius r times the slant height ℓ.	$S = B + L$ or $S = \pi r^2 + \pi r\ell$	

EXAMPLE 2   Finding the Surface Area of a Cone

Find the surface area of the cone. Use 3.14 for π.

$S = \pi r^2 + \pi r\ell$ *Use the formula.*

$S \approx (3.14)(5^2) + (3.14)(5)(9)$ *Substitute.*

$S \approx 78.5 + 141.3$ *Multiply.*

$S \approx 219.8$ *Add.*

The surface area is about 219.8 square meters.

Think and Discuss

1. Compare the formula for the surface area of a pyramid to the formula for the surface area of a cone.

Learn It Online
Homework Help Online **go.hrw.com**,
keyword MS10 10-5 Go
Exercises 1–8, 9, 11, 13

GUIDED PRACTICE

See Example 1 **Find the surface area of each pyramid.**

1.

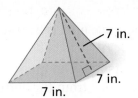

7 in.
7 in.
7 in.

2.

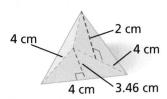

2 cm
4 cm
4 cm
4 cm 3.46 cm

See Example 2 **Find the surface area of each cone. Use 3.14 for π.**

3.

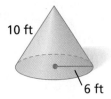

10 ft
6 ft

4.

13 m
10 m

INDEPENDENT PRACTICE

See Example 1 **Find the surface area of each pyramid.**

5.

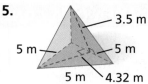

3.5 m
5 m 5 m
5 m 4.32 m

6.

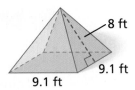

8 ft
9.1 ft
9.1 ft

See Example 2 **Find the surface area of each cone. Use 3.14 for π.**

7.

6 in.
7.5 in.

8.

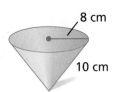

8 cm
10 cm

PRACTICE AND PROBLEM SOLVING

Extra Practice
See page EP26.

9. Construction A roof is in the shape of a square pyramid with 15 ft sides. The slant height of the roof is 14 feet. What is the surface area of the roof? (The base of the pyramid is not part of the roof.)

10. Multi-Step Game pieces are in the shape of regular hexagonal pyramids with base area 1.2 in², perimeter 4 in., and slant height 1 in. What will it cost to paint one game piece if it costs $0.05 to paint one square inch?

Find the surface area of each composite figure. Use 3.14 for π.

11.
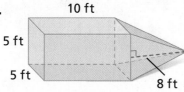
10 ft, 5 ft, 5 ft, 8 ft

12.
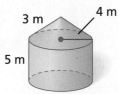
3 m, 4 m, 5 m

13. Multi-Step The surface area of a cone is approximately 282.6 square feet and the radius is 6 feet. Find the length of the slant height in inches. Use 3.14 for π.

14. Estimation A square pyramid has base side lengths of 4.1 m and a slant height of 11.8 m. Estimate the surface area of the pyramid.

15. A *teepee* is a Native American tent that is roughly the shape of a cone. Find the lateral area of the teepee. Use 3.14 for π. Explain how you found your answer.

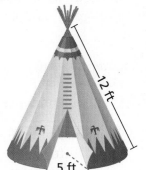
12 ft, 5 ft

? 16. What's the Error? A square pyramid is 3 feet on a side and has slant height of 10 feet. Why does $3 \times 3 + 0.5 \times 9 \times 10$ not give the surface area?

🖉 17. Write About It Explain why the surface area of three-dimensional figures is in square units while the volume of three-dimensional figures is in cubic units.

⭐ 18. Challenge The base of a square pyramid has a perimeter of 36 ft. Its surface area is 171 ft^2. Find the slant height.

Test Prep and Spiral Review

19. Multiple Choice Which expression gives the surface area of a cone with radius 6 ft and slant height 9 ft?

Ⓐ 36π ft^2 Ⓑ 54π ft^2 Ⓒ 90π ft^2 Ⓓ 135π ft^2

20. Extended Response The table shows dimensions of two square pyramids. By how much do the surface areas of these pyramids differ? Explain.

Base area	36 in^2	49 in^2
Perimeter	24 in.	28 in.
Slant height	10 in.	10 in.

Find the missing measurement of each triangle. (Lesson 9-4)

21. $b = 24$ in.

$h = 6.4$ in.

$A = $ ■

22. $b = 120$ ft

$h = $ ■

$A = 2{,}280$ ft^2

23. $b = $ ■

$h = 0.8$ cm

$A = 1.8$ cm^2

Evaluate each expression. (Lesson 9-7)

24. 16^2 **25.** $\sqrt{16}$ **26.** 1.2^2

Explore the Surface Areas of Similar Prisms

Use with Lesson 10-6

Learn It Online
Lab Resources Online **go.hrw.com,**
keyword MS10 Lab10 Go

Recall that the surface area of a three-dimensional figure is the sum of the areas of all of its surfaces. You can use centimeter cubes to explore the surface areas of prisms.

Activity 1

1 Use centimeter cubes to build the rectangular prism shown here.

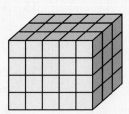

2 You can find the surface area of the prism by first finding the areas of its front face, top face, and side face. Look at the prism from each of these views. Count the exposed cube faces to find the area of each face of the prism. Record the areas in the table.

  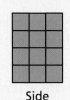

Front   Top   Side

	Front Face	Top Face	Side Face
Area	▦	▦	▦

3 Find the surface area of the prism as follows:
$S = 2 \cdot$ (area of front face) $+ 2 \cdot$ (area of top face) $+ 2 \cdot$ (area of side face)

Think and Discuss

1. Why do you multiply the areas of the front face, top face, and side face by 2 to find the surface area of the prism?

2. What are the length, width, and height of the prism in centimeters? What surface area do you get when you use the formula $S = 2\ell w + 2\ell h + 2wh$?

Try This

Use centimeter cubes to build each prism. Then find its surface area.

1.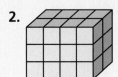

2.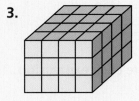

3.

Activity 2

1 Use centimeter cubes to build rectangular prism A as shown.

Prism A

2 Now use centimeter cubes to build a prism B that is similar to prism A by a scale factor of 2. Each dimension of the new prism should be 2 times the corresponding dimension of prism A.

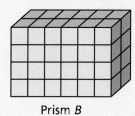
Prism B

3 Use the method from Activity 1 to find the areas of the front face, top face, and side face of each prism. Record the areas in the table.

	Area of Front Face	Area of Top Face	Area of Side Face
Prism A	▪	▪	▪
Prism B	▪	▪	▪

4 Find the surface area of prism A and the surface area of prism B.

5 Repeat the above process, this time building a prism C that is larger than prism A by a scale factor of 3. Add a row to your table for prism C, and find the areas of the front face, top face, and side face of prism C.

Think and Discuss

1. In **4**, how does the surface area of prism B compare with the surface area of prism A? How is this related to the scale factor?

2. In **5**, how does the surface area of prism C compare with the surface area of prism A? How is this related to the scale factor?

3. Suppose three-dimensional figure Y is similar to three-dimensional figure X by a scale factor of k. How are the surface areas related?

Try This

1. Find the surface area of prism R.

2. Prism S is larger than prism R by a scale factor of 4. Use what you discovered to find the surface area of prism S.

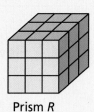
Prism R

TN SPI 0706.4.3 Understand and use scale factor to describe the relationships between length, area, and volume.
Also **GLE 0706.1.7, GLE 0706.4.3,**
✓ **0706.4.3**

Recall that similar figures have proportional side lengths. The surface areas of similar three-dimensional figures are also proportional. To see this relationship, you can compare the areas of corresponding faces of similar rectangular prisms.

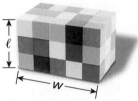

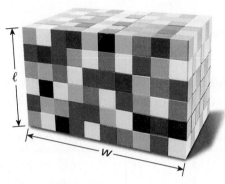

Remember!

A scale factor is a number that every dimension of a figure is multiplied by to make a similar figure.

Area of front of smaller prism

$\ell \cdot w$
$3 \cdot 5$
15

Area of front of larger prism

$\ell \cdot w$
$6 \cdot 10$
$(3 \cdot 2) \cdot (5 \cdot 2)$ ← Each dimension is
$(3 \cdot 5) \cdot (2 \cdot 2)$ multiplied by a scale
$15 \cdot 2^2$ factor of 2.

The area of the front face of the larger prism is 2^2 times the area of the front face of the smaller prism. This is true for the entire surface area of the prisms.

SURFACE AREA OF SIMILAR FIGURES

If three-dimensional figure *B* is similar to figure *A* by a scale factor, then the surface area of *B* is equal to the surface area of *A* times the square of the scale factor.

$$\begin{array}{c} \text{surface area of} \\ \text{figure } B \end{array} = \begin{array}{c} \text{surface area of} \\ \text{figure } A \end{array} \cdot (\text{scale factor})^2$$

E X A M P L E **1** **Finding the Surface Area of a Similar Figure**

A The surface area of a box is 27 in². What is the surface area of a similar box that is larger by a scale factor of 5?

$S = 27 \cdot 5^2$ *Multiply by the square of the scale factor.*
$S = 27 \cdot 25$ *Evaluate the power.*
$S = 675 \text{ in}^2$ *Multiply.*

B The surface area of the Great Pyramid was originally 1,160,280 ft². What is the surface area, to the nearest tenth, of a model of the pyramid that is smaller by a scale factor of $\frac{1}{500}$?

$S = 1,160,280 \cdot \left(\frac{1}{500}\right)^2$ *Multiply by the square of the scale factor.*

$S = 1,160,280 \cdot \frac{1}{250,000}$ *Evaluate the power.*

$S = 4.64112$ *Multiply.*

$S \approx 4.6 \text{ ft}^2$

The volumes of similar three-dimensional figures are also related.

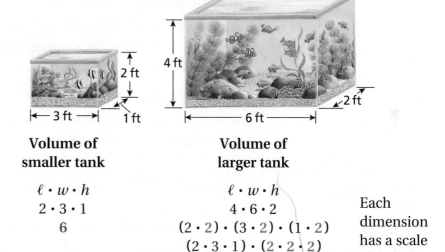

Volume of smaller tank	Volume of larger tank	
$\ell \cdot w \cdot h$	$\ell \cdot w \cdot h$	Each dimension has a scale factor of 2.
$2 \cdot 3 \cdot 1$	$4 \cdot 6 \cdot 2$	
6	$(2 \cdot 2) \cdot (3 \cdot 2) \cdot (1 \cdot 2)$	
	$(2 \cdot 3 \cdot 1) \cdot (2 \cdot 2 \cdot 2)$	
	$6 \cdot 2^3$	

Remember!

$2 \cdot 2 \cdot 2 = 2^3$

The volume of the larger tank is 2^3 times the volume of the smaller tank.

VOLUME OF SIMILAR FIGURES

If three-dimensional figure *B* is similar to figure *A* by a scale factor, then the volume of *B* is equal to the volume of *A* times the cube of the scale factor.

volume of figure *B* = volume of figure *A* · (scale factor)³

EXAMPLE **2** **Finding Volume Using Similar Figures**

The volume of a bucket is 231 in³. What is the volume of a similar bucket that is larger by a scale factor of 3?

$V = 231 \cdot 3^3$ *Multiply by the cube of the scale factor.*

$V = 231 \cdot 27$ *Evaluate the power.*

$V = 6,237 \text{ in}^3$ *Multiply.*

Estimate $V \approx 230 \cdot 30$ *Round the measurements.*

$= 6,900 \text{ in}^3$ *The answer is reasonable.*

EXAMPLE 3 PROBLEM SOLVING APPLICATION

PROBLEM SOLVING

Elise has a fish tank that measures 10 in. by 23 in. by 5 in. She builds a larger tank by doubling each dimension. There are 231 in^3 in 1 gallon. Estimate how many more gallons the larger tank holds.

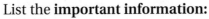

1 Understand the Problem

Rewrite the question as a statement.

- Compare the capacities of two similar fish tanks, and estimate how much more water the larger tank holds.

List the **important information:**

- The small tank is 10 in. × 23 in. × 5 in.
- The large tank is similar to the small tank by a scale factor of 2.
- 231 in^3 = 1 gal

2 Make a Plan

You can write an equation that relates the volume of the large tank to the volume of the small tank. Volume of large tank = Volume of small tank · (scale factor)^3. Then convert cubic inches to gallons to compare the capacities of the tanks.

3 Solve

Volume of small tank = 10 × 23 × 5 = 1,150 in^3

Volume of large tank = 1,150 · 2^3 = 9,200 in^3

Convert each volume into gallons:

$1,150 \text{ in}^3 \times \frac{1 \text{ gal}}{231 \text{ in}^3} \approx 5 \text{ gal}$ $9,200 \text{ in}^3 \times \frac{1 \text{ gal}}{231 \text{ in}^3} \approx 40 \text{ gal}$

Subtract the capacities: 40 gal − 5 gal = 35 gal

The large tank holds about 35 gallons more water than the small tank.

4 Look Back

Double the dimensions of the small tank and find the volume: 20 × 46 × 10 = 9,200 in^3. Subtract the volumes of the two tanks: 9,200 − 1,150 = 8,050 in^3. Convert this measurement to gallons: $8,050 \text{ in}^3 \times \frac{1 \text{ gal}}{231 \text{ in}^3} \approx 35 \text{ gal.}$

Think and Discuss

1. **Tell** whether a figure's surface area has increased or decreased if each dimension of the figure is changed by a factor of $\frac{1}{3}$.

2. **Explain** how the surface area of a figure is changed if the dimensions are each multiplied by a factor of 3.

3. **Explain** how the volume of a figure is changed if the dimensions are each multiplied by a factor of 2.

10-6

Exercises

Learn It Online
Homework Help Online **go.hrw.com**,
keyword MS10 10-6   Go
Exercises 1–8, 9, 11, 13, 15, 17

GUIDED PRACTICE

See Example **1**

1. The surface area of a box is 10.4 cm². What is the surface area of a similar box that is larger by a scale factor of 3?

2. The surface area of a ship's hull is about 11,000 m². What is the surface area, to the nearest tenth, of the hull of a model ship that is smaller by a scale factor of $\frac{1}{150}$?

See Example **2**

3. The volume of an ice chest is 2,160 in³. What is the volume of a similar ice chest that is larger by a scale factor of 2.5?

See Example **3**

4. A fish tank measures 14 in. by 13 in. by 10 in. A similar fish tank is larger by a scale factor of 3. Estimate how many more gallons the larger tank holds.

INDEPENDENT PRACTICE

See Example **1**

5. The surface area of a triangular prism is 13.99 in². What is the surface area of a similar prism that is larger by a scale factor of 4?

6. The surface area of a car frame is about 200 ft². What is the surface area, to the nearest tenth of a square foot, of a model of the car that is smaller by a scale factor of $\frac{1}{12}$?

See Example **2**

7. The volume of a cylinder is about 523 cm³. What is the volume, to the nearest tenth, of a similar cylinder that is smaller by a scale factor of $\frac{1}{4}$?

See Example **3**

8. A tank measures 27 in. by 9 in. by 12 in. A similar tank is reduced by a scale factor of $\frac{1}{3}$. Estimate how many more gallons the larger tank holds.

PRACTICE AND PROBLEM SOLVING

Extra Practice
See page EP26.

For each figure shown, find the surface area and volume of a similar figure that is larger by a scale factor of 25. Use 3.14 for π.

9.

5 ft
4 ft
3 ft

10.
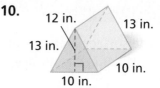
12 in.
13 in.
13 in.
10 in.
10 in.

11.
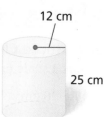
12 cm
25 cm

12. The surface area of a cylinder is 1,620 m². Its volume is about 1,130 m³. What are the surface area and volume of a similar cylinder that is smaller by a scale factor of $\frac{1}{9}$? Round to the nearest tenth, if necessary.

13. The surface area of a prism is 142 in². Its volume is about 105 in³. What are the surface area and volume of a similar prism that is larger by a scale factor of 6? Round to the nearest tenth, if necessary.

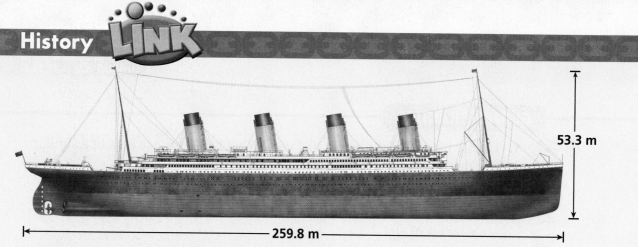

53.3 m

259.8 m

Natalie and Rebecca are making a scale model of the *Titanic* for a history class project. Their model is smaller by a scale factor of $\frac{1}{100}$. For Exercises 14–17, express your answers in both centimeters and meters. Use the conversion chart at right if needed.

METRIC CONVERSIONS	
1 m = 100 cm	1 cm = 0.01 m
1 m² = 10,000 cm²	1 cm² = 0.0001 m²
1 m³ = 1,000,000 cm³	1 cm³ = 0.000001 m³

14. The length and height of the *Titanic* are shown in the drawing above. What are the length and height of the students' scale model?

15. On the students' model, the diameter of the outer propellers is 7.16 cm. What was the diameter of these propellers on the ship?

16. The surface area of the deck of the students' model is 4,156.75 cm². What was the surface area of the deck of the ship?

17. The volume of the students' model is about 127,426 cm³. What was the volume of the ship?

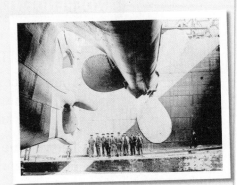

Test Prep and Spiral Review

18. **Multiple Choice** The surface area of a prism is 144 cm². A similar prism has a scale factor of $\frac{1}{4}$. What is the surface area of the similar prism?

  (A) 36 cm²   (B) 18 cm²   (C) 9 cm²   (D) 2.25 cm²

19. **Gridded Response** A cube has a volume of 64 in³. A similar cube has a volume of 512 in³. What is the scale factor of the larger cube?

Determine whether the ratios are proportional. (Lesson 4-3)

20. $\frac{7}{56}, \frac{35}{280}$ 21. $\frac{12}{20}, \frac{60}{140}$ 22. $\frac{9}{45}, \frac{45}{225}$ 23. $\frac{5}{82}, \frac{65}{1,054}$

24. Name the polygon that has ten angles and ten sides. (Lesson 8-5)

Explore Changes in Dimensions

Learn It Online
Lab Resources Online **go.hrw.com**,
keyword MS10 Lab10 Go

TN SPI 0706.4.3 Understand
and use scale factor to describe the
relationships between length, area,
and volume.
Also **GLE 0706.1.8, GLE 0706.4.3,**
✓ **0706.4.3**

You can use a spreadsheet to explore how changing the dimensions of a rectangular pyramid affects the volume of the pyramid.

Activity

① On a spreadsheet, enter the following headings:
Base Length in cell A1,
Base Width in cell B1,
Height in cell C1, and
Volume in cell D1.

In row 2, enter the numbers 15, 7, and 22, as shown.

② Then enter the formula for the volume of a pyramid in cell D2. To do this, enter
=(1/3)*A2*B2*C2. Press **ENTER** and notice that the volume is 770.

③ Enter 30 in cell A2 and 11 in cell C2 to find out what happens to the volume when you double the base length and halve the height.

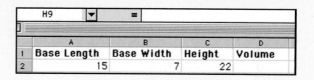

	A	B	C	D
1	Base Length	Base Width	Height	Volume
2	15	7	22	

	A	B	C	D	E
1	Base Length	Base Width	Height	Volume	
2	15	7	22	=(1/3)*A2*B2*C2	

	A	B	C	D
1	Base Length	Base Width	Height	Volume
2	30	7	11	770

Think and Discuss

1. Explain why doubling the base length and halving the height does not change the volume of the pyramid.

2. What other ways could you change the dimensions of the pyramid without changing its volume?

Try This

1. Use a spreadsheet to compute the volume of each cone. Use 3.14 for π.

   a. radius = 2.75 inches; height = 8.5 inches

   b. radius = 7.5 inches; height = 14.5 inches

2. What would the volumes in problem 1 be if the radii were doubled?

Quiz for Lessons 10-4 Through 10-6

✓ **10-4 Surface Area of Prisms and Cylinders**

Find the surface area of each figure to the nearest tenth. Use 3.14 for π.

1.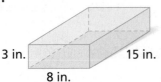
3 in. 15 in.
8 in.

2.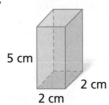
5 cm
2 cm
2 cm

3.
7 in.
15 in.

4. What is the surface area of the composite figure? Use 3.14 for π. Round your answer to the nearest tenth.

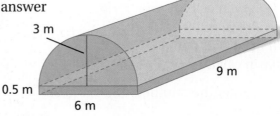
3 m
0.5 m
6 m
9 m

✓ **10-5 Surface Area of Pyramids and Cones**

Find the surface area of each figure. Use 3.14 for π.

5.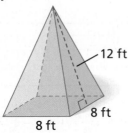
12 ft
8 ft
8 ft

6.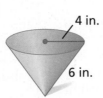
4 in.
6 in.

7.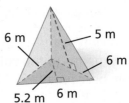
6 m   5 m
6 m
5.2 m 6 m

✓ **10-6 Changing Dimensions**

8. The surface area of a rectangular prism is 45 ft². What is the surface area of a similar prism that is larger by a scale factor of 3?

9. The surface area of a cylinder is 109 cm². What is the surface area of a similar cylinder that is smaller by a scale factor of $\frac{1}{3}$?

10. The volume of a container is 3,785 in³. A second container is larger by a scale factor of 4. Estimate how many more gallons the larger container holds. (*Hint:* There are 231 in³ in 1 gallon.)

Ready to Go On?

Bluegrass Balloon Festival The annual Bluegrass Balloon Festival in Louisville features more than 90 hot-air balloons. Although most of the balloons have the familiar teardrop shape, it's not unusual to see a balloon in the shape of a cow, a tree, or a teapot.

KENTUCKY

Louisville

1. A balloon manufacturer is making the Birthday Cake balloon shown in the table. How much material is needed to make the balloon? Use 3.14 for π, and round your answer to the nearest square foot.

2. The amount of hot air that a balloon can hold is related to the volume of the balloon. Find the volume of the U.S. Flag balloon.

3. Which of the balloons listed in the table can hold the greatest amount of air? Why?

4. A balloon manufacturer is considering making a larger U.S. Flag balloon by doubling each of the dimensions shown in the table.

    a. How does the amount of material needed for the larger balloon compare to the amount needed for the balloon in the table?

    b. How does the amount of hot air needed to fill the larger balloon compare to the amount needed for the balloon in the table?

Special-Shaped Balloons		
Balloon	**Shape**	**Dimensions**
Birthday Cake	Cylinder	Height: 80 ft Diameter: 71 ft
U.S. Flag	Rectangular Prism	Height: 53 ft Length: 78 ft Width: 29 ft
Lighthouse	Cone	Height: 115 ft Diameter: 53 ft

Real-World Connections

Game Time

Blooming Minds

Students in the Agriculture Club at Carter Middle School are designing a flower bed for the front of the school. The flower bed will be in the shape of the letter *C*. After considering the two designs shown below, the students decided to build the flower bed that required the least amount of peat moss. Which design did the students choose? (*Hint:* Find the volume of each flower bed.)

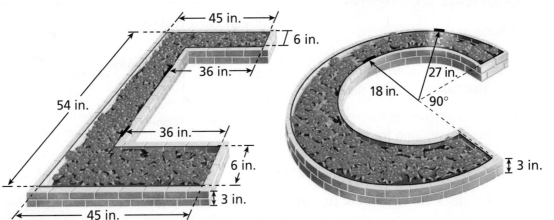

Magic Cubes

Four magic cubes are used in this fun puzzle. A complete set of rules and nets for making the cubes can be found online. Each side of the four cubes has the number 1, 2, 3, or 4 written on it. The object of the game is to stack the cubes so that the numbers along each side of the stack add up to 10. No number can be repeated along any side of the stack.

Learn It Online
Game Time Extra **go.hrw.com**,
keyword MS10 Games **Go**

Materials
- 5 CD envelopes
- hole punch
- chenille stem
- 5 sheets of white paper
- CD
- scissors
- markers

It's in the Bag!

PROJECT CD 3-D

Make a set of circular booklets that you can store in CD envelopes.

1 Stack the CD envelopes so that the flap of each envelope is in the back, along the right-hand edge. Punch a hole through the stack in the upper left-hand corner. **Figure A**

2 Insert a chenille stem through the holes, twist to make a loop, and trim the ends. **Figure B**

3 Fold a sheet of white $8\frac{1}{2}$-by-11-inch paper in half to make a sheet that is $8\frac{1}{2}$ inches by $5\frac{1}{2}$ inches. Place the CD on the folded sheet so that it touches the folded edge, and trace around it. **Figure C**

4 Cut out the circular shape that you traced, making sure that the two halves remain hinged together. **Figure D**

5 Repeat the process with the remaining sheets of paper to make a total of five booklets.

Taking Note of the Math

Use each booklet to takes notes on one lesson of the chapter. Be sure to record essential vocabulary, formulas, and sample problems.

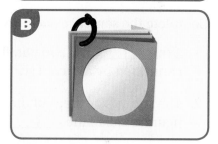

A

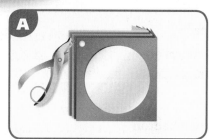

B

C

D

INTRODUCTION TO THREE DIMENSIONAL FIGURES

Vocabulary

base	588	prism	588
cone	589	pyramid	588
cylinder	589	regular pyramid	614
edge	588	slant height of a cone	615
face	588	slant height of a pyramid	614
lateral area	607	sphere	589
lateral face	607	surface area	607
net	607	vertex	588
polyhedron	588	volume	596

Complete the sentences below with vocabulary words from the list above.

1. A(n) ___?___ has two parallel, congruent circular bases connected by a curved surface.

2. The sum of the areas of the surfaces of a three-dimensional figure is called the ___?___.

3. A(n) ___?___ is a three-dimensional figure whose faces are all polygons.

4. A(n) ___?___ has one circular base and a curved surface.

EXAMPLES

EXERCISES

10-1 **Introduction to Three-Dimensional Figures** (pp. 588–591)

■ **Name the figure.**

There are two bases that are hexagons.

The figure is a hexagonal prism.

Name each figure.

5.

6.

7.

8.

10-2 Volume of Prisms and Cylinders (pp. 596–599)

■ Find the volume of the cylinder to the nearest tenth. Use 3.14 for π.

$V = \pi r^2 h$
$V \approx 3.14 \cdot 3^2 \cdot 4$
$V \approx 113.04$
The volume is about 113.0 cm³.

3 cm
4 cm

Find the volume of each figure to the nearest tenth. Use 3.14 for π.

9.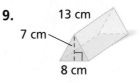
13 cm
7 cm
8 cm

10.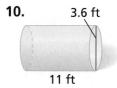
3.6 ft
11 ft

10-3 Volume of Pyramids and Cones (pp. 600–603)

■ Find the volume of the pyramid.

$V = \frac{1}{3}Bh$
$V = \frac{1}{3} \cdot (5 \cdot 6) \cdot 7$
$V = 70$
The volume is 70 m³.

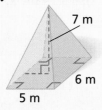
7 m
6 m
5 m

Find the volume of each figure to the nearest tenth. Use 3.14 for π.

11.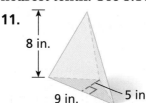
8 in.
9 in.   5 in.

12.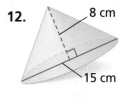
8 cm
15 cm

10-4 Surface Area of Prisms and Cylinders (pp. 607–611)

■ Find the surface area of the rectangular prism.

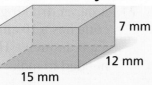
7 mm
12 mm
15 mm

$S = 2B + Ph$
$S = 2(12)(15) + (54)(7)$
$S = 738$
The surface area is 738 mm².

Find the surface area of each rectangular prism.

13.
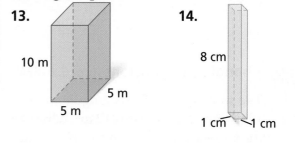
10 m
5 m
5 m

14.
8 cm
1 cm   1 cm

■ Find the surface area of the cylinder to the nearest tenth. Use 3.14 for π.

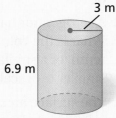
3 m
6.9 m

$S = 2\pi r^2 + 2\pi rh$
$S \approx (2 \cdot 3.14 \cdot 3^2) + (2 \cdot 3.14 \cdot 3 \cdot 6.9)$
$S \approx 186.516$
The surface area is about 186.5 m².

Find the surface area of each cylinder to the nearest tenth. Use 3.14 for π.

15.
2.4 cm
15 cm

16.
16 ft
8 ft

Study Guide: Review

10-5 **Surface Area of Pyramids and Cones** (pp. 614–617)

■ Find the surface area of the pyramid.

$$S = B + \frac{1}{2}P\ell$$
$$S = \ell w + \frac{1}{2}P\ell$$
$$S = (6)(6) + \frac{1}{2}(24)(15)$$
$$S = 36 + 180$$
$$S = 216$$

The area is 216 m².

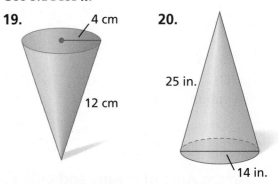

15 m

6 m
6 m

Find the surface area of each pyramid.

17.

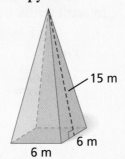

5 ft
4 ft
4 ft
4 ft   3.5 ft

18.

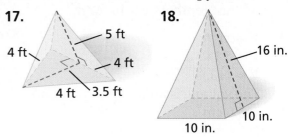

16 in.

10 in.
10 in.

■ Find the surface area of the cone. Use 3.14 for π.

$$S = \pi r^2 + \pi r\ell$$
$$S \approx (3.14 \cdot 3^2) + (3.14 \cdot 3 \cdot 10)$$
$$S \approx 28.26 + 94.2$$
$$S \approx 122.46$$

The area is about 122.46 ft².

10 ft

3 ft

Find the surface area of each cone. Use 3.14 for π.

19.

4 cm

12 cm

20.

25 in.

14 in.

21. A paper drinking cup shaped like a cone has a 10 cm slant height and an 8 cm diameter. How much paper is needed to make the cup? Use 3.14 for π.

10-6 **Changing Dimensions** (pp. 620–624)

■ The surface area of a rectangular prism is 32 m², and its volume is 12 m³. What are the surface area and volume of a similar rectangular prism that is larger by a scale factor of 6?

$S = 32 \cdot 6^2$ *Square the scale factor.*
$\quad = 1{,}152$

The surface area of the larger prism is 1,152 m².

$V = 12 \cdot 6^3$ *Cube the scale factor.*
$\quad = 2{,}592$

The volume of the larger prism is 2,592 m³.

22. A cylinder has a surface area of 13.2 in². What is the surface area of a similar cylinder that is larger by a scale factor of 15?

23. A refrigerator has a volume of 14 ft³. What is the volume, to the nearest tenth, of a similar refrigerator that is smaller by a scale factor of $\frac{2}{3}$?

24. The surface area of a model building is 2,776 in². The actual building will be larger by a scale factor of 48. Find the surface area of the actual building in square feet. (Hint: 1 ft² = 144 in²)

Study Guide: Review

Chapter Test

Classify each figure as a polyhedron or not a polyhedron. Then name the figure.

1.

2.

3.

Find the volume of each figure to the nearest tenth. Use 3.14 for π.

4.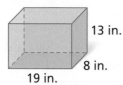
13 in. 15 in. 24 in.

5.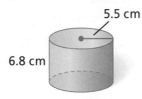
7 m 8.4 m

6.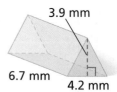
3.9 mm 6.7 mm 4.2 mm

7.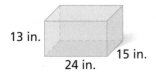
12 ft 13 ft 18 ft

8.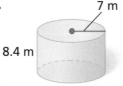
15 cm 5.6 cm

9.
1.2 in. 3 in. 2 in. 4 in. 4 in.

Find the surface area of each figure to the nearest tenth. Use 3.14 for π.

10.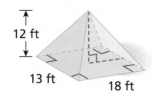
13 in. 8 in. 19 in.

11.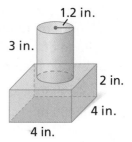
5.5 cm 6.8 cm

12.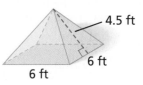
4.5 ft 6 ft 6 ft

13.
8 m 8 m

14.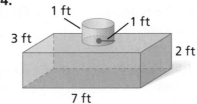
1 ft 1 ft 3 ft 2 ft 7 ft

15.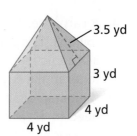
3.5 yd 3 yd 4 yd 4 yd

16. The surface area of a rectangular prism is 52 ft². What is the surface area of a similar prism that is larger by a scale factor of 7?

17. The volume of a cube is 35 mm³. What is the volume of a similar cube that is larger by a scale factor of 9?

CHAPTER 10

Cumulative Assessment, Chapters 1–10

Multiple Choice

1. What value represents the median of the data set?

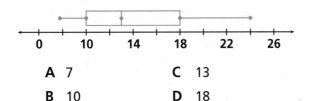

  A 7 **C** 13
  B 10 **D** 18

2. A rectangular tank has a height of 9 meters, a width of 5 meters, and a length of 12 meters. What is the volume of a similar tank that is larger by a scale factor of 4?

  F 2,160 m^3 **H** 34,560 m^3
  G 6,480 m^2 **J** 43,740 m^2

3. Clay jumps rope at an average rate of 75 jumps per minute. How long does it take him to make 405 jumps if he does not stop?

  A 5 min **C** $5\frac{2}{5}$ min
  B $5\frac{1}{10}$ min **D** $5\frac{5}{6}$ min

4. A carpenter has made a cube-shaped toy box. The cube has a volume of 343 cubic feet. If the carpenter wants to wrap the toy box to ship it, what is the minimum amount of paper he will need to cover all six faces?

  F 49 ft^2 **H** 725 ft^2
  G 294 ft^2 **J** 2,058 ft^2

5. Which ratios form a proportion?

  A $\frac{4}{8}$ and $\frac{3}{6}$
  B $\frac{4}{12}$ and $\frac{6}{15}$
  C $\frac{4}{10}$ and $\frac{6}{16}$
  D $\frac{2}{3}$ and $\frac{5}{8}$

6. Explain why the triangles are similar. What is the side length of $\overline{EG}$?

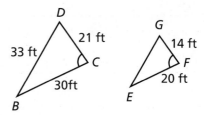

  F SAS; 21 ft **H** AA; 24 ft
  G SSS; 20.5 ft **J** SAS; 22 ft

7. Which set of ordered pairs does **not** represent a function?

  A {(1, 2), (3, 4), (5, 6), (7, 8)}
  B {(1, −2), (2, 3), (3, 4), (4, −2)}
  C {(0, −5), (3, 10), (5, −5), (6, 10)}
  D {(−3, 4), (1, 2), (2, 6), (1, 8)}

8. At approximately what point on the number line would you find the cube root of 100?

  F 2.4 **H** 10
  G 4.6 **J** 33.3

9. Which table shows the same relationship as the graph?

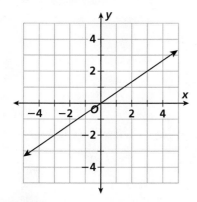

A

x	0	2	4	6	8
y	1	2	3	4	5

B

x	−1	0	1	2	3
y	−3	−2	−1	0	1

C

x	−3	0	3	6	9
y	−2	0	2	4	6

D

x	0	2	4	6	8
y	−2	0	2	4	6

 HOT TIP! Make sure you use the correct units of measure in your responses. Area has square units, and volume has cubic units.

10. The legs of a right triangle measure 9 units and 12 units. How many units long is the hypotenuse?

F 15 units

G 15 square units

H 15 cubic units

J 108 square units

11. Ali is mixing up a punch that calls for 1 cup pineapple juice for every 4 cups of sparkling water. If Ali wants to use 5 cups pineapple juice, how much sparkling water does she need?

A 9 cups **C** 22 cups

B 20 cups **D** 25 cups

Process Standards Practice
Short Response

S1. The surface area of a cylinder is 66 ft².

  a. Find the surface area of a larger similar cylinder with a scale factor of 4.

  b. Explain how the surface area changes when the dimensions are decreased by a factor of $\frac{1}{4}$.

S2. A polyhedron has two parallel square bases with edges 9 meters long and a height of 9 meters. Identify the figure and find its volume. Show your work.

S3. What is the base length of a parallelogram with a height of 8 in. and an area of 56 in²?

Extended Response

E1. Use the figure for the following problems. Round your answers to the nearest hundredth, if necessary. Use 3.14 for π.

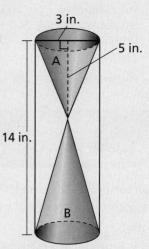

  a. What three-dimensional shapes make up the sculpture?

  b. What is the combined volume of figures A and B? Show your work.

  c. What is the volume of the space surrounding figures A and B? Show your work and explain your answer.

Why Learn This?

You can use probability to determine how likely a soccer player is to make a goal.

 Learn It Online
Chapter Project Online **go.hrw.com**,
keyword MS10 Ch11   Go

 Chapter Focus
- Understand the meaning of theoretical probability.
- Use probability and proportions to make approximate predictions.

Are You Ready?

Learn It Online
Resources Online **go.hrw.com,**
keyword MS10 Ch11 Go

☑ Vocabulary

Choose the best term from the list to complete each sentence.

1. A(n) __?__ is a comparison of two quantities by division.

2. A(n) __?__ is an integer that is divisible by 2.

3. A(n) __?__ is a ratio that compares a number to 100.

4. A(n) __?__ is a number greater than 1 that has more than two whole number factors.

5. A(n) __?__ is an integer that is not divisible by 2.

composite
  number

even number

odd number

percent

prime number

ratio

Complete these exercises to review skills you will need for this chapter.

☑ Simplify Fractions

Write each fraction in simplest form.

6. $\frac{6}{9}$ 7. $\frac{12}{15}$ 8. $\frac{8}{10}$ 9. $\frac{20}{24}$

10. $\frac{2}{4}$ 11. $\frac{7}{35}$ 12. $\frac{12}{22}$ 13. $\frac{72}{81}$

☑ Write Fractions as Decimals

Write each fraction as a decimal.

14. $\frac{3}{5}$ 15. $\frac{9}{20}$ 16. $\frac{57}{100}$ 17. $\frac{12}{25}$

18. $\frac{3}{25}$ 19. $\frac{1}{2}$ 20. $\frac{7}{10}$ 21. $\frac{9}{5}$

☑ Percents and Decimals

Write each decimal as a percent.

22. 0.14   23. 0.08   24. 0.75   25. 0.38

26. 0.27   27. 1.89   28. 0.234   29. 0.0025

☑ Multiply Fractions

Multiply. Write each answer in simplest form.

30. $\frac{1}{2} \cdot \frac{1}{4}$ 31. $\frac{2}{3} \cdot \frac{3}{5}$ 32. $\frac{3}{10} \cdot \frac{1}{2}$ 33. $\frac{5}{6} \cdot \frac{3}{4}$

34. $\frac{5}{14} \cdot \frac{7}{17}$ 35. $-\frac{1}{8} \cdot \frac{3}{8}$ 36. $-\frac{2}{15} \cdot \left(-\frac{2}{3}\right)$ 37. $\frac{1}{4} \cdot \left(-\frac{1}{6}\right)$

Where You've Been

Previously, you

- found experimental and theoretical probabilities of compound events.

- used organized lists and tree diagrams to find the sample space of an experiment.

- found the probability that an outcome will not occur.

In This Chapter

You will study

- finding experimental and theoretical probabilities, including those of dependent and independent events.

- using lists and tree diagrams to find combinations and all possible outcomes of an experiment.

- using the Fundamental Counting Principle and factorials to find permutations.

Where You're Going

You can use the skills learned in this chapter

- to determine the effect of chance in games that you play.

- to predict the outcome in situations involving sports and weather.

Key Vocabulary/Vocabulario

combination	combinación
dependent events	sucesos dependientes
event	suceso
experiment	experimento
experimental probability	probabilidad experimental
independent events	sucesos independientes
outcome	resultado
probability	probabilidad
sample space	espacio muestral
theoretical probability	probabilidad teórica

Vocabulary Connections

To become familiar with some of the vocabulary terms in the chapter, consider the following. You may refer to the chapter, the glossary, or a dictionary if you like.

1. An *experiment* is an action done to find out something you do not know. Why can we call flipping a coin, rolling a number cube, or spinning a spinner an **experiment**?

2. Several outcomes, or sometimes just one outcome, make up an *event*. For example, rolling an even number and choosing a challenge card can make up an event in a board game. What is another **event** that can occur when you play board games?

3. The word *depend* comes from the Latin word *dependēre*, meaning "to hang or to be attached." How might the probabilities of **dependent events** be linked?

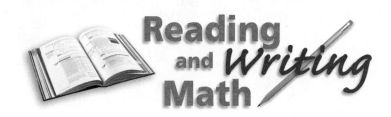 **Reading** and **Writing Math**

TN English/Language Arts
GLE 0701.6.1 Comprehend and summarize the main ideas and supporting details of informational texts.

Reading Strategy: Read Problems for Understanding

To best understand a word problem, read it once to note what concept is being reviewed. Then read the problem again, slowly and carefully, to identify what the problem is asking. As you read, highlight the key information. When dealing with a multi-step problem, break the problem into parts and then make a plan to solve it.

> **23. Architecture** The steeple on a building is a square pyramid with base area 12 square feet and height 15 feet. How many cubic feet of concrete was used to make the pyramid?

Step	Question	Answer
Step 1	What concept is being reviewed?	• finding the volume of a pyramid
Step 2	What are you being asked to do?	• Find the number of cubic feet of concrete used to make the steeple.
Step 3	What is the key information needed to solve the problem?	• The steeple is a square pyramid. • The base area of the pyramid is 12 square feet. • The height of the pyramid is 15 feet.
Step 4	What is my plan to solve this multi-part problem?	• Use the formula for finding the volume of a pyramid: $V = \frac{1}{3}Bh$. • Substitute the values for the base area and the height into the formula. • Solve for V.

Try This

For each problem, complete each step in the four-step method described above.

1. Which has a greater volume: a square pyramid with a height of 15 feet and a base with a side length of 3 feet or a cube with a side length of 4 feet?

2. At a party, each child receives the same number of party favors. There are 16 kazoos, 24 snappers, 8 hats, and 32 pieces of gum. What is the greatest number of children that may be at the party?

Probability

TN GLE 0706.5.5 Understand and apply basic concepts of probability.

An activity involving chance, such as rolling a number cube, is called an **experiment**. Each repetition or observation of an experiment is a **trial**, and each result is an **outcome**. A set of one or more outcomes is an **event**. For example, rolling a 5 (one outcome) can be an event, or rolling an even number (more than one outcome) can be an event.

Vocabulary

experiment

trial

outcome

event

probability

simple event

compound event

complement

Interactivities Online ▶

The **probability** of an event, written P(event), is the measure of how likely the event is to occur. A **simple event** has a single outcome. A **compound event** is two or more simple events. Probability is a measure between 0 and 1, as shown on the number line. You can write probability as a fraction, a decimal, or a percent.

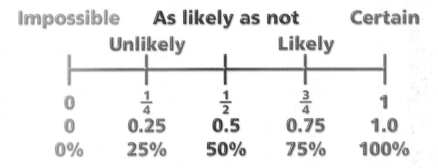

Impossible		As likely as not		Certain
	Unlikely		Likely	
0	$\frac{1}{4}$	$\frac{1}{2}$	$\frac{3}{4}$	1
0	0.25	0.5	0.75	1.0
0%	25%	50%	75%	100%

EXAMPLE 1 **Determining the Likelihood of an Event**

Determine whether each event is impossible, unlikely, as likely as not, likely, or certain.

A rolling an even number on a number cube

There are 6 possible outcomes:

Even	*Not* Even
2, 4, 6	1, 3, 5

Half of the outcomes are even.

Rolling an even number is as likely as not.

B rolling a 5 on a number cube

There are 6 possible outcomes:

5	*Not* 5
5	1, 2, 3, 4, 6

Only one outcome is a five.

Rolling a 5 is unlikely.

Video **Lesson Tutorials Online** my.hrw.com

When a number cube is rolled, either a 5 will be rolled or it will not. Rolling a 5 and not rolling a 5 are examples of *complementary events*. The **complement** of an event is the set of all outcomes that are *not* the event.

Because it is certain that either an event or its complement will occur when an activity is performed, the sum of the probabilities is 1.

$$P(\text{event}) + P(\text{complement}) = 1$$

EXAMPLE 2 Using Complements

A bag contains 6 blue marbles, 6 red marbles, 3 green marbles, and 1 yellow marble. The probability of randomly drawing a red marble is $\frac{3}{8}$. What is the probability of not drawing a red marble?

$$P(\text{event}) + P(\text{complement}) = 1$$
$$P(\text{red}) + P(\text{not red}) = 1$$
$$\frac{3}{8} + P(\text{not red}) = 1 \qquad \text{Substitute } \frac{3}{8} \text{ for P(red).}$$
$$\underline{-\frac{3}{8} \qquad\qquad\qquad -\frac{3}{8}} \qquad \text{Subtract } \frac{3}{8} \text{ from both sides.}$$
$$P(\text{not red}) = \frac{5}{8} \qquad \text{Simplify.}$$

The probability of not drawing a red marble is $\frac{5}{8}$.

EXAMPLE 3 *School Application*

Eric's math teacher almost always gives a pop quiz if the class did not ask many questions during the lesson on the previous class day. If it is Monday and no one asked questions during class on Friday, should Eric expect a pop quiz? Explain.

Since Eric's teacher often gives quizzes on days after few questions were asked, a quiz on Monday is likely.

Think and Discuss

1. Describe an event that has a probability of 0% and an event that has a probability of 100%.

2. Give an example of a real-world compound event.

3. Give an example of a real-world event and its complement.

GUIDED PRACTICE

See Example 1 Determine whether each event is impossible, unlikely, as likely as not, likely, or certain.

1. rolling a number greater than 5 with a number cube

2. drawing a blue marble from a bag of black and white marbles

See Example 2 **3.** A bag contains 8 purple beads, 2 blue beads, and 2 pink beads. The probability of randomly drawing a pink bead is $\frac{1}{6}$. What is the probability of not drawing a pink bead?

See Example 3 **4.** Natalie almost always sleeps in on Saturday mornings when she does not have to work. If it is Saturday morning and Natalie does not have to work, how likely is it that Natalie will sleep in?

INDEPENDENT PRACTICE

See Example 1 Determine whether each event is impossible, unlikely, as likely as not, likely, or certain.

5. randomly drawing a red or pink card from a deck of red and pink cards

6. flipping a coin and getting tails

7. rolling a 6 on a number cube five times in a row

See Example 2 **8.** The probability of rolling a 5 or 6 with a number cube is $\frac{1}{3}$. What is the probability of not rolling a 5 or 6?

9. The probability of randomly drawing a green marble from a bag of green, red, and blue marbles is $\frac{3}{5}$. What is the probability of randomly drawing a red or blue marble?

See Example 3 **10.** Tim rarely spends more than 30 minutes watching TV in the afternoon. If Tim began watching TV at 4:00 P.M., would you expect that he is still watching TV at 5:00 P.M.? Explain.

PRACTICE AND PROBLEM SOLVING

Extra Practice
See page EP27.

A bag contains 12 red checkers and 12 black checkers. Determine whether each event is impossible, unlikely, as likely as not, likely, or certain.

11. randomly drawing a red checker

12. randomly drawing a white checker

13. randomly drawing a red or black checker

14. randomly drawing a black checker

15. Exercise Luka almost always jogs in the afternoon when the weather is not cold or rainy. The sky is cloudy and the temperature is 41°F. How likely is it that Luka will jog this afternoon?

16. Life Science A researcher's garden contains 900 sweet pea plants. More than 700 of the plants have purple flowers and about 200 have white flowers. Would you expect that one plant randomly selected from the garden will have purple or white flowers? Explain.

17. Life Science Sharks belong to a class of fishes that have skeletons made of cartilage. Bony fishes, which account for 95% of all species of fish, have skeletons made of bone.

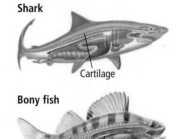

Shark

Cartilage

Bony fish

Bone   Swim bladder

   a. How likely is it that a fish you cannot identify at a pet store is a bony fish? Explain.

   b. Only bony fishes have swim bladders, which keep them from sinking. How likely is it that a shark has a swim bladder? Explain.

18. Earth Science The graph shows the carbon dioxide levels in the atmosphere from 1970 to 2000. How likely is it that the level of carbon dioxide fell from 2000 to 2010? Explain.

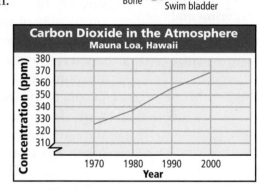

19. Write a Problem Describe an event that involves rolling a number cube. Determine the likelihood that the event will occur.

20. Write About It Explain how to tell whether an event is as likely as not.

21. Challenge A bag contains 10 red marbles and 8 blue marbles, all the same size and weight. Keiko randomly draws 2 red marbles from the bag and does not replace them. Will Keiko be more likely to draw a red marble than a blue marble on her next draw? Explain.

Test Prep and Spiral Review

22. Multiple Choice Which percent best shows the probability that Kito will randomly draw an even number from five cards numbered 2, 4, 6, 8, and 10?

   (A) 75%   (B) 25%   (C) 50%   (D) 100%

23. Gridded Response The probability of rolling a 1, 2, or 3 on a number cube is $\frac{1}{2}$. What is the probability of NOT rolling a 1, 2, or 3?

24. Short Response Describe an event that is likely to happen.

25. One of the largest lobsters ever caught weighed $44\frac{3}{8}$ lb. Estimate how much more this lobster weighed than an average 3 lb lobster. (Lesson 3-6)

26. The sales tax on a $45 DVD player is $3.38. What is the sales tax rate to the nearest tenth of a percent? (Lesson 6-5)

TN GLE 0706.5.5 Understand and apply basic concepts of probability.

During field hockey practice, Tanya made saves on 15 out of 25 shots. Based on these numbers, you can estimate the probability that Tanya will make a save on the next shot.

Vocabulary

experimental probability

Interactivities Online ▶

Experimental probability is one way of estimating the probability of an event. The **experimental probability** of an event is found by comparing the number of times the event occurs to the total number of trials. Trials can be conducted at the same time or one after the other. The results give the same information. The more trials you have, the more accurate the estimate is likely to be.

EXPERIMENTAL PROBABILITY

$$\text{probability} \approx \frac{\text{number of times the event occurs}}{\text{total number of trials}}$$

E X A M P L E 1 *Sports Application*

Writing Math

"*P*(event)" represents the probability that an event will occur. For example, the probability of a flipped coin landing heads up could be written as "*P*(heads)."

Tanya made saves on 15 out of 25 shots. What is the experimental probability that she will make a save on the next shot? Write your answer as a fraction, as a decimal, and as a percent.

$$P(\text{event}) \approx \frac{\text{number of times the event occurs}}{\text{total number of trials}}$$

$$P(\text{save}) \approx \frac{\text{number of saves made}}{\text{total number of shots attempted}}$$

$$= \frac{15}{25} \qquad \textit{Substitute data from the experiment.}$$

$$= \frac{3}{5} \qquad \textit{Write in simplest form.}$$

$$= 0.6 = 60\% \qquad \textit{Write as a decimal and as a percent.}$$

The experimental probability that Tanya will make a save on the next shot is $\frac{3}{5}$, or 0.6, or 60%.

Video **Lesson Tutorials Online** my.hrw.com

EXAMPLE 2 **Weather Application**

For the past three weeks, Karl has been recording the daily high temperatures for a science project. His results are shown below.

Week 1	Temp (°F)	Week 2	Temp (°F)	Week 3	Temp (°F)
Sun	76	Sun	72	Sun	78
Mon	74	Mon	79	Mon	76
Tue	79	Tue	78	Tue	77
Wed	80	Wed	79	Wed	75
Thu	77	Thu	77	Thu	79
Fri	76	Fri	74	Fri	77
Sat	75	Sat	73	Sat	75

Reading Math

When the frequency of a value is divided by the total number of data values, it is called *relative frequency*.

A **What is the experimental probability that the temperature will be above 75 °F on the next day?**

The number of days the temperature was above 75 °F is 14.

$$P(\text{above } 75 \text{ °F}) \approx \frac{\text{number of days above } 75 \text{ °F}}{\text{total number of days}}$$

$$= \frac{14}{21} \qquad \textit{Substitute data.}$$

$$= \frac{2}{3} \qquad \textit{Write in simplest form.}$$

The experimental probability that the temperature will be above 75 °F on the next day is $\frac{2}{3}$.

B **What is the experimental probability that the temperature will not be above 75 °F on the next day?**

$$P(\text{above } 75 \text{ °F}) + P(\text{not above } 75 \text{ °F}) = 1 \qquad \textit{Use the complement.}$$

$$\frac{2}{3} + P(\text{not above } 75 \text{ °F}) = 1 \qquad \textit{Substitute.}$$

$$-\frac{2}{3} \qquad\qquad\qquad\qquad\qquad -\frac{2}{3} \qquad \textit{Subtract } \frac{2}{3} \textit{ from both sides.}$$

$$P(\text{not above } 75 \text{ °F}) = \frac{1}{3} \qquad \textit{Simplify.}$$

The experimental probability that the temperature will not be above 75 °F on the next day is $\frac{1}{3}$.

Think and Discuss

1. Describe a real-world situation in which you could estimate probability using experimental probability.

2. Explain how experimental probability could be used for making predictions.

Learn It Online
Homework Help Online **go.hrw.com,**
keyword MS10 11-2 Go
Exercises 1–5, 7, 9

GUIDED PRACTICE

See Example **1**

1. During archery practice, Teri hits the target on 14 out of 20 tries. What is the experimental probability that she will hit the target on her next try? Write your answer as a fraction, as a decimal, and as a percent.

See Example **2**

2. **Government** A reporter surveys 75 people to determine whether they plan to vote for or against a proposed amendment. Of these people, 65 plan to vote for the amendment.

 a. What is the experimental probability that the next person surveyed would say he or she plans to vote for the amendment?

 b. What is the experimental probability that the next person surveyed would say he or she plans to vote against the amendment?

INDEPENDENT PRACTICE

See Example **1**

3. **Sports** Jack hit a baseball on 13 out of 30 tries during practice. What is the experimental probability that he will hit the ball on his next try? Write your answer as a fraction, as a decimal, and as a percent.

4. Cam hit the bull's-eye in darts 8 times out of 15 throws. What is the experimental probability that Cam's next throw will hit the bull's-eye?

See Example **2**

5. For the past two weeks, Benita has been recording the number of people at Eastside Park at lunchtime. During that time, there were 50 or more people at the park 9 out of 14 days.

 a. What is the experimental probability that there will be 50 or more people at the park during lunchtime on the fifteenth day?

 b. What is the experimental probability that there will not be 50 or more people at the park during lunchtime on the fifteenth day?

PRACTICE AND PROBLEM SOLVING

Extra Practice
See page EP27.

6. **Recreation** While bowling with friends, Alexis rolls a strike in 4 out of the 10 frames. What is the experimental probability that Alexis will roll a strike in the first frame of the next game?

7. Jeremiah is greeting customers at a music store. Of the first 25 people he sees enter the store, 16 are wearing jackets and 9 are not. What is the experimental probability that the next person to enter the store will be wearing a jacket?

8. During the month of June, Carmen kept track of the birds she saw in her garden. She saw a blue jay on 12 days of the month. What is the experimental probability that she will see a blue jay on July 1?

9. **Critical Thinking** Claudia finds that the experimental probability of her cat waking her between 5:00 A.M. and 6:00 A.M. is $\frac{8}{11}$. About what percent of the time does Claudia's cat not wake her between 5:00 A.M. and 6:00 A.M.?

10. Multi-Step The stem-and-leaf plot shows the depth of snow in inches recorded in Buffalo, New York, over a 10-day period.

Stems	Leaves
7	9 9
8	
9	1 1 1 1 8 8
10	
11	8
12	
13	0

Key: 7|9 means 7.9

a. What is the median depth of snow for the 10-day period?

b. What is the experimental probability that the snow will be less than 6 in. deep on the eleventh day?

c. What is the experimental probability that the snow will be more than 10 in. deep on the eleventh day?

11. The table shows the high temperatures recorded on July 4 in Orlando, Florida, over an eight-year period.

a. What is the experimental probability that the high temperature on the next July 4 will be below 90 °F?

b. What is the experimental probability that the high temperature on the next July 4 will be above 100 °F?

Year	Temp (°F)	Year	Temp (°F)
1994	86.0	1998	96.8
1995	95.0	1999	89.1
1996	78.8	2000	90.0
1997	98.6	2001	91.0

Source: Old Farmers' Almanac

12. ⭐ **Challenge** A toy company finds that the experimental probability of manufacturing a defective balance ball is $\frac{3}{50}$. About how many defective balls are likely to be in a batch of 1,800 balls?

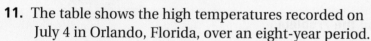

Test Prep and Spiral Review

13. Multiple Choice Darian made 26 of the 32 free throws he attempted. Which percent is closest to the experimental probability that he will make his next free throw?

(A) 50%   (B) 60%   (C) 70%   (D) 80%

14. Multiple Choice Survey results show that cheese is the favorite pizza topping for 18 out of 24 people. Which percent is closest to the experimental probability that a person's favorite pizza topping will NOT be cheese?

(F) 25%   (G) 33%   (H) 40%   (J) 75%

15. How many centimeters are equal to 6 in.? (Lesson 4-7)

Compare. Write <, >, or =. (Lesson 6-2)

16. $\frac{3}{5}$ ▢ 62%   **17.** 2.4 ▢ $\frac{12}{5}$ **18.** 0.04 ▢ $\frac{3}{10}$ **19.** 8.2 ▢ 82%

TN ✓ **0706.5.7** Use a tree diagram or organized list to determine all possible outcomes of a simple probability experiment.

Because you can roll the numbers 1, 2, 3, 4, 5, and 6 on a number cube, there are 6 possible outcomes. Together, all the possible outcomes of an experiment make up the **sample space**.

You can make an organized list to show all possible outcomes of an experiment.

EXAMPLE 1

PROBLEM SOLVING

Vocabulary

sample space

Fundamental Counting Principle

PROBLEM SOLVING APPLICATION

Lucia flips two quarters at the same time. What are all the possible outcomes? How many outcomes are in the sample space?

1 Understand the Problem

Rewrite the question as a statement.

• Find all the possible outcomes of flipping two quarters, and determine the size of the sample space.

List the **important information:**

• There are two quarters.

• Each quarter can land heads up or tails up.

2 Make a Plan

You can make an organized list to show all the possible outcomes.

3 Solve

Quarter 1	Quarter 2
H	H
H	T
T	H
T	T

Let H = heads and T = tails.

Record each possible outcome.

The possible outcomes are HH, HT, TH, and TT. There are four possible outcomes in the sample space.

4 Look Back

Each possible outcome that is recorded in the list is different.

When the number of possible outcomes of an experiment increases, it may be easier to track all the possible outcomes on a tree diagram.

 Lesson Tutorials Online my.hrw.com

EXAMPLE 2 Using a Tree Diagram to Find a Sample Space

Ren spins spinner A and spinner B. What are all the possible outcomes? How many outcomes are in the sample space?

Spinner A   Spinner B

Make a tree diagram to show the sample space. List each color from spinner A. Then for each color, list each number from spinner B.

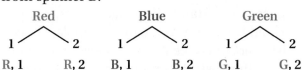

Spinner A outcomes
Spinner B outcomes
All possible outcomes

There are six possible outcomes in the sample space.

In Example 1, there are two outcomes for each coin, so there are four total outcomes.

First quarter   Second quarter

In Example 2, there are three outcomes for spinner A and two outcomes for spinner B, so there are six total outcomes.

3 × 2 = 6

Spinner A   Spinner B

The **Fundamental Counting Principle** states that you can find the total number of outcomes for two or more experiments by multiplying the number of outcomes for each separate experiment.

EXAMPLE 3 *Recreation Application*

In a game, each player rolls a number cube and spins a spinner. The spinner is divided into thirds, numbered 1, 2, and 3. How many outcomes are possible during one player's turn?

The number cube has 6 outcomes.   *List the number of outcomes*
The spinner has 3 outcomes.   *for each separate experiment.*

$6 \cdot 3 = 18$ *Use the Fundamental Counting Principle.*

There are 18 possible outcomes during one player's turn.

Think and Discuss

1. Compare using a tree diagram and using the Fundamental Counting Principle to find a sample space.

2. Find the size of the sample space for flipping 5 coins.

11-3

Exercises

Learn It Online
Homework Help Online **go.hrw.com**,
keyword MS10 11-3 Go
Exercises 1–8, 9, 11, 13

GUIDED PRACTICE

See Example 1
1. Enrique tosses a coin and spins the spinner at right. What are all the possible outcomes? How many outcomes are in the sample space?

See Example 2
2. An ice cream stand offers cake cones, waffle cones, or cups to hold ice cream. You can get vanilla, chocolate, strawberry, pistachio, or coffee flavored ice cream. If you order a single scoop, what are all the possible options you have? How many outcomes are in the sample space?

See Example 3
3. A game includes a number cube and a spinner divided into 4 equal sectors. Each player rolls the number cube and spins the spinner. How many outcomes are possible?

INDEPENDENT PRACTICE

See Example 1
4. At noon, Aretha can watch a football game, a basketball game, or a documentary about horses on TV. At 3:00, she can watch a different football game, a movie, or a concert. What are all the possible outcomes? How many outcomes are in the sample space?

5. A spinner is divided into fourths and numbered 1 through 4. Jory spins the spinner and tosses a coin. What are all the possible outcomes? How many outcomes are in the sample space?

See Example 2
6. Berto tosses a coin and spins the spinner at right. What are all the possible outcomes? How many outcomes are in the sample space?

7. For breakfast, Clarissa can choose from oatmeal, cornflakes, or scrambled eggs. She can drink milk, orange juice, apple juice, or hot chocolate. What are all the possible outcomes? How many outcomes are in the sample space?

See Example 3
8. A pizza shop offers thick crust, thin crust, or stuffed crust. The choices of toppings are pepperoni, cheese, hamburger, Italian sausage, Canadian bacon, onions, bell peppers, mushrooms, and pineapple. How many different one-topping pizzas could you order?

PRACTICE AND PROBLEM SOLVING

Extra Practice
See page EP27.

9. Andie has a blue sweater, a red sweater, and a purple sweater. She has a white shirt and a tan shirt. How many different ways can she wear a sweater and a shirt together?

10. **Critical Thinking** Suppose you can choose a ball that comes in three colors: blue, red, or green. Make a tree diagram or a list of all the possible ways to choose 2 balls if you are allowed to choose two of the same color.

11. Health For each pair of food groups, give the number of possible outcomes if one item is chosen from each group.

Group A	Group B	Group C	Group D
milk	beef	bread	vegetables
cheese	fish	cereal	fruit
yogurt	poultry	pasta	
		rice	

a. group A and group B

b. group B and group D

c. group A and group C

12. Health The graph shows the kinds of classes that health club members would like to see offered.

a. If the health club offers the four most popular classes on one day, how many ways could they be arranged?

b. If the health club offers each of the five classes on a different weekday, how many ways could they be arranged?

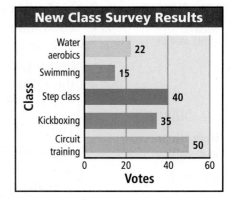

New Class Survey Results

Water aerobics — 22
Swimming — 15
Step class — 40
Kickboxing — 35
Circuit training — 50

Class / Votes (0, 20, 40, 60)

13. Recreation There are 3 trails from the South Canyon trailhead to Lake Solitude. There are 4 trails from Lake Solitude to Hidden Lake. How many possible routes could you take to hike from the South Canyon trailhead to Hidden Lake that pass Lake Solitude?

14. What's the Question? Dan has 4 face cards and 5 number cards. He shuffles the cards separately and places each set in a separate pile. The answer is 20 possible outcomes. What is the question?

15. Write About It Explain how to determine the size of the sample space when you toss three number cubes at the same time.

16. Challenge Suppose you flip a penny, a nickel, and a dime at the same time. What are all the possible outcomes?

Test Prep and Spiral Review

17. Multiple Choice Amber rolls two number cubes. How many outcomes are possible?

(A) 6   (B) 12   (C) 24   (D) 36

18. Extended Response A sandwich shop offers 3 choices of breads: white, rye, or garlic; 2 choices of cheese: American or Swiss; and 4 choices of meats: beef, turkey, ham, or pork. List the possible choices for a sandwich with 1 bread, 1 cheese, and 1 meat. How many possible choices are there?

Write each fraction as a percent. (Lesson 6-2)

19. $\frac{1}{8}$ **20.** $\frac{3}{4}$ **21.** $\frac{2}{5}$ **22.** $\frac{3}{10}$

23. Find the volume of a cylinder with diameter 8 in. and height 14 in. Use $\frac{22}{7}$ for π. (Lesson 10-2)

Theoretical Probability

BINGO!

TN SPI 0706.5.4 Use theoretical probability to make predictions.
Also GLE 0706.5.5

In the game of Bingo, balls containing a combination of a letter and a number are randomly selected. Players try to match the combinations on 5 × 5 grid cards. Of the 75 combinations used in Bingo, 15 have the letter *B* on them.

Vocabulary

theoretical probability

equally likely

fair

To determine the probability of selecting a *B*, you can randomly select Bingo balls and record your results to find the experimental probability, or you can calculate the *theoretical probability*. **Theoretical probability** is used to find the probability of an event when all outcomes are *equally likely*. **Equally likely** outcomes have the same probability.

Reading Math

You may hear probability described as "odds of winning." For more on odds, see Skills Bank p. SB9.

THEORETICAL PROBABILITY

$$\text{probability} = \frac{\text{number of ways the event can occur}}{\text{total number of equally likely outcomes}}$$

If each possible outcome of an experiment is equally likely, then the experiment is said to be **fair**. Experiments involving number cubes and coins are usually assumed to be fair.

EXAMPLE 1 Finding Theoretical Probability

Find the probability of each event. Write your answer as a fraction, as a decimal, and as a percent.

A selecting one of the 15 *B*s from 75 total Bingo balls

$$P = \frac{\text{number of ways the event can occur}}{\text{total number of equally likely outcomes}}$$

$$P(B) = \frac{\text{number of } Bs}{\text{total number of Bingo balls}} \qquad \textit{Write the ratio.}$$

$$= \frac{15}{75} \qquad \textit{Substitute.}$$

$$= \frac{1}{5} \qquad \textit{Write in simplest form.}$$

$$= 0.2 = 20\% \qquad \textit{Write as a decimal and as a percent.}$$

The theoretical probability of selecting a *B* is $\frac{1}{5}$, 0.2, or 20%.

Video **Lesson Tutorials Online** my.hrw.com

Find the probability of each event. Write your answer as a fraction, as a decimal, and as a percent.

B rolling a number greater than 2 on a fair number cube

There are four ways the event can occur: 3, 4, 5, and 6.

There are six possible outcomes: 1, 2, 3, 4, 5, and 6.

$$P(\text{greater than 2}) = \frac{\text{number of ways the event can occur}}{\text{total number of equally likely outcomes}}$$

$$= \frac{4}{6} \qquad \textit{Write the ratio.}$$

$$= \frac{2}{3} \qquad \textit{Write in simplest form.}$$

$$\approx 0.667 \approx 66.7\% \qquad \textit{Write as a decimal and a percent.}$$

The theoretical probability of rolling a number greater than 2 is $\frac{2}{3}$, or approximately 0.667, or approximately 66.7%.

E X A M P L E   2   *School Application*

There are 11 boys and 16 girls in Mr. Ashley's class. Mr. Ashley has written the name of each student on a craft stick. He randomly chooses one of these sticks to choose a student to answer a question.

A Find the theoretical probability of choosing a boy's name.

$$P(\text{boy}) = \frac{\text{number of boys in class}}{\text{total number of students in class}}$$

$$P(\text{boy}) = \frac{11}{27}$$

B Find the theoretical probability of choosing a girl's name.

$$P(\text{boy}) + P(\text{girl}) = 1 \qquad \textit{Substitute } \tfrac{11}{27} \textit{ for P(boy).}$$

$$\frac{11}{27} + P(\text{girl}) = 1$$

$$-\frac{11}{27} \qquad = -\frac{11}{27} \qquad \textit{Subtract } \tfrac{11}{27} \textit{ from both sides.}$$

$$P(\text{girl}) = \frac{16}{27} \qquad \textit{Simplify.}$$

> **Remember!**
>
> The sum of the probabilities of an event and its complement is 1.

Think and Discuss

1. Give an example of an experiment in which all of the outcomes are not equally likely. Explain.

2. Describe how the probability in Example 2 can be affected if Mr. Ashley does not choose randomly from the craft sticks.

Learn It Online
Homework Help Online **go.hrw.com**,
keyword MS10 11-4 (Go)
Exercises 1–10, 13, 15, 17, 19,
21, 25

GUIDED PRACTICE

See Example 1 **Find the probability of each event. Write your answer as a fraction, as a decimal, and as a percent.**

1. randomly choosing a red marble from a bag of 15 red, 15 blue, 15 green, 15 yellow, 15 black, and 15 white marbles

2. tossing 2 fair coins and both landing heads up

See Example 2 **A set of cards includes 15 yellow cards, 10 green cards, and 10 blue cards. Find the probability of each event when a card is chosen at random.**

3. yellow   4. green   5. not yellow or green

INDEPENDENT PRACTICE

See Example 1 **Find the probability of each event. Write your answer as a fraction, as a decimal, and as a percent.**

6. randomly drawing a heart or a club from a shuffled deck of 52 cards with 13-card suits: diamonds, hearts, clubs, and spades

7. randomly drawing a purple disk from a game with 13 red, 13 purple, 13 orange, and 13 white disks of the same size and shape

8. randomly drawing one of the 30 *G* or *O*s from a bag of 75 Bingo balls

See Example 2 **Sifu has 6 girls and 8 boys in his karate class. He randomly selects one student to demonstrate a self-defense technique. Find the probability of each event.**

9. selecting a girl   10. selecting a boy

PRACTICE AND PROBLEM SOLVING

Extra Practice
See page EP27.

Find the probability of each event when two fair number cubes are rolled.

11. *P*(total of 3)   12. *P*(total of 7)   13. *P*(total of 4)

14. *P*(total of 2)   15. *P*(total of 9)   16. *P*(total of 13)

A spinner is divided equally into 10 sectors. The numbers 1 through 5 are each placed in two different sectors. Find the probability of each event.

17. *P*(less than 3)   18. *P*(5)   19. *P*(8)

20. *P*(less than 6)   21. *P*(greater than or equal to 4)   22. *P*(3)

For 23, use the spinner.

23. Is the experiment fair or unfair for the following outcomes? Explain.

   a. landing on a 2   **b.** landing on blue

24. Recreation The table shows the approximate number of visitors to five different amusement parks in the United States in one year. Find the probability that a randomly selected visitor to one of the amusement parks visited the parks listed below. Write each answer as a decimal and as a percent.

Amusement Parks	Number of Visitors
Disney World, FL	15,640,000
Disneyland, CA	13,680,000
SeaWorld, FL	4,900,000
Busch Gardens, FL	4,200,000
SeaWorld, CA	3,700,000

a. Disney World

b. a park in California

25. Gardening A package of mixed lettuce seeds contains 150 green lettuce seeds and 50 red lettuce seeds. What is the probability that a randomly selected seed will be a red lettuce seed? Write your answer as a percent.

? **26. Choose a Strategy** Francis, Amanda, Raymond, and Albert wore different-colored T-shirts. The colors were tan, orange, purple, and aqua. Neither Raymond nor Amanda ever wears orange, and neither Francis nor Raymond ever wears aqua. Albert wore purple. What color was each person's T-shirt?

27. Write About It Suppose the probability of an event happening is $\frac{3}{8}$. Explain what each number in the ratio represents.

28. Challenge A spinner is divided into three sectors. Half of the spinner is red, $\frac{1}{3}$ is blue, and $\frac{1}{6}$ is green. What is the probability that the spinner will land on either red or green?

Test Prep and Spiral Review

29. Multiple Choice Renae pulls a marble out of the bag. What is the probability that the marble will be blue?

Ⓐ $\frac{1}{8}$ Ⓒ $\frac{1}{3}$

Ⓑ $\frac{1}{2}$ Ⓓ $\frac{1}{4}$

30. Gridded Response There are 5 red marbles, 7 green marbles, and 3 yellow marbles in a bag. A marble is drawn at random. What is the probability that the marble will NOT be yellow?

31. Find the area of the trapezoid shown. (Lesson 9-4)

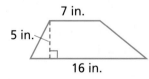

32. Dora is buying one flavor of frozen yogurt. She can choose from two sizes, small and large, and four flavors: berry swirl, vanilla, peach, and lime. How many possible choices are there? (Lesson 11-3)

Learn It Online
State Resources Online **go.hrw.com**,
keyword MS10 Lab11 Go

TN ✓ **0706.5.5** Evaluate the design
of an experiment.

A *simulation* is a model of an experiment that would be difficult or inconvenient to actually perform. You can use spreadsheets and calculators to perform such simulations as rolling a number cube or flipping a coin. These tools also can help you determine experimental probability and compare it with theoretical probability.

Activity 1

Use a spreadsheet to model rolling a number cube to calculate the experimental probability of rolling a 3.

To simulate rolling a number cube, use a spreadsheet to generate a random integer between 1 and 6. In cell A1, type **=INT(RAND()*6+1)**.

	A	B	C
1	=INT(RAND()*6+1)		
2			

To "roll the cube," press ENTER. You should see an integer between 1 and 6 in cell A1. To model 10 rolls, highlight cells A1 through A10 and choose Fill▶Down from the Edit menu.

	A	B	C
1	1		
2	2		
3	3		

The experimental probability P of rolling a 3 is $P = \frac{\text{number of 3s rolled}}{\text{total number of rolls}}$. The total number of rolls is 10. To count the number of 3s rolled, in cells A1–A10, type the formula **=COUNTIF(A1:A10,3)** in cell C1 and press ENTER.

	A	B	C	D	E
1	1		=COUNTIF(A1:A10,3)		
2	2				
3	3				
4	6				
5	4				
6	4				
7	4				
8	3				
9	2				
10	3				
11					

To calculate the experimental probability of rolling a 3, type the formula **=C1/10** in cell D1 and press ENTER.

Note: Your spreadsheet numbers will likely look different from the ones shown here.

	A	B	C	D	E
1	6		3	0.3	
2	5				
3	3				
4	5				
5	6				
6	3				
7	3				
8	6				
9	4				
10	5				
11					

Think and Discuss

1. How does this simulation compare to theoretical probability? Explain.

2. Explain how you could adapt the spreadsheet to model 100 rolls.

3. Do you think you would get the same experimental probability if you repeat the experiment? Explain.

Try This

1. Model 100 rolls, count the number of times each number 1–6 is rolled, and calculate the experimental probability of rolling each number.

2. How does each compare to theoretical probability?

3. **Make a Conjecture** Is the model better with 10 or 100 trials?

Activity 2

A school principal chooses 100 students at random to fill out a survey about cafeteria food. The school has about the same number of boys as girls. Find the experimental probability that any given survey was answered by a girl.

You can model this situation with your calculator's Coin Toss simulation. Press APPS, scroll down and select **Prob Sim**, and press any key to get past the title screen.

Then select **1. Toss Coins.** Use the keys below the screen to choose the options shown in the application. Press WINDOW to toss a coin once.

Press GRAPH and then Y= to clear the toss from the screen. Press TRACE to flip the coin 50 times. Press TRACE again for another 50 flips. Use the ▶ key to see the frequency of heads and tails.

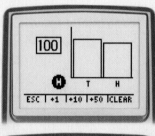

Think and Discuss

1. Explain why tossing a coin is a good model for the situation in Activity 2.

2. Compare the experimental and theoretical probability of a given survey being answered by a girl.

3. Suppose that the ratio of boys to girls was 3:2. How would this affect the outcome?

Try This

1. Suppose that the principal chooses 200 students to fill out the survey. What is the experimental probability of a given survey being answered by a boy?

2. Think of a situation that you could model with a coin toss. Explain the situation, state why a coin toss would be a useful model, conduct the simulation, and find the experimental probability.

11-5 Making Predictions

TN **SPI 0706.5.4** Use theoretical probability to make predictions.
Also **GLE 0706.5.5, ✓ 0706.5.4**

A **prediction** is something you can reasonably expect to happen in the future. Weather forecasters use several different methods of forecasting to make predictions about the weather.

One way to make a prediction is to use probability.

EXAMPLE 1 Using Experimental Probability to Make Predictions

Vocabulary
prediction

Caitlyn finds that the experimental probability of her making a three-point shot is 30%. Out of 500 three-point shots, about how many could she predict she would make?

Remember!

30% is $\frac{30}{100}$ or $\frac{3}{10}$.

Method 1: Set up an equation.

$\frac{3}{10} \cdot 500 = x$ *Multiply the probability by the total number of 3-point shots.*

$150 = x$ *Solve for x.*

Method 2: Set up a proportion.

$\frac{3}{10} = \frac{x}{500}$ *Think: 3 out of 10 is how many out of 500?*

$3 \cdot 500 = 10 \cdot x$ *The cross products are equal.*

$1{,}500 = 10x$ *Multiply.*

$\frac{1{,}500}{10} = \frac{10x}{10}$ *Divide each side by 10 to isolate the variable.*

$150 = x$

Caitlyn can predict that she will make about 150 of 500 three-point shots.

EXAMPLE 2 Using Theoretical Probability to Make Predictions

If you roll a number cube 15 times, about how many times do you expect to roll a number less than 6?

$P(\text{less than } 6) = \frac{5}{6}$

$\frac{5}{6} = \frac{x}{15}$ *Think: 5 out of 6 is how many out of 15?*

$5 \cdot 15 = 6 \cdot x$ *The cross products are equal.*

$75 = 6x$ *Multiply.*

$\frac{75}{6} = \frac{6x}{6}$ *Divide each side by 6 to isolate the variable.*

$12.5 = x$

Helpful Hint

Round to a whole number if it makes sense in the given situation.

You can expect to roll a number less than 6 about 12 or 13 times.

Video **Lesson Tutorials Online** my.hrw.com

EXAMPLE 3 PROBLEM SOLVING APPLICATION

The Wettermark family is planning a 14-day vacation. They would like to go to Pensacola, Florida, sometime in July, August, or September. Pensacola averages 19 rainy days during those 92 days. If the Wettermarks would like no rain on at least 10 days of their vacation, should they go to Pensacola?

1 Understand the Problem

The **answer** will be whether the Wettermarks should go to Pensacola.

List the **important information:**
• Pensacola averages 19 rainy days out of 92 days.
• The Wettermarks want it not to rain 10 out of 14 days.

2 Make a Plan

On average 19 out of 92 days are rainy. After finding out the number of rainy days there should be for 14 days, subtract to find the number of not rainy days.

3 Solve

$$\frac{19}{92} = \frac{x}{14}$$ *Think: 19 out of 92 is how many out of 14?*

$$19 \cdot 14 = 92 \cdot x$$ *The cross products are equal.*

$$266 = 92x$$ *Multiply.*

$$\frac{266}{92} = \frac{92x}{92}$$ *Divide each side by 92 to isolate the variable to find the number of rainy days.*

$$2.89 \approx x$$ *There will be about 3 rainy days in 14 days.*

$$14 - 3 = 11$$ *Subtract the predicted number of rainy days from the total vacation days.*

4 Look Back

Since $11 > 10$, the Wettermarks can reasonably expect at least 10 not rainy days on their vacation and should go to Pensacola.

$$\frac{19 \text{ rainy days}}{92 \text{ total days}} \approx \frac{20}{100} \text{ or } 20\% \qquad \frac{3 \text{ rainy days}}{14 \text{ total days}} \approx \frac{3}{15} \text{ or } 20\%$$

Since both ratios are about 20%, the answer is reasonable.

Think and Discuss

1. **Explain** the difference between a prediction based on experimental probability and one based on theoretical probability.

2. **Explain** whether a prediction based on a probability will always match the actual results.

Learn It Online
Homework Help Online **go.hrw.com,**
keyword **MS10 11-5** **Go**
Exercises 1–11, 13, 15

GUIDED PRACTICE

See Example **1**

1. The experimental probability of hearing thunder on any given day in Florida is 25%. Out of 730 days (2 years), about how many days can Floridians predict to hear thunder?

2. A player on the school baseball team reaches first base 40% of the times he is at bat. Out of 50 times at bat, about how many times will the player reach first base?

See Example **2**

3. If you flipped a fair coin 18 times, about how many times would you expect heads to appear?

4. A bag contains 6 white marbles and 4 black marbles. You pick out a marble, record its color, and put the marble back in the bag. If you repeat this process 35 times, about how many times do you expect to remove a white marble from the bag?

See Example **3**

5. The Escobar family is planning a 7-day vacation. They would like to go to Boulder, Colorado, in December. Based on last December, Boulder had 23 days when it did not snow. If the Escobars would like it to snow on at least 3 days of their vacation, should they go to Boulder?

INDEPENDENT PRACTICE

See Example **1**

6. The wettest U.S. city is Mobile, Alabama. The city's chance of rain is 16%. Out of a 30-day period, about how many rainy days would you expect Mobile to have?

7. A student on the basketball team makes 72% of her free-throw attempts. Out of 450 attempts, about how many free throws will this student make?

See Example **2**

For 8–9, use the spinner.

8. In 20 spins, about how often can you expect to get a number evenly divisible by 2?

9. In 150 spins, about how often can you expect to get a number less than 6?

10. A bag contains 8 white marbles, 4 black marbles, and 3 red marbles. You pick out a marble, record its color, and put the marble back in the bag. If you repeat this process 45 times, about how often do you expect to remove a red or white marble from the bag?

See Example **3**

11. Alexia wants to start taking the light rail train to work. She wants to be late no more than 5% of the time. The light rail train claims to be on time 24 out of 25 times. Should Alexia take the light rail train to work?

Extra Practice
See page EP28.

Recreation

Snow tubing has become an increasingly popular winter activity. Many ski resorts now offer downhill runs devoted solely for tubing, and tube tows to take tubers back up the hill without having to get off their tube!

12. If 12 out of 15 people recycle aluminum cans, how many people out of 1 million would you expect to recycle?

13. A spinner with equal sections has 7 different dollar amounts. Starting with $1, the amounts increase by being multiplied by 2. How many times in 84 spins are you likely to spin $16 or over?

14. **Recreation** A survey of 150 people at a ski resort were asked to name their favorite hot drink. The results are given in the table. Based on this information, if there are 500 people at the ski resort, how many can you predict would name hot chocolate as their favorite hot drink?

Drink	Number of People
Coffee	53
Tea	25
Hot Chocolate	72

15. **Critical Thinking** Roy rolls a fair number cube 18 times. Predict how many times he will roll a number that is odd and greater than 3.

16. **Critical Thinking** People exiting an electronics store were asked whether they own a laptop computer. Out of 10 people, 7 said yes. Based on this information, how many people out of 500 in the general population would you expect to own a laptop computer? Is this a good prediction? Why or why not?

17. **What's the Error?** Ella misses the school bus 1 out of every 60 school days. She sets up the proportion $\frac{1}{60} = \frac{180}{x}$ to predict how many days she will miss the bus in the 180-day school year. What's her error?

 18. **Write About It** Look up the weather predictions for your area for the week. Can you make a prediction for the year based on the information?

19. **Challenge** Two movies open in the same day. Movie A earns 40% of the total box office receipts for the month. Movie B earns $80 million, or 25%, of the month's box office receipts. If Movie A's rate of success continues, how much money will it earn over 3 months?

Test Prep and Spiral Review

20. **Gridded Response** If 4 out of 23 toys on an assembly line are defective, about how many toys out of 414 are likely to be defective?

21. **Short Response** A survey reveals that one airline's flights have an 89% probability of being on time. If this airline schedules 5,000 flights in a year, how many flights would you predict to arrive on time? Explain.

22. A sock drawer contains five pairs of black socks and seven pairs of white socks. Write a ratio showing the number of black pairs to white pairs. (Lesson 4-1)

Graph each equation. (Lesson 5-7)

23. $y = -2x + 5$ **24.** $y - \frac{1}{2}x = -2$ **25.** $y = x - 1$ **26.** $5x + y = 0$

Experimental and Theoretical Probability

Use with Lesson 11-5

Learn It Online
State Resources Online **go.hrw.com**,
keyword MS10 Lab11 Go

TN **SPI 0706.5.4** Use theoretical
probability to make predictions.
Also **GLE 0706.5.5**, ✓ **0706.5.7**,
SPI 0706.5.4

REMEMBER
- The experimental probability of an event is the ratio of the number of times the event occurs to the total number of trials.
- The theoretical probability of an event is the ratio of the number of ways the event can occur to the total number of equally likely outcomes.

Activity 1

1. Write the letters *A, B, C,* and *D* on four slips of paper. Fold the slips in half and place them in a bag or other small container.

2. Predict the number of times you expect to choose *A* when you repeat the experiment 12 times.

3. Without looking, choose a slip of paper, note the result, and replace the slip. Repeat this 12 times, mixing the slips between trials. Record your results in a table like the one shown.

4. How many times did you choose *A*? How does this number compare to your prediction?

5. What is the experimental probability of choosing *A*? What is the theoretical probability of choosing *A*?

6. Combine your results with those of your classmates. Find the experimental probability of choosing *A* based on the combined results.

Outcome	Number of Times Chosen
A	//
B	////
C	~~////~~
D	/

Think and Discuss

1. How is the experimental probability of choosing *A* based on the combined results different from the experimental probability of choosing *A* based on the results of your own experiment?

2. How many times would you expect to choose *A* if you repeat the experiment 500 times?

Try This

1. What is the theoretical probability of choosing *A* from five slips of paper with the letters *A, B, C, D,* and *E*? Predict the number of times you would expect to choose *A* if you repeat the experiment 500 times.

2. **Make a Conjecture** Based on your answers from problem **1**, make a conjecture about experimental and theoretical probability if the number of trials is great.

Activity 2

1 Write the letters *A*, *B*, *C*, and *D* and the numbers 1, 2, and 3 on slips of paper. Fold the slips in half. Place the slips with the letters in one bag and the slips with the numbers in a different bag.

2 In this activity, you will be choosing one slip of paper from each bag without looking. What is the sample space for this experiment? Predict the number of times you expect to choose *A* and 1 (*A*-1) when you repeat the experiment 24 times.

3 Choose a slip of paper from each bag, note the results, and replace the slips. Repeat this 24 times, mixing the slips between trials. Record your results in a table like the one shown.

Outcome	Number of Times Chosen
A-1	/
A-2	ЖĦ
A-3	//
B-1	/

4 How many times did you choose *A*-1? How does this number compare to your prediction?

5 Combine your results with those of your classmates. Find the experimental probability of choosing *A*-1 based on the combined results.

Think and Discuss

1. What do you think is the theoretical probability of choosing *A*-1? Why?

2. How many times would you expect to choose *A*-1 if you repeat the experiment 600 times?

3. Explain the difference between the experimental probability of an event and the theoretical probability of the event.

Try This

1. Suppose you toss a penny and a nickel at the same time.

   a. What is the sample space for this experiment?

   b. Predict the number of times you would expect both coins to land heads up if you repeat the experiment 100 times.

   c. Predict the number of times you would expect one coin to land heads up and one coin to land tails up if you repeat the experiment 1,000 times.

2. You spin the spinner at right and roll a number cube at the same time.

   a. What is the sample space for this experiment?

   b. Describe an experiment you could conduct to find the experimental probability of spinning green and rolling a 4 at the same time.

Ready To Go On?

Quiz for Lessons 11-1 Through 11-5

✓ **11-1** Probability

Determine whether each event is impossible, unlikely, as likely as not, likely, or certain.

1. rolling 2 number cubes and getting a sum of 2

2. guessing the answer to a true/false question correctly

3. The probability of Ashur's soccer team winning its next game is $\frac{7}{10}$. What is the probability of Ashur's team not winning the next game?

✓ **11-2** Experimental Probability

4. Carl is conducting a survey for the school paper. He finds that 7 students have no pets, 15 have one pet, and 9 have at least two pets. What is the experimental probability that the next student Carl asks will not have a pet?

✓ **11-3** Sample Spaces

5. Shelly and Anthony are playing a game using a number cube and a nickel. Each player rolls the number cube and flips the coin. What are all the possible outcomes during one turn? How many outcomes are in the sample space?

6. A yogurt shop offers 4 different flavors of yogurt and 3 different fruit toppings. How many different desserts are possible if you can choose one flavor of yogurt and one topping?

✓ **11-4** Theoretical Probability

A spinner with 10 equal sectors numbered 1 through 10 is spun. Find the probability of each event. Write your answer as a fraction, as a decimal, and as a percent.

7. $P(5)$　　　　　8. $P(\text{prime number})$　　　　　9. $P(20)$

10. Sabina has a list of 8 CDs and 5 DVDs that she would like to buy. Her friends randomly select one of the items from the list to give her as a gift. What is the probability Sabina's friends will select a CD? a DVD?

✓ **11-5** Making Predictions

11. Sally finds that the experimental probability of her putting a ball into a hole is 15%. Out of 20 putts, about how many could she predict she would make?

12. If you roll a number cube 25 times, about how many times do you expect to roll a number greater than 3?

Focus on Problem Solving

Understand the Problem

• **Identify important details**

When you are solving word problems, you need to identify information that is important to the problem. Read the problem several times to find all the important details. Sometimes it is helpful to read the problem aloud so that you can hear the words. Highlight the facts that are needed to solve the problem. Then list any other information that is necessary.

Highlight the important information in each problem, and then list any other important details.

1 A bag of bubble gum has 25 pink pieces, 20 blue pieces, and 15 green pieces. Lauren selects 1 piece of bubble gum without looking. What is the probability that it is not blue?

2 Regina has a bag of marbles that contains 6 red marbles, 3 green marbles, and 4 blue marbles. Regina pulls 1 marble from the bag without looking. What is the probability that the marble is red?

3 Marco is counting the cars he sees on his ride home from school. Of 20 cars, 10 are white, 6 are red, 2 are blue, and 2 are green. What is the experimental probability that the next car Marco sees will be red?

4 Frederica has 8 red socks, 6 blue socks, 10 white socks, and 4 yellow socks in a drawer. What is the probability that she will randomly pull a brown sock from the drawer?

5 During the first 20 minutes of lunch, 5 male students, 7 female students, and 3 teachers went through the lunch line. What is the experimental probability that the next person through the line will be a teacher?

TN **GLE 0706.5.5** Understand and apply basic concepts of probability.

Raji and Kara must each choose a solo from a list of music pieces to play for their recital. If Raji's choice has no effect on Kara's choice and vice versa, the events are *independent.* For **independent events**, the occurrence of one event has no effect on the probability that a second event will occur.

Vocabulary

independent events

dependent events

Interactivities Online ▶

If once Raji chooses a solo, Kara must choose from the remaining solos, then the events are *dependent.* For **dependent events**, the occurrence of one event *does* have an effect on the probability that a second event will occur.

EXAMPLE **1** **Determining Whether Events Are Independent or Dependent**

Decide whether each set of events is independent or dependent. Explain your answer.

Reading Math

Sometimes events cannot happen at the same time. These events are called disjoint events. For more on disjoint events, see Skills Bank p. SB10.

A **Erika rolls a 3 on one number cube and a 2 on another number cube.**

Since the outcome of rolling one number cube does not affect the outcome of rolling the second number cube, the events are independent.

B **Tomoko chooses a seventh-grader for her team from a group of seventh- and eighth-graders, and then Juan chooses a different seventh-grader from the remaining students.**

Since Juan cannot pick the same student that Tomoko picked, and since there are fewer students for Juan to choose from after Tomoko chooses, the events are dependent.

To find the probability that two independent events will happen, multiply the probabilities of the two events.

Probability of Two Independent Events

$$P(A \text{ and } B) = P(A) \cdot P(B)$$

Probability of both events   *Probability of first event*   *Probability of second event*

Video **Lesson Tutorials Online** my.hrw.com

EXAMPLE 2 **Finding the Probability of Independent Events**

Find the probability of flipping a coin and getting heads and then rolling a 6 on a number cube.

The outcome of flipping the coin does not affect the outcome of rolling the number cube, so the events are independent.

$P(\text{heads and } 6) = P(\text{heads}) \cdot P(6)$

$\qquad = \frac{1}{2} \cdot \frac{1}{6}$ *There are 2 ways a coin can land and 6 ways a number cube can land.*

$\qquad = \frac{1}{12}$ *Multiply.*

The probability of getting heads and a 6 is $\frac{1}{12}$.

To find the probability of two dependent events, you must determine the effect that the first event has on the probability of the second event.

Probability of Two Dependent Events

$$P(A \text{ and } B) = P(A) \cdot P(B \text{ after } A)$$

Probability of both events   *Probability of first event*   *Probability of second event given that A has occurred*

EXAMPLE 3 **Finding the Probability of Dependent Events**

Mica has five $1 bills, three $10 bills, and two $20 bills in her wallet. She picks two bills at random. What is the probability of her picking the two $20 bills?

The first draw changes the number of bills left, and may change the number of $20 bills left, so the events are dependent.

$P(\text{first } \$20) = \frac{2}{10} = \frac{1}{5}$ *There are two $20 bills out of ten bills.*

$P(\text{second } \$20) = \frac{1}{9}$ *There is one $20 bill left out of nine bills.*

$P(\text{first } \$20, \text{ then second } \$20) = P(A) \cdot P(B \text{ after } A)$

$\qquad = \frac{1}{5} \cdot \frac{1}{9}$

$\qquad = \frac{1}{45}$ *Multiply.*

The probability of Mica picking two $20 bills is $\frac{1}{45}$.

Think and Discuss

1. Compare probabilities of independent and dependent events.

2. Explain whether the probability of two events is greater than or less than the probability of each individual event.

Learn It Online
Homework Help Online **go.hrw.com,**
keyword MS10 11-6 Go
Exercises 1–10, 13, 17

GUIDED PRACTICE

See Example 1   **Decide whether each set of events is independent or dependent. Explain your answer.**

1. A student flips heads on one coin and tails on a second coin.

2. A student chooses a red marble from a bag of marbles and then chooses another red marble without replacing the first.

See Example 2   **Find the probability of each set of independent events.**

3. a flipped coin landing heads up and rolling a 5 or a 6 on a number cube

4. drawing a 5 from 10 cards numbered 1 through 10 and rolling a 2 on a number cube

See Example 3   5. Each day, Mr. Samms randomly chooses 2 students from his class to serve as helpers. There are 15 boys and 10 girls in the class. What is the probability that Mr. Samms will choose 2 girls to be helpers?

INDEPENDENT PRACTICE

See Example 1   **Decide whether each set of events is independent or dependent. Explain your answer.**

6. A student chooses a fiction book at random from a list of books and then chooses a second fiction book from those remaining.

7. A woman chooses a lily from one bunch of flowers and then chooses a tulip from a different bunch.

See Example 2   **Find the probability of each set of independent events.**

8. drawing a red marble from a bag of 6 red and 4 blue marbles, replacing it, and then drawing a blue marble

9. rolling an even number on a number cube and rolling an odd number on a second roll of the same cube

See Example 3   10. Francisco has 7 quarters in his pocket. Of these, 3 depict the state of Delaware, 2 depict Georgia, 1 depicts Connecticut, and 1 depicts Pennsylvania. Francisco removes 1 quarter from his pocket and then removes a second quarter without replacing the first. What is the probability that both will be Delaware quarters?

Extra Practice
See page EP28.

11. An even number is chosen randomly from a set of cards labeled with the numbers 1 through 8. A second even number is chosen without the first card being replaced. Are these independent or dependent events? What is the probability of both events occurring?

12. On a multiple-choice test, each question has five possible answers. A student does not know the answers to two questions, so he guesses. What is the probability that the student will get both answers wrong?

13. The tree diagram shows the probability for choosing 2 fruits from a bag containing 2 red apples and 1 green apple. To find a specific probability, follow the branches of the diagram and multiply the probabilities.

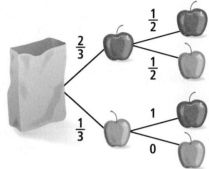

$P(\text{red, then green}) = \frac{2}{3} \cdot \frac{1}{2} = \frac{2}{6} = \frac{1}{3}$

Use the tree diagram to find the following probabilities.

a. $P(\text{green, then red})$ **b.** $P(\text{red, then red})$ **c.** $P(\text{green, then green})$

14. Write a Problem Describe two events that are either independent or dependent, and make up a probability problem about them.

15. Write About It At the beginning of a board game, players take turns drawing 7 lettered tiles. Are drawing A's on the first two tiles dependent or independent events? Explain.

16. Challenge Weather forecasters have accurately predicted rain in one community $\frac{4}{5}$ of the time. What is the probability that they will accurately predict rain two days in a row?

Test Prep and Spiral Review

17. Multiple Choice A bag contains 5 red marbles and 5 purple marbles. What is the probability of drawing a red marble and then a purple marble, without replacing the first marble before drawing the second marble?

Ⓐ $\frac{2}{9}$ Ⓑ $\frac{5}{18}$ Ⓒ $\frac{1}{3}$ Ⓓ $\frac{1}{2}$

18. Short Response José has 8 brown socks and 6 black socks in his drawer. He picked one sock and then another sock. Are the events independent or dependent? Explain. What is the probability that he will pick 2 black socks?

19. Fritz jogged $1\frac{3}{4}$ mi on Monday, $2\frac{1}{2}$ mi on Wednesday, and 3 mi on Friday. How many miles did he jog altogether on these days? (Lesson 3-8)

20. A circular fountain has a radius of 7 ft. What is the area of the fountain? Use $\frac{22}{7}$ for π. (Lesson 9-5)

Combinations

Mrs. Logan's students have to read any two of the following books.

1. *The Adventures of Tom Sawyer,* by Mark Twain

2. *The Call of the Wild,* by Jack London

Vocabulary
combination

3. *A Christmas Carol,* by Charles Dickens

4. *Treasure Island,* by Robert Louis Stevenson

5. *Tuck Everlasting,* by Natalie Babbit

How many possible *combinations* of books could the students choose?

A **combination** is a grouping of objects or events in which the order does not matter. For example, a student can choose books 1 and 2 or books 2 and 1. Since the order does not matter, the two arrangements represent the same combination. One way to find all possible combinations is to make a table.

EXAMPLE 1 **Using a Table to Find Combinations**

How many different combinations of two books are possible from Mrs. Logan's list of five books?

Interactivities Online

Begin by making a table showing all of the possible groupings of books taken two at a time.

	1	2	3	4	5
1		1, 2	1, 3	1, 4	1, 5
2	2, 1		2, 3	2, 4	2, 5
3	3, 1	3, 2		3, 4	3, 5
4	4, 1	4, 2	4, 3		4, 5
5	5, 1	5, 2	5, 3	5, 4	

Because order does not matter, you can eliminate repeated pairs. For example, 1, 2 is already listed, so 2, 1 can be eliminated.

There are 10 different combinations of two books on Mrs. Logan's list of five books.

	1	2	3	4	5
1		1, 2	1, 3	1, 4	1, 5
2	~~2, 1~~		2, 3	2, 4	2, 5
3	~~3, 1~~	~~3, 2~~		3, 4	3, 5
4	~~4, 1~~	~~4, 2~~	~~4, 3~~		4, 5
5	~~5, 1~~	~~5, 2~~	~~5, 3~~	~~5, 4~~	

Video **Lesson Tutorials Online** my.hrw.com

You can also use a tree diagram to find possible combinations.

EXAMPLE 2

PROBLEM SOLVING APPLICATION

As a caterer, Cuong offers four vegetable choices: broccoli, squash, peas, and carrots. Each person can choose two vegetables. How many different combinations of two vegetables can a person choose?

1. Understand the Problem

Rewrite the question as a statement.

• Find the number of possible combinations of two vegetables a person can choose.

List the **important information:**

• There are four vegetable choices in all.

2. Make a Plan

You can make a tree diagram to show the possible combinations.

3. Solve

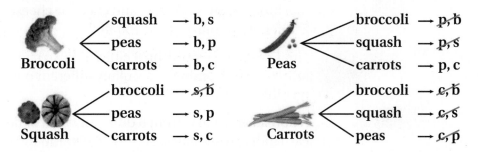

The tree diagram shows 12 possible ways to combine two vegetables, but each combination is listed twice. So there are $12 \div 2 = 6$ possible combinations.

4. Look Back

You can check by making a table. The broccoli can be paired with three other vegetables, squash with two, and peas with one. The total number of possible pairs is $3 + 2 + 1 = 6$.

Think and Discuss

1. **Describe** how to use a tree diagram to find the number of combinations in Example 1.

2. **Describe** how combinations could help you find the probability of an event.

GUIDED PRACTICE

See Example **1**

1. If you have an apple, a pear, an orange, and a plum, how many combinations of 2 fruits are possible?

2. How many 3-letter combinations are possible from *A, E, I, O,* and *U*?

See Example **2**

3. Robin packs 2 jars of jam in a gift box. She has 5 flavors: blueberry, apricot, grape, peach, and orange marmalade. How many different combinations of 2 jars can she pack in a box?

4. Eduardo has 6 colors of fabric: red, blue, green, yellow, orange, and white. He plans to make flags using 2 colors. How many possible combinations of 2 colors can he choose?

INDEPENDENT PRACTICE

See Example **1**

5. A restaurant allows you to "build your own burger" using a choice of any 2 toppings. The available toppings are bacon, grilled onions, sautéed mushrooms, Swiss cheese, and cheddar cheese. How many burgers with 2 different toppings could you build?

6. Jamil has to do reports on 3 cities. He can choose from Paris, New York, Moscow, and London. How many different combinations of cities are possible?

See Example **2**

7. A florist can choose from 6 different types of flowers to make a bouquet: carnations, roses, lilies, daisies, irises, and tulips. How many different combinations of 2 types of flowers can he choose?

8. How many different 2-member tennis teams can be made from 7 students?

PRACTICE AND PROBLEM SOLVING

 Extra Practice
See page EP28.

9. At Camp Allen, campers can choose 2 out of 8 free-time activities. Use the chart to find the number of possible combinations of 2 activities.

10. Rob, Caryn, and Sari are pairing up to play a series of chess matches. In how many different ways can they pair up?

Free-Time Activities	
hiking	volleyball
mosaics	rafting
tennis	pottery
painting	swimming

11. Gary has to write biographies about 2 historical figures. He can choose from Winston Churchill, Dr. Martin Luther King, Jr., and Nelson Mandela. How many different combinations of 2 biographies can Gary write?

12. Trina wants to select 3 of Ansel Adams's 5 "surf sequence" photos to hang on her wall. How many possible combinations are there?

13. Ms. Frennelle is teaching her art history class about famous impressionist painters. She asks her students to choose 2 artists from among Renoir, Monet, Manet, Degas, Pissarro, and Cassatt, and to find information about at least one painting made by each artist. How many possible pairs of artists can be chosen from the six painters?

Boats on the Beach at Etretat, 1883, by Claude Monet

L'Etoile, 1877, by Edgar Degas

14. Multi-Step The graph shows the number of paintings by artists of different nationalities displayed in an art book. In how many ways can you combine 4 paintings by Chinese artists?

15. ⭐ **Challenge** A gallery is preparing a show by a new artist. The gallery has enough space to display 7 pieces of art. The artist has prepared 4 paintings and 5 sculptures. How many distinct combinations of the artist's works are possible?

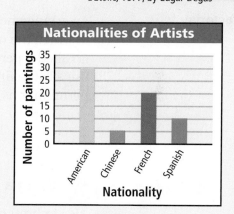

Nationalities of Artists

(bar graph: Number of paintings vs Nationality — American 30, Chinese 5, French 20, Spanish 10)

Test Prep and Spiral Review

16. Multiple Choice How many different 2-person teams can be made from 5 people?

   Ⓐ 10   Ⓑ 20   Ⓒ 24   Ⓓ 36

17. Gridded Response How many 2-letter combinations are possible from the letters *A, B, C, D, E,* and *F*?

Estimate each square root to the nearest whole number. (Lesson 9-7)

18. $\sqrt{76}$ **19.** $\sqrt{31}$ **20.** $\sqrt{126}$ **21.** $\sqrt{55}$

Decide whether each set of events is independent or dependent. Explain your answer. (Lesson 11-6)

22. A student is chosen at random from a list. A second student is chosen from the same list.

23. A girl chooses a piece of fruit from one bin. A boy then chooses a piece of fruit from a different bin.

The conductor of a symphony orchestra is planning a concert titled "An Evening with the Killer B's." The concert will feature music by Bach, Beethoven, Brahms, and Bartok. In how many different orders can the conductor arrange the music of the four composers?

Vocabulary
permutation
factorial

An arrangement of objects or events in which the order is important is called a **permutation**. You can use a list to find the number of permutations of a group of objects.

EXAMPLE **1** **Using a List to Find Permutations**

In how many different orders can the conductor arrange the music composed by Bach, Beethoven, Brahms, and Bartok?

Use a list to find the possible permutations.

Let 1 = Bach, 2 = Beethoven, 3 = Brahms, and 4 = Bartok.

Interactivities Online ▶

1-2-3-4	*List all permutations beginning with 1.*	2-1-3-4	*List all permutations beginning with 2.*
1-2-4-3		2-1-4-3	
1-3-2-4		2-3-1-4	
1-3-4-2		2-3-4-1	
1-4-2-3		2-4-1-3	
1-4-3-2		2-4-3-1	
3-1-2-4	*List all permutations beginning with 3.*	4-1-2-3	*List all permutations beginning with 4.*
3-1-4-2		4-1-3-2	
3-2-1-4		4-2-1-3	
3-2-4-1		4-2-3-1	
3-4-1-2		4-3-1-2	
3-4-2-1		4-3-2-1	

There are 24 permutations. Therefore, the conductor can arrange the music by the four composers in 24 different orders.

Video **Lesson Tutorials Online** my.hrw.com

You can use the Fundamental Counting Principle to find the number of permutations.

EXAMPLE **2**

Using the Fundamental Counting Principle to Find the Number of Permutations

Remember!

The Fundamental Counting Principle states that you can find the total number of outcomes by multiplying the number of outcomes for each separate experiment.

Three students have agreed to serve in leadership positions for the Spanish Club. In how many different ways can the students fill the positions of president, vice-president, and secretary?

Once you fill a position, you have one less choice for the next position.

There are 3 choices for the first position.

    There are 2 remaining choices for the second position.

        There is 1 remaining choice for the third position.

$3 \cdot 2 \cdot 1 = 6$ *Multiply.*

There are 6 different ways that 3 students can fill the 3 positons.

A **factorial** of a whole number is the product of all the whole numbers except zero that are less than or equal to the number.

"3 factorial" is $3! = 3 \cdot 2 \cdot 1 = 6$

"6 factorial" is $6! = 6 \cdot 5 \cdot 4 \cdot 3 \cdot 2 \cdot 1 = 720$

You can use factorials to find the number of permutations.

EXAMPLE **3**

Using Factorials to Find the Number of Permutations

Helpful Hint

You can use a calculator to find the factorial of a number. To find 5!, press 5

[MATH] *PRB 4:!* [ENTER]

[ENTER] .

There are 9 players in a baseball lineup. How many different batting orders are possible for these 9 players?

Number of permutations = 9!
$$= 9 \cdot 8 \cdot 7 \cdot 6 \cdot 5 \cdot 4 \cdot 3 \cdot 2 \cdot 1$$
$$= 362,880$$

There are 362,880 different batting orders for 9 players.

Think and Discuss

1. **Evaluate** how the permutations are listed in Example 1. Why is it important to follow a pattern?

2. **Explain** why 8! gives the number of permutations of 8 objects.

Learn It Online
Homework Help Online **go.hrw.com,**
keyword MS10 11-8 Go
Exercises 1–8, 13, 15, 17, 19, 21

GUIDED PRACTICE

See Example 1 **1.** In how many ways can you arrange the numbers 1, 2, 3, and 4 to make a 4-digit number?

See Example 2 **2.** Find the number of permutations of the letters in the word *quiet*.

See Example 3 **3.** Sam wants to call 6 friends to invite them to a party. In how many different orders can he make the calls?

4. Seven people are waiting to audition for a play. In how many different orders can the auditions be done?

INDEPENDENT PRACTICE

See Example 1 **5.** In how many ways can Eric, Meera, and Roger stand in line?

See Example 2 **6.** Find the number of ways you can arrange the letters in the word *art*.

See Example 3 **7.** How many permutations of the letters A through J are there?

8. In how many different ways can 8 riders be matched up with 8 horses?

PRACTICE AND PROBLEM SOLVING

Extra Practice
See page EP28.

Determine whether each problem involves combinations or permutations. Explain your answer.

9. Choose five books to check out from a group of ten.

10. Decide how many ways five people can be assigned to sit in five chairs.

11. Choose a 4-digit PIN using all of the digits 3, 7, 1, and 8.

12. **Sports** Ten golfers on a team are playing in a tournament. How many different lineups can the golf coach make?

13. Carl, Melba, Sean, and Ricki are going to present individual reports in their Spanish class. Their teacher randomly selects which student will speak first. What is the probability that Melba will present her report first?

14. Using the digits 1 through 7, Pima County is assigning new 7-digit numbers to all households. How many possible numbers can the county assign without repeating any of the digits in a number?

15. How many different 5-digit numbers can be made using the digits 6, 3, 5, 0, and 4 without repetitions?

16. In how many different orders can 12 songs on a CD be played?

17. **Multi-Step** If you have 5 items, and you can fit 3 of them on a shelf, how many choices do you have for the first item on the shelf? for the second item? for the third item? How many different orders are possible for the 3 items chosen from 5 items?

Literature

Since its initial publication in 1868, *Little Women*, by Louisa May Alcott, has never been out of print. It has been translated into at least 27 languages.

18. **Health** A survey was taken to find out how 200 people age 40 and older rate their memory now compared to 10 years ago. In how many different orders could interviews be conducted with people who think their memory is the same?

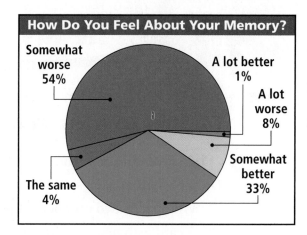

How Do You Feel About Your Memory?

Somewhat worse 54%
A lot better 1%
A lot worse 8%
Somewhat better 33%
The same 4%

19. **Literature** The school library has 13 books by Louisa May Alcott. Merina wants to read all 13 of them one after another. Write an expression to show the number of ways she can do that.

20. Use the letters *A, D, E, R*.

   a. How many permutations of the letters are there?

   b. How many arrangements form English words?

21. Josie and Luke have 3 sunflowers and 4 bluebonnets. Josie selects a flower at random. Then Luke chooses a flower at random from the remaining flowers. What is the probability that Josie picks a sunflower and Luke chooses a bluebonnet?

22. **What's the Error?** A student was trying to find 5! and wrote the equation $5 + 4 + 3 + 2 + 1 = 15$. Why is this student incorrect?

23. **Write About It** Explain the difference between combinations of objects and permutations of objects. Give examples of each.

24. **Challenge** Evaluate $\frac{11!}{3!(11-3)!}$.

Test Prep and Spiral Review

25. **Multiple Choice** Which expression can you use to find the number of 5-digit passwords you can make using the digits 1, 3, 5, 7, and 9, if you do not repeat any of the digits?

   (A) $9 + 7 + 5 + 3 + 1$

   (B) $9 \cdot 7 \cdot 5 \cdot 3 \cdot 1$

   (C) $5 + 4 + 3 + 2 + 1$

   (D) $5 \cdot 4 \cdot 3 \cdot 2 \cdot 1$

26. **Gridded Response** A school play has seven different characters. In how many different ways can seven students be assigned to the roles?

27. Use the Pythagorean Theorem to find the missing measure in the triangle at right. Round to the nearest tenth. (Lesson 9-8)

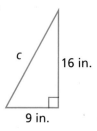

c
16 in.
9 in.

28. Margaret is traveling. She can bring two of her 9 favorite books with her. How many different combinations of 2 books can she bring? (Lesson 11-7)

 **Ready To Go On?**

Quiz for Lessons 11-6 Through 11-8

 11-6 **Probability of Independent and Dependent Events**

Decide whether each set of events is independent or dependent. Explain.

1. Winny rolls two number cubes and gets a 5 on one and a 3 on the other.

2. A card with hearts is drawn from a full deck of cards and not replaced. Then a card with clubs is drawn from the same deck.

A bag contains 8 blue and 7 yellow marbles. Use this information for Exercises 3 and 4.

3. Find the probability of randomly drawing a blue marble and then randomly drawing a yellow marble without replacing the first marble.

4. Find the probability of randomly drawing a blue marble and then randomly drawing another blue marble after replacing the first marble.

5. Marcelo has six $1 bills, two $5 bills, and one $10 bill in his pocket. He selects two of the bills at random. What is the probability that Marcelo picks one $5 bill and the $10 bill?

 11-7 **Combinations**

6. Kenny wants the guests to have 2 juice options at his party. There are 8 different juices that he has to choose from. How many different ways can Kenny choose 2 different juices?

7. Find the number of different ways that 2 out of 12 students can volunteer to organize a class party.

8. A restaurant offers entrees with a choice of 2 side dishes. How many combinations of 2 sides are available from a list of 9 side dishes?

11-8 **Permutations**

9. Four swimmers are chosen to swim in a relay race. How many orders of the 4 swimmers are possible for the relay race?

10. Six students have volunteered to help with the Spring Fest. In how many ways can these six students be assigned the following positions: concession stand, dunking booth, face-painting booth, fishing pond, ring toss, and haystack hunt?

11. Employees on the second floor have been given five 1-digit numbers from which to create a 5-digit passcode to unlock a color copier. From how many different passcodes can they choose if the passcode cannot have repeated numbers?

CONNECTIONS

The Delaware Sports Museum and Hall of Fame

Since 2002, Frawley Stadium in Wilmington has been home to the Delaware Sports Museum and Hall of Fame. The 5000-square-foot hall features artifacts, uniforms, and photos of the outstanding athletes who have been part of Delaware's history.

DELAWARE

Wilmington

For 1–3, use the table.

1. The table shows the 2007 inductees at the hall. Alison is taking pictures of the inductees. She chooses an inductee at random for the first photograph.

   a. What is the probability that the inductee played football?

   b. What is the probability that the inductee did not play football?

2. Alison chooses another inductee at random for the second photograph. What is the probability that the inductees in the first two photos both played football?

3. Alison decides to take a group picture of the inductees who played football.

   a. In how many different ways can these inductees stand in a line?

   b. Alison would like to have two of the football players seated for the photograph. In how many different ways can she choose the two inductees who will be seated?

Delaware Sports Hall of Fame 2007 Inductees	
Name	**Field**
Bernard Briggs	Coaching
Jim Bundren	Football
Bob Immediato	Baseball
Vincent Mayer	Football
Rick McCall	Coaching
Lovett Purnell	Football
Vinnie Scott	Football
David Whitcraft	Soccer
Val Whiting	Basketball

Game Time

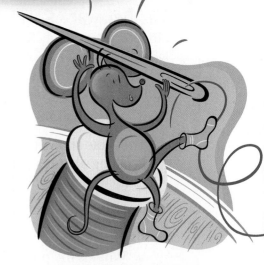

Buffon's Needle

If you drop a needle of a given length onto a wooden floor with evenly spaced cracks, what is the probability that it will land across a crack?

Comte de Buffon (1707–1788) posed this geometric probability problem. To answer his question, Buffon developed a formula using ℓ to represent the length of the needle and d to represent the distance between the cracks.

$$\text{probability} = \frac{2\ell}{\pi d}$$

To re-create this experiment, you need a paper clip and several evenly spaced lines drawn on a piece of paper. Make sure that the distance between the lines is greater than the length of the paper clip. Toss the paper clip onto the piece of paper at least a dozen times. Divide the number of times the paper clip lands across a line by the number of times you toss the paper clip. Compare this quotient to the probability given by the formula.

The other interesting result of Buffon's discovery is that you can use the probability of the needle toss to estimate *pi*.

$$\pi = \frac{2\ell}{\text{probability} \cdot d}$$

Toss the paper clip 20 times to find the experimental probability. Use this probability in the formula above, and compare the result to 3.14.

Pattern Match

This game is for two players. Player A arranges four different pattern blocks in a row out of the view of player B. Player B then tries to guess the arrangement. After each guess, player A reveals how many of the blocks are in the correct position without telling which blocks they are. The round ends when player B correctly guesses the arrangement.

A complete set of game pieces are available online.

Learn It Online
Game Time Extra **go.hrw.com**,
keyword MS10 Games Go

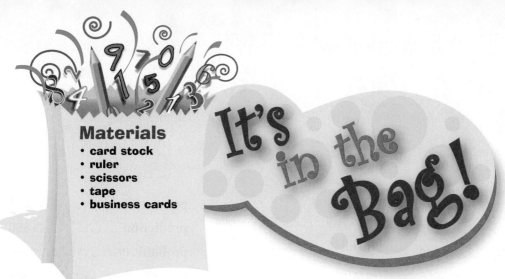

Materials
• card stock
• ruler
• scissors
• tape
• business cards

It's in the Bag!

PROJECT **The Business of Probability**

Make a holder for business cards. Then use the business cards to take notes on probability.

❶ Cut a piece of card stock to $7\frac{1}{2}$ inches by $4\frac{1}{2}$ inches. Fold the card stock in thirds and then unfold it. **Figure A**

❷ Cut out a trapezoid that is about $\frac{1}{2}$-inch tall from one end of the card stock as shown. **Figure B**

❸ Cut off about $\frac{1}{2}$ inch along the other end of the card stock. Then cut the corners at an angle. **Figure C**

❹ Fold up the bottom section of the card stock and tape the edges closed. **Figure D**

Taking Note of the Math

Use the backs of business cards to take notes on probability. Store the business cards in the holder that you made. Write the name and number of the chapter on the flap of the holder.

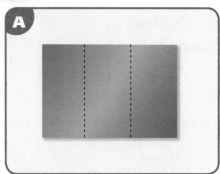

A

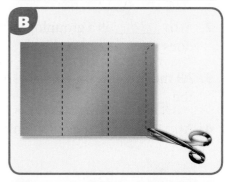

B

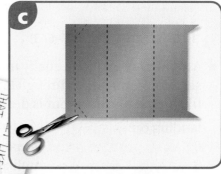

C

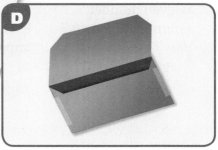

D

PROBABILITY - MEASURE...

THAT... LIKELY...

IMPOSSIBLE - IS...

EVENT -...
ONE...

EXPERIMENT - AN ACTIVITY
INVOLVING CHANCE...

OUTCOME - THE RESULT
OF AN EXPERIMENT.

CHAPTER 11
PROBABILITY

Vocabulary

Complete the sentences below with vocabulary words from the list above.

1. For ___?___, the outcome of one event has no effect on the outcome of a second event.

2. A(n) ___?___ is a grouping of objects or events in which order does not matter.

3. All the possible outcomes of an experiment make up the ___?___.

4. A(n) ___?___ is a result of an experiment.

EXAMPLES

EXERCISES

11-1 Probability (pp. 640–643)

- A spinner is divided equally into 8 sectors numbered 1 through 8. The likelihood of each event is described.

landing on:

0	impossible
5	unlikely
an even number	as likely as not
a number less than 7	likely
100	impossible

Determine whether each event is impossible, unlikely, as likely as not, likely, or certain.

5. rolling a sum of 12 with two number cubes

6. rolling a sum of 24 with two number cubes

7. The probability of rain is 20%. What is the probability of no rain?

8. The probability of the football team winning its last game is $\frac{1}{5}$. What is the probability of the team not winning the last game?

11-2 Experimental Probability (pp. 644–647)

■ Of 50 people surveyed, 21 said they liked mysteries better than comedies. What is the probability that the next person surveyed will prefer mysteries?

$$P(\text{mysteries}) = \frac{\text{number who like mysteries}}{\text{total number surveyed}}$$

$$P(\text{mysteries}) = \frac{21}{50}$$

The probability is $\frac{21}{50}$.

Sami has been keeping a record of her math grades. Of her first 15 grades, 10 have been above 82.

9. What is the probability that her next grade will be above 82?

10. What is the probability that her next grade will not be above 82?

11-3 Sample Spaces (pp. 648–651)

■ Anita tosses a coin and rolls a number cube. How many outcomes are possible?

The coin has 2 outcomes. *List the number of outcomes.*
The number cube has 6 outcomes.

$2 \cdot 6 = 12$ *Use the Fundamental Counting Principle.*

There are 12 possible outcomes.

Chen spins each of the spinners once.

11. What are all the possible outcomes?

12. How many outcomes are in the sample space?

11-4 Theoretical Probability (pp. 652–655)

■ Find the probability of drawing a 4 from a standard deck of 52 playing cards. Write your answer as a fraction, as a decimal, and as a percent.

$$P(4) = \frac{\text{number of 4's in deck}}{\text{number of cards in deck}}$$

$$= \frac{4}{52} = \frac{1}{13} \approx 0.077 \approx 7.7\%$$

Find each probability. Write your answer as a fraction, as a decimal, and as a percent.

13. There are 9 girls and 12 boys on the student council. What is the probability that a girl will be chosen as president?

14. Anita tosses 3 coins. What is the probability that each coin will land tails up?

11-5 Making Predictions (pp. 658–661)

■ Mia's experimental probability of making a free-throw is 21%. Out of 20 free-throw shots, about how many will she make?

$$\frac{21}{100} \cdot 20 = x$$

$$4.2 = x$$

Mia will make about 4 out of 20 shots.

15. Tim's experimental probability of making a soccer goal is 40%. Out of 50 goal attempts, about how many will he make?

16. If you roll a number cube 12 times, about how many times do you expect to roll an odd number?

Study Guide: Review

11-6 Probability of Independent and Dependent Events (pp. 666–669)

- There are 4 red marbles, 3 green marbles, 6 blue marbles, and 2 black marbles in a bag. What is the probability that Angie will pick a green marble and then a black marble without replacing the first marble?

  $P(\text{green marble}) = \frac{3}{15} = \frac{1}{5}$

  $P(\text{black after green}) = \frac{2}{14} = \frac{1}{7}$

  $P(\text{green, then black}) = \frac{1}{5} \cdot \frac{1}{7} = \frac{1}{35}$

  The probability of picking a green marble and then a black marble with no replacement is $\frac{1}{35}$.

17. There are 40 tags numbered 1 through 40 in a bag. What is the probability that Glenn will randomly pick a multiple of 5 and then a multiple of 9 without replacing the first tag?

18. Each letter of the word *probability* is written on a card and put in a bag. What is the probability of picking a vowel on the first try and again on the second try if the first card is replaced? (Do not include *y* as a vowel.)

11-7 Combinations (pp. 670–673)

- Tina, Sam, and Jo are trying out for co-captains of the soccer team. In how many ways can they be chosen as the co-captains?

Tina		Sam		Jo	
Sam	Jo	Tina	Jo	Tina	Sam
T, S	T, J	S͞,͞T͞	S, J	J͞,͞T͞	J͞,͞S͞

  There are 3 possible ways the girls can be chosen as co-captains.

19. How many ways can you select 2 pieces of fruit from a basket of 5 pieces?

20. How many 2-person groups can be chosen from 7 people?

21. How many combinations of 2 balloons can be chosen from 9 balloons?

11-8 Permutations (pp. 674–677)

- How many different four-digit numbers can you make from the numbers 2, 4, 6, and 8 using each just once?

  There are 4 choices for the first digit, 3 choices for the second, 2 choices for the third, and 1 for the fourth.

  $4 \cdot 3 \cdot 2 \cdot 1 = 24$

  There are 24 different four-digit numbers.

22. How many different batting orders are possible for 10 players on a league softball team?

23. How many different ways can you arrange the letters in the word *number*?

24. In how many ways can Tanya, Rika, Andy, Evan, and Tanisha line up for lunch?

25. There are 10 people playing at a recital. In how many different orders can the people play?

Chapter Test

A box contains 3 orange cubes, 2 white cubes, 3 black cubes, and 4 blue cubes. Determine whether each event is impossible, unlikely, as likely as not, likely, or certain.

1. randomly choosing an orange or black cube

2. randomly choosing a white cube

3. randomly choosing a purple cube

4. Simon tosses a coin 20 times. The coin lands heads up 7 times. Based on these results, how many times can Simon expect the coin to land heads up in the next 100 tosses?

5. Emilio spins a spinner that is divided into 8 equal sectors numbered 1 through 8. In his first three spins, the spinner lands on 8. What is the experimental probability that Emilio will spin a 10 on his fourth spin?

6. A brand of jeans comes in 8 different waist sizes: 28, 30, 32, 34, 36, 38, 40, and 42. The jeans also come in three different colors: blue, black, and tan. How many different combinations of waist sizes and colors are possible?

7. Greg is planning his vacation. He can choose from 3 ways to travel—train, bus, or plane—and four different activities—skiing, skating, snowboarding, or hiking. What are all the possible outcomes? How many different vacations can Greg plan?

Rachel spins a spinner that is divided into 10 equal sectors numbered 1 through 10. Find each probability. Write your answer as a fraction, as a decimal, and as a percent.

8. *P*(odd number)   9. *P*(composite number)   10. *P*(number greater than 10)

Find the probability of each event.

11. spinning red on a spinner with equally sized red, blue, yellow, and green sectors, and flipping a coin that lands tails up

12. choosing a card labeled *vanilla* from a group of cards labeled *vanilla, chocolate, strawberry,* and *swirl,* and then choosing a card labeled *chocolate* without replacing the first card

13. If you roll a number cube 12 times, about how many times do you expect to roll a number greater than 1?

14. How many ways can 2 students be chosen from 10 students?

15. Timothy wants to arrange his 6 model cars on a shelf. How many ways can he arrange them?

16. How many ways can you choose a 7-letter password from 7 different letters if the letters cannot repeat?

Test Tackler

STANDARDIZED TEST STRATEGIES

All Types: Use a Diagram

Sometimes drawing a diagram helps you solve a problem. When a diagram is given with a test item, use it as a tool. Get as much information from the drawing as possible. Keep in mind that diagrams are not always drawn to scale and can be misleading.

EXAMPLE 1

Multiple Choice What is the probability of flipping a coin and getting tails, and then rolling an even number on a number cube?

(A) $\frac{1}{2}$ (C) $\frac{1}{6}$

(B) $\frac{1}{4}$ (D) $\frac{1}{12}$

You can create a tree diagram to determine the sample space.

Heads   Tails

1 2 3 4 5 6   1 2 3 4 5 6

There are 12 possible outcomes but only 3 ways getting tails and an even number can occur. So the probability is $\frac{3}{12}$, or $\frac{1}{4}$, which is answer choice B.

EXAMPLE 2

Short Response Find the volume and surface area of the cylinder, and round your answers to the nearest tenth. Use 3.14 for π.

6 in.

10 in.

In the diagram, it appears that the radius is greater than the height. Remember that the scale of a diagram can be misleading. Rely on the information shown, and substitute the given values into each formula.

$V = \pi r^2 h$ $SA = 2\pi r^2 + 2\pi rh$

$V = \pi(6)^2(10)$ $SA = 2\pi(6)^2 + 2\pi(6)(10)$

$V = 360\pi$ $SA = 226.08 + 376.8$

$V \approx 1{,}130.4 \text{ in}^3$ $SA \approx 602.9 \text{ in}^2$

If you are having trouble understanding a test item, draw a diagram to help you answer the question.

Read each test item, and answer the questions that follow.

Item A
Multiple Choice The volume of a box is 6,336 cm^3. The width of the box is 16 cm, and the height is 18 cm. What is the length of the box?

Ⓐ 396 cm   Ⓒ 220 cm

Ⓑ 22 cm   Ⓓ 11 cm

---

1. What information about the box is given in the problem statement?

2. Sketch a diagram to help you answer the question. Label each side with the correct dimensions.

3. How does the diagram help you solve the problem?

Item B
Multiple Choice Janet spins two spinners at the same time. One spinner is divided into 3 equal sectors, labeled 1, 2, and 3. The second spinner is divided into 3 equal sectors, labeled A, B, and C. What is the probability that the spinners will land on 1 and A or 1 and C?

Ⓕ $\frac{1}{3}$ Ⓗ $\frac{1}{9}$

Ⓖ $\frac{2}{3}$ Ⓙ $\frac{2}{9}$

---

4. Make a tree diagram to determine the sample space. Then count the ways getting 1 and either A or C can occur.

5. Explain which answer choice is correct.

6. How does the tree diagram help you solve the problem?

Item C
Short Response Which two vats hold the same amount of liquid? Explain.

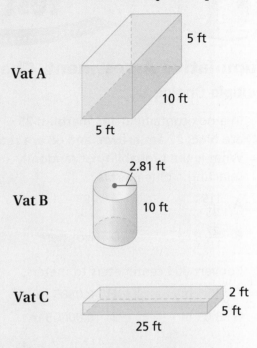

Vat A — 5 ft, 10 ft, 5 ft

Vat B — 2.81 ft, 10 ft

Vat C — 2 ft, 5 ft, 25 ft

---

7. Explain why you cannot determine the answer by comparing the scale of each diagram.

8. What formulas do you need to find the answer?

9. Explain which two vats hold the same amount of liquid.

Item D
Gridded Response Determine the surface area in square meters of a rectangular prism that has a length of 13 m, a width of 10 m, and a height of 8 m.

---

10. How do you determine the surface area of a rectangular prism?

11. Create a net for this prism and label it with the correct dimensions.

12. Use the net from problem 11 to find the surface area of the prism.

TCAP Test Prep

Cumulative Assessment, Chapters 1–11

Multiple Choice

1. In a box containing 115 marbles, 25 are blue, 22 are brown, and 68 are red. What is the probability of randomly selecting a blue marble?

A $\frac{115}{25}$ C $\frac{5}{23}$

B $\frac{22}{115}$ D Not here

2. Convert 805 centimeters to meters.

F 80.5 m   H 0.0805 m

G 8.05 m   J 0.00805 m

3. What is the value of $(-8 - 4)^2 + 4^1$?

A −143   C 145

B 0   D 148

4. The graph shows a town's high temperatures over a 5-day period. What was the average high temperature over these 5 days?

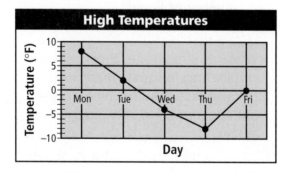

F −0.4°F   H 0.4°F

G 4.4°F   J −4.4°F

5. The cube root of 572 is found between which pair of integers on a number line?

A 7 and 8   C 20 and 21

B 8 and 9   D 23 and 24

6. What is $2\frac{5}{12} \times \frac{12}{7}$?

F $\frac{5}{7}$ H $2\frac{17}{19}$

G $2\frac{5}{7}$ J $4\frac{1}{7}$

7. A triangle-shaped wheat field has an area of 225 ft². What is the length of the hypotenuse to the nearest tenth?

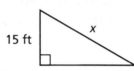

A 30 ft   C 45 ft

B 33.5 ft   D 224.5 ft

8. Which mapping represents a function?

F
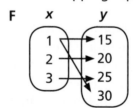

G
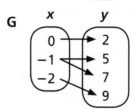

H
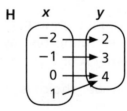

J
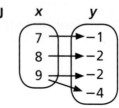

9. There are 5 dachshunds and 4 golden retrievers waiting to be groomed at the vet's office. A vet tech randomly chooses a dog to be groomed. What is the theoretical probability that the dog is a dachshund?

   A $\frac{1}{3}$ **C** $\frac{5}{9}$

   B $\frac{4}{9}$ **D** $\frac{4}{5}$

 Probability can be expressed as a fraction, decimal, or percent.

10. Mike goes for a walk. The graph shows the relationship between the amount of time spent walking and the number of miles walked.

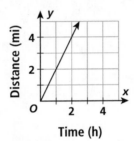
Time (h)

   What does the slope of the line represent?

   F the total number of miles walked

   G the total number of time spent walking

   H the number of miles walked per hour

   J the number of hours spent walking per mile

11. Anji bought 4 shirts for $56.80. She later bought a shirt for $19.20. What was the mean cost of all the shirts?

   A $7.52   **C** $19.00

   B $15.20   **D** $25.33

12. Which equation does <u>not</u> describe an inverse proportional relationship?

   F $y = \frac{10}{x}$ **H** $x = \frac{15}{y}$

   G $xy = 12$ **J** $y = \frac{1}{8}x$

Process Standards Practice
Short Response

S1. The diameter of the larger circle is 36 in., and the radius of the smaller circle is 6 in.

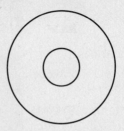

What is the ratio of the smaller circle's area to the larger circle's area written to the nearest whole percent?

S2. Rhonda has 3 different-color T-shirts—red, blue, and green—and a pair of blue jeans and a pair of white jeans. She randomly chooses a T-shirt and a pair of jeans. What is the probability that she will pair the red T-shirt with the white jeans? Show how you found your answer.

S3. Write $\frac{5}{6}$ and $\frac{3}{4}$ as fractions with a common denominator. Then determine whether the fractions are equivalent. Explain your method.

Extended Response

E1. A bag contains 5 blue blocks, 3 red blocks, and 2 yellow blocks.

   a. What is the probability that Tip will draw a red block and then a blue block at random if the first block is replaced before the second is drawn? Show the steps necessary to find your answer.

   b. What is the probability that Tip will draw a red block and then a blue block at random if the first block is not replaced before the second is drawn? Show your work.

   c. Explain how your answers to parts **a** and **b** are affected by whether or not the first block is replaced.

Why Learn This?

Scuba divers can use equations to calculate the depth of their dives or to estimate how much air is remaining in their tanks.

 Learn It Online
Chapter Project Online **go.hrw.com**,
keyword MS10 Ch12 Go

Chapter Focus
• Formulate linear equations in one variable.
• Choose procedures to solve these equations efficiently.

Are You Ready?

Learn It Online
Resources Online **go.hrw.com**,
keyword MS10 AYR12 Go

✓ Vocabulary

Choose the best term from the list to complete each sentence.

1. __?__ are mathematical operations that undo each other.

2. To solve an equation you need to __?__.

3. A(n) __?__ is a mathematical statement that two expressions are equivalent.

4. A(n) __?__ is a mathematical statement that two ratios are equivalent.

isolate the variable

equation

proportion

inverse operations

expression

Complete these exercises to review skills you will need for this chapter.

✓ Add Whole Numbers, Decimals, Fractions, and Integers

Add.

5. $24 + 16$

6. $-34 + (-47)$

7. $35 + (-61)$

8. $-12 + (-29) + 53$

9. $2.7 + 3.5$

10. $\frac{2}{3} + \frac{1}{2}$

11. $-5.87 + 10.6$

12. $\frac{8}{9} + \left(-\frac{9}{11}\right)$

✓ Evaluate Expressions

Evaluate each expression for $a = 7$ and $b = -2$.

13. $a - b$

14. $b - a$

15. $\frac{b}{a}$

16. $2a + 3b$

17. $\frac{-4a}{b}$

18. $3a - \frac{8}{b}$

19. $1.2a + 2.3b$

20. $-5a - (-6b)$

✓ Solve Multiplication Equations

Solve.

21. $8x = -72$

22. $-12a = -60$

23. $\frac{2}{3}y = 16$

24. $-12b = 9$

25. $12 = -4x$

26. $13 = \frac{1}{2}c$

27. $-2.4 = -0.8p$

28. $\frac{3}{4} = 6x$

✓ Solve Proportions

Solve.

29. $\frac{3}{4} = \frac{x}{24}$

30. $\frac{8}{9} = \frac{4}{a}$

31. $-\frac{12}{5} = \frac{15}{c}$

32. $\frac{y}{50} = \frac{35}{20}$

33. $\frac{2}{3} = \frac{18}{w}$

34. $\frac{35}{21} = \frac{d}{3}$

35. $\frac{7}{13} = \frac{h}{195}$

36. $\frac{9}{-15} = \frac{-27}{p}$

Study Guide: Preview

Where You've Been

Previously, you

- solved one-step equations.
- read, wrote, and graphed inequalities on a number line.
- solved one-step inequalities.

In This Chapter

You will study

- solving two-step and multi-step equations and equations with variables on both sides.
- reading, writing, and graphing inequalities on a number line.
- solving one-step and two-step inequalities.
- solving equations for a variable.

Where You're Going

You can use the skills learned in this chapter

- to solve problems in the physical sciences that involve comparing speeds, distances, and weights.
- to make decisions when planning events.
- to evaluate options when distributing budget funds.

Key Vocabulary/Vocabulario

algebraic inequality	desigualdad algebraica
compound inequality	desigualdad compuesta
inequality	desigualdad
solution set	conjunto solución

Vocabulary Connections

To become familiar with some of the vocabulary terms in the chapter, consider the following. You may refer to the chapter, the glossary, or a dictionary if you like.

1. What does the word *inequality* mean? How might an **inequality** describe a mathematical relationship? Give an example using numbers.

2. An example of an algebraic equation is $x + 3 = 8$. How do you think $x + 3 = 8$ would change if you were to write it as an **algebraic inequality** instead of as an equation?

3. A compound sentence is made up of two or more independent clauses joined by the words *and* or *or*. What do you think a **compound inequality** might be?

4. A solution of an equation is a value that makes the equation true. For example, $x = 5$ is a solution of $x + 3 = 8$. A set is a group of "items," such as people or numbers, that have a characteristic in common. What do you think a **solution set** might be?

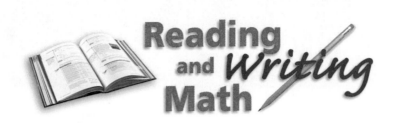 

Study Strategy: Prepare for Your Final Exam

Math is a cumulative subject, so your exam will cover all of the material you have learned from the beginning of the course. Being prepared is the key for you to be successful on your exam.

2 weeks before the final exam

- Review lesson notes and vocabulary.
- Look at previous exams and homework. Rework problems that I answered incorrectly or that I did not complete.
- Make a list of all formulas, rules, and important steps.
- Create a practice exam using problems from the book that are similar to problems from the previous tests.

1 week before the final exam

- Take the practice exam and check it. For each problem I miss, find two or three similar problems and work those.
- Look over each chapter's Study Guide: Review.
- Quiz a friend or myself on the formulas and major points from my list.

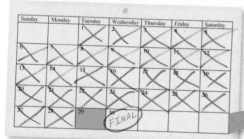

1 day before the final exam

- Make sure I have pencils and a calculator. (Check the batteries!)
- Review any problem areas one last time.

Try This

1. Create a timeline that you will use to study for your final exam.

Multi-Step Equations and Inequalities **693**

Use with Lesson 12-1

Learn It Online
Lab Resources Online **go.hrw.com**,
keyword **MS10 Lab12** Go

TN ✓ **0706.1.10** Model algebraic
equations with manipulatives, technology,
and pencil and paper.

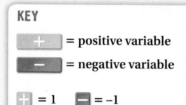

KEY

| = positive variable

| = negative variable

| = 1 | = −1

REMEMBER

- + = 0
- + = 0
- In an equation, the expressions on both sides of the equal sign are equivalent.

In Lab 2-5, you learned how to solve one-step equations using algebra tiles. You can also use algebra tiles to solve two-step equations. When solving a two-step equation, it is easiest to perform addition and subtraction before multiplication and division.

Activity

1. Use algebra tiles to model and solve $2p + 2 = 10$.

$2p + 2 = 10$

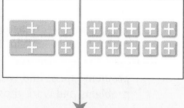

Model the equation.

$$2p + 2 = 10$$
$$\underline{-2 \quad -2}$$
$$2p \quad = 8$$

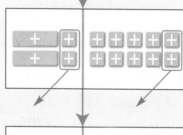

Remove 2 yellow tiles from each side of the mat.

$$\frac{2p}{2} = \frac{8}{2}$$

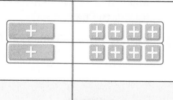

Divide each side into 2 equal groups.

$p = 4$

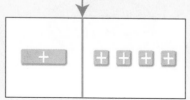

The solution is p = 4.

② Use algebra tiles to model and solve $3n + 6 = -15$.

$3n + 6 = -15$

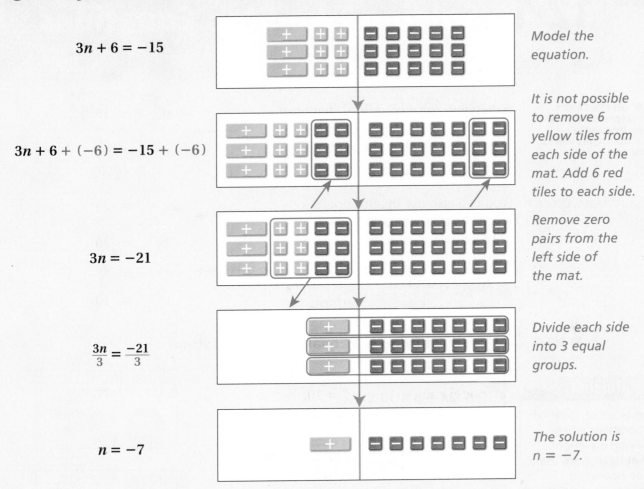

Model the equation.

$3n + 6 + (-6) = -15 + (-6)$

It is not possible to remove 6 yellow tiles from each side of the mat. Add 6 red tiles to each side.

$3n = -21$

Remove zero pairs from the left side of the mat.

$\dfrac{3n}{3} = \dfrac{-21}{3}$

Divide each side into 3 equal groups.

$n = -7$

The solution is $n = -7$.

Think and Discuss

1. When you add a value to one side of an equation, why do you also have to add the same value to the other side?

2. When you solved $3n + 6 = -15$ in the activity, why were you able to remove six yellow unit tiles and six red unit tiles from the left side of the equation?

3. Model and solve $3x - 5 = 10$. Explain each step.

4. How would you check the solution to $3n + 6 = -15$ using algebra tiles?

Try This

Use algebra tiles to model and solve each equation.

1. $4 + 2x = 20$

2. $3r + 7 = -8$

3. $-4m + 3 = -25$

4. $-2n - 5 = 17$

5. $10 = 2j - 4$

6. $5 + r = 7$

7. $4h + 2h + 3 = 15$

8. $-3g = 9$

9. $5k + (-7) = 13$

TN **SPI 0706.3.8** Solve contextual problems involving two-step linear equations. *Also* ✓ **0706.1.10, GLE 0706.3.8,** ✓ **0706.3.2**

When you solve equations that have one operation, you use an inverse operation to isolate the variable.

$$\begin{array}{rcl} n + 7 &=& 15 \\ -7 && -7 \\ \hline n &=& 8 \end{array}$$

Interactivities Online ▶ You can also use inverse operations to solve equations that have more than one operation.

$$\begin{array}{rcl} 2x + 3 &=& 23 \\ -3 && -3 \\ \hline 2x &=& 20 \end{array}$$

Use the inverse of multiplication to isolate x.

$$\begin{array}{rcl} \dfrac{2x}{2} &=& \dfrac{20}{2} \\ x &=& 10 \end{array}$$

EXAMPLE **1** **Solving Two-Step Equations Using Division**

Solve.

A $2n + 5 = 13$

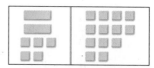

Helpful Hint

Reverse the order of operations when solving equations that have more than one operation.

$$\begin{array}{rcl} 2n + 5 &=& 13 \\ -5 && -5 \\ \hline 2n &=& 8 \end{array}$$

Subtract 5 from both sides.

$$\begin{array}{rcl} \dfrac{2n}{2} &=& \dfrac{8}{2} \\ n &=& 4 \end{array}$$

Divide both sides by 2.

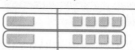

B $19 = -3p - 8$

$$19 = -3p - 8$$

$$\begin{array}{rcl} +8 && +8 \\ \hline 27 &=& -3p \end{array}$$

Add 8 to both sides.

$$\dfrac{27}{-3} = \dfrac{-3p}{-3}$$

Divide both sides by −3.

$$-9 = p$$

Check

$$19 = -3p - 8$$
$$19 \stackrel{?}{=} -3(-9) - 8 \quad \text{Substitute −9 for p.}$$
$$19 \stackrel{?}{=} 27 - 8$$
$$19 \stackrel{?}{=} 19 ✔ \quad \text{−9 is a solution.}$$

EXAMPLE 2 Solving Two-Step Equations Using Multiplication

Solve.

A $8 + \frac{m}{4} = 17$

$$8 + \frac{m}{4} = 17$$
$$\underline{-8 \qquad -8} \qquad \text{Subtract 8 from both sides.}$$
$$\frac{m}{4} = 9$$
$$(4)\frac{m}{4} = (4)9 \qquad \text{Multiply both sides by 4.}$$
$$m = 36$$

B $3 = \frac{u}{6} - 12$

$$3 = \frac{u}{6} - 12$$
$$\underline{+12 \qquad +12} \qquad \text{Add 12 to both sides.}$$
$$15 = \frac{u}{6}$$
$$(6)15 = (6)\frac{u}{6} \qquad \text{Multiply both sides by 6.}$$
$$90 = u$$

EXAMPLE 3 *Fitness Application*

Fitness LINK

A new one-year membership at Vista Tennis Center costs $160. A registration fee of $28 is paid up front, and the rest is paid monthly. How much do new members pay each month?

| registration fee | plus | 12 times monthly cost | is | $160 |

Let m represent the monthly cost.

| $28 | + | 12$m$ | = | $160 |

$$28 + 12m = 160$$
$$\underline{-28 \qquad\quad -28} \qquad \text{Subtract 28 from both sides.}$$
$$12m = 132$$
$$\frac{12m}{12} = \frac{132}{12} \qquad \text{Divide both sides by 12.}$$
$$m = 11$$

New members pay $11 per month for a one-year membership.

Labeled "the sport for a lifetime," tennis is played by people of all ages. Some tennis matches may take just minutes to complete, while others take hours or even days!

Think and Discuss

1. **Explain** how you decide which inverse operation to use first when solving a two-step equation.

2. **Tell** the steps you would follow to solve $-1 + 2x = 7$.

Exercises

Learn It Online
Homework Help Online **go.hrw.com**,
keyword MS10 12-1 Go
Exercises 1–20, 23, 25, 27, 29, 31, 33, 35

GUIDED PRACTICE

See Example 1 **Solve.**

1. $3n + 8 = 29$

2. $-4m - 7 = 17$

3. $2 = -6x + 4$

See Example 2 **Solve.**

4. $12 + \dfrac{b}{6} = 16$

5. $\dfrac{y}{8} - 15 = 2$

6. $10 = -8 + \dfrac{n}{4}$

See Example 3 **7.** A coffee shop sells a ceramic refill mug for $8.95. Each refill costs $1.50. Last month Rose spent $26.95 on a mug and refills. How many refills did she buy?

INDEPENDENT PRACTICE

See Example 1 **Solve.**

8. $5x + 6 = 41$

9. $-9p - 15 = 93$

10. $-2m + 14 = 10$

11. $-7 = 7d - 8$

12. $-7 = -3c + 14$

13. $12y - 11 = 49$

See Example 2 **Solve.**

14. $24 + \dfrac{h}{4} = 10$

15. $\dfrac{k}{5} - 13 = 4$

16. $-17 + \dfrac{q}{8} = 13$

17. $24 = \dfrac{m}{10} + 32$

18. $-9 = 15 + \dfrac{v}{3}$

19. $\dfrac{m}{-7} - 14 = 2$

See Example 3 **20.** Each Saturday, a gym holds a 45-minute yoga class. The weekday yoga classes last 30 minutes. The number of weekday classes varies. Last week, the yoga classes totaled 165 minutes. How many weekday yoga classes were held?

PRACTICE AND PROBLEM SOLVING

Extra Practice
See page EP29.

Translate each equation into words, and then solve the equation.

21. $6 + \dfrac{m}{3} = 18$

22. $3x + 15 = 27$

23. $2 = \dfrac{n}{5} - 4$

Solve.

24. $18 + \dfrac{y}{4} = 12$

25. $5x + 30 = 40$

26. $\dfrac{s}{12} - 7 = 8$

27. $-10 + 6g = 110$

28. $-8 = \dfrac{z}{7} + 2$

29. $46 = -6w - 8$

30. $15 = -7 + \dfrac{r}{3}$

31. $-20 = -4p - 12$

32. $\dfrac{1}{2} + \dfrac{r}{7} = \dfrac{5}{14}$

33. Consumer Math A long-distance phone company charges $1.01 for the first 25 minutes of a call, and then $0.09 for each additional minute. A call cost $9.56. How long did it last?

34. The school purchased baseball equipment and uniforms for a total cost of $1,836. The equipment cost $612, and the uniforms were $25.50 each. How many uniforms did the school purchase?

35. If you double the number of calories per day that the U.S. Department of Agriculture recommends for children who are 1 to 3 years old and then subtract 100, you get the number of calories per day recommended for teenage boys. Given that 2,500 calories are recommended for teenage boys, how many calories per day are recommended for children?

36. According to the U.S. Department of Agriculture, children who are 4 to 6 years old need about 1,800 calories per day. This is 700 calories more than half the recommended calories for teenage girls. How many calories per day does a teenage girl need?

37. Hector consumed 2,130 calories from food in one day. Of these, he consumed 350 calories at breakfast and 400 calories having a snack. He also ate 2 portions of one of the items shown in the table for lunch and the same for dinner. What did Hector eat for lunch and dinner?

Calorie Counter		
Food	Portion	Calories
Stir-fry	1 cup	250
Enchilada	1 whole	310
Pizza	1 slice	345
Tomato soup	1 cup	160

38. ⭐ Challenge There are 30 mg of cholesterol in a box of macaroni and cheese. This is 77 mg minus $\frac{1}{10}$ the number of milligrams of sodium it contains. How many milligrams of sodium are in a box of macaroni and cheese?

Test Prep and Spiral Review

39. **Multiple Choice** For which equation is $x = -2$ a solution?

  Ⓐ $2x + 5 = 9$ Ⓑ $8 = 10 - x$ Ⓒ $\frac{x}{2} + 3 = 2$ Ⓓ $-16 = -4x - 8$

40. **Short Response** A taxi cab costs $1.25 for the first mile and $0.25 for each additional mile. Write an equation for the total cost of a taxi ride, where x is the number of miles. How many miles can be traveled in the taxi for $8.00?

Identify the three-dimensional figure described. (Lesson 10-1)

41. 6 rectangular faces

42. 1 hexagonal base and 6 triangular faces

Find the volume of each figure to the nearest tenth. Use 3.14 for π. (Lesson 10-2)

43. cylinder with radius 5 cm and height 7 cm

44. triangular prism with a base with area 18 in² and height 9 in.

TN SPI 0706.3.8 Solve contextual problems involving two-step linear equations. *Also* ✓ 0706.1.10, GLE 0706.3.8, ✓ 0706.3.2

Jamal owns twice as many graphic novels as Levi owns. If you add 6 to the number of graphic novels Jamal owns and then divide by 7, you get the number of graphic novels Brooke owns. Brooke owns 30 graphic novels. How many graphic novels does Levi own? To answer this question, you need to set up an equation that requires more than two steps to solve.

EXAMPLE 1 **Combining Like Terms to Solve Equations**

Solve $7n - 1 - 2n = 14$.

$$7n - 1 - 2n = 14$$
$$5n - 1 = 14 \qquad \text{\textit{Combine like terms.}}$$
$$\underline{+1 \qquad +1} \qquad \text{\textit{Add 1 to both sides.}}$$
$$5n = 15$$

$$\frac{5n}{5} = \frac{15}{5} \qquad \text{\textit{Divide both sides by 5.}}$$
$$n = 3$$

You may need to use the Distributive Property to solve an equation that has parentheses. Multiply each term inside the parentheses by the factor that is outside the parentheses. Then combine like terms.

EXAMPLE 2 **Using the Distributive Property to Solve Equations**

Solve $3(z - 1) + 8 = 14$.

Remember!

The Distributive Property states that $a(b + c) = ab + ac$. For instance, $2(3 + 5) = 2(3) + 2(5)$.

$$3(z - 1) + 8 = 14$$
$$3(z) - 3(1) + 8 = 14 \qquad \text{\textit{Distribute 3 on the left side.}}$$
$$3z - 3 + 8 = 14 \qquad \text{\textit{Simplify.}}$$
$$3z + 5 = 14 \qquad \text{\textit{Combine like terms.}}$$
$$\underline{-5 \qquad -5} \qquad \text{\textit{Add −5 to both sides.}}$$
$$3z = 9$$
$$\frac{3z}{3} = \frac{9}{3} \qquad \text{\textit{Divide both sides by 3.}}$$
$$z = 3$$

EXAMPLE 3 **PROBLEM SOLVING APPLICATION**

READY TO TAKE 'EM?

I WAS BORN READY!

Jamal owns twice as many graphic novels as Levi owns. Adding 6 to the number of graphic novels Jamal owns and then dividing by 7 gives the number Brooke owns. Brooke owns 30 graphic novels. How many does Levi own?

1. Understand the Problem

Rewrite the question as a statement.

- Find the number of graphic novels that Levi owns.

List the **important information:**

- Jamal owns 2 times as many graphic novels as Levi owns.
- The number of graphic novels Jamal owns added to 6 and then divided by 7 equals the number Brooke owns.
- Brooke owns 30 graphic novels.

2. Make a Plan

Let g represent the number of graphic novels Levi owns. Then $2g$ represents the number Jamal owns, and $\frac{2g+6}{7}$ represents the number Brooke owns, which equals 30. Solve the equation $\frac{2g+6}{7} = 30$ for g.

3. Solve

$$\frac{2g+6}{7} = 30$$

$$(7)\frac{2g+6}{7} = (7)30 \qquad \textit{Multiply both sides by 7 to eliminate fractions.}$$

$$2g + 6 = 210$$

$$2g + 6 - 6 = 210 - 6 \qquad \textit{Subtract 6 from both sides.}$$

$$2g = 204$$

$$\frac{2g}{2} = \frac{204}{2} \qquad \textit{Divide both sides by 2.}$$

$$g = 102$$

Levi owns 102 graphic novels.

4. Look Back

Make sure that your answer makes sense in the original problem. Levi has 102 graphic novels. Jamal has $2(102) = 204$. Brooke has $\frac{204+6}{7} = 30$.

Think and Discuss

1. **List** the steps required to solve $-n + 5n + 3 = 27$.

2. **Describe** how to solve the equations $\frac{2}{3}x + 7 = 4$ and $\frac{2x+7}{3} = 4$. Are the solutions the same or different? Explain.

Exercises

Learn It Online
Homework Help Online **go.hrw.com**,
keyword MS10 12-2 Go
Exercises 1–20, 21, 23, 25, 29,
31, 33, 35

GUIDED PRACTICE

Solve.

See Example 1
1. $14n + 2 - 7n = 37$
2. $10x - 11 - 4x = 43$
3. $1 = -3 + 4p - 2p$

See Example 2
4. $12 - (x + 3) = 10$
5. $15 = 2(q + 4) + 3$
6. $5(m - 2) + 36 = -4$

See Example 3
7. Keisha read twice as many books this year as Ben read. Subtracting 4 from the number of books Keisha read and dividing by 2 gives the number of books Sheldon read. Sheldon read 10 books. How many books did Ben read?

INDEPENDENT PRACTICE

Solve.

See Example 1
8. $b + 18 + 3b = 74$
9. $10x - 3 - 2x = 4$

10. $18w - 10 - 6w = 50$
11. $19 = 5n + 7 - 3n$

12. $-27 = -3p + 15 - 3p$
13. $-x - 8 + 14x = -34$

See Example 2
14. $2(x + 4) + 6 = 22$
15. $1 - 3(n + 5) = -8$

16. $4.3 - 1.4(p + 7) = -9.7$
17. $3(0.6 + 2n) - 3.2 = 7.6$

18. $0 = 9\left(k - \frac{2}{3}\right) + 33$
19. $6(t - 2) - 76 = -142$

See Example 3
20. Abby ran 3 times as many laps as Karen. Adding 4 to the number of laps Abby ran and then dividing by 7 gives the number of laps Jill ran. Jill ran 1 lap. How many laps did Karen run?

PRACTICE AND PROBLEM SOLVING

Extra Practice
See page EP29.

Solve.

21. $\frac{0.5x + 7}{8} = 5$
22. $4(t - 8) + 20 = 5$
23. $63 = 8w + 2.6 - 3.6$

24. $17 = -5(3 + w) + 7$
25. $\frac{\frac{1}{4}a - 12}{8} = 4$
26. $9 = -(r - 5) + 11$

27. $\frac{2b - 3.4}{0.6} = -29$
28. $8.44 = \frac{34.6 + 4h}{5}$
29. $5.7 = -2.5x + 18 - 1.6x$

30. **Consumer Math** Three friends ate dinner at a restaurant. The friends decided to add a 15% tip and then split the bill evenly. Each friend paid $10.35. What was the total bill for dinner before tip?

31. Ann earns 1.5 times her normal hourly pay for each hour that she works over 40 hours in a week. Last week she worked 51 hours and earned $378.55. What is her normal hourly pay?

32. **Geometry** The base angles of an isosceles triangle are congruent. The measure of each of the base angles is twice the measure of the third angle. Find the measures of all three angles.

33. **Consumer Math** Patrice used a $15 gift certificate when she purchased a pair of sandals. After 8% sales tax was applied to the price of the sandals, the $15 was deducted. Patrice had to pay a total of $12 for the sandals. How much did the sandals cost before tax?

34. **Physical Science** To convert temperatures between degrees Celsius and degrees Fahrenheit, you can use the formula $F = \frac{9}{5}C + 32$. The table shows the melting points of various elements. Round to the nearest degree.

   a. What is the melting point in degrees Celsius of gold?

   b. What is the melting point in degrees Celsius of hydrogen?

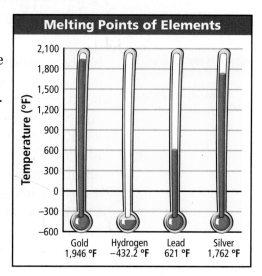

Melting Points of Elements

Gold	Hydrogen	Lead	Silver
1,946 °F	−432.2 °F	621 °F	1,762 °F

35. On his first two social studies tests, Billy made an 86 and a 93. What grade must Billy make on the third test to have an average of 90 for all three tests?

36. **What's the Question?** Three friends shared a taxi ride from the airport to their hotel. After adding a $7.00 tip, the friends divided the cost of the ride evenly. If solving the equation $\frac{c + \$7.00}{3} = \$11.25$ gives the answer, what is the question?

37. **Write About It** Explain why multiplying first in the equation $\frac{2x - 6}{5} = 2$ makes finding the solution easier than adding first does.

38. **Challenge** Are the solutions to the following equations the same? Explain.
$$\frac{3y}{4} + 2 = 4 \text{ and } 3y + 8 = 16$$

Test Prep and Spiral Review

39. **Multiple Choice** Solve $\frac{2x - 2}{4} = 7$.

   Ⓐ $x = 15$ Ⓑ $x = 18$ Ⓒ $x = 20$ Ⓓ $x = 21$

40. **Multiple Choice** For which equation(s) is $x = 3$ a solution?

   I $2x - 5 + 3x = 10$ **II** $\frac{-x + 7}{2} = 2$ **III** $\frac{-4x}{6} = 2$ **IV** $6.3x - 2.4 = 16.5$

   Ⓕ I only   Ⓖ I and II   Ⓗ I, II, and III   Ⓙ I, II, and IV

Find the volume of each figure to the nearest tenth. Use 3.14 for π. (Lesson 10-3)

41. a cone with diameter 6 cm and height 4 cm

42. a triangular pyramid with height 7 in. and base area 18 in^2

Solve. (Lesson 12-1)

43. $6x - 4 = 2$ 44. $7 = -y + 4$ 45. $5 + \frac{z}{2} = -9$ 46. $12 - 6d = 54$

12-3 Solving Equations with Variables on Both Sides

TN SPI 0706.3.8 Solve contextual problems involving two-step linear equations. *Also* ✓ 0706.1.10, GLE 0706.3.8, ✓ 0706.3.2

Mari can rent a video game console for $14.49 per week or buy a rebuilt one for $72.45. The cost of renting a game is $7.95 per week. How many weeks would Mari have to rent both the game and the console to pay as much as she would if she had bought the used console and rented the game instead?

Problems such as this require you to solve equations that have the same variable on both sides of the equal sign. To solve this kind of problem, you need to get the terms with variables on one side of the equal sign.

E X A M P L E 1 Using Inverse Operations to Group Terms with Variables

Group the terms with variables on one side of the equal sign, and simplify.

A $6m = 4m + 12$

$$6m = 4m + 12$$
$$6m - 4m = 4m - 4m + 12 \qquad \text{Subtract 4m from both sides.}$$
$$2m = 12 \qquad \text{Simplify.}$$

B $-7x - 198 = 5x$

$$-7x - 198 = 5x$$
$$-7x + 7x - 198 = 5x + 7x \qquad \text{Add 7x to both sides.}$$
$$-198 = 12x \qquad \text{Simplify.}$$

E X A M P L E 2 Solving Equations with Variables on Both Sides

Interactivities Online ▶

Solve.

A $5n = 3n + 26$

$$5n = 3n + 26$$
$$5n - 3n = 3n - 3n + 26 \qquad \text{Subtract 3n from both sides.}$$
$$2n = 26 \qquad \text{Simplify.}$$
$$\frac{2n}{2} = \frac{26}{2} \qquad \text{Divide both sides by 2.}$$
$$n = 13$$

Video Lesson Tutorials Online

Solve.

B $19 + 7n = -2n + 37$

$$19 + 7n = -2n + 37$$

$19 + 7n + 2n = -2n + 2n + 37$	*Add 2n to both sides.*
$19 + 9n = 37$	*Simplify.*
$19 + 9n - 19 = 37 - 19$	*Subtract 19 from both sides.*
$9n = 18$	*Simplify.*
$\dfrac{9n}{9} = \dfrac{18}{9}$	*Divide both sides by 9.*
$n = 2$	

C $\dfrac{5}{9}x = \dfrac{4}{9}x + 9$

$$\dfrac{5}{9}x = \dfrac{4}{9}x + 9$$

$\dfrac{5}{9}x - \dfrac{4}{9}x = \dfrac{4}{9}x - \dfrac{4}{9}x + 9$	*Subtract $\dfrac{4}{9}x$ from both sides.*
$\dfrac{1}{9}x = 9$	*Simplify.*
$(9)\dfrac{1}{9}x = (9)9$	*Multiply both sides by 9.*
$x = 81$	

EXAMPLE 3 *Consumer Math Application*

Mari can buy a video game console for $72.45 and rent a game for $7.95 per week, or she can rent a console and the same game for a total of $22.44 per week. How many weeks would Mari need to rent both the video game and the console to pay as much as she would if she had bought the console and rented the game instead?

Let w represent the number of weeks.

$22.44w = 72.45 + 7.95w$	
$22.44w - 7.95w = 72.45 + 7.95w - 7.95w$	*Subtract 7.95w from both sides.*
$14.49w = 72.45$	*Simplify.*
$\dfrac{14.49w}{14.49} = \dfrac{72.45}{14.49}$	*Divide both sides by 14.49.*
$w = 5$	

Mari would need to rent the video game and the console for 5 weeks to pay as much as she would have if she had bought the console.

Think and Discuss

1. **Explain** how you would solve $\dfrac{1}{2}x + 7 = \dfrac{2}{3}x - 2$.

2. **Describe** how you would decide which variable term to add or subtract on both sides of the equation $-3x + 7 = 4x - 9$.

Learn It Online
Homework Help Online **go.hrw.com**,
keyword MS10 12-3 Go
Exercises 1–20, 21, 23, 25, 27, 29, 31

GUIDED PRACTICE

See Example **1** **Group the terms with variables on one side of the equal sign, and simplify.**

1. $5n = 4n + 32$ **2.** $-6x - 28 = 4x$ **3.** $8w = 32 - 4w$

See Example **2** **Solve.**

4. $4y = 2y + 40$ **5.** $8 + 6a = -2a + 24$ **6.** $\frac{3}{4}d + 4 = \frac{1}{4}d + 18$

See Example **3** **7. Consumer Math** Members at the Star Theater pay $30.00 per month plus $1.95 for each movie. Nonmembers pay the regular $7.95 admission fee. How many movies would both a member and a nonmember have to see in a month to pay the same amount?

INDEPENDENT PRACTICE

See Example **1** **Group the terms with variables on one side of the equal sign, and simplify.**

8. $12h = 9h + 84$ **9.** $-10p - 8 = 2p$ **10.** $6q = 18 - 2q$

11. $-4c - 6 = -2c$ **12.** $-7s + 12 = -9s$ **13.** $6 + \frac{4}{5}a = \frac{9}{10}a$

See Example **2** **Solve.**

14. $9t = 4t + 120$ **15.** $42 + 3b = -4b - 14$ **16.** $\frac{6}{11}x + 4 = \frac{2}{11}x + 16$

17. $1.5a + 6 = 9a + 12$ **18.** $32 - \frac{3}{8}y = \frac{3}{4}y + 5$ **19.** $-6 - 8c = 3c + 16$

See Example **3** **20. Consumer Math** Members at a swim club pay $5 per lesson plus a one-time fee of $60. Nonmembers pay $11 per lesson. How many lessons would both a member and a nonmember have to take to pay the same amount?

PRACTICE AND PROBLEM SOLVING

Extra Practice
See page EP29.

Solve. Check each answer.

21. $3y + 7 = -6y - 56$ **22.** $-\frac{7}{8}x - 6 = -\frac{3}{8}x - 14$

23. $5r + 6 - 2r = 7r - 10$ **24.** $-10p + 8 = 7p + 12$

25. $9 + 5r = -17 - 8r$ **26.** $0.8k + 7 = -0.7k + 1$

27. A choir is singing at a festival. On the first night, 12 choir members were absent, so the choir stood in 5 equal rows. On the second night, only 1 member was absent, so the choir stood in 6 equal rows. The same number of people stood in each row each night. How many members are in the choir?

28. Consumer Math Jaline can purchase tile at a store for $0.99 per tile and rent a tile saw for $24. At another store, she can borrow the tile saw for free if she buys tile there for $1.49 per tile. How many tiles must she buy for the cost to be the same at both stores?

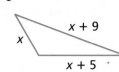

The figures in each pair have the same perimeter. Find the value of each variable.

29.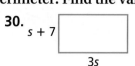

x $x + 4$ x $x + 9$ $x + 5$

30.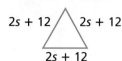

$s + 7$ $3s$ $2s + 12$ $2s + 12$ $2s + 12$

Recreation

The first indoor rock-climbing gym was built in 1987. Today, indoor rock-climbing gyms exist around the world and include ice-climbing and portable walls.

31. **Recreation** A rock-climbing gym charges nonmembers $18 per day to use the wall plus $7 per day for equipment rental. Members pay an annual fee of $400 plus $5 per day for equipment rental. How many days must both a member and a nonmember use the wall in one year so that both pay the same amount?

32. **Multi-Step** Two families drove from Denver to Cincinnati. After driving 582 miles the first day, the Smiths spread the rest of the trip equally over the next 3 days. The Chows spread their trip equally over 6 days. The distance the Chows drove each day was equal to the distance the Smiths drove each of the three days.

   a. How many miles did the Chows drive each day?

   b. How far is it from Denver to Cincinnati?

33. **What's the Error?** To combine terms in the equation $-8a - 4 = 2a + 34$, a student wrote $-6a = 38$. What is the error?

34. **Write About It** If the same variable is on both sides of an equation, must it have the same value on each side? Explain your answer.

35. **Challenge** Combine terms before solving the equation $12x - 4 - 12 = 4x + 8 + 8x - 24$. Do you think there is just one solution to the equation? Why or why not?

Test Prep and Spiral Review

36. **Multiple Choice** For which equation is $x = 0$ NOT a solution?

   Ⓐ $3x + 2 = 2 - x$ Ⓑ $2.5x + 3 = x$ Ⓒ $-x + 4 = 3x + 4$ Ⓓ $6x + 2 = x + 2$

37. **Extended Response** One calling plan offers long-distance calls for $0.03 per minute. Another plan costs $2.00 per month but offers long-distance service for $0.01 per minute. Write and solve an equation to find the number of long-distance minutes for which the two plans would cost the same. Write your answer in a complete sentence.

The lengths of two sides of a right triangle are given. Find the length of the third side to the nearest tenth. (Lesson 9-8)

38. legs: 12 cm and 16 cm

39. leg: 11 ft; hypotenuse: 30.5 ft

Solve. (Lesson 12-2)

40. $10x + 4 - 3x = -10$

41. $1.3y + 2.7y - 5 = 3$

42. $5 = \dfrac{4z - 6}{2}$

Ready To Go On?

Learn It Online
Resources Online **go.hrw.com**,
keyword MS10 RTGO12A **Go**

Quiz for Lessons 12-1 Through 12-3

✓ **12-1** **Solving Two-Step Equations**

Solve.

1. $-4x + 6 = 54$
2. $15 + \frac{y}{3} = 6$
3. $\frac{z}{8} - 5 = -3$

4. $-33 = -7a - 5$
5. $-27 = \frac{r}{12} - 19$
6. $-13 = 11 - 2n$

7. $3x + 13 = 37$
8. $\frac{p}{-8} - 7 = 12$
9. $\frac{u}{7} + 45 = -60$

10. A taxi service charges an initial fee of $1.50 plus $1.50 for every mile traveled. A taxi ride costs $21.00. How many miles did the taxi travel?

✓ **12-2** **Solving Multi-Step Equations**

Solve.

11. $\frac{3x - 4}{5} = 7$
12. $3(3b + 2) = -30$
13. $-12 = \frac{15c + 3}{6}$

14. $\frac{24.6 + 3a}{4} = 9.54$
15. $\frac{2b + 9}{11} = 18$
16. $13 = 2c + 3 + 5c$

17. $\frac{1}{2}(8w - 6) = 17$
18. $\frac{1.2s + 3.69}{0.3} = 47.9$
19. $\frac{1}{2} = \frac{5p - 8}{12}$

20. Peter used a $5.00 gift certificate to help pay for his lunch. After adding a 15% tip to the cost of his meal, Peter still had to pay $2.36 in cash. How much did Peter's meal cost?

21. A group of 10 friends had lunch together at a restaurant. The meal cost a total of $99.50, including a 15% tip. How much was the total bill for lunch before tip?

✓ **12-3** **Solving Equations with Variables on Both Sides**

Solve.

22. $12m = 3m + 108$
23. $\frac{7}{8}n - 3 = \frac{5}{8}n + 12$

24. $1.2x + 3.7 = 2.2x - 4.5$
25. $-7 - 7p = 3p + 23$

26. $-2.3q + 16 = -5q - 38$
27. $\frac{3}{5}k + \frac{7}{10} = \frac{11}{15}k - \frac{2}{5}$

28. $-19m + 12 = -14m - 8$
29. $\frac{2}{3}v + \frac{1}{6} = \frac{7}{9}v - \frac{5}{6}$

30. $8.9 - 3.3j = -2.2j + 2.3$
31. $4a - 7 = -6a + 12$

32. One shuttle service charges $10 for pickup and $0.10 per mile. Another shuttle service has no pickup fee but charges $0.35 per mile. Find the number of miles for which the cost of the two shuttle services is the same.

Focus on Problem Solving

Solve

• **Write an equation**

When you are asked to solve a problem, be sure to read the entire problem before you begin solving it. Sometimes you will need to perform several steps to solve the problem, and you will need to know all of the information in the problem before you decide which steps to take.

Read each problem and determine what steps are needed to solve it. Then write an equation that can be used to solve the problem.

1 Martin can buy a pair of inline skates and safety equipment for $49.50. At a roller rink, Martin can rent a pair of inline skates for $2.50 per day, but he still needs to buy safety equipment for $19.50. How many days would Martin have to skate in order to pay as much to rent skates and buy safety equipment as he would have to pay to buy both?

2 Christopher sells paintings at the local outdoor mall. He charges $5 for a small painting and $15 for a larger painting. In one day, Christopher earned $175. He sold 20 small paintings that day. How many larger paintings did he sell?

3 Book-club members are required to buy a minimum number of books each year. Leslee bought 3 times the minimum. Denise bought 7 more than the minimum. Together, they bought 23 books. What is the minimum number of books?

4 Coach Willis has won 150 games during his career. This is 10 more than $\frac{1}{2}$ as many games as Coach Gentry has won. How many games has Coach Gentry won?

5 The perimeter of an isosceles triangle is 4 times the length of the shortest side. The longer sides are 4.5 ft longer than the shortest side. What is the length of each side of the triangle?

6 Miss Rankin's class has raised $100.00 for a class trip. The class needs to collect a total of $225.00. How many $0.50 carnations must the class sell to reach its goal?

TN **SPI 0706.3.9** Solve linear inequalities in one variable with rational coefficients symbolically or graphically.

An **inequality** states that two quantities either are not equal or may not be equal. An inequality uses one of the following symbols:

Symbol	Meaning	Word Phrases
<	Is less than	Fewer than, below
>	Is greater than	More than, above
≤	Is less than or equal to	At most, no more than
≥	Is greater than or equal to	At least, no less than

Vocabulary

inequality

algebraic inequality

solution set

compound inequality

EXAMPLE 1 **Writing Inequalities**

Write an inequality for each situation.

A There are at least 25 students in the auditorium.

number of students ≥ 25   *"At least" means greater than or equal to.*

B No more than 150 people can occupy the room.

room capacity ≤ 150   *"No more than" means less than or equal to.*

An inequality that contains a variable is an **algebraic inequality**. A value of the variable that makes the inequality true is a solution of the inequality.

An inequality may have more than one solution. Together, all of the solutions are called the **solution set**.

Interactivities Online ▶ You can graph the solutions of an inequality on a number line. If the variable is "greater than" or "less than" a number, then that number is indicated with an open circle.

This open circle shows that 5 is not a solution.

$a > 5$

If the variable is "greater than or equal to" or "less than or equal to" a number, that number is indicated with a closed circle.

This closed circle shows that 3 is a solution.

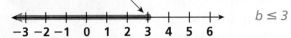

$b \leq 3$

Video **Lesson Tutorials Online**

EXAMPLE 2 **Graphing Simple Inequalities**

Graph each inequality.

A $x > -2$

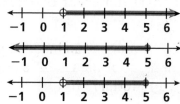
$$\begin{array}{ccccccccc} -3 & -2 & -1 & 0 & 1 & 2 & 3 & 4 \end{array}$$

Draw an open circle at −2. The solutions are values of x greater than −2, so shade to the right of −2.

B $-1 \geq y$

$$\begin{array}{ccccccccc} -5 & -4 & -3 & -2 & -1 & 0 & 1 & 2 \end{array}$$

Draw a closed circle at −1. The solutions are −1 and values of y less than −1, so shade to the left of −1.

Writing Math

The compound inequality −2 < y and y < 4 can be written as −2 < y < 4.

A **compound inequality** is the result of combining two inequalities. The words *and* and *or* are used to describe how the two parts are related.

$x > 3$ or $x < -1$	$-2 < y$ and $y < 4$
x is either greater than 3 or less than −1.	*y is both greater than −2 and less than 4. y is between −2 and 4.*

EXAMPLE 3 **Graphing Compound Inequalities**

Graph each compound inequality.

A $s \geq 0$ or $s < -3$

$$\begin{array}{ccccccccc} -5 & -4 & -3 & -2 & -1 & 0 & 1 & 2 \end{array}$$

Graph s ≥ 0.

$$\begin{array}{ccccccccc} -5 & -4 & -3 & -2 & -1 & 0 & 1 & 2 \end{array}$$

Graph s < −3.

$$\begin{array}{ccccccccc} -5 & -4 & -3 & -2 & -1 & 0 & 1 & 2 \end{array}$$

Combine the graphs.

Reading Math

1 < p is the same as p > 1.

B $1 < p \leq 5$

$$\begin{array}{ccccccccc} -1 & 0 & 1 & 2 & 3 & 4 & 5 & 6 \end{array}$$

Graph 1 < p.

$$\begin{array}{ccccccccc} -1 & 0 & 1 & 2 & 3 & 4 & 5 & 6 \end{array}$$

Graph p ≤ 5.

$$\begin{array}{ccccccccc} -1 & 0 & 1 & 2 & 3 & 4 & 5 & 6 \end{array}$$

Graph the common solutions.

Think and Discuss

1. Compare the graphs of the inequalities $y > 2$ and $y \geq 2$.

2. Explain how to graph each type of compound inequality.

GUIDED PRACTICE

See Example 1 **Write an inequality for each situation.**

1. No more than 18 people are allowed in the gallery at one time.

2. There are fewer than 8 fish in the aquarium.

3. The water level is above 45 inches.

See Example 2 **Graph each inequality.**

4. $x < 3$ **5.** $\frac{1}{2} \geq r$ **6.** $2.8 < w$ **7.** $y \geq -4$

See Example 3 **Graph each compound inequality.**

8. $a > 2$ or $a \leq -1$ **9.** $-4 < p \leq 6$ **10.** $-2 \leq n < 0$

INDEPENDENT PRACTICE

See Example 1 **Write an inequality for each situation.**

11. The temperature is below 40 °F.

12. There are at least 24 pictures on the roll of film.

13. No more than 35 tables are in the cafeteria.

14. Fewer than 250 people attended the rally.

See Example 2 **Graph each inequality.**

15. $s \geq -1$ **16.** $y < 0$ **17.** $n \leq -3$

18. $2 < x$ **19.** $-6 \leq b$ **20.** $m < -4$

See Example 3 **Graph each compound inequality.**

21. $p > 3$ or $p < 0$ **22.** $1 \leq x \leq 4$ **23.** $-3 < y < -1$

24. $k > 0$ or $k \leq -2$ **25.** $n \geq 1$ or $n \leq -1$ **26.** $-2 < w \leq 2$

PRACTICE AND PROBLEM SOLVING

Extra Practice
See page EP30.

Graph each inequality or compound inequality.

27. $z \leq -5$ **28.** $3 > f$ **29.** $m \geq -2$

30. $3 > y$ or $y \geq 6$ **31.** $-9 < p \leq -3$ **32.** $q > 2$ or $-1 > q$

33. Write About It Explain how to graph the inequality $13 \geq x$.

34. Critical Thinking The *Reflexive Property* states that $x = x$. For which inequality symbols would the Reflexive Property apply? Give examples and explain your answer.

Earth Science LINK

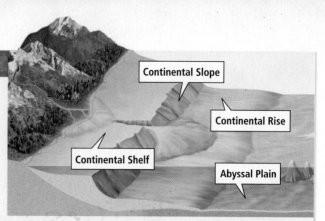

The portion of the earth's surface that lies beneath the ocean and consists of continental crust is the continental margin. The continental margin is divided into the continental shelf, the continental slope, and the continental rise.

35. The continental shelf begins at the shoreline and slopes toward the open ocean. The depth of the continental shelf can reach 200 meters. Write a compound inequality for the depth of the continental shelf.

36. The continental slope begins at the edge of the continental shelf and continues down to the flattest part of the ocean floor. The depth of the continental slope ranges from about 200 meters to about 4,000 meters. Write a compound inequality for the depth of the continental slope.

37. The bar graph shows the depth of the ocean in various locations as measured by different research vessels. Write a compound inequality that shows the ranges of depth measured by each vessel.

38. ⭐ **Challenge** Water freezes at 32 °F and boils at 212 °F. Write three inequalities to show the ranges of temperatures for which water is a solid, a liquid, and a gas.

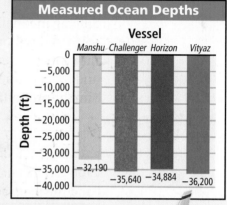

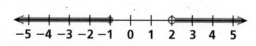

Test Prep and Spiral Review

39. Multiple Choice Which inequality represents *a number that is greater than −4 and less than 3?*

ⓐ $-4 \geq n \geq 3$ ⓑ $-4 < n < 3$ ⓒ $-4 > n > 3$ ⓓ $-4 \leq n \leq 3$

40. Multiple Choice Which inequality is shown by the graph?

ⓕ $x < -1$ or $x \leq 2$ ⓖ $x < -1$ or $x \geq 2$ ⓗ $x \leq -1$ or $x < 2$ ⓙ $x \leq -1$ or $x > 2$

41. Mateo drove 472 miles in 8 hours. What was his average rate of speed? (Lesson 4-2)

Solve. (Lesson 12-3)

42. $10x + 4 = 6x$ **43.** $3y + 8 = 5y - 2$ **44.** $1.5z + 3 = 2.7z - 4.2$

12-4 Inequalities   **713**

12-5 Solving Inequalities by Adding or Subtracting

TN SPI 0706.3.9 Solve linear inequalities in one variable with rational coefficients symbolically or graphically. *Also* GLE 0706.2.2

A high temperature of 74 °F means that the temperature that day is always less than or equal to 74 °F. You can solve problems involving temperatures by using inequalities.

Solving inequalities is very similar to solving equations. Recall from Chapter 1 that you use the properties of equality and inverse operations to solve equations. Similar properties apply to inequalities.

Addition and Subtraction Properties of Inequality			
You can add or subtract the same number on both sides of an inequality, and the inequality will still be true.			
$3 < 5$	$6 > 2$	$4 \leq 7$	$0 \geq -3$
$3 + 2 < 5 + 2$	$6 - 1 > 2 - 1$	$4 + 3 \leq 7 + 3$	$0 - 4 \geq -3 - 4$
$5 < 7$	$5 > 1$	$7 \leq 10$	$-4 \geq -7$

Interactivities Online ▶ You can use the Addition and Subtraction Properties of Inequality and inverse operations to solve inequalities.

EXAMPLE 1 Using the Addition Property of Inequality

Solve. Then graph each solution set on a number line.

Remember!
Draw a closed circle when the inequality includes the point and an open circle when it does not include the point.

A $x - 12 > 32$

$$\begin{array}{r} x - 12 > \quad 32 \\ \underline{+\ 12 \quad +\ 12} \\ x \qquad > \quad 44 \end{array}$$

Add 12 to both sides.

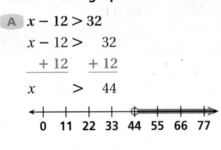

Draw an open circle at 44. Solutions are values of x greater than 44, so shade to the right of 44.

B $y - 8 \leq -14$

$$\begin{array}{r} y - 8 \leq -14 \\ \underline{+\ 8 \quad +\ 8} \\ y \leq \quad -6 \end{array}$$

Add 8 to both sides.

Draw a closed circle at −6. Solutions are −6 and values of y less than −6, so shade to the left of −6.

Video **Lesson Tutorials Online**

You can check the solution to an inequality by choosing any number in the solution set and substituting it into the original inequality.

EXAMPLE 2

Using the Subtraction Property of Inequality

Solve. Check each answer.

A $c + 9 \geq 20$

$$c + 9 \geq 20$$
$$\underline{-9 \quad -9} \qquad \text{\textit{Subtract 9 from both sides.}}$$
$$c \quad\;\; \geq 11$$

Check

$$c + 9 \geq 20$$
$$20 + 9 \overset{?}{\geq} 20 \qquad \text{\textit{20 is greater than 11. Substitute 20 for c.}}$$
$$29 \overset{?}{\geq} 20 ✔$$

Helpful Hint

When checking your solution, choose a number in the solution set that is easy to work with.

B $-2 < x + 16$

$$-2 < x + 16$$
$$\underline{-16 \quad\;\; -16} \qquad \text{\textit{Subtract 16 from both sides.}}$$
$$-18 < x$$

Check

$$-2 < x + 16$$
$$-2 \overset{?}{<} 0 + 16 \qquad \text{\textit{0 is greater than −18. Substitute 0 for x.}}$$
$$-2 \overset{?}{<} 16 ✔$$

EXAMPLE 3

Weather Application

Sunday's high temperature of 72 °F was at least 40 °F higher than Monday's high temperature. What was Monday's high temperature?

Sunday's high	was at least	40 °F higher than	Monday's high.
72	$\geq$	40	$+$ t

$$72 \geq 40 + t$$
$$\underline{-40 \quad\; -40} \qquad \text{\textit{Subtract 40 from both sides.}}$$
$$32 \geq t \qquad\qquad \text{\textit{Rewrite the inequality.}}$$
$$t \leq 32$$

Monday's high temperature was at most 32 °F.

Think and Discuss

1. Compare solving addition and subtraction equations with solving addition and subtraction inequalities.

2. Describe how to check whether −36 is a solution of $s - 5 > 1$.

Learn It Online
Homework Help Online **go.hrw.com**,
keyword MS10 12-5 Go
Exercises 1–21, 23, 25, 27, 29, 31, 35, 39

GUIDED PRACTICE

See Example **1** **Solve. Then graph each solution set on a number line.**

1. $x - 9 < 18$ **2.** $y - 11 \geq -7$ **3.** $4 \geq p - 3$

See Example **2** **Solve. Check each answer.**

4. $n + 5 > 26$ **5.** $b + 21 \leq -3$ **6.** $9 \leq 12 + k$

See Example **3** **7. Weather** Yesterday's high temperature was 30 °F. Tomorrow's weather forecast includes a high temperature that is no more than 12 °F warmer than yesterday's. What high temperatures are forecast for tomorrow?

INDEPENDENT PRACTICE

See Example **1** **Solve. Then graph each solution set on a number line.**

8. $s - 2 > 14$ **9.** $m - 14 < -3$ **10.** $b - 25 > -30$

11. $c - 17 \leq -6$ **12.** $-25 > y - 53$ **13.** $71 \leq x - 9$

See Example **2** **Solve. Check each answer.**

14. $w + 16 < 4$ **15.** $z + 9 > -3$ **16.** $p + 21 \leq -4$

17. $26 < f + 32$ **18.** $65 > k + 54$ **19.** $n + 29 \geq 25$

See Example **3** **20.** Clark scored at least 12 points more than Josh scored. Josh scored 15 points. How many points did Clark score?

21. Life Science Adriana is helping track bird populations. She counted 8 fewer birds on Tuesday than on Thursday. She counted at most 32 birds on Thursday. How many birds did Adriana count on Tuesday?

PRACTICE AND PROBLEM SOLVING

Extra Practice
See page EP30.

Solve.

22. $k + 3.2 \geq 8$ **23.** $a - 1.3 > -1$ **24.** $c - 6\frac{1}{2} < -1\frac{1}{4}$

25. $-20 \geq 18 + m$ **26.** $4 < x + 7.02$ **27.** $g + 3\frac{2}{3} < 10$

28. $-109 > r - 58$ **29.** $5.9 + w \leq 21.6$ **30.** $n - 21.6 > 26$

31. $-150 \leq t + 92$ **32.** $y + 4\frac{3}{4} \geq 1\frac{1}{8}$ **33.** $v - 0.9 \leq -1.5$

34. Consumer Math To get a group discount for baseball tickets, Marco's group must have at least 20 people. The group needs at least 7 more people to sign up. How many have signed up so far?

35. Mila wants to spend at least $20 on a classified ad in the newspaper. She has $12. How much more does she need?

36. **Transportation** The *shinkansen*, or bullet train, of Japan travels at an average speed of 162.3 miles per hour. It has a top speed of 186 miles per hour. At most, how many more miles per hour can the train travel beyond its average speed before it reaches its maximum speed?

37. **Life Science** The giant spider crab, the world's largest crab, lives off the southeastern coast of Japan. Giant spider crabs can grow as much as 3.6 meters across. A scientist finds one that could still grow another 0.5 m across. How wide is the giant spider crab that he found?

38. The line graph shows the number of miles Amelia rode her bike in each of the last four months. She wants to ride at least 5 miles more in May than she did in April. At least how many miles does Amelia want to ride in May?

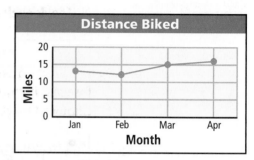

39. **Physical Science** The average human ear can detect sounds that have frequencies between 20 hertz and 20,000 hertz. The average dog ear can detect sounds with frequencies of up to 30,000 hertz greater than those a human ear can detect. Up to how many hertz can a dog hear?

40. **Choose a Strategy** If five days ago was the day after Saturday, what was the day before yesterday?

41. **Write About It** Explain how to solve and check the inequality $n - 9 < -15$.

42. **Challenge** Solve the inequality $x + (4^2 - 2^3)^2 > -1$.

Test Prep and Spiral Review

43. **Multiple Choice** Which inequality has the following graphed solution?

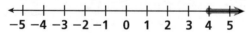

   Ⓐ $x - 2 \geq -2$ Ⓑ $x + 3 \geq 7$ Ⓒ $x - 3 \leq 1$ Ⓓ $x + 5 < 9$

44. **Short Response** The highest-paid employee at the movie theater is the manager, who earns $10.25 per hour. The lowest-paid employees earn $3.90 less per hour than the manager. Write and graph a compound inequality to show all the other hourly wages earned at the movie theater.

The surface area of a prism is 16 in². Find the surface area of a similar prism that is larger **by each scale factor.** (Lesson 10-6)

45. scale factor = 3   46. scale factor = 8   47. scale factor = 10

48. Find the probability of flipping a coin and getting tails and then rolling a 2 on a number cube. (Lesson 11-6)

Solving Inequalities by Multiplying or Dividing

TN **SPI 0706.3.9** Solve linear inequalities in one variable with rational coefficients symbolically or graphically. *Also* **GLE 0706.2.2**, ✓ **0706.3.14**

Some problems will require you to multiply or divide to solve an inequality. There are special rules for multiplying and dividing to solve an inequality.

Multiplication and Division Properties of Inequality	
Positive	**Negative**
You can multiply or divide both sides of an inequality by the same **positive number**, and the statement will still be true.	You can multiply or divide both sides of an inequality by the same **negative number**, but you must reverse the direction of the inequality symbol for the statement to be true.

$8 > 6$	$-10 \le 14$	$3 \ge -2$	$-9 < 18$
$8 \cdot 2 > 6 \cdot 2$	$\dfrac{-10}{2} \le \dfrac{14}{2}$	$3\,(-3) \le -2\,(-3)$	$\dfrac{-9}{-9} > \dfrac{18}{-9}$
$16 > 12$	$-5 \le 7$	$-9 \le 6$	$1 > -2$

Notice that you reverse the direction of the inequality symbol when you multiply or divide both sides of an inequality by a negative number. If you do not, the resulting inequality will not be correct.

$$4 < 5$$
$$4\,(-1) \overset{?}{<} 5\,(-1)$$
$$-4 \overset{?}{<} -5$$
$$-4 > -5$$

EXAMPLE 1 **Using the Multiplication Property of Inequality**

Interactivities Online ▶

Solve.

A $\dfrac{x}{11} < 3$

$$\dfrac{x}{11} < 3$$

$$(11)\dfrac{x}{11} < (11)3 \qquad \textit{Multiply both sides by 11.}$$

$$x < 33$$

B $4.8 \le \dfrac{r}{-6}$

$$4.8 \le \dfrac{r}{-6}$$

$$(-6)4.8 \ge (-6)\dfrac{r}{-6} \qquad \textit{Multiply both sides by } -6 \textit{, and reverse the inequality symbol.}$$

$$-28.8 \ge r$$

Video **Lesson Tutorials Online**

EXAMPLE **2** **Using the Division Property of Inequality**

Solve. Check each answer.

A $4x > 9$

$4x > 9$

$\dfrac{4x}{4} > \dfrac{9}{4}$ *Divide both sides by 4.*

$x > \dfrac{9}{4}$, or $2\dfrac{1}{4}$

Check

$4x > 9$

$4(3) \overset{?}{>} 9$ *3 is greater than $2\dfrac{1}{4}$. Substitute 3 for x.*

$12 \overset{?}{>} 9$ ✔

B $-60 \geq -12y$

$-60 \geq -12y$

$\dfrac{-60}{-12} \leq \dfrac{-12y}{-12}$ *Divide both sides by -12, and reverse the inequality symbol.*

$5 \leq y$

Check

$-60 \geq -12y$

$-60 \overset{?}{\geq} -12(10)$ *10 is greater than 5. Substitute 10 for y.*

$-60 \overset{?}{\geq} -120$ ✔

EXAMPLE **3** *Agriculture Application*

It cost the Schmidts $517 to raise watermelons. How many watermelons must they sell at $5 apiece to make a profit?

To make a profit, the Schmidts need to earn more than $517. Let w represent the number of watermelons they must sell.

$5w > 517$ *Write an inequality.*

$\dfrac{5w}{5} > \dfrac{517}{5}$ *Divide both sides by 5.*

$w > 103.4$

The Schmidts cannot sell 0.4 watermelon, so they need to sell at least 104 watermelons to earn a profit.

Agriculture

In Japan, some watermelons are grown in glass boxes, making them cube-shaped. These watermelons are easier to store and ship, but are also more expensive.

Think and Discuss

1. Compare solving multiplication and division equations with solving multiplication and division inequalities.

2. Explain how you would solve the inequality $0.5y > 4.5$.

Learn It Online
Homework Help Online **go.hrw.com,**
keyword MS10 12-6 Go
Exercises 1–21, 23, 25, 27, 29, 31, 35, 37

GUIDED PRACTICE

See Example 1   Solve.

1. $\frac{w}{8} < -4$

2. $\frac{z}{-6} \geq 7$

3. $-4 < \frac{p}{-12}$

See Example 2   Solve. Check each answer.

4. $3m > -15$

5. $11 > -8y$

6. $25c \leq 200$

See Example 3   **7.** It cost Deirdre $212 to make candles. How many candles must she sell at $8 apiece to make a profit?

INDEPENDENT PRACTICE

See Example 1   Solve.

8. $\frac{s}{5} > 1.4$

9. $\frac{m}{-4} < -13$

10. $\frac{b}{6} > -30$

11. $\frac{c}{-10} \leq 12$

12. $\frac{y}{9} < 2.5$

13. $\frac{x}{1.1} \geq -1$

See Example 2   Solve. Check each answer.

14. $6w < 4$

15. $-5z > -3$

16. $15p \leq -45$

17. $-9f > 27$

18. $20k < 30$

19. $-18n \geq 180$

See Example 3   **20.** Attendance at a museum more than tripled from Monday to Saturday. On Monday, 186 people went to the museum. How many people went to the museum on Saturday?

21. It cost George $678 to make wreaths. How many wreaths must he sell at $15 apiece to make a profit?

PRACTICE AND PROBLEM SOLVING

Extra Practice
See page EP30.

Solve.

22. $\frac{a}{65} \leq -10$

23. $0.4p > 1.6$

24. $-\frac{m}{5} < -20$

25. $\frac{2}{3}y \geq 12$

26. $\frac{x}{-9} \leq \frac{3}{5}$

27. $\frac{g}{2.1} > 0.3$

28. $\frac{r}{6} \geq \frac{2}{3}$

29. $4w \leq 1\frac{1}{2}$

30. $-10n < 10^2$

31. $-1\frac{3}{5}t > -4$

32. $-\frac{y}{12} < 3\frac{1}{2}$

33. $5.6v \geq -14$

34. A community theater group produced 8 plays over the last two years. The group's goal for the next two years is to produce at least $1\frac{1}{2}$ times as many plays as they did in the two previous years. How many plays does the group want to produce in the next two years?

35. Tammy is going to a family reunion 350 miles away. She plans to travel no faster than 70 miles per hour. What is the least amount of time it will take her to get there?

36. Social Studies Of the total U.S. population, about 874,000 people are Pacific Islanders. The graph shows where most of these Americans live.

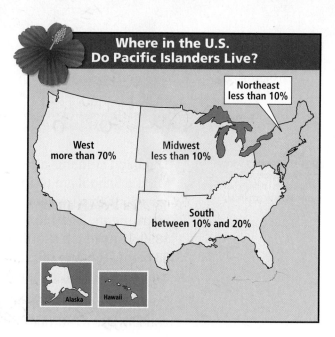

Where in the U.S. Do Pacific Islanders Live?

Northeast less than 10%

West more than 70%

Midwest less than 10%

South between 10% and 20%

Alaska   Hawaii

   a. How many Pacific Islanders live in the Midwest?

   b. How many Pacific Islanders live in the South?

   c. Critical Thinking How many Pacific Islanders live in the Midwest and Northeast combined?

37. Seventh-graders at Mountain Middle School have sold 360 subscriptions to magazines. This is $\frac{3}{4}$ of the number of subscriptions that they need to sell to reach their goal and to beat the eighth grade's sales. How many total subscriptions must they sell to reach their goal?

38. Recreation Malcolm has saved $362 to spend on his vacation. He wants to have at least $35 a day available to spend. How many days of vacation does Malcolm have enough money for?

 39. Write a Problem Write a word problem that can be solved using the inequality $\frac{x}{2} \geq 7$. Solve the inequality.

 40. Write About It Explain how to solve the inequality $\frac{n}{-8} < -40$.

41. Challenge Use what you have learned about solving multi-step equations to solve the inequality $4x - 5 \leq 7x + 4$.

Test Prep and Spiral Review

42. Multiple Choice Solve $\frac{x}{4} > -2$.

   Ⓐ $x > -8$ Ⓑ $x < -8$ Ⓒ $x < 8$ Ⓓ $x > 8$

43. Gridded Response It cost John and Jamie $150 to grow tomatoes. They sell each tomato for $0.50. How many tomatoes must they sell to make a profit?

44. In 16 tries, Sondra made 9 baskets. What is the experimental probability that Sondra will make a basket the next time she tries? (Lesson 11-2)

Solve. (Lesson 12-5)

   45. $x - 3 < -2$ **46.** $-6 < y + 4$ **47.** $z - 1 \geq 4$ **48.** $t - 12 \leq 8.4$

12-7 Solving Multi-Step Inequalities

TN SPI 0706.3.9 Solve linear inequalities in one variable with rational coefficients symbolically or graphically.

The band students at Newman Middle School are trying to raise at least $5,000 to buy new percussion instruments. They already have raised $850. How much should each of the 83 band students still raise, on average, to meet the goal?

When you solve two-step equations, you can use the order of operations in reverse to isolate the variable. You can use the same process when solving two-step inequalities.

EXAMPLE 1 Solving Two-Step Inequalities

Solve. Then graph each solution set on a number line.

A $\dfrac{x}{5} - 15 < 10$

$$\dfrac{x}{5} - 15 < 10$$

$$\underline{+15 \quad +15} \qquad \text{Add 15 to both sides.}$$

$$\dfrac{x}{5} < 25$$

$$(5)\dfrac{x}{5} < (5)25 \qquad \text{Multiply both sides by 5.}$$

$$x < 125$$

```
  ◄──┼──┼──┼──┼──┼──┼──Ο──┼──┼──►
    -25  0  25  50  75 100 125 150 175
```

B $42 \le \dfrac{y}{-9} + 30$

$$42 \le \dfrac{y}{-9} + 30$$

$$\underline{-30 \qquad -30} \qquad \text{Subtract 30 from both sides.}$$

$$12 \le \dfrac{y}{-9}$$

$$-9(12) \ge (-9)\dfrac{y}{-9} \qquad \text{Multiply both sides by } -9, \text{ and reverse}$$

$$-108 \ge y \qquad\qquad\qquad \text{the inequality symbol.}$$

```
  ◄──┼──┼──┼──┼──●──┼──┼──►
  -124 -120 -116 -112 -108 -104 -100
```

Video Lesson Tutorials Online

EXAMPLE 2 Solving Multi-Step Inequalities

Solve. Then graph each solution set on a number line.

A $3x - 12 - x > -18$

$$2x - 12 > -18$$ *Combine like terms.*

$$\underline{+12 \quad +12}$$ *Add 12 to both sides.*

$$2x \quad > -6$$ *Divide both sides by 2.*

$$\frac{2x}{2} > \frac{-6}{2}$$

$$x > -3$$

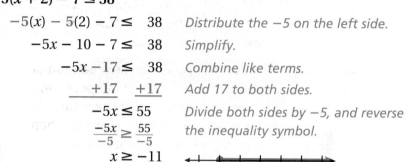

B $-5(x + 2) - 7 \leq 38$

$$-5(x) - 5(2) - 7 \leq 38$$ *Distribute the −5 on the left side.*

$$-5x - 10 - 7 \leq 38$$ *Simplify.*

$$-5x - 17 \leq 38$$ *Combine like terms.*

$$\underline{+17 \quad +17}$$ *Add 17 to both sides.*

$$-5x \leq 55$$ *Divide both sides by −5, and reverse*

$$\frac{-5x}{-5} \geq \frac{55}{-5}$$ *the inequality symbol.*

$$x \geq -11$$

EXAMPLE 3 *School Application*

The 83 members of the Newman Middle School Band are trying to raise at least $5,000 to buy new percussion instruments. They have already raised $850. How much should each student still raise, on average, to meet the goal?

Let d represent the average amount each student should still raise.

$$83d + 850 \geq 5,000$$ *Write an inequality.*

$$\underline{- 850 \quad - 850}$$ *Subtract 850 from both sides.*

$$83d \quad\quad \geq 4,150$$

$$\frac{83d}{83} \geq \frac{4,150}{83}$$ *Divide both sides by 83.*

$$d \geq 50$$

On average, each band member should raise at least $50.

Think and Discuss

1. Tell how you would solve the inequality $8x + 5 < 20$.

2. Explain why the *greater than or equal to* symbol was used in the inequality in Example 3.

Exercises

Learn It Online
Homework Help Online **go.hrw.com**,
keyword **MS10 12-7** Go
Exercises 1–18, 21, 23, 25, 27, 29, 31, 33

GUIDED PRACTICE

Solve. Then graph each solution set on a number line.

See Example 1
1. $5x + 3 < 18$
2. $-19 \geq \frac{z}{7} + 23$
3. $3y - 4 \geq 14$

See Example 2
4. $5m - 1 + 2m < 20$
5. $28 \leq 6(x + 4)$
6. $5t > 3t - 10$

See Example 3
7. Three students collected more than $93 washing cars. They used $15 to reimburse their parents for cleaning supplies. Then they divided the remaining money equally. How much did each student earn?

INDEPENDENT PRACTICE

Solve. Then graph each solution set on a number line.

See Example 1
8. $5s - 7 > -42$
9. $\frac{b}{2} + 3 < 9$
10. $19 \leq -2q + 5$

11. $-8c - 11 \leq 13$
12. $\frac{y}{-4} + 6 > 10$
13. $\frac{x}{9} - 5 \leq -8$

See Example 2
14. $4(4 - r) + 1 > 13$
15. $3j - 8 - 5j \geq -16$
16. $4d - 12 + 2d < 6$

See Example 3
17. Rico has $5.00. Bagels cost $0.65 each, and a small container of cream cheese costs $1.00. What is the greatest number of bagels Rico can buy if he also buys one small container of cream cheese?

18. The 35 members of a drill team are trying to raise at least $1,200 to cover travel costs to a training camp. They have already raised $500. How much should each member still raise, on average, to meet the goal?

PRACTICE AND PROBLEM SOLVING

Extra Practice
See page EP30.

Solve.

19. $32 \geq -4x + 8$
20. $0.5 + \frac{n}{5} > -0.5$
21. $1.4 + \frac{c}{3} < 2$

22. $-1 < -\frac{3}{4}b - 2.2$
23. $12 + 2w - 8 \leq 20$
24. $5k + 6 - k \geq -14$

25. $\frac{s}{2} + 9 > 12 - 15$
26. $2(4t - 6) - 10t < -6$
27. $\frac{d}{2} + 1 + \frac{d}{2} \leq 5$

28. Mr. Monroe keeps a bag of small prizes to distribute to his students. He likes to keep at least twice as many prizes in the bag as he has students. The bag currently has 79 prizes in it. Mr. Monroe has 117 students. How many more prizes does he need to buy?

29. Manny needs to buy 5 work shirts that are each the same price. After he uses a $20 gift certificate, he can spend no more than $50. What is the maximum amount that each shirt can cost?

30. **Business** Darcy earns a salary of $1,400 per month, plus a commission of 4% of her sales. She wants to earn a total of at least $1,600 this month. What is the least amount of sales she needs?

31. Multi-Step The bar graph shows how many students from Warren Middle School participated in a reading challenge each of the past four years. This year, the goal is for at least 10 more students to participate than the average number of participants from the past four years. What is the goal for this year?

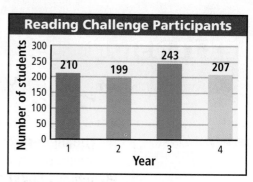

Reading Challenge Participants

32. Consumer Math Michael wants to buy a belt that costs $18. He also wants to buy some shirts that are on sale for $14 each. He has $70. At most, how many shirts can Michael buy together with the belt?

33. Earth Science A granite rock contains the minerals feldspar, quartz, and biotite mica. The rock has $\frac{1}{3}$ as much biotite mica as quartz. The rock is at least 30% quartz. What percent of the rock is feldspar?

Feldspar

Quartz

34. What's the Error? A student's solution to the inequality $\frac{x}{-9} - 5 > 2$ was $x > 63$. What error did the student make in the solution?

Biotite mica

Granite

35. Write About It Explain how to solve the inequality $4y + 6 < -2$.

36. Challenge A student scored 92, 87, and 85 on three tests. She wants her average score for five tests to be at least 90. What is the lowest score the student can get, on average, on her fourth and fifth tests?

Test Prep and Spiral Review

37. Multiple Choice Which inequality has the following graphed solution?

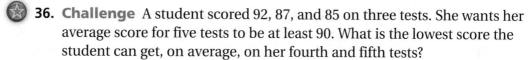

-5 -4 -3 -2 -1 0 1 2 3 4 5

Ⓐ $2x - 5 > 1$ Ⓑ $-x + 3 < 6$ Ⓒ $3x - 12 < -3$ Ⓓ $-5x - 2 > -13$

38. Gridded Response Gretta earns $450 per week plus a 10% commission on book sales. How many dollars of books must she sell to earn at least $650 per week?

39. Jamie flips a coin and rolls a number cube. How many outcomes are possible?
(Lesson 11-3)

Solve. (Lesson 12-6)

40. $6x > -24$ **41.** $-4x < -20$ **42.** $-3x \geq 18$ **43.** $\frac{x}{3} + 6 \leq 11$

Solving for a Variable

TN ✓ **0706.4.5** Solve problems using ratio quantities: velocity (measured in units such as miles per hour), density (measured in units such as kilograms per liter), pressure (measured in units such as pounds per square foot), and population density (measured in units such as persons per square mile).

The highest recorded speed of a magnetically elevated vehicle was achieved by the MLX01 on the Yamanashi Maglev Test Line in Japan. At its top speed, the MLX01 could travel the 229 miles from Tokyo to Kyoto in less than an hour.

The formula *distance = rate · time* ($d = rt$) tells how far an object travels at a certain rate over a certain time. In an equation or a formula that contains more than one variable, you can isolate one of the variables by using inverse operations. Recall that you cannot divide by a variable if it represents 0.

The MLX01 attained the record speed of 343 miles per hour in January 1998.

EXAMPLE **1** **Solving for Variables in Formulas**

Solve $d = rt$ for r.

$$d = rt$$

$$\frac{d}{t} = \frac{rt}{t} \qquad \text{\textit{Divide both sides by t to isolate r.}}$$

$$\frac{d}{t} = r$$

EXAMPLE **2** *Physical Science Application*

How long would it take the MLX01 to travel 1,029 mi if it travels at a speed of 343 mi/h?

First solve the distance formula for t because you want to find the time. Then use the given values to find t.

$$d = rt$$

$$\frac{d}{r} = \frac{rt}{r} \qquad \text{\textit{Divide both sides by r to isolate t.}}$$

$$\frac{d}{r} = t$$

$$\frac{1,029}{343} = t \qquad \text{\textit{Substitute 1,029 for d and 343 for r.}}$$

$$3 = t$$

It would take the MLX01 3 hours to travel 1,029 miles.

Solve each equation for the given variable.

1. $A = bh$ for h

2. $A = bh$ for b

3. $C = \pi d$ for d

4. $P = 4s$ for s

5. $V = Bh$ for B

6. $d = 2r$ for r

7. $xy = k$ for y

8. $A = \ell w$ for w

9. $W = Fd$ for F

10. $I = Prt$ for P

11. $C = 2\pi r$ for r

12. $A = \frac{1}{2}bh$ for h

13. $V = \frac{1}{3}Bh$ for h

14. $K = C + 273$ for C

15. $E = Pt$ for t

16. $D = \frac{m}{v}$ for v

17. $F = ma$ for a

18. $P = VI$ for I

19. $r = \frac{V}{I}$ for V

20. $I = Prt$ for r

21. $P = 2\ell + 2w$ for ℓ

22. $V = \pi r^2 h$ for h

23. **Physical Science** The formula $p = mv$ tells the amount of momentum an object has. In the equation, p stands for the amount of momentum, m stands for the object's mass, and v stands for the object's velocity. What is the velocity of an object that has a momentum of 50 kg · m/s and a mass of 8 kg?

24. **Physical Science** The Kelvin scale is a temperature scale. To convert between the Celsius temperature scale and the Kelvin temperature scale, use the formula $C = K - 273$, where C represents the temperature in degrees Celsius and K represents the temperature in kelvins. Use the formula to convert 38 °C to an equivalent Kelvin temperature.

25. **Physical Science** Density is mass per unit volume. The formula for density is $D = \frac{m}{v}$, where D represents density, m represents mass, and v represents volume. Find the mass of a gear with a density of 3.75 g/cm^3 and a volume of 20 cm^3.

26. What is the height of the cone if its volume is 8,138.88 ft^3? Use 3.14 for π.

12 ft

27. **Physical Science** The formula $E = mc^2$ tells the amount of energy an object at rest has. In the equation, E stands for the amount of energy in joules, m stands for the rest mass in kilograms of the object, and c is the speed of light (approximately 300,000,000 meters per second). What is the rest mass of an object that has 90,000,000,000,000 joules of energy?

Quiz for Lessons 12-4 Through 12-7

 **12-4** **Inequalities**

Write an inequality for each situation.

1. Gray has at least 25 blue T-shirts.

2. The room can hold no more than 50 people.

Graph each inequality.

3. $b > -1$ 4. $5 \le t$ 5. $-3 \ge x$

Graph each compound inequality.

6. $5 \ge p$ and $p > -1$ 7. $-8 > g$ or $g \ge -1$ 8. $-4 \le x < 0$

12-5 **Solving Inequalities by Adding or Subtracting**

Solve. Then graph each solution set on a number line.

9. $28 > m - 4$ 10. $8 + c \ge -13$ 11. $-1 + v < 1$

12. $5 \le p - 3$ 13. $-8 > f + 1$ 14. $-7 - w < 10$

15. A group of climbers are at an altitude of at most 17,500 feet. They are on their way to the top of Mount Everest, which is at an altitude of 29,035 feet. How many more feet do they have left to climb?

12-6 **Solving Inequalities by Multiplying or Dividing**

Solve. Check each answer.

16. $-8s > 16$ 17. $\frac{x}{-2} \le 9$ 18. $-7 \le \frac{b}{3}$

19. $\frac{c}{-3} \ge -4$ 20. $28 > 7h$ 21. $6y < -2$

12-7 **Solving Multi-Step Inequalities**

Solve. Then graph each solution set on a number line.

22. $2x - 3 > 5$ 23. $3 \ge -2d + 4$ 24. $3g - 2 - 10g > 5$

25. $14 < -2a + 6 - 2a$ 26. $3.6(1 + 2k) + 2 < 27.2$ 27. $5z - 2 - 2z \le 13$

28. A concert is being held in a gymnasium that can hold no more than 450 people. The bleachers seat 60 people. There will also be 26 rows of chairs set up. At most, how many people can sit in each row?

29. The 23 members of the Westview Journalism Club are trying to raise at least $2,100 to buy new publishing design software. The members have already raised $1,180. How much should each student still raise, on average, to meet the goal?

Real-World CONNECTIONS

CHAPTER
12

NEW HAMPSHIRE

Rock Climbing   New Hampshire is nicknamed the Granite State, so it's not surprising that it offers some of the best rock climbing in the country. For those who want to practice or take lessons, the state has more than a dozen indoor climbing gyms.

1. Ethan is planning to learn rock climbing at an indoor climbing gym. The table shows the day-use fees and cost of lessons at Indoor Ascent.

   a. Look for a pattern in the table. Let x represent the number of days. Write an expression for the fees.

   b. The total cost is the price of the two lessons plus the day-use fees. Write an expression that gives the total cost for x days.

2. A different gym has a day-use fee of $25, but the two lessons are included for free. Write and solve an inequality to find out when it is less expensive to go to Indoor Ascent.

3. Ethan's budget for lessons and fees at Indoor Ascent is $185. Write and solve an equation to find out how many days he can go to that gym.

4. Ethan saves $45 per month. For how many months must he save to have at least enough money to pay for the lessons and fees? Show how to solve this problem using an inequality.

INDOOR ASCENT CLIMBING GYM			
Day-Use Fees		Lessons
Days	Fees	Introductory Lesson $35
1	$12	
2	$24	Technique Lesson $30
3	$36	
4	$48	

Real-World Connections

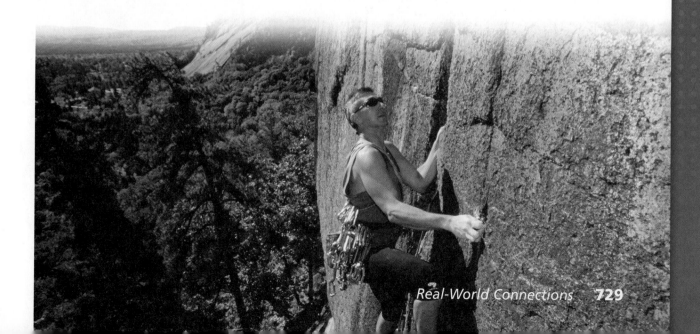

Game Time

Flapjacks

Five pancakes of different sizes are stacked in a random order. How can you get the pancakes in order from largest to smallest by flipping portions of the stack?

To find the answer, stack five disks of different sizes in no particular order. Arrange the disks from largest to smallest in the fewest number of moves possible. Move disks by choosing a disk and flipping over the whole stack from that disk up.

Start with a
stack of five.

Flip the stack
from the second
disk up.

Now flip the
stack from the
third disk up.

Finally, flip the
stack from the
second disk up.

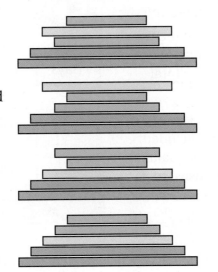

At most, it should take $3n - 2$ turns, where n is the number of disks, to arrange the disks from largest to smallest. The five disks above were arranged in three turns, which is less than $3(5) - 2 = 13$. Try it on your own.

Leaping Counters

Remove all but one of the counters from the board by jumping over each counter with another and removing the jumped counter. The game is over when you can no longer jump a counter. A perfect game would result in one counter being left in the center of the board.

A complete copy of the rules and a game board are available online.

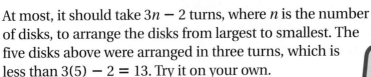

Learn It Online
Game Time Extra **go.hrw.com**,
keyword MS10 Games Go

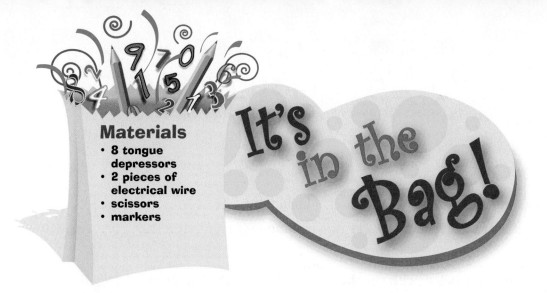

Materials
- 8 tongue depressors
- 2 pieces of electrical wire
- scissors
- markers

PROJECT **Wired for Multi-Step Equations**

These "study sticks" will help you sort out the steps in solving equations.

Directions

❶ Twist a piece of electrical wire around each end of a tongue depressor. Twist the wire tightly so that it holds the tongue depressor securely. **Figure A**

❷ Slide another tongue depressor between the ends of the wires. Slide it down as far as possible and then twist the wires together to hold this tongue depressor securely. **Figure B**

❸ Continue in the same way with the remaining tongue depressors.

❹ Twist the wires together at the top to make a handle. Trim the wires as needed.

Taking Note of the Math

Write the title of the chapter on the top tongue depressor. On each of the remaining tongue depressors, write the steps for solving a sample multi-step equation.

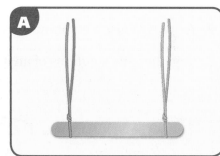

A

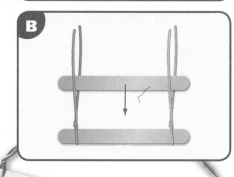

B

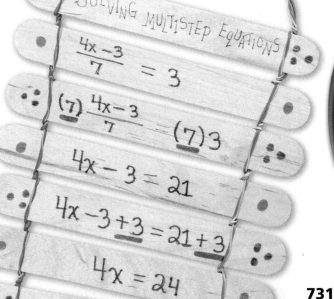

SOLVING MULTISTEP EQUATIONS

$$\frac{4x-3}{7} = 3$$

$$(7)\frac{4x-3}{7} = (7)3$$

$$4x - 3 = 21$$

$$4x - 3 + 3 = 21 + 3$$

$$4x = 24$$

$$\frac{4x}{4} = \frac{24}{4}$$

731

Study Guide: Review

Vocabulary

algebraic inequality 710   inequality 710

compound inequality 711   solution set 710

Complete the sentences below with vocabulary words from the list above.

1. A(n) ___?___ states that two quantities either are not equal or may not be equal.

2. A(n) ___?___ is a combination of more than one inequality.

3. Together, the solutions of an inequality are called the ___?___.

EXAMPLES

EXERCISES

12-1 Solving Two-Step Equations (pp. 696–699)

■ Solve $6a - 3 = 15$.

$$6a - 3 = 15$$
$$6a - 3 + 3 = 15 + 3 \quad \textit{Add 3 to both sides.}$$
$$6a = 18 \quad \textit{Divide to isolate}$$
$$\frac{6a}{6} = \frac{18}{6} \quad \textit{the variable.}$$
$$a = 3$$

Solve.

4. $-5y + 6 = -34$

5. $9 + \frac{z}{6} = 14$

6. $-8 = \frac{w}{-7} + 13$

12-2 Solving Multi-Step Equations (pp. 700–703)

■ Solve $\frac{4x - 3}{7} = 3$.

$$\frac{4x - 3}{7} = 3$$
$$(7)\frac{4x - 3}{7} = (7)3 \quad \textit{Multiply.}$$
$$4x - 3 = 21$$
$$4x - 3 + 3 = 21 + 3 \quad \textit{Add 3 to both sides.}$$
$$4x = 24$$
$$\frac{4x}{4} = \frac{24}{4} \quad \textit{Divide both}$$
$$x = 6 \quad \textit{sides by 4.}$$

Solve.

7. $7a + 4 - 13a = 46$ **8.** $9 = \frac{6j - 18}{4}$

9. $\frac{8b - 5}{3} = 9$ **10.** $52 = -9 + 16y - 19$

11. Noelle biked twice as many miles as Leila. Adding 2 to the number of miles Noelle biked and dividing by 3 gives the number of miles Dani biked. Dani biked 18 miles. How many miles did Leila bike?

EXAMPLES   EXERCISES

12-3 **Solving Equations with Variables on Both Sides** (pp. 704–707)

■ Solve $8a = 3a + 25$.

$$8a = 3a + 25$$
$$8a - 3a = 3a - 3a + 25 \quad \textit{Subtract.}$$
$$5a = 25$$
$$\frac{5a}{5} = \frac{25}{5} \quad \textit{Divide.}$$
$$a = 5$$

Solve.

12. $-6b + 9 = 12b$

13. $5 - 7c = -3c - 19$

14. $18m - 14 = 12m + 2$

15. $4 - \frac{2}{5}x = \frac{1}{5}x - 8$

16. Mercedes saves $50 each month. Ken saves $40 each month, and he started with $100. After how many months will they have the same amount saved?

12-4 **Inequalities** (pp. 710–713)

Write an inequality for each situation.

■ You have to be at least 16 years old to drive a car in New Jersey.
age of driver ≥ 16

■ Graph $x < -1$.

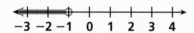

Write an inequality for each situation.

17. A bridge's load limit is at most 9 tons.

18. The large tree in the park is more than 200 years old.

Graph each inequality.

19. $y \geq 3$

20. $-2 \leq k < -1$

12-5 **Solving Inequalities by Adding or Subtracting** (pp. 714–717)

Solve. Graph each solution set.

■ $b + 6 > -10$
$$b + 6 > -10$$
$$b + 6 - 6 > -10 - 6$$
$$b > -16$$

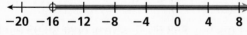

■ $p - 17 \leq 25$
$$p - 17 \leq 25$$
$$p - 17 + 17 \leq 25 + 17$$
$$p \leq 42$$

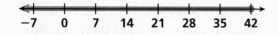

Solve. Graph each solution set.

21. $r - 16 > 9$

22. $-14 \geq 12 + x$

23. $\frac{3}{4} + g < 8\frac{3}{4}$

24. $\frac{5}{6} > \frac{2}{3} + t$

25. $7.46 > r - 1.54$

26. $u - 57.7 \geq -123.7$

27. The Wildcats scored at least 13 more points than the Stingrays scored. The Stingrays scored 25 points. How many points did the Wildcats score?

28. Gabe saved $113. This amount was at least $19 more than his brother saved. How much money did Gabe's brother save?

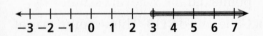
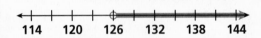

12-6 Solving Inequalities by Multiplying or Dividing (pp. 718–721)

Solve.

■ $\dfrac{m}{-4} \geq 3.8$

$\dfrac{m}{-4} \geq 3.8$

$(-4)\dfrac{m}{-4} \leq (-4)3.8$ *Multiply and reverse the inequality symbol.*

$m \leq -15.2$

■ $8b < -48$

$8b < -48$

$\dfrac{8b}{8} < -\dfrac{48}{8}$ *Divide both sides by 8.*

$b < -6$

Solve.

29. $\dfrac{n}{-8} > 6.9$

30. $-18 \leq -3p$

31. $\dfrac{k}{13} < -10$

32. $-5p > -25$

33. $2.3 \leq \dfrac{v}{1.2}$

34. $\dfrac{c}{-11} < -3$

35. It cost Carlita $204 to make beaded purses. How many purses must Carlita sell at $13 apiece to make a profit?

12-7 Solving Multi-Step Inequalities (pp. 722–725)

Solve. Graph each solution set.

■ $\dfrac{k}{3} - 18 > 24$

$\dfrac{k}{3} - 18 > 24$

$\dfrac{k}{3} - 18 + 18 > 24 + 18$

$\dfrac{k}{3} > 42$

$(3)\dfrac{k}{3} > (3)42$

$k > 126$

■ $-10b + 11 + 5b \leq -4$

$-10b + 11 + 5b \leq -4$

$-5b + 11 \leq -4$

$-5b + 11 - 11 \leq -4 - 11$

$-5b \leq -15$

$\dfrac{-5b}{-5} \geq \dfrac{-15}{-5}$

$b \geq 3$

Solve. Graph each solution set.

36. $-7b - 16 > -2$

37. $3.8 + \dfrac{d}{5} < 2.6$

38. $15 - 4n + 9 \leq 40$

39. $\dfrac{y}{-3} + 18 \geq 12$

40. $\dfrac{c}{3} + 7 > -11$

41. $32 \geq 4x - 8$

42. $18 + \dfrac{h}{6} \geq -8$

43. $14 > -2t - 6$

44. $-3 < \dfrac{w}{-2} + 10 + \dfrac{w}{4}$

45. $3\left(\dfrac{y}{21} + 1.3\right) \leq 8.9$

46. Luis has $53.55. T-shirts cost $8.95 each, and a belt costs $16.75. How many T-shirts can Luis buy if he also buys a new belt?

47. Clay, Alberto, and Ciana earned more than $475 by teaching swimming lessons together. After paying the $34 pool fee, they divided their earnings equally. How much money did each teacher earn?

Solve.

1. $3y - 8 = 16$

2. $\frac{x}{3} + 12 = -4$

3. $\frac{a}{6} - 7 = -4$

4. $-7b + 5 = -51$

5. $\frac{5y - 4}{3} = 7$

6. $8r + 7 - 13 = 58$

7. $6 = \frac{12s - 6}{5}$

8. $8.7 = \frac{19.8 - 4t}{3}$

9. $-14q = 4q - 126$

10. $\frac{5}{6}p + 4 = \frac{1}{6}p - 16$

11. $9 - 6k = 3k - 54$

12. $-3.6d = -7d + 34$

13. The bill for the repair of a computer was $179. The cost of the parts was $44, and the labor charge was $45 per hour. How many hours did it take to repair the computer?

14. Members of the choir are baking cookies for a fund-raiser. It costs $2.25 to make a dozen cookies, and the choir's initial expenses were $15.75. They sell the cookies for $4.50 a dozen. How many dozen do they have to sell to cover their costs?

Write an inequality for each situation.

15. You must be more than 4 ft tall to go on the ride.

16. You cannot go more than 65 miles per hour on Route 18.

Graph each inequality.

17. $a < -2$

18. $-5 < d$ and $d \le 2$

19. $c > -1$ or $c < -5$

20. $b \ge 3$

Solve. Then graph each solution set on a number line.

21. $n + 8 < -9$

22. $n - 124 > -59$

23. $-40 > \frac{x}{32}$

24. $-\frac{3}{4}y \le -12$

25. Rosa wants to save at least $125 to buy a new skateboard. She has already saved $46. How much more does Rosa need to save?

26. Gasoline costs $2.75 a gallon. At most, how many gallons can be bought for $22.00?

Solve. Then graph each solution set on a number line.

27. $m - 7.8 \le 23.7$

28. $6z > -2\frac{2}{3}$

29. $\frac{w}{-4.9} \le 3.4$

30. $-15 < 4a + 9$

31. $2.8 - \frac{c}{4} \ge 7.4$

32. $2\left(\frac{d}{10} - 4\right) > -4$

33. The seventh-grade students at Fulmore Middle School are trying to raise at least $7,500 for the local public library. So far, each of the 198 students has raised an average of $20. How much more money must each seventh-grader collect, on average, to reach the goal?

TCAP Test Prep

Cumulative Assessment, Chapters 1–12

Multiple Choice

1. Nolan has 7 red socks, 3 black socks, 10 white socks, and 5 blue socks in a drawer. If Nolan chooses one sock at a time and puts the sock immediately on his foot, what is the probability that he will choose 2 white socks?

   A $\frac{3}{20}$ C $\frac{2}{5}$

   B $\frac{4}{25}$ D $\frac{19}{25}$

2. Angelica has a map with a scale 1 inch = 125 miles. On her map, the distance between two cities is $2\frac{3}{4}$ miles. To the nearest mile, what is the actual distance between the two cities?

   F 293 miles   H 344 miles

   G 313 miles   J 375 miles

3. There are 126 girls and 104 boys attending a luncheon. Each person at the luncheon writes his or her name on a piece of paper and puts the paper in a barrel. One name is randomly selected from the barrel to win a new MP3 player. What is the probability the person selected is male?

   A 45.2%   C 82.5%

   B 54.8%   D Not here

4. Which inequality describes the graph?

   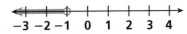

   F $-2x + 3 > 5$

   G $-2x + 3 \geq 5$

   H $-2x + 3 < 5$

   J $-2x + 3 \leq 5$

For Items 5 and 6, use the graph below.

5. The graph shows the relationship between the number of months in the savings plan and the amount of money saved.

   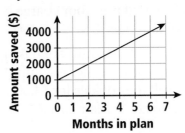

   What does the *y*-intercept represent?

   A Every month $1000 is deposited.

   B The initial deposit is $1000.

   C There is no initial deposit.

   D After the second month, there is $2000 in the savings account.

6. What does the slope of the line represent?

   F the total number of months in the plan

   G the total amount of money saved

   H the number of months per amount saved

   J the amount of money saved per month

7. Evaluate the expression $\frac{1}{3}b + 2\left(b - \frac{1}{2}\right)$ for $b = 4$.

   A $4\frac{5}{6}$ C $8\frac{1}{3}$

   B $7\frac{1}{3}$ D $8\frac{5}{6}$

8. Calculate 16.0 ft − 9.03 ft.

   F 7.0 ft   H 6.97 ft

   G 7 ft   I 6 ft

9. How would the following numbers appear on a number line from left to right?

$$\frac{3}{4}, -3.5, \sqrt[3]{125}, 2, \sqrt{16}$$

A $\frac{3}{4}, 2, \sqrt[3]{125}, \sqrt{16}, -3.5$

B $-3.5, \frac{3}{4}, 2, \sqrt{16}, \sqrt[3]{125}$

C $\sqrt[3]{125}, \sqrt{16}, 2, \frac{3}{4}, -3.5$

D $\sqrt{16}, \sqrt[3]{125}, \frac{3}{4}, 2, -3.5$

 HOT TIP! Create and use a number line to help you order rational numbers quickly.

10. A one-year membership at a recreation center costs $150. There is a $25 application fee paid at the time you sign up, and there remainder is paid monthly. How much do new members pay each month?

F $5   H $10

G $8.50   J $12.50

11. Freddy counted the number of bats he saw each night for one week. What is the median of the data set?

Number of Bats Spotted
42, 21, 36, 28, 40, 21, 31

A 21   C 31.3

B 31   D 36.5

12. What is the probability of rolling a number greater than or equal to 4 on a number cube?

F $\frac{1}{6}$ H $\frac{1}{2}$

G $\frac{1}{4}$ J 1

13. The value of n makes this equation <u>true</u>?

$$\frac{2}{3}n + 1 = 5$$

A $2\frac{1}{3}$ C $6\frac{1}{2}$

B 6   D 9

Process Standards Practice
Short Response

S1. Solve the inequality $-7y \geq 126$ and then graph the solution set on a number line. Is zero part of the solution set? Explain.

S2. Nine less than four times a number is the same as twice the number increased by 11. What is the number?

   a. Write the above statement as an equation.

   b. Solve the equation.

S3. Hallie is baking 5 batches of brownies for the bake sale. Each batch requires $1\frac{2}{3}$ cups of flour. Hallie has $8\frac{1}{4}$ cups of flour. Does she have enough flour to make five batches? Explain your answer.

Extended Response

E1. Tim and his crew trim trees. They charge a service fee of $40 for each job, plus an hourly rate.

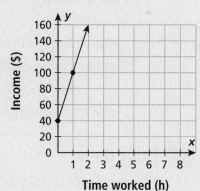

   a. Use the graph to determine the crew's hourly rate. Explain how you found your answer.

   b. Write an equation to find y, the crew's income for x hours of work.

   c. How many hours did Tim's crew work if they earned $490? Show your work.

Student Handbook

Extra Practice . . . Chapter 1

LESSON 1-1

Identify a possible pattern. Use the pattern to write the next three numbers.

1. 13, 21, 29, 37, ▨, ▨, ▨, . . .

2. 7, 8, 10, 13, ▨, ▨, ▨, . . .

3. 165, 156, 147, 138, ▨, ▨, ▨, . . .

4. 19, 33, 47, 61, ▨, ▨, ▨, . . .

Identify a possible pattern. Use the pattern to draw the next three figures.

5.

6.

7. Make a table that shows the number of dots in each figure. Then tell how many dots are in the fifth figure of the pattern. Use drawings to justify your answer.

Figure 1   Figure 2   Figure 3

LESSON 1-2

Find each value.

8. 5^3

9. 7^3

10. 5^5

11. 6^5

12. 4^1

13. 8^2

14. 12^2

15. 100^3

Write each number using an exponent and the given base.

16. 121, base 11

17. 4,096, base 4

18. 216, base 6

19. 1,296, base 6

20. 256, base 2

21. 8,000, base 20

22. Maria decided to donate $1.00 to her favorite charity the first week of the month and to double the amount she donates each week. How much will she donate the sixth week?

LESSON 1-3

Multiply.

23. $24 \cdot 10^3$

24. $20 \cdot 10^5$

25. $318 \cdot 10^3$

26. $2,180 \cdot 10^4$

27. $2,508 \cdot 10^5$

28. $5.555 \cdot 10^6$

Write each number in scientific notation.

29. 387,000

30. 2,056,000

31. 65,400,000

32. 1,560

33. 7,000,000,000

34. $206.7 \cdot 10^3$

35. The distance from the Earth to the moon is about 2.48×10^5 miles. Write this distance in standard form.

36. New York City is about 1.0871×10^4 km from Tokyo, Japan. London, England, is about 9.581×10^3 km from Tokyo. Which city is closer to Tokyo?

Extra Practice ... Chapter 1

LESSON 1-4

Simplify each expression. Use the order of operations to justify your answer.

37. $9 \div 3 + 6 \cdot 5$

38. $16 + (20 \div 5) - 3^2$

39. $(6 - 3)^3 \div 9 + 7$

40. $(4 \cdot 9) - (9 - 3)^2$

41. $5 + 9 \cdot 2^2 \div 6$

42. $6{,}842 - (5^3 \cdot 5 \cdot 10)$

43. Charlotte bought 4 shirts and 3 pairs of pants. She got the pants at a discount. Simplify the expression $4 \cdot 32 + 3 \cdot 25 - (3 \cdot 25) \div 5$ to find out how much she paid for the clothes.

LESSON 1-5

Tell which property is represented.

44. $9 \cdot 2 = 2 \cdot 9$

45. $9 + 0 = 9$

46. $12 \cdot 1 = 1 \cdot 12$

47. $1 \cdot (2 \cdot 3) = (1 \cdot 2) \cdot 3$

48. $xy = yx$

49. $(x + y) + z = x + (y + z)$

Simplify each expression. Justify each step.

50. $5 + 6 + 19$

51. $5 \cdot 10 \cdot 2$

52. $3 \cdot (5 \cdot 9)$

53. $(25 \cdot 8) \cdot 4$

54. $30 + (121 + 39)$

55. $125 \cdot (2 \cdot 3)$

Use the Distributive Property to find each product.

56. $8 \cdot (2 + 10)$

57. $3 \cdot (19 + 4)$

58. $(10 - 2) \cdot 7$

59. $15 \cdot (13 - 8)$

60. $(47 + 88) \cdot 4$

61. $5 \cdot (157 - 45)$

LESSON 1-6

Evaluate each expression for the given value of the variable.

62. $8k - 7$ for $k = 4$

63. $9n + 12$ for $n = 6$

64. $12t - 15$ for $t = 4$

65. $v \div 5 + v$ for $v = 20$

66. $3r - 20 \div r$ for $r = 5$

67. $5x^2 + 3x$ for $x = 3$

Evaluate each expression for the given value of the variables.

68. $x + \frac{15}{y} - 2$ for $x = 10$ $y = 5$

69. $3j + 4k - 20$ for $j = 12$ and $k = 2$

70. $17 + 5a - \frac{4b}{2}$ for $a = 3$ and $b = 6$

71. $s^2 - 3r + 50$ for $s = 8$ and $r = 7$

72. $\frac{m}{9} + n^2 + 5$ for $m = 36$ and $n = 6$

73. $21 + 9e - 10f$ for $e = 5$ and $f = 1$

LESSON 1-7

Write each phrase as an algebraic expression.

74. 12 less than a number

75. the quotient of a number and 8

76. add 7 to 8 times a number

77. 6 times the sum of 13 and a number

78. A music store sells packages of guitar strings. David bought s strings for $24. Write an algebraic expression for the cost of one string.

LESSON 1-8

Identify like terms in each list.

79. $2d \quad 5d^2 \quad x \quad 4x^2 \quad d^2 \quad 6x$

80. $9 \quad 5y \quad \frac{y}{2} \quad 4g^2 \quad y^2 \quad y$

Simplify. Justify your steps using the Commutative, Associative, and Distributive Properties when necessary.

81. $5b + 3t + b$

82. $t + 3b + 3t + 3b + x$

83. $8g + 3g + 12$

84. $3u + 6 + 5k + u$

85. $11 + 5t^2 + t + 6t$

86. $y^3 + 3y + 6y^3$

87. Write an expression for the perimeter of the given figure. Then simplify the expression.

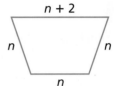

LESSON 1-9

Determine whether each number is a solution of $17 = 45 - j$.

88. 31

89. 28

90. 14

91. 22

Determine whether each number is a solution of $x + 23 = 51$.

92. 42

93. 31

94. 19

95. 28

96. Randall wants to buy a new video game. He has $53, which is $9 less than he needs. Does the video game cost $62 or $65?

LESSON 1-10

Solve each equation. Check your answer.

97. $n - 22 = 16$

98. $y + 27 = 42$

99. $x - 81 = 14$

100. $t - 32 = 64$

101. $z + 39 = 72$

102. $a + 43 = 61$

103. Raquel is hiking a 9 mile trail in the Grand Canyon. She has already hiked 4 miles. How much farther does she have to hike?

104. Mikey scored 12 points for his basketball team. The entire team scored 63 points. How many points did Mikey's teammates score?

LESSON 1-11

Solve each equation. Check your answer.

105. $20 = s \div 3$

106. $12y = 84$

107. $15 = \frac{n}{9}$

108. $\frac{m}{36} = 12$

109. $144 = 3p$

110. $72j = 360$

111. Adam is saving to buy a computer that costs $400 before school starts. If school starts in 8 weeks, how much will he need to save per week in order to have enough money?

Extra Practice ... Chapter 2

LESSON 2-1

Use a number line to order the integers from least to greatest.

1. 5, −3, −1, 2, 0   **2.** −4, −1, 3, 1, 4   **3.** −5, 0, −3, 2, 4

Use a number line to find each absolute value.

4. $|-22|$ **5.** $|9|$ **6.** $|-13|$ **7.** $|21|$

LESSON 2-2

Find each sum.

8. $8 + (-4)$ **9.** $-3 + (-6)$ **10.** $-5 + 9$ **11.** $-7 + (-2)$

Evaluate $c + d$ **for the given values.**

12. $c = 5, d = -9$ **13.** $c = 12, d = 9$ **14.** $c = -7, d = -2$ **15.** $c = -16, d = 8$

16. The temperature in Pierre at 8:00 A.M. was −33 °F . It rose 20 °F in 9 hours. What was the temperature at 5:00 P.M.?

LESSON 2-3

Find each difference.

17. $6 - (-3)$ **18.** $-4 - (-8)$ **19.** $2 - 7$ **20.** $3 - (-4)$

Evaluate $a - b$ **for each set of values.**

21. $a = 5, b = -8$ **22.** $a = -12, b = -6$ **23.** $a = 6, b = 13$ **24.** $a = 9, b = -17$

25. The highest point in the United States is Mount McKinley at about 20,320 feet. Death Valley, California, is the lowest point at about 282 feet below sea level. What is the difference in elevation between the highest and lowest points in the United States?

LESSON 2-4

Find each product or quotient.

26. $-9 \div 3$ **27.** $8 \cdot (-3)$ **28.** $16 \div 4$ **29.** $-7 \cdot 3$

30. $-2 \cdot 9$ **31.** $15 \div (-5)$ **32.** $6 \cdot 7$ **33.** $-72 \div (-12)$

Evaluate xy **for each set of values.**

34. $x = 2, y = -3$ **35.** $x = -4, y = 5$ **36.** $x = -2, y = -8$ **37.** $x = -1, y = -9$

38. A submarine descends below the ocean's surface at a rate of 75 feet per minute. How many feet below the ocean's surface will the submarine be in 12 minutes?

LESSON 2-5

Solve each equation. Check your answer.

39. $n - 25 = -18$ **40.** $y + (-13) = 61$ **41.** $21 = \frac{s}{4}$ **42.** $15y = -45$

43. $\frac{k}{-18} = 2$ **44.** $h - (-7) = -42$ **45.** $6 = \frac{z}{9}$ **46.** $68 = 4 + p$

47. On Monday, Martin deposited $76 into his bank account. On Tuesday, he withdrew $100. He then had $202 in his account. How much money did he start with on Monday?

LESSON 2-6

Write the prime factorization of each number.

48. 78   **49.** 144   **50.** 96   **51.** 95

52. 176   **53.** 156   **54.** 336   **55.** 675

56. 888   **57.** 2,800   **58.** 780   **59.** 682

LESSON 2-7

Find the greatest common factor (GCF).

60. 6, 15   **61.** 18, 27   **62.** 26, 65   **63.** 60, 25

64. 84, 48   **65.** 90, 34   **66.** 49, 56   **67.** 36, 120

68. 30, 75   **69.** 32, 68   **70.** 81, 75   **71.** 30, 70, 65, 100

72. 21, 77   **73.** 64, 84, 120   **74.** 20, 40, 80, 140   **75.** 49, 98

76. José is making identical gift bags to sell at his concert. He has 51 CDs and 34 T-shirts. What is the greatest number of gift bags José can make using all of the CDs and all of the T-shirts?

LESSON 2-8

Find the least common multiple (LCM).

77. 12, 15   **78.** 30, 12   **79.** 16, 32   **80.** 25, 40

81. 30, 75   **82.** 12, 64   **83.** 15, 50   **84.** 15, 30, 50, 100

85. 21, 28   **86.** 15, 22, 30   **87.** 20, 40, 80, 120   **88.** 42, 90

89. Kanisha shoots a basket every 7 seconds. Thomas shoots a basket every 12 seconds. They begin at the same time. How many seconds will have passed when they next shoot a basket at the same time?

Extra Practice ... Chapter 2

LESSON 2-9

Find a fraction equivalent to the given number.

90. $\frac{1}{5}$ **91.** $7\frac{2}{3}$ **92.** 96   **93.** $\frac{50}{13}$

Determine whether the fractions in each pair are equivalent.

94. $\frac{2}{7}$ and $\frac{3}{4}$ **95.** $\frac{4}{6}$ and $\frac{12}{18}$ **96.** $\frac{7}{8}$ and $\frac{20}{24}$ **97.** $\frac{5}{12}$ and $\frac{15}{36}$

Write each improper fraction as a mixed number. Write each mixed number as an improper fraction.

98. $\frac{19}{5}$ **99.** $\frac{23}{8}$ **100.** $3\frac{4}{5}$ **101.** $2\frac{13}{15}$

LESSON 2-10

Write each fraction as a decimal. Round to the nearest hundredth, if necessary.

102. $\frac{4}{5}$ **103.** $\frac{6}{8}$ **104.** $\frac{57}{15}$ **105.** $-\frac{75}{10}$

Write each decimal as a fraction in simplest form.

106. 0.85   **107.** -0.04 **108.** 0.875   **109.** 2.6

110. Brianna brought 96 CDs to sell at her concert. At the concert, she sold 84 CDs. What portion of the CDs did she sell? Write your answer as a decimal.

111. Jacob used 44 of the 60 pages in his journal. What portion of the pages did he use? Write your answer as a decimal rounded to the nearest hundredth.

LESSON 2-11

Compare the fractions or decimals. Write $<$ or $>$.

112. $\frac{8}{13}$ ▧ $\frac{5}{13}$ **113.** 0.82 ▧ 0.88   **114.** $-\frac{8}{9}$ ▧ $-\frac{11}{12}$ **115.** -1.024 ▧ 1.007

Order the numbers from least to greatest.

116. 0.5, 0.58, $\frac{6}{13}$ **117.** 2.7, 2.59, $2\frac{7}{12}$ **118.** $-0.61, -0.55, -\frac{9}{15}$

119. Brian operates an ice cream stand in a large city. He spends 0.4 of his budget on supplies, $\frac{1}{12}$ on advertising, and 0.08 on taxes and fees. Does Brian spend more on advertising or more on taxes and fees?

Extra Practice ... Chapter 3

LESSON 3-1

Estimate by rounding to the nearest integer.

1. $145.2 \cdot 6.7$
2. $26.23 + 201.86$
3. $438.57 - 129.39$
4. $55.72 \div 7.48$

5. $-5.87 \cdot 7.39$
6. $54.51 + 135.47$
7. $-87.23 - 32.62$
8. $63.38 \div 4.77$

9. Caden has $48.50. He thinks he can buy three CDs for $16.99 each. Use estimation to check whether his assumption is reasonable.

LESSON 3-2

Add or subtract. Estimate to check whether each answer is reasonable.

10. $8.79 + 45.63$
11. $-7.85 - (-34.7)$
12. $43.67 - 14.81$
13. $-18 + (-7.32)$

14. $34.43 + (-62.57)$
15. $-8.26 + 7.4$
16. $-8.75 - 5.43$
17. $-35.4 - (-24.08)$

18. Zoe gets to work in 25.5 minutes and gets home from work in 37.5 minutes. How much time does she spend commuting each day?

LESSON 3-3

Multiply. Estimate to check whether each answer is reasonable.

19. $4.3 \cdot 2.8$
20. $-3.38 \cdot 0.8$
21. $-8 \cdot (-0.07)$
22. $7.59 \cdot (-36)$

23. $-67.4 \cdot (-8.7)$
24. $5.66 \cdot (-16.34)$
25. $-43.9 \cdot (-4.7)$
26. $73.3 \cdot 6.85$

27. Griffin works after school and on weekends. He worked 18.5 hours last week and gets paid $7.90 per hour. How much did he earn last week?

LESSON 3-4

Divide. Estimate to check whether each answer is reasonable.

28. $16.9 \div (-1.3)$
29. $74.25 \div 6.6$
30. $-4.8 \div 0.12$
31. $-0.63 \div (-0.7)$

32. $-36.04 \div 4.24$
33. $34.672 \div (-4.4)$
34. $-128.685 \div 37.3$
35. $-231.28 \div (-41.3)$

36. $15 \div 2.4$
37. $70 \div -3.5$
38. $-66 \div 13.2$
39. $43 \div -8.6$

40. $-17 \div -1.7$
41. $-87 \div 5.8$
42. $-99 \div -3.3$
43. $22 \div -2.5$

44. Miley is training to run a 10K race. Miley ran 10 kilometers in 62 minutes. If she runs each kilometer at the same pace, how long did it take Miley to run one kilometer?

45. The diameter of a northern red oak tree grows an average of 0.4 inches per year. At this rate, how long will it take the tree's diameter to grow to 24.8 inches?

Extra Practice ... Chapter 3

LESSON 3-5

Solve. Justify your steps.

46. $4.7 + s = 9$ **47.** $t - 1.35 = -22$ **48.** $-4.8 = -6x$ **49.** $9.6 = \frac{v}{8}$

50. $-6.5 + n = 5.9$ **51.** $x - 1.07 = -8.5$ **52.** $-6.2y = -21.08$ **53.** $\frac{r}{13} = 3.25$

54. Billy worked 7.5 hours and earned $56.70. What is Billy's hourly wage?

55. A single movie ticket costs $7.25. The Brown family consists of Mr. and Mrs. Brown, Amy, and her two brothers. What does it cost the Brown family to go to the movies together?

56. The same cereal costs $3.99 per box at one store, $3.25 per box at another store, and $3.59 per box at a third store. What is the average price per box of the cereal?

LESSON 3-6

Estimate each sum, difference, product or quotient.

57. $\frac{3}{8} + \frac{5}{6}$ **58.** $\frac{7}{8} - \frac{1}{6}$ **59.** $5\frac{3}{4} + 2\frac{3}{8}$ **60.** $6\frac{2}{3} - 2\frac{1}{6}$

61. $4\frac{1}{12} \div 2\frac{1}{8}$ **62.** $\frac{7}{16} \cdot 2\frac{3}{4}$ **63.** $8\frac{9}{10} \div 1\frac{1}{9}$ **64.** $3\frac{2}{5} \cdot 1\frac{4}{7}$

65. A stock's price in July was $19\frac{3}{8}$ and its price in October rose to $27\frac{1}{8}$. Estimate the difference between the price in July and the price in October.

LESSON 3-7

Add or subtract. Write each answer in simplest form.

66. $\frac{1}{4} + \frac{1}{3}$ **67.** $\frac{3}{11} - \frac{3}{22}$ **68.** $-\frac{3}{6} + \frac{2}{3}$ **69.** $-\frac{1}{4} - \frac{7}{10}$

70. $\frac{3}{7} + \frac{5}{9}$ **71.** $\frac{7}{8} - \frac{2}{3}$ **72.** $\frac{7}{12} + \frac{5}{6}$ **73.** $\frac{4}{5} - \frac{9}{10}$

74. Jacob and Julius spent $\frac{1}{4}$ hour swimming, $\frac{1}{10}$ hour eating a snack, and then $\frac{1}{2}$ hour hiking. How long did these activities take Jacob and Julius?

LESSON 3-8

Add or subtract. Write each answer in simplest form.

75. $9\frac{7}{8} - 4\frac{1}{4}$ **76.** $3\frac{1}{2} + 2\frac{3}{4}$ **77.** $9\frac{5}{6} - 6\frac{1}{3}$ **78.** $5\frac{7}{12} + 2\frac{5}{8}$

79. $7\frac{1}{4} - 3\frac{2}{3}$ **80.** $4\frac{2}{3} + 3\frac{7}{8}$ **81.** $8\frac{2}{5} - 3\frac{9}{10}$ **82.** $3\frac{7}{8} + 4\frac{3}{5}$

83. The average male giraffe is about $17\frac{1}{2}$ feet tall. One of the giraffes at the zoo is $18\frac{1}{8}$ feet tall. How much taller is the giraffe at the zoo than the average male giraffe?

Extra Practice ... Chapter 3

LESSON 3-9

Multiply. Write each answer in simplest form.

84. $\frac{2}{3} \cdot 12\frac{3}{4}$

85. $3\frac{2}{9} \cdot \frac{1}{2}$

86. $\frac{5}{7} \cdot 4\frac{3}{8}$

87. $5\frac{2}{3} \cdot \frac{7}{12}$

88. $4\frac{3}{5} \cdot 3\frac{2}{3}$

89. $3\frac{1}{3} \cdot 2\frac{5}{6}$

90. $2\frac{1}{4} \cdot 3\frac{3}{4}$

91. $4\frac{1}{5} \cdot 5\frac{1}{12}$

92. $-3\frac{1}{5} \cdot -6\frac{3}{8}$

93. $-5 \cdot \frac{1}{3}$

94. $\frac{3}{7} \cdot -1\frac{1}{2}$

95. $-2 \cdot -3\frac{1}{10}$

96. Mary is $2\frac{1}{2}$ times as old as Victor. If Victor is $7\frac{1}{2}$ years old, how old is Mary?

97. Admission to a museum in 2008 was $22.50. In 1998, the admission price was $\frac{3}{5}$ of the admission price in 2008. What was the admission price in 1998?

LESSON 3-10

Divide. Write each answer in simplest form.

98. $\frac{7}{8} \div \frac{5}{6}$

99. $\frac{7}{12} \div \frac{7}{8}$

100. $\frac{2}{3} \div \frac{2}{5}$

101. $2\frac{1}{4} \div \frac{1}{2}$

102. $5\frac{7}{8} \div \frac{5}{6}$

103. $3\frac{3}{4} \div 1\frac{1}{4}$

104. $2\frac{5}{6} \div 4\frac{1}{3}$

105. $5\frac{2}{3} \div 2\frac{1}{2}$

106. $\frac{4}{5} \div 3$

107. $1\frac{1}{8} \div \frac{2}{9}$

108. $2\frac{1}{4} \div 3\frac{1}{2}$

109. $5 \div \frac{1}{5}$

110. Each serving of chicken weighs $\frac{1}{3}$ pound. Melanie bought 12 pounds of chicken for a party. How many servings does she have?

111. Jessika, Alfred, and Judith are driving round-trip to a football game that is 190 miles from their town. If each of them drives the same distance, how far will each person drive?

LESSON 3-11

Solve. Write each answer in simplest form.

112. $\frac{1}{3} + s = \frac{2}{5}$

113. $t - \frac{3}{8} = -\frac{5}{6}$

114. $-\frac{5}{6} = -\frac{1}{3}x$

115. $\frac{2}{3}w = 240$

116. $-\frac{5}{8} + n = \frac{5}{6}$

117. $x - \frac{5}{8} = -\frac{5}{8}$

118. $-\frac{2}{3}y = -\frac{3}{4}$

119. $\frac{r}{6} = \frac{1}{8}$

120. $j + \frac{4}{5} = -\frac{1}{10}$

121. $\frac{3}{4} + e = \frac{11}{12}$

122. $-\frac{1}{2}s = \frac{5}{8}$

123. $\frac{i}{7} = \frac{2}{3}$

124. Jorge owns $1\frac{3}{4}$ acres of land. Juanita, his neighbor, owns $2\frac{2}{3}$ acres. How many acres do they own in all?

125. Kyra uses $2\frac{1}{4}$ feet of ribbon to wrap each of the identical fruit baskets that she sells. How many baskets can she wrap with a 144-foot roll of ribbon?

126. Matilda uses $1\frac{2}{3}$ cup milk for a muffin recipe. If she wants to make 3 times the amount of muffins, how much milk will she use?

Extra Practice ... Chapter 4

LESSON 4-1

One day, a veterinarian saw 20 cats and 30 dogs. Write each ratio in all three forms. Make sure each ratio is in simplest form.

1. cats to dogs   **2.** dogs to cats   **3.** cats to animals

4. A compact car can travel 135 miles per 5 gallons of gas. A midsize car can travel 210 miles per 10 gallons of gas. Which car gets more miles per gallon?

LESSON 4-2

5. Danielle skipped a rope 248 times in 4 minutes. On average, how many times did Danielle skip rope per minute?

6. A serving of 8 crackers contains 128 calories. What is the number of calories per cracker?

7. Jamie's family drives 350 miles to her grandparents' house in 7 hours. What is their average speed in miles per hour?

8. A store sells milk in three different sizes. The 128 fl oz container costs $4.59, the 64 fl oz container costs $3.29, and the 32 fl oz container costs $1.99. Which size has the lowest price per fluid ounce?

LESSON 4-3

Determine whether the ratios are proportional.

9. $\frac{25}{40}, \frac{30}{48}$ **10.** $\frac{32}{36}, \frac{24}{28}$ **11.** $\frac{5}{6}, \frac{15}{18}$ **12.** $\frac{21}{49}, \frac{18}{42}$

Find a ratio equivalent to each ratio. Then use the ratios to write a proportion.

13. $\frac{72}{81}$ **14.** $\frac{15}{40}$ **15.** $\frac{24}{32}$ **16.** $\frac{5}{13}$

LESSON 4-4

Use cross products to solve each proportion.

17. $\frac{8}{n} = \frac{12}{18}$ **18.** $\frac{4}{7} = \frac{p}{28}$ **19.** $\frac{u}{14} = -\frac{21}{28}$ **20.** $\frac{3}{21} = \frac{t}{49}$

21. $\frac{y}{35} = \frac{63}{45}$ **22.** $-\frac{6}{n} = -\frac{48}{12}$ **23.** $\frac{32}{x} = \frac{52}{117}$ **24.** $\frac{56}{80} = \frac{105}{m}$

25. The ratio of a person's weight on Earth to his weight on the Moon is 6 to 1. Rafael weighs 90 pounds on Earth. How much would he weigh on the Moon?

26. In 2 weeks, a taxi traveled 2,460 miles. At this rate, how many miles will the taxi travel in one year (52 weeks)?

Extra Practice ... Chapter 4

LESSON 4-5

Choose the most appropriate customary unit for each measurement. Justify your answer.

27. the weight of 6 crackers

28. the capacity of a pond

29. the capacity of a baby's bottle

30. the length of a marathon

Convert each measure.

31. 8 pt to cups

32. 5 ft to inches

33. 6.5 lb to ounces

34. The directions on Brant's protein powder say to mix four scoops with 16 ounces of milk to make a protein drink. If Brant has a quart of milk, how many protein drinks can he make?

LESSON 4-6

Choose the most appropriate metric unit for each measurement. Justify your answer.

35. The distance from home plate to first base

36. The height of a telephone pole

37. The mass of a marble

38. The capacity of a baby bottle

Convert each measure.

39. 8.9 m to millimeters

40. 56 mg to grams

41. 900 mL to liters

42. 2 L to milliliters

43. 150 m to kilometers

44. 0.002 kg to milligrams

45. Anthony and Melinda are drinking apple juice. Anthony has 300 mL of juice left and Melinda has 0.09 L. Who has the greater amount of juice? Explain why your answer makes sense.

LESSON 4-7

46. A water fountain dispenses 8 cups of water per minute. Find this rate in pints per minute.

47. Jo's car uses 1,664 quarts of gas per year. Find this rate in gallons per week.

48. Toby walked 352 feet in one minute. What is his rate in miles per hour?

49. A giant tortoise has a top speed of 2.992 inches per second. What is a giant tortoise's top speed in meters per second? Round your answer to the nearest thousandth. (*Hint:* 1 in. = 0.0254 m)

LESSON 4-8

Tell whether the figures are similar.

50.

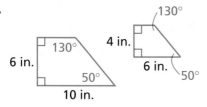

51.

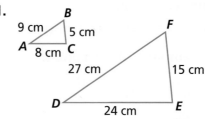

LESSON 4-9

Find the unknown measures.

52. △XYZ ~ △RQS

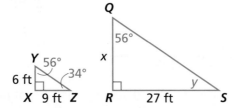

53. A 5-foot-tall girl casts a 7-foot-long shadow. At the same time, a nearby telephone pole casts a 35-foot-long shadow. What is the height of the telephone pole?

54. A 24-foot-tall tree casts a 30-foot-long shadow. A 4-foot-tall child is standing nearby. How long is the child's shadow?

55. A flagpole casts a shadow that is 26 ft long. At the same time, a yardstick casts a shadow that is 4 ft long. How tall is the flagpole?

56. An amoeba is 0.8 millimeter in length. At the science museum, there is a scale model of the amoeba that is 160 millimeters in length. What is the scale factor?

LESSON 4-10

57. A scale model of the Empire State Building is 3.125 feet tall with a scale factor of $\frac{1}{400}$. Find the actual height of the Empire State Building.

58. Kira is drawing a map of her state with a scale of 1 inch:30 miles. The actual distance between Park City and Gatesville is 80 miles. How far from Gatesville should Kira place Park City on her map?

59. On a map, the distance between the cities of Brachburg and Trunktown is 4.3 cm. The map scale is 1 cm:25 km. What is the actual distance between the cities?

Extra Practice ... Chapter 5

LESSON 5-1

Plot each point on a coordinate plane. Identify the quadrant that contains each point.

1. $M(-1, 1)$

2. $N(4, 4)$

3. $Q(3, -1)$

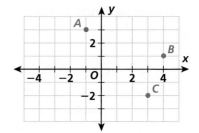

Give the coordinates of each point.

4. A

5. B

6. C

LESSON 5-2

7. Abby rode her bike to the park. She had a picnic there with friends before biking home. Which graph best shows the situation?

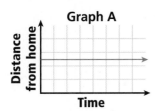

Graph A

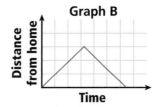

Graph B

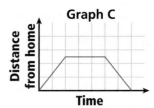

Graph C

8. Jose is selling tins of popcorn for a school fund-raiser. Each tin of popcorn sells for $12. Draw a graph to show his possible income from sales.

LESSON 5-3

Find the output for each input.

9.

Input	Rule	Output
x	3x − 1	y
−2		
0		
2		

10.

Input	Rule	Output
x	$4x^2$	y
1		
3		
5		

Make a function table, and graph the resulting ordered pairs.

11. $y = 2x - 5$

12. $y = -5x + 2$

13. $y = x^2 - 1$

14. $y = x^2 + 10$

LESSON 5-4

Tell whether each sequence of y-values is arithmetic or geometric. Then find y when $n = 5$.

15.

n	1	2	3	4	5
y	−4	0	4	8	

16.

n	1	2	3	4	5
y	2	4	8	16	

17. Tim wants to increase the number of miles he runs each week. His plan is to run 10 miles the first week, 12 miles the second week, 14 miles the third week, and 16 miles the fourth week. Write a function that describes the sequence, and then use the function to predict how many miles Tim will run during the eighth week.

LESSON **5-5**

Graph each linear function.

18. $y = 2x + 2$ **19.** $y = x - 3$ **20.** $y = -x + 2$

21. The outside temperature is increasing at the rate of 6 °F per hour. When Reid begins measuring the temperature, it is 52 °F. Write a linear function that describes the outside temperature over time. Then make a graph to show the temperature over the first 3 hours.

LESSON **5-6**

Tell whether the slope is positive or negative. Then find the slope.

22.

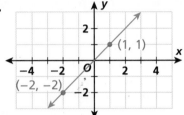

23.

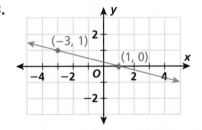

Use the given slope and point to graph each line.

24. $\frac{1}{2}$; $(2, 1)$ **25.** $-\frac{2}{3}$; $(4, 1)$ **26.** $-\frac{4}{5}$; $(-2, -3)$ **27.** 3; $(1, -3)$

LESSON **5-7**

Graph each equation.

28. $y = -\frac{2}{3}x + 5$ **29.** $y = 6x + 4$ **30.** $3x + y = -2$ **31.** $-x + y = 5$

Write the equation of each line in slope-intercept form.

32.

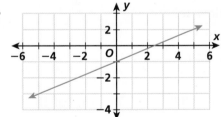

33.

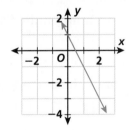

LESSON **5-8**

Tell whether each equation represents a direct variation. If so, identify the constant of variation.

34. $3x = 5y$ **35.** $y = x^2$ **36.** $y = 0.9x$ **37.** $y = 2x + 12$

38. Peter has decided to save $30 each week to buy a new stereo system.
  a. Write a direct variation equation for the amount of money d that Peter has saved in w weeks.
  b. Graph the data.
  c. How many weeks will it take Peter to save $270?

Extra Practice ... Chapter 6

LESSON 6-1

Write the percent modeled by each grid.

1.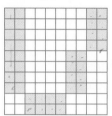

2.

3.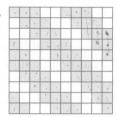

Write each percent as a fraction in simplest form.

4. 14%   **5.** 110%   **6.** 20%   **7.** 9%

Write each percent as a decimal.

8. 27%   **9.** 7%   **10.** 125%   **11.** 0.53%

LESSON 6-2

Write each decimal as a percent.

12. 0.06   **13.** 0.54   **14.** 1.69   **15.** 42.0   **16.** 0.898

Write each fraction as a percent.

17. $\frac{15}{34}$ **18.** $\frac{29}{86}$ **19.** $\frac{33}{44}$ **20.** $\frac{61}{91}$ **21.** $1\frac{2}{5}$

Decide whether using pencil and paper, mental math, or a calculator is most useful when solving the following problem. Then solve.

22. Tyler wants to donate 49% of his 50 stuffed animals to the children's hospital. About how many stuffed animals will he donate?

LESSON 6-3

Use a fraction to estimate the percent of each number.

23. 48% of 200   **24.** 27% of 76   **25.** 65% of 300   **26.** 15% of 15

27. Kel has $25 to spend on a pair of jeans. One pair is on sale for 30% off the regular price of $29.99. Does she have enough money to buy the jeans? Explain.

Use 1% or 10% to estimate the percent of each number.

28. 21% of 88   **29.** 19% of 109   **30.** 2% of 56   **31.** 48% of 200

32. Last year, Maria's retirement fund lost 19%. If the fund was worth $18,000 at the beginning of the year, how much money did she lose?

33. Every year, about 300 movies are made. Only 13% are considered to be hits. About how many movies are considered hits in a year?

Extra Practice ... Chapter 6

LESSON 6-4

Find the percent of each number. Check whether your answer is reasonable.

34. 35% of 80   **35.** 55% of 256   **36.** 75% of 60   **37.** 2% of 68

38. 17% of 51   **39.** 0.5% of 80   **40.** 1% of 8.5   **41.** 1.25% of 48

42. Ryan bought a new CD holder for his car. He can fit only 60 of his CDs in the holder. This represents 60% of his collection. How many CDs does Ryan have?

LESSON 6-5

Solve.

43. What percent of 150 is 60?

44. What percent of 140 is 28?

45. What percent of 120 is 24?

46. What percent of 88 is 102?

47. 24 is 60% of what number?

48. 9 is 15% of what number?

49. Thomas bought a desk with a retail sales price of $129 and paid $10.32 sales tax. What is the sales tax rate where Thomas bought the desk?

50. The sales tax on a $68 hotel room is $7.48. What is the sales tax rate?

LESSON 6-6

Find each percent of change. Round answers to the nearest tenth of a percent, if necessary.

51. 54 is increased to 68.   **52.** 90 is decreased to 82.   **53.** 60 is increased to 80.

54. 76 is decreased to 55.   **55.** 75 is increased to 120.   **56.** 50 is decreased to 33.

57. Abby's Appliances sells DVD players at 7% above the wholesale cost of $89. How much does the store charge for a DVD player?

58. A market's old parking lot held 48 cars. The new lot holds 37.5% more cars. How many parking spaces are on the new lot?

59. A regular bag of potato chips contains 12 ounces. A jumbo bag of chips contains $166\frac{2}{3}$% more chips. How many ounces does the jumbo bag contain?

LESSON 6-7

Find each missing value.

60. $I =$ ▮, $P = \$500$, $r = 5\%$, $t = 1$ year

61. $I = \$30$, $P =$ ▮, $r = 6\%$, $t = 2$ years

62. $I = \$168$, $P = \$800$, $r =$ ▮, $t = 3$ years

63. $I = \$48$, $P = \$300$, $r = 8\%$, $t =$ ▮

64. Shane deposits $600 in an account that earns 5.5% annual simple interest. How long will it be before the total amount is $699?

LESSON 7-1

The table shows the number of points a player scored during the last ten games of the season.

1. Make a cumulative frequency table of the data.

2. Make a stem-and-leaf plot of the data.

3. Make a line plot of the data.

Game Date	Points	Game Date	Points
Feb 7	36	Feb 25	18
Feb 14	34	Feb 27	31
Feb 18	27	Mar 1	43
Feb 20	46	Mar 3	42
Feb 23	32	Mar 4	28

LESSON 7-2

Find the mean, median, mode, and range of each data set.

4. 13, 8, 40, 19, 5, 8

5. 21, 19, 23, 26, 15, 25, 25

Identify the outlier in each data set. Then determine how the outlier affects the mean, median, and mode of the data. Then tell which measure of central tendency best describes the data with and without the outlier.

6. 23, 27, 31, 19, 56, 22, 25, 21

7. 66, 78, 57, 87, 66, 59, 239, 84

LESSON 7-3

8. The table shows the populations of four countries. Make a double-bar graph of the data.

9. The list below shows the scores on a history quiz. Make a histogram of the data.

87, 92, 75, 79, 64, 88, 96, 99, 69, 77, 78, 78, 88, 83, 93, 76

Country	1998 Population (millions)	2001 Population (millions)
Tunisia	9.3	9.7
Syria	15.3	16.7
Turkey	64.5	66.5
Algeria	30.1	31.7

LESSON 7-4

The circle graph shows the results of a survey of 100 people from Iran who were asked about their ethnic backgrounds. Use the graph for Exercises 10–12.

10. Which ethnic group is the second largest?

11. Approximately what percent of the people are Persian?

12. According to the survey, 3% of the people are Arab. How many of the people surveyed are Arab?

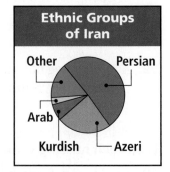

Ethnic Groups of Iran

Other, Persian, Arab, Kurdish, Azeri

Decide whether a bar graph or a circle graph would best display the information. Explain your answer.

13. the number of guitars sold compared with the number of drum sets sold for the year 2002

14. the average temperature for each day of one week

Extra Practice ... Chapter 7

LESSON 7-5

15. Use the data to make a box-and-whisker plot. 22, 41, 39, 27, 29, 30, 40, 61, 25, 28, 32

LESSON 7-6

The table shows the number of students Karen tutored during certain months. Use the table for Exercises 16 and 17.

Month	Students
Jan	5
Mar	8
May	9
Jul	12
Sep	14
Nov	18

16. Make a line graph of the data. Use the graph to determine during which months the number of students increased the most.

17. Use the graph to estimate the number of students Karen tutored during the month of October.

LESSON 7-7

Choose the type of graph that would best represent each type of data.

18. the number of participants in a hole-in-one contest for the last 10 years

19. the prices of the five top-selling MP3 players

LESSON 7-8

Determine whether each sample may be biased. Explain.

20. A bank asks the first 10 customers that enter in the morning if they are satisfied with the bank's late afternoon lobby hours.

21. Members of a polling organization survey 1,000 residents by randomly choosing names from a list of all residents.

LESSON 7-9

22. The table shows the average number of points per game that Michael Jordan scored during each season with the Chicago Bulls. Use the data to make a scatter plot. Describe the relationship between the data sets.

Year	Points	Year	Points
1990	33.6	1994	26.9
1991	31.5	1995	30.4
1992	30.1	1996	29.6
1993	32.6	1997	28.7

LESSON 7-10

Explain why each graph could be misleading.

23.

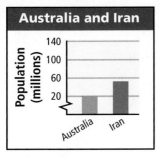

24.

LESSON 8-1

Identify the figures in the diagram.

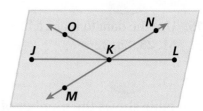

1. three points
2. a line
3. a plane

4. three rays
5. three line segments

6. Identify the line segments that are congruent in the figure.

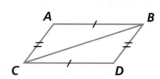

LESSON 8-2

Tell whether each angle is acute, right, obtuse, or straight.

7.
8.
9.
10.

Use the diagram to tell whether the angles are complementary, supplementary, or neither.

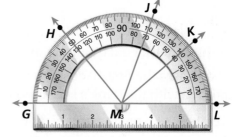

11. ∠*GMH* and ∠*HMJ*

12. ∠*HMJ* and ∠*JMK*

13. ∠*LMK* and ∠*GMK*

14. ∠*JMK* and ∠*KML*

15. Angles *Q* and *S* are complementary. If m∠*Q* is 77°, what is m∠*S*?

16. Angles *M* and *N* are supplementary. If m∠*M* is 17°, what is m∠*N*?

LESSON 8-3

Tell whether the lines in the figure appear parallel, perpendicular, or skew.

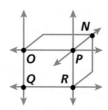

17. $\overleftrightarrow{PN}$ and $\overleftrightarrow{QR}$
18. $\overleftrightarrow{OQ}$ and $\overleftrightarrow{QR}$

19. $\overleftrightarrow{OP}$ and $\overleftrightarrow{QR}$
20. $\overleftrightarrow{PN}$ and $\overleftrightarrow{OQ}$

Line *j* ∥ line *k*. Find the measure of each angle.

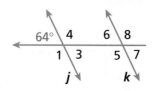

21. ∠1

22. ∠3

23. ∠8

Extra Practice ... Chapter 8

LESSON 8-4

Name the parts of circle *I*.

24. radii   25. diameters   26. chords

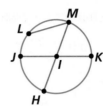

LESSON 8-5

Determine whether each figure is a polygon. If it is not, explain why not.

27.   28.   29.

Name each polygon.

30.   31. 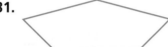   32.

LESSON 8-6

Classify each triangle according to its sides and angles.

33.    34.   35.   36.

LESSON 8-7

Give all of the names that apply to each quadrilateral. Then give the name that best describes it.

37.   38.   39.   40.

LESSON 8-8

Find the unknown angle measure in each triangle.

41.   42.   43.    44.

Divide each polygon into triangles to find the sum of its angle measures.

45.    46.    47.    48.

LESSON 8-9

Determine whether the triangles are congruent.

49.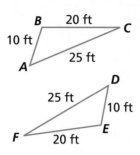

50.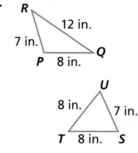

51.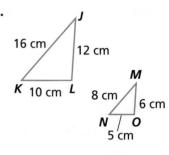

Determine the unknown measure(s) in each set of congruent polygons.

52.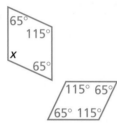

53.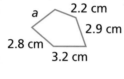

54.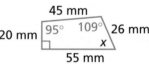

LESSON 8-10

Graph each transformation. Write the coordinates of the vertices of each image.

55. Rotate △PQR 90° counter-clockwise about vertex R.

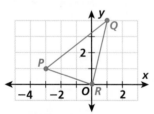

56. Reflect the figure across the y-axis.

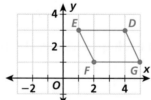

57. Translate △RST 3 units right and 3 units down.

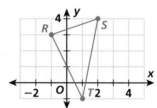

LESSON 8-11

Decide whether each figure has line symmetry. If it does, draw all the lines of symmetry.

58.

59.

60.

Tell how many times each figure will show rotational symmetry within one full rotation.

61.

62.

63.

Extra Practice ... Chapter 9

LESSON 9-1

Choose the more precise measurement in each pair.

1. 2 ft, 23 in.

2. 8.1 m, 811 cm

3. $6\frac{5}{16}$ m, $6\frac{3}{8}$ m

LESSON 9-2

Find each perimeter.

4.

4.5 cm
4 cm
3 cm
7 cm

5.

11.2 km
11.2 km
11.2 km

6.
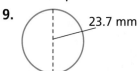
$18\frac{1}{2}$ m
$5\frac{1}{2}$ m

Find the circumference of each circle to the nearest tenth. Use 3.14 or $\frac{22}{7}$ for π.

7.

7 yd

8.
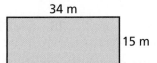
16.5 in.

9.
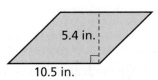
23.7 mm

LESSON 9-3

Find the area of each rectangle or parallelogram.

10.
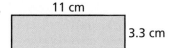
11 cm
3.3 cm

11.
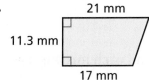
34 m
15 m

12.
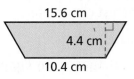
5.4 in.
10.5 in.

13. Harry is using 16 Japanese tatami mats to cover a floor. Each mat measures 3 feet by 2 feet. What is the total area that will be covered by the mats?

LESSON 9-4

Find the area of each triangle or trapezoid.

14.

13 in.
10 in.

15.

21 mm
11.3 mm
17 mm

16.
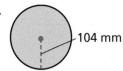
15.6 cm
4.4 cm
10.4 cm

LESSON 9-5

Find the area of each circle to the nearest tenth. Use 3.14 for π.

17. 17 in.

18. 29.8 m

19. 104 mm

20. A circular fountain has a diameter of 42 ft. What is the area of the wading pool? Use $\frac{22}{7}$ for π.

LESSON 9-6

Estimate the area of each figure. Each square represents 1 ft².

21.

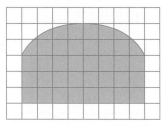

22.

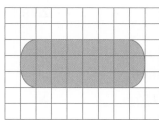

Find the area of each figure. Use 3.14 for π.

23.

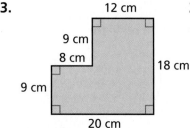

24.

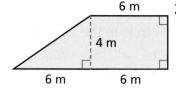

25.

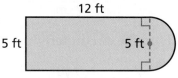

LESSON 9-7

Find each square or square root.

26. 13^2 **27.** $\sqrt{196}$ **28.** $\sqrt{625}$ **29.** 60^2

Estimate each square root to the nearest whole number. Use a calculator to check your answer.

30. $\sqrt{10}$ **31.** $\sqrt{18}$ **32.** $\sqrt{53}$ **33.** $\sqrt{95}$

34. $\sqrt{152}$ **35.** $\sqrt{221}$ **36.** $\sqrt{109}$ **37.** $\sqrt{175}$

38. A square painting has an area of 2,728 square centimeters. About how long is each side of the painting? Round your answer to the nearest centimeter.

LESSON 9-8

Use the Pythagorean Theorem to find each missing measure.

39.

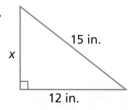

40.

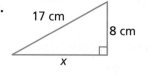

41.

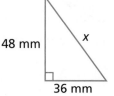

42. Ricky rides his bike 25 miles south and then turns east and rides another 25 miles before he stops to rest. How far is Ricky from his starting point? Round your answer to the nearest tenth.

Extra Practice ... Chapter 10

LESSON 10-1

Identify the bases and faces of each figure. Then name the figure.

1.

2.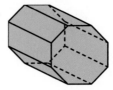

3.

LESSON 10-2

4. The back of a moving van is shaped like a rectangular prism. It is 24 ft long, 7 ft wide, and 8 ft high. Find the volume of the moving van.

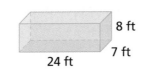

5. A drum is shaped like a cylinder. It is 12.5 in. wide and 8 in. tall. Find its volume. Use 3.14 for π.

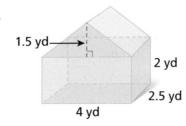

Find the volume of the composite figure to the nearest tenth. Use 3.14 for π.

6.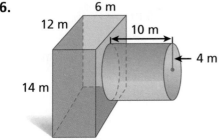

7.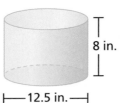

LESSON 10-3

Find the volume of each pyramid to the nearest tenth. Estimate to check whether the answer is reasonable.

8.

9.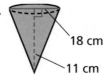

10.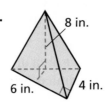

Find the volume of each cone to the nearest tenth. Use 3.14 for π. Estimate to check whether the answer is reasonable.

11.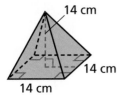

12.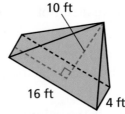

13.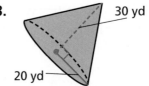

LESSON 10-4

Find the surface area of each prism.

14.

5 in.
21 in.
11 in.

15.
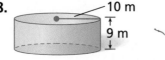
5 cm
3 cm
10 cm
4 cm

16.
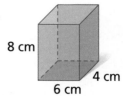
8 cm
4 cm
6 cm

Find the surface area of each cylinder to the nearest tenth.
Use 3.14 for π.

17.

2 yd
4.5 yd

18.
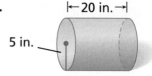
10 m
9 m

19.
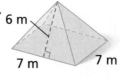
|←20 in.→|
5 in.

LESSON 10-5

Find the surface area of each pyramid or cone. Use 3.14 for π.

20.
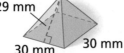
29 mm
30 mm
30 mm

21.
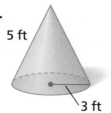
5 ft
3 ft

22.
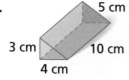
6 m
7 m
7 m

LESSON 10-6

23. The surface area of a cylinder is 49 m². What is the surface area of a similar cylinder that is larger by a scale factor of 6?

24. The surface area of a garden is 36 ft². What is the surface area of a similar garden that is smaller by a scale factor of $\frac{1}{4}$?

25. The surface area of a hexagonal prism is 65 cm². What is the surface area of a similar prism that is larger by a scale factor of 8?

26. The volume of a cube is 50 cm³. What is the volume of a similar cube that is larger by a scale factor of 7?

27. An oil drum has volume of 513 cm³. What is the volume of a similar oil drum that is smaller by a scale factor of $\frac{1}{3}$?

Extra Practice ... Chapter 11

LESSON 11-1

Determine whether each event is impossible, unlikely, as likely as not, likely, or certain.

1. flipping a coin and getting heads twelve times in a row

2. drawing a green bead from a bag of white and red beads

3. The probability of rolling a 2 on a number cube is $\frac{1}{6}$. What is the probability of not rolling a 2?

LESSON 11-2

4. Bess bowls a strike on 6 out of 15 tries. What is the experimental probability that she will bowl a strike on her next try? Write your answer as a fraction, as a decimal, and as a percent.

5. For the past 10 days, a city planner has counted the number of northbound cars that pass through a particular intersection. During that time, 200 or more cars were counted 9 out of 10 days.

   a. What is the experimental probability that there will be 200 or more northbound cars passing through the intersection on the eleventh day?

   b. What is the experimental probability that there will not be 200 or more northbound cars passing through the intersection on the eleventh day?

LESSON 11-3

6. Ronald flips a coin and rolls a number cube at the same time. What are all the possible outcomes? How many outcomes are in the sample space?

7. For lunch, Amy can choose from a salad, a taco, a hamburger, or a fish fillet. She can drink lemonade, milk, juice, or water. What are all the possible outcomes? How many outcomes are in the sample space?

8. A café makes 23 flavors of ice cream. You can get each flavor in a waffle cone, a sugar cone, a cake cone, or a cup. How many outcomes are possible?

LESSON 11-4

Find the probability of each event. Write your answer as a fraction, as a decimal, and as a percent.

9. rolling a number less than 5 on a fair number cube

10. randomly drawing a pink sock out of a drawer of 6 pink, 4 black, 8 white, and 2 blue socks all of the same size

LESSON 11-5

11. The experimental probability that it will rain on any given day in Sacramento, California, is about 15%. Out of 365 days (a year), about how many days can residents of Sacramento predict rain?

12. If you roll a number cube 22 times, about how many times do you expect to roll a number less than 4?

13. A family is planning a 7-day vacation during July at a city where there is a water park and an amusement park. The city experiences an average of 8 rainy days in July. When it rains, both parks are closed. If the family would like to spend at least 2 days at each park, should they go?

LESSON 11-6

Decide whether each set of events is independent or dependent. Explain your answer.

14. Mr. Fernandez's class contains 14 boys and 16 girls. Mr. Fernandez randomly picks a boy and a girl to represent the class at the school spelling bee.

15. There are 52 playing cards in a standard card deck. Alex draws a card and holds onto it while Suzi draws a card.

Find the probability of each set of independent events.

16. flipping 2 coins at the same time and getting heads on both coins

17. drawing a 3 from 5 cards numbered 1 through 5 and rolling an even number on a number cube

LESSON 11-7

18. Venus has decided to have a 2-color paint job done on her car. There are 6 paint colors from which to choose. How many combinations of 2 colors are possible?

19. Philip has 5 different coins. How many combinations of 3 coins can he make from the 5 coins?

20. A juice bar offers 8 different juices. You and a friend want to each try a different blend. How many different combinations of 2 juices are possible?

LESSON 11-8

21. In how many different ways can Ralph, Randy, and Robert stand in line at the movie theater?

22. Roseanne and Rita join Ralph, Randy, and Robert at the movie theater. In how many different ways could they all stand in line?

23. In how many different ways can 5 students be matched up with 5 mentors?

Extra Practice ... Chapter 12

LESSON 12-1

Solve. Check each answer.

1. $4c - 13 = 15$

2. $3h + 14 = 23$

3. $-5j - 13 = 22$

4. $\frac{e}{7} + 2 = 5$

5. $\frac{m}{6} - 3 = 1$

6. $\frac{x}{3} + 5 = -13$

7. If you multiply the number of DVDs Sarah has by 6 and then add 5, you get 41. How many DVDs does Sarah have?

LESSON 12-2

Solve.

8. $2w - 11 + 4w = 7$

9. $7v + 5 - v = 11$

10. $-7z + 4 - z = -12$

11. $\frac{5x - 7}{3} = 15$

12. $2t - 7 - 5t = 11$

13. $3(t + 2) + 1 = 8$

14. $12a - 3 - 8a = -1$

15. $\frac{2.9h - 5.1}{2} = 4.7$

16. $4(8 - s) + 6 = -2$

17. $\frac{10 - 4t}{8} = -12$

18. Erika has received scores of 82, 87, 93, 95, 88, and 90 on math quizzes. What score must Erika get on her next quiz to have an average of 90?

LESSON 12-3

Group the terms with variables on one side of the equal sign, and simplify.

19. $6a = 4a - 8$

20. $3d - 5 = 7d - 9$

21. $-2j + 6 = j - 3$

22. $7 + 5m = 2 - m$

Solve.

23. $7y - 9 = -2y$

24. $2c - 13 = 5c + 11$

25. $\frac{2}{5}g + 9 = -6 - \frac{6}{10}g$

26. $7d + 4 = 8 - d$

27. $-3p + 8 = -7p - 12$

28. $1.2k + 2.3 = -0.5k + 7.4$

29. Roberta and Stanley are collecting signatures for a petition. So far, Roberta has twice as many signatures as Stanley. If she collects 30 more signatures, she will have 4 times as many signatures as Stanley currently has. How many signatures has Stanley collected?

30. Gym members pay $3 per workout with a one time membership fee of $98. Nonmembers pay $10 per workout. How many workouts would both a member and a nonmember have to do to pay the same amount?

Extra Practice ... Chapter 12

LESSON 12-4

Write an inequality for each situation.

31. The cafeteria could hold no more than 50 people.

32. There were fewer than 20 boats in the marina.

Graph each inequality.

33. $y < -2$ **34.** $f \geq 3$ **35.** $n \leq -1.5$ **36.** $x > 4$

Graph each compound inequality.

37. $1 < s < 4$ **38.** $-1 \leq v < 2$ **39.** $w < 0$ or $w \geq 5$ **40.** $-3.5 \leq y < -2$

LESSON 12-5

Solve. Then graph each solution set on a number line.

41. $c - 6 > -5$ **42.** $v - 3 \geq 1$ **43.** $w - 6 \leq -7$ **44.** $a - 2 \leq 5$

Solve. Check each answer.

45. $q + 3 \leq 5$ **46.** $m + 1 > 0$ **47.** $p + 7 \leq 4$ **48.** $z + 2 \geq -3$

49. By Saturday night, 3 inches of rain had fallen in Happy Valley. The weekend forecast predicted at least 8 inches of rain. How much more rain must fall on Sunday for this forecast to be correct?

LESSON 12-6

Solve. Check each answer.

50. $\frac{a}{5} \leq 4.5$ **51.** $-\frac{v}{2} > 2$ **52.** $\frac{x}{3.9} \geq -2$ **53.** $-\frac{c}{4} < 2.3$

54. $13y < 39$ **55.** $2t \leq 5$ **56.** $-7r > 56$ **57.** $3s \geq -4.5$

58. The local candy store buys candy in bulk and then sells it by the pound. If the store owner spends $135 on peppermints and then sells them for $3.50 per pound, how many pounds must he sell to make a profit?

LESSON 12-7

Solve. Then graph each solution set on a number line.

59. $\frac{m}{3} - 1 \leq 2$ **60.** $7.2x - 4.8 > 24$ **61.** $-5.5h + 2 < 13$

62. $-1 - \frac{s}{3.5} \geq 1$ **63.** $-\frac{w}{1.5} - 8 \leq -10$ **64.** $4j - 6 > 16$

65. $5 - 2u < 15$ **66.** $\frac{r}{7} - 1 \geq 0$ **67.** $5 - \frac{m}{9} \leq 17$

68. Jill, Serena, and Erin are trying to earn enough money to rent a beach house for a week. They estimate that it will cost at least $1,650. If Jill has already earned $600, how much must each of the others earn?

Draw a Diagram

When problems involve objects, distances, or places, you can **draw a diagram** to make the problem easier to understand. You can use the diagram to look for relationships among the given data and to solve the problem.

Problem Solving Strategies

Draw a Diagram	Make a Table
Make a Model	Solve a Simpler Problem
Guess and Test	Use Logical Reasoning
Work Backward	Use a Venn Diagram
Find a Pattern	Make an Organized List

A bald eagle has built a nest 18 feet below the top of a 105-foot-tall oak tree. The eagle sits on a limb 72 feet above the ground. What is the vertical distance between the eagle and its nest?

Understand the Problem

Identify the important information.

- The height of the tree is 105 feet.
- The eagle's nest is 18 feet from the top of the tree.
- The eagle is perched 72 feet above the ground.

The answer will be the vertical distance between the eagle and its nest.

Make a Plan

Use the information in the problem to **draw a diagram** showing the height of the tree and the locations of the eagle and its nest.

Solve

To find the height of the nest's location, subtract the distance of the nest from the top of the tree from the height of the tree.

105 feet − 18 feet = 87 feet

To find the vertical distance from the eagle to its nest, subtract the height of the eagle's location from the height of the nest's location.

87 feet − 72 feet = 15 feet

The vertical distance between the eagle and its nest is 15 feet.

Look Back

Be sure that you have drawn your diagram correctly. Does it match the information given in the problem?

PRACTICE

1. A truck driver travels 17 miles south to drop off his first delivery. Then he drives 19 miles west to drop off a second delivery, and then he drives 17 miles north to drop off another delivery. Finally, he drives 5 miles east for his last delivery. How far is he from his starting point?

2. A table that is standing lengthwise against a wall is 10 feet long and 4 feet wide. Sarah puts balloons 1 foot apart along the three exposed sides, with one balloon at each corner. How many balloons does she use?

Make a Model

When problems involve objects, you can **make a model** using those objects or similar objects. This can help you understand the problem and find the solution.

Problem Solving Strategies

Draw a Diagram	Make a Table
Make a Model	Solve a Simpler Problem
Guess and Test	Use Logical Reasoning
Work Backward	Use a Venn Diagram
Find a Pattern	Make an Organized List

A company packages 6 minipuzzles in a decorated 4 in. cube. They are shipped to the toy store in cartons shaped like rectangular prisms. Twenty cubes fit in each carton. If the height of each carton is 8 in., what are the possible dimensions of the carton?

 **Understand the Problem**

Identify the important information.

- Each cube is 4 inches on a side.
- Twenty cubes fit in one carton.
- The height of the carton is 8 inches.

The answer is the dimensions of the carton.

 Make a Plan

You can use 20 cubes to **make a model** of cubes packed in a carton. Record possible values for length and width, given a height of 8 in.

 **Solve**

Begin with a carton that is 8 in., or 2 cubes, high. Use all 20 cubes to make a rectangular prism.

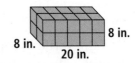

8 in.   8 in.
        20 in.

The possible dimensions of the carton are 20 in. × 8 in. × 8 in.

 **Look Back**

The volume of each carton should equal the volume of the 20 cubes.

Volume of cartons: 8 in. × 20 in. × 8 in. = 1,280 in^3

Volume of 1 cube: 4 in. × 4 in. × 4 in. = 64 in^3

Volume of 20 cubes: 20 × 64 = 1,280 in^3

1,280 in^3 = 1,280 in^3 ✔

PRACTICE

1. Give two sets of possible dimensions of a rectangular prism made up of twenty 1-inch cubes.

2. John uses exactly eight 1-inch cubes to form a rectangular prism. Find the length, width, and height of the prism.

Problem Solving Handbook

Guess and Test

If you do not know how to solve a problem, you can always make a **guess**. Then **test** your guess using the information in the problem. Use what you find out to make a second guess. Continue to **guess and test** until you find the correct answer.

Problem Solving Strategies

Draw a Diagram	Make a Table
Make a Model	Solve a Simpler Problem
Guess and Test	Use Logical Reasoning
Work Backward	Use a Venn Diagram
Find a Pattern	Make an Organized List

Shannon used equal numbers of quarters and nickels to buy an embossing template that cost $1.50. How many of each coin did she use?

 **Understand the Problem**

Identify the important information.

- Shannon used equal numbers of quarters and nickels.
- The coins she used total $1.50.

The answer will be the number of quarters and the number of nickels Shannon used.

 **Make a Plan**

Start with an educated **guess** in which the numbers of quarters and nickels are the same. Then **test** to see whether the coins total $1.50.

 Solve

Make a first guess of 4 quarters and 4 nickels, and find the total value of the coins.

Guess: 4 quarters and 4 nickels
Test: $(4 \times \$0.25) + (4 \times \$0.05) = \$1.00 + \$0.20 = \$1.20$

$1.20 is too low. Increase the number of coins.

Guess: 6 quarters and 6 nickels
Test: $(6 \times \$0.25) + (6 \times \$0.05) = \$1.50 + \$0.30 = \$1.80$

$1.80 is too high. The number of each coin must be between 4 and 6. So Shannon must have used 5 quarters and 5 nickels.

 **Look Back**

Test the answer to see whether the coins add up to $1.50.
$(5 \times \$0.25) + (5 \times \$0.05) = \$1.25 + \$0.25 = \$1.50$ ✔

PRACTICE

1. The sum of Richard's age and his older brother's age is 63. The difference between their ages is 13. How old are Richard and his brother?

2. In the final game of the basketball season, Trinka scored a total of 25 points on 2-point shots and 3-point shots. She made 5 more 2-point shots than 3-point shots. How many of each did she make?

Problem Solving Handbook

Problem Solving Handbook

Work Backward

Some problems give you a sequence of information and ask you to find something that happened at the beginning. To solve a problem like this, you may want to start at the end of the problem and **work backward**.

Problem Solving Strategies

Draw a Diagram	Make a Table
Make a Model	Solve a Simpler Problem
Guess and Test	Use Logical Reasoning
Work Backward	Use a Venn Diagram
Find a Pattern	Make an Organized List

Tony is selling dried fruit snacks to help raise money for a new school computer. Half of the fruit snacks in the bag are apricots. Of the rest of the fruit snacks, half of them are bananas, and the other 8 are cranberries. How many fruit snacks are in the bag?

 **Understand the Problem**

Identify the important information.

- Half of the fruit snacks are apricots.
- Half of the remaining fruit snacks are bananas.
- The final 8 fruit snacks are cranberries.

The answer will be the total number of fruit snacks in the bag.

 **Make a Plan**

Start with the 8 cranberries, and **work backward** through the information in the problem to find the total number of fruit snacks in the bag.

 Solve

There are 8 cranberries.   8

The other half of the remaining fruit snacks are bananas, so there must be 8 bananas. $8 + 8 = 16$

The other half of the fruit snacks are apricots, so there must be 16 apricots. $16 + 16 = 32$

There are 32 fruit snacks in the bag.

 Look Back

Using the starting amount of 32 fruit snacks, work from the beginning of the problem following the steps.

Start: 32
Half of 32: $32 \div 2 = 16$
Half of 16: $16 \div 2 = 8$
Minus 8: $8 - 8 = 0$ ✔

PRACTICE

1. In a trivia competition, each finalist must answer 4 questions correctly. Each question is worth twice as much as the question before it. The fourth question is worth $1,000. How much is the first question worth?

2. The Ramirez family has 5 children. Sara is 5 years younger than her brother Kenny. Felix is half as old as his sister Sara. Kaitlen, who is 10, is 3 years older than Felix. Kenny and Celia are twins. How old is Celia?

Find a Pattern

In some problems, there is a relationship between different pieces of information. Examine this relationship and try to **find a pattern.** You can then use this pattern to find more information and the solution to the problem.

Problem Solving Strategies

Draw a Diagram	Make a Table
Make a Model	Solve a Simpler Problem
Guess and Test	Use Logical Reasoning
Work Backward	Use a Venn Diagram
Find a Pattern	Make an Organized List

John made a design using hexagons and triangles. The side lengths of each hexagon and triangle are 1 inch. What is the perimeter of the next figure in his design?

 **Understand the Problem**

Identify the important information.

- The first 5 figures in the design are given.
- The side lengths of each hexagon and triangle are 1 inch.

The answer will be the perimeter of the sixth figure in the design.

Make a Plan

Try to **find a pattern** in the perimeters of the first 5 figures. Use the pattern to find the perimeter of the sixth figure.

Solve

Find the perimeter of the first 5 figures.

Figure	Perimeter (in.)	Pattern
1	6	
2	7	6 + 1 = 7
3	11	7 + 4 = 11
4	12	11 + 1 = 12
5	16	12 + 4 = 16

The pattern appears to be add 1, add 4, add 1, add 4, and so on. So the perimeter of the sixth figure will be 16 + 1, or 17.

 **Look Back**

Use another strategy. **Draw a diagram** of the sixth figure. Then find the perimeter.

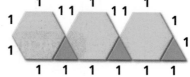

PRACTICE

Describe the pattern, and then find the next number.

1. 1, 5, 9, 13, 17, . . .

2. 1, 4, 16, 64, 256, . . .

Make a Table

When you are given a lot of information in a problem, it may be helpful to organize that information. One way to organize information is to **make a table**.

Problem Solving Strategies

Draw a Diagram	**Make a Table**
Make a Model	Solve a Simpler Problem
Guess and Test	Use Logical Reasoning
Work Backward	Use a Venn Diagram
Find a Pattern	Make an Organized List

On November 1, Wendy watered the Gribbles' yard and the Milams' yard. If she waters the Gribbles' yard every 4 days and the Milams' yard every 5 days, when is the next date that Wendy will water both yards?

Understand the Problem

Identify the important information.

- Wendy waters the Gribbles' yard every 4 days and the Milams' yard every 5 days. She watered both yards on November 1.

The answer will be the next date that she waters both yards again.

Make a Plan

Make a table using *X*'s to show the days that Wendy waters each yard. Make one row for the Gribbles and one row for the Milams.

Solve

Start with an *X* in both rows for November 1. For the Gribbles, add an *X* on every fourth day after November 1. For the Milams, add an *X* every fifth day after November 1.

Date	1	2	3	4	5	6	7	8	9	10	11	12	13	14	15	16	17	18	19	20	21
Gribble	X				X				X				X				X				X
Milam	X					X					X					X					X

November 21 is the next date that Wendy will water both yards.

Look Back

The sum of 1 and five 4's should equal the sum of 1 and four 5's.
$$1 + 4 + 4 + 4 + 4 + 4 = 21 \qquad 1 + 5 + 5 + 5 + 5 = 21 \checkmark$$

PRACTICE

1. Jess, Kathy, and Linda work on the math club's newspaper. One is the editor, one is the reporter, and one is the writer. Linda does not participate in sports. Jess and the editor play tennis together. Linda and the reporter are cousins. Find each person's job.

2. A toll booth accepts any combination of coins that total exactly $0.75, but it does not accept pennies or half dollars. In how many different ways can a driver pay the toll?

Problem Solving Handbook

Solve a Simpler Problem

Sometimes a problem may contain large numbers or require many steps to solve. It may appear complicated to solve. Try to **solve a simpler problem** that is similar to the original problem.

Problem Solving Strategies

Draw a Diagram
Make a Model
Guess and Test
Work Backward
Find a Pattern

Make a Table
Solve a Simpler Problem
Use Logical Reasoning
Use a Venn Diagram
Make an Organized List

Lawrence is making touch pools for a project about sea creatures. The pools are squares that will be arranged side by side. The side of each pool is a 1-meter-long piece of wood. How many meters of wood does Lawrence need to complete 20 square sections of touch pools?

 **Understand the Problem**

Identify the important information.

- Each square side is a 1-meter-long piece of wood.

- There are 20 square sections set side by side.

The answer will be the total meters of wood needed.

 Make a Plan

You could sketch all 20 pools and then count the number of meters of wood. However, it would be easier to first **solve a simpler problem**. Start with 1 square pool, and then move on to 2 and then 3. Then look for a way to solve the problem for 20 pools.

 **Solve**

The first pool requires 4 sides to complete. After that, only 3 sides are needed for each pool.

1 square: ▢
2 squares: ▢▢
3 squares: ▢▢▢

Notice that 1 pool requires 4 meters of wood, and the 19 other pools require 3 meters of wood each. So $4 + (19 \times 3) = 61$. The pools require 61 meters of wood.

Number of Squares	Number of Meters
1	$4(1) = 4$
2	$4 + (1 \times 3) = 7$
3	$4 + (2 \times 3) = 10$
4	$4 + (3 \times 3) = 13$

Look Back

If the pattern is correct, Lawrence would need 16 meters of wood for 5 pools. Complete the next row of the table to check this answer.

PRACTICE

1. The numbers 11; 444; and 8,888 all contain repeated single digits. How many numbers between 10 and 1,000,000 contain repeated single digits?

2. How many diagonals are there in a dodecagon (a 12-sided polygon)?

Problem Solving Handbook

Use Logical Reasoning

 Problem Solving Strategies

Draw a Diagram Make a Table
Make a Model Solve a Simpler Problem
Guess and Test **Use Logical Reasoning**
Work Backward Use a Venn Diagram
Find a Pattern Make an Organized List

Sometimes a problem may provide clues and facts that you must use to find a solution. You can use **logical reasoning** to solve this kind of problem.

Jennie, Rachel, and Mia play the oboe, the violin, and the drums. Mia does not like the drums, and she is the sister of the oboe player. Rachel has soccer practice with the person who plays the drums. Which instrument does each person play?

 **Understand the Problem**

Identify the important information.

- There are three people, and each person plays a different instrument.

 **Make a Plan**

Start with clues given in the problem, and **use logical reasoning** to determine which instrument each person plays.

 Solve

Make a table. Make a column for each instrument and a row for each person. Work with the clues one at a time. Write "Yes" in a box if the clue reveals that a person plays an instrument. Write "No" in a box if the clue reveals that a person does not play an instrument.

a. Mia does not like the drums, so she does not play the drums.

b. Mia is the sister of the person who plays the oboe, so she does not play the oboe.

	Oboe	Violin	Drums
Jennie			
Rachel			No
Mia	No		No

c. Rachel has soccer practice with the person who plays the drums, so she does not play the drums.

Jennie must play the drums, and Mia must play the violin. So Rachel must play the oboe.

Look Back

Compare your answer to the clues in the problem. Make sure none of your conclusions conflict with the clues.

PRACTICE

1. Kent, Jason, and Newman have a dog, a fish, and a hamster, though not in that order. Kent's pet does not have fur. The owner of the hamster has class with Jason. Match the owners with their pets.

2. Seth, Vess, and Benica are in the sixth, seventh, and eighth grades, though not in that order. Seth is not in seventh grade. The sixth-grader has band with Benica and the same lunchtime as Seth. Match the students with their grades.

Problem Solving Handbook

Use a Venn Diagram

You can use a **Venn diagram** to display relationships among sets in a problem. Use ovals, circles, or other shapes to represent individual sets.

 Problem Solving Strategies

Draw a Diagram	Make a Table
Make a Model	Solve a Simpler Problem
Guess and Test	Use Logical Reasoning
Work Backward	**Use a Venn Diagram**
Find a Pattern	Make an Organized List

At Landry Middle School, 127 students take French, 145 take Spanish, and 31 take both. How many students take only French? How many students take only Spanish?

Understand the Problem

Identify the important information.

- There are 127 students who take French, 145 who take Spanish, and 31 who take both.

Make a Plan

Use a Venn diagram to show the sets of students who take French and Spanish.

Solve

Draw and label two overlapping circles. Write "31" in the area where the circles overlap. This represents the number of students who take French and Spanish.

To find the number of students who take only French, subtract the number of students who take both French and Spanish from those who take French. To find the number of students who take only Spanish, subtract the number of students who take both French and Spanish from those who take Spanish.

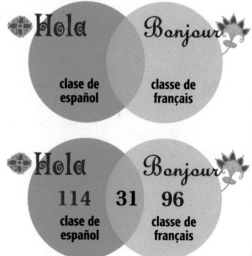

So 96 students take only French, and 114 students take only Spanish.

Look Back

Check your Venn diagram carefully against the information in the problem. Make sure your diagram agrees with the facts given.

PRACTICE

Responding to a survey, there were 60 people who said they like pasta, 45 who like chicken, and 70 who like hot dogs. There were 15 people who said they like both pasta and chicken, 22 who like both hot dogs and chicken, and 17 who like both hot dogs and pasta. Only 8 people said they like all 3.

1. How many people like only pasta?

2. How many people like only hot dogs?

Problem Solving Handbook

Make an Organized List

Problem Solving Strategies

Draw a Diagram   Make a Table
Make a Model   Solve a Simpler Problem
Guess and Test   Use Logical Reasoning
Work Backward   Use a Venn Diagram
Find a Pattern   **Make an Organized List**

In some problems, you will need to find out exactly how many different ways an event can happen. When solving this kind of problem, it is often helpful to **make an organized list**. This will help you count all the possible outcomes.

A spinner has 4 different colors: red, blue, yellow, and white. If you spin the spinner 2 times, how many different color combinations could you get?

Understand the Problem

Identify the important information.

- You spin the spinner 2 times.
- The spinner is divided into 4 different colors.

The answer will be the total number of different color combinations the spinner can land on.

Make a Plan

Make an organized list to determine all the possible different color outcomes. List all the different combinations for each color.

Solve

First consider the color red. List all the different outcomes for the color red. Then consider blue, adding all the different outcomes, then yellow, and finally white.

Red	Blue	Yellow	White
RR	BB	YY	WW
RB	BY	YW	
RY	BW		
RW			

So there are 10 possible different color combinations.

Look Back

Make sure that all the possible combinations of color are listed and that each set of colors is different.

PRACTICE

1. The Pizza Planet has 5 different choices of pizza toppings: ham, pineapple, pepperoni, olive, and mushroom. You want to order a pizza with 2 different toppings. How many different combinations of toppings can you order?

2. How many ways can you make change for a fifty-cent piece by using a combination of dimes, nickels, and pennies?

Skills Bank . . .

Read and Write Decimals

When reading and writing a decimal, you need to know the place value of the digit in the last decimal place. Also, remember the following:

- "and" goes in place of the decimal point for numbers greater than one.
- a hyphen is used in two-digit numbers, such as twenty-five.
- a hyphen is used in two-word place values, such as ten-thousandths.

EXAMPLE

Write 728.34 in words.

The 4 is in the hundredths place, so 728.34 is written as
"seven hundred twenty-eight and thirty-four hundredths."

PRACTICE

Write each decimal in words.

1. 17.238   **2.** 9.0023   **3.** 534.01972   **4.** 33.00084   **5.** 4,356.67

Rules for Rounding

To round a number to a certain place value, locate the digit with that place value, and look at the digit to the right of it.

- If the digit to the right is 5 or greater, increase the number in the rounding place by 1.
- If the digit to the right is 4 or less, leave the number in the rounding place as is.

EXAMPLE

A **Round 765.48201 to the nearest hundredth.**

765.48201   *Locate the hundredths place.*
      ↑
      The digit to the right is less than 5, so the digit in the rounding place stays the same.

765.48

B **Round 765.48201 to the nearest tenth.**

765.48201   *Locate the tenths place.*
     ↑
     The digit to the right is greater than 5, so the digit in the rounding place increases by 1.

765.5

PRACTICE

Round 203.94587 to the place indicated.

1. hundreds   **2.** hundredths   **3.** thousandths   **4.** tens   **5.** ones

Properties

Addition and multiplication follow certain rules. The tables show basic properties of addition and multiplication.

ADDITION PROPERTIES

Commutative:	$a + b = b + a$
Associative:	$(a + b) + c = a + (b + c)$
Identity Property of Zero:	$a + 0 = a$
Inverse Property:	$a + (-a) = 0$
Closure Property:	The sum of two real numbers is a real number.

MULTIPLICATION PROPERTIES

Commutative:	$a \times b = b \times a$
Associative:	$(a \times b) \times c = a \times (b \times c)$
Identity Property of One:	$a \times 1 = a$
Inverse Property:	$a \times \frac{1}{a} = 1$ if $a \neq 0$
Property of Zero:	$a \times 0 = 0$
Closure Property:	The product of two real numbers is a real number.
Distributive:	$a(b + c) = a \times b + a \times c$

The following properties are true when a, b, and c are real numbers.

Substitution Property: If $a = b$, then a can be substituted for b in any expression.

Transitive Property: If $a = b$ and $b = c$, then $a = c$.

PRACTICE

Name the property represented by each equation.

1. $8 + 0 = 8$

2. $(9 \times 3) \times 7 = 9 \times (3 \times 7)$

3. 3×5 is a real number.

4. $n \times m = m \times n$

5. $2(3 + 5) = 2 \times 3 + 2 \times 5$

6. $15 \times \frac{1}{15} = 1$

7. $3.6 + 4.4 = 4.4 + 3.6$

8. $\frac{3}{4} \times \frac{4}{4} = \frac{3}{4}$

9. $d + (-d) = 0$

10. $(5 + 17) + 23 = 5 + (17 + 23)$

11. $f \times 1 = f$

12. $p \times 0 = 0$

Skills Bank

Overestimates and Underestimates

An **overestimate** is an estimate that is greater than the actual value. An **underestimate** is an estimate that is less than the actual value.

EXAMPLE

A **Pauline has \$30 to spend on school supplies. She wants to buy a set of pens for \$12.58, paper for \$8.49, and scissors for \$6.38. Does Pauline have enough money to buy her supplies? Explain whether an overestimate or underestimate is appropriate. Then find the estimate and determine whether it is sufficient to answer the question.**

Pauline should use an overestimate for her total cost, so her actual cost is less. If she has enough for the overestimate, then she has enough for the actual cost.

$12.58 + $8.49 + $6.38

$13 + $9 + $7 = $29   *To overestimate, round each number up.*

Since the estimate is less than \$30, she can buy her supplies. If the overestimate was greater than \$30, then the estimate would not be sufficient to answer the question.

B **Lee's friend lives 245 miles away. Can Lee get to his friend's house in 5.5 hours if he drives at an average speed of 52 miles per hour? Explain whether an overestimate or underestimate is appropriate. Then find the estimate and determine whether it is sufficient to answer the question.**

Lee should use an underestimate for the distance he travels in 5.5 hours. If the underestimate of the distance is greater than 245 miles, then his actual time is less than 5.5 hours.

$52 \cdot 5.5$ *To underestimate, round each number down.*

$50 \cdot 5 = 250$

Since the estimate is greater than 245, Lee can get to his friend's house in 5.5 hours. If the underestimate was less than 245, then the estimate would not be sufficient to answer the question.

PRACTICE

Explain whether an overestimate or underestimate is appropriate for each situation. Then find the estimate and determine whether it is sufficient.

1. Raul has \$55 to buy art supplies. He wants to buy a watercolor set for \$28.45, a brush for \$12.95, and a sketch pad for \$15.75. Does Raul have enough money to buy the items?

2. Fiona's car has 8.5 gallons of gas in its tank. Her car can travel about 21 miles per gallon. Does she have enough gas to drive 158 miles?

Skills Bank

Compatible Numbers

Compatible numbers are close to the actual numbers used in a computation. Using compatible numbers allows you to use mental math to estimate easily.

EXAMPLE 1

Use compatible numbers to estimte each answer.

A 236 + 132

240 + 130   *Round to the nearest ten.*

370   *Add.*

B 16 ÷ 3.3

15 ÷ 3   *Choose numbers close to 16 and 3.3 that are easy to divide.*

5   *Divide.*

C 613 × 28

600 × 30   *Choose numbers close to 613 and 28 that are easy to multiply.*

18,000   *Multiply.*

You can also use *compensation* to make addition easier. **Compensation** is when you adjust one number up or down to make it easier to add, and then adjust the other number in the opposite way to keep the sum the same.

EXAMPLE 2

Use compensation to find the sum.

43 + 19

(43 − 3) + (19 + 3)   *Take away 3 from 43 to get 40. Then add 3 to 19 to compensate.*

40 + 22   *It is easier to add 40 to 22.*

62   *Add.*

PRACTICE

Use compatible numbers to estimate each answer.

1. 48 + 24

2. 204 − 63

3. 58 × 73

4. 6.3 × 9.8

5. 34 ÷ 7.2

6. 324 ÷ 76

Use compensation to find the sum.

7. 38 + 14

8. 19 + 24

9. 56 + 78

10. Charlie's car has 11 gallons of gas in its tank. His car can travel approximately 28 miles per gallon. Estimate how far Charlie can drive before he runs out of gas.

11. Sue drives to her friend's house at an average speed of 52 miles per hour. Her friend lives 247 miles away. Estimate how long it takes Sue to reach her friend's house.

Divisibility Rules

A number is divisible by another number if the quotient is a whole number with no remainder.

A number is divisible by . . .	Divisible	Not Divisible
2 if the last digit is an even number.	13,776	4,221
3 if the sum of the digits is divisible by 3.	327	97
4 if the last two digits form a number divisible by 4.	3,128	526
5 if the last digit is 0 or 5.	9,415	50,501
6 if the number is divisible by 2 and 3.	762	62
9 if the sum of the digits is divisible by 9.	21,222	96
10 if the last digit is 0.	1,680	8,255

PRACTICE

Determine whether each number is divisible by 2, 3, 4, 5, 6, 9, or 10.

1. 324   **2.** 501   **3.** 200   **4.** 812   **5.** 60

Significant Digits

In a measurement, all the digits that are known with certainty are called **significant digits**. The table shows some rules for identifying significant digits.

Rule	Example	Number of Significant Digits
All nonzero digits	15.32	All 4
Zeros between significant digits	43,001	All 5
Zeros after the last nonzero digit that are to the right of the decimal point.	0.0070	2; 0.0070

Zeros at the end of a whole number are assumed to be nonsignificant.

EXAMPLE

Determine the number of significant digits in each measurement.

A **120.1 mi**

120.1   *1, 2, 0, and 1 are significant.*

All 4 digits are significant.

B **0.0350 kg**

0.0350   *3, 5, and 0 are significant.*

There are 3 significant digits.

PRACTICE

Determine the number of significant digits in each measurement.

1. 2.703 g   **2.** 0.02 km   **3.** 28,000 lb   **4.** 4.003 L

5. 0.650 cm   **6.** 2,800.0 mi   **7.** 30.05 kg   **8.** 100 yd

Factors

A **factor** of a number is any whole number that divides into it without leaving a remainder.

EXAMPLE

List all the factors of 28.

The possible factors are whole numbers from 1 to 28.

$1 \cdot 28 = 28$ *1 and 28 are factors of 28.*

$2 \cdot 14 = 28$ *2 and 14 are factors of 28.*

$3 \cdot ? = 28$ *No whole number multiplied by 3 equals 28, so 3 is not a factor of 28.*

$4 \cdot 7 = 28$ *4 and 7 are factors of 28.*

$5 \cdot ? = 28$ *No whole number multiplied by 5 equals 28, so 5 is not a factor of 28.*

$6 \cdot ? = 28$ *No whole number multiplied by 6 equals 28, so 6 is not a factor of 28.*

The factors of 28 are 1, 2, 4, 7, 14, and 28.

PRACTICE

List all the factors of each number.

1. 10   **2.** 8   **3.** 18   **4.** 54   **5.** 27   **6.** 36

Roman Numerals

In the Roman numeral system, numbers do not have place values to show what they represent. Instead, numbers are represented by letters.

$I = 1$ $V = 5$ $X = 10$ $L = 50$ $C = 100$ $D = 500$ $M = 1,000$

The values of the letters do not change based on their place in a number.

If a numeral is to the right of an equal or greater numeral, add the two numerals' values. If a numeral is immediately to the left of a greater numeral, subtract the numeral's value from the greater numeral.

EXAMPLE

A   **Write CLIV as a decimal number.**

$$CLIV = C + L + (V - I)$$
$$= 100 + 50 + (5 - 1)$$
$$= 154$$

B   **Write 1,109 as a Roman numeral.**

$$1,109 = 1,000 + 100 + 9$$
$$= M + C + (X - I)$$
$$= MCIX$$

PRACTICE

Write each decimal number as a Roman numeral and each Roman numeral as a decimal number.

1. XXVI   **2.** 29   **3.** MCMLII   **4.** 224   **5.** DCCCVI

Relate Metric Units of Length, Mass, and Capacity

A cube that has a volume of 1 cm³ has a capacity of 1 mL. If the cube were filled with water, the mass of the water would be 1 g.

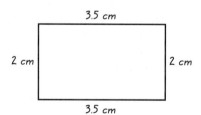

EXAMPLE

Find the capacity of a 50 cm × 60 cm × 30 cm rectangular box. Then find the mass of the water that would fill the box.

Volume: 50 cm × 60 cm × 30 cm = 90,000 cm³

Capacity: 1 cm³ = 1 mL, so 90,000 cm³ = 90,000 mL, or 90 L.

Mass: 1 mL of water has a mass of 1 g, so 90,000 mL of water has a mass of 90,000 g, or 90 kg.

PRACTICE

Find the capacity of each box. Then find the mass of the water that would fill the box.

1. 2 cm × 5 cm × 8 cm   **2.** 10 cm × 18 cm × 4 cm   **3.** 8 cm × 8 cm × 8 cm

4. 10 cm × 10 cm × 10 cm   **5.** 15 cm × 18 cm × 16 cm   **6.** 23 cm × 19 cm × 11 cm

Basic Geometric Figures

You can use a straightedge to draw geometric figures made up of segments.

EXAMPLE

Draw and label a rectangle with a length of 3.5 cm and a width of 2 cm.

Draw a horizontal segment 3.5 cm long. Next draw two vertical segments each 2 cm long to represent the vertical sides of the rectangle. Finally, draw a second horizontal segment 3.5 cm long.

PRACTICE

Draw and label each figure that is described.

1. A square with sides of 4 cm
2. A rectangle with a length of 1.5 in. and a width of 1 in.
3. A square with sides of 2 in.
4. A rectangle with a length of 5 cm and a width of 3 cm

Elapsed Time

The amount of time between a starting time and an ending time is called **elapsed time** .

EXAMPLE

A Jody drove 1 hour and 25 minutes from Lima to Trenton. Jody arrived in Trenton at 2:30 P.M. At what time did Jody leave Lima?

Time Jody arrived: 2:30 P.M.   *Think: 1 hour before 2:30 P.M. is 1:30 P.M.*

Time Jody left: 1:05 P.M.   *25 minutes before 1:30 P.M. is 1:05 P.M.*

Jody left Lima at 1:05 P.M.

B Rael ran his first lap in 2 minutes and 36 seconds. He ran his second lap in 2 minutes and 45 seconds. How much time elapsed during the two laps?

2 min 36 s + 2 min 45 s   *Find the sum of the two times.*

(2 min + 2 min) + (36 s + 45 s)   *Regroup minutes and seconds.*

(4 min) + (81 s)   *Add minutes, and then add seconds.*

(4 min) + (1 min 21 s)   *Change 81 seconds to 1 minute 21 seconds.*

5 min 21 s *Add minutes.*

The total time elapsed during the two laps is 5 minutes and 21 seconds.

PRACTICE

1. Larry was scheduled to arrive at his grandfather's house at 10:45 A.M. He was 1 hour and 20 minutes late. When did Larry arrive?

2. A train arrived at its destination at 12:15 P.M. If the trip took 2 hours and 50 minutes, at what time did the bus depart?

3. Will ran for 22 minutes and 30 seconds and then ran for 34 minutes and 54 seconds. How much time elapsed during his run?

4. Sheila completed a race in 6 hours and 6 minutes. She completed the first half of the race in 2 hours and 58 minutes. How much time elapsed during the second half of the race?

5. A movie starts at 7:20 P.M. The movie ends at 9:17 P.M. How long was the movie?

Polynomials

A **monomial** is a number or a product of numbers and variables with exponents that are whole numbers. The expressions $2n$, x^3, $4a^4b^3$, and 7 are all examples of monomials. The expressions $x^{1.5}$, $2\sqrt{y}$, and $\frac{3}{m}$ are not monomials.

A **polynomial** is one monomial or the sum or difference of monomials. Polynomials can be classified by the number of terms. A monomial has one term, a **bionomial** has two terms, and a **trinomial** has three terms.

EXAMPLE

Classify each expression as a monomial, a binomial, a trinomial, or not a polynomial.

A $43h + 14b$

   binomial   *The expression is a polynomial with 2 terms.*

B $3x^2 - 4xy + \frac{3}{x}$

   not a polynomial   *There is a variable in a denominator.*

PRACTICE

Classify each expression as a monomial, a binomial, a trinomial, or not a polynomial.

1. $5a^3 + 6a^2 - 3$ 2. $4xy^2$ 3. $7b + \frac{1}{b^2}$ 4. $6c^2d - 4$

Odds

Similar to probability, odds are a way to express the likelihood that an event will occur. The **odds** of an event are the ratio of the number of favorable outcomes to the number of unfavorable outcomes. Odds are usually written as $a{:}b$, but can also be written as a to b or $\frac{a}{b}$.

EXAMPLE

In a school raffle, 500 tickets were sold, and there were 10 winners. What are the odds of winning the raffle?

odds of winning $= \dfrac{\text{number of favorable outcomes}}{\text{number of unfavorable outcomes}}$

$\qquad\qquad = \dfrac{10}{490}$ *The number of unfavorable outcomes is 500 – 10, or 490.*

The odds of winning the raffle are 10:490, or 1:49.

PRACTICE

A bag of 20 marbles contains 9 yellow marbles and 11 purple marbles.

1. Find the odds of choosing a yellow marble.
2. Find the odds of choosing a purple marble.

Probability of Two Mutually Exclusive Events

In probability, two events are considered to be **mutually exclusive**, or disjoint, if they cannot happen at the same time. For example, rolling a 5 and rolling a 6 on a 1–6 number cube are mutually exclusive events because they cannot both happen on a single roll.

Suppose A and B are mutually exclusive events.

- $P(\text{both } A \text{ and } B \text{ will occur}) = 0$

- $P(\text{either } A \text{ or } B \text{ will occur}) = P(A) + P(B)$

To find the probability of event A or event B, add the probabilities of each event.

EXAMPLE

Find the probability of each set of mutually exclusive events.

A **rolling either a 5 or a 6 on a 1–6 number cube**

$$P(5 \text{ or } 6) = P(5) + P(6)$$
$$= \frac{1}{6} + \frac{1}{6}$$
$$= \frac{2}{6}$$

The probability of rolling a 5 or a 6 is $\frac{2}{6}$, or $\frac{1}{3}$.

B **choosing either an A or an E from the letters in the word *mathematics***

$$P(A \text{ or } E) = P(A) + P(E)$$
$$= \frac{2}{11} + \frac{1}{11}$$
$$= \frac{3}{11}$$

The probability of choosing an A or an E is $\frac{3}{11}$.

PRACTICE

Find the probability of each set of mutually exclusive events.

1. tossing a coin and getting heads or tails

2. spinning red or green on a spinner that has four equal sectors colored red, green, blue, and yellow

3. drawing a black marble or a red marble from a bag that contains 4 white marbles, 3 black marbles, and 2 red marbles

4. choosing either a boy or a girl from a class of 13 boys and 17 girls

5. choosing either A or E from a list of the five vowels

6. choosing either a number less than 3 or a number greater than 12 from a set of 20 cards numbered 1–20

Skills Bank

Inductive and Deductive Reasoning

You use **inductive reasoning** when you look for a pattern in individual cases to draw conclusions. Conclusions drawn using inductive reasoning are sometimes like predictions. They may be proven false.

You use **deductive reasoning** when you use given facts to draw conclusions. A conclusion based on facts must be true.

EXAMPLE

Identify the type of reasoning used. Explain your answers.

A *Statement:* A number pattern begins with 2, 5, 8, 11, . . .

   Conclusion: The next number in the pattern will be 14.

   This is inductive reasoning. The conclusion is based on the pattern established by the first four terms in the sequence.

B *Statement:* It has rained for the past three days.

   Conclusion: It will rain tomorrow.

   This is inductive reasoning. The conclusion is based on the weather pattern over the past three days.

C *Statement:* The measures of two angles of a triangle are 30° and 70°.

   Conclusion: The measure of the third angle is 80°.

   This is deductive reasoning. Since you know that the measures of the angles of a triangle have a sum of 180°, the third angle of this triangle must measure 80° (30° + 70° + 80° = 180°).

PRACTICE

Identify the type of reasoning used. Explain your answers.

1. *Statement:* Shawna has received a score of 100 on the last five math tests.
    Conclusion: Shawna will receive a score of 100 on the next math test.

2. *Statement:* The mail has arrived late every Monday for the past 4 weeks.
    Conclusion: The mail will arrive late next Monday.

3. *Statement:* Three angles of a quadrilateral measure 100°, 90°, and 70°.
    Conclusion: The measure of the fourth angle is 100°.

4. *Statement:* Perpendicular lines *AB* and *CD* intersect at point *E*.
    Conclusion: Angle *AED* is a right angle.

5. *Statement:* A pattern of numbers begins 1, 2, 4, . . .
    Conclusion: The next number in the pattern is 8.

6. *Statement:* Ten of the first ten seventh-grade students surveyed listed soccer as their favorite sport.
    Conclusion: Soccer is the favorite sport of all seventh-graders.

Skills Bank

Make Conjectures

Conjecture is another word for conclusion. Conjectures in math are based on observations and in some cases have not yet been proven to be true. To prove that a conjecture is false, you need to find just one case, or *counterexample*, for which the conclusion does not hold true.

EXAMPLE 1

Test each conjecture to decide whether it is true or false. If the conjecture is false, give a counterexample.

A **The sum of two even numbers is always an even number.**

An even number is divisible by 2. The sum of two even numbers can be written as $2m + 2n = 2(m + n)$, which is divisible by 2, so it is even. The conjecture is true.

B **Three points on a plane always form a triangle.**

Three points can lie on the same line. The conjecture is false.

EXAMPLE 2

Formulate a conjecture based on the given information. Then test your conjecture.

$$1 \cdot 3 = 3 \qquad 3 \cdot 5 = 15 \qquad 5 \cdot 7 = 35 \qquad 7 \cdot 9 = 63$$

Conjecture: The product of two odd numbers is always an odd number.

An odd number does not have 2 as a factor, so the product of two odd numbers also does not have 2 as a factor. The conjecture is true.

PRACTICE

Test each conjecture to decide whether it is true or false. If the conjecture is false, give a counterexample.

1. The sum of two odd numbers is always an odd number.

2. The product of two even numbers is always an even number.

3. The sum of twice a whole number and 1 is always an odd number.

4. Every pair of supplementary angles includes one obtuse angle.

5. If you multiply two fractions, the product will always be greater than either fraction.

Formulate a conjecture based on the given information. Then test your conjecture.

6. $12 + 21 = 33 \qquad 13 + 31 = 44 \qquad 23 + 32 = 55 \qquad 17 + 71 = 88$

7. $15 \times 15 = 225 \qquad 25 \times 25 = 625 \qquad 35 \times 35 = 1,225$

Trigonometric Ratios

You can use ratios to find information about the sides and angles of a right triangle. These ratios are called *trigonometric ratios*, and they have names, such as sine (abbreviated *sin*), cosine (abbreviated *cos*), and tangent (abbreviated *tan*).

The **sine** of $\angle 1 = \sin \angle 1 = \dfrac{\text{length of side opposite } \angle 1}{\text{length of hypotenuse}} = \dfrac{a}{c}$.

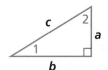

The **cosine** of $\angle 1 = \cos \angle 1 = \dfrac{\text{length of side adjacent to } \angle 1}{\text{length of hypotenuse}} = \dfrac{b}{c}$.

The **tangent** of $\angle 1 = \tan \angle 1 = \dfrac{\text{length of side opposite } \angle 1}{\text{length of side adjacent to } \angle 1} = \dfrac{a}{b}$.

EXAMPLE 1

Find the sine, cosine, and tangent of $\angle J$.

$\sin \angle J = \dfrac{LK}{JK} = \dfrac{3}{5}$

$\cos \angle J = \dfrac{JL}{JK} = \dfrac{4}{5}$

$\tan \angle J = \dfrac{LK}{JL} = \dfrac{3}{4}$

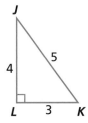

EXAMPLE 2

Use your calculator to find the length of $\overline{MN}$ to the nearest tenth.

$\overline{MN}$ is adjacent to the 58° angle. The length of the hypotenuse is given. The ratio that uses the lengths of the adjacent side and the hypotenuse is cosine.

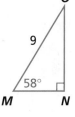

$\cos(58°) = \dfrac{MN}{9}$ *Write the ratio that is equal to the cosine of 58°.*

$9 \cdot \cos(58°) = MN$ *Multiply both sides by 9.*

9 ☒ cos 58 ENTER   *Use your calculator.*

$MN \approx 4.8$

PRACTICE

Find the sine, cosine, and tangent of each angle.

  1. $\angle D$ **2.** $\angle F$

Use your calculator to find the length of each side, to the nearest tenth.

  3. $\overline{QR}$ **4.** $\overline{PR}$

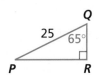

Cubes and Cube Roots

The volume of the cube at right is $5 \cdot 5 \cdot 5$, or 125 cubic units. Because 5 is a factor 3 times, you can use an exponent to write the expression as 5^3, which is read "5 cubed."

EXAMPLE 1

Evaluate 8^3.

$8^3 = 8 \cdot 8 \cdot 8$ *Use 8 as a factor 3 times.*

$\quad = 512$ *Multiply.*

Finding a cube root is the inverse of cubing a number. The symbol $\sqrt[3]{\ }$ means "cube root." For example, $\sqrt[3]{125} = 5$.

EXAMPLE 2

Evaluate $\sqrt[3]{64}$.

$\sqrt[3]{64} = 4$ *$4^3 = 4 \cdot 4 \cdot 4 = 64$, so $\sqrt[3]{64} = 4$.*

You can use a calculator to estimate cube roots.

EXAMPLE 3

Use your calculator to evaluate $\sqrt[3]{43}$ to the nearest tenth.

Press **MATH** and select **4:** $\sqrt[3]{\ }$ (from the menu.) Then enter 43 **)** **ENTER** .

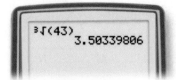

$$\sqrt[3]{43} \approx 3.5$$

PRACTICE

Evaluate each expression.

1. 2^3
2. 1^3
3. 7^3
4. 10^3

5. 6^3
6. 30^3
7. 0^3
8. 4^3

9. $\sqrt[3]{8}$
10. $\sqrt[3]{27}$
11. $\sqrt[3]{1,000}$
12. $\sqrt[3]{1}$

Use your calculator to evaluate each cube root to the nearest tenth.

13. $\sqrt[3]{30}$
14. $\sqrt[3]{68}$
15. $\sqrt[3]{100}$
16. $\sqrt[3]{3}$

17. $\sqrt[3]{260}$
18. $\sqrt[3]{1,255}$
19. $\sqrt[3]{17}$
20. $\sqrt[3]{89}$

21. $\sqrt[3]{54}$
22. $\sqrt[3]{1,728}$
23. $\sqrt[3]{25}$
24. $\sqrt[3]{3,375}$

Properties of Exponents

To multiply powers with the same base, keep the base and add the exponents.

$$x^3 \cdot x^2 = (x \cdot x \cdot x) \cdot (x \cdot x) = x^{3+2} = x^5$$

This is the *Product of Powers Property*.

To divide powers with the same base, keep the base and subtract the exponents.

$$\frac{y^5}{y^2} = \frac{y \cdot y \cdot y \cdot y \cdot y}{y \cdot y} = y^{5-2} = y^3$$

This is the *Quotient of Powers Property*.

To raise a power to a power, keep the base and multiply the exponents.

$$(5^3)^2 = 5^3 \cdot 5^3 = (5 \cdot 5 \cdot 5) \cdot (5 \cdot 5 \cdot 5) = 5^{3 \cdot 2} = 5^6$$

This is the *Power of a Power Property*.

EXAMPLE 2

Rewrite each expression as a single power of the base.

A $7^9 \cdot 7^{11}$

$$7^9 \cdot 7^{11} = 7^{9+11} \qquad \text{\textit{Use the Product of Powers Property.}}$$
$$= 7^{20} \qquad \text{\textit{Add the exponents.}}$$

B $\dfrac{x^{22}}{x^{15}}$

$$\frac{x^{22}}{x^{15}} = x^{22-15} \qquad \text{\textit{Use the Quotient of Powers Property.}}$$
$$= x^7 \qquad \text{\textit{Subtract the exponents.}}$$

C $(b^6)^9$

$$(b^6)^9 = b^{6 \cdot 9} \qquad \text{\textit{Use the Power of a Power Property.}}$$
$$= b^{54} \qquad \text{\textit{Multiply the exponents.}}$$

PRACTICE

Rewrite each expression as a single power of the base.

1. $c^{12} \cdot c^5$
2. $5^6 \cdot 5^{22}$
3. $\dfrac{y^{50}}{y^{28}}$
4. $\dfrac{6^{14}}{6^8}$
5. $(a^{11})^{12}$
6. $(8^9)^7$
7. $3^4 \cdot 3^4$
8. $\dfrac{5^7}{5^4}$
9. $(2^4)^2$
10. $x^3 \cdot x^9$
11. $\dfrac{s^7}{s}$
12. $(n^2)^5$

Absolute Value and Distance

The absolute value of a number is its distance from 0 on the number line. Since distance can never be negative, absolute values are never negative. The symbol for absolute value is | |.

EXAMPLE 1

Find the absolute value of each real number.

A 2.7

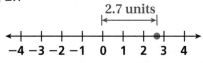

$|2.7| = 2.7$

B $-\pi$

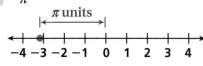

$|-\pi| = \pi$

Suppose that A and B are points on a number line that have coordinates a and b. Since distance can never be negative, the distance between A and B can be calculated as the absolute value of the difference of the two numbers. This distance can be written as $|b - a|$ or $|a - b|$.

EXAMPLE 2

Find the distance between each set of points on the number line.

A

$|-5 - 3| = |-8| = 8$

The distance is 8 units.

B

$|-7 - (-6)| = |-1| = 1$

The distance is 1 unit.

PRACTICE

Find the absolute value of each real number.

1. $-\frac{3}{4}$
2. 5.8
3. $-\sqrt{10}$
4. $3\frac{5}{8}$

5. $\sqrt{3}$
6. -0.16
7. $-1\frac{1}{10}$
8. $\frac{15}{12}$

Find the distance between each set of points on the number line.

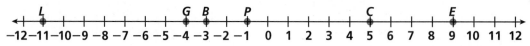

9. B and C
10. E and G
11. L and B
12. P and E

13. L and E
14. G and P
15. P and C
16. C and G

Networks and Paths

A **network** is a set of points and line segments or arcs that connect the points. The points of a network are called **vertices**. The segments or arcs are called **edges**.

A **path** is a way to travel around a network by moving along the edges from one vertex to another. In a simple path, no point is visited more than once.

EXAMPLE

The network represents the major roads connecting five cities. Each vertex represents a city. Each edge represents a road. The numbers along each edge give the distance in miles between cities.

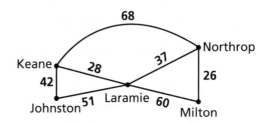

A Determine the number of simple paths from Johnston to Northrop.

1. Johnston-Keane-Laramie-Milton-Northrop
2. Johnston-Keane-Laramie-Northrop
3. Johnston-Keane-Northrop
4. Johnston-Laramie-Keane-Northrop
5. Johnston-Laramie-Milton-Northrop
6. Johnston-Laramie-Northrop

Make an organized list of the simple paths.

There are 6 simple paths.

B Determine the shortest simple path from Johnston to Northrop.

1. $42 + 28 + 60 + 26 = 156$
2. $42 + 28 + 37 = 107$
3. $42 + 68 = 110$
4. $51 + 28 + 68 = 147$
5. $51 + 60 + 26 = 137$
6. $51 + 37 = 88$

For each simple path above, add the distances between the cities.

The shortest simple path is Johnston to Laramie to Northrop.

PRACTICE

The network represents the direct nonstop train routes connecting six cities. The numbers along each edge give the time it takes in minutes to travel each direct nonstop train route one way.

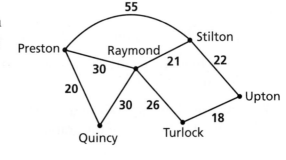

1. Determine the number of simple paths from Preston to Upton. Then determine the shortest simple path in time between the two cities.

2. Determine the number of simple paths from Quincy to Turlock. Then determine the shortest simple path in time between the two cities.

Quadratic Relationships

Quadratic relationships involve one squared value related to another value. An example of a quadratic relationship is shown in the equation $a = x^2 + 5$. If you know the value of one variable, you can substitute for it in the equation and then solve to find the second variable.

EXAMPLE

The distance d in feet that an object falls is related to the amount of time t in seconds that it falls. This relationship is given by the equation $d = 16t^2$.

What distance will an object fall in 3 seconds?

$$d = 16t^2 \qquad \textit{Write the equation.}$$
$$d = 16 \cdot (3)^2 \quad \textit{Substitute 3 for t.}$$
$$ = 144 \qquad \textit{Simplify.}$$

The object will fall 144 feet in 3 seconds.

PRACTICE

A small rocket is shot vertically upward from the ground. The distance d in feet between the rocket and the ground as the rocket goes up can be found by using the equation $d = 128t - 16t^2$, where t is the amount of time in seconds that the rocket has been flying upward.

1. How far above the ground is the rocket at 1 second and at 2 seconds?

2. Did the rocket's distance change by the same amount in each of the first 2 seconds? Explain.

3. When the rocket is returning to the ground, the distance that the rocket falls is given by the equation $d = 16t^2$. If the rocket hits the ground 4 seconds after it starts to return, how far up did it go?

4. As the rocket falls to the ground, does it fall the same distance each second? Explain.

The graph for $y = x^2$ is shown at right. Use the graph for problems 5–7.

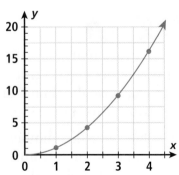

5. Find the value of y for $x = 1, 2, 3, 4,$ and 5.

6. Does y increase by the same amount for each value of x? Explain.

7. How would the part of the graph from $x = 5$ to $x = 6$ compare to the part of the graph from $x = 4$ to $x = 5$?

Exponential Relationships

An **exponential relationship** can be described by a function of the form $y = ab^x$, where a is a constant not equal to 0 and b is a positive number not equal to 1.

EXAMPLE

Create a table of values for each function, and then graph the function.

A $y = 2 \cdot 3^x$

Choose several values of x and generate ordered pairs.

x	y
−2	$\frac{2}{9}$
−1	$\frac{2}{3}$
0	2
1	6
2	18

Plot the points $(-2, \frac{2}{9})$, $(-1, \frac{2}{3})$ $(0, 2)$, and $(1, 6)$, and connect them with a smooth curve.

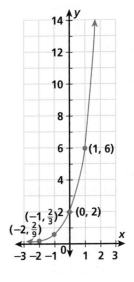

B $y = 3 \cdot \left(\frac{1}{2}\right)^x$

Choose several values of x and generate ordered pairs.

x	y
−2	12
−1	6
0	3
1	$\frac{3}{2}$
2	$\frac{3}{4}$

Plot the points $(-2, 12)$, $(-1, 6)$ $(0, 3)$, $(1, \frac{3}{2})$, and $(2, \frac{3}{4})$ and connect them with a smooth curve.

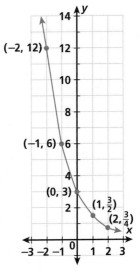

PRACTICE

Create a table of values for each function, and then graph the function.

1. $y = \frac{1}{2} \cdot 3^x$

2. $y = 4 \cdot \left(\frac{1}{3}\right)^x$

3. $y = 5 \cdot \left(\frac{2}{5}\right)^x$

4. An exponential relationship is described by the function $y = ab^x$ where $a > 0$. For what positive values of b would the graph of the function be increasing? For what positive values of b would the graph of the function be decreasing?

Skills Bank **SB19**

AAA, SAS, SSS Similarity

Two figures are similar if their corresponding angle measures are equal *and* if the ratios of the lengths of their corresponding sides are proportional. To prove that two triangles are similar, it is not necessary to show that both of these conditions are always true. They are also considered to be similar if they meet any of the following conditions:

Angle-Angle-Angle (AAA) Similarity	Two triangles are similar if all corresponding angles are congruent.
Side-Angle-Side (SAS) Similarity	Two triangles are similar if the ratios of two pairs of corresponding sides are equal and the corresponding included angles are congruent.
Side-Side-Side (SSS) Similarity	Two triangles are similar if the ratios of all pairs of corresponding sides are equal.

EXAMPLES

Explain why the pairs of triangles are similar.

A

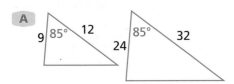

The ratios of two pairs of corresponding sides are equal: $\frac{9}{24} = \frac{12}{32}$. The corresponding included angles are congruent since they both measure 85°.

The triangles are similar because of SAS.

B

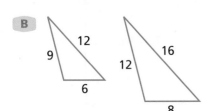

The ratios of all pairs of corresponding sides are equal: $\frac{12}{9} = \frac{8}{6} = \frac{16}{12}$.

The triangles are similar because of SSS.

C

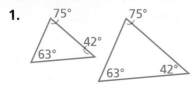

All corresponding angles are congruent since corresponding angle measures are equal: 32° = 32°, 48° = 48°, and 100° = 100°.

The triangles are similar because of AAA.

PRACTICE

Explain why the pairs of triangles are similar.

1.

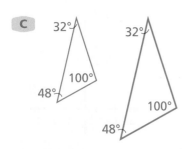

2.

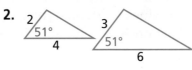

3.

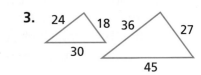

Graph Linear Inequalities on a Coordinate Plane

A **linear inequality** is a mathematical sentence of the form $y < mx + b$, $y > mx + b$, $y \leq mx + b$, or $y \geq mx + b$, where m and b are constants. The graph of a linear inequality is a shaded region with a straight-line boundary. Any ordered pair that makes the inequality true is a solution.

To graph a linear inequality, first graph the related line $y = mx + b$. If the inequality is $\geq$ or $\leq$, make the line solid. If the inequality is $>$ or $<$, make the line dashed. Then test a point not on the line to see which side of the line to shade. If the point is a solution of the inequality, then shade the side that includes the point. If the point is not a solution, then shade the side that does not include the point.

EXAMPLE

Graph each linear inequality.

A $y > 3x + 2$

Graph $y = 3x + 2$. Use a dashed line for $>$.

$$y > 3x + 2$$
$$0 \overset{?}{>} 3(0) + 2 \qquad \textit{Test the point (0, 0).}$$
$$0 \overset{?}{>} 2$$

Since $0 \not> 2$, (0, 0) is not a solution of $y > 3x + 2$.
Shade the side of the line that does not include (0, 0).

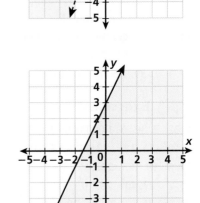

B $y \leq 2x + 3$

Graph $y = 2x + 3$. Use a solid line for $\leq$.

$$y \leq 2x + 3$$
$$0 \overset{?}{\leq} 2(0) + 3 \qquad \textit{Test the point (0, 0).}$$
$$0 \overset{?}{\leq} 3$$

Since $0 \leq 3$, (0, 0) is a solution of $y \leq 2x + 3$.
Shade the side that includes (0, 0).

PRACTICE

Graph each linear inequality.

1. $y \leq 4x - 1$

2. $y > -2x + 3$

3. $y \geq \frac{1}{3}x - 2$

4. Julia earns $10 per hour at her job. Each day, she receives a bonus of at least $20. The inequality $y \geq 10x + 20$ represents how much she earns in dollars for x hours of work. Graph the inequality.

Selected Answers ...

Chapter 1

1-1 Exercises

1. Add 8 to get the next number
3. Subtract 9 to get the next
number **5.** Equilateral triangles
each divided into six congruent
triangles with a pair of opposite
congruent triangles shaded in two
different colors so that the shaded
pairs rotate clockwise from each
equilateral triangle to the next
7. 10 green triangles **9.** Divide by
4 to get the next number **11.** Add
23 to get the next number
13. Regular heptagons sliced into
7 triangles with one triangle
shaded in each figure. In each
successive figure the shaded
triangle rotates clockwise 4
triangles. **15.** 7, 23, 39, 55, 71
17. 50, 48, 44, 38, 30 **19.** Multiply
by 4 to get the next number
21. Add 8 to get the next number
23. 134 **31.** 51 **33.** 90 **35.** 2,020
37. 100 **39.** 1,000 **41.** 23,100

1-2 Exercises

1. 32 **3.** 36 **5.** 1,000,000 **7.** 4^2
9. 10^2 **11.** 121 **13.** 512 **15.** 81
17. 5 **19.** 125 **21.** 9^2 **23.** 4^3
25. 2^5 **27.** 40^2 **29.** 10^5 **31.** 3^4
33. 8^2 **35.** 5^4 **37.** $<$ **39.** $<$ **41.** $>$
43. $>$ **45.** \$21.87 **47.** Yuma:
688,560; Phoenix: 11,370,384
49. $4 \cdot 3^3 = 108$ stars **51.** 10^1, 33,
6^2, 4^3, 5^3 **53.** 0, 1^8, 2, 16^1, 3^4
55. 8^1, 9, 5^2, 3^3, 2^5 **61.** C
63. 17 **65.** 196 **67.** Add 1 more
than the number that was
previously added.

1-3 Exercises

1. 1,500 **3.** 208,000
5. 3.6×10^6 **7.** 8.0×10^9
9. 2,000,000,000,000,000,000,000,000
11. 2,100 **13.** 2,500,000
15. 268,000 **17.** 211,500,000
19. 4.28×10^5 **21.** 3.0×10^9
23. 5.2×10^1 **25.** 8.9×10^6
27. 367,000 **29.** 4 **31.** 340
33. 540,000,000 **35.** no **37.** yes
39. 9.8×10^8 feet per second
41. 1.83×10^8 years **45.** C
49. 5^4 **51.** 2^9

1-4 Exercises

1. 47 **3.** 23 **5.** 4 **7.** \$280 **9.** 42
11. 15 **13.** 73 **15.** 588 **17.** \$139
19. 18 **21.** 20 **23.** 1 **25.** $>$ **27.** $>$
29. $=$ **31.** $4 \cdot (8 - 3) = 20$
33. $(12 - 2)^2 \div 5 = 20$
35. $(4 + 6 - 3) \div 7 = 1$ **37.** \$82
39a. $4 \cdot 15$ **39b.** $2 \cdot 30$
39c. $4 \cdot 15 + 2 \cdot 30 + 6$ **43.** C
45. D **47.** 729 **49.** 27 **51.** 612,000
53. 59,000,000 **55.** 191

1-5 Exercises

1. Assoc. Prop. **3.** Comm. Prop.
5. Assoc. Prop. **7.** 33 **9.** 1,100
11. 47 **13.** 38 **15.** 44 **17.** 208
19. Ident. Prop. **21.** Assoc. Prop.
23. Ident. Prop. **25.** 1,600 **27.** 900
29. 163 **31.** 135 **33.** 174 **35.** 92
41. 220 ft^2 **43.** 9,000 **45.** 17,500
47. 15 **49.** 0 **51.** 8 **53.** 2 **59.** H
61. 6^2 **63.** 3^2 **65.** 1 **67.** 3

1-6 Exercises

1. 12 **3.** 20 **5.** 8 **7.** 19 **9.** 22
11. 5 **13.** 11 **15.** 24 **17.** 12
19. 41 **21.** 300 **23.** 10 **25.** 22
27. 24 **29.** 13 **31.** 31 **33.** \$4.50
35. 86 °F **41.** H **43.** 6.21×10^7
45. 8×10^5 **47.** 68 **49.** 87

1-7 Exercises

1. $7p$ **3.** $\frac{n}{12}$ **5.** $\$5 \div n$, or $\frac{5}{n}$
7. $5 + x$ **9.** $n \div 8$ **11.** $3y - 10$
13. $5 + 2t$ **15.** $\frac{23}{u} - t$ **17.** $2(y + 5)$
19. $35(r - 5)$ **21.** $65{,}000 + 2b$
23. 90 divided by y **25.** 16
multiplied by t **27.** the difference
between 4 times p and 10
29. the quotient of m and 15 plus 3
31. $15y + 12$ **37.** $(104 + 19 \cdot 2)x$;
\$426 **39.** 5 **41.** 35

1-8 Exercises

1. $6b$ and $\frac{b}{2}$ **3.** $8x$ **5.** There are
no like terms. **7.** b^6 and $3b^6$
9. m and $2m$ **11.** $8a + 2b$
13. $3a + 3b + 2c$ **15.** $3q^2 + 2q$
17. $2n + 3a + 3a + 2n + 5$
19. $27y$ **21.** $2d^2 + d$ **23.** no like
terms **25.** no like terms
27. $4n + 5n + 6n = 15n$
29a. $21.5d + 23d + 15.5d + 19d$
b. \$750.50 **c.** the amount Brad
earned in June **31.** $23x^2$
35. D **37.** 2.68×10^8 **39.** 51
41. 159

1-9 Exercises

1. no **3.** yes **5.** situation A **7.** no
9. yes **11.** no **13.** situation B
15. yes **17.** yes **19.** no **21.** yes
23. yes **25.** $10{,}500 + d = 14{,}264$
29. A **31.** 1.085×10^7
33. 9.04×10^6 **35.** Identity
Property of Addition

1-10 Exercises

1. $r = 176$ **3.** $x = 88$ **5.** $f = 9$
7. 14 yd **9.** $t = 82$ **11.** $b = 67$
13. $k = 123$ **15.** $w = 43$ **17.** $s = 45$
19. $j = 76$ **21.** $q = 99$ **23.** 38 mi
25. $p = 10$ **27.** $b = 52$ **29.** $a = 45$
31. $c = 149$ **33.** $m = 199$
35. $s = 159$ **37.** $x = 839$
39. $w = 79$ **41.** $x + 65 = 315$; \$250

47. D **49.** $17 - k$ **51.** $12 + 5n$
53. $8 + 11t$

1-11 Exercises

1. $s = 847$ **3.** $y = 40$ **5.** $c = 32$
7. 9 people **9.** $k = 1,296$
11. $c = 175$ **13.** $n = 306$
15. $p = 21$ **17.** $a = 2$ **19.** $d = 45$
21. $g = 27$ **23.** $m = 110$ **25.** $x = 7$
27. $b = 62$ **29.** $f = 20$ **31.** $a = 36$
33. $d = 42$ **35.** $r = 307$
37. $7 + n = 15$ **39.** $12 = q - 8$
41. 12 toys **43.** $13,300 **49.** H
51. yes **53.** $n = 39$ **55.** $t = 578$

Chapter 1 Study Guide: Review

1. exponent; base **2.** numerical expression **3.** equation
4. algebraic expression **5.** Add 4 to get the next number **6.** Add 20 to get the next number
7. Add 7 to get the next number
8. Multiply by 5 to get the next number **9.** Subtract 4 to get the next number **10.** Subtract 7 to get the next number **11.** 81 **12.** 10
13. 128 **14.** 1 **15.** 121 **16.** 14,400
17. 1,320 **18.** 220,000,000
19. 4.8×10^4 **20.** 7.02×10^6
21. 1.49×10^5 **22.** 7,507,000 **23.** 3
24. 103 **25.** 5 **26.** 67 **27.** $55
28. Comm. Prop. of Add.
29. Identity Prop. of Add.
30. Distributive Property **31.** 65
32. 2,300 **33.** 19 **34.** 524 **35.** 10
36. $4 \div (n + 12)$ **37.** $2(t - 11)$
38. $32 \div s$ **39.** $10b^2 + 8$
40. $15a^2 + 2$ **41.** $x^4 + x^3 + 6x^2$
42. no **43.** yes **44.** no **45.** 8
46. 32 **47.** 18 **48.** 112 **49.** 72
50. 9 **51.** 98 **52.** 13 **53.** 17 h

Chapter 2

2-1 Exercises

5. $>$ **7.** $<$ **9.** $-5, -3, -1, 4, 6$
11. $-6, -4, 0, 1, 3$ **13.** 8 **15.** 10

21. $>$ **23.** $<$ **25.** $-9, -7, -5, -2, 0$
27. 16 **29.** 20 **31.** $<$ **33.** $=$ **35.** $=$
37. $=$ **39.** Aug, Jul, Sep, May, Jun, Apr, Mar, Oct **41.** -29
45. decreased by about 9% **51.** G
53. 1.8023×10^6 **55.** 8.0×10^8
57. 112 **59.** 170

2-2 Exercises

1. 12 **3.** -2 **5.** 15 **7.** -15 **9.** -12
11. -20 **13.** -9 **15.** 13 **17.** 7
19. -17 **21.** -19 **23.** -16
25. -88 **27.** -55 **29.** -14
31. -13 **33.** -13 **35.** -26 **37.** 14
39. $>$ **41.** $>$ **43.** $>$ **45.** $45 + 18 + 27 + (-21) + (-93)$; -24; Cody's account is reduced by $24.
47. -16 **49.** 3 **51.** 4,150 ft **57.** F
59. 4 **61.** 4 **63.** $>$ **65.** $>$

2-3 Exercises

1. -3 **3.** 6 **5.** -4 **7.** -10 **9.** 7
11. -14 **13.** -5 **15.** 8 **17.** 12
19. 16 **21.** -17 **23.** 8 **25.** 50
27. 18 **29.** 16 **31.** -5 **33.** -20
35. 83 °F **37.** -14 **39.** -2 **41.** 2
43. 16 **45.** -27 **47.** -17 **49.** -13, -17, -21 **51.** 1,234 °F **53.** 265 °F
57. $m + n$ has the least absolute value. **59.** 3 **61.** 19 **63.** 24

2-4 Exercises

1. -15 **3.** -15 **5.** 15 **7.** -15
9. -8 **11.** 4 **13.** 7 **15.** undefined
17. 450 feet **19.** -10 **21.** -12
23. 48 **25.** 35 **27.** 7 **29.** -8
31. -9 **33.** -9 **35.** -40 **37.** -3
39. 50 **41.** -3 **43.** 30 **45.** -42
47. -60 ft **49.** 1 **51.** -12
53. 1,400 **55.** 11 **57.** less; $-$72
59. more; $12 **63.** C **65.** $x + 6$
67. $2d - 4$ **69.** 5 **71.** -2

2-5 Exercises

1. $w = 4$ **3.** $k = -7$ **5.** $y = -30$
7. $57 million **9.** $k = -3$
11. $v = -4$ **13.** $a = 20$
15. $t = -32$ **17.** $n = 150$
19. $\ell = -144$ **21.** $y = 100$
23. $j = -63$ **25.** $c = 17$

27. $y = -11$ **29.** $w = -41$
31. $x = -58$ **33.** $x = 4$ **35.** $t = 9$
37. 3 mi **39.** $-13 + p = 8$
41. $t - 9 = -22$ **43.** oceans or beaches **49.** H **51.** multiply by 2
53. $>$ **55.** $<$ **57.** $=$

2-6 Exercises

1. prime **3.** composite **5.** 2^4
7. 3^4 **9.** $2 \cdot 3^2$ **11.** $3^2 \cdot 5$
13. $2 \cdot 5^3$ **15.** $2^2 \cdot 5^2$ **17.** $3^2 \cdot 71$
19. $2^3 \cdot 5^3$ **21.** prime **23.** prime
25. composite **27.** composite
29. $2^2 \cdot 17$ **31.** $2^3 \cdot 3 \cdot 5$
33. $3^3 \cdot 5$ **35.** $2 \cdot 7 \cdot 11$ **37.** $2^5 \cdot 5^2$
39. 5^4 **41.** $3^2 \cdot 5 \cdot 7$ **43.** $3^3 \cdot 7$
45. $2 \cdot 11^2$ **47.** $11 \cdot 17$ **49.** $5^2 \cdot 7^2$
51. $2^3 \cdot 3^2 \cdot 5$ **53.** 3^2 **55.** 5^2
57. 2^4 **61.** 7 **63.** 4 or 8 people
67. B **69.** $2^3 \cdot 3 \cdot 5$ **71.** 587
73. 14,800,000 **75.** $y = 1$ **77.** $x = 0$

2-7 Exercises

1. 6 **3.** 12 **5.** 4 **7.** 12 kits **9.** 12
11. 11 **13.** 38 **15.** 2 **17.** 26 **19.** 3
21. 1 **23.** 2 **25.** 22 **27.** 40 **29.** 1
31. 7 **33.** 3 **35.** 13 **37.** 7 shelves
39a. 7 students **45.** 7 **47.** 13
49. 81 **51.** -5 **53.** 2 **55.** 7^2
57. 2^2

2-8 Exercises

1. 28 **3.** 48 **5.** 45 **7.** 24 min
9. 24 **11.** 42 **13.** 120 **15.** 80
17. 180 **19.** 360 **21.** 60 min
23. 12 **25.** 132 **27.** 90 **29.** 12
31. 144 **33.** 210 **41.** C **43.** $5c - 2$
45. $7u + 3v - 4$ **47.** 4 **49.** 15

2-9 Exercises

9. no **11.** yes **13.** $3\frac{3}{4}$ **15.** $1\frac{4}{13}$
17. $\frac{31}{5}$ **19.** $\frac{38}{5}$ **29.** yes **31.** yes
33. yes **35.** no **37.** $6\frac{1}{3}$ **39.** $7\frac{4}{11}$
41. $\frac{128}{5}$ **43.** $\frac{29}{3}$ **51.** $\frac{11}{2}$ **53.** $\frac{141}{21}$
55. $\frac{573}{50}$ **57.** $\frac{12}{20}, \frac{6}{10}$ **59.** $\frac{9}{5}, \frac{72}{40}$
61. $8\frac{1}{3}$ ft **63.** $3\frac{1}{2}$ ft **65.** $\frac{150}{4}$ **69.** C
73. $y = 12$ **75.** $z = 80$ **77.** 45
79. 168

2-10 Exercises

1. 0.57 **3.** 1.83 **5.** 0.12 **7.** 0.05
9. $\frac{1}{125}$ **11.** $-2\frac{1}{20}$ **13.** 0.720
15. 6.4 **17.** 0.88 **19.** 1 **21.** 1.92
23. 0.8 **25.** 0.55 **27.** $\frac{1}{100}$ **29.** $-\frac{2}{25}$
31. $\frac{61}{4}$ **33.** $8\frac{3}{8}$ **35.** 8.75 **37.** $5\frac{5}{100}$
39. $\frac{307}{20}$ **41.** 4.003 **43.** yes **45.** no
47. yes **49.** no **51.** $18\frac{1}{20}$, $18\frac{1}{25}$,
$18\frac{11}{20}$ **55.** D **57.** no **59.** yes
61. $\frac{13}{4}$ **63.** $\frac{25}{4}$

2-11 Exercises

1. < **3.** < **5.** < **7.** < **9.** $-\frac{13}{5}$,
2.05, 2.5 **11.** < **13.** > **15.** >
17. > **19.** > **21.** < **23.** < **25.** $\frac{5}{8}$,
0.7, 0.755 **27.** -2.25, 2.05, $\frac{21}{10}$
29. -2.98, $-2\frac{9}{10}$, 2.88 **31.** $\frac{3}{4}$
33. $\frac{7}{8}$ **35.** 0.32 **37.** $-\frac{7}{8}$
41. sloths **47.** J **49.** > **51.** >
53. 169 **55.** 57

Chapter 2 Study Guide: Review

1. rational number; integer;
terminating decimal
2. integers; opposite **3.** > **4.** <
5. -6, -2, 0, 4, 5, **6.** -8, -3, 1, 2,
8 **7.** 0 **8.** 17 **9.** 6 **10.** -3 **11.** 1
12. -56 **13.** 9 **14.** 10 **15.** -5
16. 11 °F **17.** 6 **18.** -9 **19.** -1
20. -9 **21.** 3 **22.** 14 **23.** -50
24. 3 **25.** 16 **26.** -2 **27.** -12
28. -3 **29.** $y = 10$ **30.** $d = 14$
31. $j = -26$ **32.** $n = 72$
33. $c = 13$ **34.** $m = -4$ **35.** 18 ft
36. $2^3 \cdot 11$ **37.** 3^3 **38.** $2 \cdot 3^4$
39. $2^5 \cdot 3$ **40.** 32, 36 **41.** 30
42. 3 **43.** 12 **44.** 220 **45.** 60
46. 32 **47.** 27 **48.** 90 **49.** 12
50. 315 **51.** 1:00 PM **52.** $\frac{21}{15}$ **53.** $\frac{19}{6}$
54. $\frac{43}{4}$ **55.** $3\frac{1}{3}$ **56.** $2\frac{1}{2}$ **57.** $2\frac{3}{7}$
58. Possible answer: $\frac{8}{9}, \frac{24}{27}$
59. Possible answer: $\frac{42}{48}, \frac{7}{8}$
60. Possible answer: $\frac{16}{21}, \frac{96}{126}$
61. $\frac{1}{4}$ **62.** $-\frac{1}{250}$ **63.** $\frac{1}{20}$ **64.** 3.5
65. 0.6 **66.** 0.$\overline{6}$ **67.** < **68.** >
69. > **70.** < **71.** -0.55, $\frac{6}{13}$, $\frac{1}{2}$, 0.58

Chapter 3

3-1 Exercises

1. 63 **3.** 2 **5.** -225 **7.** no **9.** 92
11. 8 **13.** 55 **15.** 5 **17.** -120
19. 9 **21.** -7 **23.** -59 **25.** -90
27. -36 **29.** 11 **31.** -98 **33.** 225
35. 13 **37.** about 8 weeks
39. approximately 5 gallons
41. about 30 AU **47.** J **49.** -3
51. 22 **53.** -11

3-2 Exercises

1. 21.82 **3.** 12.826 **5.** 1.98 **7.** 1.77
9. $37.2 billion **11.** 18.97
13. -25.52 **15.** 10.132 **17.** -15.89
19. 9.01 **21.** 16.05 **23.** 5.1
25. 22.77 **27.** 77.13 g **29.** -4.883
31. 14.33 **33.** 1.92 **35.** 30.12
37. -1.26 **39.** -3.457 **41.** You
must keep the place value units
together. **43.** 1915 **49.** G
51. $y = 15$ **53.** $p = 39$ **55.** 22
57. 42

3-3 Exercises

1. -3.6 **3.** 0.18 **5.** 2.04 **7.** -0.315
9. 334.7379 miles **11.** 0.35 **13.** 3.2
15. -20.4 **17.** 9.1 **19.** 4.48
21. 2.814 **23.** -9.256 **25.** 6.161
27. 5.445 mi **29.** 0.0021 **31.** 0.432
33. -2.88 **35.** 1.911 **37.** 0.351
39. 0.00864 **41.** 28.95 in. of
mercury **43.** -8.904 **45.** -0.027
47. 1,224.1152 **53.** 11.3 mi
55. $5 \cdot 7$ **57.** 2^6 **59.** 8.57 **61.** -3.74
63. 19.71 **65.** -68.868

3-4 Exercises

1. 0.9 **3.** 4.6 **5.** -3.2 **7.** 2.5
9. -16 **11.** -4.8 **13.** 28 mi/gal
15. -0.12 **17.** -14 **19.** 4.2
21. 47.5 **23.** 4 **25.** -48.75
27. 2.4 min **29.** 22.5 **31.** -0.4
33. 25 **35.** 18 **37.** 6.4
39. 2,500 years **41.** 18.47 million
visits **45.** C **47.** 9.93 **49.** 9 **51.** 8
53. 5 **55.** 2.116 **57.** 18.2055

3-5 Exercises

1. $w = 7$ **3.** $k = 24.09$ **5.** $b = 5.04$
7. $t = 9$ **9.** $4.25 **11.** $c = 44.56$
13. $a = 5.08$ **15.** $p = -53.21$
17. $z = 16$ **19.** $w = 11.76$
21. $a = -74.305$ **23.** $7.50
25. $n = -4.92$ **27.** $r = 0.72$
29. $m = -0.15$ **31.** $k = 0.9$
33. $t = 0.936$ **35.** $v = -2$
37. $n = 12.254$ **39.** $j = 11.107$
41. $g = 0.5$ **43.** $171
45a. 148.1 million **b.** between
English and Italian **49.** C
53. 6.0×10^6 **55.** 1.5
57. 3 **59.** 9

3-6 Exercises

1. about 4 feet **3.** 0 **5.** 2 **7.** 3
9. 48 **11.** 1 **13.** $2\frac{1}{2}$ **15.** $\frac{1}{2}$
17. $11\frac{1}{2}$ **19.** 6 **21.** 30 **23.** 2
25. 4 **27.** $\frac{1}{2}$ **29.** 24 **31.** -8
33. 4 **35.** 11 **37.** 5 **39.** $14
41. greater **43.** 2 m **47.** D
49. $x = 27$ **51.** $m = 13$ **53.** $x = 6.5$
55. $q = -19.44$

3-7 Exercises

1. $\frac{1}{3}$ **3.** $\frac{3}{7}$ **5.** $\frac{1}{2}$ **7.** $\frac{19}{24}$ **9.** $\frac{1}{12}$ **11.** $\frac{1}{2}$
13. $\frac{3}{5}$ **15.** $\frac{2}{3}$ **17.** $\frac{1}{5}$ **19.** $\frac{1}{4}$ **21.** $\frac{3}{4}$
23. $-\frac{1}{6}$ **25.** $\frac{8}{15}$ **27.** $\frac{1}{6}$ mi **29.** $\frac{13}{18}$
31. $\frac{4}{5}$ **33.** $-\frac{1}{12}$ **35.** $\frac{1}{2}$ **37.** $-\frac{1}{20}$
39. $\frac{14}{15}$ **41.** $\frac{41}{63}$ **43.** $\frac{41}{45}$ **45.** 0
47. $\frac{91}{121}$ **49.** $\frac{5}{6}$ hour **51.** $\frac{13}{24}$ mi
53. Cai **55.** $\frac{3}{8}$ lb of cashews
61. 0.1 **63.** 6 **67.** $2\frac{1}{2}$

3-8 Exercises

1. $5\frac{1}{6}$ **3.** $6\frac{5}{8}$ **5.** $7\frac{3}{4}$ **7.** $5\frac{1}{3}$ **9.** $4\frac{9}{40}$
11. 15 **13.** $5\frac{2}{3}$ **15.** $6\frac{4}{5}$ **17.** $11\frac{7}{15}$
19. $\frac{6}{7}$ **21.** $5\frac{1}{4}$ **23.** $2\frac{7}{20}$ **25.** $\frac{9}{10}$
27. $15\frac{8}{15}$ **29.** $13\frac{5}{6}$ **31.** $6\frac{5}{24}$ **33.** $\frac{5}{6}$
35. $4\frac{1}{6}$ **37.** $10\frac{1}{24}$ **39.** < **41.** >
43. $4\frac{5}{8}$ cups **45.** $117\frac{1}{3}$ mi
47. the waterfall trail **51.** D
53. 6 **57.** $\frac{3}{4}$ **59.** $1\frac{5}{36}$

3-9 Exercises

1. -6 3. $-\frac{1}{6}$ 5. 14 7. $2\frac{1}{3}$
9. $2\frac{1}{2}$ hr 11. $\frac{1}{2}$ 13. 4 15. $\frac{1}{4}$
17. $-\frac{5}{9}$ 19. $\frac{222}{5}$ 21. $17\frac{1}{2}$ 23. $\frac{7}{3}$
25. $8\frac{1}{4}$ 27. $1\frac{2}{3}$ tsp 29. $\frac{155}{42}$ 31. $\frac{1}{3}$
33. $-\frac{1}{6}$ 35. $\frac{1}{12}$ 37. $\frac{1}{5}$ 39. $\frac{7}{10}$
41. $\frac{1}{5}$ 43. 1 45. 3 47. 5 49. 6
51. 1 53. $2\frac{1}{12}$ lb 55. $11\frac{1}{3}$ mi
59. B 61. $-7, -3, 0, 4, 5$
63. $-9, -4, -1, 1, 9$ 65. $1\frac{5}{12}$
67. $7\frac{11}{24}$

3-10 Exercises

1. 18 3. $\frac{3}{32}$ 5. $\frac{1}{4}$ 7. 2 9. 3 capes
11. 18 13. $4\frac{3}{8}$ 15. $\frac{1}{27}$ 17. -40
19. $\frac{5}{14}$ 21. -14 23. $\frac{88}{7}$ 25. $9\frac{3}{5}$
27. 6 pieces 29. -2 31. $-\frac{16}{25}$
33. $\frac{21}{2}$ 35. $\frac{1}{3}$ 37. -1 43. 87
hamburger patties 47. 11 in.
51. G 53. 30 55. 36 57. $-\frac{1}{12}$
59. $\frac{99}{28}$

3-11 Exercises

1. $a = \frac{3}{4}$ 3. $p = \frac{3}{2}$ 5. $r = \frac{9}{10}$
7. $1\frac{1}{8}$ c 9. $t = \frac{5}{8}$ 11. $x = \frac{53}{24}$
13. $y = \frac{7}{60}$ 15. $w = \frac{1}{2}$ 17. $z = \frac{1}{12}$
19. $n = 1\frac{23}{25}$ 21. $t = \frac{1}{4}$ 23. $w = 6$
25. $x = \frac{3}{5}$ 27. $n = \frac{12}{5}$ 29. $y = \frac{1}{2}$
31. $r = \frac{1}{77}$ 33. $h = -\frac{1}{2}$ 35. $v = \frac{3}{4}$
37. $d = 14\frac{17}{40}$ 39. $11\frac{3}{16}$ lb
41. 15 million species
43. 48 stories 49. G
51. $3, 3.02, 3\frac{2}{10}, 3.25$ 53. -1
55. 21

Chapter 3 Study Guide: Review

1. compatible numbers
2. reciprocals 3. 110 4. 5 5. 75
6. 4 7. about 20 weeks 8. 27.88
9. -51.2 10. 6.22 11. 52.902
12. 14.095 13. 35.88 14. 3.5
15. -38.7 16. 40.495 17. 60.282
18. 77.348 19. -18.81 20. $38.08
21. 5 22. -40 23. 800 24. -5

25. -6.24 26. 340 27. 4.5
28. -1.09 29. -15.4 30. -500
31. 2 32. 4 33. 193.0175 mi/h
34. $x = -10.44$ 38. $s = 107$
36. $n = 0.007$ 37. $k = 8.64$
38. $e = -5.05$ 39. $w = -3.08$
40. 56 hours 41. 24 42. -8
43. 3 44. 1 45. 30 46. 3
47. about $5\frac{1}{2}$ laps 48. $\frac{5}{12}$ 49. $\frac{17}{20}$
50. $\frac{5}{11}$ 51. $\frac{1}{9}$ 52. $6\frac{5}{24}$ 53. $3\frac{1}{3}$
54. $6\frac{1}{4}$ 55. $1\frac{5}{12}$ 56. $7\frac{1}{2}$ 57. $1\frac{21}{25}$
58. $17\frac{17}{63}$ 59. $6\frac{1}{4}$ 60. $\frac{4}{75}$ 61. $\frac{2}{15}$
62. 1 63. $1\frac{11}{12}$ 64. 28 slices
65. $1\frac{2}{3}$ 66. $\frac{1}{15}$ 67. $1\frac{5}{7}$ 68. $\frac{13}{28}$
69. $1\frac{3}{4}$ cups

Chapter 4

4-1 Exercises

1. $\frac{10}{3}$, 10 to 3, 10:3 3. $\frac{3}{1}$ or 3 to 1
or 3:1 5. $\frac{25}{30}$, 25 to 30, 25:30, or $\frac{5}{6}$,
5 to 6, 5:6 7. $\frac{30}{15}$, 30 to 15, 30:15,
or $\frac{2}{1}$, 2 to 1, 2:1 9. $\frac{4}{1}$ or 4 to 1 or 4:1
11. group 1 15. 3:1, $\frac{3}{1}$, 3 to 1
17. 3:2, $\frac{3}{2}$, 3 to 2 19. greater than
21. B 23. $x = -6.7$ 25. $v = 8.5$

4-2 Exercises

1. 83.5 mL per min 3. 458 mi/h
5. $7.75 per h 7. about 74.63 mi/h
9. 3 runs per game 11. $335
per mo 13. 18.83 mi per gal
15. $5.75 per h 17. 122 mi per trip
19. 0.04 mi per min
21. $\frac{1,026 \text{ students}}{38 \text{ classes}}$; 27 students
per class 23. $0.06, $0.07; $\frac{$2.52}{42 \text{ oz}}$ is
the better buy. 27. 289, 328, 609
(France, Poland, Germany)
31. D 33. 11.688 35. -1.3455

4-3 Exercises

1. yes 3. yes 5. yes 7. no 13. no
15. no 17. no 19. no 29. 3, 24, 15
39a. $\frac{1 \text{ can}}{4 \text{ hours}}$ b. No, 1:4 = x:2,080;
the class recycled 520 cans.
43a. 8:5 b. Mill Pond and

Clear Pond 49. H 51. -3.75
53. -76.25 55. $<$ 57. $<$

4-4 Exercises

1. $x = 60$ 3. $m = 16.4$ 5. 3 lb
7. $h = 144$ 9. $v = 336$ 11. $t = 36$
13. $n = 22\frac{2}{5}$ 15. 227 grams
29. about 23 dimes
31. 22 counselors 33. $\frac{4}{10} = \frac{6}{15}$
35. $\frac{3}{75} = \frac{4}{100}$ 37. $\frac{5}{6} = \frac{90}{108}$
39. 105 oxygen atoms 45. $\frac{4}{6}$
47. -20 49. 64 mi/h
51. $9.50/h

4-5 Exercises

1. feet 3. tons 5. 48 qt 7. 4.5 lb
9. 27 fl oz 11. inches 13. feet
15. 3 mi 17. 75 in. 19. $>$ 21. $<$
23. $>$ 25. $<$ 27. $<$ 29. 2.4 mi
31. 8 c, 5 qt, 12 pt, 2 gal
33. 12,000 ft, 2.5 mi, 5,000 yd
35. 9.5 yd, 380 in., 32.5 ft
37. 46,145 yd 43. A 45. $139
47. no 49. no

4-6 Exercises

1. kilograms 3. centimeters
5. 12,000 g 7. 0.07 cm 9. Sunday
11. milligrams 13. centimeters
15. 0.0014 km 17. 3,550 mm
19. 199.5 cm 21. 2,050,000 L
23. 0.37 cm 25. $=$ 27. $<$ 29. $<$
31. Mona Lisa; 4 cm 33. 1,200 mm;
130 cm; 1.5 m 35. 0.0008 kg;
1,000 mg; 9.03 g 37. Red Bat
39. 1 kg 43. C 45. 81 47. 128
49. 81 51. $a = 73.36$
53. $n = 13.5$

4-7 Exercises

1. 0.694 km/s 3. ≈ 4.02 km
5. 0.075 page/min 7. ≈ 2.7 mi
9. 360 tickets 11. 720 calls
13. ≈ 28.3 kg/ft^3 15. ≈ 11.57 days
17. 1.88 km/min 19. C 23. A
27. 10 29. 9 31. $1\frac{5}{6}$

4-8 Exercises

1. similar **3.** similar **5.** not similar
7. similar **9.** no **11.** similar
13. yes **15.** yes **17.** no **19.** no
23. C **25.** $-10\frac{1}{2}$ **27.** $\frac{3}{2}$

4-9 Exercises

1. $a = 22.5$ cm; $b = 89°$
3. 28 ft **5.** $x = 13.5$ in.;
$n = 40°$ **7.** 249.18 in. **9.** 21 m
15. B **17.** $18y$ **19.** $12 \div z$
21. inches

4-10 Exercises

1. $\frac{1}{14}$ **3.** 67.2 cm tall, 40 cm wide
5. $\frac{1}{15}$ **7.** 135 in. **9.** 16 in.
11. 75 cm; 141 cm; 240 cm
13. 2 in. **15.** about 25 mi
17. 1 mi:0.25 ft or 1 ft:4 mi
19. B **21.** 0.054, 0.41, $\frac{4}{7}$
23. $\frac{7}{11}$, 0.7, $\frac{7}{9}$ **25.** 0.064 **27.** 2.7

Chapter 4 Study Guide: Review

1. similar **2.** ratio; rate
3. scale factor **4.** $\frac{7}{15}$, 7 to 15, 7:15
5. red to blue **6.** 6 ft/s
7. 109 mi/h **8.** $2.24, about
$2.14; \frac{\$32.05}{15 \text{ gal}}$ **9.** $32/g, $35/g; $\frac{\$160}{5 \text{ g}}$
10. $7.90/h **11.** no **12.** no
13. yes **14.** Possible answer:
$\frac{10}{12} = \frac{30}{36}$ **15.** Possible answer:
$\frac{45}{50} = \frac{90}{100}$ **16.** Possible answer:
$\frac{9}{15} = \frac{27}{45}$ **17.** $n = 2$ **18.** $a = 6$
19. $b = 4$ **20.** $x = 66$ **21.** $y = 10$
22. $w = 20$ **23.** 2 pints **24.** 3,000
pounds **25.** 115 in., or 9 ft, 7 in.
27. 0.72 g **28.** 5,300 m **29.** 6 mm
30. 13.5 lb/mo **31.** 14 mi/h
32. 0.8 mi/min **33.** not similar
34. similar **35.** $x = 100$ ft; $a = 84°$
36. 8 cm **37.** about 8 ft
38. 12.1 in. **39.** 163.4 mi

Chapter 5

5-1 Exercises

1. II **3.** III
5, 7.

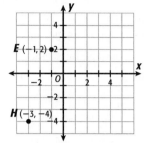

9. $(6, -3)$ **11.** $(-4, 0)$ **13.** I **15.** IV
17, 19.

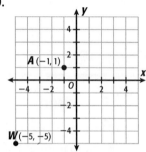

21. $(-4, 4)$ **23.** $(-5, -4)$ **25.** $(5, 6)$
27. triangle; Quadrants I and II

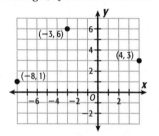

29. III
31. IV **33.** $(12, 7)$ **39.** B **41.** -6
43. -24 **45.** $6\frac{2}{5}$ **47.** $1\frac{2}{5}$

5-2 Exercises

1. A **3.** B
7.

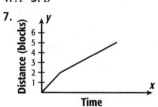

9. One of the mothers is the
daughter of the other mother.
15. 3 **17.** 0 **19.** 3 **21.** 3
23. 8.1 **25.** -2.08

5-3 Exercises

1. $-5, 1, 3$ **3.** 50, 2, 18
5.

x	-1	0	1	2
y	3	2	3	6

7. $-7, -1, 8$
9.

x	-1	0	1	2
y	$-\frac{1}{2}$	0	$\frac{1}{2}$	1

11a. $y = 11.66 - x$ **17.** J
19. -1 **21.** $x = 6$ **23.** $y = 4\frac{1}{2}$

5-4 Exercises

1. arithmetic **3.** $y = 3n$
5. $y = n - 1$ **7.** $y = 195n$
9. arithmetic **11.** $y = 7n$
13. $y = 20n$ **15.** $y = n + 0.5$
17. multiply 35 by n
19. add $\frac{1}{2}$ to n **21.** divide n by 3
23. $y = n - 0.5$ **25.** $y = 3n + 2$
27. $y = 2n - 1$ **29.** $y = 2^n$
35. 10,000,000 **37.** 729 **39.** 200
41. 105

5-5 Exercises

1.

Input	Rule	Output	Ordered Pair
x	$x + 3$	y	(x, y)
-2	$-2 + 3$	1	$(-2, 1)$
0	$0 + 3$	3	$(0, 3)$
2	$2 + 3$	5	$(2, 5)$

3. $y = 750x$
5.

Input	Rule	Output	Ordered Pair
x	$x - 1$	y	(x, y)
3	$3 - 1$	2	$(3, 2)$
4	$4 - 1$	3	$(4, 3)$
5	$5 - 1$	4	$(5, 4)$

7.

Input	Rule	Output	Ordered Pair
x	$2x + 3$	y	(x, y)
-2	$2(-2) + 3$	-1	$(-2, -1)$
-1	$2(-1) + 3$	1	$(-1, 1)$
0	$2(0) + 3$	3	$(0, 3)$

9. 8,100 cm **11a.** about 15 ppm
15. B **19.** $y = 2n - 6$

5-5 Extension

1. nonlinear **3.** nonlinear
5. nonlinear

5-6 Exercises

1. positive; 1

3.
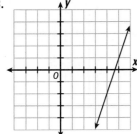

5.
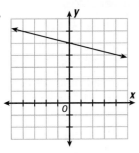

7. constant **9.** constant
11. negative; −3

13.
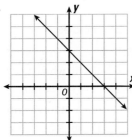

15.
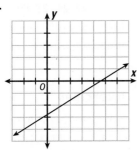

17. constant **19.** variable
21. −7 **23.** −3 **25.** $\frac{3}{2}$
29. The y-values decrease.
33. B **37.** 125 **39.** 100,000
41. add $\frac{3}{2}$ to n; $\frac{9}{2}$, 6, $\frac{15}{2}$

5-7 Exercises

1. x-int. = 6, y-int. = −4

3.
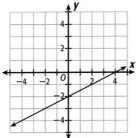

5.
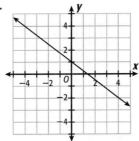

7. $y = 3x - 1$ **9.** y-int. = 280; total distance in feet that Pete has to walk; x-int. = 4; time in minutes that it takes Pete to walk the 280 ft
11. x-int. = 3, y-int. = 5

13.
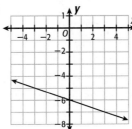

15.
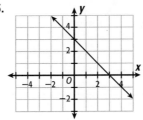

17.
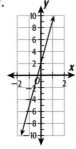

19.
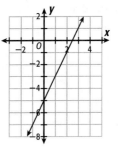

21. $y = 3x + 1$
23. $y = -700x + 35,000$
25. $y = -7x + 5$ **27.** $y = 4x + 2$
29. $y = -x$ **31.** $y = -\frac{3}{4}x - 3$;
$m = -\frac{3}{4}$, x-int. = −4, y-int. = −3
33. $y = -x + 4$; $m = -1$,
x-int. = 4, y-int. = 4
35. $y = 15x - 30$; $m = -15$,
x-int. = 2, y-int. = −30
37. $y = -x$; $m = -1$, x-int. = 0,
y-int. = 0 **39.** $y = -2.75x + 30$
45. D **47.** 50 mi/h

5-8 Exercises

1. no **3.** yes; $k = \frac{1}{4}$ **5.** no **7.** no
9a. $y = 4x$ **c.** 80 gal **11.** yes;
$k = \frac{2}{3}$ **13.** no **15.** yes, $k = 2$,
$y = 2x$ **17.** no **19.** $y = \frac{2}{7}x$
21. $y = 2x$ **23.** $y = 40$ **25.** yes;
the ratio of total pay y to number of hours worked x, is always constant, so $y = kx$ where k is the rate of pay per hour **27.** 1,800 m
33. $y = 0.65x$; \$13.65 **35.** $16\frac{1}{3}$
37. $7\frac{33}{40}$

5-8 Extension

1. direct **3.** $y = 5$

Chapter 5 Study Guide: Review

1. sequence **2.** function
3. linear function

4–7.
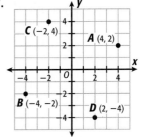

8. $(2, -1)$, IV **9.** $(-2, 3)$, II

10. $(1, 0)$ **11.** $(-4, -2)$

12.

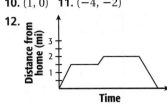

13.

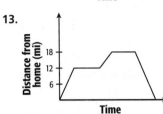

14.

Input	Rule	Output
x	$x^2 - 1$	y
-2	$(-2)^2 - 1$	3
3	$(3)^2 - 1$	8
5	$(5)^2 - 1$	24

15. $y = 25n$ **16.** $y = n - 4$

17. $y = 3n - 7$ **18.** $y = 2n + 2$

19.

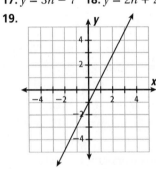

20.

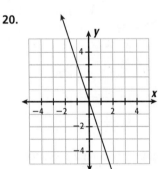

21.

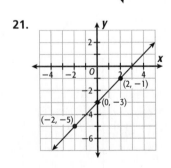

22.

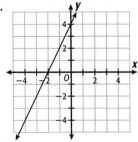

23.

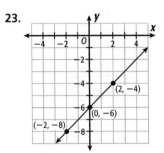

24.

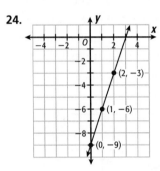

25. variable **26.** constant

27. $y = x + 3$

28.

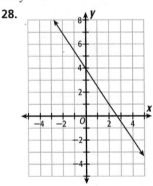

29. yes; $k = 18$; $k = 18x$ **30.** no

Chapter 6

6-1 **Exercises**

1. 79% **3.** 50% **5.** $\frac{41}{50}$ **7.** $\frac{19}{50}$ **9.** 0.22

11. 0.0807 **13.** 0.11 **15.** 45%

17. $\frac{11}{20}$ **19.** $\frac{83}{100}$ **21.** $\frac{81}{100}$ **23.** 0.098

25. 0.663 **27.** $\frac{27}{1,000}$, 0.027 **29.** $\frac{11}{25}$,

0.44 **31.** $\frac{21}{100}$, 0.105 **33.** < **35.** <

41. Brad **47.** 12 **49.** $3\frac{1}{2}$

50–53.

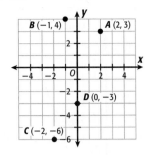

6-2 **Exercises**

1. 60% **3.** 54.4% **5.** 8.7%

7. 12% **9.** 17.5% **11.** 50%, $\frac{11}{20}$, $0.\overline{5}$

13. $-\frac{1}{10}$, 1%, 10% **15.** $\frac{35}{54}$, $0.\overline{6}$, 72%

17. mental math; 40% **19.** 83%

21. 8.1% **23.** 75% **25.** 37.5%

27. 28% **29.** -0.7, $-\frac{2}{3}$, 7%

31. $-\frac{1}{9}$, -0.1, 1% **33.** $-\frac{1}{6}$, -0.01,

2% **35.** pencil and paper; 20%

37. > **39.** < **41.** 1% **45.** $\approx 33.3\%$

49. D **54.** 0.4 m

6-3 **Exercises**

1. 30 **3.** 5 **5.** Yes; 35% of $43.99

is close to $\frac{1}{3}$ of $45, which is

$15. Since $45 − $15 = $30,

Darden will have enough money.

7. 8 **9.** 7.7 **11.** 26 **13.** 70 **15.** 216

17. 13 **19.** Fancy Feet **21.** 24

23. 12 **25.** 12 **27.** 24 **29.** 60

31. 3 **33.** 72 **35.** 15 **37.** about

26 oz **39.** about 2% more **49.** 1.2

51. 0.375

6-4 **Exercises**

1. 24 **3.** 20 **5.** 8 **7.** 423 **9.** 171

students **11.** 11.2 **13.** 3,540

15. 0.04 **17.** 18 **19.** 13 **21.** 1.74

23. 39.6 **25.** 12.4 **27.** 6 **29.** 4.5

31. 11.75 **33.** 5,125 **35.** 80

37. 120 **39.** 0.6 **41.** 4.2

43. $4.80 **45.** 2.25 g **47.** 0.98

53. C **55.** $1.75 per lb **57.** 1.25%

59. 38.9% **61.** 40.7%

6-5 **Exercises**

1. 25% **3.** 60 **5.** 18% **7.** 50 **9.** 8%

11. $33\frac{1}{3}$% **13.** 300% **15.** 225

17. 100% **19.** 30 **21.** 22 **23.** 55.6%

25. 68.8 **27.** 77.5 **29.** 158.3
31. 5% **35.** 45 pieces **39.** She
needs to make more than $22,917
per month in sales. **41.** 75
43. 3.56 **45.** 3.2 **47.** 6.6 **49.** 66.64

6-6 Exercises

1. 28% **3.** 16.1% **5.** $34.39
7. 37.5% **9.** 22.2% **11.** $55.25
13. 100% **15.** 43.6% **17.** 30
19. 56.25 gal **21.** $48.25
23a. $41,500 **b.** $17,845 **c.** 80.7%
25. about 8,506 trillion Btu **27.** A
29. $\frac{29}{9}$ **31.** $\frac{29}{4}$ **33.** $\frac{73}{3}$ **35.** 3.25 lb

6-7 Exercises

1. $I = 24 **3.** $P = 400 **5.** just over
4 yr **7.** $I = $3,240$ **9.** $P = $2,200$
11. $r = 11\%$ **13.** almost 9 yr
15. $5,200 **17.** $212.75 **19.** 20
yr **21.** $4 **23.** high yield CD: gain
$606; Dow Jones: loss $684; a
difference of $1,290 **29.** just over
$2\frac{1}{2}$yr **31.** 29.9% **33.** 93.2%

**Chapter 6 Study Guide:
Review**

1. interest; simple interest;
principal **2.** percent of increase
3. percent of decrease **4.** percent
5. $\frac{39}{50}$, 0.78 **6.** $\frac{2}{5}$, 0.40 **7.** $\frac{1}{20}$, 0.05
8. $\frac{4}{25}$, 0.16 **9.** $\frac{13}{20}$, 0.65 **10.** $\frac{89}{100}$, 0.89
11. 60% **12.** 16.7% **13.** 9%
14. 80% **15.** 66.7% **16.** 0.56%
17. −2.6, 30%, $0.\overline{33}$, $2\frac{3}{5}$
18. Possible answer: 8
19. Possible answer: 90
20. Possible answer: 24
21. Possible answer: 32
22. Possible answer: 40
23. Possible answer: 3
24. Possible answer: $3 **25.** 5%
26. 68 **27.** 24 **28.** 4.41 **29.** 120
30. 27.3 **31.** 54 **32.** about 474
33. 125 **34.** 8% **35.** 12 **36.** 37.5%
37. 8 **38.** ≈27.8% **39.** 7.96%
40. about $125 **41.** 50%
42. 14.3% **43.** 30% **44.** 83.1%
45. 23.1% **46.** 75% **47.** $208.25

48. 82.8% **49.** $I = 15
50. $t = 3$ years **51.** $I = 243
52. $r = 3.9\%$ **53.** $P = $2,300$
54. 7 years **55.** about 9 years,
3 months

Chapter 7

7-1 Exercises

1. 6 **3.** 15 **5.** 3 **7.** 4; 31 **9.** B
11. Paraguay; Colombia and
Ecuador **19.** $8.50 per hour
21. 16 points per game

7-2 Exercises

1. 20; 20; 5 and 20; 30 **3.** median
5. 83.3; 88; 88; 28 **7.** 4.3; 4.4; 4.4
and 6.2; 4.2 **9.** mean and median
11. 151 **13.** 9; 8; 12 **15.** 22.5, 23.5,
14 **21.** J

7-3 Exercises

1. grapes **3.** about 15 pounds
5.

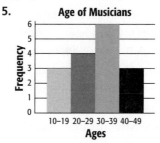

Age of Musicians

7. about 27 inches
9.

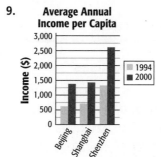

Average Annual Income per Capita

11.

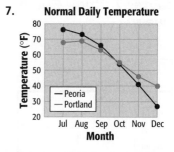

Elections of 1896 and 1900

17. 2000 **19.** no **21.** yes
23. 23.5; 23.5; 15; 19

7-4 Exercises

1. outdoor **3.** $50,000 **5.** circle
graph **7.** 30% **9.** circle graph
11. Asia, Africa, North America,
South America, Antarctica,
Europe, Australia **13.** about 25%
19. about 150 **21.** > **23.** =

7-5 Exercises

1. The range is 16, the interquartile
range is 11, the lower quartile is
35 and the upper quartile is 36.
3. airplane B **5.** The range is 16,
the interquartile is 12, the lower
quartile is 73, and the upper
quartile is 85. **7.** city A **11.** the
range **19.** 15 **21.** $3.75

7-6 Exercises

1. 1990–1995
3.

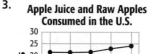

Apple Juice and Raw Apples Consumed in the U.S.

5. 1990–1995
7.

Normal Daily Temperature

9b. about 3,400 **15.** about $19
17. 136% **19.** 55%

7-7 Exercises

1. bar graph **3.** line graph
5. line plot or stem-and-leaf plot
7. bar graph **17.** circle graph
19. 90% **21.** 40.6%

7-8 Exercises

1. Daria's method **3.** biased
5. Vonneta's method **7.** not biased
9. entire population **11.** entire
population **13.** yes **17.** B
19. 0.52 **21.** 1.1 **23.** 5.5 **25.** 0.41

7-9 Exercises

1. The heart rate decreases as the
weight increases. **3.** positive
correlation **5.** The capacity
increases with time. **7.** negative
correlation **9.** no correlation
11. no correlation **17.** 75.6 **19.** 3.5

7-10 Exercises

1. graph A **3.** The vertical axis
does not begin with zero, so
differences in scales appear
greater. **5.** The scale of the graph
is not divided into equal intervals,
so differences in sales appear less
than they actually are. **7.** The
graphs do not use the same scale,
so it looks as though September
had fewer sales than October,
which is not true; redraw the
graphs using the same scale.
15. $x = \frac{1}{6}$ **17.** $x = -\frac{11}{24}$
19. negative correlation

Chapter 7 Study Guide: Review

1. population; sample **2.** mean
3.

	Frequency	Cumulative Frequency
0–9	1	1
10–19	3	4
20–29	3	7
30–39	2	9

4.

Stems	Leaves
0	8
1	4 6 9
2	5 7 9
3	2 5

Key: 1|4 means 14

5.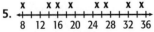

6. 302; 311.5; 233 and 324; 166
7. 43; 46; none; 25 **8.** when the
data set has an outlier
9.

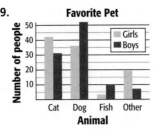

10. yellow **11.** 35 people
12. circle graph
13.

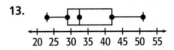

14. 13
15.

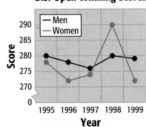

16. line graph **17.** bar graph
18. 2,500 is a reasonable estimate
based on the data. **19.** not biased;
random sample **20.** biased; it
is likely that not all teenagers
like the same type of clothing
21. positive correlation **22.** The
vertical axis is broken.

Chapter 8

8-1 Exercises

1. Q, R, S **3.** plane QRS **5.** $\overline{QU}$,
$\overline{RU}$, $\overline{SU}$ **7.** D, E, F **9.** plane DEF
11. $\overline{DE}, \overline{EF}, \overline{DF}$ **21.** C **23.** 16
25. -7 **27.** 29.4% **29.** 83.3%

8-2 Exercises

1. right **3.** straight
5. complementary
7. complementary **9.** 61° **11.** right
13. complementary
15. supplementary **17.** 95°
19. supplementary; 152°

21. supplementary; 46° **23a.** right
angle **b.** about 39° N, 77° W **27.** C
29. 5.6; 6; 6; 5 **31.** 38; 38; 41; 34

8-3 Exercises

1. parallel **3.** perpendicular
5. 115° **7.** skew **9.** parallel
11. 30° **13.** parallel
15. supplementary; adjacent
17. 45° **19.** sometimes **21.** always
23a. They are perpendicular.
b. transversal **c.** They are
corresponding angles. **29.** F
31. -1.75 **33.** complementary;
31° **35.** complementary; 65°

8-4 Exercises

1. $\overline{OQ}, \overline{OR}, \overline{OS}, \overline{OT}$ **3.** $\overline{RT}, \overline{RS}, \overline{ST}$,
$\overline{TQ}$ **5.** $\overline{CA}, \overline{CB}, \overline{CD}, \overline{CE}, \overline{CF}$ **7.** $\overline{GB}$,
$\overline{BF}, \overline{DE}, \overline{FE}, \overline{AE}$ **9.** 10 cm **11.** 151.2°
13. 60° **17.** D **19.** 45 **21.** 1
23. E, F, H, M, N, Z

8-5 Exercises

1. no **3.** no **5.** quadrilateral
7. square **9.** triangle **11.** no
13. pentagon **15.** heptagon
17. pentagon **21.** 16-gon **23.** A
25. $y = 3n + 1$ **27.** $y = n + 1.3$
29. 20.3 **31.** 25.9%

8-6 Exercises

1. isosceles right **3.** isosceles acute
5. scalene right **7.** equilateral
acute **9.** scalene **11.** isosceles
13. right **15.** 8 in., isosceles
17. isosceles acute **19.** scalene
right **21.** isosceles triangle
23. D **27.** H **29.** heptagon
31. octagon

8-7 Exercises

1. parallelogram **3.** parallelogram,
rhombus; rhombus **5.** not
possible **7.** parallelogram;
parallelogram **9.** parallelogram,
rhombus; rhombus
11. parallelogram, rectangle;
rectangle

13.

15. parallelogram, rectangle, rhombus, square

17. parallelogram, rhombus, rectangle, square **19.** true **21.** true

23. false **25.** 2 triangles, 1 hexagon, and 2 trapezoids **31.** C

33.

Stems	Leaves
1	8
2	8
3	3, 4
4	0, 3, 4, 9
5	7, 7

35. acute **37.** obtuse

8-8 Exercises

1. 77° **3.** 55° **5.** 110° **7.** 720°
9. 360° **11.** 37° **13.** 88° **15.** 101°
17. 1,080° **19.** 38° **21.** 99°; obtuse
23. 90°; right **25.** 45°, 45°, 90°
31. 80° **33.** $p = 9$ **35.** $n = 2.5$
37. rhombus, square

8-9 Exercises

1. the triangles on the game board and the holes on the game board **3.** 2 triangles; 2 rectangles; 2 green pentagons **5.** no **7.** 2.5
9. the triangles in the kite's design
11. no **13.** 112°; 8 cm **15.** the lengths of all the sides **17.** the lengths of adjacent sides in each rectangle **19.** 40 m **25.** G
27, 29.

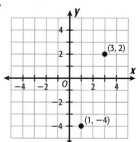

31. 25°; obtuse **33.** 90°; right

8-10 Exercises

1. rotation

3.

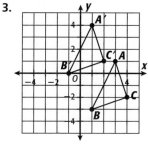

$L'(-2, 3)$, $M'(-1, -2)$, $N'(2, 1)$, $O'(-3, 1)$

5.

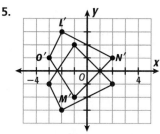

$X'(-2, -1)$, $Y'(-2, -4)$, $Z'(-6, 2)$
7. $L'(0, 0)$, $M'(3, 0)$, $N'(-1, -4)$
9. translation **13.** $A'(0, -1)$, $B'(2, -2)$, $C'(3, 0)$, $D'(1, 1)$ **17.** A
19. 38 **21.** 3 m

8-10 Extension

1. no

3.

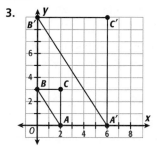

5.

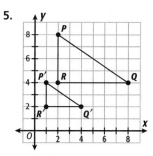

8-11 Exercises

1. The figure has 5 lines of symmetry. **3.** The figure has 4 lines of symmetry. **5.** none **7.** 6 times
9. 3 times **11.** The figure has 6 lines of symmetry. **13.** none
15. The flag has 2 lines of symmetry. **17.** 8 times **19.** regular nonagon **21.** yes; yes **27.** 8
29. $J'(1, -3)$, $K'(3, -3)$, and $L'(3, -6)$

Chapter 8 Study Guide: Review

1. acute or isosceles **2.** parallel lines **3.** chord **4.** D, E, F **5.** $\overleftrightarrow{DF}$
6. plane DEF **7.** $\overrightarrow{ED}$, $\overrightarrow{FD}$, $\overrightarrow{DF}$
8. $\overline{DE}$, $\overline{DF}$, $\overline{EF}$ **9.** acute
10. straight **11.** skew **12.** parallel
13. 74° **14.** 106° **15.** 106° **16.** 74°
17. $\overline{HF}$, $\overline{FI}$, $\overline{FG}$ **18.** $\overline{GI}$
19. $\overline{HI}$, $\overline{GI}$, $\overline{GJ}$, $\overline{JI}$ **20.** Yes; it is a square since all sides are congruent and all angles are congruent.
21. No; all sides are not congruent.
22. equilateral acute **23.** scalene right **24.** parallelogram, rhombus; rhombus
25. parallelogram, rectangle; rectangle **26.** 53° **27.** 101°
28. $x = 133°$; $z = 10$ cm
29.

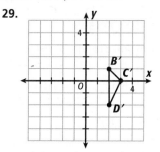

$B'(2, 1)$, $C'(3, 0)$, $D'(2, -2)$
30. 1 vertical line through the center of the flag

Chapter 9

9-1 Exercises

1. 5,281 yd **3.** 205.5 lb **5.** $2\frac{1}{2}$ in.; $2\frac{1}{2}$ in.; $2\frac{3}{8}$ in. **7.** 1.2 mm **9.** $5\frac{1}{4}$ ft

11. 5 in.; $5\frac{1}{4}$ in.; $5\frac{2}{8}$ in. $= 5\frac{1}{4}$ in.
13. about $6\frac{1}{2}$ ft **15.** oz
17. decimeters **19.** about 105°
21. mL **27.** D **29.** no correlation
31. yes **33.** yes

9-2 Exercises

1. 18 m **3.** 32 ft **5.** 20 m **7.** 37.7 m
9. 132 in. **11.** 48 cm **13.** 44 m
15. 8 ft **17.** 110 cm **19.** 32.0 in.
21. 2.8 m; 5.7 m **23.** 5.3 in.; 33.3 in.
25. 16 strands **27.** 96 ft **33.** 28 ft
35. 50.7 **37.** 21 mm **39.** 37.0 g

9-3 Exercises

1. 33.6 ft^2 **3.** 147.6 cm^2 **5.** 48 in^2
7. 28.6 m^2 **9.** 84 ft^2 **11.** 107.52 in^2
13. 6 m^2 **15.** 31.98 cm^2 **17.** 72 yd^2
19. 14 units^2 **21a.** 212 cm;
2,688 cm^2 **b.** 4,640 cm^2 **23.** C
29. obtuse **31.** right **33.** 20 m
35. $12\frac{7}{20}$ ft

9-4 Exercises

1. 28 units **3.** 39.2 units^2 **5.** 64 m^2
7. 45,540 mi^2 **9.** 7.5 units^2
11. 330 yd^2 **13.** 22.5 cm^2
15. 4.5 cm **17.** 22 in.
19. 15 units^2 **21.** 12 units^2
23. 1,282 mi; 100,740 mi^2 **27.** A
29. 90° **31.** 49° **33.** 270 ft^2

9-5 Exercises

1. 78.5 in^2 **3.** 314 yd^2 **5.** 154 in^2
7. 28.3 in **9.** 32.2 yd^2 **11.** 616 cm^2
13. 17,662.5 mi^2 **15.** 28.3 cm^2
17. 56.5 in.; 254.3 in^2 **19.** 40.2 cm;
128.6 cm^2 **21.** $r = 1$ ft
23a. 113 mi^2 **b.** 141 mi^2 **29.** A
31. 135° **33.** 45° **35.** 14 units^2

9-6 Exercises

1. 29 ft^2 **3.** 224 ft^2 **5.** 38 ft^2
7. 25 ft^2 **9.** 84.56 m^2 **11.** 46 cm^2
13. 30 ft^2; 30 ft **15.** 255.25 m^2;
65.7 m **17.** 10 **23.** 240 **25.** 44°
27. 64.5° **29.** 23.7 cm^2 **31.** 95.0 ft^2

9-7 Exercises

1. 16 **3.** 81 **5.** 20 **7.** 12 **9.** 4
11. 9 **13.** 11 mi **15.** 256 **17.** 121
19. 4 **21.** 21 **23.** 6 **25.** 10 **27.** 2
29. 12 **31.** 17 **33.** 26 **35.** 6.6
37. 9.3 **39.** 19.5 **41.** 14.2
45. 87.92 yd **47.** 1 in. **49.** $\sqrt{25}$,
$5\frac{2}{3}$, 7.15, $\frac{29}{4}$, 3^2 **51.** 151 km **57.** F
59. equilateral **61.** 69.1 in;
379.9 in^2 **63.** 18.8 ft; 28.3 ft^2

9-7 Extension

1. irrational **3.** rational
5. rational **7.** rational
9. irrational **11.** rational
13.

15.

17. 5 and 6 **19.** 3 and 4
21. 9 and 10 **23.** 8 and 9

9-8 Exercises

1. 20 m **3.** 24 cm **5.** 30 yd
7. 16 in. **9.** 9.4 ft **11.** 24.5 m
13. 22.5 in. **15a.** yes **b.** yes
c. no **d.** yes **17.** 19,153 m^2
19. 269.1 cubits **21.** 68.8 m **23.** 9.8
25. 90° **27.** 60° **29.** 8 **31.** 5

Chapter 9 Study Guide: Review

1. hypotenuse **2.** circumference
3. precision **4.** square root
5. 1.4 kg **6.** 703 ft **7.** $30\frac{1}{4}$ lb
8. 7.8 g **9.** 90 cm **10.** 204 qt
11. 83 m **12.** 81.4 cm **13.** 40.8 ft
14. 49.0 in. **15.** 50.74 cm^2
16. 826.2 yd^2 **17.** 72 in^2
18. 266 in^2 **19.** 108.75 cm^2
20. 50 yd^2 **21.** 2,163 in^2
22. 48 m^2 **23.** 36.3 m^2
24. 226.9 ft^2 **25.** 254.34 in^2
26. 34.31 ft^2 **27.** 21 m^2 **28.** 5
29. 10 **30.** 10 **31.** 12 **32.** 16 ft
33. 34 cm **34.** 60 ft **35.** 2 m
36. 60 mm **37.** 4.6 ft

Chapter 10

10-1 Exercises

1. pentagon; triangles; pentagonal
pyramid **3.** triangles; rectangles;
triangular prism **5.** polyhedron;
hexagonal pyramid **7.** triangle;
triangles; triangular pyramid
9. hexagon; triangles; hexagonal
pyramid **11.** not polyhedron;
cylinder **13.** square prism
15. triangular pyramid
19. rectangular pyramid
21. cylinder **23.** A **25.** 1 **27.** 2
29. 100 oz for $6.99 is better

10-1 Extension

1. D **5.** cylinder

10-2 Exercises

1. 240 in^3 **3.** 3.9375 in^3
5. 188.8 m^3 **7.** 192 ft^3
9. 13.44 in^3 **11.** 200 in^3
13. 288 m^3 **15.** 47.25 ft^3
21. $270 **23.** line graph

10-3 Exercises

1. 10 ft^3 **3.** 32 m^3 **5.** 16.7 in^3
7. 176 in^3 **9.** 1,350 mm^3
11. 2,375.3 cm^3 **13.** 46.7 ft^3
15. 16 in^3 **17a.** 3 **b.** 167.5 in^3
c. 502.4 in^3 **d.** yes
25. parallelogram, rectangle,
rhombus, square **27.** 110 ft^3

10-4 Exercises

1. 286 ft^2 **3.** 244.9 cm^2 **5.** 941 in^2
7. 132 yd^2 **9.** 188.4 cm^2
11b. 158.0 cm^2 **c.** 85.4 cm^2
17. 628 **19.** 79° **21.** 224 in^3

10-5 Exercises

1. 147 in^2 **3.** 301.44 ft^2
5. 37.05 m^2 **7.** 98.91 in^2
9. 420 ft^2 **11.** 305 ft^2
13. 108 in. **15.** 188.4 ft^2
21. 76.8 in^2 **23.** 4.5 cm **25.** 4

10-6 Exercises

1. 93.6 cm^2 **3.** 33,750 in^3
5. 223.84 in^2 **7.** 8.2 cm^3
9. 58,750 ft^2; 937,500 ft^3
13. 5,112 in^2; 22,680 in^3
15. 716 cm; 7.16 m
17. 127,426,000,000 cm^3 or
127,426 m^3 **19.** 2 **21.** no **23.** no

Chapter 10 Study Guide: Review

1. cylinder **2.** surface area
3. polyhedron **4.** cone **5.** cylinder
6. rectangular pyramid
7. triangular prism **8.** cone
9. 364 cm^3 **10.** 111.9 ft^3
11. 60 in^3 **12.** 471 cm^3 **13.** 250 m^2
14. 34 cm^2 **15.** 262.3 cm^2
16. 803.8 ft^2 **17.** 37 ft^2 **18.** 420 in^2
19. 200.96 cm^2 **20.** 703.36 in^2
21. 125.6 cm^2 **22.** 2,970 in^2
23. 4.1 ft^3 **24.** 44,416 ft^2

Chapter 11

11-1 Exercises

1. unlikely **3.** $\frac{5}{6}$ **5.** certain
7. unlikely **9.** $\frac{2}{5}$ **11.** as likely as not
13. certain **15.** not likely
17a. It is very likely. **b.** It is
impossible. **23.** $\frac{1}{2}$ **25.** $41\frac{1}{2}$ lb

11-2 Exercises

1. 70% **3.** ≈43% **5a.** $\frac{9}{14}$ **5b.** $\frac{5}{14}$
7. $\frac{16}{25}$ **9.** ≈27% **11a.** $\frac{3}{8}$ **13.** D
15. about 15.24 cm **17.** = **19.** >

11-3 Exercises

1. H1, H2, T1, T2; 4 **3.** 24 **5.** 1H,
1T, 2H, 2T, 3H, 3T, 4H, 4T; 8
7. 12 **9.** 6 **11a.** 9 outcomes
b. 6 outcomes **c.** 12 outcomes
13. 12 **17.** D **19.** 12.5% **21.** 40%
23. 704 in^3

11-4 Exercises

1. ≈17% **3.** $\frac{3}{7}$ **5.** $\frac{2}{7}$ **7.** 25% **9.** $\frac{3}{7}$
11. $\frac{1}{18}$ **13.** $\frac{1}{12}$ **15.** $\frac{1}{9}$ **17.** $\frac{2}{5}$ **19.** 0
21. $\frac{2}{5}$ **23a.** unfair **25.** 25% **29.** D
31. 57.5 in^2

11-5 Exercises

1. 183 days **3.** 9 **5.** No; it will only
snow 2 days on their vacation.
7. 324 **9.** 94 **11.** Yes; it is late
only 4% of the time. **13.** 36 **15.** 3
21. about 4,450 flights

11-6 Exercises

1. independent **3.** $\frac{1}{6}$ **5.** $\frac{3}{20}$
7. independent **9.** $\frac{1}{4}$
11. dependent **13a.** $\frac{1}{3}$ **17.** B
19. $7\frac{1}{4}$

11-7 Exercises

1. 6 **3.** 10 **5.** 10 **7.** 15 **9.** 28
11. 3 **13.** 15 **17.** 15 **19.** 6 **21.** 7
23. independent

11-8 Exercises

1. 24 **3.** 720 **5.** 6 **7.** 3,628,000
9. combinations **11.** permutations
13. $\frac{1}{4}$ **15.** 120 **17.** $5 \times 4 \times 3 = 60$
19. 13! **21.** $\frac{2}{7}$ **25.** D **27.** 18.4 in.

Chapter 11 Study Guide: Review

1. independent events
2. combination **3.** sample space
4. outcome **5.** unlikely
6. impossible **7.** 80% **8.** $\frac{4}{5}$ **9.** $\frac{2}{3}$
10. $\frac{1}{3}$ **11.** R1, R2, R3, R4, W1, W2,
W3, W4, B1, B2, B3, B4 **12.** 12
possible outcomes **13.** ≈43%
14. 12.5% **15.** about 20 yards
16. about 6 times **17.** $\frac{4}{195}$ **18.** $\frac{16}{121}$
19. 10 ways **20.** 21 committees
21. 36 combinations
22. 3,628,800 ways **23.** 720 ways
24. 120 ways **25.** 3,628,800

Chapter 12

12-1 Exercises

1. $n = 7$ **3.** $x = \frac{1}{3}$ **5.** $y = 136$
7. 12 refills **9.** $p = -12$ **11.** $d = \frac{1}{7}$
13. $y = 5$ **15.** $k = 85$ **17.** $m = -80$
19. $m = -112$ **21.** 6 more than a
number divided by 3 equals 18;
$m = 36$. **23.** 2 equals 4 less than a
number divided by 5; $n = 30$.
25. $x = 2$ **27.** $g = 20$ **29.** $w = -9$
31. $p = 2$ **33.** 120 min **35.** 1,300
calories **37.** 2 slices of pizza for
lunch and again for dinner
39. C **41.** rectangular prism
43. 549.5 cm^3

12-2 Exercises

1. $n = 5$ **3.** $p = 2$ **5.** $q = 2$
7. 12 books **9.** $x = \frac{7}{8}$ **11.** $n = 6$
13. $x = -2$ **15.** $n = -2$
17. $n = 1.5$ **19.** $t = -9$ **21.** $x = 66$
23. $w = 8$ **25.** $a = 176$ **27.** $b = -7$
29. $x = 3$ **31.** $6.70 **33.** $25 **35.** 91
39. A **41.** 37.7 cm^3 **43.** $x = 1$
45. $z = -28$

12-3 Exercises

1. $n = 32$ **3.** $12w = 32$ **5.** $a = 2$
7. 5 movies **9.** $-8 = 12p$
11. $-6 = 2c$ **13.** $6 = \frac{1}{10}a$
15. $b = -8$ **17.** $a = -0.8$
19. $c = -2$ **21.** $y = -7$ **23.** $r = 4$
25. $r = -2$ **27.** 67 members
29. $x = 6$ **31.** 20 days
37. $0.03m = 2 + 0.01m$; $m = 100$;
100 minutes makes the cost for
long distance from both plans
equal. **39.** 28.4 ft **41.** $y = 2$

12-4 Exercises

1. number of people ≤ 18
3. water level > 45
5.
7.

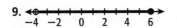

9. ◄⊕─┼─┼─┼─┼─┼─●►
  −4 −2 0 2 4 6

11. temperature < 40

13. number of tables ≤ 35

15. ◄─●┼─┼─┼─┼─┼─┼─┼─►
  −1 0 1 2 3 4 5 6 7

17. ◄━━━━━●─┼─┼─┼─►
  −5 −4 −3 −2 −1 0 1

19. ◄─┼─┼─●━━━━━━━►
  −8 −7 −6 −5 −4 −3 −2

21. ◄⊕─┼─┼─┼─┼─┼─⊕─┼─►
  −1 0 1 2 3 4 5 6 7

23. ◄─┼─⊕━━━━⊕─┼─┼─►
  −4 −3 −2 −1 0 1 2

25. ◄━━━━━●━━━━●─┼─►
  −3 −2 −1 0 1 2 3

27. ◄━━━━━━━━━━●─┼─►
  −9 −8 −7 −6 −5 −4 −3

29. ◄─┼─┼─●━━━━━━━►
  −4 −3 −2 −1 0 1 2 3

31. ◄─┼─⊕━━━━━━●─┼─┼─►
  −10 −8 −6 −4 −2

35. $-200 \le$ depth ≤ 0 **37.** $0 \ge$ *Manshu* depth measurement $\ge$ $-32{,}190$ ft; $0 \ge$ *Challenger* depth measurement $\ge -35{,}640$ ft; $0 \ge$ *Horizon* depth measurement $\ge$ $-34{,}884$ ft; $0 \ge$ *Vityaz* depth measurement $\ge -36{,}200$ ft **39.** B
41. 59 m/h **43.** $y = 5$

12-5 Exercises

1. $x < 27$ **3.** $p \le 7$ **5.** $b \le -24$
7. no more than 42 °F **9.** $m < 11$
11. $c \le 11$ **13.** $x \ge 80$ **15.** $z > -12$

17. $f > -6$ **19.** $n \ge -4$ **21.** at most 24 birds **23.** $a > 0.3$ **25.** $m \le -38$
27. $g < 6\frac{1}{3}$ **29.** $w \le 15.7$
31. $t \ge -242$ **33.** $v \le -0.6$
35. at least \$8 **39.** up to 50,000 hertz **43.** B **45.** 144 in²
47. 1,600 in²

12-6 Exercises

1. $w < -32$ **3.** $p < 48$ **5.** $y > -\frac{11}{8}$
or $-1\frac{3}{8}$ **7.** at least 27 candles
9. $m > 52$ **11.** $c \ge -120$
13. $x \ge -1.1$ **15.** $z < \frac{3}{5}$
17. $f < -3$ **19.** $n \le -10$
21. at least 46 wreaths **23.** $p > 4$
25. $y \ge 18$ **27.** $g > 0.63$ **29.** $w \le \frac{3}{8}$
31. $t < \frac{5}{2}$ **33.** $v \ge -2.5$ **35.** 5 hours
37. at least 480 subscriptions
43. 301 **45.** $x < 1$ **47.** $z \ge 5$

12-7 Exercises

1. $x < 3$ **3.** $y \ge 6$ **5.** $x \ge \frac{2}{3}$
7. more than \$26 each **9.** $b < 12$
11. $c \ge -3$ **13.** $x \le -27$ **15.** $j \le 2$
17. at most 6 bagels **19.** $x \ge -6$
21. $c < 1.8$ **23.** $w \le 8$ **25.** $s > -24$
27. $d \le 4$ **29.** \$14 **31.** at least 225 students **33.** at most 60% **37.** B
39. 12 **41.** $x > 5$ **43.** $x \le 15$

Extension

1. $h = \frac{A}{b}$ **3.** $d = \frac{C}{\pi}$ **5.** $B = \frac{V}{h}$
7. $y = \frac{k}{x}$ **9.** $F = \frac{W}{d}$ **11.** $r = \frac{C}{2\pi}$
13. $h = \frac{3V}{B}$ **15.** $t = \frac{E}{p}$ **17.** $a = \frac{F}{m}$

19. $V = rI$ **21.** $\ell = \frac{(P - 2w)}{2}$
23. 6.25 m/s **25.** 75 g **27.** 0.001 kg

Chapter 12 Study Guide: Review

1. inequality **2.** compound inequality **3.** solution set
4. $y = 8$ **5.** $z = 30$ **6.** $w = 147$
7. $a = -7$ **8.** $j = 9$ **9.** $b = 4$
10. $y = 5$ **11.** 26 mi **12.** $b = \frac{1}{2}$
13. $c = 6$ **14.** $m = \frac{8}{3}$ or $2\frac{2}{3}$
15. $x = 20$ **16.** 10 months
17. weight limit ≤ 9 tons
18. age > 200

19. ◄─┼─┼─┼─┼─●━━━━━►
  −1 0 1 2 3 4 5

20. ◄─┼─●━━━⊕─┼─┼─►
  −3 −2 −1 0 1

21. $r > 25$ **22.** $x \le -26$ **23.** $g < 8$
24. $t \le \frac{1}{6}$ **25.** $9 > r$ **26.** $u \ge -66$
27. at least 38 points **28.** at most \$94 **29.** $n < -55.2$ **30.** $p \le 6$
31. $k < -130$ **32.** $p < 5$
33. $v \ge 2.76$ **34.** $c > 33$
35. at least 16 purses **36.** $b < -2$
37. $d < -6$ **38.** $n \ge -4$
39. $y \le 18$ **40.** $c > -54$
41. $x \le 10$ **42.** $h \ge -156$
43. $-10 < t$ **44.** $52 > w$ **45.** $y \le 35$
46. at most 4 T-shirts **47.** more than \$147

Glossary/Glosario . . .

A

ENGLISH	SPANISH	EXAMPLES
absolute value The distance of a number from zero on a number line; shown by | |. (p. 73)	**valor absoluto** Distancia a la que está un número de 0 en una recta numérica. El símbolo del valor absoluto es | |.	$\|5\| = 5$ $\|-5\| = 5$
accuracy The closeness of a given measurement or value to the actual measurement or value. (p. 524)	**exactitud** Cercanía de una medida o un valor a la medida o el valor real.	
acute angle An angle that measures greater than 0° and less than 90°. (p. 454)	**ángulo agudo** Ángulo que mide más de 0° y menos de 90°.	
acute triangle A triangle with all angles measuring less than 90°. (p. 478)	**triángulo acutángulo** Triángulo en el que todos los ángulos miden menos de 90°.	
addend A number added to one or more other numbers to form a sum.	**sumando** Número que se suma a uno o más números para formar una suma.	In the expression 4 + 6 + 7, the numbers 4, 6, and 7 are addends.
Addition Property of Equality The property that states that if you add the same number to both sides of an equation, the new equation will have the same solution. (p. 48)	**Propiedad de igualdad de la suma** Propiedad que establece que puedes sumar el mismo número a ambos lados de una ecuación y la nueva ecuación tendrá la misma solución.	$\begin{aligned} x - 6 &= 8 \\ +6 \quad &\quad +6 \\ x &= 14 \end{aligned}$
Addition Property of Opposites The property that states that the sum of a number and its opposite equals zero.	**Propiedad de la suma de los opuestos** Propiedad que establece que la suma de un número y su opuesto es cero.	$12 + (-12) = 0$
additive inverse The opposite of a number. (p. 72)	**inverso aditivo** El opuesto de un número.	The additive inverse of 5 is −5.
adjacent angles Angles in the same plane that have a common vertex and a common side. (p. 460)	**ángulos adyacentes** Angulos en el mismo plano que comparten un vértice y un lado.	 ∠1 and ∠2 are adjacent angles.
algebraic expression An expression that contains at least one variable. (p. 30)	**expresión algebraica** Expresión que contiene al menos una variable.	$x + 8$ $4(m - b)$

ENGLISH	SPANISH	EXAMPLES
algebraic inequality An inequality that contains at least one variable. (p. 710)	**desigualdad algebraica** Desigualdad que contiene al menos una variable.	$x + 3 > 10$ $5a > b + 3$
alternate exterior angles A pair of angles on the outer side of two lines cut by a transversal that are on opposite sides of the transversal. (p. 461)	**ángulos alternos externos** Par de ángulos en los lados externos de dos líneas intersecadas por una transversal, que están en lados opuestos de la transversal.	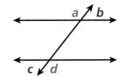 ∠a and ∠d are alternate exterior angles.
alternate interior angles A pair of angles on the inner sides of two lines cut by a transversal that are on opposite sides of the transversal. (p. 461)	**ángulos alternos externos** Par de ángulos en los lados internos de dos líneas intersecadas por una transversal, que están en lados opuestos de la transversal.	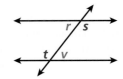 ∠r and ∠v are alternate interior angles.
angle A figure formed by two rays with a common endpoint called the vertex. (p. 454)	**ángulo** Figura formada por dos rayos con un extremo común llamado vértice.	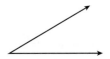
arc A part of a circle named by its endpoints. (p. 468)	**arco** Parte de un círculo que se nombra por sus extremos.	
area The number of square units needed to cover a given surface. (p. 536)	**área** El número de unidades cuadradas que se necesitan para cubrir una superficie dada.	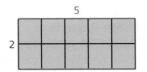 The area is 10 square units.
arithmetic sequence A sequence in which the terms change by the same amount each time. (p. 288)	**sucesión aritmética** Una sucesión en la que los términos cambian la misma cantidad cada vez.	The sequence 2, 5, 8, 11, 14 … is an arithmetic sequence.
Associative Property of Addition The property that states that for all real numbers a, b, and c, the sum is always the same, regardless of their grouping. (p. 24)	**Propiedad asociativa de la suma** Propiedad que establece que para todos los números reales a, b y c, la suma siempre es la misma sin importar cómo se agrupen.	$2 + 3 + 8 = (2 + 3) + 8 =$ $2 + (3 + 8)$
Associative Property of Multiplication The property that states that for all real numbers a, b, and c, their product is always the same, regardless of their grouping. (p. 24)	**Propiedad asociativa de la multiplicación** Propiedad que para todos los números reales a, b y c, el producto siempre es el mismo sin importar cómo se agrupen.	$2 \cdot 3 \cdot 8 = (2 \cdot 3) \cdot 8 = 2 \cdot (3 \cdot 8)$

ENGLISH	SPANISH	EXAMPLES

asymmetry Not identical on either side of a central line; not symmetrical. (p. 504)

asimetría Ocurre cuando dos lados separados por una línea central no son idénticos; falta de simetría.

The quadrilateral has asymmetry.

axes The two perpendicular lines of a coordinate plane that intersect at the origin. (p. 276)

ejes Las dos rectas numéricas perpendiculares del plano cartesiano que se intersecan en el origen.

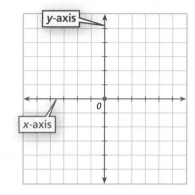

B

bar graph A graph that uses vertical or horizontal bars to display data. (p. 390)

gráfica de barras Gráfica en la que se usan barras verticales u horizontales para presentar datos.

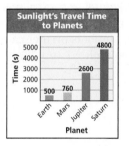

base-10 number system A number system in which all numbers are expressed using the digits 0–9. (p. 237)

sistema de base 10 Sistema de numeración en el que todos los números se expresan con los dígitos 0–9.

base (in numeration) When a number is raised to a power, the number that is used as a factor is the base. (p. 10)

base (en numeración) Cuando un número es elevado a una potencia, el número que se usa como factor es la base.

$3^5 = 3 \cdot 3 \cdot 3 \cdot 3 \cdot 3$; 3 is the base.

base (of a polygon) A side of a polygon.

base (de un polígono) Lado de un polígono.

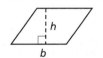

base (of a three-dimensional figure) A face of a three-dimensional figure by which the figure is measured or classified. (p. 588)

base (de una figura tridimensional) Cara de una figura tridimensional a partir de la cual se mide o se clasifica la figura.

Bases of a cylinder   Bases of a prism

Base of a cone   Base of a pyramid

Glossary/Glosario

biased sample A sample that does not fairly represent the population. (p. 419)

muestra no representativa Muestra que no representa adecuadamente la población.

bisect To divide into two congruent parts. (p. 464)

trazar una bisectriz Dividir en dos partes congruentes.

$\overrightarrow{JK}$ bisects $\angle LJM$.

box-and-whisker plot A graph shows how data are distributed by using the median, quartiles, least value, and greatest value; also called a box plot. (p. 398)

gráfica de mediana y rango Gráfica que muestra los valores máximo y mínimo, los cuartiles superior e inferior, así como la mediana de los datos.

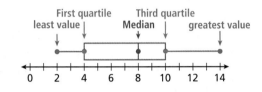

break (graph) A zigzag on a horizontal or vertical scale of a graph that indicates that some of the numbers on the scale have been omitted. (p. 428)

discontinuidad (gráfica) Zig-zag en la escala horizontal o vertical de una gráfica que indica la omisión de algunos de los números de la escala.

capacity The amount a container can hold when filled.

capacidad Cantidad que cabe en un recipiente cuando se llena.

A large milk container has a capacity of 1 gallon.

Celsius A metric scale for measuring temperature in which 0 °C is the freezing point of water and 100 °C is the boiling point of water; also called *centigrade*.

Celsius Escala métrica para medir la temperatura, en la que 0° C es el punto de congelación del agua y 100° C es el punto de ebullición. También se llama *centígrado*.

center (of a circle) The point inside a circle that is the same distance from all the points on the circle. (p. 468)

centro (de un círculo) Punto interior de un círculo que se encuentra a la misma distancia de todos los puntos de la circunferencia.

center (of rotation) The point about which a figure is rotated. (p. 505)

centro (de una rotación) Punto alrededor del cual se hace girar una figura.

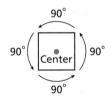

Glossary/Glosario

ENGLISH	SPANISH	EXAMPLES
central angle of a circle An angle with its vertex at the center of a circle. (p. 469)	**ángulo central de un círculo** Ángulo cuyo vértice se encuentra en el centro de un círculo.	
certain (probability) Sure to happen; having a probability of 1. (p. 640)	**seguro (probabilidad)** Que con seguridad sucederá. Representa una probabilidad de 1.	
chord A line segment with endpoints on a circle. (p. 468)	**cuerda** Segmento de recta cuyos extremos forman parte de un círculo.	

A — Chord — *B*

circle The set of all points in a plane that are the same distance from a given point called the center. (p. 468)	**círculo** Conjunto de todos los puntos en un plano que se encuentran a la misma distancia de un punto dado llamado centro.	
circle graph A graph that uses sectors of a circle to compare parts to the whole and parts to other parts. (p. 394)	**gráfica circular** Gráfica que usa secciones de un círculo para comparar partes con el todo y con otras partes.	**Residents of Mesa, AZ**

Residents of Mesa, AZ: 65+ 13%, 45–64 19%, 25–44 30%, 18–24 11%, Under 18 27%

circumference The distance around a circle. (p. 531)	**circunferencia** Distancia alrededor de un círculo.	Circumference
clockwise A circular movement to the right in the direction shown.	**en el sentido de las manecillas del reloj** Movimiento circular en la dirección que se indica.	
coefficient The number that is multiplied by the variable in an algebraic expression. (p. 38)	**coeficiente** Número que se multiplica por la variable en una expresión algebraica.	5 is the coefficient in 5*b*.
combination An arrangement of items or events in which order does not matter. (p. 670)	**combinación** Agrupación de objetos o sucesos en la cual el orden no es importante.	For objects *A, B, C,* and *D,* there are 6 different combinations of 2 objects: *AB, AC, AD, BC, BD, CD.*
common denominator A denominator that is the same in two or more fractions.	**común denominador** Denominador que es común a dos o más fracciones.	The common denom$\ldots$ and $\frac{2}{8}$ is 8.

ENGLISH	SPANISH	EXAMPLES
common difference In an arithmetic sequence, the nonzero constant difference of any term and the previous term. (p. 288)	**diferencia común** En una sucesión aritmética, diferencia constante distinta de cero entre cualquier término y el término anterior.	In the arithmetic sequence 3, 5, 7, 9, 11, ..., the common difference is 2.
common factor A number that is a factor of two or more numbers.	**factor común** Número que es factor de dos o más números.	8 is a common factor of 16 and 40.
common multiple A number that is a multiple of each of two or more numbers.	**común múltiplo** Número que es múltiplo de dos o más números.	15 is a common multiple of 3 and 5.
Commutative Property of Addition The property that states that two or more numbers can be added in any order without changing the sum. (p. 24)	**Propiedad conmutativa de la suma** Propiedad que establece que sumar dos o más números en cualquier orden no altera la suma.	$8 + 20 = 20 + 8$
Commutative Property of Multiplication The property that states that two or more numbers can be multiplied in any order without changing the product. (p. 24)	**Propiedad conmutativa de la multiplicación** Propiedad que establece que multiplicar dos o más números en cualquier orden no altera el producto.	$6 \cdot 12 = 12 \cdot 6$
compatible numbers Numbers that are close to the given numbers that make estimation or mental calculation easier. (p. 144)	**números compatibles** Números que están cerca de los números dados y hacen más fácil la estimación o el cálculo mental.	To estimate $7{,}957 + 5{,}009$, use the compatible numbers 8,000 and 5,000: $8{,}000 + 5{,}000 = 13{,}000$.
complement The set of all outcomes that are not the event. (p. 641)	**complemento** La serie de resultados que no están en el suceso.	When rolling a number cube, the complement of rolling a 3 is rolling a 1, 2, 4, 5, or 6.
complementary angles Two angles whose measures add to 90°. (p. 454)	**ángulos complementarios** Dos ángulos cuyas medidas suman 90°.	
composite figure A figure made up of simple geometric shapes. (p. 550)	**figura compuesta** Figura formada por figuras geométricas simples.	
composite number A number greater than 1 that has more than two whole-number factors. (p. 104)	**número compuesto** Número mayor que 1 que tiene más de dos factores que son números cabales.	4, 6, 8, and 9 are composite numbers.
compound event An event made up of two or more simple events. (p. 640)	**suceso compuesto** Suceso que consista de dos o más sucesos simples.	Rolling a 3 on a number cube and spinning a 2 on a spinner is a compound event.

ENGLISH	SPANISH	EXAMPLES
compound inequality A combination of more than one inequality. (p. 711)	**desigualdad compuesta** Combinación de dos o más desigualdades.	$-2 \leq x < 10$
cone A three-dimensional figure with one vertex and one circular base. (p. 589)	**cono** Figura tridimensional con un vértice y una base circular.	
congruent Having the same size and shape, the symbol for congurent is ≅. (p. 449)	**congruentes** Que tiene el mismo tamaño y la misma forma, expresado por ≅.	$\triangle ABC \cong \triangle DEF$
congruent angles Angles that have the same measure. (p. 461)	**ángulos congruentes** Ángulos que tienen la misma medida.	$\angle ABC \cong \angle DEF$
conjecture A statement believed to be true. (p. 7)	**conjetura** Enunciado que se supone verdadero.	
constant A value that does not change. (p. 30)	**constante** Valor que no cambia.	$3, 0, \pi$
constant of variation The constant k in direct and inverse variation equations. (p. 313)	**constante de variación** La constante k en ecuaciones de variación directa e inversa.	$y = 5x$ ↑ constant of variation
convenience sample A sample based on members of the population that are readily available. (p. 418)	**muestra de conveniencia** Una muestra basada en miembros de la población que están fácilmente disponibles.	
coordinate One of the numbers of an ordered pair that locate a point on a coordinate graph. (p. 276)	**coordenada** Uno de los números de un par ordenado que ubica un punto en una gráfica de coordenadas.	
coordinate plane A plane formed by the intersection of a horizontal number line called the x-axis and a vertical number line called the y-axis. (p. 276)	**plano cartesiano** Plano formado por la intersección de una recta numérica horizontal llamada eje x y otra vertical llamada eje y.	
correlation The description of the relationship between two data sets. (p. 423)	**correlación** Descripción de la relación entre dos conjuntos de datos.	

ENGLISH	SPANISH	EXAMPLES
corresponding angles (for lines) Angles in the same position formed when a third line intersects two lines. (p. 461)	**ángulos correspondientes (en líneas)** Ángulos en la misma posición formaron cuando una tercera línea interseca dos líneas.	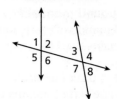 ∠1 and ∠3 are corresponding angles.
corresponding angles (of polygons) Angles in the same relative position in polygons with an equal number of sides. (p. 300)	**ángulos correspondientes (en polígonos)** Ángulos que se ubican en la misma posición relativa en dos o más polígonos.	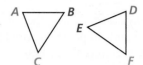 ∠A and ∠D are corresponding angles.
corresponding sides Matching sides of two or more polygons. (p. 248)	**lados correspondientes** Lados que se ubican en la misma posición relativa en dos o más polígonos.	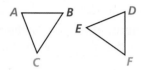 $\overline{AB}$ and $\overline{DE}$ are corresponding sides.
counterclockwise A circular movement to the left in the direction shown.	**en sentido contrario a las manecillas del reloj** Movimiento circular en la dirección que se indica.	
counterexample An example that shows that a statement is false. (p. SB12)	**contraejemplo** Ejemplo que demuestra que un enunciado es falso.	
cross product The product of numbers on the diagonal when comparing two ratios. (p. 226)	**producto cruzado** El producto de los números multiplicados en diagonal cuando se comparan dos razones.	For the proportion $\frac{2}{3} = \frac{4}{6}$, the cross products are $2 \cdot 6 = 12$ and $3 \cdot 4 = 12$.
cube (geometric figure) A rectangular prism with six congruent square faces.	**cubo (figura geométrica)** Prisma rectangular con seis caras cuadradas congruentes.	
cube (in numeration) A number raised to the third power. (p. SB14)	**cubo (en numeración)** Número elevado a la tercera potencia.	$5^3 = 5 \cdot 5 \cdot 5 = 125$
cumulative frequency The frequency of all data values that are less than or equal to a given value. (p. 380)	**frecuencia acumulativa** La frecuencia de todos los datos que son menores que o iguales a un valor dado.	

ENGLISH	SPANISH	EXAMPLES
customary system of measurement The measurement system often used in the United States. (p. 232)	**sistema usual de medidas** El sistema de medidas que se usa comúnmente en Estados Unidos.	inches, feet, miles, ounces, pounds, tons, cups, quarts, gallons
cylinder A three-dimensional figure with two parallel, congruent circular bases connected by a curved lateral surface. (p. 589)	**cilindro** Figura tridimensional con dos bases circulares paralelas y congruentes, unidas por una superficie lateral curva.	

 D ————————————————————————

decagon A polygon with ten sides. (p. 474)	**decágono** Polígono de 10 lados.	
decimal system A base-10 place value system.	**sistema decimal** Sistema de valor posicional de base 10.	
deductive reasoning Using logic to show that a statement is true. (p. SB11)	**razonamiento deductivo** Uso de la lógica para demostrar que un enunciado es verdadero.	
degree The unit of measure for angles or temperature. (p. 454)	**grado** Unidad de medida para ángulos y temperaturas.	
denominator The bottom number of a fraction that tells how many equal parts are in the whole.	**denominador** Número de abajo de una fracción que indica en cuántas partes iguales se divide el entero.	$\frac{3}{4}$ ← denominator
dependent events Events for which the outcome of one event affects the probability of the second event. (p. 666)	**sucesos dependientes** Dos sucesos son dependientes si el resultado de uno afecta la probabilidad del otro.	A bag contains 3 red marbles and 2 blue marbles. Drawing a red marble and then drawing a blue marble without replacing the first marble is an example of dependent events.
diagonal A line segment that conects two non-adjacent vertices of a polygon. (p. 486)	**diagonal** Segmento de recta que une dos vértices no adyacentes de un polígono.	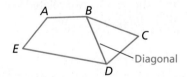
diameter A line segment that passes through the center of a circle and has endpoints on the circle, or the length of that segment. (p. 468)	**diámetro** Segmento de recta que pasa por el centro de un círculo y tiene sus extremos en la circunferencia, o bien la longitud de ese segmento.	
difference The result when one number is subtracted from another.	**diferencia** El resultado de restar un número de otro.	In 16 − 5 = 11, 11 is the difference.

dimension The length, width, or height of a figure.

dimensión Longitud, ancho o altura de una figura.

direct variation A linear relationship between two variables, x and y, that can be written in the form $y = kx$, where k is a nonzero constant. (p. 313)

variacion directa Relación lineal entre dos variables, x e y, que puede expresarse en la forma $y = kx$, donde k es una constante distinta de cero.

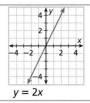

$y = 2x$

Distributive Property For all real numbers, a, b, and c, $a(b + c) = ab + ac$ and $a(b - c) = ab - ac$. (p. 25)

Propiedad distributiva Dado números reales a, b, y c, $a(b + c) = ab + ac$ y $a(b - c) = ab - ac$.

$5(20 + 1) = 5 \cdot 20 + 5 \cdot 1$

dividend The number to be divided in a division problem.

dividendo Número que se divide en un problema de división.

In $8 \div 4 = 2$, 8 is the dividend.

divisible Can be divided by a number without leaving a remainder. (p. SB5)

divisible Que se puede dividir entre un número sin dejar residuo.

18 is divisible by 3.

Division Property of Equality The property that states that if you divide both sides of an equation by the same nonzero number, the new equation will have the same solution. (p. 52)

Propiedad de igualdad de la división Propiedad que establece que puedes dividir ambos lados de una ecuación entre el mismo número distinto de cero, y la nueva ecuación tendrá la misma solución.

$4x = 12$

$\frac{4x}{4} = \frac{12}{4}$

$x = 3$

divisor The number you are dividing by in a division problem.

divisor El número entre el que se divide en un problema de división.

In $8 \div 4 = 2$, 4 is the divisor.

double-bar graph A bar graph that compares two related sets of data. (p. 390)

gráfica de doble barra Gráfica de barras que compara dos conjuntos de datos relacionados.

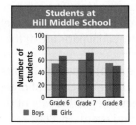

double-line graph A line graph that shows how two related sets of data change over time. (p. 407)

gráfica de doble línea Gráfica lineal que muestra cómo cambian con el tiempo dos conjuntos de datos relacionados.

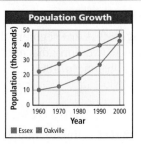

E

edge The line segment along which two faces of a polyhedron intersect. (p. 588)

arista Segmento de recta donde se intersecan dos caras de un poliedro.

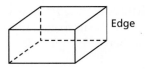

Edge

endpoint A point at the end of a line segment or ray.

extremo Un punto ubicado al final de un segmento de recta o rayo.

equally likely Outcomes that have the same probability. (p. 652)

resultados igualmente probables Resultados que tienen la misma probabilidad de ocurrir.

equation A mathematical sentence that shows that two expressions are equivalent. (p. 42)

ecuación Enunciado matemático que indica que dos expresiones son equivalentes.

$x + 4 = 7$
$6 + 1 = 10 - 3$

equilateral triangle A triangle with three congruent sides. (p. 478)

triángulo equilátero Triángulo con tres lados congruentes.

equivalent Having the same value.

equivalentes Que tienen el mismo valor.

equivalent fractions Fractions that name the same amount or part. (p. 118)

fracciones equivalentes Fracciones que representan la misma cantidad o parte.

$\frac{1}{2}$ and $\frac{2}{4}$ are equivalent fractions.

equivalent ratios Ratios that name the same comparison. (p. 222)

razones equivalentes Razones que representan la misma comparación.

$\frac{1}{2}$ and $\frac{2}{4}$ are equivalent ratios.

estimate (n) An answer that is close to the exact answer and is found by rounding, or other methods.

estimación (s) Una solución aproximada a la respuesta exacta que se halla mediante el redondeo u otros métodos.

estimate (v) To find an answer close to the exact answer by rounding or other methods.

estimar (v) Hallar una solución aproximada a la respuesta exacta mediante el redondeo u otros métodos.

evaluate To find the value of a numerical or algebraic expression. (p. 30)

evaluar Hallar el valor de una expresión numérica o algebraica.

Evaluate $2x + 7$ for $x = 3$.
$2x + 7$
$2(3) + 7$
$6 + 7$
13

even number An integer that is divisible by two.

número par Número entero divisible entre 2.

2, 4, 6

event An outcome or set of outcomes of an experiment or situation. (p. 640)

suceso Un resultado o una serie de resultados de un experimento o una situación.

When rolling a number cube, the event "an odd number" consists of the outcomes 1, 3, and 5.

Glossary/Glosario

expanded form A number written as the sum of the values of its digits. | **forma desarrollada** Número escrito como suma de los valores de sus dígitos. | 236,536 written in expanded form is 200,000 + 30,000 + 6,000 + 500 + 30 + 6.

experiment In probability, any activity based on chance, such as tossing a coin. (p. 640) | **experimento** En probabilidad, cualquier actividad basada en la posibilidad, como lanzar una moneda. | Tossing a coin 10 times and noting the number of "heads"

experimental probability The ratio of the number of times an event occurs to the total number of trials, or times that the activity is performed. (p. 644) | **probabilidad experimental** Razón del número de veces que ocurre un suceso al número total de pruebas o al número de veces que se realiza el experimento. | Kendra attempted 27 free throws and made 16 of them. Her experimental probability of making a free throw is $\frac{\text{number made}}{\text{number attempted}} = \frac{16}{27} \approx 0.59$.

exponent The number that indicates how many times the base is used as a factor. (p. 10) | **exponente** Número que indica cuántas veces se usa la base como factor. | $2^3 = 2 \cdot 2 \cdot 2 = 8$; 3 is the exponent.

exponential form A number is in exponential form when it is written with a base and an exponent. | **forma exponencial** Se dice que un número está en forma exponencial cuando se escribe con una base y un exponente. | 4^2 is the exponential form for $4 \cdot 4$.

expression A mathematical phrase that contains operations, numbers, and/or variables. | **expresión** Enunciado matemático que contiene operaciones, números y/o variables. | $6x + 1$

F

face A flat surface of a polyhedron. (p. 588) | **cara** Superficie plana de un poliedro. |

factor A number that is multiplied by another number to get a product. (p. 14) | **factor** Número que se multiplica por otro para hallar un producto. | 7 is a factor of 21 since $7 \cdot 3 = 21$.

factor tree A diagram showing how a whole number breaks down into its prime factors. (p. 14) | **árbol de factores** Diagrama que muestra cómo se descompone un número cabal en sus factores primos. | 12 / 3 · 4 / 2 · 2 / 12 = 3 · 2 · 2

factorial The product of all whole numbers except zero that are less than or equal to a number. (p. 675) | **factorial** El producto de todos los números cabales, excepto cero que son menores que o iguales a un número. | 4 factorial = 4! = 4 · 3 · 2 · 1

ENGLISH	SPANISH	EXAMPLES
Fahrenheit A temperature scale in which 32 °F is the freezing point of water and 212 °F is the boiling point of water.	**Fahrenheit** Escala de temperatura en la que 32° F es el punto de congelación del agua y 212° F es el punto de ebullición.	
fair When all outcomes of an experiment are equally likely, the experiment is said to be fair. (p. 652)	**justo** Se dice de un experimento donde todos los resultados posibles son igualmente probables.	
first quartile The median of the lower half of a set of data; also called *lower quartile*. (p. 398)	**primer cuartil** La mediana de la mitad inferior de un conjunto de datos. También se llama *cuartil inferior*.	
formula A rule showing relationships among quantities.	**fórmula** Regla que muestra relaciones entre cantidades.	$A = \ell w$ is the formula for the area of a rectangle.
fraction A number in the form $\frac{a}{b}$, where $b \neq 0$.	**fracción** Número escrito en la forma $\frac{a}{b}$, donde $b \neq 0$.	
frequency The number of times the value appears in the data set. (p. 380)	**frecuencia** Cantidad de veces que aparece el valor en un conjunto de datos.	In the data set 5, 6, 6, 7, 8, 9, the data value 6 has a frequency of 2.

frequency table A table that lists items together according to the number of times, or frequency, that the items occur. (p. 380)

tabla de frecuencia Una tabla en la que se organizan los datos de acuerdo con el número de veces que aparece cada valor (o la frecuencia).

Data set: 1, 1, 2, 2, 3, 4, 5, 5, 5, 6, 6, 6, 6

Frequency table:

Data	1	2	3	4	5	6
Frequency	2	2	1	1	3	4

function An input-output relationship that has exactly one output for each input. (p. 284)

función Relación de entrada-salida en la que a cada valor de entrada corresponde exactamente un valor de salida.

function table A table of ordered pairs that represent solutions of a function. (p. 284)

tabla de función Tabla de pares ordenados que representan soluciones de una función.

x	3	4	5	6
y	7	9	11	13

Fundamental Counting Principle If one event has *m* possible outcomes and a second event has *n* possible outcomes after the first event has occurred, then there are *m · n* total possible outcomes for the two events. (p. 649)

Principio fundamental de conteo Si un suceso tiene *m* resultados posibles y otro suceso tiene *n* resultados posibles después de ocurrido el primer suceso, entonces hay *m · n* resultados posibles en total para los dos sucesos.

There are 4 colors of shirts and 3 colors of pants. There are 4 · 3 = 12 possible outfits.

Glossary/Glosario

G

geometric sequence A sequence in which each term is multiplied by the same value to get the next term. (p. 288)

sucesión geométrica Una sucesión en la que cada término se multiplica por el mismo valor para obtener el siguiente término.

The sequence 2, 4, 8, 16 … is a geometric sequence.

graph of an equation A graph of the set of ordered pairs that are solutions of the equation. (p. 296)

gráfica de una ecuación Gráfica del conjunto de pares ordenados que son soluciones de la ecuación.

greatest common factor (GCF) The largest common factor of two or more given numbers. (p. 108)

máximo común divisor (MCD) El mayor de los factores comunes compartidos por dos o más números dados.

The GCF of 27 and 45 is 9.

H

height In a pyramid or cone, the perpendicular distance from the base to the opposite vertex. (p. 600)

altura En una pirámide o cono, la distancia perpendicular desde la base al vértice opuesto.

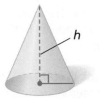

In a triangle or quadrilateral, the perpendicular distance from the base to the opposite vertex or side.

En un triángulo o cuadrilátero, la distancia perpendicular desde la base de la figura al vértice o lado opuesto.

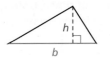

In a prism or cylinder, the perpendicular distance between the bases.

En un prisma o cilindro, la distancia perpendicular entre las bases.

heptagon A seven-sided polygon. (p. 474)

heptágono Polígono de siete lados.

hexagon A six-sided polygon. (p. 474)

hexágono Polígono de seis lados.

histogram A bar graph that shows the frequency of data within equal intervals. (p. 391)

histograma Gráfica de barras que muestra la frecuencia de los datos en intervalos iguales.

ENGLISH	SPANISH	EXAMPLES
hypotenuse In a right triangle, the side opposite the right angle. (p. 566)	**hipotenusa** En un triángulo rectángulo, el lado opuesto al ángulo recto.	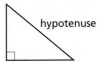 hypotenuse

ENGLISH	SPANISH	EXAMPLES
Identity Property of One The property that states that the product of 1 and any number is that number. (p. 24)	**Propiedad de identidad del uno** Propiedad que establece que el producto de 1 y cualquier número es ese número.	$3 \cdot 1 = 3$ $-9 \cdot 1 = -9$
Identity Property of Zero The property that states that the sum of zero and any number is that number. (p. 24)	**Propiedad de identidad del cero** Propiedad que establece que la suma de cero y cualquier número es ese número.	$5 + 0 = 5$ $-4 + 0 = -4$
image A figure resulting from a transformation. (p. 496)	**imagen** Figura que resulta de una transformación.	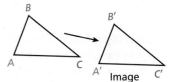
impossible (probability) Can never happen; having a probability of 0. (p. 640)	**imposible (en probabilidad)** Que no puede ocurrir. Suceso cuya probabilidad de ocurrir es 0.	
improper fraction A fraction in which the numerator is greater than or equal to the denominator. (p. 119)	**fracción impropia** Fracción en la que el numerador es mayor que o igual al denominador.	$\frac{5}{5}$ $\frac{7}{4}$
independent events Events for which the outcome of one event does not affect the probability of the other. (p. 266)	**sucesos independientes** Dos sucesos son independientes si el resultado de uno no afecta la probabilidad del otro.	A bag contains 3 red marbles and 2 blue marbles. Drawing a red marble, replacing it, and then drawing a blue marble is an example of independent events.
indirect measurement The technique of using similar figures and proportions to find a measure. (p. 252)	**medición indirecta** La técnica de usar figuras semejantes y proporciones para hallar una medida.	
inductive reasoning Using a pattern to make a conclusion. (p. SB11)	**razonamiento inductivo** Uso de un patrón para sacar una conclusión.	
inequality A mathematical sentence that shows the relationship between quantities that are not equivalent. (p. 710)	**desigualdad** Enunciado matemático que muestra una relación entre cantidades que no son equivalentes.	$5 < 8$ $5x + 2 \geq 12$

input The value substituted into an expression or function. (p. 284)

valor de entrada Valor que se usa para sustituir una variable en una expresión o función.

For the function $y = 6x$, the input 4 produces an output of 24.

---

integers The set of whole numbers and their opposites. (p. 72)

enteros Conjunto de todos los números cabales y sus opuestos.

$\ldots\ -3, -2, -1, 0, 1, 2, 3, \ldots$

---

interest The amount of money charged for borrowing or using money, or the amount of money earned by saving money. (p. 362)

interés Cantidad de dinero que se cobra por el préstamo o uso del dinero, o la cantidad que se gana al ahorrar dinero.

---

interquartile range The difference between the upper and lower quartiles in a box-and-whisker plot. (p. 399)

rango entre cuartiles La diferencia entre los cuartiles superior e inferior en una gráfica de mediana y rango.

Lower half   Upper half

18, ㉓ 28,   29, ㊱ 42

Lower quartile   Upper quartile

Interquartile range: $36 - 23 = 13$

---

intersecting lines Lines that cross at exactly one point.

líneas secantes Líneas que se cruzan en un solo punto.

---

interval The space between marked values on a number line or the scale of a graph.

intervalo El espacio entre los valores marcados en una recta numérica o en la escala de una gráfica.

---

inverse operations Operations that undo each other: addition and subtraction, or multiplication and division. (p. 48)

operaciones inversas Operaciones que se cancelan mutuamente: suma y resta, o multiplicación y división.

Addition and subtraction are inverse operations:
$5 + 3 = 8; 8 - 3 = 5$
Multiplication and division are inverse operations:
$2 \cdot 3 = 6; 6 \div 3 = 2$

Inverse Property of Addition The sum of a number and its opposite, or additive inverse, is 0. (p. 98)

propiedad inversa de la suma La suma de un número y su opuesto, o inverso aditivo, es cero.

$3 + (-3) = 0; a + (-a) = 0$

---

irrational number A number that cannot be expressed as a ratio of two integers or as a repeating or terminating decimal. (p. 562)

número irracional Número que no puede expresarse como una razón de dos enteros ni como un decimal periódico o finito.

$\sqrt{2}, \pi$

---

isolate the variable To get a variable alone on one side of an equation or inequality in order to solve the equation or inequality. (p. 48)

despejar la variable Dejar sola la variable en un lado de una ecuación o desigualdad para resolverla.

$$\begin{array}{r} x + 7 = 22 \\ \underline{-7 \quad -7} \\ x \quad\ = 15 \end{array}$$

---

isosceles triangle A triangle with at least two congruent sides. (p. 478)

triángulo isósceles Triángulo que tiene al menos dos lados congruentes.

L

lateral area The sum of the areas of the lateral faces of a prism or pyramid, or the area of the lateral surface of a cylinder or cone. (p. 607)

área lateral Suma de las áreas de las caras laterales de un prisma o pirámide, o área de la superficie lateral de un cilindro o cono.

12 cm
6 cm
8 cm

lateral face A face of a prism or a pyramid that is not a base. (p. 607)

Cara lateral Cara de un prisma o pirámide que no es una base.

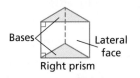

Bases — Lateral face
Right prism

least common denominator (LCD) The least common multiple of two or more denominators.

mínimo común denominador (mcd) El mínimo común múltiplo de dos o más denominadores.

The LCD of $\frac{3}{4}$ and $\frac{5}{6}$ is 12.

least common multiple (LCM) The least number, other than zero, that is a multiple of two or more given numbers. (p. 112)

mínimo común múltiplo (mcm) El menor de los números, distinto de cero, que es múltiplo de dos o más números.

The LCM of 10 and 18 is 90.

legs In a right triangle, the sides that include the right angle; in an isosceles triangle, the pair of congruent sides. (p. 566)

catetos En un triángulo rectángulo, los lados adyacentes al ángulo recto. En un triángulo isósceles, el par de lados congruentes.

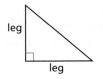

leg
leg

like terms Terms with the same variables raised to the same exponents. (p. 38)

términos semejantes Términos que contienen las mismas variables elevada a las mismas exponentes.

In the expression $3a^2 + 5b + 12a^2$, $3a^2$ and $12a^2$ are like terms.

line A straight path that has no thickness and extends forever. (p. 448)

línea Trayectoria recta que no tiene ningún grueso y que se extiende por siempre.

$\longleftrightarrow \ell$

line graph A graph that uses line segments to show how data changes. (p. 406)

gráfica lineal Gráfica que muestra cómo cambian los datos mediante segmentos de recta.

Marlon's Video Game Scores

Score: 1200, 800, 400, 0
Game number: 1 2 3 4 5 6

line of best fit A straight line that comes closest to the points on a scatter plot. (p. 427)

línea de mejor ajuste la línea recta que más se aproxima a los puntos de un diagrama de dispersión.

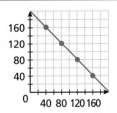

160
120
80
40
0
40 80 120 160

line of reflection A line that a figure is flipped across to create a mirror image of the original figure. (p. 496)

línea de reflexión Línea sobre la cual se invierte una figura para crear una imagen reflejada de la figura original.

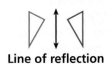

Line of reflection

Glossary/Glosario

line of symmetry The imaginary "mirror" in line symmetry. (p. 504)

eje de simetría El "espejo" imaginario en la simetría axial.

---

line plot A number line with marks or dots that show frequency. (p. 381)

diagrama de acumulación Recta numérica con marcas o puntos que indican la frecuencia.

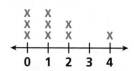

---

line segment A part of a line made of two endpoints and all points between them. (p. 449)

segmento de recta Parte de una línea con dos extremos.

---

line symmetry A figure has line symmetry if one-half is a mirror-image of the other half. (p. 504)

simetría axial Una figura tiene simetría axial si una de sus mitades es la imagen reflejada de la otra.

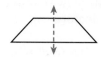

---

linear equation An equation whose solutions form a straight line on a coordinate plane. (p. 296)

ecuación lineal Ecuación cuyas soluciones forman una línea recta en un plano cartesiano.

$y = 2x + 1$

---

linear function A function whose graph is a straight line. (p. 296)

función lineal Función cuya gráfica es una línea recta.

$y = x - 1$

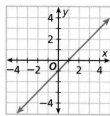

---

lower quartile The median of the lower half of a set of data. (p. 398)

cuartil inferior La mediana de la mitad inferior de un conjunto de datos.

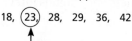

---

mean The sum of the items in a set of data divided by the number of items in the set; also called *average*. (p. 385)

media La suma de todos loselementos de un conjunto de datos dividida entre el número de elementos del conjunto. También se llama *promedio*.

Data set: 4, 6, 7, 8, 10
Mean:
$\frac{4 + 6 + 7 + 8 + 10}{5} = \frac{35}{5} = 7$

---

measure of central tendency A measure used to describe the middle of a data set; the mean, median, and mode are measures of central tendency. (p. 385)

medida de tendencia dominante Medida que describe la parte media de un conjunto de datos; la media, la mediana y la moda son medidas de tendencia dominante.

Glossary/Glosario

ENGLISH	SPANISH	EXAMPLES
median The middle number, or the mean (average) of the two middle numbers, in an ordered set of data. (p. 385)	**mediana** El número intermedio, o la media (el promedio), de los dos números intermedios en un conjunto ordenado de datos.	Data set: 4, 6, 7, 8, 10 Median: 7
metric system of measurement A decimal system of weights and measures that is used universally in science and commonly throughout the world. (p. 236)	**sistema métrico de medición** Sistema decimal de pesos y medidas empleado universalmente en las ciencias y comúnmente en todo el mundo.	centimeters, meters, kilometers, grams, kilograms, milliliters, liters
midpoint The point that divides a line segment into two congruent line segments.	**punto medio** El punto que divide un segmento de recta en dos segmentos de recta congruentes.	 B is the midpoint of $\overline{AC}$.
mixed number A number made up of a whole number that is not zero and a fraction. (p. 119)	**número mixto** Número compuesto por un número cabal distinto de cero y una fracción.	$5\frac{1}{8}$
mode The number or numbers that occur most frequently in a set of data; when all numbers occur with the same frequency, we say there is no mode. (p. 385)	**moda** Número o números más frecuentes en un conjunto de datos; si todos los números aparecen con la misma frecuencia, no hay moda.	Data set: 3, 5, 8, 8, 10 Mode: 8
multiple The product of any number and any nonzero whole number is a multiple of that number. (p. 112)	**múltiplo** El producto de un número y cualquier número cabal distinto de cero es un múltiplo de ese número.	30, 40, and 90 are all multiples of 10.
Multiplication Property of Equality The property that states that if you multiply both sides of an equation by the same number, the new equation will have the same solution. (p. 52)	**Propiedad de igualdad de la multiplicación** Propiedad que establece que puedes multiplicar ambos lados de una ecuación por el mismo número y la nueva ecuación tendrá la misma solución.	$\frac{1}{3}x = 7$ $(3)(\frac{1}{3}x) = (3)(7)$ $x = 21$
Multiplication Property of Zero The property that states that for all real numbers a, $a \times 0 = 0$ and $0 \times a = 0$. (p. SB2)	**Propiedad de multiplicación del cero** Propiedad que establece que para todos los números reales a, $a \times 0 = 0$ y $0 \times a = 0$.	$6 \cdot 0 = 0$ $-5 \cdot 0 = 0$
Multiplicative Inverse Property The product of a nonzero number and its reciprocal, or multiplicative inverse, is one. (p.194)	**Propiedad inversa de la multiplicación** El producto de un número distinto a cero y su recíproco, o inverso multiplicativo, es uno.	$\frac{2}{3} \cdot \frac{3}{2} = 1; \frac{a}{b} \cdot \frac{b}{a} = 1$
mutually exclusive Two events are mutually exclusive if they cannot occur in the same trial of an experiment. (p. SB10)	**mutuamente excluyentes** Dos sucesos son mutuamente excluyentes cuando no pueden ocurrir en la misma prueba de un experimento.	

N

negative correlation Two data sets have a negative correlation, or relationship, if one set of data values increases while the other decreases. (p. 423)

correlación negativa Dos conjuntos de datos tienen correlación, o relación, negativa, si los valores de un conjunto aumentan a medida que los valores del otro conjunto disminuyen.

negative integer An integer less than zero. (p. 72)

entero negativo Entero menor que cero.

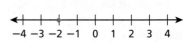

−2 is a negative integer.

net An arrangement of two-dimensional figures that can be folded to form a polyhedron. (p. 607)

plantilla Arreglo de figuras bidimensionales que se doblan para formar un poliedro.

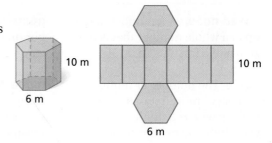

no correlation Two data sets have no correlation when there is no relationship between their data values. (p. 423)

sin correlación Caso en que los valores de dos conjuntos de datos no muestran ninguna relación.

nonlinear function A function whose graph is not a straight line. (p. 300)

función no lineal Función cuya gráfica no es una línea recta.

nonterminating decimal A decimal that never ends. (p. 562)

decimal infinito Decimal que nunca termina.

numerator The top number of a fraction that tells how many parts of a whole are being considered.

numerador El número de arriba de una fracción; indica cuántas partes de un entero se consideran.

$\frac{4}{5}$ ⟵ numerator

numerical expression An expression that contains only numbers and operations. (p. 19)

expresión numérica Expresión que incluye sólo números y operaciones.

$(2 \cdot 3) + 1$

O

obtuse angle An angle whose measure is greater than 90° but less than 180°. (p. 454)

ángulo obtuso Ángulo que mide más de 90° y menos de 180°.

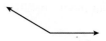

Glossary/Glosario

ENGLISH	SPANISH	EXAMPLES
obtuse triangle A triangle containing one obtuse angle. (p. 478)	**triángulo obtusángulo** Triángulo que tiene un ángulo obtuso.	
octagon An eight-sided polygon. (p. 474)	**octágono** Polígono de ocho lados.	
odd number An integer that is not divisible by two.	**número impar** Entero que no es divisible entre 2.	
odds A comparison of the number of ways an event can occur and the number of ways an event can NOT occur. (p. SB9)	**posibilidades** Comparación del numero de las maneras que puede ocurrir un suceso y el numero de maneras que no puede ocurrir el suceso.	
opposites Two numbers that are an equal distance from zero on a number line; also called *additive inverse.* (p. 72)	**opuestos** Dos números que están a la misma distancia de cero en una recta numérica. También se llaman *inversos aditivos.*	5 and −5 are opposites. 
order of operations A rule for evaluating expressions: first perform the operations in parentheses, then compute powers and roots, then perform all multiplication and division from left to right, and then perform all addition and subtraction from left to right. (p. 19)	**orden de las operaciones** Regla para evaluar expresiones: primero se hacen las operaciones entre paréntesis, luego se hallan las potencias y raíces, después todas las multiplicaciones y divisiones de izquierda a derecha y, por último, todas las sumas y restas de izquierda a derecha.	$3^2 - 12 \div 4$ $9 - 12 \div 4$ Evaluate the power. $9 - 3$ Divide. 6 Subtract.
ordered pair A pair of numbers that can be used to locate a point on a coordinate plane. (p. 276)	**par ordenado** Par de números que sirven para ubicar un punto en un plano cartesiano.	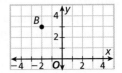 The coordinates of *B* are (−2, 3).
origin The point where the *x*-axis and *y*-axis intersect on the coordinate plane; (0, 0). (p. 276)	**origen** Punto de intersección entre el eje *x* y el eje *y* en un plano cartesiano: (0, 0).	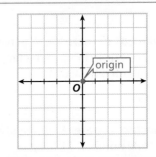
outcome A possible result of a probability experiment. (p. 640)	**resultado** Posible resultado de un experimento de probabilidad.	When rolling a number cube, the possible outcomes are 1, 2, 3, 4, 5, and 6.

ENGLISH	SPANISH	EXAMPLES
outlier A value much greater or much less than the others in a data set. (p. 385)	**valor extremo** Un valor mucho mayor o menor que los demás de un conjunto de datos.	Most of data **Mean** Outlier
output The value that results from the substitution of a given input into an expression or function. (p. 284)	**valor de salida** Valor que resulta después de sustituir un valor de entrada determinado en una expresión o función.	For the function $y = 6x$, the input 4 produces an output of 24.
overestimate An estimate that is greater than the exact answer. (p. SB3)	**estimación alta** Estimación mayor que la respuesta exacta.	100 is an overestimate for the sum 23 + 24 + 21 + 22.

P

ENGLISH	SPANISH	EXAMPLES
parallel lines Lines in a plane that do not intersect. (p. 460)	**rectas paralelas** Líneas que se encuentran en el mismo plano pero que nunca se intersecan.	
parallelogram A quadrilateral with two pairs of parallel sides. (p. 482)	**paralelogramo** Cuadrilátero con dos pares de lados paralelos.	
pentagon A five-sided polygon. (p. 474)	**pentágono** Polígono de cinco lados.	
percent A ratio comparing a number to 100. (p. 336)	**porcentaje** Razón que compara un número con el número 100.	$45\% = \frac{45}{100}$
percent of change The amount stated as a percent that a number increases or decreases. (p. 358)	**porcentaje de cambio** Cantidad en que un número aumenta o disminuye, expresada como un porcentaje.	
percent of decrease A percent change describing a decrease in a quantity. (p. 358)	**porcentaje de disminución** Porcentaje de cambio en que una cantidad disminuye.	An item that costs $8 is marked down to $6. The amount of the decrease is $2 and the percent of decrease is $\frac{2}{8} = 0.25 = 25\%$.
percent of increase A percent change describing an increase in a quantity. (p. 358)	**porcentaje de incremento** Porcentaje de cambio en que una cantidad aumenta.	The price of an item increases from $8 to $12. The amount of the increase is $4 and the percent of increase is $\frac{4}{8} = 0.5 = 50\%$.
perfect square A square of a whole number. (p. 558)	**cuadrado perfecto** El cuadrado de un número cabal.	$5^2 = 25$, so 25 is a perfect square.

ENGLISH	SPANISH	EXAMPLES

perimeter The distance around a polygon. (p. 530)

perímetro Distancia alrededor de un polígono.

perimeter =
18 + 6 + 18 + 6 = 48 ft

---

permutation An arrangement of items or events in which order is important. (p. 674)

permutación Arreglo de objetos o sucesos en el que el orden es importante.

For objects *A*, *B*, and *C*, there are 6 different permutations, *ABC*, *ACB*, *BAC*, *BCA*, *CAB*, *CBA*.

---

perpendicular bisector A line that intersects a segment at its midpoint and is perpendicular to the segment. (p. 464)

mediatriz Línea que cruza un segmento en su punto medio y es perpendicular al segmento.

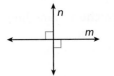

---

perpendicular lines Lines that intersect to form right angles. (p. 460)

rectas perpendiculares Líneas que al intersecarse forman ángulos rectos.

---

pi (π) The ratio of the circumference of a circle to the length of its diameter; $\pi \approx 3.14$ or $\frac{22}{7}$. (p. 531)

pi (π) Razón de la circunferencia de un círculo a la longitud de su diámetro; $\pi \approx 3.14$ ó $\frac{22}{7}$.

---

plane A flat surface that has no thickness and extends forever. (p. 448)

plano Superficie plana que no tiene ningún grueso y que se extiende por siempre.

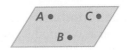

plane *ABC*

---

point An exact location that has no size. (p. 448)

punto Ubicación exacta que no tiene ninqún tamaño.

P •

point *P*

---

polygon A closed plane figure formed by three or more line segments that intersect only at their endpoints (vertices). (p. 474)

polígono Figura plana cerrada, formada por tres o más segmentos de recta que se intersecan sólo en sus extremos (vértices).

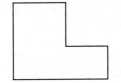

---

polyhedron A three-dimensional figure in which all the surfaces or faces are polygons. (p. 588)

poliedro Figura tridimensional cuyas superficies o caras tienen forma de polígonos.

---

population The entire group of objects or individuals considered for a survey. (p. 418)

población Grupo completo de objetos o individuos que se desea estudiar.

In a survey about the study habits of middle school students, the population is all middle school students.

ENGLISH	SPANISH	EXAMPLES
positive correlation Two data sets have a positive correlation, or relationship, when their data values increase or decrease together. (p. 423)	**correlación positiva** Dos conjuntos de datos tienen una correlación, o relación, positiva cuando los valores de ambos conjuntos aumentan o disminuyen al mismo tiempo.	
positive integer An integer greater than zero. (p. 72)	**entero positivo** Entero mayor que cero.	
power A number produced by raising a base to an exponent. (p. 10)	**potencia** Número que resulta al elevar una base a un exponente.	$2^3 = 8$, so 2 to the 3rd power is 8.
precision The level of detail of a measurement, determined by the unit of measure. (p. 524)	**precisión** Detalle de una medición, determinado por la unidad de medida.	A ruler marked in millimeters has a greater level of precision than a ruler marked in centimeters.
prediction Something you can reasonably expect to happen in the future. (p. 658)	**predicción** Algo que se puede razonablemente esperar suceder en el futuro.	
preimage The original figure in a transformation. (p. 496)	**imagen original** Figura original en una transformación.	
prime factorization A number written as the product of its prime factors. (p. 104)	**factorización prima** Un número escrito como el producto de sus factores primos.	$10 = 2 \cdot 5$ $24 = 2^3 \cdot 3$
prime number A whole number greater than 1 that has exactly two factors, itself and 1. (p. 104)	**número primo** Número cabal mayor que 1 que sólo es divisible entre 1 y él mismo.	5 is prime because its only factors are 5 and 1.
principal The initial amount of money borrowed or saved. (p. 362)	**capital** Cantidad inicial de dinero depositada o recibida en préstamo.	
prism A polyhedron that has two congruent polygon-shaped bases and other faces that are all parallelograms. (p. 588)	**prisma** Poliedro con dos bases congruentes con forma de polígono y caras con forma de paralelogramo.	
probability A number from 0 to 1 (or 0% to 100%) that describes how likely an event is to occur. (p. 640)	**probabilidad** Un número entre 0 y 1 (ó 0% y 100%) que describe qué tan probable es un suceso.	A bag contains 3 red marbles and 4 blue marbles. The probability of randomly choosing a red marble is $\frac{3}{7}$.
product The result when two or more numbers are multiplied.	**producto** Resultado de multiplicar dos o más números.	The product of 4 and 8 is 32.

ENGLISH	SPANISH	EXAMPLES
proper fraction A fraction in which the numerator is less than the denominator.	**fracción propia** Fracción en la que el numerador es menor que el denominador.	$\frac{3}{4}, \frac{1}{12}, \frac{7}{8}$
proportion An equation that states that two ratios are equivalent. (p. 222)	**proporción** Ecuación que establece que dos razones son equivalentes.	$\frac{2}{3} = \frac{4}{6}$
protractor A tool for measuring angles. (p. 452)	**transportador** Instrumento para medir ángulos.	
pyramid A polyhedron with a polygon base and triangular sides that all meet at a common vertex. (p. 588)	**pirámide** Poliedro cuya base es un polígono; tiene caras triangulares que se juntan en un vértice común.	
Pythagorean Theorem In a right triangle, the square of the length of the hypotenuse is equal to the sum of the squares of the lengths of the legs. (p. 566)	**Teorema de Pitágoras** En un triángulo rectángulo, la suma de los cuadrados de los catetos es igual al cuadrado de la hipotenusa.	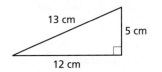 $5^2 + 12^2 = 13^2$ $25 + 144 = 169$

Q

quadrant The x- and y-axes divide the coordinate plane into four regions. Each region is called a quadrant. (p. 276)	**cuadrante** El eje x y el eje y dividen el plano cartesiano en cuatro regiones. Cada región recibe el nombre de cuadrante.	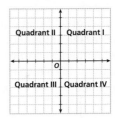
quadratic function A function of the form $y = ax^2 + bx + c$, where $a \neq 0$. (p. SB18)	**función cuadrática** Función del tipo $y = ax^2 + bx + c$, donde $a \neq 0$.	$y = 2x^2 - 12x + 10$, $y = 3x^2$
quadrilateral A four-sided polygon. (p. 474)	**cuadrilátero** Polígono de cuatro lados.	
quartile Three values, one of which is the median, that divide a data set into fourths. See also *first quartile, third quartile*. (p. 398)	**cuartiles** Cada uno de tres valores, uno de los cuales es la mediana, que dividen en cuartos un conjunto de datos. Ver también *primer cuartil, tercer cuartil*.	
quotient The result when one number is divided by another.	**cociente** Resultado de dividir un número entre otro.	In $8 \div 4 = 2$, 2 is the quotient.

Glossary/Glosario   **G25**

R

radical sign The symbol $\sqrt{}$ used to represent the nonnegative square root of a number. (p. 558)	**símbolo de radical** El símbolo $\sqrt{}$ con que se representa la raíz cuadrada no negativa de un número.	$\sqrt{36} = 6$
radius A line segment with one endpoint at the center of a circle and the other endpoint on the circle, or the length of that segment. (p. 468)	**radio** Segmento de recta con un extremo en el centro de un círculo y el otro en la circunferencia; o bien la longitud de ese segmento.	Radius
random sample A sample in which each individual or object in the entire population has an equal chance of being selected. (p. 418)	**muestra aleatoria** Muestra en la que cada individuo u objeto de la población tiene la misma oportunidad de ser elegido.	Mr. Henson chose a random sample of the class by writing each student's name on a slip of paper, mixing up the slips, and drawing five slips without looking.
range (in statistics) The difference between the greatest and least values in a data set. (p. 385)	**rango (en estadística)** Diferencia entre los valores máximo y mínimo de un conjunto de datos.	Data set: 3, 5, 7, 7, 12 Range: $12 - 3 = 9$
rate A ratio that compares two quantities measured in different units. (p. 218)	**tasa** Una razón que compara dos cantidades medidas en diferentes unidades.	The speed limit is 55 miles per hour, or 55 mi/h.
rate of change A ratio that compares the amount of change in a dependent variable to the amount of change in an independent variable. (p. 303)	**tasa de cambio** Razón que compara la cantidad de cambio de la variable dependiente con la cantidad de combio de la variable independiente.	The cost of mailing a letter increaed from 22 cents in 1985 to 25 cents in 1988. During this period, the rate of change was $\frac{\text{change in cost}}{\text{change in year}} = \frac{25 - 21}{1988 - 1985} = \frac{3}{3}$
rate of interest The percent charged or earned on an amount of money; see *simple interest.* (p. 362)	**tasa de interés** Porcentaje que se cobra por una cantidad de dinero prestada o que se gana por una cantidad de dinero ahorrada; ver *interés simple.*	
ratio A comparison of two quantities by division. (p. 214)	**razón** Comparación de dos cantidades mediante una división.	12 to 25, 12:25, $\frac{12}{25}$
rational number Any number that can be expressed as a ratio of two integers. (p. 127)	**número racional** Número que se puede escribir como una razón de dos enteros.	6 can be expressed as $\frac{6}{1}$. 0.5 can be expressed as $\frac{1}{2}$.
ray A part of a line that starts at one endpoint and extends forever in one direction. (p. 449)	**rayo** Parte de una recta que comienza en un extremo y se extiende infinitamente en una dirección.	D
real number A rational or irrational number. (p. 562)	**número real** Número racional o irracional.	

ENGLISH	SPANISH	EXAMPLES
reciprocal One of two numbers whose product is 1; also called *multiplicative inverse.* (p. 190)	**recíproco** Uno de dos números cuyo producto es igual a 1. También se llama *inverso multiplicativo.*	The reciprocal of $\frac{2}{3}$ is $\frac{3}{2}$.
rectangle A parallelogram with four right angles. (p. 482)	**rectángulo** Paralelogramo con cuatro ángulos rectos.	
rectangular prism A polyhedron whose bases are rectangles and whose other faces are parallelograms. (p. 588)	**prisma rectangular** Poliedro cuyas bases son rectángulos y cuyas caras tienen forma de paralelogramo.	
reflection A transformation of a figure that flips the figure across a line. (p. 496)	**reflexión** Transformación que ocurre cuando se invierte una figura sobre una línea.	
regular polygon A polygon with congruent sides and angles. (p. 475)	**polígono regular** Polígono con lados y ángulos congruentes.	
regular pyramid A pyramid whose base is a regular polygon and whose lateral faces are all congruent. (p. 614)	**pirámide regular** Pirámide que tiene un polígono regular como base y caras laterales congruentes.	
relative frequency The frequency of a data value or range of data values divided by the total number of data values in the set. (p. 645)	**frecuencia relativa** La frecuencia de un valor o un rango de valores dividido por el número total de los valores en el conjunto.	
relatively prime Two numbers are relatively prime if their greatest common factor (GCF) is 1. (p. 118)	**primo relatívo** Dos números son primos relativos si su máximo común divisor (MCD) es 1.	8 and 15 are relatively prime.
repeating decimal A decimal in which one or more digits repeat infinitely. (p. 122)	**decimal periódico** Decimal en el que uno o más dígitos se repiten infinitamente.	$0.757575\ldots = 0.\overline{75}$
rhombus A parallelogram with all sides congruent. (p. 482)	**rombo** Paralelogramo en el que todos los lados son congruentes.	
right angle An angle that measures 90°. (p. 454)	**ángulo recto** Ángulo que mide exactamente 90°.	

right triangle A triangle containing a right angle. (p. 478)

triángulo rectángulo Triángulo que tiene un ángulo recto.

---

rise The vertical change when the slope of a line is expressed as the ratio $\frac{\text{rise}}{\text{run}}$, or "rise over run." (p. 302)

distancia vertical El cambio vertical cuando la pendiente de una línea se expresa como la razón $\frac{\text{distancia vertical}}{\text{distancia horizontal}}$, o "distancia vertical sobre distancia horizontal".

For the points $(3, -1)$ and $(6, 5)$, the rise is $5 - (-1) = 6$.

---

rotation A transformation in which a figure is turned around a point. (p. 496)

rotación Transformación que ocurre cuando una figura gira alrededor de un punto.

---

rotational symmetry A figure has rotational symmetry if it can be rotated less than 360° around a central point and coincide with the original figure. (p. 505)

simetría de rotación Ocurre cuando una figura gira menos de 360° alrededor de un punto central sin dejar de ser congruente con la figura original.

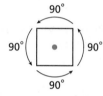

---

rounding Replacing a number with an estimate of that number to a given place value.

redondear Sustituir un número por una estimación de ese número hasta cierto valor posicional.

2,354 rounded to the nearest thousand is 2,000, and 2,354 rounded to the nearest 100 is 2,400.

---

run The horizontal change when the slope of a line is expressed as the ratio $\frac{\text{rise}}{\text{run}}$, or "rise over run." (p. 302)

distancia horizontal El cambio horizontal cuando la pendiente de una línea se expresa como la razón $\frac{\text{distancia vertical}}{\text{distancia horizontal}}$, o "distancia vertical sobre distancia horizontal".

For the points $(3, -1)$ and $(6, 5)$, the run is $6 - 3 = 3$.

---

sales tax A percent of the cost of an item, which is charged by governments to raise money.

impuesto sobre la venta Porcentaje del costo de un artículo que los gobiernos cobran para recaudar fondos.

---

sample A part of the population. (p. 418)

muestra Una parte de la población.

In a survey about the study habits of middle school students, a sample is a survey of 100 randomly-chosen students.

---

sample space All possible outcomes of an experiment. (p. 648)

espacio muestral Conjunto de todos los resultados posibles de un experimento.

When rolling a number cube, the sample space is 1, 2, 3, 4, 5, 6.

---

scale The ratio between two sets of measurements. (p. 256)

escala La razón entre dos conjuntos de medidas.

1 cm:5 mi

	ENGLISH	SPANISH	EXAMPLES

scale drawing A drawing that uses a scale to make an object smaller than or larger than the real object. (p. 256)

dibujo a escala Dibujo en el que se usa una escala para que un objeto se vea mayor o menor que el objeto real al que representa.

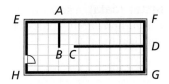

A blueprint is an example of a scale drawing.

scale factor The ratio used to enlarge or reduce similar figures. (p. 256)

factor de escala Razón que se usa para agrandar o reducir figuras semejantes.

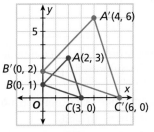

Scale factor: 2

scale model A proportional model of a three-dimensional object. (p. 256)

modelo a escala Modelo proporcional de un objeto tridimensional.

scalene triangle A triangle with no congruent sides. (p. 478)

triángulo escaleno Triángulo que no tiene lados congruentes.

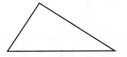

scatter plot A graph with points plotted to show a possible relationship between two sets of data. (p. 422)

diagrama de dispersión Gráfica de puntos que se usa para mostrar una posible relación entre dos conjuntos de datos.

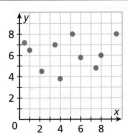

scientific notation A method of writing very large or very small numbers by using powers of 10. (p. 14)

notación científica Método que se usa para escribir números muy grandes o muy pequeños mediante potencias de 10.

$$12{,}560{,}000{,}000{,}000 = 1.256 \times 10^{13}$$

sector A region enclosed by two radii and the arc joining their endpoints. (p. 469)

sector Región encerrada por dos radios y el arco que une sus extremos.

ENGLISH	SPANISH	EXAMPLES

sector (data) A section of a circle graph representing part of the data set. (p. 394)

sector (datos) Sección de una gráfica circular que representa una parte del conjunto de datos.

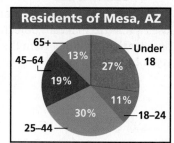

The circle graph has 5 sectors.

---

segment A part of a line between two endpoints. (p. 448)

segmento Parte de una línea entre dos extremos.

---

sequence An ordered list of numbers. (p. 288)

sucesión Lista ordenada de números.

2, 4, 6, 8, 10, ...

---

side A line bounding a geometric figure; one of the faces forming the outside of an object. (p. 474)

lado Línea que delimita las figuras geométricas; una de las caras que forman la parte exterior de un objeto.

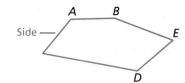

Side-Side-Side (SSS) A rule stating that if three sides of one triangle are congruent to three sides of another triangle, then the triangles are congruent. (p. 492)

Lado-Lado-Lado (LLL) Regla que establece que dos triángulos son congruentes cuando sus tres lados correspondientes son congruentes.

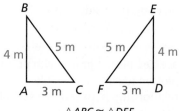

$\triangle ABC \cong \triangle DEF$

---

significant digits The digits used to express the precision of a measurement. (p. SB5)

dígitos significativos Dígitos usados para expresar la precisión de una medida.

0.048 has 2 significant digits.
5.003 has 4 significant digits.

---

similar Figures with the same shape but not necessarily the same size are similar. (p. 248)

semejantes Figuras que tienen la misma forma, pero no necesariamente el mismo tamaño.

---

simulation A model of an experiment, often one that would be too difficult or too time-consuming to actually perform. (p. 656)

simulación Representación de un experimento, por lo regular de uno cuya realización sería demasiado difícil o llevaría mucho tiempo.

---

simple event An event consisting of only one outcome. (p. 640)

suceso simple Suceso que tiene sólo un resultado.

In the experiment of rolling a number cube, the event consisting of the outcome 3 is a simple event.

ENGLISH	SPANISH	EXAMPLES

simple interest A fixed percent of the principal. It is found using the formula $I = Prt$, where P represents the principal, r the rate of interest, and t the time. (p. 362)

interés simple Un porcentaje fijo del capital. Se calcula con la fórmula $I = Cit$, donde C representa el capital, i, la tasa de interés y t, el tiempo.

$100 is put into an account with a simple interest rate of 5%. After 2 years, the account will have earned
$I = 100 \cdot 0.05 \cdot 2 = \$10$.

---

simplest form A fraction is in simplest form when the numerator and denominator have no common factors other than 1.

mínima expresión Una fracción está en su mínima expresión cuando el numerador y el denominador no tienen más factor común que 1.

Fraction: $\frac{8}{12}$
Simplest form: $\frac{2}{3}$

---

simplify To write a fraction or expression in simplest form.

simplificar Escribir una fracción o expresión numérica en su mínima expresión.

---

skew lines Lines that lie in different planes that are neither parallel nor intersecting. (p. 460)

líneas oblicuas Líneas que se encuentran en planos distintos, por eso no se intersecan ni son paralelas.

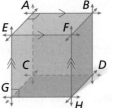

$\overleftrightarrow{AB}$ and $\overleftrightarrow{CG}$ are skew lines.

---

slant height of a cone The distance from the vertex of a cone to a point on the edge of the base. (p. 615)

altura inclinada de un cono Distancia desde el vértice de un cono hasta un punto en el borde de la base.

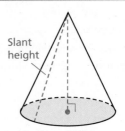

Slant height

---

slant height of a pyramid The distance from the vertex of a pyramid to the midpoint of an edge of the base. (p. 614)

altura inclinada de una pirámide Distancia desde el vértice de una pirámide hasta el punto medio de una arista de la base.

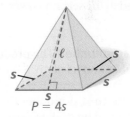

$P = 4s$

---

slope A measure of the steepness of a line on a graph; the rise divided by the run. (p. 302)

pendiente Medida de la inclinación de una línea en una gráfica. Razón de la distancia vertical a la distancia horizontal.

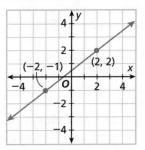

Slope $= \frac{\text{Rise}}{\text{Sun}} = \frac{3}{4}$

---

slope-intercept form A linear equation written in form $y = mx + b$, where m represents slope and b represents the y-intercept. (p. 308)

forma de pendiente-intersecciíon Ecuación lineal escrita en la forma $y = mx + b$, donde m es la pendiente y b es la intersección con el eje y.

$y = 6x - 3$

ENGLISH	SPANISH	EXAMPLES
solid figure A three-dimensional figure. (p. 588)	**cuerpo geométrico** Figura tridimensional.	
solution of an equation A value or values that make an equation true. (p. 42)	**solución de una ecuación** Valor o valores que hacen verdadera una ecuación.	Equation: $x + 2 = 6$ Solution: $x = 4$
solution of an inequality A value or values that make an inequality true. (p. 710)	**solución de una desigualdad** Valor o valores que hacen verdadera una desigualdad.	Inequality: $x + 3 \geq 10$ Solution: $x \geq 7$
solution set The set of values that make a statement true. (p. 710)	**conjunto solución** Conjunto de valores que hacen verdadero un enunciado.	Inequality: $x + 3 \geq 5$ Solution set: $x \geq 2$ 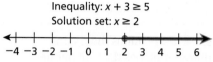
solve To find an answer or a solution. (p. 48)	**resolver** Hallar una respuesta o solución.	
sphere A three-dimensional figure with all points the same distance from the center. (p. 589)	**esfera** Figura tridimensional en la que todos los puntos están a la misma distancia del centro.	
square (geometry) A rectangle with four congruent sides. (p. 482)	**cuadrado (en geometría)** Rectángulo con cuatro lados congruentes.	
square (numeration) A number raised to the second power. (p. 558)	**cuadrado (en numeración)** Número elevado a la segunda potencia.	In 5^2, the number 5 is squared.
square number The product of a number and itself. (p. 558)	**cuadrado de un número** El producto de un número y sí mismo.	25 is a square number. $5 \cdot 5 = 25$.
square root A number that is multiplied by itself to form a product is called a square root of that product. (p. 558)	**raíz cuadrada** El número que se multiplica por sí mismo para formar un producto se denomina la raíz cuadrada de ese producto.	$\sqrt{16} = 4$, because $4^2 = 4 \cdot 4 = 16$
standard form (in numeration) A way to write numbers by using digits. (p. 15)	**forma estándar (en numeración)** Una manera de escribir números por medio de dígitos.	Five thousand, two hundred ten in standard form is 5,210.
stem-and-leaf plot A graph used to organize and display data so that the frequencies can be compared. (p. 381)	**diagrama de tallo y hojas** Gráfica que muestra y ordena los datos, y que sirve para comparar las frecuencias.	Stem | Leaves 3 | 2 3 4 4 7 9 4 | 0 1 5 7 7 7 8 5 | 1 2 2 3 *Key: 3|2 means 3.2*

ENGLISH	SPANISH	EXAMPLES
straight angle An angle that measures 180°. (p. 454)	**ángulo llano** Ángulo que mide exactamente 180°.	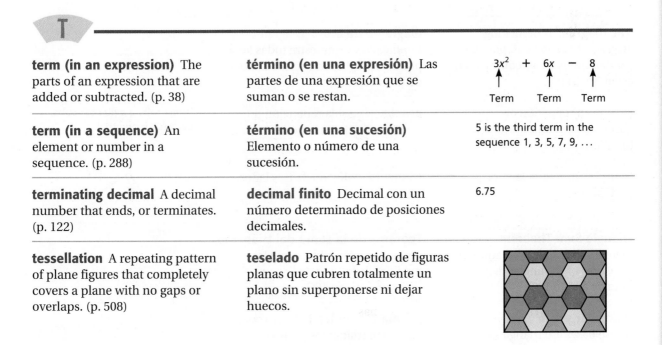
substitute To replace a variable with a number or another expression in an algebraic expression.	**sustituir** Reemplazar una variable por un número u otra expresión en una expresión algebraica.	
Subtraction Property of Equality The property that states that if you subtract the same number from both sides of an equation, the new equation will have the same solution. (p. 49)	**Propiedad de igualdad de la resta** Propiedad que establece que puedes restar el mismo número de ambos lados de una ecuación y la nueva ecuación tendrá la misma solución.	$$\begin{aligned} x + 6 &= 8 \\ -6 &\quad -6 \\ x &= 2 \end{aligned}$$
sum The result when two or more numbers are added.	**suma** Resultado de sumar dos o más números.	The sum of $6 + 7 + 1$ is 14.
supplementary angles Two angles whose measures have a sum of 180°. (p. 454)	**ángulos suplementarios** Dos ángulos cuyas medidas suman 180°.	$30°$ $150°$
surface area The sum of the areas of the faces, or surfaces, of a three-dimensional figure. (p. 560)	**área total** Suma de las áreas de las caras, o superficies, de una figura tridimensional.	12 cm, 6 cm, 8 cm Surface area = 2(8)(12) + 2(8)(6) + 2(12)(6) = 432 cm²

T

ENGLISH	SPANISH	EXAMPLES
term (in an expression) The parts of an expression that are added or subtracted. (p. 38)	**término (en una expresión)** Las partes de una expresión que se suman o se restan.	$3x^2 + 6x - 8$ Term Term Term
term (in a sequence) An element or number in a sequence. (p. 288)	**término (en una sucesión)** Elemento o número de una sucesión.	5 is the third term in the sequence 1, 3, 5, 7, 9, …
terminating decimal A decimal number that ends, or terminates. (p. 122)	**decimal finito** Decimal con un número determinado de posiciones decimales.	6.75
tessellation A repeating pattern of plane figures that completely covers a plane with no gaps or overlaps. (p. 508)	**teselado** Patrón repetido de figuras planas que cubren totalmente un plano sin superponerse ni dejar huecos.	

theoretical probability The ratio of the number of ways an event can occur to the total number of equally likely outcomes. (p. 652)

probabilidad teórica Razón del numero de las maneras que puede ocurrir un suceso al numero total de resultados igualmente probables.

When rolling a number cube, the theoretical probability of rolling a 4 is $\frac{1}{6}$.

---

third quartile The median of the upper half of a set of data; also called *upper quartile*. (p. 398)

tercer cuartil La mediana de la mitad superior de un conjunto de datos. También se llama *cuartil superior*.

---

transformation A change in the position or orientation of a figure. (p. 496)

transformación Cambio en la posición u orientación de una figura.

---

translation A movement (slide) of a figure along a straight line. (p. 496)

traslación Desplazamiento de una figura a lo largo de una línea recta.

---

transversal A line that intersects two or more lines. (p. 461)

transversal Línea que cruza dos o más líneas.

---

trapezoid A quadrilateral with exactly one pair of parallel sides. (p. 482)

trapecio Cuadrilátero con un par de lados paralelos.

---

tree diagram A branching diagram that shows all possible combinations or outcomes of an event. (p. 649)

diagrama de árbol Diagrama ramificado que muestra todas las posibles combinaciones o resultados de un suceso.

---

trial Each repetition or observation of an experiment. (p. 640)

prueba Una sola repetición u observación de un experimento.

When rolling a number cube, each roll is one trial.

---

triangle A three-sided polygon. (p. 475)

triángulo Polígono de tres lados.

Triangle Sum Theorem The theorem that states that the measures of the angles in a triangle add to 180°.

Teorema de la suma del triángulo Teorema que establece que las medidas de los ángulos de un triángulo suman 180°.

---

triangular prism A polyhedron whose bases are triangles and whose other faces are parallelograms. (p. 588)

prisma triangular Poliedro cuyas bases son triángulos y cuyas demás caras tienen forma de paralelogramo.

Glossary/Glosario

U

underestimate An estimate that is less than the exact answer. (p. SB3)	**estimación baja** Estimación menor que la respuesta exacta.	
unit conversion The process of changing one unit of measure to another. (p. 240)	**conversión de unidades** Proceso que consiste en cambiar una unidad de medida por otra.	
unit conversion factor A fraction used in unit conversion in which the numerator and denominator represent the same amount but are in different units. (p. 240)	**factor de conversión de unidades** Fracción que se usa para la conversión de unidades, donde el numerador y el denominador representan la misma cantidad pero están en unidades distintas.	$\frac{60 \text{ min}}{1\text{h}}$ or $\frac{1\text{h}}{60 \text{ min}}$
unit price A unit rate used to compare prices.	**precio unitario** Tasa unitaria que sirve para comparar precios.	
unit rate A rate in which the second quantity in the comparison is one unit. (p. 218)	**tasa unitaria** Una tasa en la que la segunda cantidad de la comparación es la unidad.	10 cm per minute
upper quartile The median of the upper half of a set of data. (p. 398)	**cuartil superior** La mediana de la mitad superior de un conjunto de datos.	Lower half Upper half 18, 23, 28, 29, (36,) 42 ↑ Upper quartile

 V

variable A symbol used to represent a quantity that can change. (p. 30)	**variable** Símbolo que representa una cantidad que puede cambiar.	In the expression $2x + 3$, x is the variable.
Venn diagram A diagram that is used to show relationships between sets.	**diagrama de Venn** Diagrama que muestra las relaciones entre conjuntos.	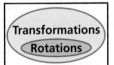
verbal expression A word or phrase. (p. 34)	**expresión verbal** Palabra o frase.	
vertex On an angle or polygon, the point where two sides intersect. (p. 454)	**vértice** En un ángulo o polígono, el punto de intersección de dos lados.	C A B *A is the vertex of* $\angle CAB.$

Glossary/Glosario

| | ENGLISH | SPANISH | EXAMPLES |

vertical angles A pair of opposite congruent angles formed by intersecting lines. (p. 461)

ángulos opuestos por el vértice Par de ángulos opuestos congruentes formados por líneas secantes.

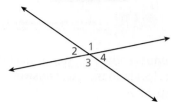

∠1 and ∠3 are vertical angles.
∠2 and ∠4 are vertical angles.

volume The number of cubic units needed to fill a given space. (p. 596)

volumen Número de unidades cúbicas que se necesitan para llenar un espacio.

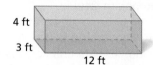

Volume = 3 · 4 · 12 = 144 ft³

x-axis The horizontal axis on a coordinate plane. (p. 276)

eje x El eje horizontal del plano cartesiano.

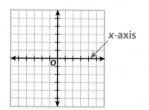

x-axis

x-coordinate The first number in an ordered pair; it tells the distance to move right or left from the origin, (0, 0). (p. 276)

coordenada x El primer número en un par ordenado; indica la distancia que debes avanzar hacia la izquierda o hacia la derecha desde el origen, (0, 0).

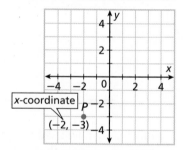

x-intercept The x-coordinate of the point where the graph of a line crosses the x-axis. (p. 308)

intersección con el eje x Coordenada x del punto donde la gráfica de una línea cruza el eje x.

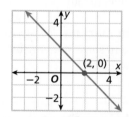

The x-intercept is 2.

Glossary/Glosario

y-axis The vertical axis on a coordinate plane. (p. 276)

eje y El eje vertical del plano cartesiano.

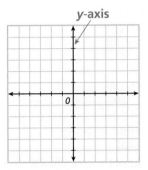

y-coordinate The second number in an ordered pair; it tells the distance to move up or down from the origin, (0, 0). (p. 276)

coordenada y El segundo número de un par ordenado; indica la distancia que debes avanzar hacia arriba o hacia abajo desde el origen, (0, 0).

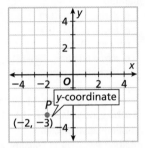

y-intercept The y-coordinate of the point where the graph of a line crosses the y-axis. (p. 308)

intersección con el eje y Coordenada y del punto donde la gráfica de una línea cruza el eje y.

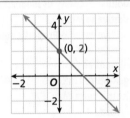

The y-intercept is 2.

Glossary/Glosario

Index

Index

Cylinders, 589
    characteristics of, 589
    cross section of, 592
    surface area, 607–609
    using nets to build, 606
    volume of, 594–597
    exploring volume of, 595

Data, displaying and organizing
    bar graphs, 390–391
    box-and-whisker plot, 398–399,
        402–403
    choosing an appropriate display for,
        412–413
    circle graphs, 394–395
    frequency tables, 380
    histograms, 391
    line graphs, 406–407
    line plot, 381–382
    misleading graphs, 428–429
    pie chart, 394–395
    populations and samples, 418–419
    scatter plots, 422–423, 426–427
    stem-and-leaf plot, 381
    using technology to display data,
        416–417
    Venn diagrams, 410–411
da Vinci, Leonardo, 238
Decagon, 475
Decimal grids, 152–153, 154, 158–159
Decimals
    addition of, 148–149
    comparing, 127
    division, 158–161
    estimating with, 144–145
    fractions and, 122–123
    multiplication of, 152–154
    ordering, 127
    as percents, 340–341, 349
    read and write, SB1
    repeating, 122
    solving equations containing, 164–165
    subtraction of, 148–149
    terminating, 122
Deductive reasoning, SB11
Degas, Edgar, 673
Degrees, 452, 454
Density, 226, 727
Department of Defense, 489
Dependent events
    probability and, 666–667
Dependent variable, 297
Design, 531
Diagonal, 486
Diameter, 468
Dilation, 502–503
Dimensional analysis, 240–241
Dinosaurs, 422
Direct variation, 313–315

Disjoint events, *see* mutually exclusive
    events
Disneyland, 655
Disney World, 655
Displaying and organizing data
    bar graphs, 390–391
    box-and-whisker plot, 398–399,
        402–403
    choosing appropriate display, 412–413
    circle graphs, 394–395
    frequency tables, 380
    histograms, 391
    line graphs, 406–407
    line plot, 381–382
    mean, median, mode and range,
        385–387
    misleading graphs, 428–429
    pie chart, 394–395
    populations and samples, 418–419
    scatter plots, 422–423, 426–427
    stem-and-leaf plot, 381
    using technology to display data,
        416–417
    Venn diagrams, 410–411
Distance
    graphs and, 280–281
Distribution, 381
Distributive Property, 25, 700
Divisibility rules, SB5
Division
    of decimals, 158–161
    of fractions, 184–185, 190–191
    integers, 90–93
    of mixed numbers, 190–191
    as multiplication by reciprocal, 190
    solving equations by, 52–53, 98–99
    solving two-step equations by, 695–696
    zero and, 93
Division Property of Equality, 52–53
Division Property of Inequalities,
    718–719
DNA molecule, 10
Dogs, 395, 717
Drawings, scale, 256–257, 260–261

Earle, Sylvia, 72
Earth, 15, 16, 89, 128, 176
    land area, 349, 397
Earthquakes, 11
Earth Science, 11, 17, 45, 74, 94, 95, 128,
    163, 196, 229, 234, 299, 351, 383, 409,
    488, 561, 643, 647, 713, 725
Earth Science Link, 11, 17, 45, 409, 561,
    647, 713
Eastern box turtle, 313, 315
Echinoderms, 394
Ecology, 224
Economics, 125, 361
Economics Link, 125, 361

Edge, 588
***Eight I* (Herbin),** 448
Elapsed time, SB8
Ellis Island, New York, 167
Ellison's Cave, 95
Endangered species in South America,
    384
Energy consumption, 361
Environment, 299
Environment Link, 299
Equality
    Addition Property of, 48
    Division Property of, 52–53
    Multiplication Property of, 52
    Subtraction Property of, 49
Equally likely, 652
Equations, 42
    addition, 48–49
    containing decimals, 164–165
    containing fractions, 194–195
    direct variation, 313–314
    division, 52–53
    integer, 96–99
    multiplication, 52–53
    multi-step, 700–701
    slope intercept form, 309
    solutions of, 42–43
    solving, *see* Solving equations
    subtraction, 48–49
    two-step, 694–697
    with variables on both sides, 704–705
Equilateral triangles, 478–479
Equivalent fractions
    decimals and, 122–123
    finding, 118–119
Equivalent ratios, 222
    finding, 223
Escher, M. C., 508, 509
Estimating, 157, 220, 235, 242, 347, 389,
    408, 527, 617
    compatible numbers, 144–145
    with decimals, 144–145
    with fractions, 170–171
    with percents, 344–345
Events
    complementary, 641
    complement of, 641
    compound, 640
    dependent, 670–671
    disjoint, *see* mutually exclusive
    independent, 670–671
    mutually exclusive, SB10
    simple, 640
Exercise, 642
Expenses, 80
Experimental probability, 644–645,
    662–663
    making predictions using, 658–659
    simulations, 656–657
Experiment, 640

Index

Index

Index

Underestimate, SB3
Unit conversion factor, 240–241
Unit rates, 218–219
Units
    customary, 232
    generate formulas to convert, 307
    metric, 236
Upper quartile, 398
Uranus, 128
U.S. Department of Agriculture, 699

Van Gogh, Vincent, 238
Vantongerloo, Georges, 451
Variable rate of change, 303
Variables, 30
    on both sides, solving equations with,
        704–705
    dependent, 297
    independent, 297
    solving for, 726–727
Variation
    direct, 313–315
    inverse, 318–319
Velocity, 727
Venn diagrams
    using, to display collected data,
        410–411
    when to use, 412–413
Venus, 14, 16, 128, 176
Vertex
    of angles, 452, 454
    of polygon, 474
    of polyhedron, 588
Vertical angles, 461
Vocabulary Connections, 4, 70, 142, 212,
    274, 334, 378, 446, 522, 584, 638, 692
Volleyball, 530
Volume
    changes in dimensions and, 625
    of composite figure, 597
    of cones, 600–601
    of cylinders, 594–597
    of prisms, 594–597
    of pyramids, 600–601
    of similar figures, 621
Vostok, Antarctica, 74

Waimea, 533
Wakeboarding, 75
Washington, University of, 482
Washington Monument, 481
Water
    buoyant force of, 50
    changes of state, 33
    density of eggs and, 151
    household use, 129
    percent of human body, 348
    pressure of, 217
Water level, 299
Watermeal, 312
Watermelons, 719
Weather, 151, 156, 196, 279, 287, 645,
    658–659, 715
Weather Link, 279
Weight
    customary units of, 232
What's the Error?, 9, 13, 27, 33, 51, 55,
    75, 95, 111, 129, 167, 197, 225, 235,
    239, 243, 279, 287, 306, 312, 317, 343,
    351, 397, 401, 409, 457, 489, 527, 539,
    543, 563, 599, 617, 661, 677, 707, 725
What's the Question?, 37, 41, 83, 229,
    299, 355, 389, 507, 549, 603, 651, 703
Whole numbers, 562
Wildfires, 409
Wind turbines, 549
Words
    translating into algebraic expressions,
        34–35
Write About It
Write About It exercises are found in
every lesson. Some examples: 9, 13, 17,
22, 27
Write a Problem, 45, 105, 121, 163, 173,
    179, 221, 253, 347, 365, 471, 485, 643,
    669, 721
Writing Math, 15, 104, 454, 641, 644,
    711
Writing Strategies. *see also* Reading and
    Writing Math
    Keep a Math Journal, 447
    Translate Between Words and Math, 71
    Use Your Own Words, 213
    Write a Convincing Argument, 275

x-axis, 276
x-intercept, 308

Yamanashi Maglev Test Line, 726
y-axis, 276
y-intercept, 308
Yellowstone National Park, 2
Yurts, 547

Z

Zero
    division and, 93
Zero power, 10
Zodiac, 104

Index

Credits ...

Staff Credits

Bruce Albrecht, Kimberly Barr, Erik Brandon, Jennifer Cassle, Tica Chitrarachis, Lorraine Cooper, Marc Cooper, Nina Degollado, Michelle Dike, Sam Dudgeon, Kelli R. Flanagan, Stephanie Friedman, Pam Garner, Diannia Green, Jennifer Gribble, Tom Hamilton, Liz Huckestein, Sarah Hudgens, Wilonda Ieans, Jevara Jackson, Simon Key, Jane A. Kirschman, Cathy Kuhles, Jill M. Lawson, Liann Lech, Leandria Lee, Jessika Maier, Jeff Mapua, Jonathan Martindill, Virginia Messler, Erica Miller, Erin Miller, Stacey Murray, Susan Mussey, Michael Neibergall, Kim Nguyen, Sara Phelps, Chris Rankin, Theresa Reding, Manda Reid, Jane Reinig, Katie Seawell, Patricia Sinnott, Patti Smith, Victoria Smith, Melinda Steele, Jeannie Taylor, David Trevino, April Warn, Kira J. Watkins, Glenn P. Worthman, David W. Wynn.

Photo Credits:

All images HMH Photo unless otherwise noted.

Real World Connection icons: ("R"), Ingram Publishing/SuperStock; ("e"), Jupiter Images/Brand X/Alamy; ("a"), imagebroker/Alamy; ("l"), Flat Earth; ("dash"), Dex Image/Alamy; ("W"), Stockbyte/gettyimages; ("o"), Jupiter Images/Brand X/Alamy; ("r"), lugris/Alamy; ("l"), Ian Andrews/Alamy; ("d"), VLO-IMAGES/Alamy

Table of Contents: (chapter one), Olivier Grunewald/Photolibrary.com; (chapter two), Gao Ming/HLJRB/ChinaFotoPress/Kyodo News/NewsCom; (chapter three), Kevin Reece/Icon SMI/CORBIS; (chapter four), Steve Winter/National Geographic/Getty Images; (chapter five), Terje Rakke/Getty Images; (chapter six), Detlev van Ravenswaay/Photo Researchers, Inc.; (chapter seven), Mark Jones/Photolibrary; (chapter eight), Richard Cummins/Corbis; (chapter nine), Jose Fuste Raga/CORBIS; (chapter ten), © guichaoua/Alamy; (chapter eleven), ©Icon Sports Media Inc./NewsCom; (chapter twelve), Prisma/SuperStock

Chapter One: 2 (bkgd), Olivier Grunewald/Photolibrary.com; 6 (tr), Digital Vision; 10 (tr), Health Head Images; 11 (cl), Manoocher Deghati/AFP/Getty Images; 13 (all), CNRI/Photo Researchers, Inc.; 14 (tr), Peter Arnold, Inc./Alamy; 22 (cr), Victoria Smith/HRW; 29 (all), Photodisc/Getty Images; 30 (t), CinemaPhoto/CORBIS; 30 (cr), LUCASFILM LTD/PARAMOUNT/THE KOBAL COLLECTION; 30 (c), Elisabetta Villa/Getty Images; 34 (tr), moodboard/Alamy; 37 (l), Eric Erbe/U. S. Department of Agriculture; 38 (tr), Digital Vision/GettyImages; 41 (l), Courtesy of the National Grocers Association Best Bagger Contest; 42 (tr), Rubberball/PunchStock; 43 (l), Sam Dudgeon/HRW/Courtesy Fast Forward Skate Shop, Austin, TX; 43 (r), Sam Dudgeon/HRW/Courtesy Fast Forward Skate Shop, Austin, TX; 45 (cr), David Davis Photoproductions/Alamy; 53 (l), © Reuters/CORBIS; 57 (b), Jon Arnold Images Ltd/Alamy; 58 (all), © Jenny Thomas/HRW; 59 (br), Victoria Smith/HRW

Chapter Two: 68 (bkgd), Gao Ming/HLJRB/ChinaFotoPress/Kyodo News/NewsCom; 72 (cr), Chuck Nicklin/Al Giddings Images, Inc.; 72 (tc), Macduff Everton/CORBIS; 75 (l), © Neil Rabinowitz/CORBIS; 80 (tr), MATHCOUNTS Foundation; 83 (l), Lee Foster; 89 (tr), NASA/Photo Researchers, Inc.; 92 (tr), Steve Boyle/NewSport/Corbis; 95 (r), Ann and Carl Purcell; 103 (b), Sam Dudgeon/HRW/Sheet music courtesy Martha Dudgeon.; 104 (tr), Directphoto.org/Alamy; 107 (t), Panorama Media/Alamy; 108 (tr), ©2007 Thinkstock/JupiterImages Corporation; 109 (tr), Victoria Smith/HRW; 111 (tl), Regina Kuehne/epa/CORBIS; 112 (tr), © Royalty-Free Corbis; 115 (b), Erich Lessing/Art Resource, NY; 115 (t), © D. Donne Bryant, DDB Stock Photography; 117 (b), Lisette LeBon/SuperStock; 118 (tr), Victoria Smith/HRW; 121 (l), Val Handumon/epa/Corbis; 122 (tr), Otto Greule Jr/Getty Images; 125 (c), © Underwood & Underwood/CORBIS; 125 (t), Image Copyright © Digital Vision; 129 (l), © Buddy Mays/CORBIS; 131 (c), Tim Flach/Getty Images; 131 (b), Joseph T. Collins/Photo Researchers, Inc.; 132 (br), © Jenny Thomas/HRW; 133 (br), Sam Dudgeon/HRW

Chapter Three: 140 (bkgd), Kevin Reece/Icon SMI/CORBIS; 144 (tr), W. A. Harewood/Gamma Presse/NewsCom; 147 (l), Darryl Dyck/iPhoto/NewsCom; 148 (tr), Novastock/Photolibrary.com; 151 (l), AP Photo/The Fresno Bee, Richard Darby/Wide World Photos; 160 (tr), Kim Karpeles/Alamy; 163 (l), JupiterImages/Creatas/Alamy; 164 (tr), Sam Dudgeon/HRW; 167 (l), © Gail Mooney/CORBIS; 169 (b), Ken Karp/HRW; 170 (tr), Michel Porro/Getty Images; 179 (l), © Anthony Bannister; Gallo Images/CORBIS; 179 (r), G.K. & Vikki Hart/Getty Images; 180 (tr), Dorling Kindersley/GettyImages; 180 (tr), Botanica/Jupiter Images; 183 (l),

Doug Pearson/Jon Arnold Travel/Photolibrary; 186 (tr), © Mark Van Doren/Florida Photo Magazine; 193 (tc), Richard Day/Daybreak Imagery; 193 (tr), Tony Freeman/PhotoEdit, Inc.; 194 (tr), vario images GmbH & Co.KG/Alamy; 195 (cr), © Charles O'Rear/CORBIS; 197 (l), James Peacock/Emporis; 199 (c), Courtesy of Civil Rights in Education Heritage Trail; 200 (b), © Jenny Thomas/HRW; 201 (br), Sam Dudgeon/HRW

Chapter Four: 210 (bkgd), Steve Winter/National Geographic/Getty Images; 214 (tr), Inti St Clair/Digital Vision/gettyimages; 217 (cr), Jeff Hunter/Getty Images; 222 (cr), © PunchStock; 222 (t), © PunchStock; 223 (l), James L. Amos/SuperStock; 225 (cr), © Lynda Richardson/Corbis; 226 (tr), © Ralph A. Clevenger/CORBIS; 229 (tl), © AP IMAGES/HO/PA; 231 (b), Sam Dudgeon/HRW; 232 (tr), Indiapicture/Alamy; 235 (l), Justin Sullivan/Getty Images/NewsCom; 236 (tr), Yoshikazu Tsuno/AFP/GettyImages; 239 (cl), National Geographic/GettyImages; 243 (tl), Corbis; 245 (bl), FRANK PERRY/AFP/Getty Images/NewsCom; 252 (tr), Image Source Limited/Punchstock; 254 (bl), NEW LINE/THE KOBAL COLLECTION/David James; 254 (br), NEW LINE/THE KOBAL COLLECTION/David James; 256 (t), Angelo Hornak/CORBIS; 257 (tr), Herscovici/Art Resource, NY; 259 (tc), Victoria Smith/HRW; 259 (cr), CORBIS; 263 (b), S. Berner/Photri; 264 (b), Randall Hyman/HRW; 265 (b), Victoria Smith/HRW; 265 (b), Victoria Smith/HRW

Chapter Five: 272 (bkgd), © Terje Rakke/Getty Images; 279 (l), © Stock Trek/PhotoDisc/Picture Quest/Jupiter Images; 280 (t), Thinkstock/Corbis; 284 (t), Rube Goldberg; 288 (t), John Foxx/Stockbyte/gettyimages; 291 (t), Friedrich Saurer/SPL/Photo Researchers, Inc.; 291 (t), Friedrich Saurer/SPL/Photo Researchers, Inc.; 293 (b), © Michael T. Sedam/CORBIS; 296 (t), Ariel Skelley/CORBIS; 299 (t), Peter Menzell/Photo Researchers, Inc.; 302 (tr), Jill Ferry/Photographers Direct; 306 (t), Stephanie Friedman/HRW; 312 (l), Ed Reschte/Peter Arnold, Inc./Alamy; 313 (tr), Sebastian Green/Alamy; 317 (l), Images&Stories/Alamy; 321 (all), Courtesy of the Alabama National Fair; 323 (b), Sam Dudgeon/HRW

Chapter Six: 332 (bkgd), Detlev van Ravenswaay/Photo Researchers, Inc.; 336 (tr), Radius Images/Corbis; 343 (l), Reuters/CORBIS; 344 (tr), Sam Dudgeon/HRW; 344 (t), Sam Dudgeon/Harcourt; 351 (cl), © Tim Graham/Alamy; 352 (tr), © Buddy Mays/CORBIS; 355 (l), © Ellen Senisi/The Image Works; 357 (b), © 1998 Joseph De Sciose; 358 (tr), Megapress/Alamy; 362 (t), United States Mint image; 365 (l), Erich Lessing/Art Resource, NY; 367 (br), Lowell Georgia/Photo Researchers, Inc.; 367 (c), ©Stockbyte; 368 (b), Randall Hyman/HRW; 369 (br), Sam Dudgeon/HRW; 369 (br), Sam Dudgeon/HRW

Chapter Seven: 376 (bkgd), Mark Jones/Photolibrary; 380 (tr), Chris Ware/The Image Works; 384 (t), Roine Magnusson/Getty Images; 385 (tr), Cartoon copyrighted by Mark Parisi, printed with permission.; 389 (l), AP Photo/Peter M. Fredin; 392 (b), Wendell Webber/Botanica/Jupiterimages; 393 (pins), © David J. & Janice L. Frent Collection/CORBIS; 393 (tc), © CORBIS; 393 (cr), © CORBIS; 394 (br), © Kathy deWet-Oleson/Lonely Planet Images; 394 (cl), SUNNYphotography.com/Alamy; 394 (tr), Photodisc/Getty Images; 395 (l), © Pat and Chuck Blackley; 398 (tr), Image Bank/GettyImages; 401 (tl), © Yiorgos Karahalis/Reuters/Corbis; 405 (b), Gerard Soury/Photolibrary.com; 406 (tc), Robert Dowling/CORBIS; 406 (tr), Robert Dowling/CORBIS; 408 (cr), © Lawrence Manning/Corbis; 409 (l), Wayne Levin/Getty Images; 412 (tr), © Volkmar Brockhaus/zefa/CORBIS; 415 (l), James D. Watt/Image Quest Marine/Alamy; 418 (tr), © Randy M. Ury/CORBIS; 421 (tl), FlyBase/Dr. F. R. Turner; 425 (tr), Kevin Shafer/Corbis; 425 (tc), Paul A. Souders/CORBIS; 429 (l), © AP IMAGES/Lynne Sladky; 433 (b), ©2008 NBAE (Photo by Melissa Majchrzak/NBAE via Getty Images; 435 (br), Sam Dudgeon/HRW

Chapter Eight: 444 (bkgd), Richard Cummins/Corbis; 448 (tr), Christie's Images/CORBIS; 450 (b), Science Kit & Boreal Laboratories; 451 (b), Copyright Tate Gallery, London, Great Britain/Art Resource, NY/© 2004 Artist Rights Society (ARS), New York/Pro Litteris, Zurich; 451 (t), © Diana Ong/SuperStock; 454 (t), Joe Drivas/Photographer's Choice/Getty Images; 460 (tr), © Frank Leather; Eye Ubiquitous/CORBIS; 467 (br), © Robert Landau/Corbis; 468 (t), © Joseph Sohm/Visions of America/Corbis; 470 (cr), © Brand X Pictures/JupiterImages Corporation; 474 (t), © Sheldan Collins/CORBIS; 477 (b), © Jacqui Hurst/CORBIS; 477 (t), John Warden/SuperStock; 477 (c), © Roman Soumar/CORBIS; 478 (tr), © Royalty-Free Corbis; 481 (l), © Craig Aurness/CORBIS; 482 (tr), UW/Mary Levin; 485 (l), Tim Davis/CORBIS; 489 (l), DoD Photo by CHESTER SIMPSON, CIV; 491 (br), Nordicphotos/Photo Library; 492 (t), © David Joel/Stone/Getty Images; 492 (br), Sam Dudgeon/HRW; 492 (bl), Peter Van Steen/HRW; 494 (tl), Peter Van Steen/HRW; 494 (tc), Sam Dudgeon/HRW; 494 (tr), Design Pics; 494 (bc), Sam Dudgeon/HRW; 494 (bl), Peter Van Steen/HRW/Courtesy International Playthings, Inc.; 494 (cr), © 2007 liquidlibrary/JupiterImages Corporation; 496 (tr), © Chris Trotman/Duomo/CORBIS;

Credits

Table of Measures

METRIC

Length

1 kilometer (km) = 1,000 meters (m)

1 meter = 100 centimeters (cm)

1 centimeter = 10 millimeters (mm)

Capacity

1 liter (L) = 1,000 milliliters (mL)

Mass

1 kilogram (kg) = 1,000 grams (g)

1 gram = 1,000 milligrams (mg)

CUSTOMARY

Length

1 mile (mi) = 5,280 feet (ft)

1 yard (yd) = 3 feet

1 foot = 12 inches (in.)

Capacity

1 gallon (gal) = 4 quarts (qt)

1 quart = 2 pints (pt)

1 pint = 2 cups (c)

1 cup = 8 fluid ounces (fl oz)

Weight

1 ton (T) = 2,000 pounds (lb)

1 pound = 16 ounces (oz)

TIME

1 year (yr) = 365 days

1 year = 12 months (mo)

1 year = 52 weeks (wk)

1 week = 7 days

1 day = 24 hours (h)

1 hour = 60 minutes (min)

1 minute = 60 seconds (s)

Formulas

Perimeter and Circumference

Square	$P = 4s$
Rectangle	$P = 2\ell + 2w$ or $P = 2(\ell + w)$
Polygon	P = sum of the lengths of the sides
Circle	$C = 2\pi r$ or $C = \pi d$

Area

Square	$A = s^2$
Rectangle	$A = \ell w$ or $A = bh$
Parallelogram	$A = bh$
Triangle	$A = \frac{1}{2}bh$ or $A = \frac{bh}{2}$
Trapezoid	$A = \frac{1}{2}(b_1 + b_2)h$ or $A = \frac{(b_1 + b_2)h}{2}$
Circle	$A = \pi r^2$